Salem Academy and College
FRIENDS of the LIBRARY

Gift of

The Friends of
the Library

Herman Melville, 1819–1851

Herman Melville

A Biography
Volume 1, 1819–1851

Hershel Parker

THE JOHNS HOPKINS UNIVERSITY PRESS
BALTIMORE AND LONDON

The Johns Hopkins University Press
2715 North Charles Street
Baltimore, Maryland 21218-4319
The Johns Hopkins Press Ltd., London

Library of Congress Cataloging-in-Publication Data will
be found at the end of this book.
A catalog record for this book is available from the
British Library.

ISBN 0-8018-5428-8

Frontispiece: *Herman Melville.*

FOR HEDDY-ANN RICHTER

Contents

Contents

Illustrations

Illustrations

Preface

Now is the very time to tackle that book about him. If this task is neglected a little longer, so that some priceless recollections of Melville, now available, are lost, and documents and other evidence of the man, which now exist, are buried still deeper beneath the litter of the years, then the book about him will be but tentative, and will leave the mystery darker than ever. And what a jolly task the writing of that biography would be! If only one lived near Nantucket.

H. M. Tomlinson, in the London *Athenæum*, 4 June 1921

This book, the first two-volume biography of the American prose writer and poet Herman Melville (1819–91), is based on long-known documents and on new caches of documents. Of the hundreds of discoveries since 1975, the year of the last biography of Melville before 1996, some came in the form of a single tantalizing letter, some came in small but explosive batches of documents. In the early 1980s the late Francis Plumeau discovered in a barn near the Gansevoort Mansion House in Gansevoort, New York, Melville family documents that proved to be all but miraculous in number and all but overpowering in significance. These were a portion of the papers of Melville's sister Augusta, running from her childhood correspondence up through 1854 (with one later year — 1863 — surviving to instill gratitude for what we have gained and awe at what is lost). Plumeau's investigations led to the acquisition of the bulk of the trove in 1983 by the New York Public Library; some of it is in private hands. In the late 1980s Anna Morewood, the widow of a grandson of Melville's brother Allan, donated a significant small trove to the Berkshire County Historical Association at Arrowhead, the Melville house south of Pittsfield, Massachusetts. Many other documents, including books from Melville's library, annotated by Melville, and long lists of other books available to him, have surfaced in the last two decades, often through the efforts of book dealers, scholars, and Melville amateurs, often in the course of ongoing work on the Northwestern-Newberry Edition of *The Writings of Herman Melville* (edited by Harrison Hayford, Hershel Parker, and G. Thomas Tanselle) and, most recently, in the course of my research for this biography.

Passages in the newly recovered "Augusta Papers" illuminate the characters of Melville's mother, brothers, and sisters to the point that one can, for the first time, make a vivid, valid thumbnail sketch of each of them, as well as of some other vaguely known members of the family and friends. The Augusta Papers also solve many old biographical problems and reveal entirely new biographical episodes. Answering a question raised by Melville's widow a century ago and asked again by all biographers, Cousin Julia Melvill of Pittsfield, Massachusetts, in a letter to Augusta provides the evidence that 1837 was the year Melville spent the "greater portion of" in Pittsfield, supposedly (but not in fact) with his Uncle Thomas. Mythical Custis cousins of Brookline, Massachusetts, turn out to be the tangible Curtis cousins of Waterford, Brooklyn, and Glens Falls, Kate Curtis being the sister of Cousin Guert Gansevoort, notorious in American naval history for his role in the *Somers* mutiny. Cousin Augustus Peebles of Lansingburgh, New York, emerges as the officious, purse-proud "Lord of the Isle," briefly Augusta's fiancé, later the decent, chastened friend who made the inventory of the house Augusta died in. Some relationships emerge momentarily into the glare of a single new document in the Augusta Papers, as when Herman Melville's self-controlled wife, Elizabeth Shaw Melville, bursts out at the folly of her selfish, snobbish, arrogant, and irresponsible new sister-in-law, Jane Dempsey Melville: "Great fool!"

Many episodes (some previously unknown) emerge from the shadows when documents are brought together from various old and new sources, including the Augusta Papers. Information in some papers of the Savage family discovered by Frederick and Joyce Kennedy lies behind part of my portrait of Melville's wife in her early years, and (when combined with the reviews of *Typee* and *Omoo* and with letters in the Augusta Papers) forced me to see that, for some years after the publication of his first book, Melville was nothing less than the first American literary sex symbol. Having discovered an autobiographical account by Clarissa Emely Gear Hobbs, daughter of the employer of Melville's Uncle Thomas in Galena, Illinois, Stanton Garner dated a dramatic episode in it to the summer of 1841, when Herman was in the Pacific; through Thomas Melvill's letters in the Shaw Collection in the Massachusetts Historical Society, I was able to date the occurrence to March 1840, and demonstrate that it affected Herman decisively. In an episode based on a shopping list, Cousin John Van Schaick, of whom we had known nothing, steps forward (in the Augusta Papers) to scour the shops of Troy for delicacies to be served (the date shows) at Maria Melville's welcoming party for her newly married son Herman and his bride (a celebration we had never heard of) and (in the Arrowhead Papers) to take Augusta, his former fiancée, for a drive after she had finished copying the book then called *The Whale*. Washington Irving's distress in 1850 at what Melville wrote about him in

"Hawthorne and His Mosses" is revealed in hitherto-unnoticed pages in Pierre M. Irving's *Life and Letters of Washington Irving* (published late in 1863), and further illuminated by young Irving's outline, which survives in the Berg Collection of the New York Public Library — but I first glimpsed the story in a hoard of new documents I was assembling about the trouble the English forger Thomas Powell was causing Irving and Melville. I discovered in the Augusta Papers that Melville completed a book called *The Isle of the Cross* in 1853 and tried to market it in New York City that June; soon Gary Scharnhorst found strong corroborative evidence, an item in the Springfield *Republican* about Melville's going to town that month with a new manuscript.

Two recently published letters from Melville to his father-in-law, Chief Justice Lemuel Shaw, in the Social Law Library and a letter from Augusta to her brother Allan, newly deposited at Arrowhead, helped to clarify Melville's borrowing $2050 from T. D. Stewart in May 1850; later Heddy Richter found perturbing new evidence in the files of grant deeds in the County Records Office in the grand Victorian building in Pittsfield which was formerly the Berkshire Athenaeum. Two letters and other records found by the Reverend Walter D. Kring in 1975 in the archives of All Souls Church in Manhattan shed tragic light on the Melville marriage, showing that in 1867 Melville's wife was convinced he was insane and her half-brothers and step-mother were urging her to take refuge with them in Boston, thus confirming rumors first recorded by Raymond Weaver in 1921. The new documentary evidence, taken together, casts light on almost every episode in Melville's life already familiar from earlier tellings (sometimes a glow as bright as the Drummond Light that P. T. Barnum installed on Broadway, sometimes only flickering, unequal crosslights). Through these archival discoveries we know much more fully people we thought we already knew; previously unknown characters now take their place with those we were familiar with; other strangers stand at the curtain backstage, indistinct. Behind them still must lurk throngs of people (significant in Melville's life) whom no biographer has yet glimpsed, but now for the first time we can see Melville living his long life in a peopled world.

Because I have worked with so much evidence, old and new, and have so many more episodes to tell, this biography is several times as long as the biographies by Raymond Weaver (1921), Lewis Mumford (1929), Leon Howard (1951) and Edwin Haviland Miller (1975). This first volume is somewhat longer than the one-volume biography by Laurie Robertson-Lorant (1996), published after my forty chapters (but not the preface) were in page proofs. Weaver based much of his biography on family documents in the possession of Melville's oldest granddaughter, Eleanor Metcalf, and on

Melville's early books, which he assumed were reliably autobiographical. In his 1929 critical biography Lewis Mumford's factual information came not from original research but primarily from Weaver's book and from Melville's own early works. Leon Howard based his biography primarily on Jay Leyda's *The Melville Log: A Documentary Life of Herman Melville* (1951), but he too assumed, at times incautiously, that he could safely take some episodes from Melville's early works as autobiography. In 1975 Miller also confused fact and fiction ("Redburn starts out from Lansingburgh"), but he had at hand the 1951 *Log* as well as the supplement in the 1969 reissue of the *Log*, and for Melville's later years he drew on new documents in a book by Eleanor Metcalf, *Herman Melville: Cycle and Epicycle* (1953), while making less use of some other recent studies, among them Alice Kenney's *The Gansevoorts of Albany* (1969). Casting a wider net than Miller, Robertson-Lorant made good use of recent publications, including the Historical Notes and other editorial information in volumes of *The Writings of Herman Melville*. She made vigorous forays into much the same archival material I have used, but she was sporadic rather than exhaustive in her study of the family letters, and not always alert to the narrative potential of other kinds of evidence, such as records of Melville's reading and his marginalia.

For four and a half decades the most authoritative source for facts about Melville's life has been Jay Leyda's 1951 *The Melville Log* and the most reliable narrative account has been Leon Howard's 1951 *Herman Melville: A Biography*, drawn from items in the *Log*, which Leyda shared with Howard as he found them throughout the late 1940s. Leyda's researches were heroic in range and sometimes little short of inspired in direction, but he (and Howard) benefited from the research of Willard Thorp in the 1930s (Thorp opened the riches of the New York Public Library Duyckinck Collection to Melvilleans) and from the ongoing research of the remarkable young scholars who were then writing Ph.D. dissertations at Yale University under the direction of the biographer of Washington Irving, Stanley T. Williams. Among these young people who became major Melville scholars and critics were Walter E. Bezanson, Merrell R. Davis, Elizabeth Foster, Harrison Hayford, William H. Gilman, Merton M. Sealts Jr., and Nathalia Wright. In addition, Leyda and Howard benefited from the work of Wilson Heflin, whose Ph.D. was from Vanderbilt but who shared his discoveries with members of the great Yale crew, and from earlier work, especially that of Charles Roberts Anderson.

Between the time Leyda went to the archives and the time I began research in 1962, restrictions had been lifted on some documents (at the New York Public Library Gansevoort Melville's London journal was handed to me almost as soon as I asked for it), and new documents had been deposited (in the Berkshire Athenaeum, new documents were housed in a new Melville Collection). Half or so of the supplement to the 1969 *Log* consists of my dissertation notes, which I sent to Leyda in East Germany; I proofread the supplement while living with Leon Howard in Los Angeles. Leon Howard and I collaborated formally on one project and informally on others, but anyone who knew Leon will realize that he would have been less than pleased at my writing a narrative biography — unless he had lived to survey the range of new documents. A would-be rationalist in an increasingly irrational world, Leon did not have a close emotional affinity with Herman Melville. Aghast at Melville's reckless excesses, he systematically tamed him down, repeatedly taking a reasonable view of quite unreasonable situations. Despite difference in attitudes and in information, my aim throughout this book has been identical to Leon Howard's: to see Herman Melville as a human being living in nineteenth-century America. In my case, that meant seeing Melville as a member of his family and a member of literary circles more complexly and intensely than Howard had done.

My book shares Leyda's (and Howard's) debts to all the scholars of the 1940s named above. Willard Thorp gave me timely encouragement for a quarter of a century. I have profited from William H. Gilman's demonstration of the fictitiousness of much of *Redburn* (which was indeed based on Melville's own trip to Liverpool in 1839) and the accumulating evidence (from Charles Roberts Anderson, Harrison Hayford, and Wilson Heflin) that much is fictional in Melville's early works that had been assumed to be autobiographical. I have profited from some of Heflin's research on the authenticity of *Omoo* which he did not live to publish, and even more from the documents about the mutiny on the *Lucy Ann* which Hayford printed in the Hendricks House edition of *Omoo*. What I say about the composition of *Omoo* follows closely what Hayford first established; what I say about the composition of *Mardi* closely follows Davis. All I say about the indenture of lease on the Fourth Avenue house is taken from Gilman's unpublished notes; some of the documents had disappeared by the time he went to double-check his own work in 1947.

My research, like that of my predecessors, has been far from systematic. Many a discovery came not in a comprehensive sweep of documents but in a purposeful foray conducted out of frustration with the available evidence. Often, at such times (as when I decided, quite belatedly, that Gansevoort Melville *must* have given speeches in or around New York City after Herman returned from the Pacific in October 1844), I was rewarded when I went where information should have been and simply put out my hand. In time someone more systematic or more shrewdly purposeful will put out a hand for the papers of Nathaniel Parker Willis, Henry T. Tuckerman, or Felix Darley, or perhaps even lay that hand on the lost *The Isle of the Cross*. Yet so much more is known today about the life of Herman Melville than even two decades ago that the existence of this book is justified on the simple level of information. The book tells, page by page, chapter by chapter, a new story about a writer we thought we had known. The abundance of new documentation affords me the extraordinary — almost unique — luxury of telling my new story without reference to other biographers, after these prefatory pages. The alternative would have been to choke the pages with modifications, corrections, and rebuttals, some significant, some quite trivial. A time or two I mention Howard's opinion on some doubtful point, as if I were continuing a discussion with the living man, but I never correct any biographer in the body of this book, and I have resisted coming down emphatically when I am quoting a document that someone else had mistranscribed or misdated. The reader who sees that my transcriptions, datings, and judgments differ from those in other biographies or criticism will have to conclude that, right or wrong, I thought I knew what I was doing.

In the 1970s, when Leyda asked me to make a new revision of the *Log*, I demurred: to Melvilleans the *Log* was sacred as Leyda's creation, however collaborative it had been. In the early 1980s, when Leyda began work on a new edition himself and I began work on a narrative biography, I kept him supplied with my discoveries, large and small. (A note in his papers: "Hershel is a faucet.") After Parkinson's disease struck him, several years before his death in February 1988, I perforce took up what we agreed to call *The New Melville Log* (by Jay Leyda and Hershel Parker). In 1988 I stopped thinking of the 1951 and 1969 editions as the *Log*: instead, the *Log* was all that, but it was also the burgeoning creature in my computer which became, over the next years, two, then three or four times its old length, old and new documents interspersed in chronological order. For five years I worked primarily on *The New Melville Log* (lighted magnifier to the right of my monitor, perpetual calendar ready at my left), creating an engorged working archive containing almost all the Augusta Papers, for instance; all the known reviews of Melville's book in full, rather than excerpts of them; and all Melville's known letters and journals.

In his last years Leyda's passion that I write a biography was intense — more intense, even, than his hopes for *The New Melville Log*. The irony is that my work on the *Log* gave the biography what strength it has. Instead of lying inert once I had put new documents into place in the *Log*, many of the items set off shock waves that forced me to move or revise old items in the neighborhood — or sometimes items far away, in different years. It was while doing yeoman's work on the progressively unruly *Log*, transcribing new documents into it (in the process, dating or redating many of them) and making new sense of surrounding old documents, that I solved many biographical tangles, some of which I was unaware of until I found myself snared in them.

Beginning in 1990, I wrote most of the first draft of this biography directly from copies of files in the working text of *The New Melville Log* (second volume first). Now that I have redone Leon Howard's task and written a biography, I can't imagine writing it if I had not acted as my own Leyda & Company, assembling documents, transcribing them, and making sense of them year by year, not least in the prolonged process of constructing a narrative from the evidence. There is little enough glamor in reading dead people's mail month after month, yet it was while transcribing letters, especially those surviving from Augusta Melville's personal archive, that I learned to listen to the yet-vibrating and vibrant voices of the Melville family. Listening to those voices holding forth in monologues and lengthy dialogues or preserved only in fragmentary phrases caught in the wind, I have remembered Ishmael's claim in *Moby-Dick* (ch. 33, "The Specksynder"): "Oh, Ahab! what shall be grand in thee, it must needs be plucked at from the skies, and dived for in the deep, and featured in the unbodied air!" If in this biography I re-create some sense of what *was* grand in Melville, if he and the other characters act out of explicable motivations, if a cumulative, implacable force propels any of the chapters, that success derives from the years I spent listening to the members of the family talk to each other while I created a chronological archive.

In the first "Knights and Squires" chapter of *Moby-Dick*, Ishmael, looking ahead to his task as biographer of the last voyage of the *Pequod*, determines not to demean his noble characters:

> But were the coming narrative to reveal, in any instance, the complete abasement of poor Starbuck's fortitude, scarce might I have the heart to write it; for it is a thing most sorrowful, nay shocking, to expose the fall of valor in the soul. Men may seem detestable as joint stock-companies and nations; knaves, fools, and murderers there may be; men may have mean and meagre faces; but man, in the ideal, is so noble and so sparkling, such a grand and glowing creature, that over any ignominious blemish in him all his fellows should run to throw their costliest robes.

It was with Ishmael's scruples in mind that I drafted the second volume of this biography first, only to find the years 1851–91 infused with the sort of valor (physical, psychological, intellectual, and aesthetic) that makes for compelling narrative. In both volumes I abjure the role of retained attorney—a decision made easier because nothing I discovered about Herman Melville impelled me to cast over him protective robes elaborately spun of forensic eloquence. More than once, I would have warned him away from a precipice, but I depict him as I see him. In an era when to write a biography is to expose a pathology, I hope I have manifested toward Melville and his family a measure of his own magnanimity and pudency, even if not (in a phrase of Hazlitt's that he copied down) his unapproachable "greatness of gusto."

Acknowledgments

In *Mardi* King Media declares that he has read Lombardo's *Koztanza* through, not once but nine times. Heddy-Ann Richter read this biography of Melville through five times, before creating the index. I have had other good critics. Harrison Hayford read a printout all through during a ten-day-and-night session. Mark Niemeyer and Steven Olsen-Smith each read a full draft. Maurice Sendak read the book before drawing the jacket and frontispiece portrait, and Alma A. MacDougall read it when she copyedited it. Others read portions: Mary K. Bercaw Edwards and Robert Madison (the nautical chapters), Michael di Capua, and Louis Zara. John Benedict, who would have been its editor, read a very early draft. Willis G. Regier, director of the Johns Hopkins University Press, read it once fast, and then again slowly, before it went to the copyeditor. I am grateful to all of these admirable readers.

Two librarians were extraordinarily helpful: Ruth Degenhardt, the curator of the local history room at the Berkshire Athenaeum, and Richard Colles Johnson of the Newberry Library, the bibliographical associate of *The Writings of Herman Melville*. I am also grateful to the magnanimous New Haven bookdealer and Melville collector, William Reese. Several times I felt that Melvilleans now dead, notably William H. Gilman and Wilson Heflin, had reached up a hand to help me; and I laid out every new episode before Jay Leyda, whether he knew it or not.

These offered timely moral support: Susan Beegel, Michael Briggs, Frederick Crews, Michael di Capua, Shirley Dettlaff, Rich Duggan, Robert and Roslyn Haber, Thomas Heffernan, Brian Higgins, Robert H. Hirst, Hiro Ichigawa, J. A. Leo Lemay, Steven J. Mailloux, Jane Millgate, Michael Millgate, Robert Newman, Dean Pearson, Noel Polk, Paul Seydor, and John Wenke. Others helped with research: Barbara Allen, Carolyn Banfield, and Edward Daunais at Arrowhead; Rick Leab, Emilie Piper, and Kathleen Reilly of the Berkshire Athenaeum; Helen Plunkett of the Berkshire County Historical Society; Dennis Marnon of the Harvard College Library; Frances Broderick, Lansingburgh archivist; Charlotte Maison of the Nantucket Athenaeum and Jacqueline Haring of the Nantucket Historical Association; Warren Broderick and James Corsaro of the New York State Library. At the University of Delaware I owe much to former provost Leon Campbell, to John R. Brunswick of Morris Library, and to Karen Pyle of Photographic Services. I am also grateful to Mrs. Paul Barden, Carl Randall Cluff, Joseph Coulombe, Chris Fauske, Stanton Garner, Adolfo Gomez, John Gretchko,

Acknowledgments

Kevin Hayes, Jeanne Howes, Frederick Kennedy, Joyce Kennedy, Richard Kopley, Alexander Moore, Joel Myerson, Thomas Osborne, Doris Sheridan, Robert K. Wallace, and Richard E. Winslow III. At the Johns Hopkins University Press, Douglas Armato, Barbara Lamb, Anita Scott, and Inger Forland all befriended the book.

Anna Morewood, daughter-in-law of Melville's first niece (the one born in 1849), showed me some of her late husband's family possessions, and William and Ruth Morewood shared family documents with me. Several descendants of Herman Melville showed me mementos and told me stories they had been told. I am grateful to Barton Chapin, Melville and Lizanne Chapin, David and Audrey Metcalf, Kitty Howe, and Jamie Whittemore. Priscilla and William Ambrose were incomparable in their encouragement.

Herman Melville, 1819–1851

The Flight of the Patrician Wastrel
and His Second Son
1830

With early Virtue plant thy breast,
The specious Arts of Vice detest.

"Allan Melvills Book," his penmanship exercise book, kept at Staniford's
School, Andover, N.H., 1796 (Reese Collection)

ON SATURDAY, 9 OCTOBER 1830, in a hastily emptied house on Broadway in lower Manhattan, Herman Melvill, eleven years old, helped his father, Allan Melvill, forty-eight, pack up a remnant of papers and odds and ends of light personal belongings that they could walk away with after dark. The boy knew they were not moving to a finer neighborhood in Manhattan, as they had done every few years. This time they were escaping the island to join his mother and seven brothers and sisters in Albany, forever. Herman may not have known that his father, a former importer of French dry goods, was three months in arrears on house rent, that other debts were unpaid, and that Melvill feared a creditor might have him arrested before he got away, but there had been no hiding from the boy the urgency of the family plight. The day before, his mother and his older brother, Gansevoort Melvill, had fled northward in charge of the family furniture. At day's end father and son abandoned the house without hindrance and made their way to the dock at 82 Cortlandt Street, up the Hudson River from the Battery, familiar territory, only a few doors from a house they had once lived in. In his diary Allan Melvill recorded, "Left New York with Herman in the Swiftsure," but in fact escape on this steamboat was neither swift nor sure. Rather than pulling away soon after they boarded, the steamboat was "detained all night at Cortlandt Sᵗ Dock by a severe Storm." There, his brother Thomas Melvill Jr.'s weeks in a debtor's prison in Lenox, Massachusetts, looming before him as a stark fate that he might himself encounter, Allan Melvill suffered through the long night hours, swaying beside his second son in the anchored *Swiftsure*.

Two decades later Herman Melville (as the name was by then spelled), in *Moby-Dick*, dramatized the biblical Jonah in his flight from God—a man with "slouched hat and guilty eye," skulking on board a ship under the suspicious looks of captain and crew (ch. 9, "The Sermon"). He finds no rest: "All dressed and dusty as he is, Jonah throws himself into his berth, and finds the little state-room ceiling almost resting on his forehead. The air is close, and Jonah gasps." Jonah's "contracted hole," sunk "beneath the ship's water-line," was foul, like the stifling sleeping cabin where Herman huddled with his father, tossed all night by the storm. At seven in the morning of 10 October the *Swiftsure* finally left the dock. Father and son were safe for the moment, however unsure their futures. That night of miserable confinement was the last night Herman ever spent in the city of his birth with his father, and the trip upriver was the last time he was ever alone anywhere with his father. Herman Melville became peculiarly sensitive to the overlayings of past and present in places where significant experiences of his life had occurred, so his father and other members of his family haunted the river and lower Manhattan whenever he walked there, even many decades later.

Far from being a run-of-the-mill defaulter and fugitive, Allan Melvill was as patrician as almost anyone in his birth city of Boston. Allan's father, Major Thomas Melvill, born in Boston in 1751, the son of a wealthy new Scottish immigrant, had been orphaned early but had attended Princeton, intending to become a minister. After his graduation in 1769 ill health led Thomas to take a restorative voyage to visit his family in Scoonie Parish, Fifeshire, Scotland, where his own grandfather, another Thomas, had been the minister. Back in Boston, young Thomas used his inheritance to become a merchant, instead of a minister. Late in 1773, when three high-pooped Indiamen of the East India Company anchored in Boston Harbor, protesters kept the heavily taxed tea from being unloaded. The cautious chairman of the Boston board of selectmen, the merchant John Scollay, also Scottish by blood, ruddy-faced and stout, led other cool-headed citizens in negotiations aimed at persuading the consignees of the tea not to accept delivery. Thomas Melvill, an intimate friend of Samuel Adams and others of the Sons of Liberty, in December 1773 took part in a tumultuous meeting at the Old South Church at Marlborough and Milk streets. Afterward, he joined a band of fellow Bostonians, some of them made up more or less like American Indians, who ran war-whooping east down Milk Street on their way across the peninsula to Fort Hill and Griffin's Wharf, where they boarded the Indiamen, hauled up crates of the heavily taxed tea, and dumped the contents into Boston Harbor.

At twenty-two Thomas Melvill did the deed that defined his life. The Tea Party precipitated the American Revolution, and no one in the revolutionary era or the next generation ever forgot the witty irony in the name quickly attached to the event at which the uninvited and indecorous guests might have paid for attendance with their lives. The next year, 1774, young Thomas Melvill married Priscilla Scollay, the daughter of John Scollay, who had tried to resolve peacefully the dispute over taxation but now was committed to defiance of British law. History and his family would remember Thomas Melvill's participation in the Tea Party, but Melvill also served the Continental cause after the Declaration of Independence. In 1776, at twenty-five, he led the firing on the British fleet which drove it from Boston Harbor. Later he commanded a detachment sent to the town of Nantasket on Hingham Bay to watch the further movements of the British fleet and was given the rank of major in the 1778 expedition into Rhode Island. Melvill's reward was an appointment by George Washington as Inspector of Customs, an appointment that was renewed by subsequent presidents — Adams, Jefferson, Madison — until in 1811 Madison named him as Naval Officer for the District of Boston and Charlestown. That also proved to be a sinecure, renewed by Monroe and John Quincy Adams. Such was the heroic paternity of the fugitive on the *Swiftsure*.

The ancestry of Herman's mother, Maria Gansevoort Melvill, was even more distinguished. Boy or man, Herman never learned very much in detail about the earliest Gansevoorts of Albany, descendants of men and women who had emigrated from Holland to Albany in the mid-seventeenth century, when that place, founded in 1624 as Fort Orange, was still in New Amsterdam. The site of Albany was strategic — the last gently elevated stretch on the western shore where the Hudson was still deep enough for oceangoing ships to navigate in the summer, even during a drought. Prospering as brewers, the Gansevoorts had married into all the best Dutch families of the colony, the Douws, the Ten Eycks, the Van Schaicks, the Van Vechtens, and even descendants of the first Patroon, Killian (or Kiliaen) Van Rensselaer, who had been granted ducal estates at the time of settlement. However little else they knew of their Dutch ancestry, Maria Gansevoort Melvill's children knew from earliest childhood that she was a cousin of the grandest living New Yorker of all, Stephen Van Rensselaer, the Eighth (or "Last") Patroon, who ruled from the Manor House at the north edge of Albany, his feudal privileges intact, until 1839, when he was succeeded by his namesake, under whom the privileges were eroded.

At eleven Herman knew that it was wholly out of character for his mother to become a confederate in a hasty and covert removal of furniture from their rented house. In the first days of October 1830, before the flight, Herman and his brother Gansevoort, three and a half years his elder, had been staying with their father in Manhattan, keeping what Allan in better times called "Bachelors' Hall," while his mother paid one of her frequent visits to her own mother in Albany (her father had been dead since 1812). This time even Gansevoort and Herman knew that "visiting" was the wrong word: she had taken refuge there with her four daughters and two younger sons. Just before their own flight, Allan Melvill had summoned Maria down to Manhattan, and she had supervised the loading of the furniture to take it to safety, away from the creditors. Herman had watched his brother Gansevoort, almost fifteen, play a man's role and escort her back up the river on the steamboat, which left without delay on the evening of 8 October for the night trip, the furniture (Allan Melvill noted in his diary for 9 October) pulled behind on the *Ontario Tow Boat* — so named because its route continued from Albany on the Erie Canal to the newer canal stretching north to Lake Ontario. There was irony for Maria in the name of the towboat, for its route north of the Erie Canal was the track of the British colonel Barry St. Leger's terrifying advance and precipitous rout — the invasion that made Maria's father, Peter Gansevoort, a revolutionary hero even greater than her husband's father.

Herman knew much about this gallant Gansevoort grandfather from family anecdotes, and he had even read about him in Thomas J. Rogers's *A New American Biographical Dictionary; or, Remembrancer of the Departed Heroes, Sages, and Statesmen, of America* (1825). That account was based on a draft supplied by Herman's uncle, Peter Jr. Born in Albany in 1749, educated at Princeton like Thomas Melvill, the older Peter Gansevoort had been a giant of a man by the measure of his time, three inches or so over six feet — about as tall as Washington himself. Before the outbreak of the Revolution he had "raised a company of grenadiers, distinguished alike for the correctness of their discipline and the grandeur of their appearance," every man being at least six feet tall in a century when the average height was several inches less. Gansevoort proved his worth in 1777, when the British attempted to cut off the New England colonies by invading the Hudson–Lake Champlain valley from both ends, north and south, while also attacking from the west. The Continental general Philip Schuyler relinquished Ticonderoga to the British general John Burgoyne and set himself to blocking Burgoyne's route south of Lake Champlain, to prevent his marching to Albany. Fort Schuyler, later called Fort Stanwix (in what is now Rome, New York), in that pre-canal century guarded the route over which goods had to be portaged from the Mohawk River, which flowed into the Hudson north of Albany, to the Oswego and thence to Lake Ontario and the St. Lawrence and the Atlantic. If it fell under early Iroquois attacks or fell to Colonel St. Leger's army, which had come down from Canada, then St. Leger could march unimpeded to join Burgoyne's army and take Albany. In August 1777 Peter Gansevoort undertook the defense of the fort and held it despite superior British cannons until Benedict Arnold (still the trusted patriot) approached with reinforcements and St. Leger retreated to Canada. On 2 September 1777 the Bostonian John Adams, cousin of Thomas Melvill's friend Samuel Adams, knowing that the fate of New England depended upon the Continental armies in New York, rejoiced in a letter to his wife: "Gansevoort has proved, that it is possible to hold a Post" (*Adams Family Correspondence*, 2, ed. L. H. Butterfield, Wendell D. Garrett, and Marjorie E. Sprague [1963]). Maria Melvill's father had defended a besieged fort and saved Albany, and therefore New York and (who cared to deny?) the Revolution, which Allan Melvill's father had helped to start at the Tea Party.

Thereafter General Peter Gansevoort was known as the "Hero of Fort Stanwix," even among his children and his grandchildren. None of the grandchildren ever saw him, but they were all taught to revere him. In the parlor of his widow, Catherine Van Schaick Gansevoort, he remained a palpable presence, not only through his array of military artifacts but also in a fine portrait, for the Hero had sat in peacetime for a portrait by Gilbert Stuart, the painter of national leaders, including Washington.

Details of the life of the Hero of Fort Stanwix, enriched for the older Melvill children by personal memories of the widow and her own children, after 1825 were supplemented by their Uncle Peter's narrative in Rogers's biographical dictionary. Herman and the other children learned that after the war General Gansevoort had taken up residence on Tory lands granted him in Northumberland in Saratoga County "and devoted his attention to agricultural pursuits" until 1790, when he was appointed sheriff of Albany County, an office his son Leonard would hold three decades later. On the Tory property, renamed Gansevoort, Northumberland, the general set up a sawmill to exploit the timber. General Gansevoort afterward "was appointed one of the commissioners for fortifying the northern and western frontiers of the state of New York, and to hold treaties with the Indians, on the part of the United States." In May 1802 President Jefferson appointed him military agent of the northern department of the United States, then, in February 1809, President Madison appointed him brigadier general in the army of the United States. In that rank he presided at the sensational court-martial of General James Wilkinson at Fredericktown, Virginia, for machinations, all but treasonous, in the new Louisiana territory. During his return from that trial, in the winter of 1812, General Gansevoort fell ill, lingering until 2 July 1812, when he died regretting that he could not serve his country in the new war with England.

Both the Gansevoorts and the belatedly arrived Melvills had been financially secure in late colonial society, and, despite the disruptions of the Revolution, that security was preserved into the first generation of independent Americans, those born during and just after the Revolution. In the new Republic both Thomas Melvill and Peter Gansevoort reaped the benefits of having been at or near the top of the colonial class system and of having served heroically in the Revolution. Still, their positions were challenged. In

1822, at the end of the Era of Good Feeling and the beginnings of the spoils system, the routine reappointment of the Hero of the Tea Party was challenged for the first time, as one of Thomas Jr.'s creditors tried to block the old major's reappointment by charging that father and son had colluded to defraud those creditors. That spring Allan had spent a month in Washington City on a rescue mission, and had secured his father's reappointment, thanks to his efforts and to the support of the Massachusetts senator Daniel Webster, with additional pressure from James D'Wolf, senator from Rhode Island (the uncle of Allan's brother-in-law John D'Wolf). In 1825 the new president, the Massachusetts man John Quincy Adams, routinely renewed the appointment of the venerable friend of his late cousin Samuel Adams.

In Northumberland through the 1820s Maria Gansevoort Melvill's oldest brother, Herman Gansevoort, confronted backwoods barbarism as he successfully struggled to keep possession of the farm and house that Congress had awarded the Hero of Fort Stanwix, intermittently challenged both by heirs of the old Tory owners and by jealous egalitarian backwoodsmen. In a letter to his brother Peter (26 January 1823), Herman Gansevoort reported that his neighbors had taken to carrying "a Gun with them on all occasions" and had spoken loudly to each other while he was standing on the front piazza: "there is old Hunks on his stoop — I want to ketch him out so as to have a shot at him." That April Herman Gansevoort reported to Peter: "My spring and piazza was last night besmear'd and the spring in a measure filled with Human Ordure — supposed to be done by the fiend old Osborn's wife." For all the uneasiness the Gansevoorts felt about the threats against their occupancy of the Tory lands, throughout Herman Melvill's childhood the family took pride when they went down the river and watched Manhattan buildings rising with roofs of hemlock that might well have come from their own lands in Gansevoort. The Hero of Fort Stanwix had sent his fourth son, Peter Gansevoort Jr. (born in 1788), to Princeton, as he had been sent. This younger Peter Gansevoort, Herman Melvill's uncle, extended himself west, speculating shrewdly in lands around the route of the proposed Erie Canal. He foresaw a great future for the Empire State, and he had the inside knowledge to keep his financial risks down, for in the late 1810s he was private secretary to Governor De Witt Clinton, the foremost promoter of the canal, and in the early 1820s he served on Clinton's military staff as judge advocate general.

While the Gansevoorts defended themselves bravely, or doggedly, when under siege, they were calculators, not gamblers. By contrast, all the male Melvills took reckless chances as well as calculated risks. After the Revolution Thomas Melvill was free to profit from trade that formerly had been controlled by the Crown. He profited, decade after decade, by his tenure as

Inspector of Customs and then Naval Officer at Boston. He had two sons who lived to adulthood, Thomas Jr., born in 1776, who attended West Boston Academy, then at fourteen was apprenticed to a West India merchant, and Allan, born in 1782 and educated at West Boston Academy and Staniford's Academy in Amherst, New Hampshire. Rather than sending his sons to college, the major, enriched by his patronage sinecure, sent them both to France, Thomas first, then, at the turn of the century, Allan. In Paris, Thomas Jr. moved among the small American diplomatic circle. He preserved a copy of a letter from Joel Barlow to Thomas Jefferson dated Paris, 15 March 1802, approving the American consul-general Fulwar Skipwith's suggestion that if he were to resign, Thomas Melvill Jr. should replace him as "our Commercial Agent" in Paris. Barlow, known to Herman Melvill's generation as an epic poet, author of *The Columbiad* (1807), had vouched for Thomas Jr.: "Mr Melvill has an excellent moral character, good talents, and sturdy republican principles. — He has established a banking, and Commercial house here, that is solid and well conducted; deserving, and enjoying an extensive credit. I doubt whether your Consulate here, could easily be placed in better hands." In the 1830s Thomas Jr. would claim to have been entrusted with "the papers of the Consulate," while "the functions of the Consular Agent" in France "were suspended, during the administration of the Elder Mr. Adams." Allan Melvill stayed almost two years in Paris with this cosmopolitan brother, learning to speak and write French fluently. He even went far afield in pre-Napoleonic Europe, crossing the Pyrenees on horseback in 1801. Major Melvill provided the capital for Allan to combine his grand tour with business, subsidizing him in importing expensive dry goods from France.

A book published in 1865 by the American Tract Society, *Records from the Life of S. V. S. Wilder*, contains an extraordinarily revealing account of Herman Melville's father. Prefaced by a quotation from Proverbs 10:4, "The hand of the diligent maketh rich," the book recounts a shrewd business transaction Wilder made in 1802. The transaction started Wilder on the road to riches, at the expense of a frantic young Allan Melvill, who had been entrusted with enormous amounts of money but lacked the calculatingly "diligent" hand that might have made him securely rich, now or later. As Wilder recollected, young Allan Melvill (Wilder used the common variant spelling "Melville") had purchased a fine cargo of French dry goods worth over thirty thousand dollars and brought it safely to the port of Boston, where he panicked about disposing of it. Wilder looked over the lot ("silks, satins, lutestrings, sarcenets, cambrics, thread laces, shawls, silk and kid gloves, hosiery, ribbons, artificial flowers, suspenders, fans, perfumery, ornamental combs, and other fancy articles") and saw at once that Melvill was asking from ten to fifteen or even twenty percent less than the going rate. Strong on business sense but short of cash, Wilder met a friend who offered to introduce him to the shipping magnate William Gray of Salem (the "King Billy" of Nathaniel Hawthorne's "Custom-House" essay in *The Scarlet Letter*), on the condition that Wilder offer Gray one-third of the profits; the friend required another third of the profits for his providing the introduction to Gray and the use of his large sales rooms, leaving the young and diligent Christian merchant Wilder a third for himself. With merely the promise of thirty thousand dollars from King Billy, not any actual cash, young Wilder "closed the bargain with Melville, had the goods delivered the following morning, and advertised and ready the same day" in State Street sales rooms, to which customers thronged. Wilder concluded his story triumphantly: "Suffice it to say, that in five days every case of goods was sold except three, which I took on my own account. At the end of a week the money was all realized, and I went at once and paid Mr. Melville. I also prepared a receipt for one third of the profits, $1,875, ready for Mr. Gray to sign."

Allan Melvill, the hapless young man in this transaction, could have rented a large sales room for a small sum and disposed of the goods himself, for a profit of some five thousand dollars beyond any profit he may actually have made — an enormous sum, enough to buy a good house on a good street in Boston or New York City. Allan Melvill possessed already, in 1802, the discriminating taste and judgment that allowed him to identify desirable lots of merchandise and the enterprise that allowed him to purchase them and see them aboard ship for the United States. He lacked, however, something he never acquired, the basic bourgeois marketing skills required if he were to compete with shrewd young entrepreneurs, professedly Christian or not. At this crisis in 1802 he inexplicably lacked as well the careful supervision that his father, so knowledgeable about commerce, ought to have exhibited in his behalf.

Even in the years following 1805, when British ships preyed on commercial shipping between the new United States and France, Major Thomas Melvill continued to subsidize Allan's voyages to France for dry goods — voyages that exposed him, each time, to possible boarding and seizure by British ships; in 1811 the British seized and sailed off to Halifax a ship of which Allan owned half the cargo, though he was not aboard it at the time. During the War of 1812, when Allan could not venture to Europe, he made buying and selling trips along the coast, and, increasingly, up the Hudson to Albany, where late in 1813 he began courting Maria Gansevoort. The Hero of Fort Stanwix had given Maria a good education at home in all that it was thought a woman should know, including years of lessons on a piano he imported from London for her. She was perfectly trained to play hostess to governors and senators, to manage as fine a household as existed in the young Republic, and to nourish children to carry on all the best family traditions. After their wartime marriage, in October 1814, Allan Melvill moved into the spacious house of his mother-in-law on North Market Street, where the Hero had died two years before, and set up a wholesale dry-goods business in town.

After 1815 Allan Melvill did not have to worry about British seizure of American vessels, but he had to try to find a niche in a new national economy that still lacked a stable system for marketing imports. In the first years after the war the Melvills prudently stayed in Albany, where their first two children were born, Gansevoort in December 1815 and Helen Maria in August 1817. Gradually Allan Melvill became restless, as he realized that New York City was destined to become the commercial capital of the country. In 1818 his desire to make a buying trip to France coincided with the chance to do some business for his father in Scotland. Major Thomas Melvill was closest surviving kin to the late General Robert Melvill, the governor of Guadaloupe in 1760, then from 1763 to 1770 the governor of Grenada, the Grenadines, Dominica, St. Vincent, and Tobago, islands France had ceded to England at the end of the French and Indian War. The value of the estate, Thomas Melvill had heard, amounted to one hundred thousand pounds. He gave Allan the responsibility of making inquiries in Scotland before proceeding to his business in Paris. On this trip, in England, Scotland, and France, Allan Melvill moved, as before, in high social circles. He dined with the poet and prose writer William Roscoe in Liverpool (Roscoe's 1795 life of Lorenzo de' Medici was standard). In Edinburgh he called upon the "famous Mr Jeffrey," founder of the *Edinburgh Review*, then dined at his country seat, as he wrote to Maria on 31 May 1818. He also passed an evening with Jeffrey and his family at their town house, where they lived "in high style" and moved "in the most exalted circles," he assured his wife. He carried away a love token, an early rose that he mailed to her from Paris on 11 June ("The enclosed Flower was plucked with my own hands in the Garden of Mr Jeffreys charming & classical retreat of Craigcrook House"). (His son Herman, when older than his father was in 1818, set himself to learn basic aesthetic concepts from some of Lord Jeffrey's exemplary early pieces in the *Edinburgh Review*.)

On 26 May 1818, Allan called on the earl of Leven and Melville at Melville House. The earl received him courteously enough, gave him a chamber overnight, informed him that the estate of his kinsman General Robert Melvill was entailed and unavailable to American claimants, then sent him on his way with an "engraved Portrait of the first Earl as a sacred Memento" and an ineffaceable memory of "the events of a day at Melville House," as Allan wrote the earl on 5 July 1818. Both men were a little awkward about their family connection, especially since Allan had not armed himself in advance with information as to his precise connection to the earl. Nevertheless, the earl obligingly gave Allan the address of his son in London, but when Allan presented himself the son coolly begged off, as Allan explained to his own father ("he informed me by note that indispensable engagements in the pending Elections prevented his calling at my Lodgings").

Unabashed, Allan did some research, and on 31 May he wrote his father of his findings in "Douglas Baronage of Scotland" and "Crawford," both of which listed their ancestors, the Melvilles of Carnbee, the founders of which line, Allan found, "were related to Queen Margaret consort of Malcolm Canmere & came with her from Hungary." Beyond that, he had news for his "good Mother" — that the Scollays of the Orkneys "sprang originally from the Kings of Norway." Allan followed the news with this reflection: "so it appears we are of a royal line in both sides of the House — after all it is not only an amusing but a just cause of pride, to resort back through the ages to such ancestry, & should produce a correspondent spirit of emulation in their descendants to the remotest posterity." From Paris on 5 July 1818 Allan wrote to the earl of Leven and Melville that he had found the Boston family was "recognized in Douglas' Baronage as belonging to the same branch of the 'illustrious House of Melville,' as the late General Robert Melvill of Strathkinness & Craigtoun," to whom his father was "Cousin German & acknowledged Heir at Law," and that General Robert Melvill and the Hero of the Tea Party were "great Grand Sons of Sir John Melvill knighted by King James the 6th as Baron of Carnbee & Grantoun in 1580, whose great Grandfather also Sir John of Carnbee was killed on the memorable field of Flodden in 1513." As an American, Allan Melvill felt obliged to justify his research to himself, if not to his kinsman: "it is always interesting to the Individual to trace back his ancestry to a noble source, & I assure you it is with no little pride of heart & elevation of sentiment, that I consider myself a Descendant of the ancient and honourable House of Melvill, & shall always entertain for your Lordship as its legitimate Head, the most profound respect & consideration." Happy as he was that the best authorities had "unequivocally established the lineage" of his family, he assured the earl of Leven and Melville that Americans had much less regard for birth than Europeans. Two generations and two wars removed from the British Isles, Allan had absorbed the prevailing ideas about the differences in American and in British attitudes toward ancestry, but his image of himself was enlivened by his sense of who his ancestors had been — the assurance that he was of royal lineage on both sides of the family.

In his letter from Paris Allan Melvill also expatiated to his noble kinsman on his financial plans:

I have been induced by the advice of my commercial Friends here & at home, & various important personal considerations, to establish myself permanently at New York, a City of unexampled growth & prosperity, & of unrivalled local resources & foreign intercourse, which must become the great Emporium of the western World — my acquaintances there are numerous and respectable, and my Wife's Family and Connexions who are among the first People in the State, (the Gansevoorts & Van Schaicks, of dutch extraction,) will afford me the same consideration I enjoy in my native town.

Armed with a loan of sixty-five hundred dollars from his father, Allan purchased in Paris dry goods in quantity sufficient for him to "re-establish" himself (as he anticipated in a draft of a letter to J. S. Cast on 31 October 1817) "on a permanent & respectable foundation" in New York City. This was his last voyage to Europe. In November 1818, about the time Herman was conceived, Allan advertised in Manhattan papers as "an importer of French goods and Commission merchant," a wholesale merchant, at 123 Pearl Street. When Herman was three, Allan Melvill did some calculations that he recorded under the title "Recapitulations of Voyages and Travels from 1800 to 1822 both inclusive": "by land 24425 miles. by water 48460 miles. days at sea, etc. 643." Small wonder that Herman and his older brother saw their French-speaking father as a dashing, romantic adventurer, a great traveler, not a stay-at-home dry-goods merchant.

The reviewer of Herman Melville's *Pierre* in the Boston *Daily Advertiser* (7 August 1852) complained that the author had taken "the Hero" of that story "from the very highest aristocracy of the country, so high one hardly knows where to look for it." Herman and his older brother and sister did not have to look for it: they knew they belonged to the very highest aristocracy of the country. In the generation of Melville's parents, family members and many friends had served in state and national legislatures, and in their young lifetimes an uncle, Leonard Gansevoort, had been sheriff of Albany County. Some of the family acquaintances, most recently the younger Adams, had become president. In Albany, Allan and Maria Melvill, through Peter Gansevoort Jr., were on intimate terms with Governor De Witt Clinton and his wife. In Boston the old major still had a few surviving cronies from the Revolution (though his special friend Samuel Adams was long dead), and friends of the family of the next generation included members of the wealthy Appleton family, the shipping magnate Daniel P. Parker, the statesman Daniel Webster, and Lemuel Shaw, the lawyer who had been engaged to marry Herman's aunt Nancy Wroe Melvill when she died in 1813, and who in 1830, shortly before Allan Melvill's flight from Manhattan, became chief justice of the Supreme Court of Massachusetts. Beyond his consciousness of a double revolutionary descent, Herman was silently reminded by the engraved portrait of the earl of Leven and Melville that the Melvill blood derived from knights and lords and kings of Scotland, and his father emphasized that descent through his tales of his stay with the earl, and reminded Herman and the other children, also, that the Scollays, even though they lacked an ancestral seat an American could visit, were descended from kings of Norway. Vaguely but powerfully, there loomed the idea (although not an engraved portrait) of Queen Margaret of Hungary far back in the family ancestry. In Herman's own generation all the heroic noble qualities of the family ancestry were concentrated in the dazzling person of his brother Gansevoort Melvill, three and a half unbridgeable years older, possessing gifts and achieving triumphs impossible to rival.

For all the glorious remote ancestry of the Melvills and the family's substantial post-revolutionary wealth, Allan Melvill, like his older brother, Thomas Jr., was helpless to augment the family fortune or even to preserve it. Through the 1820s Thomas Jr. and Allan Melvill lived deeply in debt to their father. Out of his profits from the contract for feeding British prisoners during the War of 1812 at Pittsfield, a frontier outpost in the Berkshires of western Massachusetts, Thomas Jr. had repaid his father something like fourteen thousand dollars — a fortune. During the war, in 1814, the French wife Thomas Jr. had married in Paris died in Pittsfield, and the next year he married Mary Ann Augusta Hobart (1796–1884), a daughter of Dudley B. Hobart, collector of the port of Bath, and Sophia Dearborn, whose father was Major General Henry Dearborn, secretary of war under Jefferson and, as Collector of Customs at Boston, an associate of old Major Melvill. (Hobart died young, in 1806, and Sophia in 1814.) The farm Thomas Jr. lived on south of Pittsfield, then known as the Watson place (later the Melvill place, then Broadhall, and later still the Pittsfield Country Club), was not his own but his father's, purchased in 1816. Thomas often failed even to pay the taxes on it, in 1820 cavalierly directing the collector to send the bill to the old major. His farming methods were progressive, to judge from accounts in the local papers, but unprofitable. Three months after Herman Melvill's birth Thomas Jr. gave an address to the Berkshire Agricultural Society on the trade deficit with Great Britain (Pittsfield *Sun*, 10 November 1819): "Shall we go to Europe and to India for clothing, when we have the raw materials, and of the very best quality within ourselves? In short, shall we supinely sacrifice national industry, and jeopardise our independence for the gewgaws and luxuries of other countries?" Struggling in their diverse ways to survive in the postwar economy, Thomas argued for protection of American agriculture and manufacturing even while Allan was importing from France luxuries that he had to try to persuade New Yorkers to buy despite their cost.

During the decade of the 1820s Thomas Jr. shamed his family by spending months in debtors' prison in the Berkshire shire town (or county seat) of Lenox, Massachusetts. Whatever had happened in the Melvill family during the previous two or three decades, in Paris and in this country, by the 1820s the father habitually treated the younger Allan as the good, responsible son while casting the firstborn Thomas into the role of the prodigal. Thomas Jr. in fact behaved at times with astonishing effrontery, as in presenting himself before Peter Gansevoort Jr. during his brother's absence abroad in 1818 and soliciting a loan, for which he left (as Allan wrote his father on 28 March 1820) a "Portmanteau cont'g some plate & a few Jewels belonging to his Wife," collateral that Thomas Jr. had previously pledged to Allan for a loan. (This staking of one piece of collateral for two distinct loans from different creditors recurred in 1850, the tragically disingenuous borrower being Herman Melville.) On 26 April 1820 the old major wrote Allan that he had "but one Letter from Thomas for a long time — and that was in the old way," excusing himself and begging anew. The Hero was in despair: "I have no hope that he will ever alter his conduct." On 16 April 1822, after Thomas Jr. had been released from prison, Allan hoped that he would now "enjoy the fruits of liberty in a rational manner," but realism required him to tell his father that they could "never repose confidence" in Thomas: "I pity him as a Man from my soul, & am incapable of cherishing resentment towards a Brother — but as your Friend & son, I entreat you never to put it in his power to do you an injury." The father participated in this mutual commiseration even as he advanced more money to the younger son than to the elder, and Allan's moral disapproval of his irresponsible brother went unchecked by any recognition that his own financial dealings were reckless. In the 1820s both the brothers, Thomas and Allan Melvill, while begetting numerous children, were living on money amassed before or during the Revolution or else amassed and sustained by the subsequent efforts of the revolutionary generation.

Throughout the 1820s in Manhattan Allan Melvill took responsible precautions to remove his family from the annual epidemic of cholera, typhus fever, or (in 1822) the far more dreaded "pestilential yellow fever," but in his view of the world, Fortune governed human destiny, not human design and individual enterprise. After a shipwreck in 1819 he had lamented to his father that Fortune had played him "many a scurvy trick," but he would "not complain of the fickle Goddess," who might yet be inclined to smile graciously upon him. Instead of repining, he would endeavor to merit the "future favours" of Fortune "by patience, resignation and perseverance." A month after Herman's birth Allan Melvill had assured his father: "I am neither emulous of riches or distinction, they are both insufficient to ensure happiness, or purchase health, a man may do very well in private life with a mere competency, & if I can only provide for the rational wants of my beloved Wife & children, I shall be content with my lot, & bless the hand from which all favours come." Realistically speaking, his only distinction in Boston was as the son of the Hero of the Tea Party and in New York as the son-in-law of the Hero of Fort Stanwix, and he was in truth avid for riches. A few merchants were amassing such riches even in the precarious years after the second war for independence — merchants blessed with local connections, even better credit than he, and an established clientele. Philosophy was one thing, behavior another, and "rational wants" were something Allan Melvill was always willing to provide for by irrational borrowing when money was scarce and when his own needs were pressing.

To counter pestilences that attacked human bodies and the body politic alike, Melvill depended upon ample family resources in Albany and Boston. On 20 May 1820, while she was visiting in New York, Catherine Van Schaick Gansevoort made her daughter Maria an advance against her inheritance in "the sum of Two Thousand Dollars" (a codicil to her will, in the New York Public Library). On 12 June 1820, with his mother-in-law's money in hand, Allan, once again reassuring his father that he would never involve the old man in any possible risk, declared that he had credit in New York to "command any reasonable sum" he needed, a fact he had proved by obtaining what amounted to short-term loans at low interest rates: "my Note at six months for a larger amount in payment of Goods by which I have already *realized* a handsome profit, has been freely discounted at an Insurance Office for ½ per C^t a month — no Endorser has ever been required of me in any transaction, & I am proud to believe my reputation as a Merchant firmly established throughout the City." Yet on 27 March 1821, Allan borrowed two thousand dollars from his father. Late in 1822 Allan asked his old friend the Boston lawyer Lemuel Shaw to renew a promissory note for four months, since he had "considerable money to pay next month" and was "desirous of making some immediate remittances to France." When he had not heard from Shaw by 30 December, Allan wrote a less expansive letter: now Shaw's renewal of the note "would be a particular accommodation at this season."

On 25 May 1822 Allan Melvill wrote to Lemuel Shaw: "Business . . . has suddenly declined, owing in some measure to the scarcity of money which affects everything." In his view, recovery was contingent upon events a world away, the equivalent of a whim of Fortune: "the anticipated struggle between the Ottoman & the Muscovite" might "possibly involve other parts of Europe" and enable Americans "again to profit by their folly." The immediate enemy of his security, as he lamented year after year, was the auction system, since he had to rent space on a long-term basis in order to display older as well as newer wares, whereas the auction houses could rent space, advertise widely, sell speedily at a discount, and dump any odd remainders. On 23 November 1822 he typically reported to Peter Gansevoort: "Business at private sale is rather dull, for the Auctions engross more than ever, & injure us most essentially." He wrote characteristically to Shaw on 9 December 1822: "Business which has been very brisk without much profit since our return to the City, has suddenly declined, but we anticipate its early revival in the Spring under favourable auspices." An upturn was always about to occur the next season, or in the next year. It seems never to have occurred to him that he might alter his commercial habits and merchandize his own goods as efficiently and profitably as his competitors did.

In the winter of 1823–24 Peter Gansevoort and Allan Melvill exchanged tense words about Allan's borrowing against Maria's inheritance. Peter's anxiety was linked to the death in December 1821 of his brother Leonard, recently the sheriff of Albany, who had left a widow, Mary Ann Chandonette Gansevoort, and five children (Peter, born in 1810; Guert, in 1812; Catherine, in 1814; Leonard, in 1816; and Stanwix, posthumously, in 1822). Unable to support herself and her children in a private house, Aunt Mary and her children lived for extended periods with her mother-in-law and Peter. She was forced to let her three older sons go to sea while they were boys, hardly older, in Guert's case, than Herman was when he boarded the *Swiftsure* for Albany in 1830. Peter saw to it that Mary did not gain early access to her late husband's portion of the estate: it was enough that Maria's husband was making constant inroads on *her* portion. The situation created tensions between Maria and Mary, for all their intimacy, as well as between Maria and Peter. Maria Melvill did not like to write letters, but her husband left her the task, on 11 March 1824, of broaching the subject of the estrangement between her husband and her brother: "It appears strange to me that circumstances should be allowed to change or weaken an attachment which I had every reason to suppose firmly seated on a Rock of Friendship, & supported by Pillars of consanguinity." She hoped she was "deceiv'd" but feared she was not: "their seems an indescribable something which whispers me I have lost that place in your heart & esteem which I had vainly hoped would have been mine through Life." (Never did she hint to her brother that she was in any way displeased with her husband's conduct of financial matters: tensions between her and her husband went unrecorded.)

Early in April 1826 Peter refused to renew one of Allan's promissory notes to him beyond the date it was payable, 14 April, whereupon Allan besought him not only to loan him money but to do so covertly: "I have now to request that you would forward me *immediately* your note for $2013.75 at 4 mos from 21st February, which if you could make it payable to James

Stevenson, or some other friend, might obviate the necessity of obtaining an endorsement here which I should like to avoid — & it would at the same time give it the appearance of a mercantile transaction." When he had reached the point of wanting a family loan to bear the false appearance of a mere mercantile transaction, Allan was deeply involved in financial duplicity. On 1 July 1826 Allan suddenly decided to go to Boston for a week, and not go alone. Instead, he took his wife and three daughters and his smallest son, his namesake. Word from an employee, Cyrus Chenery, followed Allan on 20 July: "Banks & Insurance offices" were failing; and it was said "that money was never so scarce in this City as at this moment." This was not a pleasure trip. Allan's purpose in displaying his wife and four helpless children was to weaken his father's resistance, and on 24 July the old man loaned him another five hundred dollars. That December Allan again appealed urgently to Peter, this time for the loan of three or four thousand dollars, which "with expectations from another quarter" would carry him "through the Winter with comparative ease." Peter obliged, once again.

Early in 1827 Allan Melvill involved himself in a vaguely recorded but dangerous scheme wherein he risked money on people who had no capital of their own; in order to participate, he all but extorted money from Peter by confessing that further advances were necessary in order to save what had already been invested. On 10 February Allan wrote Peter, explaining that the "new project," news of which had upset Peter, was set to "go into full operation on the 1st March next, with as many advantages & good prospects as ever dawned upon a similar establishment." It was "entirely a *confidential Connexion* with Persons combining every qualification but money" — and Allan had only to supply the money. Without "*seasonable & adequate assistance*" the project would be "for ever blasted in the bud," to the detriment of "those dear ones" around him. In fact, Allan had already pledged himself "to advance Ten Thousand Dollars as a Capital during three years" — capital that would have to come from his father or his mother-in-law. He did not scruple to manipulate Peter through his love of his only sister and his fondness for his nephews and nieces, including Herman:

> Therefore as you value my present welfare & future existence, disappoint me not I beseech you, in an emergency fraught with all that is personally dear to me in life, & which ever involves the present & ultimate happiness of my Family — if you do, which kind heaven in mercy avert, I shall know not whither in this World to turn for succor in the very crisis of my fate, & all, all may be lost to me forever....
>
> We are all in usual health except your little protégé Herman, who although a Monitor at the High School, is rather indisposed this eveᵍ.

Peter did not withstand this folly any more than old Thomas Melvill ever had done.

The strain so shattered Melvill's urbane facade that on 2 March 1827 he wrote Peter a febrile thanksgiving: "so vital to my hopes was the favour you have most promptly granted . . . that in spite of a fortitude of soul, firmness of purpose & energy & action, . . . my nerves were at the instant unstrung, while my heart involuntarily poured forth its ascriptions of praise to the divine Parent of all good, & my eyes betrayed the deep feeling that agitated both mind & body, & even now affects my whole frame." Whatever the stance of the "divine Parent of all good," Peter's acquiescence is difficult to understand, and, as he must have expected, he received a still more frantic letter on 30 March 1827. Now Allan beseeched Peter for five thousand dollars to fulfill his "engagements to *the concern*," on which depended all his "present hopes & future prospects." Allan begged: "as you esteem me, & *love our dear Maria*, do not I conjure you as a friend & Brother, disappoint me, in the *utmost need . . . or all will be lost even to my honour*, & I hereby pledge myself never to request your responsibility for an additional sum." The next day Allan wrote another appeal, before Peter could have answered, and on 1 April Peter did sent him a note on his order for five thousand dollars. A month later Peter was in New York, trying to see what Allan had done with all the money. From there he blandly reported to his mother that Maria and her family were in excellent health and that "Mr M." talked of going to Boston right away — to beg from his father. There he got twenty-five hundred dollars to throw after the rest.

The clever confederates who lacked only money now had received vast sums of money garnered by the Hero of Fort Stanwix and the Hero of the Tea Party, and Allan was left empty-handed. He wrote to Peter Gansevoort on 22 February 1828 that he was working for salary: "I make known to you as a Friend & Brother that I have formed a *confidential* connexion with the highly respectable general Commission House of Messrs L P De Luze & Co in the Dry Goods branch of their Business of a nature at once safe pleasant & encouraging, which will afford me a liberal compensation for my services & a certain support for my Family during the present year." On 10 March 1828 Allan wrote Peter a farrago of misplaced religiosity, well-grounded dread for his future, and apprehension for his wife and children, all infused with near-total denial of his own irresponsibility: "My humble yet ardent confidence, in the constant protection, & eventual bounty of our almighty Parent, has been strong & unwavering, this alone could have sustained me in a fearful & protracted struggle which would otherwise have overwhelmed the boldest spirit & the stoutest heart." In view of the precariousness of his situation, Allan was not merely specious but dishonest two weeks later, on 27 March, when he offered Lemuel Shaw "3 first rate Notes" to his own order, amounting to $6539.26.

With his sinecure as the Naval Officer already under siege from the Boston Jacksonians, old Major Melvill added up the money at his control, funds by which he must support himself, his wife, and three unmarried daughters, and on 19 February 1829 added a clause to his will: "Item. And whereas I have lent and may hereafter lend to my son Allan considerable sums of money, for which I have taken or may hereafter take his promissory notes, or other security, it is hereby declared that all such sums are to be considered as debts due to my estate." Later the old major's executor, Lemuel Shaw, told Maria Melvill that the Hero of the Tea Party had added the clause at Allan's insistence; in any case, on a visit to Boston from 2 through 14 July 1829 Allan must have learned that his father had put a provision into his will protecting his other children from Allan's debts. The clause itself was only fair to the other children; the question is why the old major had lent so much money to Allan, year after year, and why he was so belated in declaring those loans as debts against his estate, just now when his own position in the custom house no longer seemed invulnerable.

In 1829 the next president, Andrew Jackson, had good reason to turn out anyone his predecessor had appointed. Despite frantic efforts by Allan and others, after his inauguration in March Jackson swiftly replaced the "old Veteran of the Revolution & a vigilant dauntless & incorruptible Officer during every administration" (Allan's anticipatory words to his brother-in-law Peter on 13 February 1829). Thomas Jr. on 20 April 1829 rose to the rhetorical needs of the occasion and wrote his father unctuously, flattering himself that the Hero's "long, and meritorious services in Civil office," his "devotion to our Country during the whole period of our Revolutionary War," and his "daring chivalric deed in the destruction of the Tea," should have insured his reappointment from any president of the United States. Instead, merit and service had been sacrificed "at the shrine of party spirit, in favor of partizans!!!" Herman Melvill and his brothers and sisters heard similar lamentation at home, for Allan wrote to Peter on 26 April: "Alas poor Senate thy glory long since departed," and on 6 May Allan added his eulogy in a letter to his father: "you retired from the Custom House with the firmness & dignity of an old Roman which in rendering you if possible more than ever dear to me increases my indignation at the rude injustice of your removal, & though as a Christian I may in time forgive, as a Son I will never forget the Man, nor shall my Children while they remember you & me forget him, who might & should have prevented it—I mean General Jackson, for I cannot consider him de facto President of my Country." The older boys learned thus early that the United States might betray even the most loyal of patriots, but the vagaries of American politics and national iconography were such that Allan's firstborn later delivered a great Jackson Day oration and slept overnight as Jackson's guest in what had become a Democratic shrine, the Hermitage, and Herman in *Moby-Dick* (ch. 26) portrayed Jackson as all but deified. Herman absorbed, from family attitudes, a disdain for partisanship which he applied not just to politics but to literature, as when he commented, much later, on lines 115–31 of Milton's "Lycidas": "Mark the deforming effect of the intrusion of partizan topics & feelings of the day, however serious in import, into a poem otherwise of the first order of merit."

On 8 June 1830, shortly after Allan made a frantic visit to Albany, Peter pressured his mother to add a codicil to her will. Bowing to the weight of the evidence against her son-in-law, Catherine Van Schaick Gansevoort ordered her executors to "pay the income and profits of one equal fourth part [of the interest on bonds] thereof to my daughter Maria during her natural life for her separate use; free from the debts and controll of her said husband." The $10,250 ("or thereabouts") that Allan had borrowed remained unpaid, and "the said Allan Melvill" had declared to her "his inability to pay the said notes when they shall become due and payable." Therefore, she directed that the sum be charged against the inheritance of her daughter Maria and her children, payable to "the said Peter Gansevoort." Another provision on the same day concerned pairs of memorial spoons ("on one of which spoons shall be neatly engraved the name of my husband, the time of his death and his age, and on the other my name, the time of my death and my age, and on each shall also be engraved the initials of the name of him or her for whom such spoons are above directed to be made"). This provision became, over the next decade and a half, a source of particular bitterness within the family. Maria's spoons were "to be held in trust" by the executors, Herman and Peter Gansevoort, treated "in the same manner" that her share of her mother's "residuary real and personal estates" would be treated; the widow and her son Peter may have been afraid that Allan would pawn or auction the spoons, or they may have feared that a creditor would seize them. When he left Albany in early May, Allan must have realized that he had borrowed his last thousand dollars from Catherine Van Schaick Gansevoort.

Yet Allan Melvill still had a source of funds, his unemployed and aged father. Financial pressures pushed Allan into a hasty trip to Boston in June, sooner than he had planned, and on 15 June his father loaned him $2500. Allan was still there in Boston, or back with his son Gansevoort, on 10 July, when he borrowed yet another $1000. No one knows what he was doing with the money—perhaps handing it over to smooth business associates; he was not importing unsalable French dry goods. A letter that Lemuel Shaw wrote to Maria Melvill on 12 February 1834 exonerates Allan with cold comfort:

"In 1830, Allan's affairs were at such a crisis, that he thought it of the utmost importance in order to make a favorable settlement of his affairs, & to pay such claims as he considered to be of an honorary character . . . and his father upon that occasion, advanced him about $3500 — which relieved him from the very urgent pressure under which he was then laboring." In Shaw's account, Allan had suggested that his father treat the loans "as a debt, which should be a charge upon his expected portion of his father's estate," and he "often and strongly urged" his father to write that provision into his will, which the old man then did, but the provision in fact dated from the previous year. In 1830 the "settlement" of Allan's affairs was achieved through the expedient of his assigning to Peter Gansevoort any remaining interest he held in the dubious partnership he had formed in 1827.

In 1830, apparently, Allan raised what few dollars he could by auctioning off some of his finer books, including *The Anatomy of Melancholy*, purchased in 1816. Perhaps at last Allan Melvill learned the hard lesson he had taught his brother in August 1821, when Thomas Jr., hoping to sell an engraving in a gilded frame for a few dollars, quoted back his brother's words: "The value of a thing, is exactly what it will bring" — in such cases, a tiny fraction of the purchase price. One particular lawsuit by a creditor forced Allan to weigh some ugly possibilities, among them abject flight out of the state of New York to Boston or another city of refuge. Failing at forming a new company, he considered the necessity of taking what Peter could get him, a clerk's job in a small Albany branch of a Manhattan fur company — a vacillation recorded in a pathetic series of letters to Peter in July 1830. On 3 August, two days after Herman's eleventh birthday, Allan Melvill urgently asked Peter Gansevoort for advice: "After having commenced this suit, can they now molest me at Boston or elsewhere out of the State? — in what time can they recover judgment?" He wondered if he could give an unidentified "JM" "a Bill of Sale" for his furniture in "part payment" of his debt "& secure the use of it by a lease from him." On 11 August he did not scruple to bring Maria's health into an appeal to Peter; by now she was fully apprised of the financial realities: "[Maria's] spirits are occasionally more than ever depressed, while the family requires extraordinary attention, & unless she soon obtains relief from mental excitement, by some favorable change in our condition & prospects, I fear that her health will suffer permanent injury — she is very desirous of removing to Albany, to enjoy once more the society of her connexions & friends & feel at home & if possible happy, which she never has been, & never can be here." The boys witnessed in their father a comprehensive denial of reality in these months, for Allan at times probably treated them the way he could still treat Peter, to whom he offered a pronouncement on political affairs in this letter on 4 September:

I congratulate you in the glorious Revolution in France, & the triumph of the majesty of the People over the despotism of a Tyrant—it is a lesson which I think both Kingcraft & Priestcraft will long remember, & may not be altogether unavailable even to republican Rulers, for Men in Power are naturally prone to tyranny, & the people may be oppressed under any form of Government, for after all Pope said truly, that the one least administered was best, it may not be orthodox in Politics but it is true in Practise.

"Our friend Shaw," he added, would "make an admirable Chief justice." Dumbfoundingly, the tone was not that of a failure's abashed and hesitant allusion to a friend's remarkable success; it was the tone of a man as confident of his place in society as his friend the new chief justice.

In September Maria left for Albany with her daughters and her two younger sons, the month before Allan Melvill summoned her down to spirit the furniture up the river in the *Ontario Tow Boat* while he lingered a day longer with Herman before boarding the boat whose very name mocked him, the *Swiftsure*. From the deck of the *Swiftsure* Herman's close look at Fort Gansevoort, erected in 1812–13 a short way up the Hudson from Cortlandt Dock, was like a last farewell to the statewide and even national fame of his distinguished Albany grandfather. All day 10 October and that night they steamed upriver, arriving at Albany shortly before noon on 11 October, the terrified boy and the broken man. Herman had steamed up and down that river since he was in the womb, but this time the voyage was final: in Manhattan there was nothing to go back for and no one to go back to.

Herman Melvill's World, 1819–1830
Manhattan, Albany, Boston

Education
Forms the Mind and Manners.

"Allan Melvills Book," 1796

To outward appearances, the Herman Melvill who fled Manhattan with his fugitive father in 1830 had lived for eleven years a privileged, protected life, a patrician childhood exceptional in the rough-and-tumble young Republic. The Manhattan household of the boy's first decade consisted of loving (almost doting) and apparently wealthy parents, supported by attentive if transient nurses, tutors (at times a live-in teacher), and other servants (three or more at a time, sometimes including, besides the female cook and housemaids, an almost supererogatory male waiter). During Herman's first decade, Maria Gansevoort Melvill was a thoughtful and loving daughter, sister, wife, and mother. Herman was secure in the knowledge that there was a large and seemingly permanent cast of characters in his personal drama: three remarkable living grandparents, few uncles but many aunts, a fixed number of Gansevoort cousins (after the posthumous birth of his Cousin Stanwix in 1822), an enlarging set of seldom-seen Melvill cousins, and, most happily, at home, besides his older brother and sister, a regularly expanding set of brothers and sisters (girl, boy, girl, girl, boy), until January 1830, when there were eight children in all. The children were all part of Herman's world, once they were born, for, exceptionally, no child of Allan and Maria Melvill died at birth or in infancy. Until the flight of 1830, Herman lived in fine new Manhattan houses with progressively larger play yards (the last had an entire extra city lot on Broadway) and visited regularly the big Albany house filled with historical mementos and, less often, a big dark trophied box of a house in crooked historic Boston, as well as the house of John and Mary Melvill D'Wolf, magnificently sited on Narragansett Bay, and, as a convenient stopover, his grandfather's fine estate in the Berkshires, outside Pittsfield, occupied by his uncle Thomas Melvill and his second wife and children.

In February 1819, three months pregnant with Herman, Maria Gansevoort Melvill and her two children left Manhattan for the comfort of the Gansevoort house in Albany, 160 miles upriver. The steamboat ride still took twenty hours, so it was not a trip to be taken lightly, even by a man traveling alone. In his journal for 12 May 1819 Allan recorded: "Commenced House-keeping at No. 6 Pearl Street, New York," Maria and the children having arrived back from Albany that day, to go into the new house, one about which no details are known. Allan reported to his father on 10 July that Maria continued "well & in good spirits," although his own anxiety was increasing as she approached her time, which they thought probably would "not extend beyond the 20th." In anticipation Allan had engaged "Dr Post & a good nurse," and besought higher aid for his wife, humbly hoping "that He who has hitherto preserved will again sustain her in the hour of peril." Ten days later Maria was still (as her husband wrote his father) "remarkably well considering her situation," and attending "to the Family as usual." Allan was concerned enough for the two of them: "my anxiety increases as she ap-proaches the term of her deliverance, which cannot exceed many days — may GOD in his infinite mercy sustain her at this trying hour."

Herman Melvill was born at 11:30 P.M. on Sunday, 1 August 1819, at 6 Pearl Street in New York City. The doctor, Wright Post, attended Maria at the delivery. Although delayed beyond the date the parents had figured on, the birth was without complications. Visiting in the house when Herman was born were the father's sister Mary and her husband, Captain John D'Wolf — known as "Norwest John," and already immortalized in G. H. von Langs-dorff's *Voyages and Travels in Various Parts of the World, during the Years 1803, 1804, 1805, 1806 and 1807* (London, 1813, and Philadelphia, 1817) as the man who had crossed Siberia with Langsdorff in 1807. On 2 August 1819 Allan Melvill wrote to his brother-in-law Peter in Albany: "With a grateful heart I hasten to inform you of the birth of another Nephew, which joyous event occurred at ½ past 11 last night — our dear Maria displayed her ac-customed fortitude in the hour of peril, & is as well as circumstances & the intense heat will admit — while the little Stranger has good lungs, sleeps well & feeds kindly, he is in truth a chopping Boy." Allan Melvill announced Herman's birth to a business associate in Paris: "Mme Melvill s'est heureuse-ment accouchée le 1er courant d'un beau Garcon, et la mère et l'enfant se portent à merveilles." Allan's announcement to his father is lost, but a letter written on 13 August conveyed good news: "Maria dined below yesterday & to day, & is fast regaining her usual strength, the Babe is also doing well & is a very promising Child, I humbly trust we shall not be unmindful of these repeated blessings of Providence."

Taking no chances with Providence, however, the Melvills on 19 August had the new baby baptized — "Herman," after Maria's oldest brother, Herman Gansevoort; one or more of his sisters later thought he had been given three names, "Herman Gansevoort Melvill." The baptism was performed at home by the Reverend Mr. J. M. Mathews, of the South Reformed Dutch Church, as Allan noted in the "Family Record" section of his Bible (now in the New York Public Library). In the ceremony Mathews solemnly demanded to know if Allan and Maria understood that all children are "conceived and born in sin, and therefore are subject to all miseries, yea to condemnation itself, yet that they are sanctified in Christ, and therefore as members of his church ought to be baptised" (the words specified in the *Constitution of the Reformed Dutch Church* [1815]). They responded in the affirmative to this and other interrogations, declaring their belief that the "articles of the christian faith . . . taught here in this christian church" were "the true and perfect doctrine of salvation" and promising to see that the children "when come to the years of discretion" would be "instructed and brought up in the aforesaid doctrine." The baby's Grandmother Gansevoort, down from Albany, had purchased four gallons of rum and a supply of citron and nutmeg the previous day, makings of a punch fit for offering toasts to Maria and her baptized baby after Mathews had concluded the ceremony.

On 13 August 1819 Allan had worried to his father about the latest cholera epidemic, although he took consolation in thinking he was safer than most: "my House & Store are two of the most airy situations in New York & we therefore suffer less than many others." Every house Allan Melvill rented had to be evaluated not only in terms of price but also by its distance from the lower, unhealthy areas of the city. Each summer inhabitants of Manhattan were at risk from city-wide and region-wide epidemics. Luck, foresight, and money enough to rent in safer parts of town always kept Melvill and his family away from the worst of the contagion, but Albany was safer, and on 10 September 1819, six weeks after Herman's birth, Maria took her three children (Gansevoort, almost four, Helen Maria, two, and the baby, Herman) on the overnight boat up the Hudson to Albany, where she would stay "a few weeks" in her mother's home (as Melvill wrote his father on 14 September). They returned on 17 November, escorted by Peter, who reported to his mother in Albany that they had arrived in excellent health and that, by the nineteenth, Maria and Herman had both distinguished themselves: "Maria found her house very dirty she has already conquered much — Herman has nearly *three teeth.*"

The first winter of Herman's life passed quietly, according to his mother's recollection long afterward. A dear friend (perhaps a relative) from Albany, Caroline Yates, stayed with them, "& a delightful winter it was," Maria wrote to her niece Catherine Gansevoort, Peter's daughter, on 24 May 1866. A "charming companion ever cheerful & happy in making others so," Miss

Yates (later Mrs. Taylor) read aloud a Dumas novel in French and translated it for Maria sentence by sentence. Herman became "very fond" of his mother's friend, his first recorded preference. On 27 June 1820, Maria left with her mother, her children, and her servants to spend the summer at Albany, where the yellow fever was less likely to strike. On 14 July, while she was gone, Allan Melvill reported to the minister at Pittenweem, Scotland, the Reverend Robert Swan, whom he had met in 1818: the eldest child, Gansevoort, was "a most promising child in every respect"; their Helen Maria was "a most lively intelligent child"; and the sweet little boy baptized Herman after his eldest maternal uncle was "full as interesting as the others," although not interesting in ways which specifically differentiated him from the older two.

Herman's first birthday was spent in Albany. Maria began to become anxious to return to New York, only to have her husband urge her to stay until the threat of disease passed. On 15 August 1820 Allan relayed news of Herman to his own father: "the Babe is entirely weaned." He went on to say that Maria was talking "of going to the Springs & the farm for a few days this week with her Brother Peter in company with M^r & Mrs Clinton." That is, she was talking of going to the newly developed resort area of Saratoga Springs and then on to the property at Gansevoort, in the company of De Witt Clinton (governor, 1817–23) and Mrs. Clinton. (Part of Clinton's grand project, the Erie Canal, was in service, but the opening of the entire canal was five years away.) When Maria returned with the children on 24 September after an overnight trip on the steamboat, Allan apparently took her to a new home at 55 Cortlandt Street, which ran into the Hudson River, a few streets up from the Battery. On the twenty-sixth he announced their safe arrival to Peter, although mentioning that all three children had the whooping cough. Gansevoort had "re-commenced at a new school yesterday & obtained a Ticket of merit" already, and Allan had "hired a Cook & Nurse" and only lacked "a Waiter" to complete the "domestic establishment." On 7 October the children were still afflicted, as Melvill wrote to Peter Gansevoort: "Helen Maria suffers most with what we term the whooping cough, but which *I* am sometimes suspicious is only the Influenza, but Gansevoort & Herman are as yet slightly affected."

Around Thanksgiving 1820 Maria became pregnant with her fourth child, and on 10 January 1821, Allan described the latest illnesses to Peter. Gansevoort had "recovered from the Measles," but Helen Maria and Herman had developed cases much more severe: "they have both very bad coughs, inflamed eyes, & virulent eruptions which characterize this troublesome disorder." This severe case of the measles may have damaged Herman's eyes permanently, for even in his young manhood (as he wrote on 24 February 1849) they were "tender as young sparrows." As far as the parents were concerned, both Helen and Herman recovered in due course. By 26 May, Maria, two-thirds through her pregnancy, wrote her mother to expect her on a day steamboat, since she had decided, for once, to leave "the Children under the care of the Nurse," whom she had "reason to beleive worthy of trust." In mid-August, heavily pregnant, Maria returned to Cortlandt Street, accompanied by her mother, who remained with her. The child, born at 2 A.M. on 24 August, was named Augusta, for the month and in compliment to the second wife of Allan Melvill's brother, Mary Ann Augusta Hobart Melvill. That fall of 1821 Maria took Augusta up to Albany for a visit, again leaving the other children in New York. On 3 November 1821, Allan reported to Peter Gansevoort that "little Herman is in fine spirits & rugged as a Bear" — a robust two-year-old.

Maria went up to Albany again with Helen and Augusta in early May 1822, so she could attend her widowed sister-in-law Mary Gansevoort at the birth of her baby (Mary named the boy Stanwix, after the fort the Hero had defended), and stayed on into June. To Lemuel Shaw on 25 May, Allan complained: "myself & Boys are in the mean time keeping Bachelors Hall, which I assure you is always a sorry affair." Peter had "gone under Commission of the Legislature to investigate the operation of the Wolf Bounty in the remote Counties on the St. Lawrence, which is attended with so many abuses as to have become a most grievous tax upon the landed interest" (Allan's description to Shaw), and by 29 May Peter had heard that "Mr Melvills & little Hermans Healths are not good." Peter charitably added in his letter to his mother: "I really hope that they will come to Albany as you & Maria wish." Herman may have retained some memories of his part in the family's extensive, arduous, yet luxurious traveling in 1822. That August, a week after Herman's third birthday, all the Melvills left New York, accompanied by a nurse, in the steamboat *Connecticut* bound for Boston — the first time Herman saw the Boston Melvills. (After Herman's birth, Allan Melvill never went to see his parents unless he wanted to get money from his father.) Peter Gansevoort and his mother joined the Melvills in Boston. They all left Boston together on 1 October 1822, Allan, Maria, their four children and the nurse, and Peter and Mrs. Gansevoort, traveling in fine style in two private carriages, one rented. On their eighth wedding anniversary, 4 October, Allan and Maria stopped at the Melvill farm outside Pittsfield long enough to dine. At Albany Allan left his family and returned to New York alone, leaving Maria, three months pregnant, to visit with her mother a little longer.

In late December 1822, Maria's need for help was such that the Melvills hired a governess, Miss Adams, "a gentell, modest unassuming Girl, uncommonly mild in voice & manner which to Miss Helen Maria will be of lasting importance," Maria reported to Peter on 24 December (the family made little then of Christmas Eve and Christmas). "The Children are in fine Health," she added, and a month later the children remained as "well as Uncle or Parent could wish." On 11 March 1823, Allan wrote to Peter that Maria was "still attending to domestic concerns with more comfort & cheerfulness than usual" despite her condition, which was "always attended with painful anxiety." The children were all well, and by 29 March the three who could talk, Gansevoort, Helen, and Herman, were not only well but "quite delight'd with the Idea" of seeing their "Grandma" Gansevoort and Uncle Peter in New York, Peter having agreed to escort his mother down to be with Maria at the birth. On 7 April (Allan's forty-first birthday) the Melvills' fifth child and third son was born. Allan and Maria were agreed on naming this new child after its father, but hesitated over "Fitzallan," the new father wrote Peter on 26 April (letter in the Berkshire Athenaeum), before deciding on simply Allan. Peter had gone home after escorting his mother down, so on 8 April Allan Melvill wrote him of the birth and the responses of his other children, all of whom were "in ecstacies with the young Stranger whom they would fain have to play with them in the Garret already":

> Herman says "Pa now got two ittle Boys" & Master Gansevoort who is given to ratiocination, having asked whence he came, & being told I had purchased him of the Doctor, observed with great indignation, that "he never heard of buying Children except for Slaves" — Miss Helen Maria says "if Pa has many more children he will have to keep the rod in hand the whole time," & the Lady Augusta although somewhat jealous in disposition, smiles on the Baby with ineffable delight.

The older two children were rhetoricians in training, so Helen Maria's words cannot be taken as proof that Allan was a severe and frequent disciplinarian, although he did pride himself in his ability to curb rebellion in his children. "Pa now got two ittle Boys," the earliest recorded words of Herman Melville, curiously indicate that the boy identified with the baby nearly four years his junior rather than with Gansevoort, three and a half years his senior, whom Herman could never, at any time, rival in the esteem of the parents.

In the spring of 1824 Melvill took a four-year lease on 33 Bleecker Street, Maria wrote Peter on 11 March — a "handsome two Story house," newly built, brick, expected to be ready on 15 April, two weeks ahead of the usual moving day. Two stories meant three or four, for the basement housed the nursery (and probably the kitchen and dining room as well), and there were two bedchambers in the garret. In a letter to Peter on 11 March 1824, Maria expressed pleasure in the view of the "elegant white Marble Houses, in Bond Street," afforded from the back windows. On 1 April Allan described the house to Peter as on "an open, dry & elevated location equidistant from Broadway & the Bowery, in plain sight of both & almost uniting the advantages of town & country." The situation was no doubt better for the children, as far as air and play room were concerned, but it was too far away, as Allan had said, for him to come home for his midday meal, and although it had similarities to their present house on Cortlandt Street it was, undeniably, a two-story house rather than a three-story house: they were taking, for four years, smaller and less convenient quarters.

At the end of 1824 (29 December), Maria gave her brother Peter an account of three of her first four children:

> Gansevoort was confined to the house part of last week with a Fever. He grows very fast & does not look so robust & hearty as formerly — Herman & Augusta improve apace as to growing & talking — The former attends school regularly but does not appear so fond of his Book as to injure his Health — He has turned into a great tease, & daily puts Gansevoorts Patience to flight, who cannot bear to be "plagued by such a little Fellow."

Maria had the sense of humor in the family, so her comment on Herman as a scholar must be taken as the words of an indulgent mother who prized physical well-being in a five-year-old over abnormal dedication to scholarship. Her phrasing shows Herman had started teasing Gansevoort only recently, after her spring visit to Albany, when little Allan had begun demanding the attention due a baby of one year.

The Manhattan houses of Herman's childhood were elegantly furnished. In Melville's fourth book, *Redburn* (1849), his hero Wellingborough Redburn recalls "a large library-case, that stood in the hall" (ch. 1), tall as a small house, and other pieces of furniture brought from Europe. These were suggested by the furniture Allan Melvill had selected in France, an elegant suite of which included chairs whose arms terminated in dolphin heads, meticulously if unnaturally carved with fish-scales. Melville wrote into *Redburn* several "oil-paintings and rare old engravings" his narrator's father had brought from Paris, including two sea-pieces — all likely to have been based on real purchases of Allan Melvill. In the house there may have been "two large green French portfolios of colored prints" such as Melville's Redburn remembered as being heavier than he could lift in his childhood, when he and the other children loved them ("Every Saturday my brothers and sisters used to get them out of the corner where they were kept, and spreading them on the floor, gaze at them with never-failing delight"). At that time Maria already possessed a "set of mahogany furniture" (which her son Allan in his will dated 23 May 1868 [now in the Berkshire Athenaeum] left to his daughter, his mother's namesake, Maria Gansevoort Melville). Along with beds, chests, and other large family pieces, Maria had the piano her father had imported for her in 1801.

On the walls of the Melvill houses hung Allan Melvill's engraved portrait of the first earl of Leven and Melville, displayed "as a sacred Memento," as he had assured his noble kinsman. Copies of the Gilbert Stuart paintings of the Hero of Fort Stanwix and his wife also were prominently displayed. There was a peculiar little chair portrait the artist John Rubens Smith had painted of Allan Melvill in 1810. Herman Melville himself wrote an intensely suggestive reading of this real painting into *Pierre; or, The Ambiguities* (1852), where he adopted the offhanded descriptive style of an art critic:

> "An impromptu portrait of a fine-looking, gay-hearted, youthful gentleman. He is lightly, and, as it were, airily and but grazingly seated in, or rather flittingly tenanting an old-fashioned chair of Malacca. One arm confining his hat and cane is loungingly thrown over the back of the chair, while the fingers of the other hand play with his gold watch-seal and key. The free-templed head is sideways turned, with a peculiarly bright, and care-free, morning expression." (bk. 4, ch. 3)

(The seal in the Smith portrait of Allan Melvill, which Herman Melville owned in later years, displayed not a Melvill device but the Van Schaick coat of arms.) After the last voyage of 1818 and the removal to New York City, a propitious time, the couple hired Ezra Ames to paint new portraits of them both. Now there was no lolling in a chair: Allan sits upright, his shining coat buttons the only things that draw any attention away from the head and the mirroring white shape of starched shirtfront and cravat. The thick curling hair is brushed forward at the sides, onto the face, as in 1810, and now the hair at the ears runs into thick sideburns that grow downward until they go behind the high collar. The brows are dark and heavy. This is a solid citizen — martial looking. In *Pierre* Melville used two contrasting portraits as a way of tracing the youthful Pierre's questionings about his father's life before he was born, strong suggestion that the disparity between two actual portraits of his own father gave Melville himself early inklings of some disparity or division in Allan Melvill's nature.

Ames's companion portrait of Maria shows a young matron, oval of face, hair elaborately coiled and curled (a dark curl sits in front of each ear like a rosette), elegantly swathed in her husband's best imported French fabrics. On 30 December 1805, when she was fourteen and a half, her brother Peter Gansevoort (three years her elder) had written to their brother Leonard (eight years her elder): "Though she does not possess the Beauty of a Helen, yet that she should make up, in improving her mind in useful studies." To judge from this Ames painting and from photographs taken decades later,

Maria had not become a great beauty: a hypercritical brother could see an overgenerous mouth, a too-ample nose, and ears large enough to warrant her training curls of hair to cover them. Ames made her, at almost thirty, dignified, settled. He made her look, in fact, much like her father in the Stuart painting, which he had seen, either in the original in Albany or in Maria's copy—oval of face, ample of nose. (Ames may have done the copy from Stuart.) Another portrait of Maria from this period survives, less formal but similar. No one ever had reason to sense any disparity between Maria Melvill's outward appearance and her true nature, except insofar as her loyalty to her husband forced her to keep silent or to temporize. Maria Gansevoort Melvill was by nature straightforward, but being a dutiful wife meant that she had to be in complicity with Allan Melvill even if he threatened the interests of her children and herself.

By the mid-1820s Gansevoort and Helen, and even Herman, although probably not Augusta and Allan, were old enough to perceive that their houses in Manhattan were temporary, occupied long enough for one or two children to be born, four years at the longest, and that their father rented different quarters for his stores about as often. (While the Melvills lived at 33 Bleecker Street, Catherine was born on 21 May 1825 and Frances Priscilla on 26 August 1827.) Each time the family moved, the children would perceive the late General Gansevoort's house on North Market Street in Albany as yet more secure, and the recurrent fears of contagion in Manhattan came to make it seem a house of refuge. (The direst year of Herman's infancy was 1822, when hundreds of businessmen, including Allan Melvill, transported their goods to temporary shop quarters far north, to Greenwich Village—a flight the parents and the older two children recalled as the extreme example of what New Yorkers had to do to avoid contagion.) The Gansevoort house, the family house Herman knew best, was a capacious solid three-story structure, plus basement. With windows above ground level, the basement as usual contained the kitchen and dining room. Melville may have recalled it in *Redburn* (ch. 31), where his narrator deplores the modernity of Liverpool: "Why, no buildings here look so ancient as the old gable-pointed mansion of my maternal grandfather at home, whose bricks were brought from Holland long before the revolutionary war!" It was now occupied not only by Herman's widowed grandmother and Uncle Peter but also, part of the time, by Aunt Mary Gansevoort and her younger children. (In a draft of a letter in the New York Public Library to the British consul in Amsterdam, written in July 1818, Allan Melvill inquired about the Gansevoort coat-of-arms and motto, explaining that his mother-in-law, enthusiastically attached to "the *Fatherland*," spoke Dutch in preference to English. The Melvill children heard Dutch spoken, whether or not they acquired many words of the language.)

The house possessed "every convenience," Peter specified when advertising it for rental in 1834, and was "spacious" enough to absorb many visitors and long-term residents.

The Gansevoort house contained treasures of Dutch, colonial, and revolutionary silver and china, as well as more recent acquisitions. Throughout the house there were fine old pieces (such as mahogany wardrobes and bedsteads, including the Hero's mahogany four poster), accumulated in the distributions that recurrently took place at deaths and marriages. There were Dutch marquetry cabinets, mahogany cabinets, a Sheraton sideboard that Uncle Peter later put in his library, a mahogany rolltop desk, old couches, Dutch chairs, hall settles, and a new screen with a painting of George and Martha Washington at Mount Vernon. There were, among the multitude of treasures, many mirrors (one had views painted at the sides, including a view of the first Dutch Church in Albany; two or more were surmounted by eagles, the republican symbol). The London-made grandfather clock was probably in the house, before it was inherited by Herman Gansevoort and removed to the house at Gansevoort, where it remained for decades, until Herman Melville inherited it. There was another grandfather clock of mahogany and satinwood over eight feet tall made (with London works) in New York City by Effingham Embree in 1795. Everywhere rich details caught the eye of the children: brass andirons rested on lion stands, on the hearth were brass tongs and a poker, and on the mantel an eight-day brass clock. (For security there were five fire buckets marked Gansevoort, with the address, Market Street No. 46.) There was a very old portrait on canvas of at least one of Catherine Van Schaick's ancestors, and there were much-admired recent paintings, including a Gilbert Stuart portrait of the Hero's brother Leonard Gansevoort, who had served in the Continental Congress — the uncle of the late sheriff of the same name. There were also many other family portraits, less valued, including some now all but priceless portraits by the early eighteenth-century artist much later identified as the "Gansevoort Limner." The one of Herman's great-grandfather Harme Gansevoort (1712–1801?) hung there, and that of Harme's wife, Magdalena Douw Gansevoort (1718–96).

The house on Market Street contained, besides the Stuart portraits of the Hero of Fort Stanwix and his wife, much of his memorabilia. Grandmother Gansevoort preserved the framed certificate of the Hero's membership in the Society of the Cincinnati, signed by George Washington on 10 December 1785. She displayed some of his military trophies, such as his silver-hilted sword and banners and a brass drum captured from the British, personal prizes from the War of Independence. The general's camp bed was there still most likely (though it may have been at Gansevoort), a marvelous collapsible bed for a very tall man, like Old Pierre's camp bed that Melville wrote into

Pierre. (In the Henry Ford Museum in Dearborn, Michigan, is a collapsible camp bed, presumably a twin to his own, which Gansevoort presented to George Washington.) She had preserved many other military mementos, including trunks of uniforms and paraphernalia (some of them then or later stored in Gansevoort, in the possession of her oldest son, Herman). She displayed portraits of Washington and Jefferson (and one of William Pitt). She had a picture of the surrender of Cornwallis at Yorktown, and possessed the flag of the Third New York Regiment, which her husband had commanded, the very flag he had displayed at Yorktown, after the Third Regiment was consolidated with the Second. It was large, more than five feet square, a gorgeous thing, of blue silk with silk fringe, the New York state arms painted on both sides, like the later state arms except that the wreath was red and white, not blue and gold. The two female supporters were in costume of the time the flag was made, 1778 or 1779, in dresses of cloth of gold, with reddish mantles and sandals, blue sashes across their bodies. Grandmother Gansevoort had stories of its adventures, and perhaps even stories of its making: had she stitched "EXCELSIOR" on the scroll? (Long afterward in *Moby-Dick*, ch. 99, "The Doubloon," Melville may have associated scenes stamped on South American coins with this flag, which in the center vignette vividly depicts a spiky sun just rising over the top of a mountain.) The value of a thing, the brothers Thomas Jr. and Allan Melvill had decided, was precisely what it would bring in cash, but the old possessions in the house on North Market Street in Albany possessed value beyond cash, even to a boy like Herman, who learned early to appreciate what were known as objects of "virtu."

After he was big enough, Herman could join the two older children in venturing out from General Gansevoort's house into the fireproof stable and carriage house, the flower garden, and the bleaching yard. In the carriage house, among mundane modern conveyances there was probably the Hero's phaeton, the body painted olive green, the running gear orange, on which Melville modeled Grand Old Pierre's immense phaeton in *Pierre*. Designed to seat two people in majestic isolation, the phaeton was titanic, with a gigantic running-gear and the body attached to the gear by throughbraces that even over the roughest of backcountry roads made riding smooth. The metalwork on the top and the dash was brass-tipped, and the leather cushions deep and strong. After the Revolution the Hero had used this phaeton in his journeys from Albany to his "country-seat" at Gansevoort. At times it was kept in the carriage house there, but at Melville's death it was owned by his cousin, the daughter of Peter Jr. When the Troy *Times* described it (6 January 1894), the phaeton still was so "wonderfully well-preserved" that it argued "strongly for the substantial workmanship of the nation's early mechanics"; it had been used in the celebration of the bicentennial of Albany in 1886. In Herman's eyes it was a conveyance from an antediluvian era, when there were giants in the earth.

In 1825, the summer Herman turned six, the Gansevoort house became an even more hallowed shrine, for on his triumphal national tour General Lafayette called there upon the widow of the Hero of Fort Stanwix. In a letter to Allan Melvill on 15 June 1825 Peter described the visit his mother had received "from Gen'l La Fayette and suite" (according to a typescript of the letter, now in the Berkshire Athenaeum). Led to the sacred image, Lafayette had proved himself as a diplomat: "He recognized our departed Fathers Portrait and bore testimony to the accuracy of Stuarts Pencil in its delineations &c." Peter's historical sense and his literary sense (stimulated by the decade-old genre that *Waverley* had established) intermingled in his rhapsodic conclusion: "Posterity will be disposed to place the History of La Fayette's Year in America among the legends of romance and fiction—and even ourselves ere the lapse of many months when he shall have left our happy and peaceful shores, forever, in viewing retrospectively these Present scenes, will involuntarily exclaim 'could these things be and pass us like a Summer cloud without our Special wonder.'" (Only Shakespeare was fit to supply Peter's final flourish.) Relaying to his nephews the "romantic story of our early revolutionary existence as a People" Peter nurtured in Gansevoort and Herman a sense of the house as trophied and sacred. Henceforth, when they stood before the portrait of the Hero of Fort Stanwix, they stood on the spot where General Lafayette himself had stood. That their own uncle and grandmother had entertained Lafayette meant that the children were in the presence, every visit, of blood kin freshly linked to the nation's earliest and most glorious epoch.

Yet for the older children there were underlying tensions even in secure Albany. At some point early in the decade Peter made what amounted to a bargain that he would delay marrying and starting his own family in order to live with his mother and to do something like his duty—to his mother, his brother's widow and children, and his sister and her children. In his lawyerly view, this meant that he would hold his father's estate together as well as he could, for everyone's good, not excluding his own. Another man might have urged his mother to make provision for Leonard's widow and children, so that the sons would not have to go to sea in their childhood or youth, but, nothing if not calculating, Peter found it expedient to shelter his sister-in-law Mary Ann Chandonette Gansevoort and her smaller children in the big house, at least for prolonged periods. He also decided that he could not vociferously oppose his mother every time she insisted on making Maria an advance against her inheritance: he was, after all, living in her house, not his, and the money was hers, not his — not yet.

Having made the decision to bide his time, meanwhile holding together what he could, Peter lived with it as well as he could, but the strain became intense, for every time Gansevoort, Helen, Herman, then the younger children arrived on Market Street he could not avoid reflecting that he was himself still childless, and he could not avoid recapitulating how much more deeply his Bostonian brother-in-law had dipped into their mother's fortune since their last arrival. The children could not have known that Peter's bachelor self-denial was recurrently exacerbated by Allan's effrontery in complaining of the discomfort he experienced from sexual deprivation during Maria's prolonged stays in Albany. (Nor did Allan exempt his father from such man-to-man confidences, explicit despite the formality of the phrases, as this on 15 August 1820: "living as I do alone, you cannot imagine the sacrifice I make to their welfare.") To write in such a vein to Peter was even riskier than to his father, since Peter's ideas about a married life for himself, all that decade, were perforce put in abeyance. Peter tried to spare the children the anxiety and anger he was feeling, but he wanted to control his own money and live his own life, and by the late 1820s the older children were becoming unnerved by the tensions in the house. In the long aftermath of Allan Melvill's wastrel decade, Helen Maria (much later, in a 14 January 1844 letter to Augusta) could allude disdainfully to her Uncle Peter's besetting sin of selfishness — a judgment understandable if not entirely fair.

Through the years of Herman's childhood Allan Melvill the eighteenth-century rationalist continued to pride himself on reading the natures of his own flesh and blood, but as a practical man he did not closely inspect each successive infant for precocious signals of his or her nature. In due time, by the age of seven or so, he expected his children "to attract attention" and "disclose character" (as he wrote to his father on 20 May 1830). He had made an exception for Gansevoort, his first child, his oldest son. When the boy was four, Allan Melvill saw marks of innate character that made him suspect that Gansevoort Melvill would "imitate the civil, and heroic virtues of both his grandfathers" (as he wrote to an acquaintance in Scotland, the Reverend Robert Swan, on 14 July 1820). When Herman was small, Allan Melvill did not focus sharply on his character but defined his attitude toward Herman in relation to Gansevoort's evident genius. Then by the time Herman was seven, and old enough to "disclose character," Allan's namesake, at three, had taken second place after Gansevoort in his father's eyes. By the age of seven Herman had not yet attracted much attention from his father — and it was already too late for him to do so.

In August 1826 Herman (still "little Herman," partly to distinguish him from his oldest Gansevoort uncle) was considered big enough to be sent up to Albany in the charge of a business associate of Allan Melvill's. Herman was a "Pioneer," going before his mother and the younger children; in this letter of 9 August commending his second son to the care of Peter Gansevoort, Melvill gave his first surviving analysis of Herman's character:

> I now consign to your especial care & patronage, my beloved Son Herman, an honest hearted double rooted Knickerbocker of the true Albany stamp, who I trust will do equal honour in due time to his ancestry[,] parentage & Kindred—he is very backward in speech & somewhat slow in comprehension, but you will find him as far as he understands men & things both solid & profound, & of a docile & aimiable [amiable] disposition—if agreeable, he will pass the vacation with his Grandmother & yourself, & I hope he may prove a pleasant auxiliary to the Family Circle—I depend much on your kind attention to my dear Boy who will be truly grateful for the least favour—let him avoid green Fruit & unseasonable exposure to the Sun & heat, but having taken such good care of Gansevoort last Summer, I commit his Brother to the same hands with unreserved confidence—Have the goodness to procure a pair of Shoes for Herman, time being insufficient to have a pair made here.

This spur-of-the-moment analysis must be taken seriously, for Allan was not given to irony about his children, nor to derogating them. Herman was backward in speech, as almost anyone would have been around Gansevoort, whom Maria later that year described as "an incessant talker" (in a letter to her brother Peter on 8 December). Herman was also, his father thought, less than swift in comprehension. Yet Allan did not say that Herman was little adept at understanding "men & things" (human nature and concepts?), but merely that his understanding of them was limited. Indeed, insofar as he *did* understand them, Herman's understanding was "both solid & profound." Herman was docile, Allan had noticed approvingly, while not perceiving that docility may have been a strategy Herman had resorted to after realizing, at some level of awareness, that he had no hope of competing for attention with Gansevoort except through teasing, which he may have begun to outgrow already.

Peter Gansevoort in August 1826 mentioned Herman in what Allan interpreted as "very flattering terms," as Allan wrote on 2 September, when he added: "he will I fondly hope obey your wishes in all things & become worthy of your patronage & instruction—it affords us all sincere pleasure to hear that so close an intimacy already subsists between him & Master Stanwix, which we trust will be cherished to mutual advantage & satisfaction." This last is folderol, one of Allan's characteristic flourishes, since Stanwix

(Uncle Leonard's posthumous child) was two years' Herman's junior, only a year older than little Allan. That October Allan kept Bachelors' Hall with Gansevoort, Herman, Allan Jr., and servants. He reported to his brother-in-law in Albany that Gansevoort at once had been "appointed one of the six monitors Generals," and had soon been promoted to the senior department, where he began studying French. In that letter of 26 September (now in the Berkshire Athenaeum), Allan assured Peter that his "little Companions" were behaving remarkably well, passing "their whole time in the house, or at school," except when he allowed them to visit him at the store, for he did not "allow them to run abroad, or play in the street." There was nothing worth reporting about Herman, but Allan Jr. at three was "the cock of the walk" among the boys, "one of those sturdy champions, who bear down all opposition by the mere force of dogmatical will." Allan Jr. tyrannized over "his Brothers & his friend Billy, whose only safety is retreat to his own territories," but with his father it was otherwise ("*as Maria well knows*"). He had even become a "peaceable bed-fellow," once his father protected himself with "a large bolster" between them. Allan was taken with his namesake: "Master Allan is occasionally a little rebellious through sheer roguery, & though a mischievous wag, is indeed a most lovely, bewitching intelligent Child, he often says, 'I go Grand Ma house morrow morning, wont I Pa?'" Anyone would have been more interested in Gansevoort than Herman (that 8 December Maria marveled to Peter over Gansevoort's superiority to his older cousin, Leonard and Mary's son Peter L. Gansevoort, who did not appear to her "to possess talents or inclination for study or improvement"), but (decades of documents make clear) only a father enthralled by a namesake would have been more interested in Master Allan than Master Herman. It was natural that Gansevoort overshadowed Herman; Herman can only have felt it as wholly unfair and unpredictable that he was overshadowed by the child four years his junior.

Just before Christmas in 1826 Gansevoort achieved his greatest childhood glory, at the annual high school examination. According to the letter his mother wrote her own mother on 28 December, he "was seated on the Forum at the side of Chancellor Kent with the Lady of the Lake in his hand"—James Kent, former chancellor of New York—from which vantage point he prompted two older students in a scene from the poem. Gansevoort himself recited the new poem "Marco Bozzaris" by the Connecticut–New York poet Fitz-Greene Halleck, written in celebration of the Greek struggle for independence from the Turks. Byronic in sentiment and subject matter, it was enormously popular, since it allowed Americans to applaud resistance to tyranny without having to risk any political or economic consequences by aiding that resistance:

At midnight, in his guarded tent,
  The Turk was dreaming of the hour
When Greece, her knee in suppliance bent,
  Should tremble at his power.

. . . .

An hour passed on — the Turk awoke;
  That bright dream was his last;
He woke — to hear his sentries shriek,
  "To arms! they come! the Greek! the Greek!"

This is the first poetry Herman is known to have heard, and heard repeatedly. Having dazzled the audience, Gansevoort was crowned with a wreath and told that "the Crown was the Highest Civick Honor given by the Romans &c" (and therefore the honor most appropriate in the new Republic). Charles King, editor of the New York *American* (and son of the late Federalist leader Rufus King), "congratulated Mr Melvill said he was a promising Boy & did honour to his Father & Mother." Back in the house on Bleecker Street, the enraptured parents hung Gansevoort's crown "from his Grandfather's Picture to remain untill after the Holidays." That is, they hung Gansevoort's crown on the Ezra Ames copy of Gilbert Stuart's portrait of Peter Gansevoort, the Hero of Fort Stanwix — a telling illustration of Allan and Maria's ways of encouraging a pride of ancestry and a spirit of emulation in their sons. At seven and a half, Herman was old enough to remember the crowning, with complex emotions.

Late in February 1827, just as Allan Melvill entered into his "*confidential Connexion* with Persons combining every qualification but money," he and Maria yielded to the importunities of the winter-weary Gansevoort and Helen. Rushing spring, they planned an elaborate entertainment such as those two children had been treated to by their friends. Maria bought "confectionary & mottoes" (that is, candy wrapped together with moral sentiments or verses of poetry elegantly printed on little papers), Gansevoort and Helen having declared that "it would be no party" without them. They invited forty children, twenty-five of whom came, on a school day, despite a snowstorm, and stayed from six or seven until midnight. Allan Melvill helped by hiring the driver of the "Broadway accommodation" to pick up the neighboring children. The parents also hired a violinist, but restrained themselves on food and beverages: "nothing was handed round save Lemonade Port Wine . . . & Cakes of various kinds the sugar Plums, mottoes, Blomange, preserves, Oranges & dried fruits were displayed on a supper table." The next day, basking in the delight of their schoolmates, the children, presumably including the second son, reported to Maria that "there never was a more delightful party given." On 20 February Maria described all this to her brother in a tone that forbade him to question her right to spend money so extravagantly.

It was during this financial crisis that Allan Melvill in a letter to his brother-in-law cunningly referred to Herman as Peter's "little protégé." From his experience with his brother Leonard's orphans as well as Maria's brood, Peter knew what the phrase "little protégé" was meant to accomplish and would accomplish, for however he was being manipulated, he did love his nieces and nephews, and he could not set himself against decisions Allan and Maria might persuade his mother to make. Allan's paternal pronouncements had continued to be admirable, as in his letter of 12 September 1826 to Peter, after he had summoned Herman home from Albany so he could "resume his studies at the High School" the same day as Gansevoort (who had been summoned from Boston), thereby obviating "any feelings of jealousy or ideas of favoritism." Besides, he had continued, they might by returning "acquire a practical moral lesson whose influence may endure forever, for if they understand early, that inclination must always yield to Duty, it will become a matter of course when the vacations expire, to bid a fond adieu to Friends & amusements, & return home cheerfully to their Books, & they will consequently imbibe habits of Order & punctuality, which bear sweet blossoms in the dawn of life, golden fruits in 'the noon of manhood,' & a rich harvest for the garners of old age." It was as if Allan Melvill had no inkling that Peter Gansevoort, the man he was writing to, knew that he was recklessly imperiling his children's futures by his borrowing and his covert connections. Melvill's next surviving comments on Herman are in a letter to Peter on 22 September 1827 describing the arrival of the boys, Gansevoort from Albany and Herman from his first solo visit to Boston: "Tuesday's Boat brought us our beloved Gansevoort in charming spirits at the recollection of his visit to Albany, which will doubtless leave many agreeable traces in his tenacious memory & glowing fancy; — his more sedate but not less interesting Brother returned to us on Monday, & though less buoyant in mind, was equally delighted with his jaunt to Boston, where he became also a great favorite with the whole Family." Allan could never characterize Herman except by contrasts with Gansevoort — contrasts that in the nature of things had to be diminishing. Herman was "more sedate" and "less buoyant in mind" than Gansevoort, though his father was kind enough to insist, vaguely, that he was "not less interesting." Even when the contrast was not explicit, the implication was clear: Herman did not have such a "tenacious memory" or such a "glowing fancy."

Knowing Herman as he thought he did, Melvill was startled when he reported to Peter on 23 February 1828: "You will be as much surprised as myself to know, that Herman proved the best Speaker in the introductory Department, at the examination of the High School, he has made rapid progress during the 2 last quarters." Gansevoort of course still ranked "among the As No 1 in the senior class." Except for Herman, the children were behaving predictably: "Helen Maria is now at Mrs Whieldon & is a very smart but rather indolent Scholar, & the two Boys [Gansevoort and Herman] with Augusta attend Dancing there twice a week — the latter is esteemed a very Sylph for a beginner — & Gansevoort is said to have so much native grace (by his fair teacher Miss Whieldon) as to neglect his feet too much in the regular steps." There was no competing with a lad of such native grace as Gansevoort, but at least Herman had lessons, and presumably learned the regular steps.

Early in 1828 Melvill took a five-year lease on the house at 675 Broadway, between Bond and Jones, on a lot two hundred feet deep, running all the way through to Mercer Street, and on the fashionable side, which is to say the west side. With such news to tell, Maria overcame her "almost unsurmountable" antipathy to writing and informed Peter that since nothing had been built from Bond to Jones there was "a delightful opening & pure air for our Boys to play," in front of their house. She added: "Mr Melvill playfully says I have at last gained my point which has always been a house in Broadway." Rather than worrying herself about money, she declared that her spirits were better and that she was "a more agreeable companion" than she had been "for some time past." In Herman's early childhood, his parents had talked about living in Brooklyn, where rents were much lower, only a ferry ride for Allan to lower Manhattan. Long before 1828 Maria had known where the money had come from that they were spending, but there is no reticence in her recounting Allan's badinage about her getting what she had always wanted, a house in Broadway. Perhaps she thought her mother's money was infinite and that she was entitled to much of her portion now, while she had small children. On 10 May 1828 Allan gave Peter an account of the expedients his family was going to in order to have the new house fitted properly for their five-year occupancy — a comical vignette that puts Herman very much in his place in his family:

We have been at No 675 Broadway since the 30th Ultio, but the Painters, white washers, purifiers &c still keep us in a most distressing confusion, of which you may have an idea, when told that Maria, myself & our 7 bairns have passed the last two nights in the same chamber, Gansevoort & Herman on one side of our Bed, & Helen Maria & Augusta on the other, all in elegant negligence on the floor — Allan & Catherine point to point at the two extremities of a cot in a snug corner, & Miss Frances Priscilla on the right flank

in a cradle — surrounded on all sides by a maze of furniture belonging to this
& the 3 other Rooms which are painting.

This sounds charmingly chaotic, the sort of experience that Herman and the
other older children would remember fondly; but the older children may
have guessed that they were only a whim of the market, or a whim of a
creditor, away from losing the house and huddling in whatever refuge they
could find.

In his adult life Herman Melville knew New Yorkers who prided themselves in being living historians of the city's docks, blocks, squares, parks.
One such Manhattanite, Dr. John W. Francis, wrote Melville briefly into his
Old New York in the 1850s, where he also recalled a Manhattan cottage
occupied by the Hero of Fort Stanwix during the Revolution. But in the
surviving writings of Herman Melville there is very little to show that he
remembered much of Manhattan in the 1820s. In *Redburn* a few passages
about old New York seem based on Melville's own life. One (in ch. 1) is
Redburn's "shadowy reminiscences of wharves, and warehouses, and shipping, with which a residence in a seaport during early childhood" had supplied him, particularly a memory of standing with his father "on the wharf
when a large ship was getting under way, and rounding the head of the pier,"
a sight all the more evocative because Redburn's father, like Melville's, had
crossed the Atlantic on business several times. A little more in this passage
also sounds like Allan Melvill: "And of winter evenings in New York, by the
well-remembered sea-coal fire in old Greenwich-street, he used to tell my
brother and me of the monstrous waves at sea, mountain high; of the masts
bending like twigs; and all about Havre, and Liverpool, and about going up
into the ball of St. Paul's in London." Into the early pages of *Redburn* (ch. 7)
Melville also wrote an account of his narrator's early outing to Fort Tompkins on the Narrows, the entrance from New York Harbor to the sea: "I had
visited the place once when we lived in New York, as long ago almost as I
could remember, with my father, and an uncle of mine, an old sea-captain,
with white hair, who used to sail to a place called Archangel in Russia, and
who used to tell me that he was with Captain Langsdorff, when Captain
Langsdorff crossed over by land from the sea of Okotsk in Asia to St. Pe-
tersburgh, drawn by large dogs in a sled." The uncle was based on Langsdorff's friend John D'Wolf, so Herman himself may well have been taken on
just such a nautical outing with the brothers-in-law. Comments about old
days in New York City scattered through Melville's surviving writings (the
most evocative of which are in an 1855 story, "Jimmy Rose") are not of a
nature to suggest that he ever thought of himself as a repository of urban lore
like Dr. Francis. His reminiscences of the Manhattan of his first decade were

shadowy, blurred by the terror of fleeing the city with his father, and then by subsequent tragedies, and they did not seem to bring him joy in later life. Memory may well have suppressed many exuberant times, such as the one Gansevoort wrote to his mother about on 23 May 1829, when Maria was in Albany: "This morning Herman went to Hoboken in high spirits and returned about four o'clock." Herman had taken a ferry to what New Yorkers then called the Elysian Fields, the delightful parklike area on the Palisades from which one had incomparable views. As the decades passed, the less felicitous "Hoboken" quite supplanted "Elysian Fields" on the maps, but even in the 1840s Herman would seek refuge there, with complex emotions from the overlapping of times and conditions.

In August 1828 Melvill entrusted his friend the Boston merchant Daniel P. Parker with a letter to Lemuel Shaw offering him an investment, "two Notes drawn by Peter Gansevoort . . . for $2600 & $2650," due 18 February 1829, for which he needed to "be in funds" by 20 August: Shaw was to advance him not $5250 but a few percentage points less, so as to give Shaw six months' interest, then Shaw was to collect the entire $5250 from Peter when the notes were due. Allan also dispatched his two older sons in Parker's care, Gansevoort all the way to Boston, the nine-year-old Herman to Bristol, Rhode Island, to pass his vacation with his aunt and uncle Mary and John D'Wolf in their grand house, where he could play with his big cousin "Langs"—John Langsdorff, born in Helen's year, 1817. John D'Wolf, the most successful member of the family of his generation, was then a handsome vigorous man with a square-jawed ruddy face and deep-set eyes. Herman wrote him into *Moby-Dick* (ch. 45, "The Affidavit"), and still later the aged D'Wolf published his own account of his *Voyage to the North Pacific and a Journey Through Siberia More Than Half a Century Ago*. At nine Herman was old enough to hold a copy of G. H. von Langsdorff's *Voyages and Travels* and, in the company of Cousin Langsdorff, try to read some passages about the early adventures of Uncle John in wondrous places remote from the triangle of cities that defined his own world, Manhattan, Albany, and Boston. Gansevoort was big enough to write home himself from Boston, and on 13 August 1828 Mary Melvill D'Wolf reported for Herman, so Allan could report to Peter on 20 August: "the Boys are in good health, spirits & discipline— delighted & delighting." Herman was then passing what was probably the happiest vacation of his childhood.

Allan and Maria lived so well for so long on borrowed money that the older children, Gansevoort, Helen, and Herman, must have been slow to see any difference between the way they were living and the way a man like the merchant Daniel P. Parker lived, on Beacon Hill, or the way their mother's cousins the Van Rensselaers lived in the great Manor House at the north edge of Albany—people with secure fortunes still being augmented. Throughout the decade before the flight from Manhattan, Maria was forcing herself, day by day, to disguise her feelings, which she could refer to in words only at intervals, to her husband, her mother, and her brother Peter, and not at all, except inadvertently and obliquely, to her children. She lived every day with secret shame, fear, and unrevealable, unadmittable resentment toward her husband, wherever else she might, from time to time, deflect that resentment. She could not admit to herself or anyone else that her husband, year by year, was running through her fortune. For his part, Allan continued to conduct a stringently departmentalized life in which he could pretend that everything was normal, as he did on 21 October 1828 in describing to Peter the scene of happy chaos that ensued when Maria returned to New York with her contingent of children: "I drove round the corner of Cortland St as the Boat was rounding too at the Dock—the whole party appeared fresh from the north & much improved by a visit which they all found with the exception of the illness of our good mother & Mary very agreeable—My portion of the Children is also brisk & hearty & when they all came together again such a clatter of feet, swinging of hands & confusion of tongues were never heard this side of Babel." Even to Peter, he could keep up the pretense that nothing was wrong—except the regrettable illness of Melvill's mother-in-law and sister-in-law in Albany. In particular letters he could intermix his economic news (hapless use of money already received and pleas for fresh infusions of money) alongside his admirably paternal reports on the children or inquiries about them, if they were visiting Albany, or, less often, Boston. Skilled in the practice of shades of denial, and seeing themselves as excellent parents, Allan and Maria Melvill strove to keep their financial anxieties from their children, and they may in great part have succeeded, especially with the smaller ones. What the complicity of silence cost them in their relationship with each other is wholly undocumented.

In April 1829 there was a double disaster. While Maria was in Albany, Gansevoort "fell violently yesterday from the Wood House Roof 12 feet on to the white rail fence which broke under him." The injury, apparently to his torso, was severe, but (according to Allan's letter to Peter, summoning Maria home) Gansevoort bore all his suffering "with the mild enduring patience of a lamb, & the calm collected fortitude of a Man." On May first, while Gansevoort was recuperating, before he enrolled at the grammar school of Columbia College, Herman and Allan began the summer term at the New-York Male High School—the first time Herman had been the older brother in a school. The other disaster, in mid-April, was President Andrew Jackson's removal of Herman's grandfather as Naval Officer of the port of Boston. This terrible blow to the family finances and to the dignity of the Boston

Melvills had unexpected consequences for Herman that summer of 1829. Maria, pregnant since late April or early May of 1829, began her usual summer division, deciding where Gansevoort and Herman would vacation, and expecting as usual to hear that the boys were, in their father's phrase the previous year, delighted and delighting. During a visit her brother Herman was making her, she proposed that her son Herman should visit his Uncle Herman, where he could revel in the bucolic setting of the Mansion House. Catherine Quackenboss Gansevoort had been past the usual marrying age when Herman Gansevoort married her, and after marriage she had at once proved to be a domestic tyrant. (Later "Aunt Catherineness" became a family phrase applied to a woman determined to have her own way in domestic matters, even against the will of her husband.) Now, in 1829, although Catherine was acquainted with the admirably behaved Herman from her stays in New York City, she refused to allow her husband to receive him at the farm. Childless herself, she felt no obligation to assist Maria during her eighth pregnancy. On 15 July Maria wrote to Peter:

> I shall not be able to leave here, untill the last of this Month when I shall be accompanied by Master Gansevoort, Misses Helen, Augusta, & Miss Frances, Master Herman will go to Boston, Master Allan, & Miss Catherine being the most rebellious & ungovernable will remain at home to keep their Papa company — *Uncle*, absolutely refused to take his name-sake because Aunt would dislike it, saying it would give him great pleasure, but many of her connections were desirous of visiting them &c, &c. . . . I do not blame Herman — only he is endeavouring by an unmanly submission to indulge a woman who will ever expect more, the more he yealds.

A lesser woman might self-reproachfully have wondered what reprehensible qualities in her son had made him unwelcome, but even while smarting from the rebuff Maria declared of her brother Herman: "I am willing to bet my Ears he would feel better if he had the company of my little Son to releive his loneliness, a month hence." More of Allan Melvill's comments on little Herman's character survive than hers, but this testimony to the value of little Herman's company, however unspecific, says everything about Maria's capacity to instill in her children a sense of unshakable confidence in their worth and in her love for them.

Gansevoort, Saratoga County, was elusive, but Boston was stable, and Allan and Maria confidently sent Herman off in 1827 and 1829 (before and after his visit to the D'Wolfs) to spend the summer with his Melvill grandparents, alternating visits with Gansevoort (1826 and 1828). The Melvills lived at the northwest corner of the peninsula, on the south side of Green Street, which ran its short curving way from Bowdoin Square to Chambers

Street. The old wooden house was a simple chestlike structure, without external decoration (although the front door was deemed historic or artistic enough to be salvaged, in the 1830s, and set up in the house at the corner of Bartlett and Lambert streets in far away Roxbury). The house had been built close to the Mill Pond (already immortalized in the available texts of Benjamin Franklin's memoir). Beyond the dam (or where the dam had been in Herman's father's youth) ran the Charles River, but the river and especially the Mill Pond receded from Green Street year by year until 1824, when the last big hunks of Beacon Hill were trundled down in two-wheeled tip carts and dumped into the river for landfill. (Melville's early memory of the tip carts lies behind his remark in ch. 99 of *Moby-Dick* on the way hills about Boston are sold "by the cartload.") In Herman's childhood the adjacent house, second in from Staniford Street, was torn down and a brick church was erected there, next door to the Melvill house, and consecrated in 1826. Herman's grandfather could have afforded a much finer house, such as those the urbane entrepreneurs had put up on what was left of Beacon Hill, but he was a profoundly conservative man, content to live and die in his old house.

Like the Gansevoort house in Albany, the Melvill house in Boston had been rendered historic by Lafayette, who had called upon Thomas and Priscilla Scollay Melvill at a momentous time, during his visit to lay the cornerstone of the Bunker Hill Monument on 17 June 1825. Among the tangible treasures of the Green Street house was "a glass ship, fully rigged, modelled after the fashion of some celebrated French vessel," the delight of Herman's young eyes, very probably, as decades later a neighbor told Alexander Young, a Boston journalist, that it had been the delight of *his* own young eyes. (Melville later made use of it in *Redburn*, ch. 1.) Less spectacular but holy, shielded in a stoppered glass vial, was some "very precious tea — a part of that veritable tea which was thrown overboard when the American people resisted 'taxation without representation'" (so Alexander Young wrote, in an undated clipping preserved at the Berkshire Athenaeum). This witness also recalled that old Thomas Melvill used to display to visitors, including his grandsons, "a pair of high top Boots" — boots that caught some tea leaves as he and the other protesters were dumping it into Boston Harbor, off Long Wharf. Even in his early youth Herman may have studied the painting of the major's friend Samuel Adams, a copy of the one by John Singleton Copley, done early, before Copley left Boston for England. Paintings of the Hero and his wife were done in 1826 by Francis Alexander (who was later accorded the honor of painting Charles Dickens in Boston); the painting of the Hero went to the Bostonian Society in 1901, along with the "bottle of Tea." There was at least one more portrait of the Hero of the Tea Party, and portraits of other members of the family. On Green Street as in Albany the family portraits became objects of intense and reverent curiosity to the two older Melvill sons. There was a piano, on which stood a small painting of the Madonna and child, anomalous in a Puritanic city. There was always at least one tricornered hat, for even in the 1820s the old man knew a hatter who had not forgotten how to replace his cocked hat whenever the old one became too worn.

On his tenth birthday, at the end of the term at the New-York Male High School, his parents sent Herman to Boston again, two years after his first visit. There he got to test his father's impression that Grandfather Melvill was physically improved since his forced retirement, and bearing up with Roman dignity (the family rhetoric of the 1820s being self-consciously republican under the new American attempt to re-create a version of Roman government). The old man was always a good walker, and on Herman's second vacation, in 1829, he was unemployed, so he could multiply their strolls through the Common. The Hero could buy Herman that delicious beverage, an "egg pop" (something like an eggnog) from William Emmons, who kept his stand there. When the occasion was right Emmons would climb up and deliver an oration from the stand. Speech finished, he sold preprinted copies of his oration over the same counter where he sold his delectable drink. ("Pop" Emmons is remembered now only because Herman Melville referred to him in his 1850 essay about Hawthorne — misremembered, in fact, for Melville confused him, as many people did, with his brother Richard Emmons, author of the four-volume *Fredoniad*, an epic poem on America's naval battles in the War of 1812.) In 1829, if not 1827, the old man had time for a stroll with a grandson south and east across the peninsula to Fort Hill and South Battery and the nearby Griffin's Wharf, where he could feel again the excitement he had felt as a twenty-two-year-old on a chill December night when he boarded the Indiamen and helped to dump chests of tea into the water. The old major walked with Herman, as he did with Gansevoort, the historic route from the Old South Church at Marlborough and Milk streets to Fort Hill and Griffin's Wharf. With his cane the Hero could point out his own route to the wharf and the route of his return. (In Herman Melville's maturity, this was Liverpool Wharf, and greatly changed, like so much of the old Boston he had known.) There was no discreet blending into the throngs while taken in tow by the old major, "with whose cocked hat & small-clothes, worn to the end of his life, passed away probably the last vestige in New England of the old costume." (So Melville wrote in 1870, in a memoir of his Uncle Thomas, remembering how conspicuous a companion his grandfather had been, recognizable from afar by any Bostonian.)

Six decades later, Melville in *Billy Budd, Sailor* (ch. 8) could still recall not only some of the tales the old man could tell of the American Revolution but also the sense he had conveyed to the boy of the menace France had presented early in the nineteenth century under (a phrase Melville canceled) "the upstart Corsican": "At the height of Napoleon's unexampled conquests, there were Americans who had fought at Bunker Hill who looked forward to the possibility that the Atlantic might prove no barrier against the ultimate schemes of this French portentous upstart from the revolutionary chaos who seemed in act of fulfilling judgment prefigured in the Apocalypse." In another canceled line, Melville attributed this fear of Napoleon's designs to "venerable men" known to him "in his youth," one of whom was his Grandfather Melvill.

Among other intense feelings, sexual tension pervaded the Boston house of refuge just as it did the Albany house. The four sisters who remained in the Green Street house (three, after Lucy married in 1828) were all helpless to influence their father against advancing more money to Allan. As dutiful daughters they were expected to understand that consideration for the Melvill name required their father to support Thomas Jr.'s and Allan's children, who carried the Melvill name, rather than parting with his capital in order to dowry Priscilla (born in 1784), Jean (1788), Lucy (1795), and Helen (1798), all of them counting off the years as their hopes for marriage and motherhood were put in abeyance. Mary, long before, had been married early and well to John D'Wolf, and if she had lived Nancy Wroe would have married young Lemuel Shaw, now wealthy and married to his second wife. Thomas Melvill Jr. and Allan Melvill were free to be sexual beings, to beget children turn and turn about, while they took away their sisters' chances for marriage and parenthood. (When the old major died, late in 1832, the executors of the estate panicked, justifiably, in fear that fortune-hunters, long staved off, would descend upon the superannuated but suddenly desirable sisters.) After 1828 it was not humanly possible for the three single sisters to look upon their nieces and nephews with unalloyed affection, any more than Peter Gansevoort could look upon Mary and Leonard's brood and Maria and Allan's brood without wincing at the knowledge that his role was to be the good unmarried son and keep the household together as long as his mother lived. Allan's children had no sense, then or later, of just how deeply Allan Melvill had borrowed and just how manipulative he had become in order to further his progressively unbusinesslike purposes. In their ignorant injustice, Allan's children later came to regard their Melvill aunts as supremely selfish, much as they regarded Peter Gansevoort.

Leaving Peter to put her contingent of the children on a boat for Manhattan, in late August 1829 Maria visited her brother Herman at Gansevoort, Saratoga County, which, four months along in her pregnancy, she found to be a "land of heavenly quiet & repose" (she wrote Peter on 10 September), despite her well-justified irritation at her sister-in-law Catherine. Six children at home were enough, so Allan decided that Herman could remain in Boston until Maria came home — an acceptable plan, since the old major reported that Herman was "a decided favorite with Grand Parents, Aunts &c at Boston" (Allan wrote to Peter on 10 September). Catherine Van Schaick Gansevoort fell ill, so Maria was detained in Albany. On 12 September Allan asked his father to keep Herman a while longer, hoping that he continued "to be a good obedient Boy." On 26 September, after almost two months away, Herman returned "in charming health & spirits after a delightful visit which was equally agreeable to his friends — my Father says 'Herman has been an uncommon good Boy, & is a great favorite with us all' which commendation is fully confirmed by his Grand Mother & Aunts" (so Allan wrote to Peter). Two days later, on a Monday, Herman returned to school, this time along with Gansevoort, at the grammar school of Columbia College.

Allan and Maria Melvill's fourth son, their eighth child, was born on 24 January 1830, and named Thomas, a filial gesture toward the misused Hero of the Tea Party. The next month Lemuel Shaw during a rare trip out of Massachusetts pronounced them all flourishing. Documents for 1830 are extremely skimpy — most likely destroyed because they exposed Allan Melvill's precarious and distressing financial condition. A surviving carriage bill shows that Allan visited the Gansevoorts in Albany on 6 May 1830, plainly to consult about what could be done with his debts to his mother-in-law's estate. At this time he was forced to make an abject admission that he would never be able to repay the ten thousand and more dollars he owed her, a confession all the more shameful because she was extremely ill. We have at second hand Allan's rhetoric, for Thomas Jr., having unrealistically sought Peter Gansevoort's help in promoting him for a minor political appointment, wrote to Peter on 18 May: "We regret most deeply to learn by Allans Letter, that your excellent Mother, continues to suffer, under one of the most severe & disturbing afflictions, which can befal poor humanity." They found "great consolation to learn that she sustains her tryals, 'with the Courage of a Martyr, & the resignation of a Saint.' " On 20 May 1830 Allan wrote his father that he was planning to make a visit to Boston about 4 July, and to bring Gansevoort, who was "looking forward to pass his vacation at Boston with much pleasure." Gansevoort's injury seemed not to have retarded him, but his rapid growth at puberty was alarming his concerned father: "he is becoming a distinguished classical Scholar at the Grammar School, & is at the head of the Class in most of the English studies, but I fear is growing too fast for his health." The boy's bravery might, in fact, help to open the Melvill coffers.

Allan continued his 20 May 1830 letter with a character analysis of his next oldest children:

> Helen Maria also ranks very high at school, her natural talents are of the first
> order but like most young Girls she is rather giddy, & wants application, but
> still she continues to keep up with the list & is seldom at fault in her lessons —
> Herman I think is making more progress than formerly, & without being a
> bright Scholar, he maintains a respectable standing, & would proceed further,
> if he could be induced to study more — being a most amiable & innocent
> child, I cannot find it in my heart to coerce him, especially as he seems to have
> chosen Commerce as a favorite pursuit, whose practical activity can well
> dispense with much book knowledge.

This time Allan Melvill was comparing Herman not to Gansevoort but to
Herman himself when a little younger: the boy was making more progress
now. In his father's view, Herman was not "a bright Scholar," and perhaps not
even good enough to be what a later generation would call an underachiever.
He could improve, if he could be induced to study more — a fair indication
that there was a recalcitrant side to the boy, although not a defiant streak.
Herman was so amiable and innocent that his father hated the idea of forcing
him to study books, particularly since he seemed "to have chosen Commerce
as a favorite pursuit," his prospective pursuit as an adult. What this shows is
not any wish or aptitude manifested by Herman himself so much as Allan's
tendency to project onto the boy whatever he at the moment wanted from
him. Up to this point nothing in the surviving papers gives Allan Melvill's
notions as to any pursuit Gansevoort had chosen, but if he had made any such
decision it was apparently not one involving "practical activity." It would be a
mistake to reject this letter out of hand as wholly imperceptive and self-
deceiving. In the intensifying crisis, finding it harder than ever to concentrate on his historical and literary studies, Herman may have asserted some
degree of control over his circumstances by solving problems in arithmetic,
behavior that his father took as evidence of his choosing business as "a
favorite pursuit" in life. For his fourth child, Melvill named one accomplish-
ment: "Augusta is life and motion, but not much of a student, she has however danced herself into notice, for with scarce 2 quarters tuition, she was
pronounced by her master the most elegant Dancer at his last Ball." The
other children, he assured his father, were "too young to attract attention or
disclose character," although Allan had "a memory of Brass" and was "said to
have his full share of mother wit." If the Melvill household had continued on
its course for another decade, Gansevoort, Helen, Herman, Augusta, and
Allan might well have developed into adults with characters much like those
Allan now discerned in them; as it turned out, all the children except the
brilliant Gansevoort and the dogged Allan turned out very differently.
Both the older boys were disappointed that summer of 1830. Herman

had to give up a vacation with his recently married aunt Lucy Melvill Clark in Hadley, Massachusetts, and (as Allan wrote Peter on 27 July) Gansevoort had to decline "a very pressing invitation, to pass the vacation" in the family of Allan's cousin Prentiss near Baltimore, "which a pre-engagement to his Grand Parents prevented him from accepting." (Gansevoort had passed a vacation in 1822 with an Aunt Prentiss at Medfield; otherwise nothing is known of the Prentisses.) Herman, Allan added, was "much disappointed with regard to his visit to Hadley, but bears it like a Philosopher." Since he may have been spared the knowledge that his Uncle Herman and Aunt Catherine had refused to let him visit them, this is the first time on record that Herman had to take a child-sized portion of what he later called "a strong decoction of Seneca and the Stoics" (*Moby-Dick*, ch. 1, "Loomings"). Two weeks after Herman's birthday Allan had to quit his new store on Pine Street and work out of the Broadway house, so there was no concealing the financial disaster from the older children. Maria understandably found herself subject to "sudden depression" (as Allan wrote Peter on 21 August) and fled to Albany with all the children except Gansevoort and Herman, who remained as eyewitnesses to the disintegration of their world. The old major wrote on 30 September: "Im glad for you that your Children, are so promising, it is one of the greatest Comforts to a Parent when they Conduct well, it is our part to *Guard*, and *guide, them* with a firm and *Steady Step* — and to look to the *Parent* of all for Direction." The Hero of the Tea Party, like his two sons, was a champion at professing fine sentiments and denying reality.

One reality was that soon after Maria arrived in Albany Augusta became so sick that she was taken to the hospital — an extraordinary measure. In New York Allan and his two older sons, keeping Bachelors' Hall for the last time, prayed "night and morning" for her recovery, her father wrote her on 2 September. It was no preference for Herman that made Allan keep his second son in New York when his wife, summoned down for the purpose, and Gansevoort left with the furniture on 8 October: only Gansevoort was big enough to escort his mother, so it would be more practical for the mother to go up with the first son, the father to go up with the second son. Allan had perfected, before now, his dumbfounding ability to behave at moments as if nothing were wrong with his situation — an ability that struck his sons alternately as reassuring and unnerving. With Maria and Gansevoort present and work to be done, perhaps even Melvill hands put to unaccustomed lifting and hauling, the four may have found reassurance in action. On 9 October the terror of loss was free to stalk the man and the boy in the vacant rooms in the house on Broadway.

[3]

"The Terrors of Death"
Albany, 1831–1832

Let us improve the Time we have,
There's no repentance in the grave.

"Allan Melvills Book," 1796

WHEN THE MELVILLS FLED to Albany, Catherine Van Schaick Gansevoort had been in fragile health for many months. Since Allan's frantic visit the previous May and the subsequent necessity of reviewing and revising provisions of her will, her state of mind had been tumultuous. To spare her from fresh disruption, and to prevent the indeterminate occupation of his mother's house by a family of ten, Peter put the Melvills in a rented house nearby. In the old days, whenever Herman Melvill reached Albany he had been taken directly to the Gansevoort house at 46 North Market Street, but this time, after arriving just before noon on 11 October 1830, he and his father joined Maria and the other seven children at 338 North Market, at the southeast corner of North Market and Steuben Street. Quickly the Melvills established something that was outwardly like a normal life. On 15 October Gansevoort and Herman were registered at the Albany Academy, several blocks west, across from the state capitol. In the fourth department Herman studied geography, reading and spelling, penmanship, arithmetic, English grammar, and natural history. He was drilled in six "Catechisms" in separate small books, four on history (universal, Grecian, Roman, and English), one on classical biography, and another on Jewish antiquities. One textbook of Melville's survives, *The English Reader; or, Pieces in Prose and Poetry, Selected from the Best Writers*, by Lindley Murray (Canandaigua, 1819).

The Albany Academy was a good school for a boy with no threatening crises at home. Alexander W. Bradford, who became Gansevoort's closest friend and who later took an interest in Herman, recalled life at the academy in a commemorative oration at the semicentennial celebration of the Albany Academy a third of a century later, 26 June 1863: "Between the pleasures of study and the acquisition of knowledge, the sports of out door life, and the charms of social intercourse, there was everything to excite and animate even a sluggish nature." At the academy Herman also gained a friendship that lasted until death—with Eli James Murdock Fly, who attended from September 1829 until 1 June 1834, and thereafter became a clerk in Peter Gansevoort's law office. (Fly was born on 25 November 1817, between Gansevoort and Herman.) Neither of the Melvill boys was free to live the life of normal students that Bradford recalled so fondly. Like the others in the new Melvill household, they suffered the strains of a disrupted life, and all four older children, Gansevoort, Helen, Herman, and Augusta, knew that the family was in an undeniably chaotic financial state. Their mother was a poor relation banished from the great Gansevoort house down the street, and Allan Melvill was a hired man—not the manager of a branch office of a cap and fur store, as he liked to imply, but a clerk, a difference obvious to children who had seen him flourishing among his own employees in his own stores in New York City.

In the same month that the father and second son arrived on the *Swiftsure* the crisis became so intense that Peter Gansevoort himself made the arduous trip to Boston to discuss Allan's finances with the old major. More than three years later, on 20 February 1834, Peter drafted an answer to questions posed by Allan's friend Lemuel Shaw, chief justice of the Supreme Judicial Court of Massachusetts, in his capacity as co-executor with John D'Wolf of old Thomas Melvill's estate. In the surviving draft, Peter explained what happened during his trip to Boston in October 1830: "I had several conversations, with the good and venerable Major Melvill at that time on the subject of Allans situation & that of his family—He knew that I had brot Allan & his family to this City." The old major furthermore had been informed that with the exception "of a Clerks Hire which Allan rec^d from one of us Electors" (that is, from one of the citizens of Albany) he and his family were "dependent on us for their support"—dependent on Peter and his mother. On 3 November 1830, after Peter's return, Allan Melvill asked his father, once again, for money, and wrote him on 4 December that his situation had become "almost intolerable for the want of $500 to discharge some urgent debts" and "provide necessaries" for his family. He explained that "the daily expenses" of his family were being supplied "by occasional loans from Peter," and that he was in immediate danger of prosecution for the last quarter's rent on the Broadway house "& other demands which were unavoidably left unpaid at New York." Allan was "destitute of resources & without a shilling," but $500 would save him "from a world of trouble," and enable him "to look forward with renewed hopes," in the expectation of afterward being able to support himself, which "repeated losses & disappointments" had prevented him from doing. By this time father and son both knew that there was absolutely no prospect that the $500 could last Allan until he could become self-sufficient and a provider for his family. Yet, responding to his son's frantic state, the old major sent the money. No one knows what Allan Melvill did with it, any more than anyone knows just what he did with the more than $20,000 that his father and his mother-in-law had advanced him already, taking one large loan with another. Some of this fortune went for rent and household expenses, a few dollars (a hundred or so all told?) for tuition for the children, small amounts for servants and hired help at the store, and some of it in the earlier years, at least, went for imported dry goods that Allan could rarely dispose of at a profit. The cause, according to him, always was some downturn in the economy or some surge in popularity of the auction system that was always impossible for him to participate in — too plebeian, perhaps.

It was more than the widow of the Hero of Fort Stanwix could endure to have Allan nearby, wholly dependent on her bounty (and old Major Melvill's), and to know that her daughter and her eight grandchildren were existing on handouts from her and Peter. (In 1831 her daughter-in-law Mary Chandonette Gansevoort was out of the house, staying in Waterford much of the time to care for her uncle, Geurt, or Guert, Van Schoonhoven.) Catherine Van Schiack Gansevoort sank rapidly that autumn. The family summoned Herman Gansevoort down to his mother's deathbed, perhaps by a special messenger, but he arrived too late, after her death on 30 December 1830. Leonard's widow, Mary, phrased the news in biblical terms to Catherine Quackenboss Gansevoort: "Our dear Herman did not arrive in time to receive her last blessing." Very much "overcome," the oldest son of the Hero had asked Mary to write the letter to his wife for him:

> Oh Catherine our beloved Mother is no more; her precious soul took its departure on thursday mor^g at 9 oclk. My dear Catherine never can that comforting passage in scripture be better applyed than to her & us — Our loss is her gain; her sufferings are ended; she is now in the presence of her God. She bore her extreme sufferings with the utmost patience, & her faith never failed. She told Mr Ludlow, who asked her, if she was alarmed at the approach of death — "No, I know in whom I have put my trust, I will lay in the arms of Jesus." Blessed, comforting words. . . . Oh Cate how I wish you was here, I want you to see how calm & dignifyed she lays in death.

Maria and her husband and her eight children also saw just how calm and dignified the widow of the Hero lay — more calmly and with more dignity than anyone else could muster.

Long before his mother died, Peter was utterly disgusted at serving as surrogate father for Leonard's and Maria's children, but he had no easy way out of the role that he had been acting for a decade or more. Sometime in this period, before or soon after his mother's death, Peter Gansevoort rented a house for his sister-in-law Mary, Leonard's widow, and two of her younger children, Catherine (born 1814) and Stanwix (born 1822), so that he could be alone in the big house. Some of the family remembered little Allan's charming hope that he would "go Grand Ma house morrow morning"; now the children, especially the older ones, were left to experience the strangeness of being in Albany, near the house that had been their grandmother's, without their grandmother. Albany had been a city of refuge with a house of refuge, and now it was neither, except insofar as the familiar faces and furniture from Manhattan were in the rented Melvill house near what was now Uncle Peter's house. Helen more than a decade later remembered her Grandmother Gansevoort well; she met a relative of Lemuel Shaw's, "a dear old lady, who looked so much like Grandma Gansevoort" that she "wanted to kiss her" (as she wrote Augusta on 16 February 1842). Two decades later, just after Peter sold the house, in a letter of 16 May 1851 to Allan Jr. (in the collection at Arrowhead, the Berkshire County Historical Society), Augusta still referred to it as "Grandmamma's house." Born between the two girls, Herman was old enough to have similarly vivid memories.

Once Peter had the old mansion on North Market Street to himself and his own servants at last, in his early forties, soon after his mother's death, he felt it prudent to allow himself to fall quite passionately in love with the daughter of Nathan Sanford, who had been chancellor of the state of New York in the mid-1820s. Sanford was said to have pocketed one hundred thousand dollars a year in fees as United States attorney for the district of New York (1803–15). Even if this sum was wildly inflated (it could have supported three dozen families in comfort), the post was lucrative almost beyond imagination. This declaration of Peter Gansevoort's to Mary Sanford is undated, but written early in 1833: "My love for you, is pure and holy—there is not a particle of interest in its composition—I had never found a recipient for my heart." Here he revealed that in 1831, the year after the Melvills fled to Albany, he had suffered, at forty-three, all belatedly, something like the pangs of adolescent love: "Do you remember, that about two years since, I had the honor at table of being seated between your excellent Mother and yourself. . . . Do not be surprised when I tell you, that from that moment, I purposely avoided you—and that it was not until I had reason to hope that I was not indifferent to you, that I suffered the least manifestation of my strong partiality." Peter had never found "a recipient" for his heart because he had not been free to look for one.

Late in February 1831, Allan wrote to his brother, Thomas Jr., conveying, perhaps for the first time, word of his removal to Albany and at least guarded news of the disaster that had befallen him. Thomas Jr., in this reversal of their positions, wrote twice in the next weeks (quite unlike himself) but received no reply before 15 April, when he wrote the old major: "My good Brother Allans situation, was as unexpected to me, as it appears to have been to you, and from himself, I have learnt only, the unhappy facts; — Being now among his connexions, possessing as they do, a very considerable influence, I cannot but hope, he will yet be able, to retrieve past ill fortune. — but I have no knowledge of what may be his occupations, or prospects." This was all wishful thinking, since the only effectual connection Allan had in Albany was Maria's overburdened brother Peter.

In March 1831 the Boston family experienced an odd bit of notoriety when the *Amateur* published a poem by Oliver Wendell Holmes, a recent (1829) Harvard graduate who had studied law a year under Joseph Story, associate justice of the U.S. Supreme Court, and was now studying medicine under Dr. James Jackson. The poem was "The Last Leaf," the subject of which, everyone in the city knew at once, was the old and now unemployed Major Melvill, the Hero of the Tea Party:

> My grandmamma has said —
> Poor old lady, she is dead
>   Long ago —
> That he had a Roman nose,
> And his cheek was like a rose
>   In the snow.
>
> But now his nose is thin,
> And it rests upon his chin
>   Like a staff,
> And a crook is in his back,
> And a melancholy crack
>   In his laugh.
>
> I know it is a sin
> For me to sit and grin
>   At him here;
> But the old three-cornered hat,
> And the breeches, and all that,
>   Are so queer!
>
> And if I should live to be
> The last leaf upon the tree
>   In the spring,
> Let them smile, as I do now,
> At the old forsaken bough
>   Where I cling.

It was a cheeky performance by a young man with more wit than reverence. Whether or not it distressed its subject, everyone assumed that the notoriety would cease in a few days, but oddly enough the poem caught the whim of the public, and the poet became famous. As the decades passed the family began to take pride in the fact that the young whippersnapper, by then an eminent literary man, had immortalized the old major, and as late as the 1890s the poet, himself by then still more aged than the major had been, willingly wrote out the lines as a keepsake for one of the old major's great-grandchildren.

In Albany Allan Melvill toiled on as a clerk, but he managed to keep the three older boys in school. That summer of 1831 Herman took an arithmetic class under the care of Professor Henry and for the second time in his life surprised everyone by doing extremely well. Herman was awarded first premium in his class, a copy of *The London Carcanet, Containing Select Passages from the Most Distinguished Writers* (New York, 1831), enriched by an inscription from the principal of the academy, who did not bother to determine how the surname was spelled:

ALBANY ACADEMY.
To Herman Melville
The first best in his class
in ciphering books.
T. Romeyn Beck, Principal.

The Albany *Argus* on 9 August announced that the awards had been bestowed at a solemn ceremony in the City Hotel. This is probably the first time Herman Melvill saw his name in print, spelled Melville; later it was his first name that tended to be misspelled, as Hermann. Naturally Herman was accorded less praise than Gansevoort had received for his greater achievements in New York in 1826, but his triumph may have influenced his parents' decision to take only him and Augusta with them on a trip. The four took the noon stage for Pittsfield on 11 August—an eight-hour ride across low hills interspersed with gentle valleys, with the Catskills visible behind and the Berkshires ahead. Herman recalled this episode almost four decades later when he wrote a brief memoir of his Uncle Thomas for a history of Pittsfield. Misremembering it as the first time he had seen his uncle, he got the year right, and retained a powerful image that had been reinforced, and altered, by his later gallery-going in Europe:

It was in 1831, I think, at evening, after a summer day's travel by stage from Albany. Well do I remember the meeting, upon that occasion, between him and my father. It was in the larch-shaded porch of the mansion looking off, under urn-shaped road-side elms, across meadows to South Mountain.

They embraced, and with the unaffectedness and warmth of boys — such boys as Van Dyck painted.

The Albany Melvills stayed two nights at the Melvill place, then early on 13 August Allan and Maria left Augusta on the farm and took the stage to Hadley, a ten-hour ride, where they left Herman with Lucy Melvill Clark for his long-postponed visit, then went on to Boston, where Allan and the old major conferred and where Allan apparently promised to repay a small portion of what he had borrowed, as soon as he could. From Boston on 17 August Maria found some encouraging news about her oldest son for mention to Peter: "by the by two learned Gentlemen who saw G at Harvard university two years since when he went over it with one of his Cousins, ask^d particularly about him, they admired his intelligence & questions." She pushed her point: "if G— is noticed in Boston, where every lad is intelligent," they "should do much to preserve, foster, & increase" his talents and opportunities. On 1 September both Gansevoort and Herman returned to begin their second year at the Albany Academy, but even the tiny tuition fee seemed too much to pay, and Herman was "dismissed" (withdrawn) in October, after one year there; Allan was kept in the academy until 1 December and Gansevoort until the next March.

On 8 October 1831, a year to the day since Maria's flight from Manhattan with the furniture, the Melvill family gathered in their Market Street house to hear the baptismal ceremony together for the last time. It was performed by the Reverend Dr. Ludlow of the First Reformed Dutch Church, and, making up for neglect, it served for two babies, the last daughter and last son of Allan and Maria Melvill, Frances Priscilla (called Fanny) and Thomas. On 29 October Allan somehow prevailed upon Peter Gansevoort to loan him two thousand dollars, the whole of which he sent to his father. A month later he left for New York City to confer with Joseph Greenleaf (Allan's Grandmother Scollay had been Mercy Greenleaf, but this man seems to have been related to Herman Gansevoort's wife). At some point Greenleaf laid out a sheaf of claims against Allan for his inspection. Allan kept them for two days then returned them in much haste, on 7 December, "as he was about to go to Steam boat."

On the trip upriver to Albany the *Constellation* got as far as Poughkeepsie by the next morning. There it pulled ashore, obstructed by the ice on the Hudson, which had formed suddenly, earlier than usual. On 8 December the only conveyance Allan could take to Rhinebeck was "an open one horse waggon" (he recorded in his diary), although he was dressed to travel in a ship's sleeping cabin, not an uncovered wagon. At Rhinebeck he found some shelter overnight, and the next day, the ninth, he climbed into "an open 2 horse waggon" for the trip to the town of Hudson, where he spent the night. The next morning, 10 December, with the thermometer at two below zero, he took a covered sleigh pulled by a pair of horses and arrived at Greenbush, across the river from Albany, "at ¼ before 5"—when it was darkening fast. The clouds obscuring any light from the sliver of a moon (it was two days before the new moon), Allan Melvill crossed the frozen Hudson on foot in near pitch darkness except for what little candle and lamp glow showed ahead from buildings on the west bank of the river. There at last, he made his way to Market Street. Frantic, even fanatical nervous energy propelled him a while. Despite his exhaustion he wrote up his diary, listing the incidental expenses on the way to New York (seventy-five cents) and on his return (a surprisingly low forty-two cents). This entry concluded his diary.

That bleak month both the sons of the Hero of the Tea Party collapsed. On 22 December Thomas Jr. bemoaned his inability to visit the old major and Priscilla Scollay Melvill: "Oh, my good father—when I reflect how foolishly—nay, *more than foolishly,* I have squandered hundreds—on hundreds—and that I am deterred from visiting my aged Parents, for a few decimals—it causes a bitterness of . . . which I will not attempt to describe." It was only just that *he* should suffer, but unfair that his folly was causing those he loved to suffer from his absence. He gave no consolation to his parents by adding that he had "not heard from Allan for some time."

By the end of December Allan Melvill was, in fact, unwell, but on his feet. Not allowing himself to recover at home from his ordeal, Melvill pushed himself beyond his physical limits and thereby induced a hyperexcited state in which he could not receive the benefits of sleep. Obsessively he attempted to attend to business, both the routine tasks by which he earned his clerk's hire and the harrowing burden of dealing with Greenleaf's messages about his creditors in Manhattan. Melvill managed to write his brother one more time. In his Bible on 5 January 1832 he marked two verses of Psalm 55: "My heart is sore pained within me: and the terrors of death are fallen upon me. Fearfulness and trembling are come upon me and horror hath overwhelmed me." Maria later commented in the margin: "This Chapter was mark'd a few days before my dear *Allan* by reason of severe suffering was deprive'd of his Intellect. God moves in a misterious way." Allan was so sick on 8 January 1832 that Peter Gansevoort declined an invitation to dinner because of "the ill health of Mʳ Melvill." Allan's condition was so bad on 10 January that Peter decided it was time to summon Thomas Melvill Jr., although from his sad experience fourteen years earlier he knew that the older son of the Hero of the Tea Party would bring his own melodrama with him:

I deeply lament the painful necessity of advising you of the melancholly situation of our brother Allan.

He was unwell, when he last wrote to you But persisting in giving attention to his business — He devoted himself so closely and assiduously, as to produce a state of excitement, which in a great measure robbed him of his sleep. It is but a few days since he yielded to the wishes of his friends and remained at home. The excitement however could not be allayed and yesterday he occasionally manifested an alienation of Mind. Last night he became much worse — and to day he presents the melancholly spectacle of a deranged man — I hope it may be in your power to visit Albany *immediately* — I have purposely avoided writing to your father, fearing the effect of this intelligence upon your venerable parents — I leave to your discretion the mode of conveying the heart rending intelligence to our friends in Boston.

The letter reached Pittsfield the next day, and rather than pausing to write his parents Thomas Jr. left at once for Albany, arriving "in *six hours* after" he received Peter's letter — astonishing speed.

From the Melvill house Thomas Jr. wrote to Lemuel Shaw on 15 January that he had found Allan "*very sick* — induced by a variety of causes — under great mental excitement — at times fierce, even *maniacal.*" Thomas put upon Shaw the "painfull" task of telling the old Melvills of Allan's "afflicting situation," although the worst news was private, for Shaw alone: "in short my dear sir, Hope, is no longer permitted of his recovery, in the opinion of the attending Physicians and indeed, — oh, how hard for a brother to say! — I *ought not* to hope it. — for, — in all human probability — he would live, *a Maniac!*" Thomas Jr. was prone to experience extremes of sensibility and to indulge in extremes of expression as he analyzed those feelings, but Maria's independent testimony confirms what he wrote Shaw. Allan was raving, as well he might, for he profoundly loved his wife and his children (although he had little chance to notice the younger ones, especially the two-year-old, Thomas), and he was tortured with the knowledge that he had squandered Maria's fortune and his own inheritance, what should have been a substantial patrimony. A few days later Herman Gansevoort came down from Gansevoort and on his return noted in his "Checkbook and Remembrancer, 1823–1832" that Allan's case was "hopeless."

For all his mental wanderings, Allan Melvill knew some of what was happening around him, for on 27 January Thomas began a letter to Shaw in Peter's law office and finished it at Allan's bedside, after Allan had sent for him, perhaps his last request. In this letter Thomas wrote: "*I fear, he, will not be blessed with reason* — "; nor was he blessed with life much longer. Allan Melvill died half an hour before midnight on 28 January 1832, a Saturday.

His funeral service was held in the rented Market Street house at three in the afternoon on 31 January, preceding his burial in the Dutch Church section of the Common (that is, interdenominational) Albany Cemetery. He was a little more than two months short of his fiftieth birthday. During her husband's last illness Maria managed to keep Helen and Augusta in school. Since twelve-year-old Herman had been withdrawn from school the previous October, he was in the house all during the last weeks of his father's life. Whatever horror he and the other children saw and heard during the days before and after Allan Melvill's death was not recorded. The older children, at least, may have seen their father when he presented "the melancholly spectacle of a deranged man," after it was concluded that if he lived he might be "*a Maniac,*" and they may have heard some of whatever ravings justified the descriptions Peter and Thomas gave of his condition. Very likely they saw their mother and Uncle Thomas in throes of unrestrained grief. Gansevoort, Helen, Herman, and Augusta witnessed and remembered. Even Catherine was aware of much that went on; her grandniece Eleanor, old enough to remember her well, recorded in 1953 that she was "born with what the Yankees call 'an anxious make'"; more likely, Catherine, who would later "wear herself to an anatomy" in any crisis, was marked for life by early traumas. Allan Jr., who ought to have remembered better than Catherine, knew little of what was happening or else quickly forgot what he saw and heard, according to a diary he started in 1843.

Allan Melvill lived in Herman's memory not as an American merchant or a hired clerk. Instead, the father in Herman's memory was a cosmopolitan gentleman in whose veins coursed the blood of the earl of Melville House and the blood of remoter noble and even royal ancestors — that queen of Hungary, those kings (and surely queens) of Norway. Allan Melvill had been one of the great travelers of the world, for Herman (like Gansevoort and Helen) had seen the evidence in the little green journal with its "Recapitulations of Voyages and Travels from 1800 to 1822 both inclusive." The sums entered there were awesome: by land 24,425 miles, by water 48,460 miles, days in transit by sea or land, 643. Uncle John in empty Alaska had made friends with the great Langsdorff and had crossed empty Siberia, but on *his* travels in England, Scotland, revolutionary France (and even Spain) Allan Melvill had visited St. Paul's, Westminster Abbey, Notre Dame, the great architectural monuments depicted in his portfolios of engravings and watercolors, and he had made the acquaintance of poets, biographers, editors, politicians, statesmen, as well as great merchants, sea captains, and who knew what array of lesser folk. Above all, he had been received by his noble cousin the earl of Leven and Melville. With his amazing stories of adventures on sea and land Allan Melvill had made himself heroic in Herman's eyes. More than that, whenever a Frenchman came into his store, he had transformed himself into a man of deepest mystery, for the familiar loving "Pa" suddenly spoke a tongue as incomprehensible to the children as the Hebrew that God spoke.

The three rhetoricians among the children, the three who delighted in the English language all their lives, were the three who knew their father best, Gansevoort, Helen, and Herman. More than their mother or any of the Gansevoorts, Allan Melvill lived in their memories and imagination in elegantly structured words of the English language. All their lives they had heard him discourse fluently on all manner of subjects besides his adventures — their own character, domestic conditions, behavior appropriate for children to display toward their contemporary cousins and their elders, religion, politics, economics, foreign wars and threats of war. Allan Melvill wrote and spoke like an eloquent eighteenth-century English gentleman.

Pronouncements such as his children heard from day to day survive in Allan Melvill's correspondence, for he shared his profound opinions with friends and relatives. Bring up altruism, and he would offer his highly personal opinion "that Self Interest" was "in general the great predominative principle of human actions." Comment on the conduct of a newspaper, and he would offer his reasoned conclusion that under "all free governments the freedom of the Press degenerates into licentiousness." The previous examples are from an early letter to Lemuel Shaw, before Allan was married, but such pronouncements continued through his marriage. Allan was capable of deciding (as he wrote his father in the year of Herman's birth) that "sound practical honesty, guided by prudence & judgement," should ideally "prove an overmatch for habitual knavery" — but he could still make the thoughtful reservation: in some circumstances knavery might win out. Hearing his opinions, his children were persuaded that "Pa" knew all there was to know about world affairs: who else had solved the puzzle of which was better, a monarchy or a republic? No matter that his pronouncements were conventional opinion elegantly couched, they sounded in his children's ears as if they were products of his unique hard-won philosophical comprehension of the workings of the universe.

Herman, like Gansevoort and Helen, also knew his "Pa" as a master of persiflage when an occasion evoked it. When Uncle Peter tried to engage in extravagant verbal play, he was heavy handed; the verbal weapon *he* flourished at the heads of children (as documented late in his life) was terse ironic mockery that devastated its small victim. By contrast, "Pa" could write a letter such as one to Peter on 26 September 1826, a lawyerly letter that Maria may have asked her brother to give her, since it descended through her own lawyer son Allan before going to the Berkshire Athenaeum. Its occasion was some facetious complaint Peter had made about his guests, the sisters-in-law

Mary Chandonette Gansevoort and Maria Gansevoort Melvill, after their arrival together from New York. Addressing his response to Peter as "Counsellor at Law," Allan officially protested against Peter's disparagement:

> Your letters of the 15th & 16th inst are on file unanswered, the first however being a severe tirade or philippic against two of the gentler sex, both prodigious favourites of mine, & one of them in my eyes at least "a seeming Paragon," my own lovely wedded wife, your only beloved Sister, you will permit me in comity to glance over with a dry acknowledgement, which must not however be construed into a tacit acquiescence in its propriety, for nothing legal in the whole course of your practice, in fact or argument, could have been more manifestly improper as it regards the aforesaid fair Ladies, & in this case[,] Counsellor, silence must in no wise be tortured by law logic or professional ingenuity into consent, which it by no means implies, and I do here most solemnly protest, & beg you would enter the plea on your official record, against the injustice & indecorum of a most outrageous fulmination, which nothing could extenuate, but your being uncourteously arrested on your way to dinner, which however unpalatable to you, was a palliative to the Ladies, & the only thing which saved your bacon.

This joy in parody flourished in the speech and writing of Allan's first three children, and emerged in labored fashion in some of Augusta's correspondence, but not in the speech or writing of the younger four children.

Just as Gansevoort, Helen, and Herman, the children who heard Allan's words the longest, in adult life could imitate and even outdo him in parody, they also learned to imitate the high formal diction Allan excelled in. They absorbed the rhetoric displayed in his final instructions (27 October 1824) to his twelve-year-old nephew, Guert Gansevoort, who was about to sail on the frigate *Constitution*, on his first voyage:

> you are now fairly launched at an early age upon the great Ocean of life . . . with Honour for a compass, & Glory for a watch word, you may in peace or war, become a brave & accomplished naval Officer . . . but above all, my little sailor Boy, let me conjure you, forget not your Creator in the dawn of youth . . . neglect not the Bible, regard it as your polar star, its religious precepts & moral doctrines are alike pure & sublime, & equally inculcate obedience, patriotism, fortitude, & temperance.

Four years to the day later, Allan wrote Peter that early in the morning "Midshipman Guert Gansevoort" had done them "the favor to call on his way to Brooklyn & the Pacific Ocean." The children heard this magnificently expansive phrasing and understood it, at some level, as the formulation of a man who was not only a cosmopolitan but was at ease in the cosmos.

Memories of that phrasing, and other such formulations, emerged in "The Carpet-Bag" (*Moby-Dick*, ch. 2): "I stuffed a shirt or two into my old carpet-bag, tucked it under my arm, and started for Cape Horn and the Pacific. Quitting the good city of old Manhatto, I duly arrived in New Bedford." In such ways did the voice of Allan Melvill live on in the writing and speech of his first three children.

Toward the end of *Moby-Dick* (ch. 132, "The Symphony"), Ahab imagines his wife's telling his son about him ("cannibal old me") abroad upon the deep. About the time he wrote that passage, Herman Melville prophesied to Nathaniel Hawthorne that he would go down to posterity as "a 'man who lived among the cannibals.'" He was referring to his reputation as the man who had lived with the natives in the Typee valley in the Marquesas, but he had passed his first twelve years as the second son of a cannibal father. Allan Melvill, more some years, less some years, systematically had eaten up his children's futures, all the while indulgently providing them with luxuries paid for with other people's money, all the while professing, and feeling, the most profound concern for their welfare. It was impossible for the older children not to love Allan Melvill and impossible to understand what they knew of his behavior and his death, for he had done everything to evoke love from them all the time he was devouring their futures as day-to-day sustenance.

For her part, in January 1832 Maria learned just how a Melvill man could die when nothing was organically wrong. Having witnessed her husband's decline, she was forever after alert for signs that one or another of her sons might repeat his father's pattern. Lemuel Shaw, most likely, prepared the notice published in the 3 February Boston *Daily Advertiser and Patriot:*

> By the warmth of his affections, the purity of his principles, the undeviating integrity of his conduct, combined with great vigor of mind, and firmness and perseverance of purpose, and more especially of that equanimity arising from a firm confidence in the hopes and promises of another and better life, Mr. Melvill's character was such, as in no ordinary degree, to conciliate the affections, and to command the unshaken confidence of all those with whom he was associated, in business, in friendship, or in the nearer and more tender relations of domestic life.

A tiny portion of this tribute is verifiable by the surviving documents: Allan Melvill's affections had been warm, his mind had once possessed great vigor, and through most if not all of his life he had indeed been confident that he would live in heaven after death. The rest of the encomium might have been true of the very youthful Allan Melvill, but not of the man his son Herman knew.

Two decades later, toward the end of 1851, Herman Melville wrote into *Pierre* an account of the death of the father of his young hero, Pierre Glendinning: "His father had died of a fever; and, as is not uncommon in such maladies, toward his end, he at intervals lowly wandered in his mind" (bk. 4, ch. 2). In this novel the nurse muses over the fact that "so excellent a gentleman, and so thoroughly good a man, should wander so ambiguously in his mind," for the elder Glendinning, father of the supposed only child Pierre, calls out "My daughter! — God! God! — my daughter!" This cry is interpreted later in the book by young Pierre as an indication that he might have a half-sister, older than he and illegitimate. As far as we know, Allan Melvill did not rave about any of his daughters, Helen, Augusta, Catherine, or Fanny, but the circumstances of his death are so closely re-created in Herman Melville's novel as to suggest that as the oldest male not in school Herman was indeed very much aware of the stages of his father's decline.

Soon after Allan's death Thomas Jr. went to Boston — the older and only surviving son undertaking the sad mission of telling his aged parents details about the death and the burial of their son far from the city of his birth. No doubt he told his father what he had learned about Allan's borrowing against Maria's inheritance and tried to learn all he could about what Allan had owed the old major, although the father now, as always, withheld specific financial information from his unreliable son — the living one. Soon Thomas learned that between Allan's death and his own arrival in Boston, two women had called twice at the house on Green Street to discuss their claims against Allan Melvill's estate, both times, as it happened, missing the old major. The same two women pressed their claims again in a letter to Lemuel Shaw, written some months or perhaps a year or two later, after Shaw had undertaken his duties as executor of the estate of the old major. Shaw thereupon wrote to Thomas Jr., and, not receiving a satisfactory answer, wrote at least once more. In reply, Thomas Jr. told Shaw that if he remembered aright the women had called twice, and had seen only Priscilla Scollay Melvill and her daughter Helen. Thomas Jr. assured Shaw (as he had done in the previous letter, now lost): "I feel confident that my good father *never saw*, — or at least *never knew*, or *conversed*, either with *her* [Mrs. A. M. A.] or *Mrs B.*"

In 1832 his mother and his sister had conferred with Thomas Jr. about the "circumstance," as he called it in an undated letter to Shaw, with this result: "it was concluded that I should call on them which I did, and succeeded in dispelling the erroneous ideas they had formed of *claims*, on my father — as well as the condition of my late brothers affairs." Priscilla Scollay Melvill must have sent a sum of money along with her son, for his account to Shaw continues:

I well remember having paid some money to Mrs B — what the amount of it was, I do not remember, — nor, if it was a *part*, or *the whole* of what she may have claimed as due.

Mrs. A. M. A. — must be mistaken in stating that I *"gave her some encouragement."* — On what foundation could I give her encouragement? I had no means of my own. My brother left none — and I had strong reasons to think, that it would not be done, by those members of my own family who might have means, should the case be made known to them. — All of whom, except Helen, are to this day, as I presume, ignorant of her existence.

He added this tantalizing paragraph: "From the little I saw of her, I thought her quite an interesting young person, — that it was most unfortunate she had not been brought up different — and I most deeply regret that she too, has been called to feel the disappointments & sorrows, so generally attending our earthly sojourn."

This letter from Thomas Jr. to Shaw at some point was removed from the main Shaw archive now in the Massachusetts Historical Society and survives in the Social Law Library in Boston. The Harvard psychologist Henry A. Murray and the poet Charles Olson knew it for some years before Amy Puett found it again and published it, in 1977. The letter is susceptible to the highly melodramatic reading that Allan Melvill had sired an illegitimate daughter by "Mrs. B." long before his death, presumably before his marriage, for neither of the women, whatever their relationship, was a child. Mrs. A. M. A. (the "Mrs." not necessarily identifying a married woman) was clearly the younger, but she was grown or almost grown, since she was a "young person" who had in fact already been "brought up," however lacking in advantages and however exposed to sorrows. Upon hearing the news of Allan Melvill's death, the women had decided to press their claims at once, and had called twice to do so. Grateful that the old major had not encountered them either time, Mrs. Melvill and Helen Melvill had sent Thomas Jr. to pay them off, away from the Green Street house, so the old major would never need to hear anything about them. Thomas, himself sorrowful over his inability to educate his own children, had recognized young Mrs. A. M. A. as "quite an interesting young person" and had felt natural pity for her, but knew he could not materially assist her. As far as is known, "the case" was not made known to the rest of the family. This does not sound like a claim involving two women who had supplied Allan Melvill with something like scissors and scalloping shears on credit and now wanted to collect their business debt while there was time. If they were presenting a bill for goods delivered but not paid for, they could have pressed their claims in the courts, and if it were such a bill there would have been no need to spare the old major from learning about it.

Henry Murray may have identified the two women accurately as Ann Bent and her niece Ann Middleton Allen, importers of English and French goods, who lived at 214 Washington Street in Boston. Murray found a telling connection between Allan Melvill and Ann Bent, "a letter from Allan Melvill to his father, dated December 23, 1823, instructing Major Melvill to pay a number of debts, one of which was to Ann Bent, in the amount of $7774." However, the document in question involves $77.74, not $7774.00, and it asks the major to *collect* the money from Ann Bent, not to pay it to her. This Ann M. Allen was born in Canton, Massachusetts, on 11 April 1798, to Martha Bent Allen, who the previous December 12 had married Bethuel Allen, in Canton, when she was some five months pregnant — not an extraordinary occurrence in New England at that time. The age of Martha Bent Allen at the time of her daughter Ann's birth is unknown; Allan Melvill turned sixteen the week Ann M. Allen was born. At just past fifteen years old the summer before, he could have fathered a child: Melvill, judging from what we know of his sons, was not slow to reach physical maturity. But there is no evidence that he did father this particular child, and it is not wholly certain that the two women who called at the Melvill house in 1832 were Miss Bent and Miss Allen.

If Herman Melville had not published *Pierre*, in which the hero's father, a man very like Allan Melvill in some particulars, seems to have begotten, before his marriage, an illegitimate daughter, apparently the very woman who presents herself to the hero of the novel some years after the death of the father, then it might be easier to take the letter from Thomas Jr. to Shaw as referring to a slightly unusual business situation, where two women had pressed their claims for payment in a somewhat peculiar fashion. The tone of the letter we might then attribute to the source, Thomas Jr., a master of melodramatic rhetoric. Since *Pierre* does exist, the letter upon its belated publication became notorious, often taken as absolute proof that Herman Melville had, and knew he had, a half sister, much older than Gansevoort, uncared for, unacknowledged, and sorrowing. There is, as of now, no way of knowing. Maria Gansevoort Melvill at least was allowed to bury her husband without having to worry about the claims of anyone else with whom the adolescent Allan Melvill, in the late eighteenth century, might have shared a small early portion of what the *Daily Advertiser and Patriot* called "the warmth of his affections."

[4]

The "Cholera Year"

1832–1833

Newington. 18. Septr. 1774.

Honored Sir,

In obedience to your Commands, I send this [to] inform you what Advances I have made in my **Writing.** I find now by Experience that to write a bold free hand correctly requires no Small Care & Application[.] But this is no discouragement to me, since you have frequently told me that to write a good hand would be more serviceable to my Designs, than any other Learning, which if I attain I persuade myself you expect no more from

Your dutiful Son

Ishmael Smart

A business form-letter in "Allan Melvills Book," 1796

THE WIDOW AND HER CHILDREN were soon left to deal with their bereavement as best they might. The week after Allan Melvill's death Peter Gansevoort resumed his political life, as an avowed Jacksonian, despite the grievance the Melvills all held against the president. In the Albany *Argus* of 4 February 1832 he was among those who called for a public meeting that day where the Republican (that is, Democratic) citizens could "express their sense of the rejection of the Hon. MARTIN VAN BUREN as Minister to England, by the Senate of the United States." (Outraged at the Senate's attempt to humiliate him through his nominee, Andrew Jackson chose the New Yorker Van Buren for his running mate in that fall's election.) On 22 February, the centennial of George Washington's birth, Peter made an appropriate speech (printed in the *Argus* of the twenty-eighth) and presented to the Albany Republican Artillery "a Brass drum, *captured by his father, col. Peter Gansevoort at the siege of Fort Stanwix,*" one of the many military trophies that had remained in the Gansevoort house as well as in the Mansion House at Gansevoort. Peter was consolidating his place within the Albany Regency, the Democratic clique that now ruled the state. Never a man with a national or even a statewide reputation, Peter was well acquainted with John A. Dix, Martin Van Buren, Benjamin F. Butler, Edwin Croswell, William C. Bouck, and William L. Marcy — all the leaders of the Regency — and a power in local politics.

Anxious though he was to live his own life, Peter had to deal with family problems still. On 5 March his oldest Gansevoort nephew, Peter, son of Mary Ann Chandonette Gansevoort and the late Leonard H. Gansevoort, midshipman in the U.S. Navy, drowned in the wreck of the schooner *Increase*, lost on the south side of Long Island. Young Peter Leonard had been an inconvenience to his uncle, but he had been the oldest male descendant of the Hero of Fort Stanwix in his generation. Upon his death his brother Guert, now the oldest living son, became next in line after Herman Gansevoort for the hereditary medal of the Order of the Cincinnati. Nor could Peter Gansevoort get his Melvill nieces and nephews off his hands. Even before the body of his nephew Peter Leonard Gansevoort was in the ground (in late July, after weltering four and a half months in the ocean), Peter Gansevoort had to help set his nephew Gansevoort Melvill up in business. On 1 March, after Herman had been out of school four or five months, Gansevoort was "dismissed" (withdrawn) from the academy, and on 28 March plans for him had progressed to the point that Maria signed this memorandum (now in the New York Public Library): "This is to certify that my son Gansevoort Melvill, is carrying on the Fur, and Cap business in the City of Albany, on my account, and that I hold myself responsible for all debts contracted by my said son, in the course of said business." Peter endorsed this document, which made Gansevoort, at a little short of sixteen and a half, the man of the family. Gansevoort and his mother began spelling their surname with a final *e*, as *Melville* — perhaps for no reason other than that Gansevoort thought an extra letter afforded an aristocratic flourish, and certainly for no nefarious reason, since *Melville* was a variant spelling, in common use, which would not have misled any of Allan's creditors for a moment. (Uncle Thomas and his children retained the shorter spelling, although after Herman made *Melville* famous, his Cousin Priscilla sometimes spelled her last name with a final *e* also.) From New York City, where he went on business, Gansevoort wrote his Uncle Peter on 22 May: "I find that all the furriers in town know me; and ask me if I am the young man who lately began the cap manufacture in Albany." He was reveling in his new responsibilities as a way of submerging his grief: he would succeed where his father had failed.

On 6 April 1832 Maria was admitted as a member of the First Reformed Dutch Church in full communion, after examination and confession of her faith. She needed her church more than ever. That month, also, some late seventeenth-century buildings on the Gansevoort home lot in Albany burned down, and over the ashes Peter Gansevoort and Herman Gansevoort (summoned down from Gansevoort) planned the construction of a large stone building, to be faced in blue granite, Albany's answer to Boston's first modern hotel, the Tremont House, but designed for multipurpose use. Thereafter Peter Gansevoort single-mindedly focused on building Stanwix Hall and then guiding it through its early rentalships toward the day it could turn a large profit. Until he was satisfied that his own fortune was safeguarded, he was not willing to relinquish control of what was left of his parents' estate, and as the years went by he was slow to feel that his financial status was ever quite secure enough to warrant his taking unduly precipitous measures to settle the estate. Having never been able to say no to the wishes of his brother-in-law, Peter now proved stalwart in his denial of the needs of his nephews and nieces, unwilling to sacrifice a few dollars a year in order to educate them.

In June Herman, still twelve years old, was put to work as a $150-a-year clerk in the New York State Bank. This was Peter's doing, for he was one of the dozen directors of the bank, along with other bearers of great New York names (Douw, Townsend, Corning, King, Lansing, De Witt, Wright). All through 1832, 1833, and into 1834, at the age of twelve, thirteen, and fourteen, Herman walked south on Market Street, paralleling the river, then took State Street west toward Pearl. The bank was built on so steep a slope that the right (east) entrance had five steps to the landing and the left side only three. There were wrought iron railings at either side of each landing, then on either side was an arched doorway surmounted with ornate wrought iron. The second floor was even more distinguished, with Doric columns on either side of simple tall rectangular windows and a grand Palladian window in the center with the words STATE BANK at the top, on a semicircular piece of glass. There was a chiseled swag on the pediment, and the roof was surmounted with urns on either side and a larger one at the peak in the middle. Herman spent many months of his adolescence in this magnificent temple to Mammon and Progress.

At least 69 State Street was away from the academy, three blocks to the southeast, so Herman did not have to encounter all of his former schoolmates when they assembled for classes as he was going to work. Even so, he must regularly have caught sight of boys who had been his fellow students, including some who were blood kin to the Gansevoorts. A child's bitterness at deprivation, Melville remembered in *Redburn*, is heightened by memories of better times and is exaggerated by the awareness of more fortunate, unblighted contemporaries. Redburn (ch. 2) recalls giving up all his "young mounting dreams of glory" and learning "to think much and bitterly" before his time. When mildew has fallen on the young soul, according to Redburn, "never again can such blights be made good; they strike in too deep, and leave such a scar that the air of Paradise might not erase it." In writing these words in the summer of 1849, Melville was gently mocking his melancholy narrator, but he was remembering the blight that had once made him, like Redburn as a boy, "unambitious as a man of sixty."

In his own view, Peter had taken care of Herman, whose first duty henceforth was to show up for work at the bank; Maria, as it turned out, for a time foolishly thought her first duty still was to preserve Herman's health and even his life. Herman had hardly started work when news reached Albany of an outbreak of cholera in Canada. As early as 16 June 1832 the Albany *Argus* ran regular reports on "THE CHOLERA" and the measures being taken to prevent its being borne into town. The city marshal posted guards at the second Erie Canal lock north of the city, but passengers jumped ashore and made their way into town on foot; passengers going north evaded the guards another way, by transferring to western boats at the junction of the canals nine miles north of Albany. The populace of Albany lived the next weeks with recurrent reports of the terrible suffering in Canada and the frightening knowledge that Albany had not been safeguarded from infection. Cholera broke out in Albany after it had begun devastating New York City, and on 14 July, a Saturday, Maria fled by stagecoach to Pittsfield with all her eight children.

Having given her brother no warning she was leaving and her brother-in-law no warning that she was coming, Maria arrived in Pittsfield and, with Gansevoort's help, and the other seven children in tow, made her way out to the Melvill farm. Once she was safely arrived she wrote to Peter: "Do my dear Brother leave Albany if this weather continues, for you are the only person or Brother I should say, that I & mine have to depend upon for all things, yours is a valuable Life & not to [be] trifled with, My dear Allan often use'd to say — 'Maria you love Peter better than me or your Children,' & I can assure you his Death has not made me love you less — you are every thing to me — & for my sake take care of yourself." The haste of Maria's departure with her children is clear in a letter Helen Melville wrote to her uncle three weeks later: "We left Albany so suddenly that I hardly realised our departure until when arrived here I was surrounded by cousins most of whom I had never seen and assailed on all sides by the clamorous din of no less than 17 children." In that letter of 8 August, Helen went on to describe the phenomenal situation: "We are in no want of companions I can assure you for every child has found a cronie, and little bipeds of all ages and sizes are running to and fro, now in the house, now in the garden and making any but musical noises."

There had never been such mighty confusion in the lives of the Melvill-Melville cousins, several of whom were seeing each other for the first time. In

July 1832 Thomas Melvill Jr. had three living children by his first, French wife: Thomas Wilson Melvill, born in France on 2 March 1806 (a midshipman, then stationed in New York); Priscilla, born in France on 5 November 1810; and the mentally impaired Henry Dearborn, born 17 July 1812. Following the death of his first wife on 1 April 1814 in alien Pittsfield, Thomas had married Mary Ann Augusta Hobart on 21 November 1815, thirteen months after Allan Melvill's marriage to Maria Gansevoort, on 14 October 1814. For a decade and a half, despite all problems, financial and otherwise, including periodic incarceration, children had been born to the couples alternately, Allan and Maria having a child, then Thomas and Mary having one. In addition to the older Priscilla and Henry, all the children of Uncle Thomas and Aunt Mary were at the farm the day Maria arrived with all her children.

Perhaps only the mothers could keep track of the ages of all the children. Besides the grown-up Priscilla and Henry Melvill, Gansevoort was the oldest, followed by Cousin Robert (born 20 June 1817), Helen Maria (4 August 1817), Cousin Anne (5 November 1818), Herman (1 August 1819), Cousin Julia Maria (3 June 1820), Augusta (24 August 1821), Cousin Allan Cargill (6 January 1823), Allan (7 April 1823), Cousin John Scollay (30 March 1825), Catherine (21 May 1825), Cousin George Raleigh (30 August 1826), Fanny (26 August 1827), Cousin Helen Jean (14 March 1829), and Thomas (24 January 1830). (Mary Melvill became pregnant that summer with her last child.) Because of the curious alternation, every Melvill or Melville child had a "cronie," as Helen Maria said. (Thomas, the midshipman, returned in the fall.) The visit to the Melvill farm outside Pittsfield that cholera summer was momentous to all the Melville children, most of all to Herman, who over the next years became so passionately attached to the place that his Cousin Priscilla in a letter to Augusta (3 April 1848) referred to "his *first love* our *Berkshire* farm."

Yet Herman was granted little chance to improve his acquaintance with the farm or with his cousins on this first visit after his father's death, for on Monday morning, 16 July, Peter wrote to Maria demanding that she send Herman back to his job in the bank. Gansevoort wrote appeasingly the next day: "Your kind letter of the 16th, was received this morning; and immediately upon its reception, Mamma determined to send Herman back to Albany forthwith. He goes in tomorrow morning's stage." Accordingly, on 18 July Herman boarded the stage alone for the eight-hour ride back to Albany and his job, presumably allowed to live in his grandmother's house with his uncle. A few hours after Herman's departure, Maria Melville and Mary Melvill suddenly decided to go see their parents-in-law, whom Mary years before had despaired of ever seeing again. Thomas Jr. wrote Peter on

19 July : "You will be doubtless, somewhat surprised, my dear Sir to learn that *Maria & my wife* are just off, in the Stage *for Boston* with Gansevoort." The trip was torture to Maria, as she wrote to Peter on the twenty-fourth: "Haveing never travelled from Boston to Albany or on this road without Mr Melvill every object served to remind me of him — The absence of one to whom I ever was most sincerely attached, render'd my journey to Pittsfield, & Boston rather painful, I had need of all my fortitude to repress my feelings before Strangers." On 20 July the coach deposited the tense and exhausted travelers before the Melvill house on Green Street an hour before midnight, after everyone had gone to bed except Helen Melvill, who was still in her mother's room. Old Major Melvill "arose & came down Stairs, so over-power'd by his Feelings that he was not articulate." For her part, Maria gave way: "when I enter'd the old Mansion, it was silent & dark as night, my feelings got the better of all restraint & I wept Hysterically for some time unable to controul them." She had been a loving and beloved wife, not merely the mother of eight children; henceforth she was widow and mother, not to be thought of as a sexual being — so neatly had she and Peter ex-changed roles.

When Maria and Gansevoort got round to writing Peter on 24 July they expressed concern for both the males exposed to the cholera epidemic. Maria wrote: "Herman I have not heard of since he left us at Pittsfield — I hope he is with you, & made to occupy his time when out of the Bank in reading, & writing to me." She continued: "We have sad accounts here of the Cholera at New York — but have heard nothing from Albany since last wednesday — I am anxious about you & Herman, trust much to your prudence & leave the rest to our Almighty protector." She begged for a few lines by return mail: "It would be a great pleasure to me, to hear from you & Herman here, It will take you little time." Gansevoort added: "Give Ma's and my love to Herman, and please to tell him that his mother desires him to be particularly careful of himself." Back in Pittsfield on 2 August, the day after Herman turned thir-teen, Gansevoort wrote his Uncle Peter again: "As yourself and Herman have hitherto escaped the pestilence I pray that you may continue to escape it." They all united in love to Herman and to Peter himself.

Whatever he felt about being the only one of his family exposed to dan-ger all summer, Herman behaved conscientiously, trudging up six mornings a week to the state bank. Inside the bank, Herman filed, copied, ran errands, and made himself as inconspicuous as possible. Surrounded by money in multiple forms, state banknotes, promissory notes, mortgages, bonds, specie, he observed, week by week, the men who controlled the wealth in his world. Since this was the state bank in the capital of the Empire State, Herman became familiar, by sight, not only with the directors but with the politicians and financiers whose names recurred in the Albany newspapers. Herman had no money in his own control — probably not even his $37.50 a quarter salary. Trapped inside the bank, he still had vivid memories of the sights and smells of the docks of Manhattan. Even in Albany from many of the streets tall masts of ocean-going ships were tantalizingly visible in the Hudson except in the months when the great river was frozen.

Boys still traveled up and down that river on steamboats, as he had done all his life until October of 1830, but he was a captive clerk. In "Loomings," the first chapter of *Moby-Dick*, Melville described the compulsion of lands-men to walk toward the docks of Manhattan on Sunday afternoons in order to gaze at the water: "these are all landsmen; of week days pent up in lath and plaster — tied to counters, nailed to benches, clinched to desks." Such was his constricted life in his early teens, six days a week — a confinement always tinged with the memory of the weeks in July and August 1832 when he alone had been remanded to the plague city, where more than a thousand cases of cholera were reported and several hundred people died. The timing that summer was such that Herman probably was alone to represent the Melvilles at the funeral of his cousin Peter Leonard Gansevoort, his third Albany funeral in two years. His uncle went to take the waters at Saratoga Springs in mid-August, perhaps leaving Herman alone in the big house with the ser-vants, John and Christina, where his aunt Mary Chandonette Gansevoort occasionally looked in, as she did on 22 August, when she wrote Peter: "Do not dine out, for then you must drink wine; and *you do know* that it is very *injurious*, when taking the waters."

However much he endeavored to make himself useful that summer, in the bank and in Uncle Peter's house and garden (he could not roam the streets during the plague), Herman had time for reading. Peter had books the boy could read, and much of Allan Melvill's library remained in the rented house, although some of his more beautiful books, many in French, had been dispersed in the last terrible months in Manhattan. Among the treasures that remained in Maria's possession was Allan's eight-in-four volumes of Spenser, an 1803 New Year's gift from Obediah Rich Jr. The boy Herman may have taken the volumes up reverentially, as a memorial of his father, and then found that with a little labor he could understand much of what he read. In *Pierre* (bk. 1, ch. 2) the hero reads *his* father's copy of Spenser, with pecu-liar consequences: "Not in vain had he spent long summer afternoons in the deep recesses of his father's fastidiously picked and decorous library; where the Spenserian nymphs had early led him into many a maze of all-bewildering beauty. Thus, with a graceful glow on his limbs, and soft, imag-inative flames in his heart, did this Pierre glide toward maturity." It is as if Pierre's father is guiding him, after his death, through the early stirrings of puberty and through his simultaneously awakening literary sensibilities. Like his young hero, Herman himself in the solitude of this summer of cholera may have taken refuge in the all-bewildering beauty of the Bower of Bliss, guided into the erotic pleasures of the Spenserian text even as his body changed from that of a child. Just possibly, in the summer of 1832 the father who had been alive as Gansevoort passed through puberty may have guided Herman, by means of his long-cherished copy of *The Faerie Queene*.

Quite aside from the books in the Melville house and at Uncle Peter's, any alert twelve-year-old could absorb a good deal about literary matters from the half dozen local newspapers and the magazines and papers from other cities available in Albany. The *Argus*, for instance, on 7 June 1832 had printed a long article headed "BRYANT — IRVING," suggested by the review in the April *Blackwood's Magazine* of the English edition of William Cullen Bryant's poems, which Washington Irving had shepherded into print in London, shrewdly prefaced with a dedication to the English poet Samuel Rogers. The *Argus* reprinted the entire dedication, where Irving remarked on Rogers's "kind disposition to promote the success of American talent, whether engaged in literature or the arts." Bryant's poetical writings were "essentially American" — Americanism being defined by topography (they "transport us into the depths of the solemn primeval forest"). Reading this article in the paper owned by Peter Gansevoort's political friends, neither Gansevoort nor Herman would have been able to perceive the essential flimsiness of defining Americanism by flora, fauna, and geography, but from such articles in these years they learned that writers like Bryant, or like Fitz-Greene Halleck, whose "Marco Bozzaris" Gansevoort might still recite around the house, were part of an ongoing literary campaign to produce writings "worthy of being carefully preserved in the common treasury of the language" — worthy of being published and read in London, and around the globe. Precisely what Gansevoort and Herman read in 1832 is not known, but even if deprived of schooling no Albany boy of good family could remain ignorant of the stirrings of patriotic literary impulses.

From the plague city Herman dutifully wrote to his mother in July, apparently, and again shortly before 7 August, the second time forwarding a letter that had arrived for Maria. On 7 August Maria sent her love to Herman by Peter and described the response in Pittsfield to Herman's epistle: "His last letter was much praise'd, for its superiority over the first, the hand writing particularly, he must practise often, & daily." Helen, now fifteen, on 8 August begged her Uncle Peter to encourage Herman to reply to her last letter, and Maria added a postscript: "My best love to Herman, who I hope is a good Boy — & endeavours to make himself useful by writing — &c." Anxious though she was about her second son, Maria reveled in her Berkshire holiday. Since her marriage she had experienced very few quiet rural moments (she had exulted in the quiet at Gansevoort in 1829). As the guest of her brother-in-law, she was able temporarily to forget her fears about finances, and able at times to put even Herman's danger out of her mind, as in this letter to Peter on 7 August:

> The Family are very kind, the Children live on bread & milk, look brown & healthy — all have gain'd flesh, & my baby Tom is the picture of plenty & good nature, The air is delightful, we literally breathe sweets, the atmosphere is fill'd with fragrance from the new-mown hay, all around us, Gansevoort is employed, in raking & turning Hay, Fishing, rowing the Ladies across, & around a large pond back of the house, & in doing ample justice to the excellent Milk & delicious bread & Butter of the Farm we are happy here, but would wish to return to town [as] soon as would be prudent.

The features Maria itemized must be taken as realistic, not as fatuous rhapsody. For any inhabitant of Manhattan or even smaller Albany, the Berkshire air was pure and (visitors regularly said) palpable with benign fragrances, as Eden must have been. Gansevoort helped with the farm chores, but he also sported with the "Ladies" (his sisters and female cousins) in what Maria called a large pond and, sixteen years later, the poet Longfellow called the Tear of Heaven. (In the 1840s it was Melvill Lake, and by the early 1850s Morewood Lake.) They were in an American paradise in the height of its glorious brief summer, a decade and a half before celebrities discovered it and made it an expensive resort area. Herman missed almost all of this paradisiacal episode, and had to experience it vicariously and imaginatively as he read the letters from his mother and his older brother and sister, and perhaps Augusta as well.

The Melville children that summer learned something of the sad experience of Thomas Wilson Melvill, who suffered a "severe attack of the Asiatic Cholera at New York" that July (as Gansevoort wrote his Uncle Peter on 24 July), the only one of the family who contracted the cholera Maria had fled. The disease capped a miserable year: late in 1831, still a midshipman aboard the *Vincennes* in the West Indies, young Thomas had been suspended from duty for jumping upon the torso of an ordinary seaman, Thomas Spence, who at the time was in irons. At the court-martial, convened on 30 April 1832 (transcription in the Office of Naval Records and Library), a marine guarding Spence had testified that his drunken prisoner had called out that "Midshipman Melville, was in the habit of going into the spirit room and robbing it." Thereupon, Thomas had indeed jumped with his feet upon the breast of the prisoner, then helpless in irons. Thomas's address to the court in his own defense (on 1 or 2 May) is the best indication of the sort of education Uncle Thomas had managed to give him, and proof positive that he had absorbed the family's rhetorical extravagance: "Young as I am, I hope that I have not so soon forgotten those principles which are not only derived from a careful and affectionate education by those who brought me up and which should exist and be strengthened by a more mature age, but be my passport to future claims to advancement in a profession which is *proverbially* the test of character and which the severest scrutiny can only permit its votaries to enter." The court had found young Thomas guilty but in view of "the strong provocation given, and the general good character of Mid[n] Melvill," and "taking into consideration the long suspension from duty of Mid[n] Melvill," meted out no further punishment, merely admonishing him "to remember that no circumstances can justify an officer in forgetting his dignity, by yielding to paroxysms of passion." This lenient sentence was approved by Commodore Elliott on 4 May 1832. The legal system, which the half-French Thomas hailed in his speech to the court as derived from British law, did not permit anyone to ask if the grossly provocative accusation was true: was Thomas in the habit of sneaking into the spirit room in order to keep sufficient alcohol in his bloodstream?

Melville's Uncle Thomas made no secret of his grief over his oldest son that summer. From Boston on 24 July, after seeing his uncle in Pittsfield, Gansevoort Melville reported to Peter that young Thomas had said "that he should have died if it had not been for the attentions of two young men of New Orleans his fellow boarders at the *City Hotel.*" Young Thomas's intention, upon recovery, was to return to Pittsfield, Gansevoort reported, adding sententiously: "Pity that he had not determined on this course sooner, for he has almost broken his father's heart."

For years Thomas Wilson Melvill had been a romantic figure to Allan Melvill's older sons. Allan had read to them a letter young Thomas had written him in June 1827 from Callao Roads, from aboard the *Vincennes*, when he was expecting "to cruise among the Islands of the Pacific, & return home in May, via the Cape of Good Hope, Canton, Manilla, St Helena," with the hope of "passing his examination without going to sea again." Gansevoort and Herman knew that in July 1829 the *Vincennes* had visited the Marquesas Islands and that the crew, including Midshipman Thomas W. Melvill, had made a day's expedition into the Typee valley. (In July 1831, soon after its publication, their Grandfather Melvill purchased the printed account of that voyage by the chaplain, Charles S. Stewart's *A Visit to the South Seas, in the U.S. Ship Vincennes, During the Years 1829 and 1830;* by sometime in 1833 their uncle Thomas most likely had it at Pittsfield.) From the summer of 1832 onward, Cousin Thomas was not only a romantic but also a monitory figure to Gansevoort and Herman Melville. Early that summer they learned that a grandson and namesake of the Hero of Fort Stanwix might wash for months at sea after drowning, then they also learned that a grandson of the Hero of the Tea Party might be court-martialed for shameful behavior and then might nearly die from the cholera, far away from his father.

The "cholera summer" of 1832 ended with a new family disaster. At noon on 7 September, a Friday, a fire broke out in a brick building on Green Street in Boston, nearly opposite the Melvill house. Those were, Francis S. Drake said in 1884, "the good old times, when the fire-wards carried staves, tipped at the end with a brass flame, and marshalled the bystanders into lines for passing buckets of water to the scene of conflagration." Volunteer fire brigades were social organizations, with fees steep enough to deter unwelcome aspirants from the lower classes while welcoming younger members of the ruling class, such as the young lawyer Lemuel Shaw, who was fire warden about the time of his first marriage, 1818–22. Major Melvill had been "fire ward" of Boston from 1779 until 1825, as a friend or family member wrote in the memorial in the *Columbian Centinel* (31 October 1832), and for twenty-five of those years was chairman of the board. The memorialist continued: "On his retirement, his associates presented him with a Silver Pitcher, as a token of personal respect, and a public testimonial of his faithful services"; furthermore, the younger firemen named an engine for him.

Now, when the flames broke out so close to his dwelling, the major, eighty-one years old or not, saw his duty clear, according to the *Firemen's Advocate*: "The Major was active, and with his family were furnishing the firemen with refreshments, having an open house to all of them. But alas! by his exertions to relieve their wants at this fire, he took a violent cold, which terminated in the diarrhea; and owing to his advanced age, and the violence of the disorder, medicine had no effect in checking its progress." He died Sunday evening, 16 September, at nine o'clock, and in the next days and weeks he was mourned and eulogized as one of the city's most prominent citizens. The Boston *Evening Gazette* of 22 September recorded a significant act of homage: "The members of the 'Melville Fire Association,' attached to the Melville Engine, No. 13, met at their Engine House — attended the funeral — and voted to wear the usual badge of mourning for thirty days."

At Worcester on 12 October Daniel Webster in his address to the national Republican convention remembered Thomas Melvill as a victim of the spoils system: "He was a personification of the spirit of 1776, one of the earliest to venture in the cause of liberty. . . . His character, his standing, his Revolutionary services, were all well known; but they were known to no purpose; they weighed not one feather against party pretensions." (Webster's convention was Republican because of the shifting nomenclature: it might earlier have been called Federalist, and it might already have been called

Whig; it was the party opposed to Andrew Jackson and *his* Republicans. This same year Peter Gansevoort was running for state senator from the third district, on the Republican ticket in Albany as a partisan of Jackson.)

Daniel Webster in late August 1830 had personally battered down his friend Lemuel Shaw's reluctance to accept Massachusetts Governor Levi Lincoln's offer to make him chief justice of the Supreme Judicial Court, plying him "in every possible way" (according to Peter Harvey's 1877 *Reminiscences and Anecdotes of Daniel Webster*), while Shaw, the man who had been engaged to Nancy Wroe Melvill, "smoked and smoked," until Webster guessed that he had smoked a thousand cigars. Taking the chief justiceship meant giving up an extremely lucrative law practice, but at last Shaw accepted, after Webster made him believe it was his duty. Among his old commitments, still to be honored despite his high public office, was to be co-executor (with John D'Wolf) of old Thomas Melvill's estate. During his early years Shaw had lived in rented rooms while he mustered his forces for a successful career. Quite early, he rented from the mother of Ralph Waldo Emerson; later, he boarded with the wealthy merchant Daniel P. Parker, Allan Melvill's friend and Herman and Gansevoort's escort in 1828. In 1831, the year after he became chief justice, Shaw had moved into a house suitable for his status. It was suitable also for his status as a man who had cared for two children, the eleven-year-old John Oakes and nine-year-old Elizabeth, since his first wife died at her daughter's birth in 1822, and now had a new wife, Hope Savage Shaw, a Barnstable woman whom he had married in 1827, and, as of 15 July 1828, a new son, named for himself. During Washington's presidency enterprising Bostonians had decided that Beacon Hill was not only suitable for the architect Charles Bulfinch's splendid new State House, completed in 1800, but also was prime residential land. They formed themselves as the Mount Vernon Proprietors (a masterstroke of patriotic marketing) and set out to purchase acreage, particularly John Hancock's field and the south slope that belonged to the artist John Singleton Copley, a Loyalist who had left for London the year after the Tea Party. They employed Bulfinch to design the first structures, then cut down Beacon Hill and threw it into the Charles River and the Mill Pond, thereby extending their property. On Mt. Vernon Street the proprietors in 1803–4 built Bulfinch houses, including No. 49, on the north side, which came up for sale after the death of Stephen Higginson in 1828. When the judge acquired the property in 1831, he greatly enlarged it. Maria and Gansevoort in their visit to Boston from Pittsfield in 1832 may well have seen at least the outside of the house, enough to know that Allan Melvill's old friend now lived in one of the best houses on the best street in the best city in the hemisphere. In this house Lemuel Shaw's daughter, Elizabeth, grew up, and here she would marry Herman Melville.

Judge Shaw was in Lenox for his regular September court session when he received the news of Major Melvill's death from his wife and possibly from Thomas Melvill Jr. as well. He sent his sympathy, but felt he could not cancel his court calendar. On 23 September he forewarned his wife that some inquiry might be made of her "respecting Maj. Melvill's will," since unless it had been altered he would be one of the executors, and in fact the principal one, for John D'Wolf soon retreated into merely nominal executorship. The two (and the widow Priscilla Scollay Melvill) had been left the duty of administering the "Watson Place" in Pittsfield, lived in by Thomas Melvill Jr. but part of the old major's estate. By the terms of the will (which had not been altered since January) Allan Melvill was left nothing because advances to him amounted to more than his portion, and Maria Gansevoort Melvill twenty dollars (not $20,000 or $2,000 but $20); furthermore Allan's debts to his father, above what would have been his portion, were all to be collected; Shaw himself was left $500 to compensate him for his duties.

In Albany Maria Melville and her oldest son, Gansevoort, faced the news of Major Melvill's death together, the young man doing his best to reassure her, for most likely they had not learned the full terms of the will during their visit to Boston that summer. (Of the other children, only Herman had known his grandfather well enough to grieve for his loss.) On 24 September Maria made a memorandum from a conversation that followed the death of her father-in-law: "Gansevoort Melville says that in two years from this time he will make his Fur business worth a Net profit of $10,000 a year." Maria was still both ignorant and optimistic—ignorant of the full measure of the financial morass into which her husband had drawn her, and over-optimistic about the potential success of her firstborn simply because he was, already, at two months and more shy of seventeen, a remarkable human being. Maria was so impressed with his genuinely heroic determination that she believed him when he told her how successful he would become, as she had always believed her husband, with the difference that Gansevoort was her flesh and blood, half Dutch—and therefore to her way of thinking still more reliable than her Boston husband had been. Herman's $37.50 a quarter did not count for much in anyone's reckoning.

Despite Gansevoort's attempts to comfort her, the reality of her financial situation pressed closer upon Maria in the weeks after the old major's death. On 15 October Lemuel Shaw wrote to Peter Gansevoort that "in looking over the securities, belonging to the estate," the trustees had found "notes to a pretty large amount due from Allan, which was expected." "Pretty large amount" was a self-consciously judicious understatement: on looking over the securities, Shaw had remembered edgily the many times in the 1820s when he had taken Allan's notes himself. One particular note for $2014 was unique, for upon it, Shaw delicately commented, "Allan is promissor, payable to yourself" (that is, to Peter) "& by you endorsed, dated 29th Oct. 1831." Allan had borrowed from Peter (no one would have joked about the pro-verbial phrasing) to pay a comparatively small amount back to his father, being motivated just after his flight from New York City by some unknown exigencies — perhaps a promise made that he for once felt he had to keep if he were to borrow more in the future.

That October Maria took Catherine out of the Albany Female Academy, for even a few dollars spent on education was an unnecessary luxury. Maria's rented house on Market Street in Albany gave her no protection from agents of the Boston executors of her late father-in-law's estate. On 1 November 1832 local agents for Philip Marett, cashier of the New England Bank and the husband of a sister of Shaw's first wife, went to "the Dwelling House of Maria G Melvill" and demanded payment of one of her late husband's promissory notes, "to which demand Gansevoort Melvill the Son of the Maker of the Note answered, that the Note could not then be paid" (affidavit in the Massachusetts Historical Society). Peter also had been approached and had given the same answer, for in Boston on 8 November Marett wrote to Lemuel Shaw that the note of Allan Melvill had been returned to him "under protest for nonpayment":

> My correspondent at Albany says "Mr [Peter] Gansevoort is one of our most respected citizens & I think his word is as much entitled to credit as his oath — He requests me to say that the late Major Melvill has frequently told him that it was not his intention to charge the estate of the *wife* of his son Allan, with the repayment of the money he had lent to Allan — Mr Gansevoort says he thinks the note cannot be collected & intends to make a defence in case he is prosecuted."

In this extremely painful situation Shaw went ahead with probating the will of Thomas Melvill Sr. on 12 November 1832, thereby making its terms known. (Probably none of the Albany Melvills knew any of the Maretts on 1 November 1832, but Philip Marett's wife and daughter are continuing if shadowy figures in this biography. Decades later the daughter of the man who dispatched duns to the door of Maria Melville remembered her cousin Elizabeth Shaw Melville and Herman Melville in her will.)

In what seemed, under the circumstances, a footnote to the general ca-lamity, in those days when many families lost children (a fate Allan and Maria had been spared), nine-year-old cousin Allan Cargill Melvill, three months older than Herman's brother Allan, died on 24 October 1832. His "mortal remains were deposited in the family tomb in Pittsfield the following day." Thomas Jr., recording the death in his *Self-Interpreting Bible*, added a prayer

(Psalms 90:12): "So teach us to number our days that we may apply our hearts into wisdom." Grieving as he was for his father and his child, Thomas Melvill Jr. exploded with outrage once he learned the details of his father's will and the condition of the paternal estate. With all his "cherished hopes & anticipations" dashed, Thomas wrote to Shaw on 15 November: "Until I visited Boston, after the decease of my dear Allan [his brother, not his son], I was ignorant that my good father had made a Will; nor, was it until that Will was read, that I became acquainted with any of its provisions, except, in so far, as regarded my good mother,—of course, until Sept. last, I was entirely ignorant of what might become my situation." Thomas had been, at the age of fifty-six, so dependent upon his father that he had taken heart after the death of the old major; "knowledge" that he might inherit a competence had revived his "drooping spirits." As he wrote Shaw on 15 November: "there seemed to open to my declining years, a hope not only of maintaining my family, but that I should be able by my industry, & perseverance, indeed by economy, to do something more towards their education than I had heretofore been able to do." Furthermore, after years of intermittent imprisonment for debt in the Lenox jail, he had just been nominated by his fellow citizens as a state representative at the Worcester convention where Webster had deplored the firing of his father. Now it came home to him that some of his debts to his father would be placed against his portion of the inheritance and that his financial situation would not be altered for the better in any significant way: indeed, his family could continue to reside on the farm only by consent of his mother, his sisters, and the trustees.

On 22 November 1832 Thomas Melvill Jr. appealed to George N. Briggs, the Lanesboro (later Pittsfield) lawyer who was his representative in the state legislature. With Briggs's help, he hoped to obtain travel fare for young Thomas for the journey from Pittsfield to Norfolk, where the midshipman could "avail himself of the advantage, of the *Naval School at that place.*" Young Thomas already had official leave "to proceed to the School at New York," but Thomas Jr. knew better than to allow his susceptible son to stay there: "that is a very expensive place, a dangerous residence for young men, especially for young officers, who when not on positive active duty, are from this station & location, more subject to the banefull effect of allurements than others—and hence, I am disinclined to his going there, if possible to avoid it." At Christmas, travel funds had arrived, and Midshipman Melvill prepared to depart for Norfolk for his last chance at a career in the navy.

In December John D'Wolf in his dual capacity, co-executor and husband of an heir to the old major's estate, made the two-day stagecoach journey to

Pittsfield, where Thomas received his report about Allan's debts to the estate and reciprocated with what he knew about his late brother's affairs. Thomas wrote Peter Gansevoort on 18 December: "I availed myself of the recent short visit of Mr De Wolf to Pittsfield, to relate to him *all* the facts within my knowledge, of the state [of] my brothers affairs at the time of his decease, & of the present state of the family, as well as my opinion in respect to Maria's prospects; — with a request that he would communicate the conversation to Mr Shaw." Thomas Jr.'s own prospects were even more confused than usual. He had been elected to the state legislature, but did not have money enough to fulfill his political duties without strain. In this disturbed season Aunt Lucy Melvill Clark's husband accompanied D'Wolf in a return to Pittsfield for further discussions of the old major's will, for Julia Maria Melvill (with characteristic spelling) wrote to her Cousin Augusta, the day after Christmas: "Uncle D W'olf and Uncle Clark spent some days with us." After D'Wolf and Clark had briefed him and before he went to Boston for the legislative session, Thomas Jr. made a trip to Albany to see Maria and Peter about the terms of the will. On 26 December Julia Maria wrote Augusta: "It was my intention to write you by papa when he went to Albany but he went away so sudenly that I had not time to besides being sick We have had a sick family this winter, all have been but Ann and Priscilla." A "sick family this winter" did not begin to convey the nature of that horrible long leap year, remembered nationally as the cholera year — the literal and the metaphorical way it was remembered by the Melvilles and Melvills, for whom the year stretched on into 1833, until Priscilla Scollay Melvill joined the Hero of the Tea Party.

As Herman worked at the bank early in 1833 he had to acknowledge that he was missing irretrievable lessons at the academy. For a fraction of his small salary, his Uncle Peter, or Uncle Herman, for that matter, could have paid his tuition. He knew that his mother was being fair in keeping some of the younger children in school in 1833, Augusta at the Albany Female Academy on North Pearl, and Allan at the Albany Academy until 1 December, when he was withdrawn, probably to help Gansevoort in the store. Others may also have been in school, although Helen, the best educated after Gansevoort, had been impressed as household schoolmistress. Inevitably Herman questioned: surely it was not only the Hero of the Tea Party, now dead, and the aged Priscilla Scollay Melvill who had found him delighted and delighting in Boston? Surely the aunts had loved him too, and even Aunt Mary D'Wolf's awe-striking husband, the great voyager. Any of his Boston aunts could have paid tuition for him and doled out a supplemental allowance to Maria to make up for his meager contributions to the family exchequer. Inevitably, in the bank he saw wealthy men whose blood ran in his veins, even his kinsman, the greatest man in New York, Stephen Van Rensselaer, the Patroon. How could he matter so little to people of such wealth?

In Boston at Green Street Priscilla Scollay Melvill had failed since the deaths of her son Allan and her husband. The trustee Lemuel Shaw could not even consult the old woman about her husband's will, he explained to Maria Melville on 20 February 1833. Priscilla Melvill had been "confined to her chamber for several weeks," her mind "& especially her memory" extremely impaired, "so much so as at times to render it painful to converse with her." Priscilla Scollay Melvill died on 12 April 1833, aged seventy-seven (two weeks after the birth of her "replacement" grandchild Allan Cargill Melvill in Pittsfield). Her death left Shaw and D'Wolf with still more responsibilities as the surviving trustees. In 1833 D'Wolf moved from Bristol, where Herman had visited him, nearer to Boston, onto a rural estate (thirty-one acres, manor house, outbuildings) overlooking the Charles River and Harvard College — land now occupied in part by the Harvard Business School. Thomas Jr. as the oldest child and only surviving son pressured Shaw and D'Wolf to pass on to him paintings and pieces of furniture, regardless of the fact that his unmarried sisters, Priscilla, Jean, and Helen, were still (for a short time longer) residing in the house on Green Street, and to assist the trustees he submitted an itemized list of precisely what he wanted them to release to him. The daughters behaved as if they had some rights too. Mary D'Wolf carried off the oil painting of her father that showed him bareheaded, white hair thin on top but worn long over the ears, and she carried off the old major's last Continental hat (which when photographed in 1884 was in the possession of her son, Langsdorff D'Wolf, the cousin who was Helen Maria's age). Priscilla kept the copy of the Copley painting of Samuel Adams (and left it to Harvard in her will, not to any Melvill or Melville). Other sisters in contempt of primogeniture asserted their claims on other highly desirable and even historic artifacts. Shaw did his best to soothe feelings all around.

Out of his old affection for Allan Melvill, Shaw in his capacity as trustee proposed to the Melvill heirs that they each allot something for Allan's widow and children, and with uncharacteristic lack of caution he let Maria know what he had done. She replied on 20 June 1833: "The apparent utter desertion of the Grandparents & Aunts of my Children, since the Death of their Father, is singular, & to me seems inexplicable." The Melvills were known for their charities "to Friends & Strangers to their Blood," and now they were ignoring the needs of their own nephews and nieces. She asked: "Do you think it possible Mr Shaw that Allan's circumstances at the time of his Death, were unknown to his Parents, it can hardly be for the Major [Thomas Jr.] was here, and knew full well that my Brother was call'd upon to assist us immediately, for we had nothing—Could he have mention'd those things & been unattended to by Parental ears." Maria thanked Shaw for his efforts, and gave him heartfelt assurance of her gratitude, whatever the results of his proposal to the heirs: "you shall receive from me & mine a full tribute of praise, & the sincere prayers of the Widow & Children shall ascend for your repose here & hereafter." Unsurprisingly, Allan Melvill's brother and sisters rejected Shaw's proposal. Having brought so much anxiety down onto his aged parents, having caused his unmarried sisters grievous harm by limiting the money the old couple would spend to put them forward, Allan had forfeited any posthumous claims to consideration. The woeful Maria got nothing, not even the most meager keepsake to pass on to her children. Some items came to them eventually. What, after all, was Lucy going to do, decades later, with a cup marked "T. M." but leave it to Maria's youngest, by then the oldest living namesake of the Hero of the Tea Party?

Like Peter Gansevoort, all but one of the unmarried Melvill aunts were asserting themselves, however tardily, as women who deserved to have husbands, and even children, of their own. Lemuel Shaw had been concerned about the possibility that Priscilla (born in 1784), Jean (1788), and Helen Melvill (1798) might marry hastily and badly, since all were inheriting some fourteen thousand dollars and had no practice in managing money and weighing the character of suitors. The Green Street house was razed soon after Priscilla Scollay Melvill's death, but Jean continued to live on the block, for within a year or so of her mother's death she married a neighbor, Winslow Wright, a widower with at least one child. The Albany Melvilles probably heard belatedly and only indirectly of Jean's marriage and other events involving the Boston Melvills, but direct communication all but ceased. Allan had done so much damage that his sisters wanted nothing to do with his widow and children.

5

In the Shadow of the Young Furrier
Herman as Clerk, 1833–1835

Like negroes, these powers own [acknowledge] man sullenly; mindful of their higher master; while serving, plot revenge.

Epigraph to "The Bell-Tower" (1855), said to be "From a Private MS"

OUT OF SIGHT IN THE BANK, the second son, Herman Melville (as he now must have been spelling his name), faded out of the surviving family records except for casual, random mentions. Gansevoort, only seventeen when Herman went to work in the bank, was no child like Herman but a businessman, a young furrier with connections throughout the state and beyond. Taller than Herman and the younger brothers grew to be, oddly dark-eyed, like Augusta, in a blue-eyed family, his only surviving likeness is a watercolor miniature from 1836, showing him in profile, regular of feature and with thick brown hair like his father and brothers. The young businessman drove himself (beyond his strength, in the phraseology of the time), for he seems to have been weakened, still, by that calamitous fall off the roof onto a fence in Manhattan. Now he was fiercely determined to rescue his mother from debt and to achieve for himself a high place in his world, one way or another. The available American model for dedicated self-improvement was Benjamin Franklin. Gansevoort at seventeen had received a better education, conventionally speaking, than Franklin, one that equipped him to continue to educate himself in hours stolen from work. The difference was that the young Boston-born printer at Gansevoort's age had been saddled with no debts other than those of his own making. Gansevoort was, these years, the most powerful man in Herman's world.

All the adults, including Gansevoort, dealt day by day with momentous financial concerns. Through 1833 the New York firm of Nelson & Addoms tried to collect on some of Allan Melvill's debts. On 11 February Nelson & Addoms sent Peter Gansevoort a list of those debts "amounting to Thirty Six Hundred and Fifty One dollars and 72 Cents." Eager to reach "a final settlement," they suggested that he "purchase the Debts for the sum of Eight Hundred Dollars," twenty-five cents on the dollar. Allan's agent in New York

City, Joseph Greenleaf, now Peter's agent, on 25 May 1833 updated a list of debts. Because of the "trouble of collecting, and the expence of time and loss of interest, attending it," he thought Peter would be shrewd not to "purchase the Debts."

Freed by Catherine Van Schaick Gansevoort's death and Allan Melvill's death to try to recoup their fortunes, through most of 1833 the Gansevoort brothers Herman and Peter poured money, much of it borrowed, into their new building in Albany. In the fall their innovative and boldly named Stanwix Hall began leasing for shops, for meeting rooms, and for offices. Before that, on one day Peter achieved long-term financial security—4 June 1833, when he married Mary Sanford. The marriage began with conflict over where they would live. Mary announced to her brother: "G. [i.e., Peter Gansevoort] is going to sell his house as I will not live there." Yet from Paris on 17 September Peter's boyhood friend (and cousin, in some degree) James Stevenson (mayor of Albany, 1826–28) wrote him: "I am glad to hear you are going into the old mansion, it shows the good sense of your better half." The newlyweds had indeed moved into the mansion, temporarily.

While Allan Melvill's creditors in Boston and New York City were attempting to collect some portion of what they had loaned him, the Melville family continued to reside in the rented house at the corner of Market and Steuben in Albany until the spring of 1834. Trips to visit Melvill relatives in Boston had ceased after the summer visit Maria made with Gansevoort in 1832, but the farm south of Pittsfield became for Maria's children what it had been for her and all the children except Herman during the cholera summer, a paradisiacal haven. For Uncle Thomas, chronically short-handed, frequently in jail at times when crops needed attention, and for part of 1833 away in Boston during his term as legislator (such were the extremes of his life), the farm was more like purgatory than paradise. Despite his debts, illnesses, and griefs, Uncle Thomas still welcomed his Melville nieces and nephews to the farm, all of whom except Allan rejoiced whenever they could be there. Maria and her younger children almost always saw it at its best. Gansevoort was often there, even in winter, for he made it a base for his buying trips into the mountainous regions to the north and east where beaver and other wild fur-bearing animals were still abundant. Cousin Julia Maria, Herman's age, kept up her erratically spelled and inexactly dated (or undated) correspondence with Augusta, which provides, despite its gaps, most of the surviving information about the comings and goings of Herman and Maria's other children for two or three years. Julia even supplies a little unique evidence about the characteristic behavior and vocabulary of the Melville cousins. In those days, a decade away from cheap national mail service, the girls usually entrusted their letters to a traveler, often Gansevoort, some-

times Robert (between Gansevoort and Herman in age), Herman, or someone else. According to a letter from Julia in May 1833, while the baby, the
replacement Allan Cargill Melvill, was still tiny ("so small I cannot bear it"),
Herman had sent her a paint box (probably by "favor" of Gansevoort). She
longed for Augusta's company in the summer and enticed her by promising
fruit: "there will be a great quantity amoung which are Apples pears peaches
plumbs cheries in great abundance." In early August 1833 Helen Maria took
her brother "little Allan" to the farm for two weeks, then apparently went
home when their mother arrived for a week; on 2 September Thomas reported about Maria to Shaw: "Her health is good, & that of the children."
Herman, he added, had been there the previous week.

By the luck of their rank in their families (too young to have special privileges and too old to need special care), Herman and his "twin" Julia Maria
were of all the children most likely to miss their turns at whatever pleasure
was to be enjoyed, but now his turn had come. Helen Maria had entrusted
him with a gracious letter to "Priss and Ann" (probably thanking them for
their hospitality) which Julia (now the mistress of the epistolary tone facetious) described, in a letter to Augusta in late August 1833, as too short
("about 2 inches long and 1 broad"). This year, for the first time, Herman was
able to help with the late haying, although his description (in the memoir he
wrote of his uncle in 1870) conflates scenes from different years. His uncle, he
remembered, "never used the scythe," but frequently raked with him. "At the
end of a swath, he would at times pause in the sun, and taking out his smooth-
worn box of satin wood, gracefully help himself to a pinch of snuff, partly
leaning on the slanted rake, and making some little remark, quite naturally,
and yet with a look which — as I now recall it — presents him in the shadowy
aspect of a courtier of Louis XVI, reduced as a refugee, to humble employment, in a region far from the gilded Versailles." However much of this description may be the product of Melville's own later experiences, his uncle
powerfully appealed to his imagination, then and afterward.

Herman may have been on the farm when the adults received the news
from Hadley that Lucy Melvill's husband, Justin Wright Clark, had died,
leaving her a childless widow. Perhaps Herman spent one Sunday with his
uncle, attending morning Episcopalian service at St. Stephen's then spending
the afternoon in the tavern on the south side of the Common (where no one
drank alcohol that day), until the second service. Otherwise he was outdoors
all day helping his uncle in good weather, reveling in the freedom to stretch
his constricted limbs before resuming his duties at the bank. On a rainy day
he could climb about the barn or explore the house, which he described in
1870 as "of goodly proportions, with ample hall, & staircase, carved wood-

work & solid oaken timbers, hewn in Stockbridge." Viewed from the cellar, those timbers reminded him later, after his naval experience, "of the massive gun deck beams of the line-of-battle ship"; at the time, they awed him with their all but antediluvian size. That visit, also, he and Robert went together to Lenox one day, perhaps his first travel over the "old Lenox road" that became familiar to him (Augusta to Helen Melville, 24 January 1851), and his first sight of the shire town, where the jail stood next to the courthouse and the Little Red Inn. Pittsfield was paradise in late August, even if Herman had missed the very best season. His week there appeased him a little, but it was not enough to make up for the summer the rest of the family had passed there the year before.

As the months passed, Uncle Thomas watched his seventeen-year-old nephew warily, and wrote to Shaw on 2 September 1833: "It is hoped Gansevoort is doing pretty well — But, on acc^t of his youth, & inexperience, I cannot cease to be anxious." In November 1833 under Shaw and D'Wolf all the Melvill heirs, including Allan's eight children, banded together to resist legal action "to sell the share or proportion of the said Allan Melvill in the estate of his father the testator aforesaid, for the purpose of securing & realizing the amount due from him by notes or other securities." Allan's surviving brother and sisters were attempting to keep his creditors from plundering what remained of their parents' estate, and it was in the best interests of Maria and her children to abet the Boston family in this effort. This was the last time the whole Melvill-Melville family acted in concert in a legal matter. By the end of the year Helen Melvill, born in 1798, now bereft of both parents in a year, moaned to her "best earthly friend," Lemuel Shaw: "in the Providence of God I am left an orphan! a lonely sojourner in this cold, calculating world!" She was not so abandoned as her brother Allan's children, however, since her belated inheritance was enough to keep Shaw anxious that he might be unable to protect her from the eager hands of a fortune hunter. Unsurprisingly, the Pittsfield *Sun* on 1 January 1835 noted the marriage of Leavitt Souther, of Hingham, to Helen Melvill, daughter of the late Major Melvill of Boston; a decade younger than Jean, she was still able to bear children.

After a year of pressing their claims, Nelson & Addoms, having done the best they could expect, wrote off the majority of Allan Melvill's debts to them. Gansevoort Melville kept a diary for early 1834 that survived into the late 1940s; Jay Leyda printed part or all of it in the *Boston Public Library Quarterly* (October 1950). According to a notation Gansevoort made in this diary on 18 January 1834: "Mamma endorsed on the back of the basis of settlement between Peter Gansevoort assignee of Allan Melvill deceased and

J. G. Nelson & Mr Addoms surviving partners of the late firm of Nelson & Addoms, her approval of the settlement — Mamma has come out better in this thing than I expected, she will not probably lose over $2,750 or 3000 — Glad that the matter is settled." Peter Gansevoort on the same day wrote a letter to Joseph Greenleaf asking for his bill for services to Maria: it was Greenleaf who had persuaded Nelson & Addoms to settle on terms so favorable to the widow Melville. This was a temporary respite, as Gansevoort's diary entry for 7 March shows:

> This m'g had a note to take up of $215.40/100 in favor of Gault Biglow & Co and $375 borrowed money to pay Sheldon, Slingerland & Co. — and not a dollar to do it with; had not Uncle Peter raised Six hundred dollars for me from the bank, I could not have stood through the day — Dutcher & Harris in my mother's case against Daniel Sparks & Co. & Jno. R. Eddy which was decided in her favor in the Circuit Court made out a bill of exceptions, and intend to carry it up to the Supreme Court.

Gansevoort, through no fault of his own, at eighteen was living day to day, precariously, struggling against not one but a swarm of lawsuits and potential lawsuits, staving off creditors as best he could.

Early in 1834 Lemuel Shaw as trustee did his best to list all of Allan Melvill's debts to the senior Melvills' estates. He wrote Maria suggesting his own former student and junior partner, the indefatigable researcher Sidney Bartlett, "as a suitable person to be appointed guardian *ad litem*, in the equity suit here," and on 11 February he pressed Peter Gansevoort for specific details about a note left by Allan. The next day Shaw wrote again to Maria:

> It is probably not unknown to you, that from the time of your lamented husband's going into business at New York he received considerable sums of money from his father to be used as capital in his business, always conducting the loans as a strict, business transaction. . . . This debt went on increasing somewhat, especially about 1826 & 27. . . .
>
> I trust, Mrs. Melvill, I need not reiterate any strong assurances, to convince you of the deep interest & solicitude I feel in the welfare of your children, and the children of one of my oldest & best friends. I hope I feel the same solicitude for them, which I am sure he would feel for mine under the change of circumstances. I shall at all times & under all circumstances, do all in my power, to promote their best interests. I feel extreme regret, that there has been either in appearance or reality, any want of frank & cordial good understanding among the connexions of this family; and I trust, if it has been felt, it has been owing to some unfortunate misapprehension.

During the next few years, Shaw could have promoted the best interests of Maria's children by giving her money out of his own pocket. He did not do that, but as the decade passed he could not escape a sense of guilt at not helping them, and when occasions began to come his way a decade after Allan's death, he kept his word to Maria.

In an extant draft of a reply to Shaw's letter of 11 February 1834, Peter explained "Maria's situation" — her dependence upon Gansevoort and Peter's own liability to the state bank for "upwards of $22,000." Peter wanted Shaw to ask the Melvills not to demand that Maria pay the note he had endorsed for Allan — that is, that *he* not be required to pay it: "for if it shall be paid by me, it is virtually drawn from the little means she has, to support & educate the most lovely, interesting & promising family of young Children, you or I ever met with." Collecting from Peter in effect would be collecting from Maria. Peter was telling only part of the truth: he was indeed guarantor of Maria's enormous debt to the New York State Bank, but the main reason she could not pay off much of her debt was that he had not rushed to settle his mother's estate. Keeping Helen and Herman in school would have been a way of demonstrating that he found them lovely, interesting, and promising, but Peter did not choose so direct a way. In Boston on 19 February 1834 the debts of Allan Melvill to his father, Thomas Melvill, were itemized in an "Action by John D'Wolf and Lemuel Shaw before the Supreme Judicial Court in Suffolk County," and less than a month later the case of *D'Wolf et al. vs. Melvill et al.* was announced in the Supreme Judicial Court: all the surviving brothers and sisters of Allan Melvill had banded together in a lawsuit against his children, so as to protect their own inheritances from Allan's creditors. Earlier, all the survivors of the Boston Melvills, including Allan's minor children, had stood together against outside threats to the estate, but now all the Melvills stood together against those Melville children and their mother. The new court action was a legal necessity, but Maria and her brood could only feel it as betrayal and cruel rejection. They were worse than castaways: they were hounded outcasts.

Just turned eighteen, Gansevoort early in 1834 recorded in his diary specific details of his fur hat business, glimpses of the behavior of family members, and a good deal about his own conscientious program of self-improvement by judicious reading (and reflection on his reading) as well as by participation in the opportunities for improvement open to young men. Gansevoort's financial news mixes helter-skelter with health reports and notes on literary pursuits, for in a survival strategy he had compartmentalized his mind as tidily as a good business desk of the time. The diary is not minutely inclusive, for it does not mention that in late January the "dwelling house at the corner of Steuben and North Market Sts., at present occupied by Mrs Melville," was advertised for lease in the *Argus:* Maria was already arranging to move into one of the new houses in Clinton Square, a few blocks to the northwest. Herman does not figure largely in Gansevoort's diary: what fourteen-year-old boy matters much to an eighteen-year-old brother who has become the man of the family, with a mother and a total of three brothers and four sisters to look out for? Yet the diary provides the best evidence for the immediate circumstances of Herman Melville's life during his early teens.

Gansevoort's 1834 diary shows that he was no nominal operator of the business, but was involved, day to day, in all aspects of a complicated industry, from locating and bargaining for skins to preparing them for cutting and sewing to selling the finished products over the counter. Gansevoort then had several employees, for a diary entry on a Saturday afternoon specifies his paying "the hands off." The diary entry for 4 January 1834 describes an incidental treat Gansevoort gave his mother in the course of his work: "At 11 A M hired a horse and cutter of Kendall, and went to the mill on Norman's kill creek, (Sawyer's fulling mill) with 175 Muskrat skins to try the effect of milling them to soften the pelt and break it up, took my mother with me and left her as I went out at Whitehall." In this "cutter" (a one-horse open sleigh), Gansevoort had taken his mother a couple of miles north of town to Whitehall, the mansion that her uncle Leonard Gansevoort (1751–1810) had bought from the British general John Bradstreet, who had used it as headquarters during the French and Indian War. Now it was occupied by Maria's Ten Eyck cousins and their families, including Cousin Gansevoort Ten Eyck's bride, "a small, black eyed and rather pretty woman" who had "brought him $10,000," Gansevoort noted. Accustomed from childhood to the finest sleighs and carriages, not least the Hero's titanic phaeton, Maria had always fearlessly availed herself of chances to go about in winter. During her years in Manhattan her regular river trips had been arduous but inspiriting. Now, cooped up with her eight children in the little house on Market Street, constricted more tightly than she had ever been, Maria relished the outing to Whitehall, and professed herself "much pleased with the ride." She was prepared to take what pleasure was afforded her. Nevertheless, she and Gansevoort had to reflect, as they drove home, on just how important the $10,000 had been to Cousin Gansevoort Ten Eyck. Choices multiplied for a female of marriageable age, like Helen Maria, when she could bring such a dowry to her husband.

Herman Gansevoort, Maria's seldom-seen oldest brother, arrived in late January 1834 from Gansevoort, Saratoga County, and stayed with Maria, not with his brother and new sister-in-law. Peter on 4 February ran in the *Argus* some advertisements for rental property including one for the house of the Hero of Fort Stanwix: "TO LET — the spacious dwelling house occupied by the subscriber on North Market st., with fire proof stable and carriage house, a flower garden, bleaching yard, and every convenience for a private family, or a boarding-house. Possession if required, will be given before the first day of May next." Despite the reprieve Peter had been given on the house, the daughter of Chancellor Sanford had won, and by the spring of 1834, about the time Mary became pregnant, the Gansevoorts had bought a new house in Clinton Square, where Maria was also planning to move. As the daughter of a very wealthy man Mary felt free to express her opinions, but Peter was constitutionally dogged, and he did not sell his mother's house until 1851, having kept it as rental property since 1834. Peter was still very much in possession of the old house, but this was a good time for his brother Herman to pick up any items he wanted to carry off to the Mansion House. Herman Gansevoort was, after all, the oldest son. Some of the military gear and other relics of the Hero may have been hauled north at this time.

Herman Gansevoort passed several days with Maria and her family, long enough for Gansevoort to make a revealing judgment (in his diary for 26 January 1834) and incidentally to give news of Herman Melville: "On rising this m'g was glad to see snow. . . . Uncle Herman still remains with us, he is a very pleasant man in a family, more so than any man I am acquainted with — The snow storm prevented the female members of the family from going to church — Uncle Herman, Herman and Allan were all that went." Uncle Herman, who had no children of his own, was still tyrannized over by his redoubtable Catherine, who had forbidden him to invite little Herman to Gansevoort in July 1829. Yet at Maria's he had proved to be "a very pleasant man in a family," more so than the selfish Uncle Peter or the overwrought Uncle Thomas. While he was scouting out suitable locations for his factory, Gansevoort on 18 February got from his Uncle Herman "some good advice," which he determined to follow "if possible." In the Melville household, good advice from an adult male relative was a rarity.

Preparing for the future, Gansevoort devoured books in the years after his father's death just as he did every year of his adult life. In the process he determined, more than any other person, what books were around the house or in the store for Herman Melville to pick up and turn through — or perhaps even to devour himself, for Herman from childhood was also a compulsive reader. The diary shows that in early 1834 Gansevoort had access to at least one circulating library. He (and Herman, indirectly) made use of John Cook's reading room and the Athenaeum Library, the diary shows, as well as the libraries at the Albany Academy and (once Gansevoort joined) the Young Men's Association for Mutual Improvement. The association was open to

young men from sixteen years old to thirty-five "without distinction of pursuits, profession, or calling," according to a clipping on the Young Men's
Association in a scrapbook in the Harmanus Bleecker Library, now the Albany Public Library (noted by William H. Gilman in 1951). The association
kept a "Periodical Room," where the members might retire "to spend an Idle
hour in trying to improve their minds," although they sometimes had to try
to concentrate even while the occupants of the room beneath were creating a
ruckus by "comic songs, immoderate laughter, profane swearing, and disgusting stories" (according to the Albany *Microscope* on 5 May 1838).

On 4 January in the store Gansevoort read part of Byron's "The Bride of
Abydos" and ventured this literary judgment:

> the character of Zuleika as pourtrayed by Byron in the bride of Abydos, is the
> most sweetly beautiful female character that I have ever met with in Poetry, so
> gentle, affectionate, amiable, & ingenuous in disposition, so simply beautiful
> in her ideas, and so happy in expressing them, and appearing to possess every
> quality of heart and mind, calculated to make those around her happy, joined
> with a person, which would realize all the ideas that the Mahometan has of
> the beauty of the Houris, those dark eyed girls of Paradise, all conspire to
> make a woman as near perfection, as it is possible for her to attain.

Just turned eighteen, he was practicing the language of literary criticism. In
one drawer of his mind were literary experiences and his critical reflections
on the kind of man who might write a work he admired, for he may already
have been thinking, however vaguely, about a literary career for himself.
Within two or three years he was actively thinking of a career that involved at
least occasional literary criticism, long before anything is known for sure of
his younger brother Herman's literary aspirations or efforts.

The next day Gansevoort recorded that if anyone doubted "the truth of
the old saying, that pence get shillings and shillings pounds," he had only to
read the tale "The Founder of a Family," chapter 2 of *A Winter in London*, by
Thomas Skinner Surr, in order to be assured of its truth. The story raised the
question as to whether or not "superior talents are not essential to making
money," evoking this dictum from Gansevoort: "To make money, it only
requires a cool dispassionate disposition joined with talents even below mediocrity, and a determination to sacrifice every inclination and feeling that
may come in conflict with it." Gansevoort could justify reading *The Bride of
Abydos*, for it might equip him for light talk in elegant circles, but *A Winter in
London* was part of his pursuit of solemn and sententious financial advice that
his uncles could not be trusted to give him. In a century that glorified self-
improvement, Gansevoort was acting as many young Americans did; better
that he and Herman had been kept in school, but with his four years' advan-

tage over Herman, he could pursue his education on his own, and incidentally could keep books around where Herman would see them.

In January 1834 Gansevoort also read many novels, beginning with *The Prairie*, by Uncle Peter's boyhood friend James Fenimore Cooper, and was "well pleased with it — Characters of Ishmael Bush, Paul Hover & the trapper, well & powerfully drawn." (Maria Gansevoort Melville had known the novelist from childhood, when he would arrive from the West and stay as a guest in the house of the Hero for days at a time, playing with Peter, awaiting the breakup of the ice so he could proceed on his journey downriver.) Gansevoort had already begun to skim books for passages that might instill or confirm moral, political, or economic lessons a young man needed to learn. In the nature of things Herman gleaned after Gansevoort, who took seriously his obligation to make good books available to his younger brothers and sisters and to guide them in their reading.

In yet another way Herman followed Gansevoort, at a distance, although (the dynamics of brotherhood being what they were) he followed fast, not kept a full three and a half years behind. Gansevoort recorded spending the evening of 22 January 1834 "in listening to the debates at the Young Men's Association rooms" in the newly opened Stanwix Hall and talking to some of the young men more privileged than himself, then putting down his name on the list of active members. Noting with satisfaction that the "audience to the debates was large & respectable" and unabashed by the fact that at least some of the speakers had received more formal education than he had, Gansevoort judiciously criticized the speakers. He walked home with Alexander W. Bradford, the son of the minister who had married Allan Melvill and Maria Gansevoort, now a young lawyer, and the sort of rising young man Gansevoort would have been if his father had behaved with financial prudence instead of recklessness. Gansevoort followed up his chance the next day: "Saw Bradford, expressed himself pleased with my joining the debating society, and said that he would endeavor to have my name down among the Disputants for the next meeting." Debate and other forms of public speaking in the service of business and social contacts or in the service of a political party was another route to success which Gansevoort saw he might some day follow: though his mother may not have admitted it, he knew that his present business was precarious. Consolidating his friendship, in mid-February 1834 Gansevoort took Bradford on one of his buying trips. A few days later, in Albany, Bradford visited the Melvilles until almost midnight, strongly urging Gansevoort "to take up a course of reading, evenings." He particularly urged that Gansevoort study "Kent's Commentaries, & Blackstone," basic texts for the bar examination.

On 2 March 1834, Gansevoort avoided church all day ("going on the principle that Sunday is a day of rest"); perhaps Maria did not object because she was not in a particularly religious phase, or perhaps she simply accepted that whatever Gansevoort did was right. Her concern about the souls of her children was intermittent, affected by a variety of circumstances. That Sunday, Gansevoort "Commenced a work called 'Watts on the Improvement of the Mind'" which he determined to become "well acquainted with." Gansevoort had all his father's and Uncle Thomas's sententiousness, and despite recurrent illnesses he still possessed large stores of youthful dedication and determination. Keenly aware of the lack of a male mentor for himself, he later tried to inculcate admirable moral principles in Allan and young Tom, to whom he wrote on 19 September 1842, when the baby of the family was nearly thirteen:

> Picture to yourself, Tom, how painful it must be to be constantly aware of deficiencies in one's early education — to be oppressed in society & amid the world with a humbling sense of mental inferiority — to be forced into silence when you would speak — to listen without understanding — to distrust your own mind — to be uncertain about your own judgment — unable to sustain your own opinion — & then, too perhaps be prevented by circumstances and the want of time from repairing the deficiencies of which too late, you have become aware — If anything could add to the poignancy of feelings like these, it would be the consciousness that these thousand wants and mortifications are all owing to love of ease and pleasure and lack of ordinary industry. . . .
>
>   A boy you cannot always be, then, prepare to be a man, ere manhood is upon you unawares.

Gansevoort entreated his "dear brother" to reread the letter — "to ponder on it — to refer to it whenever your will is wavering and your endeavour weak," and then to act as Gansevoort would have him act. Allan and Tom both saved letters Gansevoort wrote to them when they were apart; Herman did not. Gansevoort labored his mightiest with Herman through the middle and late 1830s, though at times with a sense that he was wasting his breath. Yet Herman, more than the younger brothers, gleaned behind, with Gansevoort still in sight ahead of him.

    In the 1834 diary is a single vignette of Herman at work for the bank, an entry for 7 March, when Gansevoort rode to Schenectady: "This afternoon at ½ after 3 o'clock started for Schenectady (to see Hiram Haight) on horseback, accompanied by Aly Bradford. . . . I was very much surprised to meet brother Herman in the bar-room at Davis' in company with Frederick Leake, and at first could not imagine the reason of his being there, but on reflection saw that the bank must have sent them over, on enquiry I found my opinion confirmed — They came over in the afternoon car and were unable to return that eve'g there being no cars." This is Herman's first known railroad ride. Pulled by horse or steam engine (named the De Witt Clinton), the cars still were merely stagecoaches fitted with new wheels to grip the rails. Gansevoort was astonished, but as far as the entry shows, Herman was unabashed, having been found huddling in the barroom for warmth, not for alcohol. The bank considered him competent to go away on an errand, but Gansevoort's initial consternation is proof that the boy was not regularly sent out of town.

Later that month Gansevoort made one of his frequent stopovers at the Pittsfield farm. Julia Maria wrote Augusta that she had been "in hopes that he would have brought Herman with him," an altogether unrealistic wish, in view of Peter Gansevoort's determination that he not miss work at the bank. Perhaps she had sent Herman engraved pictures from some magazine with the idea that he would copy them, for she wrote: "I thought Herman would like to draw those pictures I sent him Aunt Maria said when she was here that he was very fond of drawing, his shells were very acceptable indeed." On 26 March Julia wrote to Augusta, mentioning Herman in passing: "We have not heard from *Robert* this three weeks then he was well, he has got the key to your work box and has had it since last summer when *Herman* was here I intended to write him about it but I forgot to." Robert's whereabouts are unknown, but his goings and comings in the 1830s are significant because sometimes he took Herman along (or, later, simply went with Herman).

It was most likely on 1 May, the usual moving day, that Maria took possession of a new three-story brick house at 3 Clinton Square, at Pearl Street. It was a gracious house with a brownstone porch and threshold, brownstone pillars, ceilings fourteen feet high in the front parlor and a black marble fireplace, ten-foot-high front windows, with inside shutters that fit into built-in cases. The kitchen was in the usual place, the basement. In the back was a stable where Gansevoort could keep his horses.

On 6 May, probably before they had settled into the new house completely, Gansevoort's factory (not the store) was destroyed when a fire broke out in Middle Lane about midnight, and other stores and several dwellings on North Market and Columbia were lost. The setback was devastating for Gansevoort and the rest of the family. On 14 May Uncle Thomas passed the news to Lemuel Shaw: "You may have seen by the public papers, that Gansevoorts factory, for preparing Skins was lately burnt down — by a letter from him, he estimates his loss, (over & above the insurance) at 1,500, to 2000 $." The "derangement to his business" was, as Thomas thought, "considerable." The most obvious consequence was that Gansevoort could no longer afford to keep on his hired hands, and indeed had no factory for them to work in. Under the circumstances he pulled Herman out of his job at the bank and set him to work in the cap and fur store. Almost fifteen when taken out of the bank, Herman waited on customers, but later he may have been deemed responsible enough to be trusted with fur-buying trips such as Gansevoort had sent one young man on in December 1833.

Still hoping for something from the Melvill estate, Maria arrived at Pittsfield on 7 September 1834 with Catherine and Tom, in order to waylay Lemuel Shaw during his court term in Lenox. In her anxiety Maria violated the local blue code against traveling on Sunday, as Julia revealed in a letter to Augusta on 12 September. In 1834 Augusta was allowed to visit, perhaps conveyed by Gansevoort on his way to Boston to see Shaw's associate Sidney Bartlett about the court case and about any possible inheritance that might come, however belatedly. (On 6 August Shaw wrote Peter Gansevoort that he understood Gansevoort was in Boston and depended "upon the pleasure of seeing him.") In a letter to Shaw on 9 September 1834 Thomas Jr. was explicit about Maria's purpose: "I have the pleasure to inform you that Maria, is on a visit to us for the purpose of conferring with you — she is very desirous of seeing you while you are in the County, and among other things, to communicate her Mothers will." Maria was intent on letting Shaw know that the estate of her mother had not been settled and that advances to Allan had been charged against her inheritance, so that she had no reliable income from that source, although a number of city lots were by now in her name. Around 12 September Julia wrote Augusta a letter to be carried by her Aunt Maria, who had spent her visit in the kitchen, day and evening too, " 'When on the hearth high flames the fire.' " She named the reason Herman had not come to the farm: "I was very much disappointed that *Hermans* business would not allow him to visit Pittsfield this year but *Gan* said he could not let him because he was wanted in the store."

That 9 October 1834 the Lenox *Massachusetts Eagle* in its account of the annual Pittsfield Cattle Show printed a long report "On Manufactures" signed by the committee chairman, Thomas Melvill Jr., who made a visionary declaration: "the expectation that we may raise and produce silk to advantage is no longer visionary." His term in the legislature over, Thomas Jr. in a letter to the local lawyer and U.S. Representative George N. Briggs on 9 December projected a new role for himself: "Altho' bound down, from necessity, to a farm, and almost a Hermit in a Wilderness, still I take a no less deep interest in our political affairs, than if I were in a more elevated, & pleasant situation." Herman Melville later lived out some roles projected by his uncle, and "Hermit in a Wilderness" would prove a choice role to imitate, with variations, when the time came. For the present Herman had small choice in roles available to him. He was a clerk — bank clerk, store clerk — this year forced to miss the vacation that he associated with his birth month, August. Two years before it had been Uncle Peter who determined that he needed Herman in the bank; now it was Gansevoort who needed him in the store. No one would have thought of asking him what he preferred to do.

Herman was a small human speck, perhaps not even worth $37.50 a quarter: why should Gansevoort pay him for working in the store, when Gansevoort himself got no salary? These years of relentless confinement left Herman Melville with a lifelong smoldering restlessness.

Herman had access to a little money for educational purposes, for on 30 January 1835 he paid $1.50 for his initiation fee and a quarter's dues to the Albany Young Men's Association. The year before, and even earlier than that, his brother Gansevoort had been able to goad himself on at night, improving his mind, so as to be ready when the time came to take a high place in his world. Herman, so much more poorly schooled than Gansevoort, was less equipped for self-improvement. Now, a youth confined all day in the cap and fur store, he needed the stimulation of a mutual improvement society, stimulation that often proved powerful. Boys not yet in their teens drew up elaborate constitutions for private debating societies and formally debated then-explosive political issues such as whether or not freemasonry was "injurious to mankind," along with more abstract questions such as "Which creates the greatest emotion in the human heart—fear or love?" Young Henry Sanford in 1829, shortly before Peter Gansevoort was smitten with his sister Mary, drew up such a constitution for the Philomathean Debating Society (now in the New York Public Library). After April Herman remained in the association by sufferance until 2 December 1835, when he paid up three quarters of back dues—$1.50. (That was four days before his older brother turned twenty; everyone had long forgotten that Gansevoort was still very young.) In a letter printed in the Albany *Microscope* on 31 March 1838, Herman testified to the value of debating societies:

> We ask no higher testimony in favor of its advantages, than the recorded opinions of all great men, Burke, the English Orator and Statesman acknowledged that the first spring which moved him on in a career of fame and honor, was the fostering encouraging effect of a literary club, our own Clay had revealed to him the latent powers of a giant mind in a like institution, and Franklin the philosopher and sage attributed the early development of his natural resources to the same mind stirring soul animating cause, but why specify? The learned are as one man, in their opinion of the importance of debating societies in developing the mind, and prompting to greater and higher efforts.

The training in debating techniques stayed with Herman, later allowing him, on one particular day (29 October 1849), to pass time pleasantly on shipboard: "In the evening put the Captain in the Chair, & argued the question 'which was best, a Monarchy or a republic?' — Had some good sport during the debate." More important, the training reinforced, if it did not create, the characteristic rhetorical bent that later led him to elaborate lines of thought for the sheer delight of championing a position eloquently, as he did in some of the essayistic chapters of *Moby-Dick*.

In March 1835 part of the estate of Catherine Van Schaick Gansevoort was sold, for more than forty thousand dollars, but the money was not distributed to all the heirs. Mary Ann Chandonette Gansevoort did not receive enough to stop her son Leonard, then nineteen or so, from sailing on a New Bedford whaler in July. This was an act almost of desperation, since crews of whaleships were notoriously dissipated and diseased and the required "outfits" and incidental expenses tended to eat up the expected "lay" (the portion of profits from the voyage, as explained in *Moby-Dick*, ch. 16). If Maria Melville received a trifle of the proceeds from the sale in March, that may account for Herman's being enrolled at the Albany Classical School (apparently in the spring) while working still at his brother's store. Helen in 1835 was given her last chance for advancement by being sent to the small school conducted in Lenox by Elizabeth Sedgwick, the wife of Charles Sedgwick, who was court clerk for Shaw and the other justices during their September sessions, and whose sister Catharine already had gained fame as a novelist. Elizabeth (or Eliza) Sedgwick admitted only two dozen students at a time — few enough to allow a good deal of personal tutoring. On 22 July 1835, almost eighteen, Helen wrote a motherly letter to Augusta from Lenox:

> I hope that in my absence you do all in your power to assist Mama, you know you have now a double duty to perform, be obedient kind and devoted to her, my darling, We are all in all to her in this world, and should repay her deep affection, by dutiful conduct, and prompt attention to her wishes. I never knew until I left home to be gone so long, how much I loved her, and I would now do any thing within the compass of human abilities to give her one hour of happiness.

Long before, on 23 May 1829, twelve-year-old Helen in a letter to her mother could express her sense of Maria's majestic role as the "grand spring" of the mechanism of the family. Now Helen was even more a second mother to all the children except Gansevoort. Instead of enjoying the carefree youth her birth had destined her for, she was sober beyond her years and quite removed from the marriage market that her aunts were rushing into pell-mell. Even the comparative joy of her schooling was tarnished by disgrace: while Helen was in Lenox, Uncle Thomas was also there — confined on the complaint of a creditor, M. E. Gold, in the county jail, cheek by jowl with the courthouse where Judge Shaw presided, on the other side of which was the Little Red Inn, where the judge stayed.

In Albany Herman had some freedom that summer of 1835. With his friends he swam as usual in the Hudson. The Melvilles' little cousin Henry Sanford Gansevoort, eight months old, born on 15 December 1834, was much in the house. Mary Sanford Gansevoort wrote her husband that he passed "at least half of his time with the children at Maria's," so delighted to be with them that he never wanted to come home until he was hungry. Late that August 1835 Maria was in Pittsfield with Helen (on vacation from school), again planning a visit to Lenox (once Gansevoort returned to escort her), probably to see Mrs. Sedgwick this time rather than to waylay Judge Shaw. Chances are that Thomas Jr. was home rather than in jail, for his sister Helen and her new husband were there. Helen Maria (the middle of the three Helens in the house) wrote to Augusta that "Mama" (they usually spelled the word "Mamma") was "very busy talking with Aunt Helen & Aunt Mary," and the women and the children were "all very well" and even better than that ("you would think happy if you could hear us laugh & frolic"). Cousin Anne, a mature, thoughtful, quiet young woman, sent "her best very best love to *Herman*." Helen outlined the plan: "Aunt Helen and *Uncle Souther* will return with Mama on Tuesday, and stay two or three days." This temporary resumption of family ties was infinitely poignant to Maria, since Helen Melvill, then sixteen, had accompanied her and her bridegroom during the five-day trip from Albany to Boston after her wedding in 1814. Now they would retrace together the initial part of that trip, in reverse order.

Formally or informally, some of the Melville children continued to pursue their education. In September 1835 Allan was readmitted to the Albany Academy to study Latin, arithmetic, and English grammar — a peevish boy, but one with reason to complain about being pushed into school and jerked out without regard to his progress or his wishes. Late that month Gansevoort Melville, having risen rapidly in the Young Men's Association, was named to its executive committee.

By 8 October, just after Pittsfield's annual Cattle Show and Fair, Helen Maria from the farm wrote a brave letter to the next oldest sister: "I am not homesick Augusta, but I sometimes feel very much like going home again, and would like nothing better than to join your family circle, and return to the shadow of a mothers wing, but this cannot be just yet." She continued with injunctions for the second daughter comparable to those Gansevoort must have given the second son: "Until then dear Augusta take my place as eldest daughter and fill it with becoming grace and dignity; it is rather a responsible station upon the whole, at least that was the idea Mama always wished me to take of it, you must be a model for your younger brothers and in short a 'pattern girl.'" Like Gansevoort, Helen had reading to recommend, Catharine Sedgwick's *The Lintons* ("unanimously pronounced as Miss Sedgwicks best work"). Uncle Peter was a friend of James Fenimore Cooper, but Helen was the first in her generation to know a real author, Miss Sedgwick. Robert was going to Albany, and would carry the letter. Helen enjoined Augusta to relay this message to "Mama" about Herman: "I am astonished she could withstand my anxious entreaties for a visit from Herman, and Aunt Mary now says that Mama must let him come with Robert. Oh! do beseech her to allow him to visit Pittsfield, I do want to see him so much." Helen's longing to see Herman was mingled with her uneasiness at the advancing of her first fall in the country: "Autumn is setting in apace, and the leaves are falling thick around us. The forests to be sure look beautiful, but never having been in the country at this season, I cannot avoid feeling a little melancholy sometimes, when I see the trees one by one, losing all their foliage, and standing in leafless majesty, they look bare and cold enough in some places, while in others they still retain their gorgeous robes." This was her first and last Berkshire autumn for fifteen years — and even then, in 1850, she decamped in November. Helen was and remained a city girl.

Julia Maria also wrote to Augusta on 8 October 1835, declaring they had been expecting Herman all week, and he came, in mid-October. He had glimpsed the farm in childhood and in 1832, and had spent an entire week there in 1833, but he had not been there in more than two years. Trapped indoors by the weather with all the family, he became closer acquainted with them all than ever before. Now he was old enough to appreciate the romantic history of his Cousin Priscilla, twenty-five, who had arrived in Pittsfield as a little French girl and who still remembered her mother, Françoise Raymonde Eulogie Marie des Douleurs Lamé Fleury (1781–1814). Thomas Melvill Jr. had married his French wife without obtaining the approval of his parents (an act for which his brother Allan had reproached him), and had exhausted himself in glamorizing her history. Her father, Lamé Fleury, a native of Nantes who had become a merchant in Cadiz, had been arrested by the Revolutionary Tribunal and doomed, but suddenly liberated after the death of Robespierre in 1794. Fleury then had lived, Thomas had informed his parents on 13 June 1802 (a letter now at Harvard), "a retired life at Paris on the interest of what he saved of his property." There "M. Recamier, the first and most respectable Banker in this place" (the words of Cousin David Cargill, in Paris, to Thomas Sr., 13 June 1802, also now at Harvard), had, as Thomas Jr. wrote, come to regard "the young lady in question like a child, and in the world she is looked upon and called indeed, the adopted Niece of M. Recamier," who had "acted the part of a father" in the "delicate, interesting affair" of Thomas's proposal. With her father's permission, Priscilla could show Herman a miniature of her mother which presented "a countenance of much beauty and of that kind which forcibly arrests the attention" (as Melville wrote in 1870, in his memoir of his uncle). During this visit Herman understood better, also, the lineage of his Aunt Mary, for she was not only a granddaughter of General Henry Dearborn but a descendant of other eminent New Englanders, including John Winthrop and Thomas Dudley, early governors of the Massachusetts Bay Colony and among the founders of Harvard College.

His Uncle Thomas fascinated Herman. As in his earlier visits, Herman romanticized the man: "His manners were mild & kindly, with a faded brocade of old French breeding which — contrasted with the surroundings at the time — impressed me as not a little interesting, nor wholly without a touch of pathos." This Melville wrote three and a half decades later for a *History of Pittsfield.* There he recalled the time the family spent together in October 1835, especially hours when the smaller cousins were already abed: "By the late October fire" (he meant toward the end of the evening, not late in the month) "on the great hearth of the capacious kitchen of the old farm-mansion I remember seeing the Major frequently sit, just before early bedtime, gazing into the embers, his face plainly expressing to a sympathetic observer, that his heart — thawed to the core under the influence of the genial flame — carried him far away over the ocean to the gay Boulevards." Melville as a man of fifty may have perceived some element of posturing in his uncle's broodings, but in 1835 the boy imagined his uncle as a cosmopolitan in exile, far from the scene of his social, commercial, and diplomatic triumphs in pre-Napoleonic and Napoleonic France, from 1794 to 1811. Melville recorded that his uncle had been "familiar with the stirring events which took place in that Country from the closing years of the Republic through the Consulate, and down to a period towards the collapse of the first Empire." As he inferred, his uncle had "found his way easy and delightful in the bright circles of the City on the Seine," the beneficiary of the friendliness manifested toward "any young countryman of Washington" in a country that had supported the American Revolution.

Throughout his short memoir of his uncle, Melville's own intervening experiences and judgments are intermixed with recollected feelings from 1832, 1833, and later, 1835 and 1836, most especially 1835, when the weather encouraged huddling together by the fire. Melville wrote:

> In certain departments the business of a European Banker makes it his interest to be hospitable. If his disposition coincide with his interest, his entertainments may be often extremely agreeable from the piquant mixture of the

Company. The polite Bostonian's dinner in Paris lacked not as I have been told this quality, nor the zest of a very social nature in the host. Many distinguished countrymen did he from time to time entertain at his table, together with Frenchmen of note invited to meet them. Among others, I have frequently heard him name Lafayette. . . .

Of an enterprising & sanguine temper — too much so indeed — my uncle aside from his special vocation, engaged in various tempting ventures, incident to the wars then convulsing the Continent. Naturally he shared in many fluctuations.

I remember his telling me that upon one occasion, after prosperously closing in London some considerable affair, he held in his hands, before a cheery coal fire, the proceeds — negotiable bills, and for so large a sum, that he said to himself — holding them at arms length[—]break off then, and get the[e] back to Boston Common. But a false friend — Hope by name (not one of the noted Amsterdam House) advised to the contrary.

Eventually such reverses overtook him, that recrossing the Ocean he returned to his father[s] roof.

Thomas told many such marvelous stories of unique experiences. One dealt with his taking a role, at twenty-one, in 1797, as the agent of Count de Barras in helping to negotiate a peace-at-a-price with William Pitt at the conference at Lille. Thomas had seen Napoleon with his own eyes, had welcomed Lafayette to his own table, and had conversed with all the shifting American diplomatic corps, among them Joel Barlow and Thomas Jefferson. Herman was of an age to request, "often," that his uncle describe "some of those martial displays and spectacles of state which he had witnessed in Paris in the time of the first Napoleon." Thomas responded with "pictorial" recollections that Herman "was too young & ignorant then, to derive the full benefit from."

In 1870, at fifty or fifty-one, Melville remembered only a fraction of the stories, and by that time he was bemused by what he perceived as the illustration of the psychological law that a benefactor retains a large measure of good will toward the beneficiary: having helped the colonies, the French welcomed individual Americans like young Thomas Melvill. By then, he understood some of his uncle's own limitations: "Nor though he possessed so much information, and had a good understanding was his mind of that order which qualifies one for drawing the less obvious lessons from great historic events happening in ones own time, and under ones eyes." Thomas Melvill Jr. had been an eyewitness to history, and a minor participant in it, however reduced his position in life had become, but he had not become one of "the more thoughtful" observers of his own time (a phrase from *Billy Budd*, ch. 8).

On 24 October 1835, soon after Herman returned to Albany (or perhaps while he was still on the farm to witness the degrading scene), Thomas Melvill Jr. was again arrested for debt and taken to jail in Lenox. Perhaps Helen Maria found it possible to visit her uncle in jail, perhaps not, but she lived at the school while suffering the shame of knowing where her uncle was. As in late August, when Mary Melvill and Maria Melville took tea with her, Eliza Sedgwick was obliged to overlook an indignity suffered by one of their own class, and to comfort her student. Thomas Jr. himself, by this time all but inured to the shame of his position, wrote letters to the Pittsfield *Sun* in which (as "Ben Austin") he argued against imprisonment for debt. Trouble came when he also wrote articles and responses in the Lenox *Massachusetts Eagle* until he antagonized the editor, J. Z. Goodrich, who mistakenly accused him of being "Plain Farmer" as well as "Ben Austin." In the controversy that followed, the *Sun* declared: "The Editor of the Eagle, driven to desperation, attacks Maj. Melvill in a manner unbecoming an Editor or a gentleman, but *highly becoming* a cause which cannot be sustained by creditable means." In the 19 November 1835 issue the editor of the *Sun* made a shameless appeal to hereditary patriotism (using the variant "Melville"): "The Editor of the Eagle is to be pitied. — We really believe he did not know any better than to make a base personal attack upon Major Melville! a son of one who threw tea overboard in Boston Harbor — a base personal attack, and for what? for the atrocious crime of not being a whig, for the grievous offence of being a public writer, and a poor debtor." In 1837 Herman had ample opportunity to read the files of the *Eagle* and *Sun* and see his uncle in the new light of an adept political polemicist, a likely model for an eager young nephew.

6

Clerk, Farmer, Teacher, Polemicist
1836–May 1838

Childhood is the happiest stage of our existence it is thin [then] if ever, that the cup of pleasure is sweet, then it is unpoisoned by sin and sorrow, and we may freely drink the draught unembittered with the thoughts and anxieties for the future.

Augusta Melville, a composition at the Albany Female Academy,
15 October 1836

SIXTEEN WHEN 1836 BEGAN, Herman was still working in the cap and fur store; a bill for three boys' caps survives with his name on the receipt dated 16 January. Gansevoort had continued to stock his mind with apt and readily retrievable items from what must have been, still, his daily reading, and he had devoted many evenings to improving his already formidable talents for public performance. Late in January he was elected president of the debating society in the Young Men's Association. His store now needed help on a seasonable basis rather than year in and year out; on 10 March Gansevoort advertised in the *Argus:* "Twenty Hat Trimmers — Wanted Immediately." Four days later he added to the advertisement: "Two boys as apprentices to the Hatting Business." Business was so good and portraiture so cheap that on 13 June someone painted a miniature of Gansevoort in watercolor. Three days later Maria sold for one thousand dollars one of the fifteen lots left her in her mother's will; how many of them she actually had the power to sell is not known. That summer Augusta and one or both of the two younger girls were enrolled at the Albany Female Academy on North Pearl Street. On 4 July Gansevoort played his first prominent civic role: as part of the city celebration he joined a procession by the Young Men's Association, then took the stage. As the *Argus* reported, "The Declaration of Independence was read, and well read, by Mr. G. Melville." Four days later there was cash for Herman to pay a dollar for two quarters' back dues in the Young Men's Association; he was still following close behind Gansevoort.

In Pittsfield Thomas Jr. still managed to make Maria's children welcome, in shifts, whatever his pains and strains. In 1836 Herman was allowed to go to the farm the week he turned seventeen. Helen found it hard to leave the school in Lenox, according to a letter from Julia to Augusta on 6 August: "Gan carried Helen to Lenox on Monday & she returned on tuesday of the next week then she has gone this morning with Herman to spend the day there and return after tea. I suppose she enjoys herself very much when she is at Mrs Sedgwick she wants to be there so often." (At this time Herman may have learned, without making much of the information, that Elizabeth Buckminster Dwight Sedgwick was a granddaughter of the minister Jonathan Edwards.) In the coming and going Gansevoort or Helen (or both) took charge of Fanny, almost nine, for Julia wrote: "Fanny has enjoyed herself very much, the little time she has been here, Aunt Maria will not own her when she goes home she has grown so wild and tanned Oh dreadfully." Having completed her year at Lenox and passed some time at Pittsfield, Helen returned to help her mother at home, allowing Augusta to resume the easier role of second daughter. Augusta got her visit to the farm a little later, for her fifteenth birthday. She brought with her the six-and-a-half-year-old Tom. Even Augusta, sobered early by tragedy, managed, on the farm, to feel youthful and happy.

During Herman's vacation the wealthiest resident of Pittsfield, Edward A. Newton, returned from France with his daughter, accompanying the remains of his wife, who had died in Rouen. Like the Newton family, Thomas Jr. and his family attended St. Stephen's Protestant Episcopal, the gray limestone church completed in 1832. The funeral was held on 9 August. Thomas was almost surely among the large number of "sympathizing friends" the *Sun* reported as attending the funeral, and 13 August is one of the few Sundays when Herman witnessed variations on this remarkable scene, which he recorded in his memoir of his uncle:

At that period on Sundays between services, the broad bar-room of the principal tavern of Pittsfield—long since removed—situated on the village square, was the conveniant resort, (not for unsober purposes, since the decanters were inexorably closed) of many church attendants whose dwellings were at a distance. Here too dropped in the magnates of the village. Eminent among them was the late Edward A. Newton well known as a man of fortune, who had travelled, and who lived with all things handsome about him, like the old English Squire in the play[.]

The exchange of salutations and pinches of Rappee, between this tall & stately gentleman, and my plainly clad but courtly kinsman, presented a picture upon which the indigenous farmers there assembled, gazed with eager interest, and a kind of homely awe. It afforded a peep into a world as unknown to them as the Vale of Cashmere to the Esquimaux I[n]dian.

To the ensuing conversation, also, they listened with the look of steers astonished in the pasture at the camel of the menagerie passing by on the road. It is different now. Those primitive days, with whateve[r] picturesqueness pertained thereto, are gone with the old Elm of the Green.

By 1870 Herman Melville had been, himself, the subject of such gawking by Berkshire rustics, so this memory is also overlaid by his own subsequent experiences, but across the decades persisted a sense of his uncle as a cosmopolitan surviving in rural exile amid uncomprehending hinds. In the 1830s his uncle exerted a powerful force over his imagination, and to the end of his life Thomas Jr. haunted his memory as an exiled courtier reduced to humble employment. At crises in his own life the patterns of Thomas Melvill Jr.'s life would come all too readily to hand.

Thomas Melvill Jr.'s situation on the farm—still not *his* farm, but the estate's—continued to deteriorate, but he probably put a good face on things when Daniel Webster, the friend of his father and of Lemuel Shaw, attended the Cattle Show and Fair that October. On 8 November 1836 Thomas Jr. wrote Shaw: "The weather still continues very cold, so much so, that I have to fear, we shall lose our whole crop of Russia turnips—it being impossible to get them out of the ground. We have probably 600 bushels, in jeopardy." That autumn Hezekiah Gear, an old acquaintance of Thomas's who had started up a store in Galena, Illinois, returned to Pittsfield. Built on the Galena River just up from its juncture with the Mississippi, the village (named for sulphide, the principal ore of lead) had become the major port for the Federal Lead Mine District. Just that year, 1836, the town was surveyed and the lots offered for sale, creating a boom in construction. Gear was back in Massachusetts to find (in the manner of the time) a replacement wife. Promptly enough he found Deborah Rose and married her. When he saw that Thomas Jr. was languishing on the farm, he offered him the management of his store. Thomas Jr. sent Robert out to Galena on a scouting expedition, and for a time kept his plans secret from at least the younger children, and certainly from the trustees of the estate and his creditors: like his late brother six years earlier, he was planning a flight. Around 7 November, before Thomas Jr. wrote to Shaw, Robert had arrived safe in Pittsfield "with his cargo" (according to a letter Julia wrote Augusta, by favor of Gansevoort). The cargo consisted of unidentified goods brought from the west, for she continued: "the good people thought him some young fellow coming to the east to seek his fortune I expect instead of the great western world where every one else thinks is paradise." Robert's excursion confirmed his father in the decision to go west, in due course. Robert himself undertook to teach a school that winter "some miles from home," so far away that they only saw him once a week. (Julia continued: "he likes teechin very much I should not I am shure [have] patience to do it.") As it turned out, Robert's teaching prepared the way for Herman to follow him.

On 1 September 1836 Herman was readmitted to the Albany Academy after five years' absence, and enrolled in the Latin course; at the same time he paid a quarter's dues in the Young Men's Association, fifty cents. He joined an adjunct of the association, the Ciceronian Debating Society, and when that failed, another debating club, the Philo Logos Society. It seemed that Herman might have a chance to make up some of his missed years of schooling. Perhaps this was the time Herman memorized some Shakespeare for its shock value around the younger girls, as Helen remembered when she saw the tragedian Charles Macready in Boston (and described the play in a letter to Augusta on 27 November 1843): "The witch scenes were admirably got up, and when, dancing about the 'cauldron of hell-broth,' one of the horrid creatures, puts in some terrible contribution; and enjoins it 'to make the gruel thick & slab,' I *could* not help thinking of poor Herman, who made it a favorite quotation, and talked about the 'pilot's thumb, wrecked as homeward he did come,' 'eye of newt, toe of frog,' &c." Through his teens Herman at times happily teased the girls with this indecorous passage from *Macbeth*, as he had once "plagued" Gansevoort.

Already there were ominous signs of the approaching Panic of 1837. From New York on 15 September 1836 John J. Hill wrote to Peter Gansevoort: "Money is scarce here and there is a sort of panic in Wall St & among Speculators — Now is not the time to force our property in market and I shall not do so." On 16 September Gansevoort Melville wrote to his Uncle Peter: "This morning I have been disappointed in receiving some money, on which I had calculated and which I shall not be able to get until Thursday next — This necessitates me to ask you to do me *another* favor — Will you be good enough to see the Cashier tomorrow mg & obtain permission for me to overdraw to the amt of say sixteen hundred dollars." On 22 October Herman, although underage, was pressed into service as a witness: a mortgage between Maria G. Melville and the New York Life Insurance & Trust Company (a four-thousand-dollar mortgage on eight of her remaining lots) was "sealed & delivered in the presence of Herman Melville" (records of Albany County). She was depleting the remnants of her inheritance to keep Gansevoort afloat.

For years the boom in canals and railroads had encouraged speculation in western lands, but in July 1836 President Jackson had ordered that henceforth payment for western lands must be in gold or silver. This "Specie Circular" caused sales of lands to drop and simultaneously rendered state banknotes less valuable. At the same time, gold and silver reserves were depleted by an unfavorable balance of trade with England. British banks began to call in American loans, demanding payment in gold and silver. By the start of 1837 banks had failed in some parts of the country, although New York banks held solvent for a few more weeks. The two older Melville sons had learned early to live in denial of disaster — to concentrate with excessive, even obsessive coolness on something that interested them when all around them things were falling apart. Now membership in the Albany Young Men's Association for Mutual Improvement was a way of avoiding thinking about the financial crisis, and on 5 January 1837 they each paid their dues for two quarters, one dollar. Herman had to withdraw from the Albany Academy once again on 1 March: mutual improvement rather than formal instruction was the best he could have. Both the brothers worked, read, and debated as if the world were not tumbling down around their ears. (Their Aunt Mary, Leonard Gansevoort's widow, had no such distractions. From the Van Schoonhoven house in Waterford on 4 April 1837, reduced to selling her sofa at auction, she wrote: "Peter, if you have any regard for me — pray, for pity's sake, do, in *mercy* give Stanwix the money" — $25 or so. She ended woefully: "I am half crazy.")

In January 1837, with the nation sliding into the terrible Panic, Gansevoort Melville acquired just what he needed, an easy-indexing instant-retrieval system ready-made for a young man determined to sharpen his rhetorical skills and enlarge his store of useful knowledge. This was a copy of the *Index Rerum: or Index of Subjects, Intended as a Manual to Aid the Student and the Professional Man, in Preparing Himself for Usefulness, with an Introduction, Illustrating its Utility and Method of Use* (1837). The *Index Rerum* had a long vogue and was used by many people who were already famous (one was George Bancroft) or who became famous (one was Henry David Thoreau). It was the money-coining invention of the Reverend Dr. John Todd, pastor of the Edwards Church, Northampton (already famous as the author of the widely used *Student's Manual*), and later a formidable presence on the religious scene in the Berkshires.

Todd in his introduction reviewed the human tendency to forget what is read: "much of all our valuable reading is lost, because we retain only faint impressions of it, and have no method of recalling it." A traditional commonplace book was wearisome to fill and inefficient to make subsequent use of, but Todd's improvement offered the dual advantage of rapid indexing and retrieval. Todd was wryly ironic about the fact that the body of his *Index Rerum* consisted of almost totally blank pages ("not very cheering to the fame of authorship"). In fact, the body of the sturdily bound volume *was* blank except for two-letter headings at the top of each page, a capitalized letter of the alphabet, starting with "A," followed by a lowercase vowel (also starting with "a"). The headings consisted of vowel and next vowel ("A.a.," followed by "A.e."), or consonant and first vowel ("B.a.," followed by "B.e."). Todd gave an example of an entry that would be made toward the middle of the book, in the "I's," on an otherwise blank page headed "I.i."): "INDIANS, Pequot, beautiful description of the war with: Trumb. Hist. Con. vol. 1. chap. 5." The user, in other words, would come across a passage on the Pequot Indians in Benjamin Trumbull's *A Complete History of Connecticut* (1797 or 1818), jot down the item under the general term "Indians," in which the first letter was "I" and the next vowel was also "i" (or, if he preferred, the user could jot down "Pequot" in the "P.e." section). The keeper of the *Index Rerum* would be able, months or years later, to find just where he had come across a beautiful depiction of the annihilating war against the Pequot (or Pequod) tribe. Todd's final thirty-six pages were entirely blank, to be used as a commonplace book for those stubborn users who would be disconsolate without a place to copy out at least a few memorable quotations.

In the course of the year Gansevoort indexed many dozens of books and magazine articles, along with a few newspaper items, and he strewed the blank pages at the end with quotations from the revered book that began its serialization in the year of Herman's birth, Washington Irving's *The Sketch Book*. The presence of Irving in the first entries in this appendix suggests that during their months early in the year under the same roof there had been ample chances for Herman to share Gansevoort's enthusiasm for this first great American collection of essays and fiction. Gansevoort, as usual, was reading purposefully — noting useful comments on genius, for instance, and on English writers on America. He was also reading in his set of Walter Scott. In the three years since he read Byron's *Bride of Abydos* he had become a more focused reader, no longer so concerned with passages that might help him understand male or female psychology as with passages that might directly help him toward a career.

The two volumes that survive of the four or more Gansevoort ultimately owned contain the best evidence for his — and also for Herman's — reading in the late 1830s, even though for months at a time while Gansevoort was using one volume or another of the *Index Rerum* the brothers were not living in the same house. Todd's citation of "Pequot" may be the merest of coincidences, despite the name of Ishmael's ship in *Moby-Dick*. Nevertheless, that passage and some entries Gansevoort made shed light not only on him and Herman in the late 1830s but also on Herman's later writings such as *Moby-Dick* and *Clarel*. Under "P.a." Gansevoort listed these two items:

> Parsees — of India — an excellent description of their character, & religion
> & an account of their descent — East India Sketch book p 21

Panther — encounter with an American P — and fortunate rescue — a well
drawn picture — Vol 2nd of the Pioneers

Under "P.i." Gansevoort listed:

Pirate's cabin Red Rover Vol 1 chap 6 page 84 description of.

Under "S.o." he listed:

Storm at sea graphic description of, Red Rover 1st vol c 16 p 258 good

He ran out of space under the pages labeled "S.a." so continued his list on a
page intended for "W.u.," making this entry:

Saint-Saba The convent of — the largest in the East — with a description
Incidents of travel in Egypt, Arabia Petraea & the Holy Land, v 2. c 16

When he reviewed the new edition of Cooper's *Red Rover* for the *Literary
World* early in 1850, Herman recalled: "Long ago, & far inland, we read it in
our uncritical days, & enjoyed it as much as thousands of the rising generation will when supplied with such an entertaining volume." As second sons
do, Herman read along behind Gansevoort during the early months of 1837
and intermittently thereafter. Anyone familiar with Herman Melville's writings will see in Gansevoort's *Index Rerum* books Herman must have read in
those "uncritical days" — John Lloyd Stephens's first book, *Incidents of Travel
in Egypt, Arabia Petræa, and the Holy Land* (1837), which he referred to in
Redburn and used in *Clarel* (1876), Irving's *Sketch Book* (immensely influential
on *Redburn*), William Leete Stone's *Life of Joseph Brant* (this or another copy
of which he had in hand late in 1851). Gansevoort's fascination with Parsees
and interest in the monastery of Mar Saba plainly stirred similar feelings in
his younger brother, who created the enigmatic Parsee Fedallah in *Moby-
Dick* and who eventually visited the monastery and set some scenes in *Clarel*
there.

Withdrawn from classes, Herman focused his efforts not on the Young
Men's Association but on the Philo Logos Society, a debating club "formed
for the purpose of improvement in composition, elocution and debate,"
which he joined after the demise of the Ciceronian Debating Society. Knowledge of this period comes from correspondence preserved from 1837 and
1838 in the pages of a scurrilous Albany newspaper designed for young men
about town, *The Albany Microscope Devoted to Popular Tales, History, Legends
and Adventures, Anecdotes, Satire, Humour, Sporting and the Drama.* (The New
York State Library has the unique run of the paper.) The editors depicted
themselves as savagely indignant in the true Swiftian vein, as various references to the Dean and his writings showed. Young men bought the *Microscope*

and tried to keep their families from seeing it, for it reported aspects of their life better kept from seniors — details such as just which juvenile Albanians had become publicly inebriated or had been observed emerging from a particular brothel. Older men also had reason to hope their families never saw it: in the 17 March 1838 issue (which figures later in this chapter) the paper denounced the "GAMBLING TABLE" and the "BROTHEL" in the hope of keeping some of the state legislators from transmitting "to their posterity, Pandora's box of *diseases and of death.*" The *Microscope* also offered a forum for controversies in local organizations, such as debating clubs, and it may well have been a forum for fomenting such controversies.

On 15 April 1837 a letter about Herman, signed "R," was printed in the *Microscope:*

> Mr. EDITOR: — Your paper abundantly testifies to the fact, that there is in all associations, pestiferous animals of a two-legged kind; who have crept in unawares, and scattered the seeds of dissolution in the once fair and flourishing institutions. . . . Such an animal is the P***o L***s Society cursed with. He is there known by the title of Ciceronian Baboon; and his personal appearance fully establishes the correctness of the title. He is also known as *dignitatus* melvum. . . . The society was formed for the purpose of improvement in composition, elocution and debate. . . . And it continued to flourish and spread its branches like a green bay tree, until the bohun upus melvum was transplanted into the fertile soil, from the Ciceronian Debating Society, of which he was the principle [*sic*] destroyer. . . . The reason why we cannot get rid of him is common to all associations. He, like a wary pettifogger, never considers "this side right, and that stark naught," or in other words, has no fixed principles, but can bear as the wind blows without gripings of conscience. This he considers a masterly display of his political powers.

A reference to "Hermanus Melvillian" in the same paper a year later clinches the identity of the "Ciceronian Baboon" as Herman. At seventeen and a half Herman was being assailed publicly in vituperative rhetoric, and may himself have spouted forth similar rhetoric of his own — perhaps even in print, although we have found no comment of his from early 1837.

The charges against Herman, stripped of some of the rhetoric, are that he first joined the Ciceronian Debating Society and somehow became its principal destroyer, then joined the flourishing Philo Logos Society, where his behavior reversed its "tranquil, strait forward course of doing business" and created a "continual scene of confusion." The society, according to "R," had proved unable to "get rid of him." By exposing Herman in the *Microscope,* the modern equivalent of "the *whipping post,*" "R" hoped to warn other associations against "such a character." "R" ended with the hope that he had made the truth plain and that one of two opposite things would happen — Herman would reform, or else prove so incorrigible as to be dismissed from the society. Charles Van Loon, a friend of Herman's in 1837, the next year, on 10 March 1838, claimed in the *Microscope* that the Philo Logos Society had been "fast rising to the elevation of her elder sisters" before Herman joined it: "Hermanus Melvillian entered her happy domain, and with a ruthless hand severed the ties of friendship, wantonly injured the feelings of her most estimable members, incessantly disturbed the equanimity of her proceedings, abused her unsuspecting confidence; and forever destroyed her well earned reputation. The society forbore with long suffering; reproving, exhorting and beseeching, until 'forbearance ceased to be a virtue.'" At that point in April 1837, presumably, "R" wrote his letter that was printed in the 15 April 1837 *Microscope*.

The next year, on 24 March 1838, Herman Melville published in the *Microscope* his version of his involvement in the club in early 1837: "At the solicitation of several of the Philologos Society, I became a member. Things proceeded with the utmost tranquility and order, until yourself [Charles Van Loon] indulging in a train of bitter and caustic personalities, drew upon yourself the bolts of my indignation, whereas frantic with rage, and burning with resentment, you moved that 'the conduct of H—— M—— be considered as disgraceful to himself, &c.' — Abortive attempt! Your motion was rejected, *viva voce* and yourself condemned to the pangs of mortified pride and foiled ambition." Van Loon retorted on 31 March 1838, that about a year earlier "*a resolution was adopted in the Philologos Society pronouncing the conduct of H. Melville 'disgraceful to himself, discreditable to the society, and insulting to the chair.'*" In the 24 March 1838 *Microscope*, Herman declared that in June 1837 he had left the Philo Logos Society alive and well: "Called from town for a few months, I left the society in an apparently healthful and prosperous condition." Van Loon's version (*Microscope*, 10 March 1838) was that before Herman left Albany in 1837 "Mr. Melvillian" had enervated the society by the repeated stabs of the assassin's poignard and had left it "tottering over the grave of oblivion."

The vituperation is so exaggerated as to raise the possibility that the pieces were written as high-spirited exercises in billingsgate, reflecting youthful desire to master the modern rhetoric of public slinging matches, British and American, rather than any real depth of animosity. A belated reader finds it hard to discern any practical motives for indulging in it or any real consequences. The whole thing may have been, from first to last, the quickest way at least one of the young men had for getting himself into print. It would have been natural enough if the undereducated (and, as we gather from later comments by Gansevoort, habitually unkempt) second Melville son had exploded in the Philo Logos Society from tensions quite unrelated to that debating group. Still, the accusations made by "R" are not sufficient reason to make it certain that the young Herman did so explode, or to make it incontrovertibly clear that he was ever aptly termed by his fellows the "Ciceronian Baboon" or otherwise ridiculed. The indications are that young Herman was already something of a pleasant fellow, as he demonstrably was a few years later. Chances are that the rhetoric sprang from some testosterone-driven game of one-upmanship in which sensibilities were not mortally bruised, however dire the language. As it turned out, Herman had to face up to the new economic crisis rather than to indulge himself in piquant rhetorical controversy.

In Pittsfield Thomas Jr. had fallen into his old habit of not paying the taxes on the farm, and on 28 March Shaw as trustee wrote the check on the New England Bank, Boston, of which Philip Marett was now president, not merely cashier. All this time, Thomas was secretly preparing to go to Illinois, as he at last wrote to Shaw on 16 May 1837, deputing to Shaw the duty of informing his sisters — immediately after his departure. He explained that his journey was delayed "by the effects of the commercial revolution" (the Panic), but on 3 June Thomas informed Shaw that he and his son John were planning to depart on Monday, 5 June. His going determined Herman's immediate future.

On 15 April 1837, the day the letter from "R" appeared in the *Microscope*, Gansevoort, a victim of the disastrous national economy, filed for bankruptcy, assigning to Bradford and another man all his "goods and chattels merchandizes . . . and all sums of money due owing or belonging" to him (his copy of the document is in the New York Public Library). Ten days later, on 26 April, Gansevoort resigned from the executive committee of the Young Men's Association. Two days after that Herman witnessed his mother's bond ("in the sum of Fifty thousand dollars") to the president, directors, and company of the New York State Bank; until Peter and Herman Gansevoort settled the estate of Catherine Van Schaick Gansevoort, Maria would have no way of knowing whether she would ever be free of this gigantic debt. On 10 May New York City banks suspended payments in gold and silver, paying instead in depreciated banknotes. Factories failed all over the country, foreign trade dried up, and thousands were unemployed. On 15 May Maria Melville's cousin's husband Teunis Van Vechten began his first term as mayor, but her life as a member of the Albany elite was over.

In these miserable straits on 5 June 1837 Maria held a family council in the house on Clinton Square. The first order of business was to face a traumatic disruption: sooner rather than later Maria would have to set the older three boys loose on the world and take the girls and Tom (no longer a baby) away from the state capital to some village where rents were cheap. This decision was repugnant for many reasons, not least that it meant leaving her blood relatives just when she needed their solace for herself and their solicitude in bringing her older daughters into contact with marriageable young men. Helen was about to enter her third decade, the best educated member of the family except Gansevoort, but without prospects, so marginal was their status in Albany. New York, if not the world, was all before them as choice for place of exile. For some reason, they considered Galway, some sixteen miles southwest of Saratoga Springs, a place reachable in the winter only by saddle horse (the snow could become "too deep for waggoning," Gansevoort noted in his diary in 1834, and too hard even for sleighs because the sleigh tracks got so deeply worn). Within three months they had made plans for moving there in the fall, although there was not much in the village except General Stimson's Tavern, where Gansevoort had passed a night in 1834, on his foray with Alexander Bradford.

There is no contemporary record of this distressing family council. The only account of the meeting at all is the one Allan wrote in July 1843 (now in the Berkshire Athenaeum). Characteristically, Allan remembered the session as centered on his own future: "unfortunately for me a family council was held wherein it was determined that I should be taken from the Academy & placed in my Uncles law office in Albany, which arrangement was immediately effected. I accordingly entered Peter Gansevoort's office as a student at Law." He attributed this to the need to save the expense of his tuition, since grown-ups had decided that he was "learning nothing at school." Disregarding Allan's adolescent egotism, one can see that his fate was third or lower on the agenda that day. Aside from the decision to move from Albany, whenever a suitable place was found, the paramount business was the decision that Gansevoort, rather than trying to reestablish himself in Albany, would go to New York City — to study law with his friend Alexander W. Bradford. The second item must have been Herman's fate. He would go to Pittsfield to run the farm so his Uncle Thomas could leave for Galena. In mid-June Herman left home eagerly: it would be his first time at the farm when he would not have to count the days before having to return to Albany. If he got there in time to bid farewell to his uncle, it was the only time he ever had an older male relative entrust him face to face with such a weighty responsibility, for he was expected to patrol the entire farm and cultivate what needed cultivating. At times he may have been the only competent adult male on the farm (the mentally impaired Henry Dearborn Melvill may have stayed there with his stepmother). Robert may also have been there part of that summer if he was unwilling to stay away from Susan Bates, a local woman, slightly older than himself.

When Augusta quizzed her on Herman's behavior, Julia Maria reported first that school took much of her time and that Priscilla's absence put more "household duties" upon her. There was gossip: the rich man of the village, Mr. Newton, was about to remarry after a scandalously short widowhood ("not much more than a year"). Strawberries were ripe and the wintergreens had "come 'up.' " There was news from her father: "Papa is on his way up the Missippi now I suppose We heard from him last tuesday he was at Pittsburg." At last Julia Maria gave Augusta the news about Herman she wanted to hear: "You next desire that I will tell you how Herman comes on his new line of life. Firstly you wish to know if he behaves himself with propriety, next if he conducts himself with politeness. I answer you with pleasure he is very good very polite. You need not feel uneasy about him we will try not to make him quite a savage while he resides in the country as you fear we shall." In July there was much wishful talk of Maria's taking Augusta with her on a visit to the farm, but nothing came of it.

Herman's summer passed with enough free time for him to feel an intense intimacy with the farm. Thirteen years later (4 August 1850) a literary friend, Evert A. Duyckinck, reported to his wife that Herman Melville knew "every stone & tree" of the farm. Through the property ran what a decade and a half later was called "the old Lenox Road," and near it, in the eastern part of the property, Melville claimed for his own a spot of high ground, a huge "rock," the same friend reported (on 8 August 1851), "upon which he used to linger overlooking the fair plateau on which Pittsfield rears its homes and steeples." Cousin Priscilla's reference in 1848 to the farm as Herman's first love was an observation based on Herman's profound love of the terrain during his earlier visits and especially during his long stay in 1837. Unconfined at last, he expanded physically and emotionally to match the landscape. While working in the fields he could look north at Mount Greylock whenever he paused to stretch his muscles. The U.S. Representative for the Berkshires in 1837, George N. Briggs, the old acquaintance of Uncle Thomas's, had been born in South Adams, north of Pittsfield, and now lived (when at home) just west of the village of Pittsfield. A biographer in 1866 wrote of Briggs's youth in South Adams: "Here, the majestic beauty of Greylock rose up continually before him, inspiring his heart and mind alike with lofty ambitions." Greylock's power to inspire had lost nothing in the decades since Briggs had been as young as Herman was now in 1837.

For all its lack of repair, the Melvill mansion was almost as hospitable inside as the property was outside. Since this was summer, rather than huddling in the kitchen, the warmest room, as he had done with the family during his October visit in 1835, Herman was free, on a rainy day, or after his work for the day was finished, to admire other stately, wainscotted rooms, some elegantly swathed in imported French wallpaper (selected in Paris, most likely, by his uncle, and brought back as precious cargo), and to admire the halls and large chimneys, all in all a choice specimen, already, of "mouldering rural grandeur," as the visiting Duyckinck called it in August 1850. Given the choice between modern urban comfort and mouldering rural grandeur, Herman would not have hesitated. For once in his life he was where he wanted to be when he wanted to be there.

What Herman read on the farm, deprived of Gansevoort's influence, is not known, but in the Berkshire Athenaeum, a gift of a great-granddaughter of Melville's Uncle Thomas, are several books Herman might have read, including Joseph Collyer, *The History of England, from the Invasion of Julius Caesar to the Dissolution of the Present Parliament*, 14 volumes (London, 1774), and *Quotations from the British Poets, Being a Pocket Dictionary of Their Most Admired Passages* (New York, 1836). Surviving records show that, at least between 1814 and 1824, Thomas Jr. bought books from the local bookseller Phinehas Allen, the editor of the *Sun*. In the house were probably some of Thomas's recent newspaper contributions, as well as the bulky ledgers that, Herman remembered long afterward, contained his uncle's meticulous records of crops planted and harvested. There also were files of documents, many of them signed by eminent statesmen of the early Republic (and some probably already mutilated, the signatures cut out — the devalued form in which many documents came down to subsequent generations of the family). Aunt Mary had at hand for ready display the "vial of the Boston tea," brought home in the shoes of her late father-in-law after the Boston Tea Party — a relic recently claimed by her husband as the only surviving male Melvill of his generation.

Robert, who had turned twenty on 20 June, was on the farm by summer's end (having apparently been away), and at some point that summer Herman decided to become a schoolteacher like Robert. Herman's education had been spotty, to put the matter in the best light, and little is known about Robert's schooling, but the education the two had received met (and may have exceeded) the prevailing Berkshire standards, no matter that neither of them ever learned to spell. Where Robert taught is uncertain, and not too much can be read into Julia's flippant comment about Robert to Augusta late in November 1837 that he had "commenced" teaching school again ("I intend to take my diploma next spring if he does not get discouraged 'before that time then'"). Robert may have been teaching in Pittsfield, and may even have had Julia as a pupil.

By early September Aunt Mary was, according to Julia Maria, "actually positively truely going to Albany," and soon afterward still other family visits were made. Shaw's regular second Tuesday court date in Lenox was the twelfth this year, and the judge and Hope Shaw were in Lenox at least until the nineteenth. Herman may have seen one or more of the Shaws, for Elizabeth Sedgwick took Hope to visit Mary Melvill on the eighteenth. Around mid-September Herman visited his mother in Albany, and he seems to have been there at least some of the time that Augusta had Allan with her on the farm, since Helen did not send love to Herman when she wrote Augusta with the news and a kiss for her "pet Ally," the woebegone third brother. For some reason Robert went to Albany, perhaps to accompany his mother home; then somehow Aunt Mary left town with Maria owing her a dollar. The cousins Robert and Herman seem to have taken leave of Peter Gansevoort together (some days before 25 September) when they were full of their new plan for Herman to follow Robert as a schoolteacher. Months later, on 30 December, Herman reminded his Uncle Peter that as he and Robert left Albany, in late September, Peter had "expressed a desire" that his nephew should write after his "school should have gone into operation."

On 25 September Maria wrote from Albany to Augusta in Pittsfield, after Herman's visit home. The decision to go to Galway and the prospect of implementing that decision was devastating. By rights Maria ought to have been in bed that morning with her "bad head ach," instead of writing to her dear children, including her schoolteacher son: "I have just written Herman a few lines, his conduct delights me, he has shown himself to possess an independent spirit not deficient in enterprise and willing to exert himself when necessary. I shall be delighted to see him once more, before we leave Albany." In a postscript Helen took care of one pressing financial detail: "Gus, Mama says you must request Herman to repay Aunt Mary [Melvill] that dollar, as she has not got one to send you, and she will settle with him when he comes." Plainly Maria was relieved to have Herman on his own and off her mind. She had enough to deal with in her own household, but there was worse news nearby, as she wrote Augusta on 25 September: Peter's baby daughter, named Mary for her mother, was dangerously ill, and the consumptive and pregnant Mary Sanford Gansevoort herself was almost exhausted from caring for the baby "day and night," to the point that she (the mother, apparently, not the baby) had been "discharging Blood for more than a week," and had become "very thin having lost flesh surprisingly." Risking a miscarriage even while this baby was dying, Mary Sanford Gansevoort soon left for Flushing to attend her father, Nathan Sanford, also tubercular; the eleven-month-old baby died on 10 October.

Herman's position was in the Sikes District School, on the fork of the roads leading to New Lenox and to Washington County, to the southwest of Pittsfield. The "old school house of Washington Mountain" was Augusta's description fifteen years later (in a memo on family excursions now in the

Reese Collection); "under Washington mountain" was the phrase of the Pittsfield editor and poet Joseph (J. E. A.) Smith, still later. It was "situated in a remote & secluded part of the town about five miles from the village," Herman wrote his uncle — five miles as the crow flies, perhaps, and a serious mountain hike for Herman once winter set in, if he wanted to spend Sundays with his aunt and young cousins. The schoolhouse may have been located in a sheltered spot, but Herman boarded (at least toward the end of the year) at an isolated house "on the summit of as savage and lonely a mountain" as he had ever ascended, as he wrote his Uncle Peter: "The scenery however is most splendid & unusual, — embracing an extent of country in the form of an Ampitheatre sweeping around for many miles & encircling a portion of your state [New York] in its compass." Even in the depths of the Berkshire winter, Herman must have stayed outdoors as much as possible, for in the house privacy and sanitation were rudimentary while free exchange of ideas was nonexistent: "The man with whom I am now domicilated is a perfect embodiment of the traits of Yankee character, — being shrewd bold & independant, carrying himself with a genuine republican swagger, as hospitable as 'mine host' himself, perfectly free in the expression of his sentiments, and would as soon call you a fool or a scoundrel, if he thought so — as, button up his waistcoat. — He has reared a family of nine boys and three girls, 5 of whom are my pupils — and they all burrow together in the woods — like so many foxes." The young man who had learned from Gansevoort that political ideas were, quite literally, debatable was now shut up with a man who did not look to the youthful schoolmaster for intellectual exchange. (Ironically, Melville's daughter Frances would remember him as equally free and perhaps more tyrannical in the expression of his own political sentiments.) In this environment Herman understandably became nostalgic for undoctrinaire word-lovers, and wrote longingly to Charles Van Loon, his friend from the Philo Logos debating society in Albany: "my object is to know the existing situation of the society; whether it is on the rapid decline I left it in, or whether like the Phoenix it hath risen from its ashes."

Much later Herman shared some of his "racy memories" of this term, telling stories of "a rebellion in which some of the bigger boys undertook to 'lick' him — with what results, those who remember his physique and character can well imagine." That anecdote was recorded in 1891 by Joseph Smith, who knew Melville well. In January 1852 a newcomer to Lenox who signed himself "Maherbal" gave this version in a letter to the Windsor (Vermont) *Journal*, his hometown paper: "not many years ago in a neighboring town, Herman Melville had the misfortune to exasperate to such a degree the republican spirit of two very wicked pupils in the district school of which he was teacher, as to make it incompatible with his safe continuance in the room!" ("Maherbal" was merely reporting current gossip, but the reference to the rebellious "republican spirit" of some of the students suggests that his version may have derived from some telling of the story by the schoolmaster himself, who would not have forgotten the "republican swagger" of his host.) Since the publication of Irving's "The Legend of Sleepy Hollow" teacher-tormenting had become familiar in American folklore and literature, but it was based on the realities of American education, and Herman may well have dealt with a mutiny and later made a good story of it. Something of the more workaday life in the classroom is revealed in a letter Herman wrote to his Uncle Peter at the end of December: "But now, having become somewhat acquainted with the routine of business, — having established a systim in my mode of instruction, — and being familiar with the charactars & dispositions of my scholars: in short, having brought my school under a proper organiza-tion — a few intervals of time are afforded me, which I improve by occasional writting & reading." He had been shut up in the schoolhouse with about thirty "scholars" of "all ages, sizes, ranks, chara[c]ters, & education," and presumably of both sexes. The oldest were his own age, eighteen, and some of those could not do a sum in addition, while others had been raced so fast "through the Arithmatic" that they could not "recognize objects in the road on a second journey; & are about as ignorant of them as though they had never passed that way before."

Double Thanksgivings afforded Herman the chance to go to Albany for a few days. Massachusetts celebrated the holiday properly, on the last Thurs-day in November, this year the thirtieth, but the governor of New York, where the un-Puritanic populace did not know any better, proclaimed the twenty-third as Thanksgiving. Julia wrote Augusta, by Herman, on what she called "Thursday Nov 22" but perhaps was Wednesday the twenty-second: "Herman remarked at tea this evening, that he intended to go to Albany tomorrow, therefore I thought you would like to have a few lines of my scratching." Wittily she sent a message to be disclosed to the unsuspecting bearer of the letter: "Tell Herman that I am very well indeed and have been ever since . . . he returned to Albany." In Albany, presumably for Thanksgiv-ing on Thursday, 23 November, Herman found the usual measure of dis-tress, for on the twenty-eighth Uncle Herman wrote to Peter: "I regret to hear that our Sister Maria is very unhappy on account of her creditors calling for a settlement — her situation gives me much uneasiness and trouble in mind." The troubles in Maria's household were for once overshadowed by the fresh grief at Uncle Peter's house for the dead baby. There was no occasion that grim Thanksgiving for Herman to deliver himself of his prom-ised report on his experiences with the common-school system, and Peter did not renew his request for a written report. Still, Peter thoughtfully sent him away with *Self Teacher* (1834) and John Orville Taylor's *The District School* (1835).

Back under Washington Mountain, Herman found (as he wrote his Uncle Peter) that "the variety & importance of the duties" incident to his vocation were so "numerous and pressing" that they absorbed a large portion of his time, but he read Taylor's book, and at year's end he included in his letter to Uncle Peter a formal report on it, in which he almost usurped "the province of the Edinburgh Review." Literate Americans had easy access to the *Edinburgh Review*, for enterprising American printers in even middle-sized cities regularly pirated the latest issue, and bound volumes of the *Review*, printed in the United States, were around many houses. Allan Melvill, who had plucked a rose for Maria in the rustic garden of the founder and principal writer for the magazine, Francis Jeffrey, in flush times must have had copies around, some of which may have survived the auction of his books and his removal to Albany. Any youth of Melville's class, even one with reduced opportunities, knew the magazine, and knew that it aimed not merely to pronounce magisterial judgments but also to enunciate aesthetic principles through its practical criticism. However harum-scarum his education seemed, Herman had absorbed some of the reviewer's commonplaces of the time. After giving the book "a diligent and attentive perusal" he had concluded that Taylor's was "an admirable production" which might "exert a powerful influence" of "most salutary & beneficial charactar." Herman's own spelling boded ill for the normalization of his students' idiosyncrasies of orthography: "charactar," "hystory," "difficultys," "gennerally," "intimatly." The tone, however, carried the day: "Orators may declaim concerning the universally-diffused blessings of education in our Country, and Essayests may exhaust their magazine of adjectives in extolling our systim of Common School instruction, — but when reduced to practise, the high and sanguine hopes excited by its imposing appearance in *theory* — are a little dashed." The dying fall, the fading away into understatement, was a stylistic mannerism Melville would later perfect.

In Manhattan, Gansevoort faithfully continued to set down in his *Index Rerum* salient ideas from his reading. Considering a way of attaining fame, he devoted a whole page of his *Index Rerum* under "O.a." to quotations about orators, oration, and oratory ("O" being the first letter and "a" being the next vowel). Mulling over the possibility that his literary interests might lead to a career as a writer, Gansevoort, apparently after moving to New York City, entered into his *Index Rerum* many items under "Authorship" and "Authors," including comments by Sir Walter Scott "on the subject of cutting reviewers." Under the heading "Authors" Gansevoort made note of a passage in Bulwer-Lytton's new *Ernest Maltravers* (which he had acquired in the instant Harpers reprint): "situation of an author with regard to society—a well-digested and practical view." Ignoring the ridiculous plot of the novel, Gansevoort mined the book for guidance in achieving fame. "Reputation generally aided by some peculiar circumstances" was the key idea he wrote down as the introduction to this quotation from *Ernest Maltravers*: "Few persons attain pre-eminent celebrity for anything without some adventitious and extraneous circumstances which have nothing to do with the thing celebrated.—Some qualities or circumstances throw a mysterious or personal charm about them." Gansevoort commented: "There is much truth in this remark," and set himself to embodying it in his own achievement of celebrity, which perforce would not be derived through ordinary paths.

Bulwer-Lytton's observation about persons attaining "pre-eminent celebrity" applied equally to the ways the brothers would achieve celebrity, and the likelihood is that Herman read the novel after his return to Albany early in 1838 and that it went into his thinking about his own career. He may have recalled it in a passage he wrote in January 1852: "in the inferior instances of an immediate literary success, in very young writers, it will be almost invariably observable, that for that instant success they were chiefly indebted to some rich and peculiar experience in life, embodied in a book, which because, for that cause, containing original matter, the author himself, forsooth, is to be considered original; in this way, many very original books, being the product of very unoriginal minds" (*Pierre*, bk. 18, "Pierre as a Juvenile Author, Reconsidered"). At the end of 1837 Gansevoort was heroically determined to triumph over the disasters that had crowded upon him in the past seven years; Herman was nothing like so determined, as far as anyone could see.

Herman's term at Sikes ran over into 1838. On 25 January Julia wrote to Augusta, by Herman: he was "homeward bound," to stay. He had planned to leave that day "but was not very well therefore was obliged to defer" the trip, an all-day affair in those short winter days ("You will be quite surprised to see Herman tomorrow night"). Herman arrived to a situation so dire that the owner of the house had called on Maria asking for "the Lease of the house"—the physical document, which she was reluctant to surrender unless Peter said she should. Sending her eight-year-old son Tom to Stanwix Hall with the news, she added: "Certainly this uncertainty regarding our removal, or rather the place to which we shall locate had better be settled, for longer suspense would be doubly painful now this house is given up." Despite this new crisis, just about this time, within a few days of his return home, Herman made up for lost time in the Philo Logos Society.

As with the letter by "R" the year before, the facts of Herman's involvement in a public controversy about the society are hard to disentangle. In

Herman's absence the society had languished. According to Charles Van Loon's later account in the 10 March 1838 *Microscope*, "the prodigal Melvillian returned, with the face of a saint and the heart of a devil, to grieve over the ruins of the Society, and to water his victim with the tears of a human crocidile [*sic*]." Van Loon's mention of Herman's saint-like face should not be given too much significance (perhaps he was bearded like biblical figures in illustrations), and his account of Herman's actions do not make them sound particularly villainous: "The little dispirited remnant of members were got together; a committee appointed to draft a new constitution; and it was resolved that at the next meeting the society should go into a new election. The then President [Van Loon] having signified his intention of resigning; the devoted, penitent, leisureful Melvillian was nominated by a committee of two (himself being one) to fill the chair." In the *Microscope* for 24 March, looking back at the events of early February, Herman gave a not dissimilar account. On his return from Massachusetts he had found the Philo Logos Society "in the last stages of a rapid decline." With no job to divert his attention, and starved for intellectual stimulation (matters he did *not* reveal publicly), he immediately "instituted vigorous efforts for its resusitation," with the help of "several prominent members, who all co-operated in the laudable design of reviving the ancient spark." Obstacles (such as the possibility of postponing important business until a regularly scheduled meeting) "were brushed aside." The president of the society, Charles Van Loon, having spurned these meetings, "was tacitly and virtuously deposed." Gaining a quorum to hold a new election proved harder than the insurgents had expected, so they made up new rules, deciding "that if a certain number should be present at the next session, hereafter ensuing — the election should be proceeded with." The Albany *Evening Journal* on 13 February reported the results of the election on the ninth, starting with Herman Melville's election as president.

Uncle Peter had been mocked in the *Microscope* on 27 January 1838 as a potential lecturer in a series to be offered by the "Young Men's Optimist Association For the Perfection of the Human Race." "Lecture 28: On the science of 'bowing.' P. G-nse —— t." The world saw the gentlemanly manners, and saw in them an exaggerated courtliness, but at this juncture there were enough unrented spaces in Stanwix Hall to allow Peter to behave more generously than usual, and he indulged his nephew with no harm to himself. For his part, Herman took full credit for the society's improved quarters: "Through my endeavors, a large and elegant room was obtained in Stanwix Hall, together with suitable furniture to the same, free from all expenses to the society." At the next meeting Van Loon pronounced the recent election "to have been unconstitutional and corrupt," thereby becoming, according to Herman, "rather unruly," to the point that Herman maneuvered a vote to censure his "intemperate and ungentlemanly behavior."

Van Loon in a subsequent letter disputed this account of his interruption. "Sandle Wood" joined in, declaring the society dead, and Herman, assuming that Sandle Wood and Van Loon were the same, attacked in the *Microscope* for 24 February:

> In the *van* of these notable worthies stands pre-eminent, that silly and brain-less *loon* who composed the article in your last week's paper, denying the existence of the Philo Logos Society, the legality of its recent election, and its alleged possession of a room in Stanwix Hall.
>
> I have only to remark in relation to this interesting production, that it is not more inelegant in style than wanting in truth and veracity. It is a complete tissue of infamous fabrications, and is as destitute of a single fact as is the author of parts. I refrain from enlarging upon what probable motives induced the writer to the publication of his miserable effusion. I will not say it pro-ceeded from the pique of mortified pride, or from an unhallowed and foolish envy, but will merely remark that from whencesoever it derived its origin, it is contemptible, dastardly and outrageous.

In his letter in the 10 March *Microscope* Van Loon was predictably impelled "to hold up to the scorn and execration of the good and virtuous" the author of such "a foul, dastardly attack" upon his character by the "*Ciceronian baboon*" also known "under the more romantic appellation of Her*manus* Mel*villian*":

> Hermanus Melvil[l]ian, a moral Ethiopian, whose conscience qualms not in view of the most attrocious guilt; whose brazen cheek never tingles with the blush of shame, whose moral principles, and sensibilities, have been de-stroyed by the corruption of his own blac[k] and bloodless heart. With regard to his billingsgate effusion in the Microscope, I as heartily repel its infamous allegations, as I despise the character, and detest the principles of its infamous author. . . . For the present I have done with Hermanus Melvillian. His abusive language in the last Microscope, is but the raving of an unmasked hypocrite, the "wincing, of a gall'd jade."

Van Loon was Hamlet, exposing Claudius through his rhetorical strategies in the *Microscope*, if not through "The Mouse-trap," and he had a clinching counter-accusation: Herman had falsely identified him as "Sandle Wood." Misidentification, Uncle Thomas ("Ben Austin" but not "Plain Farmer") could have told Herman, went with the territory when a polemicist took assumed names in the public prints.

Subsequently, in the 31 March *Microscope*, "in the meek and charitable spirit of Peter the Apostle," Van Loon addressed Melville directly, having made strong use of Acts 13:10: "O full of all subtilty and all mischief, *thou child of the devil*": "[I] honestly and conscientiously pronounce you Herman Melville, a 'child of the devil, full of all subtility and all mischief.' " By the issue of 7 April everyone had had enough. "Americus" tried peacemaking:

> That two individuals of their attainm[e]nts and character, who hitherto, I am confident, reciprocated the kindly feelings of a generous friendship — who mutually labored in building up and preserving an institution, whose highest honors they have respectively enjoyed; should at length so far forget the dignity of their station, the intimacy of their former acquaintance, and the well being of the common object of their care and solicitude, as to fall into a newspaper discussion; is highly reprehensible, and has been a source of deep and sincere regret to those whose good opinion neither of these "lords appellent" would be willing to forego.

What all this meant is next to impossible to say at this remove. Leon Howard's guess is shrewd (although made without realizing that the controversy had begun in 1837): "The exchanges probably marked the first appearances in print for either of the young men, and they were obviously as excited by their own rhetoric as they were by each other." Gansevoort might have checked Herman's rhetoric if he had been at home, for scurrilous invective had no place in his debater's repertory. To a belated historian the Philo Logos controversy tends to look weightier than it was because it took weeks to play out in the *Microscope*. Herman's contributions were probably dashed off in a few minutes, not labored over — that was his way. More important matters ought to have been on his mind, and perhaps were: our sense of what he was up to for months is skewed by the survival of this abusive correspondence as the only record of his activities. At the worst, the affair shows him as an aggressive youth, lashing out at easy opponents after years of being repressed, acting in a way he would conscientiously shun later in life.

To be called in print the "leisureful Melvillian" was punishment enough for any of his own reckless slurs, for it reminded the readers of the *Microscope* that in all busy, bustling America, Herman Melville had not identified a "practical activity" he could perform well. He may have "chosen Commerce as a favorite pursuit" as a child, but his pursuit of that or any other field of endeavor seemed apt to prove fruitless.

[7]

Herman in Lansingburgh
Full-grown and Useless, May 1838–May 1839

in my miscellaneous time I have been a stone-mason, and also a great digger
of ditches, canals and wells, wine-vaults, cellars, and cisterns of all sorts.

Moby-Dick, ch. 104

MARIA HAD DELAYED THE INEVITABLE as long as she could, and was now
resigned to moving to Galway, up near Ballston Spa and Saratoga Springs.
Surviving documents leave the choice of Galway a mystery, but it meant
something to the family: Gansevoort was there two and a half years later, on
2 October 1840, and had his 1837 *Index Rerum* with him, as a note in it shows.
Julia wrote Augusta on 2 April 1838, asking, "When do you go to Galway I
wish it was here that you were going to move to would it not be delightful to
have both families live in the same house." Gansevoort was supposed to be in
New York studying law, but in another letter of 17 April 1838 Julia looked
forward to her own removal to Galena (after which, she reasonably observed,
"we shall not see any of you again for an age"); understandably she wanted
Augusta to come back to Pittsfield before they left the farm: "do make Gan
bring you over to stay all the summer." Herman had made much of the baby,
Allan Cargill, and now Julia reported that this little Allan, recovering from
some recent burns, "says that he wants to see Herm." On her own she told
Augusta to relay a message: "Tell Herm that the beautiful Miss Howland is
married, did she not send him any of the wedding cake? it is customary here
to send a piece of the cake to particular friends, and I hope he was not
forgotten by her at that time." Given Julia's facetiousness, there is no reason
to think Herman had been smitten by the young Miss Howland, who had
married another, or that he was languishing for lack of a piece of the wedding
cake. In Uncle Thomas's house any full-grown but unmarried male or female
was fair game for teasing.

Uncle Peter had his own anxieties. His wife, Mary, after recklessly nursing her dying father and after suffering the death of her baby daughter, Mary,
the previous October, gave birth on 12 April 1838 to a daughter, named
Catherine for Peter's mother. Attempting to please his wife, Peter bought a

125

new home in what was then a suburban location, 115 Washington Avenue, on top of the hill northwest of the capitol. Maria Melville must have assisted as well as she could, but on 1 May, moving day, Maria went into exile with her family — though not to Galway. The last-minute choice was Lansingburgh, almost a dozen miles north of Albany, on the wrong (eastern) side of the Hudson, beyond the deep channel where large ships could safely sail — a location perhaps chosen because Mary Chandonette Gansevoort was living across the river in Waterford.

Maria rented a house on the river, at River Street and North, now River Street and 114th (in Troy), a location less bucolic than the family made it sound, since during part of the year expanses of the water were full of lumber barges and other commercial vessels. Maria was near her first cousin, the wealthy Maria Van Schaick Peebles, whose sickly husband, Gerrit, is seldom mentioned in the surviving family letters. (Maria Peebles's beauty had been of the sort people remembered and put on record.) The Peebles house was very near indeed, at the southeast corner of North and Congress, now 114th and Third Avenue (in Troy), an imposing, perfectly maintained wooden house on a stone foundation, mortar intact around every stone, every shutter perfectly hinged beside every meticulously glazed window. Like the Gansevoort house in Albany, this one contained colonial treasures, including the Van Schaick family hatchment of the great-grandfather of Maria Melville and Maria Peebles: a square hung like a diamond, points at top and bottom, bearing a shield, a bull's (or cow's) head represented on the left half, and three arrows, points up, down, and up, on the right. Young Augustus Peebles, more formidable than his father, was second cousin to Maria Melville's children. Born in 1822, in his extremely callow and prolonged adolescence he was all too aware of his wealth. Eyes too big, lips far too voluptuous, dark hair slicked down on his forehead, Augustus was a Peebles, with no touch of his mother's beauty. At this stage of his life, he gave cold welcome to the poor relations.

Herman must have helped with the heavy lifting more than anyone else in the family, but the only account of the move to Lansingburgh is Allan's, written there five years later, in 1843:

> About a year after I went with my Uncle, the family with the exception of Gansevoort my brother (who had been for some time previous settled in New York) removed to the village of Lansingburgh to a house very pleasantly situated on the bank of the Hudson (where I am now writing). Economy was the object of this change of location, and the only one which influenced my mother to forsake the "place of her heart," her early companions and old friends. But what ties are so sacred as not to be broken, or in some manner effected by the agency of gold & silver.

Julia on 31 May 1838 put the best face on the move: "How do you like your new place of residence I should think you would be glad to go from Albany, you can ramble about as much as your heart can desire, I often wish I was with you when you sail upon the river and your walks upon its banks. I am going to get ma to let me go to Lansingburgh this summer, you must think that I don't want to go for you have asked me so often & I never went, however if there is any such thing I will go this summer."

If Gansevoort was not with his mother when she moved, he soon saw the house, for he joined her as an invalid. Well before 31 May Julia knew from Helen "of the indisposition of Gansevoort was very sorry to hear he was unwell," and Anne sent "her best wishes for the speedy recovery of Gansevoort." On 9 June Maria gave this description to Peter: "Gansevoorts Ancle is about the same in appearance as when he came up he has much less pain when he moves, but is unable to bear the least weight on it, he is not able to leave his bed longer than to have it made." Presumably Herman was there, the only able-bodied man around the house. Before they made many acquaintances in Lansingburgh, Gansevoort and Herman had occasion to learn intimate details of goings on from "The Spy," the author of a series of Lansingburgh reports, "Sights from a Steeple," in the Albany *Microscope*. On 21 April 1838, the week before the move, the fifth sketch exposed "J——N——," a middle-aged Lothario. The sixth, on 12 May, attacked Mr. Y., the village poetaster. There was no escaping the *Microscope*, but it was steadily less important to the brothers as they and the others in the family met their neighbors, introduced by the Peebles.

At some time that summer Herman may have paid court to Mary Eleanor Parmelee, a granddaughter of Cornelius Lansing, the founder of the town, for in the mid-twentieth century one of her granddaughters reported to William H. Gilman that Herman and Miss Parmelee had walked together along the Hudson and that he had given her a copy of one of Tennyson's early books of poetry, which they sat on the grass and read to each other. "The Lady of Shalott" was ideal for reading along the river with islands in view, and some lines seem to have stuck in his mind for decades, perhaps in more versions than this 1833 text: "The sunbeam-showers break and quiver / In the stream that runneth ever / By the island in the river, / Flowing down to Camelot." The love of poetry was a strong recommendation, but Herman had no prospects, and Miss Parmelee was attracted to Peletiah Bliss, the son of the owner of a local bookstore. This late report to Gilman is plausible, but apparently unprovable. On 11 August 1838 in his thirteenth sketch the Spy declared that fornication in Lansingburgh was too rampant for him to refrain from denouncing it, news embarrassing to even the most innocent young admirer of Tennyson.

On 9 May 1838 Allan, now abandoned in Albany (where at least he could hope to rise in his profession), had been put to board with Maggey Wynkoop, a distant cousin of Maria's, "a very queer personage, with a very suspicious disposition, and like all old maids is very found [fond] of gossiping." Her house was in a decaying area near the basin, affording (as Allan wrote in 1843, having developed a capacity for irony) "from the front window an extensive view of a large lumber yard." (Bartleby's brick wall was closer to his window than this lumberyard to Allan's window, but there may be some faint recollection of Allan's complaints in Herman Melville's 1853 story.) In Lansingburgh Maria's situation was desperate. In a 9 June letter she asked Peter for one hundred dollars by that day's mail, since she had promised to advance her landlord half a year's rent if he would put up blinds in the front (meaning the west side?) of the house "*immediately* for the sun is pouring in with great power, & the light is intolerable." In exasperation Peter wrote their brother Herman on 12 June a letter that survives in draft:

> I am pressed by the City Bank for the $4000 & interest, I raised for Maria, after Gansevoort's failure & I have on my shoulders the weight of the enormous debt Maria owes the N.Y. State Bank— Besides all this the large debt at the Bank for Hill[']s purchases at Van Buren & our Stanwix Hall note, all which come round to morrow. — My newly purchased house and the expenses of repairs & all are in addition — And Herman, knowing my situation in these respects, you not only stay away, but maintain a deathlike silence. . . . The situation of Maria is such, that the Estate must be closed as soon as possible.

Her brothers Peter and the compliant Herman were still holding up the settlement of their mother's estate so they could control funds to pay for Stanwix Hall, as well as to make other investments. At moments when he had spent most lavishly, Peter could threaten himself and Herman that they might have to settle the estate precipitously, but whenever he felt more secure he stalled again.

By 16 June, still hard-pressed, Maria continued to urge Peter to send her the hundred dollars, specifying now that she owed a grocer for her "last Barrel of Flour." On 20 June Peter wrote his sister "plainly" — using as courier John Holme, a Lansingburgh real estate broker:

> I send by Mr Holme one hundred dollars as requested by your letter of Saturday last — You might rather have done without the blinds, than give your landlord or your neighbours the false unfounded idea that you have means to pay rent in advance — I do not object to [the] thing itself, so much as to the effect upon your comfort & peace of mind, which such an impression

may produce — Your creditors are becoming impatient. . . . You ought to be aware of your true situation. . . .

If the creditors hear that you are living handsomely at L[ansingburgh], and particularly that you pay your rent in advance, they will be inclined to annoy you by a sale of your furniture. . . .

I speak thus plainly to you my dear Maria, as I wish to avoid an occurrence, which I very much fear.

In this crisis Gansevoort got out of his sick bed (his primary problem still an ankle) to go to New York City, where on 3 July he drafted a statement to Ludlow & Osgood (New York Public Library) of his situation: "Since Mr Collier was here I have not had either the leisure or the ability to bring up our Books, but have satisfied myself upon a hasty review of our affairs since 1st January last that nothing has occurred to give them a more favorable aspect. . . . Disaster has succeeded disaster, and not a week has elapsed since 1st January 1838 (we mean to be understood *literally*) that has not brought to us additional confirmation of our over-estimate of means & resources." Gansevoort was staving off calamities, one after another. All through the summer, except for the emergency business trip to New York early in July, Gansevoort lay in bed, continuing his program of preserving the most useful points he encountered in his wide reading, keeping around him not only his latest books but his volumes of Dr. Todd's *Index Rerum* (the second, now missing, is referred to in a volume that survives).

What Herman was doing remains a mystery. Maria did not name him on 9 June 1838 as one of those joining in love to Uncle Peter, though she named the other older children, Gansevoort, Helen, and Augusta. Under better circumstances Herman might have been working at some remunerative job and thinking of supporting a family. Everyone was reminded of that on 20 June, when young Teunis Van Vechten, son and namesake of the mayor of Albany (1837–38, and again 1841–42) and of Catherine Cuyler Gansevoort Van Vechten, married Margaret Trotter Lush. Teunis was two months older than Herman, who may have had no work since the school term at Sikes ended and who had no particular prospects.

On his nineteenth birthday, 1 August 1838, the day the quarter's rent was due, Herman left for Pittsfield, according to his mother — with no indication of how long he had been with her or why he was going. Likely enough, now that one of the Boston aunts, Priscilla, was actually visiting at the farm, he went to Pittsfield to escort her and his cousin Julia both to Lansingburgh for Julia's farewell visit. Maria was concerned with getting rent money from her brother: "Presuming some mistake or miscarriage in regard to the Money I wished you to send me had occurr'd, I feel compelled by circumstances to remind you that yesterday was the first of August, and found me unprepared." After her visit to Lansingburgh Aunt Priscilla returned to the farm to see the remnant of her brother Thomas's family packed and off to Illinois. From her inconvenient vantage point Maria did the best she could to control an out-of-control situation by directing Allan to make purchases for Gansevoort, to send up his own dirty clothes to be washed, and to "attend the Sabbath School" regularly ("for be assured my beloved Boy the future usefulness of the Man depends much upon the foundation laid in boyhood"). Undoubtedly she gave similar advice in letters to Herman when he was away from her house. On 30 August Maria wrote again to Allan with near-final news of the dispersal of the Pittsfield family: "Uncle Tom has sent for Aunt Mary and all the Family to come to him to Galena, the 16th of next Month is fixed for their removal. They will be ready to begin their journey on that day, when we shall perhaps never see them more, unless you or some of your Brothers should chance to travel in that direction." (In fact, only Herman was to see his uncle again.) Gansevoort, chafing at his helplessness and isolation, also wanted the Albany newspapers if Allan could get them to him.

Around 27 August, while Cousin Priscilla was in Lansingburgh, and ailing, Cousin Julia wrote Augusta about the stage ride home to Pittsfield — good testimony as to conditions of travel encountered by females unescorted by a male, and a fair indication that Herman or another male had accompanied her and Aunt Priscilla on the earlier journey to visit Maria:

> The stage was full, one man on the back seat who seemed to have some powerful attraction which drew him with a power not to be resisted to the back seat in the stage to the great annoyance of Aunt Priscilla and myself, being determined not to give up our seats for the gentleman. We arrived safe at Lebanon, at which place we were obliged to wait about two hours untill another stage came in then we once more began our ride and re[a]ched this place about seven and was obliged to wait there a long time before we could procure a conveyance so much for not having a gentleman to take care of you.

Julia asked Augusta to tell "Priss" that they intended to turn their "faces to the 'Far West' on the *16 of September*" — Priscilla was to recover speedily and return. Julia had no desire to leave the farm: "Now Gus is it not to bad that we must go, I for one have no desire to seek my fortunes in 'A far off land and distant clime.' Pittsfield is as good a place as I wish to live in." On 30 August Julia again wrote to Augusta, via her mother, who, escorted by Robert, was visiting Maria "before starting on her long journey." Julia sent love "to Aunt Maria, Gan, Helen and the children" — not to "Herm," so she knew he was not at Lansingburgh. Anne wrote a farewell letter to "Gusey" also, jesting about the prospective suitors said to abound in the West, and sending greetings "to all, Gansevoort in particular." They were going to a land of fevers and agues, and leaving an "abundance of fruit," apples, pears, and melons "in plenty."

Herman may well have been in Pittsfield helping to pack while camping indoors amid the "many laughable inconveniences" of the disrupted household, for when Robert (on his return with his mother from Lansingburgh) married Susan Bates on 17 September, Herman was present for the ceremony. Then the Melvill party turned their faces west. Herman may well have accompanied the delayed Melvills to Hudson, where they took the boat to New York (a sixteen-hour trip), before going overland by stagecoach to Philadelphia and Pittsburgh. On 4 October Julia wrote Augusta from Cleveland, the low water on the Ohio having forced them to take a stage from Pittsburgh to Cleveland, so they could "go by the way of the Lakes." The stage had gone, she lamented, "over the worst road I ever saw in my life. . . . sometimes only two wheels touched the ground, but if I can only reach home I shall be glad it is terrible hard work to live by the wayside." She asked about Gansevoort, and added: "Herman wrote you all about the wedding I suppose"—the wedding of Robert Melvill and Susan Bates. The implication is that Herman had not gone directly home to Lansingburgh, where he could have told Augusta in person. He may have been teaching again at Sikes school. If he wasn't working, he might have been expected to accompany the party of Melvills to Galena, but he did not (as Maria's letter of 10 November shows).

At seventeen Augusta needed exposure to more refined society than Lansingburgh had to offer, so Maria sent her to visit her old friend Caroline Yates (now Mrs. Taylor) in Albany. While there, on 11 October, Augusta was admitted by profession of faith to the communion of the First Reformed Dutch Church. Maria wrote to her on 17 October, sending the letter care of Allan at Stanwix Hall. Her injunctions are of a piece with those she was sending to Allan, adapted to the needs of a young woman. One particular item of advice in this letter altered the course of Augusta's life, the advice to make friends with the Van Rensselaer cousins. An "earnest desire to please," Maria advised, could hardly fail to make her agreeable; Augusta was to "endeavor to make friends, & to keep them," guarding the while against selfishness. Coping from a distance with the reality of Original Sin, Maria warned Augusta of "the baser passions which are alas so natural to us, in our present state of depravity." Herman's later comments show that he absorbed from his mother and her church just such a sense of Original Sin. Maria did not mention Herman's whereabouts in this letter, since Augusta did not have to be told where he was.

The farm still had not been put in his name, apparently, but Thomas

Melvill Jr. felt free to make decisions about its use. He wrote to Lemuel Shaw and John D'Wolf on 26 October from Galena, letting them know that Robert, having accompanied his mother and the children to Galena, was now returning with the intention of renting the farm: "I have provisionally agreed with Robert, that he may take the farm, for 3, or 5 years, *on Rent* — the first year (from the 1st March 1839), at three hundred & fifty Dollars per year, & the succeeding years, at $ four hundred & fifty Dollars." Aunt Mary Melvill and her party had arrived in Galena the third week of October, according to another letter Thomas wrote to Shaw on 1 November, after he had contracted malaria:

> My family arrived here, safe, & in good health, about 10 days ago — they had a long fatiguing & *expensive* journey, owing to the unprecedented low State of the Water — However, it is fortunate they were detained, for had they arrived in the regular time, they would probably, most of them, if not all, [have] been subjected to the dreadful fevers that have prevailed from the source, to the outlet, of the Mississippi —
>
> Notwithstanding the good nursing, I now have, I am recovering very slowly, and am yet unable to attend to business.

If Herman had accompanied his aunt Mary Melvill, his uncle would have mentioned his presence, one would think. There is no evidence as to where he was from mid-September until early November.

That fall Peter Gansevoort was away from Albany for a protracted period in Flushing, where ex-chancellor Nathan Sanford was clinging to life. On 12 October 1838 his clerk, Eli Fly, Herman's friend, wrote Peter in incoherent anxiety: "What has become of you? for the last ten days I have been anxiously looking for you! not even a letter have I received, it's somewhat astonishing too, under all the circumstances the Circuit Court at present sitting, the Term will commence next Monday, and other matters relative to the office." Peter's absence upset Maria even more. She wrote him on 30 October, two days before the quarterly rent came due, that she had "been compell'd to borrow money to pay for Coal, and some winter Stores." Peter had in his "hands" the remainder of a small sum she had been awarded in a legal judgment, and she needed it now. Gansevoort, she said, "remains about the same, but his Symptoms are more favorable, he is less irratable and capable of more self command." She gave much the same report on 3 November to her cousin Conrad Ten Eyck: "Gansevoort's symptoms are more favorable than they have yet been, and we think him rather better this week." He was improved enough to become impatient at being out of the center of politics, the state capital, for his mother wrote Allan on 10 November: "Immediately on the receipt of this I wish you to procure for Gansevoort to day's number of the Argus, & Eve^g Journal, just put down whether Uncle Peter has come home or whether he is still absent, then mail them, also send tomorrow & Monday the same papers, your Brother is very lonely & he expresses a great desire to know all about the Election." Other than being unusually irritable, Gansevoort was "about the same but rather weaker."

On 7 November 1838 Herman arrived at Lansingburgh in the evening — from where we do not know, and added a postscript to his mother's letter of 10 November to Allan: "My complements to Eli James Murdock [Fly] tell him I shall be down in a few days." From this reference to Herman's friend, his uncle Peter's clerk, it seems that Herman had not come through Albany on his way to Lansingburgh from wherever he had been. Two days later, on 12 November, Herman paid $5.25 for the term and began a course in survey-ing and engineering at the nearby Lansingburgh Academy at North and John streets, a tidy structure, the main feature of which was a tall cupola shuttered in order to control the light and ventilation. (It still stands, at the renamed 114th and Fourth Avenue.)

Peter's prolonged absence upset Maria so much that she sent every day to the post office in Lansingburgh to look for news. As she reminded Allan on 10 November: "I am in debt, & have yet to pay my Rent. Another Barrel of Flour will be wanted next week, & many things wanted necessarily before Winter sets in. I have borrowed, & yet am again without funds." And across the Hudson from Lansingburgh, in Waterford, Aunt Mary Ann Chando-nette Gansevoort on 27 December wrote to Peter: "Surely Leonard & Stan-wix are not bastard children. . . . It is now eight years since the death of their Grandmother, who told me on her death bed, that there was enough to support me & to educate Stanwix." She added: "For the last four years I have been perfectly harrassed, for means to educate him, & to clothe him & myself, & I can do it no longer." Now she at last threatened to take legal measures, since Peter had rebuffed all her appeals to settle the estate, con-trary to his mother's promise to her. Peter stalled, blaming his brother Her-man for not bringing down the field books of the Northumberland property that was to have been sold; he could not, of course, initiate a settlement of the estate without those essential and elusive documents. Peter had disposed of his sister and his sister-in-law upriver, out of sight and almost, at times, out of mind, as if Maria were east of the sun, and Mary west of the moon.

As the winter of 1838–39 wore on, the exiles in Lansingburgh staved off disaster by one stratagem after another. The only member of the family usefully (although resentfully) employed was Allan, in Albany, serving in Peter Gansevoort's office and living in a rented room at old Cousin Maggey Wynkoop's house. Gansevoort was helpless in bed still, unable to walk as far as the fireplace (Herman had to carry him). Herman was continuing his course in surveying and engineering at the Lansingburgh Academy with the hope of having a profession at last. Tom was only nine. All four of the girls were at home that winter — Helen a woman of twenty-one, capable of teaching Tom and the two younger girls if they were not in the village school. Throughout this time Maria kept a single servant in the house at nominal wages of around sixteen dollars a quarter; the servant (her name was Rosey) left in June 1839, paid off with the last money Maria had in hand.

In Galena Uncle Tom, recovering from three attacks of fever and ague, importuned Lemuel Shaw to see that he was sent his father's personal papers and as always worried about his son Thomas, the whaleman who drank when he was ashore and avoided people who knew him. From Pittsfield Robert Melvill assured Shaw that he was not going to try to take out a loan that his father had mentioned, word that Shaw must have interpreted as less than proof positive that Robert would not change his mind.

In Albany Maria's cousin's husband Teunis Van Vechten started his second term as mayor in January 1839, but the biggest local news was the death at the Manor House, at the northern edge of Albany, on 26 January 1839, of Stephen Van Rensselaer, seventy-four year old, the Eighth Patroon, and the last of his name to govern his domain absolutely, as if it were a medieval duchy. The Melvilles were acutely aware of the contrast between the anomalous exalted position of their kinspeople and their own lowly status. Gansevoort about this time noted in an edition of *Memoirs of an American Lady* (published in 1809, just reprinted in 1836) this passage on the Patroon's singular possessions:

A gentleman of the name of Renzelaer was considered as in a manner lord paramount of this city, a pre-eminence which his successor still enjoys, both with regard to the town and the lands adjacent. The original proprietor obtained from the High and Mighty States a grant of lands, which, from the church [on the Hudson, at Oranienburgh, later Albany], extended twelve miles in every direction, forming a manor twenty-four Dutch miles in length, the same in breadth, including lands not only of the best quality of any in the province, but the most happily situated for the purposes both of commerce and of agriculture. This great proprietor was looked up to as much as republicans in a new country could be supposed to look up to any one. He was called the Patroon, a designation tantamount to lord of the manor. Yet, in the distribution of these lands, the sturdy Belgian spirit of independence set limits to the power and profits of this lord of the forests, as he might then be called. None of these lands were either sold or alienated. The more wealthy settlers, as the Schuylers, Cuylers, &c. took very extensive leases of the fertile plains along the river, with boundless liberty of woods and pasturage, to the westward. The terms were, that the lease should hold while water runs and grass grows, and the landlord to receive the tenth sheaf of every kind of grain the ground produces.

The "lady" was a little inexact, for the Van Rensselaer demesne went twelve miles along the Hudson River and twenty-four miles back in either direction, what became Rensselaer County to the east of the river and Albany County to the west. Late in 1851, when Herman worked "so long as grass grows and water runs" into his description of his hero Pierre's aristocratic heritage, he commented that the terms hinted "of a surprising eternity for a deed," and seemed "to make lawyer's ink unobliterable as the sea." The Melville sons could not escape accounts of their splendid ancestors in old books any more than they could escape accounts of their living and dying cousins in the newspapers.

In a memorable funeral, the simple casket containing the body of the "Last" Patroon was borne on men's shoulders nearly a mile from the North Dutch Church to the family vault. Apparently Maria did not go down for the services, but she and her cousin Maria Peebles weeks later were anxious that Allan bring up to them copies of the sermon Dr. William Buell Sprague had preached in the Second Presbyterian Church "on the Death of the Patroon" (the custom being that funeral sermons were promptly printed up so the mourners could have copies to cherish). Gansevoort in his *Index Rerum* recorded a "delineation of the character of this eminently good & pious man" in the "Funeral discourse on the death of[,] delivered Feb 3 1839 by Thos E. Vermilye," and made further notes on an "eloquent elogium on his character, extracted from a sermon by George W. Bethune delivered on the 3d of Feby 1839 at Phila as quoted in the Christian Intelligencer Apl 20 1839."

For years the local papers had printed news of the resentment of the Patroon's tenants against the feudal rents they owed him. On 19 October 1832, the *Argus* had reprinted from the Columbia *Sentinel* this denunciation of two "aristocrats" running for office, Carroll Livingston of Columbia, and Stephen Van Rensselaer Jr., of Albany, the son of the Eighth Patroon, and a presence in this story until his death in 1868:

> they have no feelings in common with the great majority of the people. Born to princely estates — brought up with luxurious and extravagant habits — wholly untaught and undisciplined in that knowledge which relates to the great interests of the mass of the people, and which that *enterprize* that flows from more humble beginnings in life, seems to be alone able to secure, they are as unfit to represent the democracy of America, as the bloated and purse-proud nobility of England are, to represent the commonalty of that oppressed realm. . . .

Mr. Van Rensselaer has always been a zealous and an active federalist; opposed . . . to the extension and now to the continuance of popular privileges.

The writer had gone on to indict Livingston and Van Rensselaer for their supposed control of the votes "of the numerous and respectable tenantry, which is scattered over the domains of 'The Families,'" objecting: "the tenant who pays his rent, is as independent as the lord of the soil; and pigmies are still pigmies, though perched on the fancied elevation of a manorial inheritance. Thank God, the day for the degrading influence of feudal lords has gone by! It cannot withstand the broad blaze of intelligence that now irradiates our land."

By May 1839, four months after the death of the Eighth Patroon, the resentment of his tenants was so strong that a committee of anti-renters, as the papers called them, formally called at the office of the younger Stephen Van Rensselaer. Refusing to grant them audience, Van Rensselaer instructed his agent, Douw B. Lansing ("Douw" was another of Maria Gansevoort Melville's family names), that he would communicate in writing; subsequently he rejected their claims. In Lansingburgh Maria and her children followed all these developments in the gradual disintegration of the feudal estates of their fortunate cousins: they themselves had fallen already, from a lower position, a decade earlier, and the most glorious of their kinsmen was under siege.

In his illness in Lansingburgh Gansevoort did his best to guide Allan from afar, as he later tried to guide Tom, and as he tried, with little immediate success, to guide Herman. The dutiful Allan improved his imitation of Gansevoort's superb handwriting and was rewarded by a compliment from his all-but-paternal brother. In her addition to Gansevoort's letter on 5 March 1839 Maria did her best to support her oldest son's hortatory efforts, to the extent of listing some of Allan's misspellings. She assured him: "We are much gratified by your improvement in writing, and hope you will continue to perfect yourself in that, not forgetting your spelling which requires great attention — have a Dictionary always at your side." She (and Gansevoort) routinely put on Allan the duty of paying social calls on the Taylors and the Van Vechtens so the Albany friends and relatives would be reminded of the exiles dragging out their lonely existence up the river. Determined to improve himself, and perhaps even more single-minded (though less ambitious) than Gansevoort himself, Allan acquired the *Index Rerum* maker John Todd's *The Student's Manual* in March and set himself to master it. Money was so short that Maria not only talked about selling furniture — she did so. On orders relayed by Gansevoort on 5 March 1839, Allan took ten dollars for a table (in his possession); at that very high price, it must have been a fine piece. Maria repeatedly importuned both her brothers for money, becoming frantic at one time when she could not be sure where Herman Gansevoort was. Allan seldom came up to Lansingburgh, and she instructed him to come by private conveyance whenever possible (requesting a ride with someone going upriver) rather than taking the stage. (Herman would have walked.)

Through the winter Herman tried to do his part in the family by completing the course in engineering. On 2 April Peter Gansevoort introduced Herman to William C. Bouck, a harried-looking man of fifty-three, with deep vertical ridges between sunken eyes, a jutting nose over a prim mouth, his head topped by hair upswept to the center and stabilized like meringue baked atop a pie. This was an important man, one of the five canal commissioners (and later governor of New York). The next day Peter wrote Bouck a formal letter of introduction and before sending it added a testimony from the principal of the Lansingburgh Academy as to Herman's academic status. The letter to Bouck introduced "Herman Melville, a young man of talent & good education," who was "desirous to obtain a situation in the Engineer department of the Canal" — presumably in the maintenance department rather than any project for new construction. Herman had "endeavored to prepare himself for the business of surveying & engineering," Bouck's "sincere friend" assured him. Expecting little, Peter assured Bouck that Herman "submits his application, without any pretension & solicits any situation, however humble it may be, but he indeed would prefer a subordinate station, as he wishes to advance only by his own merit." Peter Gansevoort assured Bouck that his nephew "possesses the ambition to make himself useful in a business which he desires to make his profession," and declared himself, after all, "extremely anxious" that Herman should "receive employment."

Nothing came of this request, so pallidly proffered, and in the next weeks Herman continued to be a drain on the family. While Gansevoort was assiduously filling his *Index Rerum* with key words of useful passages he read, the second son picked up some of the books, pamphlets, and newspapers that lay around his ailing brother. Herman glanced over some books by Lord Chesterfield, Sir Walter Scott, and Washington Irving, among others. From his own miscellaneous reading in the last years and from the library Gansevoort assembled around his bed, Herman ended the winter with his head abuzz with the three just named, as well as Byron, Robert Burton, Thomas Campbell, Shakespeare, Milton, Coleridge, Sheridan, and a host of other writers. Now having no classes to attend, Herman amused himself by putting his pen to paper. He had seen himself in print before, a year earlier, in the Albany *Microscope*, but as a controversialist, not a fiction writer. The Waterford *Atlas* in March 1835 had congratulated its local citizenry for living in "a reading community" and had appealed for contributions from fledgling writers: "We think Waterford contains all that is essential to raise a literary name. — Bear then in mind, *'Our Village Paper,'* — it presents a broad field for the exercise of talent; and — even as the wing of a young bird is strengthened by frequent attempts to soar to the etherial regions — practice will mature that talent, till it be found to constitute the most genial aliment of the mind." This kind of welcome to youthful talent was offered by papers of Lansingburgh and other small towns nearby all through Herman's late teens.

Within two or three weeks of his failure to hear from Bouck, Herman as "L.A.V." (an unexplained choice of initials) submitted a manuscript to the *Democratic Press and Lansingburgh Advertiser,* and had the pleasure of reading in the paper a request from the editor, William Lamb, that "L.A.V." come in for a personal interview. The result was the publication on 4 May of "No. 1" of what was billed as "Fragments from a Writing Desk" — an open-ended rubric. Melville had chosen a precious prose style — excessive enough to allow him to indulge his extravagances and just enough overdone to allow him to deny that he was taking his style seriously. The first paragraph was indicative of the allusive passages to come: "My Dear M——, I can imagine you seated on that dear, delightful, old fashioned sofa; your head supported by its luxurious padding, and with feet perched aloft on the aspiring back of that straight limbed, stiff-necked, quaint old chair, which, as our facetious W—— assured me, was the identical seat in which old Burton composed his Anatomy of Melancholy." Whether Old Burton's or the poet Thomas Gray's sofa (Melville may already have associated Gray with lounging on a sofa), the large piece of furniture was of the sort the Melville family treasured, quaint, old-fashioned, and the stiff-necked chair was still better than old-fashioned — L.A.V. said it was actually old. Old furniture, a rare old book, an anecdote of a fine old author — this was characteristic Melvillean mood-stuff.

Formerly noted for his "hang-dog modesty," the narrator has learned "what a comfortable thing is a good opinion of one's self!" Beautiful as Apollo, "dressed in a style which would extort admiration from a Brummell, and belted round with self-esteem as with a girdle," he has, all unwittingly, "provoked to an irreconcilable degree" the resentment of some of the "village beaux." The beaux are his inferiors, but not so the local belles: "this same village of Lansingburgh contains within its pretty limits as fair a set of blushing damsels, as one would wish to look upon on a dreamy summer-day!" What follows is an extended compliment to the belles of Lansingburgh, three of them in particular. The piece has the air of being a fragment à clef, meant to amuse certain male or female friends in Lansingburgh who might find the narrator's excessive posturing comically unlike the author's own manners and who might have sport claiming to have recognized each other in the characters. The arrogant and purse-proud young Augustus

Peebles, a real village beau, was the heir to Hanver Island, in the Hudson between Lansingburgh and Waterford, and later if not now among themselves the Melvilles satirically referred to him as "the Lord of the Isle," in witty allusion to Sir Walter Scott's poem about Robert Bruce, *The Lord of the Isles,* a copy of which had been at Uncle Thomas's house in Pittsfield. Herman could have been satirizing him as the village Brummell.

For all the likelihood that the piece contained topical Lansingburgh allusions, on 8 May the West Troy *Advocate and Watervleit Advertiser* reprinted it from the type set for the *Democratic Press,* resetting clumsily to make the compliment relevant across the river: "this same village of West Troy contains within its pretty limits as fair a set of blushing damsels, as one would wish to look upon on a dreamy summer-day!"

On 18 May the *Democratic Press* printed the second, disparate fragment. In it a mysterious cloaked woman drops at the narrator's feet a love note signed "Inamorata," in which he is urged to follow the messenger. She proves unexpectedly fleet of foot, but he pursues her through a grove up to a simple country villa. Summoned furtively into a large basket by his guide then pulled up to a lofty window by a pulley, he luxuriates in emotions:

> To attempt an analysis of my feelings at this moment were impossible. The
> solemnity of the hour — the romantic nature of my present situation — the
> singularity of my whole adventure — the profound stillness which prevailed —
> the solitude of the place, were enough of themselves to strike a panic into the
> stoutest heart, and to unsettle the strongest nerves. But when to these, was
> added the thought, — that at the dead of night, and in the company of a being
> so perfectly inexplicable, I was effecting a clandestine entrance into so re-
> markable an abode: the kind and sympathising reader will not wonder, when I
> wished myself safely bestowed in my own snug quarters in ——— street.

Once inside, he is ushered into an apartment as luxurious as any in the Arabian Nights, the mistress of which is a "lovely being," reclining upon an ottoman. He kneels at the shrine of her peerless charms, despite "all the vows of eternal constancy" he had sworn to another. He speaks to her extravagancies of love, and catching her in his arms he imprints "one long, long kiss upon her hot and glowing lips" before realizing that this woman whom he now so "wildly, madly" loves has a defect he is not prepared to accept: "I flung her from me, even though she clung to my vesture, and with a wild cry of agony I burst from the apartment! — She was dumb! Great God, she was dumb! DUMB AND DEAF!" The West Troy affiliate passed by the chance to reprint this second fragment.

In late April, shortly before rent day, Maria went to Albany herself and got fifty dollars from each of her brothers (Herman Gansevoort was in town) but on 23 May she was frantic. Home in midweek, Allan carried her letter back to Peter Gansevoort: "You will remember my telling you I owed for borrow'd money & Bills forty eight Dollars, my Rent fell due on the first of May which was $31.25 — leaving me $20.75 — I have been under the painful necessity of again borrowing from Mrs Peebles besides something owing the Shoe-maker. *Can you send me a remittance this week.* I think some plan must be resolved upon, or something decided about my support untill my Sons can do for me, & relieve my mind from an insupportable weight of uncertainty." In this anxious letter Maria Gansevoort Melville gave two bits of news about her two older sons. Gansevoort, she wrote, "feels well enough to go about, & will leave for New York in a few days." The other news carried a reproach that Peter had not been more effectual with Bouck the month before, when Herman was applying for a job as a surveyor on the Erie Canal: "Herman has gone out for a few days on foot to see what he can find to do."

Melville's documented jobs do not match his comment to Nathaniel Hawthorne in early May 1851 about the bodily sensations he had often felt when "a hired man," doing his "day's work from sun to sun." Between 1836 and 1840 Herman worked as a "hired man" more often than surviving records show. This time, mid-May of 1839, his efforts to find work came to nothing, as Gansevoort told Allan in a letter written the day after Maria's to Peter. Maria had retained one essential servant, as Gansevoort made clear in his letter of 24 May 1839, when he relieved Allan of the task of hiring a replacement in Albany ("Mamma expects to obtain a girl from Waterford, in a few days"). The weather had kept Gansevoort confined, and without exercise he found himself not strong enough to go to Albany "with the view of taking the steam boat for N Yk tomorrow." Instead, he would arrive the next week, planning to stay over at the Van Vechten house before going to New York. The letter reveals that great dislocation coexisted with domestic routine: "It would give me much pleasure to have your company down the river, and if Uncle has no objections to your going, you may accompany me. If he does not wish you to go, it is your duty to stay & reconcile yourself to the disappointment. The House-cleaning is progressing & everything in most delectable disorder — Herman has returned from his expedition, without success — Ma & the children all desire their love." Herman's failure was no surprise in the family, and Allan had less reason than ever to adopt any model other than Gansevoort for rising in the world.

Excited by the prospect of going to Manhattan, and perhaps deliberately taking advantage of the situation, Allan provoked his uncle (or allowed himself to be provoked by his uncle). Four years later, while visiting his mother in Lansingburgh, Allan wrote down his side of the story:

I remained in my Uncle's office doing the business which generally falls to the lot of the youngest student until the latter part of May 1839, when my Uncle wishing to rid himself of all further expences & responsibility on my account to obtain his object picked a quarrel with me, and my language (which he provoked) not being as he thought the most respectful towards him, he refused to notice me & when I afterwards begged his forgiveness *if* I had offended him he told me I must leave him.

Allan put his things together without (it seems) going up to see his mother, and was ready when his early-risen brother reached Albany. His account continues:

The next day after this occurrence with my uncle I went to New York with my brother Gansevoort who was going to the city for the first time in fifteen months. He had lain on his back at Lansingburgh during all this time sick. I remained in New York about ten days at A. W. Bradford's, a friend of my brothers. It was while I was on this visit to New York that my brother Herman sailed for Liverpool before the mast. He returned about 4 months afterwards.

This record of Herman's doings was incidental, as it usually is in the family letters of this period.

Herman's plans had been as fluid as Gansevoort's and Allan's. If he had found work on his expedition, he would have taken it. Home, there was nothing to do. The day Gansevoort left, Herman wrote him, in care of Bradford: "When I woke up this morning, what the Devel should I see but your cane along in bed with me I shall keep it for you when you come up here again." This message was written in the margin of a copy of the *Democratic Press* containing the first "Fragment," published while Gansevoort was at home in Lansingburgh, so chances are that Herman knew Gansevoort wanted to show it to Ally Bradford. Herman had expected to see Gansevoort next in Lansingburgh, not New York City, but after the failure of his expedition, Herman was making up his mind to do the one thing a poorly educated young man could do—go to sea, like Thomas W. Melvill and Leonard Gansevoort.

Two years earlier, these grown cousins had been heard from. On 27 February 1837 the whaler *Columbus* returned to Fairhaven, Massachusetts, carrying Thomas W. Melvill home from his first whaling voyage. Afraid of excesses, sexual as much as alcoholic, his father Thomas Jr. (so he wrote Shaw on 14 March 1837) had advised his son's *"immediate reshipment,* as the only means to perfect the good work, if really & truly commenced." (On 8 March 1837, Midshipman Guert Gansevoort, the family success, had been promoted to the grade of lieutenant—a high position for the boy who had sailed

as a midshipman in 1824.) On 29 March 1837 the whaler *Hercules* returned to
New Bedford with Leonard Gansevoort aboard. On 1 November 1837,
Gansevoort had written to Uncle Peter that his Cousin Leonard (born in
1816) had "sailed this m^g in the packet ship England for Liverpool — and
will probably get back by the first of January" — practical information that
Gansevoort now recalled, reminded by Leonard's presence, just then, with
his mother at Waterford.

Herman was already too old to have any hope of making a career in the
navy, like Guert Gansevoort, but he was not too old to sign on either a
merchant ship or a whaler, one almost as desperate a measure as the other, for
neither would contribute anything significant to Maria's support. A whaling
voyage was, despite everything, alluring: more than he wanted to glimpse any
part of Europe, Herman wanted to see the Pacific. In *Moby-Dick* (ch. 111,
"The Pacific"), Melville gave Ishmael a profound early longing to sail onto
that ocean: "were it not for other things, I could have greeted my dear Pacific
with uncounted thanks, for now the long supplication of my youth was
answered." The emotions Melville ascribed to Ishmael were both more complex and more particularized than his own early emotions, insofar as they are
recorded, but the South Seas may indeed have haunted his imagination since
he heard and read stories of his Uncle John's and Cousin Thomas's adventures, perhaps most especially the story of Thomas's day in the Typee valley.

8

Sailor and Schoolteacher
1839–1840

As Diamonds rough no lustre can impart,
Till their rude Forms are well improved by Art
So untaught Youth we very seldom find,
Display the daz[z]ling Beauties of the Mind
Till Art and Science are to Nature joind.

"Allan Melvills Book," 1796

ON 31 MAY 1839 GANSEVOORT summoned Herman down to Manhattan, sure that he could get him on some sort of vessel, whaler or merchant. In response, on 1 June Maria wrote a letter for Herman to carry to New York City: "Your letter of yesterday was received & preparation forthwith commenced. Herman is happy but I think at heart he is rather agitated. I can hardly believe it & cannot realize the truth of his going both my boys gone in one week." She meant both Gansevoort and Herman were gone in one week, for she expected Allan to come back up (at least as far as Albany) right away, as he did. She continued: "How uncertain & changing are all things here below — but no more of this or you will stop reading. I have put up all I had for Herman that I thought would be useful, endeavour to secure for him every thing within the range of his means that will make him comfortable, write me where his Vessel is bound, and the probable time of his Sailing." Helen had gone over to Waterford the day before with her cousins Catherine Gansevoort Curtis and the whaleman Leonard Gansevoort, and Maria foresaw how bad Helen would feel at Herman's going "without his seeing her." Since Gansevoort had summoned him in peremptory fashion, there was scant ceremony, even though Herman may have left home thinking that he might be gone three or four years.

Herman caught a boat at Albany for New York (probably the cheaper night boat) and arrived on 2 June — the first time since 1830 that the three brothers had been in New York together, and the last time until late 1844. Bradford and his wife, who lived at 105 Ninth Avenue, may have put all of them up. It developed that Gansevoort had not found a ship he could defi-

nitely recommend to Herman. Still thinking of trying whaling ports, he took
the letter Herman had brought from their mother and used blank areas of
the paper to plot out the distances between New York and two whaling ports
on Long Island — Sag Harbor (109 miles away by the "lower road") and
River Head (81 miles away by the "middle road"). Herman and Gansevoort
weighed the possibilities with perturbation — the time, expense, and uncertainty of getting to the whaling ports influencing their decision to settle on a
merchant ship sailing from Manhattan. Maybe in a few months' time (rather
than the years a whaling voyage might last) more jobs around Albany would
be open. The *St. Lawrence*, anchored at South Street, had an opening for a
boy (a green hand of whatever age, not a cabin boy) at a few dollars a month.
She was small, only 119½ feet long by 25½ feet wide, displacing 356 tons —
about the size of a whaling ship. Besides cargo, the ship would carry passengers, for an advertisement in the *Evening Post* proclaimed that a "few
more cabin and steerage passengers" could "yet be very handsomely accom-
modated at low rates" in the "splendid fast sailing packet ship." The brothers
put aside the thought of going to Sag Harbor or River Head, and Herman
signed on the *St. Lawrence*. The characteristically ambiguous *H* in his signature led to his name being transcribed onto the crew list as "Norman
Melville," but the rest was accurate enough: nineteen years old, 5'8½", of
light complexion, with brown hair. A decade later he specified that he was
5'10⅛", so perhaps now he underestimated his height, or else he was not
quite done growing, at almost twenty. Herman was, as his Ishmael was to
boast, going "as a simple sailor, right before the mast, plumb down into the
forecastle, aloft there to the royal mast-head." (Cousin Thomas Melvill the
next week sailed from Fairhaven as ship keeper at 1/135th lay — in the *Ama-
zon*, on a whaling voyage to New Zealand.)

The little that is known of the officers and crew of the *St. Lawrence* was
discovered by William H. Gilman in the 1940s and reported in his *Melville's
Early Life and "Redburn"* (1951). Gilman found that the captain, Oliver P.
Brown, was a naturalized Swede, resident in the United States for many
years. The first officer, thirty-eight years old, was Joseph M. Shaw Jr., born in
New York; the second mate was a twenty-eight-year-old Massachusetts man,
Nathan or Nathaniel Heard. The steward, twenty-three, was a black man
from the District of Columbia, Moses Walker Jr.; Perry Thomas, the black
cook, forty-six, was a Connecticut man. Among the crew was a twenty-year-
old Irish-born sailor named James Johnson, and a native of Greenland, Peter
Brown. There was a thirty-one-year-old native of New York City named
Robert Jackson (Melville used the name "Jackson" for a villainous character
in *Redburn*) and several other New Yorkers besides Herman: James McLain,
Francis Williams, William Hamilton, William Allen, James Tenell, and Lau-

rence Crawford, along with a Pennsylvanian, Benjamin Thompson, and a Maryland man, Benjamin Foy. Thompson, forty-one, 6'2", towered over the rest, but at 5'8½" Herman was taller than any of the others except Heard and Peter Brown, both 5'9". Crawford was nineteen, Herman almost twenty, and James Johnson already twenty; most of the others were in their twenties. By home state, by stature, and by age Herman was not out of place.

After the months of training for a nonexistent job on the canal then more months of fruitless job-hunting, on 5 June 1839 Herman found himself passing Governor's Island, pointed right out for the Narrows and the Atlantic. He began at once to learn the shipboard routine and nautical nomenclature—not an easy task, no matter how many sailor cousins he had. He was healthy, but nothing had prepared him for the athletic life of a sailor before the mast. Decks were to be washed down, chicken coops and pigpens had to be cleaned, and his performances of all tasks had to be as precise as possible if he were to reduce the harassment meted out to "verdant" youths fresh from inland villages. A grown man, tough enough to face down unruly youths near his own age in the backwoods of Massachusetts, wise to some shipboard ways from his cousins' stories, he concealed any agitation and fit in fast enough with the other men crowded together in the forecastle.

After a crossing for which no description has been found, early on 4 July the *St. Lawrence* arrived at Liverpool, just in time for Herman to witness a patriotic show, for all the American ships had hoisted their flags to mark Independence Day. The routine in port was probably much the same as Melville described in *Redburn* (ch. 29): "At daylight, all hands were called, and the decks were washed down; then we had an hour to go ashore to breakfast; after which we worked at the rigging, or picked oakum, or were set to some employment or other, never mind how trivial, till twelve o'clock, when we went to dinner [ashore]. At half-past one we resumed work; and finally *knocked off* at four o'clock in the afternoon, unless something particular was in hand. And after four o'clock, we could go where we pleased, and were not required to be on board again till next morning at daylight." The unloading of the cargo (mainly bales of cotton) was not part of Melville's job. Though not required to sleep aboard, he did not have the money to sleep ashore, and in any case much of what he saw ashore must have made the fetid forecastle seem almost attractive.

The Liverpool Melville encountered was already the great embarking place for immigrants, predominately young Irish men and women and other people leaving the British Isles for the United States, but also many Scandinavians, Germans, and other Europeans—a mix of people the like of which Herman had never encountered before. He had never seen docks such as these—Clarence Dock (1830), Waterloo (1834), Trafalgar (1836), Victoria

(1836), Prince's Dock (enormous — with a water area of eleven acres), then George's Dock, next the Dry Dock, then the Custom House, on the site of the Old Dock, then the Salthouse Dock, the King's Dock, and at last the Queen's Dock, and Shipwrights Yard, with large basins connecting to some of the docks, and the new (1832) Brunswick Dock. In *Redburn* (ch. 40) he mentioned Brunswick Dock as one of the most interesting because it serviced the black steamers (unlike the American boats, built to "navigate the boisterous Narrow Seas"), observing ironically: "Here you see vast quantities of produce, imported from starving Ireland." The stretch from the first large basin before Clarence Dock to Brunswick Dock took up the entire riverfront area of Liverpool.

Herman had seen foreign newspapers, French and English, in his childhood, if not later, and now he had a chance to encounter papers from some other English cities as well as Liverpool. Like every sailor, he learned of the "Remarkable Circumstance" which had befallen the ship *Priscilla*, from Pernambuco, then in Liverpool. On 6 July the Liverpool *Journal* reported that on board was being displayed (for any sailor like Herman to see) a piece of wood from the fore planks through which was stuck about eighteen inches of the bony weapon of a swordfish: "Penetrating the copper, the sword had made its way, first through the outer plank, of Scotch larch, three inches and a half in thickness, then, traversing an open space of ten or twelve inches, it had encountered another plank, of oak, and about four inches in thickness, which was also pierced, the point of the sword coming clean through on the other side." The paper commented: "The force with which it must have been driven affords a striking exemplification of the power and ferocity of the fish." When the shock occurred, the captain had thought he had struck a rock, but subsequently remembered that numerous whales "had been seen playing about the vessel the day before," so "the sword-fish, which is a deadly enemy to the whale, had mistaken the Priscilla, for one of the objects of which it was in chase; in other words, it had thought her 'very like a whale.' " This may have been the first but it was not the last story Melville was to hear of a swordfish stabbing a ship before he made ambiguous use of the phenomenon in *Moby-Dick* (ch. 54, "The Town-Ho's Story").

One of the minor pleasures available was testing what the papers said about American ships against what he knew from excited gossip among the sailors. On 17 July an American captain, Benjamin Miner, a guest aboard another American ship, the *Tallahasse* (as it was spelled), in the Victoria Dock, fractured his skull: "The hatches were open for the purpose of discharging cotton. He made a spring from the hatch to the stage on the opposite side, overbalanced himself, and fell backward into the hold. . . . Captain Miner was commander of the American ship Nonantum, which was next to the Tallahasse." His death, the *Mercury* of the nineteenth continued, was "a source of sincere regret to all the American captains in the port, the vessels belonging to whom displayed their colours half-mast on the occasion." Since the American ships flew their "colours" at half mast, Herman learned all the particulars of Miner's instantaneous transition from vitality to death, his being made immortal by brevet, in the phrase from *Moby-Dick* (ch. 7, "The Chapel").

An imaginative youth could fancy that the occasional sailor ballad-singer along the docks formed a link with an older England, but there was no denying that Liverpool was a modern town, devoid of obvious medieval charms. Up the streets from the Mersey, on higher ground, there were no awe-inspiring Druidic monuments, no imposing Roman ruins, not even a Gothic cathedral. There was one historical-aesthetic object of interest, very near the docks, in the quadrangle by the Exchange Building, behind the Town Hall, an easy stroll up Chapel Street from between Prince's Dock and George's Dock, and only a half-block from the main thoroughfare, Dale Street. This was George Bullock's enormous sculpture of the death of Lord Nelson. Victory drops a wreath on Nelson's brow even as bony Death (the ribs so deep that they seem disconnected from anything) stretches out his right hand through the drapery to clutch at the admiral's heart. Herman circled it repeatedly, scrutinizing the four symbolic captives or slaves, absorbing the moral about Death coming at the moment of Victory, and memorizing Nelson's last order, "England expects every man to do his duty." Meanwhile Death scrutinized him, for it looked not at Nelson but the viewer. This was by all odds the most impressive piece of sculpture Herman had yet seen, and so located that he saw it repeatedly over the weeks he was in Liverpool. In *Redburn* (ch. 41, "Redburn Roves About Hither and Thither") the narrator describes his rovings, observing that he had "always taken a vast deal of lonely satisfaction in wandering about, up and down, among out-of-the-way streets and alleys," and speculating upon the strangers he met. Chances are that Melville took long walks up the Mersey along Bath Street and its continuations, or north along the parallel Leeds and Liverpool Canal, or pursued his explorations along Dale Street through the city to the outskirts of the town. Most of the time he endured the lot of the sailor — seeing the most unremarkable or else the most degraded parts of any foreign city. In Liverpool his own father had stayed in the finest hotel and associated with the literary elite, only twenty-one years earlier — months before Herman had been conceived. One or another of Allan Melvill's guidebooks may have been preserved in the house at Lansingburgh, perhaps *The Picture of Liverpool; or Stranger's Guide* (1808), which Herman used in *Redburn*.

With or without a printed guidebook in mind or hand, in his rovings about hither and thither Herman, inevitably, was looking at sights he knew his father had seen — in effect, looking for his father, at times quite consciously so. That quest, and the contrast of their situations in life, gave a strange cast to Herman's whole stay in Liverpool, even mundane experiences, like going to church.

Without going to any trouble Herman found religion on the streets as well as inside churches, for street preachers were common. A New York visitor, Evert A. Duyckinck, born in 1816, son of the late New York publisher of the same name, noted in his journal on 28 July 1839 a meeting with "two street preachers, one on the steps of the exchange, with two elderly persons on each side — his audience chiefly of sailors, talking well." Herman may have been one of those sailors that Sunday, and there were occasions after Melville and Duyckinck became friends in 1846 for the two New Yorkers to compare notes with each other on their experiences in Liverpool in 1839. These clergymen in Liverpool spoke "in the open air, from the corners of the quays, or wherever they can procure an audience," so Melville remembered in *Redburn* (ch. 35), where he had his narrator say: "Whenever, in my Sunday strolls, I caught sight of one of these congregations, I always made a point of joining it; and would find myself surrounded by a motley crowd of seamen from all quarters of the globe, and women, and lumpers, and dock laborers of all sorts."

In the papers or on the streets Melville learned something about the year-old "Chartist" agitation, conducted by workingmen demanding universal suffrage for men, whether property owners or not, for the movement touched Liverpool, though not to the degree that it shook other cities such as Birmingham. One Chartist orator was so conspicuous that a correspondent complained particularly about him in the *Mercury* for 5 July:

CHARTIST ORATORS. — *W. H.* states that a stripling, about eighteen years of age, has lately been lecturing, morning and afternoon, on the Sundays, on Chartism, and he inquires whether what he regards as a nuisance ought not to be suppressed by the magistrates? We are not fond of interfering with street orators; and it does not follow that, because the young spouter calls himself a Chartist, he utters seditious harangues. As for his choosing the Sunday for his display, that is another thing, and may demand the interference of the magistrates.

This is Melville's description of a Chartist meeting that Redburn observes near the base of the equestrian statue in St. George's Square:

Addressing this orderly throng was a pale, hollow-eyed young man, in a snuff-colored surtout, who looked worn with much watching, or much toil, or too little food. . . .

In his hand was a soiled, inflammatory-looking pamphlet, from which he frequently read. . . . I was not long within hearing of him, before I became aware that this youth was a Chartist. . . .

I do not know why, but I thought he must be some despairing elder son, supporting by hard toil his mother and sisters; for of such many political desperadoes are made. (*Redburn*, ch. 41)

Here, in 1849, Melville was drawing on his memory of the stripling whose street oratory so distressed the *Mercury*.

Once away from the great docks the sailors found themselves in an urban stew. The Liverpool daily papers that summer recorded crimes and tragedies more lurid than Herman was accustomed to read about in the Albany press, frank as it was. On 28 June the *Mercury* printed a father's warning against "a biped animal that is now prowling about the town, and especially about George's Pier and the Docks," a "*monster*" (belonging "to a class for which language has not a name"). Herman probably already had a name or two for such a man who preyed on unprotected lads, luring them "to take an excursion across the river, or to the floating light, &c.," and regaling them "with wine at an hotel." On 5 July, the day after Melville's arrival, the *Mercury* reported that the biped animal had agreed to pay a five pound fine and had been advised to leave town. If he stayed and persisted in his ways, the *Mercury* recommended the treadmill. The day Melville arrived the local celebration of the Fourth of July got out of hand in a public-house at the corner of Denison Street, and a man calling himself Charles Brown (he claimed to be a Maltese but belonged to one of the American ships) was charged with having stabbed two men. The paper deplored the increase in this most un-English crime, stabbing. In the same issue there was an item headed "A Woman Strangled by her Bonnet Strings" — she having drunk gin all day then gone to bed with her bonnet on.

During Melville's first Friday in Liverpool "a young man, with more money than brains, and more liquor than either, was induced to accompany a female, who accosted him in Castle-street, to a house in Orange-street. He was there robbed of his purse . . . by the woman and a confederate." On 14 July Melville could read about "An awkward Plunge" he must have heard about already. A man had stumbled off the pier and fallen "into the George's Dock Basin, at the south-east corner, just under the sewer, where there is a channel flanked by two beds of mud, several feet deep"; he had been saved by "the gallantry of a sailor who witnessed the accident," a fellow who became an object of mingled admiration and dread among his fellow tars. The next day a man named Henry was found "under the shed, inside of the Prince's Dock," dying, a story reported under the head "Death from Drinking." On the same day the *Mercury* reported a case of infanticide in Carlton, near Worksop; Thomas Pye had impregnated his two daughters (not a specifically un-English crime, to judge from the papers) and when one of the sisters delivered her baby the other sister, still pregnant, killed it for her. On 3 August, two days after Melville turned twenty, there was another "Murder in Liverpool": a Belgian seaman of the galliot *Pauline* stabbed "a woman of disreputable character, in a house of infamy, called 'Black Wilson's' in New Brick-street."

During the weeks Herman was in Liverpool, Maria was concerned that in Albany sixteen-year-old Allan might defy his "inward Moniter Conscience" and yield to sexual temptation. She wrote Allan a little later, on 25 September: "my dear son I fear you feel too strong a confidence in your own strength — Remember God will be enquired of, and if you desire strength to overcome temptations, you must ask it from him, who is alone able to give." Allan, she knew, was "alone in a city fill'd with many things that attract but to deceive." He was still babied by Helen and Augusta, but he was sixteen, a grown man, and in need of the strength to overcome temptations. The recipient of similar "heartfelt advice" in earlier years, Herman, across the Atlantic, also needed to "strengthen the inward moniter" so he could "triumph over temptations." In *Redburn* (ch. 39, "The Booble-Alleys of the Town") Melville remembered the "pestilent lanes and alleys" such as "Rotten-row, Gibraltar-place, and Booble-alley" as being "putrid with vice and crime." The very houses, he said, had "a reeking, Sodom-like, and murderous look," so that it was just as well that the shroud of coal-smoke hid the enormities of the vice practiced there. This was a tough town, even for a young man who had knocked about a little in upstate New York and the wilds of western Massachusetts. In the city where one street was called Paradise there was no sin that could not be committed and, still worse, as Melville said in *Redburn* (ch. 36), there was "no calamity overtaking man" that could not "be rendered merchantable."

On 9 July Herman wrote his mother a letter that took until after the middle of September to reach her (as she wrote Allan on 25 September). Herman had told her what she would want to hear: "he is well, very anxious to see home, and to prove it, says he would give all the sights of Liverpool to see a corner of home." He was uncertain of the city to which he would return, appearing "to think the St Lawrence will not return to New York, this trip, but put Sail for Charleston, or one of the New England ports, it was still unsettled, depending on their Cargo." The destination was soon decided, for on 19 July the *Mercury* announced that the "fine first-class American Ship" the *St. Lawrence* was to sail on 1 August, Herman's twentieth birthday. The ship's "burthen" was five hundred tons. Coppered and copper-fastened, she was "a very desirable conveyance for goods and passengers." Delayed, the *St. Lawrence* was cleared outwards on 6 August, according to the *Mail*, and actually sailed on the fourteenth. It was far more crowded with passengers, immigrants to the United States, than on the voyage over.

One of the young men Melville frequently messed with in a sailor boardinghouse said good-bye to him "at Prince's Dock Gates, in the midst of a swarm of police-officers, truckmen, stevedores, beggars, and the like"; Melville described this parting, much later, because that messmate was aboard the Australian whaler that picked him up in the Marquesas Islands in 1842 (*Omoo*, ch. 1). The actual sailing of the *St. Lawrence* was probably much like the scene Melville described in *Redburn* (ch. 47): "After two days' work, every thing was in readiness; most of the emigrants on board; and in the evening we worked the ship close into the outlet of Prince's Dock, with the bow against the water-gate, to go out with the tide in the morning." Melville gave his narrator Redburn the word "indescribable" to express "the bustle and confusion" of the morning of sailing, the boarding of emigrants in steerage and the cabin passengers being added to "the ordinary clamor of the docks."

The voyage home was protracted — lasting almost seven weeks. On 28 September the *St. Lawrence* was off Cape Cod, on the twenty-ninth at Sandy Hook, and on the thirtieth she docked at the Howland and Aspinwall Wharf at South Street in Manhattan. The crew was released at sunrise on 1 October. Among the first news Herman heard from the pilot boat or on the docks would have been gossip about the astonishing sightings and resightings of the *Amistad*, the slave ship in the unsteady control of blacks who had risen up against their Spanish captors. One place or another, he read news reports in old and recent newspapers, such as the two-and-a-half pages in the Albany *Family Newspaper* on 12 October, copied from the New York *Evening Star*, headed "THE AFRICANS ONCE MORE!" — for the ship had made phantasmagorical appearances at various Long Island points over a period of days in late August, until it was seized and taken to New London, Connecticut, where the story gradually emerged.

At his office on Nassau Street or at his home on Ninth Avenue, Alexander Bradford had news of the Melville family, enough for Herman to reflect on as he made his way up the Hudson by himself. Herman found that Gansevoort had gone to Bath, far out in Steuben County, in western New York, to take the waters, but had returned to Lansingburgh. From Bradford, Herman also learned that Allan had returned to work for Peter Gansevoort but had found it intolerable. This is Allan's version of what happened, in his 1843 personal memoir (Berkshire Athenaeum), but close to what he told Herman in October 1839: "When I got back to Albany I went to my uncles office as usual to perform my duties, but after two or three days his conduct towards me remaining the same I finally packed up what articles I had in the office and without exchanging a word with his lordship I left him & went to Lansingburgh. Here I remained until the first of July." Maria was helpless to heal this first open break between one of her children and the uncle they regarded as a monster of selfishness. Allan had tried a second law office at "the miserable pitence of $5 per month," then had found a better situation in Dudley Burwell's office, although its location in Stanwix Hall meant that Allan and his uncle caught sight of each other more often than either desired.

In Herman's absence the family had continued to regard life in Lansingburgh as tentative. Maria thought of the First Reformed Dutch Church in Albany as hers still, for she wanted Allan to find out from Mrs. Van Vechten if the church was going to have communion and who was to officiate. She was in dread that the Reverend Mr. Thomas Vermilye was going to leave Albany for a better pastorate in Manhattan; in fact, he left, and prospered in the metropolis. As Maria reported to Allan on 25 September, Gansevoort did not seem to have benefited from his visit to the spa: "he has not gain'd in flesh but thinks his strength has increased, his cold is better than it has been." On 4 October Maria gave Allan worse news. Augustus Peebles had reported that at Troy Mr. Whipple (one of her creditors) had declared that " 'he had been played with long enough,' & could not put off the sale" — the sale of her furniture. In her letter to Allan, Maria was casting about for rescuers among her numerous relations: "I wish Mr Ten Eyck or someone feeling an interest in our concerns would come & arrange this thing. Have you been to Mr Ten Eyck — ask him not to forsake me at this time to come up & see Mr Whipple who is at Troy." Maria's ultimate question was: "Have your Uncles forsaken me." She signed herself "your distrest Mother." Among the other reasons for her distress was that Gansevoort had left for New York still unwell, his voice "very weak," planning to take the morning boat at Troy on Wednesday, 2 October. Herman had not been heard from when Maria wrote Allan early on 4 October, so the brothers Gansevoort and Herman just missed each other. As in a later year, they may have passed each other on the river, Herman going north on an Albany boat, Gansevoort going south on the Troy boat. Herman may have returned to a home despoiled of some of its furnishings.

Peter Gansevoort had not wholly forsaken Maria, but he took no heroic new measures to protect her. On 4 October he wrote to Lemuel Shaw and in the course of other business relayed some old news: "It is with the most painful feelings that I inform you, that by the failure in business, some time since, of her son Gansevoort, Mrs Melville has become entirely impoverished — mortgages are foreclosing upon her real estate & as I have just heard, her furniture is now advertised for sale." On 18 October the returned sailor, good at least as a messenger, carried a letter down from Lansingburgh to his Uncle Peter, then waited for a reply to carry back to Maria. Peter's surviving draft is detailed and defensive:

> I rec'd a few minutes since, my dear Maria, your letter by my nephew Herman, Most deeply do I sympathize in your situation and think not Maria, that I have at any time been without the most painful feelings on your account — My inability to contribute, a fixed sum for your support has arisen from the same cause by which you have been reduced — I am at this moment pressed on the Corning note, which was discounted for you after Gansevoort's failure; & which I am unable to pay, without great sacrifice — & the large debt due by you to the State Bank, the payment of which I was obliged to guaranty, remains unpaid — under the circumstances, is it reasonable that I should be heavier laden with debt & responsibility — when our brother Herman has not incurred any responsibility for you —
>
> I have been expecting brother Herman daily for some time past — I know that he sincerely laments your situation & that his kind intentions towards you are delayed by his own situation —
>
> Money has not for many years been more scarce than it is at present — I enclose payable to your order my check, for Fifty dollars & wish you to sign & return to me the enclosed receipt.

This was what Herman carried north to Lansingburgh on foot, grimly, for he knew the tenor if not the specific wording by the time he left his uncle.

About this time Herman found a job teaching in Greenbush, across the Hudson from Albany, at the Greenbush & Schodack Academy. Some idea of the school may be gained from an article on 26 October 1839 in an Albany paper, *Southwick's Family Newspaper:*

> We announce with pleasure that this highly respectable Literary and Scientific Institution, has been recently placed under the care of the Rev. Peter S. Williamson. . . . He is one of the best Mathematicians and Linguists. . . . There are two distinct departments — male and female — and every necessary preparation for the success of each. We have only to add, that the situation is a delightful one, for the enjoyment of pleasant prospects, pure air, and wholesome exercise out of doors in the summer; and in winter, an enlightened and hospitable neighborhood, for the enjoyment of social intercourse within doors.

Herman probably looked respectable enough for this job, several rungs up the academic ladder from Sikes, for his mother and Helen would not have let him teach in unsuitable garments. He seldom looked like a Christian, Gansevoort groused later, disapproving of his tendency to go unshaven and let his hair grow long and wild, but in the surviving letters no one in the family criticizes his appearance at the time. How much indoor "social intercourse" Herman had in that enlightened and hospitable neighborhood is not known, but it was probably minimal. He may not have bothered to call on Maria's cousin Mrs. Volkert Douw, who lived there in Greenbush, for she is not mentioned in surviving correspondence for this period. Eli James Murdock Fly's family lived in Greenbush, but during the week Fly (as the Melville family called him) was in Albany, in Uncle Peter's office. Herman found someone to board with, not the Fly family, on credit, but undoubtedly saved money by taking meals only five or six days a week. On Friday afternoons he went up to Lansingburgh (fifteen or so miles away), usually on foot, part way in the dark, so as to live more cheaply and be with his family. Often he went by Albany to pick up mail from any friends or members of the family, and at times took his friend Fly with him for what we would call a weekend (the term did not exist, although the conditions necessary for its invention were rapidly emerging, especially in England).

Nothing is known of any literary efforts Herman may have made in his leisure hours, although attention has been called to a sketch in the Lansing-burgh *Democratic Press* on 16 November entitled "The Death Craft" and signed "Harry the Reefer." The prose is conventionally sensational, no worse than Herman had written in the spring:

> A heavy hand was laid upon my shoulder — a loud laugh rung in my ear, it was the Mate. "See, see!" — "THE DEATH CRAFT!" He sprang away from me with one giant bound, and with a long, long shriek, that even now haunts me, wildly flung himself into the sea.
>
> Great God! there she lay, covered with barnacles, the formation of years — her sails unbent — a blood-red flag streaming from her mast-head — at her jib-boom-end hanging suspended by its long, dark hair, a human head covered with congelated [coagulated?] gore and firmly griping between its teeth a rusty cutlass! Her yards were painted black, and at each of their arms hung dangling a human skeleton, whiter than polished ivory and glistening in the fierce rays of the sun!

Whoever wrote the piece probably took no more time on it than Herman would have taken; there is no reason it could not have been his and no reason to think no one else could have written it. He was not the only literary sailor in the Hudson River valley (even assuming the author was a sailor).

Herman would have seen "The Death Craft," but unless he read it in pride of authorship he would have found more interest in the reprinting in the Troy *Budget* on 28 November from the November *Democratic Review* of a major pronouncement on the subject of an American national literature,

"The Great Nation of Futurity." He encountered this fervid appeal, now or later, from one source or another. It was in a genre that had flourished during the past decade, but this may have been one of the first such pieces Herman saw, as well as a particularly eloquent example:

> And our literature! — Oh, when will it breathe the spirit of our republican institutions? When will it be imbued with the God-like aspiration of intellectual freedom — the elevating principle of equality? When will it assert its national independence, and speak the soul — the heart of the American people? Why cannot our literati comprehend the matchless sublimity of our position amongst the nations of the world — our high destiny — and cease bending the knee to foreign idolatry, false tastes, false doctrines, false principles? When will they be inspired by the magnificent scenery of our own world, imbue the fresh enthusiasm of a new heaven and a new earth, and soar upon the expanded wings of truth and liberty? . . . Why . . . do our authors aim at no higher degree of merit, than a successful imitation of English writers of celebrity?

Rather than weighing the strengths of the argument, Herman may have assented unthinkingly to the idea that American literature should one day breathe the spirit of the democratic institutions of the United States. Later he echoed this phrasing, from this source or elsewhere; later, also, he boggled at the notion that there was an immediate and necessary relationship between magnificent scenery and magnificent prose and poetry — a notion sometimes simplified into the claim that a country with waterfalls as great as Niagara must produce a literature commensurately great.

In the fall of 1839 the anti-rent agitation, now directed against the younger Stephen Van Rensselaer, the son of the "Last Patroon," reached the point of armed resistance to the sheriff, who acted as an agent of the Van Rensselaer family. (In the first chapter of *Moby-Dick* Melville made his narrator hint that he came from "an old established family in the land," such as "the Van Rensselaers, or Randolphs, or Hardicanutes.") On 3 December the Albany County sheriff led a posse against anti-renters, but found the road to Reidsville, southwest of Albany, blocked by some fifteen hundred men mounted on farm horses; the posse retreated to Albany in the dark. On 9 December the militia called out by Governor William H. Seward marched triumphantly into Reidsville but found no anti-renters to attack. During the conflict, on 6 December 1839, the *Argus* printed a letter Stephen Van Rensselaer had written on the second, in which he quoted some of the grievances listed by "a committee of the Tenants of the Western Towns of the Manor of said Stephen Van Rensselaer, Esq." — a phrasing that bore out what the American Lady had written in the *Memoirs* Gansevoort had read, that the

Van Rensselaers really were "like German princes." These were the grievances. In the old times, a tenant could pay a year's rent on a plot of 160 acres
by giving the Patroon twenty-odd bushels of wheat, a day's services with
carriage and team, and four fowls, but now, when the soil had been exhausted, it had become "extremely difficult for many of the tenants to support their families and pay their rents, without involving themselves and
posterity in extreme peril and hardship." In addition, "the many reservations
and restrictions" in the leases ("quarter sales, all streams of water, mines and
minerals, right of ways or roads, timber, &c. &c.") were "most grievous and
burdensome."

Traveling north and south, between Greenbush and Lansingburgh, usually by way of Albany, Herman did not encounter the armed conflict, or even
blocked roads or threatening bands of men. Like the rest of the family, however, he was inevitably caught up in this political-social crisis centered on his
own living cousins and derived from the ducal privileges granted his own ancestor, Killian Van Rensselaer. For Herman the emotions were complex. He
felt pride in heroic ancestry and in the almost incredible survival of feudal terms of ownership into the democratic present. But any pride in the exalted fortune of members of the family was poisoned by the reality: his own
mother was a direct descendant of Killian Van Rensselaer, yet she was griev-
ously impoverished with no means of assuring the future happiness and
prosperity of her posterity. Herman's own Van Rensselaer blood was then
unaccompanied with Van Rensselaer wealth or any other personal intimacy
with the Van Rensselaer cousins. A decade later, some of that complex emotion went into his satirical portrayal of Redburn, where the narrator, grown
older, reflects on his younger self: "there is no misanthrope like a boy disappointed," a boy blighted into "that desperation and recklessness of poverty
which only a pauper knows" (ch. 2). Almost worse than the condition of a
lifelong pauper was the plight of a boy who had been cherished until his
"father became a bankrupt, and died," and his mother ceased to be "bright
and happy" (ch. 7). Melville in 1849 attributed these thoughts to the boy
Redburn: "what made it more bitter to me, was to think of how well off were
my cousins, who were happy and rich, and lived at home with my uncles and
aunts, with no thought of going to sea for a living" (ch. 7).

In *Redburn* (written in 1849) Melville did not mention the anti-rent disturbances, but in a part of *Pierre* written late in 1851, probably shortly before
the publication of *Moby-Dick*, Melville recalled this period from a different
point of view than the one he had held in 1839, for in the intervening years
the younger Stephen Van Rensselaer had become a second father to Augusta,
and the entire Melville family had become more or less intimate with some of
the grown-up Van Rensselaer children:

In midland counties of England they boast of old oaken dining-halls where three hundred men-at-arms could exercise of a rainy afternoon, in the reign of the Plantagenets. But our lords, the Patroons, appeal not to the past, but they point to the present. One will show you that the public census of a county, is but part of the roll of his tenants. Ranges of mountains, high as Ben Nevis or Snowdon, are their walls; and regular armies, with staffs of officers, crossing rivers with artillery, and marching through primeval woods, and threading vast rocky defiles, have been sent out to distrain upon three thousand farmer-tenants of one landlord, at a blow. (bk. 1, ch. 3)

Melville in 1851 was wrestling with the old aesthetic problem, just how to elevate American characters in literature to a status anything like as exalted as the height of their ranges of mountains, and self-pity was far from him.

That December of 1839 money woes again united the banished widows of Waterford and Lansingburgh. From Lansingburgh on 14 December Maria wrote an account to Peter of her schoolteacher son. Herman, she declared optimistically, "is now doing well and will be able to allow me from $150 to $200. a year," although, she acknowledged, he would "need nearly the whole of his first quarters salary after paying his board, to procure necessary clothing &c." Allan she hoped would soon make more than enough to pay for his clothing, and then would also be able to help her. Gansevoort she did not mention as a possible source of income, but neither did she mention him as needing funds from her. For the present, she looked to her brothers:

It cannot be possible that I am to be left by my two Brothers to struggle with absolute want, or be compelled to write painful truth-speaking letters, descriptions of our situation, to ward of[f] by a reluctant remittance, our present wants — *and how is that done,* by paying off every cent I receive to pay those I owe & in a few days to be poor again, untill necessity once more compels me to the same disagreeable duty—I can hear you say the times are hard, tis true — if I could postpone my wants untill the times become easy, I would do it with all my heart.

She added, "Shelter, food, & fuel, cannot be postponed—neither Shoes or the wearing of them to those in the habit of wearing them." Maria estimated her current expenses for herself and the five children at home as "less than fifty Dollars a month," which left "little for clothing, hardly anything." She did not keep a cook, but only "a woman of all work," at ten shillings a week, and the rest she and the children did among themselves. She added with justifiable pride, "I call myself a good manager." Without help from her brothers all she had to look forward to was to break up the family and disperse its members. "Brother Herman" she knew had no desire "of domesticating" them (his wife would have forbidden him to offer refuge to any of them), and she was blunt about Peter and his ailing wife: "you can best answer for yourself."

From Waterford on 16 December Mary Chandonette Gansevoort wrote to Peter, having "suffered every desperation" and become almost distracted — indeed, distraught, and frequently bedridden. The greatest cause of grief was having to take Stanwix out of school "for the want of means to pay his bill." Maria had lowered herself to say she was begging for charity, but Mary reminded Peter that her plight was due in large part to his keeping the estate unsettled (while he made his great investment in the ironically named Stanwix Hall): "Stanwix might certainly better have his little patrimony in his education, than any otherwise." In his own mind the widow-ridden Peter was trying to reestablish the family's financial security, which had been endangered by Allan Melvill's if not his brother Leonard Gansevoort's borrowings, but the time he needed to gain that security was precisely the time when the children ought to have been kept in school. He had to stave both the widows off — a task easier now that he had them out of Albany. Peter on 18 December offered Maria some temporary help, while pleading his own lack of funds: "You certainly, my dear Maria, are not aware of my pecuniary situation; pressed as I now am & have been for some time past, it is fortunate that thus far I have been able to prevent the commencement of suits & the foreclosure of mortgages." He told her bluntly that his disposition to aid her and her children had been "the principal cause of embarrassments" — that is, his own financial strain. Whatever he told Mary, she wrote him on 24 December asking funds for Stanwix's expenses: "He asks for his own Peter — nothing more; & not to spend for trifles — but for his bread & education."

Herman kept coming up to Lansingburgh on Friday nights, usually crossing the river (near where his father had crossed it on ice, for the last time) so as to see Allan and carry up any letters from him or others, and often he carried letters down to Albany on Sunday night before crossing the river again and walking on to Greenbush. As winter came on he equipped himself at the top, anyhow, for as Maria reminded Allan (early in February 1840), Herman had "a Fur Cap" so Allan could "put the Cloth one sent by Gansevoort in a sack to bring it up" — rather than offering it to Herman. On 6 December 1839 Herman came up with Fly, and Maria on the next day, Saturday, wrote Allan that his "Blue Coat" was ready and that she hoped Herman would carry it down, adding, "but if he & Fly walk, perhaps he will decline the Honor." In the midst of her distress she yet claimed to feel "cheered by Hermans prospects": "he appears to be interested in his occupation — he has a great charge, & deep responsibility is attached to the education of 60

Scholars, which I understand is the number usual during the greater part of the year." On 13 December Herman again walked up from Greenbush (arriving in the dark) so he could pass "Saturday and Sunday" at home (Maria wrote to Peter on the fourteenth). If all went well, Herman might live, though not thrive, as a schoolmaster. As a teacher at the Greenbush & Schodack Academy he might dream, despite his irregular education, about a future across the Hudson, perhaps even a post at the Albany Academy.

Dispersed as it was, the family kept in close communication, thanks in large part to Herman, the "family post-man," as Helen called him (5 January 1840). As 1840 began Herman was still teaching conscientiously at Greenbush, but at the end of almost every week he trekked first to Albany for mail and small necessities for his mother, then on to Lansingburgh. While there he saw the thanks William Lamb had put into the 4 January issue of the Lansingburgh *Democratic Press* for the "few literary friends who have favored us with the pencillings of their thoughts," but under the circumstances he had little time and less inclination to contribute any more fragments from his writing-desk. Because he had the enormous responsibility of sixty scholars and was in residence only during the school days, he most likely saw little of his fellow teachers outside of the academy, and indeed may have seen few people outside of school except the family of his landlord or landlady and any fellow boarders in the house. After a time Maria may have asked him to make himself known to her cousin Mrs. Volkert Douw, and he may have found in Greenbush a number of new friends with whom he spent hours valuable and pleasurable to himself and to them. Yet not a single record of his life there has been located. Curiously enough, none of his students or fellow teachers seems to have come forward with reminiscences after he became famous, unlike the Berkshire gossips who kept alive anecdotes about a student rebellion in his class at Sikes.

For the moment Gansevoort worried from afar about "the *present condition* of the family" — particularly what if anything Uncle Peter and Uncle Herman had done to relieve his mother (as he wrote Allan on 21 January 1840). More practically, he did his best to direct the lives of his younger brothers. He wrote Herman at Greenbush and sent him New York City newspapers there, and knew of course that anything he sent his mother would be retained for Herman to read also. As usual Herman was a poor correspondent and in all probability was heeding few of Gansevoort's wise injunctions; even worse, his silence made Gansevoort worry that he might not be receiving letters. Frustrated at not evoking an answer from the schoolteacher, Gansevoort analyzed Herman's character in a letter to Allan on 21 January — an analysis based on his own reading in John Gibson Lockhart's new biography of his late father-in-law, Sir Walter Scott:

Give my best love to Herman — I sometimes send him papers — Does he ever
call at the Greenbush Post Office? — Tell him, to enquire at the aforesaid
place on or before the 1st prox, as I hereby promise him a letter — I know no
other reason for his remissness but laziness — not general laziness by any
means — but that laziness which consists in an unwillingness to exert oneself
in doing at a particular time, that which ought then to be done — or, [here
Gansevoort wrote and crossed out "to speak more plainly"] — to illustrate —
that disinclination to perform the special duty of the hour which so constantly
beset one of the most industrious men of the age — Sir Walter Scott.

Gansevoort was, as usual, an acute observer of the character of his brother,
who later confessed (25 March 1848) to "a sad failing," procrastination,
though he may never have analyzed this particular failing quite so closely as
his more objective brother.

   Allan (still in Dudley Burwell's office) was altogether more tractable than
Herman, although forgetful. He flatteringly asked Gansevoort for "a course
of reading," something Herman would never have done, forgetting (despite
the memory of brass Allan Melvill had attributed to him) that Gansevoort
had given him just such a list the previous spring. Gansevoort approved his
reading "the life of Franklin — a good book," and further suggested: "I shall
be pleased to have you devote your leisure hours to reading American History. Grimshaw's Hist of the U. S. or Willards Republic of America will form
a good introduction. The former is preferable. Do not forget your Geography & Arithmetic. They are among the fundamentals, which must be
known — but above all & before all, give your attention to the business of the
office, & to your own bodily health." Gansevoort gave very specific guidance
for Allan's pursuing his legal studies, pushing him to bear in mind the wise
words "that nothing conduces so much to the desired end, in winning the
confidence & even personal attachment of one's clients as being found in
emergencies, to be 'a sound & ready Practice lawyer.'" Although Burwell
raised Allan's salary in March, Allan could not manage to repay some debt he
had incurred — probably only of a few dollars, but troublesome to Gansevoort, who out of bitter experience advised him: "Avoid all debt & pecuniary
obligation of every kind as you would pestilence." The nature of Gansevoort's lost letters to Herman may be inferred from the surviving letters to
Allan.

   Despite the fears she expressed to Peter, Maria did not have to disperse
her remaining household of four daughters and her ten-year-old son in 1840,
but she took measures to prevent her two daughters of marriageable age
from losing most by the family's exile: she redoubled her efforts to keep them
in contact with her best Albany connections. Neither Caroline Yates Taylor

nor her husband were blood relatives, as far as we know, but early in December 1839 Maria told Allan to tell her "dear Mrs Taylor" that she would promise to try "to persuade Augusta to pass the Holidays with her." From Manhattan, Gansevoort, aside from being responsible for guiding Herman, Allan, and Thomas (who would soon be taller than Kate and Fanny), like his mother was profoundly concerned about the vulnerability of the girls, who lacked opportunities for meeting suitable young men under circumstances likely to lead to marriage proposals, and in any case had no dowries at all to bring to a bridegroom, unlike the Ten Eyck bride whose ten thousand dollars had so impressed Gansevoort and his mother six years before. Reinforcing his mother's instructions, Gansevoort in his letters to Allan regularly asked to be remembered kindly to the Van Vechtens, to Cousin Maggie (the elegant Margaret Van Rensselaer Douw, not the drab Maggey Wynkoop), and to Caroline Yates Taylor. Mother and oldest son, acting in concert from opposite directions (with Herman as weekly conduit), constantly reminded Allan of his duty as representative of the family to all their Albany connections. Months later, in November 1840, Gansevoort also reminded Allan of his duty to his sisters: "You are of course uniformly kind & attentive to Helen, during her stay in Albany. In the present situation of society a lady is very much dependant upon the stronger sex for the power to pursue her own plans & render herself comfortable & at ease. Both Duty & affection conspire to render you a good & assiduously attentive brother to Helen. My best love & a kiss to her." As usual, he sent his love to the mayor's wife, Mrs. Van Vechten, and her daughter Hetty, with the message that he hoped to see them again soon. For Maria and for Gansevoort, keeping up appearances, keeping up contacts, meant being ready for a change of fortune when it came at last.

The very sick and very pregnant Mary Sanford Gansevoort had a staff of servants, but she needed the loving help the Melville nieces could give her surviving children, Henry and Catherine (Kitty), and needed their attentiveness to her in the last month of her current pregnancy. In his extremity Peter himself went to Lansingburgh, around New Year's Day of 1840, and returned with Augusta. In a letter of 5 January, Maria gave her second daughter excellent advice: "I hope you will pass your time pleasantly, endeavor to make yourself *agreeable & useful* to your Aunt Mary, I know you intend to do right, but you oftimes require a hint — you must endeavor to be promt to hear & to assist — not hurried, but easy & natural." Since Maria never wrote carelessly about her children's characters and never invented faults that needed correction, we can assume that Augusta was, at this point, good hearted but still not confident enough of her value and her skills to offer just the right service, coolly and deftly, almost before the patient knew it was needed. There was room for improvement, and improvement would assure that the family in Albany would not forget the exiles in Lansingburgh. Her own desire to improve and Maria's specific maternal criticisms worked their way, so that Augusta soon ceased to require such hints. The Albany family so important to Augusta's future included distant cousins (but cousins several times over), such as the Van Rensselaers, for under Maria's guidance Augusta was becoming intimate with Cornelia Paterson Van Rensselaer (daughter of the younger Stephen Van Rensselaer), a year and a half Augusta's junior. Early in February Peter and Mary Gansevoort's child was born—their own "little Herman," as Maria wrote to Peter on 11 February. She offered a solemn wish that the boy might "live to be a blessing" to Peter "in this life." With education of her own children so high in her mind, she managed to be a loving (and not ironic) sister in further hoping: "may God enable you to educate him in such a manner, that his mind may be early in life disciplined to pursue every good and virtuous path with instinctive knowledge."

In Manhattan Gansevoort regularly took stock of his physical condition, as people learn to do after serious illnesses (what was wrong was not simply an ailment of the "ancle"), and in the fall of 1839 or the winter he conferred with Herman on what his ocean voyage had been like, and decided that Herman had been so robust after his trip to Liverpool that an ocean voyage just might restore the older brother to vigorous health. Throughout 1840 Gansevoort brooded on the possible therapeutic benefits for himself of an ocean cruise, in warmer waters than Herman had sailed, and as a passenger, since it was inconceivable that he could survive as a sailor. There was no immediate prospect of his realizing such a hope, but Maria (writing to Augusta on 8 January 1841) referred to it as a "long anticipated plan."

In his commitment to being ready for fortune, Gansevoort in 1840 was pursuing his course of self-improvement with intense dedication. He found himself in Manhattan early in the year without his 1837 *Index Rerum* (apparently the first one he filled), and was grateful when Maria found someone to carry it down to him. Throughout 1840 Gansevoort shifted the focus of his notes in his current *Index Rerum* to legal matters, without abandoning his interest in an alternative route to fame, a literary career. Under "Authors" he made a cross reference to his 1839 volume (lost before the surviving two were deposited in the Berkshire Athenaeum in the 1950s): "Authors . . . hints to concerning the correction of their Mss I[ndex] R[erum] V 3 p 260." Purposefully, in the *Library of Useful Knowledge* he read the *Treatise on the Principles, Practice & History of Commerce*; in Roscoe's *Lives of Eminent British Lawyers* he read the life of Sir Edward Coke; he read *Civil Office & Political Ethics*, McCulloch's *Treatise on Commerce*, Jeremy Bentham's observation on the

Bankruptcy Court, Kent's commentaries on bankruptcy and insolvency laws, and many others. He scanned the papers for useful articles, noting such items as a speech of Major Auguste Davezac (a hero of the Battle of New Orleans) in "Bell's New Era" for 29 February 1840 and (in the fall) word on a rising fictionalist: "Dickens, for a scant biography of, with a criticism on his work, — see the New World Sep 26 1840 — from which it appears that he commenced writing for the Magazines in 1834 (the year in which he was married) but did not attract much attention till 1836 — showing an extremely rapid progress to the high position which he now (1840) occupies." Extremely rapid progress to high position was the only kind of ascent that would do Gansevoort himself any good, now that he had lost so many years during which his lesser contemporaries had left him further and further behind. Gansevoort was devoting himself to his duties in Bradford's office, which included such chores as making out demurrer books, but he knew that such work would not afford the extremely rapid rise to high position which he needed to make. He must have despaired by now of Herman's ever making such a rise.

In New York City on 27 March 1840 Gansevoort was in the audience when his friend Alexander W. Bradford spoke earnestly at the purportedly nonpartisan Whig meeting ("Great Meeting at Masonic Hall — Mob Law Defied and Defeated"). No one said it out loud, but the purpose of the meeting was to protest the fact that Irish aliens were voting in increasing numbers: "All power springs from the people, and their determination is manifested in their elections. 'Fraud in elections is at the root of all wickedness in the government of a republic,' and as by illegal voting the very foundation head of our institutions may be corrupted, every consideration of justice and of public policy requires that an adequate remedy should be applied where this most dangerous of all political diseases exists." This was Bradford, as reported in the *Morning Courier and New-York Enquirer* on 28 March; the full text makes it clear that Bradford had spoken ploddingly: for Gansevoort, listening would have been agonizing had his thoughts not been outrunning Bradford's stolid delivery.

Uncle Peter had run for state senator on a "toleration" ticket in 1832, and Gansevoort himself would soon take a strongly pro-Irish stand. That the anti-Irish content of Bradford's speech did not matter and that even Bradford's leaden delivery did not matter is clear from Gansevoort's letter to Allan on 31 March, which Allan would routinely have shared with Herman, the guest of the Bradfords the year before: "The meeting was riotous to a great degree for more than an hour, but finally became quiet in the Hall, altho' outside the crowd & noise were immense. . . . The noise, tumult & high excitement of the scene made it very interesting. By to-day's mail I sent to Mamma a copy of the Courier containing Bradfords address. It occupies about a column of the paper & is a very creditable production. When you next go home, it would be well to look at it." Herman also had a chance to read the full text of the speech in Lansingburgh, and surely did so out of respect for his host and hostess in Manhattan the previous spring. Herman, like anyone who knew Gansevoort's love of the debating society and his joy in reading the Declaration of Independence on the Fourth of July, would have sensed just how dangerous the noise, tumult, and high excitement were. At the Masonic Hall Gansevoort had snuffed up a whiff of grapeshot so powerful that it transformed his life.

At Greenbush Herman was not the most desirable boarder, despite his family connection with the Van Rensselaers, who had given the county its name. He was, to speak plainly (as Gansevoort would have said), not paying his board, for the simple reason that the academy was not paying him for his services. Presumably he received some payment in the fall, when he needed a wardrobe proper for a teacher in a select school near the state capital, but the school had retrenched. On 3 April 1840, when he was hoping to be home the third week of the month, Gansevoort wrote to Allan about Herman, angry and fearful enough to be garrulous:

> Herman has not yet written me — Helen informs me in her last letter that he has not yet received any money for his services during the past winter — This is very singular conduct on the part of the Trustees of the institution — They surely cannot expect that any person will devote his time & attention to their interests, without at least receiving at the regularly appointed times, at least sufficient money to enable him to pay his daily expenses, particularly his board — the amount too is constantly increasing & becoming larger & consequently more difficult to provide for, with every ensuing week — & vice versa Herman is becoming more & more indebted for his board, & should he in the end be disappointed in receiving the sum that is due him for his winter services, will be so much the more difficult to pay.

Gansevoort's fevered imagination raced down possibilities horrible to contemplate, especially when he knew that the week after his visit his mother's quarterly rent would be due on the state's moving day, the first of May.

Guiltless as well as guileless, Herman felt mounting frustration, shame, and anger as the weeks passed with his wages unpaid and his board-bill growing. Despairing of ever earning a living in New York, he and his friend Eli Fly compared notes and began talking of going west together. Fly was content enough with Peter Gansevoort's treatment of him, as Allan had never been, but he thought he might advance more rapidly in a new country.

Herman had heard favorable reports of Illinois, and in any case was lonely for his Uncle Thomas and Aunt Mary and some of his cousins, although not so very lonely as to have kept up contact with Robert, who was on the farm. At almost twenty-one he had failed repeatedly in Massachusetts and New York, so he could hardly do worse than go west to rise in the young state of Illinois with the help of his kinsman, Major Melvill.

9

West to Seek His Fortune

1840

Learning procures Preferment,
Preferment gains money, and
Money commands all things.

"Allan Melvills Book," 1796

IN LANSINGBURGH AND GREENBUSH, everything fell apart at once. The money from her brothers in December and January had given Maria some respite through to moving day of 1840, although at that time she owed her servant $60 — roughly a year's wages at $16.25 a quarter, as she wrote Peter on 16 May. Herman had given her $3 the day before, which met a small local bill, but she was $150 in debt in her household account (quite aside from her gigantic debt to the Bank of New York), and two weeks late with her rent: "Mr Knickerbocker has written me a note that he must be paid by the 20th & must not be disappointed, they are an inquisitive little Family, with very contracted minds, and the most unpleasant of all beings to be indebted to." She had still more bad news, about the Greenbush Academy: "Hermans School is to be discontinued next week for want of funds untill the winter — he thinks of going far-west, as nothing offers for him here — Oh that the Lord may strengthen me to bear all my troubles, & be pleased to sustain me under them." Having already written to her brother Herman three times without answer, Maria had intended to go to Albany, but now felt so "unequal to the exertion" that she sent her son Herman down with her letter instead, leaving him to decide whether or not to tell his uncle about the Greenbush Academy before or after Peter read the letter.

Repeatedly Herman had gone out on foot (and possibly by stage or canal boat) hunting for work, and by river to Manhattan for his ocean voyage, always taking what work he could find, surely more short-term jobs than we have record of. This lengthening list was not merely a sign of restlessness or irresponsibility. Rather, he was an unfortunate fellow who had come to maturity penniless and poorly educated, in the worst of a national depression, when many industrious and well-qualified young men could not find steady

work. Of Herman Melville's now-famous contemporaries, young Walter
Whitman lost his newspaper job in Manhattan and retreated to Long Island,
and in Baltimore young Fred Bailey, later Frederick Douglass, a slave hired
out as a caulker, was brutally beaten by white laborers who feared they would
lose work to him. If Uncle Peter had gotten him a job on the canal, Herman
might have gone through life as a surveyor and engineer. If the Greenbush &
Schodack Academy had paid him a living wage, he might have spent his life
there or in another academy, and Maria might have moved from Lansingburgh to be with him, nearer Albany. Instead, the Greenbush Academy
failed, as Maria had told Peter, without paying Herman all he was due. Even
then he did what he could, and in late May he taught at a school in Brunswick, just northeast of Troy, but he could not collect six dollars he had
earned. By then he was thinking more and more seriously of seeking whatever fortune lay in the West, and by then his friend Eli James Murdock Fly
was as keen on the venture as himself.

    Shortly after Maria reported that Herman was thinking of going far west
(that is, Illinois), perhaps after the Brunswick job proved a fiasco, Herman
and Fly made their decision. The young men were not going for an excursion
or to vagabondize a little: they were going west like thousands of other young
men, to seek their fortunes. Fly was an excellent scrivener as well as a law
clerk, and Herman might get some work with his surveying skills. Failing
that he could always teach school. Two years older than Herman, Fly seemed
to have done more with his life, having gained much knowledge of the law
during the nearly five years he had worked for Peter Gansevoort. From that
time one vignette survives of a characteristic mannerism. In 1838 little
Henry Sanford Gansevoort, with his mother in Flushing, Long Island, where
former chancellor Nathan Sanford was dying, woke up from his nap and
directed his mother what to write to his father: "he says that I must tell you
that he has a great big large stick he is showing us how Mr Fly holds his [pen]
and puts in his mouth when he is done writing." That is about the extent of
our sense of the personal behavior of Herman's closest friend, the clerk
whom Peter Gansevoort earnestly wanted to keep in his employ. Peter went
so far as to make what Fly on 2 June called a "very liberal offer," even as he
declined it: "I have had, for some weeks past a very strong desire to try my
fortune in the Western territories of this country. — I believe that a young
man, with temperance & perseverance joined with my knowledge of the legal
profession, will succeed much better in a new state, than in this." The liberal
offer must have been higher than the $75 a quarter Peter had been paying Fly
since his salary raise on 1 June 1839 — twice what the bank had paid Herman.
The decision had been made: Fly (and Herman) would "depart from Albany
on Thursday for the West." There was nothing light-hearted or frivolous in

the decision as Fly described it to his employer: "I am aware that I am taking a very singular step, and it may be a fatal one, — but I am prepared for the worst." In their daring venture Fly and Herman expected the help of Thomas Melvill, whom Herman assumed was, after three years, well established in Galena.

During the weeks that Herman and Fly had been thinking about going west together, they remained ignorant of circumstances which would have dashed their plans. Early in January 1840 Thomas Melvill had written to Lemuel Shaw that Robert "seems to think that he will be but vegetating, by remaining longer on the Farm, without capital to improve it, as is needfull, and that it will be better for him to come out to the West, next Season, instead of carrying out the Lease." There in Illinois, Thomas had reported, business was "in a most lamentable condition," but he thought nevertheless that Robert might as well come. Almost simultaneously, on 11 January, Robert had written Shaw from Pittsfield that he would "leave this place for Illinois, the ensuing summer or fall," so he could be near his "old father in his declining days who is broken down by age, and misfortune and who cannot have many more years to live." Thomas Jr. was sixty-four, and failing.

On 15 March Henry Colt, the agent appointed to rent or sell the farm, reported to Shaw that the farm was "in a very sad condition, as regards fences and buildings — A grate deal must be laid out in fencing, to make it at all tenantable." He blandly added: "I also find that there has been cut, the past Winter, not far from 100 cords of wood, which I suppose Mr Robert Melville had a *right to do*, or he would not have done it I presume. A part of which lays at the stump now. I have forbid several individuals cutting any more until I here from you." Knowing Colt would report his dishonesty to Judge Shaw, on 16 March, Robert Melvill, also shaky of spelling and syntax, confessed his shameful predicament to the trustees, Lemuel Shaw and John D'Wolf: "After I had come to this determination [to go west] I found that from the change of the times I could not raise money sufficient to carry me on to Illinois. And to raise that money I have been guilty of an act which, to say the least, must degrade me in your sight that is by selling a quantity of wood off of the farm contrary to the terms of the lease." Robert acknowledged the act "to be highly reprehensible" and "a breach of good faith between men," but offered "in extenuation" the argument that he had lost "at least two hundred dollars by the farm" and had to have money if he were to go to Illinois.

Shamelessly Robert appealed to the respect due the Melvill name: "I wish you Gentlemen by the esteem which you bear for my father and which [you] bore for my Grandfather before him that you will grant me a letter to Mr

Colt that he may give me leave to take the wood off which is yet remaining on the land and cut." Groveling, but with an eye to his object, Robert threw himself on Shaw's mercy:

> Unless this arrangement can be made (as I have already received pay for the wood) it will cause me an ammount of trouble which perhaps I hardly dream of both in a pecuniary, point of view and in the disgrace which must attend me should the circumstances of the transaction become known. it has been a lesson to me which I shall never forget. I do not wish by any means to screen myself from the payment of the wood to the estate on the contrary I wish to pay for it the amount is 108 dollars this amount I will pay in the only way which it is in my power namely by giving my note if you wish it, I have a pair of Horses and a waggon which are worth three hundred dollars I will give you a mortgage of them, and it may be placed against the share which may fall to my lot when the estate comes to be divided.

A week later, Robert wrote again, hoping to induce Shaw to believe that it was not extravagance that led him to sell the wood, but the low wages he had earned as a hired man ("9 months at 10 dollars per month") and his wife's ill health. Probably, he said, he would leave Pittsfield "about the 15th of June ensuing," three years from the time his father left. Very soon after he wrote this letter, Robert in all likelihood heard from Galena some diluted account of disastrous events that shook his resolve to go there.

Uncle Thomas had hardly started to clerk for Hezekiah Gear in 1837 before he began stealing from the till. As time passed Gear's new wife, Deborah, saw or guessed what was happening, and in 1839, if not earlier, repeatedly tried to make her husband dismiss Melvill. Gear rejected any suspicions of the son of the Hero of the Tea Party until he caught Thomas in the act, sometime in March 1840. When Hezekiah and Deborah Gear confronted the thief in the second-floor parlor of the Gear home, the following melodramatic dialogue occurred, according to Gear family tradition, recorded early in the twentieth century by a then-elderly Gear daughter:

> THOMAS MELVILL JR: "Oh, Captain, spare me."
>
> HEZEKIAH GEAR: "You must make some restitution."
>
> THOMAS MELVILL JR: "I can't, for the money is spent. It's been going on for years."
>
> HEZEKIAH GEAR: "There is nothing to do. I could send you to prison for life, but that would not bring back the money. [Dramatic pause before continuing.] Major, for the sake of your good family and for the sake of your gray hair, I'll not punish you, but I never want to lay eyes on you again."

Thereafter Thomas Melvill Jr. endeavored, however ineffectually, to avoid the eyes of his betrayed benefactor as they both went about the streets of the small town.

When Robert learned whatever he learned (at least, that his father had lost his job), he temporized further with the judge, not wanting to tell Shaw why he could not go west. On 28 July he declared that his "feelings" would carry him to Illinois, "but prudence forbids it," for the journey might kill his ailing wife. Herman may have learned in the spring that Robert was planning to go west and may even have thought of going with him, without knowing why Robert was reluctant just at that time to appear in Galena, but chances are that Herman and Robert were not in touch. Certainly Robert did not warn him away from Illinois, where his father was making what efforts he could to earn a little money. In June Thomas Jr. ran an announcement in the *North Western Gazette & Galena Advertiser,* billing himself as "Notary Public, for Jo Daviess Country, Ills. and Commissioner for taking acknowledgment of Deeds, depositions, &c. for the States of Massachusetts and Maine." He was at the same time listed as "Secretary and Treasurer of the Chamber of Commerce." True to his word, Gear had not exposed him. Thomas Jr. in a letter to Shaw on 26 June found a plausible way of accounting for the change in his condition — blaming it on the Panic:

> Here, as elsewhere, the effects of the policy & measures, of the past & present administrations, are *most severely felt* — Not the less so, for being more tardy —
>
> Few houses, doing business in 1834.5.6. & 7. have been able to withstand it. The one, with which I was, is among the Number. In March last, I found it necessary, and for the interest of both parties, to retire — & with some (to me,) considerable loss.

Unspoken was the truth, that in March Gear had fired him, and that "an agency establishment" was "the only kind of business" open to him. Thomas Jr. informed Shaw that money in Galena was "almost unobtainable in any manner, or *at any rate* — It may be said, *not to exist.*" The "political excitement" was, however, "*great,*" almost the only business at the present. He predicted "a large majority for Harrison in Illinois," where the Whigs were profiting from resentment of new immigrants, all of whom, Thomas Jr. thought, whether subversive Papists or good Protestant stock, were there taking jobs from native-born Americans in hard times. None of this was known to the New York Melvilles.

In the last rush of preparation for departure to Illinois, Herman was much in Greenbush. There was some badinage between Herman and Fly's sister Harriet, who, now or earlier, inscribed her name in different places in Herman's much-read prize volume from the Albany Academy, *The Carcanet,* in which Herman had copied three stanzas of the sixteenth air of *The Beggar's Opera* ("Over the hills and far away"). Transcribing one of her notes ("I wonder who we are to have 10 June 1840 l —— H —— ."), William H. Gilman suggested the possibility of a romance, but this is more likely teasing. The girl may have made that inscription on 3 June, a week before the tenth, just before their departure, in playful but nervous concern about what might be happening a week in the future. By then, what might have occurred to the pair of travelers? who might be at the Fly house instead of them? In his final preparations for departure Herman addressed a receipt for six dollars to the Brunswick school district and signed it, hoping someone in the family could collect the money for him, but no one ever did, and the receipt stayed in the family, dated in Herman's hand "Lansingburgh June 5th 1840," perhaps a hasty mistake for 4 June, the day he and Fly seem to have gone aboard a canal boat for the three-day journey on the Erie Canal from Albany to Buffalo.

A decade later in *Moby-Dick* (ch. 54, "The Town-Ho's Story"), Melville, creating a breathing space in his momentous narrative within a narrative, let his character Ishmael respond to demands from young Peruvian dons, who want to know what he means by referring to a Canaller. The result was one of Melville's great set-pieces of description:

> For three hundred and sixty miles, gentlemen, through the entire breadth of the state of New York; through numerous populous cities and most thriving villages; through long, dismal, uninhabited swamps, and affluent, cultivated fields, unrivalled for fertility; by billiard-room and bar-room; through the holy-of-holies of great forests; on Roman arches [the great viaducts, triumphs of engineering] over Indian rivers; through sun and shade; by happy hearts or broken; through all the wide contrasting scenery of those noble Mohawk counties; and especially, by rows of snow-white chapels, whose spires stand almost like milestones, flows one continual stream of Venetianly corrupt and often lawless life.

Ishmael describes himself as having been befriended by a Canaller when he was himself a vagabond on the canal—just possibly an indication that Melville and Fly were encouraged in some way by one of the "abundantly and picturesquely wicked" Canallers. Melville all his life remembered some of the types he met on the trip, including "the dandified Billy-be-Dam, an amusing character all but extinct" by the late 1880s, when some memory of the canal intruded as Melville was first grasping hold of his prose account of the hanged sailor he had already written a poem about, Billy Budd.

Melville left no description of his experiences on the canal, but accounts by other travelers suggest very much what he saw. Three years earlier a young New Hampshire man, Gansevoort's age, Thomas Low Nichols, had made the trip from Albany to Buffalo, and wrote about it in a book he published in London in 1864, *Forty Years of American Life*. Nichols, who later played a walk-on role that decisively altered Herman's life and saw a good deal of him for a time, made it clear that the captain of any canal-packet was expected to be ostentatious, vulgar in manners, gaudy in dress, confident of his powers to impress the female passengers he placed at table on his left and right hands. His fake diamonds were too large, his "waistcoats of too loud a pattern," but since he was an American everything would tone down as he rose in the world.

With his knack for sketching characters and settings, Nichols is a source of reliable details about a typical journey on a canal-packet the length of the Erie Canal:

> The canal-packet is out of date [in the early 1860s], and would be considered very slow in these days; but it was not a bad way of getting through the world to one who had his whole life before him, who was fond of beautiful scenery, and was in no hurry. Our sharp, narrow, gaily painted boat was drawn by three fine horses, each ridden by a smart boy, and we glided along at the regular pace of five miles an hour. A greater speed washed away the embankments, and was not permitted. But when opposition boats were running they sometimes doubled this pace, and the boats would run on the swell wave they had first created, as fast as the horses could gallop.

The routine, which varied little from boat to boat, was for passengers to rise early and make their "ablutions" in the little washroom (probably a single one, shared by gentlemen and ladies). Aghast, Charles Dickens in his *American Notes for General Circulation* (London: Chapman & Hall, 1842), described the "washing accommodations" on a Pennsylvania canal boat as "primitive": "There was a tin ladle chained to the deck, with which every gentleman who thought it necessary to cleanse himself (some were superior to this weakness), fished the dirty water out of the canal, and poured it into a tin basin, secured in like manner. There was also a jack-towel. And, hanging up before a little looking-glass in the bar, in the immediate vicinity of the bread and cheese and biscuits, were a public comb and hair-brush." Customarily, Nichols made clear, the passengers would go on deck "for fresh air and a promenade" around the luggage piled in the center of the boat; on this June 1840 trip little enough of luggage belonged to Herman and Fly. Vigorous youths could get off and take care of some of their more personal needs behind trees or bushes then trot along after the horses for exercise — brisk enough if sustained for more than a few miles.

Food was prepared in a "little closet aft," and meals were announced by an unnecessarily loud ringing of a hand-bell by the steward (a job allocated to a free Negro), and served on the long narrow table in the cabin. Breakfast according to Nichols was "hot Indian-corn bread, milk-toast, hot rolls, beefsteaks, veal cutlets, fricasseed chickens, fried potatoes, ham and eggs, apple sauce, and all the rest, washed down with many cups of hot coffee," adequate even for a young man who had stopped growing only recently. Dinner, at midday, about one, consisted typically of "Roast turkey, chickens, beef, ham, vegetables, pies, and puddings," and there was a substantial tea at six, with hours of daylight left for viewing the sunset, on a clear day. According to Dickens, breakfast and supper were identical: "tea, coffee, bread, butter, salmon, shad, liver, steak, potatoes, pickles, ham, chops, black-puddings, and sausages," and dinner varied only in the absence of tea and coffee. Writing after he had been to art galleries in England, Nichols wished that J. M. W. Turner could have seen the sunsets, for only he could have done them justice (this, in 1864, was the mark of an independent aesthetic sensibility close akin to Melville's own). The long cabin was lighted at night for reading or card-playing, while the boat glided on "with soft washing and gurgling sounds," until bedtime: "At ten o'clock a heavy curtain is drawn across the cabin, separating the ladies' portion from the rest; berths are put up along the sides of the cabin, the lights are diminished, and the wash and gurgle lull us to sleep."

Nichols recalled that there were female passengers on board, even, typically, "a pretty girl going to Wisconsin, having and needing no protector" — a comment that establishes such a girl as being of a lower social class than the Melvilles, whose female members, as Herman knew, would hardly take even a stagecoach between Troy and Pittsfield without a male escort. A girl on a canal-packet may have been quite respectable and may have behaved decorously, but she was of the new free American pioneering class, not the sort of girl Melville's mother invited into her parlor. Every farmer had the right to build a bridge low enough to crush the unwary upright passenger. For any pretty girl going to Wisconsin or elsewhere, canal-boat flirtations were unavoidable, since every few miles, at the cry "Bridge!" (or, more direful still, "Low bridge!"), masculine protectors made themselves ready to pull every young woman down out of harm's way. "What a nice journey it was!" Nichols exclaimed in 1864, thinking back two decades:

> We never forget it. A thousand landscapes fill the gallery of our memory. We have passed over dizzy viaducts, and through miles of deep-cut ravines; we have ascended steep hills through a succession of locks. At Lockport we are gently lifted up the very precipice over which Niagara pours fifty miles away, and are even with Lake Erie, whose waters have floated us up, up, up to their own level.

And so gliding along the Tonewanda Creek, and by the great rushing
Niagara river, which seemed hurrying down to the foaming rapids and the
tremendous fall below, we floated into Buffalo.

Burnt by the British in the War of 1812, by 1840 Buffalo, with some twenty
thousand inhabitants, was what visionaries like De Witt Clinton and his clerk
Uncle Peter had foreseen it would become—a western metropolis.

   Under no time constraints, able to fend for themselves, Melville and Fly
would have been drawn irresistibly to Niagara Falls, just as Melville in Constantinople sought out, almost two decades later, the most superb views, but
there is no record of a side trip to see what was regarded as the greatest
natural wonder of the continent. In Buffalo itself they saw not only the
splendor of the new city but also the slums, so bad as to come to Nichols's
mind when surveying London's squalid Wapping section, and as to remind
Melville of Liverpool. The "steam-boat men, sailors, canallers, not to say
canaille, mingled with some of the wilder young clerks from the forwarding
houses and 'stores'" who drank and danced with rouged women, Nichols
recalled. One "tall, dark, handsome young man" rode each afternoon "on a
fine iron-grey saddle-horse," enjoying his recreation as he advertised himself; this "Apollo-like beauty of form and feature, the horseman of Main-
street," was Ned Christy, who at night played the tambourine in the first
blackface band, Christy's Minstrels. Nichols is good on other American types
that Melville witnessed: "The captains, pilots, engineers, clerks, and runners
of these steamboats were characters—generous, impulsive, reckless, extravagant, they formed a very curious society." A connoisseur of powerful men,
Melville saw his Billies-be-damned on and off the canal, and he saw his
Steelkilts. Samuel M. Welch in the 1891 *Home History. Recollections of Buffalo
during the Decade from 1830 to 1840, or Fifty Years Since* . . . shows that on the
streets of Buffalo Herman also must have seen more American Indians in one
place than ever before, for their reservation was at the southeastern border of
the town. It was still "no uncommon sight during the middle hours of any fair
day to see ranging or loitering on our streets as many native American
Indians: chiefs, warriors, squaws and papooses as 'Yengeese.'" (These were
Senecas; "Yengeese" was supposedly the Indian pronunciation of "English"
later standardized as the word "Yankee.")

   Nichols remembered the sounds from the steamboats that crowded the
harbor at Buffalo: "Each boat had its band of music playing on deck to attract
the passengers as they came in on the mail-coaches or canal-boats." Once
lured aboard, passengers might have to stay overnight, until the boat had its
full load of freight and passengers and steamed off over the "sweet and pure"
waters of Lake Erie—in Melville's and Fly's case, for Toledo, on their way as

far as Detroit. There Herman and Fly had to find food as best they could. Once on ship, the passengers were "found" (supplied with meals) whether they were anchored or under weigh, so it was in their interest to book passage as soon as they could on a Lake Huron and Lake Michigan steamboat. In Detroit, as in Liverpool, Melville experienced what it was to be poor in a strange, loud, gaudy, vibrant city. The Chartist agitation in Liverpool had been tame compared to the political excitement Herman and Fly witnessed in Detroit, for this was the already frenzied "log cabin and hard cider" campaign of William Henry Harrison and John Tyler, the Whig candidates for president and vice president. On 10 June 1840 in one publicity stunt at the docks a crush of Whigs (three thousand "Federal Pilgrims," according to an ironic account in the *Daily Free Press*) boarded the steamboat *Erie* for a political pilgrimage to Fort Meigs, where Harrison had commanded the American forces against a British siege in 1813. ("Successful defence of Ft Meigs by Genl Harrison," Gansevoort noted on a list he made of battles in the late war.) On the twelfth the *Daily Free Press* jeered that the only mention one historian made of Harrison's command was "that a ball struck *a bench on which he was* SITTING during the siege." Melville witnessed also the phenomenal log cabins created for display by the Whigs at their unruly meetings. The Whigs blamed the Democrats for the disturbances, but the *Free Press* had another villain: "*hard cider* is the prime mover of the disturbances at the log cabin pandemonium." In the unruly streets and unruly newspapers of Detroit, Herman got his vivid impression of "Western Editors and log-cabin critics" — his words in a letter to an English publisher on 15 July 1846.

Any patriotic citizen remembered that in the War of 1812 the United States had done well at sea, especially in the first year, when American ships triumphed in a series of one-on-one battles. Gansevoort's list of battles of the War of 1812 included naval battles in the Great Lakes and connected waterways — "Perry's brilliant victory on Lake Erie"; "Chauncey's Superiority on Lake Ontario"; "Hull's disgraceful surrender at Detroit"; "Capture of Ft Niagara & Storming of Buffalo &c &c by the British." All this was real to Gansevoort and Herman: after all, their mother had attended a wartime ball in honor of Commodore Perry in Albany the year before her marriage. For Melville and Fly in 1840, these were storied waters, however primeval, as they were for Nichols in 1839 (two years after his canal experiences). Nichols described "the wild region of Lake Huron," covered "with shaggy firs, pines, and hemlocks, the picturesque evergreens of that northern clime," and emphasized just how striking the contrast of waters was, the Erie a deep, dark blue, and the waters of Lake Huron "clear as crystal and black as darkness in their depths." The "perfect transparency of the water" at the Straits of Mackinac was remarkable: Nichols could see large fish swimming about the anchor of the steamer. He elaborated what Melville only alludes to in a phrase in "The Town-Ho's Story" about painted Indians and their "peltry wigwams": "When I was there the beach was covered with the smoking wigwams and bark canoes of the Indians, who had come down from their wild hunting grounds to receive their Government annuities of powder, lead, and blankets, and to buy also and drink 'too much whiskey.' Soft, smiling squaws came round us to sell strings of wampum and beaded moccasins." That was Nichols; in *Moby-Dick* Melville recalled not only the Indians but also "the goat-like craggy guns of lofty Mackinaw" where American naval victories had thundered.

Lake Michigan was all but primeval. At Green Bay, Wisconsin, Nichols saw "some tall, stately, dignified warriors, in their paint and feathers — splendid savages, not quite spoiled by the pale faces and their fire-water — warriors not unworthy of the romances of Cooper or the poems of Campbell." Melville and Fly may have been on a steamer that went directly toward Milwaukee and Chicago, without putting in at Green Bay, but he saw such warriors along the lakes, as he memorably did, later that trip, on the western bank of the Mississippi. Milwaukee had no harbor and very few structures, according to Nichols: "There was a small wooden store-house on the creek, and five or six cottages on the bluff. That was Milwaukie in 1839" — and pretty much that was Milwaukee in 1840. Chicago, Nichols estimated, had five thousand inhabitants in 1839, the year before Melville first saw it. Two and a half years later, on 16 January 1843, Lemuel Shaw's oldest son, Oakes, wrote home:

> Chicago as I have said before is far from being such a place as I should make Choice of as a residence, it is a dull uninteresting place built on a dead level Prairie, built Chiefly of wood, & very sleight & unsubstantial at that, in 1832 there were only two houses in the Place, & those were only log Cabins. So you can readily Conceive that it must have been a good deal hurried, to have obtained its present Size (it has now some 8000 inhabitants) in so short a time.
>
> As to any order or Government in this State, there is no Such thing.

Melville never got over his own first impression of Chicago as a crude western outpost between an enormous lake and an endless prairie, even though he saw it again, just before the Civil War, when it had become a large city. In November 1870 or later, he reacted with exasperation to a passage in Ralph Waldo Emerson's *The Conduct of Life* on finding in Europe only things already seen at home: "Yet possibly, Rome or Athens has something to show or suggest that Chicago has not."

When Herman and Fly arrived in Galena across the prairie from Lake Michigan, it was early July. Thomas Melvill Jr. now managed to present

himself as a faded chevalier incongruously marooned on the American frontier, as if he were ready to play a part in a sequel to Cooper's *The Prairie*.
Melville was struck afresh "by the contrast between the man and his environment," as he wrote in 1870 in his memoir of his uncle. Whether or not
anyone hinted to Herman about the shameful circumstances of his uncle's
loss of his job, it was obvious at once that the old man, unable to secure the
futures of his own sons (the older two, the half-French whaler Thomas
Wilson and the mentally impaired Henry Dearborn, and the surviving sons
of his second marriage, Robert, John, George, and the replacement Allan
Cargill), could be of no help to two more youths seeking their fortunes.
Herman and Fly decided to look around a little while they had the chance,
very likely thinking that they might find some work to do.

At some point Herman, at least, may have taken an excursion up the
Mississippi to the spectacular Falls of St. Anthony and perhaps a little beyond, to judge from a passage he wrote in 1855 or 1856 as "The River,"
meant to be part of *The Confidence-Man* (1857):

> Above the Falls of St: Anthony for the most part he [the Mississippi] winds
> evenly on between banks of flags or through tracts of pine over marble sands
> in waters so clear that the deepest fish have the visable flight of the bird.
> Undisturbed as the lowly life in its bosom feeds the lord[l]y life on its shores,
> the coronetted elk & the deer, while in the walrus form of some couched rock
> in the channel, furred over with moss, the furred bear on the marge seems to
> eye his amphibious brother. Wood and wave wed, man is remote.

Yet this passage is not proof that Melville went up the Mississippi, for it
draws on a literary source, Timothy Flint's *A Condensed Geography and History
of the Western States; or, The Mississippi Valley* (1828). Judging from his later
habits, Melville would have formed a comparison of Niagara Falls and the
Falls of St. Anthony for his letters home, as he later compared Lake Como to
Lake George.

In the absence of any family letters about these weeks, we rely, perhaps
too trustingly, on what Melville said about the Mississippi in his books, such
as his description in *White-Jacket* (1850) of "a scene once witnessed in a
pioneer village on the western bank of the Mississippi" (ch. 64):

> Not far from this village, where the stumps of aboriginal trees yet stand in the
> market-place, some years ago lived a portion of the remnant tribes of the
> Sioux Indians, who frequently visited the white settlements to purchase trin-
> kets and cloths.
>
> One florid crimson evening in July, when the red-hot sun was going down
> in a blaze, and I was leaning against a corner in my huntsman's frock, lo! there

came stalking out of the crimson West a gigantic red-man, erect as a pine, with his glittering tomahawk, big as a broad-ax, folded in martial repose across his chest. Moodily wrapped in his blanket, and striding like a king on the stage, he promenaded up and down the rustic streets, exhibiting on the back of his blanket a crowd of human hands, rudely delineated in red; one of them seemed recently drawn.

Herman very likely witnessed some such striking scene, perhaps in July, although his memory of dates is always suspect, even when he is trying to write accurately about his own life. He took pleasure in inventing odd garb for his characters, including those based on himself. Some of his descriptions of western clothing in *The Confidence-Man* may be recalled from his experiences of this summer, but he himself may never have reveled in wearing a huntsman's frock, that classic fringed and beaded shirt Washington had recommended to his soldiers, with tomahawk and knife as accoutrements. More to the point, Melville witnessed many western scenes not recorded in even a semi-fictional form. The Mississippi was still frontier, and the first place where he witnessed, and began to brood upon, the process by which whites were suppressing or even extirpating people of another race.

From visual images scattered thinly through Melville's later writings, including poetry, Leon Howard plausibly plotted a course for his return to the East—down the Mississippi past St. Louis to Cairo, then up the Ohio on his way to New York City. He deduced that Melville returned in autumn, going by indications like the word "embrowned" in the first stanza of a poem Melville left in manuscript, "Trophies of Peace: Illinois in 1840": "Files on files of Prairie Maize: / On hosts of spears the morning plays! / Aloft the rustling streamers show: / The floss embrowned is rich below." No documentary evidence has been found either for the route or the month of Melville's return, but psychologically it would have been out of the question for the disappointed youths to retrace their way across the prairie to Chicago then their watery way along the lakes. As Melville wrote in his first book, *Typee* (1846), the last thing a man wants to do is to make "a right-about retrograde movement—a systematic going over of the already trodden ground" (ch. 8). Melville's nature was to see as much as he could. Once Melville and Fly found that Thomas Melvill Jr. could not help them, they may have turned back home almost at once, by the loop, very much as Howard described it.

The best evidence for the time of Melville's return lies in letters of a cousin, Elizabeth Gansevoort, one of the Bath, New York, Gansevoorts, who had been a fellow student of Augusta's at the Albany Female Academy. She spent much of the summer visiting in Albany and corresponded with Augusta in nearby Lansingburgh before she returned home. Something Augusta wrote provoked Elizabeth to make this suggestion, from Bath, on 2 September 1840: "now, dear Augusta why do you not come out and visit me this Fall I will pledge you my word that you will enjoy yourself, and as you have a Brother that I *know has nothing else to do*, and would be willing to come with you I am sure there is no excuse at all." Elizabeth specified that the brother in question was "an *elder Brother*," so she was referring to either Gansevoort or Herman. Conclusions are elusive: it seems unlikely that Elizabeth would have referred so flippantly to Gansevoort, who was at home only when he was sick; yet in fact he was the elder brother who had already visited Bath, seeking a cure for his sickness. For years now, the elder brother who had been looking for work but finding himself with nothing to do was Herman. Most likely, having failed in his western expedition, Herman was home by the end of July (he was *not* there as early as 15 July, a letter shows) or early August. Late that summer, for all we know, he may very well have looked for another job teaching school around Lansingburgh.

10

The First Year of Whaling
1841

Nature commands all men to demean themselves suitable to their several Employments.

"Allan Melvills Book," 1796

BEFORE OR AFTER VISITING Lansingburgh and Greenbush, Herman and Fly showed up in New York City, perhaps as early as August 1840, perhaps as late as November, election month. Gansevoort saw to it that they got into a cheap boardinghouse run by a Mrs. Garahan at 42 Beach Street, opposite St. John's Park, while they doggedly looked for work. From childhood or from the previous year Herman may have retained some memories of Beach, a short street running from Broadway to the Hudson River, a little south of Canal — halfway between the Battery and Fort Gansevoort. The four-acre St. John's Park, owned by Trinity Church, was "reserved for the exclusive use of the gentlemen's families who surround it, and who have keys to its iron gates" (so the *Working Man's Advocate* inveighed on 7 December 1844, outraged that the poor could only look through the exorbitantly expensive iron railing, and so Herman may have felt four years earlier).

Herman wore a beard and had allowed his hair to grow out wild, Gansevoort thought. Gansevoort prevailed in the matter of the decorum necessary in a metropolitan job applicant, and on 26 November was able to write to Allan: "Herman has had his hair sheared & whiskers shaved & looks more like a Christian than usual." That was to the good, but Herman had been and still was "a source of great anxiety" to Gansevoort. Neither Herman nor Fly had found work, so the young men were a financial as well as emotional strain on Gansevoort: "They are both in good health & tolerable spirits — & are living at a cheap rate $2.50 per week, exclusive of dinner — They dine with me every day at Sweeny's & are blessed with good appetites — as my exchequer can vouch." Sweeny's, then at the corner of Ann and Fulton, was already famous as the cheapest place to fill a stomach with food of consistent (if not remarkably high) quality. G. G. Foster in the 17 July 1848 *Tribune* described it, after it had moved to 66 Chatham. A man at Sweeny's door still proclaimed the bill of fare: "Rosebeefrosegoorosemuttonantaters." Within, everything was still utilitarian. The trick for dining there was to order a cheap dinner and to avoid extras, all of which were charged for: "Call simply for a small plate of roast beef mixed, (this means mashed turnips and potatoes in equal quantities)." This meal, followed by "bread, hard" and water, cost a shilling. The particular problem for Gansevoort was that Herman, if not Fly, was habitually ravenous, eating as if he were a still-growing lad (as there is evidence he was), and hard to keep away from the comestible extras that Sweeny's relied on for its margin of profit.

Unlike Herman, Fly had a marketable skill, his clear handwriting, and before long he found "a situation with a Mr Edwards," where he had "incessant writing from morning to Eveg" — Maria's wording in a letter to Allan, now impossible to read without thinking of a character Melville was to create in 1853, Bartleby the scrivener, who at first outdid Fly by running "a day and night line." Gansevoort's handwriting was a source of pride to the inditer and a source of joy to every recipient. Allan by this time modeled his writing so closely upon Gansevoort's that it can at a glance be mistaken for his, although at a closer look it always reveals itself as less spirited, the characters formed without informing character. Herman's handwriting was unsalable, and he could give it away only when he wrote out a letter for a truly illiterate fellow seaman (such a letter in his hand, written in 1842, survives in an archive in Sydney, Australia) or later when he answered a request for an autograph.

A job-seeker had no business loafing about with the recent autobiographical book by Richard Henry Dana Jr. (the son and namesake of the Cambridge poet famous for "The Idle Man"), but *Two Years before the Mast* was receiving much publicity, being excerpted, for example, in the October *Democratic Review* and on the first page of the *Evening Post* for 19 November. At this time Melville read some or all of the newly published book with intense feelings, remembering his own experiences at sea the year before, and wondering what it would be like to round the Horn himself and sail on the Pacific, the ocean that already haunted his imagination, judging by Ishmael's declaration that sailing into the Pacific answered "the long supplication" of his youth (*Moby-Dick*, ch. 111). On 1 May 1850 Melville wrote the younger Dana of these long-past emotions: "those strange, congenial feelings with which after my first voyage, I for the first time read 'Two Years Before the Mast,' and while so engaged was, as it were, tied & welded to you by a sort of Siamese link of affectionate sympathy." He may also have been stirred, around this time or earlier, by reading Jeremiah N. Reynolds's story in the May 1839 *Knickerbocker* about the taking of Mocha Dick, the great white sperm whale of the Pacific. Dana's new book, and very possibly the story of Mocha Dick, worked to confirm him in his resolution not only to go to sea but to go to the Pacific, while his Melvill and Gansevoort cousins' examples determined him to sign on a whaler, as he had thought of doing the year before.

Herman may have seen advertisements for whaling ships in some of the Manhattan papers. The account of the whale fishery written by "George Lightcraft" in *Scraps from the Log Book* (Syracuse, 1847) describes how owners of Nantucket and New Bedford whaleships recruited their green hands: "Shipping offices are kept in New York and Boston, over the doors of which is hung, in large letters painted on canvass, 'Whalemen wanted here,' and in such places as these the runaway young man from the country is entrapped; stories are told him, which he, from his want of knowledge readily believes, and thus becomes an easy victim to the wiles of those heartless men who get their living by selling men for a term of years, uncertain in their number, at five dollars a head." Herman was no such gullible lad, but he must have walked under such signs on canvas as he tried to determine the best whaler to take, and one of those signs may have advertised the *Acushnet*. Perhaps the brothers had that particular vessel in mind when they set out for New Bedford, most likely on a Long Island Sound steamer. Fly would sit copying in lower Manhattan, resting his long pen in his mouth during pauses, but Herman was going to sea again.

Having left Lansingburgh owing the shoemaker Henry Babcock seven dollars (according to a note from Helen to Allan on 21 December 1840), Herman, his father's son, now skipped town owing Mrs. Garahan for board; in his absence, Gansevoort or Allan paid his bill, and it remained on Allan's mind, if not Herman's, for the next four years. Gansevoort had a plan of his own taking shape or already fully in mind: he would see Herman settled on a whaler, then go on to Boston to transact some business of his own. On the Acushnet River (New Bedford to the west side, Fairhaven to the east) they saw what Frederick Douglass had encountered two years earlier, soon after his escape from slavery: "many ships of the finest model, in the best order, and of the largest size," while on shore were walls of "granite warehouses of the widest dimensions, stowed to their utmost capacity with the necessaries and comforts of life." Work went on smoothly, without men being whipped, but to the ear of the slave from Baltimore the scene was oddly silent, with neither loud curses nor loud songs. Contrasting it with Boston Harbor, from his early memories, and with New York and Liverpool, Herman may have noticed less the comparative silence than the exceptional neatness of the wharf area.

Readily enough the brothers found the *Acushnet*, a new ship, built at Mattapoisett, announced as sailing from Fairhaven. They went aboard together, probably the first time either of them had been on a whaler, since they had forgone their trip to River Head or Sag Harbor the year before. What they saw can be suggested by a description from "A Whaler," an article that first appeared in the Providence *Cadet* then was reprinted in the Washington *Daily National Intelligencer*, on 30 April 1829, that dark time of the dismissal of the Hero of the Tea Party:

> Those who have never taken the trouble or never have had an opportunity of visiting a whale-ship, fitted for a three years' cruize beyond Cape Horn, will be ignorant of what they have lost, until a leisure moment is profitably employed in that way. There, between the plank and timbers of a ship of four hundred tons, is a little world; a monarchy in miniature, with an Emperor whose power is absolute as that of the Moon's twin brother who reigns in China, and with occupations as various as are to be found in a house of industry. There is employed at his forge a blacksmith, and here, as deliberately following his vocation, a carpenter, while near at hand is to be seen the sail maker, pursuing the even tenor of his seam, and whiling away the time with a song. The whole deck, from the tafrail to the heel of the bowsprit, presents to the eye of the beholder, the idea and the picture of a community who know of nothing beyond the bulwarks, and to whom every thing further off was the same as if it never had existed. Just forward of the mainmast is seen, deeply embedded in bricks and mortar, a huge boiler, that looks as if the waters of the Pacific itself were to be heated, and the whale and misshapen walrus boiled to a jelly, and started into casks for New England consumption. Abaft this is the camboose [caboose], or "office of the doctor," as the sailors are in the habit of calling the cook, and truly it is a place that will be looked upon, for the three succeeding years, with not a little interest, as the source from whence emanates the supplies of beef and pork, but without any thing peculiar to recommend it to the attentions of strangers, who are less interested.

For Herman the contrast with the *St. Lawrence* was not so much what he saw from the dock but what he saw when stepping on the deck — a familiar space adapted for the self-contained needs of a unique industry (primarily American), all dominated by the enormous try-works, the pots in which the blubber was boiled. With Sweeny's far out of reach, Herman regarded the caboose with optimistic interest, and Gansevoort with palpable relief.

Gansevoort may have been allowed to accompany Herman on a tour of the steerage, which the writer in the *Cadet* described as "filled with implements of destruction to big fish that swim in the far off seas of other climates, and tenanted by the boat steerers, who are to make the first incision in the person of the black lord of the ocean." Here were also stored "the tackle with which his blubber is torn off his huge bones, and hoisted on board, and here is the knife and the spade that render them manageable." A "slight partition" typically separated the steerage from the captain's quarters aft, "the cabin, the seat of government, within the precincts of which no man must come with his hat on." In most ships, the cabin was "an eating, a sleeping, and a sitting room, besides being a store house of rum, tobacco, and 'slop work,' which articles are taken out by the Captain for retail, and which sometimes eat up the entire voyage of a foremast hand." The cabin could become a workshop ("the sailors aver that many a small job is done beneath the quarter deck"). Gansevoort and Herman had to take the interior of the cabin on faith, but they would have seen the forecastle, where Herman would live. It was immaculate, since it was absolutely unused, and the bedding was probably new also, as befitted a new vessel: let the men bring the fleas aboard in their hair and clothing. Gansevoort had no special reason for concern about Herman's comfort, since the space probably looked a good deal better than the forecastle of the *St. Lawrence*. Herman, in any case, was an experienced sailor already, and therefore not finicky, and in many situations not even fastidious. He would do as well as their cousins Leonard and Thomas, and perhaps better. At least he could stand in the forecastle with its six-foot ceiling — not a space his Gansevoort grandfather could have stood upright in, and so low as to make Gansevoort Melville crouch defensively at the doorway.

Gansevoort stayed on in New Bedford through Christmas Day, when he saw Herman sign a contract with the agent of the *Acushnet*. Herman's "Quality" was "Green Hand," and his "Share" (or "lay") was set at "1/175th" of the profits of the voyage. The next day, a Saturday, Herman signed his Seaman's Protection Paper, swearing with due solemnity ("So help me God") that he was born in New York (and therefore entitled to any protection that might be offered to an American seaman by a consul or other official on many a remote coast). On 27 December the brothers, still together, attended church service at the Seamen's Bethel (or chapel) on Johnny-Cake Hill, which had been built in 1831 and dedicated at a service in 1832 at which the famous Father Edward Taylor of Boston had been present. In *Moby-Dick* Ishmael says: "In this same New Bedford there stands a Whaleman's Chapel, and few are the moody fishermen, shortly bound for the Indian Ocean or Pacific, who fail to make a Sunday visit to the spot. I am sure that I did not" (ch. 7). What Ishmael found, Gansevoort and Herman found, as did thousands of sailors over the years — "a small scattered congregation of sailors, and sailors' wives and widows." The bethel was already renowned for the white marble cenotaphs on the walls eloquently memorializing local men who had died at sea, often in battle with whales. There the brothers heard a sermon by the Reverend Enoch Mudge, a notable sailor-preacher like Father Taylor. (Melville may never have learned that within a few decades his account in *Moby-Dick* had made the place a shrine, but his readers began making pilgrimages to the Seaman's Bethel even before his death, some of them not realizing that the original bethel had burnt in 1866, when many of the marble cenotaphs were saved from the fire and masoned into the walls of the replacement chapel, built at the old site on Johnny-Cake Hill.)

On Wednesday, 30 December, the *Acushnet* was registered at Fairhaven. Under oath the owners subscribed to the following description:

> that the said Ship or Vessel was built at Rochester [Massachusetts] afore-said in the year eighteen hundred and forty as appears by the certificate of the master carpenter under whose direction she was built. Ansel Weeks, appointed for the purpose of having certified that the said Ship or Vessel has two decks and three masts and that her length is One hundred four feet, eight & ¼ inches — her breadth Twenty seven feet, ten inches — her depth Thirteen feet eleven inches — and that she measures Three hundred fifty eight & $^{71}/_{95}$ tons, that she is a Ship, has a square stern no galleries and a billethead.

She was smaller than the typical craft described in the *Cadet*, a good deal lighter than four hundred tons. She was a "Ship," a technical term, meaning smaller than a steamer and larger than a bark or barque (and larger still than the progressively smaller brig, schooner, sloop, barge). The last words meant that she had no balcony-like platforms at the stern or elsewhere and did have a billethead, an ornamental carving, rather than a figurehead, as more ostentatious owners might have provided. When Melville signed the crew list the next day he was advanced "some $84, on the strength of our future services and earnings," so his shipmate Richard T. Greene recalled in the Buffalo *Commercial Advertiser* in 1846. "Lightcraft" in *Scraps from the Log Book* said that men who could not pay for their "outfits" would be advanced "seventy-five to a hundred and fifty dollars in clothing," priced "at least more than thirty per cent above their real value," and forced to pay interest and insurance on the clothing, so that even "after a protracted voyage of three and a half or four years," a sailor ("the poor victim") might come home actually in debt. Herman may have used some of his advance for his outfit and then entrusted anything left over to Gansevoort, who stayed with him "to the last." By the time the brothers parted, Herman knew that Gansevoort had decided not to return directly to New York but first to visit their father's birthplace, with the intention of calling not only on their aunts but also on Allan Melvill's old friend Lemuel Shaw, the chief justice, a man whose acquaintanceship could not help but benefit any young lawyer-to-be. Gansevoort had a particular favor to ask of the judge, for he had not gotten out of his mind the possibility that a sea voyage of his own might provide lasting benefit to his health. (Shaw obligingly subsidized what turned out to be a miserable voyage around Florida followed by a lonely frustratingly impoverished stay in New Orleans — one of the worst stretches of Gansevoort's life.)

Before 31 December 1840, Herman wrote and mailed a long farewell letter to his mother — aware that the mail would be faster than Gansevoort, even if his brother went to Lansingburgh after visiting Boston. On 8 January 1841 Maria relayed the news to Augusta, who was visiting Cornelia Van Rensselaer at the Manor House, the great ancestral seat of the Patroons: Herman had embarked "for a long Voyage to the Pacific, under the most favorable auspices, and feeling perfectly happy." Maria made no mention of receiving any money from Herman, so his advance may have been eaten up in providing his necessary outfit. Fully resigned, Maria displayed no maternal anxiety and noted complacently that "Gansevoort was with him to the last and assisted with his more mature judgement to supplying him with every comfort." Herman had shown once again his knack for telling his mother what he knew she wanted to hear, and the astute Gansevoort by then had reported to their mother that he had never seen Herman "so completely happy, as when he had determined upon a situation and all was settled." Maria was trying to master the skill that her brother Peter had perfected long before: that of putting people out of mind once they were out of sight.

Herman learned quickly enough about the living arrangements that would prevail during the voyage. Captain Valentine Pease and the mates of the *Acushnet* slept aft, and the skilled men, the boatsteerers, carpenter, cook, steward, and cooper, also slept aft, forward of the mates. All the other men inhabited the forecastle. No record of the forecastle of the *Acushnet* is known, but a forecastle was a squarish room, sometimes curving to the shape of the bows like a closed horseshoe. The bunks were arranged all along the walls and across the bulkhead. Low down along each wall from the bow to the bulkhead were four bunks, with two bunks on the bulkhead, the only ones not placed against an outer wall — ten bunks in all; then there was another row of bunks two or three feet above the lower bunks, providing living and sleeping space for twenty whalers all told. The men in the two pairs of outside bunks that started at the bulkhead slept partly against bunks built against the bulkhead, so they were closed in more than the men in the other sixteen bunks. Even though the *Acushnet* was new, the wood free of blood, blubber, and smoke from the try-pots, it took only a few hours to impregnate the timbers of the forecastle and all the bedding with tobacco fumes and a variety of strong bodily odors.

The writer in the Providence *Cadet* described the forecastle of a whaler as the most curious place of all curious places:

There, in a little room not much more than a dozen feet square are stowed, heads and points, twenty men, with their chests, their bedding, and their small stores, for a three years' cruize. There they are, through heat and through cold, day after day, and month after month, wedged into a space that would destroy so many rats; and yet living, singing, and growing fat, by far the happiest of the ship's company. With a belly full of beef, a horn of grog, and an "eighty barrel whale," they envy not the wealthy nor the great, and they fear nothing but the lance pole of the first mate. The forecastle is also a magazine of wonderful stories, and songs about "bloody loveyers." Many is the weatherbeaten tar, who, seated upon a sea chest, has recounted to his toil-worn companions stories of ghosts at sea, and wonderful sounds heard during night watches, when the billows were lashed into commotion by the tempestuous winds of an arctic sea. But a forecastle is also a place of comfort — dog comfort — where fatigued men lay themselves down and are rested — where they sing Yankee songs, and smoke Yankee segars, and are happy.

That was more than a trifle glamorized. Among other strains, whalemen had to deal with racial rivalries. J. Ross Browne in his 1846 *Etchings of a Whaling Cruise* complained that the Portuguese crewmen took all the bunks in one section and talked there only in their own language. There were "'Gees" aboard the *Acushnet* (a corruption of "Portuguese," but denoting men from the Azores of part-African blood) who may have done the same, as other groups may have done. Once claimed, by deliberate choice or default, and whether or not in an area self-selected by race, state of origin, age or another standard, Herman's bunk was his, not to be occupied by someone else, even while he was on duty. He could lie in it any direction he wanted, although the Providence *Cadet* seems to suggest that a cap-a-pie system was used. (Most men would want to sleep head forward, so their heads rather than their feet would tend to be lifted by the motion of the vessel.) Lying in his bunk the first nights, Herman may have devoted a wry moment to the memory of his lying beside Gansevoort on one edge of the bed, his father and mother in the middle, and Helen Maria and Augusta on the other edge, with Allan and Catherine stowed feet to feet on a cot in a snug corner, while Frances Priscilla lay alone in her cradle. One look into the forecastle, after a few days' habitation, was enough to make the furniture-piled temporary sleeping quarters in the house on Broadway in 1828 seem expansive. Here, like it or not, Herman Melville found his new home and his new family.

Much of what is known about the crew of the *Acushnet* was unearthed by Wilson Heflin for his 1952 Vanderbilt dissertation on "Herman Melville's Whaling Years." The crew list survives, and Melville wrote down some notes about the fates of the crew of the *Acushnet* after one of them, his "old Shipmate and Watchmate," Henry F. Hubbard, visited him in Pittsfield early in 1853. Whatever he thought of them, these were men Melville spent more hours with than anyone except the closest members of his family; these were men who knew him better, in some ways, than anyone outside his family ever knew him. Only one of them, Richard Tobias Greene (nicknamed Toby on the voyage), wrote anything about Melville for print during his lifetime, so far as is known, and aside from the captain only one other, Hubbard, left any known surviving allusion to the voyage (in a copy of *The Whale*, the English edition of *Moby-Dick*, which Melville presented to him in 1853).

Primarily from Melville's notes on what Hubbard told him, this much is known about men who sailed from Fairhaven on 3 January 1841 but did not come home on the *Acushnet*. (The ages given are those at the day of sailing.) On 2 January 1841 two members of the crew deserted before sailing from Fairhaven. Daniel or David Smith, a boatsteerer, from Philadelphia, twenty-six, with dark complexion and black hair, deserted at Santa Harbor on the coast of Peru in June 1841, while Herman was aboard; he later committed suicide at Mobile. Herman Melville, from New York, twenty-one, 5′9½″, with dark complexion and brown hair, deserted in Nukahiva in July 1842, along with Richard Tobias Greene, from Rochester, twenty-one, 5′5½″, dark of complexion and hair. After Melville and Greene deserted, the carpenter, Tom Johnson, born in Norwich, New York, twenty-two, 5′9½″, a Negro "black" of face, with "woolly" hair, went ashore with venereal disease at Maui in the Sandwich Islands. Henry Grant from Portland, Maine, seventeen, 5′8½″, with light complexion and brown hair, went ashore "half dead, spitting blood, at Oahu." Martin Brown, seaman (and boatsteerer?), Portuguese, born in Fayal, twenty-six, 5′5″, dark of complexion and hair, went ashore at Ropo (Roa-pua), one of the Marquesas, on 22 September 1842, and may have been killed there. John Wright, a Vermonter, eighteen, 5′5¾″, with light complexion and brown hair, "went ashore half dead at the Marquesas" in September 1842. The blacksmith, Ephraim Walcott, from Stow, New York, thirty-five, 5′6¼″, light of complexion with brown hair, ran away in San Francisco, long after Melville had deserted. Robart or Robert Mury or Murry, born in New York, twenty-five, 5′4″, of light complexion and brown hair, went ashore at Rio de Janeiro, "shunning fight" (with Captain Pease?); Pease's affidavit, sworn to before a notary public at Fairhaven on 13 May 1845, declares only that he deserted sometime on the voyage. Three more deserted, location or locations unknown: the carpenter-caulker, David M. White, born in Scotland, thirty-five, 5′7″, dark of complexion, with brown hair; George Eliot, from New York, twenty-five, 5′6″, dark of complexion, with brown hair; and James Williams, from Rhode Island, twenty-four, 5′7″, dark of complexion and hair. The steward, Henry Harmer (or Hayner), from

Herkimer, New York, twenty, 5'5", of light complexion and brown hair, deserted at Lahaina, on Maui, on 28 May 1843. He "ran away aboard of a Sydney ship," Hubbard told Melville; in 1856 Toby Greene reported to Melville that he had come upon him in New Orleans, keeping a hotel.

Two men did not sign the ship's papers in Fairhaven but were shipped while Melville was aboard: John Backus, the "little black" whom Hubbard identified with Pip (the boy who in *Moby-Dick* is said to be from Tolland County, Connecticut), who ran away in San Francisco, and the Irishman, James Rosman, who ran away at Salango, an island off Ecuador (Melville located it in Colombia, perhaps relying on an old map of Gran Colombia). Some five months after Melville and Greene deserted, two men went ashore at another port on the coast of Peru, Payta (or Paita) — the first mate, Frederick R. Raymond, born in Nantucket, thirty-seven, 5'7¾", dark of complexion and hair, and the third mate, "Portuguese Galvan," George W. Galvan, born in Fayal, twenty-five, 5'9", light of complexion, with brown hair. According to Melville's memorandum of what Hubbard told him, Raymond "had a fight with the Captain & went ashore at Payta" and George W. Galvan also went ashore there. Although "went ashore" was often a euphemism for "deserted," Pease in this instance paid both men when they left, $150 to Raymond and $100 to Galvan.

The following were the more stable and reliable members of the crew, or the less adventurous — the men who sailed on the *Acushnet* with Melville and who, unlike him, came home in the ship in May 1845. The captain, Valentine Pease, a Nantucketer, forty-three when he sailed on the *Acushnet*, retired after this voyage and was living at Martha's Vineyard in 1853. (Wholly by coincidence, and long afterward, Melville's daughter and son-in-law bought the Pease house, including some particularly heavy pieces of furniture belonging to the Pease family; Patricia Neal, the actress, later purchased it.) The second mate, John Hall, thirty, English-born, of light complexion and brown hair, and very tall (5'11"), came home on the *Acushnet* to Fairhaven then went to California during the Gold Rush. A boatsteerer William Barnard or Barnet (Barney), born in North Carolina, twenty-five, with light complexion and brown hair, a short man (either 5'½" or 5'5½", in different records), "came home" (the recurrent phrase Melville used). Enoch Read, a mulatto with "woolly" hair, twenty-four, 5'9", from Ohio, came home. Carlos W. (Bill) Greene, a New Yorker, nineteen, 5'5½", with light complexion and brown hair, "after various attempts at running away, came home in the end." John Adams, born in the Cape de Verde Islands, twenty-one, 5'6", dark of skin and hair, and Joseph Luis (Jo Portuguese), born in Fayal, and a resident of Portugal, twenty, 5'5", with light complexion and brown hair, came home. William Maiden, the "old cook" (thirty-eight was old to Melville in 1841), born in Philadelphia, tall (over 5′9″), a black with woolly hair, came home. Joseph Warren or Waren Steadman, the cooper, born in Boston, twenty-five, short (5′2½″), with a dark complexion and black hair, came home. A green hand, Joseph Broadnick (or Broadrick?), from Boston, eighteen, 5′6″, dark of complexion and hair, came home. (Heflin thought this sailor may have been the one called "Little Jack"; he or another man was known as "'Jack Nastyface,' from the fact that his face was as rough as a MacAdamized road" — Richard Tobias Greene, *Sandusky Register*, 13 January 1855.) Henry F. Hubbard, a green hand, from New Hampshire, twenty, a year younger than Herman, 5′9″, light of complexion, with brown hair, came home, and later looked Melville up and told him what befell their shipmates, as far as he knew.

For Herman the start of the voyage was a magical sail out of the New England winter, much as his narrator described in *Moby-Dick* (ch. 28): "for a space we had biting Polar weather, though all the time running away from it to the southward; and by every degree and minute of latitude which we sailed, gradually leaving that merciless winter, and all its intolerable weather behind us." Off the Bahama banks the *Acushnet* found whales — enough to let the captain send home 175 barrels from Rio de Janeiro in March, according to the New Bedford *Mercury* of 28 May 1841. Whales on average weighed 40 to 60 tons, were 40 to 60 feet long, and yielded around 40 to 60 barrels of oil (counting 37½ gallons to a barrel). Thus a rough rule is one barrel of oil per foot of length and per ton in weight of a whale, according to Mary K. Bercaw Edwards of the Mystic Seaport Whaling Museum. ("Barrel" was the unit of measurement: the actual container might be a cask, a hogshead, a pipe, or anything that could contain a specific fraction of a "barrel.") How long cutting up and trying out took may be seen in surviving logs. During a Pacific whaling cruise the log of the *George Washington* (at the Nantucket Historical Association) for 5 May 1843 specifies the capture of three whales at 11 A.M. and taking them to the ship and beginning to cut them. The log on 6 May seems to specify that cutting in was finished at 5 P.M. but that boiling (or trying out) had begun at midday, so the two operations proceeded simultaneously after midday. The log on 7 May specifies "Employeed in boiling." The cleaning up and stowing away was accomplished on the eighth — three whales, three days — fast work, so these were unusually small whales. David Littlefield, whaling researcher at the Mystic Seaport, confirms that it more often took about three days to cut in and try out a single bowhead whale, while it might take four days to deal with an especially large sperm whale. A hundred-barrel whale would take about forty-eight continuous hours to cut in and try out, and get some of the utensils cleaned and stowed away, while the oil might be kept on deck to cool for another day or two before the labor of stowing down was completed and the decks scrubbed to their normal whiteness. On an average voyage, according to J. Ross Browne, a whaleship might take forty whales for sixteen hundred barrels of oil.

Herman and his new shipmates by this time had experienced something very like what he described in a review of Browne's *Etchings of a Whaling Cruise* in March 1847:

> My young friends, just fancy yourselves, for the first time in an open boat (so slight that three men might walk off with it), some 12 or 15 miles from your ship & about a hundred times as far from the nearest land, giving chase to one of the oleaginous monsters. "Pull, Pull, you lubberly *hay-makers!*" cries the boat-header jumping up & down in the stern-sheets in a frenzy of professional excitement, while the gasping admirers of Captain Marryatt & the sea, tug with might & main at the buckling oars — "Pull, Pull, I say; Break your lazy backs!" Presently the whale is within "darting distance" & you hear the roar of the waters in his wake. — How palpitating the hearts of the frightened oarsmen at this interesting juncture! My young friends, just turn round & snatch a look at that whale — .There he goes, surging through the brine, which ripples about his vast head as if it were the bow of a ship. Beleive me, it's quite as terrible as going into battle to a raw recruit.
>
> "Stand up & give it to him!" shrieks the boat-header at the steering-oar to the harpooneer in the bow. The latter drops his oar & snatches his "iron". It flies from his hands — & where are we then, my lovelies? — It's all a mist, a crash, — a horrible blending of sounds & sights, as the agonized whale lashes the water around him into suds and vapor — dashes the boat aside, & at last rushes, madly, thro' the water towing after him the half-filled craft which rocks from side to side while the disordered crew, clutch at the gunwhale to avoid being tossed out. Meanwhile all sorts of horrific edged tools — lances, harpoons & spades — are slipping about; and the imminent line itself — smoking round the logger-head and passing along the entire length of the boat — is almost death to handle, tho' it grazes your person.
>
> But all this is nothing to what follows. As yet, you have but simply *fastened* to the whale: he must be fought & killed.

Variants of this scene of lowering for a whale were enacted several times in the first weeks of Melville's voyage, and whales were actually captured and tried out on a total of perhaps three or four occasions before 13 March, when the *Acushnet* came into Rio de Janeiro with a cargo of 150 barrels of sperm oil. Herman got ashore at Rio, for he met there an Englishman who had sailed on an English man-of-war and was considerably older than he. The world of international whaling was so small that it was not an astonishing coincidence that the man was on the Australian whaler *Lucy Ann* when it took

Melville aboard in 1842, making two men on that ship whom he already knew (the other a man he had met in Liverpool).

For the sake of owners of whaleships and family and friends of the crews, seaport newspapers ran regular columns of ship sightings as they were recorded and relayed by homeward-bound vessels, often with information such as the number of barrels of whale oil already filled, an indication of when the ship might start for home. In New York after three months or so Gansevoort watched for such reports of sightings of the *Acushnet* by other vessels, as the most reliable method of receiving word about his whaleman brother. Knowledge of Melville's movements through 1841 until June 1842 comes partly from these newspaper reports. It also comes from the surviving abstract log of the *Acushnet* (explained below), from logs of other vessels which mention the *Acushnet*, from subsequent comments by shipmates on the *Acushnet*, and from much later first-person and very possibly autobiographical comments in some of Melville's books and journals, as well as his extensive annotations in his copy of Owen Chase's *Narrative of the Most Extraordinary and Distressing Shipwreck of the Whale-Ship Essex, of Nantucket; Which Was Attacked and Finally Destroyed by a Large Spermaceti-Whale* (New York: W. B. Gilley, 1821). A little information also comes from reports of letters Melville wrote home. From Rio, Herman mailed a letter to his mother in which, according to what Gansevoort passed on to Lemuel Shaw, he said that the ship had put in "for the purpose of selling two hundred barrels of oil which she had taken off the Bahama banks." The figure reported in a letter from Captain Pease to someone in Nantucket was only 150 barrels, sent home "by the brig Friend." This was itself an error, for it was the *Tweed*, of Baltimore, which arrived home on 20 May 1841 carrying 150 barrels of sperm oil from the *Acushnet* (according to the New Bedford *Mercury* of 28 May 1841).

The log of the *Acushnet* has not been found, but some of its contents are known because a naval officer, Matthew Fontaine Maury (memorialized in *Moby-Dick*, ch. 44, "The Chart"), persuaded Pease along with a great number of whaling captains to "abstract" information about the directions of the winds in certain areas at certain seasons, and to supply that information on forms he provided them. From the abstract log it is known that in the South Atlantic the *Acushnet* continued to see whales, although the crew seems not to have caught any. In *White-Jacket* (ch. 28) Melville described his passage on the *Acushnet* between Tierra del Fuego to the west and Staten Land to the east:

> Upon one occasion, the ship in which I then happened to be sailing drew
> near this place from the northward, with a fair, free wind, blowing steadily,

through a bright translucent day, whose air was almost musical with the clear, glittering cold. On our starboard beam, like a pile of glaciers in Switzerland, lay this Staten Land, gleaming in snow-white barrenness and solitude. Unnumbered white albatross were skimming the sea near by, and clouds of smaller white wings fell through the air like snow-flakes. High, towering in their own turbaned snows, the far-inland pinnacles loomed up, like the border of some other world. Flashing walls and crystal battlements, like the diamond watch-towers along heaven's furthest frontier.

Through squalls the whaler made its way around Cape Horn on 15 April ("thick hazy weather") and up the coast of Chile, with pleasant weather finally coming as they approached the region of Massafuero, or Selkirk Island, where the abandonment and rescue of Alexander Selkirk had provided Defoe with the model for Robinson Crusoe, whom Defoe placed on a fictional island in the Caribbean.

The abstract log of the *Acushnet* does not show that it actually sighted Massafuero or Juan Fernandez in May 1841, but it may have done so. (Herman is known to have seen the islands in November 1843.) The log of the *William Wirt* of Fairhaven on 7 May, south of Juan Fernandez, shows that it sighted a vessel that the next day it identified as the *Acushnet*, "4 Months out 160 Bls." The abstract log of the *Acushnet* in the next weeks shows sightings of sperm whales but no captures. On 23 June 1841 the *Acushnet* "came to Anchor in Santa Harbor in 5 fathoms" — the first port she had put into since Rio. In July 1842 Gansevoort reported to Shaw that Herman had written from "Santa Martha" on the coast of Peru; he dated this lost letter from Herman as written in August, apparently an error for late June or very early July, whereas Santa Martha, not down in any map, was probably Gansevoort's reading of Herman's "Santa Harbor," much as his first name was read on the *St. Lawrence* as "Norman." From Santa, Herman reported that he was "in perfect health, and not dissatisfied with his lot," and added reassuringly (according to Gansevoort's rewording): "The fact of his being one of a crew so much superior in morale and early advantages to the ordinary run of whaling crews affords him constant gratification." Perfect health we can believe, but for the rest it is hard to disentangle what Herman told his family from what they wanted his letter to say. If in fact Herman's crew was much superior to the average in "morale and early advantages," that is not confirmed by what we know of the men he was serving with. There at Santa one man, David Smith, deserted three days before the *Acushnet* got under way.

By the time the *Acushnet* visited Santa Harbor a shifting cast of characters (many of them, to be sure, not speakers of English) had come before Herman's eyes, month by month, even while at sea. The *Acushnet* was sailing on well-trafficked routes, and once he reached the Pacific cruising grounds Captain Pease was willing enough to pause to visit with sister ships, and even to hunt in company with other American whalers. During the voyage the crew of the *Acushnet* met and exchanged stories with members of other crews with some regularity. Melville later defined a specific nautical term for one sort of visit (*Moby-Dick*, ch. 53): "GAM. NOUN —*A social meeting of two (or more) Whale-ships, generally on a cruising-ground; when, after exchanging hails, they exchange visits by boats' crews: the two captains remaining, for the time, on board of one ship, and the two chief mates on the other*." Ships might merely "speak" each other (exchange hails), or they might transfer or pick up letters without making a formal gam, but whaling captains were courteous to each other because they were so dependent on each other, if for no better reason. Herman himself visited other ships and helped play the host on his own vessel.

Always, the forecastle was, as the writer in the Providence *Cadet* had said, a magazine, an arsenal, of wonderful stories and songs. In "Midnight, Forecastle" (*Moby-Dick*, ch. 40) Melville glorified the songs and stories that simultaneously soothed and aroused the sailors, sleepy and (at least much of the time) sex-deprived. For real talk, and quiet, intimate singing, the best place was not the forecastle but on deck, during night watches. Melville said in *White-Jacket* (ch. 84) that the "long night-watches of the sailor" were "eminently adapted to draw out the reflective faculties of any serious-minded man, however humble or uneducated." Herman talked hour after hour with Hubbard, his shipmate and "watchmate," he called him later, and with Toby Greene, and perhaps with others. Greene wrote to Melville on 8 April 1861: "My mind often reverts to the many pleasant moonlight watches we passed together on the deck of the 'Acushnet' as we whiled away the hours with yarn and song till 'eight bells.'" Both of them told yarns and both sang songs. We also have Melville's recollection of his talking to the second mate, in such a way as to suggest that for all the distance usually kept between the mates and hands there was no great gulf fixed between men and mates on the *Acushnet*: Hall was approachable. As the *Acushnet* neared the Line in the Pacific, sailors inevitably told, among other stories, versions of the wreck of the *Essex* in 1820; Melville heard much about it and found much to reflect on before he saw the standard printed account of the wreck.

The story of the *Essex* that Owen Chase wrote or dictated was, as Melville called it, wondrous. West of Charles Island in the Galápagos, just south of the Line at 119 degrees west longitude, on 20 November 1820, the *Essex* had encountered a "shoal" of whales. Chase, the first mate, harpooned one that quickly stove in his boat (the second time this had happened in four days). Back safe in the ship, while the captain, George Pollard, and the second mate were in the other boats in pursuit of the whales, Chase watched as "a very large spermaceti whale" broke the surface of the water, lay quietly, spouted, disappeared, then rose, making directly for the ship:

> His appearance and attitude gave us at first no alarm; but while I stood watching his movements, and observing him but a ship's length off, coming down for us with great celerity, I involuntarily ordered the boy at the helm to put it hard up, intending to sheer off and avoid him. The words were scarcely out of my mouth, before he came down upon us with full speed, and struck the ship with his head, just forward of the fore-chains; he gave us such an appalling and tremendous jar, as nearly threw us all on our faces. The ship brought up as suddenly and violently as if she had struck a rock, and trembled for a few seconds like a leaf.

Concluding that the whale had stove a hole in the ship, Chase got the pumps going even before he noticed that the head of the ship was settling down in the water. Even in this plight he could not take his eyes off the whale: "He was enveloped in the foam of the sea, that his continual and violent thrashing about in the water had created around him, and I could distinctly see him smite his jaws together, as if distracted with rage and fury. He remained a short time in this situation, and then started off with great velocity, across the bows of the ship, to windward."

As Chase was just about to abandon the ship, a man shouted, "here he is — he is making for us again": "I turned around, and saw him about one hundred rods directly ahead of us, coming down apparently with twice his ordinary speed, and to me at that moment, it appeared with tenfold fury and vengeance in his aspect. The surf flew in all directions about him, and his course towards us was marked by a white foam of a rod in width, which he made with the continual violent thrashing of his tail; his head was about half out of water, and in that way he came upon, and again struck the ship." More than "a thousand miles from the nearest land, and with nothing but a light open boat, as the resource of safety," Chase sent the steward to save quadrants before the cabin filled, and Chase himself snatched the two compasses from the binnacle before he and twenty men aboard with him all abandoned ship. The other two boats came up, Captain Pollard's boat having been alerted by the unforgettable cry of the boatsteerer: "Oh, my God! where is the ship?" Pollard's words to the first mate were: "My God, Mr. Chase, what is the matter?" Chase's reply was, "We have been stove by a whale."

In the *Narrative* Chase described the way he and Pollard had divided men and supplies into three boats, with him at the head of one containing six men, and Pollard and the second mate each heading boats containing seven men. The boats became separated, first Chase's from the other two, later

Pollard's and the second mate's. What followed in the little book was a tale of the extremes of human suffering, from heat, starvation, and thirst, culminating in the group decision, on Chase's boat, to try to save themselves by eating the meat from the arms and legs of one (not the first) who had died. They opened the body to take out the heart (the easiest part to eat), then sewed the incision up and committed the trunk to the sea, retaining the limbs: "We now first commenced to satisfy the immediate craving of nature from the heart, which we eagerly devoured, and then eat sparingly of a few pieces of the flesh; after which, we hung up the remainder, cut in thin strips about the boat, to dry in the sun: we made a fire and roasted some of it, to serve us during the next day." The suffering on Captain Pollard's boat was so great that at last the men drew lots to determine which man would be killed so that the others could eat him, and did at last resort to murder and then to cannibalism. The second mate's boat was never heard from, but Chase and the survivors on his boat were rescued by the London brig *Indian* and taken to Valparaiso, where they were reunited with Pollard and the survivors of his boat, rescued by the Nantucket whaleship *Dauphin*. This was the story as many whalers knew it, and inevitably the subject of retellings, speculation, and allusions in any whaling voyage in the same region of the Pacific. There were other famous stories of ill-fated whaleships, notably the bloody tale of the mutiny on the *Globe* a few years after the loss of the *Essex*, but nothing to compare for terror to Chase's portrayal of the whale as the embodiment of "resentment and fury" and of the grisly aftermath in which some men from an American whaler survived by eating human flesh.

On 23 July 1841 the *Lima* of Nantucket gammed with the *Acushnet* at 4°54'S, 105°W. Melville's later memory of the name of the ship was confused, but this may have been the occasion when he met a son of the famous Owen Chase (identified as William Henry Chase), and first held a copy of Chase's *Narrative*. In 1851, when he was nearly done with *Moby-Dick*, he acquired his own copy (it was imperfect, but he prized it), and in a section of his notes in that book which he headed "What I Know of Owen Chace &c" he wrote this account of "speaking" a Nantucket craft and gamming with her: "In the forecastle I made the acquaintance of a fine lad of sixteen or thereabouts, a son of Owen Chace. I questioned him concerning his father's adventure; and when I left his ship to return again the next morning (for the two vessels were to sail in company for a few days) he went to his chest & handed me a complete copy . . . of the *Narrative*. This was the first printed account of it I had ever seen. . . . The reading of this wondrous story upon the landless sea, & close to the very latitude of the shipwreck had a surprising effect upon me." Melville's later and tantalizingly unspecific comment about the "surprising effect" the story had upon him in 1841 (due not only to the

story but to the circumstances of his reading) is one of his few known asser-
tions (outside his books) about the thoughts he experienced during the years
he was a sailor.

Melville became confused about the ship on which Chase's son sailed, and
he misremembered another ship as having been captained by Owen Chase.
He remembered, uncertainly, the second mate on the *Acushnet*, John Hall, as
claiming to have sailed on that ship on an earlier voyage with Chase as
captain. Faulty impressions and recollections permeate his notes in his copy
of Chase's *Narrative:*

> When I was on board the ship Acushnet of Fairhaven, on the passage to the
> Pacific cruising-grounds, among other matters of forecastle conversation at
> times was the story of the Essex. It was then that I first became acquainted
> with her history and her truly astounding fate.
>
> But what then served to specialize my interest at the time was the circum-
> stance that the Second mate of our ship, Mr Hall, an Englishman & Londoner
> by berth [birth], had for two three-years voyages sailed with Owen Chace
> (then in command of the whale-ship "William Wirt" (I think it was) of
> Nantucket.) This Hall always spoke of Chace with much interest & sincere
> regard — but he did not seem to know anything more about him or the Essex
> affair than any body else.
>
> Somewhere about the latter part of A. D. 1841, in this same ship the
> Acushnet, we spoke the "Wm Wirt" of Nantucket, & Owen Chace was the
> Captain, & so it came to pass that I saw him. He was a large, powerful well-
> made man; rather tall; to all appearances something past forty-five or so; with
> a handsome face for a Yankee, & expressive of great uprightness & calm
> unostentatious courage. His whole appearance impressed me pleasurably. He
> was the most prepossessing-looking whale-hunter I think I ever saw.

Melville still later corrected himself, deciding that Chase had been captain
on the *Charles Carroll* rather than the *William Wirt*, also an error, since Chase
had returned from his last voyage to the Pacific before Melville reached that
ocean. In all of Melville's life he is not known to have so intricately tangled up
so much misapprehension and misinformation as he did about Owen Chase.

Chase and his powerful story of suffering and cannibalism were in Melville's imagination for months in late 1841 and 1842. At some time in that
period he heard old news that he thought at the time was fresh, and then or
later he was sure it had recently been relayed to the man he had thought was
Chase, whether that man was captaining the *William Wirt* or the *Charles
Carroll* (neither of which Chase was in fact captaining). Here are notes Melville made, years later, in his own copy of Chase's *Narrative:* "while I was in
the Acushnet we heard from some whale-ship that we spoke, that the Cap-

tain of the '*Charles Carrol*' — that is Owen Chace — had recently received letters from home, informing him of the certain infidelity of his wife, the mother of several children, one of them being the lad of sixteen, whom I alluded to as giving me a copy of his father's narrative to read. We also heard that this receipt of this news had told most heavily upon Chace, & that he was a prey to the deepest gloom." The infidelity in fact had occurred several years before, and Lemuel Shaw in his regular court duty in Nantucket had granted Chase an uncontested divorce on grounds of adultery — something Herman Melville apparently did not discuss with Shaw before he made his notes on what he knew of Owen Chase. So much is confused in Melville's impressions at the time and his later memories that it would be easy, but wrong, to dismiss the impact on him of what he thought he had seen and heard, in 1841 and 1842, and long afterward, about Chase the captain, cannibal, writer, and cuckold. His meeting with Chase's son, his reading of Chase's book, and his sight of a man he thought was Chase — all these became powerfully mingled in Melville's imagination.

According to the list he published in his Honolulu *Temperance Advocate* in April 1843, Samuel C. Damon, the seaman's chaplain, was then holding letters for Joseph T. Chase, Joseph C. Chase, and Fred B. Chase (captain of the *Fabius*, which sailed from Nantucket on 12 July 1840). At the end of 1843 Damon listed among the whaleships that had anchored there in May two that were captained by Chases — the *Triton* of New Bedford (then twelve months out) and the *Hero* of Nantucket (then nineteen months out). The *Triton* sailed too late for its captain, Reuben Chase II, to be the man Melville thought was Owen Chase; the captain of the *Hero* was William Chase, but a meeting of his ship and the *Acushnet* is not recorded. In any case, there were Chases aplenty in the Pacific, some of them kinsmen of Owen Chase, whom Melville went to his grave thinking he had seen. Melville's multiple confusions in his impressions and recollections of this episode have so far proved unaccountable, but it is certain that he met a son of Owen Chase and read the *Narrative* fairly near the scene of the sinking of the *Essex* by a whale; afterward he saw a captain he thought was Owen Chase himself. Toward that now-unknown captain Melville had felt the emotions he thought were appropriate to feel in the presence of Owen Chase, much as years later he was capable of seeing a Raphael Madonna or the Beatrice Cenci by Guido Reni through the eyes of previous judges rather than forming for himself an absolutely independent aesthetic judgment. A key to the power of the story over Melville lies in his explicit assertion (in "What I Know") of how impressed he was by Chase after this supposed meeting ("the most prepossessing-looking whale-hunter I think I ever saw") and also how impressed he was by Pollard, after veritably meeting *him* in Nantucket in 1852 ("To the islanders he was a nobody—to me, the most impressive man, tho' wholly unassuming, even humble—that I ever encountered"). Melville was uncommonly susceptible to experiencing extraordinary, almost reverential emotions on seeing men, or even reading about men, who had endured one particular strange life experience—in this case, American men who were going about their ordinary, respectable lives after having, in their pasts, experienced fabulous adventures, endured the extremes of human suffering, and survived by eating or even murdering and then eating human beings. These white Americans had been, in their time, as cannibalistic as the natives of the Marquesas Islands, and Melville regarded them not with contempt and dread but with respect verging on awe.

In 1841 the effect on Herman Melville of reading Chase was "surprising"—powerful but not well understood. Through the months after meeting young Chase and reading the narrative, Melville retained the sense of wonder it had generated, and he may have begun to revolve upon the oddity of the story's affecting him so, catching him, as it did, off guard. One effect of reading Chase under such circumstances would have been to arouse fear at the possibility that the *Acushnet* might be sunk by a whale and the crew left to suffer as the crew of the *Essex* had suffered, isolated in a boat where the number of fellow survivors dwindled in hideous ways. The mere thought of the *Essex* could heighten the terrors of every seemingly routine encounter with a whale as the *Acushnet* went about its business. When he made his Ahab fantasize in "The Symphony" (ch. 132) that his boy wakes from his nap "and his mother tells him of me, of cannibal old me," Melville had begun to associate such devouring with the Greek myth in which Cronos swallowed his children. By then, in 1851, he had some inkling of why he had been so moved when he saw an American he thought had been a cannibal—even when he identified the wrong man.

In the next weeks after meeting the *Lima*, the *Acushnet* frequently sighted American whalers and even hunted in company with another ship for a day or two at a time. On 9 August, the *Midas* of New Bedford "spoke" the *Acushnet* (at 4°43'S, 104°47'W) and learned that the Fairhaven ship had 200 barrels on board (this the New Bedford *Daily Mercury* reported on 3 January 1842). The abstract log of the *Acushnet* shows many sightings of sperm whales but does not record kills. The 16 August log of the *Lima* shows that it had recently made a kill and was then coopering oil, before again meeting up with the *Acushnet*, speaking and boarding her. On the seventeenth the *Lima* coopered oil, gammed with the *Acushnet* in the middle of the day, then stowed down 60 barrels of oil into pipes. On the eighteenth the *Lima* spent the first part of the day gamming with the *Acushnet*. The *Acushnet* sighted sperm whales in squally weather on 30 August, but no record survives as to its success. On 25 September (5°14'S, 105°53'W) the log of the *William Wirt* reported its meeting the *Acushnet* and learning that it now had 600 barrels of oil. On 8 October the *Acushnet* "spoke" the *William Lee*, fifteen months out of Newport, with 400 barrels. On 11 October (4°27'S, 104°37'W) the *Joseph Maxwell* recorded: "at 6 P.M. spoke the ship Cuishnet of Fair-haven 9 mos. 700 b[arre]ls." On 15 October the *Alexander* of New Bedford reported speaking the *Acushnet*, which then had 550 barrels, and on 23 October the *United States* of Westport spoke the *Acushnet* ("720 bbls"). (The discrepancy in figures could mean that the *Acushnet* reported to the *Joseph Maxwell* the total she had taken since leaving home on 3 January 1841, not just the amount she then had on board.)

On 24 October 1841, during this successful period of whale hunting, the *Acushnet* crossed the Line, going to the north, at which invisible point occurred the following scene, according to Toby Greene: "We had a shipmate once, whom we called 'Jack Nastyface,' from the fact that his face was as rough as a MacAdamized road. The first time that we crossed the equator in the Pacific, 'Jack' was at the mast head looking out for whales. As soon as 'eight bells' were struck, and 'Jack' was relieved, he was informed that we had crossed the line. 'The devil we did!' says 'Jack.' 'Can't ye tell us some news? didn't I see it as well as you did, and better too? wasn't I aloft? I saw the line before any man aboard.'" American pranksters were as much alive and well on the watery frontier as in the American backwoods, and their tricks, like their stories, were of the same genre as hunting stories set in the old Southwest — stories the vogue for which was burgeoning at home while Melville was in the Pacific.

On 30 October during pleasant weather the *Acushnet* sighted the north head of Albemarle, in the Galápagos Islands, forty miles to the southeast. In 1854 Melville enthralled the readers of *Putnam's Magazine* with a series of sketches based on his landing in these "Encantadas," or "Enchanted Islands" (so called because the Spanish sailors who found them had such trouble charting them that they seemed to move or even to disappear). After being "broad upon the waters for five long months" (Sketch Second), he recalled approaching "the great outer isle of Albemarle, away from the intricacies of the smaller isles, where there is plenty of sea room" (Sketch First), where ships were not so apt to be caught in perplexing calms or impelled by the currents. At his first sight of Albemarle, some months, he said, before his "first stepping ashore upon the group," a boat's crew sent to the island returned after sunset: "I looked down over the ship's high side as if looking down over the curb of a well, and dimly saw the damp boat deep in the sea with some unwonted weight. Ropes were dropt over, and presently three huge antediluvian-looking tortoises after much straining were landed on deck" (Sketch Second). Any land creature would by then have worn "a fabulous hue to the dreamy mind," but these three tortoises, "mystic creatures," Melville wrote in "The Encantadas," affected him powerfully, and "in a manner not easy to unfold." It was that they seemed "newly crawled forth from beneath the foundations of the world," and therefore conveyed a feeling "of age: — dateless, indefinite endurance."

In "The Encantadas" Melville recounted a version of his first visit to Rock Rodondo, in the gray of the morning: "With a view of fishing, we had lowered three boats, and pulling some two miles from our vessel, found ourselves just before dawn of day close under the moon-shadow of Rodondo" (Sketch Third). This episode was based on what occurred around 31 October, when the *Phenix* of Nantucket spoke the *Acushnet* at 0°18'N, 91°50'W. On 2 November 1841 the *Acushnet* was one of four American whaleships hunting the same grounds in the Galápagos Islands, near 0°12'S, 91°42'W, the others being the *Richard Mitchell*, Nantucket; the *Henry Astor*, Nantucket; and the *Hobomok*, Falmouth. Melville seems to have multiplied this number in his *Putnam's* description (Sketch Fourth):

> The day after we took fish at the base of this Round tower, we had a fine wind, and shooting round the north headland, suddenly descried a fleet of full thirty sail, all beating to windward like a squadron in line. A brave sight as ever man saw. A most harmonious concord of rushing keels. Their thirty kelsons hummed like thirty harp-strings, and looked as straight whil[s]t they left their parallel traces on the sea. But there proved too many hunters for the game. The fleet broke up, and went their separate ways out of sight, leaving my own ship and two trim gentlemen of London. These last, finding no luck either, likewise vanished; and Lee Bay, with all its appurtenances, and without a rival, devolved to us.

On 3 November (0°43'S, 91°45'W) the *Rousseau* of New Bedford reported five ships in sight, including the *Acushnet*, 700 barrels. The *Acushnet* was sighted by the *Mary* of Edgartown on 10 November, and two days later by the *Massachusetts*, New Bedford. The *Acushnet* anchored at Chatham's Isle (0°53'S, 89°48'W) in fifteen fathoms of water on 19 November, the day the *Columbus* of Nantucket reported her as "10 Months out 500 bbls" — another discrepancy, perhaps to be accounted for by the *Acushnet's* having sent some oil home by whalers it encountered. On 25 November the *Acushnet* got under way. On 30 November, in "Pleasant Weather," it spotted sperm whales, and may have made a 70-barrel killing before sailing for the coast of Peru.

Melville carried away intense visual images from the Galápagos Islands, and the makings of his formula for creating a good replica of them, printed as the opening of Sketch First:

Take five-and-twenty heaps of cinders dumped here and there in an outside city lot; imagine some of them magnified into mountains, and the vacant lot the sea; and you will have a fit idea of the general aspect of the Encantadas, or Enchanted Isles. A group rather of extinct volcanoes than of isles; looking much as the world at large might, after a penal conflagration. . . .

But the special curse, as one may call it, of the Encantadas, that which exalts them in desolation above Idumea and the Pole, is that to them change never comes; neither the change of seasons nor of sorrows. Cut by the Equator, they know not autumn and they know not spring; while already reduced to the lees of fire, ruin itself can work little more upon them. The showers refresh the deserts, but in these isles, rain never falls.

Another feature of the isles, Melville added, "is their emphatic uninhabitableness." In "The Encantadas" he lavished upon them some of his most memorable prose, as when he described what the vegetation looked like, when it grew at all: "Tangled thickets of wiry bushes, without fruit and without a name, springing up among deep fissures of calcined rock, and treacherously masking them; or a parched growth of distorted cactus trees." Melville dramatized himself as later haunted by the islands to the point of seeming "the occasional victim of optical delusion": "For often in scenes of social merriment, and especially at revels held by candle-light in old-fashioned mansions, so that shadows are thrown into the further recesses of an angular and spacious room, making them put on a look of haunted undergrowth of lonely woods, I have drawn the attention of my comrades by my fixed gaze and sudden change of air, as I have seemed to see, slowly emerging from those imagined solitudes, and heavily crawling along the floor, the ghost of a gigantic tortoise, with 'Memento * * * * *' burning in live letters upon his back." In the weeks after the *Acushnet* left the islands, Melville's memory may well have turned to them, involuntarily, and to the giant tortoises that crawled on them.

On 2 December 1841 the *Acushnet* reached the coast of Peru and "came to Anchor at Tombez in 6 fathoms water." According to the New Bedford *Daily Mercury* (14 February 1842), Pease wrote home from Tombez that he had "570 bbls oil on board, (sent home 150.)." The keeper of the log of the *Coquette* on 15 June 1821 ventured "A Short Description of Tombus," a sample of which suggests what Melville saw as the *Acushnet* approached in "Pleasant Weather": "It is pleasantly situated on the side of a river of the same name about 9 miles from the Ponds w[h]ere the Ships lay there is a bar runs across the mouth of the river which is very dangerous in bad weather." On the banks, "covered with Bushes & brambles," at noon sailors could see "large Aligators laying basking in the Sun with their upper jaw thrown back catching flies here it is they lay their eggs which they sit on male and female in turns till they are hatched." For several miles the banks were "covered with Plantations of Banans Plantains sweet potatoes Sugar cane coconuts Oranges limes & various other plants & fruits vegatible, surrounded by flocks of goats." Sailors on this stretch "were greatly tormented by Musketoes & sand flies." The town itself made "a verry poor appearance compared to the Bank of the river, the houses are built the same as at Paita but much neater." Even the church was a disappointment, "not so handsom as might be supposed from the riches that the place contains." To a young man who had witnessed the degradation of British civilization in Liverpool, the approach to still-primitive Tombez would have seemed cleaner simply because of the lush vegetation and sparsity of population. Melville and other crewmen of the *Acushnet* may have been given shore leave. Later that month another ship spoke the *Acushnet* at sea, and by 22 July 1842 Gansevoort had seen by the papers that all had been well on Herman's vessel at the end of 1841.

Although the *Acushnet* anchored at Tombez, north of Payta, when Melville was aboard, there is no record of his ever being at Payta. However, Victor W. von Hagen in *The Four Seasons of Manuela: A Biography. The Love Story of Manuela Sáenz and Simón Bolívar* (1952) declared that the *Acushnet* anchored at Payta in the middle of November 1841 and "most of the twenty-six-man crew" stormed ashore to complain to the American consul about Pease's cruelty: "It was an acrimonious three days; there were fights in the streets which the night watch had difficulty in silencing. The second mate deserted, and the captain roared in to demand legal protection for the ship's articles. Manuela Sáenz, with experience in jails and jailings, was called in to aid in the preparation of legal documents for the local authorities. In the flickering of a burning candle, with winged termites flying in erratic circles about the flame, her scratching quill teased the salty English of the *Acushnet's* sailors into Spanish." According to von Hagen, a "quiet gray-eyed young man of twenty-two" was one of the last to give testimony: "His name, when he affixed it to the document, meant no more to Manuela than it did to his shipmates: Herman Melville." Anyone who doubts this perfervid account of the young gray-eyed Melville (his eyes were blue) and the former mistress of the Liberator is directed by von Hagen to the *Bulletin of the Colombian Academy of History at Bogotá* (February 1952), an issue that when sought out in Bogotá by Adolfo Gomez in 1996, was found to mention neither Manuela nor Herman. From von Hagen this fabulous story was picked up by the great fabulist Gabriel García Márquez in *The General in His Labyrinth* (Knopf, 1990), so it may in time prove to be one of the most memorable experiences that Herman Melville never had.

11

Whaler and Runaway
1842

I depend much on your kind attention to my dear Boy who will be truly grateful for the least favour — let him avoid green Fruit & unseasonable exposure to the Sun & heat.

Allan Melvill to Peter Gansevoort, 10 August 1826

VERIFIABLE SPIRITUAL, PSYCHOLOGICAL, OR INTELLECTUAL coordinates for Melville from the last days of 1841 through the first months of 1842 are in scant supply, but there survive spherical coordinates enough to trace the voyage of the *Acushnet*. Its abstract log recorded pleasant weather off Ecuador on 27 December, Cape Blanco in sight, Point St. Elena sighted the next day. The log for 6 January 1842 recorded the ship's approach to the Galápagos Islands from the southeast: "hazy weather Hood's Island in sight also Charles Isle." The next day ("pleasant") the crew "saw a Sperm Whale" but did not capture it. The *Acushnet* had a run of seeing sperm whales without capturing them, according to a series of notations — on 13 February at 5°31′S, 102°41′W, during pleasant weather; on 16 February at 5°28′S, 103°25′W, during hazy weather; on 3 March at 4°47′S, 105°54′W, during pleasant weather; and on 9 March at 5°35′S, 109°17′W during "rugged weather" — squalls. The *Acushnet* saw sperm whales on 12 April at 4°09′S, 122°54′W, during squally weather; on 18 April at 0°26′S, 124°19′W in fine weather; and on 1 May at 0°12′S, 127°52′W in squally weather — apparently without capturing any of these whales. On 2 May, at 0°33′N, 127°23′W the *Ontario*, of Nantucket, Stephen B. Gibbs, master, "spoke" the *Acushnet*, and was informed that it contained 700 barrels of whale oil (this news was reported in the New York *Herald* on 24 November 1842). On 4 May at 0°14′S, 128°09′W the barque *Columbus* of New Bedford, Tristram D. Pease, master, while strong trade winds were blowing, "spoke ship Achunet of F Haven got letters," according to a journal kept on the *Columbus* by Edward Smith. This may have been Herman's first chance to "post" letters in several months, and chances are that despite his constitutional procrastination he had his letters already written, ready to be handed to a homeward-bound ship.

The next day, 5 May, the *Acushnet* at 0°36′N, 128°21′W in rugged weather again saw sperm whales, and apparently caught none but took time for gamming with the *Columbus*, as Edward Smith recorded. The ships were in the same area for two more weeks. The *Columbus*, at least, was doing more than sighting whales, for at 0°27′S, 127°52′W on 7 May, Smith recorded: "Moderate trades by the wind boiling spoke Ship Acushnet of F Haven finished Boiling middle and latter part Strong Breezes Lat ᵐ16S Long 128, 16W" (the superscript *m* means meridian — they were just south of zero latitude, on the Equator). At 0°07′N, 128°26′W on 20 May, Smith noted: "Moderate trades stearing N spoke ship Acushnet of f Haven middle and latter part the same Lat ᵐ21S Long 128.25W." At 0°15′S, 129°27′W on 3 June Smith noted: "Strong trades stearing NNW spoke ship Achunet middle and latter part the same Lat ᵐ26S Long 129.52W." At 0°30′S, 129°56′W on 6 June the *Acushnet* (according to the abstract log) experienced "hazy weather saw Sperm Whales" and at 0°48′S, 130°W on 8 June saw sperm whales in fine weather. About this time, according to the journal of the *James Maury* of Salem, the *Acushnet* sighted two ships from Nantucket, the *Cyrus* and the *Enterprise*. The *Acushnet* reported 750 barrels on board (so the *James Maury* was quoted in the Boston *Daily Advertiser* for 29 November 1842). At 0°21′S, 133°W on 16 June the *Herald the Second* of New Bedford, Nathaniel H. Nye, master, spoke the *Acushnet*, which had 750 barrels on board, and sent home 200 on Nye's ship, according to the New York *Herald* of 1 December 1842.

This phase of the voyage of the *Acushnet*, judging from these contemporary records, was not out of the ordinary. How Melville experienced the voyage, day by day, is wholly undocumented. Like most whalers, the ship lowered for whales many times without killing any, but Melville's depiction of the plight of the *Dolly* in *Typee* (written three years or so later) is highly fictionalized, particularly in the implication that the ship was engaged in not only fruitless but also solitary cruising (ch. 1): "Six months at sea! Yes, reader, as I live, six months out of sight of land; cruising after the sperm-whale beneath the scorching sun of the Line, and tossed on the billows of the wide-rolling Pacific — the sky above, the sea around, and nothing else! Weeks and weeks ago our fresh provisions were all exhausted. There is not a sweet potatoe left; not a single yam. . . . there is nothing left us but salt-horse and sea-biscuit." In *Typee* (ch. 4) Melville described a long run of bad luck in a way meant to evoke the sympathy of the armchair reader or the stateroom sailor: "Although, as a general case, a ship unlucky in falling in with whales continues to cruize after them until she has barely sufficient provisions remaining to take her home, . . . yet there are instances when even this natural obstacle to the further prosecution of the voyage is overcome by headstrong captains, who, bartering the fruits of their hard-earned toils for a new supply of provisions in some of the ports of Chili or Peru, begin the voyage afresh with unabated zeal and perseverance." Headstrong such a captain might seem to a member of the crew, persistent and determined to the shipowners in Massachusetts.

Even without anything exceptional to complain about, Melville had long since realized that nothing he had learned about whaling from his cousins or their families had prepared him for the reality. Charles B. Reynolds, a foremast hand on the American whaleship *Florida,* three years later worked his experiences, more severe than Melville's because conducted in the Arctic, into a salutary little drama, replete with divisions into acts. Entitled "Cure for Romance, or A Cruise on the 'North West,'" this was written for Chaplain Samuel C. Damon's Honolulu *Temperance Advocate and Seaman's Friend,* where it was published on 1 October 1845. There Reynolds declared that all "the nostrums ever compounded by the illustrious Brandreth" (a maker of laxatives Melville also referred to in *Moby-Dick*) were nothing to the purgative powers of whaling on the northwest coast, applied to a youth's romantic notions. Reynolds offered an unidealized portrayal of forecastle life in a whaler in that frigid region:

> Curtain rises and discovers the interior of the ship's forecastle, a space of some fifteen feet square by six high, decorated with festoons of old and wet clothing, hanging in every available place, and inhabited by six Kanakas, five Portuguese, two "Gemmen ob color," two Dutchmen, one Indian, three Yankees and one New Yorker. Some are lounging upon the chests, smoking, talking, or making ineffectual attempts to master an idea, while at intervals are heard snatches of songs in some unknown tongue, mingling with execrations both loud and deep from those who chance to get pitched from one side to the other by the lurching of the vessel. — Some have sought refuge from the cold in their berths; the upper midship berth on the larboard side appears occupied by the New Yorker. . . . Time, 6½ o'clock, P. M.

About the same number of crew members shared the forecastle of the *Acushnet,* very likely in slightly smaller quarters than fifteen by fifteen. What with bodies in the upper and lower berths in each stack, and what with the grimy festoons of old and wet clothing, once fresh from the outfitters of New Bedford and Fairhaven, and the pervasive smells (unmentioned by Reynolds), as well as the sounds, Melville had every reason to think that he had learned enough about whaling for the moment.

In *Typee* Melville did not exactly blacken the name of Valentine Pease in order to justify his deserting the *Acushnet,* since he called his captain "Vangs," but in the small world of Massachusetts whaling, news of Melville's perfidious aspersions must have reached Pease, sooner or later. To Pease or any other whaleman the idea of a Pacific whaleman's making an appeal to the owners "for law and equity" was legally ludicrous, as well as logistically difficult. Equally absurd was Melville's justification for jumping ship on the grounds that the captain had been the first to break the contract between them, and had done so in "numberless instances": "The usage on board of her was tyrannical; the sick had been inhumanly neglected; the provisions had been doled out in scanty allowance; and her cruizes were unreasonably protracted" (ch. 4). Melville's heart was not in the indictment, which runs anticlimactically from "tyrannical" behavior to "inhuman" to "unreasonable," nor in his depiction of the other members of the crew, whom he had once reported (so Gansevoort said) as being superior to the general run of whalemen. This sorry lot would not rally in a general mutiny (an extreme measure for which severe consequences were set): "unfortunately, with a very few exceptions, our crew was composed of a parcel of dastardly and mean-spirited wretches, divided among themselves, and only united in enduring without resistance the unmitigated tyranny of the captain." In *Typee* Melville's analysis of the hard-heartedness of the captain modulates smoothly into reports of captains who vow to return with a vessel full of sperm oil or not return at all, and then into a tall tale about one particular ship. The *Perseverance*, a Flying Dutchman affair, had aged ungracefully with its crew decade by decade, and was still at sea, "regularly tacking twice in the twenty-four hours somewhere off Buggerry Island, or the Devil's-Tail Peak" (ch. 4). Melville got this blithe fantasy of geriatric homosexual whalemen into print in both the English and American editions, and it escaped the belated censorship that the American edition suffered, although after his death his wife made a note listing this as a passage he wanted deleted. The lightness of the tall tale effectively undercuts Melville's complaints about the fictional captain of what he called the *Dolly* in *Typee* and still more about the real Valentine Pease of the *Acushnet*.

Much of the dissatisfaction the whalemen felt was, in the nature of things, sexual. On the *Acushnet* for a year and a half, in June, Melville had lived in the forecastle with twenty or so sailors, mainly healthy men, and young—some as young as he—denied the space and privacy to touch even their own bodies without the likelihood of being observed, and, all of them, preoccupied with sex. In whaleships, to be sure, men found a degree of provisional privacy sufficient for mutually desired sexual acts. The diaries the marine drummer Philip C. Van Buskirk kept a few years later suggest that in the navy mutual masturbation was commonplace (sodomy much less so). The editor, B. R. Burg, gives Buskirk's phrase for manual, not oral, sex as going "chaw for chaw," perhaps a nautical corruption of "claw for claw," from the old phrase "claw me and I'll claw thee." Such mutually desired erotic acts usually went undetected and almost always went unpunished when discovered. Briton Cooper Busch, who scanned some three thousand logs for his *Whaling Will Never Do for Me: The American Whaleman in the Nineteenth Century* (1994), stresses that sexual incidents were recorded in logs of whaling ships primarily when one man complained against another for forcing or trying to force on him an undesired act. Then the offender might or might not be punished by flogging, fine, or discharge, depending on his rank or other circumstances. No whaling captain wanted to hear such a complaint. While undesired assaults sometimes were recorded in logs and journals of whaleships, no one, apparently, bothered to write down observed instances of practical man-to-man relief.

Nothing has survived to show that Captain Valentine Pease made life unnecessarily difficult for Melville or any other man on the *Acushnet*, but Melville was not the only man to think he might be better employed, for a time, in one lush tropical island or another, where he might eat fresh (and sometimes strange) tropical fruit and hope that the island would prove to be inhabited by natives such as he had heard of. When he later described being haunted by "strangely jumbled anticipations" before arriving at Nukahiva (*Typee*, ch. 1), Melville was indulging in fine writing, but recording something very like the mood on the *Acushnet* at the news that they were bound for the Marquesas Islands: " 'Hurra, my lads! It's a settled thing; next week we shape our course to the Marquesas!' The Marquesas! What strange visions of outlandish things does the very name spirit up! Naked houris — cannibal banquets — groves of cocoa-nut — coral reefs — tatooed chiefs — and bamboo temples; sunny valleys planted with bread-fruit-trees — carved canoes dancing on the flashing blue waters — savage woodlands guarded by horrible idols — *heathenish rites and human sacrifices.*" Melville had known long before he left home that every whaling crew was excited by the prospect of anchoring at the Marquesas, since Cousin Thomas Melvill had visited not only Nukahiva but also the Typee Valley in 1829, while serving as a midshipman on the *Vincennes*. From Charles S. Stewart's *A Visit to the South Seas, in the U.S. Ship Vincennes*, Uncle Thomas and the children in Pittsfield had known, also, of a conversation on that occasion between naval men and the Typees in which the natives had affirmed matter-of-factly, when questioned, that they were indeed in the habit of eating the bodies of their enemies taken in battle.

Melville's complaints in *Typee* lacked any substance, and any complaints he harbored or voiced in the spring of 1842 probably were mere grouses. To be sure, the food on the *Acushnet* was bad and becoming worse by the week, and, as confined men always do, Melville and the other sailors, without the distraction of productive work, came to fixate on the meals as the principal events of the days. One of the confirmed facts about Melville at the time of this voyage is that he was ruled, still, by the insatiable appetite of a healthy adolescent male. His shipmate Richard Tobias Greene on 4 January 1861 wrote him from Chicago hoping that he enjoyed good health and could even yet, in his advanced age, stow away his "five shares of duff!" If he could eat enough steamed or boiled flour pudding to feed five ordinary seamen, or even enough to justify a jest to that effect, by May and early June 1842 Melville, edgy and unhappy about the recent cruising of the *Acushnet*, was ready to taste fresh fruit. According to Melville's account in *Typee* (ch. 2), which he claimed was "the unvarnished truth," the captain all but abandoned the pursuit of whales in order to sail for the Marquesas and "recruit" (as the term was) supplies. Melville could "never forget the eighteen or twenty days during which the light trade-winds were silently sweeping us towards the islands." He went on: "What a delightful, lazy, languid time we had whilst we were thus gliding along! There was nothing to be done. . . . We abandoned the fore-peak altogether, and spreading an awning over the forecastle, slept, ate, and lounged under it the live-long day." Yet they may have paused to capture some whales in the eighteen or twenty days before they reached Nukahiva, for Pease informed the *Potomac* there that he had 950 barrels (perhaps meaning that much had been taken during the whole voyage, perhaps meaning that 950 was then on board, up two hundred after Pease had sent 200 barrels home on 16 June). In *Typee* Melville's insistence that he could "never forget" something was sometimes a good indication that the event in question never happened, and the single known record of a ship they "spoke" in mid-June neither confirms nor casts doubt on his account of the ship's heading for the islands rather than cruising for whales. There may in fact have been a yam or two still aboard the *Acushnet* in June 1842, and other delicacies besides salt-horse and sea-biscuit, but the crew had not seen land since January. They had not seen a woman in that time (unless one was aboard one of the whalers they spoke: a few captains did take their wives with them or take aboard Polynesian women), and Melville was not the only man on board who had never seen a Polynesian island. Whatever means of comforting or even regaling themselves the sailors on the *Acushnet* resorted to, most of them were, given the chance, heterosexual, and as their ship encountered the *Columbus*, the *Cyrus*, the *Enterprise*, and the *Herald the Second*, one or more of which may have just visited the Marquesas and shared stories of their reception, all the men became more and more agitated at the prospect of assisting South Sea maidens to board the *Acushnet*.

As they sailed for the Marquesas the men had ample occasion to recite horrific tales of the ferocity of some of the inhabitants of the Marquesas Islands, particularly the Typee tribe. In *Incidents of a Whaling Voyage*, published in 1841, Francis Allyn Olmsted had reported the story told him by

Captain Brown, of the whaleship *Catharine* of Nantucket, which sailed in 1839 (and which returned to Nantucket in June 1843, without Brown, who died in his boat, fast to a whale). In a conversation in the Pacific, Brown had warned Olmsted of "the treacherous character" of the natives of many of the Polynesian islands. This is Olmsted's summary of Brown's veracious tale:

> Leaving Nookaheva bay in the Island of Nookaheva, he [Brown] sailed around to the opposite side of the Island, for the purpose of trafficking with the natives that assembled in great numbers upon the beach, as his boat lay on the water, a few yards from the shore. The Tipaiis, the name of this tribe, are very ferocious, and to gratify their cannibal appetites, they are not very scrupulous in making choice of their victims. Capt. B., aware of their reputation for ferocity, disregarded all their solicitations to land, but made an agreement with them to supply his ship with a number of swine, which were to be brought down to the beach on the coming day.

Lulled by the "appearance of good faith" in the behavior of the natives, Brown went ashore, where he "was instantly seized by a party of natives, and hurried off to some distance from shore, while the swine were cut loose that the savages had collected together to decoy the captain within their reach." The natives then "thronged around him with horrid yells of triumph, and clamorously demanded of him, as a ransom, forty muskets and six kegs of gunpowder," and when he could not meet their demands they began to prepare "a dreadful doom" for him: "With awful anticipations of his horrid fate, he saw them collecting together piles of dry wood, and digging holes in the ground, to be used as ovens for roasting him, upon the following morning; and it was with the agony of despair that he found himself surrounded at night upon every side by his merciless captors." (The popular image of cannibals cooking their victims in enormous pots was a later creation, based on tales coming out of Africa, not the Pacific.) In the middle of the night the guards fell asleep, and Brown escaped to tell the tale to Olmsted, and to any other men he encountered. Even though Olmsted's book was published too late for copies to have reached whaleships in the Pacific before Melville went to the Marquesas, Brown and his crew had insured that the tale was in circulation in the whale fishery by telling it at gams and during anchorings in whaling harbors such as Lahaina and Honolulu. Tales of this sort were conscientiously made known to all whalemen in the region, since captains had a vested interest in making sure their crews knew what the natives might do with deserters. It was salutary to have every sailor know that at the Marquesas he might indulge freely in sex, feast on tropical fruit, and then be captured and eaten by cannibals.

On 23 June (according to the abstract log) the *Acushnet* reached the Mar-

quesas Islands and in squally weather "came to Anchor in Nookaheva Bay in
9 fathoms." Nukahiva Bay, or Taioa Bay (what Melville spelled "Tior"), on
the south-central coast of Nukahiva Island, was a scene of astonishing beauty.
Melville's shipmate Richard Tobias Greene in the Sandusky *Mirror* on 7 December 1854 recalled, in editorial plural, "the effect, the magnificent scenery
of Nukahiva had upon our young mind": "If Melville in his 'Typee' ro-
manced, he is to be pardoned, for when we entered that bay, and saw its
almost unearthly beauties break, as if by magic, on our bewildered eyes — the
smooth surface of that lovely sheet of water, undisturbed save by some tiny
canoe, as it shot forth from a fairy cavern, half concealed by the luxuriant
foliage which hung in graceful festoons from the rocks above, we too were
seized with the romantic." Long before Greene printed these recollections,
Melville's description of the same scene in *Typee* (ch. 2) had become one of
the most familiar passages in the young American literature:

> Towards noon we drew abreast the entrance to the harbor, and at last we
> slowly swept by the intervening promontory, and entered the bay of Nuku-
> heva. No description can do justice to its beauty; but that beauty was lost to
> me then, and I saw nothing but the tri-colored flag of France trailing over the
> stern of six vessels, whose black hulls and bristling broadsides proclaimed
> their warlike character. . . . The whole group of islands had just been taken
> possession of by Rear Admiral Du Petit Thouars, in the name of the invinc-
> ible French nation.

For Melville, not the forgetful Greene, the beauty of the bay was marred by
the presence of the huge black French flagship *La Reine Blanche* and a squadron of men-of-war with which Rear Admiral Du Petit-Thouars on 2 June
had taken possession of the Marquesas Islands in the name of France. Melville had embarked upon what became a habit — being an eyewitness to history in the making, or near enough so to make a good story.

According to *Typee* (ch. 2), as Melville's ship "slowly advanced up the
bay, numerous canoes pushed off from the surrounding shores," so that the
sailors "were soon in the midst of quite a flotilla of them, their savage occupants struggling to get aboard." As the whaler progressed within a mile and a
half of the beach, some of the islanders pointed out "a singular commotion in
the water ahead of the vessel" — a disturbance caused by "a shoal of 'whi-
henies' (young girls)" swimming out to welcome them — the wondrous local
custom that all whalemen knew to expect. The *Acushnet*, which had sailed
over known and nameless creatures of the deep, which had sailed toward
whales and slaughtered them and brought them to the side of the ship,
now under slow headway "sailed right into the midst of these swimming
nymphs," who boarded at every quarter. Since the first Spanish ships under

Mendaña touched at Nukahiva in 1595, adolescent island girls had swum out to offer themselves to the sailors. They swam naked, holding their slight garments above the water for donning after they dried their remarkably beautiful bodies (in the time before European diseases marred them), and it was the rare ship on which their sexual intentions were thwarted. Melville's description in *Typee* is facetious in its implied comparison to American or European dances, but accurate:

> What a sight for us bachelor sailors! how avoid so dire a temptation? For who could think of tumbling these artless creatures overboard, when they had swam miles to welcome us?
>
> In the evening after we had come to an anchor the deck was illuminated with lanterns, and this picturesque band of sylphs, tricked out with flowers, and dressed in robes of variegated tappa, got up a ball in great style. These females are passionately fond of dancing, and in the wild grace and spirit of their style excel everything that I have ever seen.

What took place was not in question — it was an orgy such as few landspeople could have witnessed.

For many a white whaleman new to the islands, the Marquesan welcome was their first experience with interracial sex, a fraternity of opportunity unthinkable at home, when brothels open to sailors were race-specific. Black and white members of the whaling crews tended to separate themselves, whaling logs show, but here in the Marquesas no black or American Indian sailor aboard could be denied access to brown women: sexual needs created, for the time, equality. Furthermore, the sexual urges were satisfied under circumstances where no one but the captain could ever achieve privacy. Melville wrote in *Typee:* "Our ship was now wholly given up to every species of riot and debauchery. Not the feeblest barrier was interposed between the unholy passions of the crew and their unlimited gratification." He followed his description of the orgy with a gesture toward his mother and other decent folk: he himself, the reader was left belatedly to conclude, stood aloof from the debauchery, whether from moral or religious scruples or concern about his health. He had looked on, so he later implied, fascinated but aghast. Melville's mother had told him how to resist temptation, in words similar to those she used the year before, 1841, in lecturing Allan: he was to draw on the "Celestial power" of reason to enable him "to resist the natural, depraved & consequently sinful propensities" of his nature. Original Sin had not become an outmoded theological conceit in Maria Melville's house, and till his death her second son had to resort to that concept, at times, to make sense of the world. Albany, as every reader of the *Microscope* knew, had flourishing brothels, patronized by young members of debating clubs and by members of the debating sessions of the State Assembly, and in Liverpool even Paradise Street was a stew. By now ample opportunities had come his way to yield to the sinful propensities of his nature, and he had seen enough to doubt the chances that reason, that celestial power, could conquer sexual temptation.

A thinking young man with a great deal of self-control might well have resisted temptation, although the examples of Herman's Gansevoort and Melvill cousins do not suggest that moral principle and the goddess Hygeia routinely triumphed when opportunities for sex with women came their way. On 7 January 1843, Cousin Hunn Gansevoort delivered this advice to Herman's childhood playmate Cousin Stanwix, then on the *Erie:* "I know it to be impossible at your age to abstain from pleasures that are *Moral Sins,* and I therefore tell you that where indulgence is necessary, indulge in moderation; for remember that the laws of nature admit of the abuse of no pleasure, without bringing a consequent punishment." (Cousin Hunn shared a set of great-great-grandparents with Herman and Stanwix, but he was related in other ways to Herman and particularly to Stanwix.) Hunn knew what he was talking about, for he already had a venereal disease. His language is specific: abstinence was "impossible" at Cousin Stanwix's age, and therefore, one would think, impossible for Cousin Herman, only three years his elder. Some cases of the "bad disorder" that proved the end of many of Herman Melville's shipmates must already have been apparent to him, given the close quarters of the forecastle, and if other crews that had preceded the *Acushnet* to Nukahiva Bay had been composed of men with fewer scruples than his own shipmates, as well as the fewer early advantages he purportedly had written of to Gansevoort, then the likelihood that the native women were infected with European venereal diseases was all the greater. Herman had strong reason for abstaining from pleasures that were moral sins, for such pleasures might prove, in earthly terms, mortal. Yet if Herman heeded the monitor of his conscience during the ceremonies of welcome, it may have been because he was thinking about his chances of getting inland, where the sexual welcome would be as enthusiastic and where the brown girls, if Providence were kind, would never have been touched by men from whaleships.

During the next days Melville had an opportunity to see just how impartial the girls were with their bodies, for at least one other whaler sailed in to the same reception, the *Potomac* of Nantucket, on which William Macy made this record in the ship's journal for 4 July 1842 (recording the presence of vessels which Greene later conveniently ignored): "At daylight stood in for the Bay with a very light breese & at 10 AM dropped anchor, lying here Fr frigate La Reine Blanche 54 guns frigate La Boussole & sloop of war transport La Bucephale with 200 convicts[.] the French intend to make a sort of Botany Bay of this place & are building a fort here[.] at anchor ship Acushnet,

Pease of Fairhaven 18 m[onth]s out 950 Bbls[.] in a few minutes the decks were crowded with Kanackas mostly girls swimming off like a school of porpoises." Anyone on the *Acushnet* could see the girls as they swam to the *Potomac* and belatedly consider just how many ships the girls had boarded in the last months, a sobering thought, perhaps, to a few of the men. (Any thoughtful man on the *Acushnet*, like Macy on the *Potomac*, could reflect further on the horrific implications of the French plan to make a penal colony out of what was left of paradise.)

The crew of the *Acushnet* knew well enough what might happen to deserters lucky enough to escape the natives and be recaptured by their own shipmates: they were routinely put in irons for a time. Nevertheless, at Nukahiva Bay (if not before his arrival there) Melville made the most fateful decision of his life to this point. As he put it in *Typee* (ch. 4): "To use the concise, point-blank phrase of the sailors, I had made up my mind to 'run away.'" According to *Typee* (ch. 5), one night on deck he perceived "Toby" leaning over the bulwarks, buried in thought, and, tapping him on the shoulder, broached the enterprise to him, with this result: "We then ratified our engagement with an affectionate wedding of palms, and to elude suspicion repaired each to his hammock, to spend the last night on board." In 1846 after the publication of *Typee*, Richard Tobias Greene came forward as the "Toby" of the tale. Under circumstances where it was not in his interest to quibble about details, he confirmed *Typee* as far as his own participation was concerned, and never disputed any of those details through his long life. Melville's narrative of the desertion in *Typee* is not the unvarnished truth, but true in much of its substance and grand items, truth a good deal varnished. Melville's account in *Typee* luckily is supplemented by Greene's long account in 1846 and a few slighter comments Greene later made.

When Melville and Greene were sent ashore on liberty on 9 July, they already planned to detach themselves surreptitiously and strike north toward the mountains. Their intention was not to go native (as some white men had done) but to sign on another ship after they had explored the island's terrain and its flora and fauna, it being well known that not many questions would be asked by the next American whaler short of hands. The fact that this was the wet season assisted the runaways, for, according to Melville, the rain trapped the sailors under cover of a canoe-house near the beach and the others eventually fell asleep, giving him and Toby the opportunity to steal out and plunge into the depths of a grove beyond which they began ascending a mountain. By climbing from early morning to midafternoon, the young sailors reached "what seemed to be the highest land on the island" (*Typee*, ch. 6). The first night, in Melville's version, was one of unforgettable horror, during which the rain "descended in such torrents" that their "poor shelter proved a mere mockery" (ch. 7). By noon on 10 July they were "ascending a long and gradually rising slope" and took shelter from a rainstorm in bushes near the top. Drenched again, Melville later claimed, he fell victim to chills and fevers while one of his legs swelled up so painfully that he suspected he had been bitten "by some venomous reptile." From the other side of the bushes, Melville said, he "looked straight down into the bosom of a valley" (ch. 7) cut off from them by a parallel series of ravines and ridges, and the question (as propounded in ch. 8) was which valley, the abode of the peaceable Happars or of "their enemies the ferocious Typees." (The first English readers were kept in suspense longer than American readers, since "Typee" was nowhere in the London title.) By the fourth day after leaving Nukahiva, that is, 12 July, the runaways, according to Melville, were suffering acutely from hunger; it is hard fact, reported in Macy's journal of the *Potomac*, that the *Acushnet* on the eleventh sailed, "intending to lay of[f] for a day or two & send boat in for her men who have deserted."

The runaways on 12 July performed, according to Melville, astonishing feats of climbing up and descending, such as leaping off a cliff into a treetop when the slope was too steep for them to make their way down on foot (ch. 9). On the evening of 13 July, Melville claimed, they "stood on the brink of a precipice over which the dark stream bounded in one final leap of full 300 feet," the descent terminating in the valley they had glimpsed late on 10 July:

> As it was now near sunset we determined to pass the night where we were, and on the morrow, refreshed by sleep and by eating at one meal all our stock of food, to accomplish a descent into the valley, or perish in the attempt. . . .
>
>   During the whole of this night the continual roaring of the cataract — the dismal moaning of the gale through the trees — the pattering of the rain, and the profound darkness, affected my spirits to a degree which nothing had ever before produced. (*Typee*, ch. 9)

This depression of spirits preceded the scene every reader had awaited avidly. The next day, 13 July, just before dusk, the young white men saw their first natives and soon found themselves in "a large and handsome building of bamboos" where they "held a kind of levee," at which they gave audience "to successive troops of the natives" (ch. 10). Then late at night they were left to sleep among "those who appeared to be permanent residents of the house."

The next part of the story as Melville wrote it down was dominated by the life-and-death question, melodramatically expressed at the start of chapter 11: "Was it possible that, after all our vicissitudes, we were really in the terrible valley of Typee, and at the mercy of its inmates, a fierce and unrelenting tribe of savages?" This question, Melville says, remained in their

minds during the benign experiences that followed. The runaways were fed
poi-poi, given soporific tobacco or an acceptable substitute to smoke in a
pipe, and allowed the chance to become familiar with ten or so members of
their particular household (among whom were three young men, "dissipated,
good-for-nothing, roystering blades of savages," and several young damsels,
including "the beauteous nymph Fayaway," whom Melville identified as his
particular favorite). In the next days, Melville explained, he became acquainted with the elaborately tattooed and splendidly bedecked Chief Mehevi and some hundreds of men, women, and children, notably many young
girls or women "fancifully decorated with flowers" and eagerly expressing
childish delight and curiosity about their visitors. In chapter 12 of *Typee*
Melville made much of his claim to being lame, describing the machinations
of the aged doctor and the post-manipulative dressing that left his limb
"swathed in leafy bandages." He claimed to have been carried to his "first
bath in the valley" on the shoulders of the faithful Kory-Kory, "like the old
man of the sea astride of Sindbad." He described his first sight of "the
hallowed 'Hoolah Hoolah' ground," the place of sacrifice — that is, the sacrifice of breadfruit and coconuts, if not human flesh. Among such scenes, he
summarized, "a week passed away almost imperceptibly," it being impossible
for him to think of going anywhere else until he recovered from lameness,
which resisted the herbal remedies.

The lameness sounds like a fictional device to account for the narrator's
having time and occasion for making close observations of Marquesan manners, mores, and artifacts, and in *Typee* it had the effect of encouraging any
reader with a quiet imagination to assume that an injury to any limb rendered
the narrator a sexual nonparticipant. The claim of lameness, however, is
confirmed by the medical records kept by a doctor at Tahiti and vouched for
by Toby Greene in 1846. In *Typee* Toby parts company with "Tommo"
(Melville's name for himself) in order to seek medicine for him: "At last, in
the exigency to which I was reduced, I proposed to Toby that he should
endeavor to go round to Nukuheva, and if he could not succeed in returning
to the valley by water, in one of the boats of the squadron, and taking me off,
he might at least procure me some proper medicines, and effect his return
overland" (ch. 13). Around 22 July, in fact, Toby Greene left, intending to
make straight for the beach of Typee Bay, a much less strenuous route than
he and Melville had taken in their flight. He promised to return as soon as he
could and returned very soon indeed — having been injured on the way in an
attack by the Happar tribe, as he attested in 1846 ("I have the scar on my
head which I received from the Happar spear and which came near to killing
me").

About 27 July Toby set forth again, and Melville never saw him after that until they met in Rochester in July 1846, after Toby had read *Typee* and given his own story to the Buffalo *Commercial Advertiser:*

> I left MELVILLE and fell in with an Irishman, who had resided on the Island for some time, and who assisted me in returning to ship, and who faithfully promised me to go and bring MELVILLE to our ship next day, which he never did, his only object being money. I gave him five dollars to get me on board, but could not return to MELVILLE. I sailed to New Zealand and thence home.

Then, in 1846, Toby Greene confirmed various specifics in *Typee* in the form of an open letter to Melville himself: "You recollect that I started a little after sunrise out of the valley, and with me went, Fayaway, Markeyo, Mow Mow with the one eye, and the two young Typees, living in our house, and some one hundred and fifty besides, carrying hogs, cocoa nuts, banana &c., to trade, expecting boats in the bay." When they reached the beach, he explained,

> I discovered a white man standing there, surrounded by a number of natives. This man had just arrived from Nukeheva. . . . He came on board of the *Dolly* [!] shortly after our arrival in port. He had a great deal of tattooing about his person. He was an Irishman, called Jimmy Fitch. On his perceiving me, he welcomed me to the beach, asked me if I wished to leave the bay and get a ship. I told him that I did, but that I had a shipmate up in the valley, who, on account of lameness, could not come down; that I would go up to him and get some assistance to carry him to the beach. . . . The Irishman then came to me and then told me that in all probability if I should force my way up where Melville was, we would never come down. He then made me a faithful promise [for five dollars] that he would have my companion away the next day.

Toby next described his farewell to Fayaway and his departure with Jimmy and one Typee carrying a hog on his shoulder, the rest of the company leaving their fruit on the beach and turning back toward the Typee valley even before Toby was out of sight. Reaching Nukahiva about dark that same day, Toby was powerless over what happened next:

> I was immediately hurried on board the *London Packet*, as the Captain wanted me — badly; but my sorry appearance after the loss of much blood boded no good in my favor. The Captain was loth to ship me, as he thought I was sick. — However I entered my name on the ship's articles. I told him I had a companion in Typee, and asked for a boat and crew armed that we might go and release him. But the captain had no such idea. No, he was not going to trust his men amongst the bloody cannibals, though I must say, the crew were eager for the enterprise. He told me Jimmy would have my friend on board the next evening.

In Toby's account, Jimmy betrays him, returning the next evening without Melville, provoking this rage: "So soon as Jimmy struck the beach I seized him, shouting in a voice that startled him, where is MELVILLE?" But the threats were to no avail, and the *London Packet* sailed in a day or two, about 28 or 29 July, with Toby but without his friend.

This is Melville's account in *Typee*, written some year and a half before Toby's: "Towards sunset the islanders in small parties began to return from the beach," and nowhere among the natives could he "descry" the form of his companion. His questions "appeared to embarrass the natives greatly," and to distress Fayaway: "She looked round from one to another of the bye-standers, as if hardly knowing what answer to give me. At last, yielding to my importunities, she overcame her scruples, and gave me to understand that Toby had gone away with the boats which had visited the bay, but had promised to return at the expiration of three days" (ch. 14). In *Typee*, and probably in his real experience, Melville had no certain knowledge of what had happened to Toby, and therefore could justifiably entertain the gloomiest suspicions as to his fate. He spent the best part of the next two weeks alone with the Typees, during which time his twenty-third birthday and Helen's twenty-fifth occurred. He may not have known precisely which day was his birthday.

[12]

Beachcomber and Whaler
1842–1843

Disdain not your Inferior tho' poor; since he may be your Superior in Wisdom, and the noble Endowments of the Mind.

"Allan Melvills Book," 1796

ON 7 AUGUST 1842 an Australian whaler, the barque *Lucy Ann*, a ship in which disorder approached open revolt, put into Nukahiva in order to enlist sailors. The man who passed as ship's doctor, John Troy, deserted at Nukahiva with the medicine supply but was caught and returned by the natives, according to an affidavit by Benbow Byrne, the boatsteerer. The captain, Henry Ventom, an Englishman, learning that he could exchange trinkets ("suitable articles of traffic," in Melville's words) for an American sailor detained by savages, sailed to the entrance of Typee Bay. On 9 August Melville was accordingly conveyed down the route Toby had taken, and upon reaching the beach saw (he wrote in *Typee*) an English whaleboat manned by five islanders, one of whom had been one of the regulars aboard the *Acushnet* while it was in harbor.

In short order Melville was aboard what in *Omoo* (1847) he described as "a small, slatternly looking craft, her hull and spars a dingy black, rigging all slack and bleached nearly white, and every thing denoting an ill state of affairs aboard," her four hanging boats identifying her as a whaler. A scene followed probably very like the one Melville described there (ch. 1):

> When we came alongside, a low cry ran fore and aft the deck, and every body gazed at us with inquiring eyes. And well they might. To say nothing of the savage boat's crew, panting with excitement, all gesture and vociferation, my own appearance was calculated to excite curiosity. A robe of the native cloth was thrown over my shoulders, my hair and beard were uncut, and I betrayed other evidences of my recent adventure. Immediately on gaining the deck, they beset me on all sides with questions. . . .
>
> But a few moments passed ere I was sent for into the cabin by the captain.
> He was quite a young man, pale and slender, more like a sickly counting-

house clerk than a bluff sea-captain. Bidding me be seated, he ordered the
steward to hand me a glass of Pisco. In the state I was, this stimulus almost
made me delirious. . . . After this I was asked whether I desired to "ship;" of
course I said yes; that is, if he would allow me to enter for one cruise, engaging
to discharge me, if I so desired, at the next port. . . . My stipulation was
acceded to, and the ship's articles handed me to sign.

Melville recognized two of the men, one he had met in Liverpool and another he had met in Rio. The crew list, which survives, shows that Herman
Melville, able seaman, shipped on 9 August at Nukahiva Bay at 1/120th lay,
no advance received. The next day on the *Lucy Ann* Melville saw the "blue,
looming island of St. Christina" on the horizon, and (he remembered in
Omoo) he also saw a French corvette, for him already a symbol of ruthless
colonialism.

To judge from the affidavit he swore to on 5 October 1842, before
Charles B. Wilson, Her Britannic Majesty's acting consul in Tahiti, Captain
Ventom of the barque *Lucy Ann* of Sydney was indeed a less than forceful
master at the time he took Melville aboard as an able seaman. Two months
earlier, on 7 June, when he had anchored in Resolution Bay on Santa Christina, eight crew members and an officer had deserted (the second mate,
carpenter, and seven others, according to an affidavit of the first mate). At
that time, Ventom had adjudged two more crewmen mutinous and had put
them in irons and delivered them to Rear-Admiral A. du Petit-Thouars on
board the frigate *Reine Blanche* for transportation to the English admiral
commanding at Valparaiso. (One of these men, George Lefevre, later entered oddly into Melville's life.) In August, just after Melville came on board,
Ventom hoped to pick up the deserters, who by now (*Omoo*, ch. 3) "must have
recreated themselves sufficiently," as Melville had done among the Typees,
and "would be glad to return to their duty," as he had been. Melville may
have managed to ingratiate himself easily enough with some of the crew,
particularly since he knew two of the men already. Even on the *Acushnet* he
had whiled away night watches with yarn and song, but on the *Lucy Ann* he
had even better stories to tell. As he wrote in his preface to *Typee*, "notwithstanding the familiarity of sailors with all sorts of curious adventure, the
incidents recorded in the following pages have often served, when 'spun as a
yarn,' not only to relieve the weariness of many a night-watch at sea, but to
excite the warmest sympathies of the author's shipmates." Melville was more
than ever a winsome fellow with fine yarns to tell, but the *Lucy Ann* may have
been one of the few whaling ships then in the Pacific where circumstances
were not conducive to relaxed storytelling and where even an incautious

young man might have bided his time before allying himself with one group or another in this fractious crew.

From Santa Christina Captain Ventom frustrated the expectations of most of the crew by making not for the open sea and the profits of whaling but for La Dominica, or Hivarhoo, where (the commander of the corvette had told Ventom) some English sailors had recently deserted from an American whaler. There on 26 August the *Lucy Ann* signed on a trio of recidivist deserters, John Garretson (boatsteerer) and William Bunwell and Amado Sylva (able seamen). On 20 August, when he left the Marquesas, the captain had his "full complement of able & ordinary seamen but not officers." Ventom himself was, he swore, "then perfectly well in health & strength," as were "all on board with the exception of five of the crew who were ailing & ill of the venereal." The presence of these diseased men was, for Melville, a reminder of the known venerealees on the *Acushnet*, with whom he had also slept in tight quarters, as well as an uncomfortable reminder of the infection he had every reason to be fearful of when the damsels boarded the *Acushnet*. Captain Ventom became ill on 27 August and worsened steadily, so that he was confined to his cabin on 4 September, and a few days later instructed James German, his "Chief officer" (what the Americans called first mate) to proceed to Tahiti in the Society Islands. A man not only of intimidating physical strength but of some independence of mind, German had already turned the ship toward Tahiti without waiting for orders.

The *Lucy Ann* arrived at Tahiti on 20 September 1842 but stood off, instead of anchoring at the port, thereby tantalizing the crew with an astonishing view, much like what Captain Charles Wilkes observed late in 1839. In front, Wilkes said, "the little coral island of Moto-utu forms an embellished foreground, and serves to break the regularity of the line of the harbour, while by concealing its extent, it gives it an air of greater magnitude than it in reality possesses." Behind the coral island lay "the semi-circular harbour, surrounded by the white cottages and churches of the village, embosomed in luxuriant foliage; these dwellings have a peaceful and home-like look, to the eye of an American." Beyond, the background was "filled up with a number of pinnacle-shaped mountains, jutting up in a great variety of forms." All in all, the view at Papeete was "remarkable," a "perfect picture of Polynesian scenery, enhanced in beauty by the signs of civilization, among which was the national flag of Tahiti, waving from a fortress on Moto-utu." The scenery had not changed, but the national flag may not have waved when Melville arrived: the French flag may have been flying there since 9 September.

As at Nukahiva, Melville came to Tahiti just in time to witness colonialism triumphant, symbolized for him by the ominous French ships. *La Reine Blanche* was never easy to ignore. On 8 September Admiral Du Petit-Thouars had lured the Tahitian chiefs aboard for friendly discussions. In W. T. Pritchard's *Polynesian Reminiscences* (London, 1866), one of the Tahitians, Chief Tati, recalled this exercise in international extortion: "Queen Pomare must either give him money or Tahiti, or he would fire upon the land. We were greatly afraid, and talked amongst ourselves. The Chief Utami and I said to the Regent, 'Is this the friendly meeting you asked us to attend?'" The next day the admiral sent an ultimatum: "Sign this paper, or pay ten thousand dollars within twenty-four hours; if the paper with the Queen's signature or the money be not before me within the twenty-four hours, I fire upon Papeete without further notice." *La Reine Blanche* prepared to bombard Papeete while brown Queen Pomare lay in childbirth; during her labor, "weeping and sobbing," she "signed her name to the document, and Tahiti was gone!" (This is the secondhand version of W. T. Pritchard, son of the missionary and British consul George Pritchard, who was away on a trip to London at this time, and being represented in Tahiti by Charles B. Wilson.) In the appendix to *Typee* Melville later declared: "The author of this volume arrived at Tahiti the very day that the iniquitous designs of the French were consummated by inducing the subordinate chiefs, during the absence of their queen, to ratify an artfully drawn treaty, by which she was virtually deposed." Even if not there that "very day," Melville was there in Papeete when the local resentment against the French was at its highest, and he absorbed it in full measure. He had a chance later to see a copy of the March 1843 extra of the Honolulu *Temperance Advocate and Seamen's Friend* containing Rear Admiral Abel du Petit-Thouars's proclamation of the seizure of the Society Islands. The commander of the Legion of Honor had not scrupled to make the proclamation "in the name of Her Majesty Queen Pomare." In this Gallicly smooth document the party of the first part, Pomare, and the party of the second part, the admiral, announced that they were "under the necessity of founding at Tahiti a Provisional Government to direct the affairs in that which concerns the whites, foreign relations, and to guarantee personal security, rights and public order." The document was nothing less than an assertion that "the protection of His Majesty Louis Phillippe" was thereby extended to the Society Islands.

Upon approaching the harbor on 20 September, James German took a boat to shore to bring aboard Dr. Francis Johnstone, who promptly insisted on taking Ventom off for treatment. On the twenty-second the captain was lowered down and taken ashore, after leaving word for German to keep the vessel "off and on the port." Wilson, the acting British consul, went on board and mustered the men aft, where (German affirmed) the crew told Wilson that they wanted the sick men taken ashore and a full complement of seamen and officers signed before the ship returned to sea under the chief officer. In the presence of the intimidating German, the men declined to find any fault with him, but three or four of them spoke up (as quoted just below), citing the technical point that they had signed to ship under Captain Ventom, not German. Dr. Johnstone (according to his own affidavit) went back on board, examined six crew members, apparently including Herman Melville, and ordered only two, Nicholas Utley and Henry Smyth, to be taken off for treatment, while he pronounced healthy the others who had already refused to do their duty. Even before Wilson and Johnstone were both ashore, conditions had deteriorated, to judge from German's account:

> Soon after "Garretson" — "Sylva" — and "C. Watts" [and William Bunnell, according to Wilson] said that they would do no more duty on board of the vessel — they said "We signed under Captain 'Ventom' and not under the mate and our agreement is broken by the Captain's leaving and going on shore." Shortly after Mr. Wilson left the vessel several more of the crew refused to do their duty and during the night Twelve of the crew including those who said [they] were ill were off duty — "Troy" — "Matthews" — "J. Smyth" — and "Melville" were reported by the Doctor well enough to do their duty[.] "Utley" — and "Henry Smyth" were not well enough to do duty — and "Burk" — "Garretson" — "C. Watts" — "J. Watts" — "Sylva" — and "Fraser" refused because I was to take command of the vessel.

On the twenty-third, Ventom affirmed, Wilson (not knowing anything seriously untoward was happening on the *Lucy Ann*) shipped two officers and two men, using his power as consul, but that night there was trouble. Benbow Byrne, boatsteerer and now acting third mate, had an altercation with James Watts and struck him. This is from Benbow Byrne's affidavit: "After the Acting Consul left the Ship several others refused to do their duty. I had the first watch that night, the mate told me to set the Jib and Foresail. I ordered the watch to set those sails. 'James Watts' said that he would not obey my orders and when I told him to haul down the fore tack, he replied saying 'Ask my arse'. I then struck him. 'Troy' took his part. After the quarrel 'Watts' said he would do no more duty and went below." On this night, Byrne affirmed, German was "quite sober" — given the source, a fair indication that on this occasion the chief officer was noticeably drunk.

On Saturday the twenty-fourth Wilson had a surprise: German brought the *Lucy Ann* into port, and told Ventom that "he was obliged to bring the vessel into port in consequence of Ten of the crew having refused to do any more duty, there not being left sufficient on duty to work the vessel, and to keep her at sea with safety." Wilson went on board, mustered the men aft, and separated them, placing on one side of the deck all who refused to do duty — a sorting out impossible for any well-churched young witness not to see as a separating of the sheep from the goats. In the afternoon of the twenty-fourth Wilson returned, followed by an armed boat from the *Reine Blanche*, with an officer to take away the ten who refused to do their duty, whom German itemized: Garretson, Sylva, Bunnell, and Charles Watts (the first who had refused duty, "the ringleaders in the affair"), and Burk, Fraser, and James Watts, as well as Troy, Matthews, and James Smyth. (Troy was particularly obnoxious because he had not only deserted at Nukahiva but had displayed the effrontery to take with him the contents of the medicine chest, which had been put into his keeping.) The guard took the ten off the vessel and put them into prison on *La Reine Blanche*. This ten did not include Melville.

On Sunday, 25 September, Henry Smyth, back on board the *Lucy Ann* after treatment, was seized with an urge to write to George Lefevre, one of the sailors who had been put in irons at Santa Christina and was still a prisoner aboard *La Reine Blanche*. Being illiterate, Smyth dictated this letter to the runaway the *Lucy Ann* had picked up at Typee Bay:

> On arriving here the other day I was sorry to hear that you were verry ill on board the French Frigate. — I should like verry much to go and see you but I cannot possibly as I can not be allowed to; — so I take the liberty to write you a few lines. — You know we all agreed to hang out on your account when we came aboard from the Corvette — but it so happened that those who talked loudest were the first to return to their duty. I was the last one that went forward, and would not have turned to at all, but that I found it was of no use, — so after being in double irons some time I thought it best to go forward & do my duty as usual. . . .
>
> I often think of you & I & Young Smith have often talked about you during the night watches at sea.

In this letter (which survives in the Mitchell Library, Sydney, Australia), Melville was making himself endearingly useful. Men like Henry Smyth who can't pay their scribes have to settle for basic literacy, not pedantic correctness in spelling, but Melville amused himself by putting an altogether unnecessary amount of effort into the task. Improvising, as he may already have done in the wording of portions of the body of the letter, Melville located himself and Smyth with a flourish, "On Board the Lucy Ann," and concluded with a seven-line, variably indented complimentary close and signature, a parody of the model epistles such as his father had conscientiously imitated in his exercise book, which Maria still treasured in the house at Lansingburgh. Melville then addressed the letter to George Lefevre "On Board The

French Frigate." All in all, Melville took more trouble to make this letter elegant and correct than he did with most of his own letters.

Early in the morning of Monday, 26 September, according to Wilson's notes, the prisoners were landed from the frigate and given in charge of the "Native Authorities." Then *La Reine Blanche* got under way for Valparaiso. On Wednesday the twenty-eighth Wilson examined the prisoners before Captain Ventom and in the presence of Dr. Myrick (not Johnstone this time), and heard from the men that they now refused to do their duty even if Ventom were to go on board and take command from German. Perhaps they felt it useless to complain about what everyone on board knew — German's alcoholism — but they refused to specify any reason other than that they had signed under Captain Ventom and not under the mate, a plea that contradicts the other pronouncement attributed to them, that they would not serve under either German or Ventom. It is not clear where this examination took place, but Melville was there, and spoke up, saying "that he would do no more duty and would share the same as the others who refused to do their duty." Wilson sent the men back to prison. The names of the "men who refused to do duty" Ventom now listed, including an eleventh: John B. Troy, Henry Burk, James Smyth, William Matthews, David Frazer, Amado Sylva, John Garretson, William Bunnell, Charles Watts, James Watts — and Herman Melville, who was remanded to prison along with the original ten. (Wilson noted on the twenty-ninth: "Examind Prisoners, still refused & sent back to prison & Herman Melville joined the Ten.") In the fever of affidavit-taking the good sailors who had been separated from the bad were allowed to identify themselves and finger a rebellious ten (including Melville but omitting James Watts, probably an oversight caused by their having listed one Watts already, Charles). Furthermore, the good sailors blackened the rebels by solemnly and sincerely declaring on oath that they themselves never had cause to refuse their duty and never had done so, never had aided and abetted the guilty parties, and, to clinch it all, were "perfectly satisfied with the provisions and treatment" they had received.

On 5 October Wilson brought the revolters into the British consulate, where they once again positively refused to return to duty, upon which he ordered that they all (he itemized ten, not including Melville) "be returned to prison and kept in confinement in charge of the Tahitian authorities for such *revolt* and *refusal of duty* as preferred against the before named Garritson — Bunnell — Sylva — Charles Watts — James Smyth — Henry Burke — James Watts — William Matthews — David Fraser — and for embezzlement and refusal of duty as preferred against the said 'John B. Troy.'" However, Wilson's memorandum of revolting seamen included Melville's name among the eleven. Melville had heard from the other revolters all he needed to know of imprisonment in *La Reine Blanche*, but he experienced quite another form of confinement. To get to the "Calabooza Beretanee" (i.e., the British jail), the revolters were taken a mile or so from the village of Papeete down the picturesque — indeed, gorgeous — Broom Road, not a sterile, swept-dirt path as the name might imply but a wide road overarched by foliage, originally built to connect missionary stations, with wooden bridges spanning watercourses and even stone arches spanning smaller streams. From the sea it was visible all the way from Papeete to Mataivai Bay. According to Melville's account in *Omoo*, a fat old native, shouting "Calabooza! Calabooza Beretanee!" herded the men along a fine pathway through wide groves of coconut and breadfruit trees to a large oval house, the thatch dazzling white, on the summit of a slope near the road (ch. 31). Melville described the jail as a shell, open all round, furnished with the "stocks" — the lower beam of which had semicircular spaces for at least twenty-two ankles and the upper beam of which could be lowered and fastened with an iron hoop at either end. The whole business, in Melville's account in *Omoo*, was the occasion of boisterous mirth among the natives.

Wilson had made an error in delaying until the *Reine Blanche* had sailed for Valparaiso, for by 4 or 5 October, when he asked the assistance of the French Provisional Council in deciding the "exceedingly difficult case" of the revolt on the *Lucy Ann*, he was told to try to persuade the men to return to duty and if they refused to keep them imprisoned until another warship arrived — that is, to keep charge of them indefinitely. He may have tried to intimidate the revolters by threatening to send them to Sydney for trial, as Melville alleged in *Omoo*, but without effect. Dr. Johnstone, meanwhile, was visiting the prisoners and prescribing for them. His dose book for 14 or 15 October shows he ministered to "Melvill Herman — Stocks." The next day, about the day the *Lucy Ann* sailed, the dose book showed a charge for an "Embrocation" given to Melville, a liniment-like ointment. As Melville told the story, he was most of the time only a nominal prisoner, and free with the other mutineers to run down to the beach to see the *Lucy Ann* off. There, bilged upon the beach (Melville said in *Omoo*, ch. 27), was "the condemned hull of a large ship," an old American whaler: "What were my emotions, when I saw upon her stern the name of a small town on the river Hudson! She was from the noble stream on whose banks I was born; in whose waters I had a hundred times bathed."

The days in Tahiti may have been among the most carefree of Melville's life, for he was in an island still very like Paradise, if he did not look too closely at what was happening to the Polynesian ways of life and to the bodies of the surviving Polynesians, and he had, as he seldom did, a compatible companion, Troy — whom he called Long Ghost in *Omoo*. Troy was more interesting than Toby because he was better educated, because he was unpredictably irresponsible, and because he was English (and therefore formed by different experiences than anyone Herman had known well). The *Lucy Ann* gone, Wilson soon refused to feed the mutineers, but Dr. Johnstone continued for a time to minister to their feigned needs, prescribing another embrocation for Melville on 19 October, which brought his total charge, in dollars, to $1.50. At some point he forced his patients to sign a sheet headed "This is to certify that we have received Medical assistance and attendance as herein stated," and Melville signed himself neatly after Mathews and before the illiterate Garretson, third after John Troy.

Melville's account of his adventures in *Omoo* (1847) naturally led visitors to Tahiti to want to find out what could be verified, and as early as 1851 Edward Lucett published the results of his investigations in *Rovings in the Pacific:* "I had the curiosity to search Dr. Johnstone's medical diary: the names of all the mutineers were enrolled there, and amongst them stands Herman Melville's. The whole of the doctor's charges for medicine and medical attendance amounts to but a few dollars, and the only item charged against Herman Melville is a bottle of embrocation, as the man complained of pains in his limbs: but the doctor believing him to be an impostor, which by the way I think he has clearly shown himself to have been, paid no further heed to his complaints." The likelihood that Melville was malingering in Tahiti casts doubt backward on his lameness in the Typee valley, but Greene explicitly confirmed it, and without Melville's lameness as a motivation it is hard to see why Greene would have left him in the valley. Lucett did not see the bill the medical practitioners submitted to Wilson "For Medicines & Medical assistance for the following distressed British Seamen," a document that specifies treatment of John Troy from 10 October to 19 November ($24.25) and treatment of Herman Melville from 15 October to 19 November ($19.50): the medical man had kept on padding the bill even after his patients had decamped.

For, within days of the departure of the whaler, Melville lost his zest for hanging around a free and easy jail, and in his chattings at Papeete he met Yankees (twins, he said) who had jumped ship at Fanning's Island and after much roving had settled on Eimeo, the island adjacent to Tahiti. Captain Wilkes had romanticized Eimeo (now called Moorea) from the sea as he saw it three years earlier: "Eimeo is a beautiful object in the view from Tahiti, and its beauty is enhanced on a nearer approach; its hills and mountains may, without any great stretch of the imagination, be converted into battlements, spires, and towers, rising one above the other; their gray sides are clothed here and there with verdure, which at a distance resembles ivy of the richest hue." Employed by plantation owners there, the Yankees had been dispatched to Tahiti to recruit field-laborers to be their own replacements. In *Omoo* Melville described a midnight escape with Long Ghost across the channel to Eimeo (ch. 51): "The moon was up—the air, warm—the waves, musical—and all above was the tropical night, one purple vault hung round with soft, trembling stars," while the "three great peaks of Tahiti" lorded it over ranges of mountains and valleys. On the other side "the equally romantic elevations of Imeeo" were topped by the "verdant" spire called "the Marling-spike"—("verdant" in daylight, at least). The escape as depicted in *Omoo* is fictionalized, but Melville and Troy may indeed have made some gesture toward surreptitiousness. While much of *Omoo* turns out to be quite fictional, the Yankee boys were real brothers, though not twins, one of whom, William G. Libbey, published his "Autobiography of a Quondam Sailor" serially in the *Shaker Manifesto* in 1878.

About 19 October on Eimeo Melville and Troy presented themselves before a Cockney whom Melville called Shorty in *Omoo* and a Yankee he called Zeke. Libbey gives the facts: the young Londoner was "Edward by name," and his partner was "a Yankee named James Martin"; Melville probably never learned that an English merchant, safe in Sydney, was bankrolling the two. Martin with "Yankee ingenuity" had used saplings of "Burow" wood, placed upright and tight together, to produce "a house good enough for the climate" and sufficient to keep out "the natives and pigs." Edward and Martin had hired the Libbey brothers to help them raise sweet potatoes, according to the account in the *Shaker Manifesto*, where any intention of scrupulous Shaker accuracy was undercut by typographical corruptions:

> Here we continued to work hard clearing land for a new potato piece. Our food was bread fruit, sweet potatoes, and *fars* [taro?], the latter, a vegetable shaped like a sugar beet, grown by the natives, in beds of mud, kept wet by irrigation from a brook that ran past our house. . . . We had fish every meal, and for drink, cold water from the brook. . . . Our good friends had an old flintlock musket, with which I managed to shoot several goat and wild cattle which abounded on these mountains. I made a nice hammock of the skin of one animal and suspended it in our house making a comfortable sleeping place. . . . The musquitoes were so troublesome that sometimes we were forced to go to the beach and make our beds on the sand. . . . My ram-hide [rawhide?] hammock is noticed in a book written by Hermann Melville who was at Tahiti when we were at Eimeo.

The Libbey brothers had worked cheerfully clearing away guava bushes and other shrubs with such tools as they "could procure at Affraito"—clumsy axes and mattocks, well-tested implements they bequeathed to the new recruits.

Melville and Troy were hired to work with cheerfulness to equal that of the Libbey brothers, and they may have done so, briefly, before absenting themselves from manual labor and exploring the island. In their wanderings they came to Taloo, which Melville called "the only frequented harbor of Imeeo." Anchored there in late October was the *Charles and Henry*, John B. Coleman, master. On 2 November, disgruntled in the extreme at his bad luck in overfished waters, Coleman wrote the owners, Charles G. and Henry Coffin of Nantucket:

> I arrived here a few days ago with only 350 bls of Oil after an eight months cruise, we saw whales fourteen times the cruise on the of[f] shore ground and line and only got seven which made 140 bls, whales have been very wild that I have seen and seems almost impossible to get nigh them though I can assure you that I have not got the best whaleman in the world, my boat steerers have missed two Hundred and fifty bls and there has another Hundred gone off carelessly.

He attributed the wildness of the whales to there having been "so many ships to the Eastwd," stirring them up: "it is impossible for whales to be tame when there is so many ships." He now regretted that the owners had forbidden him to take his ship to the waters off Japan, previously, and now felt even that area might have been overfished. He intended, despite his frustration, to "make a long voyage": "the Ship is good and I have plenty of Provision for four years and then I think it will be time to head towards home, the Copper has just begun to break on the ships bottom I think it has wore well for I have not been still much since I have been round here." He needed some "Potatoes or yams" and planned to "touch at some of Islands and get some" if he could.

Two men had run away at Eimeo but Coleman was confident he could get them back: "I believe the natives have taken them today, they do not allow men to stop here, so soon pick them up when they do run." At Eimeo, also, he had discharged a boatsteerer, but intended "to ship another to-morrow." Coleman had his eye on three deserters, apparently from the *J. Adams*, but they asked "great lays," so that he was afraid he would have to give them "110 lays," the natives not being inclined to ship on whalers themselves. When Herman Melville presented himself the day after Coleman wrote his querulous lament to the owners, a man who had signed on the *Lucy Ann* for 1/120th lay, the captain welcomed him, asked a minimal number of questions about his immediate past, and agreed that he could sign for the cruise only, and go ashore at the first suitable port. Around 6 or 7 November Melville said good-bye to Troy and went aboard with only what was on his back.

Ashore, in Papeete, stories were being created about Melville. One of the reprobate revolters from the *Lucy Ann* appropriated the name "Herman Melville" in a way that guaranteed it would become infamous in Tahiti. On 16 November, when Melville was far at sea, Edward Lucett, "a most respectable British shipowner and merchant" (this from Wilson's outraged account), later the author of *Rovings in the Pacific*, was kidnapped by natives, and, along with his son, manhandled. The rowdy mutineers from the *Lucy Ann* regarded the treatment of the respectable Lucetts as highly comic, and kept up a stream of "exceedingly gross and insulting remarks," which were nothing compared to what followed when the natives tried to put the Lucetts in the stocks. When the upper beam was lifted to accommodate the Lucetts, one of the mutineers, "apparently the ringleader and spokesman for the others," seized the occasion to free himself and taunt the elder Lucett with "a highly spiced dish" of ironically sympathetic oratory. Then, uttering "a volley of oaths, the dastardly dog hereupon drew his sheath knife, and threw himself" upon the helpless merchant: "Herman Melville, undoubtedly the ringleader of the mutineers, was lying in the calliboose when I was dragged there; and from the un-English way in which the ruffian who assaulted me handled his knife, I have the strongest suspicion that it was Herman Melville who threw himself upon a bound defenceless man. . . . That he was in the calliboose at the time, there is not a question; and that the man was a Yankee who threw himself upon me I will swear." So Edward Lucett wrote in his *Rovings*.

One of the unintentionally comical aspects of the story is that, like a newspaper account in Liverpool during Melville's stay in 1839, it endearingly attests to the English conviction that only vile foreigners used knives in personal combat — an illusion carried to the farthest outposts of the Empire and beyond. If Lucett had not been convinced that Herman Melville had assailed him, he might not have thought, later on, to scrutinize Dr. Johnstone's medical diary. Neither Wilson nor anyone else corrected the Lucetts' mistaken identification, and the very quietness of Melville's departure with Troy seems to have contributed to a mounting exasperation that, on 19 November, drove Wilson to address an indignant letter to the French authorities for having allowed the prisoners to go at large, to go to the other side of the island on pleasure and private business, for allowing four of them to escape the island altogether and therefore thwart the ends of justice, all in "violation of that right due to H.B.M. Government as that of the most Friendly Nation."

Happily ignorant of the outrage of the Lucetts and of Wilson's frenzy, Melville turned his mind to fitting into the crew of the *Charles and Henry* — a task made easy by his experiences in the Marquesas and Society Islands. Coleman's luckless *Charles and Henry* gained in Melville not a ruffian of a

Yankee but a modest fellow, even if he was not a great whaleman. The *Charles and Henry* also gained a storyteller. What Melville had told his shipmates on the *Lucy Ann* about his departure from Typee Bay perforce had to correspond to what they had witnessed. Anyone he met later, ashore or afloat, including the men of the *Charles and Henry*, did not have to hear the rather tame story of how Melville actually left the island, but one dramatic version or another of what settled into shape as the ending of *Typee*, where "Tommo" dashes a boat-hook into the throat of the one-eyed Mow-Mow, not an easy target, since he is swimming with his tomahawk between his teeth (ch. 34). Melville was still telling a dramatic version of the escape from the Typees, presumably a variant of the published version, as late as 1850 or 1851 (decades later Julian Hawthorne recalled Melville describing a struggle so vividly that after he went home the Hawthornes looked all about for the club he had been swinging, only to realize that it had been imaginary). For the crew of the *Charles and Henry* Melville needed to work into his repertory the several months' worth of adventures he had experienced after the *Lucy Ann* picked him up, a delightful set of challenges.

It is possible that Melville's new shipmates on the *Charles and Henry* were intensely eager to gain information about such mutually improving topics as the cannibal propensities of his hosts in the Typee valley, about the nonhuman foodstuffs, about customs governing tattooing and taboos, about the landscape, as well as edifying details of his subsequent captivity in Tahiti and his agricultural experiences in Eimeo. However, the question Melville most frequently encountered was not about one of these aspects of his recent experience, not even about the danger of his being eaten by the cannibals. In the natural course of things, American sailors wanted to know about the sexual habits of the Typeeans and about Melville's own experiences while he was their captive; some of them probably had had sexual intercourse with Marquesan islanders on ship or on shore, but not likely with any from the inland tribes. What the sailors wanted to hear were tales of how he had tested the extreme limits of his sexual capacities. Now on the *Charles and Henry* and for the rest of his time in the Pacific and on his voyage home to Boston in the Atlantic, Melville was the object of intense sexual interest and envy, a man who excited the very "warmest sympathies" of his shipmates — not merely a young man who had lived among the cannibals but the young man who had lived among a tribe notorious for sexual freedom. Whatever the quality of the crew Captain Coleman had so roundly disparaged, the men on the *Charles and Henry* must have offered Melville stories of their own that he may later have drawn on in ways now irrecoverable.

The *Charles and Henry* also offered stimulus for his mind from books. On the real *Lucy Ann* the real John Troy, Melville says in the partly fictional

Omoo, possessed books, but "a damp, musty volume, entitled 'A History of the most Atrocious and Bloody Piracies' " may be an imaginary composite of real titles such as *The History of the Lives and Bloody Exploits of the Most Noted Pirates* (Hartford, 1835). After being taken off the *Lucy Ann* Melville had spent weeks in Tahiti and Eimeo outdoors all the time, "an utter savage" (in the phrasing he used of himself in 1852, after spending weeks out of doors), reading nothing, as far as we know. Once he got aboard the *Charles and Henry* and settled into the routine of sailing without sighting whales or at least without capturing whales, he had time to catch up on his reading. The worthy Nantucket owners of the ship had supplied their craft remarkably well in every regard, not omitting the ship's library. Thanks to the surviving bill for $16.24 that the Nantucket Coffins paid on 5 April 1841, we have a good idea of what Melville could have laid his hands on — the first books we have much reason to think he read since, by his own account, he read Owen Chase's *Narrative* in his early months in the Pacific. The surviving list of the books purchased (all new, apparently) often gives only short titles and no authors; from the list Wilson Heflin identified likely editions of the books named. Following Heflin's identifications, here I sort the ship's library into rough categories. Like Heflin, I assume that most of the books shipped at the end of 1840 were still aboard after less than two years; vandalism or even careless handling would not likely have been tolerated in a well-run ship, despite the perhaps fictional bibliographical mutilation Melville describes (*Omoo*, ch. 20) as taking place on a poorly captained Australian whaler. In addition, individual sailors brought some books aboard, which in due course might have found their way into the community book-chest.

On the *Charles and Henry* when it sailed from Nantucket were several books of adventure or travel, on sea or land, among them *Jack Halyard*, by W. S. Cardell; *Visit to Constantinople and Athens*, by Walter Colton; *Shipwreck on a Desert Island; A Narrative of the Shipwreck, Captivity, and Sufferings of Horace Holden and Benj. H. Nute: Who Were Cast Away in the American Ship Mentor, on the Pelew Islands, in the Year 1832: And for Two Years Afterwards Were Subjected to Unheard of Sufferings among the Barbarous Inhabitants of Lord North's Island*, by Horace Holden; John H. Amory, *The Young Rover; Poor Jack*, by Frederick Marryat; and the *Child's Robinson Crusoe*. Heflin shows that the edition of Defoe's classic on the ship, "Carefully Adapted to Youth," was likely the one that advertised itself as "Purified from every thought and expression which might sully the mind . . . of youth." There was also a history of the American Revolution, a biography of Washington, and two books from the recent election, a campaign life of Harrison and a book called (on the cover) *Harrison versus Van Buren*.

Once a sailor like Melville got past the adventure and history, he could sample the selections in several collections and anthologies aboard the *Charles and Henry*: four volumes from the Harper's "Family Library"; *Cabinet of Literature*; "Fire Side Book" (possibly *The Fireside Book, A Miscellany*, with a plate of Abbotsford, the revered home of the revered Sir Walter Scott); and single volumes of *Abbott's Magazine* and of *Family Magazine*. There were religious works for the literate sailor desperate enough to read anything once: *The Young Christian*, by Jacob Abbott, and *Fireside Piety*, also by Abbott. In *Are You a Christian or a Calvinist?* by John Lowell (uncle of a contemporary of Melville's, the poet James Russell Lowell), Melville could have encountered this eye-catching assertion: "Jesus Christ himself was a *Unitarian*" — not, Lowell irrefutably proved, a Calvinist. The ship's library included several fictions, mainly didactic, among them *Strive and Thrive*, by Mary Botham Howitt; *Home*, by Catharine Maria Sedgwick, the sister-in-law of Helen's teacher at Lenox; *Merchant's Widow, and Her Family*, by Barbara Wreaks Hoole Hofland; the baldly titled *Moral Tales*, by Samuel Griswold Goodrich; and the popular Rousseauistic romance, *Paul and Virginia*, by Jacques-Henri Saint-Pierre, at the climax of which Virginia drowns because she is encumbered by clothing, when, naked, she might have survived — a remarkable European contrast to the Marquesan damsels. There were moral dissertations (not sugar-coated with fiction): *Victims of Gaming; Being Extracts from the Diary of an American Physician* and, most practical of all, *A Lecture to Young Men on Chastity*, by Sylvester Graham, the deviser of the popular antiaphrodisiac cracker.

Of these books, the condensed *Robinson Crusoe* (many removes from the book first published in 1719) is probably the most curiously significant for Melville's life, since it was an obvious model for a white traveler who might want to write about his adventures on a remote island peopled by "savages." (Only three years later Melville became known as "the Modern Crusoe.") In view of his portrayal of the American Amasa Delano in "Benito Cereno" (1855), it would be good to know how much of Defoe's complex portrayal of Crusoe's concept of Providence Melville ever encountered in copies that came his way: he may never have known *Robinson Crusoe* except in a form both shortened and expurgated for children. All in all, Melville found some genuine literary stimulus on the *Charles and Henry*. (He probably already knew another classic from early in the eighteenth century, Jonathan Swift's 1726 *Gulliver's Travels*, most likely in a condensed and even more rigorously expurgated form than *Robinson Crusoe*, there being so much more to expurgate. By May 1851, Augusta could casually allude to *Gulliver's Travels* to Allan [letter at Arrowhead, the Berkshire County Historical Society] when "Aztec children" were being exhibited as curiosities in Albany: "They are well called Lilliputians." Marginalia from later in Melville's life tends to

confirm what one could have guessed from the portrayal of contrasting societies in *Typee* — that from early in his life Melville was acquainted not only
with *Robinson Crusoe* but also with *Gulliver's Travels*, two examples of what we
can only uneasily call novels — about as uneasily as we call Melville's first
books novels.)

Little evidence of the route of the *Charles and Henry* has turned up. On
27 January 1843, the New Bedford ship *Roscoe*, McCleve, master, passed her
two days' sailing east of 34°10′S, 87°40′W (the position of the *Roscoe* on
25 January). In early February the *Charles and Henry* was sailing toward the
island of Mas Afuera or Massafuero, otherwise known as Selkirk Island. At
14°S, 113°42′W on 9 February the *Martha*, out of Fairhaven, Hammond,
master, spoke the *Charles and Henry*, which reported four hundred barrels of
sperm oil. The *Charles and Henry* had only one hundred more barrels three
months later, so very few of Melville's days were taken up with the work of
whaling. (Heflin cites the "Consular Returns, Lahaina" for 1 January to
1 July 1843 in support of these figures.) Melville had ample time for absorbing literary treatments of fireside piety, but he also had opportunities to
witness strange and wondrous sights, spectacles as awe-inspiring, perhaps, as
the one he attributed to his narrator in *Moby-Dick* (ch. 86): "Standing at the
mast-head of my ship during a sunrise that crimsoned sky and sea, I once saw
a large herd of whales in the east, all heading towards the sun, and for a
moment vibrating in concert with peaked flukes."

Although he seems to have done more sailing (and probably more reading) than actual whaling, Melville later claimed to a publisher to have been a
boatsteerer (a harpooneer) during one of his whaling voyages, demonstrably
not the case on the *Acushnet* and the *Lucy Ann*. There survives a letter from
Captain Coleman to the owners, written on 7 May 1843, at Lahaina, on the
island of Maui in the Sandwich Islands (that is, Hawaiian Islands), specifically
decrying his prior lack of a good boatsteerer:

> I arrived here a few days since with only 500 bls Sperm Oil bound to Japan in
> hopes to find some whales that I can get. I have seen whales six times last
> cruise and got 160 bls and [the boats] drove of[f] 100 bls I have not got a man
> in the ship that I can call a good boat steerer neither have I had this voyage;
> they have missed many whales I think about 400 bls. I am much dissatisfied
> with my officers and have been all the voyage. . . . I have got a pretty good
> crew now and the boat steerers are better than they have been. I think if we
> see whales we may get some. The Ship is in good Order tho the Copper is
> most of it of[f]. I cannot tell which way I shall go. . . . if there is no danger of
> worms getting in the ship I should like to go another season to Japan and then
> home.

Coleman's grim determination must have become common knowledge on his ship, so much so that in *Typee* the relentless Captain Vangs may owe more to him than to Captain Pease of the *Acushnet*. For his part, Herman's presence on the *Charles and Henry* had done nothing to reverse Coleman's run of hard luck, and if he ever acted as a harpooneer (as he later claimed), he never became, in the captain's opinion, a competent one.

Once the *Charles and Henry* had anchored at Lahaina, Melville had begun calculating how long he might like to stay and what he might do, for he had signed only for the cruise and knew he would be discharged. On 2 May, along with one crew member who was sick and another who was discharged by mutual consent, Melville was a free man in Lahaina, on the island of Maui.

[13]

Lahaina and Honolulu
1843

I won't believe in a Temperance Heaven.

Melville to Hawthorne, early May 1851

CAPTAIN COLEMAN ANCHORED AT LAHAINA, on West Maui, on 27 April 1843. From the harbor the *Charles and Henry* for several days afforded Melville a splendid view of the cluster of mountain peaks and ridges (the highest peak over six thousand feet above sea level). In his *A Visit to the South Seas* (1831) Charles S. Stewart had declared Lahaina by far the most beautiful settlement he had seen in the Sandwich Islands, its "wild mountains" rising "in distinct view" beyond the coconut palms on the three miles of beach. Then, a decade and more before Melville arrived, bananas, tapa (or tappa), and sugarcane were abundant, the vegetation extending, Stewart said, "almost to the beach, on which a fine surf constantly rolls." That was what Herman expected to see, after his reading of Stewart's book (which Uncle Thomas had in Pittsfield, where it had helped to stir Herman's wanderlust). In 1843 the surf still rolled, but under the rule of the missionaries and the periodic invasions of whaling crews in the next two decades this natural wealth had been squandered.

The chief seaport in the Sandwich Islands for whalers, Lahaina had become a town of some three thousand inhabitants, most of whom lived in grass houses on one street that ran along the beach for three quarters of a mile. According to the *Temperance Advocate and Seamen's Friend* (20 May 1843), between 16 February and 29 April 1843, eighty-six whaleships had arrived at the port, eighty of them American, two French, two Canadian, one English, and one Belgian. Captains favored Lahaina for "recruiting" provisions — mainly Irish potatoes, not the luscious fruits of a decade or two earlier. Captain Charles Wilkes, who had visited the port in 1841, in his *United States Exploring Expedition* (1844) emphasized that sober whaling captains particularly liked Lahaina because the crews had "not that temptation to visit the shore that is experienced at Honolulu" — the lure of grogshops and accommodating women.

The most striking man-made structure on Maui, impressive from the *Charles and Henry*, was the seminary, magnificently sited. It was still much as it was in 1841, when Wilkes saw it: "The most remarkable building to be seen as the bay of Lahaina is approached, is the seminary of Lahainaluna situated on the side of the mountain that rises behind Lahaina." There teachers for the native schools were to be instructed in "the useful arts." Wilkes had gone up there, about two miles from the town, on a road partly built by the pupils, who also made the stone walls along it. The large boys or young men, Wilkes said, were working unsystematically — like a rabble. The missionary Hiram Bingham in his *A Residence of Twenty-One Years in the Sandwich Islands* (1847) celebrated the students as "laboring at their new building, and pursuing their studies, often hungry, and with almost no shelter from the sun and the rain" — forced to build their own "truly interesting" high school. Soon after his discharge on 2 May, Melville stretched his legs by climbing up this road built with forced labor.

In *Typee* (ch. 30) Melville told a tall tale about a visit to the seminary: "In the Missionary College at Lahainaluna, on Mowee, . . . I saw a tabular exhibition of a Haw[a]iian verb, conjugated through all its moods and tenses. It covered the side of a considerable apartment, and I doubt whether Sir William Jones himself would not have despaired of mastering it." The main building of the school was still new, built in 1837, with two wings, besides the separate thatched huts where teachers lived. Wilkes had found engraving was being taught, wretchedly, for use in the missionary printing shop, when the students would more usefully have been instructed in carpentry, smithery, and agriculture. The whole school was pervaded by "an air of neglect." Spectacular as the seminary was from the sea, it was impractical, inconveniently distant from the town, and too high to afford a ready supply of fresh water. Melville poked around long enough to witness, or gather the materials for fabricating, an anecdote about the despotic power of "Kaahumanu, the gigantic old dowager queen," which he purveyed as truth in *Typee* (ch. 25): "While at Lahainaluna — the residence of this monstrous Jezebel — a humpbacked wretch was pointed out to me, who, some twenty-five years previously, had had the vertebræ of his back-bone very seriously discomposed by his gentle mistress."

After the seminary, the most conspicuous objects, according to Wilkes, were the palace of King Kamehameha III and the fort. In 1841 the palace, being constructed of coral rock, had been only half finished, but already seemed "to be in a somewhat dilapidated state," exhibiting "poverty rather than regal magnificence"; that was still its state when Melville saw it in 1843. Melville would have recognized that the reefs (to the east of the harbor) had been harvested for the palace, and were still being harvested by fishermen who piled coral in heaps before carrying it to Lahaina, where it was burnt for lime. Having seen what the Europeans had done to Tahiti, Melville was quick to grasp that Nature in another paradise had been defiled and was being eradicated piece by piece. Wilkes had dismissed the second most conspicuous object, the fort: "its form is quadrangular, the longest side facing the sea; it is of little account, however, as a defence, serving chiefly to confine unruly subjects and sailors in." It enclosed only about an acre, behind walls twenty feet high. Going there to visit the prisoners in the jail was an early order of business for Melville. As he wrote of any island port in the Pacific: "No sailor steps ashore, but he straightway goes to the 'Calabooza,' where he is almost sure to find some poor fellow or other in confinement for desertion, or alledged mutiny, or something of that sort. Sympathy is proffered, and if need be, tobacco. The latter, however, is most in request; as a solace to the captive, it is invaluable" (*Omoo*, ch. 41). Near the fort Melville saw the storehouses for the king's revenue (consisting of "large heaps of tapas"). He also saw, near the landing, the cottages of two missionaries. Alone or in company Melville made use of his time, seeing what there was to see.

By early May, from other ships in the harbor at Lahaina or from the Europeans he encountered ashore, in the fort or elsewhere, Melville and other members of the crew of the *Charles and Henry* had learned extraordinary news about history in the making in Honolulu. In the previous years, the Protestant missionaries, consolidating their power over the king and his subjects, had managed to keep Catholic priests out of the islands. At home, Samuel F. B. Morse and many like-minded Protestants were trying valiantly to alert their country to what to them was indubitable fact—Jesuits were prowling throughout the Mississippi Valley, so plausibly disguised as to have melted into the populace, but ready nevertheless to throw off their disguises and to seize power the instant they received their covert orders from the pope. Such rhetoric incited the mob that burned the Ursuline Convent School in Charlestown, across the Charles River from Boston, in 1834. Protestant missionaries in the Pacific knew that to tolerate Catholics was to risk both loss of human souls and loss of political control. Practical zealots, they realized that their de facto control of the islands would be ended if either France or England seized the islands, so, manipulating King Kamehameha III to their wishes, the missionaries, led by the back-country New York Presbyterian Dr. Gerrit Parmele Judd (1803–73), began to seek protection from the United States for their anti-European and, tacitly, their anti-Catholic stances.

In 1837 Richard Charlton, the British consul in Honolulu, had aroused Judd's hostility when he tried to prevent the deportation of two Catholic priests who had arrived in a British ship. In May 1842 the Hawaiian king and the premier appointed Dr. Judd as government interpreter and recorder. To the American Board of Commissioners for Foreign Missions Judd justified his worldly role: "The motives which induced me to take this step, were ... the absolute necessity that some one should aid the king and chiefs in conducting their affairs, and the impossibility of their procuring any other secular man with a knowledge of the native language to aid them." Captain S. Mallet of the French sloop-of-war *Embuscade* on 1 September 1842 demanded that the king give the Catholic church privileges equal to the Protestant missionaries, beginning with the granting of land for a Catholic high school to compete with the one at Lahainaluna, and including the necessary provision that "severe punishment be inflicted upon any individual, whatever may be his rank or condition, who shall destroy a Catholic church, or school, or insult the ministers of this religion." Mallet also demanded that French wines and spirits be admitted for sale in the islands at the low duty of five percent. In his nominal role as translator, Dr. Judd had written the temporizing reply for the king that Kamehameha and the chieftess Kekauluohi both signed. After Charlton left for London late in September 1842, Judd refused to accept Charlton's appointee as acting consul. Then, unsurprisingly, a missionary-controlled Hawaiian court attached Charlton's property.

In response to the pleas from Hawaii, in December 1842 President Tyler sent a message to Congress on the strategic importance of the islands: "the Sandwich Islands are the stopping place for almost all vessels passing from continent to continent across the Pacific ocean," resorted to "by the great numbers of vessels of the United States which are engaged in the whale fishery in those seas." Tyler put himself on record as warning "any other Power" not to threaten the "independent existence" of the islands. But in seizing Charlton's property Judd had been too provocative for any representative of Her Britannic Majesty to tolerate. Early in February 1843, before an American consul arrived with Tyler's message, the British ship *Carysfort* arrived in Honolulu with Lord George Paulet as captain. In his letter to Kekuanaoa, the governor of Oahu, Paulet summoned the king ("his presence will be required here"), and once Kamehameha had arrived, peremptorily demanded a private meeting with him. The reply, written by Dr. Judd and signed by Kamehameha, declined the summons and offered an insulting alternative: "In case you have business of a private nature we will appoint Dr. Judd our confidential agent to confer with you, who, being a person of integrity and fidelity to our government, and perfectly acquainted with all our affairs, will receive your communications, give all the information you require (in confidence), and report the same to us."

Paulet on 17 February contemptuously rejected this plan: "I have to state that I shall hold no communication whatever with Doct. G. P. Judd, who, it has been satisfactorily proved to me, has been the prime mover in the unlawful proceedings of your government against British subjects." Paulet demanded the immediate restitution of the property of Mr. Richard Charlton and acknowledgment that Mr. George Simpson had the right to function as Her Britannic Majesty's acting consul; he also demanded protection for British subjects in general as well as some named as having been wronged in the past. On 25 February the beleaguered King Kamehameha provisionally ceded the Sandwich Islands to Lord George Paulet in the name of Queen Victoria, at the same time secretly sending a plea to President Tyler for the United States to intercede with Great Britain on his behalf. The American residents in the Sandwich Islands were "greatly incensed," the Reverend Lowell Smith wrote in his diary (*The Melville Log*); certainly the missionaries were, but other Americans felt more ambivalent. As the next two weeks passed Smith and the other American missionaries continued to feel that they had just seen the government of the Sandwich Islands seized and buried alive (as Smith wrote on 10 March) and found only this amelioration: "perhaps the Lord has permitted the nation to pass into the hands of the English to prevent a still greater evil (viz) her passing into the hands of the French." By the time Melville climbed up the hill to the seminary at Lahainaluna, the missionaries were in a state of near frenzy over the political situation. Just then finishing up his *History of the Sandwich Islands* (with a preface dated 28 April 1843) for publication by the Lahainaluna "Press of the Mission Seminary," the mathematics teacher, the Reverend Sheldon Dibble, knew that the book would be out of date before anyone read it. He sensibly delayed publication for several months, then added an appendix, dated 4 September 1843, containing a passionate account of recent events.

The Reverend Samuel C. Damon, chaplain of the Seamen's Bethel in Honolulu, and editor of the Honolulu *Temperance Advocate and Seamen's Friend*, happened to be visiting Lahaina when Melville arrived, having left his own chapel only "partially supplied for two sabbaths." According to Damon, the seamen on Maui just when Melville arrived were behaving themselves with uncommon decorousness. The whaling fleet had subscribed for the erection of a seamen's chapel, completed in 1841, and able to accommodate two hundred men; it may have been filled to capacity on many occasions, for three dozen or more whaleships might be in the harbor at once. The Lahaina branch of the Temperance Society was six months and a week old when Melville arrived. John Stetson, the U.S. Vice Commercial Agent, whom Melville soon encountered, was the president and first signatory of the constitution of the Temperance Society ("We . . . do agree, that we will not use intoxicating liquors as a beverage, nor traffick in them; that we will not provide them as an article of entertainment, or for persons in our employment;

and that, in all suitable ways, we will discountenance their use throughout the community"). Here was no kindred spirit. On 27 April the Maui Temperance Society held a meeting in the chapel at which Damon subscribed his name to the pledge of total abstinence, along with King Kamehameha III (whose main palace was in Lahaina), the governor of Maui, "and a most respectable delegation from sea-faring men in port." Damon further reported: "Although the number of seamen, in port, at that time, was uncommonly large, yet during the season, very few have been the instances of disorderly and riotous conduct on the part of those belonging to the shipping." He listed several reasons that might account for such a "gratifying circumstance" — masters of vessels had tried to sustain the blue laws; the police and public opinion had enforced the laws relating to alcohol; the Friends of Temperance were succeeding in their campaign to "make drunkenness disreputable"; and there had been an increase in the "number of moral and religious men in the whaling fleet."

Damon encountered "at the Chapel and in the street many warm hearted Christians among the sons of the ocean," and if he did not single Melville out for notice, Melville saw him. Melville had his chances to attend the chapel on three Sundays, 30 April and 7 and 14 May, and he went at least once, as he always did in new places, whether as a devout worshiper or as a skeptical tourist taking advantage of his opportunities. "George Lightcraft" in *Scraps from the Log Book* reported that in 1834 missionaries had established a reading room for the sailors on Maui which was supplied with "both English and American papers of the earliest dates," the intention being to keep the sailors "from an association with those of the natives who were not proverbial for their morality." This reading room may have survived into the time of Melville's stay. Any papers he saw there or elsewhere at Maui would have incited him to try his luck on a more populous (and less Temperate) island sooner rather than later, for one item of news came home to him, a sensational event that had occurred in the U.S. Navy within the last year and involved his own flesh and blood.

One way or another, perhaps even while aboard the *Charles and Henry*, or there at Maui among so many whalers, some recently from Callao or Valparaiso or another major port, Melville learned from American newspapers and from sailors' gossip a great deal about the "mutiny" in late November 1842 on the U.S. brig *Somers* — a national cause célèbre in which one of the principal actors had been his first cousin Guert Gansevoort. This summary is from testimony given by Guert's superior, Commander Alexander Slidell Mackenzie: "On Saturday, the 26th of November, Lieut. Gansevoort came into the cabin and informed me that he had learned from Midshipman Wales that a conspiracy existed on board the ship to capture the vessel, to murder the Captain, bring over as many of the crew as possible, murder the rest and convert the vessel into a pirate; and that Midshipman Spencer was at the head of the conspiracy." Spencer, son of the secretary of war in President John Tyler's cabinet, was arrested, then also the boatswain's mate, Samuel Cromwell, and seaman Elisha Small as well as several other members of the crew. On 30 November Mackenzie called his officers, first of whom was Guert Gansevoort, into a council and convened a court-martial, impressing the court with the necessity of returning a verdict of guilty, which it did, on 1 December 1842, giving the formal verdict that the prisoners Spencer, Cromwell, and Small had been "guilty of a full and determined intention to commit a mutiny on board." Mackenzie promptly ordered them hanged at the yardarm. This scene ensued, according to Guert's later testimony:

> While I was standing in the gangway near Small he asked me if I would bid him good-bye, and if I would forgive him. He told me that he was guilty and deserved his punishment. I think the Commander said to him "Small, what have I done to you that you won't bid me good-bye?" Small replied "I did not know that you would bid a poor *bugger* like me good-bye sir." I think the Commander . . . told him that he was sorry he had to take the course he did but that the honor of the flag and the safety of the crew required it. . . . To which Small replied "*Yes, sir, and I honor you for it; God bless that flag!*"

(Small's speech resonates for readers of *Billy Budd*, which Melville was working on when he died; there he used similar phrasing, which he labeled a conventional felon's benediction, indicating that similar last words were commonly used by condemned men.) All this had happened not in the Indian Ocean or the South Pacific, where keeping men under indefinite restraint might have incited further disturbances, but in the Atlantic, two weeks' sail from the Brooklyn Navy Yard. Any sailor asked himself if anything could have justified the precipitous judgment and execution.

On the night of 13 December 1842 the *Somers* arrived in New York, but the next day, to general consternation, she permitted no one to board (Hunn Gansevoort naturally tried). Mackenzie had sent a dispatch to Washington and awaited orders. Rumors ran wild even before the news broke in the papers, which by the seventeenth were printing something like a full outline of the events. Ships leaving New York or Boston a week before Christmas 1842 carried with them newspapers that covered the story in detail. Whatever the character of young Spencer, his father the secretary of war was a powerful man, and in the young Republic, where naval officers were culled from the upper class, it seemed that anyone of importance in any major seaport chose sides, for or against Mackenzie. There exists no daily Hawaiian

newspaper from Melville's time there in 1843, and Damon's *Friend* did
not mention the *Somers* tragedy, but by late March or early April word
had reached the Pacific Fleet of the U.S. Navy. Three or three-and-a-half
months seems about the average time for news to reach the fleet from the
northeastern states. It was prudent policy for naval ships to board American
whalers they encountered at sea or in port in the Pacific, in order to offer any
assistance and to share news from home or from the watery world, so the
story spread very fast in the whaling fleet as well as the naval squadron, even
to many ships long out of sight of land. The tragic story of the *Somers* was
current through much of the Pacific by May and June 1843. Later, at home,
Herman learned many further details, most likely not directly from Guert
but from others.

Even though knowing only the official story as relayed by the newspapers, and possibly supplemented by nautical scuttlebutt, Herman found
much to brood upon. He had never been an intimate of Cousin Guert, seven
years his senior, though he felt a special if uneasy closeness from the fact that
everyone said that from certain angles Guert and Herman looked like brothers rather than cousins. (Oddly, given the fact that Guert lived till 1868, no
photograph of him came down in the family. One should exist, somewhere,
among the papers of naval officers.) Like Herman, Guert had lost his father
during his childhood. Herman knew that Guert had not been prepared by
early training to handle himself with quiet, manly confidence in times of
extreme pressures. No man in the family, a decade or a decade-and-a-half
earlier, not Uncle Herman, good-hearted but conveniently hamstrung by
the wife he reported to be tyrannical; not Uncle Peter with his aloof approval
of Guert's progress as opposed to the folly of Guert's older brother, the late
Peter Leonard Gansevoort; not Allan Melvill with his high-flown talk to
Guert about family honor and duty, had ever taught Guert by deed as well as
word how men acted in moments of crisis, spontaneously, from their deepest
and firmest character. Most perturbing in such reflections for Melville was
the realization that during his own adolescence the person who was nearest
to a father to him had been his fatherless older brother.

What he learned about the *Somers* in Maui made him anxious to see other
newspapers in Honolulu and to talk with men from the naval ships which
frequented that harbor. Furthermore, as far as pleasures were concerned,
Honolulu looked more and more appealing. Early in May, Paulet had uni-
laterally altered the terms of the cession so as to relax the laws against prostitution there. In a confrontation on 8 May, he declared that Dr. Judd would
no longer rule the islands, and Judd quickly protested and resigned as the
king's deputy. For a whaler wanting to find another ship, the theocracy of

Lahaina was just the place to be, but it was not the place for a young whale-man looking for excitement. In fact, Lahaina, just now, was perturbingly more constraining than Nukahiva or Papeete.

On 18 May sober John Stetson, in a report to William Hooper, commercial agent at Honolulu, Oahu, listed Melville as one of three men discharged from the *Charles and Henry*, but not as a sick man, and not his responsibility. He therefore allowed Melville and other discharged seamen to board the schooner *Star*, under Captain Burroughs, for transportation to Honolulu over the thirty-mile-wide channel between the islands, in company with seamen discharged as in need of medical treatment. Thus Melville left a sufficient number of boat lengths ahead of Captain Valentine Pease, who anchored the *Acushnet* at Maui on 27 May, carrying nine hundred barrels. On board were most of the shipmates Melville had left behind. The next day Henry Harmer deserted from the *Acushnet*, and on 29 May Pease discharged Thomas Johnson, already half dead with a venereal disease (he died at the hospital in Lahaina), and about this day he put the carpenter ashore, also "half dead with disreputable disease" — apparently David M. White, born in Scotland. On 2 June, three days before he sailed, Pease duly recited a string of old grievances and one fresh one, as Stetson recorded: "I hereby certify that Valentine Pease 2d Master of the within named ship personally appeared before me & declared that — that David Smith deserted at Santa June 30th, 1841, Richard T Greene & Herman Mellville deserted at Nukehiva July 9th, 1842 — John Wright deserted at ditto Sept 14 [1842] & Martin Brown at Rooapooa Sept 22 [1842] and Jim Rosman deserted at Salango February 3d 1843 — I also certify that Henry Harmer deserted at this Port May 28th, 1843." Stetson may have shared the information that he had encountered the name Herman Melville quite recently, but it was probably only coincidental that Pease sailed for Honolulu in the wake of the deserter. There Melville saw the *Acushnet*, and, still liable to being seized by Valentine Pease, may have spent a day or two skulking about Honolulu avoiding shipmates who might report him, until the *Acushnet* sailed for Japan on 7 June. He was then free to enjoy life in Oahu, smaller than Maui but much more populous, and he did enjoy it, for three months, four times as long as he had spent in the Typee valley and roughly twice as long as he had spent in Papeete and then Eimeo. What with the local political uproar and further news of the *Somers*, Melville had much to absorb and reflect upon as he adjusted to life on another island.

Observing Honolulu a couple of years before Melville saw it, Francis Allyn Olmsted wrote in *Incidents of a Whaling Voyage:* "Honolulu possesses a very fine harbor, and is the only one in these Islands where ships may lie in perfect safety, and undergo the repairs which may be necessary. It is formed by a coral reef extending across a recess in the Island of Oahu. Through an opening in this barrier, upon each side of which, the roaring surf beats incessantly, is the passage into the harbor of about a mile in length." The town itself was built upon a plain about a mile wide, "washed by the sea on one side and terminated by high mountains that rise up abruptly in the rear of it." Honolulu was "laid out regularly in wide streets with *adobie* walls running parallel to them," Olmsted said, the streets hard and smooth, so that "a carriage rolls along without a stone to jar it." Captain Wilkes had found those streets "ankle-deep in light dust and sand," fat old hogs wallowing in sinkholes, safe because they were tabooed animals belonging to the king. Most of the business buildings of the Europeans were made of "adobie" ("blocks of moulded clay hardened in the sun, and compacted by an admixture of grass," Olmsted explained) which was often plastered with lime and whitewashed so as to contrast with "the sombre walls and dwellings of the natives." He saw the lanai but did not use the native term: "The houses of the foreign residents are built in cottage style, with green verandahs or piazzas around them, while the adjacent grounds are tastefully laid out and planted with trees and shrubbery. Belonging to each, are several small outhouses in which the various operations of domestic economy are conducted." By contrast, the houses of the natives were "dingy looking cabins, the walls of which are constructed of *adobies.*" The roofs were of thatch, like the outbuildings of the foreigners. No one had planted trees to replace the despoiled vegetation, and the adobe walls along the streets, some six feet high, were constantly abraded by the winds, putting fine dust into the air and onto the streets. This was the unpleasant side of the natural phenomena Olmsted described, a midday cooling that any sailor like Melville would enjoy: "Before sun rise, there is usually a dead calm under the lee of the land, but soon after the sun has risen, the wind springs up, and increases until about noon, when it blows fresh, coming down in strong puffs from the mountains."

Although the streets were smooth, carriages were "rather rare articles of luxury," Olmsted observed, so the principal vehicles were "little four wheeled waggons, about the size of those which are usually appendages to a nursery at home, in which, drawn by one or two *kanakas*, a lady is seen riding in style through the streets, in going to church or making a fashionable call." Whether he had seen such sights in Lahaina or not, Melville was shocked to find in Honolulu that the missionaries and their wives had civilized "the small remnant of the natives" into draught horses, and "evangelized" them "into beasts of burden" (*Typee*, ch. 26): "Among a multitude of similar exhibitions that I saw, I shall never forget a robust, red-faced, and very lady-like personage, a missionary's spouse, who day after day for months together took her regular airings in a little go-cart drawn by two of the islanders, one an old grey-headed man, and the other a rogueish stripling, both being, with the exception of the fig-leaf, as naked as when they were born." Some of Melville's fury was based on class distinctions. In his satirical portrait in *Typee* he described this missionary's wife as a woman who "used to think nothing of driving the cows to pasture on the old farm in New England" but who now reveled in her power over the people she had been sent to help convert to Christianity, shouting at them and rapping the head of the old man with "the heavy handle of her huge fan." The Protestant missionaries — Congregationalists, Presbyterians, Methodists — were of denominations composed primarily of the lower classes (at home) and therefore (according to one of Melville's class) more apt than their wealthier, more conservative high-church brethren and sisters to abuse the natives, just as transplanted Yankees were said to become particularly cruel overseers of slaves in the American South.

Honolulu contained some ten thousand inhabitants, Olmsted estimated, of whom six hundred were foreigners. Most of these were Americans. According to Chaplain Damon's precise census, as of 1 March 1843 there were 61 males married to 61 American wives; 57 males married to 57 native wives (one wife each, a change in the past decade of missionary influence); 74 unmarried adult males; 4 unmarried adult females; 143 white children; and 576 half-caste children. If one were to deduct native wives and half-caste children, as Damon eagerly suggested, the sum was 400 American residents on all the Sandwich Islands, of whom 193, adults and white children, were connected then or formerly with the American Mission.

The foreigners, as Olmsted said, dressed in the European way, while the male natives preferred the "maro" around the waist and a piece of tappa passed over the shoulder and knotted under the other arm. Many of them showed a sense of themselves that antagonized Olmsted, who fulminated at their walking with "as much dignity and consciousness of superiority as the more favored 'lords of creation' display." Olmsted said the native women wore "long gowns like the loose morning dresses of the ladies of our country," but ludicrously bedecked: "To increase their charms, of which, judging from appearances, nature has not been very profuse, many of them tie a gay shawl tightly around the waist, which gives them a rather ludicrous gait. With a bright yellow shawl around her waist, a wreath of brilliant feathers or flowers encircling her brow, and a huge comb towering up with masses of dark hair coiled around it, a Hawaiian lady is dressed a la mode." Melville saw what Olmsted saw, but he reserved his contempt for the missionaries who bedecked the royal family (and sometimes themselves) and the native royalty in grotesquely elaborate versions of European court costumes.

Missionaries were determined to control the behavior of the natives not only in the conduct of their own lives but in their contact with the sailors.

Absolutely committed to the vindication of the Protestant missionaries, Wilkes had formed an injudicious friendship with Dr. Judd, paying Judd an excessive amount of taxpayers' money for acting as his guide and interpreter on an expedition to Mauna Loa, and in the end presenting, at taxpayer expense, a view highly prejudiced in favor of the missionaries. Wilkes took their side in regard to the "lower class of foreigners," the "keepers of low taverns, sailors' boarding-houses, and grog-shops," who were a "serious bar to improvement in morals": "Every inducement that can allure sailors from their duty, and destroy their usefulness, is held out to them here. Such men must be obnoxious in any community, and that they are not able to make more disturbance than they do, supported as they are by those who ought to know better, is, I am satisfied, mainly owing to the attention and energy of the governor, and the watchfulness of the members of the mission over the natives." In 1843 the missionaries were not only pushing the natives to take vows of abstinence from liquor — they were also discouraging tobacco smoking to the point that some of the native churches were vowing "not to receive smokers." (Hiram Bingham quoted a missionary statement in 1843 that the cultivation and use of tobacco was immoral, "tending to diffuse evil and not good in the world.")

After the sobriety of Lahaina, Honolulu, however great the power of the missionaries, afforded sights shocking even to the sailor whose ship had been boarded in Nukahiva Bay and who had lived in the Marquesas and the Society Islands. Dibble wrote in his appendix:

> The government of the islands continued under the British Commission from Feb. 25th till July 31st — five months and six days. Those were months of sorrow, sadness and gloomy forebodings. . . . Their first act is to *add* to the laws, putting on one per cent. duty to the three per cent. required by the native government. They then, call upon all foreigners holding lands by lease or otherwise to send in their titles to the commission.
>
> The next act! One's pen, for very shame, shrinks from recording it. Directly in the face of a solemn obligation clearly expressed in the articles of Cession, not to interfere with the laws of the nation, the Commission proceeds to *abrogate* a very important statute — and what statute? — the statute against fornication! making the crime punishable only when committed in the highways and thoroughfares!!

Dibble quoted Chaplain Damon, who in the extra of the *Friend* on 31 July printed a declaration dated 21 July but written, he said, early in June, and held back from print in the hope that Paulet would repudiate the cession. Knowing that his paper ultimately would reach the public in the United States as well as Great Britain, Damon summarized the laws adopted in 1841 by a Council of Chiefs. Fines and imprisonments were specified for different sexual crimes, and the law specified particular punishment for the parent who would "give up his child to whoredom or prostitution" or the man who would give up his wife for prostitution. The twelfth item made it clear that the traffic in sex included males as well as women: "whoever acts the part of a pimp in procuring either females or males, and whoever panders for prostitutes or whoremongers and whoever in any way acts the part of a pander," would be fined heavily — fifty dollars per offense, or "put to hard labor for the term of one year."

These laws were among those abrogated by Lord George Paulet, and Damon put on record his conviction that the six months previous to the abrogation had been decorous by contrast to the conditions when Melville was there: "in proportion to the number of seamen visiting this Port, a higher regard for purity and morality did not exist in any Port this side Cape Horn or the Cape of Good Hope." Paulet had reversed the situation:

> Since the force of the law has been restrained, the tide has changed — the current flows in an opposite direction. Residents in Honolulu can testify that a different state of things is fearfully rife! The influence of grog shops in their baleful effects falls far short of unrestrained licentiousness. Houses to sell wines and spirituous liquors, are under certain checks and prohibitions; but upon the pimps and panders of the brothel there are no restrictions — no tabus. They may pursue their calling without rebuke from the Public Authorities. Boat loads of lewd women have been seen going and returning from vessels which have recently touched at this Harbor for supplies. The law is prostrate — the arm of justice parylized [paralyzed] — the officers of justice permitted to witness iniquity, but forbidden to arrest the guilty offenders. The most disgusting scenes are to be seen at noon-day in the streets of Honolulu, and around certain places of resort. Report of this state of things has drawn hither scores and hundreds of simple minded and unwary females from the other Islands. Landsmen as well as seamen have taken advantage of this state of public morals.

Women prisoners were being conveyed from the fort to ships for nocturnal encounters, then taken back to prison. Dibble made sure the world knew by quoting in his book some of this earnest exposé by the genuinely grieved chaplain. Melville saw everything and made his own reflections on a despoiled paradise with "no tabus" in contrast to the intricately tabooed society in the Typee valley, an unfallen Pacific paradise.

During his stay in Honolulu Melville saw more of one missionary in particular, Samuel C. Damon, whom he had encountered in Maui, for Damon was back at his Seamen's Chapel, which Olmsted had described as (in 1840) "a plain, two story edifice, painted white, surmounted by a cupola, from the top of which, the Bethel flag waves its welcome to the shipping in the port." The flag (bearing the word "BETHEL") had once identified nonconformist churches, but now specifically identified seamen's chapels. The particular Bethel flag that Melville saw in Honolulu was the recent gift of Captain Long of the U.S. ship *Boston*, created at government expense by the sewing skills of the quartermasters. In chapter 26 of *Typee* Melville recalled this particular "spacious and elegant American chapel, where divine service is regularly performed," as a place where natives were exploited: "Twice every Sabbath towards the close of the exercises may be seen a score or two of little waggons ranged along the railing in front of the edifice, with two squalid native footmen in the livery of nakedness standing by each, and waiting for the dismission of the congregation to draw their superiors home." In Honolulu, much more than in Tahiti or in Maui, Melville had time and occasion to register the sins of the missionaries, and on the basis of what he saw in Honolulu, he subsequently blackened his portrait of what he had already witnessed in Tahiti. There was, Melville concluded then, and put onto paper some two years later, "something decidedly wrong in the practical operations of the Sandwich Islands Mission" (*Typee*, ch. 26). Not just physical nature but human nature was being defiled in the Hawaiian Islands.

Missionaries were suppressing all amusements enjoyed by the less wealthy natives. As a matter of course, the missionaries had all but done away with the traditional dances, rightly deeming some of them erotic in nature, and actively discouraged any physical exertion in sports, although they expected the natives to build roads and pull carts whenever commanded to do so. Some of the Hawaiian youths were still allowed, at times, to practice one great sport, as described by Olmsted: "I took a stroll down to the sea shore, where a party of natives were playing in the surf, which was thundering upon the beach. Each of them had a *surf board*, a smooth, flat board from six to eight feet long, by twelve to fifteen inches broad. Upon these, they plunged forward into the surf." They surfed "hour after hour, in sports which have too terrific an aspect for a foreigner to attempt." Wilkes commented that playing in the surf was "still much practiced," despite the missionaries, and decided that "the time to see a Hawaiian happy, is while he is gambolling and frolicking in the surf." Wilkes was entranced: "I have stood for hours watching their sport with great interest, and, I must say, with no little envy." William Ellis put a surf-boarding scene on the title page of the fourth volume of his *Polynesian Researches* (1833), a visual reminder Melville had seen before he celebrated the speed and balance of the surf-boarders: "Hanging over this scroll [of billow], looking down from it as from a precipice, the bathers halloo; every limb in motion to preserve their place on the very crest of the wave" (*Mardi*, ch. 90, "Rare Sport at Ohonoo"). There Melville compared surfing to "charging at the head of cavalry: you must on."

For all his being overinfluenced by Dr. Judd, Wilkes admitted and even decried the passivity of the Hawaiian boys:

> On inquiry, I learned that it had, after mature deliberation and experience, been considered advisable by the missionaries to deprive them of all their heathenish enjoyments, rather than allow them to occupy their minds with any thing that might recall old associations. The consequence is, that the Hawaiian boys are staid and demure, having the quiet looks of old men. I cannot doubt that they possess the natural tendency of youth towards frolicsome relaxations; but the fear of offending keeps a constant restraint over them.

To an impressionable young man like Melville, whose own adolescence had been stifled first inside the bank then inside the cap and fur store, the illicit happiness of the Hawaiian boys was infinitely poignant. For Melville one of the foulest sins of the missionaries was the creation of this premature sedateness in Hawaiian boys, from whom joy had been driven in the name of the crucified Jesus.

In his *Journal of a Voyage to California . . . and also of a Voyage from California to the Sandwich Islands* (1852), Albert Lyman reported on some of the amusements still pursued by the Sandwich Islanders out of the eyes of the missionaries: "gambling, either with cards or dice"; "a kind of *thimble-rigging* among them, which is called *buhenehene*, in which a stone is hidden underneath piles of *tapa* and the others guess where it is concealed"; throwing quoits; "*maiku*, which consists in hurling stones in a narrow trench dug in the ground, sometimes a mile in length, — he who can throw the furthest being considered the best player." Maiku was yielding to a more confined kindred game, bowling, for which, Lyman said, alleys had been erected at Honolulu and some of the other seaports. Even by 1843, bowling alleys had become popular. At some point early in his stay in Honolulu, Melville worked as a pin-setter in one of several bowling alleys and at quiet times picked up some skill as a bowler. Six years later from Honolulu H. R. Hawkins wrote his father in Lansingburgh (of all places) about meeting a gentleman who told him he was well acquainted with the author of *Typee* and *Omoo* "and knew him at a time when he was setting up pins in a ball alley." Hawkins added, correctly, that he thought Melville had not mentioned bowling in either of those works. Young Hawkins's information survives because his father sent the letter to the Lansingburgh *Gazette*, which printed it on 14 March 1850. It casts light on the expertise at bowling Melville was displaying in London just when Hawkins heard the story in Honolulu.

A week and a half after Herman arrived in Honolulu the *Nassau*, a New Bedford whaler, under Captain Weeks, came to anchor on 28 May and transferred a man in irons to the prison at the fort (where the Union Jack was flying), technically putting him in charge of the American consul. This was Luther Fox, whom Damon in the *Friend* for 27 June ("Bloody Affray at Sea") identified as a "native of Renselaerville, Albany Co. N.Y." — misspelled as badly as Melville himself might have done, but the town familiar from his adolescence and named for one of his own ancestors. Word of the affair swept from one to another of the American whaleships in the harbor and the sailors ashore. For swearing while aloft, Fox had been punished by being put to scraping down the masts, and the next day had been ordered to tar the bobstay and the rigging about the bowsprit. He had gone below when his watch was called to breakfast, then had refused orders to turn to, saying he would do so after he finished eating, but adding that he would die sooner than come up before he was through eating. The mate, Jepitha Jenney, had gone down to bring him up, and Fox had hit him one blow with one of the whaling implements it was his job to sharpen. When the captain demanded to know what had happened, Jenney had uttered a memorable sentence: "Fox has cut my leg off with a mincing knife." When asked if he knew what he had done, Fox had replied that he could not "help" doing it, and then had burst into tears, saying that he had warned the mate not to come down into the forecastle. Jenney had died a few hours later.

What heightened the excitement for Melville and all the other Americans in the islands, especially the sailors, was that the story of Luther Fox, remarkable as it was, came almost as an incidental horror, for the *Nassau* had lost Jepitha Jenney but picked up twenty men from Ocean Island. These were survivors of the ill-fated whaleship *Parker* of New Bedford, Captain Prince Sherman, which had sailed a year and three months before Melville. On 11 December 1841, Captain Sherman was lost, as Damon described on 27 June:

> His boat having been made fast to one of a large school of sperm whale was capsized and stove. He was thrown out either by the line "unshipping from the chocks" or by the stroke of a whale's flukes, which were seen by the crews of the other boats, frequently to pass over the boat's bows. At that critical moment a large number of whales were seen around the boat. The unfortunate captain, however, clung for a short time to the shattered boat, but before aid could arrive, he sunk to rise no more. Long. 113° W. & Lat. 00° 40′ N.

The first mate, George W. Smith, had taken command and performed well until the *Parker* encountered squalls and heavy rain near Ocean Island. On the morning of 24 September 1842 a wave (a "sea," as they said) had dashed through the cabin windows of the ship, which struck a reef about eight miles NNW from the center of Ocean Island. In three quarters of an hour she was an entire wreck: "The crew were unable to save sufficient clothes to cover them, or any provisions except 1 peck of beans and 15 or 20 lbs of salt meat, picked up after the vessel went to pieces." No water was saved. Before they reached the island, four of the crew members died — men from South Dartmouth and Boston, Massachusetts, from Payta, Peru, and from Dorsetshire, England — a representative set of victims. Twenty-four of the men, including the new captain, pieced a raft together from the remains of the *Parker* and reached Ocean Island — "after 8 days and 7 nights, of incessant labor and intense suffering from hunger and thirst." In order to make progress toward the island, they had been obliged by the currents to "warp" — that is, to swim out with a line, make it fast to coral or some other outcropping on the bottom, then haul up to it, and then repeat the process.

Once ashore, the survivors of the *Parker* had lived on seafowl and seals. They had sent off 120 seafowl "with tallied pieces of wood attached to them, hoping some one might be caught, which would in hieroglyphic language relate the situation of the crew of the Parker." Smith, now the captain, had conducted religious services every morning and evening, and on Sunday morning had hoisted "*a bethel flag*" for worship. (Of the two Bibles that had been saved, Smith presented one to Chaplain Damon.) After six months, the survivors were found by the *James Stewart*, of St. John's, New Brunswick (which took on board Captain Smith, the carpenter, the cooper, and the cabin-boy, and left provisions on the island for the other twenty, promising to return). Before the *James Stewart* returned, the twenty were rescued by Captain Weeks of the whaleship *Nassau*, of New Bedford. Seven of the rescued men signed on the *Nassau* and the remaining thirteen were landed at Honolulu, under the protection of the American consulate. From the thirteen survivors of the *Parker* who were released in Honolulu, if not from Fox or other members of the crew of the *Nassau*, Melville learned the story of the *Parker* even before he read it in the *Friend*.

The fate of the *Parker* went into Melville's memory along with many other stories he had heard, and some he was yet to hear, about disasters that befell whalemen. To judge by "The Town-Ho's Story" (*Moby-Dick*, ch. 54), the fate of Luther Fox proved even more evocative to Melville. It was clear that Fox was no cold-blooded murderer whom all decent seamen like Melville should shun. Even Damon ended his account of the "bloody affray" by observing: "When a trial shall take place before a jury of his countrymen, a full investigation will no doubt be made." Fox was a naive young man, appalled at himself, a man who had committed a hotheaded manslaughter because no one had ever taught him that he would not lose his pride of manhood if he backed down after he had boldly taken his stand. The outcome was tragic, but at bottom the affray had been a simple matter of mismanaged masculine pride, the sort of thing all other sailors could understand. Wilson Heflin, who discovered the story of Fox and still other nautical events that Melville later worked into "The Town-Ho's Story," suggested that Melville surely would have met Fox during his visits to the jail in the weeks before the U.S. frigate *Constellation* arrived in Honolulu (5 July 1843), and took Fox aboard as prisoner. Melville met members of the crew of the frigate in Hawaii and later, in January 1844, he had an opportunity to learn that Fox had escaped from the *Constellation*.

Melville had walked ashore at Honolulu with at least a few dollars left in his pockets, and not too many places to spend it all at once, but whatever Coleman paid him at Lahaina cannot have lasted long and whatever he earned as a pin-setter was not enough to live well on, so he soon thought about gaining regular employment. Isaac Montgomery was then building a store, and, having looked carefully at the emerging structure, the pin-setter presented himself as a man who in early life had acquired years of banking and merchandising experience in the state capital of New York. On 1 June he and Montgomery drew up an official indenture with mutually binding terms, obligating the party of the second part, Herman Melville, "to keep the said Montgomery's Books and Accounts, and to do and perform for the said Montgomery such other things as may pertain to the said Melville in his duties as a clerk," in recognition of which the party of the first part would pay him $150 a year. The indenture was to take effect 1 July 1843, a month away, and to remain in force until 1 July 1844. During June 1843, Melville was to receive a month's free board, lodging, and washing of his clothes, according to the fifth provision. Montgomery was willing to make this investment because food was cheap and he thought the indenture would prevent Melville from signing on a ship whenever he got the urge: for a minimal outlay, Montgomery was guaranteeing that an exceptionally competent employee, a remarkably well educated man, for a sailor, would be present in July, when his new store opened. Melville himself must have thought he had turned the tables: he the schoolteacher who had worked for months without pay was now to be paid without working so he would be available when there was work to do.

The stringently worded indenture was signed by both parties and witnessed by James Austen and A. Jenkins; it was never canceled, and a record of it survives because in August 1873 the *Friend* printed it as "A Curiosity Relating to a Literary Author." At the time he signed it, Melville must have

reflected ironically on the fact that his services were worth precisely what
they had been worth in the first quarter of 1834 (according to his mother's
account book in the Reese Collection) — $37.50. Melville's labors may have
been restricted to clerking, but Montgomery also worked as an auctioneer,
officiating on 29 and 30 June at the auction of the books of the Sandwich
Islands Institute, which had closed its doors. The indenture had not specified
when Melville was to receive his first payment of $37.50, but chances are that
since Montgomery had already staked him for a month he was not so naive as
to pay him three months' wages in advance on 1 July.

During his subsidized June, Melville dropped in at the Seamen's Bethel,
ignoring the "various religious books and tracts for gratuitous distribution"
(the *Temperance Advocate* for 10 February 1843) but devouring papers from
home. On 10 October 1856 the mate of the barque *Baltic* of New Bedford
noted that Damon's reading room contained "newspapers from most all
parts of the world" (ship's log now in the Providence Public Library, cited by
Busch, *Whaling Will Never Do for Me*). The same must have been true in
1843, and there was even the local publication, Damon's temperance paper,
to bemuse Melville, the erstwhile contributor to the *Democratic Press and
Lansingburgh Advertiser*. The March issue of the *Friend* contained a speech by
George N. Briggs, whom Melville recalled as the U.S. Representative from
the district including Pittsfield. Here Briggs was writing in his other role as
president of the congressional Total Abstinence Society. In the 20 May 1843
issue Melville had the chance to compare his experiences with Damon's by
reading the article on the chaplain's visit to Lahaina just when he had been
there himself.

Here also Melville may have encountered for the first time, quoted by
Damon, Edmund Burke's tribute to the New England whaling fleet before
the House of Commons in 1774, the year after the Tea Party:

> And pray, — sir, what in the world is equal to it? Pass by the other parts, and
> look at the manner in which New England people carry on the whale fishery.
> While we follow them among the tumbling mountains of ice, and behold
> them penetrating into the deepest frozen recesses of Hudson's Bay and Davis'
> Straits, while we are looking for them beneath the arctic circle, we hear that
> they have pierced into the opposite region of polar cold. * * * Nor is the
> equinoctial heat more discouraging to them than the accumulated winter of
> both the poles. We learn that while some of them draw the line or strike the
> harpoon on the coast of Africa, others run the longitude and pursue their
> gigantic game along the coast of Brazil. No sea but what is vexed by their
> fisheries; no climate that is not witness to their toil. Neither the perseverance
> of Holland, nor the activity of France, nor the dexterous and firm sagacity of

English enterprize ever carried this most perilous mode of hardy industry to the extent to which it has been pursued by this recent people — *a people who are still in the gristle, and not yet hardened into manhood.*

At that time, Damon pointed out, the civilized world did not know of the existence of the Sandwich Islands: "Not a Nantucket or New Bedford whaleman had doubled Cape Horn, pursuing his 'gigantic game,' along the western coast of North and South America, or upon the 'Japan ground.'" Any literary-minded sailor like Melville would understand the irony of Burke's waxing so passionate over the comparatively easy Atlantic whaling. Damon quoted Burke's speech at a propitious time, when Melville was there to exult in the rhetoric and perhaps even glory, at moments, in his own participation in what the great Burke saw as a heroic enterprise. Reading Burke's words in Hawaii meant that Melville could ponder them during the remainder of his Pacific voyaging, even if he never pursued his "gigantic game" again. It would require an even more eloquent voice than Burke's to convey the heroism of actual mid-nineteenth-century whaling in the Indian and Pacific oceans.

Melville wrote his family from Honolulu, easy to do, since Chaplain Damon took letters from sailors and forwarded them "by the earliest opportunity" (according to the April 1843 *Temperance Advocate*). The family received a letter or letters he wrote in June from Honolulu, as Allan remembered ("Your letters written in June 1843 were rec^d"), and "also a package once before that" — contents unidentified (a common gift was exotic shells) and place of posting unidentified. A year later, on 4 September 1844, the *Friend* published a notice: "To whom it may concern. . . . If Mr. Herman Melville, formerly officer on board Am[erican] W[hale] S[hip] Acushnet, is in this part of the world, and will call upon the seamen's chaplain, he may find several letters directed to his address." A possible implication is that the writer or writers of these several letters wrote when they thought Herman was on the *Acushnet* still and that their best hope of reaching him would be at Honolulu. Despite the misinformation in the paper, some of the letters may have been written in response to Melville's news that he had signed a year's indenture with Montgomery and would be at one place long enough for the family to write. It is known that in February 1844 Allan and some other members of the family sent Herman "a number of letters" (so Allan wrote Herman on 17 October 1844).

A few days after Melville began clerking in Montgomery's store, Commodore Lawrence Kearny brought the U.S. frigate *Constellation* into Honolulu Harbor. From well at sea Kearny observed the British flag flying from the fort, as it was also from less visible public places. The commercial agent of the United States, William Hooper, quickly filled Kearny in on the developments. On 10 July, writing as commander of the U.S. East India Squadron, Kearny formally reassured Hooper: "While the United States Government refrains from entangling alliances with other nations, and grasps at no power or territory abroad, it would seem but reasonable, that, having no portion of the spoils at the cutting up of the world, it should allow no infringement upon the rights of its citizens" (Carroll Storrs Alden, *Lawrence Kearny: Sailor Diplomat*). He carefully asked a leading question, knowing the answer already: "what preliminary measures were taken by the commander of H. B. M. Ship *Carysfort* for the safety of the lives and property of American citizens residing at Oahu, previous to 4 o'clock, P.M., of Saturday, the 18th of February last," just before the provisional cession. The next day Hooper replied with equal formality that "no preliminary steps whatever were taken" for the safety of the lives and property of American citizens, except the barest notification at midnight the night before. With Hooper's aggrieved letter in hand, Kearny the same day issued a formal protest against the provisional cession of the Hawaiian or Sandwich Islands and declared that he held Kamehameha III and Captain Lord George Paulet "answerable for any and every act by which a citizen of the United States, resident as aforesaid, shall be restrained in his just and undisputed rights and privileges, or who may suffer inconvenience or losses, or be forced to submit to any additional charges on imports or other revenue matters, or exactions in regard to the administration of any municipal laws whatever enacted by the 'commission.' " On 13 July, Stephen Reynolds, who for years had opposed the power-grabbing by the missionaries, excitedly jotted down the news in his journal about Kearny's action (as quoted in *The Melville Log*): "The great Document came out — a letter to Wm Hooper, and a Protest, or something of the sort, against the Cession of the Islands by His Majesty to Lord Paulet for the British Govt — ! That the commissioners (all four) he should hold responsible for all losses, damages &c that have or may happen to any American Citizen, Resident on the Islands — since the cession! and I do not know what else. Isaac Montgomery opened his new Store. Sold all calicoes at four yards for a dollar!! Had a great run!!! they all want to buy old goods!!!!" The arms stretching that calico on the counter were probably Herman's, and a busy day in the store was enough to set him remembering his youth at the cap and fur store. When a seaman from the *Constellation* was arrested for horse-racing in the streets and imprisoned in the fort, under the British flag, Kearny again protested, this time to the governor of Oahu. Kearny had intended only a brief stay in Honolulu, but two dozen Americans petitioned him to remain so as to protect many interests, including that of the American whale fishery. He kept the *Constellation* there, biding his time.

Events moved fast in the next days. On 21 July the resident Levi Chamberlain wrote to the Reverend Mr. Rufus Anderson of the "unsettled state" of affairs at the islands: "Iniquity abounds and the love of many seems to be waxing cold on account of the times. . . . The f[l]oodgates of licentiousness have been opened by the removal of law, and our streets exhibit scenes of intemperance and debauchery exceeded only by the darkest times of heathenism in the islands." On 26 July the missionary Lowell Smith recorded (quoted in *The Melville Log*): "A frigate — English! Well, what next! She proves to be the Dublin, Admiral Thomas — a peace maker. O how timely his arrival! The King has just issued his protest against Lord Paulett and Commodore Karney of the American frigate Constellation has issued his protest against Paulett and the ferment is high." Melville later recorded that the excitement the sudden appearance of the frigate *Dublin* had produced on shore was "prodigious" (*Typee*, "Appendix"). It was the flagship of Rear Admiral Thomas, the commander of the British naval forces in the Pacific. Sizing up Kearny's resources and determination, Thomas announced that he did not accept the provisional cession of the islands. Melville was there to see the Union Jack hauled down on 28 July and the flag of the Sandwich Islands hoisted "and Saluted with 21 GUNS, from each of the English Men-of-War — an equal number returned by the Fort." Then the other ships in the harbor, including the whalers and merchantmen, "fired as fast as they could with one & two guns." As Melville told it in *Typee*, three days after the arrival of the *Dublin*, on the twenty-ninth, "an English sailor hauled down the red cross which had been flying from the heights of the fort, and the Haw[a]iian colors were again displayed upon the same staff. At the same moment the long 42-pounders upon Punchbowl Hill opened their iron throats in triumphant reply to the thunders of the five men-of-war in the harbor."

The threat of British seizure ended with the formal restoration of the islands to the king on 31 July in ceremonies beginning at eight in the morning, according to Mrs. Judd's diary, quoted by Gerrit P. Judd IV in his biography, *Dr. Judd: Hawaii's Friend* (1960). Hiram Bingham described the scene:

A parade of several hundred English marines appeared on the plain of Honolulu with their officers, their banners waving proudly, and their arms glittering in the sunbeams. Admiral Thomas and the suspended king proceeded thither in a carriage, attended by the chiefs and a vast multitude of the people, who formed a line parallel with the troops. The English standard bearers advanced towards his majesty, their flags bowed gracefully, and a broad, beautiful Hawaiian banner, exhibiting a crown and olive branch, was unfurled over the head of the king and his attending chieftains, which was saluted by the English troops with field pieces, then by the guns of the Carysfort, whose

yards were manned in homage to the restored sovereign. Then succeeded the
roar of the guns of the fort, Punch-Bowl Battery, the admiral's ship, Dublin,
the United States' ship, Boston, and others.

Then was read an edict signed by Kamehameha III and Kekauluohi extending amnesty to all of their subjects for any act committed by them to the
injury of the government under the cession, ordering that all prisoners "from
Hawaii to Niihau" be "immediately discharged," and ordering all government business "suspended for ten days," so that all persons might "be
free to enjoy themselves in the festivities and rejoicings appropriate to the
occasion."

According to Melville in the appendix to *Typee*, the restoration of King
Kamehameha initiated a prolonged orgy: "Who that happened to be at
Honolulu during those ten memorable days will ever forget them! The spectacle of universal broad-day debauchery, which was then exhibited, beggars
description. The natives of the surrounding islands flocked to Honolulu by
hundreds, and the crews of two frigates, opportunely let loose like so many
demons to swell the heathenish uproar, gave the crowning flourish to the
scene. It was a sort of Polynesian saturnalia. Deeds too atrocious to be mentioned were done at noon-day in the open street." Damon's editorial in the
extra edition of the *Temperance Advocate and Seamen's Friend*, 31 July ("The
most disgusting scenes are to be seen at noon-day in the streets of Honolulu"), described scenes that had been taking place over the previous
months, not after 31 July. The missionary accounts agreed in placing the
most dissolute behavior before the restoration of Kamehameha's rule rather
than later, but Melville was there, and remembered the ten days of "rejoicing" that "were allowed to all classes of people throughout the islands"
starting 31 July. At some time during this transition of power, probably late
on the thirty-first or the next day (his twenty-fourth birthday) Melville witnessed Dr. Judd in action, for four years later, on 11 July 1847, he regaled his
friend the New York City editor Evert A. Duyckinck "with a picturesque
account of Dr Judd . . . making up his diplomacy from fat natives lolling in
the shade" (excited by the story, Duyckinck mistakenly recorded in his diary
this incident as occurring at Lahaina — not a slip Melville would have made).

On 3 August the frigate *United States*, the flagship of the Pacific Squadron, arrived in Honolulu under Commodore Thomas ap Catesby Jones. The
United States, built in peacetime when Washington was president, was the
hallowed ship in which Captain Stephen Decatur had conquered the British
frigate *Macedonian*, which he brought into New London, past the British
blockade, in December 1812. The *United States* had an awkward yaw, even a
whaleman like Melville could observe. A midshipman then on board, Sam-

uel R. Franklin, in his 1898 *Memories of a Rear-Admiral,* explained that the *United States* "was trimmed by the head, which distracts very much from the appearance of any ship," but only when seen from another ship or the shore. She was "so good in all other respects that her ugliness was forgotten," Franklin said, and the officers knew how to compensate for the yaw by positioning of the stowage. She was, properly sailed, the fastest vessel in the navy, and, some sailors thought, the fastest in the world. Sailors on the *United States* could feel the yaw, but they knew that the awkwardness was a constitutional condition of the "greyhound" of the fleet. Sailors ashore, like Melville, knowing a good deal about her reputation for speed and her service history, during the "late war" and more recently, regarded her with reverence.

Commodore Jones, like his ship a hero of the War of 1812, had recently precipitated an international incident, although it was hushed up at home. Not so much overeager as badly informed (by newspaper reports from the United States), he had disembarked at Monterey, in Mexican California, in October 1842. There he captured the Mexican vessels in the harbor and put his own crews aboard them, then seized the barracks and Government House. In effect, he seized California for the United States, for a day. For the untimeliness of this action he was being recalled by A. P. Upshur, the secretary of the navy, who sent Commodore Alexander J. Dallas out to replace him. Jones got word of his imminent recall before Dallas got sight of the *United States,* and, as the journal keeper recorded, Jones decided to sail for "some of the fairey Islands of Great Pacific," having "determined not to resign the Station untill he had visited the groups which he had not heard from since his former visit to them in 1825." Jones knew of the cession of the Hawaiian Islands to Great Britain before he reached Honolulu, for on 23 July the *United States* had anchored in Byron's Bay on the northeast of the big island, Hawaii, and had received aboard "Rev Mr Coan missionary," who "performed *Divine Service* on board" and provided the "information that the islands had been taken possession of by the *Br Hon Lord George Paulet.*" To the defused situation in Honolulu Commodore Jones brought his own news, that Great Britain and France were ready to recognize the independence of Hawaii.

Melville probably worked all day on his twenty-fourth birthday while Hawaii was preparing for public celebration. On 3 August, a Thursday, the excitement began early, hours before the arrival of the *United States.* Stephen Reynolds wrote in his diary one of his typically vivid shorthand accounts (quoted from *The Melville Log*): "Fine morn — at 10 — Everybody in motion, going and getting ready to go to Nuana to the King's Feast! A great concourse of people — Foreigners and Natives — estimated at 3000 people. Luow — Pigs — Fowls — Fish — Big hogs — Poe — and cold WATER!!! At 6 o'clock U.S.S. — U[nited] S[tates], Com^e Jones, arrived and anchored after Sunset! I was glad to see her come in!" The food at the luau was traditional ("Poe" is what Melville spelled "Poee-Poee" in *Typee*), but "cold WATER" as the beverage of the day was a tribute to the power of the missionaries. With the missionaries securely back in power, Honolulu looked less and less attractive. On the fifth the American barque *Elizabeth* arrived from a cruise, "having lost her Capt & a boats crew in taking a whale," Midshipman William H. Wilcox on the *United States* noted in the journal he was keeping — monitory news for any dissatisfied whaler ashore. Melville saw more and more Americans as the *United States* divided supplies among the fleet, sending marines' clothing to the *Cyane* on the fifth, for instance, and twenty sheets of copper on the tenth. "Lieut Avery the Purser & Master" went ashore on 11 August, "inspecting provisions" they were purchasing from local merchants, probably including Montgomery, although most of the supplies taken aboard, in the following days, were foodstuffs. If he had known himself better, Melville would have realized just how vulnerable the act of writing letters home would leave him. Now it did not take long for his acquaintance with Americans fresh from home to play havoc with his ideas of staying on in the middle of the Pacific. From the time the first sailors from the *Constellation* and then the *United States* came ashore, bringing an odd supply of old newspapers and other news from the world of his mother and brothers and sisters, if they were living still, he was overcome with homesickness.

In the end, Melville broke the indenture, by mutual consent with Montgomery or otherwise, and on 17 August 1843 he climbed aboard the *United States* and joined the navy for "3 years or cruize," according to the General Muster Roll. He thought he was done with whaling.

[14]

Ordinary Seaman on the *United States*

1843–1844

Endeavour to blend the graces & courtesy of the Gentleman, with the frankness & sincerity of the Sailor, and the precision & discipline of the Officer — having chosen a noble profession, your career may be distinguished, you have every incitement to manly enterprise & honest ambition.

Allan Melvill's advice to Midshipman Thomas W. Melvill, about to sail on the *Brandywine* for the Pacific, 28 August 1826

THERE SURVIVES IN THE NAVAL RECORDS and Library of the Navy Department a journal, "Abstract of a Cruise in the United States Frigate *United States*, under the Command of Captain James Armstrong, Esquire Bearing the Broad Pendant of Commodore Thomas Ap Catesby Jones, in the Pacific Ocean, in the Years 1842–1844," published by Charles Roberts Anderson as *Journal of a Cruise to the Pacific Ocean, 1842–1844, in the Frigate "United States"* (Duke, 1937). The author of the "Abstract of a Cruise" (his identity has not been established) prefaced his account with a description: "The United States Frigate United States is a fine Single banked Frigate, measuring 178 feet from the Knight heads to the Tafrail, 45 feet moulded beam, and 29 feet from her Kelson to Spar Deck; mounting 20 thirty two's and 2 twenty four pounders on Spar Deck, and 30 twenty four pounders on Gun Deck; and of 1750 tuns. She was built in Philadelphia, *Pa.*, in 1797 and has always been considered the fastest sailor in the American Navy." The *United States*, not even twice as long as the *Acushnet*, carried some sixteen times as many men as the whaleship. According to William M. Fowler Jr. in *Jack Tars and Commodores*, frigates like the *United States*, the "forty-fours" (a "rate" contingent on number of guns modified by other factors such as length of guns), by original regulation shipped "fifty-three commissioned, warrant, and petty officers, 245 able and ordinary seamen," making some 480 officers and men in all.

The official log of the frigate *United States* for the period of Melville's service survives in the National Archives. Three other journals of this voyage are known, one kept by Midshipman William Sharp and now held in the

Archives of the Navy Department, National Archives; one kept by Midshipman Alonzo C. Jackson, now in the Manuscript Division, Library of Congress; and one kept by Midshipman William H. Wilcox, now at the United States Naval Academy Museum, where it has been transcribed by two midshipmen, David Maxwell and Adriaen Morse, under the direction of Professor R. D. Madison.

In their journals Sharp and Wilcox both recorded for 18 August 1843 the shipping of Herman Melville and Griffith Williams, ordinary seamen, shortly after noon. Reporting to the sick-bay, Melville heard from one of the assistant surgeons an unfamiliar command, "Strip!" (*White-Jacket*, ch. 77) — unfamiliar because whaleships were less concerned to admit only healthy specimens. (The title of the book stemming from this cruise, *White-Jacket*, refers to an outlandish garment the narrator in that book makes for himself, after his ship, the *Neversink*, is unable to provide him with a regulation jacket. Nothing from the various accounts suggests that the *United States* was unable to provide Melville himself with standard equipment.) The close official scrutiny of his naked body was fresh in Melville's mind a few hours later when all hands were called to witness some official punishments on bare backs: twelve lashes on John Hall's back for striking a sentry; twelve lashes on George Clark's back for smuggling liquor; and six lashes on the backs of Joseph Stanly and William B. Ewing (apprentice boys) for fighting and for using abusive language. The boatswain, also, was "suspended" for disobedience, Wilcox recorded. On the nineteenth three more men were given twelve lashes each for drunkenness. One of them, Antonio Guavella, Melville remembered in *White-Jacket* as "Antone, the Portuguese," in chapter 33, "A Flogging," where he described the way the ritual began with "the dread summons of the boatswain and his mates at the principal hatchway — a summons that ever sends a shudder through every manly heart in a frigate: 'All hands witness punishment, ahoy!'" Melville emphasized the impossibility of not witnessing the floggings: "However much you may desire to absent yourself from the scene that ensues, yet behold it you must; or, at least, stand near it you must; for the regulations enjoin the attendance of the entire ship's company, from the corpulent Captain himself to the smallest boy who strikes the bell." On the *United States*, Melville reluctantly witnessed, all told, over a hundred and fifty floggings, each done according to "regulations."

With seven men thus adequately chastised in full view of Montgomery's former clerk, the *United States* sailed from Honolulu on 20 August ("proceeded to Sea with a fine Breeze"), bound for — the Marquesas Islands. After the first few days, she had fine weather all the way. Some events of the passage are known. On 26 August the summons by the ship's drummer called Melville to his first "General Quarters," which he described in *White-Jacket* (ch. 16, "General Training in a Man-of-war") as "a mustering of all hands to their stations at the guns on the several decks, and a sort of sham-fight with an imaginary foe." In *White-Jacket*, Melville identifies his station as at " 'Gun No. 5,' on the First Lieutenant's quarter-bill," No. 5 being "one of the thirty-two-pound carronades, on the starboard side of the quarter-deck." Whether or not he really played "rammer-and-sponger" to a "fine negro" who was "the captain of the gun," he appreciated the erotics of ramming and sponging "like a good fellow," and testified that sham-fight or not, the training left the younger men exhausted enough to appreciate what fighting a real battle might be like. The mock battle gave some of the older men occasion to tell stories from real battles they had fought, for some of them were as old as Commodore Jones (the "Flying Welshman"), whose wounds had left him unable to get his arms into his coat without assistance. Throughout Melville's service in the Pacific, all the sailors knew that sham-fight one week could be real fight the next, against Great Britain, against Mexico, there was no predicting which. Some of Melville's new shipmates who had been on the *United States* in October 1842 regarded Jones's seizure of California as an act of buffoonery: E. Curtiss Hine later made it the subject of a satiric poem in *The Haunted Barque* (1848). Promptly apologized for, the seizure had not proved to be occasion enough to create a war, but war was waiting to be triggered by some act — of buffoonery, diplomacy, or whatever. At the time Melville came aboard, Jones was still plotting just how much ocean he might traverse before Dallas managed to meet up with him and show him the letter from Upshur commanding him home.

The third was the first Sunday of September, and that morning Melville learned his tiny part in the monthly ritual: "we had a grand *'muster round the capstan*,' when we passed in solemn review before the Captain and officers, who closely scanned our frocks and trowsers, to see whether they were according to the Navy cut" (*White-Jacket*, ch. 70). Thus assured of the propriety of the men, the captain at half past ten proceeded with the rest of the ceremony, a reading of the "Articles of War" designed to terrify "a novice" standing in bareheaded awe as the captain's clerk announced the specific grave offenses for which a seaman might be punished, including more than a dozen which the seaman should avoid "on pain of death" or lest, in equally ominous wording, he should "suffer death." Some of the acts punishable by death involved improper behavior in wartime — failing to do the utmost to take or destroy an enemy vessel, giving outright aid to an enemy, or spying for an enemy. Even in peacetime on pain of death no "officer or private in the navy" should "disobey the lawful orders of his superior officer, or strike him, or draw, or offer to draw, or raise any weapon against him, while in the execution of the duties of his office." As everyone knew from the story of the

Somers, any threat of mutiny, however frivolous, was punishable by death. A deserter like Melville was warned that if "any person in the navy shall desert, or shall entice others to desert, he shall suffer death, or such other punishment as a court martial" should adjudge. Furthermore, if "any person in the navy" should "sleep upon his watch, or negligently perform the duty assigned him, or leave his station before regularly relieved," he should "suffer death, or such punishment as a court martial" should adjudge. At the end of this dramatic reading of the Articles of War, the day clear and the breezes fresh, the men remained for the eleven o'clock portion of the ceremony, when the chaplain "performed Divine Service." Anyone possessed like Herman with both a close knowledge of the New Testament and a strong sense of irony would be impelled to make reflections about a representative of the prince of peace being put to the service of a man-of-war and about the discrepancy between the apparent benignity of nature and the ferocity of man.

Once the crew knew they were headed directly for the Marquesas, any seaman who had glimpsed the islands was sure to be pumped for information, since even the green navy men had heard repeatedly the two salient reports: that the islanders (at least the men) were cannibals and that the women were almost unimaginably liberal with their sexual favors. Melville's months on the *Lucy Ann* and the *Charles and Henry,* as well as in the Sandwich Islands, had confirmed what he had realized soon after as he signed on the *Lucy Ann:* he had lived through what could be made into one of the great adventures open to a young American. Properly told, his story was an inestimable asset in any company of whalers, beachcombers, man-of-war's-men, any group of men. At this time of his life he was already becoming what the younger Richard Henry Dana called him a few years later, "incomparable in dramatic storytelling"—a compliment all the greater because Dana could compare him to the best storytellers he had heard on shipboard and in Mexican California as well as the best raconteurs among the anecdotally stocked members of the Massachusetts bar and the New England literary set. On the *United States* Melville must have weighed his opportunities for revealing that he had sailed to the Marquesas previously, and his further opportunities for revealing, to a select company, that he had seen not only how sailors were welcomed to Nukahiva Bay but also how sailors might be treated deep in the interior of the island. Later he impressed many people as a remarkably silent man, until he surprised them by talking so well. At sea, Melville did not have to rush into conversation as one might have to do at a literary salon, if one was to speak at all; he could wait to thaw, to be drawn out, a condition that encouraged his habit—already a strategy in his youth around Gansevoort, the incessant talker—of holding his silence, until the right moment came. On a long sea voyage, the right moment always came, sooner or later. Years later, he learned that at least two of his shipmates, on the *Acushnet* and the *United States*, had come so under his spell that before he became famous as an author two children were named for him, a nephew of Toby Greene and a son of Oliver Russ (who had signed the ship's roster as Edward Norton).

Once his story became known, Melville had the best possible audience — listeners who are never satisfied with one telling of the tale. These were men without women, men without privacy, mainly young men, many of them so needy for sex that they took what casual relief from each other they could manage. Far from trying to ferret out sexual acts, a sensible naval captain, like a sensible whaling captain, would ignore whatever he could. According to the marine drummer Philip C. Van Buskirk a few years later, the man-of-war *Cumberland* was a Sodom of a ship, and a corvette, the *Plymouth*, a "Sodomy den." Van Buskirk applied the term sodomy to a variety of sexual acts, making it clear that in his experience a great majority of seamen, at one time or another, practiced mutual masturbation. Even when one man forced sex upon another, the victim was a fool to complain, as Melville showed in *White-Jacket* (ch. 89, "The Social State in a Man-of-war"), where a deck officer would "turn away with loathing," refuse to hear the accusations, and "command the complainant out of his sight." There Melville generalized sententiously: "What too many seamen are when ashore is very well known; but what some of them become when completely cut off from shore indulgences can hardly be imagined by landsmen. The sins for which the cities of the plain were overthrown still linger in some of these wooden-walled Gomorrahs of the deep."

Melville had an audience whenever he wanted it, but he had to decide how much of the truth he would tell and how he would tell it. Later, when he alluded in the preface to *Typee* to his exciting the "warmest sympathies" of his shipmates by his stories, he was writing drolly. However warm the feelings he excited over his fears of being devoured by cannibals, the warmest feelings he excited were always sexual. Other sailors aboard the *United States* may have experienced the traditional welcome to the Marquesas by native women who swam out and boarded the ship and felt insulted if they were rebuffed. Melville had done more — he had gone ashore and lived in the garden of Eden before the Fall. After he was on the *United States* awhile, and perhaps even earlier, he was implying that he had lived there longer than he had. By the time he wrote *Typee*, his three weeks had become "a four months' residence," a duration which multiplied the opportunities he could claim for natural and anthropological observations, as well as for sexual observations and experiences.

A young man in Melville's situation might well have bragged to other sailors about the variety and frequency of his sexual experiences with the Typees, but the kind of yarn a man could spin from that sort of material would be apt to pall on the teller before long, as well as all but the most desperate auditors. Chances are that Melville devised other strategies for satisfying the inevitable questions. He might well have met all inquiries by acknowledging that he saw youths, hardly more than girls and boys, as well as men and women, having sex openly in interesting combinations, but rather than bragging about his own participation he may have found it more amusing to do what he did in *Typee* — to tell them, a trifle too solemnly, that he was much too sober a young man to have renounced his Christian training. Didn't they know that a decorous young man could beat down any sexual urges if he directed his thoughts toward "Home" and "Mother"? (These are the two evocative words he later soberly claimed to have taught Fayaway.) There was positive value in creating more than a little humorously teasing mystery about his experiences. In any case, his yarns were apt not to put his auditors to sleep but to arouse them by their sexual content, whatever Melville's strategy — whether he confessed, bragged, denied, or evaded teasingly.

And Melville kept telling these yarns. On 13 October 1849 the poet and journalist Nathaniel Parker Willis informed the readers of the New York *Home Journal*: "Herman Melville, with his cigar and his Spanish eyes, *talks* Typee and Omoo, just as you find the flow of his delightful mind on paper." Willis was a dapper and sensual man with much self-confessed sexual experience. Driven by charges of profligacy, he issued a "card" (a public statement) in the 18 October 1849 New York *Tribune*, five days after this comment on Melville, acknowledging that in his first residence abroad, when a single man, he "saw freely every manner of life which, by general usage, a gentleman may see." Nothing Melville said shocked Willis. Melville continued to talk *Typee* and *Omoo*, playing to his image, even in later years. In the late 1880s, there is testimony, he amused an audience in a barbershop in Glens Falls, just above Gansevoort, New York, with an indecorous tall tale about how he recognized his naked little son when his ship touched at Nukahiva on a later voyage, after his captivity and escape. Telling his adventures until he had the stories right, Melville used his experiences with the Typees to clinch his membership in the club of men among whom he had been assigned — afterguardsmen, one witness recollected, or maintopmen, among whom he placed the narrator he named only as "White Jacket."

Once he talked to men from naval vessels in Honolulu and especially after he boarded the man-of-war, Herman learned more details about the *Somers* tragedy. The direful story was one that evoked peculiar ranges of fears

1 *(left)* General Peter Gansevoort, 1794, oil on canvas by Gilbert Stuart (30 ⅛" x 25"). Munson-Williams-Proctor Institute, Museum of Art, Utica, N.Y. 2 *(right)* Catherine Van Schaick Gansevoort, ca. 1820, oil on canvas by Ezra Ames. Gansevoort-Lansing Collection, Rare Books and Manuscripts Division, The New York Public Library, Astor, Lenox and Tilden Foundations.

3 *(left)* Priscilla Scollay Melvill, ca. 1825, by Francis Alexander. The Bostonian Society.
4 *(right)* Major Thomas Melvill, ca. 1825, by Francis Alexander. The Bostonian Society.

5 Allan Melvill, 1810, watercolor on paper by John Rubens Smith. The Metropolitan Museum of Art, Bequest of Miss Charlotte E. Hoadley, 1946.

6 Maria Gansevoort [later Melvill(e)], 1814, miniature by Anson Dickinson. Gansevoort-Lansing Collection, Rare Books and Manuscripts Division, The New York Public Library, Astor, Lenox and Tilden Foundations.

7 Allan Melvill, ca. 1820, oil painting by Ezra Ames. The Henry E. Huntington
Library and Art Gallery.

8 Maria Gansevoort Melvill [later Melville], ca. 1820, oil painting by Ezra Ames.
Berkshire Athenaeum.

9 *(top)* Peter Gansevoort, engraving by A. H. Ritchie, from *Hudson-Mohawk Genealogical and Family Memoirs*, ed. Cuyler Reynolds, vol. 1 (New York, 1911).
10 *(bottom)* New York State Bank, Albany, from *The History of the City of Albany, New York*, by Arthur James Weise (Albany, 1884).

11 *(top)* Thomas Melvill Jr., ca. 1805, photograph of a now unlocated portrait. Miss Jean F. Melvill.   12 *(bottom)* "Country Life," by Thomas Melvill, 1789, from his copybook. By permission of the Houghton Library, Harvard University (bMS Am 188.6 [32]).

13 Gansevoort Melville, 1836, watercolor. Gansevoort-Lansing
Collection, Rare Books and Manuscripts Division, The New York
Public Library, Astor, Lenox and Tilden Foundations.

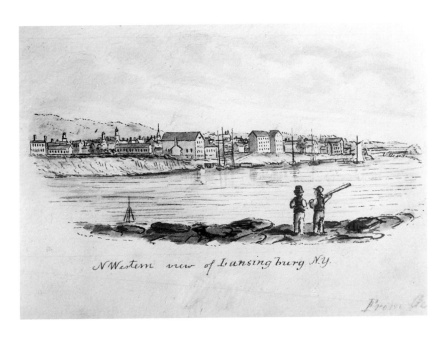

14 "N Western View of Lansingburgh N.Y.," ca. 1840, by John Barber. Collection of
Warren F. Broderick.

15 "Exchange & Nelson Monument, Liverpool," ca. 1844, engraving by Henry Lacey, from *Pictorial Liverpool*, 2d ed. (England, n.d.). The Newberry Library.

16 "The Boats of the *Acushnet* Chasing Whales," watercolor by Henry M. Johnson, from his manuscript log of the *Acushnet*, 1845–47. Courtesy, Peabody Essex Museum, Salem, Mass.

17 "Boats Attacking Whales," from *The Natural History of the Sperm Whale*, by Thomas Beale (London, 1839). The Newberry Library.

18 "An Inhabitant of the Island of Nukahiwa," engraving by J. Storer, from *Voyages and Travels,* by G. H. von Langsdorff (London, 1813). The Everett D. Graff Collection, The Newberry Library.

19 Richard Tobias (Toby) Greene, 1846, daguerreotype.
Berkshire Athenaeum.

20 *(top)* "Broom Road, Tahiti," from *Narrative of the United States Exploring Expedition*, by Charles Wilkes, vol. 2 (Philadelphia, 1845).   **21** *(bottom)* "U.S.S. *Somers*, Bound Home from the African Coast, on 1 December 1842, with the Bodies of Three Alleged Mutineers Hanging from Her Yardarm," ca. 1843, engraving. Naval Historical Center.

22 (*top*) & 23 (*bottom*) "View of Honolulu," ca. August 1843, and "Pacific Squadron: *United States, Cyane, St. Louis, Yorktown* and *Shark*" [*St. Louis* no longer visible], ca. 1843, watercolors by William H. Meyers, from his "Journal of a Cruise on the U.S.S. *Cyane,* 1842–43." Naval Historical Center.

24 "Punishment," ca. 1843, watercolor by William H. Meyers, from his "Journal of a Cruise on the U.S.S. *Cyane*, 1842–43." Naval Historical Center.

25 *(top)* "Ladies' Street Costume (Style 1846)—Lima," from *My Voyage in the United States Frigate "Congress,"* by Elizabeth Douglas Van Denburgh (New York, 1913). 26 *(bottom)* E. Curtiss Hine, from *Gleason's Pictorial Drawing-Room Companion* (3 January 1852). The Newberry Library.

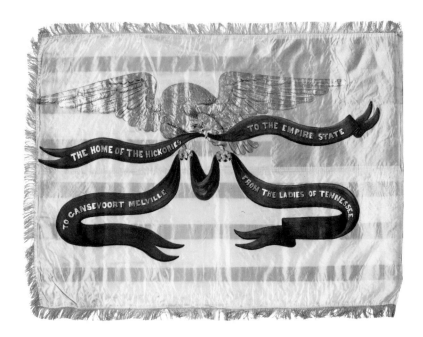

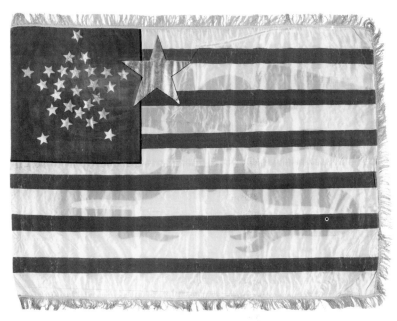

27 Commemorative banner presented to Gansevoort Melville by "the Ladies of Tennessee," 1844 (front and reverse). Albany Institute of History & Art.

and sympathies from all sailors, and one which could be endlessly speculated about. What Melville heard was garbled, one way or another, and inconclusive, as all the reporting was, but enough to set him speculating about family traits of character that contributed to Cousin Guert Gansevoort's playing just the role he seemed to have played. The wealth of family information that he could bring to bear in the analysis of the character of the second lead in the drama formed, for his special intimates, one aspect of his value as a new companion. Melville was not one to exalt himself by flaunting his kinship with a victim of American journalistic notoriety, but he was the kind of man who would share his sober reflections with well-chosen shipmates. To those who knew the history of the honorable badge of the Order of the Cincinnati, it was evocative that Guert was next in line after Uncle Herman to inherit the very badge that had belonged to the Hero of Fort Stanwix — now an ironic trophy of family pride and security. The three hangings on the *Somers*, cloaked in dense ambiguities, had been a sensation in the press, then had become a long-term matter of national conscience, well worth repeated gnawings at, during quiet meditative sessions aloft, where there was time to probe the ironies of what a later jargon would call situational ethics. Aloft there was time also for Melville to brood on his own character — how he had so far met the tests it had been subjected to, and how like or unlike Guert he might prove in whatever trials he faced.

For other matter to brood upon, Melville had access to more reading material on board the *United States* than since he left home. On the *United States* Herman found a library that dwarfed that of the *Charles and Henry*, books which charmed him and sometimes challenged him. William Sharp's journal shows that in early July 1844 Captain Armstrong transferred with him to the *Savannah* part or all of the library of the *United States*, including these particular books: William Prescott's *Ferdinand and Isabella* (3 vols.); George Bancroft's *History of the United States*; Darwin's *Voyages of H.B.M. Ships "Adventure" & "Beagle"* (4 vols.); Livingstone's *Atlas*; Hough's *Military Law Authorities* and *Courts Martial*; and Harper's Family Library (72 vols.). All those books were on board the *United States* for Melville's first ten months on the ship. The last named, the Harper's Family Library, was a nonfiction series (still being expanded in the early 1840s), mainly consisting of biography, travel, and history, with a smattering of scientific and philosophical titles, even, in the 1843 list, Cunningham's *Lives of the Painters and Sculptors* in five volumes. There were more volumes than titles, since the Harper's Family Library issued many works in two or three volumes. In the 1843 list, for example, Keightley's *History of England* comprised numbers 114 through 118, while Russell's *Polynesia* was the last, 158. That year the 158 volumes sold for $70.30. The series was primarily British, although a few books by American writers were included, among them J. K. Paulding's *Life of Washington*, W. C. Bryant's *Selections from American Poets*, Irving's *Life of Oliver Goldsmith*, and young Richard Henry Dana's *Two Years before the Mast*.

The thirst for literature in a sister ship, the *Constitution*, was described by the anonymous author of *Life in a Man-of-War, or Scenes in "Old Ironsides" During her Cruise in the Pacific, by a Fore-Top-Man* (Philadelphia: Lydia R. Bailey, 1841): "Whilst we lay in New York, three or four hundred volumes were purchased, comprising the whole of the Family Library; the works of Scott, Marryatt, Cooper, Irving, Bulwer, &c.; and when the circumstance was made known throughout the ship, the greater part of our jolly tars came forward with avidity and subscribed their mites towards repaying the purchase money." The foretopman meant that the whole of the Family Library was purchased, along with the works of fiction writers, although some nonfiction by novelists was included. The Harper's Family Library was of enormous cultural importance to the young Republic, on sea as well as on land, since it allowed a mass of pre-selected books to enter any community, including a ship's crew, all at once. The very popular series included a great many books that Melville demonstrably read, on the *United States* or at other times.

Reading may have been a solitary vice in a whaler, but not in a man-of-war. Even an ordinary seaman like Melville was expected to be an avid reader, willing to compete with his fellows for the most desirable volumes in the ship's library. Sailors read books privately, recited and read poetry and prose aloud, and retold stories of battles glorious (or ignoble) in naval history — battles they had witnessed or had heard described by actual participants. On the *United States* they read and told stories very much the way many families did at home when gathered together at the end of a day. The favorite authors of some sailors "were such as you may find at the book-stalls around Fulton Market; they were slightly physiological in their nature" (*White-Jacket*, ch. 41). In the exalted maintop there was, Melville implied, no demand for such printed pornography. The "Fore-Top-Man" offered this scene on *"Old Ironsides"*:

> just glance your eye along our ships' decks when lying in port; under the break of the poop you may observe a group of mizen-topmen, eagerly listening to some more talented shipmate, who, with voice and effect worthy the subject, is reading aloud passages from one of the splendid and romantic poems of the celebrated Byron: — In the larboard gangway a crowd are assembled, distorting their risible muscles at the trying though ludicrous scenes in Marryatt's Jacob Faithful or Midshipman Easy: — Again, on the starboard side amongst the main-topmen, a little *coterie* are gathered together, wrapped

in profound silence, every ear intent, with open mouth, swallowing some of
Cooper's thrilling descriptions of nautical life, or digesting the eccentricities
of Scott's liquor-loving Peter Pebbles, or the original and trite [*sic*] remarks of
Boz's inimitable Sam Weller; and even the hard old salts on the forecastle,
with the bronze of every climate upon their furrowed cheeks, are huddled
together around the *trunk*, hearing, with enthusiastic imagination and eyes
beaming with delight, some lettered "sheet-anchor-man" describe the glorious exploits and brilliant achievements of Columbia's ships in the last war.

Melville's depiction in *White-Jacket* of the sailors as avid readers confirms the
foretopman's account — and would confirm it even more conclusively if he
had not borrowed lavishly from the library on *"Old Ironsides"* for *White-
Jacket* (ch. 41, "A Man-of-war Library"), coolly appropriating several titles
from the "foretopman," among them *Mason Good's Book of Nature*, *Sittin on a
Rail*, and *Gumbo Squash*.

The foretopman on the *Constitution* made it clear that all the men had
access to the books without regard to rank, although with considerable regard to main strength:

> The little collection of books was put under charge of the ship's Yoeman, in
> the fore-passage, and there remained until the multiplied duties generally
> attending a vessel-of-war upon the commencement of a foreign cruise, had in
> some measure subsided, — and the first Sunday the news flew through the
> ship that books were about to be issued, an all-impatient crowd immediately
> surrounded the ladders leading to the fore-passage, and a scene of uproar and
> confusion, laughable in the extreme, took place. The several volumes had
> been numbered, and the titles placed on a catalogue, which was forcibly
> dragged from one to the other, the weakest going to the wall, to ascertain
> what books were below that might suit their several tastes.

In *White-Jacket* Melville depicted the "Man-of-war Library" as being in the
custody of one of the marine corporals, who kept the books in a large cask on
the berth-deck and had to capsize it like a barrel of potatoes when seeking a
particular volume. In that chapter Melville claims to have found less pleasure
in those books than in "a few choice old authors" whom he found "in various
parts of the ship, among the inferior officers." His examples are charmingly
tongue in cheek, and probably imagined or vastly elaborated: "One was
'*Morgan's History of Algiers*,' a famous old quarto, abounding in picturesque
narratives of corsairs, captives, dungeons, and sea-fights; and making mention of a cruel old Dey, who, toward the latter part of his life, was so filled
with remorse for his cruelties and crimes that he could not stay in bed after
four o'clock in the morning, but had to rise in great trepidation and walk off

his bad feelings till breakfast time." Yet Melville in *White-Jacket* probably conveyed something very close to what he felt as he read at least some of these books at sea, as well as what he felt in thinking about them in 1849:

> Then there was Walpole's Letters — very witty, pert, and polite — and some odd volumes of plays, each of which was a precious casket of jewels of good things, shaming the trash nowadays passed off for dramas, containing "The Jew of Malta," "Old Fortunatus," "The City Madam," "Volpone," "The Alchymist," and other glorious old dramas of the age of Marlow and Jonson, and that literary Damon and Pythias, the magnificent, mellow old Beaumont and Fletcher, who have sent the long shadow of their reputation, side by side with Shakspeare's, far down the endless vale of posterity.

Melville ended the chapter with a meditative testimony: "though public libraries have an imposing air, and doubtless contain invaluable volumes, yet, somehow, the books that prove most agreeable, grateful, and companionable, are those we pick up by chance here and there; those which seem put into our hands by Providence; those which pretend to little, but abound in much."

The foretopman on the *Constitution* stressed also the availability of newspapers: "You might perceive a bevy of *quidnuncs*, who, 'all ear,' are swallowing copious draughts of news from 'Brother Jonathan' or 'Bennett's Herald,' six or eight months old, which one of the party reads aloud occasionally, setting pronunciation at defiance altogether." *Brother Jonathan* competed directly with booksellers, because it could print an entire novel, albeit in cruelly tiny print, in a single elephant folio paper, but the New York *Herald* did not regularly offer literature, beyond the occasional poem. (*Brother Jonathan* was reduced as a threat when the persuasive Fletcher Harper, one of the Harper brothers, lobbied Congress into raising postal rates on newspapers in mid-April 1843.) On the *Constitution* reading off duty was encouraged by the officers. On the *United States* men got to read old newspapers, passed around among themselves, and every time the frigate boarded a vessel freshly arrived, or one that had recently met one that had freshly arrived, or whenever the frigate anchored at a port on the coast, then an erratic but treasured cargo of newspapers, four or eight pages each, printed on good rag paper, was brought aboard, and in due course made available to the men. Every seaman grew used to learning of important events out of perfect chronological order, and more imaginative men might find positive value in the challenges they faced when confronted with cryptic allusions to extant situations with no tracing of the events that had led up to them. (Many a seaman in the Pacific with Melville may have encountered a printed reference to President Tyler before he knew for sure that William Henry Harrison had been inaugurated.)

In *White-Jacket* (ch. 4, "Jack Chase") Melville assigns his narrator to the maintop and thereby puts him in with "a noble set of tars." The captain of the maintop was in fact named John Chase, "tall and well-knit, with a clear open eye, a fine broad brow, and an abounding nut-brown beard. No man ever had a better heart or a bolder." Chase was an Englishman, at a time when many foreigners and even American black slaves served on American ships. (All navies enlisted foreigners; Melville explains in *White-Jacket*, ch. 90, "The Manning of Navies," that he had served in the navy with at least two Englishmen who had also served in the French navy.) Chase was so much older than Melville, fifty-three or so, that in chapter 75 of *White-Jacket* Melville has him fight on the flagship *Asia* at the Battle of Navarino in 1827, when "thirty-two sail of Englishmen, Frenchmen, and Russians, attacked and vanquished in the Levant an Ottoman fleet of three ships-of-the-line, twenty-five frigates, and a swarm of fire ships and hornet craft." (Chase may have been at Navarino, but this history Melville coolly lifted from the experiences a young Scot published in Glasgow in 1829.) The midshipman Franklin could not remember Herman Melville, although he tried. Somewhat impaired by a lifetime of heavy drinking, Franklin claimed to remember Chase, through the medium of *White-Jacket*: "He was about as fine a specimen of a seaman as I have ever seen in all my cruising. He was not only that, but he was a man of intelligence and a born leader. His top-mates adored him, although he kept them up to the mark, and made every man do his share of work." According to *White-Jacket* (ch. 4), Chase "had read all the verses of Byron, and all the romances of Scott. He talked of Rob Roy, Don Juan, and Pelham; Macbeth and Ulysses; but, above all things, was an ardent admirer of Camoens." Something of a linguist, Chase could recite long passages from Camoëns's sea-epic *The Lusiad* in the Portuguese.

There is some doubt that Melville himself was a member of the maintop, especially during his early months on the *United States*, when he could hardly have possessed the skills required for that post. Wilson Heflin found that Lieutenant James Lardner, whose duty station was on the quarterdeck, read *White-Jacket* in 1850, while he was "very fresh in his remembrance of Melville," possibly from seeing him helping to handle the lower sails, and thought he had been assigned to "the After-Guard, & not in the Main top." Among the literary sailors in *White-Jacket* is a poet Melville calls Lemsford, whom he identifies as "a gentlemanly young member of the After-Guard," and whose acquaintance he had made very early: "It is curious, how unerringly a man pitches upon a spirit, any way akin to his own, even in the most

miscellaneous mob" (ch. 11, "The Pursuit of Poetry under Difficulties").
Lemsford may have been based on a seaman named E. Curtiss Hine, who
after his return wrote a novel called *Orlando Melville or Victims of the Press-
Gang* (1848). In chapter 13 Melville identifies his and Lemsford's mutual
friends, Nord and Williams, as comprising, along with Jack Chase and his
comrades of the maintop, "almost the only persons" with whom he "unre-
servedly consorted while on board the frigate." He had, he claimed, a theory:
"For I had not been long on board ere I found that it would not do to be intimate with every body. An indiscriminate intimacy with all hands leads to sundry annoyances and scrapes, too often ending with a dozen at the gang-way."
Harrison Hayford, who linked Lemsford to Hine in "The Sailor Poet of
White-Jacket" (1951), also showed that Nord was based on the man who
signed on the *United States* as Edward Norton; under his real name, Oliver
Russ, he got in touch with Melville years later. Williams was based on the
Griffith Williams, a native of Maine, who enlisted with Melville.

By 1849, when Melville was writing *White-Jacket*, he thought he would
hardly be able to recognize many of his shipmates should he happen to meet
them in the streets. The small literary society was enough. Melville may in
actuality have been assigned to the afterguard and not to the maintop, but
even if he was never a maintopman, being on duty near the mainmast, handling the lower sails, especially the mizzen and main sails, meant that Melville had opportunity to make friends with the captain of the maintop, and to
be invited aloft, when off duty.

The following passage from *White-Jacket* (ch. 11) may be greatly fictionalized, but it suggests at least the kind of books the men talked about and
the level of their discussion:

> My noble Captain, Jack Chase, rather patronized Lemsford, and he would
> stoutly take his part against scores of adversaries. Frequently, inviting him up
> aloft into his top, he would beg him to recite some of his verses; to which he
> would pay the most heedful attention, like Mecænas listening to Virgil, with a
> book of the Æneid in his hand. Taking the liberty of a well-wisher, he would
> sometimes gently criticise the piece, suggesting a few immaterial alterations.
> And upon my word, noble Jack, with his native-born good sense, taste, and
> humanity, was not ill qualified to play the true part of a *Quarterly Review;* —
> which is, to give quarter at last, however severe the critique.

(By "patronized" Melville meant that Chase acted as a patron to Lemsford.)
Melville portrayed White Jacket's own relationship with Nord as more intense than Chase's and Lemsford's, based staunchly upon the intuition that
Nord had "seized the right meaning of Montaigne." That intuition was then
verified during "a profoundly quiet midnight watch," a transformative expe-

rience: "That night we scoured all the prairies of reading; dived into the bosoms of authors, and tore out their hearts; and that night White-Jacket learned more than he has ever done in any single night since" (ch. 13, "A Man-of-war Hermit in a Mob"). On the *United States* Melville read not only more than he had recently done but more deeply than he had ever done before.

Jack Chase and the other literary men of the maintop made it manly to love literature. Gansevoort and Herman must have discussed books with each other often enough, although the books around the house at Lansingburgh were first for Gansevoort's edification, and only afterward available to Herman or Helen or others in the family. There had always been a slightly stiff air of rigorous and purposeful zeal for self-improvement in Gansevoort's reading, always a hope that what he read could be put to practical application. Now, on a man-of-war, Melville found men who knew poems by heart and liked to recite them and who, some of them, were even then keeping journals and writing poems, men who loved literature perhaps more for itself than Gansevoort did. They probably shared poetry with each other more often than they read prose aloud and discussed it, and their love of literature was endearingly sincere and unaffected. Herman could recite Byron with the best of them, and during the voyage he learned, more conclusively than on his earlier ships, that he could tell stories with the best of them. A whaleship may have been his Yale College and his Harvard, as Ishmael says in *Moby-Dick* (ch. 24, "The Advocate"), but a frigate was his Vatican Library and his Scriblerus Club. In the intervals between his watches he was a member of an ongoing symposium.

The sailing was not wholly without incident to distract Melville from his routine duties and literary pursuits. On 18 September, Wilcox recorded, the *United States* spent the day cruising about trying to find an "alleged" shoal on their chart, but encountering no bottom in several casts of the lead. On 23 September "all hands were called to '*bury the Dead*'" — the dead being Conly Dougherty, whose corpse was "brought to the Gangway by his Messmates, and, after the funeral Service being read by the Rev^d Mr Bartow, his remains were committed to the deep." That solemn occasion was followed by a dramatic occurrence on 4 October, as they neared the Marquesas, according to the "Abstract":

> at 5.22 A.M. the appalling cry of Man overboard was sung out from the cat head. The life Bouys were instantly cut away. The Ship hove to, the Barge & 4th· Cutters lashing cut, a strong breeze from S.S.E. at the time and a heavy sea running. . . . At 10.45, all search proving ineffectual, picked up the boats and made all sail on our course. . . . it appears that David Black, "Cooper," was

in the head towing his hammock and, having tied the 4 corners of it singly with lanyards, threw it over[;] the water instantly caught in the Bag, which jerked him into the sea. When making the life Bouys a few weeks before, he was told that they leaked. His answer was, "If a man cannot save himself with these, he ought to drown." Poor fellow, he little thought he would have the first chance at them.

Melville wrote this story into chapter 17 of *White-Jacket*, preserving the irony by having "Bungs" say, "I never go aloft, and don't intend to fall overboard," and by ending the chapter with this comment: " 'Bungs, is it?' cried Scrimmage, the sheet-anchor-man; 'I told him his buoys wouldn't save a drowning man; and now he has proved it!' " Searching for an elusive shoal had its amusing aspects, and the loss of the cooper was appalling, but neither of those incidents or any other event proved particularly arduous for the crew of the *United States* as it sailed toward the Marquesas.

The *United States* arrived at Anna Maria Bay, Nukahiva, 7036 miles from Hawaii after forty-seven days' sail (according to the abstract log), on 6 October, having seen no land until 5 October, when the ship reached the Marquesas and the crew successively sighted Hoods Island, Uahuga, Roapoua, and Nukahiva Tower Bluff. The author of the "Abstract" on the *United States* recorded the appearance of Nukahiva on 6 October: "The view of this steep and lofty Island is truly sublime and beautiful. It is completely covered with bright verdure & enlivened with numerous huts." He also recorded the sight of the French fleet ("the French Frigate La Reine Blanche, & Dephane, two transports, and a Barque"), the French busily building forts and "peopleing the Island" with four hundred convicts, just as the rumor had foretold in 1842. Wilcox recorded the courtesies. The *United States* "saluted the French Fort with 21 guns which was returned by the Fort with an equal number," and Admiral Du Petit-Thouars came aboard, being saluted by thirteen guns, which his ship returned. The French admiral brought a message he had been waiting to deliver if he should chance to encounter the Flying Welshman: it was, to Commodore Jones's chagrin, official notice that he was being relieved, officially delivered. The author of the "Abstract" made note of another anchorage: "Tipee Bay, about 6 miles to leeward of where we lay, is equally as safe as an anchorage, the Inhabitants of which are at contin[u]al war with the neighbouring tribes." The next day he recorded a discreet version of a royal visit: "During our visit the King & Queen visited the Ship, he being dressed in a French uniform given him by the French Admiral, and she in a red skirt which reached a few inches below the knee, about 15 years of age, with handsome features, and tattooed on all visible parts." (In ch. 1 of *Typee* Melville gave a more lickerish version of the visit, using Falstaff's vulgar pun on "cat*a*strophe" in describing how she hiked up her skirt to display tattoos in parts not normally visible: "tumbling into their boat," the "aghast" Frenchman had "fled the scene of so shocking a catastrophe." He knew such vulgarities long before he felt he had ever read Shakespeare attentively.) All amicability, the French boats towed out the *United States* from Anna Maria Bay on 7 October and sent it on its way.

From the Marquesas the *United States* made a discreet swing to the south and west to Tahiti, against the prevailing winds, rather than hastening over-eagerly to Callao, the headquarters of the Pacific Fleet and the coastal city nearest Lima. There Commodore Alexander J. Dallas might most likely be awaiting the commodore on the *United States*. Commodore Jones's decision to proceed to the Society Islands placed Melville, for a second time, in the altogether enviable position of being a man familiar with exotic coasts strange even to many of his much traveled shipmates. Now he could rehearse new stories, this time comic tales about the mutiny and the ineffectual cal-aboose, as well as tales of being generally feckless in Eimeo with his friend Troy, whom he now, most likely, began dressing up for the Smollettian role he was to play in *Omoo*. A quiet, modest young man who thawed into winning charm under good companionship, Melville consolidated the goodwill of his new acquaintances during this time when he repeatedly made the most, all ingenuously and deferentially, of his extraordinary knowledge of improbable locales. The *United States* sighted Lazereff in the Chain Islands on 11 October, then Tahiti and Eimeo in the Society Islands, arriving at Tahiti, 860 miles from Nukahiva, on 12 October. The air was so clear as they approached the Society Islands that they saw the summits of Tahiti from 45 miles away. The *United States* anchored at Matavai, outside the reef, but inside they observed H.M.S. *Dublin*, fresh from Hawaii, the French frigate *Thetis*, and several merchantmen and whalers. They were within sight of Eimeo, Wilcox noted. While they were anchored there Jones received a letter from Commodore Dallas ordering him to the United States, a message that he interpreted as justifying his sailing to Valparaiso, a port Commodore Kearny just might have reached in the *Constellation*, a likely vessel to com-mandeer for the voyage home. The author of the "Abstract" recorded that "Pigs, Poultry, vegetables, and all the tropical fruits and wyhines were found in abundance"—a fair indication that women came out on the boats bringing fresh provisions. The ship obtained water from a spring at a bluff on the south side of the bay, first sending a cutter for a load then sending two launches. They had no need to go into Papeete, visible, connected to Matavai Bay by the gorgeous green of the Broom Road. From this account it seems that Melville would have had no chance to go ashore either at Tahiti or Eimeo and confront reminders of his recent past.

After a week Melville experienced the treat of seeing another royal visitor, when the consort of Queen Pomare came aboard on 19 October, accompanied by his entourage, for a visit, before being sent on his way with a thirteen-gun salute. The *United States* stood off toward Eimeo on 20 October and lost sight of Tahiti on 21 October, bound for Valparaiso (Vale of Paradise, Melville would have learned), 5384 miles away. Much of the voyage was uneventful, but on 28 October there was an accident, as Wilcox recorded:

> In furling the Mz topsail Jas Craddock sea[man] fell from the yard and struck on the starb^d horse block smashing it and breaking an arm & leg. His fall was caused in consequence of the bunt jigger parting from the sail. It was not fitted properly in the first place being merely French Sennet stitched on the sail, very lightly. He was leaning over the yard gathering up the sail when this parted allowing the sail to drop suddenly pitching forward of the yard.

(Wilcox added a note to this entry: "He is now doing very well Jany 3 1844.") From this episode Melville fabricated chapter 46 in *White-Jacket* ("The Commodore on the Poop, and one of 'the People' under the Hands of the Surgeon"), moving the incident to Rio and blaming it on the officers who tried to make the men furl the sails faster than the other ships in the squadron and thereby glorify "the Commodore on the poop."

On 20 November the *United States* reached the Juan Fernandez chain, first sailing by Mas Afuera or Massafuera, then, after losing sight of it, approaching the island of Juan Fernandez, which Melville may have passed in the *Acushnet* in May 1841. The journal-keeper made special note of "the famed Island Juan Fernandez islands," emphasizing the prominence of its "mountain of the Anvil" which rose "3,000 feet above a shore which is formed by an abrupt wall of dark coloured bare rock." Through ravines the sailors "caught a view of verdant glades surrounded by luxuriant woodland," as well as grassy plains. Every sailor knew the story of Alexander Selkirk's solitary life on Juan Fernandez (or Selkirk Island): "Alexander Selkirk must have been a happy man when he was in this paradize and exclaimed, 'I am Lord of all I survey; my right there is none to dispute' " (the journal-keeper's fair approximation of Cowper's "I am monarch of all I survey"). Melville, like almost any seaman, was profoundly moved by the sight of the island, the emblem of man's isolation from other human beings and his triumphant survival. For Melville (in 1841 or now in 1843, or both), it was the emblem of the gap between illusion and reality. In 1857, off Patmos, he had a comparably disillusioning experience that reminded him of the Juan Fernandez islands: "Was here again afflicted with the great curse of modern travel— skepticism. Could no more realize that St: John had ever had revelations here, than when off Juan Fernandez, could beleive in Robinson Crusoe according to De Foe." Melville's analogy is imperfect, since Alexander Selkirk was real, as Crusoe was not, and in any case Defoe's story was set in the Caribbean, not Selkirk Island. Nevertheless, Melville's recollection specifically ties the emotion to the time of the experience, not to 1857, and suggests that by 1843 Melville was already becoming the kind of "pondering man" he called himself in 1849, in Cologne, one whose response to his experiences might be anything but conventional. His view of Crusoe was and remained one-sided — he saw Crusoe as the isolato, not the brisk enterprising survivor; if we knew just what abridged text or texts of *Robinson Crusoe* he ever encountered, we might better understand that view.

On 22 November, after a sail of thirty-two days, the *United States* sighted Bell Mountain in the Andes, then Point Corimilla and the Point of Angels. Some of his friends on the afterguard or the maintop must have guyed Melville about his dearth of local anecdotal detail, for he had no stories to tell about Valparaiso as they approached the harbor and the *United States* exchanged salutes with British and French ships. Herman probably saw pretty much what a later friend of his, Robert Tomes, saw in the 1850s — "flimsy white-washed houses and wooden spires, scattered about the base and sides of the cindery earthquaky hills upon which it is built," with "hardly a blade of grass or tree to be seen anywhere." As far as we know, he did not go ashore, and what happened on board was routine, if sometimes perturbing, as when on the morning of 24 November the foreyard was surveyed and found in bad shape ("the starbd half rotten & unfit for service larbd half partially decayed") then the food supplies were surveyed and "50 lbs cheese 30 lbs Raisins 350 lbs Bread" were condemned — to an unspecified fate.

There was news of the death of the U.S. Secretary of State Hugh Swinton Legaré, so at noon on the twenty-fifth the *United States*, flying colors at half mast, fired seventeen minute-guns in "consideration" of his demise (Wilcox recorded). The next morning the frigate hoisted the colors at half mast in respect to the memory of the late Commodore Hull and at noon fired a thirteen-gun salute in his memory. On 27 November 1843 the *United States* hoisted its colors at half mast in memory of "the late Commodore Porter" and at noon fired thirteen minute-guns in tribute to his memory. This was the time for someone to produce Richard Emmons's four-volume *The Fredoniad: or, Independence Preserved. An Epick Poem of the Late War of 1812*, and turn to canto 11, "Cruise of Captain Porter," and especially the exalted conclusion of canto 12, "Porter's Defence of the Essex," set there, in that very stretch of the Pacific, where Fredonia herself streams down the heavens and calls bright angels down with her trumpet as she cries: "Earth! list to the decree! Porter shall live, / Whilst Fame immortal, has a breath to give!" In the right mood, driven by Jack Chase to a temporary rhetorical excess of patriotism, Melville might have declared then, as he did in August 1850 (in the voice of a Virginian vacationing in Vermont) that America should "first praise mediocrity even," in her own poets, before praising merit in foreigners: "I was much pleased with a hot-headed Carolina cousin of mine, who once said, — 'If there were no other American to stand by, in Literature, — why, then, I would stand by Pop Emmons and his "Fredoniad," & till a better epic came along, swear it was not very far behind the Illiad.' Take away the words, & in spirit he was sound."

Whether or not the sailors paid tribute to him with epic verse, David Porter was a living presence in the Pacific Fleet, for everyone knew of the successes of the *Essex*, up to that final defeat in the late war, and knew also that as a midshipman he had helped win a glorious battle on the *Constellation*, the very ship they were half-heartedly looking for. His death in 1843 was still fresh news for patriotic sailors in the Pacific, and his treatment in the *Fredoniad* was a strong lesson for a literary youth like Melville: epic poetry was already being written on American themes. By this time Melville must have heard something about Porter's *Journal of a Cruise Made to the Pacific Ocean, by Captain David Porter, in the United States Frigate Essex, in the Years 1812, 1813, and 1814* (1815). In *Typee* (ch. 1), he declared that it was a work which he had "never happened to meet with," but unquestionably he had met with it before he finished writing that book.

Commodore Dallas had not yet caught up with Jones, that revisiter of "fairey Islands," so the conqueror of California did not hasten around the Horn, even when the *Constellation*, under Kearny, its less than epic commander, arrived on 30 November 1843, after the *United States* had been at Valparaiso a week. On 1 December the *Constellation* "hauled down the coach whip & hoisted the broad Red Penant" (according to Wilcox), the coach whip being the long narrow bunting generally flown on all naval vessels, and the broad pennant the oblong swallow-tailed flag carried at the masthead of a commodore's ship. The next day several men were transferred to the *Constellation* for return home, their terms having expired. On 5 December the *United States*, still under Commodore Jones, sailed for Callao, 1737 miles away, and arrived ten days later without incident, having not sighted land on the run until 15 December, then sighting an unidentified peak in the Andes, abeam, then successively Moro Solar and Solos Rocks, and the island of San Lorenzo. Melville's ears were battered by a great deal of deferential saluting — thirteen guns from the U.S. store ship *Relief*, thirteen guns each from the British *Vindictive* and the French *Adonis*, and return compliments from the *United States* (the *Relief* deserving only seven in return for thirteen). This was the sort of thing that led Melville to devote chapter 40 of *White-Jacket* to "Some of the Ceremonies in a Man-of-war unnecessary and injurious." On the seventeenth men from the *United States* boarded the American brig *Ontario*, a mere ninety-five days from Boston, and therefore a source of news as recent as early September. The name was enough to evoke somber memories in ordinary seaman Melville, for the *Ontario* had been the name of the towboat that carried the family furniture to Albany in 1830. Melville could flee like Jonah and still be pursued by such memories to the ends of the earth.

The journal-keeper on the *United States* dismissed Callao as "that land of foggs, Cherimoyas, and snakes" (he tried to suggest the delicacy of the cherimoya — a fruit tasting like strawberries with cream already added). The *United States* afforded a view of Callao's Moorish castle, which once had mounted 150 to 200 "beautiful" guns (reduced now, Captain Wilkes said in his history of the exploring expedition, to five), and the small fort nearer the water under construction. The population of some five thousand, according to the author of the "Abstract" (hardly two or three thousand, Wilkes thought), were "principly engaged as custom house Officers, keepers of Cigar & Dram Shops, Boatmen, fishermen, and Muleteers." The country had been "a scene of commotion and revolution for the last twenty-five years," Wilkes said in 1839, and the result was pervasive neglect, decay, decline.

From ship or boat Melville may have obtained some glimpses of old Callao, submerged after an earthquake, but not until New Year's Day of 1844 did he get a view of the present Callao from shore. As a member of the "First part Starbd Watch" he was on liberty for forty-eight hours. Between four in the afternoon and eight in the evening on 3 January Melville took one of the boats that were dispatched to bring the men back to the *United States*. All but four of the men returned on time. Only the most confirmed topers spent a forty-eight-hour liberty in Callao, where in the fortress the vultures were allowed to gorge themselves, undisturbed, on the bodies of the dead, and where the outskirts and the low places that catered to sailors were, Wilkes said, notable for their excessive filth. Eight miles away was the capital of Peru, Lima, more than ten times as large as Callao. Lima was a triangular city on the south side of the Rimac River, magnificently sited between the distant snow-capped Andes and the Pacific. The road to Lima ran straight, and near the capital went through grain fields and orchards of lemons and oranges. Even the vegetation contributed to a sense of decline, Wilkes said, for the orange groves were going from neglect into actual decay. Oliver Russ (as Edward Norton), and others, surely, went with Melville to Lima ("you probably have not forgotten all of the crew of the Old Frigate United States and more especially our visit to the city of Lima," he wrote to Melville on 4 February 1859). Midshipman Samuel R. Franklin hired a horse to carry him over that terrain, but remembered the danger from the highwaymen who infested the road. Eager to stretch their legs, and having other uses for any money at their disposal, Melville and his mates must have walked the great road rather than renting a horse, just as, when disembarked at Deal in November 1849, Melville exuberantly proposed "walking to Canterbury—distant 18 miles, for an appetite to breakfast" (and actually did walk much of the way). Late in 1846 or so, Melville wrote into *Omoo* (ch. 59) herds of panniered mules driven by mounted Indians "along the great road from Callao to Lima," a sight memorable to someone who had witnessed it from ground level himself, in company of enough stalwart shipmates to take on any robbers.

Lima was a decade more than three hundred years old, ancient even by Dutch New York standards, and was surrounded by lofty walls two and a half centuries old. It was cleaner than Callao, but buzzards, protected by law, fought over scraps in the gutter, regardless of passersby, and sat thirty or forty in a row on rooftops, Wilkes said, waiting for more food. Yet the Plaza was a noble public space such as Melville had never seen, and the Grand Cathedral on the east side was picturesque if not downright awesome to a young sailor like Melville, who had been in England but not to a medieval cathedral town. The belfries were almost filled with bells, it seemed to the author of the "Abstract," who described the "painting, carving, gilding, and decorations" of the interior as rich and magnificent, while the altar was "richly decorated with Gold, Silver, Jewels, and gorgeous drapery," with images of saints and magnificent paintings on every side. Wilkes noted the well-painted collection of portraits of the archbishops of Lima, but he also noted that "the dried-up remains" of many of these late clerics were visible in the cathedral in their open coffins—a sight Melville must have been struck by. Melville could hardly have gained access to the great library in the Museum (just the sort of place he would have gone, if he had been properly dressed and traveling with proper recommendations), but he saw enough, as a humble outsider, to create for himself, over the next years, a surrealistic vision of the city:

> Nor is it, altogether, the remembrance of her cathedral-toppling earthquakes; nor the stampedoes of her frantic seas; nor the tearlessness of arid skies that never rain; nor the sight of her wide field of leaning spires, wrenched copestones, and crosses all adroop (like canted yards of anchored fleets); and her suburban avenues of house-walls lying over upon each other, as a tossed pack of cards;—it is not these things alone which make tearless Lima, the strangest, saddest city thou can'st see. For Lima has taken the white veil; and there is a higher horror in this whiteness of her woe. Old as Pizarro, this whiteness keeps her ruins for ever new; admits not the cheerful greenness of complete decay; spreads over her broken ramparts the rigid pallor of an apoplexy that fixes its own distortions.

By 1850 or 1851, when he wrote this in chapter 42 of *Moby-Dick*, "The Whiteness of the Whale," Melville's imagination (facilitated by his reading of Wilkes and others) had associated Lima with decay, not only the tumbled white city itself but its institutions. This society was male-dominated still more obviously than the new United States, but no sailor could look at the customary outer dress of females, the saya-y-manta, which literally left only one dark eye visible, without thinking it was less a garment dictated by modesty than a disguise: were husbands paying for their own sexual predations by closing their eyes to the intrigues their wives were carrying on? In Melville's subsequent vision of corruption in Lima, religion in this ecclesiastically dominated society was reduced to a situation where freethinkers harbored under "the snug patronizing lee of churches" (*Moby-Dick*, ch. 54), although Queen Isabella's Inquisition remained a threat to reckless irreverence; by the time he wrote this passage, Melville had experienced the power of the American equivalent of the Inquisition, the religious press.

Lima was the American Venice, a magnificent and dissolute city. Melville has his Ishmael choose to tell "The Town-Ho's Story" in *Moby-Dick* (ch. 54) the way he had told it there one saint's eve to a lounging circle of his Spanish friends on the thick-gilt tiled piazza of the Golden Inn in Lima. The author of the "Abstract" records an excellent supper "provided by Mine host of the Golden Ball," the best-known house of entertainment in the capital (though Franklin remembered it as having beds like those in every hostelry in Peru — full of fleas). At such a place, Golden Ball or Golden Inn, Melville later could project himself as participant into scenes he had observed only from a lowly vantage point. What he felt at the beginning of 1844 was not as complex as what he would feel later, on more mature retrospection and reading, but he was already a judicious observer, and no other city in the Americas, not crooked old Boston, not Manhattan belted with wharves, not heavy-walled Quebec bristling with cannon, ever caught and haunted his imagination the way Lima did. The maintop's resident expert on the Marquesas and the Society Islands, he arrived at Lima without a single personal experience to recount about the city, but he left there with the setting of the telling of one of the greatest tales in the English language, "The Town-Ho's Story," and the setting of the ending of "Benito Cereno." The seeming arbitrariness of the use of Lima as a setting for the telling of "The Town-Ho's Story" (for his humor's sake, Ishmael says) may conceal a submerged connection. Steelkilt in "The Town-Ho's Story" owes much to Luther Fox, the pitiable manly murderer from Rensselaer County, whose story Melville had picked up in Hawaii. Fox had escaped from the *Constellation*, in September 1843, while it was lying off Monterey, California, so Melville learned of his escape shortly before he went to Lima, since the *United States* and the *Constellation* were together in the harbor at Valparaiso in late November and early December 1843 and at Callao in January 1844. Melville may have told his shipmates what he knew of Fox while he was at Callao, or even during the trip to Lima, where any ordinary seaman could glimpse the colorful tiles on a piazza, even if he could not afford to enter "the Bolo de Oro," as S. R. Franklin recalled in *Memories of a Rear-Admiral.*

Life back aboard the *United States* was not conducive to brooding on the strangeness of Lima, for Melville had to steel himself against flogging after flogging. Smuggling liquor aboard went on throughout the stay in Callao, and punishment for drunkenness and for quarreling became almost a daily scene. On 8 January a man took twelve lashes with the "cats" for smuggling liquor. In the succeeding days men were lashed for drunkenness (the most common offense), for gambling, for disobedience, for desertion, for drunkenness and mutinous language, for drunkenness and disorderly conduct; for fighting, for assaulting the master-at-arms, for "abuse to sentinel," for "neglect of duty on pass"; and for insolence. Each of these floggings followed quarters and prayers. Melville witnessed them all, and had the more time to brood upon them because so little work had to be done all day long.

On 21 January at three all hands were mustered and Commodore Jones gave a formal farewell to the officers and men, then left the *United States* to board the *Constellation*. The *United States* under Captain James Armstrong then hauled down the broad pennant and hoisted the coach whip, and "saluted him with 13 guns & cheered ship." The *Constellation* promptly hauled down the red pennant and hoisted the blue, which occasioned another exchange of salutes. (The blue pennant, a triangular flag, indicated that the senior officer of the two or more ships in the port was aboard it, although there was no flag officer aboard.) (The flagship of the Pacific Fleet became Commodore Dallas's frigate *Savannah*, then on its way to Callao.) After thirty-seven days at Callao, at 5:30 P.M. the *United States* weighed anchor and made sail, "standing out of the harbour in company with the U S ship 'Constellation' & HBM ship 'Vindictive.'" The *United States* was escorting the *Constellation* to sea, and the men could only assume that the *Vindictive* was "challenging" the *United States* to show its speed.

Having made a speedy run of 108 miles in honor of Commodore Jones, the *United States* returned to Callao the next day, and remained there another thirty-three days. On this short run Melville took part in the most complicated maneuvering of his naval career, in all likelihood. Wilcox wrote down an extraordinarily long description of what turned out to be a race between the *United States* and the *Vindictive*, and followed the account with some "Private" ruminations:

Although fairly (to all appearances) beat by the "Vindictive" still do we not own that she is the fastest ship. She sailed with the "Constellation" on the "China" coast and only beat her by a short dist[ance] & was to leeward. If she is the fastest ship why did she allow us to pass her at first[?] This was not meant for any trick for Capt Nicholas [of the *Vindictive*] was in the Mediterranean when this ship beat the English Squadron & consequently knew her speed & would not be apt to fool with her[.] The only way in which I can account for it on our part is that the ship was in bad trim & was not properly sailed[.] An *Englishman* had the helm when she passed us in the first watch. A young Act[in]g Lieut had the deck — the Capt was turned in confident that the ship was too far astern to come up that night[.] While I was on deck in the first watch & during the last hour of the second dog watch the ship was kept shaking a good part of the time.

The *United States* had "kept shaking" and "drifted bodily to leeward," so that Wilcox was sure "the Englishmen were as much surprized at finding themselves so close" as the Americans were at seeing them. The whole episode occasioned a good deal of chagrin and second-guessing, for months to come.

On 17 February the frigate *Savannah* came into sight under the command of Jones's replacement, Commodore Alexander J. Dallas, and bearing the broad pennant as the flagship, but after the preliminary salutes all courtesies were omitted because of the ill health of the commodore, which Dallas attributed to the discomfort of living in comparatively squalid quarters in vessels such as the *Shark*, the only American vessel he had found when he reached Callao and began his long pursuit of Jones, in the process of which he transferred to the *Erie* before taking over the *Savannah*. The next day the U.S. store ship *Erie* "came to" on the larboard quarter of the *United States*. The game of musical ships was comical to some of those in the know, but grimly serious to Dallas, who recommended that the secretary of the navy court-martial Jones. Ignorant of most of the high-level machinations, Melville would have learned that Midshipman Stanwix Gansevoort was on board the *Erie*, since names of officers were made known whenever ships met. On 11 February 1843 the New York *Herald* had announced its sailing from the Brooklyn Navy Yard, and listed Stanwix Gansevoort as a midshipman; Melville in *White-Jacket* (ch. 59) used a very similar situation involving "a torn half sheet of an old New York Herald" announcing just such a sailing, involving a sailor too proud to try to see his own brother, a midshipman, when their ships are anchored together at Rio: "I won't see him, by heaven, with this sailor's frock on, and he with the anchor button!" Melville may have had no inkling that Stanwix had become dissolute, but from Waterford on 22 March

1844 Mary Chandonette Gansevoort would write to her son: "In youth you left me; as I believe, *untainted by a vice*. After five years absence you return, to your Mothers longing heart—But oh how changed. . . . You cannot drink without the most deleterious effects upon your character—from a gentleman, you descend to a querulous, profane, & unreasonable fellow." For all we know, Melville had a chance to see his bulbous-nosed cousin at Callao (Maria Melville remarked on Stanwix's nose in 1851). If they saw each other, Herman got recent news from home—only one year old—and the cousins could not have avoided the subject of Stanwix's brother's role in the *Somers* tragedy. If they did not see each other, Guert's troubles might have been a greater factor than an anchor button in persuading Herman not to try to see his old playmate: better not to stir up painful feelings. In any case, Melville was given fresh incentive to pursue his reflections on the strange fates of the Gansevoort and Melville cousins.

A complicated exchange of supplies ensued in the next days at Callao among the *United States*, the *Savannah*, and the *Erie*. George Washington's birthday was honored with a seventeen-gun salute at sunrise and at noon, and even the French and English ships in the harbor hoisted American flags in honor of the Father of His Country—a great spectacle. Melville had seen American flags flying on ships in the Mersey and in the docks at Liverpool on the Glorious Fourth, but this was still more impressive. On 24 February, a week after his arrival at Callao, Commodore Dallas sent the *United States* off to Mazatlan, Mexico, a distance of 3698 miles, in order to obtain "money for the Squadron"—that is, Mexican silver dollars that were accepted on the coast more readily than United States money. In the months after the news of Jones's recall formally reached the *United States* at Nukahiva and Tahiti, the whole crew must have put together the various clues and realized, with some sympathy, that Jones was being punished harshly for his seizure of California.

The *United States* arrived at Mazatlan on 28 March after thirty-three days at sea, having sighted Clouds Island on 21 March and other land in the following days. As usual, being in port meant that sailors smuggled liquor aboard, got drunk, and were caught and lashed. On 2 April, according to Wilcox, some of the men got to witness an embarrassing scene:

Capt Armstrong, Mr Bartow—Lockwood—Gamble & Dr Johnson started in the whale boat on a fishing excursion—while crossing the bar on which there is generally a heavy surf the boat was upset—boats were dispatched from the "Champion" & some of the merchantmen & this ship to their relief. They all succeeded in gaining the boat & were all seen clinging to her bottom from which they were taken. Not injured but well ducked. Lost—the Capts & 1st Lieuts guns & the Profs spectacles.

(The professor was Henry Lockwood, caricatured in ch. 83 of *White-Jacket*, and the brother of John Alexander Lockwood, whom Melville encountered as surgeon on the *Constellation* years later, in the Mediterranean.) Officers sometimes collectively put on a mask of impassivity which Melville called shipping "*their quarter-deck faces*" (*White-Jacket*, ch. 66); no one had invented a special term for the straight faces that the crew knew to "ship" as the bedraggled officers were piped back aboard.

On 12 April, according to the ship's log, this ceremony was enacted: "General Mozo. — Governor of Mazatlan, and suite visited the Ship, and on leaving saluted him with 15 Guns." Then something occurred that was perturbing to any American sailor aboard. Lieutenant Avery on his own authority on 4 April had brought on board a "stranger" who was "in a state of fever," and on the fourteenth Captain Armstrong shipped him to shore into the custody of the American consul, Augustus Bell; word came the next day that he had died ashore. Armstrong did not officially reprimand Avery, apparently, but Midshipman Wilcox oddly declared that he had entered his "notice" of the transaction per order of Captain Armstrong. After remaining nineteen days, on 16 April the *United States* left Mazatlan to return to Callao. In the next two days it sighted Creston, Deer Island, the Island of Juanico (Huanico, Wilcox recorded), White Rock, and the Tres Marias. The voyage proceeded without unusual event, encountering few ships, but perhaps later Melville vaguely remembered the death on 27 April and burial at sea the next day of an ordinary seaman named Ralph W. Emerson. Between 14 and 31 May the *United States* sighted several capes, points, and islands; as they approached Callao they saw on 4 June the two Hornigas, on the fifth the island of Pescadores and San Lorenzo, and on the sixth the island of Fronton. After a sail of 5219 miles, 51 days at sea, the *United States* returned to Callao on 6 June, and stayed in port for thirty-one days. (Melville may never have calculated anywhere near exactly, but in his time on the *United States* he spent 141 days in port — almost five months; he spent 179 days at sea.)

At Callao to greet them was the *Savannah*, with its pennant at half mast, for Commodore Dallas had died on 3 June, worn down by the discomforts of the vessels in which he had pursued Jones, and the prolonged strain of that pursuit, Dallas himself had claimed, worn down also by alcoholism, others said. (The omnipresent *Reine Blanche* was also anchored there.) Taking charge of the Pacific Squadron, and moving himself to the *Savannah*, the new flagship, Captain James Armstrong bade farewell to the crew of the *United States* on 8 June. He placed Captain Cornelius K. Stribling in charge of the *United States* and ordered him to prepare to sail to Rio, and ordered the *Cyane* to prepare to return home under Captain George N. Hollins. During this stay in Callao, as usual, ships of several nations came and went, with the usual courtesies — a gaudy, noisy, crowded spectacle to the men who had had the waters to themselves, almost, on the way down from Mexico. Seventeen minute-guns were fired on the eighteenth after the news came that the secretary of the navy, William Gilmer, and others had been killed when the so-called "Peacemaker" exploded on board the *Princeton* during a trial firing. Melville recalled in *White-Jacket* (ch. 31) the irony of firing minute-guns in honor of a man "who had himself been slaughtered by a cannon." Jack Chase had a chance to expand with pride on 20 June, when "at 10. the Squadron hoisted the English Ensign at the Fore, as a mark of Respect to the Celebration of the Accession of Queen Victoria to the Throne of England" (that is, the seventh anniversary of the accession) and sent some men ashore on twenty-four-hours liberty. The sailmaker, Josiah Faxon, died on 1 July and on the second his remains were carried to the island of Lorenzo for burial — a solemn chore that all the sailors could brood about, whether or not they rowed the body and dug the grave.

The Fourth of July, as always, was celebrated with salutes from vessel to vessel, and probably with ceremonies aboard each American ship, a day that now irresistibly reminded Melville of the contrasts between Liverpool and Callao. On the *United States*, seaman E. Curtiss Hine composed a poem for the occasion: "STANZAS. Written at Callao, Peru, on the Morning of the 4th July, 1844":

> Far distant from that land of beauty,
>   I may not share her children's joys;
> Thy iron hand, relentless Duty!
>   My every hour employs.

These verses he published in 1848 in *The Haunted Barque*. Other, perhaps less lugubrious literary efforts probably marked the Glorious Fourth in Callao, and any reading of the declaration had to compete in Herman's memory with Gansevoort's magnificent performance at Albany in 1836. The *United States* fired a national salute of twenty-six guns — outdoing Albany's best efforts.

On 6 July the *United States* sailed. Among the sparse records of the voyage are an encounter on 15 July with the American ship *Natchez* and on the twenty-eighth a gale so severe that the *United States* "lay *too*, under Main & Mizen staysails & Fore Storm Staysail, for 7 hours, not being able to carry sail." Hine composed "A Vision" during "a tremendous storm off Cape Horn, on board the frigate 'United States' in 1844" (a poem good enough for *Graham's Magazine* to publish in November 1848). After forty-one days at sea and a run of 6719 miles the *United States* sighted the lighthouse on Raza Island and Sugarloaf Mountain at Rio on 16 August and arrived later that day. In the crowded harbor they found at anchor "U. S. Frigates Constitution, Congress, & Raritan, Cyane, Brig Bainbridge & Pioneer; HBM Frigates America & Alfred, & Brig Dolphin," along with French and Dutch naval vessels and an assortment of merchantmen: they had left Callao later than the *Cyane*, but had outsailed her, taking seven days fewer to make the run. Melville saw Sugarloaf again, but on this voyage he did not set foot on Brazilian soil. In sailor fashion he had seen much of the world on the *United States* and had seen little besides water.

On this voyage, more than the merchant and whaling voyages, Melville's historical consciousness was enriched as he drew out "the oldest Tritons into narratives of the war-service they had seen" (*White-Jacket*, ch. 74), stories of naval battles of the War of 1812. He heard from these men, at only second or third hand, stories of naval battles going back far into the eighteenth century, told to these Tritons by men long dead, men who had been Tritons at the end of the last century. In reflecting on a man-of-war with its authoritarian discipline as a microcosm of western civilization, Melville clarified for himself the meaning of phases of pagan life as he had witnessed it, paradise found in the valley of the Typees, paradise lost in Tahiti, the landscape and seascape desecrated by commerce, the surviving Tahitians themselves ravaged by European diseases and deprived of their ancestral customs and religion by the missionaries. In Hawaii he had seen missionaries and their wives treat the Hawaiians more like slaves than converts. In the *United States*, living not under the Bill of Rights but under the Articles of War, he had ample time to assimilate his lessons in cultural relativity.

Melville may have received no word at all from his immediate family in almost four years. He knew at Rio, if not sooner, that the hangings on the *Somers* were fading from public interest, but he could only meditate with perturbation on what he knew of the events in connection with what he would find, when he saw Guert or his sister Kate Curtis, or when he saw Aunt Mary. The *United States* was at Rio for nine days before leaving on 24 August, having arranged to race the *Raritan*, "she having been represented as a crack Ship on her keel." The *United States*, the "Old Waggon," won. The author of the "Abstract" recorded few events: on 26 August the *United States* sighted Cape Frio, on 10 September she was memorably becalmed for seven hours; she buried a man at sea on 19 September; she ran into very heavy weather on the twenty-ninth, and on the thirtieth the sailors knew they were in the Gulf Stream by the sudden warmth of the water. On 2 October the *United States* began sighting Cape Cod fishing sloops and sent a boat for a mess of fresh cod. On 3 October, after passing Cape Cod, Chatham Light, and Nausett Light, a pilot from the "beautiful and new Pilot Boat Sylph" (named from Alexander Pope?) boarded the *United States* and guided it in. From the ship

Melville had a view of Bulfinch's State House, which may have had on his homesick eyes something of the effect described in a contemporary guidebook: "It is doubtful if another single building can be anywhere found which occupies at once so prominent and commanding a position and is so perfectly adapted to its surroundings as is this capitol of Massachusetts. It is in full view of nearly one half of the inhabitants of the Commonwealth over whose destinies it presides. By land or sea, its gilded dome is the object that first meets the stranger's eye as he approaches the New England metropolis." The gilded dome irresistibly evoked memories of his grandparents and aunts. As the ship moved inward, Melville may have had a glimpse of ships at the Liverpool Wharf on the other side of Boston from the Charles and the Navy Yard, storied in his family as the place (then Griffin's Wharf) where his grandfather and the other "Indians" tossed overboard the tea. Whether or not he saw the wharf, the Tea Party once held there was fit subject for mock chauvinistic badinage as Melville began making his good-byes to that greathearted Englishman, Jack Chase, and his other special chums. The *Sylph* led them past Fort Independence and Nix's Mate into the Navy Yard in Charlestown, where orders were given to furl sails, hoist out the boats, and send ashore all men whose time had expired. They were forty days from Rio, a sail of 5937 miles.

15

Home but Not Home

October 1844

Courteous behaviour & Prudent Communications are the most becoming
Ornaments of a Young man, with which he may best be furnished by a timely
Education and the virtuous Examples of his Governors.

"Allan Melvills Book," 1796

ON 3 OCTOBER 1844 THE *United States* sailed into the Charleston Navy
Yard, which spread over sixty acres on the north side of the Charles River, the
hewn granite walls of the huge dry dock looming as the frigate approached.
To the right, rising above the Navy Yard, was Bunker Hill, capped by the
monument, at the dedication of which the Hero of the Tea Party and other
survivors of the Revolution had heard themselves eulogized by young Daniel
Webster. To the left, across the Charles, was the familiar gilded dome of the
Massachusetts State House. There Melville found himself a captive on the
warship for almost as many days as he had spent with the Typees. Melville
had enlisted for three years or the cruise, and therefore must have expected
to be discharged from the *United States* at once, but Captain Stribling held
him and some other men while awaiting a response from the secretary of the
navy to a letter he wrote on the day of arrival. The term of service of more
than half the crew had already expired, he explained, and many more would
have completed their term in a few weeks, so out of a sense of fairness, or
perhaps just to clear the roster, he asked permission to discharge, at the same
time, some fifty men who had enlisted to serve five years.

Home but not home, Herman did not have to go ashore to find some
news of one member of the family. When the first bundle of the latest Boston
dailies and recent New York papers were brought aboard (perhaps handed up
from the pilot boat, the *Sylph*), he learned that his brother Gansevoort —
what were the odds of there being a different Gansevoort Melville? — as a
Democratic orator was playing a controversial role in the presidential campaign of 1844. Herman still had, for some time, no idea whether his mother
and sisters and younger brothers were alive or dead. Three or four years

earlier, the family may have sent letters to the Pacific hoping against hope that a whaleship carrying them would gam with his whaleship, and in February 1844, after they received his letters from Honolulu, they had written him there. Most likely he had received no word of them at all since he parted with Gansevoort by the Acushnet River at the end of 1840. For a week and a half Melville remained aboard the *United States*, performing whatever chores were assigned, but mainly he marked time, something he never liked to do. "Killing Time in a Man-of-war in Harbor" (his title for ch. 42 of *White-Jacket*) was one thing when the harbor was Rio, another when the Bunker Hill Monument and the State House were tantalizingly in view. Letters must have been taken off the *United States*, but Herman did not, on 3 October 1844, post a letter to his mother in Lansingburgh — surely something Stribling's orders would have allowed, if not on the busy first day in port, then on 4 October. Nor did Herman write to her during the next week or ten days. He did not want her to know he was home, for he was youth enough to want to surprise her, which meant making as sure as he could that no one else wrote to her about his arrival.

While he was waiting there on the *United States* Melville caught up with recent events. He put on record in the appendix to *Typee* that this was when he discovered how the American press had purveyed a piece of history that he himself had witnessed, Lord George Paulet's proceedings in Hawaii: "great was the author's astonishment on his arrival at Boston, in the autumn of 1844, to read the distorted accounts and fabrications which had produced in the United States so violent an outbreak of indignation against the English." Great as that astonishment was, still greater was the future author's astonishment to see the name Gansevoort Melville not just in one or two papers but in many papers, including some that were months old. From the current newspapers he quickly pieced together the fact that Gansevoort had made a grand speaking tour in the West and was even then, in early and mid-October, making a triumphal return through Ohio and New York, speaking to tremendous crowds along the way. Free to pursue his researches, and aided by his shipmates, Herman found in one or more of the older papers an account of one particular speech Gansevoort had made in City Hall Park in Manhattan on 4 June before a throng estimated by the Democrats as more than twenty-five thousand. Gansevoort had headed a delegation of Tammany Democrats that had called on ex-president Martin Van Buren at his farm, Lindenwald (near the east bank of the river between Greenbush and the town of Hudson), after the Democratic convention in Baltimore had chosen James K. Polk as standard-bearer and George M. Dallas as candidate for vice president. Gansevoort's mission had been to invite Uncle Peter's friend Van Buren to preside over a mass meeting at City Hall Park in honor of the man just nominated by the convention that had rejected him. Herman would have understood, at least, the shrewdness Van Buren had shown in declining to attend a public humiliation. Instead, Van Buren had given Gansevoort the least that the occasion demanded of him, a letter expressing his hope that his former supporters would "merge all minor considerations in sincere and undisguised efforts to promote the success of the candidates of the Democratic party" — candidates whom he carefully left nameless. Van Buren praised the candidates' devotion to the Democratic party, but he merely concurred "in the main in the political principles by which their public lives have been hitherto distinguished," rather than "whole-souledly" approving the platform, as Gansevoort later claimed he had done.

At the meeting in triangular City Hall Park, familiar to the older Melville children from childhood, Gansevoort had gone beyond his simple duty to read aloud the letter from Van Buren. He had teased the audience with the prospect of hearing him read the letter, playing Mark Antony as he teased the Roman crowd with the will of Julius Caesar: "Fellow Democrats — I hold in my hand a letter from Martin Van Buren. (Great cheering.) Is it your pleasure that I should read it? (Shouts of approbation) With your permission I will first state the circumstances under which it was written." Gansevoort had proceeded first to "state the circumstances under which it was written," then to read in its entirety not Van Buren's letter but his own eulogistic letter, which he had "handed" the ex-president. He had seized the crowd's attention, and in what he said next he focused it upon his conversation with Van Buren:

I will now read his reply — I see that you await it with earnest attention. I know that you will repose upon it with entire confidence. It is instinct with magnanimity. It becomes the great democratic leader. It breathes a whole-souledness, a spirit of forgetfulness of self, a purity and devotion of patriotism that stirs the blood and re-animates the courage as with the sound of a trumpet. (Great cheering.) And, do you ask, how did Mr. Van Buren look when I handed him our letter? Did he look like a disappointed man? No! His countenance was radiant with satisfaction. He retired for a short time, and returning said to me, "My young friend, my reply is written, now come and let us walk over the farm." (Laughter and loud cheering.) Judge for yourselves, I will withhold it from you no longer.

By the time Gansevoort finally read the letter no one was paying much attention to just how restrained it was in support of Polk and Dallas. Having blurred Van Buren's cautious words behind his Shakespearean smoke screen, Gansevoort made the most of the last paragraph of the letter, where Van Buren paid tribute to the "lion-hearted democracy of the city and county of

New York" for coming to the Battery "in the midst of a storm of wind and rain" in order to welcome him home from Washington after Harrison's inauguration in 1841, a compliment well calculated to evoke what the New York *Daily Plebeian* on 5 June called "the most lively and oft repeated demonstrations of applause." Herman's own amazement at Gansevoort's assurance must have been heightened by the delight of watching the bemused response of Jack Chase and his other friends to his brother's Shakespearean role-playing.

Cleaving close to his English mentor in these days, prior to taking final leave, Herman found himself in the ineffable position of grasping his brother Gansevoort's motivations then explaining some ins and outs of American presidential politics to Jack Chase. Yet what the Briton and the American shipmates could have made of Gansevoort's City Hall speech must have been imperfect. Even Herman could hardly have seen much importance in Gansevoort's giving Polk a nickname: "As for James K. Polk, the next President of the United States, we, the unterrified democracy of New York will re-baptise him; we will give him a name such as Andrew Jackson [won] in the baptism of fire and blood at New Orleans; we will re-Christen him. Hereafter he shall be known by the name that we now give him — it is, Young Hickory. (Here the cheering was deafening, and continued for some moments. A voice, 'You're a good twig of Old Hickory, too!' — laughter and renewed cheering)." It took Allan, later on, or exposure to more newspapers, to explain that Gansevoort had provided a great slogan for the campaign. The Briton and the American alike, however, could relish the international appeals to political warfare: "Our signal of battle is identical in spirit and almost in language with that which animated the haughty islanders at Waterloo, when they rushed to that final and irresistible charge that sealed the fate of Europe. Let our war cry echo far and wide. The Democratic war cry is — '*Up, Democrats, and at them.*'" These quotations are from the Albany *Semi-Weekly Argus* of 6 June, as reprinted from the New York *Daily Plebeian* of the day before, but any paper Herman had hold of would have printed some variant of the description of Gansevoort's effect: "Loud and enthusiastic cheering, and 'Three cheers for Gansevoort Melville,' which were given with terrific effect." This was altogether delectable, and chances are that the remaining messmates, appreciators all of oratory, huddled around Herman and Jack Chase, and tried some of the family rhetoric out loud, if not a few Democratic cheers as well. Gansevoort's fame provided just the fillip, the rush of exciting novelty that was needed to lighten the leave-takings. Who knew? The next time Jack Chase and Herman met, Gansevoort might be president, and Herman himself the minister to the Court of St. James's. Stranger things had happened.

The sailors in the Navy Yard also learned from the papers and ship gossip that their own ship was newsworthy, for even as they lay in port the *United States* was making slave-law. The case proceeded at first without the presence of Allan Melvill's old friend Lemuel Shaw, the chief justice, who was toughing out his court session in Worcester while suffering from his "catarrh," an allergy-induced inflammation of the nose and throat, which had persisted later in the season than usual. This hereditary susceptibility became a recurrent consideration in Melville's life, for the judge suffered from it until his death, and in his daughter it manifested itself, in June rather than the autumn. (Hope Shaw on 7 October wrote fretfully to Worcester, concerned, as always, about the judge's personal grooming: "I beg you to let your hdkfs be washed you know I am particularly sensitive respecting a clean pockethdkf.") On 9 October Amos B. Merrill wrote Shaw, still in Worcester, that a writ of habeas corpus had been issued by a judge of the court of common pleas in behalf of a slave, Robert Lucas, who had come into the jurisdiction of Massachusetts by arriving on the *United States* and was being held in custody. The purser, Edward Fitzgerald, a Virginian, had enlisted his slave Lucas as a landsman drawing nine dollars a month during his service on the *United States*, wages that, by common usage, Fitzgerald collected. Shaw promptly returned to Boston, heard the case, and rendered his decision on 11 October: the moment the frigate went out of Virginia, the slave became free, and since Lucas now found himself in Massachusetts as an employee of the government, and not as a runaway, he was a free man. The sailors still on board the frigate witnessed the purser's quiet acceptance of the decision, a decency that helped confirm Herman's sense of identity with the aristocrats of Virginia. As he wrote in *White-Jacket* (ch. 34, "Some of the Evil Effects of Flogging"), "It is a thing that American man-of-war's-men have often observed, that the Lieutenants from the Southern States, the descendants of the old Virginians, are much less severe, and much more gentle and gentlemanly in command, than the Northern officers, as a class." The Lucas case also impressed Herman with the power that one man like Shaw, the man who had been engaged to marry his aunt Nancy Wroe Melvill, could exert for the liberty of the human race. In sight of the State House, he was still living under the Articles of War, but Lucas was a free man in Massachusetts.

The newspaper stories about Gansevoort whetted Herman's eagerness to see the Boston relatives and find if they knew anything about him and the rest of the family, and between 3 and 14 October he may have been given shore leave to look up some of the Melvills or Scollays. Perhaps even before he saw his aunts, Herman saw his cousin Lieutenant Guert Gansevoort, who was stationed there in the Navy Yard aboard the receiving ship *Ohio*. Although he had never been especially intimate with his older cousin, family attachment and respect for Guert's ordeal aboard and off the *Somers* required that he make an effort to see his cousin now, and the effort (whether he was allowed to go to the *Ohio* or allowed to send word so Guert could come to see him) was abundantly rewarded. Guert could tell about his own visits to Lansingburgh, including one in 1841 when everyone had been struck by his familial resemblance to Herman (Augusta wrote to Allan then: "he looks very much like Herman, we all noticed it"). Seeing the resemblance struck everyone with poignant fears for Herman, particularly since that was the day that Guert had expressed his concern, born of long nautical experience ("oh how he blames Herman for going to sea").

Moreover, Guert had particulars beyond the fact that Maria Gansevoort Melville and all Herman's brothers and sisters were alive and well. Guert — and the Melvill aunts — had very pleasing news of Herman's beloved Helen — news wholly fresh to Herman. Great had been Herman's astonishment at the news of Gansevoort's fame, and great was his astonishment at the news that in his absence his older sister had spent half of her time (it must have seemed to his aunts) visiting at the Lemuel Shaw house, in the winter both of 1841–42 and 1842–43. In turn, Shaw's daughter, Elizabeth, had spent half her time, it seemed, in Lansingburgh. From as early as 1842 Elizabeth had been keeping up a regular correspondence with the family at Lansingburgh, as none of the Melvill aunts did. Guert himself repeatedly had been Helen's courier while she was in Boston, carrying mail to and from Lansingburgh on his visits to Waterford, where his mother was again living. Eleven months earlier, in November 1843, a year after the tragic events on the *Somers*, Guert gallantly had dispatched a longboat to carry Helen and her host, Judge Lemuel Shaw, and Elizabeth to the *Ohio* — rather more elaborate a welcome to the Navy Yard than he could give Herman. As Herman learned, now and later, Guert's entertainment had been all but overwhelming. Helen had written Augusta on 27 November: "Guert came over with a Man of Wars boat, *five pr. of oars* only think!" and Elizabeth Shaw had declared that they had had a "most felicitous time." Helen had devoted a whole sheet of a letter to Augusta to the Navy Yard excursion, then had kept adding details, such as the fact that Guert had arranged to have "a fine band of music" playing all the time his guests were on board the *Ohio*.

The two cousins found that Guert's seven years' seniority meant less now that Herman had knocked about the world and had his own stories to tell — stories more pleasant than most of Guert's. Guert, his recent tragedy reminding him of the irreducible force of blood kinship, treated Herman for the first time as another man, a man so like himself that they might have been mistaken for brothers. Having learned versions of the story of the *Somers* from whalemen or naval men in Hawaii, from newspapers passed from ship to ship, and from naval gossip, now Herman let his cousin tell him as much or as little as he felt like divulging. From Guert, or later from his Uncle Peter, who had been in communication with Aunt Mary in Waterford as well as Guert, and from other members of the family, Herman learned a good deal about the *Somers* affair that he had not picked up in the Pacific. No one had been permitted on board the *Somers* when she arrived in the harbor at New York on 14 December 1842, and the next day Hunn Gansevoort, like everyone else who tried to board, had been turned away without explanation. (Hunn, Herman now learned, had been dead a year, drowned at sea.) One bleak mid-December night at nine o'clock Guert had made his way "almost by stealth" to Eleventh Street, finding his mother there with the Curtises, as Mary Chandonette Gansevoort wrote tardily (on 2 January 1843) to her brother-in-law Peter. There she had described Guert's appearance:

> He was then in such a situation from fatigue & exposure; that I sca[r]cely knew him — he had a violent cold; coughing constantly; very hoarse his limbs so contracted; that he walked like an infirm man of seventy; his eyes were red & swollen, & his whole face very much bloated — his back & sides were so sore, from the strap & weight of the huge and heavy ships Pistols; that he could not raise himself erect — Having imprisoned so many of the crew; they were short of hands & he poor fellow, did more than double duty — the eveg of which I speak, his first visit to us; he had not had even his coat off in four days.

From Guert or someone else, Herman heard a version of the story that Guert had told Hunn, who had relayed it to the Albany editor and Whig politician Thurlow Weed, who told it in his *Autobiography* (1883). The secret part of the story was that, after meeting with the other members of the council, Guert had gone on deck "and informed Captain Mackenzie that the testimony was not as strong as had been represented to him"; Guert allegedly had continued: "I thought from the indications the court did not attach much importance to it." According to this insider's version, Captain Mackenzie had directed Guert to reexamine the witnesses and, after that was done and the court still did not wish to convict, Mackenzie had informed Guert bluntly that it was his duty to impress upon the court the necessity of rendering a guilty verdict, which Guert then did, successfully.

On 21 December 1842 Guert had been ordered to Washington, to report directly to the secretary of the navy. Three days later Peter Gansevoort had written to his nephew:

> Since your return from the coast of Africa I have felt an intense interest in the development of the solemn scenes in which you have participated on board the Brig Somers —

I avoid all comment, as nothing official has been made known & satisfy myself with the remark, that I have at all times believed that your conduct throughout has been not only consistent with your manly course through life, but marked by the exercise of those generous & chivalric feelings which belong to true courage.

Peter rightly had been concerned that John C. Spencer, the secretary of war, father of the hanged Spencer, might exert influence over a court of inquiry or a court-martial, both of which in fact took place, the first convened on 28 December aboard the U.S. receiving ship *North Carolina* in the Brooklyn Navy Yard (catty-corner across the East River from Corlears Hook).

For the family Guert Gansevoort's immediate ordeal had stretched through the early weeks of 1843. On the last day of 1842 he had dined in Eleventh Street with his mother and the Curtises, Catherine just about to give birth, or perhaps with a new daughter already. (On 18 January 1843 Gansevoort Melville urged Allan: "Have you been to see Mrs Curtis, since the birth of her little girl. You should do so.") In response to Uncle Peter's letter of 24 December worrying about the effects of a public letter by the grieving father, the secretary of the war, Guert had left messages for his mother to send to Peter:

Tell him, that nothing that S. can say, can make the least change in my feelings, as regard the treatment, & execution of those mutineers. I *feel*, that we did our duty; & the consciousness of having *done my duty;* shall ever sustain me — It was not only the public property, the Flag of my country; & my own life that was in the utmost jeopardy; but the lives of the crew, (those that were true); but of those apprentices, those *children*, entrusted to the care of the Officers; for whose safety we were responsible, — to God, to their country, & to their *parents;* to many of whom, before we sailed; I had pledged myself, to extend parental care & advice — Tell him, that nothing was done in "fear or haste" — & I believe it was *approved* of God; & I have faith to trust, it will be by my fellow man.

During the court of inquiry, 28 December 1842 to 28 January 1843, Hunn Gansevoort had stayed close at hand, at the Astor House by City Hall Park, from which he had written Stanwix, on the *Erie:* "I am here with your brother attending the court and shall remain until it adjourns."

As the court of inquiry ceased taking testimony, Guert had written to a highly placed friend, Commander Samuel Francis Du Pont, at Louviers, his estate on the Brandywine north of Wilmington, Delaware. Guert wanted him to see that if Mackenzie was court-martialed he could stand trial with him, so as to be exempt from any civil trials brought by survivors of the hanged men. The court-martial had begun on 28 January, presided over by the civilian judge-advocate, Ogden Hoffman. Mary Chandonette Gansevoort on 29 January had written Stanwix in agony about the efforts of Samuel Cromwell's widow to get the judge to "issue a writ to take Guert": "It seemed passing strange to me, to have Guert, *honest & upright* as he is — keeping out of the way of the officers of Justice — & the idea of his being taken up, & lodged in prison under the charge of *Murder* — was it not awful — my blood chills when I write it, as coupling with the name of one of my beloved offspring." Mary's well-justified panic had lasted through the duration of the court-martial, the whole of February and March. As Peter had fairly said to Guert, "You & your Commander will be placed upon the defensive under unparalleled circumstances"; in the end, they were both cleared of any wrongdoing, but public opinion was fiercely partisan. James Fenimore Cooper, Uncle Peter's childhood friend, was one of many influential people appalled at the hangings.

Afterward, his health shattered, Guert had written from Waterford on 9 June to Secretary of the Navy A. P. Upshur for an extension of leave, attaching the certification of Dr. Timothy Upham that he was "suffering from an Erysipelat[o]us of the system, together with Haemorrhoids, which renders him unable to the discharge of his professional duties." The first ailment was erysipelas, the inflammation of the skin and the subcutaneous tissue caused by streptococcus, a disease poetically known as "St. Anthony's fire" — much later suffered also by his cousin Herman. The other ailment had been aggravated by his wearing the heavy horse pistols day and night while unable to maintain normal hygiene. Gradually Guert had regained some of his health and spirits and returned to duty. From his own observations, at the Boston Navy Yard in October 1844 or later, Herman learned something about Guert's way of dealing with the strain of his involvement in the *Somers* tragedy. Either he did not drink at all, while showing the strain of denying himself, or he drank, and could not keep himself from becoming at least a little sloppy.

Guert Gansevoort lived out his life under the shadow of suspicion. The oldest living grandson of the Hero of Fort Stanwix, the heir to the medal of the Cincinnati, crossed the line into dipsomania, at a time when the Washingtonians and other Temperance groups were discovering some strategies of recovery but when the medical profession knew little about the treatment of alcoholism. Guert was repeatedly saved from disgrace by his naval connections; 1843 was not the last time one sponsor, Samuel Francis Du Pont, stepped in to protect him. The *Somers* itself ended its career more rapidly, the family learned, in a storm off Vera Cruz on 6 December 1846, while chasing a blockade runner during the war with Mexico. Thirty-two crewmen were killed; seven captured by Mexican troops, and thirty-seven rescued by Americans. On 9 January 1847, the New York *Scientific American* published an unscientific report that sailors had "averred that she was haunted by the three men who were murdered by hanging at her yardarm." The writer then excoriated the officers, including Guert: "Had the cowardly officers who were thrown into such a panic as to hang three helpless men under the pretence of self-preservation, been on board at her final catastrophe, the event would have excited less regret." The wreckage was discovered in June 1986 and reported, among other places, in the Redlands (California) *Daily Facts*, 12 November 1987, and the Boston *Globe*, 1 July 1990.

Melville's later comments show that in Boston, on shore leave or after his discharge, probably after he had seen Guert, he paid his respects to his two Melvill aunts who still lived there, Jean Wright, married a decade now and living with her husband, the merchant and lawyer Winslow Wright, at 31 Green Street, the same house where Wright had lived when Herman had visited his Melvill grandparents at 20 Green Street, long before, and Priscilla, who was now boarding somewhere near the Shaws. (Herman had not been to Green Street since the old Melvill house was demolished after the death of Priscilla Scollay Melvill in 1833.) Herman may have seen other relatives, including some of the surviving Scollays. His aunt and uncle Mary and John D'Wolf had been kind to him that long ago summer on Narragansett Bay, and Herman may have retained enough affection for them to justify a long hike or a short ferry ride to Dorchester to compare nautical notes with Norwest John. He may even have gone as far as Hingham to see Aunt Helen in the days after his discharge on the fourteenth.

None of his aunts in or near Boston communicated with his mother, but they knew that she and the rest of the family were alive and well. As for their own brother, Thomas Jr., the sisters knew he was alive, but a year or two years could pass before letters went between them and Galena; Uncle John by now was only nominally a trustee of the Melvill estate. Judge Shaw, the active trustee, was still in regular contact with Thomas Jr. and his son Robert, who was on the farm at Pittsfield (and who, the aunts could tell Herman, was a father now, although at least one child had died young). Oddly, Herman had been halfway round the world and back, and yet he was the one with direct information, however old, about the Melvill family in their Galena establishment. Jean and Priscilla, it turned out, had particular news of Gansevoort and Helen Maria, the sister most like Herman in character. Gansevoort, the aunts could inform Herman, had reestablished the long-lasped intimacy with Lemuel Shaw, at a time Herman himself could date to just after his brother saw him signed on the *Acushnet*. Later Herman learned that in Gansevoort's opinion the Melvill relatives had held themselves aloof during that January 1841 visit, fearing that their ingenious and charming but impoverished nephew might appeal to their family feeling and ask for financial help that they would not supply. (Gansevoort soon afterward had confided to Shaw how his aunts had treated him that January: "None of them made anything more than the most general possible enquiries regarding the situation of my Mother, myself or any of the family.")

In the opinion of the aunts, Herman's older brother had been much more attentive to the judge and his wife than to his own blood kin during his recent trips to Boston. Indeed, they may have heard about some of the visits only after he had come and gone. Just a year before, on 30 October 1843, they had followed his doings in the public prints. At Boylston Hall at what William Cullen Bryant in the New York *Evening Post* of 3 November called an "Immense Repeal Meeting" Gansevoort had introduced to the Boston audience Horace Greeley, the editor of the New York *Tribune*. Repeal meant repeal of the union between Ireland and Great Britain — an issue with which, the Melvills thought, Americans should have nothing to do. Speaking after the editor, Gansevoort so upstaged him that Greeley said not a word about him in his report in the *Tribune* for 2 November of his own "flying trip thru the Old Bay State." On 30 October Gansevoort had gone from Boylston Hall to Faneuil Hall, where he and George Bancroft were the preliminary speakers at a Democratic meeting, well reported in the Boston *Post*, edited by Charles Gordon Greene, a prominent Democrat. At Boylston Hall and Faneuil Hall Gansevoort had been introduced as the grandson of the Hero of the Tea Party, leading the respectable papers (the Whig papers) to remind their readers (including the aunts) that Gansevoort was consorting with the blackguards who had thrown the venerable Hero out of office in 1829. Gansevoort had become an embarrassment to the Boston family, although Judge Shaw seemed to find him tolerable still. For that matter, Hope Shaw seemed partial to Gansevoort, from what the aunts heard, and for all they knew Maria Melville had begun to hope for a marriage between Gansevoort and Elizabeth, but no one told the aunts anything. They agreed readily enough not to ruin Herman's surprise by writing to Maria: they had no occasion and no desire to write to her. Stiff, astringent, habitually aggrieved against Allan's wife and children, and with cause, the aunts were freshly aggrieved against Gansevoort for being identified in Boston newspapers as the grandson of the Hero of the Tea Party but now an adherent of the tyrant of 1829, Andrew Jackson. The Melvill aunts did not make the best company for a young sailor avid for news and in a bewildered state of mind at his transition from man-of-war to an America gone mad with an election.

Good company or not, the aunts, particularly Priscilla, had much news of Herman's sister Helen Maria to supplement Guert's stories. The news set

Herman the task of focusing his memory on Elizabeth Shaw, the child he had seen on his visits to Boston, three years his junior, between Augusta and Allan in age. He had seen her, and could recall her, however vaguely. With Guert's help, and with the help of his Boston relatives and others, Herman quickly pieced together the story of how Helen had come to be a guest of the Shaws, although some information he gained later, from Elizabeth Shaw and Helen herself or others in the family. As he remembered, Gansevoort on leaving him in New Bedford or Fairhaven at the end of December 1840 had set out for Boston, planning to call on Lemuel Shaw, to see if the judge might play the fatherly role toward him that his Gansevoort uncles had never played. Herman may never have learned all the particulars, but at that time Shaw had written Gansevoort a check for $150 to pay for a therapeutic cruise to the Caribbean. Then in September 1841 Gansevoort had escorted Helen from Lansingburgh to Lenox to visit her teacher, Elizabeth Sedgwick, wife of Charles Sedgwick, clerk for the court, just before the court was due to convene, on the fourteenth, with Lemuel Shaw presiding, as usual, assisted by three associate justices, Samuel Putnam, Samuel S. Wilde, and Charles A. Dewey. When Shaw arrived at the Little Red Inn, where Gansevoort was staying, he was accompanied by his wife, Hope Savage Shaw, and his daughter, Elizabeth, who knew some of the Melvill family already, especially Aunt Lucy Clark (now Lucy Nourse), for she had passed long summer visits with the Nourses in Hallowell, Maine, and who knew Gansevoort from the previous January, even if she did not remember him from the 1820s. For all his weak constitution, women found Gansevoort intensely attractive, and it must have crossed Gansevoort's mind that Elizabeth was of marriageable age, and a great catch. His mother, or even his late father, long before, may have uttered some such injudicious hope for Gansevoort's making the alliance some quarter century after Nancy Wroe Melvill had died before she could marry Shaw. Judge Putnam was delayed, so the sheriff adjourned the court until Wednesday the fifteenth. That created time to be spent in the Little Red Inn beside the courthouse, for the justices were unwearied by court sessions. There Gansevoort had charmed the Shaws, while Judge Shaw and his "dear lady wife" (as Helen wrote Augusta on 10 October 1841) had proved "most affectionate indeed" toward Helen. Helen favored her mother, Shaw would have seen, but like all her brothers and sisters she must irresistibly have reminded him of Nancy Wroe Melvill; he did not need much reminding, since he still carried in his wallet two love letters from her. (The wallet and letters are now in the Boston Social Law Library.)

Helen had been amazed at the interest the Shaws manifested toward her, as she had written Augusta, then visiting the Gansevoort cousins in Bath, New York:

I could scarcely credit that persons comparatively strangers should take such a warm interest in Gan & myself. Gan staid at the Hotel, but spent all his evenings with us, and made all together the most delightful coterie, what with the judges, judges ladies, Miss S. & Mr [Henry] Inman the portrait painter, who was on a professional visit there. Mrs Shaw insists upon my making her a long visit this winter in Boston; both herself & husband gave me the most pressing & earnest invitations, & Mama says I may go, if there is any way for me to reach there short of Gan's taking me, which of course should not be thought of.

Whatever versions Herman heard of that meeting in the Berkshires three years earlier, he could picture the events in the always glorious terrain in the September splendor, even before the foliage made its awesome October changes. As he learned, this fortunate, and possibly even fortuitous, encounter in Lenox had brought Helen into the same household with "Miss S.," Elizabeth Shaw, with the result that the two young women (for all the five years' difference in their ages) had spent much of the last years in the same household, either in Boston or Lansingburgh.

During her first stay in Boston from 22 December 1841 until 30 March 1842, Helen had met her relatives, of whom (Herman later learned) she found only Aunt Priscilla tolerable company, even though "Aunt P." had lost her social standing, Helen had recognized, to the point that not even "Aunt Scollay" (i.e., Great-aunt Scollay) visited her. (Several years later, an acquaintance of Melville's, Joseph Smith, visited Melville's Aunt Priscilla, noting, as Merton M. Sealts Jr. recorded in his *The Early Lives of Melville*, that the house she occupied, "in furniture, interior construction, and carpentry" had remained unchanged for a very long time. The vicinity had gone down around the old woman: "the families who had been her early neighbors—and whose carriages were still sometimes seen at her door—had long before yielded their elegant mansions to a rude, and generally foreign, tenantry.") Aunt Jean was a compulsive talker, Helen had concluded, and the whole Wright household was hopelessly "uncongenial." Aunt Mary D'Wolf was "supremely selfish," Helen had decided, and Aunt Helen Souther lived much too far away in bleak Hingham.

Except for Aunt Priscilla and some of the Scollays, her relatives were hopeless, but Helen had been introduced, often on familiar footing, to visiting celebrities as well as to friends of the Shaws. She had not only shaken Charles Dickens's hand, in February 1842, she had been granted a private visit with the Shaws to the studio of Francis Alexander, the official painter of Dickens in Boston, who remembered painting her grandfather. Hope Shaw had taken Helen and Elizabeth to a sewing circle at the nearby house of the wealthy Abbott Lawrence, and had taken them to tea at the house of Philip Marett (the same Marett who had sent duns to Maria's door in 1832), Mrs. Marett being Elizabeth's aunt, her dead mother's sister. The Shaws had given a dinner party at which Helen renewed her acquaintance with Judge Wilde, who had "a most precious peice of news," that Kitty Sedgwick, Elizabeth and Charles's daughter, was engaged to William Minot, a nephew of Mrs. Harry Sedgwick. On a Saturday afternoon the judge and Hope had taken the girls to call upon Josiah Quincy, president of Harvard, and his family in Cambridge, Shaw being an overseer of the college.

On 27 November 1843, long into her second visit to the Shaws, Helen had described to Augusta her attendance with Elizabeth Shaw (Lizzie) and other friends at a performance by Charles Macready in *Macbeth*, the first time she had been to the theater since seeing Fanny Kemble in Albany. Seeing Macready (not once but twice) reminded her of "poor Herman," who had made "a favorite quotation" of the gross passages from first scene of the witches at the cauldron. To this letter Lizzie added a note addressed to her "dear Gus": "I can only add a few lines to Helens already lengthened epistle to inform you of the universal propriety & decorum with which she conducts herself, to the admiration of all beholders, except myself, and I laugh in my sleeve whenever mother holds her up as a pattern which I am to endeavor to imitate, for I think to myself it is easy enough to be a pattern when you have no temptation to do evil. Oh dear! Helen has not left me half room enough." Helen stayed on in Boston for the winter of 1843–44, until Lizzie's older brother, Oakes, escorted her to New York City on 21 February 1844, from which she, Gansevoort, and Allan seem to have written to Herman at Honolulu. Helen had met, on easy terms, the choicest families of Boston and Cambridge as well as the most sought-after visitors from abroad.

From his aunts and Guert, Herman learned some details of Elizabeth Shaw's visits to Lansingburgh — perhaps more visits than are recorded in family papers. On 30 March 1842 a Shaw friend escorted Helen and Elizabeth to Lansingburgh. Elizabeth was there again in late August, apparently, and on 5 September 1842 was about to leave. In January 1843 she had pleaded with Helen to come for another visit, as Helen wrote to Augusta:

> Speaking of Boston, Lizzie Shaw in her letter, has been so urgent in her entreaties that I would visit them soon, that if it were any way possible, it would be too bad not to accept such a heartfelt and sincere invitation. She says, "come the first opportunity," and don't "wait for an opportunity, but step into the cars, and only write beforehand, and Father and I will meet you at the dépot," and you will have come so safely and pleasantly, "that you will scarcely have been conscious of the journey." And all in this strain, for two long pages.

Lizzie was by then intimate enough to send her love particularly to Augusta as well as to Helen. Lizzie had made a long visit to Lansingburgh again, in September and October 1843, from which Gansevoort escorted her and Helen to Boston, where he made the two speeches that so offended his aunts. On 27 November 1843 Lizzie had sent Tom, almost thirteen, her deep regrets at not being able to sit down to Thanksgiving dinner with him. During her stays in Lansingburgh Lizzie had made a conquest of young Tom, who sent "sprigs" to her in token of his affection. (Helen confirmed their arrival in a letter to Augusta, 28 January 1843.)

By the time Herman returned, Lizzie Shaw felt intimate with Maria and all her household, and Oakes felt so free with them that once he stopped unannounced to dine on his way to Chicago, where he was planning to settle. With Augusta becoming a cherished inmate of the Van Rensselaer Manor House and Helen being urged to return to Mt. Vernon Street, Maria had good reason to hope that her two eldest daughters, although without dowries, would find suitable husbands in the houses they were visiting; then by the time Kate and Fanny were older and in more immediate need of husbands, her mother's estate might be settled and Gansevoort might be making more money. Some of this Herman picked up in Boston, some after his return to Lansingburgh, but the fact of Helen's and Gansevoort's intimacy with the Shaws and Lizzie's intimacy with Maria and her household was on the lips of all his kinfolk. Later, as he heard stories of Boston from Helen and the rest of the family, Herman became still more grateful for the opportunities the Shaws had given his sister to move in the society to which she belonged by birth. Now, to judge from the way Aunt Jean had treated Helen two years earlier, and how "uncongenial" the still-embittered Helen had found the whole Wright household, Aunt Jean wasted little time tartly directing her nephew to inquire about his family at 49 Mt. Vernon Street, the Shaw mansion. From Priscilla, more kindly, Herman received the same advice: the one person in Boston who knew all about his family was Elizabeth Shaw, grown up and intimate with his whole family, except Allan, who was probably in New York at the times she visited Lansingburgh.

One way or another, what with reiterated news from his Gansevoort cousin and his Melvill aunts and the newspapers, in the days before his discharge Melville had much to mull over, some of which he could share with his friends, from whom he was preparing to part. He said good-bye to them, in small groups or one at a time, probably last of all to Jack Chase, that "great heart" whom he never forgot, and to whom he dedicated *Billy Budd*, the book he was working on when he died. At last, on Sunday, 13 October, Herman wrote a letter — not to his mother or to his older brother but to his brother Allan in New York, because he knew from the papers that Gansevoort was still on his stumping tour. Even then Herman did not mail the letter promptly: he had learned that the family was alive and well, and he was, all uncharacteristically, biding his time for reasons of his own. Herman's letter is not known to be extant, so its contents must be inferred from Allan's reply. Herman had made it clear to Allan that he had not written to anyone at Lansingburgh: he wanted his surprise. Furthermore, he counted on going to New York City before going home. He explained that "the circumstances connected with the ship" (his words, quoted back to him by Allan) had prevented his "immediate presence" (Allan's words) among the family. Herman's failure to specify just what "the circumstances" were caused Allan to feel vague alarm mingled with specific exasperation: not even home yet, his brother was causing unnecessary concern by his thoughtless failure to convey all the requisite information when he had the chance. Herman also mentioned having seen at least one account of Gansevoort's oratory, the speech at the "ratification meeting" on 4 June.

Stribling's authorization came, at last, on 14 October, when the log recorded: "Completed breaking out & clearing out ship. Paid off her crew & turned her over to the officers of the yard." Melville was discharged, with enough money in his pockets to get him home. He later claimed to have tossed the non-regulation white jacket into the Charles River, a comedown for the grandson of an "Indian" who had dumped tea into the water on the other side of the peninsula, but he may not have possessed such a jacket. (Melville was a truthful man, even what he called in *Pierre* an "Enthusiast to Truth," except when cornered into defending the veracity of his partly fictional books.) Stribling's scruples about discharging some of the men before others had given Melville time to adjust slowly, but he was nevertheless suspended, waiting to be born again into the family and to shore life, born out of the watery element into life on land.

Melville's own comments on his experience are not recorded, but a passage in young Richard Henry Dana's autobiographical sketch (published in 1953 then again in the three-volume *Journals* in 1968) is relevant to Herman's experience with his Melvill relatives and with the Shaws: "Safe am I in saying that rarely has mortal felt the delights of refined & affectionate social intercourse, especially with cultivated females, more than I did during this week. To be transferred in a day from a forecastle, the contact of none but rough & vulgar men, servile duty, blasphemy, obscenity & tyranny, to perfect freedom & leisure, literary conversation, refined language & manners, with all the arts & ornaments of polished life, added to a personal affection not to be doubted, was a change wh. has not befallen many." Dana had lived in huts with one Indian woman after another up and down California, but once home he reverted to the conventionally religious sensibility and high Bostonian refinement into which he was born. Because he had been so sheltered before going to sea, and because he was instantly absorbed into his old world when he returned, Dana experienced the shock of transition more briefly but more violently than Herman did. Herman had experienced on whaleships, especially the *Lucy Ann*, all that Dana described, but the last year and more had oddly introduced him as well to "literary conversation" and some of the "arts & ornaments of polished life." On the *United States*, after all, Herman had made friends who could speak of literature without resorting compulsively to "blasphemy, obscenity & tyranny." Being kept on board in the harbor for some days, whether or not he had shore leave, lessened the shock of transition for Herman, yet despite all the buffering Stribling unintentionally gave him, the transition from ship to shore, for a sailor so long at sea, was always little short of magical.

There are no contemporary records of Herman's days in Boston, no hard evidence of why the most restless of the Melvilles did not, after his discharge, make his way at once to Lansingburgh or New York City. Herman was eager to see his mother, sisters, and younger brother in Lansingburgh, eager also to see Allan in New York City and (he could guess by published accounts) be there to welcome Gansevoort home from the West. Nevertheless, he lingered in Boston after his discharge. Another sort of sailor might have made his way with Jack Chase and other shipmates to the nearest doggery and there have drunk himself blind until his companions hoisted him upon a train for the first leg of his journey to New York, but Herman did not disappear for days into the netherworld of the Boston waterside. He behaved, later documents make clear, as a responsible grandson of the Hero of the Tea Party, calling upon his aunts, perhaps calling upon the escort of his youth, the great merchant Daniel P. Parker (for their intimacy seems likely to have been resumed at this time), and finding out all he could about his family from the best possible source while not rushing to find out in person.

Lacking more documentary evidence from October 1844, Herman's delay in Boston is inexplicable except in terms of subsequent events. In 1846 he dedicated *Typee* to Judge Shaw ("affectionately" in the English edition, "gratefully" in the later American edition); in 1846 he became engaged to Elizabeth Shaw; and in 1847 he married her. Taken with other evidence, these events make sense only if he saw the Shaws in Boston in October 1844. Seeing them, after all, was the most natural thing in the world. Having sought information from Guert and his Melvill aunts, the only reasonable thing for Herman to do was to act on their advice and make his way to Beacon Hill, for Elizabeth would know recent particulars that no one else would know, such as just where the older sisters were, that month.

Herman knew crooked old Boston, and he remembered Lemuel Shaw, not then chief justice, but he had never been to the Shaw house at 49 Mt. Vernon Street on Beacon Hill. Even if he had walked many times on that street with his grandfather, he had not seen the house as it was, since upon purchasing it in 1830 Shaw had almost doubled its size. It was brick, not wooden like his grandfather's, and it was three stories high, four counting the basement where the kitchen and the dining room were located. The basement had large windows on the street, so high above the floor that a cook did chores sitting in a rocking chair on a table so she could see out. Shaw had taken the tall narrow building with its symmetrical front, each floor having two large double-hung windows with shutters, and had built on to the west, where the entrance had been. He had built, facing the street, a large new brownstone entrance supported by elegant pillars, next to the old part of the house. There was also a new entrance to the basement on the street behind a wrought-iron fence and gate. The upper two floors had another pair of double-hung windows, closer together than in the old house, and on the ground floor a single window, for the new entrance doorway was imposing. Seven steps led from the street to the first landing at the protruding archway leading into a sheltered recess, and one step led up to the landing before the new door, with its narrow side lights. A man who had not spent much time inside any building since Honolulu and, briefly, Lima, Herman must have appreciated that this was Boston living at its finest.

Luckily, as events show, Herman was also appreciated. However he was rigged out, most likely in sailor's gear still, as Allan assumed, he must have made a sensational impression, especially on Elizabeth Shaw. Like most of the Melvilles, he was handsome, and he was young — twenty-five. Just now darkly tanned, he was in all likelihood the most athletic young man she had ever seen in her house, and one who more or less unconsciously combined athleticism with eroticism in his gait, since he could not have gained his land legs yet. Sailors liked to exaggerate the roll, knowing it was perceived as erotic and knowing that they could protest, in all innocent indignation, that they were merely walking as they had to walk. (Richard Henry Dana Jr. liked to affect it, long after he had stopped involuntarily compensating for the pitch of a ship.) Elizabeth Shaw had shared the concern of Helen and the whole Lansingburgh family about his fate until his letters from Honolulu arrived. Then she had become party to whatever he had written his family about his stay among the Typees and his subsequent adventures in Tahiti and Eimeo, besides his whaling experiences. It had been impossible not to be caught up in his family's feelings about the wanderer, and Herman's arrival must have had something of the magical in it for Elizabeth.

The evening of the fourteenth, the day of Melville's discharge, is not one he could have spent with Judge Shaw and his wife, for that night they, along with the rest of the cream of Boston society, were attending the English actor Charles Macready's benefit performance in *Macbeth*, with the American Charlotte Cushman as Lady Macbeth. For the event, his farewell to his Boston friends, Macready had hired Papanti's Hall (hallowed locally as the site of a ball for Dickens in late January 1842). According to the dazzled entry Richard Henry Dana Jr. made in his diary, there were "about 300 people of the highest fashion & intelligence in the city, & a great part of the clergy," among them "Mr. Webster, Mr. Choate, Ch. Jus. Shaw, Pres. Quincy, Abbott Lawrence, Nathan Appleton, & other distinguished public men, the Ticknors, Eliots, Dwights, Nortons, Searses, Otises, Quincys, &c. &c., & Longfellow, Felton, Hillard &c. &c." Macready read Dryden's song for St. Cecilia's day, Wordsworth's "Old Cumberland Beggar," "O'Connor's Child," and "ended with the scene from Henry the 4th part 2nd, beginning where the king asks Clarence where the Prince is, & going through to the death." Herman, more dazzled than young Dana, must have heard about this reading after it took place. It is possible that he spent the evening with Elizabeth and her younger half-brothers, Lemuel Jr. (born 15 July 1828) and Samuel (born 16 October 1833), along with the housekeeper, Ellen Sullivan, and the rest of the staff, which always included Shaw's waiter, Canning. For it was Elizabeth whom Herman needed to consult, more than the judge or Hope, since she was the one who had visited Lansingburgh the year before, and also had in her possession very recent letters, as she always did, from Helen, and probably from Augusta as well.

Lemuel Shaw himself must have urged the sailor to remain a day or two in Boston, perhaps while he equipped himself in "duds" (Gansevoort's word) appropriate to a landsman. He may have been invited to stay at the Shaw's. After all, Oakes's room was free (if young Lemuel Jr. had not already claimed it, as he later did), and there were guest rooms and at worst space in the servants' quarters fit for him to sleep in. Aunt Lucy's stepson stayed there at will, so why not his old friend Allan's second son, blood nephew to Nancy Melvill?

The judge remembered Herman as a boy very well, but had not seen him for a decade and a half, and as always, when he saw one of the Melvilles, he was stirred by memories of his first choice for a wife and by memories of his affection for Allan Melvill and others in the family. Furthermore, Shaw, for all his well-governed disposition, may have felt a welter of regret and even irrational guilt. In doing his duty to the old Major Melvill, acting as trustee of the estate, Shaw had been forced to aid and abet the Melvill family in abandoning the widow and eight children of his friend Allan. On 12 February 1834 Shaw had written to Maria Melville of the "deep interest & solicitude" he felt for her children, who were also the children of one of his "oldest & best friends." He had made a promise: "I shall at all times & under all circumstances, do all in my power, to promote their best interests." If he had not felt something like guilt, however unjustified, he would not have been quite so recklessly generous to Gansevoort and Helen when he met them in Lenox in the fall of 1841, not quite so eager "to promote their best interests." He had not felt himself able to help the Melvilles when they most needed his help, but when they came into his ken as young adults, he would do what he could.

From Elizabeth, Judge Shaw knew that Herman had written home from Oahu, and when it was clear that he had visited Maui as well, Shaw had particular reason for giving the informative and entertaining sailor his most alert attention. Shaw's friend Captain John Percival as recently as four years earlier had given him information from the second mate of a New Bedford whaler concerning a cousin of his, John Shaw, born like him in Barnstable, whom the mate met "at the Island of Mowhee." By this report John Shaw "was an intelligent & educated man, had married a native female & had several children, the oldest son was brought out by the 1st mate whose name he unfortunately had forgot, that said lad was active & intelligent & returned home in the Ship." Pathetically and endearingly, John Shaw from his exile in Maui had "made many enquiries" respecting his kin in Barnstable and environs. Percival had directed Judge Shaw to John Coffin Jones Jr., "late Consul of the Sandwich Islands, & long a resident there," but (in November 1840) residing in Boston. Now Shaw could ask Herman if by any chance he had encountered this lost cousin on Maui. Chances were good, really, since there were only some seventy-five or so "foreign residents of Maui," and when D. Baldwin, the secretary of the Maui Temperance Society, sent Damon his report on 1 March 1843, less than two months before Herman arrived there, he had included John Shaw among the thirty-six foreigners who had signed his abstinence (not really temperance) pledge (a letter printed in the April 1843 *Temperance Advocate, and Seamen's Friend*). Herman knew that the person for Shaw to write to for information was Damon, the de facto postmaster-general of the Sandwich Islands. In any case, such an inquiry would have opened floodgates. Since Herman at this period was a remarkable young man, personally alluring and filled with boundless enthusiasm as he told his adventures, Shaw would have listened receptively, his serious mind assimilating new information, and revolving it.

Besides the family connection, the older and the younger man shared an area of personal history, for in 1800 Shaw had taught school in Lexington — better paid, as a Harvard graduate, than Herman had been. That pedagogical experience in Herman's past may have made Shaw reflect on the extraordinary fame young Dana had gained with one book. After a session or two Shaw would quite naturally have been moved to discuss with Herman the possibility that he might write up his adventures, as any good schoolteacher ought to be able to do. Literature had private value, Shaw believed; after he graduated from Harvard he had written to a classmate about his resolve not to neglect his literary interests: "Literature in my opinion is almost the only resort of a man who wishes to render his enjoyments independent of others" ("Lemuel Shaw," in *Memorial Biographies of the New England Genealogical Society* [1885]). Yet there was no reason literature could not have public value as well. In the last few years the younger Dana (no one in Boston could forget the still hearty senior Richard Henry Dana, the poet) had reclaimed his family status and become a lawyer whose literary fame obviously had enhanced his opportunities at the bar, even though, as the judge probably knew, the Harpers had all but stolen the copyright from the young man. Whether or not Herman followed his older and younger brother into the law, to write a book even remotely comparable to *Two Years before the Mast* would be of service to him for the rest of his life, whatever else he might do. This was not pie-in-the-sky advice but common sense, based on Shaw's personal knowledge of young Dana's recent success in his profession. Some such advice, some sort of assistance or encouragement, lies behind the dedication of *Typee* to Shaw.

Herman had found that time had blurred the facial differences between one aunt and another and had accented the family bone structure; time had also transformed the small Shaw daughter he vaguely remembered into a young woman of twenty-two. Biographers have been led astray by an awkward early daguerreotype of Elizabeth Shaw, as well as by crude contemporary jokes from newspapermen about her putative resemblance to her father. (As late as 1900 Samuel Adams Drake in *Old Landmarks and Historic Personages of Boston* repeated from *Bench and Bar* a story about Rufus Choate and Shaw, "who was by no means a handsome man": "Choate addressed his Honor in these words: 'In coming into the presence of your Honor I experience the same feelings that the Hindoo does when he bows before his idol, — I know that you are ugly, but I feel that you are great.' ") Elizabeth Shaw must have been a handsome young woman. One sharp photograph from 1872 shows that she was still handsome, even then, fair, regular of features, level of brow, with a slightly full lower lip, and delicately formed ears (as Herman would have noticed, aware of his mother's sensitivity about the size of her own ears). At twenty-two, we know from Helen's letters and her own, Elizabeth was youthful still, even girlish in the unaffected way carefully protected young women can be. Allowing for the possibility that white women shoppers in Honolulu may have exchanged commonplaces with him in Montgomery's store, Lizzie had a major incidental advantage in her meetings with Herman: she was most likely the first young white woman he had conversed with in a familiar way since December of 1840, almost four years earlier. And like Herman, Elizabeth was so placed as to make an impression: she had the news he wanted to hear.

First, Herman had to ask her not to communicate with his mother or sisters and Tom in Lansingburgh: he wanted to surprise them. Then, perhaps in a series of interviews during the days after his discharge while he lingered in Boston, Lizzie told Herman what she knew of his family. Lizzie had treasures of news about the minutiae of daily life in Lansingburgh and about his beloved Helen's visits to Boston, some of it supplementing what he had already heard from Guert or his aunts. Some of her anecdotes were charming—how after meeting the young English sensation Charles Dickens, Helen had vowed that her right hand would go henceforth unwashed, and some, such as her visit to the *Ohio* with Helen and her father, deeply poignant, since everyone had known how much it cost Guert to put on his old gaiety. She knew what he may have learned earlier from Guert, that in his absence not only Gansevoort but also Allan had become a lawyer. She had anecdotes of his Aunt Lucy, whom she knew much better than he did, and his Uncle Amos, whom he may never have met (a comical situation for them to joke about), and stories of Gansevoort's visits to Boston. In the course of conveying four years' information to him, Elizabeth must have found it natural to talk intimately about herself as now all but a member of the Melville family. What she said revealed that she and the other Shaws had followed his fate almost from the day of his sailing, since Gansevoort had called at Mt. Vernon Street just after seeing him aboard the *Acushnet*. They had received further news of Herman in July 1842, when Gansevoort had written Shaw of being "in receipt" of a letter from him on the coast of Peru. Elizabeth, if not the other Shaws, had seen his letters from Honolulu on her last visit to Lansingburgh, so she knew already whatever he had told the family about his experiences in Typee, Tahiti, and much else. She knew more, before seeing him, than any biographer has known of episodes of his life, such as his first experiences on the coast of South America and the Galápagos—whatever episodes were striking enough for him to have described them in his letters from Honolulu. Through occasional bulletins and especially through her conversations with Helen and later with all the Melvilles (except Allan), Elizabeth had come to share the anxiety all the Melvilles felt about the fate of the sailor, last heard from, probably, when he was in the Sandwich Islands. She had read Helen's letter about Herman's quoting *Macbeth*, and even added her own note to a sheet of that letter. Now Herman must have listened to her with more avidity than anyone had ever done, simply because never in her life had she possessed so much intimate information that another person so eagerly wanted to hear. Elizabeth in turn must have responded powerfully to the evidence of her new power to compel an audience. By his attentiveness, he may have made her feel, for the first time in her life, bewitching (a few years later she regularly took pains to make herself "look as bewitchingly as possible" before seeing him at dinner, as she wrote her stepmother on 23 December 1847). According to her oldest grand-daughter, Eleanor Melville Metcalf, in *Herman Melville: Cycle and Epicycle*, long after his death Elizabeth was "fiercely proud" that she had been Her-man Melville's wife — emotion that dated from a time the two young people were intensely attracted to each other during the days they united themselves in a strangely intimate complicity to keep his arrival a secret from anyone who might write to Lansingburgh.

In exchange for her stories of his family, Herman told her some of his wondrous adventures, and judicious testimony is clear that he was a remark-able talker, once his lips were opened. Lizzie was not the greatest belle of Boston, but she was one of the most privileged — the only young woman that October to hear from the bearded lips of a brilliant, dark, muscular, hand-some young man enthralling accounts of his adventures, foremost of which was a wondrous tale of his indulgent captivity among a cannibal tribe in the Marquesas — by now, after so much practice, a far better story than he had told in his letters from Hawaii, which she knew all about. Herman must have conveyed, as well, amazing incidental insights and observations about great whales and other beasts of the sea and about peoples and places she could never hope to know. Their meeting had a Shakespearean precedent: Othello-like, he told her of "moving accidents" by flood and field (or Typee vale) and of "hair-breadth 'scapes"; Desdemona-like, she loved him for the dangers he had passed, and he loved her that she did pity them. Lizzie had no taste for the "wealthy curled darlings" of her nation, the Harvard graduates whom Hope and the judge had introduced to her. Conventional, methodical, prudent, she was old enough already to have married a safe man from Boston's elite, but she had waited for something different, and this adven-turer, a subject of her thoughts at intervals for two years, now proved enor-mously alluring and, almost literally, enthralling. Except where it counted most for felicity in this life, Elizabeth Shaw was a cautious young woman.

Lemuel Shaw and his daughter together had the power to delay Herman a day or two, but lingering would be folly if he wanted his surprise, now that so many people knew he was home. In New York, Allan received the letter from Herman on the morning of Thursday the seventeenth but could not take time to answer it until eight that evening, when he wrote a four-page reply beginning with purest fraternal joy:

I need not express to you my feelings when I opened your letter. . . . You can imagine that they overcame me. I was indeed unprepared for such good fortune and trembled while perusing your epistle—a prayer of gratitude played upon my lips — & I thanked the Giver of all good for your safe return. Herman! we are once more all together & I pray God that we may never be seperated more — Let these hasty lines be the forerunner of the hearty & true welcome you will receive when we can take you by the hand, look upon you, and embrace you. Oh! hasten your departure that my words may be soon confirmed. — But I will not keep you in suspense as to the situation of affairs at home. The family are still at Lansingburgh where you left them. All well. & when I was there and saw them all, some two weeks since our kind mother spoke of her far distant son & expressed a hope that before many months she should see him[.] But how little does she expect to be so soon comforted with your presence!

The bulk of the letter, quoted below, dealt with the family, especially Gansevoort. At the end, Allan's mood changed from ecstatic rejoicing to profound ambivalence: his impulse was to leave at once for Boston, but he had appointments; he still might leave Friday afternoon and be with Herman in Boston on Saturday morning, if he could "fix things accordingly." Distracted already, he added a skittery series of postscripts, including this command: "Come here before you go to L. that we may rig you out with clothes" and reassurance that Herman's "bill" to Mrs. Garahan had "been paid." Carelessly, Herman had not given Allan his whereabouts, so Allan had to send the letter general delivery and would not have known where to find Herman even if he showed up in Boston; frustrated, he added: "Be at the Tremont House at 9 oclock on Saturday mg. You will probably see me. if not you will find a letter in the P.O." (Allan was aware that Herman knew the Tremont as the country's first modern hotel, Uncle Peter's inspiration for Stanwix Hall, John Jacob Astor's for the Astor House.) On Herman's hint, Allan offered assurance: "I have not yet written home yet but will wait for a reply from you before doing so ie if I don't see you at Boston." The double "yet" construction preserves the frantic ambivalence Allan was feeling, ambivalence that carried through into still another qualification: if he did not go to Boston and if Herman came immediately to New York City, then Allan could be found "either at the house No. 7. Greenwich St near the Battery or at the office No 1. Nassau st."

Herman received the letter from Allan on Saturday the nineteenth and left the same day. He had plenty to reflect on as he traveled by train and boat to New York City, and he had reading material, including such newspaper accounts of Gansevoort's speeches as his relatives and friends had thrust upon him for his immediate delectation (perhaps knowing he could pass them on to Allan the archivist). He also had Allan's four-page letter (addressed to his "Beloved Brother") to read over and over. In writing this document meant to cover four years in at least a cursory fashion, since the family in the United States did not know whether or not Herman had ever received word from any of them, Allan had forgotten that Lizzie knew everything of importance, or had been too excited to realize that Herman would have consulted her:

Tom has grown to be quite a man & is at the Academy in L[ansingburgh]. G[ansevoort] was admitted in Dec. 1841 & practiced with some considerable success until May 1843 when he rec^d an appointment of Examiner in Chancery who's duty consists in taking the testimony of witnesses in writing when attended by counsel in suits in Chancery—a very fair office and one which pays quite well. This appointment is conferred by the Governor of the State & G—— continued to perform the duties under his appointment until May last (1844), when he resigned & succeeded in obtaining my appointment in his place just ten days before I was myself admitted as an Attorney of the Supreme Court & a solicitor in Chancery, I having passed my examination & obtained my sheepskin on the 17. of the same month. So brother mine when you next me you see a "member of the bar" having his suit of offices at No 1. Nassau street opposite the Custom House. I must say that so far I have been favored. — Now for G. About two years since he made his first attempt at a political speach before a meeting of the Democrats of one of our wards & from that time to the present his course has been singularly triumphant. Never probably in the political annals of our country has so young a man in so short a time earned for himself so prominent a position before the public. In March last he delivered an address on the occasion of Genl. Jacksons birth day to some 5000 persons assembled in the Tabernacle in Broadway (including a large number of ladies) A fine report of his effort appeared in the city papers & was universally copied by the Democratic press of the Country. His first appearance since the nomination of Mr Polk was at the ratification meeting to which you refer as having seen an a/c. In the latter part of July he left this city to attend the great Nashvill (Tenn.) Convention which was held on the 15 Aug. Here he followed Genl Cass who was the first Speaker. Since then he has stumped it through Tennessee, Kentucky & Ohio & he is now passing through this State on his return. Tomorrow the 18. he speaks at Troy, his last appointment. To day he was to have spoken at Schenectady as I presume he did. I now expect him in New York about the 23rd. He was advertised at all the principal points from Buffalo down. I wish you were here. I would show you a bushell of news papers containing notices of him such as the "orator of the human race" the "eloquent Melville" "the great New York orator" "the Champion of the New York Democracy" for to him belongs the honor of christening Polk "Young Hickory" He made a visit of some days at Mr Polks residence Columbia Tenn. & also with the "old man of the Hermitage" under his own roof. The opposition have of course made their attacks upon him & some of them are very severe. Prentiss the witty editor of the Louisville Journal was right down upon him. In Ohio they dubbed him Col! that is the Democratic papers.

Allan had miscellaneous news of family and other connections, all piled out helter-skelter. Aunt Mary Sanford Gansevoort had died in February 1841, just after Herman sailed on the *Acushnet*, but before her death had "lost another child, a boy" (Allan was forgetting that Herman would remember this death) and had left two children, both still living, "Henry & a beautiful little Girl — Kate." Allan worded the news from his usual self-centered stance: "I regretted her loss very much as I was a favorite of hers." In December 1843 Uncle Peter had married Susan Lansing, "a sister of Christopher Y. Lansing of Albany an exceedingly fine woman & no doubt they are a very happy couple." Aunt Mary Chandonette Gansevoort and her daughter Kate and Kate's husband, Mr. Curtis, were all well, but "Old Mr Peebles" (Gerrit Peebles) had been "gathered to his fathers." In his excitement Allan mixed important news with comparatively trivial detail:

> Guert you will find at the Charlestown Navy Yard near Boston on the ship Ohio. Do you know that an attempt was made to procure a bill of indictment for Murder against him & Com McKenzie & after an argument of some four days before the United States Court here it was denied[.] The excitement here at the time was very great. Edward Sanford uncles brother in law has been nominated for Senator from this District[.] Alley Bradford published a book in 1841 called 'American Antiquity & the History of the Red Race' which took very well.

Herman's friend Eli Fly had worked in Gansevoort's office about a year then in April 1844 had gone "up to Rhinebach Dutches Co in this State & formed a law connection with a Mr. Armstrong," whence he reported himself as doing quite well. The hasty letter is an epitome of recent family history as filtered through Allan's very partial and subjective lenses.

As he watched the autumn foliage of the tame New England routes of his childhood travels, Herman had time to sort out some of the sequences of events he had been told about, although even after he had heard the same stories from two or more sources, in Boston, in Manhattan, and in Lansingburgh, he could never have gained more than a general impression and some vivid vignettes of those years. The details he had heard in Boston were soon overlaid by what Allan told him and what his mother and other members of the family would tell him in Lansingburgh, and Gansevoort's still subsequent stories of what had passed in the nearly four years of his absence. This information came in jumbled form—the way he had been learning about world events over the last few years, highly detailed accounts of the later phases of events which presumed knowledge of prior occurrences of which he was wholly ignorant. One thing was sure. Allan, he knew before the boat arrived in lower Manhattan, would know all there was to know about "the orator of the human race."

16

The Sailor, the Orator, and the Grand Contested Election

1844

They [the owners of a menagerie, stopping in Albany] had a gigantic saddle for the male elephant. . . . In ancient times they must have been a terrible weapon in the hands of an army, by giving loose rein to Imagination I could almost fancy to myself the army of Pyrrhus King of Epirus when he invaded the Roman Territory, what an awful, fear inspiring sight to see 100 Elephants drawn up in line, each carrying 5 or 6 armed men on his back.

Gansevoort Melville's diary, 27 February 1834, after riding an elephant

HERMAN AND ALLAN WERE REUNITED late Saturday the nineteenth of October 1844 or early Sunday the twentieth. Greenwich Street, the second street in from the Hudson, which it paralleled, was familiar to Herman from childhood, and Allan's rooming house there was near the Battery, convenient for anyone arriving by water. Edgy, anxious, talking and listening to Allan, even while thinking intermittently about Elizabeth Shaw and her father and his relatives in Boston, Herman spent the first hours he had ever passed with Allan as one man with another man. It was a reenactment in reverse of his time with Guert.

Allan was justifiably full of himself, as well as of the orator. He was, after all, a lawyer. Furthermore, from James K. Polk's own house in Columbia, Tennessee, on 1 September, Gansevoort had entrusted Allan with a secret assignment, which he had been carrying out faithfully:

This m^g I have had a long conversation with Gov Polk in the course of which I offered to have some of the N Yk opposition papers sent to him. He accepted the offer with pleasure. So from the receipt of this I wish you to mail *daily* to Gov Polk either the Tribune, Herald, Courier & Enquirer, American, Republic or Express—more frequently one of the first three named & twice each week send the Eve^g Post. Do not let any person see the direction of the papers—put them up *uniformly* in the brown envelope paper, direct them in your largest legible hand and drop them in the P. O. yourself—Exercise your judgment in sending those which contain interesting political matters. Send the Herald not less than twice a week.

With concealed ostentation Allan may have let Herman see him wrap up a bundle of journals in standard brown envelope paper and direct the package to "Hon James K Polk/Columbia/Tenn." Allan, Herman could see, had a place in history, too, as a discreet courier.

Since as an examiner he had public or private news from Albany twice or more a day, Allan knew that Gansevoort had spoken at Troy on the eighteenth (where, according to the *Argus* on the twenty-second, the Democrats overflowed the hall, despite a downpour that left the streets knee-deep in mud). This meant Gansevoort had seen the family in Lansingburgh before speaking across the river at Waterford on the nineteenth, Saturday evening, and probably had spent part of Sunday with them before going to Albany on the twenty-first. He had needed fresh clothing and the ministrations of loving fingers to repair his campaign gear, and he had carried handbills, letters, and other trophies to show them, but he had not stayed long. Allan may have learned that Gansevoort would leave Albany for New York City on the twenty-second. He probably did not know that the orator would stop at Kinderhook to report to Martin Van Buren before veering halfway across the wide state to Elmira, where Gansevoort had accepted an urgent invitation to speak on the twenty-third, making him later in reaching New York than he had told Allan.

At the tip of Manhattan island, Herman and Allan took stock of the situation. There was a chance that Herman could reach Albany or Lansingburgh in time to see Gansevoort for a moment before the orator raced to his commitments, whatever they were, but only a small chance. The sensible thing to do was for Herman to go home as fast as possible then return to rendezvous with Gansevoort and Allan in Manhattan. Allan would normally have been avid to hear of Herman's adventures in the Pacific, but time was short, and the election was all-consuming. In his turns at telling stories and displaying newspapers from the "bushell" basket he had written Herman about, as well as recent letters in the familiar perfectly formed script of their older brother, Allan could at least give Herman a sense of just how their brother had become so famous an orator.

As Allan had written to Herman, Gansevoort had been admitted to the bar in December 1841. Now what Allan told Herman supplemented the letter and what he had learned in Boston. On 10 January 1842 Gansevoort had hung out his shingle as an attorney at law, "at 51 William St, a few doors from Wall," as he wrote Shaw on the twenty-fifth. There he had "a desk and the use of a library in offices occupied" by two friends of his, Alexander W. Bradford and Theodore E. Tomlinson, and was therefore "constantly with Allan, who is a student with Bradford and takes charge of his Attorney's business." (Bradford, a prominent Whig already, had not let politics divide him from Gansevoort.) By July 1842 Gansevoort had begun to earn a little money (he wrote Shaw that during the past six months he had "received $210, in cash, and charged $165 more, against good men, all for professional services, making $375"), but simultaneously, from the time he hung out his shingle, he had "also mingled somewhat in politics, avoiding committee work, and eschewing any connection with the complex wire-pulling machinery which unfortunately is so prevalent here" (thus Gansevoort wrote to Shaw). He had begun making political speeches, "the first before some 400 persons at the Shakespeare Hotel, the second before about 2000, in the open air, and the third at the head quarters of our party, Tammany Hall before a crowded auditory of between 3 & 4000 men." On receiving this distressing news, Lemuel Shaw, Whig only because the Federalist party was dead, had warned him against the seductions of party politics, and Gansevoort had placated him, but had kept on speaking.

In 1843 Gansevoort had come into his own. As the effects of the Panic of 1837 faded, and as his post of examiner in chancery began to bring in small regular sums, he felt freer to seek glory as an orator. With his physical presence, his talent, and access given by his politically influential Democratic relatives, all he needed, if he were to bypass the "committee work" and "complex wire-pulling" that made rising to political prominence so tedious, was a spectacular issue with which he could identify himself. By the middle of 1843 (which Daniel O'Connell had proclaimed the "Year of Repeal") Gansevoort seemed to have found that issue in the agitation for repeal of the union between Great Britain and Ireland, and the reestablishment of a national Irish Parliament. (There had been recent Irish famines, but the "Great Hunger" was just ahead, 1845–49.) In the United States the repeal agitation also was at its most intense, led by fiery Irishmen as young as Gansevoort himself, who could see on the docks that the immigrants from Ireland were overwhelmingly and heartbreakingly young—in their teens, in their early twenties, the surviving youth of Ireland, sent singly across the Atlantic, not arriving, like stalwart German immigrants, as intact families. Always of necessity an opportunist, it was no wonder that Gansevoort responded powerfully to the young Irish and took their cause as his own, regardless of the fact that he and his family had no special interest in Ireland. From Galena, in letters to both Shaw and to Gansevoort, Uncle Thomas growled his resentment about this unseemly meddling with the Papists, and Shaw mildly pointed Gansevoort toward steadier pursuits; Gansevoort temporized, then did what he wanted.

By 20 September 1843 Gansevoort had advanced so far that at a "Great Repeal Meeting" in New York City he was one of the five leading speakers who, "for two or three hours with great animation, ability, and zeal," kept up the initial debate over the method of choosing officers (William Cullen Bryant's Democratic *Evening Post,* September 21). The next night he made an extraordinary speech. After entertaining the audience with witty mockery of a straw man — the editor of the Whig *Journal of Commerce,* who two months before had announced that the repeal movement was dead — he declared that repeal was a cause "Vital in every part, / And cannot but by annihilating die," a less than apt Miltonic passage that may have been quoted around the house, for it stuck in Herman's mind too, at least later on. In his peroration (as printed in the *Evening Post* on 29 September) Gansevoort turned from a survey of the progress of repeal abroad to the progress of the movement in Ireland:

> And now, when we turn to Ireland itself, what eye is there that does not sparkle? What bosom that does not heave as we call to mind the million of Repealers on the hill of Tara? [Great Cheering.] "Tara of the Kings"; Tara hallowed by a thousand recollections; the seat of Ireland's early royalty; before the hoof of the Saxon profaned the sod; when Ireland was a nation — [profound silence and a marked sensation in the meeting, while after a pause, the speaker resumed] — she is not one now. But her time is coming. She is going to take her place. To avail ourselves of the vivid imagination of John Bunyan — Ireland has just toiled from out the Valley of the Shadow of Death. The sunshine is around her and upon her. She is standing upon the top of the Delectable Mountains, and the shining city is in full view. That shining city is Repeal — the total repeal of the miscalled, tyrannical, and accursed union between Great Britain and Ireland.

When Gansevoort declared that, "having consumed much time, he would no longer trespass on the attention of the audience," he was met "with cries of 'Go on,' 'Go on,' from a thousand throats — one ardent repealer shouted 'Speak on — speak forever.'" Accordingly, Gansevoort resumed his speech. Small wonder that he began to harbor political ambitions of more than trifling seriousness, for with this speech Gansevoort had proved himself a masterful crowd-swayer and a hero to the New York Irish. On the strength of it he had been invited to Boston in October 1843, the time he had gone up to Lansingburgh first so as to escort Elizabeth Shaw home, along with Helen.

Gansevoort's first major address to the Democracy of New York in 1844 had been at the Tabernacle on 15 March, Andrew Jackson's birthday. In a portion directed to the women in the audience he made direct complimentary comments on the women of his family:

> I come from a stock, the women as well as the men of which have, from the first organization of parties, manifested a preference for and a sympathy with the democratic cause. [Loud cheers.] If any man wishes more proof than is derived from his own personal knowledge, let him look around him. Those galleries will settle the question. [Tremendous applause and nine cheers for the ladies.] The wild flowers of feminine delicacy, beauty, and grace, that honor us with their presence here to-night, and whose exceeding loveliness might lure an anchorite from his cell, were never plucked from the prim and artificial gardens of modern whiggery. [Shouts of laughter and tremendous applause.]
>
> Show me a woman who can sympathise with the magnificent mother of the Gracchi—who, when asked by the aristocratic dames of ancient Rome to exhibit her store of ornaments of gold and precious stones—answered, that she had none of these, but at the same time produced her two glorious sons, exclaiming, "these are my jewels." Show me a woman who can understand this and feel it, and that woman is at heart a democrat. [Cheers.]

Confident of his own eloquence, he portrayed himself as a blunt fellow pestered with popinjays:

> Now, my fair countrywomen, with your permission, a word with you. I grant ye that the whigs have the advantage of us plain-spoken democrats in scented hair, diamond rings, and white kid gloves—[roars of laughters,] in the language of compliment and the affectation of manner, and most particularly, in their style of dressing. If one of these exquisites wished to express the idea contained in the home-spun adage, "There is the devil to pay and no pitch hot," he would say, "There is a pecuniary liability due to the old gentleman, and no bituminous matter, of the proper temperature, wherewith to liquidate the obligation."

At this, there was uproarious laughter and applause, "in which the ladies joined."

Soberly alluding to the troubled life of the late Rachel Jackson, Gansevoort compared Jackson's memories of her to Fitz-Greene Halleck's "beautiful lines to the memory of Burns—lines that will live forever." He closed with a tribute to Jackson as the heroic survivor of "obloquy and contumely":

> Picture him now in the Hermitage. The sun is setting. Its declining rays fall through the casement on the bowed form of one who, had he been a Roman, would have been the noblest Roman of them all. Silent and alone, he falls into a reverie. His eyes involuntarily close, and the days of his youth come back upon him. His countenance saddens as he feels that the voice of her who is in heaven, falls no longer on his ear. . . . He is conscious that his sun is going

down in peace. — The air around him is laden with the blessings of a grateful people, and every breeze is vocal with his praises

> All things bear in him
> An aspect of eternity — his thoughts,
> His feelings and his passions, good or evil,
> Have nothing of old age; and his bold brow
> Bears but the scars of mind, the thoughts of years,
> Not their decrepitude.

When Andrew Jackson died, Gansevoort assured the throng, he would have left

> A deathless lesson,
> A name which is a virtue, and a soul
> Which multiplies itself throughout all time.

This speech was promptly printed up in the form of a pamphlet, which Gansevoort must have sent to Judge Shaw, among others. Uncle Thomas saw the speech, in a newspaper or the pamphlet, and felt such disgust toward it that he seems to have stopped writing to Gansevoort. Herman may already have seen it in Boston. Now he learned that it had consolidated Gansevoort's reputation with the emerging leaders of the new Democratic party of the Empire State.

Allan was ready to explain what lay beneath the surface of another speech, the one at City Hall Park which Herman had read in Boston. On 27 April 1844 letters from both Henry Clay, the leading Whig candidate for the presidential nomination, and ex-president Martin Van Buren, the leading Democratic candidate, had been published in Washington, each man explaining, with varying scruples, his own opposition to the immediate annexation of Texas. Although a majority of the delegates to the national Democratic convention, to be held in Baltimore at the end of May, were already committed to Van Buren, the expansionist delegates, especially those from slave states, began looking for a way to vote for someone else. Van Buren's supporters, like Benjamin F. Butler, then district attorney of the Southern District of New York, frantically sought to prevent his being dropped in favor of some expansionist like Lewis Cass of Michigan. This situation had profound repercussions in New York state politics, for it destroyed the Albany Regency, the Democratic clique which, to Peter Gansevoort's benefit, had ruled the state for almost twenty years. Assured that the governor would appoint Allan in his place, on 7 May Gansevoort had resigned his appointment as examiner in chancery. The governor had promptly appointed Allan to succeed him, and Allan had promptly passed his examination so as to validate the appointment. In Tammany Hall the Central Van Buren Committee met on 15 May to issue an address to "the Democracy of the Union" denouncing the "intrigues in Washington" and defending Van Buren as the strongest candidate the Democrats could nominate. One signer was Allan Melville, who thought, still, the future was with the former president; Gansevoort had not signed. Intending to be no one's tool, Gansevoort had daringly freed himself to seize his great chance in life, whatever precise form it might take.

On the morning of 30 May, New York City received news of the nominations of James K. Polk and Silas Wright at the Baltimore convention. Wright, a sturdy, round-faced man who combed his remaining hair forward on his face above his ears and pushed the hair at the top of his forehead into a topknot, promptly removed his name out of loyalty to Van Buren, and the convention had to reassemble to nominate the Pennsylvania George M. Dallas in his place. Late on the thirtieth the Whig diarist George Templeton Strong speculated wryly on how soon the news would reach Van Buren: "The tidings went northward by this evening's boat and they'll reach the cabbage gardens of Kinderhook in an hour or two" (*The Diary of George Templeton Strong*, 1, ed. Allan Nevins and Milton Halsey Thomas, 1952). The next day New Yorkers knew that Wright had refused the nomination, and on the night of 1 June the Democrats met in Tammany to see what face to put on the new situation. They resolved to dispatch "a special committee of four" to pay respects to Van Buren and to invite him to preside at a mass meeting at City Hall Park on 4 June to endorse the Baltimore nominees. Gansevoort, whom Van Buren knew as Peter Gansevoort's nephew, was made chairman of the committee. The emergency forced Gansevoort to break a speaking engagement before the Boston Democracy in Faneuil Hall, but even when writing in haste after the Tammany meeting on 1 June he knew what his tactics should be. Explaining that "an unforeseen and imperative summons to a distant portion of the state" compelled him to cancel his trip to Boston, Gansevoort continued with what was to be his message for five months, the "cheering fact, that throughout the city and state of New York the great republican [i.e., Democratic] party are animated by one impulse and have but one aim," that rival Democrats, "ALL TO A MAN," had pledged their support to the Baltimore nominees. The Boston *Post* published the letter on 5 June, the day after the park meeting on the fourth, which drew a crowd that the Democratic newspapers generously estimated at over fifteen thousand or over twenty-five thousand. Gansevoort had savored his first moment of national glory.

In Albany, Uncle Peter had been busy overseeing an enlargement of Stanwix Hall, topping it with the gilt dome it had always deserved (it re-opened on 10 June 1844), but he had time for a practical political switch, and he signed a resolution inviting the Democrats to a meeting on 6 June to endorse the Baltimore nominees, regardless of their previous "personal preferences" for Van Buren. Edwin Croswell, at this time a deceptively timid-looking man in his mid-forties with a triangular head accented by short whiskers running from ears down to under the chin like a strap to a hat, observed in his Albany *Argus* on 6 June that it was "confidently hoped that Gansevoort Melville, esq., of New York" would address the assemblage. Gansevoort was in fact speaking elsewhere, and in the next months the *Argus* printed many of his letters of regret to the Democrats of various towns. With the Whigs eager to prove that the Democrats were divided into the expansionist Polk men and the anti-annexation Van Buren men, and with many Van Burenites reluctant to vote for Polk, Gansevoort and his letter were invaluable. The letter from Van Buren in hand, Gansevoort was the orator best capable of setting the rank and file of the "Democracy" to cheering loudly enough to forget the temporarily concealed split in the party.

For Gansevoort more truly than for Polk, 1844 was a dark-horse year. Before his Jackson Day and his City Hall Park speeches, Gansevoort had been known in the Northeast as a repealer, and his name had appeared even in some western papers in accounts of repeal meetings, but he was hardly a national figure. When Polk began looking for eastern Democrats to cooperate in the campaign—and specifically to convey to his home state of Tennessee the loyalty of the Van Buren men to the party's nominees, he first hoped to enlist the Massachusetts Democrat George Bancroft, who had written a campaign biography of Van Buren that was now undistributable. Bancroft was thrown into confusion when he received a letter from J. George Harris, the editor of the Nashville *Union*, in which Harris announced that he would be forwarding biographical material on Polk, and concluded blithely: "It is a matter of great joy with us that you have consented to exercise your fresh, vigorous, and polished pen upon the pure character of the Governor"—that is, Governor Polk. Before Bancroft could reply that he had consented to nothing of the kind, Harris wrote again, on 24 June, sending the material on Polk under Old Hickory's frank and informing Bancroft that "the old Hero," Andrew Jackson, had expressed "a wish that you would write the history" of Polk's life. Somehow Bancroft explained his reluctance to write the biography, and Polk wrote him on 20 July expressing a high regard for Martin Van Buren and declaring that he understood Bancroft's reasons for declining.

The northeastern Democracy had no sooner failed to cooperate with the new southwestern leadership in the matter of the campaign biography than another test of loyalty presented itself. On 22 July, Gideon J. Pillow, the Tennesseean who had helped stage-manage the Baltimore convention, wrote

Bancroft from Polk's home in Columbia, urgently pleading with him to attend the "great mass meeting in Nashville on the 15th of August next," which was being planned as a demonstration of Democratic solidarity. Bancroft again refused, and Polk's men turned to Senator Silas Wright—who in turn found reasons for remaining in New York. Their refusals left Gansevoort as the logical choice. He was uncompromised by recent support for Van Buren, and he was the possessor of the magical Van Buren letter—or at least of the magic that made the letter say what the Polk Democrats wanted it to say. As early as 21 July William E. Cramer wrote Polk from the *Argus* office with a strong suggestion: "Your great Mass Convention is approaching. Has *Gansevoort Melville* of New-York been invited? He would feel the Compliment and he is deserving of it, As he is one of the ablest Stump Orators we have in the Northern States. His voice is so powerful that he can easily be heard by thousands. Perhaps he may come." After this, as Maria wrote to Augusta on 8 August, "several invitations" promptly came from Tennessee, "one in particular from Cave Johnson, urging him particularly to come on saying some very flattering things to induce him—&c." Johnson, a bald-domed U.S. Representative from Tennessee and one of Polk's managers, may have offered the ultimate inducement, the prospect that Andrew Jackson himself would preside at the meeting.

There was some doubt whether the seventy-seven-year-old Andrew Jackson would be able to preside at the great Nashville convention. His doctors urged him to stay home, fearing, in Gansevoort's report (the New York *Herald*, 5 November 1844), "that the great rush and shouting of the people as they pressed to look upon him, would be dangerous to him in his present feeble state." More than once Gansevoort implied that Jackson nevertheless had presided over the mass meeting, and he claimed to have been at the Hermitage when Jackson made his decision, saying, according to Gansevoort, "I am very old; I cannot stay here much longer; I can do little or no good by remaining, so if I can do any good by presiding at that Convention of the Democracy, carry me there! Place me in the chair and I'll die in my seat!" Recent research by Randall Cluff suggests strongly that Jackson remained at home. According to two letters Jackson wrote on 15 August, he was "panting for breath," too ill to attend, and remained alone ("entirely alone," he emphasized in one letter), while even his servants went "to the Mass meeting at Nashville." The site of the meeting was, after all, on the banks of the Cumberland, hard miles away from the Hermitage.

In the Nashville *Union* for 16 August, Harris hailed the substitute speaker from New York: "There were two miles of table on which the GREAT DINNER was served. Gov. [Lewis] Cass made the first speech; and it was one of unsurpassed eloquence and power. Mr. Melville, of New York, followed with a thrilling, edifying and instructive speech — eliciting the most rapturous applause at the turn of every period." The heavy-featured, thick-necked Cass and the tall young Melville played to different needs in the same crowd, each successfully. In this initial report on the 15 August meeting Harris promised at least an outline of Gansevoort's speech from his reporter's hasty notes, but for the meantime observed that Gansevoort had assured the crowd that the New York Democrats were united, "whatever the voice of misrepresentation might say to the contrary" — or the voice of truth. Gansevoort was precisely what the Polk Democrats needed in the West that summer — a cultured Easterner who could piously lay Van Buren in his political tomb while assuring his auditors that Van Buren's former supporters were now wholeheartedly for Polk. On 27 August Croswell commented in the *Argus* on the Whig reaction to Gansevoort's "most thrilling and effective speech at Nashville" and rejoiced in "the sincere, noble and zealous support" Van Buren and Silas Wright were giving to the nominees. Wright was even then "traversing the state, rousing up the democracy." But rousing up the Democracy was something no one could do like Gansevoort, so whatever his plans had been, the Westerners refused to let him return directly home after his speech.

From Polk's house in Columbia, Gansevoort reworked his itinerary at the same table where the candidate was working. He could not be a major player on the political scene and at the same time act as his own historian, so he gave Allan specific instructions: "Be particular in preserving those newspapers which you think will be interesting to me, & also take memorandums of the dates of those at the news room which you can not procure so that I may refer readily to them." (These news rooms survived through the century, maintaining files of major papers and offering current papers for purchase.)

The news of Gansevoort's stay in the Hermitage, whether he read it first in the papers or in Allan's letter, impressed Herman profoundly, enough so that in 1849 he wrote about it and about Gansevoort's visits to Polk in *White-Jacket* (ch. 70), contrasting his own status during August 1844 with his older brother's: "By the main-mast! then, in a time of profound peace, I am subject to the cut-throat martial law! And when my own brother, who happens to be dwelling ashore, and does not serve his country as I am now doing — when *he* is at liberty to call personally upon the President of the United States, and express his disapprobation of the whole national administration, here am *I*, liable at any time to be run up at the yard-arm, with a necklace, made by no jeweler, round my neck!" Gansevoort had in fact, in his time, called personally upon more than one former president and president-to-be at their homes — John Quincy Adams, Martin Van Buren, James K. Polk. But for glamor he could parlay into power, nothing compared to this stay with Andrew Jackson at the Hermitage. Traveling light, except for weighty stories to be cherished by his audiences and his family, Gansevoort left Nashville on 8 September for what became a triumphal return to New York.

Before the mass convention in Nashville, even, Gansevoort's friend Levi Slamm, the editor of the New York *Plebeian*, had broken the news of treachery in the party, William C. Bryant's "confidential" circular-letter, a request to three dozen prominent Democrats that they support the Baltimore choices but reject the resolution favoring annexation of Texas and also unite to elect non-annexationists to Congress. Polk wrote to Andrew J. Donelson about the circular on 3 August, concerned, but hopeful that the Democrats' main trouble in New York would be over the governorship. (As it happened, the much respected Silas Wright was popular enough to win the governorship and pull the less popular Polk to victory with him.) All through August and September Polk knew, and Gansevoort knew, that the primary function of the representative of New York in the West was to assure the faithful that the party was unified. Gansevoort's safest strategy was to ignore all dissension and to persist in bland praise of Van Buren and in denials of disharmony.

On 2 October, at Elyria, Ohio, Gansevoort assured his audience "that the Democracy of the Empire State were united as one man in support of Polk, Dallas and Texas." Exhaustion and the fever-pitch of mass adulation caught up with him, and incited by his theme, Gansevoort could not leave well enough alone:

> W. C. Bryant, editor of the *Evening Post*, George P. Barker, Attorney General, and a half dozen other prominent men of the party, who were and are opposed to the Annexation of Texas, did throw a missile into their [the Polk-Dallas] camp which was intended to do mischief, in the shape of a secret circular, but that it exploded, doing no injury but to the authors. *They had been met by a storm of indignation that had driven them back to their holes*, and *now they sued for mercy*, and promised, if forgiven, to go the whole for Polk and Dallas, but wanted to protest against Annexation. They had not now more than two hundred followers in the whole State, and the Democracy had *consented that all the rebels, captains and privates, might vote for Polk and Dallas, for their votes were all they wanted, and they might protest when and where and as long as they pleased. Give us Polk and Dallas, and we shall have Texas in spite of all the protests of all the conspirators, and thousands more like them.*

On 12 October in the New York *Tribune* Horace Greeley recommended Gansevoort's words "especially to the regard of the *Evening Post* clique, who are hostile to the Annexation of Texas, and profess to believe that the election of James K. Polk will not ensure that result." Greeley then maliciously quoted a long account of Gansevoort's speech at Elyria from the Cleveland *Herald* of 8 October. Gansevoort's reckless reminder embarrassed Polk by giving the Whigs dangerous ammunition; Polk had been as angered by the circular as Gansevoort, but was shrewd enough to know he must not say so in public. Gansevoort's indiscretion haunted the Democratic party for the next two years and had wholly unpredictable literary consequences, for it soured the long-lived and powerful Bryant toward any member of the Melville family, including the sailor who took up the profession of authorship.

In the second week of October, Gansevoort progressed to western New York. His speech at Buffalo on 7 October was a triumph, which he shared on 9 October in a letter to "Friend Cramer," a victory report marked "Private of course & as usual." Although there had been only twelve hours' notice, the crowd was larger than had been mustered, after a week's notice, to hear a speech by Auguste Davezac, one of the authentic heroes of the Democratic party, now a New Yorker, but, at the end of 1814 and the first days of 1815, the Louisianian who had advised General Jackson about the New Orleans terrain, before the battle. Gansevoort permitted himself this exultation in his letter to Cramer:

> It was a raw cold gusty eve^g — The arrangements were very deficient. No lights were provided on the stand from which I spoke — so that when some tar barrels which had been set on fire had burnt out we were left in entire darkness. The crowd *could not see me & I could not distinguish a single feature or individual in the mass* before me. . . . The odds were 25 to 1 against Olympian Pericles himself holding that crowd together. It was so cold that overcoats were indispensable and the wind swept through the square moaningly and in gusts — Everything was against me — and I felt it — but that consciousness only seemed to give me added energy and to steel my courage for the strife. Thanks to the Most High, I was enabled to triumph over all. For two hours & a quarter that crowd stood attentive, silent & save when manifesting their appreciation wrapt in the subject & the speaker — And at the close there was a perfect sea of long continued cheering followed up by three cheers for Melville! Three more! —— Three more! and so on — . . . . That's the true style — the western style — energetic — fair open & above board.

Gansevoort got out of town just in time, for on 12 October a phenomenal storm stranded canal boats in Seneca Street and lifted sail vessels onto the docks and onto Main Street. Even while swollen with pride, he kept one eye on practical Albany politics: "Do not let one friend add an appointment for Albany without my *full previous concurrence.*" He knew that his friend Cramer, assistant editor on the *Argus,* was at the paper on sufferance, sure to be fired by Edwin Croswell if Polk did not win the election (so Cramer wrote to Polk on 13 November). As he wrote Allan on 13 October, Gansevoort was receiving more than ordinary courtesies, for at nearly every point across the state he had been "waited on by deputations from points in the adjacent counties bearing invitations of the most pressing character." Allan had been saving all Gansevoort's letters, and saving newspaper printings of his speeches and other accounts of his triumphs (as well as scornful Whig refutations); about this time he gave up controlling the pile of little four-page papers (so small that a tar like Herman could hide a *Herald* under his hat) and began stacking them in the bushel basket he mentioned in his letter to Herman.

Horace Greeley watched his fellow repealer with mounting glee, and at last on 12 October put a stinging little editorial in the *Tribune:* "GANSE-VOORT MELVILLE ON TEXAS. We have had several letters from the West, intimating rather broadly that our friend *Gansevoort Melville,* who is repre-senting the Polk Democracy of New-York through that region, does not understand human nature well enough to stump in that quarter. He devel-opes too much gas and glory — talks too much of himself, Mr. Van Buren and Gen. Jackson — and says too little of the great questions before the People." When Gansevoort was talking about Van Buren and Jackson and himself, his gas and glory, Greeley surely knew, was just what the Democrats needed. The one thing Gansevoort had done wrong was to attack Bryant and his co-conspirators.

On 14 October, the day Herman was discharged, the Albany *Argus* ("At-tention Democrats!") gave a partial schedule of Gansevoort's appearances on his way home from Buffalo: the fourteenth at Ithaca; the sixteenth at Utica; the seventeenth at Schenectady; and the eighteenth (a Friday) home at Troy. Gansevoort's Utica speech was reported in the Oneida *Chief* as "a splendid affair" at the end of which "long, loud and many times repeated hurras were given for POLK, DALLAS, VICTORY and MELVILLE." At Schenectady (accord-ing to the *Reflector*) Gansevoort touched on the aims of the British: "He showed that England was, as she ever has been, painfully alive to, and jealous of, the stately steppings of our young and growing Republic, and that she is insidiously attempting to check our territorial extension, and to increase her colonial possessions in America." At Troy on the eighteenth Gansevoort played to his strength, for the Irish were "very strong" there, as William E. Cramer wrote Polk on 22 October, and remembered worshipfully Ganse-voort's repeal orations from the year before. On Saturday evening, the nine-teenth, Gansevoort gave a short talk at Waterford, across the river from home (and, not coincidentally, the home of John Cramer, former U.S. Rep-resentative and father of William E. Cramer). Sunday he must have spent, in part, with the family, but on Monday, 21 October, he was down in Albany with young Cramer. There Gansevoort may have received the news of Her-man's return. Gansevoort kept silent if he knew about Herman when he saw his mother, but from some stopping place he sent instructions for Allan to relay to the sailor if there was time: Herman was to shave and make himself presentable before showing himself to their mother.

Cramer's letter to Polk on 22 October specified that Gansevoort "left this morning for New York as he is very anxious to understand the full aspects of this new Coalition with Nativism" — that is, the alliance of Whigs and rabid anti-Catholics ("church-burners," the *Argus* called the Nativists on 12 October), which in fact led to the election of James Harper (of the Harper & Brothers publishing firm) as the Nativist mayor of New York City. Cramer expected that Gansevoort might "speak at Philadelphia and Baltimore before the canvass is over" and then go back to speak at Albany. On his way down to New York City, according to Gansevoort's letter to Polk on 26 October, he stopped at Lindenwald ("Mr Van Buren is in excellent health and evidently growing fat"), but he made a detour to Elmira, where he spoke on the twenty-third. In his letter to Polk on 26 October, Gansevoort reported: "Our gatherings are more largely attended than those of our opponents, and in the more than a dozen meetings which I have addressed since my return home [to New York State] the attendance has been in every case far greater than had been anticipated and the enthusiasm more obvious than I have elsewhere witnessed." In this letter Gansevoort wrote:

> Political excitement in this state has reached a high and almost fearful point. . . . It is unexampled in the history of New York politics. Coming from one theatre of action into another and still stormier one . . . I have kept both eyes and ears open, have conversed with prominent men of the respective parties. . . .
>
> For the views here-in expressed I am alone responsible. They conflict in some particulars of importance with the views of older more experienced and more sagacious men. Mr Croswell, Mr Cramer, Gov Bouck, Mr Van Buren, and all our other friends feel a greater and some of them a *much* greater degree of confidence than I do.

The names are of Albany area politicians, but Gansevoort had been back in Manhattan a day or two already, surveying the metropolitan scene and very likely speaking to the Democracy. Gansevoort was relieved to know that his sailor brother was alive and well, but he still had a president to elect.

The timing of Herman's return to Lansingburgh is known from two notes. One is from Allan to his mother on Monday evening, 21 October: "Herman has arrived & you may expect him every hour after tomorrow. In great haste . . ." There survives another note, in very similar handwriting, saying "Herman has arrived & you may expect him every moment." Herman himself wrote it, with Allan's note in front of him. Herman probably took the cheaper night boat up on Monday, 21 October, reaching Albany Tuesday morning. Early on 22 October the brothers just missed each other—indeed, their ships most likely passed in the dark, Gansevoort going downriver to see Van Buren before making his way far west and south to Elmira. In Lansingburgh, acting out a variation on his role as the family postman, Herman managed to slip Allan's note and his own note to Tom or one or more of the girls. Herman knew his mother. When Maria was shown the note from Allan she would fall to her knees to give thanks to God. Then when she was handed Herman's own note she—no fool—would stride toward the front door, clutching his note to her breast. Herman was mature enough to want his mother to be forewarned about an emotional situation so she would not suffer too great a shock, but boyish enough to want to jump sideways into the door-frame and say something like, "Mamma, I'm home" (a great chance to use two words he later claimed to have taught Fayaway). That was Herman's homecoming. He had been away four years and was still a great tease, as Gansevoort had complained in 1824.

Once the tumult had faded, anyone who wanted to could go outside and look up in the sky. Members of the Millerite sect, who had proselytized across the river in Waterford, were expecting the return of Jesus, not to the Holy Land but to the United States, and many of them had been waiting all night in encampments, thinly clad, so as to be awake when He descended. (Children died from exposure in such a camp in Pennsylvania.) On 13 October, before Herman's discharge, Jesus had left the Mercy Seat, they said, and, traveling at divine but not magical speed, was due to appear in the heavens on this day, the twenty-second. Herman's homecoming had been overshadowed by the return to the Empire State of Gansevoort Melville, the "orator of the human race," but it could have been overshadowed by the Second Coming.

Maria, to her son's blinkered eyes, was unchanged and changeless, "Mamma." Helen and Augusta had changed little. Helen was maturer, having moved in august circles in the Athens of America, but she was what she had been for almost two decades, the second mother of the family. Augusta from her many visits at the Manor House had developed, in conversations with her host and hostess, not only greater social skills but also an ever stronger devotion to the tenets of the Dutch Reformed Church. She was a second mother herself, to Allan for years now, and to the three younger children. These three took getting used to. Kate at nineteen and Fanny at seventeen had changed more than the older sisters, and Tom at almost fourteen was, as Allan had warned, quite a man, and manly in a fashion Herman must have found unsettling at first, but then oddly comfortable, for he looked and behaved remarkably like Herman himself.

Once the family realized that Herman and Gansevoort must have passed each other on the Hudson, they compared notes and told Herman some details about Gansevoort's supposedly therapeutic sea-voyage, paid for by Lemuel Shaw, on the *Teasel*, bound for New Orleans by way of Jamaica. Putting the schedules together, Herman and the others realized that for a time in early February of 1841 the brothers had been near each other off the Bahama banks, after their wintry parting—their curious fate being to pass each other repeatedly by water. Herman heard, for the third time or more, piecemeal, the history of the last years, including the circumstances of their receiving letters and at least one package from him, and details of what reports they had read of the *Acushnet* and perhaps of the *United States*. (The *Acushnet* may have been the only ship they had known he was on while he was still on it.) He and Helen could compare notes on the aunts they had both seen and the ones Helen had visited although he had probably not.

For the older sisters, Herman was a wonder, but sartorially speaking he was a woe. Allan had been concerned to rig Herman out in civilian clothes for his voyage upriver, but now Helen and Augusta had a greater challenge: to assemble a wardrobe to complete whatever he had acquired in Boston or Manhattan. Once they took Herman's measurements and compared them with Tom's, there was no absolute need for him to be there for fittings, and waiting for that wardrobe would have meant spending days there. Having seen everyone, talked to everyone, having been measured up, down, and sideways, Herman became restless fast. He had the one acceptable excuse for leaving his mother and going back to New York City: he had not yet seen Gansevoort. He longed to see Gansevoort, and once again, recalling 1840, he longed to see the climax of the grand contested election for the presidency in the gaudiest possible city, where his brother would be a conspicuous performer. After his wanderings in the Pacific, he wanted, this once, to be in the center of the action, at the climax of the campaign. He knew well enough that for Gansevoort the great day of the month was 5 November, election day, not the day he would rejoin his brother, but Herman wanted to be there, part of history. Gansevoort had gone to New Bedford to see him off on his voyage to the Pacific, and now Herman would be in Manhattan for the last moments of Gansevoort's triumphant campaign.

During the last week of October Herman must have gone back down to New York. The boat trip gave him privacy for reflection. Going to the metropolis was always more exciting than going north, and suggestive of possibilities. He had to do something with his life, and since Gansevoort had so amazingly succeeded, despite all his disadvantages, perhaps he too could make a name for himself. Gansevoort's speeches filled whole columns of newspapers, so why shouldn't the stories he had been telling his shipmates be good enough to print? One brother's political success fired the other's literary ambition.

In Manhattan Herman got less than total attention from his older brother, as he had expected, but in other ways he got more than he bargained for. Gansevoort was exhausted, but he was still a whirlwind. He had shown Maria and his sisters a gorgeous banner he had carried back from Nashville, but he had not left it with them at home as he would ordinarily have done. He had a use for it in Manhattan. While briefing a reporter from the *Herald* he displayed it, and on 30 October the paper published an item on "COURTESIES OF POLITICS," which described the banner as "chaste and beautiful," like the "fair hands" that sewed it. For a hastily produced tribute, it was remarkable: "On one side is emblazoned an eagle with a scroll, on which is inscribed — 'The Home of the Hickories — to the Empire State: to Gansevoort Melville — from the Ladies of Tennessee.' On the reverse are the 'Stars and Stripes' and the 'Lone Star' of Texas. The possessor of such a gift is indeed a fortunate man." (The family saw this, for the *Argus* picked it up on 2 November.) All the Gansevoorts knew how to preserve historic textiles (think of the flags at Uncle Peter's and Uncle Herman's), but banners belonged in tissue paper in chests only after they had flown or streamed at historical events, and the Democrats had the perfect occasion. On Friday, 1 November, a notice dated 31 October was published in Bryant's *Evening Post:* "The undersigned Members of the Bar of the City and County of New York, respectfully invite their fellow citizens, especially those of their profession, to unite with them in the Democratic Demonstration on the 1st November next and to assemble for that purpose in the corridor of the city Hall on the afternoon of that day, at 6 o'clock." Among the 130 signers were Gansevoort Melville and A. Melville. Following this notice were instructions on how to recognize the officers in charge of leading the grand "Torchlight Procession."

It was late in the season for a parade, but the "evening was beautiful, the sky serene, and not a breath of air to extinguish a light or tear a banner" (the *Herald* said the next day, 2 November). All the Democratic clubs and associations gathered at different points before converging on City Hall Park. The *Plebeian* printed the route:

> Leaving the Park at the entrance opposite Tammany Hall, the procession will march up Chatham street to Bowery, up Bowery to Grand street, through Grand to Columbia, up Columbia to Houston, through Houston to Bowery, up Bowery to Astor Place, through Astor Place to Broadway, down Broadway to Fourth street, down Fourth street to Sixth Avenue, down Sixth Avenue to Carmine street, down Carmine street to Hudson, down Hudson to Spring,

through Spring to Broadway, down Broadway to Barclay, down Barclay to Greenwich street, down Greenwich to the Battery, round the Bowling Green up Broadway to Tammany Hall.

In the early darkness the procession began winding its way around the lower streets before ending at midnight, when the last of the procession reached Tammany Hall.

The New York *Plebeian and Democrat* of 21 October 1844 named Thomas Low Nichols as the "President" of the "Central Convention of Democratic Associations — Grand Torch Light Procession" — its chief organizer. Nichols gave this account in his autobiography:

> The night before the election [a memory lapse], Captain Rynders, mounted on a white charger, headed the Empire Club, one thousand strong, and his club headed a torchlight procession of twenty thousand New York Democrats, with twenty bands of music, and thousands of torches, Roman candles, rockets, and transparencies [images in windows or doorways, painted on cloth or paper, and backlit from within], with never-ending hurrahs for Polk and Dallas, Texas, Oregon, Fifty-four-forty-or-fight. A torchlight procession of twenty thousand men, pouring like a vast river of flame through the streets of a great city — broad streets which stretch away for miles in straight lines — with abundant music and the shouts of an excited multitude, enthusiastic, yet orderly in its enthusiasm, is a grand spectacle.

Nichols was an active member of the Empire Club that year (*Plebeian*, 13 August 1844), and an ally of the rowdy Isaiah Rynders, five years later a fomenter of the Astor Place riots. Rynders was no friend of Gansevoort, who on 26 October wrote Polk about Rynders's hooliganism at the recent Whig procession: "A Democratic association started here within a few months known as 'the Empire Club' (one of those fighting and bullying political clubs which disgrace our city politics) some of the leading officers and members of which including its President are men of reputed and believed suspicious and *criminal* character, and which owing to its reckless boldness and activity in the contest has been over-much petted by the Democratic press has of late committed some unprovoked outrages upon Whig processions and meetings." Rynders's irresponsibility made Gansevoort's role in the procession all the more valuable, for he had to whip up enthusiasm while helping to prevent outright vandalism and hooliganism.

For the parade all the various clubs and associations (in an American equivalent of medieval guild processions) outdid themselves. The *Post* singled out one work: "One of the most beautiful things in the procession was a ship of about twenty-five feet in length, fully-rigged and equipped with sails,

&c.—the sails bearing appropriate mottoes. The hull, which was of a most perfect model, was entirely composed of young hickory saplings, secured entirely with pieces of hickory instead of nails. She is named the 'young Hickory,' and was manned with a most gallant crew. The boatman, with his whistle, was continually piping all hands." This float, according to the *Herald* on the second, was pulled by the "Sailors," while the "Pilots made a splendid display, and exhibited several beautiful models of their skimmers of the seas, and various banners and devices. The boatmen of Whitehall and Staten Island made a strong show with several beautiful models and boats fully manned with crews in uniform" (this Whitehall was the dock on the Hudson near the Battery, close to Allan's lodgings; Herman wrote it into the first chapter of *Moby-Dick*). Here was a spectacle for the Melville brothers, Gansevoort who had named Polk "Young Hickory" and had slept under the sacred roof of the Hermitage, and Herman himself, who would have regarded the ships with purest joy, for they had no distracting imperfections, nautically speaking, and were marvels of workmanship. He had witnessed log cabin demonstrations by hard-drinking Whigs in Detroit four years before, but this was sublime, this was the way a grand contested election for the presidency should culminate. (Nothing was sacred: for months at the northeast corner of Prince and Broadway men could buy for a dollar a box of "Young Hickory Tobacco" containing forty plugs, with a portrait of Polk on each plug; ads ran in the *Plebeian*.)

Many of the marchers carried banners with mottoes—"Free Trade and Sailors' Rights"—"Where's that Roast Beef?"—"Albany Basin Rattlers"—"Germans by accident; Americans by choice; Democrats by principle." Auguste Davezac marched with banner and hallowed trophy: "This Flag was at the Battle of New Orleans, 8th January, 1815." Gansevoort would have affronted the "beautiful ladies" of Nashville if he had not paraded with their "very splendid silk banner." He belonged on an elephant again, as in 1834, but he probably settled for a horse: he deserved to ride, after his campaign. Allan must have marched, since he signed the public invitation. Herman stuck with them: lose sight of his brothers for a moment, lose them for hours. Whig and Democratic counters estimated twenty-four hundred horses were in the procession, ridden or pulling conveyances of one sort or another, and the most grudging estimate of the marchers was twenty thousand people and a generous estimate thirty thousand. By one timing the procession took three hours and ten minutes to pass the Bowery Theatre (the *Plebeian* said four hours), but on 2 November, spoilsport Horace Greeley, his teeth set on edge, called it "the richest joke of the season," and maliciously alleged that the same marchers looped past certain points more than once until "the spectators began to ask the showmen *how many times more they were coming round.*"

Hostile as ever to the Tammany Hall faction of his party, Bryant in the *Evening Post* on Saturday, 2 November, nevertheless took satisfaction in the Democrats' proving once again that they managed such spectacles better than the Whigs. James Gordon Bennett in the *Herald* gave enormous attention to the "Democratic Demonstration" as "one of the grandest, greatest, roughest, wildest, and most original displays that ever took place in this country." Bennett waxed Miltonic: " 'It looked' as a poet said, 'like all hell itself let loose, with Satan at their head and his hottest devils at their tail.' " Nathaniel Parker Willis in the *Weekly Mirror* of 2 November commented on the unusual enthusiasm displayed by onlookers, including many ladies, and rejoiced that the affair included "a large mixture of *fashionable young men*, which is a new feature in public processions of this city." (Willis had a knack for seeing political issues as more ephemeral than fashions.) The occasion was historic: "The *quality of the general feeling*, to our thinking, was more nearly up to the warmth of the Lafayette Ovation, than any procession that has taken place since." On this same day, 2 November, Gansevoort wrote Polk with considerable relief: "The Democratic procession of last evening was a surprising turn-out. It was a magnificent demonstration of the *man-power* — full of life, energy and enthusiasm. Our voters are eager for the contest. The Whig procession of Wednesday last was far less numerous but more costly and imposing in its splendor. It was an exhibition of the strength of the Money-power. Ours, of that which after all controls the wealth, the masses." He enclosed for Polk the grudging *Tribune* for 2 November and "one of the Native American prints" (that is, the rabid anti-immigrant newspapers), letting Polk see the worst.

Even after the marching and speech-making on 1 November, the Manhattan lawyers Gansevoort and Allan, like other Democrats, had important electoral work to do, such as signing up new voters by the simple expedient of making citizens of any alien they could lay hands on. As Gansevoort reported to Colonel Samuel Medary, the editor of the Columbus *Ohio Statesman*, on Monday the fourth, a letter plainly meant to consolidate good feelings beyond the election, Tammany Hall those last days was "a perfect jam from 8 AM till after midnight" — "Naturalization going on among our friends to an immense extent. On Saturday 260 — *all Democrats* — recd their papers." The atmosphere was electric: "Little knots of men at every corner. The political headquarters of the different parties thronged." In his letter to Polk on 2 November Gansevoort explained that he was leaving "town in a few moments" in order to speak at the "last rally of the Democracy of the powerful Whig county of Essex in New Jersey" — all but surely with both Herman and Allan in tow.

At that rally in Newark's Washington Hall, Gansevoort delivered a magnificent speech that ran over three hours. Bennett lavished most of a column to the speech on 5 November 1844 under these synoptic heads: "Great Meeting of the Democracy at Newark — Speech of Gansevoort Melville — The Men and Women of the West — Whigs taking Possession of Salt River — A Scene at the 'Hermitage' — The Spirit of the Old Man Still Lives." Gansevoort had "commenced by stating the issues involved in the present contest," explaining first the disastrous consequences that would follow the election of Clay and the reestablishment of a national bank. He defended the maintenance of the president's veto power against the Whig Henry Clay's "avowed opposition to it." He spoke about the "history, geographical position, and undeveloped resources of Texas, and defended at length the constitutionality and expediency of re-annexation." He broached a divisive subject: "He then entered into a very ingenious and lucid argument for the purpose of demonstrating that the annexation of Texas would necessarily lead to the gradual extinction of slavery in the slave-holding States, and their consequent vastly increased prosperity." Then, having dealt with issues much more closely than he had done early in the campaign, Gansevoort put on a show for the assembled Democrats and his astounded brothers.

Gansevoort roused his audience in extended compliments to the ladies and the men of Tennessee:

> Why, here, if a gentleman offers his hand to a fashionable lady she receives it in a sort of minimy pinimy, don't touch me sort of an air, that may perhaps affect him unpleasantly; but these Tennessee girls take right hold as if they meant it, and in a way that is really delightful to a plain, backward, bashful man like myself. (Great laughter and cheers) And then the Tennesseans of the man sex have peculiarities of manner which are decidedly interesting and characteristic. One of these peculiarities is, that they make a man talk such an unconscionable time. If a man gets up to speak, and they don't happen to like him, they soon shout out — "Hello, stranger, you've mistaken your vocation — slope!" (Roars of laughter.) And if he won't slope, they make him. (Renewed laughter) Tennessee is, indeed, the land of social democracy. I have seen men clad in linsey-woolsey garments, and with unshod feet, setting in Colonel Polk's parlor, and at the table of Andrew Jackson. (Loud cheers) They are ever frank and free in expressing their opinion, be it pleasant to the hearer or the reverse. On one occasion, after I had addressed a large popular assemblage, a sturdy frontier's man, who was about six feet high, without a superfluous ounce of flesh upon his stalwart frame, one of your men who never turn their backs on either friend or foe, and who looked as if he could whip his weight in wild cats, (laughter) strode up to me and grasped my hand with an iron energy that . . . reminded me forcibly of a vice [vise], and

suddenly withdrawing his grasp, slapped me on the back with tremendous force, sung out — "Old horse — I love you!" (Roars of laughter, repeated again and again.)

The peroration was an extended, powerful eyewitness testimony to the daily courage of Jackson the failing warrior, designed in part to refute Whig charges that his nephew Andrew Donelson was writing letters without Jackson's knowledge and signing the former president's name to them: "They were each and all either written by his own hand, or dictated by him and written under his own eye by Major Donelson. . . . To them all he has affixed his signature with his own hand."

Caught up in his own rhetoric, Gansevoort claimed to have been at the Hermitage when Jackson made his decision to preside at the mass meeting on 15 August. But Jackson had not left the Hermitage that day, and Gansevoort did not claim in so many words that the old warrior had in fact been carried to the meeting on the banks of the Cumberland. Having offered a vision of Jackson as willing martyr to the Democratic cause, Gansevoort exalted his audience with a patriotic vision of the manner in which the old Hero would die, when his time came:

> When Andrew Jackson dies, he will not drivel his path to the grave like a slobbering dotard, as the whig press falsely call him; but when HE dies — when the great soul within shall have utterly consumed its outer tenement of clay — why, then, a MAN will die! And our children, and children's children, will go up to that corner of the little garden at the Hermitage, where his wife now lies — and by whose side he will sleep in death — and that will forever be to us and our descendants, next to Mount Vernon, the holiest and most sacred spot on American soil.

As Gansevoort drew to a close the "manifestation of feeling amongst the audience" was "great." When Herman heard the speech in Newark, or when he read it, as he indubitably did a few days later in the *Herald* or another paper, amid his intense feelings, already, was the conviction that if he chose his topic wisely, he could write as eloquently as his older brother could speak.

Recognizing the historical value of Gansevoort's tribute to Andrew Jackson, the Washington *Globe* printed about the last half of the speech (more than half of what the *Herald* printed) under the heading "Scene at the Hermitage" on 8 November, three days after the election. There was a final rally on 3 November, Sunday, at Tammany Hall, with many speeches, in which a sprig of Young Hickory probably gave his last harangues of the campaign. (The wonder would be if Gansevoort had not marched Herman to the polls, for the only time in his life.) On Monday the fourth late in the evening "the dismal rain cleared away; the wind went round to the northwest, and the weather became suddenly cold," according to the *Evening Mirror*; election day was sunny and "glorious."

Six years and some months later, when he wrote his first "Knights and Squires" chapter (26) for *Moby-Dick*, Herman recalled Gansevoort and that magnificent night in Newark. This chapter justified Melville in advance if he were later to "ascribe high qualities" to "meanest mariners, and renegades and castaways" — that is, to ennoble American whalemen to the stature of tragic heroes. If he were to do that, "all mortal critics" might denounce him (as in fact the reviewer in the New York *Albion* had denounced him for just that kind of democratic idealism in *White-Jacket*), so his aesthetic justification could come only from the "Spirit of Equality":

> Bear me out in it, thou great democratic God! who didst not refuse to the swart convict, Bunyan, the pale, poetic pearl; Thou who didst clothe with doubly hammered leaves of finest gold, the stumped and paupered arm of old Cervantes; Thou who didst pick up Andrew Jackson from the pebbles; who didst hurl him upon a war-horse; who didst thunder him higher than a throne! Thou who, in all Thy mighty, earthly marchings, ever cullest Thy selectest champions from the kingly commons; bear me out in it, O God!

This passage is infused with disparate provocations, beginning with Melville's simple delight in his own exalted elaboration of the whimsical invocation in his source passage in Laurence Sterne's *Tristram Shandy* (bk. 9, ch. 25: "Gentle Spirit of sweetest humour," "Thou who . . . didst cast thy mystic mantle o'er his [Cervantes'] withered stump"). Still more, it was infused with anger at one particular reviewer; with inspiration from literary nationalists who had called for an American Shakespeare; and with ecstasy at his own knowledge of the grandeur of his achievement in his manuscript. But far behind it were the "mighty, earthly marchings" in Manhattan on 1 November 1844 (all the mightier for Greeley's ridicule). Behind it was the family model of Gansevoort's forging a high rhetorical style with literally a "mass" appeal (one in which he could celebrate the barefoot men in linsey-woolsey garments at Polk's table and at Jackson's table, and all but deify the man of the Hermitage as the American of all Americans capable of reluming "the fires of democratic impulses" in others). Behind it and infusing this magnificent passage in *Moby-Dick* was the bewildering, uplifting, almost supernaturally exciting night in Newark, New Jersey.

17

Catching Up

1844

in Saba here remain
Ten years; then back, the world regain —
Five minutes' talk with any one
Would put thee even with him, son.
Pretentious are events, but vain.

The abbot to Derwent, *Clarel*, bk. 3, canto 23

ON THE NIGHT OF WEDNESDAY, 6 November 1844, the impression was widespread in Manhattan that Henry Clay had won, and some incautious Whigs began celebrating. "Tammany Hall looked bleak," the *Evening Post* said the next day. The *Herald* on 7 November proclaimed: "EXTRAORDINARY EXCITEMENT! NEW YORK STILL IN DOUBT!" The *Post* of the eighth announced that the Democrats had won New York: the popular Silas Wright, candidate for governor, had carried the ticket. The *Plebeian* on 8 November bragged: "All is Well! The City of New-York has Saved the State, and perhaps the Union." The national election still was undecided, although Polk needed to win only one of the states that had not yet reported election figures — Georgia, Tennessee, Louisiana, Mississippi, Indiana, or North Carolina. The *Post* for 9 November had the news that North Carolina had gone for Polk, so the Democrats could at last rejoice.

Acquaintances in New York now had the chance to see the three Melville brothers together. Alexander Bradford, at least, knew the brothers from Clinton Square in Albany, a decade earlier, and now Gansevoort and Allan had a host of new acquaintances, some of whom later figured in national life, among them Sam Tilden, who had grown up in the interminable stretch between Albany and Pittsfield. Some of the friends of the lawyer brothers made a point of getting to know Herman as well, and at least Theodore E. Tomlinson and his wife became intimate with him. The brothers were memorable as a trio or in one or another pairing. Gansevoort, utterly driven by his ambition, focused, physically imposing (taller than Herman and Allan), was febrile and, beneath the courageous force, feeble. Herman was hopeful, but

not consumed by ambition and not settled on a way of making a living. He
was muscular, athletic, even gymnastic, constitutionally restless, and was
himself (as he wrote to Nathaniel Hawthorne on 29 June 1851) the victim of
"a very susceptible and peradventure febrile temperament." Much like Herman in appearance, Allan was an imitator of Gansevoort, of less towering
ambition but, like Gansevoort, absolutely focused, determined to be a well-
to-do lawyer, and willing to do whatever necessary to attain his less extravagant goals; physically inhibited if not actually lazy still, he would condescend
to take salt water baths near the Battery in the heat of the summer for the
sake of the exercise his mother advised, but never joyously, exuberantly.

Work in the office in Nassau Street was anticlimactic for Gansevoort,
who missed hustling Irishmen from dock to voting booth, addressing mass
meetings, and accepting adulation. He faded out of the news, although as late
as 28 November N. P. Willis and his associates at the *Evening Mirror* put into
"To-Day's floatage of News" a choice passage, probably picked up from the
Herald of 5 November: "Mr. Melville the democratic orator, was very much
surprised, after one of his speeches in the West, to be saluted by one of his
audience with a punch in the back and the exclamation of 'Old horse, I love
you.'" By this time, most newspapers had lost interest in an orator who was
no longer orating and an election that was won and lost. Deflated, Gansevoort waited to hear from Polk. Meanwhile, the lawyers had work to do.
With time on his hands, not looking for a job, as he had done at this season in
1840, Herman must have gone to Sweeny's to see if the same barker stood at
the entrance proclaiming "Rosebeefrosegoorosemuttonantaters" and if the
all but identical chops were available at the same cheap price. Sweeny's remained the restaurant where the "unwashed democracy" took their "six-
penny cuts" — Hiram Fuller's sneer in his New York *Evening Mirror* (19 September 1849, but just as true of 1840 or 1844). As always, Herman lived
frugally, but he was the sort of brother who had signed on a whaler without
paying his board at Mrs. Garahan's, and, under the circumstances, he may
have been a distraction and a drain on resources, as he had been four years
earlier. Soon he was more than a little in the way.

During these weeks Herman picked up from Gansevoort and Allan, busy
as they were, some information on topics too peripheral for Allan to have put
in his hasty letter to Boston. He could not hear enough of Helen's intimacy
with the Shaws. The previous February Lizzie had been extremely reluctant
to let Helen leave Boston, as Helen wrote: "Lizzie insists upon it, that she
will not let me until March; and that if I will *stay until June!*, she will go back
with me!" Helen had hoped that Gansevoort could come round by Boston
and take her with him on his way to Lansingburgh, but as it turned out Oakes
Shaw had escorted Helen to New York City on 21 February 1844, for a visit

to the Curtises before returning to Lansingburgh. While Helen was there members of the family had sent Herman "a number of letters," missives hopefully dispatched toward Honolulu. Oakes may have deceived his father about his reason for going to New York, but he had confided in Gansevoort, and on 10 May 1844 Gansevoort had done Judge Shaw an incalculable disservice.

Obliging Oakes, Gansevoort had written him an introduction to the Reverend Dr. Thomas E. Vermilye, the minister much respected by Maria, now removed to Manhattan. On 14 May Vermilye married John Oakes Shaw and the inopportunely pregnant Caroline Sarah Cobb — a covert, hasty wedding with no relative of the bridegroom present. (Vermilye prospered: the 1868 *Sunshine and Shadow in New York* said he was "in possession of a handsome fortune" and dwelt "in metropolitan style in the upper part of New York" — a far cry from his first position in a small Congregational church in Massachusetts. In 1872 he presided at Maria Gansevoort Melville's funeral, with John Oakes Shaw's sister, Elizabeth, among the mourners.)

Very likely ignorant of Gansevoort's role in Oakes's marriage, Shaw on 28 May 1844 had drafted a wounded but dignified letter to his oldest son: "unwilling as I am, to cast the slightest shade on the joyous feeling . . . yet I must be allowed to say . . ." Then he strove for a more conciliatory tone:

> Before this time, I presume you have arrived at your place of destination, which I earnestly hope, will prove a happy home. Your letter from New York, announcing your marriage, & your intended immediate departure, was duly received. On the same day it was received, we saw Mr Henry Connor, who gave us some further particulars. I was a little disappointed in not seeing you on my return from Worcester; I reached home on the evening of the same day, on the afternoon of which you left Boston. I thought you would either write to me or come by the way of Worcester and see me. As it was, the fact came upon me, at the time, with some surprise.

The judge's struggle for control left his syntax imperfect, but he wanted to say that it would certainly have given him "great pleasure to have become personally acquainted" with the lady whose destiny in life was now indissolubly connected with Oakes's. Shaw continued with his characteristic magnanimity in which, although being abused, he simply would not sound long-suffering: "I shall ever feel the most affectionate regard to one who is dear to you. I hope at some time to have an opportunity to express . . . this sentiment to your wife personally. I most earnestly hope & pray for the blessing of Heaven on you both, and on the union you have thus formed, that it may largely contribute to the happiness of both."

On 11 August Oakes wrote his father from Chicago with political news:

"We have just got through an Election Municipal & Congressional, in which the Whigs were whipped badly the Locos carrying everything but this is nothing new it always has been & always will be so, as long that foreigners & Paupers are allowed to vote & not only give one but half a dozen votes if they please, & when votes can be bought by any one who will condes[c]end to do it." Oakes was obliged to his father for his "kind remembrance" of Oakes's wife, and the wife also gratefully acknowledged the remembrance. Gansevoort had part of this story to relay to Herman, and Herman later learned a good deal about how the Shaws felt about their daughter-in-law, and once his and Oakes's paths crossed, Herman found himself in a not unfamiliar situation—becoming acquainted with someone who had known Gansevoort first and known him well. (Usually, the people who had known Gansevoort were themselves worth Herman's knowing; Oakes, the failed firstborn of a great man, may have resented the appealing young Herman even before he met him; later he seems to have hated him. In the 1920s Oakes's daughter took much trouble to blacken Melville's memory.)

Herman may have had a little money left from his discharge after the costs of his civilian clothing and his traveling, but he was, after all, another mouth to fill, and a capacious one. He went back home to Lansingburgh for a while soon after the election. There was room for him. If nothing else was empty, the unheated garret had headroom enough, but he could share a bed with Tom now, at a need. Gansevoort's room had been in the main part of the house because of his illnesses, and Herman had slept in the same bed with him at times, if not regularly. (Herman observed later, in *Moby-Dick*, perhaps with the obstreperous leg-flailing and snoring Allan uppermost in mind, that a man would a good deal rather not share a bed, even with his own brother.) If it had been April, Herman could have set to work in the garden alongside Tom, but this was the end of November, most likely, or early December, and there was nothing for him to do in particular, since Tom, quite a man, could chop whatever wood they needed to heat the house and do other chores. At home, not looking for work, Herman steadily caught up on more of the news.

The events of Melville family life had not been strange or tumultuous during Herman's own absence, aside from Guert's tragic experience, for the deaths in the family were to have been expected, even Mary Sanford Gansevoort's. After her death, Herman learned, Augusta had begged to be allowed to raise Kitty, but Peter had declined, preferring to keep Henry and Kitty with him. In a closer family, a widower such as Peter might have invited a beloved sister to come with her brood (in Maria's case four girls and an eleven-year-old boy) to take up residence in his house and care for his two children. That did not happen. A practical man, he knew he would remarry and that he could remarry well. His own two children filled the house to his satisfaction, and besides being concerned about them he was worried about some of his creditors, who in April were making threats to foreclose on Stanwix Hall.

In 1841 Maria had been left to worry about day-to-day expenses as well as the quarterly outlay for rent. Her older sons were no help: Gansevoort had been horribly seasick in the gulf, then stranded for some wretched weeks in New Orleans (without money to buy items he needed and to visit places of interest nearby); Herman had been even farther out of touch, whaling off the Bahamas. On 5 April 1841 Maria had written Peter that their Cousin Maggey could "no longer accommodate" Allan, who was "in her debt for several months board." She said Allan had been "very desirous" of staying with Peter — apparently staying in Peter's house for a time, although she may have meant merely working in his office:

> Mercenary help is not always true, & Peter you have known me from Childhood and have often heard Mamma say that we must always cling to each other as brothers and an only Sister should do — my dear brother I know you are in trouble and my heart is sad at the thought. . . .
>
> This world is fleeting, changing, & most uncertain. Allan is now growing up his habits & manners are forming, make a firm friend of Allan he has many, many good points about him, he may be of service to your Children when you are in the grave.

Peter had been unresponsive, and on 1 May (rent-payment day) Maria had consoled Allan for Peter's refusal to advance him some money. Now toward his Uncle Peter, Allan must show Christian restraint:

> As to your Uncle Peters indifference on last Sabbath Evening to your situation, I can have nothing to say, but I have felt that he perhaps did as he would not wish to be done by. May God forgive him as freely as I do. . . . I forgot to mention that you must not speak about your Uncles strange conduct nor even allow yourself to speak of him when you are angry. When you meet him bow to him politely but do not speak unless he first speaks to you, bear him no ill will, make it a principle to forgive others as you wish God to forgive you.

Young Allan and his uncle tried to tolerate each other, but both were stubborn, and neither wanted to be around the other for long.

Kate Gansevoort, Guert's sister, had married George Curtis, a lawyer able and willing to try to force Herman and Peter Gansevoort to settle the estate of Catherine Van Schaick Gansevoort. In Albany on 23 December 1841, Herman Gansevoort had responded to a bill of complaint in the suit brought in the New York state court of chancery by the widow and children of Leonard Gansevoort against Herman and Peter Gansevoort, executors of the estate of Catherine Gansevoort. Uncle Herman (responding for himself and his brother Peter) made an ugly, specious defense, as transcribed by Mabel C. Weaks from legal papers in the New York Public Library ("Some Ancestral Lines of Herman Melville as Traced in Funeral and Memorial Spoons"). Yes, he and his brother had not fulfilled the seventh clause of their mother's will regarding silver memorial spoons, but Mary Ann Chandonette Gansevoort and her children, including Kate (now Catherine Curtis), had made "no demand" for those spoons; furthermore it was his intention and Peter's that "as soon as the said estate should have been so far closed up and settled as to enable this defendant and the said Peter Gansevoort to take measures on a final distribution thereof to cause all the said spoons to be manufactured and delivered to the said Complainants." Herman had added gratuitously, if not cynically: "this defendant supposing from the fact that several of the legatees entitled to the said Spoons led a sea-faring life, and that the said Mary A. Gansevoort and the said Catharine Curtis were not permanently at house keeping that such delivery at the time of the said final distribution of the said residuary estates would prove satisfactory to the said Complainants."

Had Herman and Peter promptly settled their mother's estate, of course, Mary Ann Chandonette Gansevoort and her children might have had a permanent address and her sons might have gone to school, not to sea, and then might have gone into one profession or another. At year's end, 1841, Peter and Herman had successfully fought off legal efforts to force them to settle their mother's estate, and stalled another half decade at the cost of the permanent estrangement of Mary Ann's children from their Uncle Peter and Uncle Herman and at the cost of a long coolness between Maria's children and, at least, Uncle Peter (the one whom they blamed for keeping the estate unsettled). On 28 December 1841 Peter had turned his mind quite away from the distressed women and orphaned children: he had hosted at Stanwix Hall a celebration of the completion of the Western Railroad, which linked Albany directly with Boston along the stage route the Melvills had traversed many times, so slowly. Without Peter's protection, his Melville nephews and nieces had been beginning to lead their own lives: Gansevoort had been newly admitted to the bar; Helen had been launched in Boston society, for whatever good it might do her (she had attended a large ball the night Herman Gansevoort responded to that bill of complaint); Allan was in New York, less resentful, now that Gansevoort was there too; Augusta was in Bath, New York, visiting Gansevoort cousins; and Maria and her four younger children were in Lansingburgh. At the end of 1841, Herman was leading "a sea-faring life" in the Pacific, only God knew where.

From Gansevoort and Allan, and from the family at Lansingburgh, Herman gathered soon enough that the family finances were slightly improved. There had been a crisis late in 1841, during which (on 17 November) Peter drafted a letter to his sister: "The enormous note for upwards of Twenty thousand dollars, which I was compelled to give to the New York State Bank for you, falls due this day." Presumably he renewed the note and Maria went along as before. Early in February 1842, Gansevoort had written Helen the good news that "he had enclosed the greater half of a small fee, to Mama," and Helen had commented to Augusta, "small though it may have been, it was an earnest of better things for the future, and it is so long since there has been *anything* coming in, so long since we have had any one to look to for anything, that it glads my heart, to find that Gan is at last in the receipt of money, the avails of his own exertions. He says that his fees have so far paid his board." She continued: "May God bless him, and keep him from every evil, for we are all dependant on his exertions." Gansevoort on 13 July 1842 had written Lemuel Shaw a letter which must have reminded the judge of the letters Allan Melvill had written him in the 1820s. Gansevoort had hoped at best to do business enough to make four hundred dollars, the first year, eight hundred the second, then twelve hundred the third, but the results so far had surpassed his "humble expectations." "Moderate" or even "pitiful" as the actual figures were "in comparison with the emoluments of a long established and widely extended professional connexion," Gansevoort regarded them "with thankfulness as the first fruits of a soil" that he would till to the best of his powers. In November 1844 the lawyer brothers in New York were sending at least a little money home.

A year after Peter was left a widower, Maria may have heard a report that reached as far as Gansevoort, Saratoga County, a rumor disconnected from any proven pattern of Peter Gansevoort's behavior. Her brother Herman on 8 January 1842 wrote Peter that he had heard rumors "that Peter Gansevoort was broken down and not worth anything and that he was in the habit of frequent if not daily inebriation." Peter may have resorted to solitary drinking during which he distanced himself still further from Maria. Whatever the mixture of old and new causes, in the years of Herman's absence Maria's family had grown so estranged from Uncle Peter that when he finally decided it was time to marry Susan Yates Lansing, Helen took a high tone in a letter to Augusta from Boston (1 December 1843): "So a day has been at last fixed upon for Uncles wedding! I would like to be present, and I hope for your sake that he will have the politeness and consideration to ask our family at least" — if not Mary Chandonette Gansevoort's family. It seemed to her that Peter could not "do less." After she received Augusta's eyewitness account of the wedding, Helen wrote: "You must have had a very pleasant time at that wedding Gus. I should have liked to have been there. When I return home, or rather on my way, I want to stay a day in Albany, that I may call upon our new Aunt Susan, and upon Kate Yates. I have no doubt that Mrs Peter Gansevoort will be a great acquisition to the family and modify Uncles selfishness, if she cannot entirely eradicate his besetting sin. I long to see her." As far as Peter Gansevoort was concerned, he was a man who had been grossly abused by his brother-in-law over the period of a decade and more and since 1832 had been laboring single-mindedly to safeguard the remnant of his father's once great estate and to set the foundation for his own future security. The Melville children, and the late Leonard Gansevoort's children, knew only that he had failed to help them when a pittance would have kept them in school and given them chances in life. His "besetting sin" was, and remained for years, selfishness, and Herman, three and a half decades later, sounded very much like Helen in attributing a remarkably generous act of his uncle's to the benign influence of the spirit of Aunt Susan. Until his mother and Allan Melvill had both died, Peter had not had a life of his own, and he had found that he liked having one.

Now in late 1844 Herman quickly accustomed himself to the changes in the Lansingburgh household. Physically maturing already, promising to be stalwart, Tom was drawn to the sea. He all but worshiped Herman, it seemed, and he was easy with Maria and the girls. Healthy like Herman, he did not know what physical suffering was, as Gansevoort did, and never had an occasion for whining, such as Allan still found. He had never known anything but poverty, so he had never been embittered by the fall from riches and privilege. He had no memory of any father but Gansevoort. Having been adored for a decade and a half by his mother, brothers and sisters, and assorted cousins, he was what he had been at one and two years old — loving, confident, adorable, destined to be for his generation what Uncle Herman was for his, the most "pleasant man in a family."

Nineteen-year-old Kate was a frequent visitor to Maria's cousins the Van Vechtens in Albany, where she was great friends with young Catherine. (The lady of the house, Catherine Gansevoort Van Vechten, wife of Teunis Van Vechten, mayor when the Melvilles moved to Lansingburgh and again 1841–42, was Maria's first cousin, a daughter of the Leonard Gansevoort who was brother to the Hero of Fort Stanwix.) More nervous than the other girls, and more critical, Kate already had begun to manifest a curious variation on a pattern in her mother's behavior. In any especially dire financial crisis Maria put her mind to controlling all her children's behavior much more minutely than usual. Lacking Maria's scope, Kate asserted order in a disordered universe by arranging her part of the world meticulously. Before long, her need to have the castor at just the right angle to the napkins was obsessive, uncomfortable to watch, even to those who loved her, and a great strain on those with no special duty to love her.

Seventeen-year-old Fanny had grown into a young woman of middle height, slender, with brown hair, blue eyes (like Helen and Kate), a pert upturned nose, rosy lips, a wide mouth, and quite large white teeth (her own description in an essay entitled "Myself," which she let Augusta keep and which was among the papers acquired by the New York Public Library in 1983). She was a reader, like the rest of the family ("Of reading I am extravagantly fond and desire no better companion than a book"). She was afflicted with a "retiring" disposition to the point of being almost pathologically shy, although she thought of herself as being sociable, as manifesting the sort of sociability, she decided, that consisted in taking pleasure in sitting and observing others rather than taking part in conversations. Almost a liability when it came to entertaining strangers, Fanny was easy for members of the family to be around.

The older sisters were the least changed, to outward appearances. Helen had been capable of fulfilling any role in life open to a woman, if she had been given her chance in time. To all appearances she had not profited from her opportunities in Boston, as far as Maria was concerned, since she had not received a proposal from one of the young Bostonians to whom she had been introduced. Augusta's adventures were easily told. She had been away so much that Helen referred to her as the gypsy sister, or her dark gypsy sister (from her eyes, brown instead of the usual blue). Visiting the great Van Rensselaer Manor House when Herman left for the Pacific, she had become, as the years passed, an intimate of Cornelia (Nilly) and Justine (Teny), especially. Augusta had also made one or two long visits to distant Gansevoort cousins at distant Bath, in western New York, but she was more often at the Van Rensselaer house, where she had become indispensable to the comfort of Stephen Van Rensselaer and his wife, Harriet Elizabeth Bayard Van Rensselaer, both of whom shared her quiet piety. No one at the Manor House put menial duties upon her, but Augusta was unsurpassable in a sickroom, and Maria's training had equipped her to direct servants in all aspects of husbandry. Soon one of the many chambers was simply designated as "Gus's room," waiting for her whenever she would come. The Van Rensselaers saw that she enjoyed outings, including one to Beverswick, the seventy-two-room mansion built above Rensselaer for William P. Van Rensselaer, the heir to the manor land east of the Hudson. (Helen wrote her from Boston: "I have always had a great desire to see the interior of that spacious mansion, and your description, has given a new zest to my curiosity.") A more unworldly young woman than any of her sisters except Fanny, Augusta made the friends of highest rank and the most durable friends of all the girls.

Over the next years Herman escorted Augusta several times to the Manor House and got his own sense of the almost Old World splendor of the place. Without complaint he had slept hundreds of nights in crowded forecastles, but at some level he felt that by birth he was entitled to live out his life in a house such as the Market Street mansion or Whitehall. The first time Herman saw the manor after his return was a shock, since the transformation of the eighteenth-century structure had been completed in 1843. As Cuyler Reynolds described the renovation in the *Hudson-Mohawk Genealogical and Family Memoirs* (1911), the "wings had been torn down, the whitestone had been removed and replaced with brown New Jersey sandstone, and the great wings and porch in front had been added." The exterior brick was covered with "sanded mastic," and "the new stone-work was for the most part of a strictly classical design; but in gables and belt courses a distinctly Gothic tendency prevailed." The great hall, twenty-four feet wide, ran a full forty-six feet front to back, and there were deep window seats on either side of the front and rear doors. The walls were still decorated with frescoes from Holland first installed in 1768, and the stairs were lit by a window displaying the family coat-of-arms, in colors, like the window a member of the family had placed in the Albany Dutch church in 1656. In the main hall were two alabaster urns a few inches taller than Herman (he acquired a smaller one before he died), and two large bronze equestrian statues, one depicting Chevalier Bayard. What with carved wood, oil paintings, and a vast library, this was very much the sort of place Herman would have liked to live in.

One of the Van Rensselaer daughters, Margaret (Maggie) had married a cousin of hers, John De Peyster Douw, and had set up housekeeping in what Gansevoort (in January 1843) had described to Allan as their "beautiful home on Clinton Square" in Albany (where Maria had lived before moving to Lansingburgh, and where Peter had lived). In Gansevoort's admiring eyes, there were "few more agreable, stylish or high-bred women" than Cousin Maggie. The Douws (both cousins of Maria's) had two children and seemed happy. What a mere man like Gansevoort was oblivious to at the Douw house, Augusta had learned a good deal about from her intimate visits with Maggie's family. That fall she wrote Helen at the Shaws' about the situation, alluding to it rather than describing it, for whatever Cousin John had done wrong or wanted Maggie to do, it was sexual in nature, and it could not be written down. Cousin Maggie's plight concerned Augusta and Helen for the next several years, and at more dramatic moments engaged Maria's objective attention. Helen at one point (14 January 1844) seemed to have the most reliable information:

The night we passed in Albany, Mrs Van Vechten told me the true state of the case between Margaret Douw & her husband. I do pity her from my heart. It is another sad warning to all girls, not to marry men so far inferior to them in intellect, that they cannot understand the workings of a really noble and generous mind, nor appreciate the motives that actuate the conduct of a really pure hearted woman. God help her! poor girl, she will have little more comfort in this world. Her despicable husband less, for if he has a conscience it will smite him 'till his dying day.

What horror John had committed remains unnamed, but Nilly, at least, thought it did not amount to grounds for a separation. The tragic estrangement and its aftermath surfaced repeatedly in the letters of the next years, and reached one of its climaxes during the composition of *Moby-Dick*, a few months before Melville wrote the Patroons into *Pierre*. (Maggie and John's marital distress eventuated, decades later, in family books and papers, including letters from Augusta, being inherited by a Van Rensselaer grandson, Cousin Walter Berry, remembered now as the consort of Edith Wharton. Some of the papers and books, taken to Paris, passed into the possession of a great-grandson of Augusta's patron Stephen Van Rensselaer, mad Cousin Harry Crosby, the subject of Geoffrey Wolff's *Black Sun*.)

Herman was slow to piece together any recent account of his Uncle Thomas, since he remained the one who had last been to Galena. With no good news to relay, Lemuel Shaw could have hinted to Herman that his uncle was still in severe financial straits, and he could indicate a general dissatisfaction with the state of affairs on the farm without telling Herman confidences better left unshared. In the matter of Uncle Thomas's thievery, who knew what, and when, and who knew what others knew is quite obscure. When Shaw saw Robert in Lenox in September of 1840, Shaw probably did not know that Thomas Melvill Jr. had been fired for stealing from his employer in Galena, but Robert probably did know, and took that into account in delaying his promised move to Galena. However, he did not scruple to accept money from Shaw to help him meet the expense of moving. Shaw's magnanimous behavior to Gansevoort early in 1841, when he advanced him $150 to pay for the voyage to New Orleans, had occurred at a time when he was wholly unaware that Robert had taken the money but had not left Pittsfield. Just afterward, on 27 January 1841, Shaw had drafted a furious letter to Robert: "From a gentleman whom I met in the street today, I learned with equal surprise and disappointment, that you were still in Pittsfield." Shaw was angry enough to make demands he knew could not be met: "I must . . . pray you to write me immediately, & clear up this seeming mystery, & also return me the money, which I advanced solely for the purpose of enabling you to take that journey, which you regard as so interesting to your father's family and your own." On 31 January Robert replied with a characteristically garrulous, querulous letter about his "prepperations" to go west, in which confession and repentance mingled with defensiveness, a letter written under the severe disadvantage of defending himself for not going to Galena without telling Shaw the main reason he was reluctant to go — his father's disgrace.

Soon afterward Shaw's agent in Pittsfield, Henry Colt, had weighed in with discouraging news about repairs on the Melvill "Mansion" and outbuildings. Toward the end of April Thomas Melvill Jr. likewise poured bad tidings out to Shaw. For nearly seven months he had been "confined to the House," in the course of which the physicians discovered and removed a painful abscess in the abdomen. He had not heard from Robert for over half a year, but had heard from his younger son John, also in Pittsfield, of a misunderstanding between the brothers. Thomas reported that John honorably had expressed "a disinclination to return to Illinois, untill he can earn the means to pay his passage out *himself*," news Shaw must have taken skeptically. In the meantime, Thomas enlisted Shaw's help in finding John scope for his "very considerable *mechanical genius*," but attempts to place him in a "*Machine making Shop, at Lowell*," failed, and not from any fault of John's. In the summer Thomas reported bad news from Galena: "We continue to be frequently annoyed with Fever & Ague — rarely a fortnight elapses, without one, or more of us being down with it. — Julia, has suffered the most, by reason of an inflamation of the eyes, supposed to have been caused by it." Robert soon wrote Shaw that Thomas Melvill Jr. was in precarious health and that his brothers in Galena could not find work; he asked for Shaw's assistance in bringing the family back to Pittsfield.

In July 1841 Shaw held court in New Bedford. He later learned that young Thomas Melvill, the alcoholic midshipman and whaler, had caught sight of him there in time to dodge out of the way and even leave town for several days, explaining, prideful dissolute as he was, "that he would never see any of his friends until he could see them in better circumstances." The informant said, nevertheless, that he thought Thomas was "less intemperate than usual," although as a matter of course the whaleman "had spent all the proceeds of his former voyage." As Shaw learned a few months later, Thomas had sailed out again on 21 July in the *Oregon*. Repeatedly, Shaw had reason to justify his sponsorship of the purposeful Gansevoort Melville even as he felt wrung by the importunities and excuses of the Melvills, who justified year by year the pronouncement the Reverend Mr. Edward Ballard made on 4 September 1841: "Calamity appears to be the lot of that family."

In September 1841 Helen and Gansevoort had brought back to Lansingburgh from Pittsfield news from Robert about the family in Galena —

news so bad that, despite their own financial straits, Maria and her children took on the task of heartening the Galena contingent (so Helen wrote to Augusta on 10 October): "We were very busy last week in preparing a large package to send Uncle Tom's family at Galena, Mama wrote Aunt Mary, Cousins Priss & Anne will have immense letters from me, Kate wrote a note to Julia, and Fanny to Helen. We have sent remembrances to each in company with the letters, and I hope that they will prove acceptable." In Galena the disgraced Thomas Melvill Jr. had begun 1842 with a pitiable appeal to Shaw that he solicit fifty dollars from each of the four Melvill sisters; without waiting for permission, he had drawn thirty-five dollars on Shaw's account, an action he justified with the knowledge that Shaw could eventually reimburse himself out of income received by the estate of the old major. Thomas was ill, unemployed, contemplating taking in "4, 5, or 6 day boarders, as a resource in aid of the support of my family — which by reason of the low price of provisions, (Bread & Meat) can be done to advantage." To that end, he expected the chief justice to go down to the wharfs and select "some *pickled fish* — as per note at foot, to be shipped *to New Orleans*, for *Th Melvill, Galena Ill.*" He lamented not hearing from the D'Wolfs for years ("I take it for granted they are willing to forget us"). Anxious lest his appeal had miscarried, and probably more anxious lest Shaw ignore it for a time, Thomas had written again on 14 January 1842, now acknowledging that he had been nearly two years ill, with family members ill, and "without steady employment." In this letter he indulged in wishful thinking about an object of value he had left at the farm, "a miniature Ship, which was made by my Prisoners in the last War — & for which I was induced to pay them, about what they considered the value of it — namely $75." Ideally he could have presented it "to the Seamans friend Society — but, '*circumstances alter cases,*'" and he wanted to sell it for twenty-five dollars to a citizen of Pittsfield, but another townsman (in the sort of complication Thomas Jr. mired himself in) was claiming "*that the Ship is his,* — on what authority I know not." According to the definition of value worked out by Thomas and his brother Allan in 1821, the value of the ship, whoever owned it, was exactly what it would bring, not what Thomas long before had been induced to pay for it.

In a letter on 17 January 1842 Shaw had reproached Robert again for taking $250 on the pretext of using it for his removal to Galena; ten days short of a year, Shaw's outrage had not abated. On 2 February 1842 (about the time of the birth of his son, Allan Ezekiel, who lived only until 21 August), Robert wrote to Lemuel Shaw, abasing himself but not returning the money. On 15 March 1842 from Galena Thomas Melvill Jr. placed Robert's behavior as the last item in a woeful litany: "I acknowledge that his having given up his journey, West, after being fully prepared for it, would evince an unstable disposition—Still I think great allowances are to be made for his peculiar situation, owing principally to the health of his wife." In the strain of keeping the disgrace secret, the Galena Melvills had fallen silent, and had lost touch with the Melvilles: on 29 June 1842 Julia Maria, woeful now but still bravely facetious, wrote Augusta that for the last year her time had been "fully occupied in shaking, and recovering from the ague." She had not known that Herman had been at sea for a year and a half, but after learning it "quite accidentally" she decided that "the Melvill family resemble the Jews in one particular, they are to be found in every part of the world."

Early in November 1842 Cousin John Scollay Melvill had arrived in Galena from a trip to Pittsfield with a report of decaying outbuildings on the farm as well as damage to the house, which Thomas Melvill Jr. described to Lemuel Shaw on 30 November as being "occupied by 3 famillies," "two at least, of the inner rooms" being used "for cooking purposes"—an evident danger. Henry Colt, Shaw's man in Pittsfield, wrote on 31 July 1843: "Mr Robert Melvill left Pittsfield a few days since rather *suddenly*," leaving his family there—a discreet way of implying that Robert had left a trail of debts. He had left, in particular, a mortgage deed for six hundred dollars with Colt, in favor of Shaw and D'Wolf as trustees, for his interest in the Melvill estate, which Colt had at once sent to Lenox to be recorded. In Galena, with Robert on his hands by early August, Thomas Jr. ran for justice of the peace, an effort he described to Shaw on 6 September 1843 as undertaken only "at the earnest solicitations of some valued friends of the Whig party who were anxious there might be one business man, in that office, altho' I was confident there was but little chance of success." He lamented, with a lamentable pun, that in the primary he was crushed by "the overwhelming force, of the whole *Catholic alien vote*, which can be brought to bear *in a mass* in all our elections, on the side of the self-styled democratic party—or more properly Jacobins, thro' the influence of the *Priests*." He added: "Success, would have been both gratifying, and interesting to me. *The people* in Illinois, may yet find out that Irish & German rule, is neither pleasant, profitable, or republican, and learn wisdom from experience." This was a losing battle, outside the family and within it. By the time Herman returned, the contact between Maria's family and Uncle Thomas's family had faded away again, so that oddly enough Herman remained the one who had seen Uncle Thomas and Aunt Mary most recently.

Gansevoort and Herman knew Washington Irving's already classic New York story of Rip Van Winkle, who took some time after his long sleep before he could get into the regular track of gossip, or could be made to comprehend the bewildering events that had taken place during his absence. Little by little in the weeks after the election, in New York City and in

Lansingburgh, Herman caught up on the most momentous family events that had occurred in his absence, and got into the regular track of gossip, though chances are that for years someone would make a remark that bewildered him because it took for granted that he knew what the rest of the family knew. His face would have been worth watching the first time someone alluded, offhand, to the arrival of the spectral syphilitic and alcoholic remittance man Uncle Wessel in the fall of 1842, prepared to spend the winter with his loving sister Maria. Herman had been away a long time.

18

The Sailor at the Writing-Desk
1844–1845

Each goodly thing is hardest to begin

Checked by Melville in *The Faerie Queene*, I, 10, vi
(Priscilla Ambrose Collection)

MELVILLE HAD SPUN HIS YARNS about the Typees for two years, but "it was entirely being urged by his family to write about his wonderful [adventures] especially his sister Augusta, that he began to write." This family version of how he became a writer was recorded by his niece Charlotte Hoadley, daughter of Kate Melville, on 14 February 1944, a century after Melville's return from the Pacific. Her assertion is the more believable because Charlotte as a young woman overheard many private conversations between her mother and her aunts, and because after he wrote *Typee* Melville in fact gave Augusta (rather than another member of the family) the first draft, carefully labeling it for the personal archive she had been assembling for a decade, since her early childhood. Melville's first biographer, his friend Joseph (J. E. A.) Smith, who after 1850 met all the family except Gansevoort, gave this account in the 21 November 1891 Pittsfield *Evening Journal*:

> He was now 25 years old and, with little disposition to return to the sea, was considering what pursuit in life he should choose. . . . One could not well see to what profession he was adapted. A chance word decided it.
>
> The family had given their interesting wanderer a warm welcome home, and one day one of them, or one of their intimate friends said to him: "Why don't you put in book form that story of your South Sea adventures which we all enjoy so much?" He at once accepted the suggestion.

When the poet and editor Nathaniel Parker Willis, a friend first of Gansevoort's and then of Herman's, reviewed *Redburn* in the *Home Journal* (24 November 1849), he asserted as a fact that Melville had "beguiled the long winter hours of his own home circle" with the incidents of his Marquesan adventures, later "printed at their request."

Whatever the exact timing of Augusta's importunities and the appeals of other family members and the advice of others such as Lemuel Shaw, Herman may have decided before reaching home, on the basis of the demand for his stories on shipboard, that his adventures among the cannibals would make a good book. He had been, after all, a published author on both sides of the Hudson even before his first voyage to Liverpool, and four years at sea had left him less prepared than ever to earn his living ashore. Now, by virtue of having a "rich and peculiar experience in life" (*Pierre*, bk. 18) to write about, and having nothing better to do ashore, Herman decided to take up authorship — perhaps for the nonce only, mindful of the author of *Two Years before the Mast*.

Financially speaking, there was no good reason for Melville to think of writing more than one book. In the New York *Weekly Mirror* for 12 October 1844, a copy of which must have lain around more than one house or office Melville entered, Willis had printed, on the basis of becoming his own publisher, an article on "Authors' Pay in America." The gist of his argument was that publishers exploited their authors, "the seller of the book being paid *from twice to five times as much* as the author of it!" Still more dismaying was Willis's "The Pay for Periodical Writing," in the *Weekly Mirror* for 19 October 1844, just when Herman reached New York City. Authorship, knowledgeable people must have told Gansevoort, Allan, and Herman, was not a way of making a living in America. However, the reputation as a man who had written a book might be very useful in advancing a career in some other area of life, as Shaw had probably advised Herman in Boston.

While the final decision to write up his adventures may have been made in Lansingburgh, Herman did not act on that decision there, for he later specified that he began writing *Typee* in New York City during the winter of 1844–45. He had returned to Manhattan by late November or early December 1844. In Gansevoort's and Allan's law office at the head of Nassau Street there was paper, pen, and writing surface to spare, so Herman most likely wrote there, doing his best to ignore the occasional client or one of Gansevoort's political visitors (he recalled some of the odder ones nine years later in "Bartleby" as the ward politicians who came calling on Nippers). Inevitably, he was caught up in his older brother's anxiety. Gansevoort waited until 17 December to congratulate president-elect James K. Polk: "Being well aware that the favorable result of the Presidential canvass would cause you to be for a time fairly overwhelmed with letters of congratulation and business from all parts of the country I have purposely abstained until the present moment from tendering my warm political and personal congratulations." To let himself fade from the mind of the president-elect was a calculated risk, and Gansevoort at this time was nothing if not calculating. The next day he wrote to William E. Cramer: "Today is the day of the election in the different wards for delegates to the Committees at Tammany Hall. I was a member last year having carried my ward at 24 hours notice by over 60 majority in a poll of 310 votes. This year I have positively declined running." Gansevoort now wanted a national office. As Gansevoort played his waiting game and passed slowly from exultation to controlled panic, Herman did his best to focus on his manuscript.

Herman's education owed more to what he had absorbed in a literate family and to the haphazard acquisitions of an alert mind than to his catch-as-catch-can months of formal schooling after his father died, but in his quiet way he had his share of the family confidence that Gansevoort so histrionically displayed. He had the advantage of having rehearsed some episodes of his story many times, and promptly enough he made sure that printed sources would be helpful, particularly a book with the strongest family connection, G. H. von Langsdorff's *Voyages and Travels*. Herman's first cousin Langsdorff D'Wolf by his very name was a constant reminder that Uncle John had spent the winter of 1805 in primitive, leaky quarters in Norfolk Sound, Alaska, with the famous scientific traveler. There the two had become "almost inseparable, participating both in each others' pleasures and troubles," according to the memoir D'Wolf published decades later. In Melville's childhood Uncle John had told him stories of his own voyage and land travel in Russia with Langsdorff, and he probably told stories of his friend's other adventures as set out in the book that lay in a place of honor in the house on Narragansett Bay when Herman summered there. D'Wolf would have owned the 1813 London edition, which contained awe-inspiring engravings of tattooed Polynesians. Soon a Philadelphia company reprinted the book, without the fine engravings, so the Melvills of Green Street and Herman's father may have had either edition around the house. Herman may well have seen a copy at his Uncle Thomas's in his adolescence, just when certain passages would have proved remarkably titillating. Before he got very far into the composition of *Typee*, Melville had a copy of Langsdorff's book in his hands.

A connoisseur already of the psychological phenomenon of overlapping images, Herman had remembered Langsdorff in 1842 as the *Acushnet* approached Nukahiva. Now, late in 1844, in the light of what he had witnessed himself, he reread Langsdorff's account of the welcome the ship received at "Nukahiwa" in 1804:

A number of the islanders, a short time after came from the opposite shore of the harbour, which was to the north-west, and swam to the place where we were anchored, a distance of three miles. At first we could only see a shoal of black-haired heads just above the water; but in a short time we had the very extraordinary spectacle presented us of some hundred men, women, girls, and boys, all swimming about the ship, having in their hands cocoa-nuts, bread-fruit, and bananas, which they had brought to sell.

The cries, the laughter, the romping of these mirthful people, was inde-scribable, and made a very novel impression upon us. . . . The young girls and women were not more clothed than the men, and were collected even in greater numbers. They were above all loud and noisy, and, according to our European ideas, immodest. They burst into a loud laugh at the most trifling things; and as we did not understand a word of the many comic effusions addressed to us, their oratory was illustrated with pantomimic gestures, by which we were sufficiently given to understand that they were making us the most liberal and unreserved offers of their charms. The men who were with them did not shew the slightest symptoms of jealousy, but rather seemed pleased and flattered when a wife, a daughter, or a sister, attracted our particu-lar attention.

Perhaps a bit more restrained than the crews of American whaling ships, the sailors had taken stock of the situation momentarily, while Langsdorff, at least, made what he called "philosophical observations upon our new Ven-uses." Then those Venuses had "vanished, hand-in-hand with the sailors, to the interior of the ship, while the goddess of night threw her dark veil over the mysteries that were celebrated." Melville knew that Langsdorff did not mean that they waited for night; he meant that the sailors sought partial privacy with their Venuses in the dark interior of the ship rather than coup-ling with them on the deck, as often happened.

After his own Pacific voyaging, Melville looked with a would-be profes-sional eye at Langsdorff's other chapters on the Marquesas Islands. All in all, Langsdorff offered a vast amount of material ready for Herman to use — elaborate accounts of tattooing, for instance. Herman knew of still other accounts of the Marquesas, even if he did not have them immediately at hand, so he was confident, from the start of his work on *Typee*, that he would not have to rely on his own unaided memory or printed sources still wholly unknown to him. Writing this book would be something he could do.

By the start of 1845 Herman had been in New York City for some time, judging by Helen's letter on 2 January 1845 to Augusta, who was back at the Van Rensselaer Manor House. Herman remained there, writing, for he was in New York City on 20 January when he wrote a long letter to his next-to-youngest sister, Kate, who was making a prolonged visit to her cousin Kate Van Vechten in Albany. The pretext for the visit had been that Kate was pallid and needed a change of scene: that spring she would turn twenty, and perhaps she could find a husband in timely fashion, even if it meant leaving two older sisters still unmarried. Mindful of the Catherines of different generations in the Van Vechten house, Herman began his letter with an elaborate jeu d'esprit on his love of the name "Kate" and all persons who bear the name. There is nothing in this Shakespearean literary exercise that directly relates it to the manuscript he was already writing, except for an appreciation of feminine beauty and charm which links his sister and her friends to the nymphs of the Marquesas Islands ("What! Face, neck & bosom all bathed in glowing floods of vermillion! — Verily, Modesty is the cheifest attribute of the Kates"). One offhand and perhaps self-mocking comment indicates that he may have begun taking himself seriously as an author: "You know you can put this letter of mine, among your things — Can't you?" The implication is that Kate had followed Augusta's, and probably Helen's, example and had begun to preserve her correspondence, as a young lady should do.

For months the three brothers were together in New York City, Herman writing. As the days passed, Gansevoort chafed more and more to receive his reward from Polk. In late January he "paid a flying visit to Washington" to try to establish his claims for a political appointment (as he informed William E. Cramer on 7 February). There Gansevoort had "quite a talk" with old John Quincy Adams, on whom he had called with his father two decades before. Making and keeping contacts, as always, he managed to speak confidentially with "other celebrities" (such as Andrew Stevenson of Virginia, the former Speaker of the House). As a result of his neglect of his legal business he was in such bad financial straits that on 1 February a creditor, George P. Nelson, accepted $17.54 — ten cents on the dollar — as settlement of what Gansevoort owed him. Herman witnessed the legal document that Allan drew up — a miserable duty that reminded him of the time he witnessed a similar document for his mother in 1837, her bond "in the sum of Fifty thousand dollars" to the New York State Bank. In mid-February Gansevoort left his brothers for a trip to Albany, where he fulfilled his promise to William E. Cramer of "an old fashioned confab." Then, while Allan took care of what legal business there was and Herman continued to write up his experiences with the Typees, Gansevoort went to Washington City (this time on a less rushed visit) to attend the inauguration on 4 March and to collect his spoils. From there he handled some business — sending Lemuel Shaw a note for $500 which the judge discounted, so that on 24 April Gansevoort had $487.75 to send to Allan. Cousin Guert was also seeking a favor from Washington; on 2 April Uncle Peter asked his old friend William L. Marcy, the new secretary of war, to rescue Guert from his purgatorial station on the receiving ship *Ohio* in the navy yard at Charlestown and let him go to sea again, now that the hangings on the *Somers* were more than two years in the past.

When James K. Polk became president he ignored "the orator of the

human race." Back in New York, Gansevoort began waging a carefully coordinated wire-pulling campaign. First he assiduously collected letters recommending him for the post of marshal of New York. When he had the letters
in hand, Gansevoort made a "Memorandum list of letters relative to Gansevoort Melville of the City of New York," thirty-two letters from an eminent
group. Among them was Uncle Peter's brother-in-law (by his first wife)
Edward Sanford, young Henry and Kate's uncle, still close enough to the
family that Allan had included him in his round-up informational letter to
Herman, as if he were their blood uncle also. "For several years Member of
the Legislature & candidate in Nov '44 for the State Senate from the city
of N. Yk.," according to Gansevoort's list, Sanford now reminded Polk of
Gansevoort's high qualities of "head and heart," and said he knew "of no
gentleman who in the same space of time, has, by the exercise of superior
cleverness established a more sure foothold in the confidence and esteem of
the Democratic party in the City of New York." Sanford like Gansevoort was
pushing himself, rather than coasting through life on his position as the son
of a former chancellor. Young Oakey Hall (later New York district attorney
and then mayor), who had clerked in the Sanford office, said a few years later
that Sanford's "chrome yellow skin and sunken eyes admit that the proud
station which he occupies at forty years of age was not reached without weary
climbing" (the New Orleans *Commercial Bulletin*, 13 February 1850).

Other letters were from Horatio Seymour, "Speaker of the Assembly";
Auguste Davezac, "Late a member of the Legislature" (Jackson's death at the
Hermitage on 8 June 1845 would leave Davezac the best-known living hero
of the great Battle of New Orleans); Lewis Cass of Michigan, who reminded
Polk of Gansevoort's "high moral and intellectual qualities"; William C.
Bouck, former governor of New York, who had not given Herman a job on
the Erie Canal when he needed one; and Stephen Cambreling, master in
chancery in New York City. Charles O'Conor ("*The* leading democratic
lawyer of the N. Yk. bar") wrote: "Mr. Melville has held a public office
requiring the employment of patient attention and sound discrimination in
legal questions. In the performance of his duties these qualities were displayed in so large a degree as to excite general approval and to overwhelm
him with occupations." O'Conor added: "As a public speaker Mr. Melville
has given to his fellow citizens throughout the union ample proofs that he is
possessed of talents of the highest order; and by uniform courtesy and kindness in his private and official intercourse has secured the good will of all
parties here." Stephen A. Douglas (congressman from Illinois) reminded
Polk that Gansevoort's appointment would be "gratifying to those of us
whose good fortune it was to canvass the western country with him," and (he
added in a postscript) "would be particularly gratifying to the young Democ-

racy of the country." Marcus Morton, former governor of Massachusetts, now the newly appointed collector of the port of Boston, wrote on Gansevoort's behalf, perhaps because he had met Gansevoort at the Shaw house, where his daughter Susan Morton had wintered, just as Helen had. District attorney Benjamin F. Butler gave his support, despite any lingering resentment for Gansevoort's exposure of the secret circular, and Edwin Croswell wrote the president that Gansevoort had "made his own way by the force of his fine powers & his just perceptions of character & duty, to a position of high respectability & deserved prominence"—a fair account of Gansevoort as a self-made man. As he witnessed Gansevoort's efforts, Herman could take some satisfaction that in his less spectacular way he was himself attempting now to rise to a position of respectability by the force of his own "fine powers" with words.

Of Melville's initial efforts at *Typee*, sixteen leaves are known to survive, at least fifteen because Melville gave his first draft to Augusta, who died in 1876—on Staten Island, but when her home and Fanny's was what had been Uncle Herman's house at Gansevoort. No one claimed her papers, and sometime after Fanny's death they were apparently pushed from the living areas of the house to make room. Some of them survived for a century in the area (although a great mass was probably hauled to a local dump in the 1950s). In 1983 the New York Public Library acquired a remnant stored in a nearby barn, including the fifteen leaves from the draft of *Typee*. A single leaf (two pages) from the same draft had long been owned by the New York Public Library, perhaps removed from Herman's bundle as a gift from Augusta to Uncle Peter's daughter, Kate (the "Kitty" whom she had volunteered to raise when Aunt Mary Sanford Gansevoort died).

The sixteen leaves (thirty-two pages) are from three chapters, 12, 13, and 14 in the final numbering. Their content (even at this draft stage) is already pretty much the content summarized in the synoptic headings used in the first edition: chapter 12—"Officiousness of Kory-Kory. His Devotion. A Bath in the Stream. Want of Refinement of the Typee Damsels. Stroll with Mehevi. A Typee Highway. The Taboo Groves. The Hoolah Hoolah Ground. The Ti. Time-worn Savages. Hospitality of Mehevi. Midnight Misgivings. Adventure in the Dark. Distinguished Honors paid to the Visitors. Strange Procession and Return to the House of Marheyo"; chapter 13—"Attempt to procure Relief from Nukuheva. Perilous Adventure of Toby in the Happar Mountain. Eloquence of Kory-Kory"; and chapter 14—"A great Event happens in the Valley. The Island Telegraph. Something befalls Toby. Fayaway displays a tender heart. Melancholy reflections. Mysterious Conduct of the Islanders. Devotion of Kory-Kory. A rural Couch. A Luxury. Kory-Kory strikes a Light *à la* Typee." If Melville had retained the spellings in the draft, the book might have been called *Tipii* (absolutely unpronounceable); and if he had not begun changing his "u" to "oo," *tabu* might have become the standard English spelling of *taboo*, since no one gave the word (in the spelling *taboo*) more currency than he did. Melville's name for himself would have been Tomo, not Tommo; Kory-Kory would have been Kori; and Fayaway would have been impossibly named Faaua or Faawa and then, in her unpronounceable state, might not have become the most famous character Melville ever created, in the judgment of his century.

Melville's handwriting was lamentably unlike Gansevoort's, still. He could form letters clearly if he concentrated letter by letter or word by word, but as he became engrossed in any topic he formed letters carelessly. Nevertheless, he knew how to prepare a manuscript so that it could be copied out legibly, by himself or preferably by someone else, perhaps the sister who had importuned him to write out his adventures. No one in the impoverished and provident Melville family ever wasted paper in these years (Allan later, in the era of cheap postal service and personal prosperity, once shockingly drew wavy lines across a page to simulate news he was decidedly not taking time to write to Augusta). The *Typee* leaves are from a fluently written first draft. Saving paper by not indenting for paragraphs, Melville inserted clear paragraph symbols as he went, and enough of that paragraphing survives into the first printed version of the work for us to be sure it remained pretty much his. He did not throw away a page if he thought of something else to say in a passage he had just completed and gone beyond. When he thought about making such an insertion before he finished the page, he stopped at the end of whatever sentence he was on, put down an "insert above" symbol there and where the insertion was to start, and continued on the same line with the words to be inserted until he finished and indicated that he was now resuming his narrative at the later point. Later he or his copyist would encounter the symbol where the insertion was to be made, and then look down and pick up the addition so everything was copied out in the sequence he intended. On one of the pages Melville employed a sequence of "insert" symbols for successive afterthoughts, first a cross inside a circle, with a dot in each of the four wedges; then a diamond, elongated horizontally, with three dots centered horizontally.

If he thought of making an addition *after* he had filled a page, Melville wrote the belated material on little pieces of paper salvaged, most likely, from leaves so messy they had to be discarded. One paragraph in chapter 14 (p. 110 in the Northwestern-Newberry Edition of Melville's *Writings*) begins "Every evening the girls of the house gathered about me on the mats," and describes the girls anointing his body. Above "Every evening" Melville wrote: "(See slip)"—a reference to the piece of paper upon which he had written an addition. Although the slip did not survive with the manuscript leaf, prior to "Every evening" in the first edition of chapter 14 occurs a little paragraph not in the draft: "But the tranquillizing influences of beautiful scenery, and the exhibition of human life under so novel and charming an aspect, were not my only sources of consolation." At the end of 1845 Gansevoort used the same phrasing when he said that Herman had sent him "pages & slips of paper." (In composing *Billy Budd* at the end of his life Melville was still following the same frugal practice of cutting off a "slip" of the right size and attaching it to another leaf.) In drafting *Typee*, Melville, for all his frugality, was making the manuscript such that another person could follow it, albeit with some effort. No one later had to intervene to change the sailor's incoherent and illiterate manuscript into acceptable English prose: aside from the most minor sort of editorial or compositorial changes, *Typee* is Melville's own.

As he wrote the draft, Melville was forced to grapple with some basic problems in narratology. He made this stab at accounting for his telling what Toby told him while not able to recall it verbatim: "As I cannot remember the words made use of by Toby on this occasion, I shall accordingly relate his adventure in my own language tho' in the same [?] putting the words in his mouth." He marked that out and tried again: "Though I can not recall to mind anything like the precise phraseology employed on this occasion, I shall still for the sake of unity permit my companion to rehearse his own adventure in the language that most readily occurs to me. — After leaving the house with Marheyo — began Toby — we struck across the valley, & ascended the opposite heights." By the time he prepared the fair copy for the first edition (ch. 13, p. 100), Melville had decided he was wasting his effort; he dropped all the preliminary explanations and began instead with: " 'After leaving the house with Marheyo,' said Toby, 'we struck across the valley, and ascended the opposite heights.' " How best to tell someone else's story without pretending to use that person's words was a problem in narratology that bedeviled Melville all his career, although he learned to turn it to advantage.

To judge from the discrepancies between the draft pages and the printed book, Melville's most pressing difficulty had nothing to do with how to construct a narrative and get it down on paper in an intelligible way. His problem was how to present himself as author in proper relationship to his presumed readers. In the draft, he was handicapped by writing (first of all) for an audience that consisted of his family and perhaps some friends who knew him well. The fun of writing his first "Fragment" in 1839 had lain, partly, in planting private allusions for the subsequent delectation of Gansevoort, Helen, and others, probably including friends we know nothing about. Now in 1844 and early 1845 he did much the same thing. Throughout the surviving pages of the draft are passages meant to amuse those in the family who would read the manuscript or hear passages read aloud. Once sufficient amusement had been derived, Herman could remove some of his words and shape the book to fit some larger audience that still remained quite nebulous to him.

A "great tease" at the age of five who had daily put Gansevoort's "Patience to flight," now Herman "quizzed" (as the term was) Gansevoort by writing into the draft satirical comments on orators. In the draft of what became chapter 13, Melville wrote a passage with obvious application to his older brother:

> As he continued his harang[u]e however, Kori like more polished orators
> [then Melville deleted the previous four words and continued:] in emulation
> of our more polished orators, began to branch out rather diffusely into his
> subject, enlarging perhaps upon the moral reflections that it naturally pro-
> duced [Melville deleted "produced" and replaced it with "gave rise to"] &
> proceeding in a strain of unintelligible gibberish, in the peroration [he de-
> leted the previous word and replaced it with "course"] of which he reminded
> me of a man with his mouthful of chub spluttering choking & spitting the
> bones out in every direction. Such a horrific unedifying merciless jargon
> never surely was heard before. All these mad sounds seemed to be served up,
> in a fricasee of vowels & consonants coated [?] with a spice of cayenne —
> Heaven defend me from such another infliction! It gave me rheumatic pains
> in every joint in my body. What it all meant I could not for the life of me
> conjecture without the speaker was improving the occasion to enlarge upon
> the transitory nature of all human enjoyment[s?] & the vanity of terrestrial
> expectations.

The indelicacy of what happens to the mouthful of chub could be paralleled many times in the backwoods humor stories that appeared in newspapers and such magazines as *The Spirit of the Times*, so it was, strictly speaking, publishable, but Melville cannot have meant this particular fraternal satire to be published. It was planted in the draft for his family to spot as they read it. Everyone would enjoy it, according to his or her lights, and even Gansevoort would be brought to see that, if reduced, the passage might delight other readers while still being perceived by the family and their intimates as an affectionately teasing allusion to the orator of the human race. The passage in fact survives, in a greatly condensed form, as the last paragraph of chapter 13 (p. 103), where Kory-Kory emulates "our more polished orators" so well that he gives the narrator "the headache for the rest of the day."

One or more other members of the family also had their turn at seeing themselves at least temporarily immortalized in the manuscript. The missionary-minded Augusta was probably the loving target of a passage for chapter 14. Just before the first-edition paragraph beginning "Frequently in the afternoon" (p. 110), Melville wrote in the draft a much-revised section in which the lame Tomo (Tommo, in the printed version) being carried by Kori Kori reminds the narrator of a picture of a boy, Little Henry, being carried by his bearer, Boosy, in colonial India. As Melville indicated, this picture decorated the title page of Mary Martha Sherwood's ubiquitous "Little Henry and his Bearer," which Herman drolly referred to as "that pleasing and popular religious tract." On the cover of the tract the turbaned servant Boosy carries a little Henry of quite an early age, perhaps three years (although the caption declares that when Henry "was only ten months old, he used to put his arms" round Boosy's neck and kiss him). Little Henry dies early, as good children have a way of doing in such fiction, but in dying he gains a soul for Jesus — Boosy, hitherto a relativist who had speciously argued that "there are a great many religions, but they all lead to heaven." Herman was hopelessly ironical about sentimental racist religiosity; Richard Henry Dana Jr. recalled the same story as provoking a profound although evanescent religious experience in his childhood. The first edition of *Typee* contained no sign of Little Henry or Boosy, and far from being strikingly apt, the analogy of Kori Kori carrying a full-grown Tomo to Boosy carrying little Henry was considerably strained. Augusta seems the target for this funning because, certainly by 1846, and probably earlier, she carried just such tracts to the Irish in the "Hill" region of Lansingburgh, pious activity that bemused Herman with the gulf between what he had seen of missionary efforts to convert brown Apollos in the islands of the South Seas and Augusta's earnest distribution of Protestant tracts to immigrants from an exhausted isle off the European continent.

Herman delighted in titillating all four of his sisters with his daringly risqué comparisons between the loose tappa or frank nudity of the Polynesian girls and the heavy clothing that swathed fashionable maidens of America like themselves. Such comparisons ran through the draft pages and the book as published, but some did not reach print. In the description of the narrator's being bathed (ch. 12, p. 90), the draft described the naked girls as "looking like so many mermaids sparkling in the billows that washed the sea weed covered sides of their lurking places" — a passage not in the first edition.

At points in the draft he described more sensuous scenes than anyone in the family could have read with absolute comfort. In print in chapter 14, (p. 110), the paragraph beginning "Every evening" ends: "and I used to hail with delight the daily recurrence of this luxurious operation, in which I forgot all my troubles, and buried for the time every feeling of sorrow." In the draft a new paragraph had started with an earlier variant of those words, then continued at length:

> I used to hail with delight [changed to "transport"] the daily recurrence of this luxurious operation in which I forgot all my troubles & buried for the time every feeling of sorrow or of care. With Captain Macheath in the opera I could have sung "Thus I lay like a Turk with my doxies around," for never certainly was effeminate ottoman in the innermost shrine of his seraglio attended by lovelier houris with more excess of devotion than happened to me on these occasions I have mentioned. — Sardanapalus might have experienced such sensations — but I dou[b]t whether any of the Sultans ever did.

In the draft Melville marked out the lines about Macheath and his doxies and began a new sentence with "Never certainly"; he also deleted "than happened to me on the occasions I have mentioned."

Melville may never have wanted to get such sensual language into print, but his writing it is revealing, for again, as when he copied out verses from one of the airs in *The Beggar's Opera* in his youth, he was comparing himself to Captain Macheath. Nor was it the last time he compared himself, directly or obliquely, to a Turk surrounded by his harem: in 1850 at the Melville house outside Pittsfield, after a morning spent drafting most of an essay on Nathaniel Hawthorne's *Mosses from an Old Manse*, Melville dressed as a Turk for a costume party. In the years before the publication of *Moby-Dick*, Herman Melville had sometimes seen himself as Macheath, or Lord Byron, or a Turk — a self-image that affected how he behaved and how others perceived him.

Some of Melville's early teasing survives into the published book, and some of it he must have been sure his sisters would not understand. Knowing he could get away with what no one imagined anyone could put into print in the mid-nineteenth century, Herman went far indeed in planting not just sensuous but actually obscene passages in his decorous manuscript. Having deleted the passage about Captain Macheath and his doxies, Melville left in the draft the passage immediately following, a description of Kory-Kory's ministrations to him after the "girls of the house" had left them alone. Before lighting his pipe for him, Kory-Kory would sometimes be "obliged to strike a light for the occasion," a process involving a stick about six feet long and three inches in diameter. Knowing that no one would dare to describe Onanism in a book offered for popular reading, a reader could only reproach himself or herself for any fleeting suspicions that more might be involved than making fire: "At first Kory-Kory goes to work quite leisurely, but gradually quickens his pace, and waxing warm in the employment, drives the stick furiously along the smoking channel, plying his hands to and fro with amazing rapidity, the perspiration starting from every pore." Approaching "the climax of his effort," Kory-Kory "pants and gasps for breath, and his eyes almost start from their sockets with the violence of his exertions." This operation, Melville drolly observed, seemed to him "the most laborious species of work performed in Typee." The sexual innuendo may have been obvious to Gansevoort, from his knowledge of the author, but baffling to any gentleman or lady who read the printed book. One of the striking oddities about the reception of Typee was that a number of readers put on record their sense that Melville had worked upon them insidiously, so that only upon rereading did they recognize the immorality of the work.

While the fire-starting passage was retained in the first edition, Melville retrenched at several points from the rambunctious humor of the draft. In chapter 12 (p. 95), it would have been funnier to have retained "salubrious," which stood before "morning" in the draft: the first edition less jauntily reads "and all to make a fat meal for a parcel of bloody-minded cannibals one of these mornings." (Here the word "minded" was not in the draft.) A few paragraphs further, Melville cut an identification of the source of the meat as "the mutilated remains of a prematurely deceased porker"; in the first edition this becomes "the mutilated remains of a juvenile porker" (p. 95). In the draft for the beginning of chapter 13 (p. 97), where Toby is worrying about the natives being cannibals, the narrator grants that fact but then insists: "a more humane gentlemanly & amiable set of epicures in that particular, do not probably exist in the Pacific"; the first edition dropped "in that particular" — thereby losing a charming specificity.

In the draft of chapter 13 (p. 102) Melville amused himself with the Polynesian words he puts in Kori Kori's mouth — a speech, he says, "a liberal interpretation of which would signify — Terrible fellows, those Haapaas — devour an amazing quantity of men — Oh shocking bad." In the first printed version Kory-Kory's speech flatly "signifies" the English words that follow — an assertion that the narrator understood the words and was translating them exactly. Melville's more diffident, and humorous, manuscript reference to "a liberal interpretation" thus had already been built into the foregoing part of the chapter when he wrote this later passage that survived in the published version (p. 103): "Which, liberally interpreted as before, would imply"; in the draft, this reference to what had occurred "before" made perfect sense, but in the first edition, it does not. The loss is minor, but it is a double loss — of a little humor, and a little coherence.

In the first edition of chapter 14 (p. 111) is a passage about how Kory-Kory "bustled about" Tommo "and employed himself at least twenty minutes in adjusting everything" to suit Tommo's personal comfort. Then, in the next paragraph, begins the passage describing how Kory-Kory would get him his pipe and light it for him. The draft had a little more of Kori Kori's officiousness, marked out, before the occurrence of the word "bustled" mentioned above; it continued, before the paragraph about the pipe, in this longer version: "He then bustled around me and employed himself for at least 20 minutes in adjusting everything that affected my personal comfort to his own satisfaction; — for in these matters he never heeded in the least my own humble wishes, thinking doubtless that as I was the interested party & consequently prejudiced in favor of my own whims and inclinations that I should not by any means be permitted to have my own way in the matter." Such amusing passages may have been cut while Melville was getting rid of passages he never intended to keep, such as part of the comparison of Kori Kori to a polished American orator: getting rid of private jokes, he retrenched more than he needed to do.

To a large degree, Melville's uncertainty about which humorous passages had to be cut and which could be retained sprang from his failure to formulate a clear sense of who might read *Typee* after members of his family had read or heard parts of it. He had not defined an ideal general audience for himself at the outset, and he had not decided just what such an audience might think an American sailor would be capable of writing. From his youth he had filled his writing with historical, literary, and artistic allusions, and such allusions came naturally to him as he wrote the draft. The variants between draft and book show that he became aware, at least at times, that such allusions might make readers suspicious of his claim to be both adventurer and writer of the adventures, and at some point he cut some of them, but almost as erratically as he had cut some of the humorous passages.

In the last paragraph in what is now chapter 12 (p. 96), the first edition retained a reference to a "superannuated warrior" doing "the honors of his mansion with all the warmth of hospitality evinced by an English squire when he regales his friends at some fine old patrimonial mansion." The draft, rather more perplexingly, had more elaborately asserted that the "superannuated warrior" did "the honors of his mansion with all the warmth of hospitality evinced by an English squire, who with a heart like a mastodon's regales his visiters at some fine old patrimonial mansion in the country" — a passage that would have sounded peculiar enough, coming from the mouth of a writer who identified himself as an American sailor.

Melville removed a reference to Europe near the end of chapter 14 (p. 111). There, in the printed version, before the paragraph beginning "A straight, dry, and partly decayed stick," the narrator declares that since Kory-Kory's way of lighting a fire was entirely different from any way he had ever seen or heard of, he will "describe it." In the draft that passage is worded differently, and more fully. Instead of "describe it," the words were first "record it": "I shall here record it for the benefit of Europe & posterity & incidentally for the comfort of those who may hereafter get lost in the woods at night & be desirous of building a fire." This whimsy is all the more peculiar because Melville probably wrote the passage before English publication became a real possibility.

Other learned-sounding references were cut. In chapter 12 (p. 93) the draft had a good description of the natives "running to & fro before the flames, while others dancing & capering about looked like so many demons tending the tartarean furnaces." In the first edition, the sentence ended with "demons." (The passage anticipates "The Try-Works," ch. 96 in *Moby-Dick*, where the "Tartarean shapes of the pagan harpooneers" stand on the hatch, and seem fiendlike.) In chapter 12 (p. 96), between the next to last and last paragraphs, Melville in the draft wrote this little paragraph, not present in the first edition: "This picturesque procession carrying along such glorious specimens of tropical vegatation [?] moving with wild chants through the sylvan defiles of the valley might have been taken for a throng of the ancient devotees of Ceres wending their way with votive offerings towards the alters [altars] of the goddess." In the draft for what became chapter 14 (p. 111), Melville wrote a passage that stood between "kitchen cupboard at home" and the paragraph beginning "The islander": "Having said this much in brief introduction, I here take Kori Kori by the hand & introducing him to the reader I have no doubt but that the former is perfectly willing to go through the Promethean ['Promethean' was interlined] operation of striking a light for his particular gratification." The passage did not survive into the first edition.

Another deletion involves a biblical reference. In the first paragraph of chapter 13 (p. 97) the second sentence read, in the draft: "The natives actuated by some mysterious impulse day after day redoubled the assidulty of their attentions & like the heavenly visitants of Lot of old we seemed in their eyes worthy of their utmost devotion." This sentence got printed: "The natives, actuated by some mysterious impulse, day after day redoubled their attentions to us." The cut may have been made because any biblical comparison could have been regarded as flippant, but the comparison had also seemed dangerous because it would irresistibly remind some readers of the way the men of the city of Sodom had treated their heavenly visitors. The deletion of a sentence from the draft for chapter 13 (p. 101) could possibly have been part of an attempt to avoid the use of God's name, or even the word "Providence." There Toby eludes the bad Happars by running down a mountainside, and later reports seeing them recover their weapons and turn back, while he continued his descent as fast as he could. After the words "abandoned the chace" (Melville's habitual spelling, even in the name Owen Chase), the draft continues with this sentence: "Gratefull to Providence for this signal preservation from a shocking death [Melville marked out the four preceding words, 'from a shocking death'] I continued my descent, renouncing all thoughts of resuming a journey attended by such unlooked-for perils." Deleted here (with the entire sentence), "Providence" occurs in *Typee* a very few times as a safe synonym for God, as in chapter 17 (p. 124); in the same context "God" is used in chapter 26 (p. 196); most other times "God," "gods," or "godship" are applied only to a heathen deity or deities.

Even some of the cultural commentary was removed. In the draft and in the book (ch. 14, p. 112) is a sentence about the possibility of setting up a college of vestals to be charged with keeping a fire alive so no one would have to repeat Kory-Kory's stick-rubbing method. In the draft Melville elaborated the topic a bit: "What a striking evidence this, of the difference between the extremes of savage & enlightened life." Then he marked those two lines out and wrote six lines of commentary on his own attitude toward women (lines left not quite coherent): "One difficulty however would present itself in the way of this benevolent enterprise which as it might be considered in the light of a slanderous aspersion on the fair fame of the gentle damsels of the vale I courteously beg to be excused from more distinctly pointing out." This passage did not appear in the first edition. In the draft Melville continued with this: "What a striking evidence does this example furnish of the wide difference between the extremes of savage and enlightened life! A gentleman in Tipii . . ." This passage beginning "What a striking evidence" survived in the first edition (ch. 14, p. 112), where Melville went on to stress that in "Tipee" (as the draft spelled it) food might be had simply by reaching out a hand to pluck fruit from the branches of any surrounding tree. In the draft another passage followed: "This single practical illustration is, I insist upon it, worth volumes of learned disquisitions on the nature & theory of the respective pretensions of the various forms of social life & I accordingly commend it to the consideration of all the political economists & public spirited Philosophers who are engaged in putting to rights this most imperfectly constituted planet of ours." This Melvillean philosophical flourish did not appear in print.

In trying to make the book believable as the work of a man who had sailed before the mast, Melville did not excise learned allusions and commentary systematically. The first edition still presented the sailor-author as a man who could allude casually to Trajan's columns, Captain Marryat, and Teniers, and make at least mock-philosophical reflections. As it turned out, in 1846 some readers in London (more than in the United States) were perturbed even by such passages that survived the pruning.

At some time Melville wrote a note on the cover of a bundle of paper (probably after the book was published—certainly after December 1845): "First Draught of Typee—After which much was added & altered. Written in the Spring of 1845—Begun in New York in the winter of that year [1844–45] & finished in Lansingsburgh in the early part of the summer [1845]." Perhaps he was labeling the draft for himself, having learned that real authors keep their archives for posterity, but more likely he labeled it specifically for Augusta, who had implored him to write it, and into whose possession it (or the bulk of it) went, whether at once or subsequently.

While he was writing during the early months of 1845 Herman gained some sense of what there was of a literary life in New York City, although at this stage he was still putting the names of the younger writers together with their works and with some of their faces. The great Irving was in Spain, and Cooper was only briefly in New York City and Philadelphia while arranging the publication of *Satanstoe* (a book in which a character was named Guert Ten Eyck, from family names of Cooper's friend Peter Gansevoort). Many of the lesser metropolitan writers were at work in several blocks south of City Hall, the area overlapping with Lawyers' Row, and therefore approachable. There was no walking on or near Nassau Street without passing newspaper and magazine offices. Writers were constantly finagling reviews or other items from each other, starting up papers, selling them, renaming them, sabotaging them, and watching them wither away under their hands. The literary sensation of the season was "The Raven," which Edgar Allan Poe published under the pseudonym "Quarles" in the February 1845 issue of the new Whig magazine, the *American Review*, out in late January. Willis reprinted it in the *Evening Mirror* of 29 January 1845, and Poe himself reprinted it in the new *Broadway Journal*, which he was editing with Charles F. Briggs (a man with some nautical experience behind him) and Henry C. Watson. Poe was inescapable in the little publishing world. (Gansevoort picked up a copy of the English edition of *Arthur Gordon Pym* within the year. Herman later gave his wife a copy of Poe's poems, later lost in a fire; he made references to Poe in *Pierre* and *The Confidence-Man*, and an annotation in a copy of Spenser that had been his father's shows that he knew Poe's works well enough to cite a line from "Ulalume" as a borrowing from Spenser.) In the 28 February 1846 issue of the London *Athenæum* that reviewed Melville's first book there was also a review of *The Raven and Other Poems*. Poe and Melville for some time before Poe's death had a mutual friend, Evert A. Duyckinck. There happens to survive no known record of Melville's ever having seen Poe, although he describes Poe to the life in *The Confidence-Man* (ch. 36).

A fixture of another sort on the literary scene was Gansevoort's friend and

Herman's host in 1839, Alexander W. Bradford. Gansevoort on 7 March 1842 had sent Shaw a copy "of a work on American Antiquities with Researches into the Origin and History of the Red race" by his "former schoolfellow and most intimate friend, Alexander W. Bradford." Poe took Bradford seriously enough to announce in the *Broadway Journal* on 25 January 1845 that he had "a work nearly ready for publication on the Manners and Customs of the Ancient Mexicans" — a work never printed, at least in book form. For years Gansevoort and Herman had known some of the writings of the poet and writer of society fiction Nathaniel Parker Willis, who was then editing the New York *Evening Mirror* at 4 Ann Street (with George Morris, the author of the immortal "Woodman Spare that Tree"). Charles Fenno Hoffman was then editing the New York *Gazette and Times* (at 47 William Street, near Wall Street). Gansevoort had been reading and making notes both on Willis and on Charles Fenno Hoffman's novel *Greyslaer* late in 1840, while Herman was in New York City with him. In reading *Greyslaer* Gansevoort had been struck by the hunter Balt's praise of oratorical power. He had noted Hoffman's quoting of a Bryant poem, and had copied out a passage of *Greyslaer* into his current *Index Rerum*, where he also frequently commented on Willis's works and copied out a satirical poem about Willis. At this time Gansevoort may already have been acquainted personally with Willis (who in November 1845 called upon him, at least twice). Gansevoort seems to have been on good terms, through his political activities, with Hoffman, whose older half-brother, Ogden Hoffman, had been judge advocate at the court of inquiry that convened on 28 December 1842 on the alleged mutiny on the *Somers*. (Ogden Hoffman had served on the *United States* during its still-celebrated capture of the British frigate *Macedonian* in the War of 1812.)

These American writers pursued their activities defensively, under the pall of Sydney Smith's scornful words in an article on "America" in the *Edinburgh Review* (1820) — "In the four quarters of the globe, who reads an American book?" In 1845 Poe's editor at the publishing house of Wiley & Putnam, Evert A. Duyckinck, was just initiating a new Wiley & Putnam series as a self-conscious rebuttal to the *Edinburgh Review*, the "Library of American Books" — not "an" American book but a whole library of American books, each worthy to be read throughout the country, and even abroad. Duyckinck did not intend to have future generations of Americans "make it their chief boast, for many generations to come," merely that they were "sprung from the same race with Bacon and Shakespeare and Newton" (Smith's disdainful proposition). The "Library" was a wildly optimistic bit of entrepreneurship, but it became at least a small source of national pride as the scope of the contributors widened to the northeast, south, and west. The first volume, Nathaniel Hawthorne's edition of his friend Horatio Bridge's *Journal of an*

African Cruiser, published about 20 June 1845, was quickly followed by Poe's *Tales.* (Evert A. Duyckinck shamelessly reviewed the *Tales,* anonymously, in the *Morning News* on 28 June 1845.) Poe in turn noticed in the *Broadway Journal* for 27 September Duyckinck's friend Cornelius Mathews's *Big Abel, and the Little Manhattan,* the fifth volume in the "Library," following J. T. Headley's *Letters from Italy* and William Gilmore Simms's *The Wigwam and the Cabin.* After these came the Reverend George B. Cheever's *Wanderings of a Pilgrim under the Shadow of Mont Blanc,* Caroline Kirkland's *Western Clearings,* and Poe's *The Raven and Other Poems* (published 19 November).

Anonymity cloaked most of the partisan boosting and boasting, but even a newcomer like Herman, with a little guidance from Gansevoort and from Bradford, could see that the local literati, inordinately prone to self-promotion, to mutual admiration, and to erratic backstabbing, were stirred by literary patriotism as well as personal ambition. Such patriotism was displayed, however awkwardly, by Duyckinck, Mathews, and others who, in the early 1840s, had fatuously applied to themselves the term "Young America," thereby vaingloriously comparing themselves to Benjamin Disraeli's "Young England" group of democratic-minded Tories. Underlying all the sycophancy, arrogance, and pettiness was a pervading hope that the literary men and women of lower Manhattan could somehow create a national literature. Even while Melville labored away on *Typee,* he was gaining a realistic sense of the New York literary world he might become a part of. The manuscript, after all, was good enough to become a book. Yet to think of the book as one in an imposing series like the Library of American Books might be too much to hope.

19

A Manuscript but No Publisher
1845

Honor and Fame, with Diadems & Empires are the Aims of ambitious Men;
but he that is Master of an excellent Pen, transcends them all.

"Allan Melvills Book," 1796

EARLY IN 1845 GANSEVOORT STAYED in the new six-story Astor House, built with "the rich dark-colored Quincy granite of Massachusetts" (as Jefferson Williamson pointed out in *The American Hotel*), not in the cheap boarding house at 7 Greenwich, where Allan and perhaps Herman were staying. It fronted on the west side of City Hall Park (early in the twentieth century the Woolworth Tower went up on part of the land it occupied), so it kept him at the political center of New York. There Hunn Gansevoort had stayed on long-term rates through the court of inquiry on the hangings on the *Somers*. John Jacob Astor, the richest man in America, had built the Astor House in 1836 to surpass Boston's first luxury hotel, Tremont House; it had gaslight from the start, and even before Croton water was piped into Manhattan, it had baths for guests in the basement and water closets on every floor, though not in private rooms. In this splendid setting Gansevoort began to despair, as the weeks passed after the inauguration, and on 7 May 1845 he wrote the president. The "entire failure" of his application for public employment had injured him "both in the present and the future" and had fallen upon him "with stunning force."

In Boston Elizabeth Shaw weighed her brother Oakes's invitation of 29 April to pack up her "duds" and come to Chicago for the summer to visit him and his wife (whom Lizzie probably had never seen), and their baby. Oakes was so freely hospitable because he had resorted to an illegal and immoral way of getting money (as Judge Shaw learned after Oakes's partner, Joseph B. Henshaw, wrote him on 24 December 1845 that Oakes had not only been lax at the business but had been cheating him). During May, Lizzie vacillated because she did not have a suitable escort. Not reassured by Oakes's suggestion that she go with Mr. Henshaw, in her cautious way she applied to her father for his counsel while he was away at Lenox on his court circuit: "I do not feel, even if it were left to me, competent to decide . . . and then again when I think of the long and perhaps perilous journey, and the idea of going out with Mr Henshaw almost a stranger to me, without any female companion, as would probably be the case, my courage and resolution fails, and I think I had better not go. I have not yet seen Mr Henshaw, (he is expected today I believe)." Recognizing that this character trait of Lizzie's was meritorious conscientiousness, not something negative like procrastination, which in his own youth had been a debilitating fault, the judge advised her to wait until he returned to Boston, then on 25 May he escorted her to Lansingburgh for a visit to the Melvilles and arranged his affairs so he could return a little later and travel to Chicago with her. Lizzie may have been in Lansingburgh still when Gansevoort came home in June — the occasion when he gave Fanny a volume of poetry by the Harvard professor Henry Wadsworth Longfellow, *Voices of the Night*. Herman had made a point of being there for Elizabeth's visit, and he "finished" *Typee* in Lansingburgh in the early part of the summer, perhaps while she was still there. Like the sisters, she was intrigued and impressed that he had actually written down a narrative of some of the adventures he had told her, and he was alternately optimistic and doubtful about the possibility that it would become a printed and bound book that he could present to her and the judge.

Having begged Herman to write out his adventures, Augusta may have copied the pages out for him in her tidier, consistent handwriting, but he may have prepared his fair copy himself, perhaps salvaging some of the cleaner pages from the draft. At this final stage, if not before, Herman swept through the manuscript eliminating many of the private references that had served their purpose of entertaining members of the family and himself. He also made the style as good as he could make it. However much he improved it, the work was still rife with the stock language of various subliterary genres and of the popular novel, for much of that language persisted from the surviving draft pages into the printed book. He kept assuring the reader that he, the author, had had many unforgettable experiences. He could "never forget the eighteen or twenty days" as the *Dolly* (his name for the *Acushnet*) swept toward the Marquesas (ch. 2); he could "never forget" (ch. 4) a comment about the cannibals in the Typee valley his shipmate Ned made (he had shuddered at the comment but "little thought" that he should be "a captive in that self-same valley"); the glen of Tior had produced an impression upon his mind that would "never be obliterated" (ch. 4); a view from the heights down at the lovely bay of Nukahiva (misprinted in the first edition as "lonely") "formed altogether the loveliest view" he ever beheld, and were he to live a hundred years, he "should never forget the feeling of admiration" which he then experienced (ch. 6); no description could "do justice" to the beauty of the bay of Nukahiva (ch. 2), and — pages later — nothing could exceed its "imposing scenery" (ch. 4); the five streams and gorges formed a sight that would "ever be vividly impressed" upon his mind (ch. 7), but sleeping in the ravine was unpleasant ("Shall I ever forget that horrid night?"); and he could "even now" recall his first glimpse of the Typee valley "with all the vividness" of the first impression (ch. 7). No one had drilled into Melville the rule that a good writer does not insist on how unforgettable he found certain scenes but instead describes scenes so vividly that the reader can never forget them. Novelistic clichés (e.g., in ch. 12, "A cold sweat stood upon my brow, and spell-bound with terror I awaited my fate!") occurred throughout the book as published, although they diminished in the later and surely later-written sections. No reviewer protested against such banalities: after all, the language was not worse than that in many popular books. The prose of *Typee* began to strike people as amateurish only well into the twentieth century, when, for the first time, readers began to come to *Typee* after reading *Moby-Dick*. Eventually, almost no one read *Typee* before reading *Moby-Dick*, "Bartleby," *Billy Budd*, and other examples of Melville's later writing, so that it gradually became almost impossible for an educated reader to recapture anything like the effect *Typee* had on its first audiences.

A lover of Melville's great prose or a lover of his poetry, working backward, can find, even amid the clumsy passages of *Typee*, faint hints and even strong suggestions of the great individuality to come. Such passages tend not to come in set descriptions and other heightened rhetorical passages, but in odd moments. When Melville contemplated something he could "only describe" as "a hash of soaked bread and bits of tobacco, brought to a doughy consistency by the united agency of perspiration and rain" (ch. 7), he had marked a small but distinct stage in his journey toward originality in observation and expression. The authentic Melville way of generalizing about human traits is present in this passage: "There is scarcely anything when a man is in difficulties that he is more disposed to look upon with abhorrence than a right-about retrograde movement — a systematic going over of the already trodden ground" (ch. 8). Not only is there the good phrase (one does not tire quickly of "a right-about retrograde movement"), there is a foretaste of Melville's later habit of capping one phrasing by another passage that restates it ("a systematic going over of the already trodden ground"). A hint of the essential Melville is in the passage in which the native physician after pounding Tommo's sore leg stoops over it "either whispering a spell, or having a little confidential chat with some imaginary demon located in the calf" (ch. 11). There are moments that anticipate the character of Ishmael with the acknowledgment, however superficial, of the mystery in human perceptions: "Whenever in the course of my rambles through the valley I happened to be near the chief's mausoleum, I always turned aside to visit it. The place had a peculiar charm for me; I hardly know why; but it was so" (ch. 24). The subsequent musings in this particular passage show a good deal of the unique personal charm of what became the distinctive Melvillean style. Melville learned by doing, but the contemporary reviewers who delighted in the style of *Typee* were not grossly deficient in aesthetic sensibilities. When Melville decided it was time to show the fair copy of his manuscript to a publisher in New York, he had nothing to be ashamed of.

In the "early part of the summer," by which he may have meant late spring, late May, or any part of June, but most likely well after Lizzie Shaw's arrival, and perhaps after her departure, Melville took the fair-copy manuscript to the Harper brothers' publishing house in Cliff Street, near the lower tip of Manhattan. It was a bad time for the oldest Melville brother, for Gansevoort was almost despairing of receiving a political reward, but Herman had good reason to hope that the Harpers would take his manuscript, since they were the publishers of the highly successful book Melville saw as most nearly comparable to his own, Dana's *Two Years before the Mast*. He wanted the Harpers, also, because they were well known to have developed not only the facilities for publishing works in what passed as handsome format but also to have developed better strategies for advertising and distributing their books than any other American publisher. Frederick Saunders was then a "copy reader" for them, "reading manuscripts and afterwards sending in written reports to the firm as to their literary value" (the manuscript "Recollections of Frederick Saunders," in the New York Public Library). Later he said that Melville "sent" the Harpers the manuscript of *Typee;* "delivered" to them, would have been more plausible. This is from Saunders's third-person description: "Mr. Saunders read the same with great interest and gave his opinion that 'this work if not as good as Robinson Crusoe seems to me to be not far behind it.'" Despite Saunders's advice, the Harper brothers held a council at which they decided to reject the manuscript, "on the ground that 'it was impossible that it could be true and therefore was without real value.'" Saunders's story that the Harpers rejected *Typee* is corroborated by the very late source, Melville's niece Charlotte Hoadley, who on 14 February 1944 recalled hearing her mother (Kate Melville Hoadley) and aunts talk about Melville's enduring hostility toward the Harpers for the rejection of *Typee:* "One thing I do know, the Harpers refusing it calling it a second 'Robinson Crusoe' embittered his whole life."

Charlotte Hoadley in her letters to Victor H. Paltsits (of the New York Public Library) emerges as a conscientious woman who would not have invented any part of such a story. The bitterness she emphasizes makes good sense if we realize that Melville took the Harper rejection as final, as the opinion he could expect to get from any other publisher. He was not the sort of man to hawk the manuscript aggressively from publisher to publisher once the doors of the best firm had been closed in his face. (He did hawk *White-Jacket* down Publishers' Row, late in 1849, in London, but that behavior was uncharacteristic, done under a compelling exigency.) Having spent his first months out of the navy writing a manuscript, he now spent weeks or even months thinking that the manuscript was wasted effort, unpublishable. In disgust and despair now, Herman left the manuscript bundled up at Gansevoort's and Allan's law office and returned to Lansingburgh, empty-handed, and with no prospects of income. For a period of several weeks he and Gansevoort were similarly despondent, Gansevoort in New York City "stunned" by the crushing force of Polk's failure to repay him, Herman in Lansingburgh numbed by the crushing force of the Harpers' arbitrary rejection.

It was mid-July, after he had all but given up hope of a political appointment, that Gansevoort received a letter from Secretary of State James Buchanan, dated 9 July, naming him "as Secretary of the Legation of the United States of America near her Brittanick Majesty." The letter also contained "a passport, letter of credit on Baring Brothers & Co and printed personal instructions." (This was a diplomatic passport, which means that it lacked the physical description recorded on passports and in the Register of Passports for private citizens traveling abroad.) Gansevoort accepted the appointment on 16 July and began making plans for immediate departure. Allan would be left in charge of the law office. Herman was in Lansingburgh, and if he returned to New York he would have to sponge off Allan or find something else to do, since his venture at authorship had failed. He had experience in teaching school—more experience teaching than being paid for teaching, and he could always go back to sea, as his cousins had done. As it turned out, the fate of the manuscript Herman had abandoned in New York was directly affected by Gansevoort's good fortune. Thomas Low Nichols, the "Empire Club" Democratic journalist from New Hampshire who had organized the great torchlight parade of 1 November 1844, called on Gansevoort in Wall Street just after he had been appointed secretary of legation to the American embassy. Nichols had frequently heard Gansevoort speak, he wrote in his autobiography, and, the implication is, he simply came by to congratulate his ardent friend. This was also a fence-mending visit, since Gansevoort had been opposite sides of the party from Nichols and Levi D. Slamm, the editor of the *Plebeian*. Nichols knew Gansevoort's appointment had been very late in coming, probably knew that Gansevoort's stirring up the secret circular controversy had made it hard for Polk to reward him, and knew that the job was a mixed blessing: "It was a step upward and forward in the public life to which he aspired; but he was poor, and the salary was scarcely enough for his gloves and cab hire."

In 1864 Nichols (by that time a physician resident in London) included in *Forty Years of American Life* an account of that visit to Wall Street. In Gansevoort's absence (very likely he was away on his farewell visit to the family in Lansingburgh), Allan had confidentially informed Nichols that he and Gansevoort had a third brother: "He had been 'a little wild,' and some years before had run away to sea, sailing first to Liverpool and then in a whaler to the South Pacific. This was nothing strange — what followed was." According to Nichols, "He got home a few months ago," Allan had said, "and has been writing something about his adventures among the cannibals. Would you like to look at it?" Allan was officious by nature, but he was concerned about the way Herman had taken the Harpers' rejection, and he may have sensed that a practical journalist like Nichols might help somehow. Nichols recalled:

> I had a couple of hours to spare, and at once sat down and opened the package of the sailor boy's manuscript. It was "Typee," and the runaway brother of my Wall-street friends was Herman Melville.
>
> I read "Typee" at one sitting, and had, of course, no doubt of its success; but the better to assure it, I advised the diplomatic brother to take a copy to London, and have it issued there simultaneously with its publication in New York. I felt sure that the reviewers of the English press would make its American success, and I was not at all sure that the process could be reversed.

The family had been so excited about Gansevoort's appointment and his plans for an immediate departure that no one had thought about Herman's manuscript, but once Nichols made his suggestion everyone recognized its obvious brilliance. Perhaps forwarding the suggestion to Gansevoort and Herman in Lansingburgh, Allan wrapped the bundle up a little tighter and put it in Gansevoort's chest along with his essential *Index Rerum* volumes, so that it remained in New York, out of Herman's reach, through the last week of July. In Lansingburgh, or later in New York as well, Gansevoort and Herman talked over Nichols's suggestion and Herman gave his brother authority to depart with the manuscript (probably the only form of the book other than the draft) and power of attorney to sell it. The possibility of publication was so dubious and the means of duplication so onerous that neither brother felt particularly uneasy about the arrangement. That summer Gansevoort's mind had been on his own career, not on his brother's, and Herman had been easily deterred by one flat rejection. He had tried New

York, Gansevoort would try London, and together they would have exhausted the biggest publishing centers.

In New York Gansevoort wrote Shaw to warn that Allan might have to renew the five-hundred-dollar note again in September. He sailed on 31 July, carrying with him the "manuscript" of *Typee* — the full fair copy made from the draft Herman had completed in the late spring or early summer, since Gansevoort needed to have with him the best and fullest copy of the work. (The manuscript may already have been "affectionately inscribed" to "Lemuel Shaw, Chief Justice of the Commonwealth of Massachusetts," changed to "gratefully inscribed" in the American edition; the dedication, whenever it was written, marks an intimacy between Herman and Shaw not fully explained by other surviving contemporaneous documents. The implication is that the judge had made a forceful impression on Herman in Boston in October 1844 and again in late May or early June 1845, when he escorted his daughter to Lansingburgh and then returned to accompany her to Chicago.) Gansevoort's promise to try to arrange the publication of the work was as good a present as Herman had known in a long time. The day after Gansevoort sailed, Herman celebrated the first birthday he had spent with members of his immediate family since 1838, or possibly 1840.

Perhaps Herman saw Gansevoort aboard the *Great Western*, then stayed on in New York City through September, for he was there a good deal in the next months. In Allan's office or elsewhere, he soon met Thomas Low Nichols and saw him frequently, from then into 1846 and probably beyond. To Nichols, four years his senior, Melville behaved with the respect due to Gansevoort's friend and to his own potential benefactor, grateful for the mere idea of sending the manuscript to London, even if nothing were to come of it. On the basis of these meetings Nichols later gave a brief impression of Melville at this time: "He was a simple-hearted, enthusiastic man of genius, who wrote with the consciousness of an impelling force, and with great power and beauty." Nichols's praise is unique, for it is based not only on later knowledge of Melville's published writings but on knowledge of the unpublished manuscript, of which he was the first known reader outside the family or the Harper establishment. Simple-hearted may seem an odd bit of praise to prefix to the words "man of genius," but Herman *was* simple-hearted in comparison with the brother Nichols knew best, Gansevoort, and even in comparison with the calculating Allan. (Nichols had no way of knowing it, but no male in the family possessed young Tom Melville's stores of simple-heartedness.)

One piece of slightly dubious evidence puts Herman in New York City late in September 1845. One of the Ten Eycks, Anthony Ten Eyck (perhaps the one of that name who had been a fellow member of the Albany Young Men's Association for Mutual Improvement), was appointed as U.S. Commissioner in the Sandwich Islands. Ten Eyck and his wife and children were then living in Detroit, and passed through New York City on their way to Norfolk, where they were to sail at the end of September 1845 on the U.S. frigate *Congress*. (As it turned out, the sailing was delayed a month, which the Ten Eycks spent in rented quarters in Portsmouth, Virginia.) By 29 September the Ten Eyck family had reached Baltimore on the way to Norfolk, so it probably was a few days before that, around the previous Friday, the twenty-sixth, or Saturday, the twenty-seventh, that they left New York City. After Herman became not only famous but notorious, and furthermore suspected of writing under a nom de plume, Ten Eyck spoke up in the Honolulu *Polynesian* (18 March 1848): "We can state for the information of the reviewers in Blackwood, that we actually met the gentleman in New York a few evenings previous to our embarcation for this place in the spring of 1845." "Spring" is a slip: good dates are available in Elizabeth Douglas Van Denburgh's long-belated recollections, *My Voyage in the United States Frigate "Congress"* (1913). Presumably Ten Eyck saw Herman in New York in late September, and saw him because he knew through the family gossip that Herman had been to Hawaii (the Ten Eycks and Gansevoorts had intermarried, and intermarried some more). Ten Eyck knew Herman was the brother of the Tammany orator whose appointment to the Court of St. James's had been in all the papers. (No Ten Eyck living in Detroit in 1844 could have failed to see the family patronymic Gansevoort used as a Christian name in all the papers along with a decidedly un-Dutch surname.) When he met Ten Eyck in New York, Herman's perspective on Lahaina and Honolulu was not the vantage point that the commissioner was to hold, but the ex-sailor was, as always, amusing. He may have kept silent about his literary aspirations, however, since he had finished the first draft of his book some months before and still had no prospect of seeing it in print.

That summer word reached the family, most likely through Shaw or Lizzie, that Uncle Thomas had died in Galena, on Herman's twenty-sixth birthday. One of Uncle Thomas's last acts had been to obtain from Judge Shaw an advance of two hundred dollars designated for "a decent outfit and the necessary expenses" for the wedding of his daughter Anne to John Dean, in Galena. Within a week or so of the funeral, Robert in Pittsfield wrote Shaw a characteristically convoluted letter expressing the desire of the family in Galena to return to the East and their lack of money to do so, and on 1 September the widow, Mary Melvill, wrote Shaw of her plans to spend the residue of the last check from Shaw to pay for the wedding, which was to take place before she returned to the farm at Pittsfield, leaving some of her children in Galena. The Melvill and Melville children, each of whom had had a cousin for a crony in 1832, were now dispersed, and only Priscilla ever reclaimed the privileges of cousinship for any sustained period. Focused on the attempt to build a life of his own, at last, Herman may not have grieved sharply for his uncle; years may have passed before he acknowledged the power the example of his uncle would exert over his later life. Sometime in 1845, also, the Melvilles learned that Cousin Thomas Wilson Melvill had died at sea on the whaleship *Oregon* on 26 September 1844, of "inflammatory Rheumatism & Scurvy" — not, of course, dipsomania or "mania-a-potu" (*White-Jacket*, ch. 58) or another name for alcoholism. He died the day before the ship reached Maui. Chaplain Samuel C. Damon in what he by then called the *Friend of Temperance and Seamen* recorded that Melvill's "remains were brought to Lahaina, and interred on shore Sept. 28th." Paradise for Cousin Thomas was not Lahaina, ravaged since his first glimpse of it from the *Vincennes*, but a spirit-room to which he possessed the key, where there was no wretched Spence to insult him for covertly visiting it as often as his comfort required. Lemuel Shaw as trustee of the estate of Thomas's grandfather received a report in early June 1845, perhaps the first news in this country: "Capt Sherman (master) enquired of him if he had any message for his friends, he answered no, the few clothes he had which were very poor he gave the crew." At this time, in 1845, Thomas's fate became entangled in Herman's mind with Guert's fate, another cousin, from the other side of the family, wholly destroyed by alcohol.

A vignette survives of Herman's behavior one Sunday in 1845, most likely in the summer, before or after Gansevoort's departure. In it Herman avoids social awkwardness by telling stories — not from his Marquesan experiences but his adventures in Tahiti or Eimeo. While she was entertaining Augusta's friend Augusta Whipple, Maria Melville took advantage of Herman's momentary presence to excuse herself and leave him to keep the young woman company. On 14 January 1846, the guest, by then a matron, Mrs. Augusta Whipple Hunter, recollected the scene in a letter to Augusta Melville: "I frequently think of the intermission which seemed so short to me Poor Herman when your mother, left the room with the request that he would entertain Miss Augusta, until 'Church going' time his countenance spoke, his thoughts, & he e'enmost despaired of entertaining, I should say of accomplishing the task of 'making himself agreeable' to his sister's dull friend — I laugh to myself frequently, when this picture rises — But he succeeded admirably." This description of Herman's body language is, from this time, unique, and valuable despite its facetious exaggeration. Still later, on 6 October 1847, after she had read both *Typee* and *Omoo*, Mrs. Hunter wrote Augusta: "I have read Herman's last publication & like it equally as well as

Typee. At first I did not, but the interest increased as I advanced & I closed
the volume not knowing to which to give the preference — I recognised in
Omoo some incidents related to me by Herman one *short* Sunday noon."
Mrs. Hunter made it clear that Herman's rollicking narratives were acceptable for female company even on the Sabbath, and that before there was any
firm chance for seeing *Typee* in print, he was rehearsing tales from a later
phase of his adventuring, tales which he may have begun to think about
writing down, if there were any prospect of his having a career.

After the devastating rejection by the Harpers, Herman did not get a job,
as far as we know, and did not try to write up another adventure. He may well
have remained most of the time in Lansingburgh, where he could help Tom
take care of their mother's garden and wait out the end of the summer.
Wherever he was, Lansingburgh or New York, Herman suffered two months
or so more of anxiety, hoping to hear that Gansevoort had arrived safely, and
then hoping that his brother had found time to take the manuscript to a publisher who might read it and respond differently from the way the Harpers
had done. Lacking a full duplicate of the final version, Herman had nothing
fit to show anyone, even if he were predisposed to try to find another American publisher after the Harpers had so firmly rejected the manuscript. During this long period of suspense his anger toward the Harpers settled into the
lifelong bitterness his niece recalled, for the final manuscript was out of his
hands, who knows where in London, in Gansevoort's room or in a drawer at a
publisher's, and he had nothing to build any plans on.

Meanwhile, London was a fool's paradise for Gansevoort. The Dela-
warean Louis McLane, Polk's new minister to Great Britain, assuming he
would select his own secretary of legation, had leaked the announcement to
the Baltimore *Sun* of 8 July that his choice, John Randolph Clay, had received
the appointment, the day before Buchanan signed Gansevoort's commission
and wrote out his passport. Then McLane had been humiliated when the
president named Gansevoort, not Clay, as the secretary. His vanity so affronted, as early as September Louis McLane began badgering Secretary of
State James Buchanan to transfer Gansevoort to another post — chargé d'affaires in Constantinople, for instance, somewhere out of Christendom, at the
ends of the earth. On the Oregon question Gansevoort was much closer to
President Polk's position than McLane, as John Munroe showed in *Louis
McLane: Federalist and Jacksonian*, and, far from being a happy representative
of Polk's policy, McLane spent his first months as minister complaining
about his predecessor, chafing at his impotence to make policy, annoyed at
credit being bestowed on Daniel Webster for diplomacy rather than on him,
suspicious that he was being left in the dark, and frustrated at being hamstrung by the president. McLane was so frustrated that he came "close to

intrigue," as Munroe delicately says — in fact, he treacherously went behind the backs of the secretary of state and the president and at first indirectly then directly tried to work his way through John C. Calhoun, secretary of state in Tyler's cabinet and now back at home in the Senate. McLane roiled, these months, in one long ferocious stew of frustration, resentment, and rage. Inside the McLane household, as in McLane's letters to Buchanan, Gansevoort was transformed into a monstrous caricature, a vulgar, lower-class Northerner.

Knowing nothing of McLane's machinations (and just possibly planted by Polk to check the minister's ability to affect policy), Gansevoort wrote his mother on 16 September about family affairs. He had tried to impress upon Allan's mind "the sacred priority of the monthly payment" to her — a payment that Gansevoort himself most likely had been making faithfully during the months before his appointment. The embodiment of fiscal probity as he described his penurious habits, he was in fact wholly responsible in fulfilling his promise to the second son in the family. By early October Gansevoort took a sample of Herman's manuscript to John Murray, the son of Byron's publisher, born in 1808, only seven and a half years older than Gansevoort. On 17 October Murray wrote to Gansevoort a letter now lost, although its contents can be inferred from the reply to it. He was uneasy about what he had read, since it seemed so much like the work of "a practised writer" that it did not seem possible that the narrative could be authentic. According to the history of the firm, *At John Murray's* (1932), the publisher "was attracted by the dramatic interest of the narrative and the raciness of the style, but he scented the forbidden thing — the taint of fiction." Nevertheless, he was interested enough to ask to see the remainder of the manuscript in the possession of Gansevoort, who responded on 21 October:

> Immediately on the receipt of your note of Friday the rest of the MS was put up to your address, but owing to the carelessness of a servant to whom it was committed, yet remains with me. It is herewith forwarded in compliance with your request.
>
> The Author will doubtless be flattered to hear that his production seems to so competent a judge as yourself that of "a practised writer" — the more so as he is a mere novice in the art, having had no experience; for it is within my personal knowledge that he has never before written either book or pamphlet, and to the best of my belief has not even contributed to a magazine or newspaper.

Here Gansevoort was prevaricating, or else he had forgotten the "Fragments from a Writing Desk." He could be firm on Herman's identity at least: "In regard to the other point to which you allude I can only give you the assurance of my full and entire belief that the adventurer, and the writer of the adventure are one & the same person." On 17 October, therefore, Murray was interested, though skeptical. He wanted to be reassured, but he was willing to see "the rest of the MS." Along with his assurances, good for what they were worth, Gansevoort was able to send the rest of the manuscript at once. The interchange pretty clearly implies that Gansevoort had what he considered to be all the manuscript with him in London at the time he had left a portion with Murray.

During November Gansevoort seems to have marked time as far as *Typee* was concerned, but there was a new complication: by now he had been told to watch for more material from Herman. On 18 November he wrote Allan: "I shall write Herman a note as to 'Typee,' in regard to which I am estopped from making any movement until I hear from him again & receive the additional Mss chapters." The question is how Gansevoort knew there were to be more chapters coming and when Herman had told him so. The obvious suspicion is that Gansevoort wrote Herman that Murray doubted the authenticity of the narrative (doubted that the writer had ever stayed among the Typees) and that Herman then began writing some passages that supplied what was or would pass as eyewitness detail. However, the timing makes it clear that Murray did not ask that the distant author supply certain kinds of chapters, and that the author did not then write them up to satisfy a demand or request from London. A letter from Gansevoort to his mother dated 3 November shows that he took advantage of the opportunity to write by the *Britannia*, which left Liverpool on 4 November: "By this steamer (that of tomorrow) you will receive 3 nos. of the 'Illustrated News,' two of 'Punch' and some other papers. I have written Herman a long letter about his Mss. I entertain good hopes of its success. If it succeeds it will pave the way for anything he may do in that line hereafter — 'Ce n'est que le premier pas qui conte.' "

The newspaper shipping notices show that the *Britannia*, the first steamer on which Gansevoort could have relayed any hypothetical demand from Murray, arrived at Boston on 20 November. For Gansevoort to have received the additions to the manuscript when he did (apparently on the *Caledonia*, which arrived at Liverpool on 28 November with "advices" from New York and Boston as late as 14 November, or, less likely, on the *Fidelia*, which arrived on 4 December with advices to 17 November), Herman would have to have mailed them by early or mid-November. The shipping schedule simply does not allow time for Herman to have received any request from Murray, then written up several chapters and parts of chapters, fiddled with the manuscript in various other ways (making do with the early draft of the manuscript, an imperfect representation of the manuscript Murray had), then send them off soon enough for Gansevoort to have received them by late November or very early December.

The inference is that Herman by late October had put Gansevoort on notice that more chapters would be coming, before he heard from his brother about Murray's comments on what he had read. Around the end of September Herman learned that Gansevoort had been active on his behalf, for in a letter to their mother from London on 16 September Gansevoort referred to the contents of his letter to Herman of the previous day. There he had spoken "at some length" about his personal expenses in London "& also as to 'Typee.'" The specific purport of the letter is unknown, but presumably he was reassuring Herman that he would take it to a publisher as soon as he got settled into his new life. In the meantime, Herman had thought about the manuscript he had entrusted to his brother, and had decided that he had more to say. He could not revise what he had written, not without a copy of the manuscript, but he could write new sections. Very likely the impulse to elaborate the manuscript began during his frustration at not being able to make a thorough new revision before Gansevoort's precipitous departure. Vague as the prospect of publication in London was, it was his only hope, and it was enough to lead Herman, beginning in August or September, to invest some days in trying to enhance the believability of the book.

From the beginning of his work on *Typee*, Melville had put himself into a bind. He had decided that no one would take seriously his claim to any expertise if he admitted that he had remained with the Typees only three weeks, so he had multiplied the length of his stay to four months, which gave him enough time to make many more observations and to progress some way in making sense of the more baffling customs of the islanders and to acquire, plausibly, some rudiments of the language. If he admitted that he knew only a handful of words in the Typee language, he complicated his narrative possibilities, since he could not plausibly introduce into the work anything he had not puzzled out on the basis of what he saw or what he was able to comprehend from the natives' words and gestures. As he had gotten farther into the manuscript he had described scenes in which he managed with a minimum of words and a maximum of gestures both to convey complex thoughts and to understand complex ideas offered by the natives. In claiming to write almost entirely from his own observations and experiences, he had cut himself off from the possibility of citing any great range of previous publications on the subject of the Marquesas Islands. The more he alluded to such publications, the less likely his account was to be taken as a true personal narrative containing valuable firsthand information. Now, for a number of new additions, to be incorporated into the book largely as his own observations and reflections, Melville turned to source books he had assembled, before or after Gansevoort left for England, especially Captain David Porter's *Journal of a Cruise Made to the Pacific Ocean, in the U.S. Frigate Essex;* Charles S. Stewart's long-familiar *Visit to the South Seas;* and William Ellis's *Polynesian Researches* (London, 1833). Melville may well not have seen Porter's *Journal* when he wrote down his claim not to have seen it (*Typee,* ch. 1), but now he had it in hand and used it in new chapters and parts of chapters, which he soon began forwarding to his brother. The relatively small number of pages Herman added at this time, being based on published sources that had to be assimilated if he were to avoid either outright plagiarism or the appearance of writing only from books, not from his own experiences, were harder to write than the same number of pages of simple narrative, and making any additions at all by trans-oceanic mail was difficult without an exact copy of what Gansevoort had. Still, the draft gave him the chapters in rough form, so Herman could describe to Gansevoort where to insert or append new passages — at the easiest places, the ends of chapters.

Melville later had a way of writing new public or private events into his already finished manuscripts, as when, early in 1852, he wrote his new rage against the same Harper brothers into the finished manuscript of *Pierre.* The Harpers were, proudly, famously, Methodists. J. Henry Harper, in his 1912 history of the family business, repeatedly emphasized the Methodist milieu from which the brothers sprung and in which they flourished all their lives. In accounting for their becoming "just the men they were," J. Henry Harper ascribed the cause primarily "to the influence of Methodism, and still more to the impress of Methodist preachers." Just possibly, it may have been the rejection of the manuscript of *Typee* by the Methodist Harpers that led Melville to write the scathing appendix, his eyewitness account of and his subsequent reflections on a great historic episode of the previous year, the "cession" of the Hawaiian Islands to Her Britannic Majesty and the subsequent restoration of sovereignty to King Kamehameha. The whole appendix (a violation of the unities, Melville knew) is informed by hatred of the Methodist missionaries:

High in the favor of the imbecile king at this time was one Dr. Judd, a sanctimonious apothecary-adventurer, who, with other kindred and influential spirits, were animated by an inveterate dislike to England. The ascendancy of a junto of ignorant and designing Methodist elders in the councils of a half-civilized king, ruling with absolute sway over a nation just poised between barbarism and civilization, and exposed by the peculiarities of its relations with foreign states to unusual difficulties, was not precisely calculated to impart a healthy tone to the policy of the government.

Resentful, as the family testimony says that he was, Melville may well have seized the chance to accomplish two purposes at once: to tar the Methodist Harpers with the same brush he was using on Dr. Judd and to propitiate whatever English publisher Gansevoort would show the manuscript to. The appendix is not mentioned among the sections that Melville sent to London, but its defense of Lord Paulet makes it look like a late addition, written after English publication seemed a possibility.

Murray gave Gansevoort some informal assurances of the seriousness of his interest on 3 December (or earlier), since on that day Gansevoort wrote Herman that *Typee* was "going to have a fair chance for favor in the literary world." That night Gansevoort received the publisher's formal offer: "I have carefully examined the MS. placed by you in my hands entitled 'Typee' and am willing to publish it — making a few slight omissions — which on the score of taste I have no hesitation in saying will be for the benefit of both author and book." (Murray surely never had to read the passage about the orator trying to talk while eating chub.) We cannot identify these slight omissions, since the fair copy does not survive and so few leaves of the draft are known to be extant. Murray thought he was accepting "the" manuscript when he offered to pay one hundred pounds "at Six Months from the day of publication" for the right to print one thousand copies and for the English copyright. Now or later Murray made the decision to put the book in his series, the Home and Colonial Library.

Sometime before 6 December (in their "last conversation") Gansevoort broke the news to Murray that the "last steamer from the U.S." had brought "some corrections & additions to the Mss in your hands." On 6 December he sent them to Murray:

> The bulk of the new matter consists of three new chapters, numbered respectively 20 — 21 — & 27, which are in my humble opinion less amenable than the others to the faults you have pointed out, and from their subject matter, especially that of Chapter 27, will go far to give a more life-like air to the whole, an[d] parry the incredulity of those who may be disposed to regard the work as an ingenious fiction.
>
> There are also two schedules of minor corrections & additions relating chiefly to the Taboo, the cause of Missions, and the religious belief of the Marquesans, to which I beg leave to invite your attention.

Chapter 20 ("History of a Day") began as an easy expansion which formalized information that had already been suggested in a scattered way, then included a new section on "dances of the Marquesan Girls" — a section which displeased Murray so much that he removed it. Herman took chapter 21, on the spring of Arva Wai and the great stone pi-pis, largely from Porter, while chapter 27, "The social Condition and general Character of the Typees," also derives from Porter, although Herman managed to give it the somewhat spurious air of an eyewitness account. The additions did not materially alter the nature of the work that Murray had already seen, but they did tend to help establish the narrator as a genuine observer of what he described.

The minor corrections and additions Gansevoort referred to cannot all be identified, but most likely they included three substantial additions at the ends of chapters. The new footnote defining "arva" and "wai" in chapter 21 (p. 153) made redundant the definition of arva which survived in a later chapter (23, p. 165), but which had been written earlier. The minor addition at the end of chapter 24 (p. 177) began with "But in sober seriousness, I hardly knew what to make of the religion of the valley"; this was redundant, since Gansevoort had carried with him this passage that stood earlier in the chapter (p. 171): "For my own part, I am free to confess my almost entire inability to gratify any curiosity that may be felt with regard to the theology of the valley." The new insertions made both chapters 24 and 26 intrude awkwardly upon the sequence of chapters concerning the Festival of the Calabashes. Furthermore, the addition on the taboo in chapter 30 weakened the suspense over whether or not Tommo would be tattooed. Thus for greater believability Melville paid the cost of introducing some stylistic and structural weaknesses, the inevitable result of tinkering at long distance without recourse to a perfect copy.

Gansevoort got possession of the manuscript from Murray in order to incorporate into it the new chapters and smaller changes, then wrote to Murray on 20 December: "Herewith I return the Mss with the exception of the 11th & 12th chapters which with your permission I will retain until Monday. Four or five pages & slips of paper cont'g for the most part corrections by the author accompany it. He seems to regard them as of importance & I should be sorry to have them overlooked." This last stage of making large insertions and making small insertions and alterations was tedious for Gansevoort, and possibly annoying for Murray, who hired a young man named Henry Milton to clean up the manuscript, paying him twenty-nine shillings for the job on 31 December. (Milton was a nephew of the travel writer and novelist Frances Trollope, and cousin of the later novelist, Anthony Trollope.) The decent state of surviving pages of the draft, surely messier than the fair copy Gansevoort took to London, shows that Milton did not deserve any more than that — he was just tidying up the manuscript a little, not rewriting it.

Before he knew that Murray was determined to censor the passages which he thought were in bad taste, Herman already had sent to Gansevoort the passage describing the dances of the Marquesan girls (ch. 20), which

Murray duly censored, although he allowed the American sailor to go very far indeed in describing the girls as dancing "all over, as it were," in such a way that watching them was "almost too much for a quiet, sober-minded, modest young man" like him. This was the family style of humor, and may even be an echo of Gansevoort's speech in Newark on 2 November 1844: "these Tennessee girls take right hold as if they meant it, and in a way that is really delightful to a plain, backward, bashful man like myself." This, Herman remembered, had evoked "Great laughter and cheers." (At some point in the next months, Herman learned that Murray had rejected his erotic addition; he regained possession of it, possibly, or, more likely, hung on to his draft of it, and reused it in his next book.)

Gansevoort's services to Herman in regard to *Typee* were over, for the moment, as the year came to a close. He was almost surely oblivious of the fact that he had been the subject of highly undiplomatic political and personal backstabbing. James Buchanan wrote a personal letter to Minister McLane from Washington on 3 December: "I have presented Mr. Melville's case strongly to the President; but without effect. He does not know where to send him. Carr will not be removed from Constantinople." While that was going on secretly, Gansevoort became embroiled in diplomatic controversy. In October the extent of the potato blight in Ireland had become clear, and the British prime minister, Sir Robert Peel, had distributed emergency supplies of Indian corn the next month (even while much more food was leaving Ireland), then on 5 December resigned when he could not push through Parliament the repeal of the Corn Laws. On 4 December, in the midst of the British and Irish crisis, Gansevoort explained to Murray that he was "more than usually occupied," because McLane was in Paris.

One of the matters occupying Gansevoort that week was a charge in the London *Morning Herald* on 8 December that McLane had planted in the *Times* a story designed to influence the debate about "the tariff question" in the United States. On 9 December Gansevoort wrote to the editor of the *Morning Herald*, with a copy to the *Times*, which printed his letter on 10 December:

> Thirty years of high public service, and a probity in private life which is proverbial, have placed Mr. M'Lane beyond the reach of attacks like these....
>
> We do not suspect Mr. M'Lane of such indirect practice, but whether he has or has not resorted to it, the guilt of *The Times* is the same; for that journal ought not to publish what it knew to be false upon the suggestion of any one, least of all upon the suggestion of a foreign Minister.

More details about these weeks came in some recollections the publisher George P. Putnam printed in his revived *Putnam's Magazine* for December

1869; he was a little askew on the sequence, but his memory was basically sound about what he had been told, however flawed his source may have been:

> When Mr. McLane was a second time Minister to England, I was honored with some intimacy with his amiable family. . . . Mr. [Washington] Irving, who had been Secretary of Legation, with Mr. McLane at the same post in 1830, and was now Minister to Spain, visited his old friend when he came to London, about the time the Oregon question was most hotly discussed. During Mr. McLane's visit to Paris, when this negotiation was in the most delicate condition and a war seemed to many inevitable, I was told that the Minister was invited by Lord Aberdeen to a formal diplomatic dinner, given to the leading foreign Ministers. In his absence, the Secretary, Mr. M——, appeared in his place. Replying to a formal toast, "The President of the United States," the Secretary electrified the diplomatic circle by a Tammany speech, winding up somewhat thus: "I was one who helped to place Mr. Polk where he now is, and I know that he will not *dare* to recede from 54.40!"

What with Herman's aggressively pro-British appendix and Gansevoort's aggressive pro-expansionist speeches (which went round London diplomatic and publishing circles), John Murray may have been not a little bewildered by what he had gotten himself into.

Whether Polk was horrified by what McLane and others reported from London or whether he thought the British might be thrown off guard by so fiery a secretary of legation, Gansevoort was enunciating, in extreme fashion, Democratic national policy which in a small way he had helped to shape. Until the Mexican government gave the United States some pretext for seizing California, the only Pacific territory within the grasp of the United States was Oregon, ideally construed as a region stretching northward to 54°40′ or beyond. Herman had learned from firsthand experience in the Marquesas Islands, the Society Islands, and the Hawaiian Islands just how predatory a set of colonialists the French and the British were, although he could congratulate himself on Great Britain's ultimate refusal to seize the Hawaiian Islands. He knew that the Pacific Fleet had not been anchored at Callao merely to bore him intolerably—it was also there to respond to any threat to American interests from the French or the British. Herman could not forget that Commodore Jones on the frigate *United States* in 1842 had actually seized California, for a few hours, in an incursion at Monterey that could be treated as comic but was an altogether serious manifestation of the intention of the United States either to seize California for herself or at the least to keep any European power from seizing it from Mexico. Whatever their personal differences about the relative benignity of the French and the

British in the Pacific, Herman and Gansevoort took American expansion as inevitable, however ironical Herman could treat the subject. Like other Democrats, they had grasped the significance of the "Pacific Rim" a good century and a half before the phrase entered the language.

The dire implication of Putnam's story is that the secretary of legation, with a little help from irrational Britons, just at this juncture, might have helped to start a war. Yet a vignette from 14 March 1846, three months later, may represent more fairly Gansevoort's characteristic tone. The witness was Captain E. Knight, who along with a Philadelphian and a South Carolinian had made an excursion to Cambridge with Gansevoort:

> During the month of March last, I had the pleasure of riding many miles, visiting many places, and spending many days and nights, in his company. I shall never forget our visit to Cambridge. Passing under the same archways, along the same walks, through the same doors and halls, which were so familiar once to many great men, we finally arrived at the Library rooms, when Mr. M, walking up to an immense terrestrial globe suspended in the centre of one of the rooms, and placing his hand upon it, said, Look here, gentlemen, and see if any American can carefully examine the map of our globe, and not feel a gratitude and just pride at seeing the geographical position our country holds upon its face. Here lies Asia and the whole East, with its immense wealth. There is the mouth of the Columbia River, almost as near Canton as London is to New York. Now here is a little speck called Europe, upon the Eastern shores of the Atlantic, and a smaller speck on its Western shore called New England, including New York city, which have ever held the trade of this immense region, at the expense of passing Cape Horn, or the Cape of Good Hope, the South Atlantic, Indian Ocean, &c. &c. "Look here," said he, "and tell me if any American can give up, or barter away the valley of the Columbia, and not, Esau like, sell his birth-right?"

The family read this notice in the Albany *Argus* of 4 June 1846, reprinted from the New York *Journal of Commerce*, where others in the family already had seen it. Anyone who knew Gansevoort could see him walking up to the globe and placing his hand on it, and anyone who knew him could hear his voice speaking the words recorded by Captain Knight. Knowing nothing of the London gossip about Gansevoort's intrusion of Tammany politics into London diplomacy, anyone in the family could read those words and think of him as a policy-maker, not just an implementer of policy. Herman, in particular, could reflect upon Gansevoort's pronouncements until he himself was ready to offer the world what he called (in a letter of 5 June 1849) "the peculiar thoughts & fancies of a Yankee upon politics & other matters."

A Modern Crusoe

1846

Since the joyous moment when we first read Robinson Crusoe and believed it all, and wondered all the more because we believed, we have not met with so bewitching a work as this narrative of Herman Melville's. . . . Like Robinson Crusoe, however, we cannot help suspecting that if there be really such a person as Herman Melville, he has either employed a Daniel Defoe to describe his adventures, or is himself both a Defoe and an Alexander Selkirk.

John Bull (London), 7 March 1846

ON 1 JANUARY GANSEVOORT TOOK Murray's note for one hundred pounds directly to his fellow American Joshua Bates at Baring Brothers and asked him to discount it — to give him about the equivalent of five hundred American dollars minus a percentage to cover their commission and their carrying the note to term. In a letter of 3 January Gansevoort sent five pounds to Herman with the news that Murray had formally purchased his manuscript; he also sent three letters to Allan "together with a dft for £100" — a sum that sounds peculiar, for he would not have received the full hundred pounds from Baring Brothers, and may be an error for one hundred dollars. Herman later reported that Allan had sent a hundred dollars to Lansingburgh, money Herman thought was from Allan's "collections" but money that Gansevoort thought (when Herman brought the subject up) was money he himself had "sent out by the Jany steamer." Gansevoort tried to straighten things out in a letter to Herman on 3 April. Allan, he complained, seemed "to find it entirely too much trouble" to send him "the monthly accounts of receipts & disbursements," none since the end of November, so that Gansevoort consequently was "in a state of almost entire ignorance as to what is transpiring at No 10 Wall St" (Allan's new address) and all because of Allan's selfish behavior: "This is very unthinking in him for my thoughts are so much at home that much of my time is spent in disquieting apprehensions as to matters & things there. I continue to live within my income, but to do so, am forced to live a life of daily self denial." The details are muddy, but from the English edition of his first book Herman must have received somewhat more than four hundred dollars, at a time when a small family could live modestly on one thousand dollars a year in a city in the United States.

Through a combination of personal charm and sheer accident Gansevoort was able to do Herman another service that not only gained him an American publisher but established the pattern that was to prevail for the next several years: he would receive a sizable sum of money for first publication in London, followed rapidly by publication in New York, and payment from the American publisher (unless he had already received an advance). On 6 January 1846, while Gansevoort was taking care of his correspondence at No. 1 St. James's Place, Washington Irving, the newly resigned minister to Spain and the most popular American writer, walked in, fresh from Paris, "lamenting Mr McLane's absence from town" at Lord Ashburton's estate (as Gansevoort wrote in his new journal). Irving was miffed, for, having resigned knowing that Polk would not reappoint him, he had sought out the legation in the certainty that, Polk-appointee or not, his old friend McLane would be hospitable. McLane's absence was Herman Melville's gain, for McLane did not have a chance to warn his friend against the secretary of his legation. Collegial old boy that he was, Irving turned to the secretary as the best available American and "fell into an interesting conversation which lasted two hours," as Gansevoort recorded in his journal. Having pored over *The Sketch Book* eight or nine years earlier and copied out many passages from it (and having read parts of it and other works by Irving at other times), Gansevoort was highly gratified "to see the obvious frankness" with which Irving was treating him—a courtesy he quite wrongly assumed that he owed to kind words from McLane. Flattered and delighted by the older man's openness and ingenuousness, Gansevoort invited Irving to breakfast the next morning, and as he walked home he stopped by Albemarle Street to invite John Murray to come also. The breakfast on 7 January was a triumphant occasion, for characters in the old volumes of his *Index Rerum* (he had at least some of the volumes with him) came to life: "Washington Irving & Mr Jno Murray the publisher breakfasted with me. Mr I seemed very happy to meet the son of his old friend. They talked of old times, of old Mr M, Scott, Rogers, Wilkie, Gifford, Lockhart &c &c. I listened. At 12 Mr M —— went away & I read to Mr Irving various parts of the first 10 chapters of Herman's forthcoming book. He was very much pleased—declared portions to be 'exquisite', sd the style was very 'graphic' & prophesied its success—This delighted me." The breakfast extended three hours, and after that Gansevoort and Irving "walked arm in arm to Wiley & Putnam's" London office, where they parted. Two hours later, at three, they met again and walked together in Regent Street.

The next day, 8 January, Gansevoort breakfasted pleasantly with three

Americans, including "Mr Putnam of the firm of Wiley & Putnam," Irving's American publisher, and an important man already, although only a year older than Gansevoort. (He had a literary connection himself, for he was a first cousin of Sophia Peabody Hawthorne, the wife of Nathaniel Hawthorne, some of whose stories Gansevoort and Herman had seen, without his name signed to them, in local papers in the late 1830s.) Just the past month, Putnam had heard that Gansevoort Melville's temperament was dangerous when loosed on the real world of international politics, so he was more forewarned than Irving. Later that day, McLane got back to London, but at first his presence did nothing to interfere with Gansevoort's new intimacy with Irving. After dinner at McLane's that night Irving exerted his prerogative of dozing in his chair while Gansevoort and the minister "talked for a couple of hours about Canada, Mexico & the future of the U.S.," McLane, from a slave state, Delaware, going so far as to acknowledge his fear that "an enlargement of the power of the North" would threaten "the safety of the Union."

The next day, McLane and Irving naturally excluded Gansevoort from some of their pleasures, such as breakfast "with old Mr Rogers the poet," but on the day after that, Saturday the tenth, Irving came by the legation and for more than an hour talked to Gansevoort "with much unreserve of his affairs & his literary labors, manner of working &c" — a remarkable experience for the secretary. Now, Gansevoort learned that the great author had informed George P. Putnam about the exquisite and graphic adventure story written by the brother of the affable and respectful young secretary of legation. Even though he knew that Gansevoort was regarded in some circles as an incendiary, Putnam also knew that there was no better judge of literature than the author of *The Sketch Book*, and no author he more wanted to please, so he expressed his willingness to see what the fuss was about. Accordingly, on Saturday night Gansevoort handed "the first 107 pp proof sheets of Hermans Mss to Mr Putnam to read."

Sunday night, 11 January, at McLane's, where Washington Irving and others were present, Gansevoort had a moment with Putnam and got this response about *Typee:* "He expressed himself much pleased, in fact delighted with the opening chapters, sd that they kept him from church, that it had all the interest of Robinson Crusoe, superadded to that of being a work of fact. He expressed his desire to publish it in N Yk in Wiley & Putnam's Library of choice Reading." As energetic as the secretary himself, Putnam had worked out the full terms of his offer before he called on Gansevoort the evening of 12 January:

He sd that he should like to publish Herman's Mss in their "Library of Choice reading" and would publish it on joint a/c, or allow the author 12½% on the retail price of the book on each copy sold, making a settlement each July & January, & leaving it optional to settle with the author to select either mode of settlement when the time shall arrive. He will publish it in March at 50 cts — This would on the 12½% principle give Herman 6¼ cts on each copy sold. I anticipate a sale in the U. S. of not less than 5000 copies in 12 mos. He is to make his offer in writing tomorrow.

Putnam did make the offer in writing on Tuesday the thirteenth, asking for a copy of the proofs to be ready for the steamer on 4 February, so that the book could be published simultaneously in both countries. On the fourteenth, lawyer that he was, Gansevoort called upon Putnam "to get him to alter the terms of his proposal to publish Herman's Mss in the U. S." — perhaps just to specify that Gansevoort was giving him rights only for the United States. On the sixteenth at 4:15 they concluded the agreement: Putnam was to bring *Typee* out "in 2 nos at 3/ ea in the 'Library of choice reading.' " The plan was that the first number would be published on 28 February or 1 March, in order, they thought, to assure the copyright by simultaneous publication.

In the absence of an international copyright, for another half century American publishers blithely reprinted any book shipped across the Atlantic. British publishers were more selective, being disdainful of most books that appeared in the United States, but they also were free to reprint any book that was imported. In the mid-1840s a few British publishers paid some American authors for what purported to be copyright, maintaining the fiction that if a book appeared simultaneously in the two countries no other British firm would pirate it. They were acting as if they could imbue their gentlemen's agreements with the force of law. This fiction was exploded by an unambiguous legal decision in 1849, after which American writers could hope only to be the beneficiary of the occasional reckless generosity from British publishers, the same publishers who were being pirated at will anywhere in the United States. In the mid-1840s no American author could reasonably expect to profit, from year to year, by offering his or her wares to British publishers, all of whom were free to reprint any American book without paying a shilling for it. Yet more than financial gain, some British publishers wanted the honor of publishing worthy American books and encouraging American literature in general. Melville's father as a schoolboy had been taught that magnanimity was the rare quality by which heroes maintained their tranquility and preserved the free use of their reason. Magnanimity in the 1840s was hardly a rare quality among British publishers who set themselves to encourage the spirit of literature in states which had so rudely cast off allegiance to the Crown.

When Gansevoort saw Murray an hour later, at 5:15 on 16 January, he learned that Irving had spoken "most favorably" about the book. Murray told Gansevoort it would run from 220 to 240 pages (to be published in two numbers) and promised "the whole proof sheets by the 3rd prox, without fail," so Putnam could have a full set to send to the United States on the "Despatch day," 3 February. By midnight on 16 January Gansevoort had "revised" the proof sheets of *Typee* up through the 107 pages he had shown Putnam. He spent part of the morning of Sunday the first of February correcting the Murray proof sheets "of Herman's 'Typee,'" finding that his "opinion of its intrinsic merits" was "raised by this careful perusal." On 3 February he "corrected the *last* proof sheets of 'Typee,'" which he had just received. Afterward he wrote formally to Wiley & Putnam to complete the arrangements ("Herewith you have the corrected proof sheets of 'Typee' complete in full time to send by the steamer tomorrow. I trust that the dedication to Judge Shaw will not be overlooked in the hurry of the publication"); then he carried a complete set of proofs of the work to Putnam "for transmission to the U.S." He also wrote Herman "a long letter," a letter each to Helen and Allan, and several other letters, and sent out his usual supply of newspapers to family, to Judge Shaw, and to political friends in several cities. The now-lost letter to Herman was received by the family in Lansingburgh with the profoundest excitement, since it contained an account of Washington Irving's providential arrival in London and his role in arranging for the American publication of the book by Wiley & Putnam. The greatest American writer had played fairy godfather to *Typee*. It also contained detailed information about the state of international copyright—enough, as it turned out, to alarm Herman when something seemed not to proceed on the schedule Gansevoort had laid out so meticulously.

On 3 February, that busy day, Washington Irving (back from a visit to Birmingham) stopped by the legation where he "read the Preface & Appendix to Typee" in proof and "expressed himself highly pleased—prophesied its success," clearly not seeing anything incendiary in the appendix. (Grateful, the next day Gansevoort in a letter to Henry William Ellsworth [1814–64], the chargé d'affaires to Sweden and Norway, described Irving as "a most kind hearted excellent man.") There were still details about the book to handle, for on the ninth Gansevoort wrote Murray "a note covering dedication of Typee, Appendix &c." On the evening of 24 February Murray sent Gansevoort "6 bound copies of Herman's book," *Narrative of a Four Months' Residence Among the Natives of a Valley of the Marquesas Islands; or, A Peep at Polynesian Life*, and Gansevoort exulted in his diary: "It looks well—God speed it." Murray had arbitrarily rejected Melville's own main title, *Typee;* the "Peep" subtitle was probably Melville's, meant to warn the reader about the casual, unexhaustive nature of the account they were to read, but since that word was having a vogue in titles and subtitles of travel books it was less a disclaimer than it now appears. Gansevoort wrote Allan the next day, and most likely sent at least one copy of the book to Herman. Never mind the title — the book was out.

G. P. Putnam had been the right man (an American publisher) in the right place (London) at the right time (January 1846) to listen to his prize author Washington Irving's advice that he help launch young Gansevoort Melville's still younger brother's literary career with *Typee*. Putnam did what Irving suggested, with no quibbling over the details of the book, and no consultation with his partner, John Wiley. Putnam himself dealt with Herman from time to time for another quarter century, on courteous terms, but his first exposure to the Melvilles was ineffaceable — Gansevoort in person, Herman in proof sheets. In London, Putnam became privy to Irving's abrupt retrenchment once Louis McLane had expressed his views on Gansevoort's dangerous behavior in London, and undoubtedly he knew why Irving, the consummate old boy of the political and literary establishment, immediately and irrevocably washed his hands of the Melvilles. Before McLane got to him, Irving had propelled the young whaleman-author into American celebrity. If he had not been turned against Melville, Irving might have sought him out on his return and befriended him in ways that would decisively have altered his life. As it was, in the copious letters written during the rest of his life, most of it spent at Sunnyside, soon to be only a short commute by train to Manhattan, Irving expressed interest in many new American writers but never (so far as anyone has found) let the name Melville pass his lips or be formed by his pen.

The previous November, Gansevoort had seen a good deal of another American author, Nathaniel Parker Willis, when this highly successful imitator of Washington Irving had showed up at the American legation in early November 1845, on his way to Berlin, where he was to be an attaché to the legation there. Willis had called twice upon Gansevoort that month, complaining of eye troubles. He was too decorous to have slapped Gansevoort on the back and exclaimed, "Old horse, I love you," but the men recalled his putting that vignette into the *Mirror* and shared the oddity of their reminiscing about it now that they were both so far from New York, not to say Tennessee. The men were on such easy terms that Gansevoort must have told him about his brother's manuscript, which was still being considered at Murray's. Willis then left for the Continent, from which he sent home a series of letters to the New York *Evening Mirror*. After Hiram Fuller took over as owner in January any letters should have gone to George P. Morris for the new *National Press* instead, but none have been found. (Although he wrote long letters to the *Mirror* from the Continent, apparently Willis did not write from London at a time when he would naturally have made grist for his journalistic mill from Gansevoort Melville's efforts on behalf of his brother's manuscript.)

In early January 1846, Willis was back in London. On the ninth the Bostonian bookseller Charles F. Dennett called upon Gansevoort, as an available American, to ask him to be his groomsman at his wedding; his other groomsman would be Willis, whose late sister had been Dennett's first wife. Willis called on Gansevoort at half past ten on Sunday the eleventh to second Dennett's request and to make a closer friend of Gansevoort, who recorded in his journal: "We had a long, friendly & I may almost say intimate conversation. He gave me many details of his literary life — the reason that he has of late years written in such a light & almost trifling manner." Gansevoort shared with Willis the momentous news of the progress of the Murray edition and of Washington Irving's and G. P. Putnam's interest in *Typee*, and perhaps even gave Willis what he had just given Irving four days earlier, a private reading of various early parts of the forthcoming book. Gansevoort on 19 January stood up for Dennett along with Willis at St. Mary le Bow. Then he attended the "very sumptuous déjeuner" afterward (as he wrote in his journal), and at the conclusion "walked away together" with Willis. In the last week of January, Willis, his daughter Imogen (named from *Cymbeline*), and the Dennetts sailed for the United States, where Willis soon transferred his intimacy to Herman, as friend and journalistic ally. Through the next half decade of Manhattan literary life, Willis always saw Herman partly in the subdued light of the ceremony at St. Mary le Bow, an unshakable memory, something else Herman owed to Gansevoort.

In promoting *Typee* (the only title Herman and Gansevoort had used, although Gansevoort soon picked up *Marquesas Islands* from the reviews as the short title on the spine) Murray had sent advance sheets to the *Athenæum*, which on Saturday, 21 February, gave it (as Gansevoort was pleased to see): "7½ columns of extracts, mingled with favorable criticism & closing with a promise to continue." On March first Gansevoort saw "the rather favorable critique in yesterday's 'Spectator' on Herman Melville's Marquesas Islands" — and now was relishing the mouthful of author's name and London short title. By the steamer of 4 March Gansevoort sent his usual letters (three to Allan, one to Herman), newspapers ("Mother 14. Augusta 1. Herman 6. . . . Mrs Polk 1. . . . Ch Jus Shaw 1"), and this time books (" 1 copy Hermans Marquesas to Mother, 1 Do — to Mrs Bancroft" — Mrs. George Bancroft, second wife of the historian, the man whose refusal to lead the delegation to Van Buren and whose later refusal to address the Democracy at Nashville had cleared the way for Gansevoort to take his place both times. Bancroft had gallantly run for governor of Massachusetts in 1844, attempting to hold the party together, and after his loss had been consoled with the office of secretary of the navy; briefly on intimate terms with Gansevoort, he seems never to have made any overture to Herman or to have taken any particular interest in his writings).

On 4 March Gansevoort had dismaying news from Murray: "He tells me that the genuineness of the Residence in the Marquesas is doubted, some thinking that it is an invention, & not a narrative." Murray was concerned, for doubt of the authenticity of the *Marquesas Islands* impeached the reputation of the entire Home and Colonial Library (which included Borrow's *Bible in Spain* and Heber's *Indian Journals*), but in fact relatively few reviewers let their skepticism mar their pleasure in the book. Gansevoort was overcome by a strange lassitude that evening, and could do little about the suspicions. On 13 March he noted that six days earlier both the *Critic* and the *Examiner* had praised the book. On 18 March, dispatch day, Gansevoort selected three newspapers for President Polk's wife and bundled up thirty-seven other papers ("principally Examiners & Critics contg notices of Herman's Marquesas Islands"): "9 papers to Mother, 3 to Herman, 2 Mrs [Andrew] Stevenson, 2 Mrs Shaw, 2 Croswell, 3 S D W Bloodgood, 1 ea to Mrs Bancroft, [Eugene A.] Casserly, Allan Fawcett, [Elisha P.] Hurlbut [a political ally who later married Melville's cousin Catherine Van Vechten], Jno Hone, Mrs [Maggie Van Rensselaer] DePeyster Douw, Mrs [Teunis] Van Vechten, W E Cramer, Mrs Tomlinson [wife of Theodore E. Tomlinson, the young New York City lawyer, Alexander Bradford's partner], Miss Fanny Mason, James Taylor, Peter Gansevoort & N P Willis."

These names, familiar and unfamiliar, show how widely Gansevoort had cherished his old ties even while forming new friendships. In Washington he had met the Virginians Mr. and Mrs. Andrew Stevenson, he the former Speaker of the House, once appointed to the Court of St. James's but rejected by the Senate, she a woman with much of the force and charm of her cousin Dolley Madison. Mrs. Bancroft was likewise notable in her own right, as the immensely wealthy widow Bliss when she married George Bancroft; Gansevoort had charmed her during his October 1843 visit to Boston. Hope Shaw was notable mainly as the wife of Lemuel Shaw, but she fits the pattern: Gansevoort was attentive to many women married to powerful men, women somewhat older than he, and some of these women found Gansevoort's deferential attention immensely attractive. The reviews he sent the women would please them, whether they were wives of public figures or members of the Gansevoort family like Maggie Douw. Edwin Croswell of the *Argus* and William E. Cramer, Croswell's assistant, would know just what to do with the reviews, as Nathaniel Parker Willis would. When Willis went back to work with Morris (who on 14 February started the weekly *National Press*, later renamed the *Home Journal*), he had inside information on Herman's book from Gansevoort's mouth and English papers selected by Gansevoort himself. This odd lot of relatives, friends, politicians' wives, political allies, and journalists could be counted upon to help, indirectly or directly, with the launching of the Wiley & Putnam edition of *Typee*, as well as simply to rejoice in Gansevoort's brother's success. The pity was that no one in the family was on the spot in London to witness the phenomenal spectacle of Gansevoort suffused with uncritical pride in his brother Herman.

As Murray had planned it, the *Athenæum* on 21 February, on the basis of the sheets supplied by Murray, had set the tone for the British reception: "we are sure no one will refuse thanks to the contributor of a book so full of fresh and richly-coloured matter. Mr. Melville's manner is New World all over; and we need merely advert to the name of [John Lloyd] Stephens, the foremost among American pilgrims, to explain our epithet." The *Spectator* a week later had defined the value of the work: "it is the first account that has been published of a residence among the natives of the Polynesian Islands, by a person who has lived with them in their own fashion, and as near as may be upon terms of social equality: for although hundreds of mariners have lived and died upon these islands, and some of them — as Christian the mutineer — were perhaps capable of writing a book, none of them that we remember have ever done so." Sea captains, scientists, missionaries had written down their observations, but Melville had given the first eyewitness account on the basis of actual life with the natives. (There languished, unpublished, an account by William Pascoe Crook for the period 1797–99 and one by Edward Robarts for 1798–1806, now available as *The Marquesan Journal of Edward Robarts, 1797–1824*.) On 7 March the *Critic* made the same point: the picture "of Polynesian life and scenery is incomparably the most vivid and forcible that has ever been laid before the public."

Many of the early London reviewers acknowledged their delight, but were not at all convinced that the book was what it purported to be — an account of personal experiences written by the adventurer himself. From what he knew of national differences, the reviewer in the *Spectator* accepted the narrative as authentic: "Had this work been put forward as the production of an English common sailor, we should have had some doubts of its authenticity, in the absence of distinct proof." In the United States, he asserted, it was "customary with young men of respectability to serve as common seamen," as Cooper (he supposed) and Dana had done. Besides, the "wide-spread system of popular education also bestows upon the American a greater familiarity with popular literature and a readier use of the pen than is usual with classes of the same apparent grade in England." The reviewer had received special assurance that "the narrative is the *bona fide* production of a brother to one of the gentlemen officially attached to the American legation in this country, and his alone." The *Examiner* on 7 March took a similar line on its authenticity: "Mr Melville, like Mr Dana, is a young and educated American, who had signed articles as a common seaman on board an American South-Sea whaler. The precise meaning or drift of this custom, we confess we cannot arrive at; unless it be to qualify for the writing of interesting books." The *Critic* on 7 March was certain that the writer "though filling the post of a common sailor, is certainly no common man," and explained that his doubts had been allayed upon learning that the writer was the brother of a member of the American legation. Young Americans, like young Germans, were more apt to go out and see the world for themselves than young Englishmen. On 7 March *John Bull* also expressed both delight and skepticism. The London *Mirror* on 7 March sounded the name of "Herman Melville" and declared it rang "marvelously like the fanciful appellation of a hero of romance," but was "a true cognomen," most likely. On 21 March the London *Atlas* acknowledged "certain doubts" that had to be overcome, and some lingering uneasiness: "Now the pleasure we derive from Mr. Melville's narrative would be much diminished, did we suppose that its contents reached us at second-hand, after being largely modified in their passage through the mind of a professional *littérateur.* But this we will venture to say is not the case." Even if the manuscript had been "revised by a European," it had not, internal evidence suggested, "been rewritten by any other hand than the author's." Edgy but open-minded, the reviewers in the great London papers were remarkably judicious and tolerant.

The earliest London reviewers took a decidedly unprudish view of the scene in which mermaids swim out to board the whaleship, and more than one of them printed, deadpan, Melville's blithe fantasy that the *Perseverance* might still be "regularly tacking twice in the twenty-four hours somewhere off Buggerry Island, or the Devil's-Tail Peak." There was at first little criticism of Melville's descriptions of the nudity of the islanders and their un-English (and un-American) sexual behavior, although *John Bull* delicately observed that a few passages were liable "to the same censure which was bestowed upon Dr. Hawkesworth for his account of Otaheite, in Cook's Voyages," and in April *Simmonds' Colonial Magazine and Foreign Miscellany* commented that "one or two voluptuous scenes might well have been expunged, and the high strain of admiration for savage life and uncivilized customs somewhat moderated, before the book was sent forth for circulation in family circles, to fascinate the minds of inexperienced youth."

The *Critic* on 14 March departed from the early pattern by offering an extremely long argument with Melville on the relative merits of savagery and civilization: "Seldom have savages found so zealous a vindicator of their

morals; rarely, too, has Christianity owned so ungrateful a son. What ROUS-
SEAU, in his famous Dijon thesis, traced out in theory, MR. MELVILLE endeavours to exhibit in practice. Both are wrong." Rousseau had backed his
views "by a remark of DIDEROT's; and though he supported them in a strain
of fervid and bewildering eloquence, it afterwards became known that they
were as contrary to the deliberate convictions of his judgment as they are
specious, imaginary, and unsubstantial." Melville now failed in his attempt
"from a want of comprehensiveness in argument." The *Critic* also objected
to Melville's treatment of the missionaries: "it is remarkable that he never
speaks of them but in terms either of downright disrespect, of ridicule as
often as he can, or to charge them with gross and wilful exaggeration in their
statements, or with credulity and blindness in their dealings with the natives." Melville's slurs against the missionaries were compounded by his taking "a light tone" toward the natives' being "idol-worshippers" and their
having defective (and downright un-English) notions of chastity and family
relations. The reviewer was not put off by Melville's disclaimer in the preface, which itself was objectionable for its "despicable and mischievous" tone
of mock respect. Clearly, Melville did not have "the real interests of Christianity very seriously at heart." Others saw the tone as expressing a whole-
some bonhomie, but the reviewer in the *Critic* identified a quality of the book
that bothered other readers (particularly Americans) even more on subsequent reflection than during the first reading: the tone was insidious.

Returning to the subject the next week, 28 March, the reviewer in the
Critic drew support from a book it had located in the interval, John Coul-
ther's *Adventures in the Pacific*, which displayed a correct attitude toward
Christian triumphs in the South Seas. The London *Eclectic Review* for April
also condemned Melville: "The missionary of the gospel has been the friend,
the advocate, and the defender alike of the Polynesian islander, the Caffree,
the Hottentot, the Bushman of Africa, and the Negro Slave of our western
colonies. Whilst humanity survives, who will cease to hold in grateful reverence the names of Williams, Philip, and Knibb." Still, these reviews were
anomalous, and the *Times* spoke for the majority in saying Melville had
written "with a laudable and Christian purpose": "Let it be regarded as an
apology for the Pagan; a plea for the South Sea Islanders, governments, and
missionaries, who understand so little the sacred charge which God commits
to them, when He places in their hands the children of His favoured sunny
regions; may they learn from fiction a lesson which experience has hitherto
failed to teach them — viz., that if it be needful for Christianity to approach
the Heathen, it is equally necessary that it should approach him *reverently and
tenderly.*" Most English reviewers, one can safely assume, were Church of
England men (or men and a few women), not apt to be wholly sympathetic

with the cause of missions, which was, in their country, primarily the activity of dissenters, most often Methodists. Still, it took only a few prudes and militant supporters of the missionaries to shake Murray's confidence, since he himself had doubted the authenticity of the narrative and had tried to be beforehand in eliminating the most glaring examples of bad taste.

The review in the *Times* on 6 April marked a more cautious stage in the reading of the book. Delighting along with Melville in the depictions of "the houris," the reviewer exclaimed (in a phrase that proved highly quotable): "Enviable Herman! A happier dog it is impossible to imagine than Herman in the Typee Valley." Yet delighted though he was, the reviewer had all along been gathering evidence that the narrative had to be a piece of fiction, not fact. Melville's education had betrayed him: "In his own province, the voyages of Cook, Carteret, Byron, Kotzebue, and Vancouver are familiar to him; he can talk glibly of Count Bouffon and Baron Cuvier, and critically, when he likes, of Teniers." Furthermore, the reviewer saw that the "book betrays itself," and pointed out some inconsistencies that other reviewers had missed: "After a week or two's sojourn the guest, ignorant of the Typee language when he first set foot in the valley, with most unaccountable facility understands all that is said to him, although the discourse of the chiefs comprehends abstruse points and very complex reasoning; and yet at the end of two or three months, forgetting what happened before, he informs us that gesticulation is required to enlighten him on the most ordinary subjects." This skepticism influenced some subsequent reviewers, and perturbed the already nervous John Murray. Objectors, however, could not halt the instant popularity of the book. The unknown sailor had become the famous author, the modern Defoe, and through Murray's remarkably effective marketing of his Home and Colonial Library the sailor's fame was rapidly carried throughout the British Empire.

Meanwhile, during the first months of 1846 Herman seems to have been more at Lansingburgh than Manhattan. By New Year's 1846 or shortly afterward, Melville knew that Murray was going to publish *Typee*, and he decided that he had other stories to tell. He had, to be specific, the rest of his first story to tell—what happened in the weeks of 1842 after the Australian whaler had picked him up in the Marquesas and put him ashore in the calaboose at Tahiti, and on to the time that he left Eimeo. He had been telling parts of the story aloud ever since Coleman took him aboard the *Charles and Henry* there. In the preface to *Omoo*, probably written near the end of 1846 or very early in 1847, he referred to the frequency with which the incidents in the book had been "verbally related"—his point being that his own tellings and retellings had stamped the events "upon the memory" so that as he wrote them down they were almost as fresh in his mind as if he had kept a journal to prompt his "simple recollection." What Melville did not say in the preface to *Omoo* is that the frequency with which he had verbally related the incidents in his narrative now greatly facilitated the speed and relative painlessness with which he wrote those incidents into his second book. A little of the work was already done before he started *Omoo*: Murray had rejected the description of the erotic dance, and the passage (in a draft form, or in the fair copy Gansevoort had sent back from London) was at hand for possible salvage in the course of the composition of the new book.

During those first winter weeks of his work on the new book in Lansingburgh, Herman made great progress by sticking closely to those incidents he had already told and retold. The calm was violently interrupted by a letter about *Typee* that arrived from Allan on the morning of Monday, 23 February. It had to do with the arrival in New York of the *Cambria*, which had unloaded mail but may or may not have yet unloaded packages, including the proofs of *Typee* from which Wiley & Putnam were to set the American edition. The consternation in Lansingburgh ensued because Allan had written hastily and carelessly. As Maria explained to Augusta on Saturday the twenty-eighth, none of them could understand the letter from Allan, it was "so contradictory in its information." In the face of this confusion, Maria tried her best to let Augusta know what was happening with the book:

> Herman was very desirous of having it come out in Wiley & Putnams "Library of Choice Reading," and from Allans letter, the thing was not determined, and indeed the arrival of the Book itself by the Cambria by the reading of Allans letter was more than uncertain.
>
> If the book was not got out by the first of March he would lose the Copy right in America, so Gansevoort wrote. Herman had no Idea of that you may suppose, to have the copy right was all to Herman — so he concluded to go to New York, altho Gansevoort particularly requested him to remain here — but too much was at stake and he went down — to assure himself that all was safe.
>
> Gansevoort wrote Helen by the Cambria, he also wrote Herman that he believed the book would have brilliant success, and do you believe Augusta — he even went so far — *was so very kind* as to offer him some advice about not being too much elated — with his success — and the numerous advances, complimentary &c — that would be made to him.

Exactly what Gansevoort wrote is not known, but he and Putnam had agreed to an overly tight schedule in their wish to achieve simultaneous publication. Panicked at the possible loss of American copyright for *Typee*, and very likely mindful of the horror story of Dana's loss of copyright to *Two Years before the Mast*, Herman dropped all work on *Omoo* and made plans to go to Manhattan at once: there was no point working on his second book if he was to lose the

American copyright on his first. Herman wrote Helen, who was visiting the Shaws. She was to stay a week or a little longer, and he "would take Boston in his way back and escort her home," on his own way home from New York. He left that Monday, the day Allan's letter arrived, going down to Troy in the evening (to stay with the Van Schaick cousins?) so he could catch "the early Cars" to Manhattan.

What Herman found when he reached New York City was reassuring. Even before he saw John Wiley, he probably saw some of the "showbills" for *Typee* that were pasted up around town, even on Broadway (for the Wiley & Putnam office was at No. 161, by the Rathbun Hotel). The showbills may have given Herman the first news that his book was to be published not in the Library of Choice Reading but, instead, in the Library of American Books, the Wiley & Putnam series edited by Evert A. Duyckinck — a change no one at the American publisher's office thought had to be legally negotiated. (It was just as well Melville got to enjoy the showbills, for he had paid for them, he learned from the publisher's statement of 7 October 1846.) Two years earlier Gansevoort had walked about the village of Honesdale, Pennsylvania, smiling at the sight of his "name conspicuous on every corner in letters an inch long & heralded in terms that would make Demosthenes blush." Herman's response to the showbills for *Typee* is not recorded, and none of them, any more than Gansevoort's, seems to have survived. (Now one of them, however bedraggled and repaired, might well fetch more at auction than Herman Melville earned in his lifetime.)

Herman was in New York City from 24 February until 3 or 4 March. At Wiley & Putnam's he saw the proofs that Putnam had sent, and chances are that he had to deal with John Wiley's anger about parts of the book. What happened, apparently, is that under the great pressure to attain simultaneous publication Wiley had sent the English proofs to compositors at once, without reading them, and within a very few days had received a complete set of new proofs. The haste of setting caused the New York edition to contain a good many careless errors along with a sprinkling of Americanizations in spelling. Wiley or someone else may have softened some language on the proofs (changing, for instance, "absence of the marriage tie" to "looseness of the marriage tie"), but such changes could have been made during a phase of alterations for which the printers charged, claiming three pages had been reset, probably pp. 6, 8, and 17 of the New York edition. Textual variants between the English and American editions as well as some physical evidence (p. 6 was stereotyped a line short) make it clear that the purpose of the resetting was to make some expurgations, and that it was done right away, probably as soon as Wiley saw the first proofs of his own edition, at the end of February or the beginning of March.

The passages in question are in chapters 1 and 2 (pp. 7, 8, and 15). The first occurs in an anecdote of how the natives, thinking the fully clothed wife of a missionary must be a divinity, managed to ascertain her sex then angrily stripped off all her clothing as punishment for deceiving them. The English edition continues: "The gentle dame was not sufficiently evangelised to endure this"; the American edition said simply that she "could not endure this." The second expurgation is in the passage about what happened when the island queen, the wife of Mowanna, escorted by the French in a gig "gaily bedizened with streamers," made a formal call upon the flagship of the American squadron. Fascinated by a heavily tattooed old sailor, she "gazed with admiration at the bright blue and vermilion pricking," then reciprocated: "all at once the royal lady, eager to display the hieroglyphics on her own sweet form, bent forward for a moment, and turning sharply round, threw up the skirts of her mantle, and revealed a sight from which the aghast Frenchmen retreated precipitately, and tumbling into their boat, fled the scene of so shocking a catastrophe." Wiley removed her turning sharply round and throwing up the skirts of her mantle, but ignorantly left in Melville's play on "I'll tickle your cata*s*trophe." Then, from the description of the naked Marquesan women doing their toilettes after swimming out to the *Dolly*, the first American edition was altered, after being set, so as to delete these words: "What a sight for us bachelor sailors! how avoid so dire a temptation? For who could think of tumbling these artless creatures overboard, when they had swam miles to welcome us?" A few paragraphs further, as the scene closed on the "riot and debauchery" on board the ship, the following sentence was also cut: "Not the feeblest barrier was interposed between the unholy passions of the crew and their unlimited gratification." Wiley was probably adamant about making these cuts, and it is quite possible that he made them with the young author's helpless acquiescence. As time passed and Elizabeth Shaw stayed in his mind, Melville had more of his own reasons than the year before to be wary of indelicate sexual references.

On 28 February Herman wrote Gansevoort a calm letter declaring that the news in Gansevoort's letter of 3 February about *Typee* was "gratifying enough" (the news that Gansevoort had delivered the entire work to Putnam for "transmission to the U. S." and that Washington Irving had that day, 3 February, "prophesied its success" again). Herman also informed Gansevoort that he was continuing busy (presumably on *Omoo*, which on 15 July he described, somewhat inaccurately, as "nearly completed"). Herman mentioned that there was something that he intended to write Gansevoort about but had decided to defer: "What do you allude to," Gansevoort asked — a question that stayed in Herman's mind as a poignant reminder about the folly of procrastination. There was also a crisis about Tom, for at the age of sixteen he wanted to go awhaling; Gansevoort's friend Cramer, removed to Wisconsin, in an article on *Omoo* wrote in the *Daily Wisconsin* (in August 1847) that Tom's family had been "most reluctant to part with him, but were finally induced to let him follow the bent of his adventurous spirit." Even before Augusta went to the Manor House in February it had been determined that "he should go" — to sea. Maria wanted Augusta to rejoice "that matters came to light as early as they did" (Tom's attachment to a girl — quite a man, Allan had called him, even in October 1844 — or a girl's attachment to him?). Whatever it was, the situation would remain "just so," at least "until Hermans return." Augusta was allowed to stay with the Van Rensselaers until mid-March, but Maria would write her so she could come home to meet Herman and Helen on their return. Gansevoort had given little news about himself: "Gansevoort says nothing more about himself — than that he was present at the opening of Parliament 'in Sword and Gold embroidery,' about fifteen feet from the Queen, who he says is 'lamentably fat & plain, but read her speech with right Queenly grace'" — that was on 22 January.

Herman arrived in Boston on 4 March, Hope Shaw recorded, giving his point of departure as Lansingburgh, though he came directly from New York City. Nominally, he was there to escort Helen home, but he wanted to see Lizzie. Perhaps he carried a set of Wiley & Putnam proofs, or perhaps he had been given the superseded set of proofs of the English edition, but he did not have in hand what he would have wanted to bring Judge Shaw, a printed and bound copy of the book. About the time he arrived word came from Chicago that Oakes's first child, Frank, the precipitant of the hasty wedding in New York City, had died; Shaw's letter of condolence was dated 6 March. There were social events for the young author-to-be, surely, as well as family visiting, especially to Aunt Priscilla. Helen had made friends earlier with the brothers Abbott and Amos Lawrence (owners of textile mills in Lawrence and Lowell) and their wives. Now the elder of the wealthy brothers inscribed "With the kind regards of Amos Lawrence March 9, 1846" in a copy of *Sketches of Bunker Hill Battle and Monument* by G. E. Ellis (Charlestown [Mass.], 1843); then or later Herman wrote his name above Lawrence's inscription and "Boston" below it. This was an altogether appropriate gift to a grandson of the Hero of the Tea Party, since, as everyone knew, the old major had been a host of Lafayette during the laying of the cornerstone of the Bunker Hill Monument two decades earlier; furthermore, much of the money for the monument building fund had been donated by Amos Lawrence himself. Rather than departing at once, Herman and Helen remained in Boston until Thursday, 12 March.

On 18 March, in the excitement of being an author, Herman inscribed a copy of *Typee* to the wife of Gansevoort's friend Theodore Tomlinson, rather than saving all the first copies for older acquaintances and family. The next day, he wrote his Aunt Priscilla that copies of *Typee* for each of his aunts would "soon be forthcoming": he was mending relationships as best he could, even with the aunts who had paid Helen less attention than she deserved when she first had visited the Shaws. Herman's courtship of Lizzie was now intense, although his bread-and-butter letter to Shaw, also on 19 March, was a formal acknowledgment that he had passed an "agreeable visit." He declared truthfully that he should "not soon forget" that visit, and asked to be remembered "most warmly to Mrs Shaw & Miss Elizabeth," and to all Shaw's family. With that formal note went "one of the first bound copies of 'Typee'" Herman had been able to procure. The dedication probably came as a surprise to the judge: "To Lemuel Shaw, Chief Justice of the Commonwealth of Massachusetts, THIS LITTLE WORK IS GRATEFULLY INSCRIBED BY THE AUTHOR." The wording was "very simple," Herman wrote him, "for the world would hardly have sympathised to the full extent of those feelings with which I regard my father's friend and the constant friend of all his family." Perhaps Herman had expressed those "feelings" more openly in the Murray edition, where the adverb was "AFFECTIONATELY," not "GRATEFULLY."

[21]

International Author
and the Man of the Family
1846

He most improves who studies with delight,
And learns sound Morals while he learns to write.

"Allan Melvills Book," 1796

AT LANSINGBURGH IN THE SECOND HALF of March the Melvilles luxuriated in Herman's new fame even while he reapplied himself assiduously to his new manuscript. A notice in the April issue of a New York City monthly, *Illustrated Magazine of Literature and Art*, was succinct about *Typee:* "This is one of the most interesting, amusing, and original books of adventure we have read for many a day. Get it and read it, by all means, as we are willing to risk the price of the book that you will find in it something that you never read of or thought of before — besides, it is by an American sailor." The family collected that sort of praise rapidly, for on 6 April Augusta wrote her second cousin in Troy, Catherine Van Schaick, offering to send her "some of the Reviews and complimentary notices" from both "English and American Journals." That month Augusta was also much excited by a special honor for herself, for Cornelia Van Rensselaer rode up on 17 April to ask her to be a bridesmaid at her wedding in June to Nathaniel Thayer, a Bostonian. This was to be a grand wedding at the Manor House, so the trousseau had to be selected in New York (with a week or ten days allotted for making the necessary purchases). Mr. Thayer was to meet the Van Rensselaers in Manhattan and return with them, after which Nilly (as she was called) and her fiancé would pay Augusta the compliment of riding up to see her together.

Between Nilly's engagement and her marriage, Tom left, around the end of April, for Westport Point, Massachusetts, where he signed on the *Theophilus Chase*. At sixteen, he was five feet six-and-a-half inches tall, and had not done growing; his complexion was given as light and his hair brown. (He claimed five feet seven, despite the ship's papers, after Helen guyed him that he would return six feet tall from his eighteen months of whaling.) Despite his attendance at the academy, Tom always found correct spelling harder to achieve than any of the family, even Herman, but on 3 May he struggled to

409

write proper letters to his sisters Helen and Augusta (Dut) before sailing. He was homesick already, the way Herman had been ("I miss the sight of home and all the pleasent faces"), but full of plans to make the best of a likely stop in the South Atlantic for the ship to "recruit," St. Helena: "Before I come back I will proberably visit the Grave of Napoleon, that Ceaser of Modern history and you may tell Miss Lyzy Shaw that I will fetch her a peace of one of the willows (that droope their heads over the spot hounoured by being chose as the resting place of one of the greatest men that ever lived) to put in her collection of ods and ends." Since his early adolescence, he had been in the habit of sending tokens to his favorite grown-up female friend, Elizabeth Shaw, who was indeed a conscientious collector of odds (as she would have spelled it) and ends. Tom sailed on 5 May, leaving one matter unresolved — an errand Gansevoort was planning to discharge for him in London. Perhaps no one in the family was there to stay with young Tom "till the last," but Herman's involvement in the composition of his second book and in the reception of the first was intense indeed if it kept him from accompanying Tom to Westport as Gansevoort had accompanied *him* to New Bedford.

Thomas Low Nichols had been right when he assured Allan and Gansevoort that the reviews of their brother's book in the English press "would make its American success." Not every American reviewer felt it necessary to mention the British reception, but the importance of that reception is easy to demonstrate. On 26 March Edwin Croswell announced in the Albany *Argus* that he had "favorable notices of the work in London papers, to which we shall hereafter allude." He had in hand early London reviews (in four papers) directly from Gansevoort on the steamer that had left England on 4 March. On 21 April the *Argus* quoted a favorable extract from the London *Critic*, which it said expressed "the general current of the London Press." Much later, on 9 July, the *Morning Courier and New-York Enquirer* commented that in England, so far as it could "judge from the criticisms of the press," the "general opinion" seemed to be favorable as to the authenticity of *Typee*, while there had been more skepticism in the United States. Readers in the United States soon gathered, accurately enough, that the London critics had dealt rather kindly with *Typee* — enough to make the earliest American critics respectful of the book.

The two volumes in the Wiley & Putnam Library of American Books were published on 17 March, and American reviews appeared immediately. Evert Duyckinck, who was in charge of the series (although in this instance superseded by one of the owners), reviewed it for the New York *Morning News* (a paper edited by the Democratic leader John O'Sullivan) on 18 March. He pronounced *Typee* "a happy hit whichever way you look at it, whether as travels, romance, poetry or humor," for it had "a sufficiency of all of these to be one of the most agreeable, readable books of the day." He ended with a nod to some celebrated dancers of the time:

> Curiosity is piqued, good sense flattered; there is a dash of romantic Rous-seauism, with now and then a shadow of the Cannibal as a corrective. The peculiarity of the book, to us, is the familiar and town life of the author among a race of naked savages. He goes down every day from his hut to a lounging shed of the chiefs, the Ti he calls it, as if he were walking from the Astor House to the Saloons of the Racket Club. He could not admire Celeste, or Ellsler, or Augusta with more gallantry than he celebrates the attractions of the delightful Fayaway. The *bonhommie* of the book is remarkable.

In his review, Duyckinck caught the tone Melville had used in portraying himself among the men of the island—"a good fellow among a club of good fellows whose sole infirmity was the occasional eating of human flesh." Duyckinck himself was the center of such a club of good fellows, who met in his basement retreat in Clinton Place just north of Washington Square, near Broadway. "This modern Crusoe," Duyckinck called Melville on 21 March, when the *Morning News* printed extensive excerpts, including the "Buggerry Island" fantasy. (He made a curious slip in his description of Melville in the South Sea paradise: "the gentle Fayaway, a beautiful nymph, slept at night by his side," he said, although according to the book it was Kory-Kory who slept there, not Fayaway.)

Duyckinck was an Episcopalian—not Dutch Reformed, as his old New York name might have suggested. His father, the elder Evert Duyckinck, had been a prominent local printer, and with wealth the family had stepped up socially from the Dutch Reformed church. Earnest a Christian as he was, Duyckinck was not infused with the sense of a duty to convert all heathens (including Catholics) to true evangelical faith. In the notice on 21 March he took Melville's criticisms of the low-church Protestant missionaries as very likely valid:

> Our author represents the missionary rule in the Sandwich Islands as for the most part a vulgar and miserable misgovernment. We have no respect what-ever for a vulgar missionary. He is probably as odious and injurious a creature as was ever "dressed in authority," and we say, Show him up by all means, but (and our author *does* make this admission) we are not to charge all the evils arising from the conflict of two races and ten eras of society in those islands exclusively upon the missionaries.
>
> Undoubtedly the missionaries have had a difficult task, but it would be well

to inquire, at the suggestion of Mr. Melville, whether the best and wisest men have always been sent to occupy this post of the Christian world.

More concerned with literary than religious matters at the moment, he added a bit of musing about the evocative power of the sailor's first book: "It was some such material as this that set the brain of Shakespeare working on the Tempest." What he meant was that Melville had produced some wonderful raw material that a great writer subsequently might seize upon and work into some masterpiece. He may have been thinking of his boyhood schoolmate Cornelius Mathews, whom he fondly believed was emerging as the great American writer. Such a writer's brain could be set aworking by Melville's raw and clumsily presented material. (In an odd coincidence he alluded to Isabel's speech on "authority" in *Measure for Measure*, a play just then on Gansevoort's mind in London.)

Hiram Fuller, since January the sole owner of the New York *Evening Mirror*, with which Willis and Morris had been associated, on 4 April showed a similar cosmopolitan spirit. *Typee*, to begin with, had "all the *vraisemblance* of Robinson Crusoe — we hope it is at least as true. Certainly, if it is *not*, we shall set the writer down as second only to De Foe." Melville's style had "a careless elegance which suits admirably with the luxurious tropical tone of the narrative," so that the reviewer suspected "the author to be at least as well acquainted with the London club-houses, as with the forecastle of a merchantman." Of the other reviews, three were by Americans who were to become better known. Duyckinck sent Nathaniel Hawthorne a copy of the book deprecatingly ("a Frenchy coloured picture," he called it). Hawthorne surprised Duyckinck by quite liking it, and praising it in his anonymous review in the 25 March Salem *Advertiser*:

> The book is lightly but vigorously written; and we are acquainted with no work that gives a freer and more effective picture of barbarian life, in that unadulterated state of which there are now so few specimens remaining. The gentleness of disposition that seems akin to the delicious climate, is shown in contrast with traits of savage fierceness; — on one page, we read of manners and modes of life that indicate a whole system of innocence and peace; and on the next, we catch a glimpse of a smoked human head, and the half-picked skeleton of what had been (in a culinary sense) a *well-dressed* man. The author's descriptions of the native girls are voluptuously colored, yet not more so than the exigencies of the subject appear to require. He has that freedom of view — it would be too harsh to call it laxity of principle — which renders him tolerant of codes of morals that may be little in accordance with our own; a spirit proper enough to a young and adventurous sailor, and which makes his book the more wholesome to our staid landsmen.

Now or later, Hawthorne's wife also read the book, so imaginatively that when she met Melville in 1850 she saw Fayaway in his face — saw a man unlike her husband, a man with a history of sexual conquests.

A New England cousin of Hiram Fuller's, Margaret Fuller, then a pioneering newspaper woman, reviewed *Typee* in the 4 April New York *Tribune*. Like some British reviewers, she was reminded of *Rasselas*, and she brought other exposés of missionary operations to bear on her reading of Melville's criticisms. On the basis of her unconventional theological beliefs she recommended that ladies find out what use their charity was put to: "With a view to ascertaining the truth, it would be well if the sewing societies, now engaged in providing funds for such enterprises, would read the particulars, they will find in this book beginning p. 249, vol. 2d, and make inquiries in consequence, before going on with their efforts." Familiar with exceptional liberated and literary-minded women in Boston, she generalized, without irony, that "the sewing societies of the country villages" would "find this the very book they wish to have read while assembled at their work." As editor of the Brooklyn *Eagle*, Walter Whitman (years away from shortening his first name) probably wrote the 15 April notice: "A strange, graceful, most readable book this. It seems to be a compound of the 'Seward's Narrative,' and 'Guidentio de Lucca,' style and reading. As a book to hold in one's hand and pore dreamily over of a summer day, it is unsurpassed." The first known poetic parody appeared on 27 March in the *Morning News:*

> I never shall forget the place
> Where *poor old Toby* died.
> Of mince pies I am very fond,
> But of them I shall never eat
> Without thinking of these cannibals,
> Of *Toby*, poor *Toby*, and mince meat!

Parody was a sure sign of incipient fame. So was becoming a source book: in the summer, at Walden Pond, Henry Thoreau read *Typee*, making notes on experiments in living successfully tested by the Polynesians.

In the *Harbinger*, the organ of the socialists at Brook Farm in West Roxbury, the young Fourierist Charles A. Dana on 4 April gave *Typee* a long, learned review, the sort of journalism that soon led Horace Greeley to hire him for the *Tribune*. Already the London *Spectator* (28 February) had noted that Melville portrayed a society where "a community of goods, and an absence of anything like jealousy or female restraint," made a reality of "the Pantisocracy which Southey, Coleridge, and others, fancied the perfection of society during the phrensy of the French Revolution." Passionately dedicated to Fourieristic views, Dana quoted extensively from several sections where the "social state" of Typee was described. The secret of happiness in Typee, he decided, was *"abundance for every person"*: "Give them [laborers] such an abundance of material things as bountiful nature in Typee bestows upon her children, and then when you bid them love each other, your words will not fall dead and unmeaning upon their ears. The peace and good will of that South Sea valley are as possible here as they are there; they are possible here in a far higher degree, on account of our greater refinement and intelligence, and our higher religious development." The way to achieve *"universal abundance"* in western societies was to arrange "the organization of industry and the distribution of its products according to principles of exact justice." Given his skepticism about the present organization of society, Dana was not surprised to learn what Melville exposed about the operations of the missionaries in Hawaii: "It is proper to say in behalf of the author, that he does not impeach the honesty with which this mission was planned, or the Christian character of the Missionaries in general. He merely avers that their designs have often been injudicious and that other influences than that of the New Testament have operated on the natives, which are undoubtedly the facts." Melville was receiving a more serious response, all in all, than he could have bargained for, especially in this essay by a radical Transcendentalist on the lookout for innovative ways to reform a corrupt society.

The *Times* of London on 6 April had looked attentively at what Melville said about "the houris of whom he had dreamt on board the Dolly," before bursting out with its exclamation of envy for Herman, that happy dog. Numerous reviewers in both countries chose for their extracts passages in which Marquesan women were unclothed. The *Spectator* praised as "too natural to be invented by the author" the section in chapter 18 which it called "The Bath of the Nymphs," a scene that "but requires us to call the savages celestials, to suppose Mr. Melville to have dropped from the clouds instead of 'bolting' from the skipper Vangs, and to fancy some Ovidian graces added to the narrative, in order to become a scene of classical mythology." Most of the first American reviewers took a tolerant, worldly tone toward the sex in *Typee*. The New York *Subterranean* chose for an extract what it called "Description of a Typee Beauty." The London *Atlas* (28 March 1846) quoted as a "very pretty cabinet picture" Melville's description in chapter 18 of Fayaway's using her tappa as a windsail. Charles Fenno Hoffman quoted the same scene in the New York *Gazette and Times* (30 March 1846), introducing it by saying: "With this wood Nymph Fayaway by name, and a Man Friday called Kory-Kory, our American Crusoe revelled in all sorts of out-of-doors felicities." Melville's romantic portrait of Fayaway provoked the reviewer in the London *Gentleman's Magazine* (July 1846) to exclaim: "Ah! thou gentle and too enchanting Fayaway, what has become of thee?" Throughout the spring and summer of 1846, critical response to the sexual teasing Melville had indulged in had not yet careened out of control.

On 4 April, Gansevoort sent Herman copies of the business correspondence he had conducted with Wiley & Putnam. His accompanying letter, which Herman probably received around the first of May, was manly and restrained:

> The climate is too damp & moist for me. I sometimes fear that I am gradually breaking up. If it be so—let it be—God's will be done. I have already seen about as much of London society as I care to see. It is becoming a toil to me to make the exertion necessary to dress to go out, and I am now leading a life nearly as quiet as your own at Lansingburgh—I think I am growing phlegmatic & cold. Man stirs me not, nor woman either. My circulation is languid. My brain is dull. I neither seek to win pleasure or avoid pain. A degree of insensibility has been long stealing over me, & now seems permanently established, which, to my understanding is more akin to death than life. Selfishly speaking I never valued life much—it were impossible to value it less than I do now. The only personal desire I now have is to be out of debt. That desire waxes stronger within me, as others fade. In consideration of the little egotism which my previous letters to you and the family have contained, I hope that Mother, brothers & sisters will pardon this babbling about myself.

This news of Gansevoort's illness, written in the familiar masterful hand and worded in elegant prose that echoed Hamlet's, caused more concern than alarm, particularly since Gansevoort was preparing further advice on Herman's career: "I am glad that you continue busy, and in my next or the one after that will venture to make some suggestions about your next book." (Preserved with this letter and perhaps originally contained within it is a longer quotation from Shakespeare in Gansevoort's hand, Claudio's speech on death in *Measure for Measure*.) The day he wrote Herman, Gansevoort made his last entry in the diary he had started on New Year's Day. To judge from his correspondence with Henry William Ellsworth, the chargé d'affaires to Sweden and Norway, he remained oblivious to McLane's mounting frenzy toward him, and continued to treat the minister with genuine respect and cordiality.

By the time Gansevoort's letter arrived, Herman found himself battling for his book against two enemies. The one that struck him at the time as the least threatening was the one that damned his literary career in the end—the Protestant press. The April issue of the New York *American Review* (or *American Whig Review* or *Whig Review*, the official Whig organ) took exception to the "remarks concerning the Missionaries of the Sandwich Islands which we think are prejudiced and unfounded," but made no further denunciation.

The turning point in the American reception of *Typee* came with a review in the 9 April New York *Evangelist*, the principal organ of the Presbyterian church, and as such a fervent promoter of Protestant missions. The writer capitalized on the book's appearing first in London; no wonder it had: "The work was made, not for America, but for a circle, and that not the highest, in London, where theatres, opera-dancers, and voluptuous prints have made such unblushing walks along the edge of modesty as are here delineated to be rather more admired than we hope they are yet among us. We are sorry that such a volume should have been allowed a place in the 'Library of American Books.' It can only have been without reading it beforehand, and from deference to the publisher on the other side." This last sentence sounds very like a reassurance John Wiley had hastened to give his friend the reviewer. What the reviewer added was even more damaging than what he had just said: "We have long noted it as true in criticism, that what makes a large class of books bad, immoral, and consequently injurious, is not so much what is plainly expressed, as what is left to be imagined by the reader. Apply this rule to the work in hand, and while everybody will admit it is written with an attractive vivacity, and (except where it palpably lies) with great good humor, it cannot escape severe condemnation." This was a self-righteous pronouncement, but there was in it a measure of truth. Melville had, on shipboard, developed a strategy of saying less and letting his auditors imagine more, on indelicate topics, and the evidence of the draft pages shows that he was pushing the bounds of good taste in his jokings with members of his family. Melville could hardly have been writing with a London "circle" in mind, but he was still what he had been long before to Gansevoort, a great tease, as the reviewer so hostilely perceived.

Not all reviews in the religious press have been located, and many of the numerous daily four-page New York papers have simply disappeared, but the currency of the opinion of the *Evangelist* is clear in a letter written to Mrs. Edward Baker on 14 April by George Long Duyckinck, younger brother of the editor of the Wiley & Putnam series in which *Typee* had appeared: "The religious papers here haul it over the coals for its treatment of the missionaries and some other points." (Older New Yorkers, perhaps even Maria Melville, would hear this young man's name and smile, realizing that one pioneer printer, Evert A. Duyckinck Sr., had paid a high compliment to his fellow printer George Long.)

Once the *Evangelist* had spoken, John Wiley, the devout Presbyterian, hastened to appease the missionary interests — which meant merely to act on his own religious convictions. In April, when a new printing of the book was called for, Herman was rather naively delighted at the idea of correcting some of the errors that had crept into his text. From Lansingburgh on 7 May he sent Wiley & Putnam a corrected copy of *Typee*, along with a note: "Besides correcting mere typographical errors, I have made two or three slight alterations. — I do not know exactly to what extent you can, without incurring much expence, alter the plates — But I hope that you will see, that all my alterations are attended to, except such as would be attended with any considerable trouble or expence. Of course, all the mere verbal corrections can be easily made." He learned, within the next weeks, that Wiley had in mind not merely a new printing (which is what Melville thought) but instead an expurgated edition that would be called the "Revised Edition." He still did not know what Wiley had in mind when he wrote Gansevoort on 29 May that a second edition (that is, a second printing) was "nearly out."

The other enemy of the reputation of *Typee*, and of the author himself, was the charge that it was a fraud, an outright fiction, or else had not been written by the adventurer himself, or in a variety of other ways was not what it purported to be. Herman could not forget that the Harpers had rejected the work on the grounds that it could not be true, and that at the start Murray had been suspicious. By the end of March or early April Herman had learned from Gansevoort about Murray's concern over doubts about the "genuineness" of the book, so that news was worrying him well before he saw the review of *Typee* in the *Morning Courier and New-York Enquirer* for 17 April.

This reviewer in the *Courier and Enquirer* had convictions, not mere doubts: "in our judgment, in all essential respects, it is a *fiction*, — a piece of Munchausenism, — from beginning to end." The reviewer had "not the slightest confidence in any of the details, while many of the incidents narrated are utterly incredible." The trouble was that in *Typee* falsehoods were "put forth as a simple record of actual experience":

> It professes to give nothing but what the author actually saw and heard. It must therefore be judged, not as a romance or a poem, but as a book of travels, — as a statement of facts; — and in this light it has, in our judgment, no merit whatever. Parts of the work claim to be historical, in giving an account of the missionary labors in the Islands, the proceedings of the French, &c.; but the spirit of fiction in which the whole is written deprives these of all reliability.

In his fear and anger Herman took direct action. He went to see Croswell at the Albany *Argus*, and on 21 April the paper dutifully described the book as "having a deservedly great run," but also having been misjudged: "There seems to be an impression in some quarters, that the events are too strange to be true, and the book *has* been designated as a beautiful fiction. The author desires to state to the public, that Typee is a true narrative of events which actually occurred to him. Although there may be moving incidents and hair-breadth escapes, it is scarcely more strange than such as happen to those who make their home on the deep." Presumably the echoes of *Othello* are Herman's own, for he knew the way to get what he wanted into print was to write out something for Croswell to use rather than to put the burden of composing the item on an editor, however facile he might be. Then Herman went down to New York City to do what he could to contain the damage.

Nothing shows that Gansevoort had prepared the way for Herman to approach the new owner of the *Mirror*, but in any case Hiram Fuller responded to Herman's request to put a statement in the *Mirror* of 9 May, part of which may be in Melville's own words:

> We are requested to state, on the authority of the writer himself of this universally read, though suspected book, that the work is a genuine history of actual occurrences, and not by any means the fiction it has been represented. The misbelief in the story arises from the actual poverty of most persons' imaginations. A cold Yankee, shivering and sneezing on Cape Cod, finds it very hard to believe in the existence of a region where a perpetual summer smiles on fields shaded by the bread fruit — where the ground yields its spontaneous treasury, and spades and dunghills are entirely unappreciated — where the inhabitants sleep sixteen hours out of the twenty-four, and feast and make love the other eight. It is difficult to realize, but it is so. It is unfair to class Mr. Melville with Sir John Mandeville, because he has had the good luck to live with Fayaway in Typee, while other mortals have grown wizen over anthracite in New York.

Fuller at times was rabidly hostile to various of Melville's friends, later on, but he never damned Melville for his associations.

Concerned for Gansevoort as he was, Herman focused in the next week on writing his second book and attempting to manipulate what the papers said about his first one. If, under such pressure, he let Tom sail early in May without a last embrace on the dock at Westport Point, he certainly could not focus, a week or two later, on President Polk's making an executive's war on remote Mexico. Having already consulted with Alexander Bradford in New York City, on 23 May, from Lansingburgh, Herman sent an article he had written, which he wanted Bradford to run anonymously in the New York *Morning Courier and New-York Enquirer*:

> I have endeavored to make it appear as if written by one who had read the book & beleived it — & moreover — had been as much pleased with it as most people who read it profess to be. Perhaps, it may not be exactly the right sort

of thing. The fact is, it was rathar an awkward undertaking any way—for I have not sought to present my own view of the matter (which you may be sure is straitforward enough) but have only presented such considerations as would be apt to suggest themselves to a reader who was acquainted with, & felt freindly toward the author.—Indeed, I have moddled some of my remarks upon hints suggested by some reviews of the book. . . .

What I have written embodies some thoughts which I think will tell with the public if they are introduced thro' the proper channel.—That channel is the C[ourier] & Enquirer, as it contained the obnoxious review.—I feel confident that unless something of this kind appears the success of the book here as a genuine narrative will be seriously impaired. I am told that, that malicious notice (for it certainly has that sort of edge to it) has been copied into papers in the Western part of the state.—It will do mischief unless answered. . . . You have been so kind as to express your willingness to do what you can in this matter. . . . Now that I think of it, however, if they should demur at inserting the accompanying article on account of its contradicting a previous notice, you might in that case procure its insertion as a communication.

Melville's concerns were genuine, even though the narrative was not entirely so, for he was fighting for nothing less than a chance at a literary career. Bradford seems to have failed him, for this article, so cunningly prepared, has not been located in the daily, semi-weekly, or weekly editions of the *Courier and Enquirer.*

Gansevoort seems not to have told his family, but by the middle of March he had been losing vision in his left eye and suffering excruciating headaches. On 25 March he rose and went about his business: "Dressed, dull pain in the head, no appetite, little or no feeling of uneasiness or pain in the left eye, a mist still before it & quite unable to read even large type with the right eye closed." He underwent a botched dental extraction and was told that his mouth "should be rid of all unsound teeth & fitted out with masticators," this after going to the legation but doing "little or nothing." Predictably, McLane observed this inefficiency with ferocious disdain. During the next days the minister's private secretary, McHenry Boyd, a young man with independent means enough to justify independent behavior, decided it was his duty to take a hand. He could hardly do less as a decent man and an American in London, but he also had a duty to befriend any cousin of his friend Nilly Van Rensselaer. The conscientious Gansevoort had always thought him dumbfoundingly lazy, but Boyd between 11 and 19 April bestirred himself to write a careful letter which informed the family that Gansevoort was ill—too ill to write himself. Boyd followed with another written around 20 April, shortly after the doctor called in as a consultant had decided that in a few days Gansevoort could be removed to the country to recuperate. The first of these letters arrived a week after Gansevoort's letter of 4 April, the second two or three weeks later. Neither is known to survive.

During the period when McHenry Boyd was behaving so considerately, Gansevoort's superior was working himself into a frenzy. On 4 May, McLane wrote Secretary of State Buchanan this outraged letter accusing Gansevoort of malingering:

> Now, that I am writing *you* a letter, that you will have no occasion to show to any one, I may tell you frankly, that in not giving any heed to the allusion I early made to a functionary of this Legation, you have not treated me as I deserve, and you have exposed the P[resident] and his admn, to no amiable commentaries, in many important quarters in this great metropolis. I confess that I have never before met with precisely his parallel; and, with a rhetorical extravagance of speech & manner, and truthlessness the most extraordinary, he is constantly doing things that I will not venture now to hint at. The President himself is rather freely handled, as I learn, in places where his name ought never to be and, except in terms of respect; and altogether, unless now the fact that I had been somewhat known here before, the Legation would occupy no enviable position. These will gradually work their cure, and ultimately, no doubt, he will find a level at which he will be comparatively himself. For the last month he has been confined to his house, with what he represented to me as an affection of the eyes, and a consequent *loss of sight!* From his physician, however, I learn that his sight is not materially affected, & that his disorder is in some degree connected with the brain, and a state of nervous derangement, which if it should now come would not surprise me. I have never seen him since he came here that he was not in a mood painfully extravagant, as to all Men & all things; and now at this day if I had no option but to remain here, I would *myself force a departure.* So it is I have discharged my duty, & leave it to others to discharge theirs. Be assured of one thing; the P[resident]. will suffer more from his continuance here than *I* will. —

Ill himself, McLane was behaving with appalling cruelty, a secret that he and James Buchanan carried to their graves.

Melville had already interrupted his work on *Omoo* to defend the authenticity of *Typee* when the letters arrived from McHenry Boyd. Herman had heard no further reports by 29 May, when he wrote Gansevoort from Lansingburgh. He was profoundly moved by Gansevoort's letter of 4 April, and further disturbed by the conflicting reports of Gansevoort's condition and by the family's inability to help nurse him. Herman put himself out not to be a plaguy fellow to his big brother:

I look forward to three weeks from now, & think I see you openning this letter in [one] of those pleasant hamlets roundabout London, of which we read in novels. At any rate I pray Heaven that such may be the case & that you are mending rapidly. Remember that composure of mind is every thing. You should give no thought to matters here, until you are well enough to think about them. As far as I know they are in good train.

Mr Boyd's second letter announcing your still continued illness was a sad disappointment to us. Yet he seemed to think, that after all you were in a fair way for recovery — & that a removal to the country (then it appears intended shortly) would be attended with the happiest effects. I can not but think it must be; — & I look for good tidings by the next arrival. — Many anxious enquiries have been made after you by numerous friends here. ——

The family here are quite well — tho' very busy dressmaking. Augusta is one of the bridesmaids to Miss C[ornelia]. Van. R[ensselaer]. & her preperations are now forwarding.

People here are all in a state of delirium about the Mexican War. A military arder pervades all ranks — Militia Colonels wax red in their coat facings — and 'prenticeboys are running off to the wars by scores. — Nothing is talked of but the "Halls of the Montezumas" And to hear folks prate about the purely figurative apartments one would suppose that they were another Versailles where our democratic rabble meant to "make a night of it" ere long. — The redoubtable General Veile "went off" in a violant war paraoxysm to Washington the other day. His object is to get a commission for raising volunteers about here & taking the feild at their head next fall. — But seriously something great is impending. The Mexican War (tho' our troops have behaved right well) is nothing of itself — but "a little spark kindleth a great fire" as the well known author of the Proverbs very justly remarks — and who knows what all this may lead to — Will it lead to a conflict with England? Or any other great powers? — Prithee, are there any notable battles in store — any Yankee Waterloos? — Or think once of a mighty Yankee fleet coming to the war shock in the middle of the Atlantic with an English one. — Lord, the day is at hand, when we will be able to talk of our killed & wounded like some of the old Eastern conquerors reckoning them up by thousands; — when the Battle of Monmouth will be thought child's play — & canes made out of the Constitution's timbers be thought no more of than bamboos. — I am at the end of my sheet — God bless you My Dear Gansevoort & bring you to your feet again.

Herman reserved a bit of "egotism," as the family would have said, for the postscript. "Typee is coming on bravely — a second edition is nearly out. — I need not ask you to send me *every notice of any kind* that you see or hear of."

The envelope survives in the Berkshire Athenaeum, postmarked Lansingburgh, 29 May, and marked by Herman *"For the Boston Steamer."*

What had happened to Gansevoort in the days after 4 April is imperfectly conveyed in what McLane wrote to Buchanan on 18 May, only twelve days after his most recent denunciation. This time the minister presented an elaborate account that may at first have struck the secretary of state as tragi-comical prelude to the most recent evidences of Gansevoort's malingering. On 7 April, McLane reported, while he was himself confined to his bed "with severe illness," Gansevoort had sent him a message that "he was threatened with a total loss of sight." Dr. Quinn, whom Gansevoort misrepresented as being "a celebrated occulist," had advised that the secretary of legation "withdraw immediately from his official duties and give entire rest to his eyes." McLane had "promptly acquiesced," he now avouched to Buchanan, only to learn that Gansevoort was not following orders (instead, three days in a row visiting the office but not doing any work there, and being seen elsewhere in London). Then on 11 April McLane had learned from his own doctor that Gansevoort was disobeying the instructions not of an oculist but of a *"homeopathist."* McLane thereupon had sent Gansevoort a message that he was on to the misrepresentation and was ready to select "proper medical aid" for the secretary himself, so (he did not tell Buchanan) he would not be the victim of Gansevoort's fabrications. Gansevoort then assured McLane that he had called in "a *Doctor Waters*," whom he would ask to call on McLane. In the meantime, McLane (who had his sources) received daily reports that Gansevoort was not in fact confined to his bed, but was continuing "to walk about his parlour, occasionally lying on his sofa," and in general loafing while McLane was prostrate with his own severe illness. When Dr. Waters at last called on McLane on 17 April, he "represented that when first called to see Mʳ Melville he found him in a state of great nervous derangement, and that although his sight was in some degree impaired he thought it proceeded from no defect in the eye, but from other causes. He said that although he had promptly composed his system, and checked the most unpleasant symptoms of the case, Mʳ Melville did not get better as he had expected." Dr. Waters now requested authorization to bring in a consulting physician, a request to which the minister readily acceded.

The eminent Dr. W. F. Chambers began treating Gansevoort, who continued to drive out "once or twice, for exercise," and McLane was able to call at his secretary's lodgings and "personally inspect his situation," so he could conclude that there appeared to be not even "the least ground of alarm." After a few days Dr. Chambers called upon the minister to report that the secretary "would soon be able to get out and go to the country for a change of air."

Having sufficiently emphasized the extent to which he had put himself out to see that Gansevoort received the attention an American diplomat deserved, McLane proceeded to the point of his letter, which was not, Buchanan now saw, a new request that the painfully extravagant Gansevoort be banished from Christendom:

> On the 4th of May, however, after one of his rides, he was attacked with bleeding from the gums, which made it necessary, in the opinion of Doctor Chambers to call in Sir Benjamin Brodie an eminent Surgeon. During the night of the 9th May the bleeding was arrested, but the stomach became so irritable as to be able to retain nothing, and by the 10th all his symptoms assumed a typhoid character. He rallied a little early on the night of the 11th but soon after 9 o'clock an unfavorable change ensued. From that time he rapidly sunk and at 2 o'clock in the morning of the 12th ceased to exist.

Dr. Edwin D. Moore, who was present when Gansevoort died, had informed McLane that by midnight, when he arrived, he "found a most sudden and rapid change had taken place, more fresh blood had been brought up and he was cold and his eyes fixed," insensible to sound or light. Now McLane wrote to Buchanan: "He expired at his lodgings in this city at two o'clock on the morning of the 12th instant after an indisposition of more than a month." Throughout the month of Gansevoort's final illness, the secretary of state was to understand from this account, McLane had acted at all times out of a superabundance of charitable concern for his secretary of legation. Indeed, he had exerted himself to see to Gansevoort's needs, even despite his own severe illness. No one could have been kinder.

On 14 May, two days after Gansevoort's death, Moore gave McLane more details, specifying that on occasion after the sixth of May Gansevoort had been conscious, and composed of mind: "He spoke to me in confidence of his family and it may be cheering to them to know that of his mother and brothers and other members of his family he talked with the deepest feelings of affection and that if he lived he should tell them how tenderly he had been nursed and attended, he spoke also of your Excellency's great care for his comfort, and assistance under his malady, and with great gratitude at your having sent Dr Chambers to see him." The day before, 13 May, Dr. Chambers had submitted to McLane a report on the autopsy: "The examination after death exhibiting disease of three essential organs namely the heart liver and kidneys, to all of which our attention had been directed, must be so far satisfactory as to prove that no human skill could have been effected in saving his life." The wording is curiously self-serving in its lack of specificity, and McLane went on to quote Sir Benjamin Brodie as declaring sententiously "that for a considerable time Mr Melville must have labored under organic disease beyond the reach of art."

On 18 May a pathetic funeral service was held in Westminster Abbey, attended by a woebegone dozen, mainly Americans, one of whom was Henry Stevens, a Vermont bookman resident in London. On that day McLane wrote of Gansevoort's death to Allan, as he also wrote to Buchanan: "I have in a letter to Mr Allan Melville of New York communicated a more full and detailed account of the illness and death of his brother, and have also transmitted to him not only the full report of the post-mortem examination, but also letters from Sir Benjamin Brodie, and Mr Moore, and Doctor Chambers." (The "full report" seems not to have survived.) McLane continued: "I caused his effects, except the private papers, to be taken charge of, and an inventory of them to be made by Mr John Miller, the agent of the Legation, by whom they will be forwarded to Mr Allan Melville by the packet-ship Prince Albert, Captain Sebor, to sail from this port for New York on the 20th instant. The private papers have been collected, under my direction, by Mr Boyd, and will be sent home to the same person by the same ship." Gansevoort's body was sent home in "a leaden coffin with an appropriate case," on board the Prince Albert. Gansevoort's death was, to McLane's knowledge, the first time in the nation's history someone of his rank in the diplomatic service had died abroad, so the minister properly asked Buchanan to arrange a special provision for covering the expenses incurred during Gansevoort's illness and the costs of shipping the body home, and pointed out the need for creating regulations to govern such cases in the future.

Within a week of his writing to London on 29 May, Herman learned that Gansevoort had been dead since 12 May. The news was in the New York Herald on 4 June, but the family may have heard from McLane or Boyd before the papers had the news from their London correspondents or from London papers. At the time they heard of the death, or very soon afterward, the family heard that McLane was recommending that a quarter's pay be granted to help cover the expenses of the illness and transportation of the body, so despite their grief they forced themselves to second his request. For the family, Edwin Croswell wrote to Polk on 5 June that Gansevoort's brother Herman Melville, "a young gentleman of talents & genius, the author of 'Typee,'" would be writing to ask that "a quarter's salary be allowed the representatives of his brother." (That month during a condolence call Croswell's young associate Cramer gave Augusta "24 Letters written by dear Gansevoort to W. E. C."; on 6 June Judge Shaw wrote Maria a "sincerely sympathizing letter.") Also on 6 June, Herman wrote directly to President Polk asking that McLane's recommendation be carried out, or else the "great part of the expenses attendant" on the illness and funeral would have "(for some time at least) to remain unpaid": "The claims of a widowed mother, four sisters, and a younger brother, are paramount even to the duties we owe the dead. — I should feel most bitterly the reproach, to which the country in some measure, and the memory of my poor brother would be subjected, should these debts remain long uncancelled. But I can not think that this will be the case." Recalling Polk's long aloofness in the first half of 1845, Herman felt it necessary to assert the family's claims as well as Gansevoort's own: "The services which so many of my family in many ways have rendered the country — my noble brother's own short but brilliant public career, and the universally-acknowledged and signal services he rendered the Democratic party in the last memorable general election — all these, Sir, will surely lend great weight to the urgent claims of the case itself." This passage survives because Melville copied it into another letter he wrote to James Buchanan in his position as secretary of state. Herman felt easier writing to William L. Marcy, secretary of war, whom the family knew as governor of New York (1833–39); he could make a "personal appeal of a mourning family, to whom Providence has brought unspeakable & peculiar sorrows." There was no delay: on 6 June, Buchanan, privately aghast now at McLane's earlier charges that Gansevoort had been feigning illness, authorized McLane to pay the funeral expenses, and on the ninth wrote Herman what he had done.

Herman on 13 June conveyed to Uncle Peter the news he had received from Buchanan. He was greatly relieved that the expenses would be covered, with a little left "to bestow some testimonial" of their esteem upon the landlady or housekeeper "& to remunerate the colored man who tended Gansevoort during his illness." He was going to wait in Lansingburgh several days, until 17 June, before going to New York City to meet the *Prince Albert* and claim the body. William E. Cramer published a memorial article in the Washington *Daily Union* of 13 June slanted to those incidents connected with Gansevoort's life and character which would be "deeply interesting to the young men of our country," who might emulate him:

Gansevoort Melville, though young in years, with the disadvantages of a self-education, had already acquired an eminence and a reputation given to few young men of our republic.

As an orator he was peculiarly gifted. His imagination was rich and brilliant, but strong and just, combined with that extraordinary command of language which gave peculiar power to his burning thoughts and earnest manner. His heart was warm and noble, as an orator's would be, to move the masses. . . . His voice was expressive, and yet its deep tones could be distinctly heard by thousands. His figure was majestic — some might say colossal; his eye, large and black, with the glance of a Webster, and with a head and forehead whereon was stamped, by "the seal of Nature," the elements of a great and commanding character. . . .

But it was beautiful to see Mr. Melville in the family of his mother and sisters. He was not loved, but rather idolized, with a love "passing that of earth;" and he reciprocated that attachment with an intensity few "can wot of."

There is no record of Gansevoort's height other than this word "colossal" (if he had not been given a diplomatic passport, a physical description would have been filed in the Department of State). This is also the only indication that he did not have the blue eyes characteristic of the family (except the "gipsy" Augusta).

The family all knew that Gansevoort had made enemies by his opportunistic use of the letter from Van Buren, knew that he had left wounded pride and envy in his wake (the mighty William Cullen Bryant was unforgiving, and the Irish-born Tammany politician Mike Walsh, editor of the New York City workingman's paper, the *Subterranean*, for some reason was all afroth against him). As far as the family was concerned, Gansevoort's diplomatic appointment had vindicated him. None of the family ever knew that Gansevoort's superior in London had considered him a firebrand and had been moving heaven and earth (easier than moving President Polk) in his efforts to get Gansevoort out of London. They could think of Gansevoort as what Herman called him in his letter to Polk, his "noble brother."

Peter Gansevoort's abiding selfishness had left Maria unwilling to ask favors of him and almost ashamed to tell him that she felt she had to hold a funeral for her son. She explained the modest scale of her plans: "Not an expensive one, that we think not of, but merely to give the friends of my dear son, an opportunity of paying their last tribute to his memory." Carefully informing Peter that Mrs. Van Vechten had offered the use of her house for the services and that she would accept, she proceeded: "Many may think that your house would be more proper but that you did not offer & I would not ask a favor, which would bring gloom & sadness into your dwelling." In another paragraph she added: "That Mrs Van Vechten lives nearer the Boat is reason enough for others." Under this pressure Peter unbent enough to offer to hold the funeral from his house — not the house of the old General Peter Gansevoort, which he was renting out, but his new house on Washington Street. Poor Augusta on 23 June wrote to her cousin Kate Van Schaick, in Troy: "You know how I loved him, how I idolized him, how my very heart strings were entwined about him, oh Gansevoort, my brother, my darling brother, how hard it is, to feel that I never, never can see you again." For Nilly's sake she had been sorry to have to miss the wedding at the Manor House on 15 June, but she was not the sort of selfish girl who would regret not being a bridesmaid when she was in deepest mourning.

On 27 June Herman (and Allan?) saw that Gansevoort's coffin was transferred from the *Prince Albert* to the *Hendrik Hudson*, and sat up with it through the night on the way to Albany. On that miserable journey Herman could reflect bitterly on a small irony of the situation: for once, he was not either following Gansevoort up or down the Hudson, or else passing him, going north as Gansevoort went south. The brothers would never pass each other by water again; this time, for the last time, they were together. Herman, probably accompanied by Allan, saw the body conveyed to Peter's house early on the twenty-eighth. The funeral was at five in the afternoon, and afterward the body was taken to the Common Albany Cemetery, near the grave of Allan Melvill. One small consequence of Gansevoort's death was that the survivors felt freer to associate with Peter despite their rankling resentments.

The family clung to their trophies of Gansevoort. In his thoughtful way, he had left some papers all packaged up, long before. On 28 June 1847 Maria wrote to Augusta: "Just one year to day, that we committed our ever loved Gansevoort to the Grave. It added much to my distress accidentally opening a trunk which had not been look'd in since last May 1846, I saw a bundle of Miscellaneous papers which he had given me to place safely, with his own well known characters on the Face of the Package, & '24 July 1845' — *his last visit to us*, I had forgotten all about it. I have been looking them over, and now turn to my desk to write you."

McLane had itemized a few possessions found at Gansevoort's death: "The only effects left by Mr Melville, at the time of his death, in this country, consisted of £19.0.6 in the hands of the bankers, being his salary, as Secretary of Legation, from the 30th of April to the 12th instant; £1.10.0 in a purse found in his room; a court-dress, including hat and sword; a watch, and two small rings, a few books and his ordinary wearing-apparel." The court-dress McLane had sold for eight pounds, a great loss, which he explained was "unavoidable." The books, watch, rings, and ordinary wearing-apparel were sent home to Allan — memorabilia to be dispersed within the family. Allan intercepted some items in New York, some books, surely, and the now infinitely poignant instant-retrieval *Index Rerum* volumes Gansevoort had taken to London. The women had in their hands the "very splendid silk banner" the ladies of Nashville had presented to Gansevoort, one side emblazoned with an eagle clutching a scroll. They must have kept handbills advertising some of Gansevoort's appearances, such as those that had been affixed to trees in the wilds of Wayne County, Pennsylvania. In the summer of 1846, Maria sorted through Gansevoort's possessions that had been returned from England and gave Herman her late husband's watch fob with a seal on the end. He retained it all his life (as his widow wrote to Uncle Peter's daughter, Kate, on 9 November 1903). Now or later, Maria Melville took out Gansevoort's memorial spoons provided for in her mother's will (but cast only in 1845), and had the one in memory of her father, Peter Gansevoort, the Hero of Fort Stanwix, further engraved with the date of Gansevoort's death, 12 May 1846.

Augusta was given Gansevoort's law-office sign and retained it until her death, after which it survived all vicissitudes until it was found among the remnants of her possessions in an upstate barn and brought to the New York Public Library in 1983. Gansevoort left many books, which family members divided among themselves and cherished; most of them were probably left, long afterward, in the house at Gansevoort and later trashed (in the 1950s the alert Mrs. Paul Barden retrieved, from a load on its way to the dump, several books bound together, one of them Gansevoort's last present to Fanny, Longfellow's *Voices of the Night*). Allan got a scrap of paper in Gansevoort Melville's hand, now in the *Index Rerum* for 1837 and possibly there when Allan took possession of at least two of the four or more volumes, some or all of which had gone to England. On this scrap Gansevoort had written these words:

> The sword is broken in its sheath
> The armor hath rusted on the wall
> The knightly housings cumber the ground
> & the banner is trailing in the dust
> I had hoped to shout my war cry & draw my blade
> in many a stricken field — but the blade is
> broken & the war cry shall ne'er be heard[.]

The family kept letters about Gansevoort written in his golden childhood, and Fanny gave one of them to Kate's almost eleven-year-old son, Frank, in the centennial year, 1876, in remembrance of "Uncle Gansevoort" — Uncle Gansevoort, who never saw a niece or nephew, who had been dead two decades before the lad's birth, but was still a vital presence in the family. Until the day she died Maria Gansevoort Melville had eight children, the noblest and dearest of whom was still Gansevoort Melville. If he had lived, Maria knew, most of her subsequent tragedies surely could have been averted, or mitigated.

Herman Melville had grown into manhood with no expectations of having to support his family. After their father's death in 1832 it was his older brother, Gansevoort, who was made the man of the family, and whose debts their mother stood good for. In the opinion of the family Herman had been doing well enough when he barely supported himself. Had he seen himself as breadwinner, he would never have signed on a whaler. He had left Gansevoort to fulfill the role (however inadequately) and sailed for the ends of the earth, where for three or four years he would be helpless to assist his mother, four sisters, and two younger brothers, and from which at best he would return with only a few dollars in his pocket. This was the behavior of a young man who felt and was made to feel responsible only for himself. Gansevoort was responsible. Even when he seized his chance for glory in 1844, he left competent, dogged Allan in charge of the legal business; dying, he had worried when Allan failed to keep him abreast of his financial condition. Long before he passed the bar exam, Gansevoort knew who he was and what his role in the family had to be. Herman had not come into a sense of himself until he was in the process of writing *Typee*, to judge from a frank statement he made to Nathaniel Hawthorne in 1851, that until he was twenty-five he had had no development at all. Such a man, belatedly come into a sense of himself, was just the sort of man to wince under the weight of sudden new responsibilities.

Gansevoort's death did not have the devastating economic impact on the family that Allan Melvill's death had created in 1832. He had barely been supporting himself, while Allan Jr. was doing the day-by-day legal work in New York, and Allan was the one making the sacred remittance to Maria each month. Early in March Gansevoort had used a page of his diary to make an "Abstract" of "Allan's business for 13 weeks — 3 mos — prior to 24*th* January: Oaths 169; Folios 3,343; Exhibits 249" and rejoiced: "This amt quite exceeds my most sanguine anticipations, and if sustained in like ratio for 9 mos more will lead to a splendid result." He fretted, however, over Allan's unwillingness to take the time to keep him supplied with the latest financial figures, so his mind could be more at peace. Herman had received a large sum from England and a lesser sum from Wiley & Putnam. Being a Melville, Herman counted on a large income from a book that was proving so newsworthy. The estate of Catherine Gansevoort was finally about to be settled, long after Maria had used up her portion in the dribs and drabs that Peter had doled out to her.

The family was in sore straits, but the immediate economic effects of Gansevoort's death were nothing to the psychological damage it did to the family. Now, when Allan received the medical reports from London about the autopsy, the family looked back at Gansevoort's strange collapses in a different light. None of them had ever accused him of malingering, but now everyone could reproach himself or herself with not being solicitous enough, with not being appreciative enough, with not being cooperative enough, with not sufficiently acknowledging the stoicism that had infused Gansevoort's determination to continue his self-education, and with not suffi-

ciently appreciating the courage it took for Gansevoort to drive himself so
relentlessly in the pursuit of a political career. The members of the family
grieved for Gansevoort as long as they lived.

Everyone in the family had ifs to torment himself or herself with. If Polk
had promptly given an appointment to Gansevoort, their lives would have
been different. He could have been in London before Herman finished the
manuscript, and Herman might or might not have sent the manuscript after
him. Gansevoort himself might have died as prematurely in New York as in
London, but if he had not gone out so late, after Herman's manuscript was
finished, rather than just after Polk's inauguration, Herman's literary career might never have been launched, and certainly would not have been
launched in the best possible way, by acclaim in London prior to publication
in America. It was Gansevoort who had scouted out the most likely of all
London publishers to accept a book of adventures in the South Pacific, and it
was Gansevoort who handled all the negotiations, so that only after his death
did Herman have any occasion to write a letter to John Murray. It was
Gansevoort, in London, who arranged the American publication. No one
ever said it, but everyone could reflect privately that if Gansevoort had not
driven himself in his last months to launch Herman's career, he might have
recuperated in some pleasant village outside London and survived his illness,
which had attacked, the doctors said, so many organs of his body. He was like
those fallen angels in the passage he had quoted from *Paradise Lost:* vital in
every part, no one disease could kill him. Gansevoort could not but "by
annihilating die."

[22]

The Resurrection of Toby
1846

The early part of the volume, narrating the author's escape from the prison ship — with his strange comrade Toby, whose mysterious fate, after baffling our curiosity and speculation, is yet to be developed — for the best of all possible reasons, that the author himself has not found it out! — is full of vivid excitement.

Douglas Jerrold's Shilling Magazine, April 1846

WHILE HE WAS IN New York City in late June waiting for the arrival of the *Prince Albert*, Melville saw some of the attacks on *Typee* in the new July issues of religious magazines and other magazines with a squad of clerical reviewers. At this painful time for Melville the evangelical press seemed to have mustered its forces to haul and rehaul *Typee* over what George Duyckinck had referred to as coals — and he might have specified red-hot coals. One latecomer to the group-torture inflicted upon the book was the reviewer in the July issue of the New Haven *New Englander*. After saying he had at first thought to ignore *Typee*, he declared: "On reading farther, however, we entirely changed our views; for it is difficult to believe that the author was not actuated, either by a perverse spirit of intentional misrepresentation, or that he is not utterly incapable, from moral obtuseness, of an accurate statement." Melville had manifested "moral obtuseness" whenever he had "an opportunity for exhibiting a correct spirit." He had let no opportunity slip by "for giving a glowing description of savage life, and for launching quips and small anathemas" against civilization:

> For missionaries and missionary labor, — except in *general*, — he has a special abhorrence. The cause of Missions is a good thing — except where it raises man from cannibalism to civilization. . . . Of truths of general history he seems to know nothing. The fact of the depopulation of the Sandwich Islands, seems to him to be something new; and this is specially brought about by the efforts of missionaries and their hypocrisy. The fact that wherever civilization comes in contact with savage life, there the savage wastes away; or at least that

this has been so, wherever the Saxon stock comes into contact with it; he never thought of; — and now for the first time seeing the fact he gives his own crude explanation of it, and would have the world then receive his volume as a work of authority.

The readers of the *New Englander* were told flatly that Melville was incapable of giving "an accurate statement of moral facts," having never known "a course of life calculated greatly to improve his moral eye sight." The complication was that the book was "not without literary merit," even "very companionable," and therefore insidious, and necessary to be condemned rather than to be ignored.

The July New York *Christian Parlor Magazine* printed a ten-page denunciation. In the ferocity of the opening even Melville might scarcely have noticed the error about the British publisher:

> An apotheosis of barbarism! A panegyric on cannibal delights! An apostrophe to the spirit of savage felicity! Such are the exclamations instinctively springing from our lips as we close a book entitled "Typee: a Residence in the Marquesas," lately published in Wiley & Putnam's interesting "Library of American Books." It is even so, reader! A work coming from the press of one of the first houses in this country, and published simultaneously by the same house in London, gemmed with enthusiastic descriptions of the innocent felicity of a savage tribe — tinselled with ornate pencillings of cannibal enjoyments — drawing frequent contrasts between the disadvantages and miseries of civilization, and the uninterrupted paradisiacal bliss of a tribe which has traced in ominous characters of blood on the outer battlements of its natural fortresses of rock and mountain that omnipotent and talismanic "TABU."

The reviewer warned that his article was not an example of literary criticism but an exposé of a malignant book "wherein the cause of MISSIONS is assailed, with a pertinacity of misrepresentation and degree of *hatred*, which can only entitle the perpetrator to the just claim of traducer." The writer, like some other religious reviewers, was genuinely in conflict, unwilling to publicize *Typee* yet afraid not to condemn it: "To give circulation to such statements as our author makes may seen unwise, but as extracts from it of the nature we condemn are obtaining a channel through the public journals, we have determined to do our part in the work of making him known to the public." Ferociously, obsessively, he denounced Melville's "undisguised attempt to decry the missionary work in its every feature" and ranked Melville as a specimen of the writers who "condemn, under assumed pretexts, the ripening fruit of the gospel of Christ."

Presumably the writers of these last reviews did not know that John

Wiley had already acted, following his own moral urgings and the comments of early readers, and had arranged for *Typee* to be expurgated, under the mediation of the series editor, Duyckinck, since at this juncture Melville's fraternal grief and Wiley's religious outrage were running too high for the men to meet with each other about the expurgations. It was distasteful to Wiley to have to deal directly with a man who had caused such consternation among his Presbyterian friends. Dealing with authors in the series was what he had hired Evert A. Duyckinck for, and now Duyckinck would have to deal with an author who had been foisted into the series with not even a pretense of consulting its editor.

Melville's first introduction to Duyckinck, a literary man himself, may well have been from the words of Edgar Allan Poe, one of Duyckinck's authors in the Library of American Books. Once Melville had let it be known that he would be seeing Duyckinck, Bradford or another New York acquaintance would have pointed him to the July 1846 issue of *Godey's Magazine and Lady's Book*, available in Manhattan in the last week of June. There in the third installment of his "The Literati of New York City" Poe profiled Duyckinck along with Fitz-Greene Halleck and others. Poe was predictably flattering. "Mr. Duyckinck has slyly acquired much fame and numerous admirers under the *nom de plume* of 'Felix Merry,' " he wrote, and then he gave an impressionistic character analysis. Duyckinck was "distinguished for the *bonhommie* of his manner, his simplicity and single-mindedness, his active beneficence, his hatred of wrong done even to any enemy, and especially for an almost Quixotic fidelity to his friends," and seemed to be "in perpetual good humor with all things." Poe described him as "light" of hair and eye, five feet eight, "somewhat slender," "scrupulously neat but plain" in dress. A momentous fact for Melville, not revealed in *Godey's*, was that Duyckinck was the possessor of one of the greatest private libraries in the country. He was only three years older than Melville, and his younger brother George was Allan's age, a fact that later encouraged intimacy between the sets of brothers.

Duyckinck's immediate task was to prepare Melville for what Wiley had decided on — a drastic expurgation of *Typee*. The men met while Melville was waiting to meet the *Prince Albert* and unload the coffin containing the body of the brother who had also been his literary intermediary. Resentful of having Putnam force *Typee* into his Library without asking him, its initiator, Duyckinck had deprecated the cuckoo in his nest, superciliously calling Melville's book "lively and pleasant," "not over philosophical, perhaps," to Hawthorne. He had conveyed his irritation to his brother, George, who in a letter on 14 April dutifully declined to take *Typee* "all for sober verity," commented smugly on its treatment in the religious papers, and reveled a little in the implausibility of some of Melville's scenes ("His exploits in descending the waterfalls beat Sam Patch" — the most famous daredevil of the day). Evert Duyckinck struck the sailor-author as polite but somewhat prissy, to judge from the way Melville defined the editor's manner when he wrote him a little later: "There was a spice of civil scepticism in your manner, My Dear Sir, when we were conversing together the other day about 'Typee.' " Duyckinck had been "politely incredulous" about the authenticity of the book — a point that was already an open sore. Melville alluded to the reviewer of the *Evangelist* as being a conspicuous man "of little faith," while Duyckinck had been another, only less egregious. But the business could wait: even in his outrage, Wiley was willing to let the young author bury his brother before making him butcher his book.

Late on Thursday, 2 July, four days after Gansevoort's burial, Herman received astonishing news. Edwin Croswell as editor of the *Argus* regularly exchanged copies of his paper with many other editors across the state and beyond its borders. Late on 1 July he received the Buffalo *Commercial Advertiser* of that date, and he saw to it that it reached Herman in Lansingburgh the next day, 2 July. There the author of *Typee* read the article entitled "How strangely things turn up!" It began with an introductory paragraph by the editor, Dr. Thomas M. Foote:

> One of the most curious and entertaining books published last season was a work entitled *"Typee, a residence in the Marquesas."* We read it with great interest, but the impression it left on the mind was that the incidents and mode of life it described were too extraordinary, and too much at variance with what is known of savage life, to be true, and that like the fabled *Atlantis* or the travels of *Gaudentio di Lucca*, though without their philosophical pretension, it was the offspring of a lively inventive fancy, rather than a veritable narrative of facts. This impression, we believe, was very general.

That was all buildup for Foote's revelation:

> The readers of *Typee* therefore can imagine, and will share, our surprise, at hearing that here, in Buffalo, is a credible witness to the truth of some of the most extraordinary incidents narrated in the book. *Toby*, the companion of Mr. MELVILLE in the flight from the whale ship, and whom in his book he supposes to be dead, is now living in this city, following the business of a house and sign painter. His father is a respectable farmer in the town of Darien, Genesee Co. We received from *Toby* this morning the subjoined communication. His verbal statements correspond in all essential particulars with those made by Mr. MELVILLE respecting their joint adventures, and from the assurances we have received in regard to Toby's character, we have

no reason to doubt his word. His turning up here is a strange verification of a very strange and, as has hitherto been deemed, an almost incredible book.

All this was Foote, who knew how to package a story.

In the letter that Foote then printed, as a proper climax, "Toby," Richard Tobias Greene, explained that he had read a review of *Typee* only belatedly (in a most ironic place, the *Evangelist*): "The *Evangelist* speaks rather disparagingly of the book as being too romantic to be true, and as being too severe on the missionaries. But to my object: I am the true and veritable 'Toby,' yet living, and I am happy to testify to the entire accuracy of the work so long as I was with Melville." Greene thereupon asked Melville to send him his address if the article "should chance to meet his eye." This was, of course, nothing like sealing a message in a bottle and entrusting it to the Trades, or attaching pieces of wood to seafowls, as the crew of the *Parker* had done. The telegraph was still experimental, but railroads had made the editorial fraternity close-knit and efficient.

With a copy of the *Commercial Advertiser* in hand, Herman immediately wrote to Toby and then wrote Duyckinck on 3 July. He knew from the article in the *Commercial Advertiser* that Greene was set to vouch for *Typee* as far as it concerned what both men had experienced. He was not worried about Greene's exposing the most serious fraud he had perpetrated in *Typee*, since his friend had no way of knowing that he had not in fact spent a total of some four months with the Typees before escaping. Melville hastened to enlist Duyckinck in the best strategic use of the news:

> Seriously, . . . this resurrection of Toby from the dead — this strange bringing together of two such places as Typee & Buffalo, is really curious. — It can not but settle the question of the book's genuineness. The article in the C.A. with the letter of Toby can not possibly be gainsaid in any conceivable way — therefore I think it ought to be pushed into circulation. I doubt not but that many papers will copy it — Mr Duyckinck might say a word or two on the subject which would tell. . . . I have written Toby a letter & expect to see him soon & hear the sequel of the book I have written (How strangely that sounds!)
>
> Bye the bye, since people have always manifested so much concern for "Poor Toby", what do you think of writing an account of what befell him in escaping from the island — should the adventure prove to be of sufficient interest? — I should value your opinion very highly on this subject.

In response to this letter, Duyckinck may have "pushed" some items into print in New York City, but he did not need to push very hard, given the inherent newsworthiness of Toby's reappearance.

In the meantime, Melville pushed as hard as he could. He went down from Lansingburgh to Albany on Saturday, the fourth of July. He called at the *Argus*, but Croswell had better things to do on the Glorious Fourth than sit in his office. Melville himself had no desire to join the celebrations, which could only remind him of Gansevoort's reading the Declaration of Independence there, so he lingered to write a letter to Croswell on the spot, explaining that "the 'Toby' of the Buffalo Commercial Advertiser is all that he says he is. — Of this there is no mistake — allusions are made in his letter to matters which no one else could know anything about except himself." On Tuesday, 7 July, Croswell paraphrased part of the letter Melville had left for him: "Mr. MELVILLE says that he can readily account for what may seem to be inexplicable in 'Toby's' statement, viz: the five dollars paid the Irishman for assisting him on board the ship: and he adds, 'I have written to my old comrade, and expect soon to hear from him and see him.'" Even before this article appeared, the original article in the *Commercial Advertiser* was being widely reprinted. It appeared locally in both the Albany *Argus* and *Evening Journal* on 3 July, in the *Morning Courier and New-York Enquirer* on 9 July, in the London *Athenæum* on 8 August, and many other papers, and it was excerpted in dozens more, with a range of introductory comments.

Thurlow Weed, the editor of the Whig *Evening Journal*, was not yet converted on 3 July: Foote would not tell an outright falsehood, but he just might have lent his columns to what he thought was an amusing hoax:

> while we give our belief freely to the existence of the gentle "Fayaway," the devoted "Kory," the royal "Mehevi," and even of "Toby" himself, yet the appearance of either of them, in *propria persona*, would excite suspicions of their identity. We do not believe, therefore, that the mysterious, and mysteriously absent "Toby," is a Sign Painter at Buffalo! And of course we are bound to believe that our friend FOOTE, of the Commercial Advertiser, though a gentleman of strict veracity, is romancing with us in the following article. Perhaps, however, he will say as another of the Editorial fraternity was accused of saying — "This is a good-enough 'Toby' until you produce a better one."

This last was an allusion to the phrase "good-enough Morgan," a reference to a sensational political event a decade and a half earlier, when Masons were accused of murdering a man named Morgan, and a body was discovered that the anti-Masonic party identified as the missing man. If the body was not Morgan, it was nevertheless a "good-enough Morgan" until after the election, and this Toby at Buffalo would be a good-enough Toby until the vogue of *Typee* had quite faded away.

In making his rounds of newspaper offices on the fourth of July Melville came to Weed, a conventionally handsome, somewhat foppish fellow with arching brows, a sensuous-looking mouth (bowed upper lip, full lower lip), and hair long in the manner of European poets and musicians: no one had ever had to tell this man to shave and look more like a Christian. Weed saw Herman not as an individual but as one of a clan—Gansevoort Melville's brother and, more than that, Hunn and Guert Gansevoort's cousin. Weed knew them all, and other kinfolk of Herman's. Hunn was dead now, drowned at sea in 1843, but in Philadelphia at Christmas in 1842 he had waxed extremely confidential to this friend of the family about Guert's revelation to him in his hotel room the night before, during Guert's stopover on his way to Washington. Hunn then had repeated Guert's damaging version of events on the *Somers*. Now Weed listened to Herman, dubiously, as a friend of the family. He obligingly printed this in the *Evening Journal* on 6 July: "Mr. MELVILLE, the Author of 'Typee,' who was in town on Saturday, says that he has no doubt but that the Buffalo Sign Painter is his veritable Ship-Mate and Companion 'Toby.' If this be so, it furnishes a strong exemplification of the seeming contradiction that 'Truth is stranger than Fiction.'"

Delighted at Weed's skepticism, Dr. Thomas Foote, the "gentleman of strict veracity," on 6 July quoted extensively from the article in the Albany *Evening Journal* and cited new testimony received on that busy fourth of July:

> We acknowledge the romance, but it is the romance of truth. Our friend of the *Journal* may dismiss his doubts. There is no mistake whatever. The father of *"Toby"* called upon us last Saturday, and confirmed his son's story in every essential particular. *"Toby"* went on a whaling voyage at the time mentioned in Mr. MELVILLE's book, and on his return related his strange adventures precisely as they are told in *Typee*. He supposed, till lately, that Mr. MELVILLE was dead, or yet remaining on the island, and as a proof of regard for his friend—which we mention for the benefit of the author of *Typee*—induced a married sister to name her boy MELVILLE.

Showing again that he knew a good thing when it fell into his lap, Foote continued: "We hope ere long to be able to place '*Toby's*' adventures before our readers"—good news to everyone but the author of *Typee*. This article of the sixth was duly picked up in its turn, and nothing less than a brief media sensation ensued. New York newspapers (with or without encouragement from Duyckinck) took up the story, the *Morning Courier and New-York Enquirer* and the *Morning News* on 9 July printing some of the documents, along with commentary. The "resurrection of Toby" became a publicity windfall, so much so that there were those who at first declared it all a publicity gimmick. Every paper that had mulled over the question of the authenticity of *Typee* now had to inform its readership of the appearance of Toby, and to follow the story through several days. Even skeptical editors gave *Typee* good new publicity, and sooner or later most of these skeptical editors publicly ate crow, so that their readers were forcefully reminded, over and over again, that truth is stranger than fiction. Weed the holdout finally recanted on 8 July, after the new testimony had reached him, and the recantation itself was newsworthy.

Upon his receipt of Melville's letter, Greene responded with a letter to "*Friend 'Tommo'* " containing an account of his own departure from the Typee valley, his crossing through the territory of the Happars, his embarkation, and his subsequent nautical adventures; then he gave the letter in much the same form to Foote, who published it in the *Commercial Advertiser* of 11 July — taking up almost a full column. A peculiarly constructed but otherwise skillful piece of writing, it started with Greene's arrival on the beach and his finding a white man standing there, Jimmy Fitch the Irishman. Then Greene described subsequent events in sequence, until he got two thirds of the way through the letter, when (after eloquently describing his sailing away on the *London Packet* — "the good ship was ploughing the billows like a thing of life, while the mountains of Marquesas were 'hull down' in the distance") he reverted to his departure from the Typee valley. Melville remembered, he was sure, his departure from the valley, accompanied by "Fayaway, Markeyo, Mow Mow with the one eye, and the two young Typees, living in our house, and some one hundred and fifty besides," and laden with hogs and fruit. The rest Melville had not witnessed: "We arrived on the beach in about three hours and found no one there but the Irish Jimmy, who had escaped from an English Man of War, and who I have since learned was captured by the English after this event. Here ensued the above conversation." The "above conversation" was by now inexplicably far "above," preceding a section on Greene's arriving at Nukahiva and signing on the *London Packet* in the expectation that Jimmy would bring Melville aboard the next day. Greene concluded his account with weighing anchor and setting sail, and the ships he subsequently sailed on, the last of which landed at Fairhaven somewhat over a year after he left Nukahiva.

In Albany on 13 July the *Evening Journal* reprinted "Typee — Toby's Own Story." Melville could have asked Weed later, but it would not have been clear to him at once whether this opening paragraph was by Foote or by Weed: "The following communication from the *'Toby'* of *'Typee,'* giving an account of the manner of his escape from the Typee valley, will be read with interest. It is a mere sketch, however, and in a new edition of *Typee*, which we see has been called for, will be doubtless given with all necessary details." This paragraph was in fact by Weed, and it was influenced by Melville's own efforts on 4 July to manage the story, and also influenced, apparently, by publicity coming from Wiley & Putnam in New York City. Melville had not yet learned that news was not something he could manage, and the wording of this first paragraph set him into something of a panic, since it opened the possibility that Toby's "mere sketch" would be filled out (by Toby? by Melville?) for publication in the new edition of *Typee*. Mindful of the importance of writing his own sequel, Melville was helpless to keep "Toby's Own Story" from being widely reprinted.

The second paragraph in the article as published in the *Evening Journal* of 13 July began *"Friend 'Tommo' "* — possibly evidence that the Typees really referred to Herman as Tommo, but also, under the circumstances, a clear wink to Herman that Greene was set to back up his story without quibbling over details. Of even more crucial importance was Greene's simple confirmation of "Fayaway" as the name of a Typee maiden. Melville must have noticed at a glance that Greene had adopted his spellings of Polynesian names as if they had been standard, lifted from the Marquesan census rolls: "Fayaway"! "Mow-Mow"! "Tinor"! (Following the misreading of Greene's hand in the Buffalo paper, Weed misprinted one of them as "Markeyo.") That was all confirmation to thrust before the skeptics, but Weed's printing of Greene's description of his parting from Fayaway was enough to make Melville edgy:

> I sat there [in the tabooed house on the Typee beach] for half an hour before
> we started when Jimmy called the Typee, and me, and then the fair Fayaway,
> our Typee dulcinea, came up to me and shook hands with me and said, "how
> you do," in English, as you recollect we taught her a few words of English,
> such as "good bye" and "how do you do," and she mistook the words and said
> for good bye *"how you do,"* and then the Typee shouldered his ho[g], and we
> started off, the natives still looking, talking, and leaving their fruit on the
> beach, left for the valley before we were out of sight.

If Fayaway was Toby's Dulcinea as well as Tommo's, who was Sancho and who was the hero of the romance? (If he ever compared this to the *Commercial Advertiser* printing of the article carefully, Herman would have seen that Toby had said "your Typee dulcinea," going along with his friend's story, not "our Typee dulcinea.") There was another wrinkle. As he read the *Evening Journal* it was clear to Melville that this sample of Greene's literary style (aside from that odd placement of the scene on the Typee beach) was not obviously inferior to his own — a disturbing fact, especially since if "Toby's Own Story" had been picked up by the *Evening Journal* it was sure to be picked up by other papers. (Hiram Fuller, for one, put it in the 1 August New York *Weekly Mirror.*) Melville grew increasingly nervous that Greene was undercutting his prospects for using "Toby's Own Story" in shaping his own sequel.

For all this uneasiness, Melville must have regarded the timing of this resurrection of his shipmate as providential. It offered him a much-needed distraction from his grief, and it promised to vindicate him in the eyes of those who thought *Typee* was a fiction. Now, rather than staying in Lansingburgh to go through Gansevoort's possessions with his mother and his sisters, Herman could go down to Albany and try to manage the news. It seems odd that Herman did not take the train west at once for a reunion with his comrade, but Wiley, having calculated the amount of time a younger brother required to grieve for a Democratic orator, was insistent that he return to New York City. Wiley was so determined to scotch the appearance of any new articles like those in the July magazines that he dealt personally with Melville this time. On 11 July Wiley & Putnam paid $150 to Melville on his Typee account — a timely coolant, for over the next days Melville suffered not only from the summer but also from the heat of what he called on 15 July "the fiery ordeal of Mr Wiley's criticisms." (Infernal imagery came naturally to Melville's mind, just as it had to George Duyckinck's.) It was bad enough to have to agree to tone *Typee* down, but now it was much worse to allow Wiley to show him, point by point, just what was going to be expurgated. As usual, Melville repressed his feelings, but his resentment rankled all his life, just as his resentment toward the Harpers did. His niece Charlotte, born in 1859, often heard her mother, Melville's sister Kate, and her aunts talk about the fact that Melville "was very cut up that in all later editions — all mention of the Missionary's [*sic*] was omitted. He saw how much evil they were doing and thought it should be known."

The sessions with Wiley left Melville with a grudge against his Presbyterian accusers and tormenters which he settled in wondrously ecumenical fashion in chapter 10 of *Moby-Dick*, where Ishmael justifies his worshiping Queequeg's god: "I was a good Christian; born and bred in the bosom of the infallible Presbyterian Church. How then could I unite with this wild idolator in worshipping his piece of wood? But what is worship? thought I. Do you suppose now, Ishmael, that the magnanimous God of heaven and earth — pagans and all included — can possibly be jealous of an insignificant bit of black wood? Impossible!" Even in 1850 or 1851, when he wrote this scene, he had not learned that he had no chance of winning against supporters of the missionaries. At the time, unpleasant as it was to cooperate in chopping up his book and suppressing his opinions, Melville had something to rejoice about: he did not have to deal with the publisher's uneasiness about the authenticity of the narrative. Toby's reappearance allowed Melville to focus on his vindication in the metropolitan press as the author of a genuine narrative. Secure in that vindication he could, with a freer spirit, capitulate to the religious press and delete his comments on the missionaries as well as some of the more sexually suggestive passages. In short, the news about Toby allowed him the chance to think of himself as in some sense having won one battle for his book, even when he was losing the battle to say his say about the missionaries.

Duyckinck had been out of the negotiations this time, but Melville reported to him around 15 July, itemizing his topics. He had agreed with Wiley not only on the expurgations but on what else remained for him to do for the "Revised Edition," and he had resolved to tell himself that *Typee* was the better for the omissions. He would go to see Toby and "obtain all the materials for the proposed Sequel." He would also work on "the new preface" and would assemble some of the most favorable reviews of the book so that they could "be prefixed" to it in the new printing, he said. Apparently Wiley had proposed adding a cluster of reviews at the back of the book. For some reason, instead of these reviews, Wiley & Putnam actually inserted advertisements for other books, starting with William Hazlitt's *Age of Elizabeth* and concluding with the Reverend Dr. Benjamin I. Land's *The Mysteries of Tobacco* (congenially entitled, but in fact an exposé of the evils of the weed, bolstered here by a sympathetic review). However, in an 1847 reprinting of the "Revised Edition" Wiley & Putnam included an advertisement containing what seem to be the quotations Herman had gathered earlier. It began with an introductory paragraph adapted from *Typee* (the "*heathenish rites, and human sacrifices*" passage from chapter 1), then continued with quotations from the New York *Mirror, Morning News, Courier and Enquirer,* the Baltimore *Western Continent,* the New York *Tribune,* the Cincinnati *Herald,* the New York *National Anti-Slavery Standard,* the Richmond *Republican,* the Albany *Argus,* the New York *American Review,* the Philadelphia *Graham's Magazine,* the New York *Hunt's Merchant's Magazine,* and a second notice in the *Courier and Enquirer.* Following this section were "Notices of the English Press," including quotations from the *Times* (in which was that wonderful "Enviable Herman!" passage), *Douglas Jerrold's Shilling Magazine, Beckett's Almanack of the Month,* the *Sun,* and shorter quotations from the *Athenæum,* the *Examiner,* the *Spectator,* the *Critic* (first and third notices), and the *Eclectic Review.* Most of these Gansevoort had sent; the *Times* review of 6 April appeared two days after his last diary entry, but he probably had managed to mail it. The notices are of special interest since Melville may have selected not only the reviews he wanted to "prefix" to *Typee* but also the parts of them he wanted to quote.

On that same Wednesday, 15 July, Melville for the first time wrote directly to John Murray, a very long letter, for which he apologized, remembering Maria's sage maxim that first letters, like first visits, should be kept short. Acutely aware both of Murray's initial skepticism and his recent worry about the skepticism of some readers, Melville triumphantly broached the subject of the authenticity of his book: "In the first place I have to inform you that 'Toby' who figures in my narrative has come to life — tho' I had long supposed him to be dead. I send you by this steamer several papers (N.Y. Courier & Enquirer, N.Y. Morning News, & Albany Argus) containing allusions to him. Toby's appearance has produced quite a lively sensation here — and 'Truth is stranger than Fiction' is in every body's mouth." That was the unalloyed good news; then Melville had to slant the next portion so as not to alarm Murray. What he sent was the initial report, *not* "Toby's Own Story," although he acknowledged that such a narrative was in print ("I was sorry for this on some accounts, but it could not be helped"). Murray, he went on, "would be greatly diverted to read some of the comments of our Western Editors and log-cabin critics" — an example of the kind of diffident jocular subservience that tinged his letters to his next English publisher as well, even four or five years later. Melville moved to the point: "I am now preparing a short Sequel to Typee containing a simple account of Toby's escape from the valley as related to me by himself," a sequel that he said would be "bound up with all subsequent editions of the book" in the United States. He excused himself for not delaying the publication of the sequel until Murray could print it as well: "there is a present demand for the book which the publishers can not supply — a new edition is in preperation — & after what has happened, this can not come out very well without the story of Toby." (Preparation was a word both he and Cousin Robert had trouble with.) In this context Melville did not mention the expurgated nature of the "new edition," but focused on copyright concerns: he would take care that Murray received a copy of the sequel "by the earliest possible op[p]ortunity" so no other publisher would interfere.

In the next paragraph a very subdued Melville recited the rationalizations he had settled upon to justify his expurgating his book, some of them pretty clearly echoed from the more temperate dicta of John Wiley. Melville knew that Murray had omitted a few passages on the score of "taste," and might be sympathetic with more such changes, but he also knew that the British critics were not, for the most part, fervent champions of the missionaries, and that no British critic had found anything objectionable in the appendix, that resounding vindication of Lord Paulet. He explained carefully that the revision would exclude "those parts not naturally connected with the narrative" and include "some slight purifications of style":

> I am pursuaded that the interest of the book alone wholly consists in the *intrinsick merit of the narrative alone* — & that other portions, however interesting they may be in themselves, only serve to impede the story. The book is certainly calculated for popular reading, or for none at all. — If the first, why

then, all passages which are calculated to offend the tastes, or offer violence
to the feelings of any large class of readers are certainly objectionable.—
Proceeding on this principle then, I have rejected every thing, in revising the
book, which refers to the missionaries. . . . Certain "sea-freedoms" also have
been modifyed in the expression—but nothing has been done to effect the
general character & style of the book—the narrative parts are untouched—In
short—in revising the work, I have merely removed passages which leave no
gap, & the removal of which imparts a unity to the book which it wanted
before.

He was quoting the term "sea-freedoms" from the 28 February *Spectator*,
which had said that such expressions might better have been removed before
publication. Melville enclosed a document justifying the excisions, a now-
missing draft of the preface for the "Revised Edition." He did not specifically
mention the deletion of the pro-British appendix, which because it dealt with
the missionaries did not have to be singled out.

With much to convey and no desire to be confessional, Melville circled
about his reasons for wanting Murray to issue a "Revised Edition" as well,
based on the copy to be forwarded him by the first steamer, hotly followed by
the sequel. "Hang policy," Gansevoort had cried: "My blood is up!" Now a
chastened Herman wrote, "Depend upon it Sir, that it will be policy so to
do"—that is, to issue a "Revised Edition": "Nor have I decided upon this
revision without much reflection and seeking the advice of persons every way
qualifyed to give it, & who have done so in a spirit of candor." Duyckinck, at
least, had candidly advised him to do whatever John Wiley suggested, and
Melville had brooded bitterly about the expurgations, although he may never
have been able to devote calm "reflection" to the topic.

His emotions were ferocious and contradictory. Pushing him one way
was the determination to do what he had to do to keep an American publisher
and solidify an American reputation (so that he might establish some sort of
career based on his authorship, and so that he might marry, if he were lucky
enough to persuade the right young woman to accept him). Pulling him the
other way was the impulse to expose the practices of the missionaries in the
new book, even more graphically than in the first. He wrote to Murray as a
modest, practical young author concerned with the unity of his narration,
even if that meant excluding the sections on the missionaries. Shortly afterward he wrote into his next manuscript new and aggressive criticisms of the
missionaries, passages which he may very well have seen as more nearly
unified into the work than such passages had been in *Typee*, but passages
which made it clear that he had meant everything he had said in the first
edition of *Typee*.

Mentioning the "most flattering success" of the book in England, Melville reminded Murray of his having assured Gansevoort "that in case the book met with 'unusual success' he would still further remunerate the author." Now if Murray felt "every way warranted in so doing" Melville would be gratified by his "early consideration of this subject." There was another pecuniary matter: "altho' you will not be bound to pay me any thing for the Sequel, still, should you make use of it, I rely not a little upon your liberality." He devoted a longish paragraph to the title. From the first he had "deeply regretted" that Murray had not used the title he had "always intended for it." He was on weak grounds in arguing that the title in America had anything to do with making the book "a decided hit," since he knew it had been a "hit" in England under a most cumbersome title, but he had an author's affection for his own title: " 'Typee' is a title *naturally suggested by the narrative itself*, and not farfetched as some strange titles are. Besides, its very strangeness & novelty, founded as it is upon the character of the book — are the very things to make 'Typee' a popular title. The work also should be known by the same name on both sides of the water." This last was a reasonable request enough, easy to effect.

Toward the end of this letter Melville offered Murray his next book. On 15 February 1846 he had informed Gansevoort that he was "continuing busy," and on 3 April Gansevoort had promised that "in my next or the one after that" he would "venture to make some suggestions about your next book." Herman had been deflected from constant application to *Omoo* by delighting, distressing, and devastating events, among which was his courtship of "Miss Elizabeth," who had contributed to his having had such an "agreeable visit to Boston" the previous March. Now he offered Murray an optimistic account of the status of the book and its likely progress: "I have another work now nearly completed which I am anxious to submit to you before presenting it to any other publishing house. It embraces adventures in the South Seas (of a totally different character from 'Typee') and includes an eventful cruise in an English Colonial Whaleman (A Sydney Ship) and a comical residence on the island of Tahiti. The time is about four months, but I & my narrative are both on the move during that short period." He hastened to assure Murray that his "new M.S.S." would be "in a rather better shape for the press" than the previous one: "A little experience in this art of book-craft has done wonders." It would be ready "the latter part of the fall — *autumn* I believe it is with you." But before he could get back to the "nearly completed" manuscript he had some other writing to do.

To keep the momentum going, and to get Greene's story into the "Revised Edition" in something like unvitiated freshness, before Greene had solidified his own proprietorial rights to it, Melville went west to get the story from his shipmate directly, so he could make it his own in the retelling. He met Greene in Rochester, apparently, rather than Buffalo, for the next year, in his commentary on *Blackwood's* review of *Omoo*, Thurlow Weed admitted his own skepticism about the existence of Toby, recalled the amazing announcement in the Buffalo paper, then declared: "These Marquesan adventurers subsequently met at Rochester to assure themselves as well as a doubting public, of their respective identity and existence." Whatever the rendezvous point, Herman traveled light, as always, but probably carried a copy of *Typee* for Greene and surely carried the problematical "Toby's Own Story" in the *Commercial Advertiser* printing and the *Evening Journal* reprinting.

It was strange for Melville, taking the train over a route (past the site of General Gansevoort's revolutionary triumph) that he had traversed on foot and by canal, with excruciating slowness, six years before, then not quite twenty-one, hoping to make his fortune in the West. Now he was still a young man, but for four months or so a famous one, even if sometimes vilified. He surely had formulated for himself already the comparison to the overnight fame of Lord Byron, which he used in a letter to an autograph seeker on 24 July ("You remember someone woke one morning and found himself famous. — And here am I, just come from hoeing in the garden, writing autographs"). He had never thought to be the oldest living son, and Gansevoort had been the one to consider a literary career, years before, but now Gansevoort was dead, he was the writer, and his own new manuscript on the South Seas was in progress. His hopes of making the right marriage, to Elizabeth Shaw, depended upon his redeeming *Typee* and succeeding with the new manuscript. There was no shortage of topics to meditate upon as he thundered along parallel to the "tempestuous" canal (his joke, decades later, in *Billy Budd*), at forty miles an hour, and this was the year that Melville began to articulate a sense of himself as a "reflective man." There is no account of the meeting, but tokens of it remain — a daguerreotype of Toby and "a lock of those ebon curls." Melville had something practical to do in the cars on the way home: he could work on the sequel. (On 2 September he promised to send John Murray by the next steamer an account of the manner of his hearing of Toby and "our interview &c," but if he did so, that letter is not preserved in the Murray archives.)

By 20 July, or the twenty-first at the latest, Melville was back in Lansingburgh, for Allan had a letter from him by Wednesday, 22 July, part of the contents of which he relayed to Evert Duyckinck: "My brother desires me to see Mr Duyckinck & say that he has reached home after having seen 'Toby' & that he will be in town on Monday with the sequel. He further more wished me to say to Mr Duyckinck that the advertizing [of] the Revised Edition had better be delayed until his arrival in town for reasons (very good ones I suppose) which he was in too great a hurry to enumerate." Before going to New York City Melville probably had a good draft of what was published as the "Preface to the Revised Edition." There he said in public what he had been practicing in private: "The reception given to Typee has induced the author to believe it worthy of revision. And as the interest of the book chiefly consists in its being the history of a remarkable adventure, in revising it, several passages, wholly unconnected with that adventure, have been rejected as irrelevant."

Melville also must have written the sequel by the time he arrived in New York. Toby's prior publication of his own version of the escape from the Typee valley complicated matters, for Melville could not merely repeat his friend's story if he hoped to be paid for it by Murray and to make it a salient feature of the new Wiley & Putnam edition. Before he returned to Lansingburgh, Melville had written a little "Note to the Sequel" stating that he had heard the story from Toby himself, "not ten days since," literally true if he wrote the note before 29 July or so. In the sequel he took extreme care to avoid repeating the substance of "Toby's Own Story." He got from Toby or invented or dressed up a new episode about the procession to the beach, an elaborate, time-consuming practical joke on Toby in which the natives pretended to be evading a Happar ambush while Toby prepared to do battle with his bare fists, since they refused him a spear. Then Melville enriched the encounter with Jimmy by specific details: "He wore a Manilla hat and a sort of tappa morning gown, sufficiently loose and negligent to show the verse of a song tatooed upon his chest, and a variety of spirited cuts by native artists in other parts of his body. He sported a fishing rod in his hand, and carried a sooty old pipe slung about his neck." He even stalled the action while he related (as from his own earlier experience at Nukahiva) two of Jimmy's stories about natural prodigies on the island, a hermit out of whose temples grew a great pair of horns and a lad who was marked for the priesthood by the rooster-like comb that grew on his head and his cock-like prideful crow.

With a graceless "But to return to Toby" (a formula he employed all his life after digressions) Melville put the discussion between Toby and Jimmy in the form of dialogue, dramatized Toby's attempt to return to the Typee valley (Toby had said two or three hands restrained him, Melville made it an even dozen), and prolonged his struggle to free himself from the natives who were restraining him. He elaborated Toby's description of being approached, despite the taboo, by an old woman, as well as the description of how Jimmy got Toby away from the natives. Toby had specified that he and Jimmy got something to eat in the Happar valley, but Melville ballooned that into a detailed account of their stopping at Jimmy's house there, where he kept two Happar wives, and Toby's enduring a suspenseful meal of "fish, bread-fruit, and bananas," during which he stayed close to Jimmy while trying to recognize the man who had wounded him. Melville carefully emphasized that Toby saw the French men-of-war still lying in the harbor ("as Toby looked down upon them, the strange events which had happened so recently, seemed all a dream"). In the newspaper article Toby had told a dramatic story of signing on the *London Packet* in Nukahiva harbor in the hope that Jimmy would return the next day with his companion: "The next evening came, and found me on the beach waiting to welcome my shipmate. I could descry his form seated in the stern sheets as the boats approached the shore. But alas! he was not there. My brain grew dizzy, the savage villains have killed him, but I will be revenged on the scoundrel that took me from the valley. So soon as Jimmy struck the beach I seized him, shouting in a voice that startled him, where is MELVILLE?" In the sequel Melville moved the encounter to shipboard and told it this way: "Towards evening he [Toby] was on the watch, and descried the boats turning the headland and entering the bay. He strained his eyes, and thought he saw me; but I was not there. Descending from the mast almost distracted, he grappled Jimmy as he struck the deck, shouting in a voice that startled him, 'Where is Tommo?' "

Stock constructions like "Little did Toby then think" and "Well must the old sailor have known" or "Vain were all Toby's ravings, — they were dis-regarded" (common in *Typee*, rare in *Omoo*) and the peculiar ballooning of two episodes are signs of Melville's extreme uneasiness with what he called "The Story of Toby." Greene's own account had been tauter, more powerful, despite its peculiar construction, a fault that Foote could have corrected in a moment. Melville later made himself a master of turning other men's narra-tives into his own, but he was too inhibited to do that with "Toby's Own Story." By writing such a strong narrative Greene had established what Mel-ville could only see as unwelcome proprietorial rights. Aware that in his earlier letter he had pumped up the significance of the sequel, Melville ex-plained diffidently to Murray on 2 September that it was "written as simply as possible," merely "to satisfy the reader's curiosity as to Toby's escape."

The sequel remained worrisome even after Melville turned it over to Wiley & Putnam. At the end of July, as he prepared to return to Lan-singburgh, he left a note for Duyckinck: "You remember you said something about anticipating the piracy that might be perpetrated on the 'Sequel', by publishing an extract or two from it—which you said you would attend to." This was "a matter of some little moment" to him, and he relied on Duy-ckinck also to handle the larger problem of promoting the new edition just the right way: "The *Revised* (Expurgated? — Odious word!) Edition of Typee ought to be duly announced — & as the matter (in one respect) is a little delicate, I am happy that the literary tact of Mr Duyckinck will be exerted on the occasion." On 30 July, probably the same day that he wrote to Duyckinck, Melville sent a copy of the sequel (probably proofs rather than manuscript) to John Murray with the explanation that the "Revised Edition" where the sequel would be published was not yet ready, so he would have to send a copy later. Wiley & Putnam printed five hundred copies of the "Revised Edition" the next day, 31 July, a week before the official publication date of 6 August. In Albany on 15 August Melville left a copy of the "Revised Edition" at the *Evening Journal* for Thurlow Weed, which means he probably left a copy for Croswell at the *Argus* as well. Such obligations taken care of, *Typee* was pretty much off Melville's hands and in Duyckinck's, and Murray's.

Winning Elizabeth Shaw
and Winning the Harpers
1846

The own heart's choice of every youth, seems ever as an inscrutable witch to him; and by ten thousand concentric spells and circling incantations, glides round and round him, as he turns: murmuring meanings of unearthly import; and summoning up to him all the subterranean sprites and gnomes; and unpeopling all the sea for naiads to swim round him; so that mysteries are evoked as in exhalations by this Love; — what wonder then that Love was aye a mystic?

Pierre, bk. 2, ch. 4

IT TOOK MELVILLE A FEW WEEKS to clarify all the details about the expurgation, the preface, and the sequel to *Typee*. Murray wrote him on 3 August, sending condolences for Gansevoort's death and offering fifty pounds at year's end for the "*corrections*" and the "Sequel" (sight unseen), and promising "as liberal an offer" as he could make for the new work, after seeing it. This letter, forwarded from New York City, reached Melville before the end of the month, "a few days" before he replied on 2 September, and it made him joyous, for it confirmed that his international literary career would continue. Murray's letter was perfectly timed, for on 31 August Elizabeth Shaw, escorted by her young half-brother Samuel, arrived by train at Greenbush. Herman (and perhaps Helen or others of the family) met them, probably in a carriage borrowed from the Lord of the Isle, Augustus Peebles. The guests had seen none of the Melvilles since Gansevoort's death, and conveyed their condolences at once, though Lizzie had done so long before, by mail. As he prepared to escort them north to Lansingburgh, Herman pointed out the scenes of his life as a youthful pedagogue, letting the guests reflect on the contrast between that status and his present fame. The Shaws had stories to tell of the Boston earthquake of the week before, more than enough to match any local laments about the drought in the Hudson Valley. In the Lansingburgh house Maria and her four daughters (Tom was still awhaling) welcomed the visitors, especially Lizzie, as family. As Lizzie wrote her stepcousin Samuel H. Savage a year later (September 1847), she felt at home there in Lansingburgh because she had visited "so many times before at this season of the year" — in the summer of 1842, early October of 1843, and the end of May 1845, if not other times as well, before this long visit in 1846.

It was all to the good that Lizzie felt at home there in Maria's house, but her ease with the family made it hard for Herman to get her away from the others. The letter from Murray had given Herman the confidence to commit his future to Elizabeth Shaw, but gaining any privacy with her took planning. He could have walked along the Hudson with her, as he is rumored to have done in 1838, when he was said to have courted Miss Parmelee by sitting beside the river and reading some of Tennyson's early poems with her. In May 1842 "Tommy" at Gansevoort's request had borrowed a boat and taken Eli Fly out rowing and fishing, with Augusta, all the way to Little Falls, an excursion that took two and a half hours. The Lord of the Isle maintained the makings of a flotilla, for he and various employees had to reach his watery domains, so now Herman may have borrowed a boat from him and rowed Lizzie upriver. He may, before this, have demonstrated to her that as a veteran of whaleboats he retained some minimal competence with a pair of oars. Escape on the river was preferable to walking along the banks, for the weather up and down the Hudson was excessively hot and dry. The Troy *Northern Budget* on 31 August reported: "The River is very low. It is with difficulty that the steamers pass the overslaugh. — Rain is much needed." North of Lansingburgh the river, even when shallow, was perfect for respectable privacy. Given the limited range of possibilities, a reasonable guess is that Herman rowed Lizzie away, then after a few hours brought her back to the house refreshed from a salubrious voyage, her future sealed. They may not have told the other people in the house what had happened, but he proposed on 31 August, the day Lizzie arrived, and she accepted. She had received at least one proposal of marriage before, in April of 1833, when she was eleven, from her half-brother Lemuel, almost five, but even then she had been a cautious girl, and nothing had come of it. Now Murray's letter, as important to her as it was to Herman, gave her the assurance she needed to commit her future to him.

The dating of the engagement hangs on Maria's observing on 30 May 1847 that in July of that year Lizzie and Herman would have been engaged for eleven months — meaning that they became engaged in August of 1846. This could be true only if they became engaged on 31 August (under no circumstances would the vigorous, tactile Herman have proposed by mail). Maria may have been referring, a little inexactly, to the last day of August or very early September, but given her record for accuracy, 31 August is safe enough. In any case, the two were engaged before many hours had passed, since the engagement was a settled matter before Herman replied to Murray on 2 September. There, thanking Murray for the promise of fifty pounds, he observed discreetly that "circumstances" would "make it peculiarly acceptable." Circumstances always made money welcome to Maria's household, but, given the timing, this is the self-satisfied allusion of a young lover giving a transatlantic hint at news that may not even have been told inside the family.

Writing hastily, so as to catch the mail for Boston, Melville was diffident about the sequel and justifiably concerned that he might have raised Murray's expectations about it too high. He rejoiced "that the magic, cabilistic, *taboo-istic* 'Typee'" would "hereafter grace the title-page of all subsequent English editions of the book," Murray having agreed to put "Typee" before the title he had previously used. Despite reading the newspaper accounts about Greene that Melville had sent, Murray — harassed by skeptics — had asked for "documentary evidences" of Melville's having been in the Marquesas, to which Melville responded jocularly:

> Dear Sir, how indescribably vexatious, when one really feels in his very bones that he has been there, to have a parcel of blockheads question it! — Not (let me hurry to tell you) that Mr John Murray comes under that category — Oh no. . . . He only wants something to stop the mouths of the senseless sceptics — men who go straight from their cradles to their graves & never dream of the queer things going on at the antipodes. —
>
> I know not how to set about getting the evidence — How under Heaven am I to subpeona the skipper of the Dolly who by this time is the Lord only knows where, or Kory-Kory who I'll be bound is this blessed day taking his noon nap somewhere in the flowery vale of Typee, some leagues too from the Monument.

He claimed to have written to the owners (i.e., of the *Acushnet*) "asking if they could procure" for him "a copy of that part of the ship's log which makes mention of two rascals running away at Nukuheva." He wanted Murray to accept *Typee* on the terms that most Americans took it: " — they beleive it here now — a little touched up they say but *true*." In furtherance of that aim, he enclosed "a paper (formerly conducted by N P Willis) which contains an article with regard to the genuineness of Typee which I wish you to observe" — that is, Fuller's notice in the 9 May New York *Evening Mirror*.

Melville had nothing to say about what he had described (in his even longer mid-July letter) as his nearly completed second book, except this shipbuilder's image of the state in which he had abandoned it: "Concerning the book on the stocks (which bye the by must'nt fall to peices there, since I have not done much to it lately) I will forward you enough of it to enable you to judge therof. — (Perhaps the whole) — However, you must not Dear Sir expect another Typee—The fates must send me adrift again ere I write another adventure like that exactly." The promise to send part of the book was ill advised, in the present state of understanding of copyright law (when it might have been pirated), and was never fulfilled. The warning not to expect another *Typee* proved off the mark, for in Murray's Home and Colonial Library *Typee* and *Omoo* became, as commentators later said, the Siamese twins of Pacific adventuring. Melville's whole "terrific scrawl" is permeated with important matters left unspoken, notably those astonishing "circumstances" that made the prospect of an additional fifty pounds so "peculiarly acceptable." The beachcomber was no longer adrift, and not apt to be set adrift again.

How soon the engagement was revealed to the family is uncertain, but Herman and Lizzie did not burst upon the assembled Melvilles and young Sam Shaw with irrepressible news. Innately cautious, Lizzie asked Herman for time. After witnessing her father's grief at Oakes's hugger-mugger marriage in Manhattan, she would never have let him hear of her plans from anyone but her, and she wanted, for her own comfort, to consult Hope Shaw, whom she loved as her mother, not her stepmother. At some point during her two-month visit they may have confided their plans to Maria, but no announcement was made. As late as the next January, Helen was instructing Augusta on what she was to say about her knowledge of it if Lizzie were to bring the subject up.

The weather was miserable those days after Lizzie's arrival, the earth very dry and the river very low, the Troy *Northern Budget* lamented on 3 September. How the Melvilles entertained Lizzie outside the house is not known, but anyone in the vicinity of Troy was being notified that for twenty-five cents apiece they could see "Titian's Venus" ("Those who do not intend visiting Europe had better take advantage of this opportunity"). Melville saw enough of such putative masterpieces, early and late, to ridicule them in *Pierre*. Herr Alexander, the magician, was performing there that week, as well, and they probably witnessed his feats, since Melville alluded to him familiarly in *Moby-Dick*. (He performed there the next year, at a time less likely for Herman and Lizzie to have seen him.)

With Lizzie in the house with him, Herman began assembling information about his financial status. He asked Allan (now by default his lawyer) to inquire at Wiley & Putnam about the costs and profits on *Typee*. On 7 October they replied with an account that showed Melville had earned only $86.26 on the 2000 copies of the first edition, after the costs of "composition, stereotyping, paper, showbills, binding" and the publisher's half profits, $86.26, had been deducted from the sales of 1286 copies in paper and 428 in cloth. These figures indicate that *Typee* had not been a bestseller, by the standards of the time—a famous book, much talked about, even notorious, but not in fact a runaway success. Herman was at the mercy of Wiley & Putnam's sales figures, always the case, as Willis had complained in the 12 October 1844 *Weekly Mirror*, and subject to skepticism about them, in the light of the enormous publicity the book had received, little thanks to the publishers.

Whoever answered Allan's query boasted a little: "As to those copies given to Editors, the Press in the City, (almost all of them) receive all our books. Those sent into the Country go to the principal Cities and towns throughout the Union." That claim was less than veracious, for *Typee* went pretty much unreviewed by newspapers in the two other publishing centers, Philadelphia and Boston, and the lack of reviews in Boston was a serious embarrassment to the author, where his aunts and the Shaws were watching for notices. Not Wiley & Putnam but the Harpers were known to control the only truly national system of distribution, to outlets from Augusta to New Orleans to young Chicago. They still used ships for sending books to coastal cities in the South, as other publishers did, but they shipped books to the West by rail much earlier than the unaggressive Boston publishers did. Under the crushing pressures of the summer, with Gansevoort's grave still bare to the Albany sun, Melville had submitted to the expurgation of *Typee*, and had even rationalized that it improved the unity of the book, but Wiley was no man for a good fellow like Melville to form an enduring business relationship with. He could do better with the book that had been too long on "the stocks" and now, with the spur of Lizzie's presence, was nearing completion.

When Melville informed Murray that a little experience in the art of book-craft had done wonders for the condition of the manuscript, he meant that the compositor would find the manuscript easier to set from since it would have, for instance, fewer "slips" pinned to the pages. (He was thinking that Murray would set the book from manuscript, which did not happen.) He had learned more than the mechanics of manuscript preparation since *Typee*. There he had been diffident about expressing his thoughts, as in chapter 4, where he punctured his sententious mood, confessing that even while he was revolving portentous ideas about "long centuries of progressive civilization and refinement" in Europe, contrasted with the static societies of the islands, he had been partaking of a "golden-hued bunch of bananas." In the preface to *Omoo* he similarly disclaimed any "pretensions to philosophic research"; if reflections were "occasionally indulged in," they were "spontaneous, and such as would, very probably, suggest themselves to the most casual observer." Yet in *Omoo* he began to elaborate his reflections in a personal way, as when (ch. 9) he described the inevitable revery that would occur when, at night, the ship headed "right out into the immense blank of the Western Pacific"; then he would lean over the side and think of the strange objects they might be sailing over, the dangers of uncharted or ill-charted regions being enough "to cause any reflecting mind to feel at least a little uneasy." At the end of chapter 17 he described his "dreaming of the endless grottoes and galleries, far below the reach of the mariner's lead" — alliterative, poetic, and unclichéd. In his new unselfconscious use of metaphor, albeit indebted to books about early explorations, Tahiti seemed "a fairy world, all fresh and blooming from the hand of the Creator," the landscape "like something seen in a dream" (ch. 18). And now he could quote Bougainville — "I thought I was walking in the Garden of Eden" — without puncturing the mood with self-deprecating humor. Melville's recent experiences (among which were the composition and publication of his first book and the death of the most important man in his life) had stimulated his psychological growth beyond anything evidenced in *Typee*.

One of the characteristics of his mature style was Melville's powerful portrayal of images from different times and places which alternate rapidly in the mind, merge with each other, and (in later examples) disentangle again. In *Pierre* and in *Clarel*, he made profound use of this psychological phenomenon, but it appears in most of its essentials in *Omoo* (ch. 27), where he described the sensations of seeing on the stern of the beached whaler in the harbor at Tahiti the name of a town on the Hudson: "In an instant, palm-trees and elms — canoes and skiffs — church spires and bamboos — all mingled in one vision of the present and the past." In chapter 17 the onward gliding of the ship preceded his reveries; later, in *Moby-Dick* and *Pierre*, the gliding would be explicitly transferred to the mental processes, but even now, in chapter 31, he described "sliding from one revery into another" — simple enough, but destined to eventuate in the sliding, gliding, images of thought-progression in *Pierre*. The narrator of *Omoo* proved powerfully attractive, for all the jocoseness of attitude, for all the comicality of the events he described: a unique sensibility was emerging. Melville was on his way to what he described himself as being while he was in Cologne late in 1849 — "a pondering man."

Book-craft was evident in Melville's new command of language — particularly in the way his descriptions of events and actions were now saturated with the Scriptures. The mate (ch. 2) "abhorred all weak infusions, and cleaved manfully to strong drink" (Romans 12:9). The crew (ch. 3) "gave themselves little thought of the morrow" (Matthew 6:34). Lem Hardy's tattooed face was far worse than Cain's (Genesis 4:15); indeed, "all the waters of Abana and Pharpar, rivers of Damascus, could never wash out" the blue shark on his forehead (II Kings 5:12). Hardy had "a sort of Urim and Thummin engraven upon his chest" (Exodus 28:30). A luxury on the *Julia* (ch. 10) was the molasses, and bread dipped in the liquid, "thus prepared and eaten in secret," could not be other than pleasant (Proverbs 9:17), despite the rat found in one can. Nobody liked a landlubber such as Rope Yarn (ch. 14); "a sailor has no bowels of compassion for him" (I John 3:17). In the same chapter there was danger to Ropey if he looked too eagerly at his food ("Woe be unto him" — as in Jeremiah 23:1 and elsewhere); yet Ropey had managed in Sydney the biblical-like action of taking "unto himself a wife." Imprisoned on the *Reine Blanche* (ch. 29), "the sailors asked for meat," and the Frenchmen "gave them soup" (Matthew 7:9–10). In chapter 39 the departing companions told Captain Bob "to give no thought as to wherewithal" they should be clothed and fed (Matthew 6:31). Kooloo (ch. 40) was "as sounding brass and a tinkling cymbal" (I Corinthians 13:1). A question for casuistical debate (ch. 42) was "whether it was right and lawful" for any native to keep the European as opposed to the missionary sabbath (Matthew 12:2). Ten times out of eleven, a "respectably dressed European" would shun Melville and Long Ghost (ch. 43) "by going over to the other side of the road" (Luke 10:29–37). Queen Pomare's consort (ch. 65) besought an auctioneer "to leave all and follow him" (a biblical mélange). Melville's mind was Bible-soaked, and this sort of writing to many people is enormously appealing, enlarging as it does the frames of reference, creating an effect not unlike Milton's comparisons of small things to great (or great to small). Yet there were many pious people who kept a wary eye out for the use of God's word in vain, and who would find such submerged allusions blasphemous. This was risky writing, for a man who had been denounced by the *Evangelist* and other right-minded papers.

Melville claimed in the preface (which he wrote in December, probably) that every occurrence had been put down "from simple recollection," reinforced by frequent verbal repetitions. Charles Roberts Anderson in *Melville in the South Seas* (1939) found that Melville had not relied merely on his memory, and after a detailed study of the sources Anderson had located, Harrison Hayford in the Hendricks House edition of *Omoo* (1969) summed up Melville's actual practice: "He had altered facts and dates, elaborated events, assimilated foreign materials, invented episodes, and dramatized the printed experiences of others as his own. He had not plagiarized, merely, for he had always rewritten and nearly always improved the passages he appropriated. Yet he had composed . . . in a way he had not really acknowledged, and in a way that even his most suspicious contemporary critics had never dreamed." Hayford showed that Melville repeated the process he had followed in *Typee*, first writing out the narrative based on his recollections and invention, then using source books to pad out the chapters he had already written and to supply the stuff of new chapters that he inserted at various points in the manuscript.

For *Omoo* Melville's "major prompt-book," Hayford showed, was William Ellis's *Polynesian Researches, During a Residence of Nearly Eight Years in the Society and Sandwich Islands* (New York, 1833), in the "Harper's Stereotype Edition," a book he had mentioned in *Typee* but had made only slight use of. He used extensively someone's set of Charles Wilkes's *United States Exploring Expedition. During the Years 1838, 1839, 1840, 1841, 1842. Under the Command of Charles Wilkes, U.S.N.* (Philadelphia, 1844) — although he apparently bought his own set, in the 1845 reprint, only in 1847. He used Michael Russell's *Polynesia: or, an Historical Account of the Principal Islands in the South Sea*, published in Harper's Family Library (1843). He again used Charles S. Stewart's *A Visit to the South Seas*, which he had drawn on late in his work on *Typee*, and made some new use of Langsdorff's *Voyages and Travels*, that familiar book in which his Uncle John figured.

Now, in these months after the engagement, Melville used, misused, and downright abused his sources as he worked his "expository borrowings into the manuscript," as Hayford says — "insertions designed primarily to load it with solid information." (Hayford is the source of the examples in this paragraph.) In chapter 6 Melville invented Captain Guy's shooting a native as a way of illustrating a passage in Stewart. In the next chapter he invented the renegado Lem Hardy as a voice for information from Langsdorff, then in chapter 8 used Hardy to dramatize a section in Langsdorff on tattooing. In chapter 26 he inserted facts about Papeete Bay from Wilkes, then in chapter 30 took Tahitian scenery from Wilkes and Stewart. In chapter 33 he took Tahitian maladies from Ellis. In chapter 39 he took information from Ellis which he attributed either to his own observations or to Captain Bob. In chapter 44 the church Melville "attended" was one described by Ellis as existing two decades before, on another island. Ellis also provided the missionary's sermon in chapter 45 (here Melville claimed to have been "forcibly" moved by a Tahitian psalm at the divine services). In chapter 47 he took the "horrid" native women's hats from Ellis, amusing himself by relaying a scandalous report that they had been "first contrived and recommended by the missionaries' wives" — Mrs. Ellis having in fact helped to make them. The wild-cattle hunting in chapter 54 came primarily from Wilkes, although William Libbey, one of the "twin" Yankees Melville mentions as having worked for Zeke and Shorty, testified that he himself hunted goats and wild cattle in the mountains, so Melville may have done so also. In chapter 55 the trees and the depopulation were from Ellis. In chapter 67 Darby and Joan were invented from Ellis's descriptions of Polynesian hospitality. Most dishes at the banquet in chapter 68 had been served to Ellis on one occasion two decades before, and other dishes had been served to him at other times. Hayford's detailed account of Melville's depredations on his sources conveys something of the reckless fun Melville must have had during the commission of the purloinings and adaptings. He even had fun with the clichés he had used uncritically in *Typee*: now in chapter 70 he declared that the nocturnal spear-fishing was unforgettable ("I shall never forget the night"), but the memory was wholly Ellis's, not his at all.

After Anderson and Hayford had worked on Melville's sources in *Omoo*, Wilson Heflin came upon a curious volume in the St. John's College Library in Annapolis, a first edition of *Omoo* annotated, he was able to establish, by Samuel Marcy, son of the secretary of war, William Marcy. Young Samuel, who visited Tahiti in November 1848 as a midshipman aboard the *Independence*, took this copy of *Omoo* ashore with him to check its descriptions against the things described, then carried it to Eimeo, where he was allowed to inspect another copy of *Omoo*, one that had been annotated by someone who arrived in Tahiti long before, in 1827, and in late 1847 or early 1848 had been enraged by Melville's inaccuracies. Heflin decided that this annotator was Alexander Simpson, a brother-in-law of the missionary-consul George Pritchard. Marcy copied Simpson's annotations, some of which I quote from Heflin's transcriptions. Three dozen of the annotations, according to Heflin, "challenge Melville's competence in the Tahitian tongue." Others are concerned with historical fact. At the end of chapter 35, where Melville described a visit by "Dr. Johnson" to the Calabooza Beretanee, Simpson wrote: "There is no one who knows Dr. Johnstone but will concur in saying that the preceding chapter . . . is an entire tissue of misrepresentation."

Mainly, Simpson corrected part 2 (ch. 40 to the end), aided by a reliable source about the actual damage Melville and Long Ghost had done to the fauna of Eimeo: "Shorty says all the preceding chapters on bullock hunting are false." Simpson subjected chapter 58 to verification: "I asked Mr. Howe if he had preached from the above text. After referring to his Tahitian bible he replied No." Where Melville described a long pathway to Tamai (ch. 61), "a solitary inland village," Simpson declared that the path was "along the beach and partly through the sea ankle deep," while Tamai was only a quarter of a mile from the beach. Melville described the women of Tamai as "the most beautiful and unsophisticated women in the entire Society group," but Simpson admitted that (no fault to Melville and his friend) most of the women had long been "the most abandoned and consequently diseased upon the islands." Of chapter 68, where Melville described a reception by Chief Marharvai at the village of Loohooloo, Simpson declared that there was "no hamlet bay or village by the name of Loohooloo" and that Marharvai was "not a native name."

In chapter 73 Melville described the welcome by "Ereemear Po-Po" or "Jeremiah-in-the-Dark." Simpson fruitlessly devoted "great pains" to trying to identify this man. In chapter 75 Melville claimed to have seen in the settlement of Partoowye a block of two-story houses "fast going to decay"; they had been built, Melville claimed, by "a veritable Yankee," a house carpenter. Simpson was outraged: "I know of but one two-story house in Faatoai, the dwelling of E. Armitage a missionary artisan who left in 1837. The house was demolished in 1838." There had been no such Yankee: "It is utterly hopeless to expect any information on which dependence can be placed from a man so destitute of even a shadow of truth in his statements. I have lived 20 years here and there has not, in that period, been a single house erected by a 'Yankee' nor has there ever been a saw mill on this island." As to the sugar plantation of Mr. Bell (ch. 78) and the spicy sherry he served the wanderers out of halves of fresh citron melons, Simpson again took a deposition: "Mr. Bell informed me that the whole statement about the wine was false and that he knew nothing of the individuals." According to Simpson, there was no Captain Crash, the seducer Melville portrayed in chapter 79, and Melville's call upon the court of Queen Pomare evoked a frenzy of denunciations; one paragraph, Simpson said, was "concocted from the lively though crazy imagination of the author." As to the adventurers' tour of the queen's apartment, of course no one "could have obtained admission in the way stated." Young Marcy thus profited from the investigations of a previous reader, the first American besides Melville to realize that *Omoo* was a mixture of fact with much more fiction than most readers were assuming. Many of these matters his informant denounced were independently rejected as factual by Hayford on the basis of an examination of Melville's printed sources.

The manuscript undeniably had been much-interrupted. Part of it was the product of his ebullient winter, after he knew Murray would publish his first book. Part had been written at odd moments during the excitement over the early London reviews Gansevoort sent. He had continued it, with lesser or greater application, during the panic over the possible loss of copyright in the United States; during Wiley's initial expurgation of *Typee*; during the controversy over the authenticity of the book; during young Tom's going awhaling; during news of Gansevoort's illness and death and after his burial; during the onslaught from the religious papers; during Toby's reappearance; during Wiley's full-scale expurgation of *Typee*; before and after his trip to Rochester and the composition of the sequel; and during a hot August while waiting to hear what Murray would say about the sequel to *Typee* and his new book and while waiting to know just when Lizzie would come to visit — that is, to visit Helen. In August, most likely, at the end of which Lizzie arrived and he proposed to her, but also in September and October, while Lizzie, having accepted him, remained at Lansingburgh, and in early November,

Herman worked, making more progress, most likely, than he had made since the late winter.

What Melville put together was not the obviously disjointed thing that might have resulted from such a series of traumatic interruptions as he had suffered all through 1846. He had, after all, a happily episodic tale to tell, comical and melodramatic voyaging on an ill-captained whaleship, a seriocomic mutiny in Tahiti, followed by a little beachcombing there and on the neighboring island of Eimeo before signing on another whaler. In the actual John Troy he had material to transform into a figure of "fantastic raffishness," as Hayford says, an unselfconsciously lustful companion whom he could depict as satisfying his sexual urges while depicting himself as altogether more staid and self-disciplined, albeit envious. He was adept enough at sexual innuendo to be able to quote (ch. 34) Long Ghost's opinion on keeping "a small leather wallet — a 'monkey bag' " ready for use: "it behooves a stranger, in Tahiti, to have his knife in readiness, and his caster slung." Melville himself took great joy in writing much of the book, pleasure that glistens in his portraying the desirable Mrs. Bell then depicting his own hopeless sexual envy of her husband — "Mr. Bell (happy dog!)" He had read and passed on to Wiley the review of *Typee* in the *Times* of London, and had rejoiced in that reviewer's exclamation — surely one that had become the subject of badinage in the family: "Enviable Herman! A happier dog it is impossible to imagine than Herman in the Typee Valley." Herman *was* a happy dog, his fame achieved, internationally, by one book; his literary competence growing amazingly in his second manuscript; his physicality and his high moral character triumphant in Lizzie's consent to marry him; and his sexual urges in a fair way to be gratified, with the blessings of society, in holy wedlock. Meanwhile, his knife in readiness and his caster slung, there were hours when it was impossible to imagine a happier dog than Herman in the Hudson Valley.

By this time evidence was mounting as to how the "Revised Edition" would succeed. As early as the September issue, the New York *Christian Parlor Magazine* commented: "The most objectionable parts of the first edition, to which we took exception in a review in this Magazine, are omitted in this — an evidence that, for some reason, the counsels of truth and decency have been regarded." Policy was paying off. Gradually, critics also came to terms with the evidence for the book's authenticity. The friendly London *Athenæum* on 3 October reviewed the "Sequel" (issued as a "separate," like a pamphlet) with great sophistication: "If the whole be an invention, however, it has been determined to 'play out the play.' Mr. Herman Melville is called in to attest the discovery of the Editor of the *Buffalo Commercial Advertiser* —

just as it has been suspected that the Editor was called in to attest the discoveries of Herman Melville. There is a kind of 'handy-dandy' in this mode of presenting the matter — a sort of illogical evidence — a series of affirming in a circle — which increases the puzzle. We do not undertake to light our readers through the mystery." Murray had packaged the sequel admirably, as the *Athenæum* explained: "We have only to add, for the sake of the purchasers of the former narrative, that this tale of Toby is printed as a few pages of addition — the paging continued on from the last of the original volume; and that they may complete their possession of this true history, or pleasant romance, (as the case may be,) for the small supplementary charge of three-pence." But Murray was still beleaguered by skeptics of the most annoying kind — charming literary people adept at brilliant and all but unforgettable phrase-making. As late as 12 December the London *Literary Gazette* concluded a little exercise in irony about the mysterious author of *Typee* "(Master Hermann Melville of ****, *****!)" by comparing him to Sinbad the Sailor and inviting Melville to a small, select party on April Fools' Day 1847: "we intend to ask only . . . Mssrs. Crusoe, Sinbad, Gulliver, Munchausen, and perhaps Pillet, Thiers, Kobl, and a few others." A daguerreotype said to depict Richard Tobias Greene and a lock of ebon curls purporting to be from his head might well have been passed around the table as authentic relics.

In Massachusetts that summer and fall the *Typee* fever caught up young Ellery Channing (nephew of the great minister William Ellery Channing) and his friend Henry Thoreau, then beginning his second year of residence in his cabin at Walden Pond outside Concord. Sober young Thoreau had ignored the naked maidens so as to focus on the supposedly solid anthropological information about the communication system ("when a ships boat approaches the bay . . . the news is shouted from man to man — from the tops of cocoanut trees," Thoreau noted) and the readily available items of commerce (the coconuts and breadfruit gathered and carried to the beach to sell). Feckless, self-indulgent Channing rewrote *Typee* into a poem of some two hundred lines, "The Island Nukuheva," a testament to his envy of "Adventurous Melville." There Channing retold Melville's book in detail. Typee as a place where one did not have to work for food appealed to him strongly ("No dusty Ploughman breaks the heavy clod, / But crops in native clusters freely nod"). He devoted an elaborate description to "Mehevi tall," but still more lines to "the sweet shape of Fayaway." For Channing, as for many other readers, Melville's book was not only a modern *Robinson Crusoe* but, more important, a modern *Paradise Found.* By November or December, at the latest, Channing had his Melville poem in proofs, for it appeared in his *Poems* published in Boston early in January.

In the first months after the publication of *Typee* and even during the next year, Melville's alleged sexual immorality had by no means been a major theme in the early reviews. Most of those who most deplored the book, even among the reviewers for the religious press, did not dwell on the sexual behavior and sexual opportunities Melville had described; what bothered them most was his attack on the missionary operations — an attack that they thought would affect donations. After *Omoo* appeared, but before a copy got to the Sandwich Islands, the Honolulu *Friend* (1 June 1847) acknowledged that Wiley & Putnam had done well to suppress, in the "Revised Edition" of *Typee*, Melville's criticisms of the missionaries, but wished the sensual passages had been as thoroughly excised:

> If the author had erased other passages, we think he would have shown good judgment and exhibited "a sober second thought." Such a course would certainly have led him to suppress some of those glaring facts respecting his habits of gross and shameless familiarity not to say unblushing licentiousness, with a tribe of debased and filthy savages of Marquesas. In chapter XIII, revised edition, he refers to an anointing process, performed every evening, when the girls gathered about him on the mats. "I used," he remarks, "to hail with delight the daily recurrence of this luxurious operation, in which I forgot all my troubles, and buried for the time every feeling of sorrow!" In Chapter XVII, revised edition, there is the following remark, "Bathing in the company of troops of girls formed one of my chief amusements!!" — Scores, aye, hundreds of passages might be quoted, showing that the writer sunk lower than the debased people among whom he took up his temporary abode.

This writer for the *Friend* went farther in condemning the book than the religious press had originally gone. With the worst offenses removed, it was easy to see what else should have been expurgated from *Typee*. When was Melville going to expurgate the expurgated edition?

After the best of that beautiful autumn had passed, Sam Savage (Hope Shaw's nephew) left Boston on 31 October to escort Lizzie home, and on 1 November Maria wrote to Lemuel Shaw that his daughter and young Savage were leaving "this Evg for Troy, where they will pass the night, to secure her going in the early morning train of Cars." (They may have slept at the Van Schaick house; no one stayed in inns or hotels if there was an alternative.) For half a year, Maria had felt unable to respond to Judge Shaw's letter of condolence, but now she thanked him for it and expressed her present feelings: "To time alone can I look forward to bind up by its soothing influences my wounded heart, to raise from their present state of depression, my lost spirits. . . . My dear Gansevoort — this early in life to die — he was deeply belove'd by us, yes bound up in our very hearts." She ascribed his death to his long fatherless struggle to help lift the family out of financial misery: "His gigantic efforts to overcome more than ordinary obstacles, his too long and continued exertion both bodily & mental — I have no doubt occasioned his early & melancholy death." Maria never attributed to her second son any such "gigantic efforts" at overcoming obstacles, but she had drawn her conclusion, once again, as in her husband's fate, as to the consequences of "too long and continued exertion" of body and mind, and she would apply it, later, to Herman's case.

In New York City, Allan's life was also changing. Still renting a room at 7 Greenwich, near the Battery, he had formed an attachment to Sophia Thurston, daughter of the banker Charles Myrick Thurston, who had died on 6 May 1844, at the age of fifty-two — comparatively young, but older than Allan Melvill had been. Sophia, a little over four years younger than Allan (born 22 August 1827), still lived with her mother and some of her family in the house at No. 7 Bond Street — that short and exclusive street of brick houses, some of them marble-fronted, that Maria had wistfully glimpsed from the back windows of one rented house. Richard Lathers, a commercial merchant who married Sophia's sister Abby on 9 July 1846, and who had an avid interest in art and architecture, later recalled fondly that the houses were all "of the most ornate character." Behind each house a stable faced on an alleyway for the use of the carriages and the servants: Bond Street residents never had to enter or descend from carriages in view of their neighbors. In 1846, according to Lathers, Bond Street was almost exclusively a social center, not yet invaded by businesses: "It extended from Broadway to the Bowery, a single long block in which lived Dr. John W. Francis; Rev. Dr. Spring; C. M. Thurston [Jr.], the banker; General Dix; Ex-Postmaster Coddington; Ex-Collector of the port of New York Morgan; the Pell family; the Ward family (including the celebrated Julia Ward Howe, daughter of the banker and society leader Samuel Ward); the Sampson family, among the first to have a picture gallery in New York; the brothers Parmly; the popular Guilbert Davis, called by his sporting friends 'Governor of Coney Island'; and George Griffin, a lawyer whose talented daughter married General Veile." (The general whom Teresa Griffin married was Egbert Viele, born in Waterford in 1825, just Kate Melville's age, who had attended school in Lansingburgh. Their divorce in 1872 was scandalous.) Lathers had the pleasantest recollection of his "relations with the statesman and soldier, General John A. Dix, and his accomplished wife, who were the intimate and valued friends and neighbors" of the Thurstons, and among the particular guests at the wedding breakfast for Abby Thurston and Lathers. The Dixes were also intimate friends of Uncle Peter, and Catherine Dix had helped prepare the funeral for Mary Sanford Gansevoort. Even on Bond Street, where many were artistically minded (and all were wealthy enough to indulge artistic tastes), the Dixes' "fine collection of pictures and cultivated household" were such as to be memorialized by Henry T. Tuckerman, the young art historian and literary man whom Herman may have encountered by late 1846. (In the decline of Bond Street in the late 1850s the Reverend Dr. Spring's house went first, demolished to be replaced by a stove factory.)

Allan could not have formed higher social connections than by winning a Bond Street girl. Nothing is known about how Allan met Sophia Thurston and attracted her interest — probably not through old connections, for the Thurstons were relative newcomers, from Newport. After the engagement was formalized, Sophia met Augusta sometime in the fall at Hell Gate, on the northern tip of Manhattan, during a visit Augusta made to the Blatchfords, wealthy connections of the Lansingburgh Blatchfords. Richard M. Blatchford, the father of Augusta's special friend Mary, was a lawyer, an agent of the Bank of England, and a leading Whig. He was an intimate of Philip Hone, mayor of New York in 1825 during the official opening of the Erie Canal, and himself a leading Whig. After Hone's death Blatchford took as his second wife Hone's daughter Catharine. Augusta probably found the Blatchford estate as invigorating as Hone did in another autumn, in October 1844, when he contemplated "the delightful scene" on arising: "the clumps of fine old trees clothed in the gorgeous foliage of autumn, the lawn still bright and green, the mild, refreshing breeze, the rapid waters of Hell Gate covered with sailing vessels and steamboats — all combined to present a picture of consummate beauty" (*The Diary of Philip Hone, 1828–1851*, ed. Allan Nevins [1927]). The night before Hone wrote this, John Jacob Astor, the richest man in the United States, had been one of the dinner guests. In September and October 1846, Augusta was well situated for receiving a visit from a Bond Street girl. Augusta gave her visitor a little rose, which afterward reminded Sophia of their "pleasant walk and ride together" at Hell Gate. Behind the lovers, Allan as well as Herman, the family was mobilizing.

Sophia wrote Augusta on 9 December a letter that shows she had been intimately aware of Allan's circumstances before the 2 November 1846 election; he had moved up town from near the Battery and his time had to be measured out: "Ever since Allan moved up town, he has reserved three evenings in the week for the purpose of reading. But until last week, I imagine he has read little or nothing. But there is some excuse for him. He has been very busily engaged at his office, often till a late hour, and then that horrid Election business. The idea of sitting up all night to count the votes, after such a . . . day, is really too bad. Poor Allan was quite exhausted; of course I was not so unfeeling as to press him to persist in his resolution of reading at such a time." Sophia herself was conducting a course of reading, as a well-trained young woman, in particular one marrying into a literary family, was expected to do. She had just finished reading Prescott's *Conquest of Mexico* with much interest and had gone on to Thompson's *Recollections of Mexico* for information about "what Mexico is in the nineteenth-century, which is more interesting to read at the present time, on account of the existing state of hostilities between that country and our own." (The war was barely touching Herman and the family, except through news of Guert, who was or soon would be on duty on the *John Adams* in the Gulf of Mexico.) The four evenings Allan did not devote to reading were devoted to attendance upon the lady: "Time passes so swiftly that it seems as if every fourth day was Sunday. Indeed I have only four days in my week, which are those, the evenings of which, Allan devotes to 7 Bond Street. The other three are only blank spaces between, and not days." This courtship in Manhattan, simultaneous with the courtship in Lansingburgh, impelled momentous decisions before either marriage could occur.

Meanwhile, a perturbing aspect of Herman's fame made its presence known. During her visit to the Blatchfords at Hell Gate Augusta met an Englishwoman, Ellen Astor Oxenham, and in escorting or visiting his sister Herman met Mrs. Oxenham also. This woman pursued the acquaintance-ship with a letter to Augusta in October 1846:

> I rejoice in a kind of instinct that always tells me of the spirits that will harmonise with mine, very few are they in number & great therefore is my grief when I find the happiness of their society is not permitted to me. I would take such pleasure in you & love you so dearly. Why don't you live in New York & then I could see your bright eyes, & mayhap a small ray of Typeeian felicity might fall on me from Tommo's. . . .
>
> Mr [Fitz-Greene] Halleck says he knows your brother Mr Allan Melville but I think he said he had not the pleasure of knowing Typee of pleasant memory . . . you know I long to see you & *Typee*. . . . Typee, you dear creature, I want to see you so amazingly.
>
> [P.S.] I present Typee with the fortunate words that rescued him from becoming too entirely one of the gentle savages — There is food for reflection in those two words.

On 12 December she wrote again: "I do not wish to appear rude by letting yours remain unanswered or unmindful of the honor conferred on me by Typee — you might think too my friendship was meteor like, instead of which it is burning as evenly as a well-trimmed solar lamp." Helen, the most perceptive of the sisters, thought even the seal on Mrs. Oxenham's letters was unduly aggressive. If he saw these letters, Herman may have taken some indefinite alarm, but he would not have known yet quite how to interpret them in relation to what was happening to his reputation, where readers perceived him in terms of his presumed sexual experiences. He could move beyond his first book, but many readers would always identify him not only as "Tommo" but as "Typee." (Even members of the family referred to him for years as "Typee.")

It was not peculiar that Allan had met the revered poet Fitz-Greene Halleck before Herman did: Allan frequented Bond Street, where all the neighbors sooner or later encountered the poet, most often at Dr. John Wakeman Francis's home at No. 1. Halleck, born in 1790 and famous since he published his "Byronic" society-satire *Fanny* in the year of Herman's birth, had published little since the Burnsean *Alnwick Castle* in 1827. He enjoyed an exalted national fame, and his reputation was very high among some British lovers of poetry, as members of the American literati were quick to assure their readers, themselves, and Halleck himself. In 1844 Gansevoort had quoted Halleck's lines on Robert Burns in his Jackson Day address, and in 1826 he had memorized Halleck's then-new "Marco Bozzaris" while Herman was his captive if not fully comprehending audience, so that no doubt a few lines stuck ineffaceably in Herman's brain. That poem was still much admired. The English banker-poet Samuel Rogers "was fond of reading it to his guests at his famous breakfasts," saying, "it is better than any thing we can do on this side of the Atlantic" (according to James Grant Wilson's 1869 biography of Halleck). Melville probably never became intimate with Halleck, but they were much at the same places, and he came to know well the "square, firmly-set jaw" that watchers thought gave Halleck's face both a decisive and a satirical look. That July of 1846, Poe in his "Literati" series for *Godey's* (preceding the sketch of Duyckinck) had described Halleck as about five feet seven, and settled into mature shape: "He *has been* stout, but may now be called well-proportioned." According to Poe, Halleck conversed "fluently, with animation and zeal," and was "choice and accurate in his language, exceedingly quick at repartee and apt at anecdote." He was also sharp of tongue, even unkind in his wit. By the time Melville was a young writer in New York, Halleck had long passed the stage in which he had to worry about the consequences of his satirical jabs: his victims were expected to feel honored by the source of the wit that stung them. The literary use Melville made of Halleck is pretty much limited to writing him into a late section of *Mardi* (ch. 177) as "Marko," Bardianna's scribe — that is, John Jacob Astor's secretary — "Marko" being a then-obvious allusion to Halleck's "Marco Bozzaris," and a private reference to Gansevoort's recitations of it.

In Lansingburgh Herman had agreed to lecture sometime that season to the Troy Young Men's Association, as the *Northern Budget* announced on 28 November. Before then, Herman had gone to New York City with his manuscript, but prepared to deal first with more important matters in Bond

Street then in Mt. Vernon Street in Boston. He was introduced to Sophia the day before Thanksgiving. The house on Bond Street was more or less in disarray because (as Sophia wrote to Augusta) "carpenters masons painters etc." had been at work, in one of the earliest of the major renovations that owners of better homes in town then faced — the necessity to retrofit with gas fixtures and indoor plumbing. Confusion in some of the rooms or not, the Thurston widow and her family entertained Allan and his author brother for Thanksgiving dinner on the twenty-sixth. Rather than showing his manuscript to a publisher right away, Herman left it "with a particular lady acquaintance" of his who resided "up town," as he rather cryptically told Duyckinck on 8 December. A newly engaged man with little excuse for coyness, he may simply have left it "up town" with Mrs. Bradford at 105 Ninth Avenue, off Nineteenth Street, for she had treated him kindly in 1839, and he had sought Bradford's help earlier in the year in managing the reception of *Typee*. Or he may have left it with Sophia Thurston, where Allan could see it if he had time. Bond Street was uptown, for, as Henry T. Tuckerman wrote in 1865, in the 1840s Bond Street still "formed the 'up-town' centre of the most eligible private residences" and was "the scene of the choicest social enjoyment."

Having left the manuscript off with a woman who would keep it safe, Melville departed for Boston, where he arrived on Saturday night, the twenty-eighth, carrying not a manuscript but a Bible as a gift to Hope Shaw from Helen. There is no record of what Herman brought to his affianced and her father, other than high hopes for his second book. When the lovers told the judge of their engagement is unknown. On 31 August, the day Lizzie had arrived in Lansingburgh, the judge had been in Lenox for the September court session, there early because he was hoping to alleviate his suffering from his annual affliction by alternation in atmospheric pressure: "a change from the air of the sea-coast to the atmosphere of these mountains, has proved highly beneficial." Then he had hoped to escape "the worst form of the disease" and to be able to stay for the meeting of the full court on 15 September. On his mind, when he wrote his wife that 31 August, was Oakes's future, not Lizzie's.

Oakes had been visiting in Boston, disgraced but not threatened with jail, a young bereaved father, and the judge particularly wanted to avoid letting his daughter-in-law conclude that he blamed her for any of Oakes's troubles. Shaw wrote to Hope on 31 August: "I am very sorry to be absent during so large a part of the visit of Oakes & his wife, especially at the time of their departure, & nothing but a regime for my health would induce me to do it. I believe Caro. knows & will always feel, that I have a great affection for her, and take a great interest in her welfare." (From Chicago in mid-December

Oakes put the best face on his disgrace, declaring that he felt "much more inclined for agricultural life than any mercantile pursuits" — this while doing nothing to achieve that sort of bucolic life.) In the Massachusetts Historical Society this letter is filed under the year Shaw very legibly miswrote on it, 1836, and it appears in the Shaw microfilms under that date. "Caro." the judge had to make the best of, but Herman he could welcome into the family with open heart, although with undisguised concern.

For despite Murray's overtures, Herman still had no publisher for the new book, in either New York or London — an unsatisfactory state of affairs for everyone. Shaw may have taken Herman aside and talked of his seeking a patronage job such as the old major had held, perhaps in New York, now the publishing center of the country. Herman's fame from *Typee* marked him as a candidate for a patronage job, even aside from Gansevoort's recent services to the administration and the noble services of the revolutionary generation to the nation. Whoever had the idea that Herman should look for a regular job, there was no gainsaying that it was wise to find one and hold on to it, at least for the foreseeable future. In his restless state, happy to be with Elizabeth, hopeful and agitated about his uncertain future and unable to promise the Shaws anything, Herman cannot have passed an easy week.

Soon after his arrival Herman called on the Shaws' new neighbor at 89 Mt. Vernon Street, Mrs. Nathaniel Thayer, the former Nilly Van Rensselaer, at whose wedding Augusta was to have been a bridesmaid. Good cousin and decent soul that she was, probably just aware that she was pregnant with her first child, Nilly at once planned a dinner for Herman. Through her husband and through her father, even before her own character became known in Boston, Nilly was a powerful hostess with access to the very best people, such as the historian William H. Prescott, author of the book Sophia Thurston had been reading, *History of the Conquest of Mexico* (1843), and Professor Charles Thomas Jackson, a pioneer of modern anesthesia (and brother-in-law of Ralph Waldo Emerson), and she invited both of them as well as others ("distinguished & agreeable literary characters") to meet Herman. Melville had a little research to do, if he could, for on 3 December there was charged on Lemuel Shaw's membership at the Boston Athenæum Otto von Kotzebue's *A New Voyage round the World* (London, 1830). Herman had already lifted a quotation from Kotzebue that he had found in Michael Russell's *Polynesia*, but now he apparently copied out another quotation and took down the full title to put in a footnote (thereby disguising his debt to Russell). Perturbed, beyond his habitual restlessness, by the need to settle with a publisher and make some longer-range plans, he abruptly decided to go back to New York. He called at Nilly's house the night of 6 December to apologize to her for missing the dinner, but she was not at home. He traveled down on the seventh, reflecting on how greatly his life had changed since he last made the journey two years earlier and on just how uncertain it remained.

The next day, 8 December, Melville wrote to Evert Duyckinck not as a man connected to Wiley & Putnam, he specified, but "confidentially & as a friend": "As I hinted to you some time ago I have a new book in M.S. — Relying much upon your literary judgement I am very desirous of getting your opinion of it & (if you feel disposed to favor me so far) to receive your hints." That night or the next day he gave a portion of the manuscript to Duyckinck, then on 10 December sent him the rest, with this explanation:

> Herewith you have the remaining chapters. Those marked in the Table of Contents as Nos V. VII. & XVII. have been rejected altogether — but this does not break the continuity of the book. I have not as yet altered the numbers of the chapters as thus affected.
>
> I beg you to pay particular attention to the following chapters — Chapters 33. 34 — & 45. 46. 47. 48. 49. 50. — They all refer more or less to the missions & the condition of the natives.

The clearest explication of the letter is Hayford's:

> Since Melville may not have permanently rejected V, VII, and XVII, and may have cancelled or rearranged other chapters, we cannot be sure which published chapters are referred to in the second group. Chapters V and VII would have fallen on either side of the present Chapter 5 (which is a postdated version of ship's affairs that had taken place in the southern Marquesas prior to his coming aboard), and just before the present Chapters 6, 7, 8, which are fictitious. Chapter XVII would have followed the present Chapter 14, where there is no obvious gap. Melville's "*33, 34*" may have been the present Chapters 32 and (less probably) 33, and his "45, 46, 47, 48, *49, 50*" were certainly the present Chapters 44–49, the heart of his exposure of conditions at Tahiti under missionaries.

It is uncertain just what Melville had in mind when he asked Duyckinck to pay particular attention to chapters that dealt with the missions and with the effect of the missions on the present conditions under which the natives lived, but the two could not have discussed such chapters without recalling the grounds for the expurgation of *Typee*.

The obvious question is why, having just agreed to the expurgation of *Typee* and having tried to persuade Murray to adopt the expurgated text for the English market, Melville attacked the missionaries anew, and attacked them more systematically than before. Hayford considered the possibilities. Perhaps Melville "was stung to perversity by the imputations of pious reviewers." Perhaps he persuaded himself that the attacks in *Typee* had been irrelevant to the narrative ("after all, there were no missionaries" in the Marquesas), while in *Omoo* his attacks were "organic parts of his subject," since "in Tahiti everything he saw seemed to be conditioned" by the presence of the missionaries. Perhaps he was furious that even his expurgations had not appeased the missionary forces.

As a good Episcopalian and Wiley's employee, Evert Duyckinck may have been surprised by Melville's renewing his attacks on the missionaries, but he was not shocked at the portrayals of the unsupervised doings of low-church religionists at the ends of the earth. On 15 December he wrote to his brother George, who had left on his grand tour of Europe: "Melville is in town with new MSS agitating the conscience of John Wiley and tempting the pockets of the Harpers. I have read it. His further adventures in the South Seas after leaving Typee. He owes a sailor's grudge to the Missionaries & pays it off at Tahiti. His account of the church building there is very much in the spirit of Dickens humorous handling of sacred things in Italy." How Melville was agitating the conscience of John Wiley is not certain. Wiley had merely done his duty as a Presbyterian in hastening to align himself with his fellow religionists on the *Evangelist,* and had nothing to repent. Presumably Duyckinck meant that Wiley was too shrewd a businessman, or too greedy, not to want to hold on to a profitable author, even if that author had at first brought the firm notoriety and even opprobrium. The phrase "sailor's grudge" does not mean that Melville's grudge was primarily against anything actual missionaries did to him when he was a sailor but against the missionary press for what it had just done to him as a writer — and was continuing to do. Duyckinck was writing facetiously, and he was still (and long remained) a literary snob who could not accept Melville simply as a writer, but merely as a sailor who had written a book, and then more than one book. It sounds as if Melville had waved the manuscript before Wiley's nose and then quickly called on the Harpers, hoping for a small bidding war.

Duyckinck may have wished he could have had *Omoo* in the Library of American Books, which needed another popular volume in it after the slam the series had received in the *North American Review* for October ("with the exception of a few of the volumes," the series was "not likely to do much honor" to American literature). In the November *Knickerbocker* Lewis Gaylord Clark happily quoted the jibing at Cornelius Mathews in the *North American,* then floated the rumor that Wiley had offered Mathews "a cheque for a hundred dollars" if he would withdraw *Big Abel, and the Little Manhattan* from the series after it had been announced. Clark went on to praise Melville and others at Mathews's expense:

A library however which includes among its volumes such excellent and attractive works as CHEEVER'S "Wanderings of a Pilgrim under the Shadow of
Mont-Blanc and the Jungfrau," "Western Clearings," by Mrs KIRKLAND,
"Mosses from an Old Manse," by HAWTHORNE, "The Wilderness and the
War-path," by Judge HALL, "Typee," by MELVILLE, and the like, should not
be tabooed on account of two or three worthless or uninteresting publications, from which, at the buyer's option, they can be made to "part company,"
without derangement of the series.

The Library of American Books was in trouble, but now Melville was consulting Duyckinck as a friend, not as the editor of the series, and *Omoo* would
neither threaten nor rescue the Library.

Just when Melville tempted the pockets of the Harpers is not certain, but
the temptation scene is on record, and it was remarkably brief. According
to Frederick Saunders's "Recollections" (in the New York Public Library),
Melville walked into his room in the Harpers building with the manuscript in
hand and remarked tentatively, "Saunders, I suppose there is no use of offering this to the house?" Saunders recalled that he told Melville to wait a
minute: "Mr [Fletcher] Harper is in his carriage now at the door about to
start to Europe. I'll go and ask him." Here is the rest of the encounter:

> I hurried out of the building without waiting to put on my hat and came to
> him just in time.
> "What is it?" said he.
> "Oh another manuscript from Herman Melville," said I. "He is offering it
> to us. What do you say?"
> "Take it at once," said Mr. Harper, jumping into his carriage and driving
> off.

Thus began Melville's long, edgy connection with the Harpers, the pious
Methodists who actively promoted Methodism in some of their publications.
They were not closely allied with the cause of foreign missions, and they had
been berating themselves for months over losing the chance to publish the
most sensational book of the year. On 18 December Melville signed an
agreement with Harper & Brothers "to publish a certain manuscript, entitled
'Omoo: a Narrative of Adventure — in the South Seas,'" the company and
the author each to receive half profits, after the publisher had recouped the
costs of publication. To seek out the Harpers as publishers for *Omoo* was
practical, given their reputation, but there was in it a perverse element, a
desire to vindicate himself from one rejection at the cost of making a bad
permanent relationship — almost like willingly going into marriage with a

partner who had once refused him and against whom he therefore held a grudge, and held it with good cause.

During the Thanksgiving visit or the December visit to Manhattan, Herman may have made or improved his acquaintance with Charles Fenno Hoffman and Nathaniel Parker Willis. Both recent acquaintances of Gansevoort, Hoffman and Willis were such intimate friends that a decade and a half earlier Willis had set up a workroom in the garret of the Hoffman house. On 3 February 1846 Gansevoort had primed the novelist and editor Charles Fenno Hoffman with a letter "regarding 'Typee.' " In his review in the *Gazette and Times* on 30 March, Hoffman mentioned Gansevoort's current occupation and the brothers' maternal grandfather, long familiar to him since he was a serious student of New York history and had used the half-breed Joseph Brant or Brandt, a foe of the old Peter Gansevoort at Fort Stanwix, as a character in his *Greyslaer*. Gansevoort Melville had most likely given Herman explicit instructions to present himself before Hoffman at the *Gazette and Times* on William Street and make a useful friend. Whenever Herman showed up, he encountered there just the sort of literary man he was prepared to like, a burly outdoorsy man of extraordinary vitality, despite his being one-legged as a result of an accident as a lad in 1817, at the Cortlandt Street Dock, that luckless place for Herman as well as for him. Here is William Keese's contemporary description: "A fine head, with dark brown hair, quite decidedly inclined to wavy curl; whiskers of the same color and character quite surrounding the face, though with the lips and chin clean-shaven; a good and rather firm mouth; nose slightly low, though of fair length, and the reverse of acquiline; and pleasant eyes, well browed, but always hidden behind the glasses made necessary by short-sight." Hoffman's latest, and patriotic, poem, "Monterrey," had been printed in the 13 November *National Press*. Melville read it at this time, and remembered it all his life.

On 18 March 1846 Gansevoort had thoughtfully followed up his intimacy with Nathaniel Parker Willis in London by forwarding him critiques of *Typee* in the *Examiner* and the *Critic* and perhaps other papers. Willis (in his "ringlets") and his old partner George Morris ("the beaming, rosy, perspiring face of the 'American Körner,' " Thomas Low Nichols remembered) were running the *National Press*, and their former associate Hiram Fuller seems to have been in sole command of the *Mirror* before February 1846. Gansevoort did not comment on Willis's dress in his diary, but Herman would have thought Willis a Brummell. In 1849 a correspondent sent home for the Oneida *Herald* an account of a phenomenon in Broadway; the *Herald* is lost, but the item survives in the Portland (Maine) *Daily Advertiser* for 13 June 1849:

See that fellow in drab pants, greased and begrimed with ink, with his bag-like drab coat to match, slouched hat and old boots — all of which look as if they might have belonged to his great-great-grandfather — and with a careless, rollicking gait. On his arm hangs a prim fashionable, perfumed and brushed, with white kids, all and in every respect as neat and as delicate as a nice new doll from the band-box. You ask a by-stander who these strangely mated men can be? They are Horace Greeley of the Tribune, and Nat. Willis of the Home Journal.

Herman Melville and Nat Willis would have presented almost as peculiar a pairing. Melville was still athletic, and in his knockabout life he had formed the habit of dressing a little askew, prizing comfort over elegance, and ignoring subtleties of color. Willis was just as the correspondent to the Oneida paper described him, except that the delicacy was partly a result of physical weakness, a touch already of consumption. According to his passport description, he was brown haired, blue eyed, thin lipped; his round face was marked by a scar near the right eye. Melville had to look up to him, for he was six feet tall. In the New York publishing world almost everyone had long histories with everyone else: Hoffman had his own memories of Gansevoort, and always Willis carried the memory of Gansevoort at the wedding in St. Mary le Bow. By the end of 1846, Melville was fast making himself part of that little world.

In Lansingburgh, Manhattan, and Boston, the family began to adjust to Herman's engagement to Elizabeth. In mid-December Elizabeth paid a call on Nilly, her Mt. Vernon Street neighbor, and a few days later Nilly returned the call. Lizzie was out but Hope was home, and delighted to have a chance to quiz the impeccable Mrs. Thayer about the Gansevoort side of her prospective son-in-law's relations. Nilly reported to Augusta on 22 December that "her Mother entertained us very pleasantly, she is still quite a pretty woman & seems to be very kind hearted, we had a mutual topic to discuss, your family & of course I could be most eloquent." Nilly had been eager to help introduce Herman into Boston society, she made clear. She was sorry not to have seen more of him and disappointed that he could not dine with her, but she accepted the excuse that Herman had been drawn away by the new book, and anxiously asked when it would appear, being "quite impatient to see it." Nilly was as good a representative of the Gansevoorts as Herman could have wanted. Gansevoort Melville had always behaved deferentially to Hope, perhaps had even played the gallant to her, and Herman was undeniably famous, and personally attractive. Still, the present generation of Melvills and Melvilles were all short of money, so it was good to be reminded that one of the Gansevoort clan, better than that, a Van Rensselaer, could move, as a bride, into a house on the best street in Boston, the Shaws' own Mt. Vernon Street. Hope herself owed her social position wholly to the status of her husband. Nothing in the Shaw or Savage background touched the splendor of the Melville descent from the lords of Leven and Melville and the Patroons of Rensselaer and Albany counties in the Empire State, and Nilly was eager to do her best for her Cousin Herman with all the best Boston society, most particularly Elizabeth Shaw and her family.

At Lansingburgh that Christmas for the first time there was no Melville male present: Tom was still on his whaling voyage, Herman and Allan were in New York City, and, everyone had to acknowledge with renewed sorrow, Gansevoort was never going to preside at the table. Maria invited her cousin Maria Peebles for their reduced gathering. Augustus Peebles, the Lord of the Isle, came without his mother and "carved the Christmas turkey inimitably, and presided with great dignity behind the huge fowl, which on first sitting down almost screened him from view," in the ironic account Helen wrote later Christmas Day to Augusta, who was at the Manor House. Augustus and the women amused themselves that evening by reading aloud the eighth chapter of *Dombey and Son*, which Edwin Croswell had printed in the *Argus* (as American editors did, whenever the latest installment was put ashore — often before the passengers disembarked):

> Fanny & I laughed until we almost cried over poor little Paul, and "Miss Pankey, the mild little blue-eyed morsel of a child," and lugubrious Mrs Wickam, who "was a waiter's wife, which is equivalent to being any other man's widow" — and old Mrs Pipchin in her black bombazine — "Whom gas itself couldn't light up after dark, and whose presence was a quencher to any number of candles" and who took such pains to impress upon the minds of her young charges "that nobody who *sniffed* before visitors ever went to Heaven," and who "always made a point of being particularly cross Sunday nights." Oh! it is too funny, and is worth all the rest of the book together, except dear lovely Florence, and good nurse Polly, the "temporary." But you must read it yourself.

Helen, as usual, brought out the best in the family, making even Fanny laugh uncontrollably. Herman did not hear this Dickens reading, though he was present for the reading of at least one other Dickens novel, later on, and probably others.

Augusta's missionary zeal in Lansingburgh was such that in one absence from home she persuaded the diffident Helen to distribute tracts for her. On 2 January 1847, a year and a half or two years after Herman wrote Little Henry into his draft of *Typee*, Helen wrote Augusta about the efforts she had made a few days earlier:

I went out Tuesday morning, the first good walking we had, and distributed all the tracts you gave me, in the "hill region," with tolerable success. One daughter of Green Erin, with two beautiful little black eyed children, said "that she had taken two or three of *them things* from Miss Melville, but she was going to stop *right short off* now, and not have anything more to do with the things." I spoke my prettiest, and smiled my sweetest; but all to no purpose and was fain to put the offered tract back into my muff, for the lady manifested as supreme a contempt for "Fashionable Amusements" as our good pastor himself. Another family said — "that Miss Melville had tried to make her take them many a time, but she had never been in the habit of taking them, and shouldn't begin now." It was all in vain that I tried to entice the children with the bright cover, and the stern-looking mother with the allegorical picture, of a card-table on the edge of a rock, and a lady in the extreme of undress, waltzing with a gentleman in mid-air, — she would have none of it — and quite crest-fallen I withdrew.

Helen's ironical tone corresponds closely with Herman's tone about "Little Henry and his Bearer" in the *Typee* draft. Both Helen and Herman looked askance at their pious younger sister's missionary efforts, but they would not willingly have hurt her feelings. In the draft passage about Little Henry, Herman probably wanted merely to tease Augusta before apologizing and ostentatiously removing his choice literary allusion. After the heroic exposure of her person to the Irish up the hill at Christmas and New Year's, Helen had declined making additional "tract efforts" for Augusta. When Herman returned to Lansingburgh Helen would have regaled him with her description of the "lady in the extreme of undress," knowing that he shared her sense of what was ludicrous.

At some point that winter Richard Tobias Greene wrote Melville a "cursed letter," which he later claimed his officious and misguided friends had drafted for him to copy out. In it he applied "to Herman for his share of the profits, in the immense Sale of Typee!" (so Helen wrote Augusta about 19 February 1847). Herman's reply was "so beautifully gentle & noble, without any spice of anger or contempt for his unworthy conduct," that it brought Toby "to his senses," and evoked this apology, which Helen quoted in her letter to Augusta: "I find on consideration that I have no right to any such thing. You must my dear friend forgive and forget all, as an old shipmate and friend, you must remember human nature is liable to err. I am heartily sorry, that I ever penned that infernal scrawl." In Herman's absence Helen had opened the letter because she recognized the superscription, but she would with equal aplomb have opened it if a strange superscription required attention to the contents: how could the family at home know whether or not to forward news unless they opened all letters that came for absent members? Even before she wrote to Herman, Helen went on to sum up the situation for Augusta: "Are you not glad? I could not bear that a cloud should come between such old and tried friends." No one wanted any new clouds, for at the holiday season, Thanksgiving, Christmas, and (vastly important to old New York families) New Year's were all painful days — the first the family had to live through knowing they would never share them again with Gansevoort. Herman was "very busy" in New York City, Maria said in a postscript to Helen's letter to Augusta, doing two things. One was "correcting Omoo" — reading through the manuscript for the last time in order to be sure that the absence of any chapters that had finally been "rejected altogether" did not "break the continuity of the book," and in order to spot any minor infelicities. He was not reading proofs already, for in a letter on 30 December to John R. Brodhead, the current secretary of legation in London, Melville declared that the book had "just gone to press." He was also doing something else "at the same time," Maria wrote to Augusta: "endeavoring to procure employment in the C H." — that is, in the family tradition, a patronage job in the Custom House, one lasting, with luck, as long as the one to which George Washington had appointed the Hero of the Tea Party.

[24]

Office-Seeker and Reviewer

1847

> But where's Guert Gan? Still heads he the van?
> As before Vera-Cruz, when he dashed splashing through
> The blue rollers sunned, in his brave gold-and-blue,
> And, ere his cutter in keel took the strand,
> Aloft waved his sword on the hostile land!

Melville, "Bridegroom Dick," in *John Marr and Other Sailors*, 1888

IN DECEMBER 1846 MELVILLE FACED FACTS: he was engaged but not married, and not apt to be married until he had a steady job or else showed that he might reasonably expect to make a living as a writer. Apparently neither Lemuel Shaw nor Herman realized just how nearly impossible it was to make a living as a writer. Only two American writers, Washington Irving and James Fenimore Cooper, were reported to earn enough from their writings for a family to live on (family in Irving's case comprising mainly nieces). In fact, Cooper's earnings had dropped ever since the 1820s, to the point that in the early 1840s "no stratagem Cooper could devise — not even a return to the approved form of romance or a greatly increased productivity — could surmount the harsh conditions of the trade," as James Franklin Beard observed in *The Letters and Journals of James Fenimore Cooper.* Beard went on: "A severe national depression together with a plethora of popular foreign novelists (including Dickens, Bulwer-Lytton, G. P. R. James, Dumas, and Sue) and of cheap formats for exploiting them (especially the 'extras' or 'supplements' of the mammoth weeklies) made fiction virtually unsalable."

A fair sample of important American writers are those Melville was to list in August 1850 in his essay on Hawthorne's *Mosses from an Old Manse:* Hawthorne, Emerson, Whittier, Irving, Bryant, Dana, Cooper, Willis. Of these, Hawthorne's only real money came later, from his appointment in 1853 as consul at Liverpool; Emerson lectured but he could have lived on his early legacy from his deceased bride; Whittier worked as a newspaper man and never made money from his writings until *Snow-Bound* was a surprising success in 1866; Irving had family money and also had received magnificent sums in London for some of his early writings, from Byron's publisher, John Murray, the father of Melville's publisher; Bryant was a working newspaper owner and editor; Dana (bitter about his mistake in signing away the copyright of *Two Years* to the calculating — or avaricious — Harpers) was comfortable from family money but worked as a lawyer; Cooper's wife was wealthy, and like Irving he had been lavishly paid for some of his earlier writings; and Willis struggled as a journalist and editor. There were no secrets in the small literary milieu. By December 1846 Melville knew that Charles Fenno Hoffman was a working journalist, the poet Fitz-Greene Halleck was a clerk for John Jacob Astor, and the poet Longfellow was a professor at Harvard whose second wife was an Appleton (a name synonymous with wealth in Boston). Herman knew from Gansevoort that the second Mrs. George Bancroft had been the rich widow Bliss, while Bancroft was himself widely known as a wealthy man.

Long afterward, memorializing the recently deceased Fitz-Greene Halleck in the February 1868 *Putnam's Monthly Magazine*, Evert Duyckinck reflected on authorship in America:

> It happens, rarely, . . . in America, that the few persons whom, in the higher sense of the word, she is privileged to call her authors, have not pursued some other occupation than that of literature. It is only in recent years that authorship has afforded a profitable means of support, and the dependence is still inadequate and precarious. A few writers may live by the proceeds of their books, but they are the lucky exceptions to a general rule. Irving, in the better literature of the country, is, perhaps the most favorable example of an author profiting by his writings; but he was a merchant, though an unsuccessful one, in his youth, and his resources in age were materially aided by his government employments. Prescott is to be regarded as a man of wealth, independently of his profitable books. The same may be said of Longfellow and of Bancroft, who has besides held high official stations; while the historian, Motley, has probably been as well rewarded by the nation as by the booksellers.

Duyckinck had known Halleck well when the poet had toiled at a humble salary, personal clerk to the wealthiest man in the United States. He had, in fact, known almost all the aspiring American authors, and in December 1846 he was the representative of the publishing world to the sailor-author. If Melville received a government job, preferably a sinecure that left him some free daylight hours, he could continue to dash off occasional pieces that would keep up his literary friendships and keep his name before the public. Never would Duyckinck have urged him to stake all on a literary career.

Paramount for Melville was the fact that the New York literary world could offer only an inadequate source of income, but there was a further consideration, brought home by Lewis Gaylord Clark's comments in the

November *Knickerbocker*: this was an unpleasant place for a decent man to find himself. Melville had gained, long before this, some idea of the malicious infighting that characterized the New York literary scene (quite aside from the vicious righteousness of the religious press). The Philo Logos controversy, however serious or joking it was, had given Melville his fill of vituperative articles in the public prints. He was still willing to manage the news if he could, as it concerned his books, but he did not brawl in the public prints any more. His friend Duyckinck, for all his geniality, at times did entangle himself in public feuds, and the wonder is that no one, not Hiram Fuller, not Nathaniel Parker Willis, not the editor of the *Knickerbocker*, Lewis Gaylord Clark, ever tarred Melville with the brush they used on Duyckinck and his close friend Cornelius Mathews, even though they all knew of his association with Duyckinck and, after a time, with Mathews.

While Melville was worrying about *Omoo* and a patronage job, Duyckinck was much involved with Mathews and the critic Richard Grant White (two years Melville's junior) in planning *Yankee Doodle*, one of the several short-lived periodicals which testified to the lure of that will-o'-the wisp, an American *Punch*. In this they were associated with George G. Foster, an expert on low-life in the city (Melville probably encountered him the first year of his return from sea, while he was writing *Typee*, for Foster's office was at 160 Nassau, near Alexander Bradford's). By 16 January 1847 *Yankee Doodle* was embroiled in street-fighting tactics, attacking Hiram Fuller, the new editor of the *Evening Mirror*, for *his* attacks on Edgar Allan Poe, the controversial but valuable author in Duyckinck's Library of American Books:

> We have been inexpressibly delighted with the considerate delicacy and forbearance with which the temporary misfortunes of a distinguished author have been recently dragged before the public by the newspapers. Every mean-spirited cur, who dared not bark when his tormentor had strength, feeds fat his ancient grudge, now that he sees his enemy prostrate and powerless — with heart crushed and brain shattered by the sickness and suffering of those most dear to him in life. This shows in a just and flattering light the prudence and discrimination of the press, and is a pregnant commentary on the blessings of the type-metal.

What this really showed was Duyckinck's willingness to descend to the level of vituperation that had already proved comfortable to Poe and his critics, or at least to associate himself with men who were willing to do so. Having mired himself in that foul arena in 1838, Melville stayed clear of it now.

In keeping his distance early in 1847, Melville was encouraged by something Fuller was serializing in the *Weekly Mirror*, *The Trippings of Tom Pepper*, generally known to be written by Charles F. Briggs, who had been Poe's co-editor on the *Broadway Journal*. Some of Melville's new city friends figured among the satirical portraits in the book, to the delight of those literary folk who were being spared, installment by installment. Lewis Gaylord Clark took disingenuous notice of it in the February 1847 *Knickerbocker*, wondering, oh wondering about the real-life model for a character:

> We wonder who is "Mr. FEROCIOUS," a literary lawyer, in whose office "TOM" is, and whom he introduces to us while engaged in denouncing certain "piratical barons" in Cliff-street, and other "marauding" bibliopolists, and especially sundry critical "assassins," who are envious of his literary renown. "Mr. FEROCIOUS" hands "TOM" one of his entertaining "works" to read; directing him to "dive down into the mysteries of his author; grapple with him; bring up the pearls and diamonds of his fancy, and play with his leviathan thoughts." "TOM" makes a beginning upon the book, but experiences such a soothing effect from the perusal of a few sentences that he falls directly into a sweet slumber, with his head resting upon the open page.

This was designed to send Clark's readers scrambling for back copies of the *Weekly Mirror*, since Mr. Ferocious was patently Clark's bête noire, Cornelius Mathews, the author of *Behemoth: A Legend of the Mound-Builders* (1839), a man preternaturally proud of his own prose and poetry. In his own mind he was the leading American nationalist, "the originator of the 'Young America' Party in the United States" (as Perry Miller quoted him in *The Raven and the Whale* [1956]), an outgrowth of the Tetractys Club, which he, Evert Duyckinck, William Alfred Jones, Jedediah B. Auld, and Russell Trevett had founded in 1836, in their youth.

In the 27 February installment of *Tom Pepper* Duyckinck got his comeuppance too, along with another of his stars in the Library of American Books, in a description of what went on at a fashionable salon like that of the literary hostess Anne Lynch. "Mr. Ferocious" along with his friend Tibbings (Evert Duyckinck) enter, "followed by a gentleman who was announced as the celebrated critic, Austin Wicks [Edgar A. Poe], author of the 'Castle of Duntriewell,' a metaphysical romance, and a psychological essay on the sensations of shadows":

> The literati conducted themselves with great propriety during the evening, doing nothing worse than saying the most ill-natured things they could utter about all their acquaintances who were not present, and complimenting each other in the most fulsome and laughable manner, until the refreshments were introduced, when Mr. Wicks, having drank a glass full of wine, the little spirit that it contained flew into his weak head, and he began to abuse all present in such profane and scurrilous terms, that all the ladies went into hysterics.

This, as even Duyckinck would soon witness and record in his diary, was an only slightly exaggerated depiction of Poe's transformation from gentleman to monster after imbibing a small quantity of alcohol.

Briggs's most telling attack came in the 6 March installment — cruelly honest in its depiction of the self-delusion of the editor of the Library of American Books. It was, in truth, not only Mathews but Duyckinck who associated the fate of the writings of his schoolfellow Mathews with the fate of American literature as a whole:

> Mr. Ferocious began to unfold his gigantic scheme.
>
> The countenance of Mr. Ferocious beamed with delight while that of his friend and follower, Mr. Tibbings, was suffused with purple pleasure, convinced, probably . . . that the object of their call was within their grasp.
>
> "I will read you all about it, sir," said Mr. Ferocious, taking a tape-tied bundle from his coat pocket, and, unfolding it, he began to read: "Whereas, a national literature being essential to nerve the bold right arm of a nation's glory — ". . . .
>
> Mr. Tibbings clapped his hand to his mouth and held his breath, but Mr. Ferocious rolled up his manuscript and replaced it in his pocket. He then began again to unfold his plans.
>
> "A certain author, I shall name no names, now; it is not necessary," said Mr. Ferocious, with more seriousness than before, and a little less of glowing satisfaction in his countenance, "proposes to dispose of the copyright of his various writings, consisting of novels, plays, essays and romances, for a certain sum, to be paid yearly, or in one amount, as the parties may agree; provided that a company can be formed of high-toned lovers of their country, a national literature, and with sufficient means, and willing to undertake to circulate a certain number of copies of that author's works in these United States, and in the various countries of Europe."

Briggs here ruthlessly caught the single-minded intensity of Duyckinck's desire to exalt Mathews's literary career. It seemed to the literati who watched Duyckinck's fascination with his old friend that if Duyckinck had been imaginative enough to think of such a far-fetched scheme, he might very well have gone so far as to form a joint-stock company to subsidize Mathews's literary career, convinced that he would with that single stroke support an entire American national literature at home and abroad. The truth to glean from such satires was that Duyckinck would never promote Melville's books as doggedly as he would promote Mathews's: Mathews was his man.

The downright irrational nature of Duyckinck's attachment to Mathews became clearer than ever after Wiley & Putnam allied with Appleton in January 1847 to sponsor a magazine modeled on the format of the London

Athenæum and to be edited by Duyckinck. This was the *Literary World: A Gazette for Authors, Readers, and Publishers*. Duyckinck would be paid a thousand dollars annually for contributions and five hundred for his services as editor. He was to stuff the paper with newsworthy reprints of pieces from British books, magazines, and papers, but he was to write a great many of the columns himself and fill many others with (usually) unpaid contributions from his literary acquaintances. Since, as in the *Athenæum* and other journals, pieces were to be anonymous, he could call upon the resources of a few of his trusted literary friends for a disproportionate number of columns. It was essential that he keep the back pages for a list of forthcoming books, advertisements for books just published, and other publishing news, the feature that caused the aroused Willis on 23 March 1850 to call the *Literary World* a *"journal of disappointed authors who have turned booksellers' hacks."* The first issue, which appeared on 6 February 1847, contained the announcement that the Messrs. Harper were preparing for publication "a new work from the graphic pen of Mr. Melville, of Typee celebrity."

Almost at once, the owners became unhappy at just how much of the magazine was devoted to the works of or the suspected contributions by "Mr. Ferocious." All this would come sharply to Melville's attention, but at the end of 1846 and the beginning of 1847, he was focused on the publication of *Omoo*, not on the journalistic enterprises of the editor who had advised him on expurgating *Typee*. He needed someone to help arrange its publication in England, but young rich and lazy McHenry Boyd was no longer at the American legation in London. Adjusting to the new situation, and taking care of business, on 30 December 1846 Herman wrote to John Romeyn Brodhead, the newest secretary of legation in London, and the son of Jacob Brodhead, who in 1826 had become pastor at the Dutch Reformed Church on Broome Street, which the Melvills had attended in their last years in New York City. John R. Brodhead, born in 1814, knew the Melville children from the 1820s, as Herman reminded him:

The long-standing acquaintance between our families, and particularly that between my late brother Mr Gansevoort Melville and yourself, induce me to solicit a favor which my own slight acquaintance with you would not perhaps warrant. By granting it, as I think you will, you will confer that which I shall not forget.

I have recently made an arrangement with the Harpers to bring out a new work of mine. But altho' it has just gone to press, they are to defer publication until I have concluded arrangements to bring out the work in England. This is for the express purpose, as you will perceive, of securing a copyright there. — Now, I have no correspondent in London who can act for me — is it too much to solicit your friendly offices? — There is little to be done — a mere sale to effect.

By the same mail he sent news to John Murray that the new book was at last finished, and he should "much prefer" that Murray publish it in England rather than someone else: "I think that as it has a certain connection with 'Typee' you will be desirous of so doing. The two books will sell together." One way or another, as full-time author or as government employee and part-time literary man, his future would be secure, he could tell himself.

The sale of *Omoo* to John Murray went forward speedily. Brodhead wrote Melville on 14 January 1847, agreeing to act as his London agent, and on 29 January Melville wrote Murray that proof sheets of *Omoo* were being sent to Brodhead:

> The stereotype plates are cast, & publication held *here* in suspence. . . .
>
> Of the book itself, of course, you will judge for yourself. So I will not say, what opinions of it have been given here by persons competent to judge of its merits as a work calculated for popular reading. — But I think you will find it a fitting successor to "Typee"; inasmuch as the latter book delineates Polynisian Life in its primitive state — while the new work, represents it, as affected by intercourse with the whites. It also describes the "man about town" sort of life, led, at the present day, by roving sailors in the Pacific — a kind of thing, which I have never seen described anywhere.

Here Melville was recalling Duyckinck's comments in the *Morning News* about the way "Tommo" would go down every day from his hut to a lounging shed of the chiefs, the Ti, "as if he were walking from the Astor House to the Saloons of the Racket Club." He acknowledged that the title of the work, *Omoo*, might "be thought a curious one — but after reading the narrative no one will doubt its propriety as explained in the Preface." Melville was carrying on his old argument with the man who had rejected *Typee* as the title of the first printing of his previous book: "It gives a sort of Polynisian expression to its 'figure-head.' — At any rate, no one questions the right of a parent to dub his offspring as he pleases; — the same should be accorded to an author." In another passage Melville was disingenuous about a genuinely problematical feature of the manuscript, his reuse (on a different island, with different natives) of a rejected portion of *Typee*: "You will perceive that there is a chapter in the book which describes a dance in the valley of Tamai. This discription has been modified & adapted from a certain chapter which it was thought best to exclude from Typee. In their dances the Tahitians much resembled the Marquesans (the two groups of islands are not far apart) & thus is the discription faithful in both instances." The letter to Murray behind him, on 30 January Melville deposited the title of *Omoo* at the copyright office of the Southern District of New York, and appointed John Romeyn Brodhead his attorney to dispose of *Omoo* in the United Kingdom of Great Britain and Ireland. Then he packed up the proof sheets of *Omoo* for shipment in the *Hibernia* on February first.

The only hitch came in Liverpool, where officious customs agents seized the proof sheets as a piracy of *Typee*. On 18 February Brodhead wrote what he called "a pretty sharp letter" of protest to the Harnden express agency: "I have just received your letter of yesterday in which you state, that by the 'Hibernia' Steamer, you received from your Boston house, a parcel addressed to me, 'which on being examined at the Customs, was found to contain an American reprint of an English Author, entitled 'a Narrative of a voyage to the north seas by Melville,' and as such — was seized by the examining officer." North seas, South seas, Brodhead rose to the occasion, as tough as Gansevoort would have been: "The Custom's Officer therefore, who in the superabundance of his zeal without knowledge made the deliberate seizure of *the proof sheets of an original and unpublished American work*, under the pretence of its being an American reprint of an English work, has not only displayed great ignorance but has most unjustifiably transcended his duty." The letter (quite sharp enough) elicited a humble apology, and on 20 February Brodhead sent the sheets to Murray "with a note requesting his early attention."

Brodhead saw Murray "again" on 25 February and recorded that the publisher "spoke favorably of Melville's Book" and promised to write him "in a few days." Murray did better than that, writing the next day that he was "much pleased" with *Omoo*: "Though it has not the novelty of the former, it is full of talent & interest." He was "happy," in fact, to pay £150 for the English copyright, a generous sum. Brodhead wrongly thought the terms not "liberal" enough, but took a practical attitude: "I shall have to take them I suppose." On 27 February Brodhead looked so dubious about the terms that Murray was blunt with him: "He said that so far from Melville's first Book helping the sale of the second, he hoped the reverse would be true, for he had not yet sold enough of the first to pay expenses. It was then agreed that I should write to him & he would reply as to cash payt." On 28 February Brodhead accepted the £150 but asked that it be paid in cash, so on 1 March Murray agreed to pay £144.3.4 — in cash, on publication. On 31 March Melville wrote Brodhead from New York, gratefully drawing only £140 so as to allow more than four pounds for expenses his agent might have incurred and might yet incur if he agreed "to cause to be collected" and sent to Melville, "in their original form, whatever notices may appear of the book." He wanted papers, clippings at least, not some clerk's longhand transcription of the reviews. What with Brodhead's competence and Murray's generosity, everything about the sale had been handled as well as Gansevoort himself could have done. Melville on 2 April expressed his satisfaction to Edwin Croswell of the Albany *Argus*, saying that Murray had spoken of the book to Brodhead "in a very high strain of compliment," then had paid the work "a still better & more satisfactory compliment in the offer he made for it." The Harper publication went forward with equal expedition, and their early copies were ready by 23 April or so.

In the meantime, Melville continued his endeavors to get a government job. When he heard that under the New Loan Bill some jobs were "to be at once created in the Treasury Department at Washington," he decided to go there at once to apply for one, and, if he failed, to find some other job. Already by 3 February, when he wrote asking his Uncle Peter (then in his last year of a four-year term as first judge of the county courts of Albany County) to help him with "another letter to Gen: Dix," he had "obtained several strong letters from various prominent persons" in New York City, addressed "to the most influential men at the seat of government." He left for Washington, with Allan, the next day, after writing his mother a long letter. Maria (in a letter to Augusta) was pleased to see in it that Herman was manifesting a degree of perspicacity and good judgment he had hitherto lacked:

> He seems to feel that if he succeeds at all in getting an appointment it will be brought about by his own personal exertions at head-quarters, I am glad that he is at last convinced of this important truth.
>
> It is worth a fortune to any man to understand this, and act it out, it is a lesson Herman has been long in learning, but he is young enough to profit by it still, I hope *God* will see fit to bless his endeavours, and if it is for his & our good that he may succeed.

Maria was clear-sighted, as usual. Gansevoort had made the most of his connections, but he had gotten ahead, finally, by "his own personal exertions" at whatever "head-quarters," a debating room in Stanwix Hall, a repeal platform, Tammany Hall, or an improvised western platform (never, perhaps, an actual tree stump).

Herman had indeed been "long in learning" that he had to act in his own self-interests. So far, none of his father's generation had acted for him effectually, not Uncle Peter in 1837, not Uncle Thomas in 1840 — only Gansevoort in 1845 and 1846. Herman was twenty-seven, old to be learning the lesson that he had preferred not to learn, and Maria and her daughters had paid the cost for his failure to learn it. But on 8 February, when she wrote this to Augusta, Maria expressed only optimism. Herman seemed "to be in good spirits," and he had "provided himself with many good letters from prominent men at New York to influential characters in Washington."

Within a day of reaching the capital, Melville called at the Washington house of Senator John A. Dix. The New York home of the Dixes was beside the Thurstons on Bond Street, so Allan was a frequent caller there (carriage-less, he had to come to the front door), and Allan remembered Mrs. Dix's helping prepare Mary Sanford Gansevoort's body for the funeral. In his tardy reply to Herman, Uncle Peter particularly emphasized how Herman was to behave toward this friend: "When you are introduced to Mrs Dix, please present my respects to her & as she is an excellent sensible & charming woman you must make yourself very agreeable to her, which will greatly aid you in carrying out your views at Washington." As it happened, Mrs. Dix paid more attention to Allan than to Herman, partly because Allan put him-self out to talk to her while Herman tried to talk to the senator. Writing to a friend who also had a hand out for one of the new "offices" created in Washington, the "Mr Melville" she said had interested her very much was Allan, "from his connections with Typee, and the lovely Fayaway, as well as from the prospect of a closer tie, which seemed likely to take place between himself and one of the sweetest of our Bond street girls." The senator, a lank-haired, harried man, added a message to his wife's letter explaining that there were fewer appointments to be made than the papers had indicated: "Mr. Gillet had only one clerk to appoint, as the additional number created was to be divided between him & the Treasurer & he had supernumeraries in his office temporarily employed on acting permanent places." Herman's hopes had been unrealistic.

From Washington by the middle of February Herman wrote his mother that he had received letters from both Murray and Brodhead, and that the former had sent £50 (about $250), the payment for the sequel to *Typee*. Herman wanted her to pay a doctor named Nelson what he owed him, then give his sisters ten dollars each as a "very slight testimonial of his love & remembrance of them." In early February Augusta and Fanny had visited the Van Rensselaers at the Manor House, then Augusta had gone for a shorter stay with Uncle Peter and Aunt Susan, where on 17 February she received her mother's letter. Not content with quoting Herman's description of the ten dollars as a "very slight testimonial," Maria prefaced the quotation with two words, this way: "a small 'very slight testimonial.'" She was following his instructions to let the girls, as she quoted his letter, "do with the money as they will." The money was welcome, and properly disposed of: "This money enables dear Herman to pay all his little debts, to retain fifty dollars for himself and the remainder, I am to have, of course deducting the beautiful gift of forty — to his belove'd Sisters — he begs I will lay 'no restraint what-ever on the disposition of it.'" Maria went to observe, quite candidly: "The whole sum of £50, is small, but the proper disposition thereof is beautiful, it

at once shews his love of justice in paying his debts, his affection and gratitude to his Sisters, and his filial love to his Mother." She was too worldly wise
not to recognize that however admirable was Herman's respect toward her
and however amiable was his devotion to his sisters, he was dealing with a
very small total sum of money. The appreciative family was helping him with
his career. Before he left New York Herman had sent Augusta "the remainder of the Proof Sheets of 'Omoo.'" Now Maria wanted her to send
them on to Lansingburgh when Fanny returned from the Van Rensselaers.

In Washington Herman and Allan found time to go to an art exhibition
together, where they saw Thomas P. Rossiter's painting *Ruth and Naomi* (as
Sophia wrote to Augusta on 24 June, when that work was on exhibit in New
York City). Both of them would have been struck by the comparative youth
of the painter — twenty-eight. The painting was recorded as *Ruth and Naomi*,
but this may be the piece Rossiter had done in Rome, *The Parting between
Ruth, Orpha, and Naomi*. In the brothers it set up odd reverberations involving Maria Melville and each young man's fiancée and perhaps each man's
prospective mother-in-law as well, reverberations all arising from the theme
"Whither thou goest." Able or not to articulate to each other any responses
to the painting in relation to Maria and their brides-to-be, Herman and Allan
discovered that they shared an interest in the visual arts, and they were so
impressed by this particular painting that they described it enthusiastically to
the family at home.

In Washington, Herman was also stimulated by being at the center of
political power, where he could chat on equal social terms with Commodore
Thomas ap Catesby Jones at a ball at the Russian ministry (*White-Jacket*,
ch. 69). This was a quintessentially American bit of leveling, possible once
the well-born able seaman had become a civilian and an author. He also
carried home from Washington a grim vision that he put to use in his third
book a year and a half later, a slightly sanitized depiction of "the grand
council of Vivenza," the Twenty-ninth Congress, in glorious session:

> Entering the temple, we beheld an amphitheatrical space, in the middle of
> which, a great fire was burning. Around it, were many chiefs, robed in long
> togas, and presenting strange contrasts in their style of tattooing.
>
> Some were sociably laughing, and chatting; others diligently making exca-
> vations between their teeth with slivers of bamboo; or turning their heads into
> mills, were grinding up leaves and ejecting their juices. Some were busily in-
> serting the down of a thistle into their ears. Several stood erect, intent upon
> maintaining striking attitudes; their javelins tragically crossed upon their
> chests. They would have looked very imposing, were it not, that in rear their

vesture was sadly disordered. Others, with swelling fronts, seemed chiefly in-debted to their dinners for their dignity. Many were nodding and napping. . . .

But heedless of all, in the midst of the amphitheater, stood a tall, gaunt warrior [Senator William Allen of Ohio], ferociously tattooed, with a beak like a buzzard; long dusty locks; and his hands full of headless arrows. He was laboring under violent paroxysms; three benevolent individuals essaying to hold him. But repeatedly breaking loose, he burst anew into his delirium; while with an absence of sympathy, distressing to behold, the rest of the assembly seemed wholly engrossed with themselves; nor did they appear to care how soon the unfortunate lunatic might demolish himself by his frantic proceedings. (*Mardi*, ch. 158)

On any given day a session of the American Congress in that decade did not constitute an entirely edifying spectacle, other witnesses testified; whatever laws they were meditating, all too many of them did it while smoking or else masticating tobacco and expectorating in the direction of spittoons, and all too many of them played to the galleries.

Melville went home disappointed, but his reputation was rising. Aside from advertisements in his publishers' books, he had not seen his name in a book other than *Typee*, but from Washington he had written his mother about a new stage in his fame, his appearance in a volume of poems by William Ellery Channing as "the bold/Adventurous Melville." The book, which Allan sent up to Lansingburgh, contained the poem called "The Island Nukeheva," which was, Maria wrote to Augusta, "poetically descriptive of Tipee and is very pretty." Among its almost two hundred lines was this description of Fayaway:

> The Typee maiden with her olive skin,
> Through which a soft vermilion shines within,
> Her dazzling teeth, like arta's milk-white seeds,
> Her soft smooth form contrived for fairy need.
> Upon her naked shoulders flowed her hair
> Of deepest brown, which like a mantle rare
> In natural ringlets dressed her in its pride,
> Her hands as soft as Countess', — she, the bride
> Of Nature, who in captivating mood,
> Sculptured this maiden for this solitude.
> Her dress at home was a slight belt of bark,
> With some leaves, like those Fig leaves (save the mark),
> Which our first Parents found, but in this she
> Moved like a creature wove of sanctity,

Fell like a sunbeam in that summer world,
Beneath those skies her native grace unfurled.

Melville might have taken warning from this sensuous warmth, or from
Ellen Astor Oxenham's odd letters, if Augusta shared them with him. He
seems to have been oblivious at the senator's house that Allan Melville had
interested Catherine Dix partly "from his connections with Typee, and the
lovely Fayaway." A few months later, in the summer of 1847, Melville understood, at last, that he was being defined in terms of his sexuality, but he could
have had no inkling that he would be defined that way for years to come. On
his way back from Washington the last thing on his mind may have been the
burden any intelligent male celebrity feels when he is perceived only in terms
of his past sexual adventures and his present physicality.

Apprehensive that his failure to gain a government job would delay his
marriage, Melville returned home to glance over the proofs of *Omoo* himself,
secure in the knowledge that Augusta and others in the family had thoroughly scrutinized them for typographical errors. He also soon realized that
he was eating up his earnings in the purchase of books — partly gifts (James
Andrews's *Floral Tableaux*, probably for Elizabeth Shaw), and partly tools of
the trade (*Curiosities of Modern Travel* and Bayard Taylor's *Views A-Foot*). The
8 February 1847 statement from Wiley & Putnam, waiting for him on his
return, showed that almost twelve hundred copies of *Typee* had been sold
(twice as many paper as cloth) and had produced $661.94 of income. The
publisher had deducted $439.18 in expenses, leaving Melville with $111.38.
After his book purchases of $103.57 were deducted, he received $7.81 — not
an encouraging sum for a man engaged to be married.

As he cast about for alternatives to government office, Melville saw lecturing as a possible way of earning money — one first offered him in the fall of
1846. Having learned that a Schenectady association had invited Melville to
lecture, Hooper C. Van Voorst had invited him to lecture before the Albany
Young Men's Association. In his reply to Van Voorst on 19 January 1847,
Melville had explained that the Troy Young Men's Association had advertised his lecture on the strength of his only provisional promise, and that he
had declined the invitation from Schenectady. Furthermore, he could not be
in Albany on the day Van Voorst wanted him to lecture. Melville was polite in
his conclusion, but he was not setting himself up to receive renewed invitations from Albany: "But in case I lecture anywhere, or at all, I shall be most
happy to lecture before your association in Albany." Maria was dismayed that
he passed by these opportunities, but there was really no reasoning with her
second son, despite his fine pre-Washington avowals. She knew that lecturing *ought* to have been irresistible for him, since he had developed into so

enthralling a storyteller. At crucial moments in his subsequent career Melville was to make almost perversely self-destructive decisions; at this stage there was no apparent reason he did not accept the invitations to lecture which were coming his way, for the money would have been easy to earn, and an engaged man who had just paid off his little debts might have wanted to think about amassing a nest egg before his marriage.

Circumstances conspired to offer Melville another literary outlet — one that did not pay, but might pay in the future. "Articles" and poems might be sold to magazines, he probably remembered from Willis's "The Pay for Periodical Writing," which he had had a chance to see in the *Weekly Mirror* on 19 October 1844, the day he reached New York City, or thereafter. Reviews were often not paid for, but there were exceptions, and for a man whose disposable income seemed to go to bookstores, writing about a book he wanted to own seemed like an easy way of paying for it. Before the first issue of the *Literary World* appeared on 6 February, Duyckinck had asked Melville to review just the sort of book the editor thought fell within the former sailor's genuine but limited capacities, a new Harper book by J. Ross Browne, *Etchings of a Whaling Cruise*. Duyckinck had been shrewd enough to know the sort of thing Melville, the deserter from the "Dolly," would say: "When the brutal tyranny of the Captain of the 'Styx' is painted without apology or palliation, it holds up the outrageous abuse to which seamen in our whaling marine are actually subjected, a matter which demands legislation." Melville was also taken with a reminder of his own search for a vessel, an "irresistably comic" scene in which Browne and his companion are inveigled into enlisting by a wily old shipping agent lurking like a spider in a dark loft above Front Street. Before or after thumbing through the book, Melville told Duyckinck he should "find much pleasure in making it the basis of an article." He may have carried the book in the cars to Washington, for he picked it up just before leaving. There is no indication that Duyckinck offered even nominal compensation for the review: he was helping out by giving Melville a chance to become more of an all-round literary man. (Melville had his own preoccupations, but Duyckinck and his friend Mathews as well as Willis all were distressed that week about the death of Virginia Poe on 30 January; on 2 February these three took the noon cars up to Fordham from City Hall for the funeral, returning, grim and chilled, at four.)

Long before, at the end of 1837 Herman had almost usurped "the province of the Edinburgh Reveiw" in his comments on John Orville Taylor's *The District School*. Now on 6 March his first professional piece of literary criticism appeared, anonymously, in the *Literary World*. He or Duyckinck had added a new book, *Sailors' Life and Sailors' Yarns*, by Captain Ringbolt (pseudonym of a Boston captain, John Codman), to the Browne book, which was already several months old. Melville's review of *Etchings of a Whaling Cruise* identifies a stage in his aesthetic development. In his early work on his own whaling book three years later, he defined his current problem as the need to tell the truth about whaling while not losing the poetry in the theme. In the review of Browne he was already beginning to articulate the elements of what became a complex aesthetic problem for him:

> From time immemorial many fine things have been said and sung of the sea. And the days have been, when sailors were considered veritable mermen; and the ocean itself, as the peculiar theatre of the romantic and wonderful. But of late years there have been revealed so many plain, matter-of[-]fact details connected with nautical life that at the present day the poetry of salt water is very much on the wane. The perusal of Dana's Two Years Before The Mast, for instance, somewhat impairs the relish with which we read Byron's spiritual address to the ocean. . . .
>
> Mr J Ross Browne's narrative tends still further to impair the charm with which poesy & fiction have invested the sea. It is a book of unvarnished facts; and with some allowances for the general application of an individual example unquestionably presents a faithful picture of the life led by the 20 thousand seamen employed in the 700 whaling vessel[s] which pursue their game under their American flag. Indeed, what Mr Dana has so admirably done in describing the viscicitudes of the merchant sailor's life, Mr Browne has very creditably achieved with respect to that of the hardy whaleman's.

In the original preface to *Typee* Melville had expressed "his anxious desire to speak the unvarnished truth" (just perhaps a recollection of Othello's "round unvarnish'd tale" — which Gansevoort had quoted from memory in a letter to Henry Ellsworth as "plain unvarnished tale") and in his recently written preface to *Omoo* he presented himself as "an unbiased observer" of Tahitian traits and an equally unbiased observer of "missionary operations," which he commented on only through "a strict adherence to facts" and "an earnest desire for truth and good." Melville's comments on the effect of realistic accounts of the sea upon poetic attitudes at this time did not go beyond declaring that realistic descriptions impaired "the charm with which poesy & fiction have invested the sea." Later in the review he recurred to the "lamentable delusion" under which "shore-disdaining, ocean-enamored youths" go to sea: "We shudder at all realities of the career they will be entering upon."

When he came to talk of "the whaling part of the business," Melville burst the bounds of the review with the dramatic passage already quoted in chapter 10 above (" 'Stand up & give it to him!' shrieks the boat-header at the steering-oar to the harpooneer in the bow"). Getting fast to the whale was nothing, Melville explained, to what follows: "As yet you have but simply *fastened* to the whale: he must be fought & killed." Restraining himself, he decided that the reader's "imagination" would have to "supply the rest," but he could not quite stop himself from putting before the reader some scenes the imagination should supply: "the monster staving the boat with a single sweep of his ponderous flukes; — taking its bows between his jaws (as is frequently the case) & playing with it, as a cat with a mouse. Sometimes he bites it in twain; sometimes crunches it into chips, & strews the sea with them." Finally he stopped himself: "But we forbear." His own imagination had been caught, long before. In the still unpublished preface to *Omoo* he had explicitly disclaimed any pretense "to give any account of the whale-fishery (for the scope of the narrative does not embrace the subject)," though he still intended "to convey some idea of the kind of life" experienced by the reckless seamen who made up the crews of the sperm whale fishery in the South Seas. The subject was on his mind, and perhaps he even thought he was ready to take it on in his next book. With no government job forthcoming, he would have to write a third book. His shore experiences in the South Seas were all but exhausted, unless he wanted to write about setting bowling pins and keeping mercantile accounts and selling yards of cloth in Honolulu, so it might be time for a genuinely nautical book.

In his tagged-on comments about the Codman book, mainly a collection of banal romantic tales, Melville like a practiced reviewer skipped to the last chapter, "Sailors' Rights and Sailors' Wrongs," where Codman (writing just after Browne's book came out) allowed that some officers might be guilty of "tyranny and maltreatment," but less frequently than writers were leading people to believe:

> I do not wish to deal in hints, but much prefer to speak out plainly. Such books as Mr. Dana's "Two Years Before the Mast," and Mr. Browne's "Whaling Cruise," however interesting in many particulars, convey very wrong impressions as to the general treatment of seamen. They do not assert in so many words, that sailors are always abused (for they acknowledge instances of the contrary,) but they give people to understand that sailors are rather maltreated by their officers than otherwise. The reverse is the truth. I do not profess to know much about whale ships; but no one can read Mr. Browne's experience, without seeing plainly that he has overshot the mark, and without being amused at his project of establishing a democracy at sea.

This was enough to make Melville erupt, somewhat unfairly:

> Captain Ringbolt almost denies that the sailor has any wrongs and more than insinuates that sea-captains are not only the best natured fellows in the world but that they have been sorely maligned. Indeed he explicitly charges Mr

Dana & Mr Browne with having presented a decidedly one sided view of the matter. And he mournfully exclaims that the Captain of the Pilgrim — poor fellow! — died to[o] soon to vindicate his character from unjust aspersions.

— Now as a class ship owners are seldom disposed partially to judge the captains in their employ. And yet we know of a verity that at least one of the owners of the Pilgrim, — an esteemed citizen of the good old town of Boston — will never venture to dispute that to the extent of his knowledge at least Mr Dana's captain was a most "strict & harsh disiplinarian" which words so applied by a ship owner, means that the man in question was nothing less that [than] what Mr Dana describes him to have been. — But where is Browne's captain? He is alive & hearty we presume. Let him come forward then.

In Boston during December 1846 Melville had talked to one of the owners of the *Pilgrim*, perhaps the wealthy Abbott Lawrence or his father's old friend the State Street merchant Daniel P. Parker, resident of Beacon Street. Melville brought local Boston gossip to the Codman review and a whaleman's experience to the Browne review, and he had showed to himself that this sort of literary work was something he could do, if he needed to, as part of a New York literary life. However, Duyckinck could make no more demands for articles for the *Literary World* just then, for with the 1 May issue the owners fired Duyckinck for abusing their trust by devoting far too many of his columns to writing by his oldest friend and most intimate, Cornelius Mathews. They replaced him with Charles Fenno Hoffman. Hoffman may have made overtures to Melville, in respect for Gansevoort, but as far as we know Melville wrote nothing for the *Literary World* during Hoffman's editorship.

At Lansingburgh Augusta and Fanny were away in February, leaving Helen and Kate with their mother. When a letter from Lizzie to Augusta arrived, it was opened as a matter of course. Helen wrote to Augusta: "Knowing the superscription we read it, as there is nothing particular in it only a long two pages of wonderment about 'that engagement,' I will not send it by mail. I may have a private opportunity. She wont believe it yet hardly, and applies to *you* for the *truth* of the matter. When you write all you have to say *remember* is, 'I know nothing about it, except the engagement.'" What delicate shades of discretion lay behind Helen's injunction are now irrecoverable, but the wondrous engagement was Lizzie's own, acknowledged only very slowly. The whole subject of marriageability was much on the minds of all the girls, including Helen, who had not sufficiently improved her opportunities in Boston to have attracted a suitable man. (If Helen had only sent it on, Elizabeth Shaw's letter about "that engagement" might have been properly filed and then survived as part of the Augusta Papers.)

On 17 February Helen wrote to Augusta vivaciously about Saint Valentine's Day in Lansingburgh. Part of the game was to send anonymous valentines, though when the identity was suspected or known, missives had to be "duly answered." Several of the replies, including some poetical ones, were excellent. Augustus Peebles, the Lord of the Isle, had participated, as well as Mary Parmelee:

> Gus Peebles showed me one that *I think* Mary Parmelee wrote (in answer to his poetical Valentine) that was capital! He sent me a very pretty one, which I detected by means of comparing it with your *mark-book*, and I strung off some rhymes in answer forthwith, which were very fine I can assure you; both passed duly through the P.O. and neither of us "let on" that we know anything of the authors. — And that aint all, Miss Augusta, I have had *two* others, most beautiful ones, in every respect, the most "chaste" possible, in ideas — expression — chirography — paper — envelop — and seal. — Kate has had one beauty, besides the one Cuyler [Van Vechten] sent her, so I think for two modest, retiring young ladies, who have not been to a party, or any other merrymaking for a year, and so have done nothing to remind the young gentlemen of our existence, we have fared very well.

What happened within the Melville house before and after Valentine's Day 1847 was intimately tied to what was going on in the village. Just as the Melvilles arrived in the village in 1838, the "Spy" had informed the readers of the *Microscope* that fornication in Lansingburgh was too rampant for him to refrain from denouncing it. Now, nine years later, due to war fever, a clumped group of marriageable young folk, or whatever cause, there was an outbreak of flirtatiousness and other forms of romantic emotionality involving members of the family, stirred by outright eroticism involving some of their neighbors.

Time had not yet passed any of the Melville daughters by, but Aunt Lucy, Aunt Jean, and Aunt Priscilla were monitory figures: marriage should not be indefinitely postponed. Even before Gansevoort's death, Augusta had been engaged to her witty, deferential, and obliging second cousin John Van Schaick, who lived in Troy. A year before, on 14 January 1846, Augusta Whipple Hunter had reminded Augusta (also Gus or Guss, or Dutty, among other names) of her own partiality to Van Schaick: "Guss you were kind in mentioning John Van Schaick — An old flame of your ladyship's — The only wonder in my mind has been, how you could so cruelly treat him — For my part I never liked it much for John was always a great favorite of mine." A charming, ebullient slight fellow with a full measure of the family's verbal wit, Van Schaick remained on good terms with Maria, his father's first cousin, and with all the Melville children. Early in 1847, while engagement was fueling engagement in Lansingburgh, Augusta became engaged again, to Gus Peebles, like John a second cousin — and a second cousin of John's. Only Herman remembered, even if he had not comprehended, the state of agitation that had vibrated through the Green Street house in the late 1820s; now when he was home, intermittently, he may have felt tensions not unakin to that belated suppressed tumult.

Augusta Whipple Hunter and the Gansevoort cousins in Bath, New York, heard something of the unwonted romantic excitement in the village, for early the next year (on 3 January 1848) she wrote to Augusta Melville from there about the rumors of romances emanating from Lansingburgh throughout 1847. Elizabeth Albro had run off with Edward Martin Jr. of New York City, but he had married her in London on 27 July 1847, so Mrs. Hunter, although grieved to hear the details, still hoped that all might "end well." Neighbors in Lansingburgh could behave as they would, but Elizabeth Shaw, safely at home in Boston, and not even considering a new visit to the village on the Hudson, remained a model of decorum and caution. In late January 1847 Lizzie had written (probably to Helen) that Herman was expected at Boston if only for one day, on his way home from Washington, an indication to Maria that "this visit to Washington must be a very sudden affair." It was 9 March before Herman got to Boston (unless he had been there in February); he may have been the one who charged out Washington Irving's *History of New York* on Shaw's membership at the old Boston Athenæum on Pearl Street that day (the fine new building opened two years later). When he first planned the visit to Boston, it had been with the hope of presenting Shaw and his daughter with details of employment at the Custom House and, most likely, with ideas about how he might continue his literary career, in a modest way, so that he could consolidate his place as an American author without being wholly dependent on what he could earn from writing. Having failed in Washington, Herman was in no position to press aggressively for an early wedding, and, however persuasive he managed to be, Elizabeth did not set a wedding day.

Herman was probably back in Lansingburgh soon after 12 March, when Augusta wrote Aunt Susan that they were "expecting him every day." On the same day, not worrying about a long-delayed breakup of the Hudson that year, Sophia Thurston sent Augusta an invitation to visit her in New York: "It seems to me that there can be no obstacles to prevent your coming. The river is now closed it is true, but it will be open in a few days, and Herman is coming to New York about that time I hear, so there will be no difficulty about an escort." Herman did go down, but he went alone, hovering near the Harper establishment on Cliff Street. He was in New York when news came of the fall of Vera Cruz to the American forces at the end of March, and could celebrate with Allan the fact that poor tormented Guert had distinguished himself in the nautical phase of this first major amphibious campaign in the history of the young nation.

John Van Schaick must have been very familiar with his second cousin Augustus Peebles, who was now contemplating a marriage that would create an Augustus-Augusta partnership. Born in 1822, a year or so younger than Augusta, this Cousin Augustus (he was not the only one of that name), no longer the heir but the owner of Hanver Island, in the Hudson between Lansingburgh and Waterford, had remained, for the years the Melvilles had known him at Lansingburgh, in a prolonged phase of adolescent and post-adolescent arrogance. On 8 February 1847, Maria made a few astringent observations to Augusta, punning as they always did on the title of the familiar Scott poem: "The Lord of the 'Isle' is well I saw him yesterday, with cross'd legs on stool: — cutting his nails, ever & anon, most leisurely throwing away the minute particles to the distance of exactly two feet, two inches from him. 'Dutty, Dutty' I know not what to say." What Maria left unspoken, and what Helen may have implied by reference to the bookmark Augustus had inscribed, Maria still left unspoken in a letter to Augusta on 30 May 1847: "Augustus Peebles is in fine spirits & looking very well, & moreover getting some very extravagant Ideas 'would be happy to go abroad if he had a wife, & she had a taste for these things,' and many other astonishing remarks such as eating off of 'Silver being far preferable to eating off of China,' now do you not think he is getting rather lofty in his notions, he is very polite to Helen, bringing her flowers, whenever she 'asks for them,' he took Fanny to the 'May day' too, but he ask'd her to go." Whatever the precise import of Maria's comments on her first cousin's son, Hope Shaw explicitly recorded in a letter to her nephew Sam Savage on 13 August 1847, "Augusta Melville is to be married to Mr. Augustus Peebles of Lansingburgh this autumn," and Lizzie needlessly reported to the same youth in September the latest news about "Dutty": "She is engaged to Augustus Peebles and will probably be married before the end of the winter."

When Sam Savage reached New York City on 27 April, Augusta was still in Lansingburgh. He went to see his "friend Allan" on Wall Street and "found Herman there also," and glad to see him (as he wrote to Hope Savage Shaw on 30 April): "They inquired particularly abo all & Herman a little more particularly abo my coz Eliz." After considerable chat Herman took him off "to the Harpers to see his book & their immense printing Establishment and it was quite a curiosity to see too." Sam Savage later met the Melville brothers and started with them "for Hoboken on the Jersey shore a beautiful place" (the bucolic Elysian Fields of Herman's boyhood), but the outing was doomed: "we got on the boat and it blew a gale and when we arrived over there the dust blew in such clouds in our faces that we were forced to beat a retreat & made a rush for the boat & sailed to N York again." This was merely bad luck. Dana Jr. in June 1851 wrote in his journal that he never saw a view in his life to surpass the view from Hoboken "for beauty & interest": "You wander in the woods, on the banks of the Hudson, under the shade of the noble trees, with the great city stretched along for miles before you, its hum of trade & work just audible across the still broad river at your feet, the shutting in of the Highlands visible up the river, & down the river the opening to the Ocean at the narrows, the whole scene enlivened by countless sails, pleasure boats, & vessels of burden, with every few minutes a huge steamer darting out with a scream & deep-drawn breathing from the slips of the city." As Herman had discovered, this extraordinary beauty was still accessible, on a good day, a little less than two thousand yards away by ferry from the Christopher Street dock.

When Allan happened to mention to Sam that he wished he had time to go up the river and bring Augusta down for the proposed visit with Sophia Thurston, Sam responded: "as I had nothing in the world to do & should like to see the Melvilles much I volunteered my services A & H having more to do now than they can attend to. Allan poor fellow is overrun with business & Herman has to be on hand abo his book which requires his constant attention." Sam spent the day of 28 April very pleasantly with Maria and her household, then took the night boat down with Augusta. When Herman returned to Lansingburgh he proved to be no good at systematic narrative of social doings, however good a storyteller he was, and Maria was left to pick up what she could, as she wrote Augusta on 17 May, after her second daughter had progressed to Boston: "You must have passed your time very pleasantly at the Thurstons, every day Herman by accident as it were, tells us something that happened while you were together." One item is known: on 4 May Herman escorted Augusta and Sophia to the Gallery of the Fine Arts in John Vanderlyn's Rotunda on Chambers Street, near the jail and City Hall, where for their three dollars they bought a certificate of membership which included lifetime free admission to the gallery. They saw several paintings by Asher B. Durand and still more by Thomas Cole, whose *Course of Empire* and *Voyage of Life* series were on exhibition.

These months Lizzie had considered herself engaged to Herman, without thinking that marriage was an immediate reality. The engagement was nebulous because Herman as yet had shown no capacity to earn a living, but some complicating awkwardness may have sprung from the fact that the parties held different regional expectations. As a Bostonian, Lizzie would normally have made the engagement public, according to the usages that the Bostonian George Griggs reviewed to Augusta on 19 October 1853:

You know it is not customary here to have an engagement remain a secret, unless for special reasons. In New York and further South I believe such an event is only known to the immediate families of the parties. . . . I think the New York custom must require a strict guard upon one's self for we have high authority that "out of the abundance of the heart the mouth speaketh." If you wish to exercise your metaphysical faculties consider this question and let me know to what conclusion they lead your mind.

The Melville brothers and sisters, half Bostonian though bred in Dutch New York ways, may have acted in a fashion that some outsiders found inexplicable. Only Allan and Sophia were comporting themselves like happy and unabashed young lovers.

Triumphant Author, Triumphant Lover

1847

I had heard as you supposed of Elizabeth Albro's hasty marriage, but if I understood you correctly, She has returned to England which I did not know. Do you imagine any reason for the steps she took? What was the character & condition of her husband? — But the most laughable of all love affairs, is Elizabeth Alvord's, husband & no husband. I think her mind must have been shattered, which is surely a most charitable view of her freaks. Guss suppose you write a novel founded on facts, a sufficient number of which you might gather from events that have transpired in Lansingburgh for a little more than a year past.

Augusta Whipple Hunter to Augusta Melville, 22 April 1848

HAVING FAILED TO PERSUADE LIZZIE to name a wedding day during his brief visit to Boston in the middle of March, Melville spent the next weeks in New York City. There he handled the last financial details for the English edition of *Omoo* and helped to shepherd the Harper edition into print. On 31 March he wrote Murray: "If 'Omoo' succeeds I shall follow it up by something else, immediately," thereby implying that if it failed he might not follow it up with anything else. It is possible that he was trying to find some sort of steady job, but it looks as if he was doing all he could to assure that *Omoo* would indeed succeed. On 2 April he sent an early copy of the next day's *Literary World* to Edwin Croswell so he could refer in the *Argus* to the announcement running there about the imminent publication of *Omoo*. On the strength of a great success the Shaws just might agree that the time had come for him and Lizzie to marry. In his own mind, he had given up hope of finding another occupation any time soon. However cautious he sounded to Murray, and however practical a tone he may have taken with his mother and the Shaws, by early April he had made up his mind to write another book, and to write it immediately, without waiting to learn whether or not *Omoo* had succeeded.

The evidence is in his book purchases. Melville's known purchases of books from Wiley & Putnam during his work on *Omoo* (source books and otherwise) had taken on such proportions as to threaten his profits from that work, and (as Merrell R. Davis showed in 1952) Melville began his plans for *Mardi* (1849) by purchasing an expensive group of potentially useful books. On 10 April 1847 at Gowans's antiquarian bookstore Melville picked up a copy of Robert Burton's *Anatomy of Melancholy* (not noticing that his father had owned that very copy). On that same day, the Harpers announced the publication of *Omoo* and gave him a line of credit upon which he began charging books at the Harper bookstore: a copy of Webster's dictionary for $2.80; Benjamin Morrell's *Narrative of Four Voyages* for $1.20; Thomas J. Jacobs's *Scenes, Incidents, and Adventures in the Pacific Ocean*, $1.00; Darwin's *Voyage of H.M.S. Beagle*, $.72; and three unidentified volumes of Harper's Family Library at $.36 each. The Wiley & Putnam bill for his very expensive ($21) six-volume set of Charles Wilkes's *United States Exploring Expedition* is dated 17 April 1847; the year before he had drawn on Wilkes for *Omoo* without having his own set. On 7 May from the Harpers he bought *Voyage of the United States Frigate Potomac* (1835) by Jeremiah N. Reynolds, author of the sensational article on the whale Mocha Dick in the May 1839 *Knickerbocker,* and the same day he acquired an 1845 New York edition of Oliver Goldsmith's *The Vicar of Wakefield*, which he had known since childhood.

From his work on *Omoo*, he still had at hand William Ellis's *Polynesian Researches*. For this book, if not for the previous one, he also drew on Daniel Tyerman and George Bennet's *Journal of Voyages and Travels* (1832). At Bartlett and Wellford's shop in the Astor House he paid three dollars for the source Davis called most useful for the start of *Mardi*, Frederick Debell Bennett's *Narrative of a Whaling Voyage round the Globe, from the Year 1833 to 1836. Comprising Sketches of Polynesia, California, the Indian Archipelago, etc., with an Account of Southern Whales, the Sperm Whale Fishery, and the Natural History of the Climates Visited* (London: Bentley, 1840). (Melville wrote "New York, June 1847" on the front free flyleaf of the first of the two volumes, the only evidence that suggests he was in the city that month.) At least one current publication proved useful. The May 1847 *Blackwood's Edinburgh Magazine* (probably available even in Lansingburgh or Troy, in one reprint or another, by early June) contained an article entitled "Belisarius, — Was He Blind?" Here Melville found comparisons of the duke of Marlborough to the Roman general Belisarius and Sarah, duchess of Marlborough, to Lady Antonina, hints which (Davis showed) he made the "basis for his characterization" of Samoa and Annatoo, a feuding South Sea couple introduced early in *Mardi*. In New York City through April and early May, Melville continued to prepare for serious work on the new book. Now that he was a professional writer, he could afford to start his book more efficiently than before. Instead of writing out a basic narrative then assembling printed sources to help him fill it out, he would assemble at the outset what he thought would be his essential sources.

Before he could think about putting pen to paper, as eldest living son he had to try to soothe and encourage various of his aggrieved or ailing kinspeople. Long before he sailed for the Pacific, the silver memorial spoons that Peter Gansevoort's widow had wanted distributed to her descendants had come to symbolize discord within the family. The law's delay had been remarkably long, but George Curtis (representing his wife and her brothers, including Guert Gansevoort) early in 1847 at last secured a judgment against the Gansevoorts of Gansevoort, Saratoga County, in his attempt to force Peter and Herman Gansevoort to settle the estate of their mother, even if it meant evicting Herman Gansevoort from his home. With a sheriff's sale looming, Herman's wife, Catherine Quackenboss Gansevoort, wrote anxiously to Peter on 28 March 1847 to enlist "all the sympathies and humanity" of his nature in behalf of Herman Gansevoort, his "honourable and manly brother, whose suffering from wounded feelings must now be total": "Yet I will make one remark. When alone with me then the strong man gives way, and upbraids himself for injustice done himself and to me who left a thrice happy home to share with him the solitude of a then desert, and now when we have by every prudent exertion been enabled to erect two neat buildings for Public Worship to be degraded by a sheriff's sale, that is too humiliating, even to minds of much lower grades than ours."

Subsequently the brothers resorted to evasive maneuverings. Herman Gansevoort assigned his property to Peter, to protect it from their brother Leonard's children, and Peter bought out Herman's interest in Stanwix Hall. Allan Melvill, Peter and Herman Gansevoort's brother-in-law, had never seen a thousand dollars he couldn't throw away, and his third son and namesake never saw a deed to property he didn't want his name on. On 1 May Allan drafted an assignment of decree by which Peter Gansevoort would assign to Allan and Herman Melville all moneys due on the recovery of Herman Gansevoort's suit in the court of chancery. Peter Gansevoort noted on the draft: "This paper I refused to sign." A year and a half later, in December 1848, Peter and Susan Gansevoort did sign a document, as did Herman and Allan (according to the "true copy" in the Berkshire Athenaeum). In it the Gansevoorts conveyed to the Melville brothers their "lands and premises situate in the town of Northumberland county of Saratoga and state of New York," in trust for the use of Herman Gansevoort during his life and after his death for the use of Maria G. Melville. Because they were always conscious that Herman Gansevoort had married a woman older than himself who would therefore die before him, they overlooked the possibility that Catherine Quackenboss Gansevoort might outlive her husband. Peter's "besetting sin" was still selfishness, but for his sister's sake he was persuaded to sign this document, which removed him as an heir to whatever family properties were held by his brother Herman Gansevoort.

For the Melville family the practical significance of Uncle Herman's sufferings lay a decade away, but for his writer nephew a literary consequence was immediate. During the late winter or early spring of 1847 Herman Melville realized that he could do something to salve the wounded feelings of his uncle, so he put into both the London and the New York edition of *Omoo* this dedication: "To Herman Gansevoort, of Gansevoort, Saratoga County, New York, this work is cordially inscribed by his nephew, the author." Nicely spaced, in graduated type, it looked stately, and Herman sent up an early copy, inscribed: "Gen. Herman Gansevoort from his nephew the Author. New York, April 31st 1847" (perhaps 1 May?). Nephew Herman must have seen Uncle Herman before this, after his return from the South Seas, but this summer for the first time there is a surviving record of Herman's visiting the uncle distinguished by his "portly figure & substantial Dutch bearing" (as Melville referred to him in a letter to Murray in October). Proud of the achievements of his namesake, Herman Gansevoort made this formal notation in his "remembrancer" for 21 July: "The Author of Typee & Omoo came here this evening (Mr Melvill) and his mother Mrs Melvill"; they left on the morning of 23 July. This was a healing visit, but also a long-range planning session for at least Uncle Herman and Maria: what would happen if Catherine, his querulous, domineering, and aging wife, still cursed with an intact memory of her deprivations in exile from Manhattan, could no longer take care of him?

Acting again as a conscientious kinsman even before the unlikely thirty-first of April, Herman had asked the Harpers to bind up an advance copy of *Omoo* for him to put on a ship headed to Rio, where his ailing second cousin Augustus Van Schaick had been sent to recuperate, after stopping by Lansingburgh. There during Herman's last visit Maria Peebles (born a Van Schaick) had read him a considerable portion of one of Augustus's letters, and in the letter of 26 April 1847 that accompanied his book Herman wrote cheerfully to his "Dear Augustus":

> I was much pleased to see that you had by no means lost that pleasantry of humor you had when here—From this I infer that you are not quite cast-down & indeed I think you have no reason to be, seeing that the beautiful climate of Rio must reinvigorate you & make you a robust fellow after all. That this will prove to be the case is my sincere & fervent wish. If you will take the advice of one who loves you you will keep up a valiant heart—Nil Desperandum—so as to come back to us again & send a challenge across the

water to fight Bendigo for the Champion's Belt of all England. — All whom I see desire much happiness for you & send regard[s].

("Bendigo" was William Thompson, a boxer from Nottingham.)

A valuable member of the extensive Van Schaick–Gansevoort family, now that his fame almost made up for his poverty, Herman wrote Augustus Van Schaick another letter on 11 June, again offering jocular comfort, and assuring him of shared knowledge of distant climes: "I have heard many of your letters read — & your descriptions & the names of various localities you mention are quite familiar to me. Preya Grande &c &c. — Rio harbor you must certainly confess the most glorious sheet of water in the universe. As a sailor 'I can not sufficiently admire it.' " This was in Herman's best manner of dealing with downcast members of the family when he was himself in good spirits — very like encouragement he was to give Sam Savage in 1851. It is not known just where all the Van Schaick cousins hung on the family tree, and sometimes only an isolated reference survives to show that intimacy existed among third, fourth, or fifth cousins who in that era, in that stable locality, were not thought of as "distant." Whatever their earlier contacts with this other Augustus, Herman was now doing his part, and others in the family were doing theirs, by sending him letters, gifts, and healing good wishes. The female members of the family, just at this time, may have been far more upset about troubles between John De Peyster Douw and his wife, Margaret Van Rensselaer Douw, than they were about the illness of Augustus Van Schaick, but Maggie's troubles, as always, were of the sort that a gentlewoman could not quite put down on paper. (On 11 June Helen wrote Augustus Van Schaick a long letter. Ailing though he was, Augustus was now the adventurer: "Our village remains very much as you left it, few startling events occur to break the monotony & our days pass in a quiet dearth of excitement very healthful no doubt, and conducive to longevity.")

Meanwhile, having made elaborate plans for the book, or at least having assembled a working library before starting it, Herman apparently decided that it would be unwise to begin writing before he learned how *Omoo* was faring in London and how it would do at home. The book was published in London on 30 March as *Omoo: A Narrative of Adventures in the South Seas; Being a Sequel to the "Residence in the Marquesas Islands"* — not *Being a Sequel to "Typee."* Murray was holding to his antipathy to the look and sound of "Typee," despite his previous agreement that in future printings Melville's first book would bear his barbaric main title. Not knowing the exact date of the publication of *Omoo*, Melville on 31 March expressed his hopes to Murray: "I trust that the reception which has been predicted for 'Omoo' may be verified by the event." Melville saw, all in all, many of the British reviews, through the good offices of Brodhead and through re-publications of English reviews in this country and comments on British reviews in American newspapers. As early as 12 May Thurlow Weed quoted the London *Spectator* of 10 April in the Albany *Evening Journal*, so chances are that before then other early London reviews, such as those in the *Athenæum*, the *Britannia*, and the *Critic*, had reached New York and Boston. Weed entitled his article " 'Who Reads an American Book?' " — jibing at Sydney Smith's notorious question in the 1820 *Edinburgh Review:* "It is but a few years since this question was sneeringly asked in English Reviews! But such questions are no longer asked. American Books, 'that *are* Books,' have not only readers but admirers in England." Melville had to wait until late April and early May to be sure that the British reviews of *Omoo* were as favorable as he could have hoped.

As Melville should have expected, reviewers had to confront their prejudice against a sequel, which all experience showed was bound to be inferior to its predecessor. On 10 April the London *Spectator* gave its verdict: "Unlike most sequels" *Omoo* was "equal to its predecessor," despite there not being "the same novelty of subject." On 24 April the alternative verdict on *Omoo* went out in the London *Home News; A Summary of European Intelligence for India and the Colonies:* "Though good, it is not nearly so good as its predecessor, partly because it offers rather 'the rinsings of the cup,' and partly for the cause which makes the first bumper of champagne taste better than those that follow. Typee gave us the cream of the author's experience or fancy, and had, besides, the freshness of novelty: Omoo has more the flavour of skimmed milk, a more homely and familiar beverage, but still very pleasant and refreshing, and by no means to be despised." On 26 April the London *Sun* professed to have been so charmed by *Typee* ("It came upon us with the freshness of a treasure discovered where one was least expected") that *Omoo* was "nothing in comparison": " 'Typee' is as pure gold to the lacquer of 'Omoo.' Yet 'Omoo' is lively, sparkling, humourous, conversational, diversified with little episodes of ocean life and vivid descriptions of southern scenery." *Omoo* was comparatively deficient "in romance and incident," but agreeably penned, "and evidently written with the utmost truthfulness." On 30 April a provincial paper, the *Nottingham Review and General Advertiser for the Midland Counties*, pronounced it "just one of those works which, once commenced, so fascinates the reader, that he finds it difficult to lay it down until he has devoured every page"; it was a "worthy sequel," and "destined to become as great a favorite with the adventure-loving public." The London *Guardian* on 16 June saw no reason "why 'Omoo' should not be popular," though it was, "perhaps, not equal to the work that preceded it"; *Typee* had broken ground in a new direction ("which is a great thing with the many who read for amusement, and to supply whose appetite all the remote corners of the world are laid unto contribution, just as earth, sea, and sky were ransacked to supply the tables of Roman epicures or Lord Mayors of London"). On 12 April the London *Bell's Weekly Messenger* anticipated for the new book "a popularity even surpassing that of 'Typee.'"

British reviewers frequently summarized the action of *Omoo* at considerable length and quoted many sections of the book with great relish. Extracts were most often devoted to Dr. Long Ghost, not only the initial account of him, but scenes in which he played a large part, such as the dinner-party in Eimeo (ch. 68), a visit to a Partoowye family (ch. 73), and the visit to Queen Pomare (ch. 81); his being an amorous rogue escaped the attention of no British reviewer. The reviewers also quoted passages in which Bembo the Mowree, Jermin the mate, Kooloo, and other characters figured. The reviewer on 29 May in *Chambers's Edinburgh Magazine* relished the cast of characters on the *Julia* so much that he was not about to be fully appeased by the reduction to two: "we longed to know what became of this strange crew when they sailed away from Tahiti; and we do not care to hide our discontent at having palmed upon us, as substitutes for the whole batch, merely Doctor Long Ghost and the author." Reviewers manifested strong interest in cockroaches, rats, mosquitoes, coconut trees, tattooing, and the general aspect of Tahiti (the *Times* of London exclaimed on 24 September: "How surpassingly beautiful must that island be! How enviable the rude sailor's hand which can trace its form so sweetly clear upon the canvas!"). Almost the worst anyone said was in the *Spectator.* The reviewer of *Typee* there had complained of "certain sea freedoms" that might have been removed, and now the same reviewer noted: "As in *Typee*, there are a few free passages, that might as well have been omitted." Misled by a bibliographical anomaly in its copy of *Omoo*, the *Economist* made this wistful assumption about the fate of the two companions: "Shortly after this rebuff to the Doctor's love-making efforts, our adventurous couple, we are led to believe, joined another whaler, but the last sheet of the volume being absent, their ultimate fate is unknown to us." He retained his goodwill: "as the story is interesting, we hope none of the readers of the Home and Colonial Library will be in a similar predicament."

Naturally the British reviewers approved of Melville's hostility toward the French seizure of Tahiti (a sign that the author was in fact British?) and his hostility toward the missionaries, and often treated the two topics in the same passage. *Bell's Weekly Messenger* declared that Melville's testimony was "little favourable to the smartness and seamanlike qualities" of France. The *Economist* underwrote Melville: "The moral and religious condition of the inhabitants of Tahiti is touched upon at some length, and we have no doubt that Mr Melville's views with regard to the conduct and influence of the missionaries, are quite correct." *John Bull* on 17 April took Melville as criticizing the missionaries out of a sense of the need to tell the truth: "At Tahiti the author resided for a considerable period, and his account of the island, of the natives, of the proceedings of the French, and of the conduct of the missionaries (whom he is not inclined to spare), form by far the most valuable and interesting portions of the work." The reviewer wished "he had spoken with more respect of the missionaries, and that the names of individuals had not been so openly mentioned; for instance, that of the acting British Consul at Tahiti." These were lapses "excusable in a young American, who appears to be more than usually endowed with the roving disposition of his country-men." In its belated (24 September) review, the *Times* combined its com-ments on the French and the missionaries in the Pacific as dual polluters:

> Lovely land, happy people! — and doomed to be defaced and polluted by the foot of civilization; people left to be brutalized, corrupted, and destroyed by the professors of Christianity. Strange that the boasted triumphs of five cen-turies' ardent prosecution of science, art, and noble deeds, and the mildest, holiest faith the world has ever seen, can be transplanted to the antipodes only to bring havoc to innocence and misery to unoffending virtue! Shall we sum up the good that France has effected in Oceania, or that English missionaries have produced in the benighted islands which, under their half-spiritual, half-civil government, have become far more gloomy?

The writer continued with an eloquent and elaborate discussion that in-cluded this declaration:

> Mr. Melville's account of missionary doings agrees with all that has reached us from trustworthy travellers. . . . Subscriptions raised in Exeter Hall, under the influence of provincial eloquence, will hardly purchase the poor heathen's soul or effect one *bona fide* conversion, let the money be spent as it may. Before attempting the conversion of the savage it would be wiser to reclaim him from his savageness. We have invariably, with our murderous strong drinks and lamentable practices, rendered him a greater brute than when we first dis-covered him.

The word "provincial" is telling: a major difference between American mis-sionary work and British was that the effort was perceived in London review-ing circles as low church and provincial, while in the United States it was low church, indeed, but the most popular churches were low church, and the most successful fundraising occurred in the metropolitan areas. In these British reviews Melville was taken seriously as an informed observer and a cautious social commentator.

Once again the British reviewers compared Melville to other nautical writers and adventure writers. The *Spectator* thought Dana and his imitators had already taken some of the freshness from Melville's portrayal of "nautical life and character as seen from the foremastman's point of view," while many writers had described the natives of Polynesian islands "*au naturel.*" Dana and Melville were equal authorities in depicting little "ill-treatment of the natives by the sailor or the outcast." The *Britannia* thought that "without being a copyist" Melville had "caught the spirit of Cooper's nautical style." *Douglas Jerrold's* made the first new comparison to Defoe, saying that *Omoo* possessed "much of the charm that has made Robinson Crusoe immortal — life-like description," then compared the book to Cooper's *The Red Rover* in depicting a ship's crew "composed of seamen from most of the maritime people of the world." The *Literary Gazette* took the book wholly as fiction, "carrying on Mr. Melville's imaginary adventures in the Pacific in the same Crusoe-ish vein" as before, and dashing off "his feats and exploits by sea and land in a style worthy of Philip Quarles or Robinson Crusoe, as aforesaid." *Blackwood's* declared Melville to be "the phoenix of modern voyagers, sprung, it would seem, from the mingled ashes of Captain Cook and Robinson Crusoe." Kept from "light literature" by a "long session of Parliament and a general election," the *Times* weighed in on 24 September with a comparison to Irving worth Melville's waiting for:

> Herman Melville is as clever and learned as ever. Sailor before the mast as he is, he discourses as pleasantly and humorously of Nature in her hundred aspects as the gentle Washington Irving himself, the Prince of story-tellers, the most delicate and touching of painters. Melville professes to be born in the same region as Irving, and we are bound to believe him. But the man puzzles us. Common sailor he is not. If he be an American, he is quite as familiar with English literature and London streets as he is with Bryant and Longfellow, Broadway and Long Island. If he needs an illustration, Regent-street occurs to him as it would to Mr. Dickens; the cockney not the Kentuckian is the subject of his satire, and King John and George IV. supply matter for discussion which Washington and Jackson fail to furnish. To say the least, these are suspicious facts.

Although quite "as fascinating a production as *Robinson Crusoe,*" *Omoo* was "twenty times less probable." Even when narrating unlikely incidents, Defoe had maintained a convincing "air of wild reality." Melville had not kept out the "hitches" that alert even children to something doubtful about the authenticity of the narration: "The illusion is not perfect. The artificial is mixed with the natural; the *vraisemblable* with the utterly improbable; the craftsman peeps out where the untutored traveller should alone be visible; the man of letters writing for Mr. Murray clashes alternately with the sailor frisking at his ease with the natives of the Southern seas." There were conspicuously fewer of such comparisons to other writers than in the reviewing of *Typee*, partly because the situation in that book was more strikingly close to the one in *Robinson Crusoe*, partly because although still a center of speculation, or even controversy, as to his authenticity, Melville was no longer quite the novelty he had been early in 1846.

From first to last the British reviews stressed the pleasures Melville offered in *Omoo* — "sufficient freshness," as the *Spectator* said, a "fluent vivacious style" that created interest, and "a natural aptitude for describing a scene or telling a story." The *Spectator* put a finger on what it called the "true characteristic of the book," its "nautical pictures" and "the glimpses it gives of the strange characters that are to be found scattered over the South Seas":

> The outcasts of all nations would seem to congregate there. The little law anywhere, its total absence in some of the islands, the readiness with which a subsistence may be procured, and the *dolce far niente* indulged in a climate where fuel and clothes may both be dispensed with, are all attractions to the runaway convict or the broken-down adventurer. . . . Yet it seems wonderful what a sense of right and wrong obtains among them towards Europeans; and if they do not extend the same feeling to the natives, it seems owing to ignorance, and the example of their superiors: nor indeed has this catholic morality long prevailed even in England, as it does not yet in many nations of Europe. Little ill-treatment of the natives by the sailor or the outcast, however, appears either in Dana or Melville; and perhaps little takes place, unless in a brawl. Polynesian hospitality satisfies their wants; the general licentiousness gratifies their passions; and they lead an easy and uncontrolled life, removed from all temptation which requires violence or crime to indulge in.

Looking beyond Melville's comments on the evils of French colonialism and the devastating effects attempted Christianizing had wrought on the natives, the reviewer responded deeply to Melville's suggestive portraits of the kind of lives hundreds, or thousands, of Britons were then living on the fringes of the Empire, Britons oddly mixed in with the outcasts of all nations. Throughout Victoria's Empire, *Omoo* from the start had personal resonances for many British readers.

Doubts of authenticity, the old bugbear, reappeared as a problem for the reviewer in the *Athenæum* (10 April): "As a roving sailor the author spent, he says, about three months in various parts of Tahiti and Imeeo; and under circumstances most favourable for correct observations on the social condition of the natives. The authenticity of his statements is thus asserted incidentally and as of course — but without any direct answer being given to the doubts which have been thrown on the reality of his former narrative." The *Economist* on 10 April made an unusual claim to personal knowledge of life on shipboard in the South Seas: "the characters of some of the sailors are exceedingly well drawn, and we can venture, from our own knowledge, to vouch for the correctness of many of Mr Melville's descriptions." The *Britannia* on the same day suspected "perhaps some romantic licence in dealing with facts," but took seriously Melville's "melancholy" comments on the fate of the natives of Tahiti. In Edinburgh the June *Blackwood's Magazine*, under the heading "Pacific Rovings," devoted fourteen pages to *Omoo*, taking the occasion as a chance to display scintillating verbal pyrotechnics, almost irresistibly quotable. *Omoo* was "of the order composite, a skilfully concocted Robinsonade, where fictitious incident is ingeniously blended with genuine information." "Melville" had visited the South Seas, but not as a sailor, least of all as a whaler: "His speech betrayeth him"; "his tone is refined and well-bred; he writes like one accustomed to good European society, who has read books and collected stores of information, other than could be perused or gathered in the places and amongst the rude associates he describes. These inconsistencies are glaring, and can hardly be explained." Perhaps Melville was an educated British lad driven to sea by some "wild freak or unfortunate act of folly, or a boyish thirst for adventure." The very name of the author was cause for suspicion: "Herman Melville sounds to us vastly like the harmonious and carefully selected appellation of an imaginary hero of romance. Separately the names are not uncommon; we can urge no valid reason against their junction, and yet in this instance they fall suspiciously on our ear. We are similarly impressed by the dedication. Of the existence of Uncle Gansevoort, of Gansevoort, Saratoga County, we are wholly incredulous." The reviewer set down poor Herman Gansevoort, "the gentleman with the Dutch patronymic," as "a member of an imaginary clan." In December the *Dublin Review* (taking twenty-three pages) found *Omoo* full of " 'wonders' " — the first being how such a book could have been written by one who had sailed before the mast. Simply claiming to be an American was grounds for suspicion: "Then again, the fact that Mr. Melville 'hails from' Yankee Land, (for he dedicates his work 'To Herman Gansevoort, of Gansevoort, Saratoga County, New York,' with whom he claims consanguinity,) is a circumstance which excites suspicion. Not that we would be supposed to hold the bigoted theory, that every Yankee tale is like 'that 'tarnal sea-sarpint' of which there is neither end nor beginning — as we opine. Far otherwise, but we do mean to say that the 'States' are a very large country, and it is very difficult to identify our author by his tone, habits, or thoughts, with any of the peculiar classes into which the land is divided." All this, especially the earliest skepticism, was perturbing to Murray, especially a few months later, when he was pressured to remove the books from the Home and Colonial Library.

Around November 1847 Sir Walter Farquhar wrote to Lord Ashley: "My dear Ashley, I am anxious that you should speak to Mr. Murray on the subject of two volumes in the Home and Colonial Library, entitled *Typee* and *Omoo*, by Herman Melville. In the original prospectus of this series it is stated to be the publisher's intention to publish a number of useful and entertaining volumes — the utmost care being at all times exercised in the selection of the works, *so that they shall contain nothing offensive to morals or good taste.*" Murray had broken his pledge in publishing these two books: "By a rather unsparing editorial pruning both these volumes might have been less objectionable — under any circumstance their tone is, I think, reprehensible throughout." Farquhar's further comments on tone fit with some comments that American reviewers had by this time made: "They are not works that any mother would like to see in the hands of her daughters, and as such are not suited to lie on the drawing-room table." He wanted assurance from Murray that there should not appear in his series another volume similar in character, for without such assurance he should "be reluctantly compelled to cease subscribing to the series." This letter was forwarded to Murray, who accepted it as one more in a litany of complaints first about *Typee* then about *Omoo* also. But he left the volumes in his library.

The "Home and Colonial Library" (also called "Colonial and Home Library") was more than a mere title: all the books in the library did indeed sell together, at times, and furthermore sold together or singly at the ends of the earth, which is to say at the farthest outposts of the British Empire. Murray packaged *Typee* and *Omoo* with other books in the library, shipped them around the country and around the world with other books, promoted them in ads in other books, all the time creating respect for Melville by the mere act of listing him along with well-known writers. This was not only highly flattering but also beneficial for sales and reputation. Melville was not in any position to understand just how significant for his worldwide fame his inclusion in the library was. He did not have ready access, for instance, to the *China Mail*, the official organ of all government notifications in Hong Kong, which on 25 November 1847 listed as available at Mackay & Co., in both Hong Kong and Canton, twenty-two volumes in "MURRAY'S COLONIAL LIBRARY":

Heber's Indian Journal, 2 vols. — Irby and Mangle's Drinkwater — Barbary's Baltic — Amber Witch, Cromwell, and Bunyan — Drake's New South Wales — Ripa's China, and Lewis's West Indies — Malcolm's Sketches of Persia — Agiers, the Jesuits — Bracebridge Hall — Darwin's Naturalist's Voyage — Life of Condé — Livonian Tales, Missionary in Canada — Sale's Brigade, Madras — Borrow's Bible in Spain — Ford's Gatherings from Spain — Melville's Marquesas Islands — Borrow's Gypsies of Spain — St John's Highland

Sports — Sketches of German Life — Head's Pampas — Seiges of Vienna —
Adventures in the South Seas.

In the course of things many a young man must have been sent forth into
outposts of the Empire with a set of the library, an obvious choice for a
durable, educative gift, assertively expensive but not outlandishly extravagant. If an Englishman sailed from home without the library, it might pursue
him a year or two later, the ideal present from any Uncle Reginald or Aunt
Agatha to any young Algernon in Calcutta or Canton. Over the decades
Melville's presence in the library insured the fame of his first two books with
two or three generations of English readers all around the world. The fact
that no subsequent book of his was included in the library limited his widest
fame to his first two books, but it made those two undeniable classics of
literature in the English language.

The British reviews, many of which Melville saw, did not influence the
earliest American reviews and did not immediately influence Melville himself, for this time the publication was more nearly simultaneous than the
publication of *Typee* had been. Reviewers of the Harper edition (available
earlier, but officially published about 1 May, a Saturday) encountered a book
with a shorter title than the English edition, *Omoo: A Narrative of Adventures
in the South Seas*. Once again Melville tried to manage the local reception of a
book by planting information in Croswell's Albany *Argus*. Gansevoort's loyal
friend responded with an item on 7 April, "New Work by the Author of
'Typee,'" in which he relayed Melville's boast about "the high price readily paid for the copyright by the great London publisher." The announcement in the 10 April *Literary World* may have given an authentic early title:
"Messrs. Harper & Brothers have just ready Mr. Melville's new publication,
'Omoo, or South Sea Rovings.'" Two weeks later, using proof sheets supplied by Melville, Duyckinck printed "The French Priests Pay Their Respects" (ch. 37) and "A Dinner-Party in Imeeo" (ch. 68). Since the British
critics had established Melville as a serious writer the year before, subservient American journalists did not need to be told now that he was worth
reading, and were free to react to *Omoo* with prompt superficial and patriotic
praise. The New York *Spirit of the Times* on 24 April recommended *Omoo* on
the strength of "the peculiar characteristic power and brilliancy of the author's former work." On 1 May Weed in the Albany *Evening Journal* was
equally hopeful: "favorably impressed with 'Typee,' the reading public will
take up 'Omoo' with alacrity." The New York *Evening Mirror* on 1 May had
the book "in advance of its publication," courtesy of the Harpers, and opined
that the author had "lost nothing of the freshness and vigor of style, which, as
much as the novelty of his subject, gave so great a popularity to Typee."

On 2 May the New York *Atlas* was brief and friendly, but the New York *Sunday Times & Noah's Weekly Messenger* was fulsome: "Melville is the greatest writer of the age, in his way, and has deservedly been styled the 'De Foe of America.'" "In his way" was a serious check on the opening words, but some of the family must have amused themselves reading the first eight words in various intonations. On 2 May Weed described what he had read so far (half of the first volume) but glanced ahead at something controversial: "The second Volume, we understand, gives an unfavorable account of the character and labors of Missionaries in the Polynesian Islands. In this respect, the Book will probably give offence. If, however, Missionaries in that portion of the World are less faithful and devoted than the hundreds of pious and self-sacrificing Christian Philanthropists who teach by example as well as precept, in China, India, Birmah, &c., it is well that the fact be known." On 3 May the *Argus* praised "the clever and pleasing style of narration and remark for which the author is distinguished," and announced its approval of the dedication to "Herman Gansevoort, of Gansevoort, Saratoga county, uncle of the author." Local interest suffused the conclusion of the notice in the Troy *Northern Budget* on 4 May: "More might be added to this notice, but the readers of 'Typee,' who comprise the whole reading community, will require no more."

The writer in the Boston *Post* on 5 May was skeptical of Melville's veracity, but acknowledged that "Columns on columns of pleasant extracts might be given." He had two quibbles: "One wishes that Mr Melville had not been quite so chary of relating his own adventures with the fair Tahitians. We hope his next book may have a Christian title." Walter Whitman probably wrote the unsigned note in the Brooklyn *Eagle* on 5 May, a recommendation of *Omoo* "as thorough entertainment — not so light as to be tossed aside for its flippancy, nor so profound as to be tiresome." In New York on the fifth someone in Bryant's *Evening Post,* still resentful toward Gansevoort Melville, allowed stiffly that *Omoo* seemed "to have all the liveliness of Mr. Melville's other work *Typee,* which was so popular, and like that will probably be much read." In Troy on 5 May the *Daily Whig* had an enthusiastic review by someone who had found time to read much of the book: "'OMOO' is *not* inferior to Typee. The same fascinating style of narration, the same fresh unhackneyed, ingenuous mode of conveying the author's impressions to the reader, and a series of incidents and adventures just as exciting and amusing as those which occurred to the hero of Typee, render this work quite as interesting as its popular predecessor." On 6 May the Boston *Daily Chronotype* saw there might be trouble:

Instead of the primitive valley of stark paganism, and unsophisticated nature, the mongrel mixture of savagism and Christianity is here the subject. There is no lack of scenes, however, that are wholly Captain Cookish, and painted in the liveliest colors. — The author seems not to be a prejudiced witness, yet in describing the results of the Missionary operations he pitches his tune a full octave below the Missionary Herald's — indeed, he tells some stories which would not have a very happy effect upon the contribution box at a "Monthly Concert."

On 8 May the reviewer (probably British-born) in the New York *Albion* (the paper catering to the colony of expatriate Britons in New York) was charmed: "Omoo and Typee are actually delightful romances of real life, embellished with powers of description, and a graphic skill of hitting off characters," which it declared "little inferior to the highest order of novelist and romance writers" — remarkable praise to put next to "Melville is the greatest writer of the age, in his way." On 8 May the New York *Anglo-American* prophesied: " 'Omoo' is destined to create a prodigious sensation in the literary circles." That same day in New York the *Christian Inquirer* was extraordinarily charitable in saying the reader must overlook Melville's sailor excesses and "be content with very good picture-writing, no little shrewdness and causticity of remark, and a ceaseless and abounding flow of animal spirits."

The New York *Literary World* on 8 May 1847 declared that few American books had awakened the "lively interest" excited by *Typee*. Duyckinck had lost control of the magazine to Charles Fenno Hoffman the week before, so the likelihood is that the older man, Hoffman, was the author of this review of *Omoo*, which draws on a long urban memory:

> To many, the theme was entirely new; to others, Commodore [David] Porter's once famed, and now nearly forgotten journal, had long since commended it, and they seized upon Mr. Melville's book with the avidity that children take up any new volume which purports to be a continuation of Robinson Crusoe. In the city of New York, especially, from which the three or four of Porter's surviving officers hailed originally, Typee was remembered in years far back as the theme of many a dinner-table yarn, when men used to tell longer and *stronger* stories over their Madeira than is now the fashion among modern sherry drinkers. And while the world abroad were showing their acuteness in detecting Mr. Melville as a veteran bookmaker, who, being master of a brilliant style, had ingeniously fashioned a most readable piece of Munchausenism while sitting in his library, his work was at once recognised as a genuine narrative in the city where it was published.

The writer said Melville's description of the bay at Tahiti would remind his readers of a panorama exhibited in the fall of 1840, Frederick Catherwood's

"Bay of Islands." (The New York *Mirror* on 5 September 1840 had called it "one of the boldest and best representations of savageism, and of a scenery best befitted to represent it in, that was ever looked upon"; it is possible Melville saw it then, before signing on the *Acushnet*.) Though it was probably Hoffman who wrote this review, Duyckinck was becoming steadily more important to Melville. The year before, the intricacies of defending and expurgating *Typee* had led Melville to leave a note behind for Duyckinck every time he left town, it seemed, but now early in 1847 he formed a new pattern, becoming "a frequent visitor at No 20," as Duyckinck wrote to George on 14 May — 20 Clinton Place. (Trusting that the new neighborhood would be stable, the conservative Duyckincks had moved to 20 Clinton Place from Bleecker in 1841 even though it was at the far edge of town, north of Washington Square, near Broadway.) An obituary writer long afterward grandly compared Duyckinck's house at 20 Clinton Place to that of Samuel Rogers, the English poet, whose hospitality in St. James's Square Melville would sample in 1849. There was no true comparison architecturally between the London house and the New York one, or in art works (Rogers's collection was magnificent, paintings a prince would have been proud of), yet in number and rarity of books there was a genuine similarity, and indeed both houses were "always the resort of the most eminent literary men of the country."

Another knowledgeable review appeared in the Newark *Daily Advertiser* for the next Monday, 10 May. The writer was in a position "to judge of the truthfulness as well as of the picturesqueness" of Melville's "descriptions of life and manners in the South Seas," having survived a "career of nautical vagabondism" not unlike that described in Melville's "bewitching yarns," except that he had not experienced a "paradisiacal sojourn in the wondrous valley of Typee." Confirming all that Melville said about "the character of the Tahitian nation, as developed under the two-fold influence of sailors and missionaries," he offered this personal affidavit: "It being my hap to be thrown in very much with the well-meaning supporters of the latter institution, I have been often mortified by their evident incredulity when I stated facts with respect to the present condition of these interesting converts, which, with the missionary Heralds and Intelligencers before them, in the face, we may say, of Moses and the prophets, were not to be believed, though one should rise from the dead." Understanding fully that Captain Wilkes had been little but a tool of the missionaries, co-opted into writing the history of the exploring expedition as a celebration of the Pacific missions, the writer had rejoiced when *Typee* appeared: "We were glad therefore to see a plain and honest statement of things with which a month's stay in Tahiti had made us too well acquainted. How the public have received Mr. Melville's 'experience' I do not know — but for ourselves, a whilome cosmopolite and impartial observer of things in the South Seas, we do not hesitate to give him a grip of approval, and repeat the oft-pronounced but, till his genial spell awakened old associations, the almost forgotten encomium *'matai.'* " This encouraging reinforcement was not picked up by other papers, as far as is known, and there is no record of Melville's seeing it.

There was a third intelligent review, on 11 May, in the New York *Gazette and Times*, which Hoffman probably had some connection with still, enough to assign the review, perhaps, if not write it himself. Among other thoughtful comments, the author linked the natives of the South Sea islands to the American Indians:

> The statements which are made in relation to the missionary establishments, and the labors of these religious emissaries must inevitably attract great attention. Evils, barely hinted at in Typee, are openly detailed in the present work, and as the testimony of an unbiassed intelligent witness, the facts and the results which the writer adduces, must make a deep impression. As with the Indian of our own continent, contact with the white man, has only served to entail upon the primitive, simple and happy people of the South Sea Islands, the worst vices, and to introduce diseases, from the ravages of which the race is becoming gradually but surely extinct. This is a melancholy subject of reflection, but it is one nevertheless, which can neither be denied nor extenuated.

In his purely literary comments, the reviewer observed that there were in *Omoo* enough "original characters dashingly and concisely hit off, to set up a score of modern novelists."

By mid-May, before some of the most favorable reviews appeared, Melville was home in Lansingburgh, just at the wrong time for any peace. As Maria explained on 17 May to Augusta, who was visiting her pregnant cousin Nilly Van Rensselaer Thayer, on Mt. Vernon Street, she and her other daughters had spent three weeks in the relentless rigors of her annual Dutch housecleaning. The upheaval was so dire that it prompted the self-absorbed Augustus Peebles to take pity on Herman and carry him "out to the Island" one day, Herman paying his way by rowing. After the cleaning, Maria said, she had nothing to do but prepare Kate and others for the large wedding planned for 8 June — that of Kate Van Vechten to Elisha P. Hurlbut. Kate was the special friend of young Kate Melville, who therefore had to be much in Albany. As always, plans for one wedding reminded everyone of other weddings that might take place soon, if things went well, and the Van Vechten plans, one way or another, stirred up the Lansingburgh cousins, including the one who thought he might be ready to find a quiet place for writing.

Acknowledging that Herman needed a room of his own to write in, Maria devoted the last phase of the housecleaning to setting up a proper work space for the author of the now undeniably successful *Omoo*. Maria, like Herman, had a strong sense of the importance both of physical comfort and of symbolic ambiance:

> Herman just left the room & sends his love to you. We have been particularly busy to day in assisting him, in embellishing the small front room as a Library and Study. The walls have been colored, the bed-sted removed a new carpet, and curtains, the library has been remove'd and placed before the door leading into the next room, a great box & two trunks have been unpacked filld with books, and handsomely disposed together with the Ship and miniature Anchor — his Desk &c, together with three ancient mahogany Chairs from the attic, he looks, and his Study looks, ready to begin a new work, on the "South Seas" — of course.

As to his second book, *Omoo* was having, she assured Augusta, "an unprecedented run — the papers are very flattering in their notices" (a fact that Augusta had already gathered from the Boston papers). She sent her "best love to Judge & Mrs Shaw and daughter Lizzie" — the "daughter Lizzie" tacitly acknowledging that all the unpacking and pushing and hauling might be provisional, subject to disturbance again when and if Lizzie became her daughter-in-law.

Trying to seem as settled as his "Study," Herman began his new book, around the middle of May. Very likely he had the title *Mardi* in mind already. Merrell R. Davis in *Melville's "Mardi": A Chartless Voyage*, his 1952 volume in the Yale Studies in English, cited Charles Anthon's 1845 *Classical Dictionary* for the proper noun "MARDI" as the name for "a people of Asia, near the northern frontiers of Media," a likely source for the title, since "Media" is a name Melville used for one of his characters in the new book. Or Melville may simply have taken "Mardi" from the legend spread over a stretch of the waters and archipelagos of the South Seas on an old map or globe, Mar di Sud — that is, Sea of the South, or South Sea. The legend occurs sometimes with "Mar di" on one line and the word "Sud" centered underneath — a design that would have made it easy for Melville to compress "Mar di" into one word.

The book as Melville began it involved a situation reminiscent of *Typee* — an escape from a whaleship in the South Seas by the narrator and his companion, this time not a youthful confederate like Toby but an old sailor from the Isle of Skye, Jarl, and this time not by land but in an open boat. The deserters pursue a course toward the western Kingsmill Islands, during which they board an apparently deserted brigantine, the *Parki*, which proves to be inhabited by a South Sea couple, Samoa and his wife Annatoo. She is swept off the brigantine shortly before it sinks, and Samoa joins the narrator and Jarl on the *Chamois*, the open boat. The adventures to this point take up just less than a fifth of what was eventually published as *Mardi*.

Nothing in his later comments on *Mardi* suggests that Melville at the outset thought of it as different in kind from *Typee* and *Omoo*, except (a big exception) that he may already have intended the South Sea adventures to be wholly fictional, although it derived loosely from his cruise on the *Charles and Henry*. Allowing for revisions and interpolations (some of which thickened the literary allusiveness) in the opening section as it was finally published, it is clear that he was writing in those early weeks of May and June of 1847 some of the essayistic chapters that would make this book a cult favorite with some English readers forty years later. What he had in hand in the early weeks of his writing was remarkable for confident expansiveness of style and subject, as in chapter 1, where the sailor-narrator regards the Pacific "as one mighty harbor," so "what matters it, though hundreds of miles from land, if a good whale-boat be under foot, the Trades behind, and mild, warm seas before?" Chapter 2 is devoted to an attempt to convey the impressions felt in a calm at sea, "certain nameless associations" that can yet be evoked to the wonder and delight of the reader. In chapter 3 Melville's own alluring ingenuousness shone through his account of the impossibility of disguising human nature at sea: "You wear your character as loosely as your flowing trowsers." He was elegant in his generalizations about human subjectivities: "To ourselves, we all seem coeval with creation," he asserted in chapter 3. In chapter 4 he expatiated on another feeling: "Now this standing upon a bit of stick 100 feet aloft for hours at a time, swiftly sailing over the sea, is very much like crossing the Channel in a balloon. Manfred-like, you talk to the clouds: you have a fellow feeling for the sun." In chapter 9 he declared: "For the consciousness of being deemed dead, is next to the presumable unpleasantness of being so in reality. One feels like his own ghost unlawfully tenanting a defunct carcass." In chapter 10 the narrator mentions but does not enumerate "the tragico-comico moods which at times overtook" him. In chapter 11 Melville offered an anatomy of reveries, his theories about his companion's states of being: he had seized as his own the theme of the riddling nature of the universe and every creature and object in it. In these early chapters Melville was evoking precisely some of the most unnameable moods, states of mind and body, states of consciousness — one of his greatest strengths.

Page by page, Melville was laying down delights for the readers of *Typee* and *Omoo*. Knowing where this writer had come from, in two years, three years, the reader (as some actual reviewers later testified) rejoiced at encountering writing still more gorgeous than that which had graced some pages in those earlier books. This sample is from chapter 19, a scene where the hero and Jarl explore that strange and seemingly unmanned brigantine, the *Parki*:

> Unfastening the cabin scuttle, we stepped downward into the smallest and murkiest den in the world. The altar-like transom, surmounted by the closed dead-lights in the stern, together with the dim little sky-light overhead, and the somber aspect of every thing around, gave the place the air of some subterranean oratory, say a Prayer Room of Peter the Hermit. But coils of rigging, bolts of canvas, articles of clothing, and disorderly heaps of rubbish, harmonized not with this impression. Two doors, one on each side, led into wee little state-rooms, the berths of which also were littered. Among other things, was a large box, sheathed with iron and stoutly clamped, containing a keg partly filled with powder, the half of an old cutlass, a pouch of bullets, and a case for a sextant — a brass plate on the lid, with the maker's name, London. The broken blade of the cutlass was very rusty and stained; and the iron hilt bent in. It looked so tragical that I thrust it out of sight.

That self-mocking last sentence (not so far from Ishmael's hastily disengaging himself from the mysterious poncho-like garment in the bedroom of the Spouter Inn in *Moby-Dick*) wraps one of Melville's "tragico-comico" moods around some rich nautical gothicism. Today some readers hitherto unfamiliar with *Mardi* will respond with a frisson to this just-quoted paragraph and to the evocations of moods and consciousness quoted from the previous chapters. That sort of reader may be responding to a concentrated essence of what was so astonishingly alluring about Melville at this time of his life, in his person and in his books, for in these passages he wore his character as loosely as his flowing trousers. For a few weeks — two, three, or a month, he quieted his turmoil about his thwarted romance in the composition of some of the happiest and most evocative pages he ever wrote.

Even in Lansingburgh there were interruptions. The whole family continued to see all the important reviews, since everything came to Allan's attention in Manhattan and entire papers were cheap for him to send up. Intermingled with welcome attention to Herman was unwelcome attention to an uncle of Lizzie's, Philip Marett. The New York *Weekly Mirror* on 22 May contained a reprinting of an essay on Melville's two books and the notice that *Omoo* was selling well and carrying off stacks of *Typee*. It also carried an article, "SOMETHING NEW IN THE FINANCIAL WORLD," about disclosures that followed Marett's resignation as president of the New England Bank: "Since the resignation of Mr. Marett, it has been discovered that he had for many years been in the habit of using the funds of the Bank for shaving purposes, and after paying in the legal interest on the money used, pocketed the surplus. Now it appears that the directors were unable to make

so large a dividend as they had sometimes done in consequence of this financial cunning of Mr. Marett, and when they discovered that he had pocketed
the usury, they made him disgorge to the amount of about 65,000 dollars,
leaving him still a very handsome balance." This news aroused complex
feelings among those in the family with the longest memories, for Maria
remembered the name from the time duns came knocking at her door in the
fall of 1832. The Maretts took refuge in what they called Long Island but
everyone else knew was simply Brooklyn. Once the Maretts were only a ferry
ride away, Allan learned the value of a Boston connection in New York, and
the pleasures of being near a "handsome balance."

In the weeks after Herman began work on his new book, extraordinary
reviews of *Omoo* came out at short intervals, just long enough apart for the
family not to grow jaded with the previous one before a new one was published. In the 21 May New York *Evening Mirror* under the heading "Polynesian Life. — 'Typee' and 'Omoo' " appeared yet another of these brilliantly
written essays. The author, someone high up in the journalistic establishment with a special zeal to defend Melville, knew that it was not mere reality
that gave Melville's books their value:

> It is not altogether the truthfulness of these sketches, however, that con-
> stitutes their great charm — a daguerreotype could be merely accurate; it is
> the warmth, the tropical luxuriance, the genial flow of humor and good-
> nature — the happy enthusiasm, gushing like a stream of mellow sunshine
> from the author's heart — all these, and a thousand nameless beauties of tone
> and sentiment, are the captivating ingredients of "Omoo." Who can follow
> our young adventurer in his wanderings through those quiet valleys and leafy
> glens, and listen to his pleasant discourse, without feeling completely regen-
> erated? Ushered gradually into a world of primitive beauties, enveloped in
> a spell of delicious enchantment, humanized and spiritualized at the same
> time — the reader unconsciously yields to the charm and finds himself a
> dreamy inhabitant of the sunny South Sea Isles.

"Charm" is a word that recurs in such tributes, charm that Melville at this time
effused effortlessly and unconsciously, in person as well as in print. The writer
in the *Mirror* went on to imagine just what sort of reader could fail to respond to Melville: "Cold, indeed, must be his heart, if it does not inspire him
to grasp the hand of his roving cicerone in the very intensity of right-down
cordial good-fellowship." (On 1 June Nathaniel Parker Willis in the *Home
Journal* paid a similar tribute to the style and the man: "His vivacious manner,
the animal spirits which his style overflows, and the novelty of the scenes to
which he introduces the reader, throw a peculiar charm around these records
of life among the wild savages and tropical fruits of the North sea." North,

South, a curious error to recur this year in unrelated contexts; but what counted was the sheer physical vitality of Herman's alluring manner.)

In the course of his remarkable tribute in the *Evening Mirror*, the reviewer gave an elaborate rebuttal to the *Evangelist* of the year before and all those who had joined in the attack on Melville's treatment of the missionaries:

> The moderation and forbearance with which he treats of clerical despotism and evangelical tyranny, cannot fail to produce a deep impression on the minds of all reasonable men. Such testimony, bearing intrinsic evidence of candor and impartiality, will for that very reason be unpalatable to the mass of our church-bigots, who regard these things as too sacred to be placed in the category of worldly matters. It is not a question to be classed with human imperfections and ordinary realities. Of course Mr. Melville can no longer claim to be a Christian — he has taken the part of the poor savage, and questioned the propriety of scourging him into the traces of fat Missionary ladies and Christianity — and is therefore an Atheist. Thus, having proved him, out of his own mouth, to be an enemy of religion, because he is opposed to evangelizing the natives into draught horses and beasts of burden, the corollary is irresistible — is he entitled to credit? Assuredly not!

The writer ironically placed himself with those so far steeped in wickedness "as to exercise the gift of reason" and to admit the inadmissible: "It too often happens that the prostitution of the natives is indirectly made as source of revenue to the clerical establishment; and although this charge has been denied, it is none the less true." He had read books, but he also had talked to men who had been in the Pacific:

> Nearly every intelligent traveller who has visited the islands of the Pacific bears verbal testimony to the fact, though few have the hardihood to commit their views to print. It is always a thankless task to expose abuses of this kind. The American public have become so accustomed to one side of the question, that the bare intimation of another is an outrage not to be tolerated. In sober truth, these deluded philanthropists have, by deluding others, built up an immense institution, requiring annually several hundred thousand dollars to support it; and now they are deluding the natives with the idea that it is all for *their* good. This talk about glorious revivals among the heathens, is the veriest nonsense that ever emanated from the muddled brains of madmen. A few ignorant islanders are harangued into a state of mere animal phrenzy, frightened into the grossest absurdities, and finally reduced to a state of slavery — and all this is heralded as a grand triumph of religion!

His conclusion was a sturdy endorsement of both *Typee* and *Omoo*: "We consider them, in a word, the best works on Polynesian life yet published, either in this country or England; and no work within the range of our nautical reading can compare with them in the spirit and vividness of their forecastle revelations."

Such defenders had faced up to the possibility that a portion of the religious press could destroy Melville's budding career, and were speaking out while they might yet do some good, while they might forestall or counteract denunciations from the religious papers. On 27 May high praise appeared in the Washington *National Era* and the Washington *National Intelligencer* (which began as a remarkable review of *Typee*, written without a copy of the book at hand, then moved to *Omoo*). Even the reviewer in the New York *Evangelist*, that last week of May, fell under the spell of *Omoo* and admitted that the "lively sketches steal one's favor and approbation in spite of himself," and had to remind himself to warn his readers that Melville's "mendacity" was "sometimes flagrantly visible, as well as his spite against religion and its missionaries." What with some of his enemies sounding almost genial and his admirers writing more philosophically than ever, taking him seriously, by late May Melville's American triumph seemed sealed.

That fame was rambunctiously enhanced when American editors and the Melvilles and Gansevoorts found indubitable evidence that there was no dupe like a snobbish and superior Britisher. On 25 June in the Albany *Evening Journal* Thurlow Weed happily printed an article headed "Blackwood's Review of 'Omoo,'" based on "SCOTT's republication of BLACKWOOD's MAGAZINE for June" (that is, a local pirating of the whole issue by an Albany printer named Scott). Weed sympathized with the editor of *Blackwood's* for being "puzzled and bewildered" in his efforts to analyze *Omoo*, since he himself could not "decide how much this delightful book owes to the Author's imagination." Admitting he had been one of the many "who, in reference both to 'Typee' and 'Omoo,' commenced by distrusting much, ended in believing all," now Weed seized the occasion to make public amends for his own prolonged skepticism: "That there is something alike poetical and suspicious in the conjunction of the name of 'HERMAN' with that of 'MELVILLE,' must be admitted, but they both belong, rightfully and legitimately, the one by birth, and the other by baptism, to the same individual — an individual who has a 'local habitation' in addition to 'a name.' And of the existence, identity, and veritableness of 'HERMAN GANSEVOORT, of Gansevoort, Saratoga Co.,' to whom 'Omoo' is dedicated, we are quick witnesses." In New York the *Eclectic Magazine* reprinted the *Blackwood's* review in the July issue, then the Boston *Littell's Living Age* reprinted it in the 24 July issue. It became the most widely reprinted of the early British reviews, and by all odds the one most talked about.

The editors of the Albany papers, all of whom knew Herman Gansevoort, especially delighted in exposing such British fatuity, and all the Melvilles and Gansevoorts and their connections relished the review. On 23 June Sophia Thurston had "sat up till nearly one o'clock to read a notice of Omoo 14 pages long in 'Blackwoods' " (as she wrote Augusta the next day), savoring the reviewer's conviction that Herman Melville's name was "too romantic to be real" and delighting in his declaring "his entire disbelief of the existence of any Uncle Gansevoort of Gansevoort &c." On 11 July from school at Chatham (near Poughkeepsie) Uncle Herman's young nephew Henry Gansevoort, Peter's son, wrote to his sister, Kate: "Tell Mother that I read the remarks of Blackwood which were marked in the Evening Journal respecting Omoo & its author I think if John Bull doubts there being such a man as Herman Melville they had better take a trip across the Atlantic & satisfy themselves by calling on some of that family which they think existed only in the imagination of the writer &, though they may not find quite such lordly men, they will find them quite as good, & worthy, as any of their english blood." The Melville cousins were noble Scots themselves, not figments of someone's imagination, but a word needed to be said for the Gansevoorts, cousins of the Patroon! All the family found great amusement, not to say pride, in the review.

Having his own workroom with its nautical ambiance encouraged Melville to write industriously for a time, but he was growing more and more restless and lonely. Every time a new batch of favorable reviews arrived from Allan (or from Augusta or others), there seemed less reason to hunker down to a long summer's celibate work on the manuscript. During these weeks, also, while the girls were agitated over pairings and possible pairings involving neighbors, cousins, and members of the immediate family, it was impossible for Herman not to think of his sisters, even if momentarily and involuntarily, the way he thought of Allan and himself, as sexual beings. At this time he may already have been able to recognize and articulate to himself, however imperfectly, some of the sexual ambiguities inherent in any family relationship. By the time he wrote the beginning of *Pierre* in late 1851, he could openly identify "that strange license which a perfect confidence and mutual understanding at all points" could breed between son and mother — or, he might have said, between brother and sister. If he were married, of course, tabooed thoughts, however evanescent, could be banished instantly the moment they intruded, and he would be able to focus entirely on the book, when he was not with his wife. Herman had been passionately in love with Lizzie from their first sessions together in Boston in mid-October 1844, it now seemed, and it was time to try yet again to persuade her to name a wedding day. In an earnest and decorous confidential session with his mother he conveyed the difficulty of his situation. Maria was all sympathy, remembering how restless her husband had become whenever he was apart from her. Now she wanted nothing more than to have her son happy and the connection with the Shaws made permanent.

Augusta was still at the Thayer house on 30 May, when Maria forewarned her (in a letter for Herman to carry): "Herman is going on to Boston, his visit is one of much importance to himself and every member of our family, it is nothing more or less than to have Lizzie name an early day for their marriage." She continued with an analysis of Herman's emotional state and suggestions for dealing with Lizzie:

> He is very restless and ill at ease very lonely here without his intended, I can see no reason why it should be postponed any longer, if Lizzie loves Herman as I think she does with her whole heart & soul why, she will consent to live here for the present, and she can be happy too — all the elements of happiness are thick around us if we only will hold them to us, and not wantonly leave them. I want you to say nothing to Herman until he speaks to you, on this subject — which he will do soon. This is our pleasantest season & you must tell Lizzie she must consent. In July she will have been engage'd eleven months, a long time now a days — Herman is really depress'd because if Lizzie loves she can be as happy here with him as elsewhere, and you must tell her so, Herman is able to support her here now, and to wait for an uncertain future, which none of us can penetrate, would be unwise, he is really unsettled and wont be able to attend to his "Book" if Lizzie does not reflect upon the uncertainty of the future, & consent to name some day say in July.

She thought Augusta "had better return home with Herman he will most probably come back next Saturday" (5 June); then she reiterated that Augusta "had better return with Herman," so she could be at the Van Vechten wedding on Tuesday the eighth.

These Van Vechten festivities were to be elaborate, and for once they were in the nature of a rehearsal for the family. The bride, Cousin Kate Van Vechten, and her "Groom elect," Elisha P. Hurlbut, had come up to carry Kate Melville down with them to Albany, so her dress could be fitted there. Augusta could attend a ceremonial "introduction" on Monday (Maria wrote her on 30 May), then others in the family would be involved: "Helen, & Fanny have prepared themselves to go down with Herman on *the* day of the wedding which is to take place on the 8th of June. I suppose you know that your friend Catherine V. R. is to be one of the Bridesmaids." (Here were Kates enough even for Herman.) For some reason Maria was portioning out daughters for Allan's wedding and other daughters for Herman's: "Remember that Helen, & Fanny, are to attend Herman's wedding, and you Allan's, dont forget together with Kate." She ended her letter to Augusta by reiterating: "I shall expect you back with Herman" and in a postscript she commanded: "You *must return* with Herman."

Herman arrived at Boston on 1 June, carrying for Hope Shaw a gift, a copy of *Omoo*. The Shaw house was as always intimidatingly massive without. In the warmth of early June, Herman was alert to the beauty of the tall elm trees that made Mt. Vernon Street, a guidebook declared, "the most elegantly shaded street in the city." This time, Herman was resolute. He may have echoed his mother in urging that Lizzie live in the house in Lansingburgh after their marriage. In her quiet way Lizzie may have resisted, seeing, as Herman did not see, how awkward it might be to live as a daughter-in-law in a house where she had been perfectly at ease as a guest of Helen. Very likely Shaw analyzed his daughter's hesitation into its constituent parts before deciding that he could allow her to marry while making it unnecessary for her to live in the house Maria was renting in Lansingburgh. No details are known of Herman's talks with either Shaw or his daughter, or with Hope Shaw about the book he had brought her or the ancestry and connections she had checked on, but this time the Shaws capitulated to Herman's insistence that a wedding day be set. Leaving the great Shaw house triumphant this time, he returned to Lansingburgh on the seventh or so. But he left Augusta on Mt. Vernon Street with Nilly, who needed her badly as the warm weather approached and she entered the eighth month of her first pregnancy.

Before the Van Vechten wedding Kate Melville, as one of the prenuptial party, went down to New York, where she visited the Thurstons. Allan, the son who had made dutiful calls on the Van Vechtens after Maria had moved to Lansingburgh, came up for the wedding, which went off in great style. Cousin Maggie Van Rensselaer De Peyster Douw (kin to Mrs. Van Vechten through the Van Schaicks — and in other ways) came despite her infinitely distressing but unnameable troubles, and "look'd beautiful" (Maria wrote Augusta on 15 June — knowing that Augusta would relay this information to her hostess, Maggie's sister Nilly). Maggie, in fact, outshone the bride, so much that Cousin Leonard, Guert's brother, said "she was the handsomest woman in the room." (The bride's grandfather was the Leonard Gansevoort who was a brother of the Hero, and a representative under the Articles of Confederation, what Herman in *Redburn* called the Old Constitution.) Writing to Augusta on 15 June, Maria still could not speak of her brother Peter without protective irony: "But I must not forget your friend the Peter — he really look'd handsome in his white cravat. I could not refrain from telling him so, *that is*, that his 'White Cravat was particularly becoming' — Aunt Susan &c send love to you." ("Your friend the Peter" was a phrasing that masked heartache.) The fact that Peter wore a white cravat was in itself hilarious proof of his conservatism, for only the oldest of fogies, or fogiest of oldsters, like Dr. John Wakefield Francis, of Bond Street, still wore them instead of fashionable colored ones. Maria knew Augusta would comprehend her satiric undertone even while sharing her long-persisting pain.

On 11 June, three days after the Van Vechten wedding, Helen gave the news to Augustus Van Schaick, the cousin they hoped would recover his health in Rio de Janeiro: "Herman has returned from a visit to Boston, and has made arrangements to take upon himself the dignified character of a married man some time during the Summer, about the first of August. Only think! I can scarcely realize the astounding truth!" Without connecting the success of the new book to the plans for the wedding, Helen gleefully gave Augustus news about the book, an advance copy of which he already possessed: "Herman's 'Omoo' has been wonderfully successful. In one week after it was issued the whole edition of 3000; or 3,500 was disposed of and another was put in progress. It has been more highly spoken of on both sides of the Atlantic than its predecessor even, as containing, more instructive matter." Helen's comments on *Omoo* were based on the 12 May Albany *Evening Journal* article, and probably on other newspapers that gave quotations from the English reviews. As for the triumphant author and suitor, Herman was hoeing his tomatoes, having done his duty by the corn the day before, she told Augustus — evidence that he was bearing himself "very meekly under his honors." It may have been at this time, flush with success, that Herman granted the Albany portraitist Asa Twitchell the privilege of painting his portrait ("gratis," he specified in his 1849 journal), the only surviving image of Melville before 1860.

After the Van Vechten wedding Maria let herself become caught up in Allan's wedding plans. She also set herself to taking a strong hand in Herman's less definite plans, despite the arrival of a Lowell paper that contained "a rather serious account of Judge Shaws illness." Following hard upon Herman's success in pressing the issue at Mt. Vernon Street, it seemed as if the illness might disrupt Herman's plans, but Augusta soon had good news in that regard. Her mother responded: "poor Herman felt very bad — but your letter had the effect of recalling his spirits & he is again as he has been since his return from Boston, perfectly happy." Perfectly happy turned out to be a state worth commenting on, for it lasted less than two weeks.

[26]

Scandal and Marriage
1847

Contaminated Minds mind mundane Things;
But virtuous Minds mount with celestial Wings.

"Allan Melvills Book," 1796

NOW THAT HERMAN AND ALLAN were engaged to wealthy young women
from Mt. Vernon Street and Bond Street and were talking about wedding
dates, Maria Gansevoort Melville began to push out from the poverty that
had constricted her for almost two decades. Little or nothing had been left
for her at the long-delayed settlement of her mother's estate, but now, one
way or another, through Allan's efforts perhaps more than Herman's, her lot
would be better. In her own mind she worked everything out in considerable
detail, without consulting the other principals. Allan's living in Manhattan
was out of her control, but Herman had written much of *Typee* and almost all
of *Omoo* there at home on River Street, and he had started his third book
there under improved conditions, and Lizzie had visited there while he was
at work, so Herman and Lizzie did not need to rent a house for themselves.
Herman, comparatively docile once he was married, and Lizzie, always com-
plaisant or downright compliant, would have their own room; otherwise
Maria's household would function as it had done the previous autumn, but
surely with augmented resources.

Recognizing the need to brush away anything that might delay Herman's
marriage, on 15 June 1847 Maria took advantage of Augusta's presence at the
Thayer house on Mt. Vernon Street. The deferential Augusta was to convey
some fairly blunt instructions to Hope Savage Shaw:

Remember me to Mrs Shaw, & say that in my opinion Lizzie had better leave
things as they are, and when she becomes domesticated with us, she will be
able to know whether she wants any thing more, perhaps a wardrobe or something of the kind, but she can herself procure any thing she finds missing at
Lansg. Your half sheet containing Lizzys note came in. thank Lizzy for her
very sweet note, that she must not fatigue herself with much preparation for

she will have so much leisure time during the winter that she will need some
friendly employment to engage the time not devoted to Herman, reading, and
visiting, which latter duty is not very arduous in our matter of fact Village.

Brimming with Christian charity, and expansive as she had been early in her
marriage, Maria behaved as if her hard-hearted sisters-in-law had done nothing she needed to forgive. In her letter of 15 June, Maria sent her particular
love to "Aunt Priscilla" as well as to her other sisters-in-law, and even to
"Aunt Scollay & her Family," so ready was she to rebuild severed Boston
connections. Helen and now Augusta were familiar figures in Boston, and
Maria herself would be making visits there, even more often than in the
1820s, thanks to rail service direct from Troy to Boston.

Maria sent Augusta local news. Cousin Maria Van Schaick Peebles was
well "& the Lord of Isles quite happy & cheerful," having "bought a Poney,
the first animal he has owned since he made such a sweep last fall & sold off
his horses." Helen, Fanny, and Maria, while missing Augusta, were "busily
employed in preparing Herman for his 'debut' in July," so much so that
Helen sent word that she was too much engaged in preparing Herman's
"Trusseau" (as she spelled it) to write. Maria was lonely for her, but Augusta's
presence in Boston was in its way providential. The much lamented late
Stephen Van Rensselaer, father of Augusta's patron, had not sought out his
Cousin Maria in 1832 and settled a competency upon her, as such a ducal
kinsman might have done, if he had recognized her plight: such fantasies
sprang up unbidden in Melville brains, to judge from *Redburn*. Unlike the
Melvills, the Van Rensselaers had done nothing Maria needed to forgive,
and, thanks to Augusta, their acquaintance with the family of the Last Patroon was changing into outright intimacy delightful to all. At the Van
Vechten wedding, Mrs. Van Rensselaer had given Maria a good account of
Augusta's health. Subsequently Stephen Van Rensselaer had escorted Maggie to Boston, and Maria had assumed that Augusta would return with him
when he concluded his visit to Nilly: Maggie was a mother twice over, and
could care for her sister far better than Augusta could. Maria needed to have
her second daughter with her in these tumultuous weeks, but she could see
that Nilly's installation on Mt. Vernon Street was abetting her own liberation: her cousin Stephen Van Rensselaer, from time to time, would escort her
to Boston for visits to the Shaws, Melvills, and Scollays.

On 21 June, Maria continued her string of instructions and injunctions to
Augusta, whose return was now linked to Maggie's return from Boston, the
Van Rensselaers having decided that at least one person from the Manor
House had to be in attendance during the last weeks of Cornelia's pregnancy.

Maria wanted Augusta back with Maggie: "I almost forget how you look." She was to do the social niceties: "thank aunt Priscilla kindly & say that she must try to come on to Lansingburgh 'for the Silk' I mean, my love to all who enquire." Augusta was to give Lizzie instructions: "Before I forget it I wish you to tell, or rather advise Lizzie to get her Hat at New York, Cousin Kate [Curtis] will kindly assist her — to a fashionable Milliner, or Sophia either I have no doubt will accompany her." Her horizons broadening day by day, she sent word to Aunt Scollay that it was "more than probable" that she should "now be induced to visit Boston," and that it would "be a pleasant anticipation, to meet her, and Catherine." Furthermore, Augusta was to get word to Dorchester: "Tell Aunt D'Wolf and Uncle, it is my intention to pass a day or two with them before I leave Boston, if they can come for me to the City." Augusta was to give Maria's love to Aunt Jean (on Green Street) and Aunt Helen (in Hingham) as well. The family at Lansingburgh was rejoiced to hear of Judge Shaw's full recovery, and sent love to him, and to Hope Shaw. Allan had promised to return: "Allan is not here, but will be up next month, to make us quite a visit." Helen once again begged off writing, since she, along with Fanny and her mother, was "very much engag'd preparing for Herman's wedding," without the help of Kate, who was probably still with the Thurstons. Maria enclosed a note to Cornelia, which she assumed Augusta would read: "You will find Cornelia's note somewhat Poetic — perhaps it will recall many a reminiscence — all true, however, except the Garden was the scene of 'Archery['] instead of the bank of the river." Maria had waxed poetical (presumably in prose) about Cornelia's visit to Lansingburgh in April 1846, when all eight children were alive and Augusta was to be a bridesmaid at the Manor House.

On 24 June, Allan's fiancée, Sophia Thurston, wrote from New York to Augusta, who was still at Nilly's in Boston. She and Allan had been surprised by the 1 August wedding date for Herman and Lizzie: "I had no idea it would be so soon. This will be the first wedding, in your immediate family. Now that the ice is broken, more will follow, and the next thing, that I shall hear perhaps, will be that Miss Dutty has concluded to follow her beloved brother's example. . . . But is it not strange that however dearly one may love her brother, yet they never would love such a man for a husband. You will never marry a man like either Herman or Allan."

On 28 June, Maria wrote to Augusta again, grieving: "Just one year to day, that we committed our ever loved Gansevoort to the Grave." This time she was insistent that Augusta return with Maggie, and firm that Augusta must not accept a new invitation to move to a room in the Shaw house up the street:

you must come home, and think not of making Lizzie a visit at this time, for
she can do no less in common politeness than urge you to make her a visit, but
you should remember that her time for preparation is very short, & you must
not allow yourself to be overpersuaded to do that which your own good sense
would condemn, were you to give full time to reflection, Lizzie's letter receive'd last saturday tells Helen, "Augusta['s] visit to me commences the last
of this week," now how is this, some mistake there must be for we have been
led from your last letter to us to believe that you would be with us this week
without fail.

Maria sent "Particular love to daughter Lizzie." The plans were for Mrs.
Thurston to bring Sophia up for a visit the next week, "escorted by Allan &
her son Henry." Mrs. Thurston and young Henry (born in 1832, two years
after Tom) would stay for a day or two, then Sophia and Allan would stay on,
in full expectation of seeing Augusta there in Lansingburgh.

Herman was to be in Boston but could not escort Augusta back, Maria
explained, since he was returning by New York City, where he would "remain a week on business—besides providing his wedding suit &c." The
business may have had to do with the comic magazine *Yankee Doodle*, which
Cornelius Mathews took hold of, shortly before 14 July according to a letter
Evert Duyckinck wrote his brother George. More likely, it had to do with
news he had received from Boston. In June, if not earlier, the compliant,
hesitant Lizzie, the young woman who had never defied anyone in her life,
had begun to confide in her father her scruples about going to live in Maria's
rented house in Lansingburgh, where she would be merely one of five young
women. The judge, just as quietly and soberly, had begun to work out an
alternative arrangement, without consulting the dowager Maria. No one
acknowledged that they were facing another impasse, but Herman's visit to
Manhattan may have been under Shaw's instructions. According to his plan,
the two brothers and their brides and their mother and sisters would all live
together in New York City, in a house to be provided by the father-in-law
of one, Herman, and perhaps to be maintained with some help from the
mother-in-law of the other, Allan, or from Allan's earnings. The last thing
Lizzie wanted was to pit her will against Maria's, so Herman and Allan
needed to consult and work out details before anyone broached the matter to
Maria and dealt with the stages of her reaction. Although the plan would
challenge her absolute domestic authority, Maria could have no reasonable objection to it, and when had she been unreasonable? Indeed, as Nilly
acutely observed to Augusta later, on 15 December, "I should think she
would be happier for Lansingburgh always seemed to me rather a limited

sphere for her, though she was a lesson of contentment to all." Her installation in Manhattan would end almost two decades of exile.

These weeks Allan was euphoric during his regular calls on Sophia at tree-lined Bond Street, where the ten-foot-high lamps that gleamed amid the leaves reminded the traveler of Paris (so Henry T. Tuckerman recalled, years later, after the illusion had been quite destroyed by commercialization). Sophia was not only openly in love with Allan, but also rich and well trained in social forms. Around 1 July she very properly wrote to Augusta, by then finally home at Lansingburgh. Sophia mingled formality with just the right familiarity, such as Allan's pet name for the sister next older than he:

> I suppose your Mother will receive a note from mine before you read this accepting her invitation to accompany me to Dutty's home, where we expect to be Monday evening. I anticipate a great deal of pleasure in seeing your Mother and sisters. . . . I wonder if they will like me or not. I wish to be loved for my own sake and not merely because Allan is —— I do not know what to say next, so I will leave a blank there, to be filled up by your imagination.

Monday was 5 July; Sophia's visit was postponed a few days or a week. In the attempt to coordinate plans Allan had written a long letter that missed Augusta in Boston, but he wrote her another with a pleasant command: "N.B. See Dutty dear that every thing is done to make Totie's visit a pleasant one." It was not yet clear whether he would accompany Sophia up or follow her. Augusta did her duty so well that she had her second chance to be a bridesmaid, for Sophia would formally ask her in a letter of 7 September to stand up with her "some day between the 20 and 25th of this month, in the church of the Ascension."

In the midst of all this politesse, about the end of June 1847 and the beginning of July, Melville's public reputation took a strange turn. From this time through the next years Melville's fame was always tinged with notoriety because of new accusations brought against him — not accusations of lying about the missionaries, but of being sexually dangerous, and even depraved. The first sign of the shift in critical opinion was an article in the New York *Tribune* of 26 June 1847, written on 8 June 1847 from his vacation spot "Up the Lakes" by the editor himself, Horace Greeley, Gansevoort's fellow repealer. Greeley's zeal could burst out in quirky and irresponsible ways, as in 1842, when he gleefully hounded the exasperated James Fenimore Cooper into a self-destructive libel suit, selling papers by making the great author a comic butt. Or it could burst out in profane displays on what should have been solemn national occasions, as in 1845, when at Andrew Jackson's death he denounced Old Hickory as a jobber in human flesh and a slave-trader.

The second sign was George Washington Peck's essay in the July *American Whig Review: A Whig Journal of Politics, Literature, Art and Science.*

These two attacks became available almost simultaneously, since the July issue of the magazine was out several days before the end of June. Peck, immediately and publicly identified as the author of the attack in the *Whig Review*, was an assistant editor on the *Morning Courier and New-York Enquirer.* Peck was known in Boston legal circles as a former law clerk of Richard Henry Dana Jr. and a crony of his younger brother, Ned Dana. It was common knowledge among his remaining friends that he was deteriorating physically and morally in New York, the sort of dipsomaniac who sinks fast into absolute addiction rather than going down slowly plateau by plateau. Already he was borrowing money from anyone who would still lend it to him and living in successively more squalid conditions. (By June 1851, one of the last times Dana Jr. tracked him down, Peck had taken refuge in "the cock-loft of a house in Anthony st." between City Hall Park and Canal, a room "sufficiently poverty stricken, to suit the taste of any poor-author fancier.") The article in the *Whig Review* was the work of a well-educated but sexually disturbed and pathologically jealous young alcoholic. Together these two men, Greeley and Peck, further reinforced by news reports of Melville's engagement and marriage, flushed out into the open something that had happened almost without anyone's noticing: *Typee* had made Melville the first American author to become a sex symbol. Herman was a man whose experiences fueled diverse sexual fantasies of many men and some women.

Yet Greeley and Peck did not initiate their charges. No one had seemed to notice it at the time, the religious attack was so stern, but the reviewer in the 9 April 1846 New York *Evangelist* had gone beyond simple denunciation of the voluptuousness of *Typee*. This reviewer even then had defined the problematical quality of the book as residing less in what Melville said than in what he hinted. As many readers remembered, the reviewer had identified *Typee* as belonging to the large class of books that are "bad, immoral, and consequently injurious" not so much by "what is plainly expressed, as what is left to be imagined by the reader." Whether influenced by this notorious review in the *Evangelist* or not (they certainly knew it), both Greeley and Peck a year later used the opportunity of their reviewing Melville's new book to echo its point about the special prurience in Melville's writing. They charged Melville not merely with sexual license but with a strange sexual perversity that was not recognizable at first reading but that wormed its way into the reader's consciousness insidiously, as time passed.

Greeley's article in the *Weekly Tribune* for 26 June was a revisionist's look at *Typee* in the light of *Omoo*:

"Typee" and "Omoo," doubtless in the main true narratives, are worthy to
rank in interest with Robinson Crusoe and in vivacity with the best of Stephens's Travels. — Yet they are unmistakably defective, if not positively diseased in moral tone, and will very fairly be condemned as dangerous reading
for those of immature intellects and unsettled principles. Not that you can
put your finger on a passage positively offensive; but the tone is bad, and
incidents of the most objectionable character are depicted with a racy lightness which would once have been admired but will now justly be condemned.
A penchant for bad liquors is everywhere boldly proclaimed, while a hanker-
ing after loose company not always of the masculine order, is but thinly
disguised and perpetually protruding itself throughout the work.

Greeley, the erratic utopian reformer, who during a running debate the previous winter had defended Fourierism in the *Tribune* against Henry J. Raymond in the *Courier and Enquirer,* took an unusual stance toward Melville's
exposure of the missions, regretting that Melville's defective tone would
prevent his testimony as to "the effect and the defects of the Missionary
labors among the South Sea Islanders from having its due weight with those
most deeply interested." But what most tantalized in the commentary sent
down from the lakes was Greeley's attempt to put his finger on something
elusively wrong with Melville's tone. The review hurt Melville, for all the
family saw the *Tribune,* which went throughout the region.

The virulent prurience of Peck's attack in the July *American Review* (or
Whig Review) will remain not quite imaginable to anyone who does not read
the entire lengthy document. Peck began with thoughts on reading then on
rereading *Omoo* — reading "with interest, and yet with a perpetual recoil."
Confessing an inability to match cause and effect, he resorted to the familiar
rhyme "I do not like thee, Doctor Fell," then he proceeded with a minutely
argued discussion of the failure of earlier reviewers to get at their "causes of
dislike" of *Typee* and *Omoo:* "They are evidently not pleased with the book;
but — as most writers would, sitting down to write a hasty notice of it immediately after running it through — the daily critics find nothing worse to say
respecting it than that they do not believe it." They had missed the evidence
that Melville was "what a plain New Englander would call 'a *smart scamp*' ":

The phrase is a hard one, but it is certainly well-deserved. Here is a writer
who spices his books with the most incredible accounts and dark hints of
innumerable amours with the half-naked and half-civilized or savage damsels
of Nukuheva and Tahiti — who gets up voluptuous pictures, and with cool,
deliberate art breaks off always at the right point, so as without offending
decency, he may stimulate curiosity and excite unchaste desire. Most incredible, we style these portions of his stories, for several reasons.

First: He makes it appear always, that he was unusually successful with these poor wild maidens, and that his love-making was particularly acceptable to them. Now, if this had been so, we fancy we should have heard less of it. A true manly mind cannot sit down and coin dramas, such as these he gives us, for either others' delectation or its own. It is nothing new to hear conceited men boast of their perfect irresistibleness with the sex. "Oh, it is the easiest thing in the world," we remember, one of these gentry used to say, a la Mantalini; "a woman is naturally cunning, now only you keep cool and you'll soon see through her; a man must look out for himself, a woman for herself," &c. This very person, as we happen to know, through a confidential medical friend, could no more, at that very time, when his conversation was in this lofty strain, have wronged a woman, than Charteris could have committed the crime for which he was hung. Since then, and confirmed by various other experience, we have always doubted when we hear a man, especially on a short acquaintance, and most especially in a book that goes to the public, pluming himself on his virility—letting it be no secret that he is a "very devil among the women." Once, in a refectory in ——, we were supping with a friend, when, the tables being full, there came a little, long-knecked, falling-shouldered, pumpkin-faced young man, and took the end of ours. We exchanged a few words, and presently he dashed, without previous preparation, into a full confession of what he styled his "peculiar weakness," in which, if we were to believe him, he let out enough to show that he might have out-bidden the Satyrs, in Spenser, for the favors of Helena. Our friend, who has command of visage, drew him on till he could not help smiling at his own lies. We made inquiry, and learned afterwards that he was a sheriff's clerk, or some such sort of thing, and that his name was Joseph.

Now, with a thousand such instances sleeping in the memory of years, we have no sort of confidence in the man who paints himself the hero of voluptuous adventures. Suppose any one of us—you, or I, gentle reader—had been through the scenes Omoo depicts, we might—yea, even the best of us—have done as badly as he represents himself to have done; cast away from home and country, drifting about on the rim of the world, surrounded by license, and brimfull of animal health, we should very probably have made sad deviations from the "path of rectitude," but should we have come home and told of it? On the contrary, we should have kept as dark about the matter as possible; and nothing but some overmastering passion or motive could ever have made us reveal it. Native manhood is as modest as maidenhood, and when a man glories in his licentiousness, it raises a strong presumption that he is effete either by nature or through decay.

And this remark leads to our second reason for doubting the credibility of these amours. Taking the evidence of imbecility afforded by the reason just given, in conjunction with all that Omoo would have us believe he did (for he does not speak out in plain words like old Capt. Robert Boyle), and it cannot be possible, without Sir Epicure Mammon's wished-for elixir, that he could have the physical ability to play the gay deceiver at such a rate among those brawny islanders. This body of ours is very yielding it is true, and if a man resolutely sets his mind to imbrute himself he may go a great way; but a half year of such riotous life would have sufficed for one so proud of his exploits (if, indeed, this very display is not rather the result than one of the causes of a blase condition — perhaps it is both).

Thirdly. We do not believe these stories, for the reason that those poor savage maids could not possibly have been such as Omoo describes them; they are not half so attractive.

There was much more, all in the same vein — a public psychological analysis of Melville's sexual pathology on the basis of his two books.

Things got worse in the press before they began to get better. On 14 July J. Watson Webb went out of his way to champion Peck in his *Morning Courier and New-York Enquirer*, without mentioning that Peck was connected with his paper: "*Omoo* and *Typee*, two books which have attracted a great deal more of attention and of comment than they have deserved, are reviewed in a just and highly interesting paper by G. W. Peck, whose contributions to the Review we have hitherto characterised as exceedingly valuable. This article evinces uncommon critical acumen and a clear-sighted, discriminating sympathy with what is sound and healthy in literature and morals." Just as the neighbors in Pittsfield later gossiped that *Moby-Dick* was "more than Blasphemous," the word was out in the weeks before Melville's wedding that *Typee* and *Omoo* were more than licentious, licentious in a peculiarly effective and perverse way. Melville and his family could tell each other that there was some political component in this, perhaps some residue of hatred for his brother the great Democratic orator, for Peck's article had appeared in the official magazine of the Whig party and the *Courier and Enquirer* was now in the Whig camp. Since April, J. Watson Webb had been promoting the candidacy of a general in the field, the hero of the February battle at Buena Vista, Zachary Taylor. Given Greeley's fun with Gansevoort's slip about the secret circular, there *must have been* a political component, but telling each other so did not make the existence of the review less painful. Politics, however, was not enough to account for Greeley's stern disapproval and Peck's frenzy. Something not quite identifiable was at work.

Around 8 July Duyckinck sent over to Melville a favorable London review of *Omoo*, one of a good number Melville had seen by that time (not the much hooted-at review in *Blackwood's*). Perhaps he did so to console Melville for the attack in the *American Review*, though it was 10 July before Duyckinck noted that piece in his diary as "grossly abusive." Melville in an immediate response called the English review "frankincense": "Upon my soul, Duyckinck, these English are a sensible people. Indeed to confess the truth, when I compare their reception of Omoo in particular, with its treatment here, it begets ideas not very favorable to one's patriotism. But this is almost being too frank." This is subdued, even muted, in Melville's best stoic vein, an indication that he had decided how to comport himself in the wake of Greeley's and Peck's denunciations. Greeley he could shrug off, but all his female relatives would in due course see the piece in the *American Review*. Hope Shaw and even Lizzie would have to read some of Peck's prurient allegations that he was, among other horrors, impotent — not the best recommendation for a bride's family to encounter in print in the official magazine of the judge's political party, the one carrying on, in diluted fashion, his Federalist principles. Under no circumstances could Maria Gansevoort Melville give her second son unqualified support in the face of such onslaughts: if he had only written differently, discreetly (as Gansevoort would have done — never mind his lapse about Bryant and the secret circular), such humiliating attacks could never have been mounted. In the summer of 1847, the sudden, unexpected, and flagrantly public analyses of the sexual experiences and capability of the bridegroom disastrously disrupted the prenuptial mood in which the principals pursued their wedding plans.

Before he left New York for Lansingburgh and what was to have been a triumphal advance of the wedding party across Massachusetts, Melville took some consolation in the company of Duyckinck and his friends. By that spring, at the latest, Melville had formed the habit of dropping by the Duyckinck house. He took tea with the Duyckincks there on 4 May, for instance, before Evert wrote to George about his becoming a frequent visitor. On 11 July, after both men had confronted the *Whig* calumnies, Melville had regaled Duyckinck with that "picturesque account of Dr Judd" making up "his diplomacy from fat natives lolling in the shade." Over the months Duyckinck introduced Melville to many of his friends. (Duyckinck's Wiley & Putnam author Edgar Allan Poe made a trip south in July, during the early popularity of *Omoo*. Half a century later, Robert DeUnger recorded that as an apprentice printer he had come out of a Baltimore bookshop in 1847 carrying *Omoo* and de la Motte Fouqué's *Undine, and Sintram and His Companions*. Poe met him, looked at the books in his hands, then discoursed to him for a time on *Undine*, but said not a word about *Omoo*.) Among those whom Duyckinck did introduce to Melville, probably by early in 1847, was his closest friend, Cornelius Mathews, whom the Melville family soon began to refer to as the Centurion, from the Cornelius in Acts 10.

Meanwhile, *Yankee Doodle* under Mathews had afforded amusement to its editors and their friends for the months of its existence, although the points of its jokes are now so blunted, the topicality of its reference so esoteric and so trivial (we perhaps ignorantly assume), that the wonder is that intelligent people spent as much time on it as they did. For several days, or even a week or so, Herman Melville was much involved in discussing it and writing for it. Duyckinck recorded a meeting in his study on 14 July in which Mathews and "Typee" shared in the general laughter over the woodcuts in No. 41 of the paper, the point being that the "literary matter" was "really good in the inverse ration of the wood cuts," or so Evert deluded himself in a letter to his brother George, who was still traveling in Europe with a friend, young William Allen Butler (born in 1825), son of the New York Democrat Benjamin F. Butler of the secret circular. Duyckinck wrote George, "Herman Melville will probably in some shape or other take care of the sea serpent," a reference to news reports about sightings of a monster off Nahant. Melville may well have written some of the squibs that appeared in the magazine about the sea serpent, and he certainly wrote a series of "Authentic Anecdotes of 'Old Zack,'" reported for *Yankee Doodle* "by his special correspondent at the seat of War," the last three words punning on the datelines in newspapers for dispatches from "The Seat of War."

In *Yankee Doodle* the Duyckinck group was satirizing the expansionistic and nationalistic notion of Manifest Destiny then promoted by John O'Sullivan in the *Democratic Review* — a political vision that had proved alluring to Gansevoort and was not without a strong appeal for Herman. Much in the spirit of arch-Whigs like Philip Hone, the former mayor, these Democratic satirists acquiesced in the prosecution of the war in Mexico without ever pretending to justify it. That summer of 1847 Jedediah Auld, a lawyer and essayist, a long-time friend of the Duyckincks, wrote to George and young William Allen Butler, still on their grand tour, of his dread "that this horrible war will continue yet some time." In September (neither letter is precisely dated) he wrote: "The Mexican War still drags its slow length along. I wish it was over for the sake of humanity and the interest of every section of the country but I suppose that a military occupation of the northern portion of Mexico will be inevitable till we fill it up with the Anglo Saxon & the Saxon stock not forgetting the Gael from old Ireland." After mid-July, at the latest, the friends were free to express in *Yankee Doodle* their indignation at Polk's aggressive, and undeclared, war and their quite contrary fear that the Democratic war was producing a hero for the Whigs to capture the presidency with the next year. Perhaps some of the Duyckinck crowd knew that Charles Fenno Hoffman had amused himself the year before, in September 1846, by writing (but apparently not publishing) some spoof letters between General

Zachary Taylor and William L. Marcy, the secretary of war, in which the satire was built on Polk's presumed desire to prolong the war so as to make the most political capital from it and Taylor's presumed desire to gain the Whig nomination for the presidency. The danger "Marcy" points out, in Hoffman's satires, is that if Taylor conquered Mexico and the United States annexed it (or just Texas?) the Whigs might run the Mexican general Santa Anna as "the best expediency candidate."

Whether or not they knew what Hoffman had written, the Duyckinck circle felt a very similar impulse, and they would have the advantage of satiric illustrations. Taylor was notoriously no beauty, and the jut-browed, turtle-mouthed Marcy was one of the homeliest Americans in public life, a boon to a caricaturist. Clever people saw that the situation and the personalities were rife with possibilities for the right American humorist. Melville was not the right one. He probably dashed off his nine "Old Zack" anecdotes in two or three sittings that third week of July, but Mathews parceled them out through issues from 24 July through 11 September, making a weak thing last as long as possible. The first target of Melville's satire was the press (especially the Whig press), the "anecdote-making editors of the North," who had been peppering their papers with innumerable personal anecdotes about General Zachary Taylor, the general in charge of conducting the ground war in Mexico.

The Whig party had at first accurately denounced the Mexican War as an "executive's war," and therefore unconstitutional, but before long the more alert Whig leaders had realized that out of the illegal Democratic war they might pluck a Whig presidency, and the Whig press had set itself the pleasant task of exalting Taylor into the status of a military hero they could use in a domestic campaign in 1848. After Taylor failed to demand unconditional surrender at Monterey in September 1846, Polk had lost all confidence in him, but the Whig press glossed over his military ineptitude. Some in the series of anecdotes Melville wrote for *Yankee Doodle* may have had specific reference to more egregious Whig celebrations of the noble Roman simplicity of the unostentatious general's habits, for Melville portrayed him as washing his own garments at the camp-kettle, not with hard soap ("an unsoldier-like luxury") but with "soft soap" — a typical example of the punning Melville indulged in throughout the anecdotes.

The consistent object of Melville's satire was Taylor's single-minded concern for his reputation with the voters. The "special correspondent" from the "seat" of war in Anecdote 2 reported that Old Zack sewed up his own garments (he was, after all, a "*Taylor*"), and very frequently had to repair the bottom of his ample pants "owing to the constant practice, and the habit the old hero has of violently slapping his person when excited." That anecdote contains a reference to the "ire-provoking and dastardly conduct of the Illinois regiments," a careless error for the Second Indiana, which had broken ranks at Buena Vista, not an error readily traceable to Melville's handwriting: maybe a good deal of the news from Mexico was washing over him without deeply engaging his consciousness. Anecdote 3, about the general's repairs to his "inexpressibles," snagged by a tack, built toward Secretary of War Marcy's reaction to the news about the tack. Marcy suggests that Taylor "keep dark about the matter, since he (Secretary MARCY) knew by experience that any thing touching one's inexpressibles was calculated to provoke vulgar mirth." Aside from the sure-fire comedy in the reference to underwear (the same euphemism used in "The Big Bear of Arkansas"), this was a satirical reference to something everyone knew. Years earlier, having been guaranteed that his expenses on a trip would be refunded, the meticulous Marcy had quite legally charged the state of New York fifty cents for having his pants patched: he had paid out that fifty cents, and he damned well expected to be reimbursed. His enemies had pilloried him, charging him with gross misuse of public funds.

Melville's boisterous response to the Whig attempts to build up the unqualified General Taylor as presidential material was fueled by his genuine disgust at Taylor's specious reluctance to discuss either his candidacy to be president or his stand on particular political issues. A year later the Webster Whigs were still infuriated by the general's persistent refusal to declare himself a Whig and to champion the principles of the Whig party. For Melville, who had ridiculed American chauvinism at the outbreak of the war, it was a congenial task, particularly since it allowed him to pay off a personal score against Marcy for not helping him effectively when he had gone office-seeking in Washington.

William Gilmore Simms, a fellow author with Melville in the Library of American Books, wrote his friend Duyckinck that *Yankee Doodle* would surely fail; he had "no faith in the humour of a single man" among the contributors. The episode may well have taken Melville back to some happy moments during his raucous (and only apparently vituperative?) literary efforts in his Albany youth, and it undoubtedly provided him some momentary relief from the great strain caused by the *Whig Review*, strain compounding his confusion of emotions about the wedding day fast approaching. The kindest way of looking at the Old Zack anecdotes is to see them as what Melville's New York friends gave him instead of a bachelor party. (At the close of the year Evert Duyckinck confessed to his brother that *Yankee Doodle* was rapidly evaporating: "After three months well applied labor Mathews gets nothing from Yankee Doodle, nor Melville, nor Bangs.")

Even as Melville was laughing at wretched woodcuts (perhaps a rudimen-

tary stage he had to pass through before he could become a genuine connoisseur of engravings) and writing that series of anecdotes, Duyckinck's friends
in the New York literary establishment, notably Jedediah B. Auld, were
mobilizing in defense of *Omoo*. Other editors occasionally took on the idiosyncratic Greeley in print. The equally egregious Scot, James Gordon Bennett, editor of the still-scandalmongering *Herald*, was always eager to do so.
Even William Cullen Bryant could be pushed into a dogfight with him. (On
15 January 1850, the newly-decorous *Herald* reproached both Bryant and
Greeley after Bryant said Greeley in his enthusiasm for Taylor had decided
that extension of slavery into some of the new territories was acceptable
and Greeley had replied, in the *Tribune*, "You lie, villain! wilfully, wickedly,
basely lie!") Usually, no one bothered much with denouncing Greeley, who
was always twisting up some peculiar position (conservatives thought) about
repeal of the union between England and Ireland or Negro slavery or wom-
en's rights or copyright reform. But Peck's attack in the *Whig Review* had to
be responded to.

On 21 July Hiram Fuller's paper, the New York *Evening Mirror*, published Jedediah B. Auld's comments on that month's *Whig Review*, the editor
of which, the man who had published Peck, was George H. Colton:

> In all nature there is not a single animated object to be found without at least
> one parasitical annoyance; in the literary kingdom the same rule holds, and
> critics and snarlers are the crawling and creeping things of the world of
> letters. How was it possible for Mr. Colton, who has the credit of literary
> discrimination, to admit so execrable an article into his magazine as the
> disgusting and spiteful review of *Omoo*? We should have supposed that the
> voice of the public would have outweighed the captious snarlings of any small
> clique even if accompanied by what Mr. Colton might consider a gratuitous
> advertisement.

Auld testified to having read *Omoo* without sexual arousal, not even dreaming
"of sensuality in the perusal": "But if Omoo is free from the guilt of pander-
ing to a depraved taste, so is not the reviewer. Finding a fair chance to
disgorge on the public a little of his own filth, in the pleasant disguise of a
moralist and conservative, he launches forth as much disgusting loathsome-
ness and personal blackguardism as could be crammed in the compass of his
few pages." It was peculiar in the extreme that Peck's foul article had been
praised in the *Morning Courier*: "strange as it may seem, this affected jumble
of smuttey morality and personal abuse finds favor in an austere morning
paper famous for stern conservativism. Or is it possible to account for the
high praise bestowed on this atrocious specimen of falsehood, silliness and
nastiness, on the supposition that there exists among the numerous writers

for that journal a *societe d'admiration mutuel,* and that one of their fellows is the savage Juvenal of the Whig Review." In short, according to Duyckinck's friend Auld, the attack on *Omoo* may have sprung from some journalistic cabal in which men of mediocre talent exalted each other's stature by well-planted items of praise — a dangerous allegation that might boomerang back on the Duyckinck camp, already dubbed the Mutual Admiration Society by Lewis Gaylord Clark in the *Weekly Mirror* (6 December 1845).

Melville left town, and by 21 July he had arrived at Gansevoort with his mother for his long-postponed visit to Uncle Herman, leaving his friends in New York City to try to control the damage from the Whig attacks. In *Yankee Doodle* on 24 July Duyckinck disclaimed any "superior morality" for that paper but he too was forced to speak out in order to keep respect for "the decencies of life" and to help preserve "the proprieties of language":

> A writer, whose initials (G. W. P.) make him known as one of the assistant editors of the *Courier & Enquirer* newspaper, takes Mr. HERMAN MELVILLE to task, in the last number of the *American Review* in high parsonical style, for the freedom of his "Omoo." Mr. P. is not entitled to the throwing of the first stone, and if he had made up his mind to lynch "Omoo," he should have selected cleaner shot than the following to pelt it with. Are we reading a miscellaneous magazine, for the study and the drawing room, or have we come upon a stray leaf in physiology, bound in among the pages of the *"American Review, a Whig journal,"* by mistake!

He quoted, as printable in a masculine magazine, the passage running from "It is nothing new to hear conceited men" down through "his name was Joseph." *Yankee Doodle* was seen in the publishing area of Manhattan, but the *Tribune* went everywhere and the *American Review* got into important libraries and stayed on the shelves. (Maria and the others could only wince at the sight of a copy of any issue of the magazine. It died in the next decade with the dissolution of the Whig party, but bound copies were always around in private libraries, as long as any of the family lived.)

Melville returned to Manhattan, for a day or two. On 31 July, the day before his twenty-eighth birthday, he dined with Duyckinck at the "magnificent saloon" of the Astor House, "100 feet by 52, supported by pilasters of the Corinthian order, on the sides, and by a beautiful colonnade at each end," under a ceiling "richly painted in fresco" (as described by Williamson in *The American Hotel*). Duyckinck later effaced his diary entry, but he had recorded a personal and literary judgment: Melville was "cheerful company" without being very "[a word or words here have not been deciphered]" or "original"; specifically, Melville modeled "his writing evidently a great deal on Washington Irving." The effacing has withstood infrared scrutiny, leaving a mystery of just what Duyckinck wrote, and another mystery of whether he ever said anything to Melville about his literary debts to Irving, which were real and which were to deepen. After that dinner, Duyckinck and Melville strolled into the bookshop of John R. Bartlett (later famous for his *Quotations*) and Charles D. Welford in the ground floor of the Astor House. (In 1849 Melville was good enough friends with the owners for Mrs. Welford to give him a letter of introduction to Joseph Munt Langford, of the London branch of Blackwood & Sons.) Bartlett was always ready to receive his literary friends and show them the latest magazines and new as well as old books. Charles Fenno Hoffman was a regular there, and Halleck was among the "most constant visitors." This afternoon Duyckinck, presumably still with Melville, "met Halleck at Welfords" and heard his latest chat about his hobbies, "monarchy and war," and Duyckinck declared him "very pleasant, anecdotical withal with a spice of worldly indifferentism." Halleck also relayed, from the mouth of William Wordsworth, an appallingly bad pun — "the suggestion of the question of whether the high arched bridge at Keswich, in the shape of the Letter *A* was named after the river Greta (Great — A) or the river after the bridge." There were occasions for other meetings between the author of *Typee* and the author of "Marco Bozzaris," and long before this Melville had begun dropping by the bookshop to sample the old books and to look for his name in the magazines and newspapers.

Melville could do nothing about the attacks in the *Tribune* and the *American Review*, and Duyckinck and his friends could do little, even as the attacks prompted a burst of private and public comments on Melville's presumed sexual past. In Cambridge Henry Wadsworth Longfellow and his second wife, Fanny Appleton Longfellow, had read *Omoo* aloud in July, and on 3 August Fanny wrote to her father, the wealthy Nathan Appleton, at 39 Beacon Street, a near neighbor of Shaw's: "We have just attacked Prescott [*The Conquest of Mexico*], after skirmishing through Omoo which is very inferior to Typee, being written not so much for its own sake as to make another book, apparently. I understand the author is engaged to a daughter of judge Shaw. After his flirtations with South Sea beauties it is a peculiar choice (in her)." (Long before, Nathan's brother Eben had been one of the young Shaw's closest friends, in a group Appleton had styled the three "merry men," he the Falstaff to Shaw's Bardolph, as Samuel S. Shaw related in an 1885 memoir of his father.) The announcement of Melville's approaching wedding also evoked this more decorous comment in an unidentified New York paper saved by a member of the family: "Herman Melville, Esq., author of 'Typee' and 'Omoo,' we are happy to learn, is likely to find more happiness in civilization than he ever enjoyed in the romantic Valley of the Marquesas. We expect to find the full particulars in a few days under the proper head, in some Boston paper." Some comments, in public as well as private, were far less subdued.

In the glare of the new notoriety, and of the gossip they knew it had caused, the Shaw family took stock of the situation as the day of the wedding approached. George Washington Peck would not return to Boston and storm the New South Church like a Savonarola, but no one in the family felt at ease about what Herman's admirers might do. Reflecting on the changing circumstances, and putting in abeyance her own deepest desires, the cautious Elizabeth abandoned her plan of being married in the church. In September, when she explained her decision in a letter to Sam Savage, she characteristically minimized her discomfiture:

> At first I had some idea of being married in church and ordinarily I think it the most appropriate place for such a solemn ceremony — but we all thought if it were to get about previously that "Typee" was to be seen on such a day, a great crowd might rush out of mere curiosity to see "the author" who would have no personal interest in us whatsoever, and make it very unpleasant for us both — So I determined to have it in the house, as privately as possible inviting only our relatives, and a very few intimate friends.

At least she was pretty much out of reach on her honeymoon when items like this appeared: "BREACH OF PROMISE SUIT EXPECTED. — Mr. HERMAN TYPEE OMOO MELVILLE has recently been united in lawful wedlock to a young lady of Boston. The fair forsaken FAYAWAY will doubtless console herself by sueing him for breach of promise." This piece of journalistic wit (lamely justified by the current vogue of breach of promise suits by aggrieved ladies) was in Greeley's *Daily Tribune* on 7 August 1847. Thanks to such items in the press, everyone knew that the daughter of the chief justice of the Supreme Court of Massachusetts had married the man who had dallied with Fayaway then deserted her — so that in a peculiar way Elizabeth, both before and after her marriage, stood in Fayaway's shadow.

At the beginning of August 1847, no one in the family had come to terms with this perverse new way of seeing Herman, but the publicity meant that neither the Melville relations in and around Boston nor the Shaw family volunteered or were encouraged to make overmuch of the approaching wedding. The one person who by inclination, duty, proximity, and resources would have behaved splendidly on behalf of the young couple did nothing, for Nilly Van Rensselaer Thayer was nine months pregnant, and gave birth, the day before the wedding (the new father wrote Augusta), to "a strong healthy little fellow," stoutly named Stephen Van Rensselaer Thayer. Ida Russell, who lived a few miles south of the center of Boston, in Milton, put herself out on 9 July to introduce Herman to her cousin Richard Henry

Dana Jr. ("he would like to meet you," she wrote Dana on 8 July) and others, including "Mr. Hudson" and "Dr. Vinton." She included Melville again in a larger party, perhaps the day before the wedding. Dana toward the end of August recorded some of those who had attended: "Present, the Russells & Geraldine Rivers, Henry Wheaton (late Emb. to Prussia), Chas. Sumner, R. B. Forbes, Hermann Melville (Typee), Coolidge Shaw, Ch. Jus. Shaw & fam. R. G. Shaw & family, Mrs. Augira & Miss Rotch, Mrs. Jno. Forbes, the [E. T.] Channings, Bishop Fitzpatrick &c. &c — A good many men of note & very pretty women." This was Melville's first introduction to many prominent people whom Elizabeth Shaw had known all her life.

Melville had arrived in Boston on 2 August with his mother, Helen, and Fanny; the women stayed at the Shaws and Melville stayed elsewhere, perhaps with his father's old friend Daniel P. Parker, possibly with an aunt. Scraps of evidence survive about the Shaws' preparations for the wedding. Hope Shaw was in no position to obstruct any of Lizzie's plans, since the young woman's behavior had been eminently reasonable, unlike Oakes's reckless and huddled up wedding in New York City. Lizzie's half-brother Lem, just turned nineteen, was opposed to her wedding and wrote his cousin Sam Savage that it would not have "done any hurt to have waited a year or two" (as Sam quoted his words back to Lem). Cousin Sam assumed there was "a great hubbub in the family & a great tearing & slashing of linen" (as he wrote to Lem on 18 July), but no details are known. The Shaws almost surely invited all of Melville's aunts in the Boston area, including Mary, whose husband, John D'Wolf, was still legally a co-trustee of the Melvill estate with the judge. Amos Nourse and Aunt Lucy came down from Maine (Bath, now, not Hallowell), the doctor having responded emotionally to his old friend Shaw: "I have no need to speak of the interest we both feel in the event & ceremony which you so kindly invite us to witness — Lucy has always felt a peculiar attachment to her nephew, & Elizabeth has so established her claims upon the affectionate regards of both of us, that the prospective marriage of a sister or a child would hardly interest us more — Nothing therefore could give us more heart-felt pleasure than to become witnesses of the interesting ceremony you advert to, the prelude, we fondly hope & trust, of abounding happiness."

Despite the confusion preceding the wedding, Shaw had kept his mind on ways to protect Elizabeth. On 2 August he had drafted this note concerning legal work he had just given to Benjamin R. Curtis, who first had the job of clarifying who the "you" and the "I" were meant to be:

As you [Curtis] have this day executed an instrument jointly with myself, in which Herman Melville is the party of the first part, my daughter Elizabeth K

Shaw is party of the second part, & you & myself parties of the third, is contemplative of a marriage between the said Herman & Elizabeth, in which we as parties of the third part, have acknowledged the receipt of the sum of three thousand dollars, to hold manage & dispose of, according to the trusts therein declared. Now this is to stand as an acknowledgment & observance, that I [i.e., Curtis] have received the said sum of three thousand dollars, & am responsible for the same, & shall so continue until some further & different arrangement is made between you & myself.

In giving Curtis charge of three thousand dollars to invest, the judge was assuring that Lizzie would receive somewhat more than a hundred dollars twice a year, so she need never be dependent on Herman for small personal expenses.

On 4 August, a very pleasant day, Herman sallied out early in the forenoon for his last vagabondizing as an unmarried man. He had known the Common from childhood, when the old man in the tricornered hat took him there in tow, and now he walked under the tall elms, and saw again near the center of the Common the Great Tree, the largest and oldest tree in the vicinity. By some wayside within the Common he found a four-leaved clover. Later he "yearly" reminded Lizzie of the coincidence of his "chancing on such a specimen" on their wedding day (as he wrote in his dedication to "Weeds and Wildings Chiefly," drafted in the year of his death). Meanwhile, before the ceremony, Lizzie received communion from the Reverend Mr. James Freeman Clarke (1810–88), an original member of "Hedge's club," or the Transcendental Club, a Unitarian, minister of the Shaws' church, the New South Church. The Reverend Mr. Alexander Young performed the ceremony at about eleven in the morning (his son and namesake four decades and more later wrote newspaper articles that recorded details about the Boston Melvill family and the old house on Green Street).

Herman and Lizzie were married downstairs at the Shaw house, great pocket doors opened between the two parlors, in the presence of "relatives, and a very few intimate friends," as Lizzie wrote to Sam Savage in September. Relatives and a very few intimate friends amounted, all told, to about a hundred persons, by Hope Shaw's count. Those present included Judge Shaw and Hope, Lemuel Jr. and Samuel, Maria Melville and Helen (who turned thirty this day), Fanny, and Allan, Sophia and her mother, Rachel Hall Thurston, and the Nourses. The presence of the Nourses at Mt. Vernon Street (Aunt Lucy had brought a Bible as her wedding gift to Lizzie) and the presence of Maria, Helen, and Fanny reminded Lizzie that she had spent summers or falls in her childhood and young womanhood with Herman's relations, so that his family felt almost like hers. Herman remembered Lucy and her first husband from his visit at Hadley, but he may never have met Nourse before. For his part, Shaw as always saw hints of young Nancy Wroe Melvill in the family faces, and took solemn satisfaction in seeing his daughter marry into the aristocratic family he had hoped to marry into himself, and as always he carried in his wallet two love letters from the aunt Herman had never seen.

From Albany young Cuyler Van Vechten (Tom Melville's "twin") came with his sister Kate, the new bride of Elisha P. Hurlbut (without her bridegroom?), and from Lansingburgh came Helen's and Herman's friend Tertullus D. Stewart. (This man's large role in Herman's life was more than three years away; earlier, he may have been attentive to Helen, but by now he was probably engaged, for on 19 October 1847 he married a young Lansingburgh woman, an acquaintance of the Melvilles, Augusta Hitchcock.) Among the guests must have been some other members of the Scollay and Melvill families (Aunt Scollay and her daughter Catherine, Aunt Priscilla, Aunt Jean and Uncle Winslow, Aunt Helen and Uncle Souther, Aunt Mary and Uncle John D'Wolf, young Langsdorff D'Wolf, and his sister, now Nancy D'Wolf Downer). Some of Lizzie's relatives — the Heywards, the Dows (especially her Aunt Lucretia), and the George Waleses — must have come. Daniel P. Parker and his wife were probably invited. Some of the judge's oldest friends on the bench must have been there, Judge Wilde, at least, who was fond of Helen, and some of Hope's and Lizzie's friends, including some of the young women such as Susan Morton, daughter of the former governor, who, like Helen, had wintered there. Canning, the Shaws' waiter, and Ellen Sullivan, the housekeeper, as long-term employees must have witnessed the wedding, if only from a discreet alcove.

Confident in the rest of his wardrobe that Helen had stitched, Herman was soberly dressed in the wedding suit he had "provided" for himself in New York (as his mother had written to Augusta on 28 June). Lizzie wore whatever she and Hope had managed to achieve without Augusta's help. A month later Lizzie described the scene to Sam Savage as best she could:

> I am the least competent of any to give you any account, for saving the knowledge of what Mr. Young said to me, and I said to him, it is all dreamy and indistinct to me — a vision of Herman by my side, a confused crowd of rustling dresses, a row of boots, and Mr. Young in full canonicals standing before me, giving utterance to the solemn words of obligation, is all I can recall when I think of it — They said however that I acquitted myself inimitably, and to all appearances (saving perhaps a more than usual paleness) went through the ceremony with the utmost calmness and composure.

Lem, also writing to Sam Savage, confirmed this claim: "Everything went off well, the weather was very pleasant, Lizzie behaved very well — did not cry or anything of that sort — there were no bridesmaids."

After the ceremony the hundred drank their toasts to the bride and groom then dispersed, except for the more intimately connected (Lem said there was "a party of about twenty five at dinner"). These two dozen or so sat down to dinner, perhaps as early as one o'clock. The Van Vechten cousins and Tertullus Stewart must have stayed, having come so far, as well as the Nourses. Counting four Shaws and six Melvilles (including Lizzie), and two Thurstons, and some aunts (and an odd uncle or two) and cousins, we pretty much know who was there. They had, Hope later wrote, "a very pleasant time." Aunt Lucy probably remarked on a coincidence that bettered Herman's finding of a four-leaved clover: on that same day Amos's daughter Mary was acting as a bridesmaid in Needham at the marriage of a daughter of the judge's classmate Mr. Kimball, Charlotte Sophia Kimball, to John Chipman Hoadley, a civil engineer in charge of the construction of mills and of steam and water-power plants at Lancaster, Massachusetts. (Some of the family recognized the name when they encountered Hoadley as a young widower in Pittsfield three or four years later. It was July 1851 before he met the woman who became his second wife, Kate Melville.)

While almost fourteen-year-old Sam gorged himself on wedding cake until the taste of it was "disgusting" and his cheeks became the resplendent hue of his blue jacket, the maturer guests had plenty to talk about. As to the honeymoon trip, especially, the father of the bride, now a very large man who did not indulge himself in arduous vacationings, could marvel at how much easier travel had become in the last decades, for in June 1816 the judge himself, accompanied by Dr. Jacob Bigelow, had made a memorably difficult excursion to North Conway, a stopping point for the newlyweds. Shaw's party had ascended Mount Washington, and then with the help of guides and men carrying provisions and baggage they had reached "the celebrated natural passage through the mountains known by the name of the Notch," as Shaw had written to his mother, who later had mothered Lizzie until her son's remarriage. Stories of that heroic climb had been part of Elizabeth's childhood. Now the newlyweds were to go through New Hampshire to Canada and back down Lake Champlain to Lansingburgh. Then all the Melvilles would prepare for the great move to New York City — in November, if Hope heard the plans right. Lizzie, who had never even visited New York, needed to hear some cheerful accounts of life in that alien metropolis where Herman and Allan and their brides and their mother and their sisters would all live happily together in one big house.

Newlyweds in New York City

1847

> The audacious immortalities of divinest love are in me; and I now swear to
> thee all the immutable eternities of joyfulness, that ever woman dreamed of,
> in this dream-house of the earth. A god decrees to thee unchangeable felic-
> ity; and to me, the unchallenged possession of thee and them, for my inalien-
> able fief.

Pierre to Lucy, *Pierre*, bk. 2

THE ITINERARY OF THE HONEYMOON is recorded, but little about anything
more personal, other than Lizzie's 6 August admission to her stepmother
that she had left home under the bewildering influence of "commingling
thoughts." Hope Shaw wrote to her nephew Sam, "Mr. & Mrs. Herman
Melville left" (by railroad train) "in the afternoon for Concord on their way
to the White Mountains & Montreal"—first stop, Concord, New Hampshire. To Sam Savage in September Lizzie described the journey to the
White Mountains as "very pleasant." On 5 August they reached Center
Harbor "after a pleasant ride from Franklin the present terminus of the
Northern Rail Road," Melville wrote his father-in-law (apparently having
taken a stagecoach all the way from Franklin, not changing to a steamer at
Weir's). Lizzie also wrote: "We are now at Center Harbor, a most lovely and
romantic spot at the extremity of Winnipiscogee lake, having arrived last
evening from Concord—and we intend to remain until tomorrow. One
object in stopping so long and indeed the principal one was to visit 'Red
Hill.' . . . But today it is so cloudy and dull, I am afraid we shall not be able to
accomplish it." Red Hill was just to the northeast of their location at the
northwest end of Winnipiscogee, and Melville earnestly wanted to climb
it and look back at the "carvings and adorning of its curiously scalloped
shores"—Thomas Starr King's description in his *The White Hills: Their Legends, Landscape, and Poetry* (1862). They were five or six weeks too early to see
Red Hill with its maples all scarlet, but the June colors would have been
already "deepened and enriched," by this time, according to King (whom
Herman later met). To their northwest was the Saco River, which entered

Moby-Dick (ch. 1, "Loomings"). In the postscript to his wife's letter Herman staunchly declared that he trusted "in the course of some two weeks to bring Lizzie to Lansingburgh, quite refreshed & invigorated from her rambles." Cloudy weather or not, the newlyweds had glimpsed an American paradise to rival the Berkshires, and singly or together they returned to it repeatedly in later years.

On 7 August Herman and Elizabeth Melville took the stagecoach for Conway, near Mount Washington, and from there into the White Mountains, where they crossed over into Canada. Melville apparently wrote his mother from Conway. By 18 August Herman and Lizzie were in Montreal, where they proved conscientious sightseers ("The Convents, Cathedral and Parliament House," as Elizabeth wrote to her stepmother, 21 August). They arrived at Quebec on 20 August, and from there Lizzie explained to Hope that her time was so "taken up" that she could scarcely "enter into a description" of all she had seen: "Both cities, Montreal and Quebec impress a stranger very curiously. . . . I like Montreal much the best though — Quebec looks so cold and forbidding and comfortless with its heavy walls and gates, and its huge citadel bristling with cannon. Yesterday we visited the fortification and strolled about on the ramparts." Herman was struck strongly enough by the fortified aspect of the town that two years later he worked the city into an elaborate comparison (*White-Jacket*, ch. 18): "a man-of-war is a lofty, walled, and garrisoned town, like Quebec, where the thoroughfares are mostly ramparts, and peaceable citizens meet armed sentries at every corner." They wanted to get out to the falls, knowing that the British major general James Wolfe's camp in 1759 had been at the mouth of the Montmorenci, but a heavy rain prevented their going, and all in all they were not happy with Quebec, as Lizzie wrote to her stepmother:

> were it not for some scenes of interest in the vicinity we should have left here before this — particularly as our accommodations are not of the first order. The House at which we are staying, the best one in the place, is a great rambling, scrambling old castle of a thing, all stairs and entries, and full of tawdry decorations. A forbidding *strangeness* pervades the place and makes one want to get out of it as soon as possible.
>
> There are no travellers scarcely, and but one or two ladies in the house. The table is mostly filled with English officers who are not always as refined and elegant as they might be.

They got out in the morning of the twenty-first between showers and visited the Plains of Abraham, where the British general James Wolfe had defeated the French general Louis Montcalm at the cost of his own life. They were hoping to be able to see the Indian village Lorette, nearby, the next day, and they found opportunity to buy presents and souvenirs — for Herman, a small meerschaum pipe he kept all his life.

On 24 August in the evening they started home, by way of Lake Champlain, sailing pleasantly down the slender length of "that beautiful piece of water" (as Lizzie wrote to her stepmother), disembarking at Whitehall, the town at the southern foot of the lake, on the afternoon of the twenty-fifth. They had thus far traveled by railroad, stagecoach, and sailboat, that we know of, and now faced another decision, as Lizzie explained:

> The next question was whether we should proceed to Lansingburgh by stage or take the canal boat. We thought stage riding would be rather tame after the beautiful scenery of New Hampshire, and as I had never been in a canal boat in my life, Herman thought we had better try it, for the novelty. This would expedite our journeying too, and having once set our faces homeward, we were not disposed to delay. Being fully forewarned of the inconveniences we might expect in passing a night on board a canal boat — a crowded canal boat too, and fully determining to meet them bravely we stepped on board — not without some misgivings however, as we saw the crowds of men, women and children come pouring in, with trunks and hand boxes to match.

The four-leaved clover had been auspicious, but the canal boat was a disaster, as Herman should have known:

> Well, night drew on — and after sitting on deck, on trunks or anything we could find, (and having to bob our heads down every few minutes when the helmsman sang out "Bridge!" or "*Low* Bridge!") it became so damp and chilly that I was finally driven below. . . . [Herman] also passed a weary night, though his sufferings were of the opposite order — for while I was suffocating with the heat and bad atmosphere, he was on deck, chilled and half-frozen with the fog and penetrating dampness — for the gentlemen's apartment was even more crowded than the ladies . . . so Herman preferred to remain on deck all night to being in this crowd.

On the damp deck Melville could warm himself with thoughts of the last three weeks. The suffocating Lizzie had been sitting up in the cramped women's cabin for two hours when Herman came for her at five "with the joyful intelligence that we were actually approaching Whitehall — the place of our destination" — the town of Whitehall, not the Ten Eyck family estate. There on the morning of Friday, 27 August, they caught the cars for an hour's ride to Lansingburgh and rousted the family up at six o'clock. They were so "very warmly welcomed and cared for" that they soon forgot the "tribulations of the canal boat." Helen had returned to Lansingburgh the day after the wedding, probably escorted by Tertullus Stewart and the Van Vechtens, but

Maria and Fanny had stayed on with the Shaws until 20 August, when both Lem and Sam Shaw escorted them to Lansingburgh, then took their leave. Augusta was probably home, although Kate may have been with the Thurstons in New York. Lizzie would have looked around for Tom, but there were enough Melvilles to give the newlyweds a hearty though sleepy reception.

The black-bordered columns of the Saturday, 28 August, issue of the Troy *Northern Budget* proclaimed direful news, the death of the former governor Silas Wright. Even Herman, then fresh from the ocean, recalled that all Gansevoort's oratory in 1844 would have been in vain if Wright by his personal popularity had not pulled Polk to victory in the state. Wright had been generally admired and even beloved, but Maria could not alter her personal plans. She had a little money — perhaps one of Herman's thoughtful but small donations — and she had a resurgence of ambition. She had all but forgotten how to give a party, for the last was the one she gave for Gansevoort and Helen, the big children, in February of 1827 in Manhattan, more than twenty years earlier. Resigned to God's will in adversity, a model of patient acceptance, Maria was ready to break the long limits on her social activity. Summoning up her mother's superb lessons in household management and her early experiences as a hostess, she planned a suitable welcoming party for her second son and his bride, to be held on 31 August 1847. Perhaps she noticed that the thirty-first had a special meaning as the anniversary of Lizzie's arrival one impossibly busy year before; perhaps she knew it had a still more special meaning as the anniversary of Herman and Lizzie's engagement. With the scribal help of Helen and Augusta, Maria agitated the nearer reaches of the Hudson River valley and the Mohawk valley with requests for assistance and with invitations. She cast her net broadly. Augusta saved a note from an unidentified E. F. Bullan, across the Hudson in Waterford, acknowledging the very kind invitation of Mrs. Melville and explaining that an unexpected engagement out of town would deprive him of the pleasure which he anticipated, and which he doubted not the guests would realize on the happy occasion. Allan may have come up from Manhattan. Maria must have invited the Gansevoorts of Gansevoort and the Gansevoorts of Albany and New York City, as well as assorted Van Rensselaers, Curtises, Douws, Van Vechtens, Van Schaicks, Taylors, and others, as well as the local Peebles and Stewarts. Lizzie remembered many of them from her several visits between 1842 and 1846.

John Van Schaick, Augusta's rejected fiancé, who worked in Troy, received a shopping list from Maria. He wrote a charmingly uncousin-like heading on his response (dated only Monday, 30 August): "Commercial!" Augusta had rejected a man with a large measure of the family wit, for John's nothing-but-business tone to Maria was worthy of Helen or Herman:

Pine apples are out of season; not *one* in market.

Smoked Salmon — *none* to be found to-day. One *dealer*, however, who receives a box once a week, will be able to afford a supply to-morrow morning at 15¢! the pound. Will await your *further orders*, before purchasing.

Cocoa nut cakes, sugar plums & almonds, the "pair" selected on Saturday as a *present*, and 2 pounds Lemon powder, accompany this, which with the two exceptions, "above referred to," completes your order thus far; and hoping you will receive them safely and in season, I remain, Very truly, Cousin John.

He asked her to be kind enough to tell Helen "that *those invitations* were duly delivered, and the *General* promises to smile upon you to-morrow evening." The general would, Cousin John added, "be accompanied by a smaller planet. (That's me)." The "General" is unidentified. John's father, the sun he as planet should have revolved around, was dead, but he may have meant Peter Gansevoort, who had "General" available as one of his honorific titles that he might put on the way he would choose one or another from among his white cravats.

This was a festive celebration in high Gansevoort style. No one in the family was deluded into thinking this was anything but the matriarch Maria's party, but Herman, Lizzie and the others were free to take from it all the incidental pleasure they were capable of experiencing. They had waited, all of them, even Lizzie, for an occasion to celebrate. When it came time for the ritual toasts, everyone had to think of those who should have been there, Lizzie's own mother, Allan Melvill, the father of the bridegroom (who would have been only sixty-five, younger than his friend, Lizzie's father), and above all Gansevoort Melville, who by reestablishing the family intimacy with Lemuel Shaw had made this marriage possible. Even while grieving afresh for Gansevoort, the Melvilles celebrated, and for Herman the party was a personal vindication, fittingly held in the place of exile at the end of exile.

After these festivities, the family could pay attention to some recent developments in the reception of Melville's second book. They could feel quietly pleased that some friend of Melville's, perhaps Evert Duyckinck, had commented on the *Blackwood's* review in an article entitled "De Tocqueville" in the August *United States Magazine and Democratic Review* (the New York magazine that functioned as the more or less official organ of the Democrats, the counterpart to the *American Whig Review*). The writer had seized on the *Blackwood's* review to crow about the British skepticism that the name "Herman Melville" could be real and that Herman Gansevoort was a genuine patronymic, but he also made some points about British delusions of superiority to Americans and about social mobility in America. John Bull's firm conviction "that under any circumstances he cannot be 'humbugged'" had marked him for hapless gullibility. The ordinary Briton was gullible enough, but worst of all were "the public writers," so convinced of their "wonderful sagacity." The American reviewer used the Scot's pompous praise for *Omoo* to emphasize just how "exceedingly rare" it was for British reviewers to take American writers seriously. The writer understood how American humor worked — by piling up truths amid improbabilities, until the audience believed the fantastic and doubted the simple truth. No one had even tried to trick *Blackwood's* — the reviewer had tricked himself:

> Here is genuine Bullism. The improbabilities are cheerfully swallowed; but the plain matter of fact excites suspicion; like the elderly lady, who reproved her sailor son for telling such monstrous stories as his accounts of whale catching; but readily believed the raising of one of Pharaoh's chariot wheels on a weighed anchor in the Red Sea, because she knew that they had been lost there. The Review is incredulous that a man of Mr. Melville's great capacity should have been a seaman; and in expressing such doubts, betrays that utter misunderstanding of American character, which makes American people and institutions so utterly incomprehensible to Englishmen.

The writer gave John Bull a lesson in American social history. The American commercial fleet was surpassing the English because of the "superior class of men that man the vessels" — an opinion quoted from testimony "before the committee of Parliament." That was natural, since the "young seamen in the merchant vessels of America" were to "a considerable extent well educated young men of good families" — news to any American whaleman.

The writer then turned the analysis into a spirited celebration of opportunities open to enterprising American youths:

> The restless enterprise, which impels the agriculturalist and trading youths of the Atlantic states to push into the remote west, reclaiming the wilderness, overrunning the virgin soil, and building up cities like magic, is by no means confined to those classes, but urges as strongly the young man of the seaports to seek adventure on the ocean — not to be or to remain a sailor, but to seek an outlet for the fiery energy within him burning for advancement.

English youths who went to sea were locked into that station for life, whereas an American youth of the same age would go on board "comparatively educated, intelligent and active," advancement on his mind:

> There are few wealthy merchants, or eminent commercial men in New-England, that have not at some time in their lives taken "a trick" at the wheel. Nothing would be more hazardous, when a boy is going into the forecastle of

an American vessel as a "green hand," than to predict any thing in relation to him. Because he begins by "slushing a topmast," "furling a royal," or "taking in the slack of the topsail halyard," it is by no means safe to aver that he will not speedily astonish the literati of Europe in the line of their own occupations; that he will not revolutionize the first country he lands in, or suddenly turn up member of Congress from some western state.

Furthermore, Melville was not the only American man who had sailed before the mast then had written books: "Mr. Dana, of Boston, and Mr. Brown [J. Ross Browne], of Kentucky, have, among others, acquired considerable reputation as authors." The writer had worked *Blackwood's* into a discussion of issues he had already pretty well thought out, and the result was a complex contemporary attempt (perhaps the first such attempt) to use Melville to make a point in a significant argument about American national culture.

The farewell visit was unpleasant, for September was the ugliest Lizzie had ever experienced in Lansingburgh. "Rain! Rain! Rain!" fell all the twelfth and into the thirteenth, then by the seventeenth the nights and mornings were "cold enough for Jack Frost to commence his revels," so that the days felt like November (according to the Troy *Northern Budget* on 13 and 17 September). Herr Alexander, the magician Melville wrote into *Moby-Dick*, was back in Troy from 20 to 22 September, but Herman and Lizzie probably saw him the previous year, not now. Lizzie adjusted to the oddity of being in a familiar place in unfamiliar circumstances. Her very familiarity with the house now created strange sensations, for at times, as she wrote Sam Savage in September, it seemed exactly as if she were there for a visit — until Herman's casual, if not thoughtless, behavior reminded her that she was on different footing: "The illusion is quite dispelled however when Herman stalks into my room without even the ceremony of knocking, bringing me perhaps a button to sew on, or some such equally romantic occupation. Just imagine 'a bride' (as the girls joking call me altogether) mending an old black coat or a pair of stockings — What a picture! But the romance of life must sometimes give place to the realities, unless we can be etherial and dispense with food and raiment." The Shaws witnessed some of this domesticity, for in early September they arrived at Lansingburgh, together intending to go down the river to Red Hook to see Sam Savage's stepmother, Hope's sister-in-law, but the judge was so ill with his devastating annual catarrh that Hope left him there "for a couple of days" and went without him. Maria and Augusta were, after all, incomparable at nursing, and the judge and Maria could always play chess with each other. (Allan Melvill had written Shaw on 6 April 1815: "Maria often speaks of our friend Shaw, but would be no less delighted to best him — at Chess, in which she finds me rather a stupid scholar.")

As usual, the family divided up responsibilities. Herman had begun a new book and needed to get back to it, although he may have been banished from the study that had just been set up for him. Allan was obviously better equipped than Herman for scouting out a house in New York City and sizing up its qualities. For years he had lived in wretched rented rooms, beginning with the grim one at Maggey Wynkoop's that he had occupied in Albany in 1838, where his chamber afforded "an extensive view of a large lumber yard," an affront to his sensitivity that made even the commercial docks of Lansingburgh look bucolic. He had a higher standard now. He had moved uptown from Greenwich Street, nearer the Thurston house in Bond Street, where he spent half his evenings in the back parlor, reading or playing chess with Sophia. By early September Allan had discharged his commission of "looking out for a house in N. Y." — able at last to satisfy some of his lust for real property, even if vicariously. Shaw was on hand in Lansingburgh to approve Allan's selection and advance Herman the money he would need in order to obtain it. Melville could not buy a suitable house with Shaw's two thousand dollars, even in the remote stretches of uptown just south of the new Union Park, but the money was enough for him to take over an indenture of lease on the house newly renumbered as 103 Fourth Avenue, between Eleventh and Twelfth streets, catty-corner to the northeast behind Grace Church. The family always located the house in relation to this recently completed landmark, which occupied 200 feet on Broadway between Tenth and Eleventh (the church property stretching 150 feet from Broadway eastward). Fourth Avenue until quite recently had been called the Bowery, for it was a continuation of that old Dutch trail out to the wilds of Manhattan Island. The structure was probably a row house, since the entire property was only 25 feet wide (by just under 94 feet deep). The property was administered by Gerard Stuyvesant, Hamilton Fish, and Lewis M. Rutherford for Rutherford Stuyvesant, and Melville was forbidden to sell his indenture of lease without the consent of the administrators. Apparently a speculative venture done for the ultimate benefit of a minor, this was a recently built house (as its neighbors were), perhaps just new enough to have Croton water piped into the kitchen and just old enough to have been built without an indoor toilet or gas pipes.

On 9 January 1845 the administrators had signed a previous, and probably the first, indenture of lease with Hannah L. Morley, spinster. Now, on 10 September 1847, with their permission she transferred her indenture of lease to Herman Melville of New York, gentleman. In consideration of six thousand dollars paid by Herman Melville to Hannah L. Morley, the property was his to have and to hold from 10 September 1847 until 10 September 1868, subject to the payment of "the rent," in an unspecified amount, and to a mortgage on the indenture of lease for five thousand dollars. Hannah

Morley and Herman Melville signed the indenture, and Allan Melville deposed that Herman Melville had signed it in Allan's, the deponent's, presence, all according to the book of conveyances of the city of New York. This means that Melville put down one thousand dollars, received from Judge Shaw, and that within the next weeks, if not already, he had possession of at least one thousand more, for Shaw specified in 1860 that he had advanced Melville a total of two thousand dollars for the purposes of obtaining the house. Therefore in the early fall of 1847 Melville had a thousand dollars of Shaw's money to pay for moving and settling in. Fairness would have dictated that Allan's contribution would be to make the mortgage payments and to pay the annual rent (a few hundred dollars?), at least for the first two or three years — perhaps with the help of Rachel Thurston.

In her letter to Sam Savage, written between 12 and 18 September 1847, after the judge's departure from Lansingburgh for his regular duty at Lenox, Lizzie went to some pains to convey to Sam that she had not deliberately deceived him about her plans when he left for Illinois in the spring: "I little thought that before I saw you again I should have passed such an important era in my life, and changed my home and my name for another. Indeed it was as much of a surprise to myself as to any of my friends for you know when you went away it seemed very indefinite, indeed almost unthought of." Now the plans had changed again. Far from setting up housekeeping at Lansingburgh (as Sam had been left to assume from what he had heard in August) the whole family was "on the eve of leaving Lansingburgh and removing to New York":

> We have already taken a house there and shall probably be settled there in three or four weeks. Allan is to be married next week on Wednesday, and we are all to reside together in one large family. We are going down to the wedding and that will be my first appearance in New York. We shall return in a day or two and begin immediately to make arrangements preparatory to the grand move. I don't know how I shall like living in New York. I'm afraid no place will ever seem to me like dear old crooked Boston, but with Herman with me always, I can be happy and contented anywhere. "Tis home where the heart is" you know, and as long as mine is where it is, outward scenes will make little difference to me.

She was still the only bride in the immediate family, and she had made a love match. Allan's wedding would give her a glimpse of her new life so she could be prepared for the move around the first or second week of October.

In this letter to Sam, Lizzie had a delicate message for him to convey when he was in Chicago, but "*only*" (she emphasized) if "a good opportunity" were to arise: "tell Mr. McIlroy for yourself, *not from me*, that my marriage was very unexpected, and scarcely thought of until about two months before it actually took place. I have some reason for wishing him to know this fact but I want you to mention it casually on your own account." "Scarcely thought of" is a curious phrasing that reinforces the possibility that the engagement existed without Lizzie's being sure that it could soon eventuate in marriage. Brought from Ireland when young, Daniel McIlroy had been educated at Harvard, after which he clerked for Judge Joseph Story, through whom he presumably met the Shaws. In 1844 he had left Boston for Chicago, where he was soon much admired for knowledge of the law and for exceptional oratorical skills. Elizabeth saw him there when she visited her brother Oakes Shaw in 1845. McIlroy's attentions had stirred her to the point that she felt some obligation to pass word to him, in a studiedly offhand fashion, rather than let him see a report in the papers, if he had not already seen one.

Herman escorted Lizzie, Maria, and the bridesmaid, Augusta, down to Allan and Sophia's wedding on 22 September in the Church of the Ascension at Fifth Avenue and Tenth Street. Kate was probably already staying with the Thurstons or the Curtises (now a ferry ride away, in Brooklyn), to be present for the wedding. The widow Thurston and her children attended, even Sophia's older sister Abby Pitman Thurston (born in November 1821) and her husband, Richard Lathers, besides Sophia the member of the Thurston family who proved most important in the lives of the Melvilles. After their marriage on 9 July 1846 the Latherses had moved to Georgetown, South Carolina, on the coast between Charleston and the North Carolina border, a location that had reduced their occasions for making any particular acquaintance with Herman, a letter of 1848 shows. Now Lathers and his wife paid Maria the attention she deserved.

Many of the Bond Street neighbors attended. Evert Duyckinck wrote his brother that the redoubtable obstetrician Dr. John W. Francis, of No. 1 Bond Street, was there, happily squelching a captain who was bragging about the valor of American field officers: no one remembered, Francis was sure, the names of even the generals at the capture of Tippoo Sahib — the momentous capture that ended the second Mysore War in 1783. Allan ought to have invited Aunt Mary Chandonette Gansevoort, Guert, and the Curtises, and perhaps the Bradfords, if not the Maretts, and Maria may delicately have been requested to invite a few of her own special friends from the 1820s — the Joseph Greenleafs, perhaps. (Allan had special reason to be polite to Aunt Mary, because Guert or Geurt Van Schoonhoven had died in Waterford on 17 July 1847, ten years and a month after willing a house in Albany to Aunt Mary Chandonette Gansevoort as well as a cash bequest to her, two thousand dollars, and property to be divided among her children. The will is in the Manuscript Room, New York State Library.)

One of the invited who did not attend the wedding was Cousin Priscilla,

long exiled to Galena, now back in Pittsfield, and still grieving for her father
(dead on Herman's birthday in 1845) and for her sister Julia Maria (dead on
18 July 1846). In the early 1830s Cousin Priss had been rumored, at least by
Julia Maria, to have had a suitor, but she was now confirmed in spinsterhood,
and unaware of Augusta's own romances. In a note to Augusta she played
upon the name of the church in which Allan was married: "We received
Allan's wedding cards in due season — In imagination, I saw them at the
altar — attended by those nearest & dearest to both — and afterwards — as a
happy bride & groom — the centre of a joyous circle — tell me, 'Gus — (for I
believe *you* were present) — Did they not look like Divinities? — & of *course*
they left *New-York* for a short time — for space & freedom to enjoy the dawn
of their wedded bliss — was their love as ethereal, (like *Hermans* & *Lizzie's*)
that it bore them *upward*, towards a *heavenly* Paradise — or did they seek one
among the lovely beauties of earth?"

What Priscilla wrote is very curious in the light of *Pierre*, the book in
which Herman made use of her history and situation in life. There (bk. 3,
ch. 3) Herman's narrator exults at the way the setting sun bathes Lucy's
"whole form in golden loveliness and light," so that her "flowing, white, blue-
ribboned dress, fleecily invested her." All her aspect to Pierre was "touched
with an indescribable gayety, buoyancy, fragility, and an unearthly evanescence." After marriage, Pierre decides, "one husbandly embrace would break
her airy zone, and she exhale upward to that heaven whence she hath hither
come, condensed to mortal sight." "By heaven," he concludes, "but marriage
is an impious thing!" The Gansevoorts and Van Schaicks were highly self-
conscious users of the language, but to a remarkable degree the Melvilles
lived not in their actions so much as in their words. Herman's strangely
extravagant ironical style in *Pierre* begins in his responses to the idiosyncratic
and excessively mannered style of his tragedy-struck Cousin Priscilla.

Duyckinck was impressed with the ceremony as well as the prospects for
another civilized house in Manhattan, for Melville had never before been
able to entertain him during his stays in Manhattan: "Last evening passed an
hour or two very pleasantly at wedding of Allan Melville (a brother of Typee)
who has married a Miss Thurston in Bond St. Herman was there with his
Boston bride and the two brothers in a few days commence housekeeping
together in this neighborhood. It promises to be an agreeable house to visit
at. Miss Melville — a sister — was as kind and impressive, with more softness
than the East Hampton ladies" (friends of George, a family named Miller).
Duyckinck had the news that Melville was preparing a third book which
would "exhaust the South Sea marvels" and presumably close the career that
the sailor had so oddly managed to draw out beyond that first book. A

comment on the contrasting images of Herman Melville proved irresistible: "Typee in a worked satin vest was a pleasing contrast to Typee — the wanderer Omoo &c." Herman himself probably witnessed another contrasting spectacle that Duyckinck recorded in his diary that day, a "dull procession of Irishmen" all "celebrating" the delayed funeral of Daniel O'Connell, the "Liberator," champion of the repeal movement. There were occasions enough that day to set Melville reflecting on the vicissitudes in his life that had made him the outsider looking in and now the insider looking out, while others had perished — including Daniel O'Connell and the great American orator in the cause of repeal, Gansevoort Melville.

Soon after the wedding Melville and Lizzie returned to Lansingburgh to begin serious packing, but Herman was back in town in early October. There he wrote his father-in-law a letter in which he evinced his constitutional inattentiveness to business detail. Hope forwarded the letter to Worcester, where Shaw was holding court, and from there Shaw wrote her the next day, 10 October, saying, "He [Herman] seems not very well to have understood me, but I believe there will be no difficulty." In case anyone called at Mt. Vernon Street to present a bill of exchange drawn by Herman on the judge, all Hope had to do was "to ask the person to call on Mr Clark, cashier of the New England Bank," to whom the judge had already written on the subject. By that time, Sophia and Allan may have returned from their honeymoon, but Allan's presence in his capacity as a lawyer was apparently not necessary for these final steps.

In the midst of the preparations for the move, a new attack had appeared in the *Tribune*, not in the daily but in a supplement, on 2 October 1847. J. Parton in his 1855 *Life of Horace Greeley* observed that during the "fighting years" of the *Tribune*, 1845, 1846, and 1847, if the paper "was not at war with all the world, all the world seemed to be at war with it, and it was kept constantly on the defensive." Nevertheless, Greeley was, in sober truth, constantly on the offensive, as in this article in the supplement. The author, W.O.B., was understood at once to be William O. Bourne, a journalist Melville's age, but a close friend of Horace Greeley already. Bourne claimed that he wrote his article only because he had seen news that Melville was "preparing another work for the press," and therefore, as a Christian who devoutly believed in the righteousness of missionary work, he was obligated to lay the truth before readers of Melville's first two books and prospective readers of his third. Bourne mustered a formidable array of numbered topics and alphabetized subtopics on the theme of Melville's lack of credibility as a historian and his unscrupulous condemnation of the missionaries. He then offered these general thoughts:

From a consideration of the whole subject I pronounce Mr. Melville's book [*Omoo*], so far as its pretended facts are concerned, a tissue of uninformed misrepresentations, of prejudiced ignorance, and of hostility characteristic of one who loves South Sea adventure for South Sea abandonment and "independence." His caricatures of the Missionaries, whether in the pulpit or surrounded by a crowd of gaping natives — his contempt for constituted authorities and the consuls and officers — his insubordination — his skulking in the dark where he could not be seen by decent men — his choice of low society — his frequent draughts of "Pisco" or other liquors — his gentle associations with Tahitian and Marquesan damsels — and the unsullied purity of his life and conversation, all entitle him to rank as a man, where his absurdities and misstatements place him as a writer — the shameless herald of his own wantonness, and the pertinacious traducer of loftier and better men.

The "unsullied purity of his life and conversation" was mere sarcasm rather than some attempt at an ironic reference to Melville's tendency to distance himself from the reprehensible behavior of others, notably Long Ghost, since Bourne went on to call Melville "the shameless herald of his own wantonness."

Someone in the literary circles Melville had moved into took it upon himself to write a long rebuttal for the *Evening Mirror* of 6 October. Early in the year, in *Yankee Doodle*, the Duyckinck clique had been openly feuding with the new editor of the *Mirror*, Hiram Fuller, a Whig and the man whom Poe had immortalized on 21 February 1847 when he won a long-delayed libel suit against him. Repeatedly expressing his loathing for Duyckinck and for Mathews, Fuller still showed no sign that he associated Melville with them. Whoever wrote the article showed unusual knowledge of the vicissitudes of Melville's short career and a great deal of genuine concern for the young author. "If Omoo were nearly forgotten," as W.O.B. asserted, "why should this indiscreet defender of the missionaries, be at so much pains to prolong the memory of that book by making such an assault upon its author as he has done?" The truth was that *Omoo* was "daily becoming more widely known, and its author more universally admired." The writer made a remarkable assertion: "No American book, since the appearance of Stephens' travels in the Holy Land, has been so popular as Omoo."

The defender of Melville in the *Evening Mirror* went on to assert that the reception of *Omoo* was even more favorable in England than here. Cheerfully admitting that the books were not faultless, he insisted that Melville had a right to express his views on the missionaries, and concluded with an elaborate comparison:

The merits of his books consist in their pleasant narrative style, and the vividness with which he produced impressions of scenes that more learned, grave, and pious men had not been able to do with all their correctness and respectability. There was no lack of books on Polynesia, but until Melville's lively volumes appeared, we were completely in the dark about that remote and very peculiar region, except the enlightenment we had received from oral testimony. . . . Such books are just as necessary to give us correct notions of distant countries, as are the reports of statistical compilers and topographical engineers. They are to such works what landscape paintings are to maps. One gives us particulars, and the other general truths. A landscape drawing of Tahitian scenery might be untrue in all its particulars, and yet enable us to form a perfectly correct idea of the general characteristics of that region, but a map would be utterly useless if not strictly correct in all its lines. . . . Ellis, Williams, Stewart and Ruschenbugn [Ruschenburg], supplied us with maps of Polynesia, but Mr. Melville has given us bright and beautiful landscapes. None but a dunce and a bigot would quarrel with him for not intruding upon the province of map-makers and making his book the half and half work which is so obnoxious to God, men and critics.

The tone of this defense was admirably restrained and the basic premise well taken, but there was no winning against virulent attacks like Bourne's, any more than against Peck's and Greeley's.

The *Evening Mirror* was probably on Duyckinck's table on 6 October when Melville dropped by to see him. Later Richard Lathers decided on the basis of what he knew of Charles Lamb's works and reputation that Duyckinck as host "much resembled" the English essayist "in his constitutional shyness, unctuous and quiet wit, sententious and clever conversation, and slight hesitation in speech," mannerisms of Duyckinck's that Melville came to be extremely familiar with. On this occasion Melville got swept along to the opening of the new rooms of the Art Union at 497 Broadway for "an elegant entertainment, at which were present, during the evening, at least five hundred invited guests" (according to the account in the *Evening Express* the next day); the "assembly was composed of clergymen, literary men, editors and artists." Melville had a good chance to observe Duyckinck in action as the editor shepherded him about. This is Evert's account to his brother: "The Art Union opened its new rooms to night in its Broadway quarters in the rear of Mr Cram's former dwelling house — a long hall, well lighted, the walls covered with paintings by Cole, Page, Brown, Gignoux, Hicks, &c the floor well sprinkled with good fellows, the artists generally of fine personal appearance, a selection from the Press." According to the *Evening Express*, a "feast was spread out, and wine, 'that maketh the heart glad' flowed freely."

There was formal entertainment ("A number of admirable stories were told by Mr. Matteson, the artist, and other distinguished story tellers, and several songs were sung by one or two gentlemen") but the guests were able to mill about as they wished. Duyckinck introduced Melville to several men, including William Cullen Bryant, the author of "Thanatopsis" but more to the point the man whom Gansevoort had jeered at in the speech at Elyria just three years before, when he gloated that Bryant and his friends had been driven "*back to their holes*" and had "*sued for mercy.*" Bryant's memory being particularly keen, he got away from Melville as soon as he could, and thereafter continued his policy of saying as little about him in the *Evening Post* as possible. (About the most attention he ever gave anything of Melville's was when he quoted extracts from Melville's essay on Hawthorne in 1850, not knowing who the author was.)

After parting from the sour Bryant, Melville had a better time. Someone told him and Duyckinck that one of Thomas Sully's bathing nymphs looked like Fayaway, so they had to go see for themselves. Charles Lanman, the art critic, introduced Duyckinck to Sidney Mount, "the humorous painter," who struck him as possessing "a fine and even beautiful countenance." "Mount and Melville were delighted with the living tableaus," Duyckinck noted, and clearly were delighted with each other, especially since Mount's paintings were modern versions of Dutch genre painting, wholly congenial to Melville's taste and familiar from childhood on walls in Albany houses. A great many people in this milieu still remembered Gansevoort, with good will or ill will, and Herman's new enemies Greeley and Peck may have been in the rooms, but the number of accomplished men who wanted to make Herman's acquaintance boded well for his move to the city. All in all, the former country schoolteacher and sailor had spent hours in less appealing company, and the evening gave him something to think about on his way back up the river to Lansingburgh.

The exact day or days of the grand move is uncertain. Augusta left for a short stay, probably at the Manor House, and during her absence a letter arrived from Augusta Whipple Hunter written on 6 October and another that Cousin Priscilla had completed on 8 October. Someone at Lansingburgh wrote a hasty note on the back of Mrs. Hunter's letter: "I herewith send you Priscilla's letter, and this one, which arrived this morning. We have two letters from Tom. He is well & will be back in May. The small hymn book and bible we will bring if possible. *Dont forget the spectacles.* and we shall expect you Tuesday morning." This note is signed "N." — that is to say, an "H" which looks for all the world like an "N," so it is either Helen's or Herman's, more likely hers. Tuesday would have been 12 October, and the implication is strong that packing was going on even while Augusta was away—perhaps away by design: she was inordinately pained by household confusion, a persisting reminder of the traumatic move to Albany in 1830, when she was nine. The Melvilles probably left Lansingburgh that week and were settled in New York City by mid-October.

For the first time since 1837 all the Melville children would live under one roof. No one could forget an old story Maria told to inculcate the virtue of family unity. Allan had even saved the version of it she had written to him on 7 August 1842:

> You must recollect the Story of an old man who on his death bed called his Sons around him, and handed them a bundle of Sticks, requesting them each in turn to endeavour to break them, they all tryed but were unsuccessful, he then requested them to undo the bundle and try the Sticks singly. They were then found to break easily, there was then no difficulty in snapping them assunder.
>
> You will understand from the above Illustration the great importance of unity and attachment between the different members of the same family, there are Eight of you, and acting together, each anxiously and deeply feeling towards each other one interest you will be happier and wiser than each to [go] separate ways.

No one had to be reminded that there were only seven of them to provide beds for in the house on Fourth Avenue. If anything, Gansevoort's death had strengthened the depth of feeling the others felt toward each other. Lizzie had been one of the family before Herman returned from the Pacific. Sophia was comparatively a stranger, but she had not been required to enact the biblical scene that had so moved Herman and Allan in Rossiter's painting they had seen in Washington. She was going where Allan went, to what was in effect Maria's house, but Bond Street was close enough by that her marriage did not shatter the "unity and attachment" of what remained of the Thurston household.

After old Major Melvill's death there had been no occasion for distribution of any furnishings to Allan's widow, and even the smaller personal items were kept by Allan's brothers and sisters (Mary D'Wolf was the one who had walked off with her father's last cocked hat). Peter and Herman Gansevoort had possession of most of the military clothing and the furniture of the Hero, still. What Maria now owned was what had been huddled out of Manhattan aboard the *Ontario* and now was returning, almost intact, despite the recurrent threats that her furniture might be seized by her creditors. The table her son Allan sold for her may have been the only piece she had to relinquish, for in Lansingburgh there had been surplus furniture stored away in the garret. Now Maria had quite enough furnishings for the bedrooms and parlors of the new house on Fourth Avenue, perhaps supplemented with a few pieces from the families of the brides. (In a letter to Helen on 5 December 1850, Augusta implied that Sophia had brought comparatively little Thurston furniture with her.) A few of the pieces survive, in the family, and others are known by nineteenth-century descriptions. The piano, later discarded by the irreverent Allan, was Maria's, the one imported from London and given to her by the Hero of Fort Stanwix when she was ten. There was an elegant set of small French armchairs with smooth dolphin heads where anyone's palms would fit, but scaly bodies for human forearms to rest on. The "ancient mahogany Chairs" brought down from the Lansingburgh garret in the spring (as Maria had written to Augusta on 17 May) were available for use downstairs, if needed. There were copies of some paintings of ancestors (Uncle Peter still had the Gilbert Stuart originals), and original portraits of Maria and Allan Melvill, as well as Asa Twitchell's portrait of Herman, and a watercolor of the young Gansevoort that was the only image they had of him—a painful reminder that if he had just spent his money on himself, instead of being so self-denying, he could have been daguerreotyped in New York or London.

Herman, a man who had traveled light, and would do so again, delighted in living among elaborate old furnishings, as he made plain in a passage he wrote two years later, at the Fourth Avenue house (*White-Jacket*, ch. 76):

> Out on all furniture fashions but those that are past! Give me my grandfather's old arm-chair, planted upon four carved frogs, as the Hindoos fabled the world to be supported upon four tortoises; give me his cane, with the gold-loaded top—a cane that, like the musket of General Washington's father and the broad-sword of William Wallace, would break down the back of the switch-carrying dandies of these spindle-shank days; give me his broad-breasted vest, coming bravely down over the hips, and furnished with two strong-boxes of pockets to keep guineas in; toss this toppling cylinder of a beaver overboard, and give me my grandfather's gallant, gable-ended, cocked hat.

Gamesomely remembering possessions in the Melvill house on Green Street and the Gansevoort house on Market Street, Melville found quite enough old-fashioned charm in what the women made of the Fourth Avenue house. Recognizing that he needed some atmospheric touches, he probably duplicated most of the nautical cast Maria had helped to give to his workroom in Lansingburgh after the tumultuous upheaval of the spring housecleaning. Like his mother and Helen, and perhaps even the younger Augusta, he must have had the feeling, at moments, that Allan and Maria Melvill had moved once more, from the Broadway house out to what had been a remote stretch of the Bowery but was now called Fourth Avenue. He was home for the first time since 1830.

Maria and Lizzie, at least, were keenly aware that the house was architecturally undistinguished. Lizzie described it as being very convenient, although "without any pretensions to style or elegance," unlike, she did not have to specify, the Mt. Vernon Street house. In this letter, written early in April 1848 to invite Sam Savage to visit, she stressed the space: "Notwithstanding our family is so large, we have *two* unoccupied bedrooms, and each of us plenty of rooms besides." (Tom, when he returned, would take one of the bedrooms.) Herman and Lizzie had a small suite of rooms—a workroom with a desk or table for him and the bedroom, which, in the custom of the time, doubled as Lizzie's own room and their private sitting room. American dinnertime was at two, but the Melvilles dined late, at four, to accommodate Herman's need to concentrate on his manuscript for one sustained stretch of hours. (The normal time for tea in America was six, a "massive" meal, in effect, supper, according to the British observer Mrs. Felton, but for the Melvilles tea was delayed, and less substantial.) After dinner Lizzie and Herman customarily retired to "their" room, and in the evening all of them gathered in "the" parlor, which means that there was a family parlor as well as a more public parlor, for Evert Duyckinck on 15 November in a letter to George referred to two parlors. The house was at least two stories high, probably three, not counting the basement, where the dining room and kitchen would have been, as usual in the city—shallow enough in the granite of Manhattan so that there were windows at ground level. There were rooms (probably in the basement or the garret) for at least one resident servant (when Sam Shaw arrived early one Sunday in June 1848, nobody "was up but the girl," he wrote to his father). It was not Mt. Vernon Street and it was not Bond Street, but it was undeniably large and "convenient"—to Maria's old friends, to shopping, to Allan's office in Wall Street, to Duyckinck's house at 20 Clinton Place. It was handy to the single omnibus line, which ran from a point in Broadway opposite Bond Street down to the Astor House, fare ten cents—no straps for passengers, and no one allowed to enter when seats were full.

Again drawing Melville into their projects, Duyckinck and Cornelius Mathews saw him on the evening of 23 October and "discussed a possible weekly newspaper which should combine the various projects of the kind" Mathews "had entertained for the last few years" (Evert wrote in his diary). By November the hospitality was not all one-sided, for the Melvilles were entertaining, as Evert Duyckinck wrote to George: "Melville has got into a happier valley than the Happar not far from here and wife and I have looked in at the Ti—two very pretty parlors odorous of taste and domestic felicity.

He is a right pleasant man to pass an evening with and I think I may promise you some pleasure from his society." Purblind to the value of any youngish male writer besides Mathews, Duyckinck continued to think of Melville as a sailor-author, not simply an author, but now, after a Bond Street wedding and a glimpse, with his wife, Margaret Panton Duyckinck, in tow, of a most elegantly furnished (if merely convenient and not ornate) house and highly refined female family members, he was ready to concede that Melville was "right pleasant company." On 23 September three years later, 1850, George Duyckinck wrote to a friend, Joann Miller, that the Fourth Avenue house was "one of the pleasantest to visit at" that he ever came across. The Melvilles were indeed all pleasant company, even Allan, who was easier to take when he was one of a number of people in the party.

To all outward appearances, it was Duyckinck who exerted influence upon Melville, three years his junior, and Melville visited Clinton Place far more often than Duyckinck visited Fourth Avenue. Yet there is a curious possibility that Melville was having a strong effect on the older Duyckinck, that he was proving genuinely fresh, and refreshing, to this editorial friend accustomed to a certain safe level of achievement and ambition. Melville may have been proving so original that Duyckinck actually felt that some of his basic attitudes might bear reexamination, for he wrote George on 15 November:

> I am getting less fastidious about many things, realizing that we have only a life interest and not a fee simple in the things of this world, finding more good in common enjoyments, thinking a good digestion infinitely better than an elegantly bound library. I have never enjoyed extraordinary fine weather more than this season. You must not think because American publishers are not the choicest fellows in the world and since newspapers are quicksands and trade a rat trap that there is no living in America. There are cakes and ale even if Griswolds, Wileys, Appleton &c &c are not virtuous.

This is rather less than a conversion. Duyckinck could never say, with Melville, that anyone who has been a sailor is not in the least fastidious. Before long the attraction of an elegantly bound library would reassert itself with Duyckinck. But the young Herman Melville made a profound impression even on people temperamentally antipathetical to him, and it would be excessively skeptical to assume that Duyckinck's ruminations had nothing to do with being so much in Herman's presence. Words such as "winning," "alluring," and "charming" do not quite suggest the effortless power Herman emanated at this confident phase of his life.

[28]

Mardi as Island-Hopping Symposium
1847–1848

> My cheek blanches white while I write; I start at the scratch of my pen; my
> own mad brood of eagles devours me; fain would I unsay this audacity; but
> an iron-mailed hand clenches mine in a vice, and prints down every letter in
> my spite.

Mardi, ch. 119

PREOCCUPIED WITH IMPORTANT MATTERS, *Mardi*, marriage, and the move
to New York, Melville let months pass without writing to the English publisher of *Typee* and *Omoo*. At last, on 29 October 1847, a week after the
session with Duyckinck and Mathews about a polemical newspaper, he felt
settled enough to write to Murray, as he might in courtesy have done at any
time over the previous months. The letter was long and disingenuous, if not
devious. Melville began with the easy target, *Blackwood's* skepticism about
Uncle Herman's very existence as well as the identity of "Herman Melville."
He declared that he was "engaged upon another book of South Sea Adventure (continued from, tho' wholly independent of, 'Omoo')." It would "enter
into scenes altogether new" and would "possess more interest than the former; which treated of subjects comparatively trite" — remarkable disparagement to the publisher of his two works, the first of which no one had declared
trite, and the second of which had rarely been perceived as anything but
fresh. The warning was of the sort Melville later called ambidexter. The
words "continued from" implied that he was thinking of a book that would
recount some of his adventures on the *Charles and Henry* (a ship which
Gansevoort would likely have mentioned to Murray, however vaguely, as
part of his informal affidavit that the author of the manuscript of *Typee* was
his brother and a bona fide sailor who had been in the South Seas). Yet it was
"wholly independent" of *Omoo*, more interesting, and entering "into scenes
altogether new." Everything in this description could fit closely enough a
fictional account of adventures of two whale hunters who touch at islands
other than those in the Marquesas and the Society group.

Melville let Murray know that he had "recently received overtures from a house in London concerning the prospective purchase of the English copy-right of a third book" — an offer he was sure would be "liberal." Treading more than a little clumsily, he asked what Murray might offer in advance for the book, which was not, he now seemed to think, by an author whose previous subjects were "comparatively trite": "I can not but be conscious, that the feild where I garner is troubled but with few & inconsiderable intruders (in my own peculiar province I mean) — that it is wide & fresh; — indeed, I only but begin, as it were, to feel my hand." The year before, he had been fairly specific about when *Omoo* would be ready (saying on 1 July 1846 that it was "nearly completed" and would be ready the latter part of the fall — which in fact it was). Now, on 29 October 1847, he was much more vague: "I can not say certainly when the book will be ready for the press — but proba-bly the latter part of the coming Spring — perhaps later — possibly not until Fall — but by that time, certainly."

In his brash attempts at pushing for the best deal, Melville was estimating the sales of *Omoo* in England by the praise in the British notices that had come to his attention. Now he expressed his dissatisfaction that "there was no reservation for the benefit of the author as in 'Typee' " — that is, no promise that Murray would give more than bargained for if the book proved very successful. Showing no comprehension of how important his presence in Murray's Home and Colonial Library was to the building of a lasting reputation for him throughout the British Empire, Melville suggested that if Murray took the new book he should publish it independently of the library, so as to sell it at double the price at first then later in a cheap edition. Whatever his mood when he wrote, he sounded arrogant: "With regard to the new book, let me say that my inclinations lead me to prefer the im-primatur of 'John Murray' to that of any other London publisher; but at the same [time] circumstances paramount to every other consideration, force me to regard my literary affairs in a strong pecuniary light." Like many an author whose books are widely reviewed, Melville had convinced himself that he was enriching his publishers, and he hated having to take the publisher's word for how many copies were printed and sold. Rankling now in Melville, also, was the resentment that he was not being taken at his new valuation of himself — a quite irrational feeling, since no publisher had been given the chance to discover in the new manuscript evidence that the sailor had mastered the art of fiction. Indeed, in his letter Melville carefully avoided letting Murray know that the new book was different in kind from *Typee* and *Omoo*.

On the next day, 30 October, there was good news even in the *Tribune*, a letter from its London correspondent dated 4 October, quoting the praise of *Omoo* in the *Times*. Nathaniel Parker Willis had a full copy of the *Times* when he quoted extensively from it on 13 November in the *Home Journal*, under the heading "FOREIGN APPRECIATION OF MELVILLE," beginning with the praise that Willis, some years earlier, while assiduously imitating Irving, would have exulted to hear applied to himself: "This journal says that Mr. Melville is as clever and learned as ever, and 'sailor before the mast as he is, he discourses as pleasantly and humorously of Nature, in her hundred aspects, as the gentle Washington Irving himself.'" On 18 November William Cramer, Gansevoort's friend, in his Milwaukee *Daily Wisconsin* expressed his gratification that *Omoo* was "received with the highest encomiums in England," and that in particular the *Times* had spoken "of it in the most unqualified commendation"—commendation that Cramer picked up from the *Home Journal*, most likely. He went on to comment on a "quaint remark of a reviewer, that the author woke up one fine morning and found himself a great man"—a reference to the June issue of the New York *Columbian Magazine*. Cramer concurred: "In truth, Mr. M. seems to have 'vaulted' into greatness; for probably no author in so brief a time, has ever acquired so wide a name." Melville was not only the American Defoe, he was also the American Byron. Accounting himself among Melville's "earliest friends," Cramer rejoiced "in every manifestation which evinces that he is likely to hold that position in the literary world, worthy of his abilities, his family, and his country."

On 18 December in a column on "HARPERS' BOOKS" in the *Home Journal* Willis went out of his way to compliment Melville while working in allusions to British praise:

> If there is anybody who has not submitted to be enchanted by the books of *Herman Melville*, we commend to him to seize, therefor, the first rainy day, or sleepless night, the first leisure, in short, if leisure there be this side the water. Douglas Jerrold says of Omoo, that it is "a stirring narrative, possessing much of the charm that has rendered Robinson Crusoe immortal—life-like description." And Blackwood says, Melville is "the phoenix of modern voyagers, sprung, it would seem, from the mingled ashes of Captain Cook and Robinson Crusoe. The book is excellent, quite first rate—the 'clear grit,' as Melville's countrymen would say."

This fall some of Melville's earliest and latest friends were rallying to consolidate his reputation and to assure him of a welcome to the city of his birth, the city that now promised to be his permanent home.

At Fourth Avenue during late October and early November 1847 Melville quickly settled into a routine. A long letter Lizzie wrote to her stepmother on 23 December is the most valuable surviving record of their routines, including Melville's work habits. The short days (just then the shortest of the year) flew by her, Lizzie wrote. Breakfast was at eight, after which Herman went out into the cold for a walk, one direction or another (they were a quarter of a mile north of Washington Square and just south of Union Park, that almost treeless plot surrounded by a high iron railing). In his absence Lizzie flew up one or two flights of stairs "to put his room to rights," so that he could "sit down to his desk immediately on his return." Inexperienced with husbands, she availed herself of some of the attitudes she had displayed toward young Lem and younger Sam: "Then I bid him good bye, with many charges to be an industrious boy, and not upset the inkstand." Afterward she went to her own room, the bed-sitting room, to "flourish the duster, make the bed, &c." Before she knew it, "ding-ding" went the bell for luncheon, at half past twelve, and afterward the ladies had to be dressed to receive any callers. Herman insisted upon her "taking a walk every day of an hours length at least," so it was two o'clock or later when she returned, and then she had a wifely duty (as quoted earlier), to make herself "look as bewitchingly as possible to meet Herman at dinner."

After their late dinner of four (or even four-thirty, young Lem said the next March), Herman and Lizzie went upstairs to their room (the bed-sitting room, not the workroom, for Lizzie could never have sat with him in a disordered room, although she might leave it as it was until he went out for his morning walk). There they enjoyed "a cosy chat for an hour or so," or he would read to her some of the chapters he had been writing in the day. Then he went downtown for a walk, looked "at the papers in the reading-room &c," the "&c" covering other possibilities, such as his dropping in at one or another house on the way. He returned, customarily, "about half past seven or eight":

> Then my work or my book is laid aside, and as he does not use his eyes but very little by candle light, I either read to him, or take a hand at whist for his amusement, or he listens to our reading or conversation, as best pleases him. For we all collect in the parlor in the evening, and generally one of us reads aloud for the benefit of the whole. Then we retire very early—at 10 o'clock we are all dispersed—indeed we think that quite a late hour to be up—This is the general course of daily events—so you see how my time is occupied but sometimes—dear me! we have to go and make calls! and then goodbye to everything else for *that* day! for upon my word, it takes the whole day—from 1 o'clock till four! and then perhaps we don't accomplish more than two or three, if unluckily they chance to be in—for every body lives so far from every body else, and all Herman's and Allan's friends are so polite, to say nothing of Mrs M's old acquaintances, that I am fairly sick and tired of returning calls.

And the round was endless: "no sooner do we do up a few, than they all come again, and so it has to be done over again." Excepting formal calls, she wrote, she had scarcely visited at all.

For Elizabeth life in New York was constricting. As November arrived her spirits had sunk at the thought of facing the great New England holiday away from the dear old crooked streets of her own Boston. New Yorkers might make polite social calls, but they were Maria's and Sophia's friends, not her Boston friends, and while New Yorkers might be well intentioned about observing Thanksgiving, celebrating the Puritan holiday properly was not something that could be done out of sight of the State House.

Accordingly, Lizzie and Herman arrived at Mt. Vernon Street on Wednesday the twenty-fourth and stayed until the thirtieth. Nilly reported to Augusta on 15 December: "I was very happy to have seen Mrs. Herman, she was looking remarkably well & seemed quite happy again to be among her own friends, though she seems to like the city of her adoption very much." "How could she," Nilly sagaciously asked, "be otherwise than happy in N. Y.?" She hoped that Lizzie had taken back "good reports" of her little treasure, who was being called simply Rensselaer: "you cannot imagine what a never failing source of comfort & amusement the dear little fellow is to us." Always thoughtful of Augusta's feelings, Nilly wrote in this self-satisfied vein only because she was confident that Augustus Peebles was making a weekly pilgrimage down from Lansingburgh to pursue his courtship of Augusta. Nilly was in fact confident enough to think that this mild winter was "peculiarly favorable for Mr. Peebles, no ice barriers to chill ardent wishes; in fancy I imagine once a week a young gentleman seated by your side, with a tender arm entwined around your waist & breathing all kinds of tender loving vows. After all there is no happiness compared to the love giving & love receiving heart, is there cara mia?" She wanted to know when the happy event was to take place, but her letter may already have struck the recipient as ironic, for sometime this fall or winter the engagement was broken (Augusta broke it, the story went). Thereafter, Augusta's life was an adjunct to other people's—her mother's, her brother Herman's, her sister Fanny's, and the Van Rensselaers'.

Thanksgiving over, Herman and Lizzie returned to their new routines. Herman was "not fond of parties," Lizzie explained to her stepmother in the long letter on 23 December, and she didn't "care anything about them" there in New York, her words carrying not only a sense of lost familiar acquaintances and practices but also an awareness of the social distinctions between Boston and New York, such as Nilly Thayer, in Boston, had mentioned to Augusta a year and a day earlier (22 December 1846): "We are very gay, and there seems no end to it at present we have five or *six* invitations ahead, the gentlemans society is particularly good, the young men are more substantial & less frivolous than in N. Y. & their mind & morals are much more attended to. A dissipated young man in Boston cannot gain admittance into society as elsewhere." Other forces worked to keep the Melvilles very private. Sophia's ultra-high Episcopalian principles forbade her going to the opera or the theater, so when a great treat was proposed for 24 December, it was Herman, Lizzie, and Fanny who went to the new Astor Place Opera House around the corner to hear Donizetti's *Lucia di Lammermoor,* sung by Ferdinando Beneventano as Lord Henry Ashton and Teresa Truffi as Lucy, and conducted by Rapetti. It was "the first place of public amusement" Lizzie had attended since her arrival in New York, but "somehow or other" she was not pining for public amusements.

Herman had his own amusements. When he sallied out during his evening freedom between six or six-thirty and seven-thirty or eight, a great walker since childhood, he may have headed directly for the wharves or the Battery, perhaps still rolling in his gait a little, more likely striding with the erect carriage that became characteristic, and for decades drew eyes to him. These late autumn months, he found it convenient to drop in, after walking, at one reading room or another, as Lizzie said, or some other public place where he could sample social intercourse. In his strolls Melville may have looked into a French café in Warren Street, opposite City Hall. According to Henry T. Tuckerman, by now a friend of his, its appointments and aspect "closely resembled similar places of rendezvous and refreshment in the provincial old towns, where retired officers, village notaries, and political quid-nuncs, year in and year out, hold impromptu *soirées* over snuff, dominoes, and their *demi-tasse.*" Here or elsewhere, Melville often encountered Thomas Low Nichols, Gansevoort's friend, the first godfather to *Typee,* and very likely Fitz-Greene Halleck.

Another accustomed stop for Melville may have been Frank's (Francis Monteverde's), an Italian hostelry at No. 5 Barclay Street, where "came many celebrities well known in the artistic, literary, fashionable, and theatrical circles of the city." James Grant Wilson in his biography of Fitz-Greene Halleck listed among the regulars the journalists A. D. Paterson of the *Anglo-American,* Dr. J. S. Bartlett of the *Albion,* the conspicuously tall William T. Porter and his four brothers of the *Spirit of the Times,* and George W. Kendall of the New Orleans *Picayune.* Halleck, William Henry Herbert, George Morris, and Edgar Poe "were among the *habitués* at Frank's," which was perhaps a little too rowdy a place for Melville, given over, toward the end of the evening, to a fast theater crowd, the sort that sees the first half of the play and adjourns to drink. In his review of *Moby-Dick* in the 6 December 1851 *Spirit of the Times,* Porter referred to "our friend" Melville — a conventional phrase that in this case may indicate a personal acquaintanceship and affection between the publisher of the "Big Bear" school of American literature and the author of *Moby-Dick*. At the office of the *Spirit of the Times*, at Frank's, or elsewhere, Porter and Melville very likely met and talked.

Because Duyckinck was an obsessive diarist and hoarder of paper, and one of the few hoarders with enough prescience to see that suitable repositories received his own great library and his papers, we tend to think of Melville as a satellite of Duyckinck's during his early career in New York. Melville may indeed have known Duyckinck best, but he probably dropped in, with some regularity, at the homes of other literary men for whose social gatherings no records have survived. Willis, for one, lived nearby, on Washington Square. After his death, many of Willis's papers were destroyed, or were lost, so we tend to forget that when Willis arrived home from London early in 1846 he took up with Herman just where he had left off with Gansevoort, and their intimacy had grown as Willis defended and promoted the young author in the columns of the *Home Journal*.

There is documentary evidence for two regular stops Melville made in his nocturnal socializing — at Clinton Place and at Bond Street. Here were the two houses in all of New York where one could hear the best conversation. Duyckinck knew everyone worth knowing. Richard Lathers in his *Reminiscences* celebrated the regular informal Saturday night supper parties that Duyckinck ("the prince of good fellows," Lathers called him) held in the great dining room in his basement. Lathers gave a typical guest-list during William Makepeace Thackeray's lecture tour in 1855–56. His memory had a way of conflating experiences, and Melville was probably not present when Thackeray was, but the list conveys a sense of the sort of men whom Melville did meet there, beginning in 1846 or 1847: "such kindred spirits as Dr. J. W. Francis, Rev. Dr. Hawks, the poet Fitz Greene Halleck, the comedian Hackett [who became a special friend of Allan Melville's], the novelist Herman Melville, and the poet and traveler Bayard Taylor."

Melville also became a regular at Dr. John Wakefield Francis's house at No. 1 Bond Street, the "center for the intellectual galaxy of this metropolis," according to an 1850 letter a New York journalist wrote to a New Orleans newspaper. Another regular at Dr. Francis's was Henry T. Tuckerman, who may have written that account; at the least, he filed it away for safekeeping, then quoted it extensively in his own 1865 memoir of the doctor:

> Occasionally this position [Francis's centrality in the intellectual galaxy of the city] is held in public, when the distinguished are gathered together in solemn conclave, and daily at his hospitable board may be seen some visitor in New York. But of an evening one may drop in, and find a genial gathering, surrounded by the smoke of their own cigars. One is at home here — and so is the

> Doctor, if not professionally engaged. T. [Tuckerman] keeps his classicality
> for his Addisonian books, and is full of anecdote and humor; G. [Rufus Gris-
> wold], fiery, sarcastic, and captious; D. [Duyckinck] critical; M. [Melville]
> (when in town) taciturn, but genial, and, when warmed-up, capitally racy and
> pungent; painters and sculptors, men of deeds, not words, and among them,
> rarely seen abroad, the friend of Shelley and Byron. The Doctor himself is
> glorious, when no lumbago or fresh bronchial attack dispirits.

(Scholars of the Romantics have not yet identified the aged friend of Shelley and Byron, resident in Manhattan about 1850.) Enthralled with "the commerce of select intelligences, celebrated by Boswell and other literary annalists," Dr. Francis had created the nearest New York could come to such gatherings of extraordinary people as the lucky visitor could still find in London. Duyckinck, in a memorial tribute to Tuckerman, wrote of often witnessing "the delight with which Mr. Tuckerman was welcomed in that hospitable home in Bond street." Melville, welcomed with the same delight, became fond of Dr. Francis — enough so as to send him in 1852 a rare book he knew the doctor would enjoy, Alexis Marie de Rochon's *Voyage to Madagascar and the East Indies;* to that gift Francis responded with a courtly compliment about Melville's having "seen the whole world" and possessing "graphic powers" of description denied to him. For a man who had spent months in the forecastle of whaleships, the level of social intercourse at Duyckinck's and Francis's was high.

At Duyckinck's and Francis's, and perhaps in other parlors, Melville frequently found himself in the company of Henry T. Tuckerman, only six years his senior, but already one of the country's leading critics of both literature and painting. Born into a wealthy Massachusetts family, cherished, destined to graduate from Harvard until he was sent to Italy out of fear that the harshness of the New England climate would shorten his life, Tuckerman returned home ready to publish his first book, *The Italian Sketch Book*, in 1835, at twenty-two (the title an obvious tribute to Irving). He returned to Italy in his mid-twenties for a longer stay that resulted in his book on Sicily, in which a thread of fictitious adventures united his descriptions of "the scenery, antiquities, and manners of the island." Returning home again, he had "passed some seven years devoted to mental cultivation in Boston" before coming to New York in 1845, so he was as new to the city as Melville, though with immediate easy access to the art world as well as the literary circles. Willis in reviewing his *Painters of America* in the 20 November 1847 *Home Journal* described him then as twenty-seven (he was thirty-four), a man who "wears all his beard, (and a very handsome chestnut growth it is), has the slight stoop of a scholar, winning manners, and no wife." He was an odd companion for the athletic Melville, it might seem, as odd as the foppish Willis, but Tuckerman and Melville developed a mutual respect for each other that lasted until Tuckerman's death at the end of 1871.

One way or another, through his business connection with the editor of the Library of American Books, through the accident of Allan's having courted and married a girl from Bond Street, through his own marriage and move to the city, in late 1847 Melville at twenty-eight found himself in a literary society where many American editors and writers, some hardly older than he was, hoped and plotted to rival the British in every aspect of literary production. Some of the more nationalistic like Duyckinck or even chauvinistic like Cornelius Mathews were obsessed with creating a rival to *Punch*. Melville had participated in *Yankee Doodle* to that end, and even talked about yet another paper partly inspired by *Punch*. Much more important, the new literary patriots needed to create great long poems in the English language, better than Barlow's, better than Emmons's. Mathews had tried for recognition as the great American poet with his *Wakondah; The Master of Life* (1841) and his *Poems on Man, in His Various Aspects under the American Republic* (1843), and as the great American prose writer with his strange works of fiction such as *Behemoth: A Legend of the Mound-Builders* (1839), *The Career of Puffer Hopkins* (1842), and *Big Abel, and the Little Manhattan* (1845), all set in American locales. Early in November 1847 the papers began assessing Professor Longfellow's self-consciously North American epic, *Evangeline* (parts of it uncertainly sprinkled with names of flora lifted from source books on the Mississippi Valley). In the Washington *National Era* of 25 November 1847 the abolitionist journalist and poet John Greenleaf Whittier exclaimed: "EUREKA! — Here, then, we have it at last! An American poem, with the lack of which British reviewers have so long reproached us." (This review was reprinted in Boston in *Littell's Living Age* on 25 December, and so became widely available.) Whether Longfellow had succeeded or not with *Evangeline*, he focused attention on the possibility of someone's writing a great American poem — and as British reviews of *Evangeline* reached the United States the respectful treatment of the poem suggested that the genre in which the great American literary work was to appear was probably not drama, which Mathews had also attempted, or fiction, but epic poetry, or at least the long poem, not the lyric. Melville took due note of the high rank afforded the long poem by the best contemporary authorities (aside from Edgar Poe). At this stage of his career Melville's realistic hope was that he could write poetic prose that might make a London or Edinburgh critic exclaim something like "EUREKA! — Here, then, we have it at last! An American poetic fiction!"

As he worked through late 1847 and into 1848 Melville began to feel that he was more than a sailor who had mastered the techniques of book-craft with amazing swiftness. For years he had possessed a capacity for profound responses to what he read, though he remained slow to define just what aspects of what he read most powerfully stirred him. Owen Chase's "wondrous story" had exerted a "surprising effect" when he read it "upon the landless sea, & close to the very latitude of the shipwreck," he recalled, much later, without defining the effect. The powerful if inchoate literary response Melville experienced in 1841 was matched by the powerful but inchoate literary aspirations he began to experience during and after the traumatic, ecstatic summer and early autumn of 1847. Now, there were times when, excited at what was happening in his manuscript, exalted by the evidence of his achievement, he allowed himself the dangerous thought that he might be becoming a truly great writer.

Why a young man with an education as deficient as his could decide that he might be writing greatly, albeit with two successful books behind him, requires a good deal of explanation. Leaving untouched his great model Washington Irving (and leaving aside the great novelist Cooper, against whom, oddly enough, he never had to rebel), Melville had seen many American writers for himself and taken their measure. Americans since the revolutionary generation had striven to be great epic poets, among them, notably, his Uncle Thomas's acquaintance Joel Barlow. In Melville's youth the air had been thick with projects for a great independent national literature designed to match the physical and political grandeur of the young nation that had achieved and confirmed its independence by twice defeating the British. Even before he had published a book, Melville had begun meeting some of Gansevoort's literary friends, and subsequently had formed friendships with writers of celebrity, including Hoffman and Willis. It was now apparent to him that these writers, as well as Halleck, so revered as a poet, had missed their chances to produce the great literature of the present or the future. If he had taken the measure of Halleck and Hoffman and others of the older generation, he had also taken the measure of the younger Longfellow and Mathews. He could become a better writer than either of them, not to mention a better than Richard Emmons and the other writers of national epics. Melville's mood owed something to the terrible abuse he had taken in the papers over the past two years — from the "man of the Evangelist," from Greeley, from Peck, from Bourne, and others, singly or in cohorts. Instead of being crushed by cruel denunciations, he would rise higher than ever.

The timing is not certain, but within weeks of his resuming his work on the book, perhaps shortly after writing to Murray at the end of October, very possibly before Thanksgiving 1847, Melville decided to change the basic nature of the work he was writing. Around this time, clearing the way for his new plot, Melville wrote a scene in which the surviving, and more or less realistic, characters encounter a large double-canoe manned by stalwart sons of an old priest, Aleema, carrying a maiden to sacrifice to the gods of Tedaidee. In a violent rescue, the narrator kills the priest, and he, Jarl, and Samoa sail on with the maiden, the infinitely mysterious and unimaginably beautiful Yillah, white of skin, golden haired, blue eyed, and allegorical — representing something like a state of early consciousness, the time when celestial visions seem to steal transparently over the face of a slumbering child (as in ch. 49, "Yillah"). They sail on, the narrator taking the name of a god, Taji, and are welcomed by Media, king of the island of Odo (imaginary islands having begun to appear among real ones). Soon mysterious damsels, emissaries of the dark Queen Hautia, land on the beach and offer ambiguous gifts. After an idyllic interlude with Taji on an islet, Yillah disappears, and three of Media's subjects are introduced: Mohi, or Braid-Beard, the historian; Babbalanja, the philosopher; and Yoomy, the poet. With Taji, they sail away in nominal quest of Yillah. What follows is an island-hopping symposium in which Melville was free to bring up on a new island whatever subject he wanted to expatiate on at the moment, and free to sail off to another island and take up a new topic of conversation. The narrator continued, nominally, but his companion Jarl and the native Samoa dropped away in chapter 102, "They depart from Mondoldo," so that they need not compete with Media, Babbalanja, and the other members of the floating symposium. In his rough and ready way, Melville had decided he could alter the nature of his book in what remained to be written while retaining the bulk of what he had already written. At least this decision saved rewriting.

By the end of December 1847, Melville had received John Murray's 3 December reply to his truculent letter of 29 October. Driven to bluntness, Murray forcibly disabused Melville of the idea that his books had been profitable:

> Of Typee I printed 5000 Copies and have sold 4104. Of Omoo, 4000 and have sold 2512 — Thus I have gained by the former 51 — 2.3. & by the latter am a loser of 57 — 16 — 10. I do not willingly enter into such details but this is bona fide the state of the Case. I shod not have entered into such details with an Author but that it is evident from your Manner of Writing that you and your friend[s] suppose me to be reaping immense advantages in which you ought to be participating — understand I pray that I do not eventually expect to be a loser but *I cannot anticipate* from what has occurred that I shall be any great gainer except in credit as the publisher of these two Books.

Sheltering Melville from knowledge of the private complaints he had received about *Typee* and *Omoo*, Murray magnanimously offered to read the new work in sheets and, if he thought he could make profit for both of them, to advance Melville one hundred guineas on publication and then after the costs had been recouped to pay Melville thereafter half profits from every printing. In closing, he groused, once again, that there had so far been no means of proving to the English public that Melville's books were "not fictions imitations of Robinson Crusoe": "T'is this Feeling of being tricked which impedes their Circulat^n here."

The tradition of making New Year's calls survived, so Maria may have gotten abroad or else stayed home and received guests on 1 January 1848, but Herman devoted part of the day to replying to Murray. Still aggressive, he demanded that the suggested advance of one hundred guineas be doubled, at the least. In this letter a canceled phrase as well as the final text indicates pretty clearly that already, during the fall, after the move to New York, his book had become something other than a continuation of *Typee* and *Omoo*, and therefore was not to be thought "barren of novelty": "But the plan I have pursued in the composition of the book now in hand, clothes the whole subject in new attractions & combines in one cluster all that is romantic, whimsical & poetic in Polynisia. It is yet a continuous narrative. I doubt not that — if it makes the hit I mean it to — it will be counted a rather bold aim; but nevertheless, it shall have the right stuff in it, to redeem its faults, tho' they were legion." He had first written "it will be counted a rather" (the word looked like "rathar") "bold aim; & its authentic" then canceled "& its authentic." The unnamed new book was not, by the end of 1847, "authentic" in anything like the way he had wanted *Typee* and *Omoo* to be perceived as being — that is, as true narratives of his own adventures. The manuscript had "a continuous narrative," but it combined all that was "romantic, whimsical & poetic" about Polynesia — a far cry from what Murray valued. Clear, at least, is Melville's ambition: this was the book by which he took bold aim at high literary stature. He proposed the only reasonable course — that barring something unforeseen (like an unsolicited and unconditional offer from another London publisher), they would let matters rest until he had a book to show Murray.

After he had been settled for weeks in New York City in the fall of 1847, Melville bought P. P. Cooke's edition of Froissart's *Ballads and Other Poems* (\$.75) — a cautious outlay of funds in what seems to have been a period of stringent avoidance of unnecessary expenditures. Allan may have been paying part or all of the "rent," but whatever was left of Shaw's second thousand dollars must have been steadily diminishing for household expenses. Early in 1848, as months passed without any substantial new income from *Typee* and *Omoo*, Melville began trying to borrow books instead of buying them. On 17 January he became a member of the New York Society Library, then situated conveniently at 348 Broadway, when he purchased from Evert Duyckinck his brother George's share (George himself had purchased it from Jedediah B. Auld). Melville promptly put his membership to use by withdrawing "Bougainville Voyage" in the 1772 English translation (*A Voyage round the World. Performed . . . in the Years 1766, 1767, 1768, and 1769*) and three volumes of "Hartley on Man" (David Hartley's 1801 *Observations on Man, His Frame, His Duty, and His Expectations*). The next day, however, he bought on his Wiley account a calf-bound edition of Shakespeare (not in type that he found easy to read) and a Montaigne, for a total of $9.25. Around the end of January, Melville borrowed from Duyckinck "Rabelais vol 2"; he also apparently borrowed from Duyckinck a book owned by someone else (George Tomes, brother of Robert Tomes, the writer, both perhaps already friends of Melville's): Charles H. Barnard's *A Narrative of the Sufferings and Adventures of Capt. Charles H. Barnard, in a Voyage round the World* (the 1829 or perhaps the 1836 edition). On 8 February from Wiley he bought Defoe's *Roxana* for $.75, Coleridge's *Biographia Literaria* for $1.50, and another copy of Burton's *Anatomy of Melancholy* for $2. In March he borrowed from Duyckinck a volume of Sir Thomas Browne, another volume of Rabelais, Esais Tegner's *Frithiof's Saga*, then perhaps on another day two more volumes of Browne and yet another volume of Rabelais. During 1848, probably early in the year, he acquired Seneca's *Morals* and James Macpherson's *Fingal, An Ancient Epic Poem*. On 22 June 1848 he bought a copy of Carey's translation of Dante from Wiley for $2.12, and five days later, for $.65, *An Inquiry into the Authenticity of Various . . . Portraits of Shakespeare*. Of this partial list for which evidence survives, not all the works have any relevance to *Mardi*, but some of them are directly relevant to it.

In those early months of 1848, Merrell R. Davis showed, Melville began not only to be more frugal in gaining access to books but also to employ a wider range of source books than ever: "Now Melville, though continuing his reading of travel literature with Barnard or Bougainville, ranged far afield with Shakespeare, Montaigne, Seneca, Browne, Ossian, Coleridge, and Rabelais." Davis puts the situation pithily:

In an early chapter on the "Chondropterygii," based on various travel books, Melville could now interpolate a paragraph citing Sir Thomas Browne as his "ensample; who, while exploding 'Vulgar Errors,' heartily hugged all the mysteries in the Pentateuch." By an ingenious combination of an anecdote from Ellis and a footnote in Browne he could compound a traveler's tale of a trepan operation with Atahalpa's receipt for hatching a fairy. Instead of going to Bennett's *Whaling Voyage* for the basis of a chapter on the phosphorescence of the sea he could now turn to Seneca's *Morals* for the substance of a chapter on Oh-Oh, the antiquarian, and to Rabelais ("Rabeelee roared, — let us") in order to parody the long catalogues of "rarities" or of books, "old ballads . . . Tarantula books . . . theological works," all with comic titles. Instead of relying on his personal experience (however changed or assisted by South Sea books) for his characterization of the captain of the *Arcturion* he could turn to Ossian or *Frithiof's Saga* to interpolate or revise a chapter characterizing Jarl. "My life for it, Jarl, thy ancestors were Vikings . . . Ah! how the old Sagas run through me!" With Hartley and Coleridge in mind he could parody the conflicting discussions of the "doctrine of Philosophical Necessity" or permit his Babbalanja to disclose Hartley's vibration theory or Coleridge's "All-Plastic Power." For Babbalanja's ontological heroics and his comic battle of words with the sage Doxodox ("Tetrads; Pentads; Hexads; Heptads; Ogdoads; — meanest thou those?"), Melville could rely on Thomas Taylor's translation of Proclus.

Davis cautions that Melville "did not neglect to use his books of South Sea voyages," William Ellis's *Polynesian Researches* in particular, which along with Tyerman and Bennet's *Journal of Voyages*, Wilkes's *United States Exploring Expedition*, and Bennett's *Narrative of a Whaling Voyage*, continued to suggest episodes and incidents. The difference, according to Davis, is that now Melville was using Ellis with the eye of a satirist as he turned "the material into bizarre and humorous, oftentimes whimsical accounts that satirize lawyers, doctors, or religion." The difference at times may have been more in degree than kind, for Harrison Hayford points out quite similar satirical uses of Ellis in *Omoo*. So often as to show that he must have owned a set, Melville was also plundering the *Penny Cyclopædia of the Society for the Diffusion of Useful Knowledge* (London, 1833–43) for all sorts of arcane information, not least the entry on "Squalidae," from which he may have picked up "Chondropterygii," as Mary K. Bercaw has shown.

Melville had room in his manuscript to record news from his emerging sense of himself, as in "Dreams" (ch. 119). There he celebrated his belated intoxication with great writing and great thinking:

Like a grand, ground swell, Homer's old organ rolls its vast volumes under the light frothy wave-crests of Anacreon and Hafiz; and high over my ocean, sweet Shakespeare soars, like all the larks of the spring. Throned on my seaside, like Canute, bearded Ossian smites his hoar harp, wreathed with wildflowers, in which warble my Wallers; blind Milton sings bass to my Petrarchs and Priors, and laureats crown me with bays.

In me, many worthies recline, and converse. I list to St. Paul who argues the doubts of Montaigne; Julian the Apostate cross-questions Augustine; and Thomas-a-Kempis unrolls his old black letters for all to decipher. Zeno mur-

murs maxims beneath the hoarse shout of Democritus; and though Democritus laugh loud and long, and the sneer of Pyrrho be seen; yet, divine Plato, and Proclus, and Verulam are of my counsel; and Zoroaster whispered me before I was born. I walk a world that is mine; and enter many nations, as Mungo Park rested in African cots; I am served like Bajazet: Bacchus my butler, Virgil my minstrel, Philip Sidney my page. My memory is a life beyond birth; my memory, my library of the Vatican, its alcoves all endless perspectives, eve-tinted by cross-lights from Middle-Age oriels.

Rather than forging stronger alliances with members of the New York Democracy or the New York literati, for many months past he had been fastening himself with hoops of steel to more durable associates: "my . . . friend Stanhope," "my old uncle Johnson" (ch. 13); "my Right Reverend friend, Bishop Berkeley" (ch. 20); "my fine frank friend, poor Mark [Antony]" (ch. 22); "my . . . ancestor, Froissart," "my friend and correspondent, Edmund Burke" (ch. 24); "my . . . friend Thucydides" (ch. 32).

The routine that Melville established before Thanksgiving of 1847 continued through the first half of 1848. Family letters give a sense both of the routine and of the sort of breaks he took to fulfill his obligations as host or simply to recreate himself beyond his daily walks. The test came on 27 January 1848, when Lizzie's half-brother Lem, nineteen-and-a-half, and a Harvard student, presented himself to be pampered for a month. He "had been studying very hard and needed the relaxation" (so Lizzie wrote to Sam Savage on 3 April). On 28 January, a Friday, Herman and Allan, both of whom had been working very hard themselves, took Lem "to the top of Trinity church steeple," which afforded a superb view from almost three hundred feet high. From that vantage point, down to the east the Corinthian columns on several of the temples to Mammon on the northern side of Wall Street looked almost like a row of diminishing-sized pencils. But looking down, in any direction, was not the true point of the climb. On a clear day nothing interfered with the vistas: the bay, filled with steamers, ships, brigs, schooners, sloops, and barges; the East River, the Navy Yard, and Brooklyn Heights, and, above them, New York Sound; the farms and wild stretches of Manhattan beyond the new cross streets in the Thirties; the grand Hudson River, Fort Lee, Hoboken, and the stretch down toward the Navasink Highlands (which, C. F. Briggs had said in *Trippings*, could "loom up across the bay like a great lump of lapis lazuli bathed in liquid gold"); and the ever-varying bay again.

After the manful climb and descent were over, Helen and Lizzie took Lem as their escort over the ferry to Brooklyn to call on "a Mrs Gansevoort" (Aunt Mary Chandonette Gansevoort) and on Lizzie's relatives the Maretts, as Lem wrote to his mother on 30 January. Lem saw "Aunt Marett" (no blood kin to him) and "Mr. Marett" but not Lizzie's first cousin the ailing Ellen (who was "very much fatigued by a walk, the first she had taken for a great while"). That evening "little Mr. Dana from Boston called"—young Ned, son of the "Idle Man" (the senior Richard Henry Dana) and brother of the sailor-writer; unmentionable at Fourth Avenue was his intimacy with the abominable George W. Peck, whom he was visiting. Having decided that his way of playing the amiable host without betraying his frustration was to wear out his guest with physical activity as fast as possible, on Saturday morning Herman tramped off with Lem all the way up to 174th Street "to see the Aqueduct bridge over the Haarlem river." The stone aqueduct supported by fifteen Roman arches, just being completed as part of the permanent route of the city's blessing, water from the Croton Reservoir, was notable as the new country's longest bridge. Herman probably also took Lem on one of his regular walks down to the Battery on a suitable day, for even from there the view down the coast of New Jersey toward the Navasink Highlands (popularly corrupted into "Neversink," which Melville later made use of as the name of his man-of-war in *White-Jacket*) could be as colorful as the inside of Grace Church. As a resident of Manhattan, Melville had to content himself weeks on end with occasional glimpses of natural beauty, or nature being straddled with an awe-striking antique-looking aqueduct, but he retained his love for open spaces. He was still the sailor who had swayed aloft with his ship, and had seen, in his time, in two oceans, tumultuous nautical views that might be said to rival those from Trinity's steeple.

There were things Melville simply would not be party to. A massive torchlight parade with the bannered Gansevoort was unforgettable, but one such was enough. Early in 1847 Melville had seen the Congress in typically disreputable session. Now he did not need to witness the local Democrats as they whipped themselves into frenzy, so on the first Saturday night of the visit he turned Lem over to Allan for "a great Democratic war meeting in Tammany Hall," a crowd such as the sheltered Whig youth had never been exposed to in all his nineteen years. Bryant's *Evening Post* commented that after an early hour the hall was so crammed that no further access could be obtained, "and the neighboring streets were filled with a dense crowd." Those inside, including Allan, "unanimously and enthusiastically" denounced the Whigs for attempting to discredit Polk's excellent reasons for making war by executive action. The crowd resolved virtuously that "the present war was commenced by an unprovoked and inexcusable attack made by the Mexican army on our forces upon American soil; that it was the highest duty of the Government to repel this attack." Allan voted cheerfully for the fifth resolution of the night, a charge that Whigs were unpatriotic: "That the reproaches and lamentations poured out, as to the origin and conduct of the war, evince little patriotism, and still less sense; that the only object of a large portion of those who pursue this course, and the only real tendency of all who adopt it, is to distract the minds of our people, to enfeeble their energies, and to offer to the world the same spectacle of a divided, disgraced and degraded country that Mexico now presents to us." After the resolutions, Lem was privileged to hear "the celebrated General Houston of the U.S. Senate and also Mr. Foote of the Senate" (as he wrote to his mother on 30 January). Sam Houston assured the Democrats not only that Texas was theirs by right but (what was more to the point) that Texas was "a country blessed with fertility and richness of soil, variety and beauty of climate," and was therefore well worth winning. Bryant in the *Evening Post* dryly reported that the Hero of San Jacinto "concluded amidst rapturous and vehement acclamation" after declaring that he "believed that as surely as the sun il-lumined the firmament so surely was it destined by Divine Providence that the great and glorious institutions of the United States would be spread over the entire southern portion of the continent." This was Manifest Destiny with a vengeance, as Herman heard in due course.

Then there were "loud and repeated calls for Foote, Foote, cheers, hur-rahs, &c. &c." (according to the *Post*). This was "General" Henry S. Foote, whom Greeley on the thirty-first identified as the man a mere Mississippi faction had "sorely taxed the omnipotence of the People in attempting to make a Senator of." Now Foote boldly claimed that opponents of the war were traitors and that the United States had the inalienable right to wage wars of conquest: "He combatted the doctrine preached by their enemies, that they should not pursue a war of conquest, that they had no more right to the acquired territory than a parcel of robbers. He said that two jurists but the other day broached that doctrine in Congress, Messrs. Clayton and Webster. (Loud groans and hisses.) He contended that almost every land, country and nation, were held by the right of conquest. He instanced En-gland, conquered by William of Normandy—Greece by the Pelasgians—America itself torn from George the Third." Furthermore, if the United States did not seize Mexico, England would. At which a voice from the crowd was heard: "If England attempts to annex Mexico, we shall annex Ireland to be even with her." This was orgiastic pandemonium for a young Harvard Whig, who had lived much of his life without knowingly dining with a Democrat besides Gansevoort Melville. Senator Webster, now ridiculed with Miltonic groans and hisses, was Lem's father's old and dear friend.

On Monday, 31 January, the *Tribune* piously reported that "the advocates of more Butchery and Subjugation among us convened per order at Tam-many Hall to rekindle, by lies and liquor, the fainting, flickering flame of infernal War"—and the Democrats had done so, almost sacrilegiously, on Saturday evening, "when the Christian's thoughts turn naturally to the coming day of worship as well as rest, and to the Prince of Peace whose terrestrial birth it commemorates." Christians, those identifiable by "moral principle, religious precept or humane feeling," Lem could have told Greeley, were not in attendance at Tammany that night. The Democrats had no way of knowing that Polk's secret peace commissioner Nicholas P. Trist was then, without authority, negotiating the Treaty of Guadalupe Hidalgo, which he signed on 2 February. Polk declared an armistice on 29 February, several days after the treaty reached Washington. The Senate duly ratified it on 10 March, after defeating a proposal to apply the Wilmot Proviso to the new territory. This territory—which might be carved into slave states—was substantial, for Mexico relinquished claims to any part of Texas above the Rio Grande and ceded to the United States what became the states of California, Arizona, Nevada, and Utah, along with the bulk of New Mexico—the rest of which was purchased in 1853—and part of Colorado and Wyoming. James Buchanan, still the secretary of state, thought the United States should take all of Mexico while it had the chance.

Herman had a fair sense of what he was avoiding firsthand exposure to, and cheerfully turned what he heard about the meeting into notes toward the theory articulated in *Moby-Dick* of American imperialism in terms of "fast fish and loose fish." In the set of Shakespeare he bought the next year, he marked the passage in *Julius Caesar* about the "rabblement" hooting and clapping their chapped hands, and throwing up "their sweaty night-caps," the "tag-rag people" clapping and hissing the speaker "according as he pleased and displeased them," then he identified the Roman scene with a familiar Manhattan locale: "Tammany Hall."

Protecting Herman both from Lem and from religious services, members of the family took the collegian on a round of church-sampling as varied as the island-hopping in Herman's manuscript. On Sunday morning Allan and Sophia escorted Lem to the new Church of the Ascension, in the Gothic style, like a smaller Trinity, with an exterior of polished stone, at the northwest corner of Fifth Avenue and Tenth Street, which was about Allan's notion of a Sunday hike, counting there and back. In the afternoon Augusta had Lem escort her to Calvary, a "very magnificent church" in brownstone, only two years old, on the northeast corner of Fourth Avenue at Twenty-first Street. Mrs. Thurston had Lem (and others) to dinner, so he sampled Bond Street, the only street in Manhattan that could even begin to compare with Mt. Vernon Street. Mrs. Thurston continued to repay the judge's and Hope's hospitality by having several of the family (including Herman and Lizzie) with Lem on Wednesday evening, until late. On 3 February Lem went to a masquerade party, "masked of course" (Lizzie wrote to her stepmother the next day) and decked out by the women "in a court dress of the time of Louis fourteenth." After garbing Lem (the source of "a deal of fun"), Lizzie and Herman (and others?) went to another party, a very pleasant one where Lizzie "passed off for Miss Melville and as such was quite a belle!!," as she reported to her stepmother on 4 February, by which time it had become clear that a Bostonian round of such merriment was not appropriate under the present circumstances:

> We have resolved to stop after this though and not go out at all for while Herman is writing the effect of keeping late hours is very injurious to him — if he does not get a full night's rest or indulges in a late supper, he does not feel bright for writing the next day and the days are too precious to be thrown away — and to tell the truth I dont think he cares very much about parties either, and when he goes it is more on my account than his own. And its no sacrifice to me, for I am quite as contented, and more — to stay at home so long as he will stay with me.

But they went out that night, taking Lem to the Astor Place Opera House, where they heard Teresa Truffi and Settimio Rosi in Donizetti's *Lucrezia Borgia*.

As Lizzie confessed to her stepmother, by their standards they had been not merely social but "very dissipated" the week of the ball and the opera ("for usually we are very quiet"). They had tried to hold to some schedule, for Lem reported on their odd dinner hour: "They dine at half past four; and Herman usually stays in his room writing until that time, then he has done for the day; he never writes in the evening." Not writing in the evening was one thing and not being able to put himself in a frame for writing the next morning was another. By this time Herman was suffering, and they had to call quits to night life. In the next days Herman worked off the poisonous influences of the interruption, and he seems to have let Lizzie and the family do the honors of entertaining Lem through the rest of his four-week visit, having some of the others accompany Lem or else letting the lad take himself to "nearly all the theatres" and to other parties besides the masked ball. Before he left Lem gave Augusta "*Jane Eyre. An Autobiography*. Edited by Currer Bell." in the new Harper edition, so the sensational book was in the house, early, whether or not Herman read it right away. Lem learned before he left that Augusta had broken her engagement to Augustus Peebles. By 22 April 1848, Augusta Whipple Hunter was urging Augusta not to be coy with her friend from Bath: "should you purpose *surprising* me just remember that Madam Rumor often spoils surprises." By that time, Madam Rumor had reported Augusta's second broken engagement all across the wide state. Did

Augusta see herself, early in 1848, as somehow akin to the heroine in Jane Eyre's narrative?

Valentine's Day in this decade was still an occasion for calculated flirtations, even in larger cities; and among constricted Northerners it could be an occasion for defiant to-hell-with-winter parties. Herman had to make something like a command appearance this year at the home of Anne Lynch, who was outdoing herself as literary hostess at 116 Waverly Place. (Named for Scott's novels, although spelled without a second *e*, the street had provoked chauvinist developers to name a nearby locality Irving Place.) Miss Lynch enlisted young Bayard Taylor, as he wrote to Mary Agnew on 29 January:

> Anne Lynch is a perfect jewel of a woman. She is going to have a grand Valentine party on the coming 14th and showed me a list of the invited lions; among them are Halleck, Bryant, Willis, Morris, Hoffman, Parke Godwin, Lanman, Tuckerman, Dr. Dewey, Page, Inman, Darley, Healy, Durand, Mrs. Kirkland, Grace Greenwood, Mrs. Smith, Miss Sedgwick, Mrs. Osgood, Mrs. Ellet, Mrs. Hewitt, and a host of others. What a constellation! . . . Miss L. made me promise to write a number of valentines; and this is the list she allotted to me: — Mrs. Godwin, Miss Kate Sedgwick, Mrs. Kirkland, Mrs. Seba Smith, Hoffman, and Willis. I shall be kept busy in hammering out stanzas, up to the eventful day; and I intend dipping into some book of metres for a variety in that line, at least.

Melville may not have made the initial list, but by 13 February he had accepted an invitation and Taylor was "obliged to write a valentine for him." Anne Lynch may have been slow to realize who the author of *Typee* was, but she had overlapped with Augusta as a student at the Albany Female Academy in 1833, and just after she graduated from there in May of 1834 she had been hired back as a teacher. From her early youth Augusta had kept up her connections with relatives and friends (as she kept up her friendly meetings with her two cousins who were also ex-fiancés); she and Miss Lynch had gone quite separate ways, but now they reunited under auspicious conditions, and resumed their friendship. Herman Melville's first claim on Miss Lynch's hospitality was that he was a brother of Augusta Melville.

In a letter of 23 February, Bayard Taylor wrote: "Well, the grand Valentine party came off at last, and a very pleasant one it was. Nearly all the author-tribe were there, but several lions of a different class — among whom were Rossiter [whose painting Herman and Allan had admired in Washington], Cushman, Darley [later, if not already, a good friend of Melville's], and Dubourjal, artists; Gen. Gaines and Capt. Reid, of the army; Biscaccianti, and others. I became acquainted with Herman Melville's sister and with Mrs. Mary E. Hewitt, the poetess, — a lovely woman. It fell to my lot to read a part of the valentines." The sister Taylor met was Augusta, who thereafter saw Anne Lynch during daytime calls, independent of her brothers. Melville, who had Ellery Channing's poem on *Typee* for comparison as well as unpublished valentines from his Lansingburgh years, now had no cause for complaint about Taylor's effort:

> Bright painter of these tropic isles,
>> That stud the blue waves, far apart,
> Be thine, through life, the summer's smiles,
>> And fadeless foliage of the heart:
> And may some guardian genius still
> *Taboo* thy path from every ill!

The poem appeared in the *Home Journal* for 4 March, where, in Bath, New York, Augusta's friend Augusta Whipple Hunter read it. She relied on the paper for news of New York City, where, as she said, everyone knew Herman. It seemed as if everyone did, indeed, when she could read a poem about her Sunday entertainer in the *Home Journal*. The poem was in the lengthy article "The Valentine Party" by "G. G." (G. G. Foster): "During my present visit to New-York, it has been my good fortune to attend the Valentine party in —— Place, where was a great gathering together of the notables of your city — of its beauty and its genius — an evening's renovation of Athenian life — a drawing-room conclave of muses and divinities, 'for one night only.' " ("For one night only" was a witty use of a phrase from theatrical advertising.) By anyone's standard the evening was a success. Melville had met Manhattan's literati and artists in grand assembly before, and he had met a good many of his fellow celebrities elsewhere, in smaller groups, notably at Dr. Francis's and at Duyckinck's. No comment survives on his impressions of this soiree at Anne Lynch's.

Melville's next known socializing after the Valentine's party was with Duyckinck. One night in the first week of March he carried over to Clinton Place a bundle of manuscript from *Mardi*, part of which he read to Duyckinck, or perhaps merely left off for Evert to read later. These were early chapters, first drafted months before, among which was "A Calm," chapter 2 in the final numbering, if not at this time. Melville invited Evert Duyckinck on 8 March to "come round and make up a rubber of whist — about 1/2 past seven," and as it turned out Evert "played the longest rubber of whist last night at his house" he had ever encountered: "It was like his calm at sea — in the new book," he wrote George the next day, adding that in "poetry and wildness" the new book would be "ahead of Typee & Omoo." This last was probably a masculine occasion, like most of Duyckinck's evenings, with Allan and some other man for the other two players. Another occasion, perhaps requiring little or nothing from Herman, was a visit from Justine Van Rensselaer (she married Dr. Howard Townsend on 2 February 1853) before 14 March; she duly reported to her sister Nilly, who relayed the word to Augusta from the Manor House, where she was displaying her son: "Teny tells me that you have such a nice house & are so very delightfully settled."

By then, Melville was restless, his muscles cramped, and tension building because of the letter he had received from Murray around the end of January. Instead of answering it, he procrastinated, trying to decide what to say to his publisher about what *Mardi* had become.

29

Dollars Be Damned
"The Red Year Forty-Eight"

> O men,
> Since Science can so much explode,
> Evaporated is this God? —
> Recall the red year Forty-eight:
> He storms in Paris; thence divides;
> The menace scarce outspeeds the fate:
> He's over the Rhine — He's at Berlin —
> At Munich — Dresden — fires Vien;
> He's over the Alps — the whirlwind rides
> In Rome; London's alert — the Czar:
> The portent and the fact of war,
> And terror that into hate subsides.

Clarel, bk. 3, canto 1

BY MARCH 1848 THE HOUSEHOLD had learned not to invade Melville's mornings and not to expect to keep him out late at night. Still, he remained available for brief therapeutic excursions. Melville had met Duyckinck's friend Robert Tomes and perhaps his brother George Tomes. The Tomes brothers were kin to the great pulpit orator Dr. Francis Hawks, who made occasional triumphant visits home to Manhattan from Mississippi and Louisiana in the late 1840s. Having signed as ship's doctor on the new ocean steamer the *Hermann*, plying between New York and Southampton-Bremen, Robert Tomes invited Evert and Herman aboard for a tour on 18 March, the day the *Post* printed the schedule and guaranteed that there was an "experienced surgeon on board." Evert punned in a letter to George Duyckinck ("I visited her with Melville another representative of the old Arminius") and added some startling news about the sailor: "By the way Melville reads old Books. He has borrowed Sir Thomas Browne of me and says finely of the speculations of the *Religio Medici* that Browne is a kind of 'crack'd Archangel.' Was ever any thing of this sort said before by a sailor?"

In 1846, before George's departure, and even through 1847, the Duyckincks had not known Melville as a reader of "old Books," though Melville may have been such a man all along. Now Melville not only read old books, he was capable of making perceptive offhand judgments on them worth writing down and sending to a brother on the grand tour. He was phenomenal, for a sailor. In a letter to George on 13 June 1848 Evert mentioned Hogarth's depiction of a man-of-war's man in "those traditional stage petticoats which no living tar (and I have questioned my Bunsby—Melville) remembers." In alluding to the vacuous, self-important, and physically grotesque seaman in Dickens's *Dombey and Son*, the installments of which Americans had been reading in newspapers since 1846, Duyckinck meant that Melville was his ultimate authority in things nautical, but the comment conveyed a lack of genuine respect. Despite whatever he had learned about Melville's distinguished ancestry, and despite what he had learned about Melville's literary abilities from *Omoo*, if not from *Typee*, Duyckinck never quite got over his Johnsonian attitude toward Melville: the wonder was not that he wrote so well but that he wrote at all.

On 18 March the first news of the February Revolution in France arrived in Manhattan. Before noon Evert Duyckinck wrote of the sensation to his brother George, then opportunely in Paris: "A Walk in Broadway to-day is a thing of excitement, the news of the Revolution in Paris having imparted to every one that vivacity of eye, quickness of intelligence and general exhilaration which great public events extend to private ones. . . . You have fairly shaken hands with History. . . . People all here say it is a fine thing, some varying the phrase with the epithet 'glorious.' " Melville witnessed the tumultuous public scenes and Duyckinck's immediate enthusiasm for the revolution, since it was that day that he went with the editor to see the *Hermann*. He may have waited at the dock with Evert for George's letter describing the revolution, which Evert was expecting, and which in fact arrived that afternoon. Melville had seen himself as a political commentator when he described British and French imperialism in the South Seas, and as more news of the European revolutions reached New York in March and April he was more and more tempted to discourse on international politics in his new and capacious book. For the moment, he resisted temptation, but he observed carefully what was going on around him, and saw ways that might make him as important an actor on the political stage as Gansevoort had been, albeit in a very different way.

Aliens and naturalized citizens of New York made the third of April their "Revolutionary Jubilee," but despite Duyckinck's initial impression, the American response to the news was not altogether joyous. There were many to agree with the doughty old Whig Philip Hone, who was willing to "let the

French rejoice in the overthrow of monarchy, in their own country," but condemned the error by which Americans participated in "public demonstrations of joy." Evert himself by the middle of April exhibited a tardy skepticism:

> If France does not learn the lesson, which all things human *must* be taught, that much is to be endured[,] she cannot but fail. Society is not exempt from the laws of individual life. Nations must be patient and endure as well as individuals. . . . A choice of governments is a choice of evils though there is a better and a worse. If the French will only know the wisdom of old Hesiod's maxim that "the half is better than the whole," they will prosper. If like the dog in the fable they want shadow and substance both they will lose all.

Later that year, having yielded to temptation and delayed his book, Melville wrote into his manuscript (*Mardi*, ch. 161) a description of the varying American responses to the news of the European revolutions: "With the utmost delight, these tidings were welcomed by many; yet others heard them with boding concern." He continued: "Those, too, there were, who rejoiced that the kings were cast down; but mourned that the people themselves stood not firmer. A victory, turned to no wise and enduring account, said they, is no victory at all. Some victories revert to the vanquished." The image of an erupting volcano that Melville used in this chapter ("all Porpheero's volcanoes are bursting!" — Porpheero meaning Europe, from the Latin for "purple," the royal color) was one that had occurred to other commentators. The Washington *National Intelligencer* used it on 27 March 1848: "A Republic in France has, we say, been but a sort of social volcano, rocking and blasting with its convulsions its own foundations, and sending forth its streams of lava to desolate abroad all that they reached."

Melville delayed until 25 March 1848 before replying to Murray's letter dated 17 January — a remarkably fast response to his of 1 January. Though Murray's letter is now lost, some of its contents can be inferred from Melville's allusions to it in his of 25 March. Murray had expressed his desire (in Melville's satirical echoing) "to test the corporeality of H—— M—— by clapping eyes upon him in London" — the seed of an idea that Melville let fall to the fallow ground. He had also requested, not for the first time, "documentary evidence" of Melville's "having been in the South Seas, wherewithall to convince the unbelievers." Melville in the 25 March letter at last corrected the misleading impression he had given Murray in his "last but one" letter that the new work was "a bona-fide narrative" of his adventures in the Pacific, continued from *Omoo*. On 1 January he had first vouched for its authenticity then inked through that claim, but now he had to admit that there had been a change in his "determinations":

To be blunt: the work I shall next publish will in downright earnest [be] a "Romance of Polynisian Adventure" — But why this? The truth is, Sir, that the reiterated imputation of being a romancer in disguise has at last pricked me into a resolution to show those who may take any interest in the matter, that a *real* romance of mine is no Typee or Omoo, & is made of different stuff altogether. This I confess has been the main inducement in altering my plans — but others have operated. I have long thought that Polynisia furnished a great deal of rich poetical material that has never been employed hitherto in works of fancy; and which to bring out suitably, required only that play of freedom & invention accorded only to the Romancer & poet. — However, I thought, that I would postpone trying my hand at any thing fanciful of this sort, till some future day: tho' at times when in the mood I threw off occasional sketches applicable to such a work. Well: proceeding in my narrative of *facts* I began to feel an invincible distaste for the same; & a longing to plume my pinions for a flight, & felt irked, cramped & fettered by plodding along with dull common places, — So suddenly abandoning the thing alltogether, I went to work heart & soul at a romance which is now in fair progress, since I had worked at it with an earnest ardor. Start not, nor exclaim "Pshaw! Puh!" — My romance I assure you is no dish water nor its model borrowed from the Circulating Library. It is something new I assure you, & original if nothing more. But I can give you no adequate idea, of it. You must see it for yourself. Only forbear to prejudge it. It opens like a true narrative — like Omoo for example, on ship board — & the romance & poetry of the thing thence grow continuously, till it becomes a story wild enough I assure you & with a meaning too.

Here Melville detailed a psychological history, one which must have been, at the time, at least subjectively true.

According to his account, Melville might have continued to write basically autobiographical works if those works had been believed; because they had not been believed, he had been provoked into showing the critics what a piece of fiction by Herman Melville would really look like. That was not the only motivation: he had "long" thought (since 1842?) that only a romancer and poet could do justice to the matter of Polynesia, but, at that early time, he had also taken a long view of his own development: he had thought that later, when he was older and more experienced, he might be the one to show just how richly poetical the material was. Now he felt himself ready. Quite incidentally Melville asserted in this letter something about his development as a writer not otherwise documented. He may have meant that before writing *Typee*, or between writing that book and *Omoo*, or between writing *Omoo* and *Mardi*, he had tried writing other things: "at times when in the mood" he had thrown off "occasional sketches," short pieces of romantic, poetical fiction dealing with Polynesian places and peoples, apparently — sketches for which we have no record other than this letter, although he may have meant that he had incorporated such sketches into *Mardi*.

Then Melville proceeded to enunciate a dangerous theory of creativity — one which would lead him to the creation of at least one masterpiece of world literature but which would destroy his career. It might be impolitic to put forth "an acknowledged *romance* upon the heel of two books of travel which in some quarters have been received with no small incredulity," but that, he arrogantly proclaimed, was a question for which he cared little, "really": "My *instinct* is to out with the Romance, & let me say that instincts are prophetic, & better than acquired wisdom — which alludes remotely to your experience in literature as an eminent publisher." In Melville's theory at that point, instinct did not have to be reconciled with acquired wisdom, did not have to be harnessed and put to the service of conscious rational purposes. Yet the result of yielding to instinct would have a utilitarian purpose, if a childish one: an outright romance might "afford the strongest presumptive evidence of the truth of Typee & Omoo by the sheer force of contrast." Unable to conceive of an artistic compromise for his reckless impulses, Melville tried to be politic with a pecuniary compromise, suggesting now that if Murray liked the manuscript he would pay Melville at once not double the one hundred guineas he had suggested but only half again that much, on acceptance, and half profits thereafter. "If upon the receipt of the sheets you should agree to this, then, without waiting to communicate with me, you might consider the matter closed at once & proceed to business at once; — only apprising me immediately of the very earliest day upon which I could publish here. This would save time." Saving time at this late stage, given the time he had taken on the book, can only have sounded a little peculiar to the publisher. (Unsurprisingly, the tenor of Murray's reply to this astonishing letter, according to Melville's own belated reply on 19 June, was "Antarctic." Nevertheless, Melville indulged in sheer wishful thinking, knowing Murray did not publish fiction: "I fear you abhor romances; But fancy nevertheless that possibly you may for once relent.")

Weary and nervous after a winter's writing on a book that his English publisher had not liked the sound of, and stirred up about the possibility of abruptly shifting the plan of his book, for a second time, so as to accommodate his thoughts on politics, Melville became more and more restless. He knew he had reached a sort of crisis such as he had never experienced during his work on *Typee* and *Omoo*. There he had voyaged through the composition guided by his own experiences and his previous tellings of his story, while now he was seeking a new world, "the world of mind" (ch. 169, "Sailing on"):

"Oh, reader, list! I've chartless voyaged. With compass and the lead, we had not found these Mardian Isles. Those who boldly launch, cast off all cables; and turning from the common breeze, that's fair for all, with their own breath, fill their own sails. Hug the shore, naught new is seen; and 'Land ho!' at last was sung, when a new world was sought." This is part of his apologia, written months later. He had cast off cables already, but in March of 1848 he may not have been able to admit what the consequences might be — that in voyaging chartless he might end "an utter wreck." The immediate provocation of the crisis was a simple conflict between his impulse to work the latest news from Europe (and from the United States) into his manuscript (in the form of allegorical satire) and the urgent need to get the book to the publisher. In early April Lizzie wrote to her step-cousin Sam Savage: "His frequent exclamation is — 'Oh Lizzy! the book! — the book! — what *will* become of the *Book!*'" Tormented as he was, he was desperate for physical activity. In the last four months he had taken only one out-of-town trip we know about, at Thanksgiving, and had "dissipated" a few nights by staying out so late that he did not feel fresh the next morning, but he had held rigorously to his writing routine. The nocturnal socializing he did with his male literary friends was kept within manageable limits, so that it stimulated him for his work rather than distracted him from it. He needed a sharp break in his routine.

Winter left so early that on 27 March the *Herald* printed a celebratory article "THE SPRING," Bennett having learned that the public wanted not just to experience weather but also to read about it: "The spring is now fairly opening upon us with all its beauty, fully three weeks before the usual time. The Hudson river is navigable to Albany, in advance of the regular season, and the weather is more bland and beautiful than we have ever seen it in the United States at this time of the year. It is really more beautiful than it is in Italy." The twenty-ninth was "by far the most delightful day of the season," "indeed a spring day." The thirtieth was "perfectly delightful": "The sun rose from a clear horizon, and pursued his course uninterrupted by even a single passing cloud." The weather, and the talk about the weather, became too much for Melville, who decided that he had to get out of town, alone, and loosen his constricted limbs in some Berkshire vagabondism, now that spring had come.

Free to take a boat up the unfrozen river to Hudson or Albany if he liked, and a stage from there, Herman arrived in Pittsfield expecting to wander all over the hills, but he was betrayed by a snowstorm — unseasonable, but not extraordinary, as any year-round resident knew. The storm kept Melville locked up for many hours with Robert and his family at the Melvill place (there were at least two living children, Robert's namesake, around eight, and another baby son, Julian, a year or so old and named for Herman's contemporary, Julia Maria, dead since 1846). He took what physical pleasure he could in negotiating the mile or so between the farm and the rented room in the village, where he sat for hours with his older cousin Priscilla.

French-born, French-speaking in childhood, four when her mother died in backwoods Massachusetts in 1814, Priscilla now pursued, year after year, what was referred to as the "French claims," repeatedly asking Judge Shaw to depute travelers to Paris to seek out her unknown kindred and establish her right to an inheritance. Already she may have begun to hope that she would be able to buy or at least rent a tiny place of her own in Pittsfield. Four and a half years later, on 7 October 1852, she wrote to Augusta: "I often dream of blissful solitude — freedom from care — & a *crust* & *water*, in the 'Brown Cottage' — which quiet retreat from some of the vexations & anxieties of Life, Helen assures me looks as *'enticing as ever.'* " She dared then to hope of possessing, even by rental, that "little paradise." In April 1848, Priscilla was already deeply sensitized to the discrepancy between her ancestry and early training and the drudgery that seemed destined to be her lot. She reflected in 1852 on what it was like, for one "in the station to which by birth & taste" she felt herself to belong, to be "cast upon the world, to depend upon their own exertions, with a less galling sense of the yoke": "It is *more this* circumstance of *birth* & *taste* that causes my spirit to chafe *thus* under the burden than ought else — & doubtless I should consider my lot a most admirable one — did not my *native* aristocracy rebel." This passionate woman by then was reduced to constant sewing as an alternative to dragging along an existence far from any of her blood. She was more optimistic in 1848 than in 1852, and less weakened by tuberculosis, but her plight was already tragic in the eyes of her cousin, who knew himself what it was like to be an aristocrat cast upon the world as a pauper. As always happened when he met again some remarkable character last known in his youth, Melville responded profoundly to this woman. His new insights into her history and psychology led him, in the following months, to insights into himself as blood of her blood. These hours when he was fortuitously, and at the time frustratingly, marooned with Priscilla, as much as any other single experience of his life led to his composition of *Pierre*.

During his visit, Priscilla improved the opportunity and wrote a letter for Herman to carry to Augusta, the letter that tells all that is known about this trip. Then rooming with the Tyler family, who taught school in the village, and able to sound enthusiastic about her difficult situation, she reminded Augusta of the old habit Maria had of sending her children to Pittsfield in the summer:

We were confirmed in the belief that you felt exalted, by a residence & *great* establishment in New York — far above the condition of your country cousins, & had concluded to forget them — but we knew that the return of summer would certainly bring you to your senses, & to Pittsfield — unless Herman should chill you with his account of the cold reception he recieved in Berkshire — but you must allow for the difference between our bracing mountain air — & the soften'd atmosphere that surrounds you in the city —. I believe that Herman has arrived at the conclusion that the country is not *always* beautiful — but it will very soon wear a more attractive appearance & you will be tempted to leave the home that possesses so many charms at present to enjoy for a season the pleasures of the country.

Herman's frustration evoked from Priscilla the first surviving direct statement of the strength of his feelings for the Berkshires in general and for the family farm in particular:

I am really sorry that Herman has been disappointed in his plans for passing the time during his short stay with us — especially since he has manifested so much constancy toward the object of his *first love* our *Berkshire* farm — as to *tear* himself from the idol of his heart to indulge again in the unfetter'd freedom of Batchelor days — but his appearance in our midst, gave us an agreable surprise & we have enjoyed the opportunity for enquiring into each others welfare & prospects & a mutual interest is raised in our hearts — he has drawn for us, a pleasing picture of *your* family arrangements.

This offhand assertion that his "first love" was their Berkshire farm sounds hyperbolic, as excessive as Uncle Thomas's own rhetoric, but it expresses what Priscilla knew as an obvious truth. From adolescence Herman had loved the farm, his unbounded haven in the rare days of freedom from the temple to Mammon and from the constricting counter of the cap and fur store, his vantage point for surveying Mount Greylock, the base for his explorations of the surrounding terrain, and the one accessible place he knew where the geography matched his spirit.

His hopes of free unfettered wandering shattered, Herman returned to Fourth Avenue reporting the "divers *other* particulars" Priscilla had promised, such as the news that Robert at the moment, in advertisements running in the Pittsfield *Sun*, was proclaiming: "MAKE WAY FOR THE DEVONSHIRES" — his way of luring farmers to pay him a dollar, cash, for a chance to breed their cows to his Devonshire bull. The biggest news was about the house: "Robert is making preparations for opening his house for a large family during the summer months — & I hope he may succeed in making it profitable." The next month, 17 May, Robert began running an advertisement in the *Sun:* "PRIVATE BOARDING HOUSE," headed by the paper's wood-cut symbol of a three-story house:

> THAT FINE OLD MANSION known as the Melvill House, situated one mile south of the Village of Pittsfield, Mass., having been put in order for the accommodation of persons who are desirous of spending the summer months in the country, the subscriber would say to such, that they can hardly fail to be pleased with the House or its situation. The rooms are very large, with many conveniences not usually found in ordinary boarding houses, and the situation is unrivalled either for the beauty of its scenery or the salubrity of the air. A carriage will be in attendance for those who may wish to avail themselves of the many pleasant drives in the vicinity.

In fact the "Melvill House" was a fine old mansion, if needing repair, and in an all but incomparable location. Word got out fast, and that summer the Longfellows, both of whom remembered the old Major Melvill, came from Craigie House in Cambridge.

In April, Sophia and Allan heard the challenging news of the birth of a daughter, Abby Caroline, to Abby Thurston Lathers and her husband, Richard Lathers, still in Georgetown, up the coast from Charleston. Allan wrote a teasing letter that evoked a graceful reply from Lathers, a torn portion of which survives in the Berkshire Athenaeum: "Accept my thanks for your brotherly congratulations on the birth of our little girl, and I would reciprocate your kind expressions of this new relation to which this event has introduced me by hoping soon to have the same pleasant office to discharge toward yourself—Indeed I do feel 'my responsibility' and were it not for the *quizzical* propensities of her Uncle, many rare qualities should be set forth as discoverable in '*Abby Caroline*' peculiar only to *one's first child.*" Abby and Richard promised "*all* at Fourth Avenue an early visit from this *our* prodigy to all her Aunts and Uncles therein located," an indication of how solidly Lathers had already enclosed the Melvilles within the compass of family; an immigrant child with almost no blood relatives in the United States, he made all the Thurston connections his family, including all the Melvilles, even, later on, Cousin Priscilla: kin to Allan, kin to him. ("Prodigy" thus entered the family vocabulary in reference to a new baby.)

At Fourth Avenue, more anxiety was expressed about Tom than about the book. In late April Herman wrote the owners of Tom's ship in Westport hoping for news, since the papers had reported sightings of the homeward-bound *Theophilus Chase*. Herman was told that the ship was expected the first of May, a day that came and went without news. Lizzie wrote her stepmother on 5 May that once the whaleman arrived, Herman would "have to go over to Westport for Tom and see that he is regularly discharged and paid, and bring him home." Maria was "watching and counting the days with great anxiety for he is the baby of the family and his mothers pet," so Lizzie wrote, but the truth was that Tom was everyone's pet, including Lizzie's. (Augusta Whipple Hunter a little later inquired about him from Augusta as a favorite of *hers*.) Tom's ship had in fact arrived on the fourth at Westport Point, where he may have learned from the owners that Herman had been inquiring for him from New York — not from Lansingburgh, where he would have expected to make his way to. Herman may well have gone to Westport to accompany Tom back, a journey fraught with memories of his own whaling voyage, and told him the story of the past year on their way back. Once in Fourth Avenue, oddly situated with mother, four sisters, two brothers, and two new sisters-in-law (one, Sophia, a stranger to him), Tom absorbed the changes quickly, then proved to be as restless as Herman. The first week or two he was home, he looked "for a place in some store," Lizzie wrote her stepmother on 6 June, but after repeated disappointments over a several-day period, he determined to go back to sea as soon as he could. Herman had already written to his father's and Shaw's friend Daniel P. Parker to see if he could send Tom out in one of his ships, under the idea that Parker would be likely to "take an interest in him and promote him." (The idea that Chief Justice Lemuel Shaw had ever been a struggling young man who boarded frugally with the Parkers or anyone else seemed odder every year.)

Hope Shaw wanted Lizzie to come home just after the annual house-cleaning, but in her letter of 5 May Lizzie explained humorously that she might have to wait until the house would be ready for yet another (if less rigorous) cleaning, July or August. The reason was "the book," which she declared was "done," but still requiring great attention:

> Herman of course will stick to his work till "the book" is published and his services are required till the last moment — correcting proofs &c. The book is done now, in fact (you need not mention it) and the copy for the press is in far progress, but where it is published on both sides of the water a great deal of delay is unavoidable and though Herman will have some spare time after sending the proof sheets to London which will be next month sometime probably he will not want to leave New York till the book is actually on the booksellers shelves.

Lizzie explained that she could not write a longer letter because she was very busy copying and could not spare the time. In explaining the oddity of the size of her writing paper she revealed a little about the way the manuscript looked: "I tore my sheet in two by mistake thinking it was my copying (for we only write on one side of the page) and if there is no punctuation marks you must make them yourself for when I copy I do not punctuate at all but leave it for a final revision for Herman. I have got so used to write without I cannot always think of it." Some oddities in punctuation in *Mardi* may derive from Lizzie's following Herman's instructions and Herman's not filling in the spaces she had left.

Although the war with Mexico had been winding down since February, there was no escaping politics — not only European but American — and no escaping the recurrent thought that Gansevoort should have been taking part in the campaign of 1848, passionate, driven, febrile, still "the orator of the human race." In the same house with Allan, the sort of politician who was willing to do the tedious work of counting ballots since he was unable to enthrall crowds, Herman inevitably heard more than he wanted of the split in the Democratic party in New York between those who wanted not to alienate white Southerners (the Marcy-Croswell wing, the Hunkers, who had won out in 1844) and the antislavery Barnburner wing loyal to Van Buren, who in 1844 had opposed immediate annexation of Texas. Early in 1847, the year before, it had become known that Van Buren himself supported the Wilmot Proviso, which would have stipulated that "as an express and fundamental condition to the acquisition of any territory from the Republic of Mexico," slavery should be excluded from that territory. At the state convention in Syracuse on 29 September 1847, the Hunkers had tabled the Barnburners' resolutions, amid intense rowdiness. The Albany *Atlas* had denounced the Hunkers for "Capitulation to Slave Power," and the Barnburners had met separately in Herkimer on 26 October 1847, where the dazzling scion of the Fox of Kinderhook, John Van Buren, known as Prince John, had dominated the convention with a vehement attack on Edwin Croswell for betraying the party (and incidentally for buying votes for his Hunker candidates at fifty cents a head in the ninth ward of Albany). On 16 February 1848 a Barnburner convention in Utica had selected national delegates and issued an address that supported the prosecution of the Mexican War (otherwise they all would have been labeled traitors) but insisted on excluding slavery from any territory ceded by Mexico — the proposal trounced in the Senate on 10 March.

After the Baltimore national convention of the Democratic party in May 1848, where the opposing delegations from New York presented their cases, Duyckinck wrote to George, on 23 May, that young William Allen Butler had been an active Barnburner at Baltimore (Butler having preceded George home from Europe): "He relies a great deal on a certain 'political capital' movement of John Van Buren — introducing the Wilmot Proviso into the New York democratic party — 'barnburners' they call them — but I have an instinct they will all be shelved as a parcel of May bodies. Let slavery take care of itself. It will. New York might reestablish slavery again but who thinks of it." (This was conservative. Gansevoort had expressed a much more progressive belief about the ultimate extinction of slavery in his Newark speech.) The Baltimore convention voted to admit both sets of delegations, giving each delegate half a vote, but, rather than compromise, the Barnburners withdrew to New York to oppose the nominee, Lewis Cass. In Albany Uncle Peter, always a practical party man, took the side of Marcy and Croswell against the Van Burenites, and wrote a long resolution enthusiastically supporting the Democratic candidates and eulogizing General Cass. In New York City, Allan Melville was rewarded for his services to the Hunkers by being nominated for a seat in the New York State Assembly. (That year Gansevoort's friend the Whig Alexander W. Bradford was elected surrogate of the city and county of New York, a post he held for a decade, during which his decisions made him a creator of American ecclesiastical law. From this point there is no record that he kept up his friendship with the Melvilles, except that he recommended Melville for a consulship in 1861.)

In early June the Melvilles had Tom in one of the spare bedrooms and Sam Shaw in another, for Sam arrived on the fourth after travel by railroad, boat, and carriage, the last a ride that cost "only" fifty cents, as he reported to his father that day. That was a Sunday, so Sam promptly embarked on the tour of churches, going first "down to Trinity," where he got a bad seat from which he could not see its features to advantage, then in the afternoon went "to the Dutch church with Mrs. Melville," and after those services Augusta took him to Grace Church, which impressed him as "a most magnificent edifice, the brilliant stained windows of which cast different hues upon the walls." A Bostonian accustomed to chaste ecclesiastical settings, he was agog at the almost heathen decor: "There are also some windows with beautiful pictures, there are many small statues, in the walls, of the Apostles. The organ looks more like a Chinese temple than a musical instrument." How Herman, Allan, and Tom entertained Sam is not known, but his expectations must have been high after the way they had pampered Lem. Lizzie took him out to Brooklyn to see the Maretts, she wrote to her stepmother, revealing to Hope that his presence in Manhattan was inopportune: he had arrived just when Herman thought he was a week away from finishing the book. Torn between responsibilities, Lizzie needed to catch up with her copying before taking Sam across the East River.

Melville seems to have written a letter to Richard Bentley, the London publisher, on 19 June 1847 ("seems," for the year may have been 1848). In this confidential letter Melville thanked Bentley for a note of 17 May (1847, or 1848) and its "friendly overtures" and regretted that he had already "a partial understanding with another publisher," but he asked, just in case anything occurred to alter his "present views and arrangements," at what value Bentley "would hold the English copy right of a new work of South Sea adventure," occupying "entirely fresh ground." What Melville could have meant by "fresh ground" in 1847 is not at all clear; if the letter is from 1848, it clearly and accurately refers to his landing his narrative on fictional islands.

On 6 June, Lizzie wrote to her stepmother again, during Sam's visit, that they were nearly through with the book, that they would "finish this week." She now broached the possibility of her returning without Herman, hesitating, characteristically, as she had hesitated about going to Chicago to see Oakes without satisfactory escort, or as she had hesitated about naming a marriage date as long as she was expected to live in Lansingburgh. Lizzie's problem was threefold. One was Herman's unreliable nature. The second was her annual allergy attack. The judge's catarrh came in the fall, but the miserable season for her was June, and this year she may have been suffering worse than usual because, whether she knew it or not, she was three or four weeks pregnant:

> My cold is very bad indeed, perhaps worse than it has ever been so early, and I attribute it entirely to the warm dry atmosphere so different from the salt air I have been accustomed to — and Herman thinks I had better go back to Boston with Sam to see if the change of air will not benefit me. And he will come on for me in two or three weeks if he can — and then in August when he takes his vacation he will take me there again. But I don't know as I can make up my mind to go and leave him here — and besides I'm afraid to trust him to finish up the book without me! That is — taking all things into consideration I'm afraid I should not feel at ease enough to enjoy my visit without him with me.

She was jesting in earnest about being afraid to trust Herman to finish up the book without her, for she understood already that he was strangely involved with this manuscript, inordinately ambitious for it, and determined to follow his instincts with it wherever they led him, and however long they held him. The upshot was that she went home with Sam, taking Kate, and arriving in the morning of 18 June, by that time most likely conscious that she was pregnant. (Sophia was also pregnant, having conceived about the same week as Lizzie.)

Daniel Parker may have taken a hand in Tom's career by late June; in any case "Tommy" had signed on a merchant ship on a voyage to China, due to depart within a week of the Fourth of July. On 3 July Guert returned "the Melvilles call" on the Curtises and his mother in Brooklyn, and while there invited "Helen & Tommy, (who has returned from whaling) & Augusta to accompany them to the Oppera House, to see the Viennese children dance" (as Guert wrote his mother). Guert Gansevoort was "in the van" of those returning homeward, for the last United States troops did not leave Vera Cruz until early August. On the morning of 3 July 1848 Allan and Sophia had left for a trip accompanied by the shyest Melville sister, Fanny. Tom had helped them aboard a boat on the Hudson and said a solemn good-bye. The travelers had taken the day boat to Albany. Rain had prevented their stopping at West Point, which Fanny wanted particularly to see. In Albany they made their way up the Washington Street hill, perhaps the first time Allan and Fanny had been there since Gansevoort's funeral. None of them felt quite comfortable with selfish Uncle Peter, but at least "Aunt Susan was or appeared to be" glad to see them, and the Gansevoorts entertained them on the Fourth "very pleasantly."

Inside the new house Sophia may have found the old paintings on the walls dark and depressing, but Allan was on his way to becoming something of a connoisseur of art, and he must have looked now with different eyes at objects familiar from 46 North Market Street in their unfamiliar Washington Street surroundings. At some point a very red *Morning* by Frederick Edwin Church, painted that year, 1848, entered the house — perhaps much later; but the new house on Washington Street was already a lived-in museum of colonial and revolutionary artifacts, as well as more recent trophies. After breakfast on the Fourth the visitors went about their other calls, Fanny to the Taylors, Allan and Sophia to the Van Vechtens, where Fanny joined them. Then all three went to Cousin Maggie's — not Maggey Wynkoop but Maggie Van Rensselaer Douw, who was still suffering unnameable marital woes caused by her cousin-husband. Allan was being just the sort of son Maria wanted, keeping up ties with old and loyal friends and relatives, and even, with Sophia's help, testing the possibilities of patching over old differences with Uncle Peter. There was a document Allan wanted Peter to sign; and Peter and Susan Gansevoort, in December, in fact deeded the farm and house at Northumberland, Saratoga County (or perhaps their part of it) to Herman and Allan Melville. This was a stratagem for insuring that Uncle Herman could leave the Saratoga County property to his sister Maria, rather than leave it jointly to his surviving sister and brothers — Peter and the all but forgotten Wessel, who had to be taken account of, in such legal exigencies.

On 6 July Fanny wrote Tom from Black River, New York. The travelers had taken a variety of conveyances — steamboat, some sort of horse-drawn conveyance to the Gansevoort house, the cars for Utica, the stage for Alder Creek, a carriage there on the way to Black River — to the house of a Gansevoort cousin descended from the Hero's Uncle Pieter (1725–1809). She lamented: "I can hardly believe that you will not be at home when I come back." He would sail for China around 9 or 10 July, and might miss Fanny's letter. Herman had seen Tom off before he left for Boston on 12 July, by which time the judge and Hope had become accustomed to Lizzie's condition, and everyone had found leisure time to wonder why Herman had not given the book to a publisher. The next day Shaw invited Richard Henry Dana Jr. to a small party to see Lizzie and Herman — a party that grew to thirty or so, and Dana reciprocated at once by inviting Melville to the Parker House on 17 July ("I thot I ought to do something for him," he explained to his absent wife).

Physically Dana was not prepossessing, for his hair already receded on his round head, and he accentuated the circularity by wearing his hair long at the back, sideburns down to his chin line. He was of enormous interest to Melville, who may have been privately amazed at just how many years a former sailor could affect a rolling nautical swagger in his walk. To join him and Melville, Dana invited some of his usual intimates. Edwin Percy Whipple (1819–86), then superintendent of the Boston Merchants' Exchange, later was editor of the Boston *Globe* and famous as a critic. Horatio Woodman (1821–79), a founder of the Saturday Club, was a near-nonentity among luminaries — an "alert red-headed and bewhiskered Boston lawyer," the Emerson biographer Ralph L. Rusk called him. (Whipple and Woodman are paired in several of Dana's lists of men attending gatherings of one sort or another, and in 1857 Dana noted in his journal that Woodman had really no claims to be a member of the Saturday Club except that of being a founder: "a bachelor, a literary quidnunc & gossip, or as [B. A.] Gould says, 'a genius broker.'" Woodman lived at the Parker House and had "got into the habit of entertaining" Emerson, the Unitarian minister John Sullivan Dwight, Whipple, and others there, "from which the club grew.") At the Parker House to meet Melville were also an older man, Thernon Metcalf (1784–1875), a lawyer, known for his *bon mots*, who had been on the state supreme court under Shaw since 25 February 1848, and Allen Crocker Spooner, a Harvard classmate of Dana's and Boston lawyer born in 1814. Dana recorded: "We sat from 9 to 12, & I believe they had a good time. I gave them cold birds, fruit champagne & hock."

In New York it was said to be possible for gentlemen to dine together without talking politics, and in Boston Dana may have restrained himself, but he had been talking little else for weeks. The day before Melville's arrival in Boston he had relayed the latest news to his father, the old Federalist-Whig whose real sympathies were still royalist, like those of Halleck. As far as the younger Dana was concerned, the Whig party had dissolved itself at the Philadelphia convention in June by nominating Zachary Taylor, a man who had "always refused to be the candidate of a party, to be the exponent of the principles of a party." (In May the Democrats had nominated for president Lewis Cass, Gansevoort's stumping partner.) Dana was still hoping that

Daniel Webster would openly oppose Taylor, weeks after the Whig convention. The antislavery faction of the Democratic party, the Barnburners, had held their own convention at Utica on 22 June 1848, nominating Martin Van Buren for president, and calling for a national Free-Soil convention in Buffalo on 9 August—a convention that Dana had decided to attend. Melville (presumably with Lizzie) returned to New York in the last week of July well informed about the Whig split between Webster and Taylor and about the new faction of Whigs that had joined the Democratic Barnburners and was now amalgamating with other factions under the Free-Soil banner.

Now it was clear to everyone that the book was nowhere near finished, yet Melville felt enough disengaged from it, a week or so after returning, to take an outing with Duyckinck to Fort Lee. This, as Duyckinck must have told him, was Fitz-Greene Halleck's favorite spot, and getting there was part of the pleasure. In the summer you took a boat, and in the winter crossed on the ferry to Hoboken and took a carriage up to Fort Lee, where, Tuckerman later testified, Halleck's favorite vantage point during the years of his clerkship for Astor was a high bluff commanding a noble prospect of the city and bay of New York, as well as of Manhattan Island, the East River, and Long Island Sound. The other commanding height there was Flat Rock, and Duyckinck could be counted on to get Melville to one or both of the best spots, although Duyckinck's record of the day in his diary consisted only of derisive comments on some plebeian picnickers.

Melville still held on to his manuscript as the family scattered on vacations. In early August Sam Shaw accompanied his mother, and probably the judge as well, to Niagara Falls, where they took rooms at the Cataract House. Dealing with Hope's usual pathetic protestations, Sam wrote the housekeeper, Ellen Sullivan: "You know Mother said before she came that she should not go on the suspension bridge, nevertheless she went as well as any of us." Lizzie and Herman had said so much about their honeymoon that the Shaws now went home by way of Montreal, to see for themselves, then took a cruise down Lake Champlain, to Hope's terror, and continued through Saratoga. By mid-September Augusta was at the Manor House. Aunt Mary Gansevoort had returned to Waterford, and Guert had been to see her three times, for very brief visits, sober all the time he was around her: "I never saw so great a change, as there is in him—he says he is resolving it shall be radical, & permanent—he reads all day long; & I know he will soon feel the good effects of improving his mind." Reading all day did not conquer the obsession to drink, but it distracted him, for a time, around his mother.

Neither a trip to fetch Lizzie from Boston nor an outing to Fort Lee nor forays around Manhattan constituted a vacation for Herman, but this year, despite the fact that he still retained the manuscript, he was planning one for

August, as in most years of his adolescence; he would take Lizzie to the Melvill house. First the Longfellows had to come and go. On 28 July Fanny Appleton Longfellow wrote her brother-in-law Samuel Longfellow from "Melville Hall, Typee Valley," comparing it favorably to Craigie House: "We have a grand old mansion here, in the style of ours, with immense halls, a porch in front & a stoop with blinds behind, built by a wealthy Dutchman of Kinderhook. It is very spacious & comfortable, & very well kept by Typee's cousin, an intelligent farmer." Less formidable, less to be considered, was Susan Bates Melvill, Robert's "very quiet, timid, little wife," the wealthy Fanny Appleton Longfellow decided. Longfellow himself also found the Melvill place comparable to Craigie House, and luxuriated in poetic emotions at the lake where Gansevoort had rowed the girls; when the locals heard that the poet had referred to the lake as "the Tear of Heaven," that term vied with the more sensible Melvill Lake.

When she wrote to Augusta in April, Priscilla had been boarding in Pittsfield with the Tylers, who were "principals" of a "school for Boys" in the process of taking over the Ontario Female Seminary in Canandaigua. That June Priscilla accompanied them there, perhaps as housekeeper, perhaps as a teacher. Canandaigua was still a village with "an air of neatness, of ease and elegance about it" (as a writer said in the New York *Commercial Advertiser* a decade before, in July 1836), and the female academy made a good appearance: "Its buildings, pleasure grounds, and every thing connected with it, are on a scale truly magnificent." "Nothing" surpassed the place, the visitor reported in 1836, but it became a place of exile to Priscilla, isolated as she was from her blood kin, and obliged to work so severely as to weaken her health. On 20 August, from Canandaigua, Priscilla wrote to Helen Maria that by deserting again "the home of her early days" and turning "her face toward the setting-sun" she was "sacrificing the pleasure of introducing" her Cousin Lizzie to the haunts "*dear* to the memory" of the rest of them:

> though *she* cannot visit them with the same feelings of interest that those scenes would awaken in *our* bosoms, & will perhaps wonder when she sees them, what great charms they possess, for I presume she has heard them described again & *again*, in glowing colors, for before New-York with its glare & show had caused a distaste for natural beauties, *our* rural retreat, with all its *in*-animate & *animate* objects were regarded with *sincere admiration* — but *perhaps* I judge you harshly, Helen.

She was not clear about the timing, and thought Herman might already have gone "to rusticate in Pittsfield." She was sure the "*old place*" looked "very pleasant & cheerful this season" and hoped that some of the others accompanied Herman and Lizzie: "Susan will give you a cordial welcome — & I presume the *Longfellow's* & *McIntoshes* are still there." In New York Herman and Lizzie were poised to replace the Longfellows, not to join them. In honor of their plans, their own Fanny, back from Black River, may have taken down her final gift from her brother Gansevoort, an inscribed copy of Professor Longfellow's *Voices of the Night:* everything, in this election year, reminded someone in the family of Gansevoort.

There is additional although belated testimony that Herman and Lizzie vacationed on the farm in 1848, from Joseph (J. E. A.) Smith in his book on Dr. Oliver Wendell Holmes, *The Poet among the Hills* (1895): "In 1848, shortly after his marriage, and the brilliant success of his first books, 'Omoo' and 'Typee,' he passed the summer in the same old broadhalled mansion, which was then a boarding-house, where, among other agreeable fellow-boarders, he found the poet Longfellow with his wife and children." Biographers have tended to assume that 1848 was an error for 1850, but Herman and Lizzie were expected, after the Longfellows rather than at the same time, so they probably did pass a week or two in late August at the *"old place."* Let Allan worry about the repercussion of the great Buffalo convention of 9 August. Lizzie could sit in the shade of the larch trees and inhale pure air, and Herman could tramp and climb twenty miles a day if he wanted to. His body demanded strenuous exercise, for as a sailor at a desk job he was an athlete whose limbs were deprived of motion for hours at a time.

Each new national event meant Melville might write more current history into his manuscript. That late summer and early fall, with no one talking any more as if the book were finished, Melville continued his work on new sections of political satire, roughly chapters 145 through 168 in the book as published. (One of them, ch. 166, was based on the news that Greeley published in the 19 August *Tribune*—the discovery of gold in California, now happily American territory, or, if you asked some inhabitants of Monterey, twice-American.) In these chapters King Media, the voice of both authority and mediation, the philosopher Babbalanja, the poet Yoomy, and the hero, Taji, pass through allegorically renamed countries of Europe and North America in their increasingly perfunctory search for the maiden Yillah. The central chapter in the political section of *Mardi* is chapter 161, "They hearken unto a Voice from the Gods." The travelers have reached a "great valley" in northern Vivenza—recognizable as the Erie Canal route where the Van Burenites had been holding their conventions. Here the travelers encounter "a clamorous crowd gathered about a conspicuous palm, against which, a scroll was fixed." After much preliminary stump-speaking, the scroll is read aloud by a "fiery youth." The authorship of the scroll is left elaborately in doubt—an early use of Melville's recurrent device of inserting into a work an extremely phrased document which is either anonymous or else so dubiously pieced together that no one can quite be assigned full responsibility for its views.

The doctrines the scroll propounds consist of Melville's indictments of the errors of America and his prescriptions for the future conduct of the country, all provocatively phrased. The scroll attacks the Puritan idea of America as the chosen land and of Americans as the chosen people, an idea that had recently given credence to the extra-legal notion of Manifest Destiny. The American "sovereign-kings" are warned that the grand error of the nation is the conceit that the world was in the last scene of the last act of its drama, and that "all preceding events were ordained, to bring about the catastrophe you believe to be at hand, — a universal and permanent Republic." The grandson of Federalists, Melville in the scroll reminded his fellow countrymen: "Your nation enjoyed no little independence before your Declaration declared it." (Older contemporaries said the same thing. The renowned Dr. Francis L. Hawks, long an intimate friend of Duyckinck's, expounded the same idea to the New-York Historical Society in February 1858, when Duyckinck paraphrased the topic in his diary: "It was because America was freeborn and elevated in freedom before the separation from England, that she was free afterwards.") Finally, the scroll denounced American aggression against Mexico and echoed the Whigs in attacking Polk for beginning an executive's war: "Delegate your power, you leagued mortals must. The hazard you must stand. And though unlike King Bello of Dominora [Great Britain], your great chieftain, sovereign-kings! may not declare war of himself; nevertheless, has he done a still more imperial thing: — gone to war without declaring intentions. You yourselves were precipitated upon a neighboring nation, ere you knew your spears were in your hands." For the perspective he needed to integrate commonplace ideas into a coherent statement, Melville owed something to his reading of Edmund Burke's "Reflections on the Revolution in France." He had read it in his boyhood, and judging from the reference in chapter 24 of *Mardi* he had reread it recently. Especially, Burke's sense of the colonies' "entailed inheritance" of English liberties seems to inform Melville's irritation at those Americans who disregard their debts to the past. Whatever his intentions when he began writing current events into *Mardi*, Melville in these political chapters was freeing himself from the political factions and parties to which his acquaintances, friends, and relatives were vehemently allying themselves.

Melville's distancing himself from political factions may have led to his distancing himself from the literary cliques, although what set him off may have been an article in the *Tribune* of 27 September 1848, "The Literary

Soirees," by Mathews's sour acquaintance, G. G. Foster. Number twenty-six in a series of journalistic glimpses of the city, "New-York in Slices" (as in the phrase "a slice of life"), this article contained a description of a Valentine's party at a literary salon, plainly Anne Lynch's. In the article were portraits Melville would have recognized, such as those of John Inman, the brother of the recently deceased painter Henry Inman (whom Helen and Gansevoort had met in Lenox in 1841), and Melville's acquaintance from evenings at Dr. Francis's, Rufus Griswold ("a thin, nervous man, his gray eyes looking shyly about like a girl's, and his mouth twitching every now and then, with the conception of a new biography").

Most disturbing for Melville, this article in the *Tribune* contained a devastating portrait of the protective way Evert Duyckinck behaved toward the egregious egotist Cornelius Mathews, behavior Melville had witnessed frequently:

> On the sofa, with his plump, handsome feet piled up on the footstool and his round face illuminated by a pair of green spectacles, above which rises rather conceitedly and knowingly a capacious brow, buttressed by two very respectable organs of ideality, sits a gentleman [Cornelius Mathews] listening earnestly to the reading of the Valentines, fearful lest, by some unaccountable mishap, he should have been overlooked. Beside him is a handsome, intellectual-looking young man [Evert Duyckinck], evidently of the old aristocratic Knickerbocker blood, who seems to be watching for *the* Valentine quite as intently as his companion. He, however, has no misgiving — he knows it will come — for he wrote it himself, lest his friend should be forgotten. These two personages are in some respects remarkable. Both are men of high intellectual powers — one of them entirely ambitious and ready to dispute his rights on the instant with any rival or pretender; the other as entirely and eminently unselfish — thinking ever only of his friend and how to promote his interests and advance his fame. They are the Castor and Pollux of Literature — the Gemini of the literary Zodiac — the Damon and Pythias of the drama of real life. One of them has produced books which have at least been read, and have furthermore received the compliment of being heartily abused. — The other does not write books, but he is a delicate appreciator of the books of others, and for a certain kind of amiable and tender criticism has no rival. Both these men — for they are never apart — form a work in two volumes well worth the studying.

Whether or not a scene much like this happened at Anne Lynch's Valentine party under his own observation, this description, in the ugly narrow columns of the *Tribune*, forced Melville to reevaluate scenes he had indeed witnessed, and it entered into his rethinking of the values of the literary clique into which he had been dropped by the mere fact of Gansevoort's arranging for his book to be published by Wiley & Putnam, where Duyckinck was the editor of the Library of American Books, the series into which *Typee* had been deflected.

Months before, early in 1848, when he was preoccupied by creating a fictional symposium in his manuscript and worried about how he was going to explain himself to John Murray, Melville may have made his observations at Anne Lynch's without analyzing them and without making many judgments. The consciousness of his own powers had already burgeoned within him, and was about to burst out in his declaration to Murray that he meant to make a hit, that he was taking bold aim. While he was living such an intense inner life he may have missed much of what went on around him at the Valentine party. The *Tribune* article forced Melville, perhaps for the first time, to reflect on the peculiarly protective, subservient manner Duyckinck always displayed toward Mathews. Now Melville had to acknowledge the irony of the situation. Duyckinck thought himself lucky enough to be the friend of the greatest American poet and the greatest American fiction writer, all embodied in one man with a round face, a capacious brow, and tender sensibilities, whose name began with an *M* — not Melville, but Mathews. Foster may have forced Melville to see that Duyckinck might always take him far less seriously than he took Mathews, a bitter acknowledgment for him to make.

If the *Tribune* did not cause Melville to look afresh at the behavior of his friends, something else did. Less than a month later, on "October, the 21st day, in the year '48," the brash Harvard-educated punster James Russell Lowell, Melville's age, came forth with *A Fable for Critics*, the rhyming title page of which ended "G. P. Putnam, Broadway" (to rhyme with "21st day"). (Lowell's name did not appear on the book, but his authorship was public knowledge at once, part of the joke.) Lowell's close New York friend (and Poe's associate editor on the defunct *Broadway Journal*) Charles F. Briggs had fed him inside information on the New York literary scene and actors that went into the poem, along with suggestions for ways of sizing the actors up. In the *Fable* Melville himself escaped notice, yet again (unless he inspired the putdown of the prescriptive critic who "shrieks out *Taboo!*"), but Mathews and Duyckinck, as in Briggs's *Trippings of Tom Pepper*, were not so lucky. Mathews was twice-whipped, once in the shape of the critic who lobbies Apollo "to get up a subscription, / Considering that authorship wasn't a rich craft, / To print the 'American Drama of Witchcraft.' " Apollo flees, shrieking "Help!" when the "Hero" offers to read him a scene. Then Evert Duyckinck intrudes on Apollo, who has been going over sonnets:

> So, condensing the strength here, there smoothing a wry kink,
> He was killing the time, when up walked Mr. —— ;
> At a few steps behind him, a small man in glasses,
> Went dodging about, muttering "murderers! asses!"
> From out of his pocket a paper he'd take,
> With the proud look of martyrdom tied to its stake,
> And, reading a squib at himself, he'd say, "Here I see
> 'Gainst American letters a bloody conspiracy,
> They are all by my personal enemies written;
> I must post an anonymous letter to Britain,
> And show that this gall is the merest suggestion
> Of spite at my zeal on the Copyright question[."]

Duyckinck himself came out relatively unscathed. Apollo greets him:

> Good day, Mr. —— , I'm happy to meet
> With a scholar so ripe, and a critic so neat,
> Who through Grub street the soul of a gentleman carries, —
> What news from that suburb of London and Paris
> Which latterly makes such shrill claims to monopolize
> The credit of being the New World's metropolis?

The only news Duyckinck has to tell the god is of an attack on Mathews, who is still lurking behind him:

> Why, nothing of consequence, save this attack
> On my friend there, behind, by some pitiful hack,
> Who thinks every national author a poor one,
> That isn't a copy of something that's foreign,
> And assaults the American Dick —

Apollo cuts Duyckinck off, knowing Mathews's habit of carrying hostile criticisms of his works around with him and forcing them on other people's attention, and weary of Mathews's promoting himself as the American Dickens. Unfazed, Duyckinck offers the god a copy of a book by Mathews (the forty-fourth copy given him), along with the promise of space in the next issue of the *Democratic Review* for Apollo to review it (Duyckinck having been associated, for a time, with that magazine).

Toward the end of his long struggle to make a great book of *Mardi*, Melville in "Some pleasant, shady Talk in the Groves, between my Lords Abrazza and Media, Babbalanja, Mohi, and Yoomy" (ch. 180), described the process by which the genius Lombardo created his masterwork, his *Koztanza*: "When Lombardo set about his work, he knew not what it would become.

He did not build himself in with plans; he wrote right on; and so doing, got deeper and deeper into himself; and like a resolute traveler, plunging through baffling woods, at last was rewarded for his toils." Lombardo had, he decided, "created the creative" — at the cost of renouncing those captious nymphs "the unities" and yielding himself to "one autocrat within — his crowned and sceptered instinct." In this chapter Melville lashed out at the New York literati, represented by the Job's comforters to whom Lombardo showed the work: Zenzori "asked him where he picked up so much trash"; Hauto "bade him not be cast down, it was pretty good"; Lucree "desired to know how much he was going to get for it"; Roddi "offered a suggestion" — that he "had best make a faggot of the whole; and try again"; and Pollo took notes on the manuscript all night, then professed to have run through the sheets carelessly: "You might have done better; but then you might have done worse. Take them, my friend; I have put in some good things for you." With such good reason did Lombardo despise the critics: "Critics? — Asses! rather mules! — so emasculated, from vanity, they can not father a true thought. Like mules, too, from dunghills, they trample down gardens of roses: and deem that crushed fragrance their own. — Oh! that all round the domains of genius should lie thus unhedged, for such cattle to uproot! Oh! that an eagle should be stabbed by a goose-quill! But at best, the greatest reviewers but prey on my leavings." Here Melville in his own *Fable for Critics* explicitly declared his literary independence from the New York literati, not only the ones who had attacked him, but also the Duyckinck clique. Declaring independence was easy; winning it, his grandfathers could both have told him, was another matter.

Life for others in the house went on, but Herman kept writing. In the election, 7 November, the Whig candidate R. Brewer won the seat in the State Assembly from the Fifteenth District, Seventeenth Ward, with 1496 votes to Allan's 857 (according to the *Tribune* of the ninth). In mid-November Anne Lynch, now a neighbor at 45 Ninth Street, near Fifth Avenue, gave a party for the visiting celebrity Fredrika Bremer, to which she invited "the Misses Melville," Lizzie being much too far in her pregnancy to go out; with her usual ungraciousness, Miss Bremer complained that she was required "to act the parrot in a large crowd till toward midnight." (At least Charles Dickens, the ungrateful author of *American Notes*, had behaved politely as long as he was in the United States.)

Everyone knew Melville's book was not finished, and some people assumed he had time for other work. The Duyckincks had bought the *Literary World* and resumed editing it in early October, after seventeen months, and within a few weeks Evert sent Melville a book for review, Joseph C. Hart's *Romance of Yachting*. At first Melville was amenable: "I will look over the book with pleasure. And will contrive to write something about it, but being much engaged just now, wont be able to say a great deal. — I will see you before long." He was just then engaged in negotiating with the Harpers for the publication of *Mardi, and a Voyage thither* (finally, that title and subtitle are given in a document that survives). On Allan's draft of the contract, Melville himself drafted an additional clause: "In case it is hereafter agreed between us, that it would be profitable to illustrate the book, Messrs Harper will defray the expences of the engravings, without charging any portion thereof to the account of H.M. But H.M. shall receive half the profits as before." He was thinking big when he signed the actual contract on 15 November, even though that clause was excluded. (No edition in English of *Mardi* or any of his other books was issued with illustrations, although many of his books were eminently eligible candidates for that treatment.) Most likely, Melville delivered the bulky manuscript at the signing.

Melville wanted to oblige Duyckinck, but in his long-awaited freedom from his manuscript he was not about to return to his old flippant level of reviewing Browne and Codman in the *Literary World.* The Hart book Duyckinck had sent him was a most strange affair, in sober fact, containing among other oddities the first appearance of the bizarre news that Shakespeare had not written Shakespeare's plays. No wonder that instead of writing a review Melville wrote a letter (14 November) about how impossible it would be to write one:

> What the deuce does it mean? — Here's a book positively turned wrong side out, the title page on the cover, an index to the whole in more ways than one. — I open at the beginning, & find myself in the middle of the Blue Laws & Dr O'Callaghan. Then proceeding, find several extracts from the Log Book of Noah's Ark — Still further, take a hand at three or four bull fights, & then I'm set down to a digest of all the commentaries on Shakspeare, who, according "to our author" was a dunce & a blackguard — Vide passim. . . .
>
> . . . And as for Mr Hart, pen & ink, should certainly be taken away from that unfortunate man, upon the same principle that pistols are withdrawn from the wight bent on suicide. — Prayers should be offered up for him among the congregations, and Thanksgiving Day postponed untill long after his "book" is published. What great national sin have we committed to deserve this infliction?

"Seriously," on his "bended knees," and with tears in his eyes, Melville begged Duyckinck to be delivered "from writing ought upon this crucifying Romance of Yachting." He could not "publicly devour" Mr. Hart, and he could not gloss "over his book with a few commonplaces." Now there were things Melville would not do for Duyckinck; he was not breaking with him, but he had taken the measure of his literary friend.

In the course of writing *Mardi* Melville had caught the vision of becoming a great writer, and taking a great theme in his immature hands, he had tried to write something more than a mere romantic narrative of adventure. He had voyaged into a new world, he was sure, "the world of mind" — the world of ideas. In "Dreams" (ch. 119) he had celebrated reading great old books until he had become his own Vatican Library, where in him "many worthies" could recline and converse. Neither there nor elsewhere did he define his growth in terms of aesthetics: he had not voyaged into the world of art (and he did not even tell himself he had voyaged toward the mastery of artistic techniques). Nor had he voyaged more than tentatively into the world within. To use an image that came to his mind early in 1852, he had not yet dropped an angle — a fishhook — into the well of childhood. Into the well of the present, of his early manhood, he had looked deeply enough to write his own new creative life into his account of the way the great poet Lombardo created his masterpiece. In *Mardi*, Melville hoped, he had written his own *Koztanza*, a genuinely Rabelaisian book fit to stand on a shelf beside Burton's *The Anatomy of Melancholy* and Swift's *Gulliver's Travels*.

30

Malcolm and the Fate of *Mardi*

1849

I suppose you are long since informed through the family of the birth of an
heir to my fame & fortunes, which is truly a most "joyful event" to Mrs M &
myself, & especially as he is pronounced by all to be a most noble Boy, which
we are very willing to believe, without calling in question the taste or
sagacity of a shrewd & enlightened publick.

Allan Melvill to Lemuel Shaw, 20 January 1816, on the birth
of his son Gansevoort

ON 2 JANUARY 1849 MELVILLE accompanied his very pregnant wife on the
arduous and even dangerous midwinter journey home to Mt. Vernon Street,
leaving the proofs of *Mardi* in the hands of Augusta. She struggled with them
through the month, with some tardy help from the author. In an interval Augusta entered into her commonplace book, *Orient Pearls at Random Strung*, a
poem, "The Rights of Women," by Mrs. E. Little, that sufficiently conveyed
her sense of the question being agitated in the aftermath of the Seneca Falls
convention in 1848. It read, in part:

> "The rights of women," what are they?
> The right to labor and to pray;
> The right to watch while others sleep,
> The right o'er others' woes to weep;
>
> . . . .
>
> The right to shed new joy on earth,
> The right to feel the soul's high worth,
> The right to lead the soul to God
> Along the path her Saviour trod.

(The poem satisfied a popular need, judging from its reprinting in the Portland [Maine] *Daily Eastern Argus* so late as 21 August 1866.) Having conducted researches into the family genealogy, Augusta pressed Lizzie to accept her choice of a name for a boy, Malcolm, from the Scollay family. She

left it to Lizzie to propose the name to Herman, who gave it his unqualified approbation, knowing *Macbeth* from his youth, whether or not he knew the Scollay ancestry: if the baby was a boy, in due course he would become king. The coincidence of approaching birth and approaching publication was lost on no one, and in her letter to Lizzie on 27 January Augusta mingled her fantasy about the baby with a report on the proofs:

> — *Malcolm Melville!* how easily it runs from my pen; how sweetly it sounds to my ear; how musically it falls upon my heart. — Malcolm Melville! — methinks I see him in his plaided kilt, with his soft blue eyes, and his long flaxen curls. How I long to press him to my heart.
>
> There, I can write no more. The last proof sheets are through. "Mardi's" a book! — "Ah my own Koztanza! child of many prayers." Oro's blessing on thee.

As the member of the family who had first encouraged Herman to write down his adventures in the Marquesas, Augusta retained a special concern for his career, but everyone in the Fourth Avenue house was caught up in the process of bookmaking as well as babymaking.

Back in New York to work on the proofs, Melville on 28 January wrote John Murray another aggressive letter to accompany the sheets of *Mardi:*

> After full consideration, I must explicitly state, that I can hardly consent to dispose of the book for less than 200 guineas, in advance, on the day of publication, & half the profits of any editions which may be sold after the book shall have paid for itself. . . . Upon these terms should you feel disposed to undertake it, I should feel exceedingly gratified to continue our connection, & should equally regret to be obliged to leave you.

Closing his mind to the value of tying the new book to the reputation he had earned, he made this preposterous request: "Unless you should deem it *very* desirable do not put me down on the title page as 'the author of Typee & Omoo'. I wish to separate '*Mardi*' as much as possible from those books." He had, already, a capacity for impractical behavior that verged on the self-destructive. On 6 February Allan mailed the proofs to John R. Brodhead for delivery to Murray. Herman had put a truculent little preface (dated January 1849) into the Harper edition, so chances are it was included in what Allan sent:

> Not long ago, having published two narratives of voyages in the Pacific, which, in many quarters, were received with incredulity, the thought occurred to me, of indeed writing a romance of Polynesian adventure, and

publishing it as such; to see whether, the fiction might not, possibly, be received for a verity: in some degree the reverse of my previous experience.

This thought was the germ of others, which have resulted in Mardi.

Murray's dismay and disdain if he saw this note can be imagined. On 30 January, Melville was back in Boston, finished with *Mardi* except for selling it abroad.

Less frantic now than in December 1846, when he was finishing *Omoo*, Melville called on his Cousin Nilly, who still lived only a few doors from the Shaws. Comparatively a free man, he heard Ralph Waldo Emerson lecture on "Mind & Manners in the Nineteenth Century" around 5 February at the Freeman Place Chapel on Beacon Street. Journalists had been outdoing each other in quotations demonstrating the unintelligibility of all Transcendentals, Bronson Alcott worst of all, but Emerson as well, so Melville was pleasantly surprised at finding him both comprehensible and challenging. At some point on this visit (4 and 11 February were likely Sundays), he probably went over to the blue-flagged Seaman's Bethel in North Square, where Father Taylor preached. Dickens had made the obligatory visit and recorded in his *American Notes* what was generally known, that the preacher's imagery "was all drawn from the sea and from the incidents of a seaman's life," and for a seaman-author the chance to hear Father Taylor was not to be missed. On 12 February Melville went to a reading by Fanny Kemble Butler of *Macbeth* at the Masonic Temple, a sufficient reminder of the majesty of the ancestral name Malcolm, whether or not she read passages in which that name appeared. No name for a girl appears in the surviving family papers, but there was no need for one, for the baby, born at "half past 7 o'clock in the morning" on 16 February, was a son, duly named Malcolm.

Two mornings later, on the eighteenth, Sophia Thurston Melville gave birth to a daughter, dutifully named Maria Gansevoort Melville. The fathers stayed in character. Allan, who had complained about being sent on an errand to the village during the paradisiacal summers at Uncle Thomas's, now resentfully left the house at six o'clock (to make things worse, it was Sunday) to take the ferry to Brooklyn to get a nurse for the baby, and for years he lost no opportunity to tell the child just how cold and uncomfortable a journey he had made of it, while she had remained indoors, newly dried and warm, cared for by her mother, aunts, and one or two grandmothers. In that era of fast mail service, Herman responded to the news of the birth of the new Maria Gansevoort Melville with his own exultant letter on 20 February:

> I have yours of yesterday. I am rejoiced that Sophia is well after her happy delivery.
>
> Lizzie is doing well, also the phenomenon, which weighs I know not how

many pennyweights, — I would say, hundred-weights. —— We desired much
to have him weighed, but it was thought that no hay-scales in town were
strong enough. It takes three nurses to dress him; and he is as valiant as Julius
Cesear. —— He's a perfect prodigy. —— If the worst comes to the worst, I
shall let him out by the month to Barnum; and take the tour of Europe with
him. I think of calling him Barbarossa — Adolphus — Ferdinand — Otho —
Grandissimo Hercules — Sampson — Bonaparte — Lambert. —— If you can
suggest any thing better or more characteristic, pray, inform me of it by
the next post. —— There was a terrible commotion here at the time of the
event. — I had men stationed at all the church bells, 24 hours before hand;
& when the Electric Telegraph informed them of the fact — such a ding-
donging you never heard. — All the engines came out, thinking the State-
House was on fire.

Of course the news was sent on by telegraph to Washington & New Orleans. — When Old Zack heard of it — he is reputed to have said — "Mark me:
that boy will be President of the United States before he dies." —— In New
Orleans, the excitement was prodigious. Stocks rose & brandy fell. —— I have
not yet heard from Europe & Pekin. But doubtless, ere this, they must have
placed props against the Great-Wall. —— The harbor here is empty: — all the
ships, brigs, schooners & smacks having scattered in all directions with the
news for foreign parts. — The crowd has not yet left the streets, gossiping of
the event. — The number of calls at 49 Mt Vernon Street is incalculable. Ten
porters suffice not to receive the cards; and Canning the waiter, dropped
down dead last night thro' pure exhaustion. —— Who would have thought
that the birth of one little man, when ten thousands of other little men, &
little horses, & little guinea-pigs & little roosters, & the Lord only knows
what, are being born — that the birth of one little phenomenon, should create
such a panic thro' the world: — nay, even in heaven; for last night I dreampt
that his good angel had secured a seat for him above; & that the Devel roared
terribly bethinking him of the lusty foe to sin born into this sinful world.

Herman addressed Allan companionably as "The Reverend Father in Wedlock" in the superscription of this letter, which so dazzlingly reveals Melville's state of mind. First child, first son: everything was going his way, and
he had a publisher in reserve if Murray continued to behave in an Antarctic
fashion two winters in a row. In his best contradictory fashion, now with
everything to live for, this man had just asked Murray not to advertise *Mardi*
as by the author of *Typee* and *Omoo*.

Writing still from Boston, knowing that Evert Duyckinck had heard the
family news (and probably having received a discreet note of congratulation),
Melville omitted mention of either baby in his relaxed letter of 24 February.

He had asked Duyckinck about "The Colonel's Club" in the *Literary World* and had been told that it was being written by young William Allen Butler, George Duyckinck's companion on the grand tour. Melville was beyond praising such journalistic maunderings: "Mr Butler's a genius, but between you & me, I have a presentiment that he never will surprise me more." Young William Butler would never surprise him, but William Shakespeare had just surprised him — had all but overwhelmed him, as he explained with rising excitement:

> I have been passing my time very pleasurably here. But chiefly in lounging on a sofa (a la the poet Grey) & reading Shakspeare. It is an edition in glorious great type, every letter whereof is a soldier, & the top of every "t" like a musket barrel. Dolt & ass that I am I have lived more than 29 years, & until a few days ago, never made close acquaintance with the divine William. Ah, he's full of sermons-on-the-mount, and gentle, aye, almost as Jesus. I take such men to be inspired. I fancy that this moment Shakspeare in heaven ranks with Gabriel Raphael and Michael. And if another Messiah ever comes twill be in Shakespere's person. —— I am mad to think how minute a cause has prevented me hitherto from reading Shakspeare. But until now, every copy that was come-atable to me, happened to be in a vile small print unendurable to my eyes which are tender as young sparrows. But chancing to fall in with this glorious edition, I now exult over it, page after page.

The edition was *The Dramatic Works of William Shakspeare* in seven volumes (Boston: Hilliard, Gray, 1837), which he marked extensively, then and later. Melville "knew" his Shakespeare as well as most educated people, already, but now he was able to make "close acquaintance" with the Shakespeare whom he found to be a profound thinker on human nature and the place of human beings in the universe.

Now or later, in *The Tempest* Melville boxed and scored Miranda's famous "brave new world" speech and Prospero's reply, "'Tis new to thee," then commented: "Consider the character of the persons concerning whom Miranda says this — then Prospero's quiet words in comment — how terrible! In 'Timon' itself there is nothing like it." In *The Winter's Tale* he scored Polixenes' speech: "Yet nature is made better by no mean, / But nature makes that mean," and commented: "A world here." In *King Lear* he marked Edmund's speech: "What in the world he is / That names me traitor, villain-like he lies. / Call by thy trumpet; he that dares approach, / On him, on you, (who not?) I will maintain / My truth and honor firmly." Melville commented: "The infernal nature has a valor often denied to innocence." He scored Hamlet's "Why, then 'tis none to you; for there is nothing either good or bad, but thinking makes it so; to me it is a prison," and noted: "Here is forcibly shown the great Montaignism of Hamlet." He was seeing in the plays his own serious thoughts articulated memorably. The annotations show that he thought of Shakespeare in terms of the tragedian's dark meanings, not the way those meanings were expressed; Melville was, after all, self-taught, and technical features simply were not uppermost in his consciousness at this time. For years to come, as far as his comments reveal, Shakespeare to him was the profound thinker, the deep psychologist, not primarily the master of the English language and master of poetic and dramatic techniques; by no coincidence, he thought of himself the same way, as thinker first, rather than artist.

In that letter of 24 February Melville gave a favorable report on the lecture he had heard Emerson deliver: "Say what they will, he's a great man." He also reported on Mrs. Butler, whom Pierce Butler was divorcing for abandonment: "She makes a glorious Lady Macbeth, but her Desdemona seems like a boarding school miss.—She's so unfemininely masculine that had she not, on unimpeachable authority, borne children, I should be curious to learn the result of a surgical examination of her person in private. The Lord help Butler. . . . I marvel not he seeks being amputated off from his matrimonial half." There ensued a foreboding little exchange. In response to this 24 February letter Duyckinck apparently sent Melville a clipping from the *Tribune* of 6 February, a cartoon which portrayed Emerson swinging in an upside-down rainbow, meaning it as a personal reproach to the sailor who just might be naive enough to become one of Emerson's disciples. Duyckinck had dealt with some of those disciples already, notably the young Henry David Thoreau, whom the erratic Greeley had decided to promote in the *Tribune*, but whose *Week on the Concord and Merrimack Rivers* Duyckinck had rejected for inclusion in the Wiley & Putnam Library of American Books in very late July or early August 1847, despite Emerson's recommendation (Thoreau had pressed Duyckinck for a decision on 27 July, just before Melville's wedding). On 3 March 1849 Melville defended himself, forthrightly declaring that he did not "oscillate in Emerson's rainbow," but insisting that he had been "very agreeably disappointed" by Emerson's performance: "I had heard of him as full of transcendentalisms, myths & oracular gibberish; I had only glanced at a book of his once in Putnam's store—that was all I knew of him, till I heard him lecture.—To my surprise, I found him quite intelligible, tho' to say truth, they told me that that night he was unusually plain." What appealed to him was a quality he now recognized in himself, intellectual daring: "I love all men who *dive*. Any fish can swim near the surface, but it takes a great whale to go down stairs five miles or more"—as not just

Emerson but "the whole corps of thought-divers" had kept doing "since the world began." Melville had a new category for himself, thought-diver, though he identified himself only as one who loved such men.

That late winter and spring Melville made other major purchases besides the Shakespeare. One was *The Complete Poetical Works of John Milton* in two volumes (Boston: Hilliard, Gray, 1836), in the same format and legible print—a momentous purchase. In the prefatory "Life of Milton" Melville scored a passage on Milton's "wanderings in religious belief" and commented: "He who thinks for himself never can rema[i]n of the same mind. I doubt not that darker doubts crossed Milton's soul, than ever disturbed Voltair. And he was more of what is called an Infidel." Reading farther in the description of Milton's ceasing to attend public worship and his retiring "within himself, in the dignity of age, to employ the unimpaired energies of his intellect on the most important and awful subject of inquiry," Melville scored this passage on Milton's religious practice: "It was to dwell alone in its holy meditations, cloistered from public gaze, and secluded within the humbler sanctuary of the adoring heart. If the believer felt it to be his duty to attach himself to any particular church, that church was to be unconnected with the state"; in the margin Melville commented (apropos of himself and Milton): "A singular coincidence."

Another purchase, charged to him at Wiley's on 16 February, while he was still in Boston, was a set of the *Modern British Essayists* in several volumes for eighteen dollars. This set has not been located, but it included volumes of essays by Thomas Babington Macaulay, Sir Archibald Alison, Sydney Smith, John Wilson (Christopher North), Thomas Carlyle, Francis Jeffrey, and (together) Sir James Stephen and Sir Thomas Noon Talfourd; it may have included a volume by Sir James Macintosh, and still less likely a volume of Sir Walter Scott's essays. This was another momentous purchase, since it meant that for the rest of his life Melville had on his shelves a library of classic literary criticism of the previous half century. Almost surely, his edition was printed in double columns of small print (the Jeffrey volume running to more than 750 pages), which he might need a magnifying glass to use, but in which he did read widely. This Jeffrey volume, perhaps the most important for him, contained the early reviews of the English Romantic poets printed in the *Edinburgh Review* as the volumes of poetry appeared year by year—*Manfred, The Lady of the Lake, Endymion, Childe Harold's Pilgrimage, The Excursion,* among others—the magazine having started a little too late for *Lyrical Ballads.* As he used the volume in the next decades Melville slowly came to understand the significance of Jeffrey's prefatory claim that the *Edinburgh Review* from the beginning had "professed to go deeply into *the Principles* on which its judgments were to be rested" — which was to say that it consciously dealt in problems of aesthetics or what is now called literary theory, not merely in practical criticism.

Meanwhile John R. Brodhead was once again acting energetically as Melville's London agent. Around the beginning of the fourth week of February he presented the sheets of *Mardi* to John Murray, who promptly declared that the book did not suit him, being "a *fiction.*" With the package back in his possession on 24 February, Brodhead read the sheets himself preparatory to offering them to Richard Bentley, according to Melville's instructions. Bentley rushed the sheets to his reader and before the end of the month received a hasty report, starting with a plot summary based on a reading of the Harper first volume as well as the first quarter and last twenty pages of the second. The reader was delighted by the "first half of the first volume, say, two thirds": "There is such a form of language, (a little Carlylish, by the bye), such a prodigality of description — such a vivid picture of things that may be, however extraordinary, — that I began to hope, nay, to assure myself, — that now at last there was a book whose publication I could confidently urge." That expectation was dashed by what followed, and the reader singled out the chapter on "Dreams" as seeming almost "to have been written by a madman," while the last few pages were "quite delirious." Nevertheless, Bentley called on Brodhead on 1 March and accepted Melville's offer. A few days later he wrote Melville agreeing to pay "the sum of Two Hundred and ten Pounds" as advance and as assurance of Melville's "moiety of the profits that may accrue" — an astonishingly generous offer, in view of the uncertain state of the copyright law as well as the strong reservations advanced by the reader.

Pressing on after the manuscript was accepted, the reader supplied Bentley with this blunt comment: "The Author wrote the first third of the work to seduce the reader into reading the rest; but the reader will loudly complain that the work does not turn out to be what, after reading no small quantity, he had a right to expect." "I fancy not one in a score will discover what it's all about," the reader predicted, "and as to the tale of Babbalanja, the sage, who is by far the most loquacious, *none* will arrive *at* all he means." In spite of all this, on 5 March Bentley wrote Melville a "frank & friendly letter" (as Melville called it in his 3 April response), and set the compositors to work so fast that he published the book, in three volumes, in an edition of one thousand copies, on 15 March. It lacked the preface that appeared in the Harper edition, but the dedication to Allan made it into both.

While this was all proceeding without his knowledge but to his great benefit, Melville made a brief business trip back to New York on 3 March, probably in order to settle some matters with the Harpers. Having closed his eyes to the sailor's report of his fresh ecstatic reading of Shakespeare (an exceptional sailor could read old books, but could not really read Shake-speare), Duyckinck seized Melville during his brief trip and got him to write a review of Francis Parkman's *The California and Oregon Trail*. What else was a travel expert for? The hasty essay shows Melville's irritation — perhaps deflected from the condescending editor of the *Literary World* to the Bosto-nian Parkman who so disdained his many inferiors:

> It is too often the case, that civilized beings sojourning among savages soon come to regard them with disdain & contempt. But though in many cases this feeling is almost natural, it is not defensible; and it is wholly wrong. Why should we contemn them? — Because we are better than they? Assuredly not; for herein we are rebuked by the story of the Publican & the Pharisee. — Because, then, that in many things we are happier? — But this should be ground for commiseration, not disdain. . . . When we affect to contemn savages, we should remember that by so doing we asperse our own progeni-tors; for they were savages also. Who can swear that among the naked British barbarians sent to Rome to be stared at more than 1500 years ago, the ances-tor of Bacon might not have been found? — Why, among the very Thugs of India, or the bloody Dyaks of Borneo, exists the germ of all that is intellec-tually elevated & grand.

This was the voice of the man who in *Typee* (ch. 26) had declared: "The Anglo-Saxon hive have extirpated Paganism from the greater part of the North American continent; but with it they have likewise extirpated the greater portion of the Red race."

Melville scanned *The Oregon Trail* with pen in hand, pausing at passages that struck him, as in this episode, on "the verge of the wilderness," across the Mississippi:

> They visit a man in whose house is a shelf for books, & where they observe a curious illustration of life: they find a holster-pistol standing guard over a copy of Paradise Lost. We presume, then, that on our Western frontier, when a man desires to soar with Milton, he does so with his book in one hand, & a pistol in the other; which last, indeed, might help him in sustaining an "armed neutrality" during the terrible but bloodless battles between Captain Belzeebub & that gallant warrier Michael.

Charmingly offhand, Melville confessed that he could not attempt to follow Parkman and his companions "thro' all their wild rovings," and then gave evocative hints at the sort of novelties the reader would encounter, from killing buffalo to meeting "veritable grandsons of Daniel Boon." (He pri-vately noted the title of ch. 24, "The Chase," and the implied characteriza-tion of the bison as "Mightiest of all the beasts of chase" in the epigraph to the chapter, from Sir Walter Scott's "Cadyow Castle.") Even in his hurry, Melville was taken with the characterization of the hunter and guide Henry Chatillon: "He belongs to a class of men, of whom Kit Carson is the model; a class, unique & not to be transcended in interest by any personages introduced to us by Scott. Long live & hunt Henry Chatillon!"

Melville noted also, for the bemusement of the Mt. Vernon establishment, the portrayal of the dashing, picturesquely attired Quincy A. Shaw, an acquaintance if not a connection: "He sported richly worked Indian leggins, a red tunic & sash; and let loose among a herd of bison, did execution like our feirce friend Alp in Byron's 'Seige of Corinth' — piling the dead round him in semicircles." He added some fresh gossip he had picked up in Boston: "Returned from his hunting tour across the Western hemisphere, Mr Shaw, we learn, is now among the wild Bedouins of Arabia." The book, he pronounced, had "the true wild-game flavor," and would amazingly tickle the palates of all "who are so lucky as to read it." Melville commented on the "two pictorial illustrations by the well-known & talented artist Darley, one of which is exceedingly good." (He may already have made the acquaintance of Felix Darley, who lived far away from the metropolis — in Claymont, Delaware — but was becoming the nation's favorite illustrator.) There was no point copying out an extract of the book himself: at the end of his comments Melville wrote, "Among numerous fine & dashing descriptive chapters we have only room for the following," and made a note for the printer: "(Beginning at the paragraph 'We had scarsely gone' etc on page 390 to the end of the chapter)." Duyckinck fiddled a little with the ending, substituting the one word "select" for Melville's "have only room for," and published the piece, anonymously, as usual, in the 31 March issue under the title "Mr. Parkman's Tour." This sort of thing Melville could dash off on demand, given a reasonably quiet corner of a table, at Clinton Place or the *Literary World* office at 157 Broadway, or at Allan's office in Wall Street.

By mid-March Melville was back in Boston, where the Shaws would have commented on Parkman's pursuit of a distant connection of Herman's, Catherine Scollay Bigelow. On 17 March Hope Shaw reported to her nephew Sam Savage that "Lizzy continues improving" and that Herman was "very happy," even though his book was not out. He was waiting for the steamer from London, she explained, so both books, "the one in London & the one here" could be published the same day. Melville met his new friend Richard Henry Dana Jr. at the Parker House on two different nights. Dana brought a cousin along one time, probably the James Dana who became a professor of natural history at Yale that year, and on the other night Melville met a young Cabot who had "just come from sea." When Melville was "very happy," he was dazzling, and it was at this time that Dana wrote his brother Edmund

(Ned), then in Heidelberg, that Melville was "incomparable in dramatic story telling."

Melville took care of business, from Boston on 27 March asking the Harpers to furnish the sheets of *Mardi* so Duyckinck could print extracts and a review in the *Literary World*. Informing Duyckinck of this arrangement the next day, he added a tribute to the weather: "Rain, Rain, Rain — an interminable rain that to seek elsewhere than in Boston would be utterly vain — Rhyme by Jove, and spontaneous as heart-beating. — This is the Fourth Day of the Great Boston Rain, & how much longer it is to last the ghost of the last man drowned by the Deluge only knows. I have a continual dripping sensation; and feel like an ill-wrung towel — my soul is damp, & by spreading itself out upon paper seeks to get dry." He signed himself "Yours well saturated / H Melville." He was making himself at home, familiar now with the workings of the Shaw house, and no more restive there than he would have been in the late winter in Manhattan. Shaw may have turned over to him, for daytime use, the large study adjoining the judge's bedroom, for the high, wide-corniced room was fitted with bookcases floor to ceiling on one wall and on another from the ceiling down to cabinets some three feet high. Melville always required a proper writing surface, and in this study the main piece of furniture was a large circular table (fitted with at least four drawers) supported on a triangular pedestal base with scrolled feet. The fireplace was exceptionally well protected by a screen that pulled out on each side as well as at the top. A set of eight Chippendale chairs that had belonged to Dr. Samuel Savage of Barnstable, the judge's second father-in-law, was arranged along the bookcase walls; at his table Shaw sat in a Directoire armchair. There were Turkish rugs on the floor and, over the table, an elegant chandelier, perhaps already converted to gas.

While thus comfortably ensconced in Boston, Melville read in the newspapers that Charles Fenno Hoffman had gone insane and had been confined. He wrote Duyckinck on 5 April:

> Poor Hoffman — I remember the shock I had when I first saw the mention of his madness. — But he was just the man to go mad — imaginative, voluptuously inclined, poor, unemployed, in the race of life distanced by his inferiors, unmarried, — without a port or haven in the universe to make. His present misfortune — rather blessing — is but the sequel to a long experience of morbid habits of thought. —— This going mad of a friend or acquaintance comes straight home to every man who feels his soul in him, — which few men do. For in all of us lodges the same fuel to light the same fire. And he who has never felt, momentarily, what madness is has but a mouthful of brains. What sort of sensation permanent madness is may be very well imagined — just as

we imagine how we felt when we were infants, tho' we can not recall it. In both conditions we are irresponsible & riot like gods without fear of fate. — It is the climax of a mad night of revelry when the blood has been transmuted into brandy. — But if we prate much of this thing we shall be illustrating our own propositions.

Melville's characterization of Hoffman was the result of close and sympathetic contact. His mother and others in New York read the reports, also, and a few years later the family recalled the specific language of the newspaper articles in their concern about Melville himself. Many years afterward, in the "Burgundy Club" pieces unpublished at his death, looking back at his early New York City friends, Melville remembered the long-incarcerated writer: "my chivalric friend, Charlie Fenno Hoffman — remember Charlie, sir? No, no; you don't go back so far." Melville remembered, all his life, Hoffman's poem "Monterrey," which he read upon its publication late in 1846. In the balances of Fortune, Hoffman was down and Melville was up, married, father of a son, havened in Mt. Vernon Street, and writing to a man whose approval of *Mardi* he looked forward to savoring.

Yet as he lounged on a sofa, reading, Melville felt himself changing, growing — growing beyond *Mardi*, he was sure, as he wrote Duyckinck in that letter of 5 April. Melville envisioned a summer of thoughtful reading. He had ordered more Macaulay from the Harpers on 2 April, and about the same time he had bought, in Boston, Pierre Bayle's *An Historical and Critical Dictionary* in four or more folio volumes, a skeptic's partisan guide to the history of philosophy and religion. To Melville's delight, Bayle mocked Platonism, ancient and Renaissance, in terms which he could readily apply to the Transcendentalists, who were just then soothing Boston and environs with what he began to see as their specious denial of the existence of evil. As he wrote Duyckinck, he was looking forward on his return to laying the "great old folios side by side" and going "to sleep on them thro' the summer, with the Phaedon in one hand & Tom Brown in the other." Specifically, he was looking forward not only to luxuriating in his books but also to beginning a fourth one of his own, as he hinted in his letter to Duyckinck:

> I am glad you like that affair of mine. But it seems so long now since I wrote it, & my mood has so changed, that I dread to look into it, & have purposely abstained from so doing since I thanked God it was off my hands. — Would that a man could do something & then say — It is finished. — not that one thing only, but all others — that he has reached his uttermost, & can never exceed it. But live & push — tho' we put one leg forward ten miles — its no reason the other must lag behind — no, *that* must again distance the other — & so we go till we get the cramp & die.

Melville was plotting out his summer in the full expectation of pushing beyond *Mardi*, in a still more ambitious book.

In a letter to Sam Savage on 6 April, Hope Shaw recorded Melville's restless activities: "Herman ranges about, to day he is exploring the Navy yard and enjoying Leutenant Melville's—his cousin—society with much interest—Commodore Downs moves to Charlestown as he now has the Superintendance of the Navy yard—I regret that Percival could not have it though I know Downs is a very popular officer." "Leutenant" or Lieutenant Melville was Hope's slip for Guert Gansevoort, stationed there again, in peacetime. During this stay in Boston Melville probably spent some time with Captain John Percival, a Barnstable native, and a childhood friend of Lemuel Shaw's. Before Melville returned from the Pacific, Percival had formally escorted Lizzie to a reception, and Helen had met him and his wife at Mt. Vernon Street. Percival had been away when Melville arrived on the *United States*, taking the *Constitution* on its only around-the-world cruise, which ended back in Boston on 27 September 1846. Passed over in favor of a younger man, he had reluctantly retired to Barnstable, but he visited Shaw, and Melville became familiar with this stalwart balding-domed man who brushed his remaining straight white hair at a forty-five-degree angle on the sides of his head, down to join his white sideburns—a wide-mouthed, aquiline-nosed, gray-eyed man. Melville paid attention to his appearance, as he had paid attention to the man he thought was Owen Chase, for this gentle man, the droll fellow who had charmed Helen, the man with stories of the old Thomas Melvill, was "Mad Jack"—famous as the hero of the *Globe* mutiny, and notorious for brutal treatment of his men and for the vulgarity and even blasphemy of his language. The rogue captain had outraged the missionaries on Sandwich Islands almost two decades before Herman did, and had done a better job at it, for he had emptied a school for female natives so they could service his men. Herman's own offenses to the missionaries were mere annoyances by comparison. Percival was the sort of man Melville could happily kill time with, and on one or another phase of his long visit they may have done some "ranging" together such as he did with Guert.

Tearing himself away from such manly pleasures, Melville helped assemble his party (doubled in number) for the trip to New York by steam packet on 10 April. (Hope allowed the housekeeper Ellen Sullivan to go with them to help care for Malcolm until they were settled.) The day was "rather stormy," the judge wrote Peter Gansevoort on the eleventh. Once Melville was in New York, Duyckinck enlisted him to review for the 28 April *Literary World* Cooper's *The Sea Lions; or, The Lost Sealers: a Tale of the Antarctic Ocean*, just published in two volumes by Stringer & Townsend. Melville was taken with Cooper's depiction of the sealers in the Antarctic seas, which reminded him of "walled in by 'thrilling regions of rock-ribbed ice'" — a line from *Measure for Measure* that Melville could never forget, once he had seen Gansevoort's transcription of Claudio's speech containing it, labeled "*Death.*" in that incomparable hand. (Melville's new edition read "thick-ribbed.") The descriptions reminded him of Captain Wilkes's and also of William Scoresby's in his *Journal of a Voyage to the Northern Whale Fishery; Including Researches and Discoveries on the Eastern Coast of West Greenland . . . in . . . 1822* (Edinburgh: Constable, 1823):

> Few descriptions of the lonely & the terrible, we imagine, can surpass the grandure of many of the scene[s] here depicted. The reader is reminded of the ap[p]alling adventures of the United States Exploring Ship in the same part of the world as narrated by Wilkes, & of Scoresby's Greenland narrative. — In these inhospitable regions the hardy crews of the Sea Lions winter, — not snugly at anchor under the lee of a Dutch stove, nor baking & browning over the ovens by which the Muscovite warms himself — but jammed in, masoned up, bolted & barred, & almost hermetically sealed by the ice. — To keep from freezing into chrystal they are fain to turn part of their vessels into fuel.

In looking through the book Melville was bemused by Deacon Pratt, "a hard-handed, hard-hearted, psalm-singing old man, with a very stretchy conscience; intent upon getting to heaven, & getting money by the same course of conduct, in defiance of the scripitral [scriptural] maxim to the contrary" — a hint for the Quaker owners of the *Pequod* in *Moby-Dick*. He was pleased to encounter Stimson, the "old Kennebunk boatsteerer, & Professor of Theology." Writing a little about himself, he offered ironic praise of the romantic subplot involving "the timely conversion" of Roswell Gardiner from his "too latitudinarian view of Christianity to a more orthodox, & hence a better beleif" — a conversion that fitted him for "the moist rosy" hand of Mary Pratt, "the reward of his orthodoxy." By "latitudinarian" Melville meant Unitarian, the church of the Shaws, and of his Melvill grandparents. He and Lizzie had rented a pew at Henry Bellows's All Souls Unitarian Church in Manhattan; the earliest notation of payment of pew rent is 18 February 1849, while they were in Boston. (Bellows, a great pulpit orator, lived nearby at 30 West Union Place.) Melville restrained himself to this comment: "Somewhat in the pleasant spirit of the Mahometan, this; who rewards all true beleivers with a houri." At the end he deplored the way Cooper's name had been tarnished: "even those who more for fashion's sake than any thing else, have of late joined in decrying our National Novelist, will in this last work perhaps recognize one of his happiest."

By 30 April Ellen Sullivan had returned to Boston, and Lizzie reported to her stepmother that she had been taking Malcolm out "every pleasant day" to Union Park, which he seemed to enjoy; she added, "he is a great pet in the house, and behaves himself as a prince should do." (Nobody forgot that Malcolm had become king of Scotland.) By then enough reviews of *Mardi* had appeared for Lizzie to become apprehensive: "I suppose by this time you are deep in the 'fogs' of 'Mardi' — if the mist ever does clear away, I should like to know what it reveals to *you* — there seems to be much diversity of opinion about 'Mardi' as might be supposed. Has father read it? When you hear any individual express an opinion with regard to it, I wish you would tell me — whatever it is — good or bad — without fear of offence merely by way of curiosity."

The earliest New York reviews of *Mardi* were written by personal friends of Melville's. Evert Duyckinck in the *Literary World* (7, 14, and 21 April) and N. P. Willis in the *Home Journal* (21 April) had the privilege of writing from advance proof sheets of the novel, and the writers in the New York *Evening Mirror* (13 April) and the *Spirit of the Times* (14 April) pretty clearly were also friends. Duyckinck's announcement on 7 April 1849 was extravagant:

> From a perusal of a part of the proof sheets, it is evident to us that so far from any flagging from the interest of his previous works, "Mardi" is, as might have been anticipated, an onward development, with new traits, of all the fine literary qualities of those productions. The invention is bolder, the humor as strong, sometimes more subtle, while the felicitous descriptive power at once tells the story, and insinuates a thousand compliments to the reader's under-standing, by putting him in communication with so much beyond, — in brief, a right enjoyable brace of volumes.

The New York *Evening Mirror* itemized some of the pleasure in store for readers: "Mardi, with all its fascinations, its unique style, its beautiful lan-guage, its genial humor, its original thoughts, its graphic descriptions, its poetic flights, its profound reasonings, its philosophic reflections, its gentle religious teachings, its inimitable whole, stretches before us like a new world, and the mental eye can never weary of gazing upon its strangely beautiful landscape." William T. Porter or one of his staff in the *Spirit* said: "This writer is one of the choice spirits of the day. May he long live and write among us." The reference to choice spirits evoked the word "master" in those who caught the allusion to *Julius Caesar:* Melville was among the choice and master spirits of the age.

On 14 April Duyckinck elaborately reviewed Melville's three-book ca-reer and the question posed by it: "Was there anything more in the author of 'Typee?'" The answer was yes, for *Mardi* was "not only a very happy, genial production, in the best mood of luxurious invention, but a book of thought, curious thought and reflection." The next week Duyckinck continued his lavish quotations, despairing at "any way of giving an account of the multi-fold contents of this well filled book, laden deep as a Spanish argosy with many an ingot of gold and silver in the hold, many quaint articles of antique workmanship, men and women moving about on the deck with strange dresses, but with hearts and heads of the universal make, while around in the winds is blowing a steady life-giving breath of good earnest heart." He concluded with praise of this "extraordinary book": "Mardi is a species of Utopia — or rather a satiric voyage in which we discover — human nature. There is a world of poetical, thoughtful, ingenious moral writing in it which Emerson would not disclaim — gleams of high-raised fancy, quaint assem-blages of facts in the learned spirit of Burton and the Doctor. Mardi exhibits the most various reflection and reading." *Mardi* would "undoubtedly add to Mr. Melville's reputation," but just how it would, Duyckinck was a little uncertain: "The public will discover in him, at least, a capital essayist, in addition to the fascinating novelist and painter of sea life."

On the same day as this third *Literary World* notice, 21 April, Willis in the *Home Journal* recalled "the ecstacies into which the London press was thrown on the publication of 'Typee,'" and concluded that *Mardi* would "increase the wonder," being "an exquisite book, full of all oriental delights." (Willis had sailed from London at the end of January 1846, before these ecstatic reviews appeared, but Gansevoort had forwarded some to him in New York.) One of Edward Sanford's former law students, Oakey Hall, was now a young lawyer who picked up some money by writing a weekly letter to the New Orleans *Commercial Bulletin*. A friend of Duyckinck and Mathews and a frequent contributor to the *Literary World*, he sent by ship a comment printed in the Crescent City on 3 May:

> Now summer is coming on; . . . rusticaters would do well to provide them-selves . . . with Willis's new book [*Rural Letters*]. . . . A dip into it will spice a morning omelette, or drive away that heavy, drowsy feeling, which will come on you after a glorious country dinner, unless some magician, with potent wand, be there to spell it off! The same may be said of Melville's Mardi — a regular Mardi-gras of a novel, to judge from the richness of its prose. Prose! It is a poem; and you can pencil out of its pages blank verse enough to set up an hundred newspaper poets, for the balls of bowling critics to roll at.

Hall was using the pseudonym "Croton," from the reservoir that now sup-plied New York City's excellent water. "Mardi-gras" was a nice touch for the city, which knew how to celebrate even if it had to do so without Croton water. The members of the Duyckinck circle, and Willis, on his own, were doing as much as Melville could have hoped for.

Yet what Melville saw in papers from London and Boston was disturbing for a young writer who intended to support his family by his books. On 24 March 1849 the *Athenæum*, which had been so delighted with his first two books, sorted out the "many madnesses" Melville had mingled in *Mardi*. The reviewer alluded to Benjamin Disraeli's *Alroy* (1833) as being in a similar Cambyses vein (or Hercules vein) that the author brazenly called a new style; he alluded as well to the former poet laureate Robert Southey's miscellany, *The Doctor* (1834), which began with a peculiar "Prelude of Mottoes," extracts from an odd assortment of books:

> Some pages emulate the Ercles' vein of the "Wondrous Tale of Alroy": — not a few paragraphs indicate that the author has been drinking at the well of "English bewitched" of which Mr. Carlyle and Mr. Emerson are the priests. Here and there, in the midst of a most frantic romance, occur dry little digressions showing the magician anxious half to medicine half to *bamboozle* his readers after the manner of "The Doctor." In other passages of his voyage, where something very shrewd has been intended, we find nothing more poignant than the vapid philosophy of Mr. Fenimore Cooper's "Monikins."

The reviewer in the London *Literary Gazette* on 24 March used the word "puzzle," a notion that Melville picked up and employed later in regard to *Mardi*:

> Our author, it may be remembered, took in many of the knowing ones in his former work; but we fancy the present will puzzle them more. At least it has posed us, and is a 3 vol. metaphor into the applications of which we can only now and then catch a glimpse. It has struck our head like one of those blows which set everything glancing and dancing before your eyes like splintered sunrays; and amid the sparkle and glitter you can discern nothing distinctly. Yet the images are brilliant, and upon the whole you wonder how aught so luminous can be so dark. We never saw a book so like a kaleidoscope. As for giving any idea of it, we have none ourselves. As far as we can make out, Mardi is a group of islands in the Pacific Ocean; perhaps on the way to California! The author is thereabouts, in a good old ship, the captain of which resolves to proceed to Arctic regions, a-whaling; on which our friend resolves to leave, and persuading an ancient tough Skyeman sailor, one Jarl, to accompany him, they cut and run in a boat by night, and trust themselves to the wide expanse of waters, tolerably well provided for a few weeks' chance to fall in with land. Their adventures are superb. The sharks and other fish of the sea are described in the style of Coleridge's *Ancient Mariner*.

The London *Examiner* on 31 March called *Mardi* an outrageous fiction, a transcendental *Gulliver*, or *Robinson Crusoe* run mad, and decided that for "examples of thoughtful writing, and very extensive reading, much in the manner of Sir Thomas Browne, and with a dash of old Burton and Sterne, we think the best chapters in the book are those on subjects apart from its ostensible purpose; such as the essays interposed on Time and Temples, on Faith and Knowledge, on Dreams, and on Suppers." The reviewer in the Boston *Post* of 18 April said *Mardi* reminded him "of the *talk* in Rabelais, divested of all its coarseness, and, it may be added, of all its wit and humor," in fact, "Rabelais emasculated of every thing but prosiness and puerility." Taking off angrily from Melville's preface, the *Post* gave stern advice in certainty that the young author would read it: "He had better stick to his 'fact' which is received as 'fiction,' but which puts money in his purse and wreathes laurels round his head, than fly to 'fiction' which is not received at all, as we opine will be the case with 'Mardi,' in a very short time, and in spite of the all extending and pervading influence of his publisher." This last was a slap at the distribution powers of the Harpers, who, as it turned out, were not able to overcome bad press and bad word-of-mouth. The reviewer was exasperated enough to blast the brother of the late Democrat Gansevoort Melville, but he was not a hangman, despite the pain his review caused Melville. The early reviews of *Mardi* manifested a great deal of goodwill and simple human decency. Even those Melville called attacks were from reviewers who were disappointed, not hostile — not like the attacks by G. W. Peck or W. O. Bourne in 1847.

On 23 April Melville faced up to the reviews of *Mardi* and wrote defensively to Judge Shaw, naming the four papers just quoted:

> I see that Mardi has been cut into by the London Atheneum, and also burnt by the common hangman in the Boston Post. However the London Examiner & Literary Gazette; & other papers this side of the water have done differently. These attacks are matters of course, and are essential to the building up of any permanent reputation — if such should ever prove to be mine — "There's nothing in it!" cried the dunce, when he threw down the 47th problem of the 1st Book of Euclid — "There's nothing in it! — " — Thus with the posed critic. But Time, which is the solver of all riddles, will solve "Mardi."

In 1846 and 1847 Melville would never have put in writing anything about the building up of a permanent reputation; even in 1847, the writing of a third book was contingent on the success of the second. Now in 1849, after having devoted two years to *Mardi*, Melville was ready, in one mood, to leave its solution to Time. He did not in this letter apologize for what he had written and the length it had taken him to write it, and he never did.

The reviews continued to be more ambivalent than hostile. There was an occasional throwing up of hands, as when the writer in the London *Literary Gazette* (24 March) confessed his inability to give an idea of the book, or when the writer in the London *Weekly Chronicle* of 1 April dramatically bemoaned his efforts: "As for ourselves, we have turned the book over, like a dog might a jellyfish, without being able to make it out, for the life of us." The London *Atlas* on 24 March called it "a compound of 'Robinson Crusoe' and 'Gulliver's Travels,' seasoned throughout with German metaphysics of the most transcendental school." The London *Critic* on 1 April said: "In the various islands he visits the author typifies and satirizes men, manners, and institutions at home, somewhat after the plan of *Gulliver's Travels*, to which, indeed, *Mardi* bears a resemblance." Much later, on 19 May, the London *Morning Chronicle* weighed in: "In fact, if we were asked to define the manner and the matter of 'Mardi,' we should say that the book was a wonderful and unreadable compound of Ossian and Rabelais — of Moore's 'Utopia,' and Harrington's 'Oceana' — of 'Gulliver's Travels,' and 'Cook's Voyages,' spiced with rhetoric from Mr. Macaulay's essays, and sarcasm from Mr. Disraeli's perorations." Most reviewers, these quotations show, knew perfectly well what sort of book they had in hand, frequently identified the literary ancestry of *Mardi* with a good deal of accuracy, and might well have been content if they had considered it a worthy companion to the books it evoked comparisons to.

Frequently recalling the controversy over authenticity that had dogged *Typee* and *Omoo*, the reviewers now were willing to concede Melville's existence and even the reality of his South Sea adventures, and they were, for the most part, genuinely tolerant, knowing he was still a young man and hoping for better from him. Every reviewer enjoyed the opening, what the *Athenæum* called "the good pages of this provoking book"; but soon after this, the reviewer lamented, "the romance ends, and the harlequinade begins." The *Literary Gazette* enjoyed the narrator and Jarl at the beginning: "Their adventures are superb." The Boston *Post* declared "The Voyage Thither" (that is, the opening of the book) to be "interesting enough," though even it was "almost spoiled by the everlasting assumption of the brilliant, jocose and witty in its style." A good many reviewers were willing to take some pleasure in the latter portions of the book as well — in England, this meant in the second and third volumes of the triple-decker. The April *Bentley's Magazine* gave the work a review, not a puff. The story was "the least part of the work," which consisted "of an infinite number of episodes and digressions, descriptions and speculations, theories and commentaries sometimes immeasurably fantastical." In these sections Melville was almost as "discursive" as Rabelais, having "something to say on every imaginable topic," and with a purpose in view: "The thing to be achieved is no less than the reconciling of the mind to the creation of an Utopia in the unknown latitudes of the Pacific, to call into existence imaginary tribes and nations, to describe fabulous manners;

and to glass them so distinctly in the fancy that they will appear to have been implanted there by memory." The London *Examiner* (31 March) was typically forgiving: "Altogether we regard this as a remarkable book. When a man essays a continual series of lofty flights, some of his tumbles will be sufficiently absurd; but we must not be thus hindered from admiring his success when he achieves it." The London *Morning Post* on 30 April surrendered and let Melville conduct him "through a gorgeous dream," and found "in every page of the work, such a commingling of learning and imagination and of shrewdness and quaintness as entitles it to the designation of a useful as well as entertaining production." Some "moral or social meaning" could be extracted even from "the crudities of each of the author's fabulous descriptions." Reviewers could have been crueler toward a provoking book that started off as a narrative of adventures and ended as something very different, but the reviews and word-of-mouth comments were enough to slow down the sales and make Melville give up the idea of writing another ambitious book.

The best professional critic in the United States, the Transcendentalist George Ripley, a cousin of young Dana's wife, brooded for weeks over the review he had to write for Greeley's New York *Daily Tribune*. During that time Ripley shared his bafflement and irritation with the elder Dana, who wrote to his son Richard on 16 April: "Hasn't Melville written an absurd book? Mʳ Ripley read me a very absurd passage from it yesterday, & speaks of it as a strange compound." The review finally appeared on 10 May, and Melville at least must have taken it to heart: "If we had never heard of Mr. Melville before, we should soon have laid aside his book, as a monstrous compound of Carlyle, Jean-Paul, and Sterne, with now and then a touch of Ossian thrown in; but remembering our admiration of his former charming productions, we were unable to believe that the two volumes could contain so little of the peculiar excellence of an old favorite, and only mock us with a constant sense of disappointment." Ripley recollected the great delight all classes of readers felt in reading Melville's first two books, which had been "written under the immediate inspiration of personal experience." He understood that Melville now had literary ambitions:

> The present work aims at a much higher mark and fails to reach it. It professes to be a work of imagination, founded on Polynesian adventures, and for a portion of the first volume maintains that character with tolerable success. In the description of the escape of the "Ancient Mariner" and himself from the whale ship — their strange voyage in an open boat over a thousand miles of ocean — of their gaining unexpected possession of a new craft, MELVILLE is himself — and this is saying a great deal. There are passages in this part of

the work, which, taken as separate pictures, display unrivaled beauty and power — the same simple, unaffected grace — the same deep joy in all the rare and precious things of nature — and the same easy command of forcible, picturesque language, which in his former productions called forth such a gush of admiration, even from the most hide-bound reviewer.

Ripley was dismayed by what happened after the voyagers reached Mardi: "We are then presented with a tissue of conceits, fancifully strung about the personages of the tale, expressed in language that is equally intolerable for its affectation and its obscurity. The story has no movement, no proportions, no ultimate end; and unless it is a huge allegory — bits of which peep out here and there — winding its unwieldy length along, like some monster of the deep, no significance or point. We become weary with the shapeless rhapsody, and wonder at the audacity of the writer which could attempt such an experiment with the long-suffering of his readers." Melville had "failed by leaving his sphere, which is that of graphic, poetical narration, and launching out into the dim, shadowy, spectral, Mardian region of mystic speculation and wizard fancies." Ripley had earnest advice: "Let the author return to the transparent narration of his own adventures, in the pure, imaginative prose, which he handles with such graceful facility, and he will be everywhere welcomed as one of the most delightful of American writers."

This was the most widely distributed of any American review, but the general reading public could hardly savor it, for events at nearby Astor Place drove everything else out of the minds of New Yorkers and the rest of the nation. On 7 May a mob of ruffians attempted to stop the performance of Charles Macready in *Macbeth*, alleging it to be unfair competition to the performance of the American Edwin Forrest at a Bowery theater. The Shaws had been among Macready's select guests the week Herman was discharged from the *United States* in 1844, so the Melville house had special reason for choosing sides in this unseemly conflict. Without thinking of the implications (who expected anything to follow from an expression of principle?), Melville signed a petition the next day urging Macready to proceed with the play rather than to take the night off. On 9 May the *Herald* printed the petition, which by that time had been signed by forty-seven citizens, including Washington Irving, Evert Duyckinck, and Cornelius Mathews, besides Melville: "The undersigned, having heard that the outrage at the Astor Place Opera House, on Monday Evening, is likely to have the effect of preventing you from continuing your performances . . . take this public method of requesting you to reconsider your decision, and of assuring you that the good sense and respect for order, prevailing in this community, will sustain you on the subsequent nights of your performances." James Fenimore Cooper, too much a man of the world to sign such a thoughtlessly contrived letter, wrote to his wife that he was not about to volunteer a broken head, and he pointed out the implications of what people who signed it had done: "Some of the literati have put themselves forward and won't stand 'the hazard of the dye.' " Persuaded by the signatures and personal reassurances, Macready went on stage in *Macbeth*, and in the ensuing riot in the square outside the theater, just blocks from the Melville house, twenty-two people were killed and thirty were wounded in clashes between some twenty-five thousand people and the militia. The Melvilles heard the gunfire, and the men may have ventured out to see what was going on — Herman, Allan, and perhaps Tom, who returned from his voyage to China around this time.

Among the casualties was Tertullus D. Stewart, one of the few guests at the Melvilles' wedding who was not a family member, who had been struck by a large bullet while descending from a railroad car on the Bowery line. In the 8 July issue, the Lansingburgh *Democrat* marveled at his surviving: "The ball entered the neck and passed between two of the main arteries which lie within the one hundredth part of an inch of each other, and lodged in the back about two inches from the surface, from which place it has been ex-tracted. The attending surgeon says that the arteries were separated by the force of the ball, and thus escaped being severed, a thing which would proba-bly not occur more than once in a million cases." (Melville may have had occasion, in the last decades of his life, to reflect that his career had been destroyed, indirectly, by Stewart's miraculous survival.) *Mardi* was already old news, so the riots did not affect its fate in any way, except in making sure that few people troubled to think about Ripley's serious review in the *Tri-bune*, but the riots may well have helped turn Melville inward toward his next project. The riots also kept Lizzie and Malcolm out of Union Park for some time and more indoors than she would have liked, although at this season she could expect to do little anyway but suffer from her allergies.

In these weeks after the riots the reviews of *Mardi* dwindled to a halt. On 9 June, after the initial rush of reviewing was over, the New York correspon-dent in his "Gossip from Gotham" column reported to Elizur Wright's Boston *Weekly Chronotype*: "HERMAN MELVILLE's new work has greatly dis-appointed his old admirers. . . . We cannot afford to let so vigorous and fascinating a writer in his own sphere become an imitator of Carlisle or of some fantastic German. Come back, O Herman, from thy cloudy, super-mundane flight, to the vessel's deck and the perfumed i[s]les, and many a true right hand will welcome thy return." Many an ordinary reader would have echoed the correspondent: "Come back, O Herman"! In the July *United States Magazine and Democratic Review* one of the Duyckinck circle offered a lengthy and sometimes eloquent defense of *Mardi*: "The beginning of the book is accepted by most, perhaps all, readers. It is in the style of Omoo and Typee — books that made the multitude crazy with delight. These works were to Mardi as a seven-by-nine sketch of a sylvan lake, with a lone hunter, or a boy fishing, compared with the cartoons of Raphael." He then proceeded to blame the reviewers:

> The fact that Mardi is an allegory that mirrors the world, has thus far escaped the critics, who do notices for the book-table on a large scale. Pilgrim's Progress and Gulliver's Travels were written so long ago, that they seem to have dropped through the meshes of the memory of critics, and they have ceased to think any reproduction or improvement of that sort of thing possible in the future, because they have forgotten its existence in the past. . . . Portions of Mardi are written with this divine impulse, and they thrill through every fibre of the reader with an electric force.

For all his near adulation, the reviewer had scruples about Melville's attitude toward Christianity: "Mr. Melville seems to lack the absolute faith that God had a purpose in creating the world. He seems to think that the race is in a vicious circle, from which we cannot escape — that what has been must be again forever." The reviewer declared, "We believe in God, and therefore we cannot accept the doctrine that this world can be a failure." This elaborate review in a political magazine concluded with evangelical fervor: "Mr. Melville must emerge from this evil state, with those for whom he has labored in bonds, bound with them."

Only a few more comments appeared in the next months. One, from Edinburgh, in the August *Blackwood's*, denounced Melville as the creator of a new school of novelists whose style "seems a compound imitation of Gulliver, *Munchausen*, *The Arabian Nights*, and *Robinson Crusoe*; the ingredients being mixed in capricious proportions, well stirred, seasoned with Yankee bulls and scraps of sea-slang, and served hot — sometimes plain, at others with a *hors d'oeuvre* of puffs." *Mardi* was "a rubbishing rhapsody," trash, "mingled, too, with attempts at a Rabelaisian vein, and with strainings at smartness — the style of the whole being affected, pedantic, and wearisome exceedingly." In October the reviewer in the Charleston *Southern Quarterly Review* found Melville's political stance unforgivable: "he spoils every thing to the Southern reader when he paints a loathsome picture of Mr. Calhoun, in the character of a slave driver, drawing mixed blood and tears from the victim at every stroke of the whip."

Indeed, *Mardi* left a bad taste in many a mouth, as the summer and autumn passed. Through the spring of 1849 and long afterward, Melville was defensive about *Mardi* and secretly hopeful that sooner or later it would be recognized as a great book. Some of his comments suggest that he regarded the whole book as an allegory, a riddle that would be appreciated once some-one guessed the meaning. "Time" (he had said on 23 April 1849) would "solve" *Mardi,* and on 2 February 1850, he suggested two possibilities: it might "flower like the aloe, a hundred years hence — or not flower at all, which is more likely by far, for some aloes never flower." So far, its only flowering seems to have been not a century but four decades later, when for a time it became something like a cult favorite among a small coterie of British admirers of Melville — centered not in London but in Leicester.

[31]

Redburn and *White-Jacket*

Summer 1849

> How like a flash that life is gone —
> So brief the youth by sailors known!
>
> Agath, in *Clarel*, bk. 4, canto 2

ON 5 JUNE 1849, after it was clear that *Mardi* had failed, Melville justified himself to Richard Bentley with no apparent sense that he was writing to a man who would lose a great deal of money because of him: "You may think, in your own mind that a man is unwise, — indiscreet, to write a work of that kind, when he might have written one perhaps, calculated merely to please the general reader, & not provoke attack, however masqued in an affectation of indifference or contempt. But some of us scribblers, My Dear Sir, always have a certain something unmanageable in us, that bids us do this or that, and be done with it — hit or miss." Melville's pride in yielding to the "certain something unmanageable" in him could only have struck Bentley as arrogant in the present and ominous for the future. Yet Melville had been humbled by the reviews of *Mardi* (however much incidental praise he could glean from them) and was genuinely alarmed at the implications of its economic failure, to the point of determining on a sacrifice: he would interrupt his progress toward greatness manifested by unmanageable impulses and step backward toward, if not all the way to, the picaresque, quasi-autobiographical, and distinctly less ambitious level of *Typee* and *Omoo*.

Abandoning whatever he had been thinking about doing, if his thoughts had begun to congeal already, he may have cast about a little for unused segments of his experience which he could work up speedily and painlessly. Whaling was not a choice for a simple book, and no one would want to read about schoolteaching in the backwoods of Massachusetts. What determined his choice of subject may have been the fact that Tom had returned from China and, as if the land seemed scorching to his feet, began looking for another ship. He found the *"Navagator"* (as he spelled it in his journal entries, which Augusta preserved in her papers), technically a "ship," smaller than steamships and larger than barks, brigs, schooners, and sloops. The

Tribune on 28 May reported her as cleared for Canton. The "Ship Navigator of Boston," Captain William Putnam (Tom spelled it "Putman" in the diary he started), first mate "Mac Gown," left the pier at the foot of Maiden Lane at eleven o'clock on Monday the twenty-eighth of May and anchored in the East River for three days, "puting on chaffing gear," according to ordinary seaman Thomas Melville. Henry Thurston, sixteen and a half years old, fatherless at eleven, had found in his sister Sophia's youngest brother-in-law, almost three years his senior, both a chum and a hero, and on Wednesday, 30 May, Henry and another friend, Jack Hall, went aboard to see Tom. On Thursday "Herm and Henry came aboard" for a last farewell before the steamboat came to tow the *Navigator* down the bay. About a year later, the family learned that the mate had taken "a fancy" to Tom. "Offered to learn me navigation and setts me about all the sailor Jobs he can," Tom wrote in his diary, and a month later added: "The mate still continues to treat me as an able seaman and the other night when I went out to furl the jib, he called me back and said that he did not want me or the rest of the men to furl any of the light sails when the greenhands were on deck. I told him that I shiped as a boy, that makes no difference said he, as long as you do a mans work you nede not do boys." There was a purposeful, eager air about Tom, as about Gansevoort and Herman, that made people superior to them by circumstance take notice of them and offer to "learn" them things.

Herman lost sight of the ship almost at once in the thick fog, but in imagination he followed his nineteen-and-a-half-year-old brother out the bay and through the Narrows, reexperiencing his own youthful sailing to Liverpool. As in 1848, he played the roles of both Alexander Bradford and Gansevoort Melville while his youngest brother played the role of the young Herman. Tom was perfect in the role. For Herman, looking at Tom was apt to be hallucinatory, like looking into a mirror and seeing not himself but the image of the youth he had been, and, at least since the time he wrote *Omoo*, he had been conscious of his own vulnerability to that particular psychological experience where different places, times, and people seem to overlay until they merge. The previous year, the still-burgeoning *Mardi* was on his mind when Tom sailed, but this year he was between books, and indeed was in need of a subject for a quick and easy new one. He may almost have felt that the decision was made for him, perhaps two or three weeks before Tom actually sailed, when he was looking for a ship, or between the time he found the *Navigator* and his sailing: the book would be a fictional account of his own voyage to Liverpool an even decade earlier, the summer he turned twenty. The dedication this time may have been devised before much of the book was written: "To my younger brother, Thomas Melville, Now a Sailor on a Voyage to China, this volume is inscribed."

The man who had proved himself a master of book-craft with *Omoo* could take new pride in showing just how professional he could be if he set his mind to it. He would have preferred to write something else, but outlining *Redburn* was easy—he would get his hero to sea, subject him to a comic initiation, expose him to the evils of Liverpool, and get him safely home. Melville picked up the Scottish name "Redburn" from an anonymous poem, *Redburn or, the Schoolmaster of a Morning*, which had appeared a few weeks after his return from the South Seas, an imitation of Oliver Goldsmith's still-popular *The Deserted Village*. The New York *Morning News*, with which Duyckinck was then connected, had offered the author of the poetic *Redburn* kind advice on 28 December 1844: "If the author, whom we suppose to be a young man, would improve . . . let him study the tales of Crabbe." The name Redburn probably evoked for Melville the image of a flustered, red-faced youth—at the stage of inexperience then usually designated as "verdant" rather than red. The poem was by a New Yorker named John Carroll, but ignorance of that fact misled some twentieth-century critics into attributing the poem to Melville, no matter how wretched it was. The most Melville may have taken from Carroll's book (or a sight of its title) was the appealing name Redburn.

Melville's first surviving allusion to his new manuscript is in the 5 June letter to Richard Bentley, where he attempted to persuade his publisher that his new manuscript would sell better than *Mardi*. The tone of his description was detached: "I have now in preparation a thing of a widely different cast from 'Mardi';—a plain, straightforward, amusing narrative of personal expe-rience—the son of a gentleman on his first voyage to sea as a sailor—no metaphysics, no conic-sections, nothing but cakes & ale. I have shifted my ground from the South Seas to a different quarter of the globe—nearer home—and what I write I have almost wholly picked up by my own obser-vations under comical circumstances." The "personal experience" was his hero's (colored by his own), and the observations were his own (except what was borrowed from his source books). Such experience and observation would speed the composition along; in this letter Melville estimated that the book would be "perhaps a fraction smaller" than *Typee* and would be ready for the Harpers "two or three months hence, or before." To judge from this letter, Melville had little trouble at first holding to his cool resolve to be practical rather than "unwise" or "indiscreet" and to control that "certain something unmanageable" in him long enough to write a book "calculated merely to please the general reader, & not provoke attack." For most of the chapters up to the arrival of Redburn in Liverpool, Melville followed fairly closely the chronology of his own experiences in 1839 and seems to have composed in something of a "straightforward" fashion. He should in fact have enjoyed much of his early work on the book, for it must have flowed easily and given him, day by day, satisfaction at holding so steadily to his plan. Besides that, it was good writing, for he was now the master of precise detail as well as the master, for many pages, of technical control of a dual narrative perspective, that of the youthful and the older Redburn, such as he had never attempted before.

In writing a fictionalized version of his first voyage Melville could keep research down by recalling his own situation as the impoverished son of a dear dead father, a gentleman. He could make his hero, like himself, a younger son in a large family exiled to a village on the Hudson, driven to sea as a sailor by a "naturally roving disposition" after experiencing sad disappointments in other plans for his future life. He could keep some distance by skirting maudlinity in portraying the relationship between the fictional boy and his mother: "It was with a heavy heart and full eyes, that my poor mother parted with me; perhaps she thought me an erring and a willful boy, and perhaps I was; but if I was, it had been a hardhearted world, and hard times that had made me so. I had learned to think much and bitterly before my time; all my young mounting dreams of glory had left me; and at that early age, I was as unambitious as a man of sixty" (ch. 2). There was considerable release for Melville in being able to make his self-pitying narrator recall such emotions, as well as satisfying control in being able to have the narrator make a mature reflection: "there is no misanthrope like a boy disappointed." For Melville there was also danger in writing fluently about the bitterness of youth ("never again can such blights be made good; they strike in too deep, and leave such a scar that the air of Paradise might not erase it"). That danger was not uppermost in his mind as he wrote, for he was writing too fast to let himself think much about what feelings he was stirring up. Melville's characters were easy to portray, since Redburn's father and other members of his immediate family were modeled on Melville's own. He brought Gansevoort back in his role as officiously concerned elder brother; his hero's late seagoing uncle was based on Melville's uncle John D'Wolf, who had indeed sailed with Langsdorff but was very much alive still; and the Joneses provided the sort of hospitality to Redburn that the Bradfords had offered to Melville. Paraphernalia from his own household and the households of other relatives, such as European books and a glass ship, was ready to be boldly appropriated. He could privately indulge his old habit of making comparison of time against time, situation against situation, in this instance summing up for himself the contrast between the anonymous green hand of 1839 and the beleaguered literary celebrity of 1849. Making this clash of perceptions artistically challenging by inventing a hero sufficiently different from what he had been, he characterized Wellingborough Redburn as a self-pitying boy, instead of the tougher and more experienced grown man he himself had been in 1839, and he distanced himself from the narrator (Redburn when a good many years older, after he had become a sentimental and sententious bachelor very much in the mode of Irving's bachelors).

Melville may have thought when he started that he would not need his accustomed array of sources, but that favorite of his and Gansevoort's, Washington Irving's *The Sketch Book*, was much in his mind. He made his narrator resemble Irving's Geoffrey Crayon in the mixture of sentimentality and gentle irony with which he comments on his longing for travel that begins in childhood and increases with adolescence. Both narrators are given to romantic reveries and to musing about the "associations" of the names of remote places. This following of Irving's model could have been done with little or no reference to the familiar book, but Melville probably had a copy at hand as a pattern for incidents at sea on a voyage to Liverpool and incidents ashore in that port. Details in Irving's book (and in Melville's) included sea-reveries, the sighting of "the monsters of the deep at their uncouth gambols," the sighting of a wreck, an anecdote about a collision at sea, a visit to the reading room of the Liverpool Athenaeum, a chapter on the poet Roscoe, sections on rural life in England (including Sunday visits to country churches), a dismissal from a library, and even a ringing visionary passage on the future of America. Evert Duyckinck's comment in his diary two years before was more apt than ever, for Melville was now quite consciously modeling his writing a good deal on Irving's, not merely reflecting Irving's pervasive influence.

Short as the time was that he devoted to *Redburn*, it was long enough for Melville to become weary of the rapid pace of composition, especially since he compressed his work on the book into the next three or four weeks after 5 June, rather than taking the two or three months he had allowed. He pushed along on his plan (mentioned in ch. 40) to "group together" the parts "concerning the Liverpool docks, and the scenes roundabout," including "What Redburn Saw in Launcelott's-Hey" (ch. 37), a powerful description of the boy's ineffectual attempts to help a dying woman and her dead and dying children, in the course of which attempts Redburn asks a quintessentially Melvillean question: "What right had any body in the wide world to smile and be glad, when sights like this were to be seen?" Melville had written his way fairly far into the Liverpool chapters before bogging down from a shortage of memories that could be readily fictionalized. When his memories failed him, he started to plunder a source, *The Picture of Liverpool; or Stranger's Guide*, for information on areas he remembered less clearly than the area around the docks. While plundering it he realized that he could write a good many pages on what he called, in the title of chapter 31, the "Prosy Old Guide-Book." In the process of patching together chapters from the guidebook, Melville lost some of his sense of distance from the older Redburn, the writer-down of the adventures, and with that loss of aesthetic distance he lost some of his pride in what he was doing. Turning to whatever other source was at hand, he gleaned from the *Penny Cyclopædia* odd bits of information, including the entries on the Gulf Stream and the Atlantic Ocean, as Mary K. Bercaw showed.

At several points Melville took on the role of social reformer, partly in response to current events. This summer James Harper (of Harper & Brothers) was waging a successful campaign as the Nativist mayor of New York City, playing to anti-Catholicism, a sentiment which Uncle Thomas had expressed in Galena. "Church-burners," the Albany *Argus* later that year (12 October 1849) called the Nativists, in allusion to events of 1834 and 1844, especially. Stirred into disgust by the rhetoric of the Nativists, and still resentful toward his own publishers, in *Redburn* (ch. 33) Melville praised the "sober Germans" such as he had observed in Liverpool, their main port of embarkation, and denounced the bigoted patriotism that was proving so popular. "You can not spill a drop of American blood without spilling the blood of the whole world," he announced, and continued in a vatic tone summoned up from his work on *Mardi:*

> For who was our father and our mother? Or can we point to any Romulus and Remus for our founders? Our ancestry is lost in the universal paternity; and Cæsar and Alfred, St. Paul and Luther, and Homer and Shakspeare, are as much ours as Washington, who is as much the world's as our own. We are the heirs of all time, and with all nations we divide our inheritance. On this Western Hemisphere all tribes and people are forming into one federated whole; and there is a future which shall see the estranged children of Adam restored as to the old hearth-stone in Eden.
>
> The other world beyond this, which was longed for by the devout before Columbus' time, was found in the New; and the deep-sea-lead, that first struck these soundings, brought up the soil of Earth's Paradise. Not a Paradise then, or now; but to be made so, at God's good pleasure, and in the fullness and mellowness of time.

At the end of chapter 58 he returned to his anti-Nativist theme:

> Let us waive that agitated national topic, as to whether such multitudes of foreign poor should be landed on our American shores; let us waive it, with the one only thought, that if they can get here, they have God's right to come; though they bring all Ireland and her miseries with them. For the whole world is the patrimony of the whole world; there is no telling who does not own a stone in the Great Wall of China.

The first ecstatic passage, and the second one, more hortatory but still employing heightened rhetoric, both embody Melville's ambition, despite the failure of *Mardi*, to carry on Gansevoort Melville's role as national propagandist, or even orator of the English-speaking peoples, and behind all his other feelings about Americanism lay the determination not to kowtow to his publishers.

Melville apparently concluded the manuscript in a shortish form toward the end of June, then counted pages with an eye to its publication in England in two volumes and hurriedly "enlarged it somewhat" by various insertions until he estimated it as the size of *Omoo* or perhaps "a trifle larger," as he wrote Bentley on 20 July. The best guess as to how he enlarged the manuscript is that he added the character of the specious dandy Harry Bolton, after having first gotten Redburn safely back to New York City without his dubious companionship. Melville probably had, at one point, a manuscript without the most highly colored scene (ch. 46) of the final book—the trip the melodramatic Bolton and Redburn make to London (where their sightseeing consists of a nocturnal tour of a flamboyantly decorated gambling-hell, in which Redburn drinks a pale yellow wine that he later suspects was drugged). This lurid and wholly unconvincing London scene has from the time the book appeared demanded an amount of attention disproportionate to its brevity and lack of artistic interest. Reviewing the book in the *Literary World* on 17 November 1849, Duyckinck put his finger on that episode as the only one violating the general realism: "we are introduced to a fancy young gentleman who gets up with Redburn a hurried, romantic night visit to London, which is enveloped in the glare of a splendid gambling establishment. The parties, however, soon get back to duty, and find nothing whatever lurid or romantic in the discipline under Captain Riga." Other reviewers and later readers reacted, most often, even more strongly than Duyckinck did to this strangely intrusive episode.

William H. Gilman in 1951 pointed out that the "mythological oil-paintings" Melville described as hanging in one chamber of the strange London building were all pornographic—"such pictures as the high-priests, for a bribe, showed to Alexander," "such pictures as the pontiff of the sun strove to hide from Cortez," "such pictures as you may still see, perhaps, in the central alcove of the excavated mansion of Pansa, in Pompeii," "such pictures as Martial and Suetonius mention as being found in the private cabinet of the Emperor Tiberius," among others. This is peculiar stuff, for Melville, whose normal comical tone toward dandies like Harry Bolton is that of chapter 6 of *White-Jacket*, where the commodore's secretary, a particularly precious exquisite, furnishes his quarters as if it were "the private cabinet of Pelham," with "alabaster statuettes of Venus and Adonis, tortoise-shell snuff-boxes, inlaid toilet-cases, ivory-handled hair-brushes and mother-of-pearl combs, and a hundred other luxurious appendages scattered about." Striving to account for the peculiarities of this episode in *Redburn*, Gilman tellingly mustered a series of verbal parallels between Melville's second installment of "Fragments from a Writing Desk" (1839) and the London gambling-house in *Redburn*, citing "tonal" qualities ("Oriental atmosphere") as well as "parallels in physical details and in phrasing."

Gilman did not mention a London story called "The Gambler's Fate," which appeared in the 22 July 1837 issue of the Albany *Microscope*, the paper in which Herman had been assailed on 15 April 1837. No other paper was credited, so presumably this story was by a local writer. (July was the month after Herman left for Pittsfield to run the farm.) In this piece, much of it set in a London gambling-hell, occurs the following passage:

> "Another glass of Curacca — and then for St. James's," said Russell to his friend. "Has lengthened residence on the continent, embued you with taste for ecarte or roulette?"
>
> "No," replied Melvil, "ever opposed, both by inclination and education, to the vice of gambling, I have studiously avoided entering the magic circle in which the fickle goddes[s] enthrals her votaries. Surely you do not play?" . . .
>
> The Curacca was drunk, the cab was ordered, and the scene was changed. One hour afterwards he [Russell] was deeply engaged in the mysteries of play, and Melvil occasionally looking on, and anon chatting to some young lordlings to whom his friend had introduced him, patiently awaiting the termination of an amusement for which he entertained no small degree of distaste.

In the end Russell loses his "high pile of gold" to Hawkes, "one of those professed players, who nightly haunt the gaming table," a wretch whom he identifies to Melvil as the man who "married Blanche Vane: — she, with whom it was said by village gossips, you once had an *affaire de coeur* in early life." Later Melvil accuses Hawkes of cheating, and a duel ensues. The dying Hawkes confesses in order to vindicate Melvil: " 'You,' addressing Melvil, 'you were right — I did use false dice last night; but hear my justification, such as it is. I have a wife — children — I shall never behold them more.' "

There is no particular reason, other than the name Melvil and the similarity to *Redburn*, for thinking Herman Melville wrote this farrago in the *Microscope*, even though it is much in the vein of his "Fragments." The name Melvil was, at the least, eye-catching to young residents of Albany like Gansevoort and Herman Melville and their friends in the improvement societies, so someone may have sent Herman "The Gambler's Fate" while he was on the farm or saved a copy for him, so he could see the family name "Melvil" in print. This piece of fiction at least suggests that Gilman was on the right track in seeing some relationship between the London episode of *Redburn* and Melville's early literary milieu — not just his "Fragments" but the larger local milieu. Some memories of participation in a series of deliberately outrageous prose exercises, memories involving long-suppressed psychosexual feelings from Albany and Lansingburgh in the 1830s, may lie behind the creation of Harry Bolton and this implausible London scene. If the primary purpose of the Harry Bolton section was to pad the story, once he decided to bring the size of the manuscript up to the equivalent of two of the three Bentley volumes of *Mardi*, Melville could have padded with any amount of other kinds of material, but he chose Harry Bolton and the London gambling-hell. What he thought he was doing in it, as a young married man and a new father, is an unanswered question.

When he finished the book Melville had every reason to be proud of himself, since everyone in the household, not to mention his literary friends, must have been astounded at the speed with which he had written it. Writing *Redburn* in a month or two was all the proof he needed that he had become a professional writer. He may have been a little contemptuous of some of the parts he had stuffed into the manuscript toward the end of his work on it, but he probably had a strong sense of just how good a comic initiation story he had written and just how admirably, through much of the work, he had held to the point of view of his created character rather than writing, as he instinctively did, in his own person. Despite his abandoning the point of view he had created, and despite his intrusion of the lurid Harry Bolton and the London gambling-hell, he had made, in the earlier portions, a notable aesthetic advance.

And the book was easy to sell. The Harpers had taken over *Typee* from Wiley & Putnam and had reprinted it from the old plates (that is to say, the plates after the expurgation), so they had to recoup their costs before giving Melville any more royalties from his first book. Nevertheless, it was pleasant for Melville to see reviews of their *Typee* appearing a week or two before he took *Redburn* to the Harpers. On 2 July the Harpers agreed to publish the book (then entitled "My First Voyage &c") and advanced Melville three hundred dollars. Melville handed the manuscript over on that date and the Harpers promptly sent it to the printer.

In a 20 June letter Richard Bentley explained to Melville with great kindness that the sales of the English edition of *Mardi* had all but stopped as a result of "the nature" of the book: "the first volume was eagerly devoured, the second was read — but the third was not perhaps altogether adapted to the class of readers whom 'Omoo' and 'Typee', and the First Volume of 'Mardi' gratified." Bentley continued in an exceptionally gentle tone: "The effect somehow or other has been decidedly to check, nay I may almost say, to stop the sale of the book." He went on to describe a serious alteration in the copyright situation: "To complicate matters still further, our sapient Sir Fred^k Pollock with Justices Platt & Rolfe have decided that a foreigner has *no copyright*. This drivelling absurdity can scarcely be suffered to remain, I trust, but in the mean time this decision will expose publishers like myself, who am so largely engaged in this department of publishing to the risk of attack from any unprincipled persons who may choose to turn Pirate." In view of "the want of success of Mardi and the stupid decision, at present with regard to copyright," Bentley magnanimously offered Melville £100 for *Redburn*, sight unseen — not the £150 he had asked for, but more than generous, under the circumstances. Melville was realistic enough to accept the offer, on 20 July, when he told Bentley that the work was then going through the press and that he could send complete proof sheets to London "in the course of three weeks or so." Although the sale to the Harpers and to Bentley went smoothly, in retrospect Melville could regard *Redburn* not only as a book he had not wanted to write but also as a book that had earned him less money than he had expected.

Even aside from intruding the flaccid Harry Bolton into his realistic book, Melville had behaved, as it turned out, recklessly: only a young and still naive man could have thought that he could write a kind of psychological autobiography (as he had done in the early pages, however lightheartedly) without suffering any consequences. By the next year or year and a half, the act of writing the early quasi-autobiographical chapters of *Redburn* had caught up with him, changing him profoundly. Melville knew about the Come-Outers, the sect whose members followed Paul's injunction in II Corinthians 6:17 ("Wherefore come out from among them, and be ye separate"). William Lloyd Garrison had headlined the term in the *Liberator* while Melville was in Boston in October 1844, and later Melville punned on the name of the sect, relishing its metaphorical significance, in *The Confidence-Man*: come-outers were people who came out publicly with information about themselves that should have been kept private. In the summer of 1849 Melville was working too hard to notice that he had unwittingly joined the psychological equivalent of this new American religious sect; in mythological terms, he had opened Pandora's box when he thought he was merely describing the lid.

In the four hot months of the summer of 1849 Melville may have socialized a little or taken his usual expeditions to scenic spots in easy reach of Manhattan, but the surviving letters and the sheer quantity of writing he achieved suggest that he shut himself up as he wrote, first *Redburn*, and then another book, *White-Jacket*. He would have been better off not making the one new literary acquaintance we know about, Thomas Powell, who had arrived in New York City from England sometime in the spring. During that summer of 1849 the term "Confidence Man" was coined in New York City to identify the *modus operandi* of a native rogue, a kindred spirit to this English crook. Forty years old, Poe's age, a poetaster, dramatist, editor, and journalist, Powell was also a thief, a forger of commercial and literary documents, and a compulsive, accomplished, and grandiose liar and all-round blackguard. In his social climbing among the heights of the London literati (Wordsworth, Leigh Hunt, Elizabeth Barrett, R. H. Horne, Robert Browning) Powell had formed the habit of sealing his new intimacies with gifts (the more ready since he paid for them with stolen money, which also subsidized the publication of his own plays and poems from year to year) and with flattering comments on his new acquaintances' literary productions. Powell met Robert Browning and became an intimate of Browning's father. He added Charles Dickens to his list of friends and was invited to dine at Devonshire Terrace. Powell's London career unraveled in 1846 when it became known that he had embezzled on a grand scale from his (and Dickens's brother Augustus's) employer, Thomas Chapman. In quintessential Victorian fashion, for the sake of Powell's family Chapman did not prosecute him. Caught stealing again, Powell committed himself to a lunatic asylum at Hoxton, frustrating the magistrates, who suspected that his insanity "had been produced by artificial means—by the excessive use of opium, and resorting to the expedient of igniting charcoal in his bedroom—the object being to produce a temporary state of delirium, in the expectation by that means to evade justice." Early in 1849 he fled with his wife and children to the New World.

Upon his arrival, the portly Powell lightly resumed his career of crime, finding it good to be shifty on a new island. He cashed forged letters of credit at a local banking house even as he burst into the Anglophiliac New York literary world, claiming to be (as he once had been) on friendly terms with almost everybody who was anybody in the London literary milieu. Powell gravitated at once toward Evert Duyckinck, who welcomed him as a representative of the great world of English literature. His intimate anecdotes of literary London charmed the Duyckincks and their friend Cornelius Mathews. Powell sealed his friendship with Duyckinck by a brilliantly contrived gift, a volume of Tennyson's poems containing what he modestly described as some "trifling" revisions in the poet's own hand. (The volume does not survive in the New York Public Library, where Duyckinck's books went, so there is no being sure that the "revisions" were forged.) Through Duyckinck, Melville met Powell soon after his arrival and talked with him on a number of occasions that summer.

One occasion was on 28 June, following the baptism of little Maria

Gansevoort Melville by the Reverend Mr. Bedell in the Church of the Ascension. Bedell's routine Episcopal sign of the cross over the baby so horrified Cousin Kate Van Vechten Hurlbut (a member in good standing of the Dutch Reformed church) that she could not bring herself to go afterward to the Romish establishment at 103 Fourth Avenue for ice cream and brandy-peaches. The party turned out to be a memorably dull occasion for some of the women and perhaps a momentous occasion for some of the men present. Tertullus Stewart, recovered from his gunshot wound, attended, as did "the Duyckincks and Mr Powell," Sophia wrote to Augusta. Powell did not need the food, for the New York heat was causing him to swelter in his fat — like Niobe, all tears, he wrote in a note to Duyckinck. That may have been the day that Melville bestowed upon Powell a copy of *Mardi*, dating it only "June," thereby distracting him a moment from the desserts. In her letter to Augusta on 1 July what Sophia stressed was how boring the men were, not how reckless. "St John" (she meant "St George" — George Duyckinck) had been his reticent self: he "opened his mouth and spoke once I did not hear what he said, but I doubt not that it was the concentration of wisdom." The literary men became so exceedingly boring that the ladies "at last went in the other parlour with Mr Stewart" (Helen always found him entertaining) and "left the other gentlemen to knock their heads together, the English egotist (alias Mr Powell) being spokesman." Melville himself may have held forth a little on this occasion, for long afterward, in the New York *Daily News* on 14 April 1856, Powell claimed that Melville had once named to him the plan of a work "intended to illustrate the *principle* of *remorse*, and to demonstrate that there is, very often, less real virtue in moral respectability than in accidental crime" (Steven Olsen-Smith, "Herman Melville's Planned Work on Remorse," *Nineteenth-Century Literature*, 50 [1996]). In her letter Sophia made it clear that the women had seen through Powell, recognizing intolerable egotism if not criminality. Sophia was a Bond Street girl, who did not have to listen to egotistical pronouncements from rotund sweaty Britons, or even to reckless talk from her brother-in-law.

That summer Evert Duyckinck found himself paying for the gift book of poems purportedly containing revisions in Tennyson's own hand. Powell began asking Duyckinck for loans, invariably promising to repay each one in full, and soon. Melville cannot have followed each episode in Powell's adventures, although he would have known that G. P. Putnam, suddenly alerted to something dubious about Powell, had repudiated his agreement to publish *Living Authors of England*. There were other occasions when Melville might have talked about a projected work on remorse, for he had intermittent contact with Powell in the succeeding months and was fairly well acquainted with him by October.

Mainly, Melville kept on writing. In a section added to *Pierre* early in 1852, after it had been completed and a contract for it had been agreed to, Melville described the kind of obsessive state in which a writer can toil on at his manuscript: "From eight o'clock in the morning till half-past four in the evening Pierre sits there in his room; — eight hours and a half!" Outside, city life goes on:

> From throbbing neck-bands, and swinging belly-bands of gay-hearted horses, the sleigh-bells chimingly jingle; — but Pierre sits there in his room; Thanksgiving comes, with its glad thanks, and crisp turkeys; — but Pierre sits there in his room; soft through the snows, on tinted Indian moccasin, Merry Christmas comes stealing; — but Pierre sits there in his room; it is New-Year's, and like a great flagon, the vast city overbrims at all curb-stones, wharves, and piers, with bubbling jubilations; — but Pierre sits there in his room. . . .
> He will not be called to; he will not be stirred. (bk. 22, ch. 4)

That summer of 1849, Melville would hardly be stirred. Lizzie and Malcolm seem to have stayed on in New York that intense summer, she suffering from her allergies in June. Vulnerable, distrusting her own literary judgment about *Mardi* but less eager than at the end of April to hear what her father or her stepmother or "any individual" thought about it (as she wrote to Hope Shaw on 30 April), she loyally did her best to keep Herman at peace in the hours he was away from his desk. Because he was locked up for hours at a time, not seeing his son, Melville created a game to play with Malcolm after his writing stint was done. When the boy was four, five, six, and seven months old Melville (to judge from entries in a journal he kept that fall) would pretend that Malcolm had spent the day interrogating his mother and the rest of that household about his absent father: "Where dat old man?" "Where dat old man?" When he picked up Malcolm, he would remind the prodigy what question he had been pestering the women with all day, and once Malcolm's eyes were focused on his face, the father would give the triumphant reassurance that *here* was dat old man, *here* with more ink on his fingers, ready to play with "little Barney." (Malcolm was a wee bairn of a Scot; Helen used "bairns" for "children," so it was in the family vocabulary.) The game may have had a second part: "Where's Orianna?" — Orianna being Malcolm's mother, the faithful heroine of *Amadis de Gaul.* But daytime, Melville kept on writing.

Sophia put little Maria into shorts at the end of June, about when Kate's canary bird died and the Thurstons entrusted the family with three canaries and four goldfish. A new city ordinance prohibited fishmen and fruiters from hawking their wares from door to door, depriving the older Maria of the pleasure of bargaining on the stoop for fish of "doubtful" freshness, as Sophia wrote Augusta. Intermittently that summer Malcolm and little Maria were teething noisily. The cholera struck the city again early in June, and by the end of the month Allan had taken Sophia and Fanny to Bergen Point to test the possibility of Sophia's summering there, but Sophia was "frightened" at being where Allan could not return home until very late each afternoon, and decided she could not spend the season. Augusta's friend Anne Lynch had moved again before July, and was taking in boarders; Allan passed on the rumor that she gave the boarders nothing to eat. The miraculously recovered Stewart with his wife went off to Huntington before the Glorious Fourth, just when Allan took Sophia on an excursion to West Point and on to Albany and then Saratoga, where Sophia stayed while Allan went up to see Uncle Herman, an errand relating to the deed to the Northumberland property. At some point in the summer the matriarch Maria, the heir to that property, suffered an illness which "reduced her" very much (Nilly remembered the next year, 23 August 1850, in a letter to Augusta), and from which she was slow to recover her strength. But while babies teethed, goldfish swam, canaries sang or died, and fish and fruit came no more to the door of 103 Fourth Avenue, while the progenitive former President Tyler and his young wife vacationed at the Melvill place within sound of the Devonshire bull, Melville kept on writing.

Melville's later comments on the hastily written *Redburn* were colored by events that occurred between the time he completed it and the time it was published. He managed to supervise the proofreading of *Redburn* rather carefully, most likely with Helen's help, for Lizzie was off duty as Herman's copyist and on duty as Malcolm's mother. Minor typographical errors got into the printed book along with a few inconsistencies in the plotting. He altered the title from "My First Voyage &c" in a gesture toward avoiding the question of authenticity, which had been an annoying aspect of the reception of *Typee* and *Omoo*. About the middle of August Melville sent a set of the Harper proofs to Bentley, who prepared his edition rapidly, to avoid any possible piracy, and published it on 20 October as *Redburn: His First Voyage. Being the Sailor-Boy Confessions and Reminiscences of the Son-of-a-Gentleman, in the Merchant Service*, a stuffy title Melville had taken pleasure in crafting. Melville's contract with the Harpers called for their holding their plates for four months to allow him to arrange prior publication in England, but it also provided that within those four months they would publish immediately if he instructed them to. They published, promptly enough, on 10 November.

Throughout the fall and early winter Melville's comments on *Redburn* were uniformly negative. On 6 October he wrote his father-in-law:

For Redburn I anticipate no particular reception of any kind. It may be deemed a book of tolerable entertainment; — & it may be accounted dull. — As for the other book, it will be sure to be attacked in some quarters. But no reputation that is gratifying to me, can possibly be achieved by either of these books. They are two *jobs*, which I have done for money — being forced to it, as other men are to sawing wood. And while I have felt obliged to refrain from writing the kind of book I would wish to; yet, in writing these two books, I have not repressed myself much — so far as *they* are concerned; but have spoken pretty much as I feel. — Being books, then, written in this way, my only desire for their "success" (as it is called) springs from my pocket, & not from my heart. So far as I am individually concerned, & independent of my pocket, it is my earnest desire to write those sort of books which are said to "fail."

So far his only failure had been the big one, *Mardi*, but he was to get his wish. On the same day he referred to the book in a postscript to a letter he wrote Dana: it was a "little nursery tale" of his. Melville's later comments were in the same vein. He had started *Redburn* under financial compulsion, pushed it onward hurriedly. His attitude toward it shifted during his work on it and again during the following months, in which it was published and reviewed. He disparaged it repeatedly after completing it, probably never admitted to himself how interesting a book he had written, and, in a 14 December letter to Duyckinck, expressed the hope that he would never have to "write such a book again."

Melville did not glamorize the feat of writing *Redburn* in two months. In his letter of 14 December he told Duyckinck: "when a poor devel writes with duns all round him, & looking over the back of his chair — & perching on his pen & diving in his inkstand — like the devels about St: Anthony — what can you expect of that poor devel? — What but a beggarly 'Redburn!'" Melville saw what he had done as slave labor, not heroic dedication, and allowed himself no public exulting at how hard he had pushed himself to write the book in such a short time. But some of his excessive truculence toward the book in the next months ("a thing, which I, the author, know to be trash, & wrote it to buy some tobacco with"; "the thing called 'Redburn'"; "beggarly 'Redburn'") may derive from his having begun to understand just how naive he had been in thinking he could write a semi-autobiographical book about childhood and walk away from it unscathed. Two years later Melville understood all too well just how significant *Redburn* was when he noted a temporary stage in the interior development of another young hero, Pierre: "Not yet had he dropped his angle into the well of his childhood, to find what fish might be there; for who dreams to find fish in a well?" (bk. 21, ch. 1).

28 John Murray III, ca. 1843, calotype by Hill & Adamson. Scottish National Portrait Gallery.

29 The Harper brothers: (*top, left to right*) James and John, (*bottom, left to right*) Joseph Wesley and Fletcher, from *The House of Harper: A Century of Publishing in Franklin Square*, by J. Henry Harper (New York, 1912).

30 *(left)* Charles Fenno Hoffman, from *Cyclopædia of American Literature*, by Evert A. Duyckinck and George L. Duyckinck (New York, 1855). 31 *(right)* Nathaniel Parker Willis, from *Cyclopædia of American Literature*, by Evert A. Duyckinck and George L. Duyckinck (New York, 1855).

32 Evert A. Duyckinck, photogravure. Portrait File, Miriam and Ira D.
Wallach Division of Art, Prints and Photographs, The New York Public Library,
Astor, Lenox and Tilden Foundations.

33 *(left)* Cornelius Mathews, from *Cyclopædia of American Literature*, by Evert A. Duyckinck and George L. Duyckinck (New York, 1855).   34 *(right)* George L. Duyckinck,
engraving. Portrait File, Miriam and Ira D. Wallach Division of Art, Prints and Photographs, The New York Public Library, Astor, Lenox and Tilden Foundations.

35 Herman Melville, ca. 1847, oil on canvas by Asa W. Twitchell.
Berkshire Athenaeum.

36 Elizabeth Shaw Melville, ca. 1847, daguerreotype.
Berkshire Athenaeum.

37 *(top)* Allan Melville, ca. 1847, daguerreotype. Berkshire Athenaeum.
38 *(bottom)* Sophia Thurston Melville, ca. 1 847, daguerreotype, from *The Melville Log*, by Jay Leyda, vol. 2 (New York, 1951).

39 Richard Bentley, from *Richard Bentley & Son* ([Edinburgh], 1886). The John M. Wing Foundation, The Newberry Library.

40 Lemuel Shaw, 1851, daguerreotype by Southworth & Hawes.
The Metropolitan Museum of Art, Gift of I. N. Phelps Stokes, Edward S. Hawes,
Alice Mary Hawes, Marion A. Hawes, 1938.

41 Hope Savage Shaw, ca. 1863, photograph. By permission of the Houghton Library, Harvard University (bMS Am 188.7 [2], no. 21).

42 Elizabeth Shaw Melville and Malcolm Melville, ca. 1850, daguerreotype.
Berkshire Athenaeum.

43 "Chief Justice Shaw's Study at 49 Mt. Vernon Street, Boston," from *Bulletin of the Society for the Preservation of New England Antiquities* (December 1916).

44 *(top)* Thomas Powell, from *Frank Leslie's Illustrated Newspaper* (22 January 1887). The Library Company of Philadelphia. 45 *(bottom)* "Dr. Holmes in 1850," from *Life and Letters of Oliver Wendell Holmes*, by John T. Morse Jr. (Boston, 1896). Berkshire Athenaeum.

46 *(top)* Sarah Huyler Morewood, ca. 1850. Berkshire Athenaeum.
47 *(bottom)* Nathaniel Hawthorne, 1851, engraving by Thomas Phillibrown after a
portrait by Cephas G. Thompson. Berkshire Athenaeum.

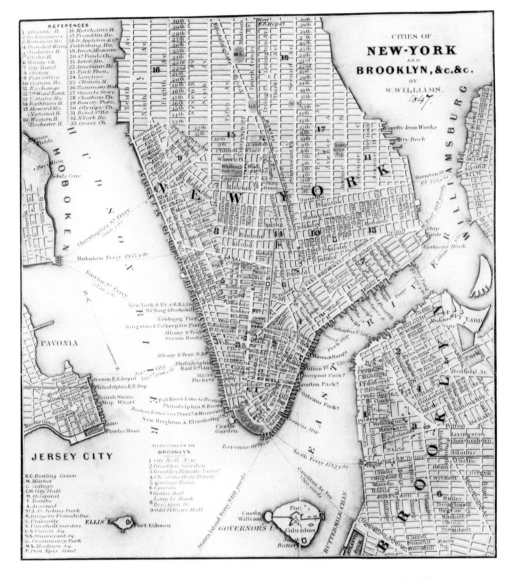

48 "Cities of New-York and Brooklyn, &c. &c.," 1847, engraving by W. Williams. Collection of the New-York Historical Society.

49 Detail from "Cities of New-York and Brooklyn, &c. &c.," 1847, engraving by
W. Williams. Collection of the New-York Historical Society.

50 "Melville's Residence," woodcut by W. Roberts, from *Cyclopædia of American Literature*, by Evert A. Duyckinck and George L. Duyckinck (New York, 1855).

Melville may have thought in May that he could redeem himself by dashing off a new book in record time, but as the weeks passed he saw that *Mardi* was not being "solved" to his satisfaction and was not selling, and that *Redburn* would not redeem him. He would need to write another book, even as he dealt with the proofs of *Redburn*. Having proved just how fast he could write, he would to do it all over again. In the sixty or so days from early July to late August Melville wrote all of this second book of the summer, an awe-inspiring achievement. Based on his own voyage home from the Pacific in the frigate *United States*, *White-Jacket* was set on a similar man-of-war called the *Neversink*. The name of the narrator, and the book, he took from a non-regulation jacket the narrator claims to have been issued at Callao, when the purser's steward is said to be fresh out of gregos, or pea-jackets. Near the opening the narrator makes a good story of his alterations to the white duck frock he was issued, describing how he bedarned and bequilted the inside until it became as "stiff and padded" as "King James's cotton-stuffed and dagger-proof doublet." Rather than being waterproof, it is so spongelike that it makes him "a universal absorber," in a happy double meaning. Melville lavished some of his best early prose on his description of the narrator's providing the jacket "with a great variety of pockets, pantries, clothes-presses, and cupboards" (ch. 9). When his shipmates raid his pockets he at last masons them up, all but two to stick his cold fingers in. The loss of pockets becomes the loss of privacy, the loss of individuality.

Melville did not write *White-Jacket* the way he wrote *Redburn*, plunging on through many chapters guided by his memory, then running short of material. Nor did he encounter the same sort of temporary impasse where the memory ran low and he had to turn to one big convenient source book. Instead, he proceeded in professional fashion, having truly learned much about book-craft, as he had prematurely boasted to Murray in the fall of 1846. A copyist was no problem. Helen served as his copyist for most of the summer of 1849, for on 1 July, while she was "deeply engaged in copying" *Redburn*, she sent word to Augusta, who had prolonged a visit to the Van Rensselaers at the Manor House then had transferred herself to Nilly's house on Mt. Vernon Street. Helen, according to Sophia, wanted Augusta to know that she need not come "home to assist": Helen and Herman were getting "along very well" without her. Even the late-written surviving fair copy of a preface for *White-Jacket* (which, he later decided, too frankly acknowledged his sources) is in Helen's hand, so she had made herself available all through this summer of intense achievement.

For *White-Jacket* Melville shrewdly settled on a structure in which he could write several sequences of related chapters—such as chapters dealing with the introduction of the jacket, chapters about regulations and routines on a man-of-war, chapters about flogging, chapters about Rio. He gathered up a pile of reference books, no doubt giving them some preliminary scanning as he laid them out. Hot from its use in *Redburn*, Melville had at hand the *Penny Cyclopædia* and drew on it frequently, often in order to make fun of serious articles, as Kendra H. Gaines, Wilson Heflin, and Mary K. Bercaw have demonstrated. The "Beards" entry helped him with chapters 84–87, for instance. In chapters 60–63 on Surgeon Cuticle's amputation of the leg of a foretopman, Melville used the articles on "Amputation," "Anatomy," "Gun-Shot Wounds," "William Hunter," "Skeleton," and "Tourniquet" — all involving matters and medical men brought freshly to his attention by Dr. Francis. To Melville, probably more than most of Dr. Francis's non-professional guests, it proved important that Francis as a medical student in London, Edinburgh, Paris, and even in German cities, had met or heard the lectures of the most eminent scientists. As Henry Tuckerman later wrote, Francis had heard "John Hunter, Cuvier, and Denon," at Paris; he had "listened to Bell's anatomical illustrations, talked with Herschell, joined in the levees of Sir Joseph Banks, heard Horner speak in the House of Commons, attended the meetings of the Royal Society, and saw Gall dissect a human brain." Francis saw John Hunter's new anatomical museum in Edinburgh at the time when, Tuckerman wrote, "physiological studies had begun to modify metaphysical theories." Francis saw or heard almost every notable scientific, literary, and artistic figure, Tuckerman emphasized: "No American physician better appreciated the anatomical triumphs of Hunter and Bell, the cerebral discoveries of Gall, the physiological investigations of Cuvier, the surgical achievements of Dupuytren, or the common sense applied to medical practice that made John Abernethy so famous." Young Herman Melville had lived with the cannibals, but his scientific reading had just begun, and he was now only one voluble host away from the best British and Continental minds of his century. The Hunters, Bell, Gall, and Cuvier — men Dr. Francis talked about — were men whose writings Melville would use and misuse in the next years. In *White-Jacket* he tempered his use of the article on "William Hunter" in the *Penny Cyclopædia* with awareness of Dr. Francis's particular respect for that pioneer anatomist and his brother John. Perhaps now, from Gansevoort's edition of William Hazlitt's *Table Talk*, he copied this tribute into Bennett's *Narrative of a Whaling Voyage*: "John Hunter was a great man. He would set about cutting up the carcass of a whale, with the same greatness of gusto, that Michael Angelo would have hewn a block of marble."

Francis Jeffrey's review in the May 1828 *Edinburgh Review* of *Correspondence of Vice-Admiral Lord Collingwood* supplied hints for scattered chapters — 27, 36, 52, 74, 90. Melville could have consulted a copy of the *Review*, but he had the essay in its reprinting in the Jeffrey volume in *Modern British Essayists*, which he had bought earlier in the year in the set that was proving a treasure-trove. Samuel Leech's *Thirty Years from Home, or A Voice from the Main Deck* (Boston, 1843) supplied Tawney's recollections in chapter 74, "The Maintop at Night," as well as parts of other chapters (16, 33, 88, 90). William McNally, *Evils and Abuses in the Naval and Merchant Service Exposed* (Boston 1839), gave Melville many factual details in chapters 37 and 75 as well as the basis for the portrait of Bland in chapter 44 and for the near-mutiny in chapter 85. Melville drew heavily on *Life in a Man-of-War, or Scenes in "Old Ironsides" during Her Cruise in the Pacific, by a Fore-Top Man* (Philadelphia, 1841), so much so that in his long version of the preface (published in 1970) he frankly credited that book with "recalling to his memory several minute man-of-war technicalities & humorous phrases, that otherwise might have escaped his memory" as well as for "supplying corroborative, or additional hints for two or three scenes in the following chapters." Nine chapters derive from this source: 14, 23, 32, 37, 41, 43, 47, 90, 91, including several comic episodes.

Melville used further sources more locally than the ones just cited. In chapters 70–72 he used the Articles of War from the *United States Statutes at Large*. He supplemented the actual articles with a piece available from the last days of July, John A. Lockwood's "Flogging in the Navy" in the August 1849 *United States Magazine, and Democratic Review*, especially as he wrote chapters 71 ("The Genealogy of the Articles of War") and 72 ("Herein are the good Ordinances of the Sea"). (This was the next issue after the magazine had so eloquently defended *Mardi*.) In chapter 75, "Sink, Burn, and Destroy," Jack Chase's exploits at the Battle of Navarino are in reality those of a young Scot, the author of *Life on Board a Man-of-War; Including a Full Account of the Battle of Navarino* (Glasgow, 1829). Chapter 90 ("The Manning of Navies") contains a direct allusion to *The Life and Adventures of John Nicol, Mariner* (Edinburgh, 1822), by Nicol, who had to skulk "for whole years in the country round about Edinburgh, to avoid the press-gangs." Melville also used Nicol for passages in chapters 37 and 75. Information for chapter 90 also came from Thomas Hodgskin's "Abolition of Impressment" in the October 1824 *Edinburgh Review*. One of the most spectacular pieces of writing in *White-Jacket*, the fall from the yardarm in chapter 92, was adapted from Nathaniel Ames's *A Mariner's Sketches* (Providence, 1830) and from Bulwer-Lytton's translation of Schiller's "The Diver." Melville used Ames as well for some of chapter 81, "How they Bury a Man-of-war's-man at Sea."

Whatever his frame of mind as he reorganized his shelves for the new book, Melville worked out in advance a basic writing-plan for *White-Jacket* as he had never done before. He planned it better and held more closely to the plan than he did with any subsequent book except *Pierre*, and possibly the lost *The Isle of the Cross* (written in 1853) and *Clarel*. The next year (9 April 1850), after *White-Jacket* was published in America, young Oakey Hall, still special correspondent to the New Orleans *Commercial Bulletin*, gave his southern readers the inside story on how Melville wrote it: "This last work of his was dashed off in a score of sittings, yet possesses the air of Irving's elaboration." Hall was still intimate with the Duyckincks and especially with Mathews, so he was in a position to know the truth about the composition of *White-Jacket* or what passed for fact in the Duyckinck circle. "Dashed off" is easily said, and books like *Redburn* and *White-Jacket* are not easily written, but Hall had no reason to say anything about a "score of sittings" unless he thought it to be true.

The flat assertion that Melville wrote *White-Jacket* in (roughly or precisely speaking) twenty sittings is enough to stimulate reflexive skepticism, but what Hall said may very well be almost if not quite literally true. In July and August Melville wrote systematically, holding to a rigorous routine. Oakey Hall's claim would be literally true if Melville set up and pursued a system by which he spent two days or so laying out a set of sources for the next narrative sequence and planning how he would use them (and perhaps getting out for some vigorous striding around town), then on the third day wrote furiously — wrote the equivalent of twenty pages in the standard Northwestern-Newberry edition. That process would account for the tightness of the many different sections of the book and would account for Hall's astonishing claim as perhaps literally true. One odd result of the speed in which Melville wrote *White-Jacket* was that it was a mere interlude in his career, a lengthy book which he could almost forget having written.

In writing both *Redburn* and *White-Jacket* Melville felt he was refraining from writing the kind of book he would wish to, though he had "not repressed" himself much but had "spoken pretty much" as he felt, as he wrote to his father-in-law on 6 October 1849. Financial considerations aside, it was his "earnest desire to write those sort of books which are said to 'fail,'" he insensitively added. In *White-Jacket* by virtue of his genre and subject matter Melville had less need to hold himself in check than in *Redburn*. In no earlier book had he given the reader so much credit for scope of reading, depth of understanding, and liberality of views. Despite this new stance of democratic camaraderie with the reader, Melville had arrived at an elitist view of reading, in which the best reader, like his friend "Nord" in *White-Jacket*, can seize the right meaning of Montaigne; by implication, most others, failing to seize that right meaning, would proceed through life imperceptive, content with a wrong reading. Not explicit in this passage was the theory that the author might have hidden his deeper meanings, but that notion emerged later, as Melville refined his theory of the writer-reader relationship.

While adopting the voice of Christian reformer as the best means for urging remedy of naval abuses, flogging in particular, and in that voice speaking pious words he would hardly have endorsed outside his book, Melville nevertheless was not so duplicitous as he had been in *Typee:* sincere in his advocacy, he was willing to adopt Christian rhetoric if it would advance his cause. Passionately he argued that the United States should abolish flogging at once, making precedents for the future rather than being bound by the "lumbering baggage-wagons" of old precedents:

> Escaped from the house of bondage, Israel of old did not follow after the ways of the Egyptians. To her was given an express dispensation; to her were given new things under the sun. And we Americans are the peculiar, chosen people — the Israel of our time; we bear the ark of the liberties of the world. Seventy years ago we escaped from thrall; and, besides our first birth-right — embracing one continent of earth — God has given to us, for a future inheritance, the broad domains of the political pagans, that shall yet come and lie down under the shade of our ark, without bloody hands being lifted. God has predestinated, mankind expects, great things from our race; and great things we feel in our souls. The rest of the nations must soon be in our rear. We are the pioneers of the world; the advance-guard, sent on through the wilderness of untried things, to break a new path in the New World that is ours. In our youth is our strength; in our inexperience, our wisdom. At a period when other nations have but lisped, our deep voice is heard afar. Long enough have we been skeptics with regard to ourselves, and doubted whether, indeed, the political Messiah had come. But he has come in *us*, if we would but give utterance to his promptings. And let us always remember that with ourselves, almost for the first time in the history of earth, national selfishness is unbounded philanthropy; for we can not do a good to America but we give alms to the world. (ch. 36)

Here in his role of passionate advocate of the rights of man-of-war's-men Melville spoke in the prophetic-philosophic voice he had used in *Mardi*, but now without violating the narrative consistency of the new book. Yet he was reckless at times, as at the end of chapter 76, "The Chains," where he allowed that in "view of the whole present social frame-work of our world, so ill adapted to the practical adoption of the meekness of Christianity, there seems almost some ground for the thought, that although our blessed Savior was full of the wisdom of heaven, yet his gospel seems lacking in the practical wisdom of earth."

White-Jacket was the most coherent book Melville had written. Sufficiently praised by its first reviewers early in 1850, it has been neglected ever since. Merely as a book about occupations, the affinities between man and job, and the effects of jobs and surroundings upon human nature, Melville had created a satisfyingly and seemingly complete nautical anatomy. Free of the hampering persona of a shipboard naif grown older, he was able throughout *White-Jacket* to adopt the sophisticated vocabulary and views of an educated, well-read man at ease with himself and confident in his reader. In it the narrative voice he employed was not immeasurably inferior to that of Ishmael, which is to say that this time, unlike what he had done in *Redburn*, he let the narrator speak with a voice indistinguishable, at times, from his own. He was writing as well as he could write, and in *White-Jacket* the sweetness, the verve, and the charming idiosyncrasies that drew people to him are fully displayed. Charles Lamb and other essayists lay behind some of the most endearing passages in the book, notably the recurrent celebration of creature comforts. Melville celebrated companionship: "Now, the tops of a frigate are quite spacious and cosy. They are railed in behind so as to form a kind of balcony, very pleasant of a tropical night. From twenty to thirty loungers may agreeably recline there, cushioning themselves on old sails and jackets. We had rare times in that top" (ch. 4). In chapter 12 he had excellent advice on driving off a "blue fit" by pleasant sounds from an Aeolian harp or a conch shell. Pleasant sights were also effectual: "a gay-painted punch-bowl, or Dutch tankard — never mind about filling it — might be recommended. It should be placed on a bracket in the pier. Nor is an old-fashioned silver ladle, nor a chased dinner-castor, nor a fine portly demijohn, nor any thing, indeed, that savors of eating and drinking, bad to drive off the spleen." Still better was "a shelf of merrily-bound books, containing comedies, farces, songs, and humorous novels. You need never open them; only have the titles in plain sight. For this purpose, Peregrine Pickle is a good book; so is Gil Blas; so is Goldsmith." For all his depictions of sociability, Melville celebrated throughout the book the quiet pleasures of meditation in small snug places like the chains, the small platform outside of the hull ("After hearing my fill of the wild yarns of our top, here would I recline — if not disturbed — serenely concocting information into wisdom" — ch. 76). He had his lists of snug places in the chains: "little chapels, alcoves, niches, and altars, where you lazily lounge." He claimed that his jacket, "like an old castle, was full of winding stairs, and mysterious closets, crypts, and cabinets." Like a "confidential writing-desk," it abounded in "snug little out-of-the-way lairs and hiding-places, for the storage of valuables" (ch. 9).

This celebration of snug places was not without some suggestive innuendo. Philip C. Van Buskirk, a marine drummer starting in 1851, in his diaries details a picture of common homoerotic behavior on a man-of-war, the *Cumberland*. He referred to the storeroom on a second ship, the *Plymouth*, as a "Sodomy den," and also identified the "boom cover" on deck as a favorite place for assignations. Melville does not mention the boom cover, but in chapter 30 he describes *"the ship's Yeoman's store-room"* in Gothic detail, and describes the Yeoman himself, *"Old Revolver,"* as "a somewhat odd specimen of a Troglodite," a "little old man, round-shouldered, bald-headed, with great goggle-eyes." His "incessant watchfulness and unaccountable bachelor oddities" drove away a succession of young sailors billeted with him, leaving White Jacket the object of his attentions, a likely candidate, just the sort of "steady, faultless young man, of a literary taste" that he desired. Melville whimsically describes his, or White Jacket's, alarm at the man's "goggling glances," lest he should drag him "down into tarry perdition in his hideous store-rooms." In chapter 89, "The Social State in a Man-of-war," Melville for a moment alluded to "the close cribbing and confinement of so many mortals in one oaken box on the sea" as producing evils "so direful that they will hardly bear even so much as an allusion." What he said about the sins of the cities of the plain lingering on in "wooden-walled Gomorrahs of the deep" fits with what current naval historians have found — that officers did not want to hear complaints about sexual assaults: "the deck officer would turn away with loathing, refuse to hear them, and command the complainant out of his sight." On shipboard were "even worse horrors" than were to be found in Horace Walpole's *Mysterious Mother,* Sophocles' *Oedipus Tyrannus,* and the story dramatized by Shelley in *The Cenci.* It was forcible rape that evoked such portentous citations, but rape, from the evidence of Van Buskirk, was extremely rare, while mutual assistance of casual "chaw for chaw" (or "claw for claw"?) was very common in snug places aboard ship. Denouncing in one place, teasing in another place, Melville was employing again the characteristic elusiveness that had so enraged G. W. Peck in 1847.

For the first time in his short career, Melville had to let go of a manuscript as soon as he finished it, without going back for his usual belated interpolation of chapters and parts of chapters here and there. As indicated by a letter from Evert Duyckinck to his brother, Melville was "hard at work" reading proofs on the Harper edition of *White-Jacket* on 5 September, even before the contract was signed on the thirteenth. Many weeks later he did get in some last licks, for he enhanced the English edition with a few small changes and an extended interpolated passage about the cook, Old Coffee, but otherwise he pretty much left good enough, or great enough, alone. On 10 September the Harpers' account showed Melville owing the brothers $832.29 — then on the thirteenth they advanced him $500 for *White-Jacket.*

Bentley's description of the shifting rulings on copyright in Great Britain, in regard to *Redburn,* may have set Melville to thinking about the possibility of going to London himself, so as to bargain in person for the best price. The idea of going had been planted by Murray, long before. We do not possess a letter from Melville to Bentley offering him *White-Jacket*, nor do we possess a letter from Bentley declining to purchase it. Possibly such an exchange of letters took place before Melville made his momentous decision. If the idea had occurred to him so soon, then from some point early in the composition Melville may have approached *White-Jacket* not merely as if he were entering a new period of drudgery. Rather, he may have seen *White-Jacket* as his payment in advance for a suitable reward for the summer's slavery — nothing less than the sort of grand tour that some of his new city acquaintances in their early manhood had been given by their wealthy families. By late August or early September, Melville had definitely decided to take the work to London, in the form of the Harper sheets. (With them he carried Helen's fair copy of a preface, which he had composed too late for the Harpers to set and which, as it turned out, he did not use in full.) Lizzie was expected to reconcile herself to the trip by the realization that she could settle into Mt. Vernon Street long enough to let her family and friends learn to appreciate her princely son.

Whenever he made his decision, Melville had stirred himself into a state of wanderlust by writing about his months on a man-of-war in the Pacific and Atlantic: "Oh, give me again the rover's life — the joy, the thrill, the whirl! Let me feel thee again, old sea! let me leap into thy saddle once more. I am sick of these terra firma toils and cares; sick of the dust and reek of towns" (*White-Jacket*, ch. 19). He was physically exhausted from writing *Mardi* and then from the double ordeal of writing *Redburn* and *White-Jacket*, and he was psychologically strained by the failure of *Mardi* and by all the emotions involved in writing the two very different books of the summer. A sea voyage would restore him, as one had not restored Gansevoort.

If he succeeded in selling *White-Jacket* for a large sum, Melville could then embark on an eleven additional months of travel, journeying that he would not have to excuse as a vacation but could readily justify as a source of new experiences to be written into new literary works. The time was right to lay in new stores. Melville may have been revolving the possible work on the theme of remorse, but he had one literary project in mind that would require research into locales in London and Paris. He was already thinking about making a book of his own from an odd pamphlet about an American of his grandfathers' generation, *Life and Remarkable Adventures of Israel R. Potter* (Providence, 1824). The real Potter had been in those cities during the Revolution, and afterward had suffered the strange fate of being unable to return to the United States until his extreme old age. The long exile struck an odd chord, reminding Melville of his Uncle Thomas, an exile from the court at Versailles. More obviously, Melville saw that in fictionalizing the narrative he could bring Potter into contact with famous revolutionary figures who appealed to his own imagination for one reason or another. All in all, it seemed like a practical project, not a highly ambitious one, but at some levels the story of Israel Potter appealed deeply to him. All practical reasons aside, he had itchy feet. The sailor who had returned from the South Seas only five years before had now set his heart on seeing the wonders of Europe and the Mediterranean.

Around the end of August, despite the fact that he was still hard at work on the proofs of *White-Jacket*, Melville set about the early arrangements for his trip with the giddy exhilaration of a man just released from bondage. He asked Shaw, Dana, and others for letters of introduction to literary men in London and Paris. As an afterthought he asked Shaw to request from his acquaintance Ralph Waldo Emerson a letter to Thomas Carlyle; he received no such letter, and therefore had no chance to multiply the political and social fulminations and nicotian fumigations emanating from Cheyne Walk. However, Shaw got Edward Everett, in his last year as president of Harvard, to write a letter addressed to Samuel Rogers, the banker-poet, and to Richard Monckton Milnes and to Gustave de Beaumont, the son-in-law of Alexis de Tocqueville; Dana wrote an introduction to the publisher Edward Moxon (now coasting into old age on his well-publicized intimacy with Lamb). Early in September Melville put Evert Duyckinck into "a flutter" by asking him along "on a cheap adventurous flying tour of eight months, compassing Rome!" Evert was sufficiently tempted to say he would not go without George (a suggestion Melville "relished") and to ask to delay a decision until George came back from East Hampton, so the brothers could "get the benefit of at least a dream out of the project."

George Duyckinck took the general line toward Melville's planned trip: the journey would be of "great service to him" — not as physical and mental therapy but as a source of observations and information that would be worked into his next literary projects. Thomas Powell officiously gave Melville parting advice, sound enough, on asking the price of anything alcoholic before drinking it and assured him that in England "he would find no low press or publisher to abuse him, & no respectable persons to believe them if they did" — a reference to the recent New York City newspaper reports of his own arrest for forgery. Melville noted Powell's advice about inquiring the price of liquor, but he had more urgent business to attend to, such as having Malcolm baptized at home by the Reverend Doctor Henry W. Bellows on the last Sunday in September. Reconciling Lizzie to the separation was a hard matter, but she took the view (as Melville expressed it to his father-in-law) that she could bear it better "especially as she will have Malcolm for company," and Melville took the view that "when she finds herself surrounded by her old friends in Boston, she will bear the temporary separation with more philosophy than she has anticipated." Melville was in a mood to push all difficulties aside, although in writing to Shaw he allowed for contingencies: "It is uncertain, now, how long I may be absent; and, of course, my travels will have to be bounded by my purse & by prudential considerations. Economy, however, is my mottoe." He also laid down a line of defense against the attacks he expected *White-Jacket* would incur. On 6 October he wrote Dana that he expected to be away "for some months" after its publication and diffidently suggested that, if reviewers took hold of it in "an unfair or ignorant way," Dana might make public comment on its truthfulness, on the basis of his own "peculiar experiences in sea-life." He was still planning a tour lasting many months. The New York *Tribune* may have been well informed when it reported that he intended "to spend a twelvemonth abroad."

He almost didn't go. Gansevoort had identified Herman's perverse sort of procrastination, that sort which consists in a "disinclination to perform the special duty of the hour," and now Herman waited until 1 October to request a passport from John M. Clayton, the secretary of state. Then he wanted fast action: "As the vessel sails on the 8th Inst: may I beg, that the passport will be forwarded in time — to my address — Nº 14 Wall Street, New York City" — Allan's office. On that page he listed "the items of personal description" which he thought were required, starting with "Heighth" — 5'10⅛". Clayton's clerk responded promptly with a request for proof of citizenship, so on 4 October Allan wrote out an affidavit for himself and his brother to sign in the presence of a notary public ("Herman Melville being duly sworn says that he is a citizen of the United States . . . that he was born in the city of New York"). In his new letter to Clayton on 4 October Melville was still edgier than before: "I sail on Monday. May I hope to receive the passport by return mail." In a new "Description of person" he gave his "Stature" again as 5'10⅛". Most of the other items were the same as those on 1 October, his hair still dark brown, his eyes still blue, but in three days his "medium prominent" nose had become "prominant" (he wrote "medium prominant" and marked the "medium" out). His height when he sailed on the *Acushnet* was given as 5'9½", five-eighths of an inch less than nine years later. There would be more comedy in his measuring his height in eighths of an inch if in 1856 he had not listed his height as 5'8¾". In October 1849 Melville had proved himself a formidable writer, despite the fate of *Mardi*, one justified in crediting himself with every last eighth of an inch of height. Procrastinator or not, he got his passport.

32

London and a Peek at Continental Life
Fall 1849

Aristippus, being asked wherein the Learned differed from the unlearned,
said send them naked unto Strangers and you will then see.

"Allan Melvills Book," 1796

WITH THE PROOFS OF *White-Jacket* and letters of introduction stowed away
and his passport safe at hand, on 10 October 1849 Melville said good-bye to
Lizzie and Malcolm and the other members of his family, expecting to see
them again late in 1850, and boarded the *Southampton* in the North River
(that is, the Hudson). The weather prevented the ship from departing (it was
a sailing vessel, not one of the new transatlantic steamers like the *Hermann*),
so he had to return anticlimactically to Fourth Avenue. There he responded
to a note from Duyckinck, who had heard he was home: "Having taken so
dramatic a farewell of my kindred this morning, and finding myself among
them again this evening, I feel almost as if I had indeed accomplished the
tour of Europe, & been absent a twelvemonth; — so that I must spend my
first evening of arrival at my own fireside. Release me from my promise then,
and save what you were going to tell me till tomorrow when we glide down
the bay." The next day "the last familiar faces" he could see from the ship
were those of George Duyckinck and Allan, and his thinking of what the
family "might be doing at home" modulated rapidly into other memories as
the Narrows prompted a recollection of his childhood visit with his father
and Uncle John D'Wolf to Fort Tompkins as well as his own voyage to
Liverpool, about which he had just written.

In keeping with his determination to gather material for future works, he
kept a journal, perhaps for the first time of his life. It is the basic source for
this chapter, which follows it day by day, for some stretches, then at other
times treats topics extracted from it. Here Herman Melville presents himself
openly — as openly as a man is likely to do when he is self-consciously writing
the journal for later perusal by his wife, as he seems to have done. Nevertheless, despite any conscious or unconscious reticence about putting down his
experiences and his responses to them, the document offers a far more inti-

mate portrait of Melville than even the most autobiographical passages of his presumably autobiographical books like *Typee, Omoo, Redburn,* and *White-Jacket.* The journal provides, for this period of his life, a unique intense record of his particular way of viewing the world, just as the pages from the draft of *Typee* provide a unique glimpse of his early compositional methods.

Once aboard, Melville at first panicked that he might be cabined with the young son of the rich merchant Robert H. McCurdy (a lad he described as "a lisping youth of genteel capacity," unfortunately "quite disposed to be sociable"). Theodore Frelinghuysen McCurdy was twenty-one, six feet tall, with dark eyes and hair and a light complexion, according to the description his father provided in the letter to the secretary of state in which he requested a passport for the lad. The senior McCurdy also asked Clayton to enclose "a few lines introducing him to Mr Cass at Rome" (Lewis Cass, Gansevoort's stumping companion). His son, McCurdy assured Clayton, was "a graduate of our University & studied law at Cambridge, & now visits Europe for the benefit of his health & general improvement." Despite Melville's trepidation, the captain, R. H. Griswold (a cousin of the McCurdys), in fact gave him the only single-occupancy cabin, a space almost as big as his "own room at home." He had asked in advance for private accommodations, but what he got was splendid: "a spacious birth, a large wash-stand, a sofa, glass &c &c," with "plenty of light, & a little thick glass window in the side," which he could and did open in fine weather. As he learned, he had celebrity status, the only passenger "thus honored with a room to himself."

After his first restful night at sea Melville, a sailor who had been long ashore, rose early and went aloft, "to recall the old emotions of being at the mast-head," needing to renew the physical experience in order to "recall" the old emotions. On the thirteenth through his bull's eye window he saw the sun just rising, the horizon red, a "familiar sight" reminding him of old times, and he "went up to the mast-head, by way of gymnastics." That afternoon he was the first to see a man in the water and to shout "Man overboard!" Then he "dropped overboard the tackle-fall of the quarter-boat, & swung it towards the man," who caught it, only to let go. On deck the crew and passengers warned Melville not to fall over, himself. The man drifted astern, a merry expression on his face, and sank, having succeeded in a bizarre suicide. ("The man drowned like a bullock," the shocked Melville wrote in his journal.) Later a "terrific gale" came up, prostrating most of the passengers. At midnight Melville went on deck and in the cuddy found the captain, Robert Griswold, who directed his attention "to those fellows"—a sight he had never seen, corposant balls on the yardarms and mastheads, like "large, dim stars in the sky."

The fourteenth of October was a "regular blue devel day," everyone sick, saloons deserted, and "all sorts of nausea noise heard from the state-rooms," including that of the lisping youth, so Melville read with pleasure in Caroline Kirkland's new "European tour," *Holidays Abroad*. At the rail a man, a victim of delirium tremens "consequent upon keeping drunk for the last two months," disconcertingly directed him to look for nonexistent steamers. When convalescent passengers emerged on the fifteenth they regarded Melville "as a hero, proof against wind & weather" and his "occasional feats in the rigging" they admired "as a species of tight-rope dancing." He had been showing off (as he continued to do for at least another two years), but he was also simply enjoying the fact that he still had some gymnastic prowess at thirty, after years of sedentary labor, and he was taking pleasure not only in climbing to the masthead but in being there, looking out at the ocean again. On the sixteenth he surrendered to a "temporary effect" of the sea, which made him "for the time incapable of any thing but vegetating" and mooning about Malcolm and Lizzie ("What's little Barney about? Where's Orianna?"). The sea continued to fascinate him, particularly moonlight sailing on the twenty-fifth, such as he had never seen before. He enjoyed the "moonlight midnight" on the twenty-ninth, and the next night he found "magnificent."

At first Melville was reserved with the captain (having formed a poor opinion of him) and most of the passengers. A "Scotch artist" introduced himself as a friend of the Albany painter, Asa Twitchell, who had done a portrait of Melville "gratis," but he turned out to be the husband of the woman Melville had observed holding a copy of *Omoo* and looking up at the author now and then, "as if comparing notes," and Melville did not pursue their acquaintanceship. Nor was he interested in several Frenchmen and Englishmen, one of the latter bearing back "two glorious pairs of antlers (moose) as trophies of his prowess in the woods of Maine." Luckily, Evert Duyckinck had introduced him to a friend of his who happened to be on the ship, George Adler, a scholar of German philosophy and literature who taught modern languages at New York University and was the author of a German-English lexicon which Melville decided was "formidable." Melville wrote in his journal that Adler was "full of the German metaphysics, & discourses of Kant, Swedenborg &c." Only twenty-eight, a naturalized citizen, Adler was a slight fellow (5'5"), with (as his self-description for his passport continued) "forehead, high: — Eyes, brown: — nose, straight. — hair, light-brown & thin; complexion, light; face, smooth." Also aboard as ship's doctor was Frank Taylor, a cousin and former traveling companion of Bayard Taylor, the young writer who had written Melville a valentine and whom he identified in the journal as "the pedestrian traveller." Frank may have been Taylor's middle name, for he seems to be the Philadelphian who applied for a

passport on 21 September as John Taylor, thirty years old, 5′6¼″ tall, with
light complexion, light brown hair, gray eyes, a high forehead, and a small
mouth in a round face. Identifying Adler and Taylor as boon companions,
Melville had as little to do as possible with anyone else.

With Adler, Melville had long talks on "Fixed Fate, Free-will, fore-
knowledge absolute" — Milton's list of topics debated by the fallen angels,
and Melville's favorite way of indicating the scope of any serious philosophical discussion he engaged in as well as his awareness of what opinion conventional society held of anyone willing to debate such topics: the topics were fit
speculation only for fallen angels. His journal entries show him as the novice
learning from the professor, making sure he gets philosophical niceties
clearly in mind and clearly recorded; they also show him as what he called
himself a few weeks later, a "pondering man."

The early talks with Dr. Taylor were less philosophical than those with
Adler, but in their way momentous, particularly one on 15 October:

> This afternoon Dr Taylor & I sketched a plan for going down the Danube
> from Vienna to Constantinople; thence to Athens in the steamer; to Beyroot
> & Jerusalem — Alexand[r]ia & the Pyramids. From what I learn, I have no
> doubt this can be done at a comparativly trifling expence. Taylor has had a
> good deal of experience in cheap European travel, & from his knowledge of
> German is well fitted for a travelling companion thro Austria & Turkey. I am
> full (just now) of this glorious *Eastern* jaunt. Think of it! — Jerusalem & the
> Pyramids — Constantinople, the Egean, & old Athens!

In this journal Melville never wrote without some caution. Here, the parenthetical "just now" acknowledges the evanescence of moods, but it does not
disguise his rapturous enthusiasm for a glorious jaunt through storied terrain
with at least one congenial and experienced male traveling companion.

On 18 October Melville got his new friends aloft, this time including
Adler in some of the travel plans: "Spent the entire morning in the main-top
with Adler & Dr Taylor, discussing our plans for the grand circuit of Europe
& the East. Taylor, however, has communicated to me a circumstance, that
may prevent him from accompanying us — something of a pecuniary nature.
He reckons our expenses at $400." Of the three, Taylor was now the doubtful
party. Melville himself seemed to be the most committed to the tour, which
still involved a sweeping loop, through Europe and the Middle East and back
(to England?) by some unspecified route, presumably through Spain. The
night of the twenty-first the three caroused in Melville's room:

> it was proposed to have whiskey punches, which we *did* have, accordingly.
> Adler drank about three table spoons full — Taylor 4 or five tumblers &c. We

had an extraordinary time & did not break up till after two in the morning. We talked metaphysics continually, & Hegel, Schlegel, Kant &c were discussed under the influence of the whiskey. I shall not forget Adler's look when he quoted La Place the French astronomer — "It is not necessary, gentlemen, to account for these worlds by the hypothesis" &c. After Adler retired Taylor & I went out on the bowsprit — splendid spectacle.

The discussions about the tour continued, not without vacillations, as Melville recorded on 26 October: "For a few days passed, Adler & I have had some 'sober second thoughts' about our grand Oriental & Spanish tour with Taylor. But tonight, the sight of 'Bradshaw's Railway & Steamer Guide' showing the marvellous ease with which the most distant voyages may now be accomplished has revived — at least in *my* mind, — all my original enthusiasm. Talked the whole thing over again with Taylor. Shall not be able to decide till we get to London." The decision hinged on Melville's selling *White-Jacket* for a good price, payable in advance of publication. He would need cash in hand. Meanwhile, on 20 October he read the "account of Venice" in Murray's guidebook, just in case.

Toward the end of the voyage Melville changed his mind about the captain, deciding that he was "a very intelligent & gentlemanly man — converses well & understands himself." He noted his own fault: "I never was more deceived in a person than I was in him." He also began to unbend a little with some passengers besides his favored two, a difficult maneuver, for one Englishwoman was "flat" and a Miss Wilbur of New York, "of marriag[e]able age," habitually talked "about 'winning souls to Christ,' " and ostentatiously kept a diary (not known to survive). Yet the gilt saloon, brilliantly lighted, seemed like an elegant parlor ashore, a place to be sociable. On the twenty-seventh Melville "played Shuffle board for the first time," and later whist. In the afternoon of the twenty-ninth while some of the passengers had succumbed to the weather again he "tried to create some amusement by arraigning Adler before the Captain on a criminal charge," and that evening "put the Captain in the Chair, & argued the question 'which was the best, a monarchy or a republic?' " — one of the standard questions for debating societies in his youth. There was some "good sport during the debate," but the Englishmen were too stiff to take part in it. On the thirtieth he included "the ladies" along with Taylor at "Shuffle Board."

The greater sociability kept pace with greater access to alcohol. At first, remembering Thomas Powell's advice to ask the price of everything before consuming it, Melville was nervous about how much they would charge for his "small bottle of London Stout" for dinner (he thought it did him good), but he soon stopped worrying. He had "*mulled wine*" supplied by McCurdy, in Melville's room, of course — a subtle way for McCurdy to make his way into the sanctum; a "good deal of wine & porter on table"; and more "mulled Sherry" from McCurdy. There was a return of McCurdy's civilities, in which Captain Griswold joined, ordering "a pitcher of his own," enough to lead Taylor to play "a rare joke upon McCurdy" that evening ("passing himself off as Miss Wilbur, having borrowed her cloak &c.," even walking with the lisping youth, taking his arm to do so). There was a rowdy party in the gentlemen's cabin on 3 November (in which Melville did not join), everyone mistakenly thinking it was the last night of the voyage, and the roisterers paid the price the next day: "long faces at dinner — no porter bottles." Melville "cracked some Champaign" with McCurdy on the night of the fourth, however. In these last days of the voyage Melville was letting his arduous summer wash out of his consciousness, but he carefully recorded his thoughts of home (20 October: "Where's Orianna? How's little Barney?"; 28 October: "Where dat old man?"; 30 October: "Where dat old man?" again). He kept up a long letter to Lizzie, which he finished on 4 November after adding the last entry to his *"log"* on the *Southampton:* " 'Where dat old man?' — 'Where books?' " (Allan wrote Evert Duyckinck in mid-January 1850 that Lizzie had relayed a portion of this letter in which Herman reported himself as homesick already, on the voyage out.)

Melville's excitement soared merely from knowing, on 30 October, that the Scilly Islands were there to the north, though out of sight. On 1 November, well up the Channel, he saw a great number of ships and possessed enough historical imagination to brood on the significance of the waters through which "Blake's & Nelson's ships once sailed." They made the Isle of Wight early on 3 November and took aboard the pilot (who brought London newspapers for the past two weeks), but they had to tack all day and were still in sight of the Isle of Wight the next morning, before striking away for Dover. The night of the fourth, making his last entries, Melville identified the overwhelming emotion as he prepared to land. He was feeling triumphant vindication, however much defensive self-deprecation he set up: "This time tomorrow I shall be on land, & press English earth after the lapse of ten years — *then* a sailor, *now* H.M., author of 'Peedee' 'Hullabaloo' & 'Pog-Dog'." The contrast understandably suffused him with pride as he reflected on the discrepancy between hopeless youth and buoyant young manhood, between the greenhorn required to keep his distance from the paying travelers and the author given the best cabin in the ship and eyed by a lady over a copy of a book he had written.

Captain Griswold awakened him at five in the morning on the fifth — Guy Fawkes's Day — so he could get onto a cutter, already alongside. After a "comical scene," the boon companions Melville, Adler, and Taylor were beached at Deal, not Dover, having left their baggage to go by ship to London. The champagne still in his system early this "fine autumnal morning," he was ecstatic, as if he were touching English soil for the first time. Liverpool, where he had been dock-bound, counted for little: this at last was the England of history, poetry, and fiction. When he wrote up his account of going ashore at Deal he kept his geographical and historical fervor tamped down: "Some centuries ago a person called Julius Caesar jumped ashore about in this place, & took possession." His page proofs safely en route to London on the ship, he and the other two men "wholly unincumbered," Melville "proposed walking to Canterburry — distant 18 miles, for an appetite to breakfast." Taking possession of the island in his own way, he strode with his companions through Deal to open country then breakfasted in Sandwich "at a tumble down old inn," finishing with "ale & pipes." Thus cheered, they visited a Roman fortification, "Richboro' Castle," then being excavated — for Melville, a marvelous introduction to lower layers of history. They saved sightseeing time by taking the railroad cars to see the cathedral at Canterbury, "on many accounts the most remarkable in England." Unselfconsciously Melville commented in good tourist fashion: "Henry II, his wife, & the Black Prince are here — & Becket. Ugly place where they killed him." They dined at the Falstaff Inn then went to the theater, laughing at themselves and the performance, then slept all three in one room at the inn.

The next morning, 6 November, they swallowed a glass of ale and took the cars to London, third class, and therefore "exposed to the air — develish cold riding against the wind," but passing in sight of Philip Sidney's Penshurst on the way. They crossed London Bridge at noon, went past St. Paul's, and after eating in a chop house secured rooms at a guinea and a half a week ("Very cheap"). Already having written into *Redburn* an absurd fantasy of a London visit, he was actually there, and within hours of his arrival he inquired of *Redburn* in a bookstore and was offered a copy for a guinea. In a reading room he saw the review of it in the November *Bentley's Miscellany*. Reviewers of Bentley books in Bentley's own magazine did not always write puffs, but this one was at least very kind: "Indebted less for its interest to the regions of the fantastical and the ideal, than to the more intelligible domain of the actual and real, we are disposed to place a higher value upon this work than upon any of Mr. Melville's former productions. Perhaps it is that we understand it better, and the fault is not in Mr. Melville, but in ourselves, that we appreciate more satisfactorily the merits of a story of living experience than the dreams of fancy and the excursions of a vivid imagination." In a sentence written, it seemed, to be quoted, the reviewer declared: "In the Dutch fidelity and accumulation of the incidents, it is a sort of Robinson Crusoe on ship-board." The "episode of Harry Bolton" was, perhaps, "a little in excess," but it was like "a dash of romance thrown in amongst a cluster of familiar and homely incidents." There was even, at the end, a compliment to the "idiomatic peculiarities of the style," identified by the reviewer as due to the nationality of the writer, not to his own genius.

This was pleasant, but it was nothing to what Melville soon encountered in Julien's bookstore: "Blackwood's long story about a short book," fourteen pages, which he skimmed through. The reviewer had opinions on all four of Melville's books, the best of which was *Omoo*:

> after a decided and deplorable retrogression, Mr Melville seems likely to go ahead again, if he will only take time and pains, and not over-write himself, and avoid certain affectations and pedantry unworthy a man of his ability. Many of the defects of *Mardi* are corrected in *Redburn*. We gladly miss much of the obscurity and nonsense that abound in the former work. The style, too, of this one is more natural and manly; and even in the minor matter of a title, we find reason to congratulate Mr Melville on improved taste, inasmuch as we think an English book is better fitted with an English-sounding name than with uncouth dissyllables from Polynesia, however convenient these may be found for the purposes of the puff provocative.

Amid extensive summary and extracts were some sharp criticisms. The scenes in Launcelott's-Hey were "exaggerated exhibitions of the horrible." The London episode, the reviewer assured the author, was "in the very stalest style of minor-theatre melodrama," a genre not without its pleasures: "We perfectly remember our intense gratification when witnessing, at country fairs in our boyish days, a thrilling domestic tragedy, in which the murderer rushes on the stage with a chalked face and a gory carving-knife, howling for 'Brandy! Brandy!!' swallows a goblet of strong toast and water, and is tranquillised." Now "surely Mr Melville had no need to recur to such antiquated traditions." The whole of the London expedition was "utter rubbish": "Why will not Mr Melville stick to the ship? There he is at home."

The reviewer knew he was not writing merely for British readers of *Redburn*:

> When this review of his last work meets the eye of Mr Herman Melville, which probably it will do, we would have him bear in mind that, if we have now dwelt upon his failings, it is in the hope of inducing him to amend them; and that we have already, on a former occasion, expended at least as much time and space on a laudation of his merits, and many undeniable good qualities, as a writer. It always gives us pleasure to speak favourably of a book by an American author, when we conscientiously can do so. First, because Americans, although cousins, are not *of the house;* although allied by blood,

they are in some sort strangers; and it is an act of more graceful courtesy to
laud a stranger than one of ourselves.

The second reason was that the reviewer hoped "to encourage Americans to
the cultivation of literature — to induce some to write, who, having talent,
have not hitherto revealed it; and to stimulate those who have already written
to increased exertion and better things." He went on with high solemnity:
"For it were false modesty on our part to ignore the fact, that the words of
Maga [*Blackwood's Magazine*] have much weight and many readers throughout the whole length and breadth of the Union — that her verdict is respectfully heard, not only in the city, but in the hamlet, and even in those
remote back-woods where the law of Lynch prevails." The third reason was
that he hoped by praising good American books that America would pass an
international copyright law: "For surely it is little creditable to a great country to see her men of genius and talent, her Irvings and Prescotts, and we will
also say her Coopers and Melvilles, publishing their works in a foreign capital, as the sole means of obtaining that fair remuneration which, although it
should never be the sole object, is yet the legitimate and honourable reward
of the labourer in literature's paths." Later, Melville took the time to reflect
on this sober advice, but now he only marveled at its high seriousness in his
journal: "the wonder is that the old Tory should waste so many pages upon a
thing, which I, the author, know to be trash, & wrote it to buy some tobacco
with." Together these two reviews afforded a hearty welcome, particularly
since the one in *Blackwood's* was so oddly directed to him as its chief reader, as
if it were a personal letter awaiting his arrival in London. Having read *Blackwood's*, Melville stopped in at the American Bowling Saloon in the Strand —
thereby opening himself to strangely juxtaposed images from his time as a
pin-setter near another strand, in Honolulu six and a half years earlier.

On 7 November, after "infinite trouble with the cursed Customs," all
three men had their trunks in their lodgings, so they went to see Madam
Vestris and Charles Mathews at the Royal Lyceum Theatre, Strand, where a
fellow went round "with a coffee pot & mugs — crying 'Porter, gents, porter!'" Next day, on 8 November, Melville called at Bentley's offices in New
Burlington Street, but his mission to sell *White-Jacket* got off to a bad start,
for the publisher was at Brighton. Welcoming him, the staff pulled out the
reviews of *Redburn* they had collected, so Melville stayed awhile there in
Bentley's office, looking through the reviews he had not already seen. Many
of them, like *Blackwood's*, summarized the story and extracted favorite passages, usually from the comic initiation scenes or the somber scenes such as
the death of Jackson — all space misspent, according to the author. The *Literary Gazette* on 20 October had resolved the issue of Melville's identity: "that

he is really an American may be credited by his use of the Yankee words realizing, loaning, and others not yet transferred to the English vocabulary." The *Britannia* (27 October) announced that "fierce and swaggering exaggeration of the genuine Yankee style is forcibly and, if truth must be told, unpleasantly conspicuous in this work." The "staple of the book" was "coarse and horrible," and oddly mingled "with much that is tediously minute." The reviewer called attention not to the scene in Launcelott's-Hey but to the chapter called "A Living Corpse" and the death of Jackson. Melville had "been spoiled by partial success." In *Redburn* as in *Mardi* Melville's talent was "running to seed from want of careful pruning." *John Bull* (27 October) was sure that Melville's faults were growing "less conspicuous" while his "excellencies" remained undiminished. Melville had "happily steered clear" of the "slippery scenes" of the earlier works where he exhibited "vice scarcely veiled, for the amusement of his readers." The future was open to him: "With such works as this, Mr. Melville bids fair to fill the void left in the marine part of our novel literature by the death of the late Captain Marryatt."

The *Spectator* (27 October) thought that *Redburn* was "even more remarkable than his stories 'founded on fact' descriptive of native scenery and life in the islands of the Pacific," since this book sustained interest without the advantage of "novelty and interest of subject." The London *News* (29 October) worried inconclusively about the aesthetic distance between Melville and his narrator: "There is discrepancy felt at first between the author and the biographer. Herman Melville and 'Redburn' are two distinct personages; thus when 'Redburn' does a silly action, which he does frequently, though he knows better afterwards, we find him envelop it with rich thought and keen observation. How can we admit the fool in action with 'the wit in mind?' " Without distinguishing the younger from the older Redburn, the reviewer contented himself "with highly lauding a work so much out of the common." The *Morning Post* (29 October) thought Melville had told "old stories" and dressed up "old objects" and presented "old incidents so as to look quite fresh — at least, fresh enough for the passing entertainment of one who reads for amusement." There was a problem of genre: "This is not a novel, for there is neither plot nor love in it; it is simply what it professes to be, the narrative of a voyage from New York to Liverpool and back by a sailor boy." The *Morning Herald* (30 October) commented that Melville had developed "a story of maritime life somewhat in the style and spirit of Captain Marryat." Finishing his survey of a representative sample of reviews, very likely including several others from London dailies, he decided, ungratefully, that they were "laughable."

Later on 8 November Melville called on his other publisher, but Murray was also away. From there he went to the National Gallery, the first time he had been in a great museum. He dined with Taylor and Adler, and then began his night and day rambles about the London of Shakespeare, the London of the wits of Queen Anne's time, the London of Goldsmith, Lamb, Dickens (whose *Pickwick Papers* he had been reading on shipboard), and the city of his own literary godfather, Irving, whose *Sketch Book* contained loving tributes to "London Antiques." On 9 November, after he "went into Cheapside to see the 'Lord Mayor's Show' it being the day of the great civic feast & festivities," he recorded a thought that recurred to him on one of the bridges, "that a fine thing might be written about a Blue Monday in November London — a city of Dis (Dante's) clouds of smoke — the damned &c — coal barges — coaly waters, cast iron Duke &c its marks are left upon you, &c &c &c." He had come on business, to sell one book and gain material for others, including the story of Israel Potter, who had lived out a long exile in London after the Revolution. In his journal he conscientiously recorded impressions that he was sure he could use, one place or another, and in fact he did draw on the journal, a few years later, for short stories as well as for the Potter book. This passage on the city of Dis he used to help him fictionalize the story of Potter, and he found, before he left, further tangible help in a historical map of London.

On his sixth day ashore, Saturday the tenth, Bentley's message was awaiting him at breakfast. The men arranged that the publisher would come up to meet his American author at his office on Monday. That Saturday, Melville continued his saturation in London by "sauntering thro' the Temple courts & gardens, Lincoln's Inn, The New Hall, Gray's Inn, down Holborn Hill thro' Cock Lane (Dr Johnson's Ghost) to Smithfield (West)," and "so on to the Charter House," where he chatted with an old pensioner who guided him "thro some fine old cloisters, kitchens, chapels." An officer of the Fire Department led him through squalid lanes, alleys, and closes to "a dirty blind lane" identified as Dick Whittington's birthplace, then the man led him "thro cellars & anti-lanes" (ante-lanes) "into the rear of Guildhall, with a crowd of beggars who were going to receive the broken meats & pies from yesterday's grand banquet (Lord Mayor's Day)." Melville saw comical possibilities in the "heaps of fowls hams &c &c," and imagined a character who would proclaim, "I could tell who had cut into this duck, or that goose." In short, a "good thing" might be made of it. In the next days, surrendering himself to London, he proved himself an indefatigable tourist, with his friends or alone, all guiltlessly, since any impression he recorded or remembered might be put to use in a future work.

In his office Richard Bentley received Melville on 12 November very kindly, despite having lost so much money on *Mardi*, and, as he had promised, he gave Melville his note for one hundred pounds at sixty days for

Redburn. (Melville then had to find someone to discount it for him so he could deposit some of the proceeds for Allan to draw on.) Despite "much anxiety & vexation at the state of the Copyright question," Bentley also made a generous offer for *White-Jacket*, two hundred pounds for the first thousand copies, on publication. Melville could not wait for that; he needed an advance on *White-Jacket* if he were to be able to make the tour with Taylor and Adler. Bentley's note for *Redburn* did not enter into his calculations as funding for the trip; if he made the trip, he had to do so with money from the newest book. On 14 November Melville found Murray in. His first publisher treated him very civilly and "seemed decidedly pleased" at what Melville said about *White-Jacket* and sent to Melville's lodgings for the sheets; that same day, 14 November, Melville dined with Taylor, young McCurdy, and Adler and learned that the sickly McCurdy was to have the privilege of going forth the next day with Taylor, without Melville and without Adler, bound "for the East—Jerusalem, &c." If Murray had accepted the book and given Melville a sufficient advance then and there, he might have set out in pursuit of the pair, but having examined the sheets, on the sixteenth Murray politely informed him that it "would not be in his line" to publish *White-Jacket*. Nothing in his journal explicitly records a shift in plans under which Melville decided that Paris (and possibly even Rome) were realistic destinations even after the tour of eastern Europe and the Levant was renounced, but on hearing then of Melville's suddenly scaled-down plans, Murray sent two guidebooks from his famous series to Melville's lodgings, the "Book of the Continant & for France," as Melville listed them. The particular two guidebooks which Murray gave him, taken with his journal entry for the next day, show that some such retrenchment had occurred, as does Melville's belated acceptance on 17 November that he would not see Rome. An excursion to Paris Melville could make without selling *White-Jacket*, he thought. Having come so far it would be improvident not to gain at least a glimpse of the Paris his father and uncle had known so well.

Reserved by nature, unfitted to play either the brash salesman or the suppliant author (despite his display of epistolary arrogance toward Murray), Melville overcame all his distaste for what he was doing and in the next days canvassed one publisher after another. (This dogged salesmanship was observed and later aptly described in the columns of the *Times*, with unpleasant aftereffects in New York City.) He called on Henry Colburn, and then successively on the Longmans, on David Bogue, on Chapman & Hall, and on H. G. Bohn. The result was always "No go." During this time he was on tenterhooks: if the next publisher, Bogue, Bohn, whoever, accepted *White-Jacket* and paid him in advance, he would set off after Taylor and McCurdy on some version of a grand tour culminating in the Mediterranean countries, perhaps even rendezvousing with them at some exotic location they had named before parting. At the least, he would see Paris.

By day and by night striding the streets of London in quest of historical and literary sites and shrines, Melville saw storied public monuments from outside and, whenever he could, from inside. He walked streets, lanes, alleys, and closes, by day and far into the evenings (typically, on 18 November, wandering "among a labyrinth of blind alli[e]s & courts," then threading "more allies, lanes, & courts"). He was game for anything: he went on 13 November to Horsemonger Lane, Borough, to see George and Marie Manning hanged for murder. The papers estimated that thirty thousand spectators witnessed their deaths, and another eyewitness, Charles Dickens, made a great to-do in the *Times* with his emotional journalistic accounts of the event. Melville bought a broadside of the hanging to send to Lemuel Shaw, and recorded: "All in all, a most wonderful, horrible, & unspeakable scene." He walked through the gigantic Thames Tunnel to Rotherhithe, and came back by boat. At the Temple Church he saw "the 10 Crusaders — those who had been to the Holy Land, with their legs crossed," and the fine heads of the damned. He saw the royal gardens at Kew, and saw where James Thomson (like everyone, the Melvilles knew his *Seasons*) and Alexander Pope had lived. Many nights, he dropped in at theaters, often astonished at the behavior of vendors, watchers, and actors. English actors and actresses he could see at home, but the whole experience of theatergoing in the metropolis was a wonderment, and he learned to make discriminations as the days went on, and remembered particular actors for many years.

Acutely aware that few great paintings, pieces of sculpture, and other art works had made their way to the United States, Melville avidly looked at many private and public collections, usually on his own or with Adler. (Before he left for Europe, Taylor had proved less interested in art than Melville.) On 11 November Melville inspected the paintings at Hampton Court. He went to the National Gallery briefly on 12 November, on his way to see Bentley. On the fourteenth he admired the statues in Westminster Abbey. On the sixteenth at the British Museum he saw some fragments of colossal Roman sculpture ("big arm & foot") and "Ninevah sculptures" as well as the Rosetta Stone, the significance of which he had understood since childhood. The next day he and Adler went to the Dulwich Gallery, well worth the five-mile horse-pulled bus ride: "The gallery is full of gems — Titians, Claudes, Salvators, Murillos. — The Peasant Boys — The Venus — The Peasant Girl — Cardinal Beaufort — The mottled horse of Wouvermans — St John — The Assumption — The old man & pipe — Mrs Siddons as Tragic Muse." On the way back Adler and a Yankee they had met carried "on a spirited discussion concerning the merits of the various paintings," a conversation he did not feel qualified to join. On the nineteenth on Albemarle Street, John Murray took him upstairs to see his private gallery of portraits of Murray authors: Byron, Moore, Campbell, Borrow, and many others, not including the author of *Typee*. During the days after Taylor and then especially after Adler left for Paris on the nineteenth, he was much alone, and most of the time happily so — by day "victoriously" running "that painted gauntlet of the gods" in the art galleries (as he said in *Pierre*, bk. 26, ch. 1).

From his first hours in London, Melville was a habitué of reading rooms and bookstores, as well as publishers' offices. There he probably saw some of the last reviews of *Redburn*. On 7 November the *Home News: A Summary of European Intelligence for India and the Colonies* acknowledged that "the writer, who conceals himself under the dark disguise of Herman Melville possesses great descriptive talents." Previously Melville had wasted his powers on "wild and fantastic themes," but now his "mixture of simplicity and distinctness" reminded the reviewer "occasionally" of Defoe. Everyone Melville encountered had seen the *Athenæum*, which on 10 November identified the humour of the book as borrowed from Marryat's *Peter Simple* and pronounced that *Redburn* was "better written" than either *Typee* or *Omoo* and was in some respects a striking improvement upon *Mardi*. But Melville by now was not looking for his notices. He was a man who not only read old books but loved to encounter old books appropriately printed and bound. In the Strand he saw a folio of Beaumont and Fletcher in the window and went in, finding "the shopman to be an old acquaintance of young Duyckinck's — Mr Stibbs." He bought the "B & F" and a folio Ben Jonson and looked longingly at a Chapman's Homer. In one bookstore he "turned over some noble old works, & chatted with the bookseller — a very civil, intelligent young man," then bought a quarto of Davenant and "a little copy of Hudibras." On 20 November he called on Edward Moxon, Dana's publisher. The old man was clammy at first, but warmed up, and told him stories about Charles Lamb ("he had often put Lamb to bed — drunk"), and sent him a copy of his edition of Lamb's works. In Holborn he found "Lavater's Phisiognomy" for ten shillings sterling. In the previous years in New York Melville had made friends with Bartlett and Welford in their Astor House bookshop and had made himself at ease in Duyckinck's great library, but after the dispersal of his father's library he had been surrounded by cheaply printed and ugly American books — indeed, for long periods immured on shipboard with nothing but a few of the very cheapest of books and pamphlets. London was a bookman's paradise.

Without quite defining another mission, Melville turned his need to dine into a quest for the perfect snuggery. One of the first, on 15 November, was the best: "At half past 5 (P.M.) went with Adler to the 'Edingburgh Castle' a noted place for its fine Scotch ale, the best I ever drank. Had a glorious chop & a pancake a pint & a half of ale, a cigar & a pipe, & talked high German metaphysics meanwhile. Home & to bed by 10'o'clock. The 'Castle' is the beau ideal of a tavern — dark walled, & like a beef-steak in color, polite waiters &c." Whenever possible, he ate and drank at houses associated with great writers. On 16 November he met Adler "at the 'Mitre Tavern', Mitre Court, Fleet Street — the place where Dr Johnson used to dine." He inspected the bust of Johnson by Joseph Nollekens and savored the stewed rump steak, bread and cheese, and ale. He smoked a cigar in the cozy upper room, grateful that the tavern had no "cursed white walls." They also stopped for ale at the "Dr Johnson Tavern" nearby, the rival claimant to Johnson's favor, which had in Melville's mind the advantage of being "the *darkest.*" They also stopped for stout at the Cock Tavern that night, in honor of Tennyson: "Dark & cosy," he commented, comparable to the "Edinboro'." On the eighteenth he and Adler found the Rainbow Tavern, which he also associated with Tennyson, and enjoyed a "Terrific bumper of Stout." The Edinburgh Castle remained the tavern par excellence.

The delays between publishers gave Melville intervals in which to continue his exploration of London, for some of the publishers were kind enough to take the sheets and look them over for a day or two before making a decision. He would have made the most of his days in London under any circumstances, but he looked intently these mid-November days because he never knew how many more he would have there. If any one of the publishers had accepted *White-Jacket*, he might have left at once for the Continent on his way to Vienna, the Holy Land, Rome, who knows where, and might never have seen London again. On 17 November, after Colburn had rejected his demands for *White-Jacket* (still two hundred pounds for the first thousand copies), he wrote: "Bad news enough — I shall not see Rome — I'm floored — appetite unimpaired however — so down to the Edinburgh Castle & paid my compliments to a chop. Smoked a long pipe." Melville's terse notation about the results of his calls on publishers ("No go") in effect became the epitaph for the trip with Taylor. Rarely had Melville put himself on record as wanting anything so much as he wanted this prolonged trip to eastern Europe, the Holy Land, and the entire Mediterranean region. He was careful to note in his journal that he was homesick for his wife and son, but for weeks he had been wild to have his *Wanderjahr,* and he did not want the journal to record the full misery of his relinquishing that trip.

For a few days after Taylor and McCurdy departed, Melville lived even more provisionally, still trying to place his book (he saw one of the Longman brothers on the nineteenth), and spending much time with Adler before the scholar's departure for Paris. On 19 November, accepting the fact that he

would be alone in London the next day, Melville tried to present his letter
from Evert Duyckinck to Thomas Delf and then tried to present "Young
D's" letter to Wiley's agent, David Davidson, but neither was in. Melville
successfully presented a letter of introduction from Mrs. Welford (the English wife of the partner of Bartlett in the Astor House bookstore) to J. M.
Langford, the drama critic for the *Observer* and head of the London branch
of Blackwood & Sons. Langford received him very cordially and invited him
to the theater to see Macready (safe on stage, on this side of the Atlantic) and
"to sup with him & meet Albert Smith, the comic writer who has just returned from the East & purposes writing something 'funny' about it." At
Bentley's were "two budgets" (packets) from home, and also other letters,
but before he saw any of them he was accosted by an awed "clark," who
announced, "Lord John Manners has been here for you, sir!" Manners had
just received word from N. P. Willis that Melville was in London, and had
promptly written two introductions himself, which he had left at Bentley's,
one to "Monckton Miles" (as Melville misspelled the name of Richard
Monckton Milnes) and one to Manners's sister, Lady Elizabeth Drummond.
One of the letters from New York was Willis's, enclosing a letter to Manners
and another to the immensely popular poet Martin Farquhar Tupper, the
author of *Proverbial Philosophy*. Melville felt sufficiently at ease at his publisher's to go "into B's private room" to read his "home letters," where he
found that all were well, "& Barney a bouncer." After that emotional interlude, he pulled himself together and acknowledged the new shift in his situation — not what he had wanted, but also not without its benefits. Calling on
Murray, Melville informed him that "people here having anticipated" him,
he "should stay awhile now, & make some social calls &c."

Accordingly, on the next day (rebounding from a rejection from Longmans awaiting him atop his blackened boots) he took out his letters and
"resolved to go at it, like a regular job, which it is, this presenting letters of
introduction"; then he went out to present them in a businesslike fashion.
First, he left a letter and card at the palatial residence of the banker-poet
Samuel Rogers in St. James's Place, then crossed to the American legation on
Upper Belgrave Street. There he found both the new minister, Abbott Lawrence, and the new secretary of the legation, John Chandler Bancroft Davis.
Remembering him as Lemuel Shaw's son-in-law and Helen's brother, Law-
rence received him "very kindly" and gave him the news that "the Duke of
Rutland (father of L J Manners & L Emmeline) had been seeking" his ad-
dress. Invited to dine that evening at the minister's temporary residence in
the Clarendon Hotel, Melville went there (freshly "rigged up") and found
Mrs. Lawrence so hypocritical, so disdainful and hateful, that he raged

against her in his journal then subsequently decided he had been unjust and tried to efface what he had written.

On 21 November, downriver at Greenwich Hospital, the British equivalent of the Sailors' Snug Harbor (New York's rest home for sailors on Staten Island), he went into "the Painted Hall," where he saw sea-pieces and portraits of naval heroes as well as relics worshipfully preserved: "coats of Nelson in glass cases." Later, he found George Duyckinck's friend David Davidson in Paternoster Row and quickly made friends with him. That night he called at Langford's lodgings and found one young fellow already there and more expected:

> Snug place enough. At last there came in four or five young fellows — sociable chaps. And in the end, Albert Smith the comic writer & Tom Taylor the Punch man & Punch poet. Smith was just from the East, & sported a blazing beard. A rattling, guffaw, cockney — full of fun & a little malice perhaps. — Nice plain supper — no stiffness. Porter passed round in tankards. Round table, potatoes in a napkin. Afterwards, Gin, brandy, whiskey & cigars. Smith told funny stories about his adventures in the East, &c. Gave me his address &c. Came away about 2 A.M.

Nursing a hangover on 22 November, Melville toured the state apartments in Windsor Castle, remarking on the mast of the *Victory* and the bust of Nelson, as well as a Cellini shield and "miraculous" Gobelin tapestry.

On 23 November, a Friday, Melville met with David Davidson, who assured him that he could get Bentley's note for *Redburn* cashed, a great relief to him. Furthermore, Davidson suggested publishers he could show *White-Jacket* to, telling him to "keep pushing," and even accompanied him to Bogue's to propose the book. That night at Murray's house Robert Francis Cooke, a cousin of the publisher, showed him portraits on the walls, commenting all the while on what John Gibson Lockhart, Scott's son-in-law, thought of them. Lockhart was present, the chief guest, but in what Melville felt was only a ghostly way. Long before, Herman as well as Gansevoort had read his biography of Walter Scott, and now the man wore "a prodigious white cravat" which Melville decided had been made from Walter Scott's shroud. Lockhart's disdainful behavior astonished and amused Melville rather than outraging him: "He stalked about like a half galvinized ghost — gave me the tips of two skinny fingers, when introduced to me — or rather, I to him." The "stiffness, formality, & coldness of the party" left Melville feeling like "knocking all their heads together." He sat next to Lockhart at dinner, or at least after dinner, when the ladies withdrew; then three decanters, "Port, Sherry & Claret," went the rounds "with great regularity." Others were playing the "snob" to Lockhart (that is, fawning over him), but Melville refrained, and was rewarded when the man famous as a son-in-law grinned at him "his ghastly smiles." Melville concluded: "Such is a publisher's dinner. A comical volume might be written upon it. — Oh Conventionalism, what a ninny, thou art, to be sure."

On the morning of 24 November Melville went out into an "oldfashioned pea-soup London fog — of a gamboge color," but it lifted and he peddled his book as the fog floated in midair. He left his note with Davidson, who had promised to cash it. The Anglo-American banker Joshua Bates (who had reluctantly discounted Murray's note for *Typee* for Gansevoort on 1 January 1846) had invited Melville to dine at his home in East Sheen that evening and to stay on till Sunday. Melville unexpectedly received a call in his fourth-floor room from Henry Stevens, his own age, a Vermonter long resident in London. He was a great bookman, a dealer and book-agent who already was buying for some of the finest American libraries. He had met Lizzie in Boston, and had befriended Gansevoort in London and been one of the pathetic handful who attended his funeral services in Westminster Abbey. Melville responded to him powerfully, and time ran so fast that after Stevens finally left he had to rush to get "rigged" and out to catch an omnibus to St. Paul's and from there a Richmond stage to East Sheen, nine miles away.

Bates, who turned out to be "quite a jolly old blade," received him cordially in his "large & noble" house, where the rooms were immense, the decorations brilliant ("statuary, vases, & all sorts of costly ornaments," and one cheap decoration, a copy of *Typee* on a table). At Bates's the chambers were "sumptuous," the welcome "courteous," the lords and ladies and baroness and merchants, half of them foreigners, were all "free, easy & in good humor — all talkative & well-bred — a strong contrast to the miserable stiffness, reserve, & absurd formality of Mr Murray's, the tradesman's, dinner last night." Melville the putative descendant of kings and queens and the veritable cousin of the current lord of Leven and Melville had his categories at hand — stiffness and pretension were the marks of the tradesman. At Bates's the "sundry mysterious French dishes" and the free-flowing wine were marvelous.

At Bates's Melville fell into conversation with the American George Peabody, the Massachusetts-born banker and philanthropist, quickly judging him to be "a very fine old fellow" ("old" being four years younger than Maria Melville). The benevolent Peabody described to him Gansevoort's solitariness in London shortly before his death. A third party to the conversation was Davis, Brodhead's successor in what had been Gansevoort's job, and a nephew of George Bancroft. Davis also had known Gansevoort. Caught off guard by memories of his brother, and far more perturbed than he at first recognized, Melville impetuously decided to return to London with the two Americans rather than to stay the night, as he had been invited to do. Before departing he took "a cup of prodigiously strong coffee & another of tea" — a reckless act, what with his susceptibility to caffeine and his feelings of guilt, remorse, and love toward Gansevoort. Remembered by Murray, Stevens, Bates, Peabody, and others, Gansevoort was now a palpable presence in the city where he had launched his sailor-brother's career. Reflecting alone in his room after midnight, Herman revealed an odd inability to acknowledge how long his brother had been dead (three and a half years): "No doubt, two years ago, or three, Gansevoort was writing here in London, about the same hour as this — alone in his chamber, in profound silence — as I am now. This silence is a strange thing. No wonder, the old Greeks deemed it the vestibule to the higher mysteries." What with the excitement of the party, the caffeine, and the intensity of his memories, Melville suffered "a most extraordinary night — one continuous nightmare till daylight" — enough to exempt him from purgatory, he thought.

Sunday night Melville dined at Morley's Hotel with Stevens and Davis, who both lived there, then smoked a cigar with Davis before calling with him on the Lawrences at the Clarendon Hotel, where Mrs. Lawrence was so very pleasant that he took back the bitter things he had written about her. Then on the way home the author of humanitarian passages in *Redburn* and *White-Jacket* was pleasantly surprised by Davis: "I was struck with his expressions concerning the poverty & misery of so large a portion of the London population. He revealed a heart." The next day, 26 November, he had to wait for Davidson but ultimately walked away with a check that he could cash, and deposited forty pounds for Allan to draw in New York, keeping enough to finance his own travels. That afternoon Stevens took him on a personal tour of the treasures of the British Museum: "Endless galleries & three-deckers of books. Saw many rareities. — Maps of London (before & after the Great Fire), Magna Charta — Charlemagne's bible — Shakespere's autograph (in Montaigne) &c &c &c. Went into the Manuscript room — saw the famous Alexandrian Manuscript & many Saxon M.S.S. of great value." In this, the climax to Melville's museum-going in the first phase of his London visit, Stevens, through the Keeper of Printed Books, Antonio Panizzi, had gained him access to parts of the museum few tourists — and few residents — ever saw. Early the next morning he was on his way down London Bridge stairs to catch the boat to Bologne, bound for Paris.

On 28 November Melville found Paris still a "garrisoned town" in the aftermath of the latest revolution. After hunting a bit for Adler, he took a room on the rue de Rivoli then sallied out to "subscribe" at Galignani's reading room, where Americans and Englishmen rendezvoused. The next day, still hunting for Adler, he followed the recommendation of his New York friend the literary doctor Augustus K. Gardner, author of *Old Wine in New Bottles: or, Spare Hours of a Student in Paris* (1848), and took lodgings at Madame Capelle's (where he took notes that he later used in *Israel Potter*). Then he went to Livingston & Wells's in the place de la Bourse, "the place where our countrymen most congregate on the arrival of every steamer" (said a correspondent from Paris in the New Orleans *Picayune* of 12 November 1849). The next day, 30 November, he spent three hours at the Louvre, seeing "Heaps of treasures of art of all sorts," including what he approved as an "Admirable collection of antique statuary" which beat that in the British Museum. Then he read a new batch of American newspapers at Galignani's, where (amid new astonishing stories about discoveries of gold in California) he found that "the thing called 'Redburn'" had just been published. On 1 December he admired the "Fine monument of Abelard & Heloise" and "tombs of generals &c" at Père Lachaise cemetery. On 2 December he saw the captured flags and gallery of military paintings at the Hôtel des Invalides.

On 4 December, his seventh day in Paris, Melville met Adler at the "Bibliotheque Royale" and looked over "plates of Albert Durer, & Holbein," and walked through the "halls of books" seeing Persian and Coptic manuscripts and a letter of Benjamin Franklin's. He later bought a copy of *Telemachus* near the Louvre—perhaps an English translation of François Fenelon's new *Aventures de Telemaque*. On 5 December he soothed a lifelong curiosity about abnormal human anatomy by going to the Museum Dupuytren, recommended by Dr. Francis, who knew the founder of the collection of "Skeletons & things without a name." Some Melville could give names to, readily enough—a French miser's heart fatally clogged with a French gold piece, or French babies (this one betailed, that one two-headed), all three, heart and babies, pickled in transparent bottles. From Dupuytren's edifyingly pathological collection Melville made his way through the Latin Quarter to the Hôtel de Cluny, "the princely fifteenth-century city residence of the abbots of Cluny" (Howard Horsford's description in *Journals*) "built in flamboyant Gothic style over vast Gallo-Roman ruins." Then as now a museum, it contained hundreds of works of medieval art, but for Melville its greater importance was below ground. From the chapel "a winding staircase led down to the vestibule of the Roman palace, thought to have been Julian the Apostate's residence when he was proclaimed emperor" (as Horsford says). The remains of the Roman baths, partially excavated, overwhelmed Melville with a sense of antiquity and recurred in a powerful image of the subconscious (ch. 41, *Moby-Dick*) in the next book he wrote. He wrote in his journal: "The house is just the house I should like to live in. Glorious old cabinets—ebony, ivory carving.—Beautiful chapel. Tapestry, old keys. Leda

& the Swan. Descended into the vaults of the old Roman palace of Thermis. Baths &c." It was overweening for an American to declare, even in the privacy of his journal, that the Hôtel de Cluny was just the house he should like to live in, but he had been sheltered in the houses of the Hero of Fort Stanwix and the Hero of the Tea Party, was a kinsman of the Van Rensselaers of the Manor House, and had married the daughter of Judge Shaw on Mt. Vernon Street. The Hôtel de Cluny was just the house he should like to live in, and during his travels on the Continent he would continue his quest for a snuggery like the Edinburgh Castle, but even darker, more tobacco-saturated, and more cheerfully manned by yet more polite waiters serving darker and stronger stout. On 6 December he took the cars to Versailles, where he admired the architecture as well as the enormous paintings in the Salle de Batailles. (Like his friend Tuckerman, he surely paused ironically under the one in which the French lieutenant general Rochambeau accepts the surrender of Cornwallis at Yorktown while Washington stands by in humble gratitude: where was Peter Gansevoort and the blue flag of his regiment?) He was unequivocally impressed by the sculptures: "Titan overthrown by thunderbolts &c. Apollo & the horses on the fountain."

On 7 December Melville took a second-class car to Brussels, a "dull dreary ride all day over an interminable flat pancake of a country." He put up in a "fine chamber," and thought obligatory thoughts of Byron, but heard "no sound of 'revelry' now, heaven knows." Waterloo, eight miles away, was out of the question ("Can not visit it — & care not about it"): he was off to Cologne, anxious as to whether or not ice would keep him from steaming on the Rhine, an evocative river to any good American Romantic. On the ninth he had only to look up to see Cologne's "famous cathedral, where the everlasting 'crane' stands on the tower" — an image he wrote into his next book as a symbol of the difficulty of completing any great project. There was no Sunday morning boat, so he spent the day there in Cologne, a "not altogether unpleasant" experience. He went through the cathedral, during a service, and saw the skulls of the three wise men. In the museum he was impressed by "some odd old paintings," particularly a "splendid one (a sinking ship, with the Captain at the mast-head — defying his foe)." He concluded that: "In this antiquated gable-ended old town — full of Middle-Age, Charlemaigne associations, —— where Rubens was born & Mary De Medeci died — there is much to interest a pondering man like me." That phrase "a pondering man like me" is as clear an assessment as he gave of himself at this time of his life.

On the night boat Melville shivered all the way down to Coblenz, but consoled himself by glimpsing "tall black cliffs & crags" each time he went on deck, a "grand sight." At Coblenz he crossed to the "famous Quebec fortress" of Ehrenbreitstein on the heights, which he found a "magnificent object, truly," particularly since the day was clear enough for him to gain a "superb" view from the summit. At the precise confluence (the meaning of Coblenz, he probably learned), where the Moselle and the Rhine meet, across from the Eck, he drank Moselle self-consciously, having drunk Rhine wine in Cologne. Reminded of the fortress of Quebec, which he had seen with Lizzie on their honeymoon, he set up a strange polarity: "Opposite was the frowning fortress — & some 4000 miles was America & Lizzie. — Tomorrow, I am *homeward-bound!* Hurrah & three cheers!" He took a mid-afternoon boat from Coblenz to Cologne on 11 December, chilled from the intense cold but glad to see by daylight "Drachenfells & the Seven Mountains, & Rolandseck, & the Isle of Nuns." Much in the spirit in which he had written to his mother, ten years earlier, that he would give all the sights of Liverpool to see a corner of home, he now sentimentalized in the journal, in part for Lizzie's eyes: "The old ruins & arch are glorious — but the river Rhine is not the Hudson." In Brussels he went at once to the hotel to reclaim the shirts he had left to be washed, but the "insidious landlady & the rascally waiters" pretended the garments "were not come home yet" so as to keep him for dinner there, if not an overnight stay. In no mood to be harassed, he had "a few comical scenes with the landlady & started off in a pet & went dodging about town to get a cheap dinner." The long, dreary, and frigid ride to the coast threw him into such a "fit of the nightmare" that at a "way-place" he all but got off the train, thinking he had reached Ostend. At midnight, he "went down into a dog-hole in the bow" of the waiting boat "& there sat & smoked, & shivered, & pitched about in the roll of the sea" all night, arriving at Dover before daylight on the thirteenth.

The British customs agents seized the fine copy of Thomas Hope's *Anastasius: or, Memoirs of a Greek* Melville had bought at the Palais Royale and told him "it was food for fire." He was rightly enraged by this action, the more capricious and arbitrary since the book had originally been published in London — in 1819, under the imprimatur of the elder John Murray. ("Anastasius is a sort of oriental Gil Blas," the *Edinburgh Review* had said, though the Greek was the greater villain because he acted "in a worse country, and under a worse government." The *Quarterly Review* had called the profligate seducer "a scoundrel of the deepest dye, with no mixture of the milk of human kindness to blend with the harsher ingredients of his character.") His load thus lightened by a book putatively written in a time of greater frankness ("at the close of the 18th Century," according to the subtitle), Melville reached London at noon, "after posting all the way from Coblentz, without cessation." (Richard Bentley soon gave him a copy of his inferior reprint of *Anastasius*—a generous gift, but not a replacement for his fine French English-language edition.)

Back in his lodgings on Craven Street in the "villians garb" he had traveled in, and not having shaved in a week, he was told by the overawed chambermaid that "a gentleman from St: James" had come in his coach—the venerable and wealthy banker-poet Samuel Rogers; he was also handed "with a meaning flourish" a note from the duke of Rutland sealed with a coronet. The duke had invited him "to visit Belvoir Castle at any time after a certain day in January," which he knew he could not do: "I am homeward-bound, & Malcolm is growing all the time." What with his disappearance to the Continent for a time, he had been an elusive man to make contact with, even if a Briton knew to seek him at Murray's or Bentley's, and from the outset he seems to have been uneasy about his appearance, repeatedly mentioning that his green coat played "the devel" with his respectability there. At last, on the fourteenth, he purchased a more discreet "Paletot," and had his hair cut, for it had become "as long as a wild Indian's." There were setbacks. When he called, Rogers was out of town, and John Forster of the *Examiner*, Dickens's friend (and later his biographer), was simply out, but he found himself, after a while, taken up by remarkable people, hospitably received into English literary and artistic circles (which as always overlapped with commercial and political circles). From this point his socializing escalated, for people now knew he was in town, and knew that he would not be there for long.

On 13 December he found letters from Lizzie and Allan when he called at Bentley's, and later from the legation he received not only letters from them but from Allan a bundle of newspapers also, full of scandalous news about Thomas Powell, most astonishing of which was a letter from Charles Dickens, printed in the *Tribune*, labeling Powell a scoundrel and a thief. Melville went off to the Edinburgh Castle to wash down what he referred to as the "Powell Papers." Good-hearted and probably still deluded, Melville lamented in his diary, "Poor fellow—poor devel—poor Powell!" Later, on 17 December, his acquaintance Henry Stevens told Melville that "certain persons" (Britishers speaking from sad experience) "had called upon him denouncing Powell as a rogue." (These same days, there in London, Charles Dickens panicked, fearing a suit for libel, and gathered, in his own defense, affidavits attesting to Powell's criminal past which he printed in a pamphlet labeled "PROOF.")

On 15 December Bentley relented—far too late for Melville to go on his eastern trip—and promised to give his note for *White-Jacket* the next day, two hundred pounds at six months, in anticipation of publication of one thousand copies on 1 March 1850, profits from any subsequent editions to be shared between author and publisher. "Hurrah & three cheers!" Melville wrote in his journal. The worst of leaving as he was now about to do was having to decline the invitation of the duke of Rutland to visit him in Belvoir Castle (he probably knew to say it like "beaver"). Having renounced the eastern jaunt that was to culminate in a sweep back through the Mediterranean and Spain, then having renounced the consolation prize of Rome, Melville made this very different renunciation. Seeing Europe and the Levant as a tourist could have been wonderful, although he would have been dependent on polyglot foreigners and the occasional speaker of English. Staying in a castle as the cherished guest of a duke was a once-in-a-lifetime opportunity, he recognized.

On 15 December, after Bentley had made his magnanimous offer, Melville read over the duke's invitation, which he had "not fairly perused before," and found it "very cordial," but naming a date impossibly far ahead, in what he took to be the custom "here for these sort of invitations into the country." On Sunday the sixteenth he was in turmoil:

> It is now 3. P.M. I have had a fire made & am smoking a cigar. Would that One I know were here. Would that the Little One too were here —— I am in a very painful state of uncertainty. I am all eagerness to get home — I ought to be home — my absence occasions uneasiness in a quarter where I most beseech heaven to grant repose. Yet here I have before me an open prospect to get some curious ideas of a style of life, which in all probability I shall never have again. I should much like to know what the highest English aristocracy really & practically is. And the Duke of Rutland's cordial invitation to visit him at his Castle furnishes me with just the thing I want. If I do not go, I am confident that hereafter I shall upbraid myself for neglecting such an opportunity of procuring "*material.*" And Allan & others will account me a ninny. — I would not debate the matter a moment, were it not that at least three whole weeks must elapse ere I start for Belvoir Castle — three weeks! If I could but get over *them!* And if the two images would only *down* for that space of time. —— I must light a second cigar & revolve it over again.

At half past six he wrote again: "My mind is made; rather, is irrevocably resolved upon my first determination. A visit into Leicester would be very agreeable — at least very valuable, in one respect, to me — but the Three Weeks are intolerable." On 16 December, the day he renounced the opportunity to visit the duke of Rutland in Belvoir Castle, Melville resolved to book "a state-room on board the good ship Independence," a sailing ship. Bitterly ambivalent, he wrote in his journal: "Would that I could go home in a Steamer — but it would take an extra $100 out of my pocket. Well, its only 30 days — one month — and I can weather it somehow."

Making use of the time he had left, on 17 December he went to the National Gallery "& spent an hour looking at Rembrandt's Jew & the Saints of Taddeo Gaddi, & Guido's Murder of the Innocents," then looked in at the Vernon Gallery. On the nineteenth he went back to the British Museum and "wandered about for a couple of hours," and on the twentieth he got into the House of Lords to see the frescoes through the courtesy of the artist John Tenniel, a friend of Murray's, who held him for two hours of enforced art appreciation, including a look at a "very fine" Cordelia and Lear and Tenniel's St. Cecilia, illustrating Dryden's poem. Melville was absorbing impressions, fitting familiar names of artists and works of art to the tangible objects, reconciling smudged and careless reproductions to the veritable, or less than verifiable, originals, all the while recording titles of favored objects, often straight from the guidebooks. His journal entries are short of original judgment; indeed, idiosyncrasy emerged mainly in humorous reactions, as when he noticed in Westminster Abbey a chapel where a knight rested with a wife on his right side and a vacant place on the left, "the vacant lady refusing to be put there," thereby providing a "serio-comico moment about Death." Nothing in Melville's journal indicates that he had within him the makings of a notable connoisseur of art works, engravings in particular, still less the makings of an earnest student of aesthetics, but it does show him looking, looking — intently eyeing, to use one of his phrases.

On 18 December Melville dined with Bentley ("a very fine frank off-handed old gentleman," he decided now; old meant born in 1794) in a party of fourteen or so "in a fine old room hung round with paintings (dark walls)" — a good sign: "There was a Mr Bell there — connected with Literature in some way or other. At all events an entertaining man and a scholar — but looks as if he loved old Port. Also Alfred Henry Forrester ('Alfred Crowquill') the comic man. He proved a good fellow — free & easy — & no damned nonsense, as there is about so many of these English." Having warmed toward Bentley and members of his family, he walked away with Forrester, who invited him to the theater.

The next night, 19 December, was memorable. Robert Francis Cooke, Murray's cousin and factotum, whom Melville decided he had misjudged, revealed himself a great host: "Last night dined in Elm Court, Temple, and had a glorious time till noon of night. A set of fine fellows indeed. It recalled poor Lamb's 'Old Benchers'. Cunningham the author of Murray's London Guide was there & was very friendly. A comical Mr Rainbow also, & a grandson of Woodfall the printer of Junius, and a brother-in-law of Leslie the painter. Leslie was prevented from coming. Up in the 5th story we dined. The Paradise of Batchelors." Samuel Stone, the brother-in-law of the absent Charles R. Leslie, the painter, so strongly pressed Melville to spend Christmas with him and Leslie in St. John's Wood, that he could "barely resist," but his voyage home on the *Independence*, under Captain Fletcher, had been settled, and there was no staying. Tearing himself away from that memorable dinner, Melville arose early on the twentieth to accept the honor of breakfasting alone with Samuel Rogers, whom he found a "remarkable looking old man truly," and whose paintings he found superb. Rogers paid him the high compliment of inviting him back to meet some ladies on Sunday. That night, with Rogers's hospitality and his magnificent art collection still fresh in his memory (there were some Turners in oil, watercolor, and pencil), Melville dined at the Erechtheum Club on St. James's Square, with Cooke's brother William Henry Cooke as host. There were nine at the "fine dinner"— Rainbow, a Mr. Cleave ("a fine fellow"), all making up an "exceedingly agreeable company."

The next morning Melville called on Cleave in his rooms in the Temple and got a tour of "the Library — Hall of the Benchers — Kitchen — rooms — Dessert room & *table*," and saw portraits of the benchers and manuscripts of kings and queens and chancellors hundreds of years old. Then they were on to Lincoln's Inn, where Melville melted at the sight of the "Sublime Kitchen — *chimney place*" — for heaven on earth was a sublime kitchen with a cosy inglenook where he could drink and smoke while preparation of foods went on in his sight. Among other sociable encounters, he dined again at the Erechtheum Club on Saturday the twenty-second in a party of eight: "Charles Knight the author of London Illustrated &c & the Publisher of the Penny Cyclopedia & concerned in most of the great popular publications of the day; — Ford the Spanish Traveller & Editor of the Guide Book — Leslie the painter — Cunningham the London Antiquarian & author of the London Guide published by Murray; — & Mr Murray the Albemarl Street man — together with Cooke & a youth whose name I forget. — We had a glorious time & parted at about midnight." The next morning, 23 December, he breakfasted again with Samuel Rogers, and "there met 'Barry Cornwall' otherwise Mr Procter; & his wife — and Mr Kinglake (author of Eothen?)." He passed a very pleasant morning, and left at quarter past one. Later that day Melville walked with Captain Fletcher on the Strand, deciding that he seemed "a very fine fellow," and later dined with H. G. Somerby of Newburyport, his "future fellow passenger" on the *Independence*. Christmas Eve, Bentley took him to the Reform Club, where he admired the superb hall of pillars and was thoroughly interested in the working arrangements of the whole establishment. With conflicting emotions, homesick but miserably aware of what he was forgoing, Melville boarded a train for the five hours' ride to Portsmouth, accompanied by Somerby (who left no known record of his encounter with the celebrity). At Portsmouth on Christmas Day Melville had a chance to see (but not to go aboard) Nelson's *Victory*. Months later he wrote Bentley that he had made "a prosperous passage across the water last winter; & embarking from Portsmouth on Christmas morning, carried the savor of the plumb-puddings & roast turkey all the way across the Atlantic." In London he had met people who could have been lifelong friends, in other circumstances, and he had been inside many a fine old building where he could happily have lived out his life.

33

The Breaching of Mocha Dick

January 1850

As I spoke, the fury of the animal seemed suddenly to die away. He paused in his career, and lay passive on the waves, with his arching back thrown up like the ridge of a mountain. "The old sog's lying to!" I cried, exultingly. "Spring, boys! spring *now*, and we have him! All my clothes, tobacco, every thing I 've got, shall be yours, only lay me 'longside that whale before another boat comes up! My *grimky!* what a hump! Only look at the irons in his back! No, do n't *look* — PULL ! Now, boys, if you care about seeing your sweethearts and wives in old Nantuck! — if you love Yankee-land — if you love *me* — pull ahead, *wont* ye?"

> J. N. Reynolds, "Mocha Dick: or, The White Whale of the Pacific,"
> *Knickerbocker Magazine*, May 1839

ONTO THE *Independence* MELVILLE CARRIED (along with the savor of English Christmas cooking) many choice books, and carried with him, too, irrepressible curiosity about what else he might have done had his tour not been truncated. On 29 December 1849, after five days of good sailing in which nothing seemed to be happening, Melville declared his journal closed. For a time he sorted and fondled his trove of books, making memoranda from Rousseau's *Confessions*, Boswell's *Johnson*, Sir Thomas Browne's *Vulgar Errors*, and the *Works* of Ben Jonson. Even during all the bustle of his travels, Melville had found some time to read. Notably, in the middle of December, in London, he absorbed Sterne's *Tristram Shandy* for the first time, then that "most wondrous book," De Quincey's *Confessions of an English Opium Eater.* Cannibals were on his mind, as always. In London, perhaps just before leaving for France, he noted "Cannibals/Execution/Terrapin," and in London or on the *Independence* he glanced at a marginal gloss in his new Browne on "Eating of Man's Flesh" (about the hounds tearing Actaeon's body), which he mistook as an "Allusion to *Cannibals.*" He also made this unexplained notation: "Indian (Gay-Head) Sweetheart flogged." In his short "Memoranda of things on the voyage" Melville included anecdotes from Captain Fletcher about a "pirate & the missionary," about smuggled grog, and about a catamount pursuing a "runaway sailor thro' the horrible woods of Perue along the sea-coast," leaping "from bough to bough" (this runaway "slept with his knife in his hand," a detail that "Recalled the 'Opium Eater' & 'crocodile' "). Having misjudged Captain Griswold at first, Melville made no such mistake with the congenial Captain Fletcher, whose anecdotes provided marginal glosses to the great book still reverberating in his mind.

On shipboard, Melville worked up his list of "Books obtained in London," which, besides copies of his own books from Bentley and books given him by Murray and Moxon, consisted of a remarkable array: folios of Ben Jonson, Davenant, Beaumont and Fletcher, and Sir Thomas Browne, copies of *Hudibras*, Lavater, Rousseau's *Confessions*, Walpole's *The Castle of Otranto*, "2 plays of Shakspeare," Mateo Alemán's *Guzman de Alfarache*, Chatterton, Godwin's *Caleb Williams*, Beckford's *Vathek*, Mme. de Staël's *Corinne*, Mary Shelley's *Frankenstein*, *Aristocracy of England* (probably William Howitt's), Marlowe's plays, the autobiography of Goethe and his *Letters from Italy*, and *Confessions of an Opium Eater*, besides books obtained in Paris (*Telemachus*, the *Anastasius* seized and then replaced in London, and *Views of Paris*) and in Germany (three books about the Rhine). He was careful to put down what he paid for the books, or to give his best guess if he had forgotten the exact price. He had learned the hard way by early 1848 that if he blithely charged books against his account with Wiley & Putnam or with the Harpers, he paid for them all at the next accounting. Some books, he had learned, should be borrowed. Now, he had indulged his love of fine old books with marvelous words inside, and also had assembled a working library of both standard and peculiar modern European and British books he knew he wanted to have at hand in New York. Some of these books would go on the shelves with his father's eight-in-four Spenser, his seven-volume set of Shakespeare, his two-volume Milton, and his not-yet-plundered treasure, the seven or eight-volume *Modern British Essayists*. He would never write another book like *Redburn*, where the primary literary influence was an American—Washington Irving.

Yet Irving was on his mind, for self-consciously, as he approached and walked through Temple Bar, Melville had retraced Irving's steps in a memorable section of *The Sketch Book*, "London Antiques." In reading De Quincey, especially, he had recognized his own affinities with a modern writer of greater power than the charming literary man he had, at times, too much modeled his own style on. In London, Melville had seen in the "Powell Papers" Allan had sent him the consequences of Thomas Powell's daring to speak truthfully, although disrespectfully, about Irving's habit of appropriating other people's work. On the *Independence* he had time to brood over those newspapers, whether he still had them with him or whether he was reflecting on his memory of what they said and his memory of what Henry Stevens and others had said to him about Powell.

There was much for him to sort out, still, despite his session with the "Powell Papers" at the Edinburgh Castle. From the newspapers Allan had sent, he knew that in November 1849, a month after his departure on the *Southampton*, and simultaneous with the American reviewing of *Redburn*, scandals had erupted over two parts of Powell's hastily written *Living Authors of England*, the book Appleton had unwarily taken over after Putnam shrewdly had disentangled himself from it. George Ripley in the *Tribune* (16 November) had denounced the passage in *Living Authors of England* where Powell called Washington Irving "an agreeable essayist, and a very successful imitator of the level style of Addison and Pope." Powell had gone on to describe Irving's new life of Goldsmith as "so glaring an instance of unscrupulous appropriation of the labor of another, that it is utterly impossible to avoid arraigning the offender." This was "outrageous calumny," Ripley declared. To speak disparagingly of Irving's habitual blithe commandeering of the work of lesser writers was simply not permitted in the United States.

Other reviewers and editors were still joining in the denunciation of Powell as a traducer of Irving when a separate and more dramatic controversy ensued as a consequence of the first, this time involving Charles Dickens. Innocently, Bryant in the New York *Evening Post* of 6 September had printed, before publication, part of Powell's chapter on Charles Dickens from *Living Authors of England*, omitting, without comment, the fulsome comparisons of Cornelius Mathews to Dickens. Someone sent a copy of the paper across the Atlantic to the famous address on Devonshire Terrace. Spared the comparisons of him to Mathews, Dickens nevertheless was outraged at the publication of this unauthorized "life" of him, and fired off to his acquaintance Lewis Gaylord Clark, still the editor of the *Knickerbocker*, a letter exposing Powell. Clark, coincidentally the inveterate enemy of the Duyckinck-Mathews clique, knew that Powell had exalted Mathews to equal stature with Dickens (but probably did not know that Dickens had *not* seen that part of the chapter). The letter from the great novelist came too late for Clark to get it into the December issue of the *Knickerbocker*, and by the January 1850 issue the information in it would have lost some explosive power. Scorning delay, Clark marched over to the *Tribune* offices with Dickens's letter.

Greeley and his partner McElrath gleefully printed Dickens's letter about Powell on 20 November under the heading "A Scoundrel Branded":

> He is a Forger and a Thief. He was managing-clerk to an eminent merchant's house in the city of London, and during a series of years forged and altered

checks until he had defrauded them to the extent of thousands upon thousands of pounds. His robberies being discovered one day, he took up his hat, went to a chemist's, bought some laudanum, walked off to a warm bath, and was found in it insensible. . . . After some months' endurance of the misery and shame of his position, he was taken up at Croydon (ten miles from London,) for passing several forged checks to divers trades people in that neighborhood; was stated to the magistrate to be mad; and was actually confined for some time in a lunatic asylum, that the prosecutions against him might not go on. From the lunatic asylum he found his way to New-York.

In the glare of nationwide publicity, Powell had brazened the situation out. He even had one or two editors arrested for reprinting the Dickens letter, while numerous enemies of Duyckinck and Mathews seized the opportunity to lambast them as the "Mutual Admiration Society," for American editors, unlike Dickens himself, knew the full Dickens chapter where Powell had compared Dickens and Mathews at length, and not to Dickens's favor.

James Gordon Bennett of the lurid New York *Herald* in late November had plied Powell with food and drink, if not a few coins, and in ample return Powell had spun him an elaborate set of lies which Bennett spread out in the *Herald* of 26 November 1849 under a two-line head: "FRIGHTFUL ROW AMONG THE LITERATI — A SPLENDID PROSPECT FOR BLACKWELL'S ISLAND" — Blackwell's Island being the site of the prison in the East River. According to this article, Powell's lamentable experiences in England all resulted from his innocent participation in a railway bubble which had burst as calamitously as that notorious speculative scheme, the South Sea bubble. Misspelling Clark's name, the *Herald* rejoiced in Powell's "criminal prosecution against Mr. Clarke, and all parties concerned in this city," including Greeley and Hiram Fuller, who had become the new Whig Naval Storekeeper (a plum appointment) while remaining the editor of the *Evening Mirror*. The *Herald* containing this farrago was among the newspapers which Allan had bundled up and sent to London, and which Melville read, in London if not also on the voyage home.

For Melville there was no shutting his eyes: it was as if all hell had broken loose in the literary cliques of Manhattan soon after he left. An ocean away when the controversies began, he was affected by it in London, then on the way home. The whole affair, including the warnings he had received in England, colored his natural eagerness to see all his New York literary friends. Such journalistic scandals seemed all the more petty on that "certain day in January" (after which Melville might any day have driven up to a cordial welcome at Belvoir Castle). That day can hardly have passed on shipboard without giving Melville a twinge for his renunciation of a chance of a lifetime, and by contrast it emphasized the insignificance of the literary circles he was sailing toward. What he knew from the "Powell Papers" confirmed him in a determination to distance himself from the Manhattan literary cliques and feuds, as he had been doing since late in 1848. He could lock himself up and work, as he had done the previous summer.

At sea, at the end of 1849 and the beginning of 1850, his journal closed, and apparently not intruded upon by his fifty fellow passengers, none of whom left a known record of the voyage, Melville faced up to his obligation: he had to prepare to write another book, as soon as possible. He had not written a word for publication since September, except for brief passages he added to the proofs of *White-Jacket* on the voyage out or after his arrival in England. His trip had been justified not only as a means of selling *White-Jacket* to best advantage and then, if he succeeded, of making a grand tour that he might work up into at least one book. On a humbler level a purpose of the trip had been to gather experiences and observations for the story of Israel Potter. He had bought an old map of London on 18 December, noting: "I want to use it in case I serve up the Revolutionary narrative of the beggar." The phrase "serve up" suggests that the book was to be written as *Redburn* had been, in the literary equivalent of chopping wood. A few months earlier, Melville had talked to Powell of writing a work on remorse, and in at least an inchoate fashion he may have envisioned any number of possible subjects for books, for, at the end of 1850, he professed to have so many ideas for books that he facetiously requested "fifty fast-writing youths" to help him get them down. If he had been able to conduct a sweeping (and commendably economical) tour to the Mediterranean, keeping his journal all the way, he might have written one or more books based on his new travels. If he had bought passage home in a steamer and arrived in New York late in the first week of January 1850, he might have spent the short voyage reflecting mainly on his recent experiences and on how he might serve up the story of Israel Potter.

Instead of a fast trip, the voyage home on the *Independence* was inordinately drawn out, even for a sailing ship, so Melville had time to conclude that he wanted to put off work on the Potter book. Assessing his English and Continental experiences, he decided that, however useful those experiences might prove in the future, they could not form the basis of a book the way periods of comparable length in his life had gone into *Omoo* and *Redburn*. He had been successful in gaining an advance on *White-Jacket*, in the teeth of the copyright ruling, but he had learned just how hard selling his next book in England might be. His own reiteration of "No go" was hard to forget. He had no option: he needed to settle before he got home upon a new subject worthy of a pondering man like him. Full of his latest enthusiasms for *Tristram Shandy* and *Confessions of an English Opium Eater*, laden with precious

books, old and new, in the weeks on the ocean Melville confirmed the growth
in acuity or profundity which he had been watching in himself, over the past
year, when his head had been abuzz with Shakespeare and Milton and
Browne, and now was newly teeming with passages in Sterne, De Quincey,
and other writers, contemporary and older.

Furthermore, the writing of two autobiographical books under such intense pressure the previous summer was ready now, after the lapse of a few
months, to wreak its consequences. Melville had been naive not to know how
dangerous it was for any thoughtful man to write about the early loss of his
beloved father and the loss of a fine home and education in fine schools.
Easily written, *Redburn* was now exacting its psychic price in forcing Melville
to confront soberly what he had seized upon merely as handy materials for a
quickly written narrative. Finally, experiences on the voyage out (talking
metaphysics, plotting forays on Constantinople, Cairo, Rome) and in England and the Continent had flooded in upon him, bearing him up hopefully
at times, dropping him into miserable disappointment at others, but educat-
ing him, all the while. Beachcombing in Eimeo and Lahaina had not made
him a man of the world, nor, even, had the writing of *Mardi*. Now, especially
now that he had bought a more respectable coat than the green one, Lord
Chesterfield himself would have acknowledged him as a man of the world, a
cosmopolitan. He had been undergoing, by the time of this voyage and
return, an accelerated unfolding within himself which he could now begin to
take stock of. The prolonged Atlantic voyage of five and a half weeks gave
Melville the time he needed to reflect on the book that he would begin as
soon as he greeted his family and friends and settled into a late winter's work.
He was ready to use the part of his Atlantic Ocean and South Sea experiences
he had so far shied away from — whaling. He had been so good a husband,
living cheaply, selling *White-Jacket* against all odds, renouncing his tour, that
he deserved to take the financial risk of writing a book he wanted to write, not
merely an anatomy of the whale fishery (one comparable to the book he
underestimated as a mere anatomy of life on a man-of-war), but a book as
comprehensively informative as *White-Jacket* yet also as ambitiously literary
as *Mardi*. If he had felt free to spend that extra hundred dollars on a steamer,
if he had reached home so promptly, Melville might never have written
Moby-Dick.

At sea Melville could brood about his story without any whaling sources
in hand, since to some extent the book that took shape on the voyage home
was autobiographical. As a whaleman Melville had participated in one of the
most extraordinary physical experiences then available: he had helped hunt
whales, had lost whales, had caught whales, cut whales up and tried them out,
cleaned up the bloody and greasy decks (which he had seen heaped with parts

of whale heads and other recently living debris), he had stowed away the signs of trying out, had met and gammed with other ships in the remotest of waters, had known men lost to death and desertion and had himself deserted. As a whaleman he had also participated in one of the most remarkable literary phenomena of his time, the frontier-training of untutored writers, in which ordinary Americans (men, usually, although Caroline Kirkland did something of the sort) confronted natural horrors and wonders, far from home, and came back, when they were lucky, to tell tall tales about their experiences, to tell truthful tales so extraordinary that stay-at-home people might take them as false. Melville was to tell Richard Bentley that he had based the narrative in his next book upon certain wild legends of the whale fishery, but he could as well have based it on tales that his own careful inquiries had established as true stories, however wild. Some such stories, to be sure, were passing into legendary status, among them a number of stories of hunting great white whales in the Pacific. Simply by being months at a time on a whaleship Melville had heard (along with sailor songs, jokes, proverbs, and miscellaneous tall tales) a range of whaling stories from the other members of the crew, some stories surely more than once, and — starved for news — avidly heard fresh stories or fresh versions of old stories from crews of other whaling ships encountered in the open waters or ports of the Pacific.

One story current throughout the whaling fleet in the Pacific when Melville arrived there was the horrific tale of the Martha's Vineyard whaler the *Globe*, which in 1824 had picked up several new hands in Hawaii then cruised in the Line Islands, far to the south. A Rhode Island man, Samuel Comstock, plotted with three new hands to take over the ship. Comstock sneaked below while the captain was sleeping and nearly severed his head with an axe. He killed the first mate in a similar way, then shot the third mate before stabbing the second mate several times with a bayonet, then finished off the third mate. The conspirators threw all four bodies overboard, but the second mate, still alive, managed to cling to the edge of the deck, where Comstock stomped on his hands until he fell. After more murder and threat of murder, the ship sailed west through the Kingsmill group, and finally to the Mili Atoll, in the Marshall Islands, where at last one of the mutineers killed Comstock. Six men, including George Comstock, Samuel's brother, cut the cable of the *Globe* secretly and, abandoning the other mutineers, sailed toward Chile, some seventy-five hundred miles away, and months later reached Valparaiso. Some of the mutineers left on Mili Atoll were so brutal to the natives that they rose up and killed all but two young men, William Lay and Cyrus M. Hussey, who probably had taken no part in the mutiny. When the owners at last heard some details of the catastrophe by way of the fleet in Valparaiso, the secretary of the navy ordered Commodore Isaac Hull to take his flagship *United States* to hunt the surviving mutineers. Instead, Hull sent Captain John Percival on the *Dolphin*. Late in 1825 Percival took Lay and Hussey alive in a real-life rescue not unlike the fictional ending of *Typee*, and (as Melville knew when he prepared the "Extracts" to *Moby-Dick*) in sincere gratitude Lay and Hussey dedicated their 1828 *Narrative* of the *Globe* mutiny to this man, "Who, under the auspices of Government, visited the Mulgrave Islands, to release the survivors of the Ship *Globe*'s crew, and extended to them every attention their unhappy situation required." The story of the *Globe* was familiar to all Pacific whalemen, but for Melville it now had special significance from Percival's intimacy with the Shaws and from (most likely) his own acquaintance with "Mad Jack."

Melville could combine his previous reading with his own memories of whaling scenes and with oral tales he remembered, all without source books at hand. Before he went whaling — even before he went to sea on a merchant ship — he had read and heard many facts and stories about the whale fishery, mainly from newspaper and magazine items devoted to what in those pre-kerosene years was a major segment of the national economy as well as a regular source of newsworthy events. Melville's reading of his whaling sources for *Moby-Dick* may have dated from as early as 1839. On 27 May 1839 the Albany *Argus* had printed "Method of Taking the Whale" from the British surgeon Thomas Beale's *The Natural History of the Sperm Whale to Which Is Added a Sketch of a South-Sea Whaling Voyage in Which the Author Was Personally Engaged* (London: Van Voorst, 1839), an excerpt that included the powerful passage about the death flurry of the immense creature, mad with his agonies. If Melville somehow missed that sample of Beale, he had another chance to read it when the West Troy *Advocate* devoted two columns to it on 23 October 1839 (only a few months after it had reprinted one of his own "Fragments").

Just before Melville had sailed to Liverpool, the May 1839 issue of the new popular New York magazine, the *Knickerbocker* (edited by both Lewis Gaylord Clark and his twin, who died a little later, Willis Gaylord Clark) had published J. N. Reynolds's "Mocha Dick: or, The White Whale of the Pacific: A Leaf from a Manuscript Journal," an account that many readers found enthralling — and memorable, for people alluded to it in print over the following years. Reynolds told the somber story of an obsessive hunt in a classic "frame story" situation, where the man who had killed Mocha Dick, a first mate, some time after the event, recounted the tale to a group that included the man who wrote it down for publication — an oceanic equivalent of the technique T. B. Thorpe used a few years later in the quintessential *Spirit of the Times* story of a comic-mythic hunt, "The Big Bear of Arkansas." Mocha Dick was a great white whale, known by name to his hunters: "This renowned monster, who had come off victorious in a hundred fights with his pursuers, was an old bull whale, of prodigious size and strength. From the effect of age, or more probably from a freak of nature, as exhibited in the case of the Ethiopian Albino, a singular consequence had resulted — *he was white as wool!*" He had crushed many boats, and once "came off victorious from a conflict with the crews of three English whalers" at once. His back was "serried with irons," and "from fifty to a hundred yards of line trailing in his wake, sufficiently attested, that though unconquered, he had not proved invulnerable." His celebrity was such that when whaleships met in the broad Pacific the whale's name "seemed naturally to mingle with the salutations": "the customary interrogatories almost always closing with, 'Any news from Mocha Dick?' " The whale evinced great intelligence combined with a fore-bearing disposition: his "malicious disposition" or "lurking deviltry" was evinced only after attacks upon him. Before he is at last killed, a young harpooneer, having "imbibed a sort of superstitious dread of Mocha Dick," thinks of the whale as "some ferocious fiend of the deep," rather than a "regular-built" whale: "Judge then of his trepidation, on beholding a crea-ture, answering the wildest dreams of his fancy, and sufficiently formidable, without any superadded terrors, bearing down upon him with thrashing flukes and distended jaws!" This harpooneer wavers, and misses his chance. Later on that occasion the first mate kills Mocha Dick. A reviewer of *Moby-Dick* was to recall that every "old 'Jack-tar' " knew the story of Mocha Dick in one form or another, and in 1839 through 1843 the young jack-tar Herman Melville had found good chances to know it, or part of it, from print or from sailors' yarns, and perhaps even then had chances to retell it.

Merely from Reynolds, Melville could plan a book about the pursuit of a great white whale famous in the fishery by the name of Mocha Dick, or some similar name. But Melville also had been deeply stirred by reading Owen Chase's account of the wreck of the *Essex* in the Pacific, in that copy loaned him by one of Chase's sons. Chase's narrative offered Melville, ready made, a stupendous catastrophe. Reynolds vividly described the death of Mocha Dick, but Melville's white whale, rather than being killed, could sink a ship deliberately and revengefully, and then swim triumphantly away.

A little more than five years earlier, looking at Langsdorff and other possible sources ready for the plundering, Melville had decided that *Typee* was a book he could write. Now, remembering his reading of Reynolds, and recalling even more vividly his reading and reviewing of J. Ross Browne's *Etchings of a Whaling Cruise* early in 1847, Melville knew he could write the story of the white whale. He had J. Ross Browne and other source books in his workroom at home. He could get hold of Thomas Beale's book and any other scientific books of whaling he learned of. He would have, to start with, some marvelous writing to imitate or to spark his own ideas. From printed sources already available to him, once he reached home, he knew he would lay hand on many set scenes, de rigueur in whaling books. If he wanted, he could borrow from Browne a description of the chicanery by which lands-men lured green youths to sign on a whaling voyage. Once the ship was launched, Melville could find vivid descriptions of captains, mates, harpoon-eers, and other members of a crew, such as Reynolds's introduction of the first mate who killed the white whale: "He had probably numbered about thirty-five years. We arrived at this conclusion, however, rather from the untamed brightness of his flashing eye, than the general appearance of his features, on which torrid sun and polar storm had left at once the furrows of more advanced age, and a tint swarthy as that of the Indian." He could find any number of vivid descriptions of rowing after whales, like this in "Mocha Dick," in these reported words of the mate: " 'There he blows! An old bull, by Jupiter! Eighty barrels, boys, waiting to be towed alongside! Long and quick — shoot ahead! Now she feels it; waist-boat never could beat us; now she feels the touch! — now she walks through it! Again — *now!*' Such were the broken exclamations and adjurations with which I cheered my rowers to their toil, as, with renewed vigor, I plied my long steering-oar." (In his *Literary World* review, Melville had quoted a dramatic passage from Browne on the chase.)

Any whaling story would have to describe the successive encounters with other whaling ships, and from "Mocha Dick" Melville had a model of what his ship could call to another: "Any news from Mocha Dick?" Once he had that question (improved to "Hast seen the white whale?"), he had a plot — a pursuit of a particular whale, by a single-minded captain whom he could make as melodramatic or tragic as he chose. All whaling books would give him accounts of how whalemen died horrible deaths or were saved from death at considerable cost to the profits of the owners. A shipmate of Mel-ville's on the *Acushnet*, Henry F. Hubbard, later identified Pip, the black cabin-boy in *Moby-Dick*, with Backus, an actual crew member on the *Acush-net*, and saw Pip's jumping overboard as a recollection of Backus's panicky leap from a whaleboat headed by the real second mate, John Hall. Still, the decision to cut a line — thereby saving the life of a seaman but losing a whale — was one many whalemen faced, and forms a dramatic moment in "Mocha Dick" ("we must not see them drown, boys, . . . cut the line!"). In Beale and elsewhere Melville had seen powerful depictions of whale killing, and in particular of the final death flurry. Any whaling story would have to depict the try-works fully fired, and preferably at night, when they looked most hellish. Browne's book, which compared the scene to Dante's descrip-tion of the inferno, was ready for improving, but he would do his own try-works scene all the better if he looked at Browne again before writing it. Melville could have planned and later written many of such set scenes wholly from memory of his own experiences or from tales he had been told, but always he felt more comfortable letting himself be reminded and inspired by other men's accounts of experiences similar to his own.

Melville's reading, in his frigate's library in 1843 and 1844, and in libraries ashore, had exposed him to more whaling information, and during his work on his first three books he acquired or became familiar with several of the works which were to become his source books for his whaling story. Around the first of February 1847 he had gotten his copy of J. Ross Browne's *Etchings of a Whaling Cruise* in order to review it for the *Literary World*. During the early stages of his work on *Mardi* he had bought a copy of Frederick Debell Bennett's *Narrative of a Whaling Voyage round the Globe*. By 28 April 1849, Melville knew at least one of William Scoresby Jr.'s works on the North Atlantic fishery, the *Journal of a Voyage to the Northern Whale Fishery*, the source for the "level lodestone" passage in "The Needle" (ch. 124); he made offhand mention of it in his review for Duyckinck's *Literary World* (28 April 1849) of Cooper's *The Sea Lions*. In that review he also referred knowledgeably to the "appalling adventures" in the Antarctic related in Charles Wilkes's *United States Exploring Expedition*. Having already used a copy of Wilkes for *Omoo*, Melville had purchased his own copy in April 1847 for work on *Mardi*, so he had it available for use in *Moby-Dick*. As he planned the book, he did not necessarily have in mind particular uses for these books, but their being in his library was comforting.

For information about whaling as an industry, facts necessary as ballast for the book, Melville could search in a number of accounts published in the previous decades. As for relaying such information to the reader, Melville could describe the whaling processes in order, from killing the whale through pulling it alongside, cutting it up, trying it out, and on to stowing down and cleaning up. If he paced the information a little at a time, as he proceeded with his story of the whaling voyage, the reader would never have to be told in detail about the try-works, say, more than once, and he would be free to expatiate from time to time on any of the whaling processes in one or more of his little essayistic chapters that he had perfected in *White-Jacket*. The book would have to contain fictional or highly fictionalized characters, but Melville may have postponed any elaborate planning of the more dramatic or even tragic of his personae (for the catastrophe of the *Essex* would not befit anything less than tragic).

The writer of five books, he knew that even he could not predict what usable tidbit had lodged in his memory already or would catch his eye during the composition. Somewhere, sometime, he may have seen this passage from William Cobbett's *Life and Adventures of Peter Porcupine:* "From the top of Portsdown, I, for the first time, beheld the sea, and no sooner did I behold it than I wished to be a sailor. I could never account for this sudden impulse, nor can I now. Almost all English boys feel the same inclination: it would seem that, like young ducks, instinct leads them to rush on the bosom of the water." Was this in his mind as he wrote "Loomings," chapter 1 of *Moby-Dick* ("If they but knew it, almost all men in their degree, some time or other, cherish very nearly the same feelings towards the ocean with me")? Some books "that prove most agreeable, grateful, and companionable," Melville had said in *White-Jacket* (ch. 41), seem that way because they are picked up "by chance here and there"; "those which seem put into our hands by Providence; those which pretend to little, but abound in much." Melville could trust in his extraordinary ability to turn to good use books not generally recommended as essential reading, and to turn to good use in a proposed whaling narrative books on quite other subjects.

The books that meant most to Melville as he planned his whaling book on shipboard (far more of which were in his mind rather than in a sea chest in the *Independence*) were primarily the sort of old books that he had surprised Duyckinck by borrowing, then had commented on with acuity unexpected in a sailor. These included the Bible and classics of English literature, along with some European classics, in translation. Melville imposed his habitual way of weighing books even upon the classics, for he tended to take hold of them providentially, as when he discovered a large-print edition of Shakespeare just when he was both intellectually ready to grapple with the plays and just when he had many days in Boston with not much else to do besides look in on his wife and newborn son, and read. It had been because he found the text of Shakespeare suddenly visible to his weak eyes as well as congenial to his new psychological burgeoning that he immediately sought out an edition of Milton in the same format, and soon he was rereading *Paradise Lost.*

For Melville it is risky to attempt to systematize the routine and sometimes idiosyncratic uses he made of his literary sources. Yet some influences indisputably made their presence obvious in parts of *Moby-Dick* during the next year and a half. The book was pervasively influenced by the Bible (in particular the Book of Job, which provided an analogue for Ahab's quarrel with God, and the Book of Jonah, which provided an analogue for Ishmael's less defiant method of coming to terms with the universe); by Shakespeare's plays (where King Lear and other tragic heroes provided models for Ahab); by Milton's *Paradise Lost* (from which Melville took some of Ahab's qualities as Satanic opponent); by Marlowe's *Doctor Faustus* and Goethe's *Faust* (where he found analogues of demonic temptation and heroic obsession); by Robert Burton, whose *Anatomy of Melancholy* served as his sonorous textbook on morbid psychology; by Sir Thomas Browne, that "crack'd Archangel" (for seductive and filchable prose rhythms that Browne had put to the service of a dumbfoundingly self-possessed idiosyncrasy); by the book he had to buy in two editions in order to bring home one of them, Thomas Hope's *Anastasius; or, Memoirs of a Greek* (where he found hints for his character Ishmael's twists of mind and actions, not least a ceremonial marriage between men); by Lord Byron, the hero of his brooding adolescence (for the character of Bulkington, so important in his initial concept of his whaling book); by Mary Shelley's *Frankenstein* (for a prolonged revenge pursuit); by Dante (for an anatomy of human sinfulness); by Pierre Bayle's dictionary and Montaigne's essays (for their worldly-wise skepticism, which braced him against the superficial pieties demanded by his time); by Coleridge's lecture on *Hamlet* (for the crucial definition of the Shakespearean hero that he worked, at a late stage, into "The Ship," ch. 16); by Carlyle, especially *Sartor Resartus* but also *Heroes and Hero-Worship* (for a sardonic verbal playfulness and a depiction of the physical universe as emblematical, but also for the depiction of Cromwell, which gave him hints for his tyrannical captain); by Laurence Sterne's *Tristram Shandy* (for its liberating gamesomeness toward the lofty task of book-making); by De Quincey's *Confessions* (for the Malay whose Asiatic associations were infused into Fedallah and his boat's crew, and for the apparently inimitable prose style which to Melville was as natural as his own voice).

Such a list, even cursorily annotated, has at least the virtue of emphasizing what should be kept most obvious — that in Melville's resolve "to give the world a book, which the world should hail with surprise and delight" (words already ironic when he wrote them for *Pierre* two years later), that wondrous book would itself be the original product of the assimilation of many other books. In *Pierre* (starting a new subplot after the manuscript had been completed) he defined the nature of his hero's adventures with books: "A varied scope of reading, little suspected by his friends, and randomly acquired by a random but lynx-eyed mind, in the course of the multifarious, incidental, bibliographic encounterings of almost any civilized young inquirer after Truth; this poured one considerable contributary stream into that bottomless spring of original thought which the occasion and time had caused to burst out in himself" (bk. 21, ch. 1). However arch this description, it defined his own early career as a reader of books against the memory of Gansevoort's public display of industrious, systematic reading (Irving or Scott or Brandt in one hand, Todd's *Index Rerum* in the other).

The river of Melville's reading had long flowed into his conscious mind (indeed, it had overflowed there in the more bookish parts of *Mardi*). Now his profounder reading not only flowed on the surface but was partly diverted into a subterranean river that flowed into the spring of original thought, a spring ready to burst out, under the pressure of the occasion and the time, into *Moby-Dick*, once the interminable voyage was over.

34

Hiding Out on the Cannibal Island

February–June 1850

Critics? — Asses! rather mules! — so emasculated, from vanity, they can not father a true thought. Like mules, too, from dunghills, they trample down gardens of roses: and deem that crushed fragrance their own. . . . Oh! that an eagle should be stabbed by a goose-quill! But at best, the greatest reviewers but prey on my leavings.

> Babbalanja, quoting Lombardo on a conclave of professional critics,
> *Mardi*, ch. 180

IN THE LAST DAYS OF JANUARY 1850 the whole family, except for Tom, was home at 103 Fourth Avenue, Sam Shaw having escorted Lizzie and Malcolm down from Boston in anticipation of her husband's arrival. The growing babies were about to have their first birthdays, Malcolm on 16 February and little Maria two days later. Sophia was two months pregnant. When Melville disembarked from the *Independence* on 31 January the reunion must have recalled to the Melvilles the noisy reunions of the 1820s. Herman needed to hold his wife and son, give everyone the gifts he had brought, and tell them, unsystematically, about his experiences, unless he had worked up a few stories for proper telling. Promptly enough he gave the gifts, a few of which are recorded. In Cologne he had bought mementos, including "a little medal (not silver)" for Lem. He sent to Hope Shaw an old-fashioned wooden bread trencher and bread knife he had bought in London for her to use on ceremonial occasions, such as Thanksgiving. (For him, the trencher was a powerful symbol of student life at Oxford or Cambridge in centuries gone by.) Precious trophies were the Bentley volumes of his *Mardi* and *Redburn*, which he gave away rather than hoarding for his own shelves. A set of the three-volume English *Mardi* went to Allan, the dedicatee.

Melville had been thoughtful of his friends as well as his family. A gift for Duyckinck, similarly redolent of England, was the "fine old spicy duodecimo mouthful in the shape of 'Hudibras,'" containing the signature of a former owner whom Melville in inscribing the book envisioned as "Mr Miles the old

Englishman, in silk small clothes." He accompanied the book, which he delivered the day after he reached home, with an evocative commentary not only on the man who had owned it eighty-five years before but also on the publisher, "John Baker, at the Black-Boy in Pater-Noster-Row": "Did the late Mr Baker have a small *live* Nubian standing at his shop door, like the moccasined Indian of our Bowery tobacconists? . . . I perceive no possible affinity to books — unless, by the way, Mr Baker dealt altogether in black-letter, — Thomas the Rhymer, Lydgate, & Battle Abbey Directories. — Are they not delicious, & full flavored with suggestiveness, these old fashioned London imprints?" Denied a university education, Melville had been granted weeks in which to absorb the suggestive odors of bookstalls, bookstores, and the great library of the British Museum, and the trencher and the *Hudibras* were full of significances for him. He presented a set of the two-volume English *Redburn* to Dr. Augustus Gardner, who had recommended that he take lodgings with Madame Capelle in Paris.

Melville had destined a set of the three-volume *Mardi* for Duyckinck, since the great library at Clinton Place was "a choice conservatory of exotics & other rare things in literature," where the three volumes would survive into future generations, at which time *Mardi* might "flower like the aloe, a hundred years hence — or not flower at all." *Mardi* was an Ishmael of a book, or, in contemporary terms, an adherent to that new religion divinely revealed in upstate New York: "Again: (as the divines say) political republics should be the asylum for the persecuted of all nations; so, if Mardi be admitted to your shelves, your bibliographical Republic of Letters may find some contentment in the thought, that it has afforded refuge to a work, which almost everywhere else has been driven forth like a wild, mystic Mormon into shelterless exile." Aside from a self-mocking comment during the Civil War, this stands as his last recorded look backward at the only one of his first five bibliographic children which he deeply cherished. After months of being confident that the "riddle" of *Mardi* would be solved in his time, Melville was ready to consign *Mardi* to the sanctuary of Duyckinck's great library. He was through looking for someone to solve the riddle of *Mardi*, for he was, once again, going to try to write a great book.

In his journal Melville had recorded, over and over again, his anticipation of reunion with Lizzie and "Barney." Now, friends as well as family clamored for their undue share of his attention. Even Allan, in the midst of his brotherly welcome, wanted to talk business. He had shown Herman his "bushell" of newspapers about Gansevoort in 1844; now he had a pile of papers containing American reviews of *Redburn*, as well as other papers, most likely, such as "Powell Papers" he had not sent to England. The reviews could wait, and the worn-out scandals of November could wait, but now Herman had to confront the very latest Manhattan maliciousness sprung from the buzzing brain of Thomas Powell — new slander.

After the international furor in November and December, Duyckinck and his brother had distanced themselves further and further from Powell despite the crook's continuing flow of begging letters. For all their earnest morality and their profound loyalty to Washington Irving, neither of the Duyckincks could bring himself to break openly with Powell, for their appetite for intimate details about English writers still could overcome their scruples. Just before Melville returned, the brothers were still reveling in each new installment of *David Copperfield*, awed by their certainty that they were personally acquainted with the original of one of Dickens's characters. George wrote to his East Hampton friend, Joann Miller, on 28 January 1850: "Mr Micawber in Copperfield is I think there is no doubt taken from Powell. His tight shirt collar and eye glass and the description of his person are verbatim and the character and conversation of the two are almost identical except that Powell was always telling capital stories. I never saw a man who had such a fund. He made them answer as a fund in a double sense for I believe every one who heard them suffered in pocket to their full value." Almost any malefaction could be glossed over so that they could continue to be titillated by direct contact, practically, with the most exalted members of the London literati. They had even been able to interpret as praise what Powell had said of their cherished Centurion Cornelius in *Living Authors of England*, although more objective people would have seen at once that Powell had set Mathews up for ridicule by so elaborately comparing the self-denominated "American Dickens" to the real one.

Rebuffed by Duyckinck, however politely, Powell had taken his first revenge on the Duyckinck circle in the hastily written and hastily printed *Living Authors of America*, published by Stringer & Townsend in January, while Melville was on the Atlantic. There in the chapter on poor Edgar Allan Poe (dead in Baltimore as Melville was packing for his trip) Powell had identified Melville and Irving as "the worst enemies of the national mind":

> It is a curious fact that the worst enemies of the national mind have been a few of her own sons. These are authors who till lately have entirely enjoyed the monopoly of the English market; now they will be obliged to join the body of native authors, and hurry to the rescue. So long as they could trespass on the mistaken courtesy of the British publishers, and get four thousand guineas for this Life of Columbus, and two hundred guineas for that Typee, there was no occasion for any interference; in fact, they were materially benefited by this

crying injustice to the great body of authors. Now their own rights are in
jeopardy, and they must join the ranks of International Copyright.

The Duyckincks might have forgiven this slur against Melville and even
against Irving, but Powell had gone even further, as George Duyckinck
wrote Joann Miller on 28 January 1850: "After over puffing Mr Mathews in
the other book he abuses him in this, and has also an insulting insinuation
against the 'Adelphi of a literary Journal' to use his phrase"—meaning the
Literary World. The slurs had come home to Clinton Place. George assured
his friend, "All Dickens['] charges are I hear substantiated by other witnesses
in London, who have written out here."

Once Melville was home, Allan or Evert Duyckinck promptly saw to it
that he looked through *Living Authors of America* long enough to see with his
own eyes the calumnious way the English scoundrel had linked his name
with that of the great Irving. Also awaiting Melville on his return was Evert
Duyckinck's review of *Living Authors of America* in his "Adelphi of a literary
Journal" for 2 February 1850. Under the heading "Enemies of the National
Mind (A dead lift for the copyright question)" Duyckinck had quoted and
had attempted to laugh off Powell's attack on Irving and Melville. Unable to
correct Powell's lie about what he had earned from *Typee,* Melville took no
pleasure in looking through Powell's new book, but he held it long enough to
read this theory of literary influence in the Longfellow chapter, based on a
reading of *Groatsworth of Wit:* "Imitation has been charged on all poets, and
we know that the indignation of Robert Green was so soured by the appro-
priations of Shakspeare, that he denounced him 'as a jay strutting about in
our feathers, and fancying himself as the only *Shakscene* of the country.' This
charge is always more or less true of a young author, and it is in the very
nature of things." Every poet, Powell had concluded, "commences with
more or less of some predominant mind, the most assimilant to his own."
This passage struck Melville so strongly that it worked its way into his
ambitious broodings in the next months, then burst out in an essay he wrote
on Hawthorne that summer.

Almost before Allan and Duyckinck could tell Melville about the other
recent additions to the "Powell Papers," the *Herald* of 6 February maliciously
welcomed Melville home with a very long article headed "Fruits of Literary
Appropriation," unsigned, but by Powell. The title referred to the vast sums
he declared that Irving had received from his British publishers for works
which he had cynically plagiarized from genuine scholars whose work he
scarcely acknowledged. Cooper also, although no plagiarist, had "received
immense sums" from his British publishers. The roll call went on: "Prescott,
Bancroft, and other distinguished American writers, have been richly remu-

nerated by the London houses which have brought out their books. Even the flippant, kaleidescope, polka-dancing Melville has been enabled to line his pockets pretty substantially by the revenues accruing from his English editions." "Hitherto," these few "American writers have been almost as generously rewarded, by the publishers of London, for the works they have brought out, as they would have been if their books had been covered by the shield of a copyright."

Powell was no longer concerned with the unfairness of it all — a few writers like Irving and Melville taking advantage of an interpretation of the copyright law so as to profit abroad while most American writers earned little or nothing! Instead, he gloated that Irving, Melville, and the elite handful would profiteer no more from this unjust condition, that "the golden streams which were flowing from the great London houses into the pockets of our popular American authors" suddenly had been checked, just in time to thwart one author:

> Mr. Melville started, we are told, some time ago, for England, with the early proof sheets of his last book, intending, on the avails of it, to make the fashionable tour over the continent, and luxuriate in the capitals of Europe, upon the fruit of his labors. The revulsion came on. He was coolly informed, by his former London publisher, that he could pay no more copyrights; and the aforesaid intellect quits the great metropolis in despair, with empty pockets, and turns his face once more towards his native land.

Powell rejoiced that English publishers had discovered the folly of paying out large sums to American writers when they could "legally publish any American book in their market, without paying one copper to the writer." American publishers, growing rich by pirating the British books, had "opposed most strenuously the passage of an international copyright law," and now "the same joke" was being played on American writers by British publishers.

In a great stroke of scoundrelism, the beneficently patriotic Powell, writing anonymously, quoted his own calumny from *Living Authors of America*, discreetly omitting the name of the author of that admirable work:

> It is neither to be disguised nor palliated, that the effect of these piracies on the part of our publishers, has been, and will continue to be, injurious to the morals, the principles and national spirit of the country. By flooding this nation with the myriad works which bear the name of popular foreign authors, every man of sense must know that American productions, for the most part, are crowded from the market, and our readers are compelled to buy the works of foreign writers, or have nothing to read. The consequences of this

system of policy are pretty clearly shown up, in a book, which has recently been published, entitled the "Living Authors of America." In the article on Mr. Poe, the celebrated toper and poet, he [Powell himself] uses the following bold language, in attributing the success of Poe, as a writer, to the fearlessness of his criticisms: —

. . . "It is a curious fact, that the worst enemies of the national mind have been a few of her own sons. These are the authors who, till lately, have entirely enjoyed the monopoly of the English market. Now they will be obliged to join the body of native authors, and hurry to the rescue. Now their own rights are in jeopardy, and they must join the ranks of international copyright."

Gleefully Powell acknowledged the "force in these remarks made by a foreigner": "They are the fruit of his own observation; and it would be well for Americans to bestow a thought on the subject, and make a 'note of it,' to use the language of the immortal, eloquent, learned, and distinguished Captain Cuttle."

This was, take it all in all, an onslaught to rank with frantic young George W. Peck's. So ferocious an assault in one of the two most popular papers in the city ought to have stirred up all the combatants in the Powell-Irving affair, but no responses have been located. The day after it was published sixty or more men were blasted to death in a machine shop in lower Manhattan when a boiler in the basement blew up. (A blacksmith died with a hammer still raised in his clenched hand, like Tashtego at the end of Melville's next book.) This horrific disaster — forty more people died of their injuries the next day — filled the newspapers for many days, and may simply have pushed Powell's petty allegations out of mind until such a time that a reply would not have been topical. Perhaps also by this time the New York literati of all camps had decided that the way to contain Powell was to ignore him. In any case, with this article Powell's grosser attacks on Irving and Melville ceased, as far as we know, and Melville was left to make what sense he could of Powell's malignity as he caught up on how he had been treated in the American press in his absence.

At some point Melville pieced enough of the sequence together to realize that, just about the time the English scoundrel published *Living Authors of America*, Nathaniel Parker Willis had written a pleasant piece on Melville in the *Home Journal* on 12 January 1850, "Light Touchings," on the topic of international copyright: "Our friend Herman Melville is one of the first and most signal realizers of the effect of the recent English repudiation of copyright. . . . Melville went abroad, about the time that this retaliatory system came first into action — but knowing nothing of it, and relying on the proceeds of the English editions of his books, for the means of prolonged travel. He writes us that he has abandoned his more extended plans, with this disappointment, and will return sooner than he expected." Thereupon Willis printed a portion of the letter that Melville had written him on 14 December, including a sentence in which Melville doubted that "Gabriel enters the portals of Heaven without a fee to Peter the porter—so impossible is it to travel without money"—a wonderful fragment known only because Willis printed it. Cruelly distorting this open-hearted letter, which Willis had endearingly entrusted to the readership of the *Home Journal*, Powell had based on it some of his slander in "Fruits of Literary Appropriation." Poor Willis saw the *Herald* and knew just what evil had been wrought with his innocent publication of the passage from Melville's letter.

Melville had no time for recriminations. To finish catching up on the state of his career, he had to spend two or three hours looking through the American reviews of *Redburn* that Allan had collected, a task that reminded him forcibly of the hours in Bentley's office when he looked over the British reviews. As he could have expected, reviewers frequently had compared *Redburn* to *Typee* and *Omoo* (considered together) and *Mardi*. The Boston *Post*, which had been so contemptuous of his third book, on 20 November had found in *Redburn* "no glimmer of the levity, coxcombry, affectation, inconsistency and *hodge-podge* of 'Mardi.'" Signing himself "R," the Transcendentalist George Ripley in the New York *Tribune* (1 December) found *Redburn* a "decided improvement" over his previous book, even though Melville had not "worked himself entirely free from the affectations" and pretentious spirit "which had gained *Mardi* such an unlucky notoriety." Yet Ripley missed "the freshness, the gayety, the natural frolicsomeness" which had given "such a charm to the fragrant descriptions of Typee, and to a certain extent, to the off-hand, picturesque sketches of Omoo." In the *Home Journal* (24 November), Willis, proving himself a genuinely sympathetic friend, took the boldest minority stand: "The popularity of this work we think will far exceed any of the previous ones, though it will not perhaps raise the author's literary reputation from the pinnacle where Mardi placed it." Months later, when Melville was well into the writing of *Moby-Dick* and when reviews of *White-Jacket* were already appearing, the *Southern Quarterly Review* (April) held that, "wild, improbable and fantastic" as it was, *Mardi* gave more proof of "real powers in reserve" than *Redburn*. The majority, however, were sure that after what *Blackwood's* had called the "decided and deplorable retrogression" of *Mardi*, Melville had returned successfully to his "own peculiar walk" or his "own peculiar element" (as the New York *Albion* said on 24 November), even though *Redburn* lacked "the brilliant and bewitching scenes" of *Typee* and *Omoo* (the December New York *United States Magazine and Demo-*

cratic Review). Willis's brief comments came closest to giving Melville the reassurance that he plainly needed still in regard to *Mardi*, the book that he had been slow to abandon to its fate.

Even though Melville wanted to be known as more than the author of picaresque travel books like *Typee* and *Omoo*, it was reassuring to be told (in a variant of the phrasing in the *Albion*) that he possessed his "own peculiar vein" (the *Democratic Review*), in which he reigned as the modern Defoe. In the *Literary World* (10 November) Duyckinck called Melville "the De Foe of the Ocean," and the *Southern Literary Messenger* (December) began its comments by saying, "If this volume be an imaginary narrative then is it the most life-like and natural fiction since Robinson Crusoe's account of his life on the island of *Juan Fernandez.*" In the rare qualifications to this distinction, *Graham's* (January) acutely identified "a bit of deviltry" in Melville that was not to be found in Defoe, and *Holden's* (January 1850) rejected the comparison altogether, insisting that "there is hardly an English writer" whom Melville so little resembled as Defoe: "The charm of de Foe is his simplicity of style, and artistic accuracy of description; the author of Redburn on the contrary is, at times, ambitiously gorgeous in style, and at others coarse and abrupt in his simplicity." Most reviewers concentrated (like the Boston *Post*) on the Defoe-like "truthfulness and vividness of detail" that made *Redburn* seem "to be *fact* word for word" ("bating a little that is melo-dramatic and exaggerated in the hero, at the outset").

Ripley in the *Tribune* had cannily declared that *Redburn* had "something about it which savours more of the bookmaker by profession, and shows that it is not the product of any innate necessity." Other reviewers, less bold and perceptive but more tolerant, found it noteworthy that Melville had sustained so much interest in what was, after all, unpromising and commonplace material, compared with adventuresome nautical fiction they had read. Several reviewers thought the book's passages on Redburn's comical naïveté better than they would have expected from the subject matter, and quoted at length from chapter 14, "He Contemplates Making a Social Call on the Captain in His Cabin." The evil Jackson struck several reviewers as impressively described, and several reviewers quoted scenes he appeared in, most often his death scene, which the *Literary World* on 17 November called one of the "most striking" in nautical fiction.

Melville had been contemptuous of *Redburn* himself, knowing better than anyone how little it accorded with his ambitions as a writer. He had grown beyond it even in the summer of 1849, in the process of writing *White-Jacket*, and had grown immeasurably beyond it during his trip to England and the Continent. Nothing suggests that he ever thought of it as more than hackwork, but he could take satisfaction that reviewers as diverse as Duyckinck, Willis, and Ripley had united in liking *Redburn*, for such approval had encouraged lovers of *Typee* and *Omoo* to give him another chance, after the general disappointment with *Mardi*.

Now more than ever a private pondering man who wanted nothing more than to focus on his next book, Melville suffered under yet another public airing of his efforts to get a substantial advance for *White-Jacket*. It began in London. On 22 January 1850 the *Times* printed a letter from an importer of foreign books asking how it happened "that the author of *Typee*, &c., who recently made a voyage to this country on purpose to sell the 'right' of his unpublished *White-Jacket*, wearily hawked this book from Piccadilly to Whitechapel, calling upon every publisher in his way, and could find no one rash enough to buy his 'protected right.' " Three days later the *Times* printed a letter from Richard Bentley, an attempt to put the best face on Melville's efforts ("the work was in the first instance offered to me by the author himself, and I have become the purchaser of what I firmly believe to be the copyright, for a considerable sum").

Duyckinck printed the letter from the "importer" in the *Literary World* on 23 February, then on 2 March under the heading "Mr Melville and Copyright in England" he reprinted Bentley's letter ("Mr. Bentley, by the way, protects Mr. Melville from the random allusion of 'An Importer' ") and included another by "K," a New Yorker, who offered this defense:

> I believe injustice may be done Mr. Melville as well as his publisher, by allowing the statement that the former "wearily hawked his unpublished *White Jacket* from Piccadilly to Whitechapel, calling upon every publisher in his way," &c., to pass uncontradicted. It is simply untrue. But that is not all. Mr. Melville had not the slightest difficulty in making an arrangement for the publication of *White Jacket* with Mr. Bentley, the publisher of Mr. Melville's previous work, and what is more, such arrangement was concluded promptly, without impediment or finesse. Mr. Melville is not the man to "hawk" his wares in any market, and Mr. Bentley not the publisher to allow so capital a book to escape him.

On the voyage home Melville had been justifiably proud that he had avoided the worst consequences of the copyright situation, and more than noble about renouncing first the grand tour of the classical world and second the invitation to Belvoir Castle. Melville could not but be dampened by the persistent public hoopla about his exploitation of his fame at the expense of his fellow writers and about his weary hawking of *White-Jacket* on Publishers' Row. Every time he thought the newspapers must be done with trumpeting misinformation, half-truths, and lies about him, he had to confront some new outrage. The time was not propitious for starting a new book, but very soon after his return Melville must have started it, and fought hard to shut out all distractions, never mind how viciously personal and sensational they were.

Between February and June of 1850, while *Moby-Dick* was first taking shape (growing to what he described as half done on 1 May), Melville's work habits were indulged by the family much as they had been for three years. He had his privacy and no household duties that we know of, and he had Helen (it seems) as his regular copyist. He marked the children's birthdays, surely, and made himself available for whatever readings aloud took place in the evenings. At no time had Allan served as an intellectual companion (the way George Duyckinck, silent around other people, seemed to serve Evert), but now his lawyer-brother kept him from being the only man in the house, evenings. In these weeks there was pleasant anticipation. Maria Melville on 13 March wrote to her brother Peter that the family had heard from Tom lately and expected him "some time next month" (carrying "Susans Chess Board," which Uncle Peter had commissioned him to bring back from the Orient). He was "coming home by way of London," she added, having rounded the world. Tom's arrival would give Melville companionship for his walks and would add to his privacy during the day, since whenever he was in the house Tom was naturally the focus of his mother's and sisters' attention, except for whoever was serving as copyist.

For Herman the challenge of the manuscript can hardly have been far from all-absorbing, and he pretty much dropped out of sight. Having been received into a veritable Paradise of Bachelors, a fine sample of London literary and artistic society, he could treasure his memories and resist, most nights, even the temptations of Dr. Francis's house on Bond Street. Evert Duyckinck still made overtures, asking him to write reviews and otherwise reminding him that he was part of the *Literary World* brotherhood. Making an exception, on 27 February Melville went to Duyckinck's for brandied peaches and homemade ice cream. Besides the Saint (as the Melville household continued to call George Duyckinck), there were present the senior Dana, young William Allen Butler, Mathews, "and a few others of less literary note," as George wrote to Joann Miller on 1 March. Duyckinck was able to give him an advance look at Richard Bentley's reply to "An Importer," and that night may have been the time Melville borrowed Smollett's *Roderick Random*.

Socializing, however, was not going to become habitual. On 6 March 1850, Melville was unable to use some tickets Duyckinck had sent him: "having been shut up all day, I could not stand being shut up all the evening — so I mounted my *green* jacket & strolled down to the Battery to study the stars." The "homeless loafers on the Battery" regularly "outslept the watching of the stars, winking at their pale echoes in the placid waters," G. G. Foster observed in a book published that year, *New York by Gas-Light: with Here and There a Streak of Sunshine*. Along the Battery his green jacket would not play the devil with his respectability, but Melville could never be wholly alone in that part of New York at any time of night, for, along with the living homeless, he might encounter other spirits from the past—himself as a child, his father, or the bannered ghost of Gansevoort winding through the packed streets in the great torchlight procession. High among the changes rapidly taking place in him was a new openness to memories, even shadowy recollections of his childhood in a vanishing Manhattan.

Melville's underlining "green" in his note, a play on his forthcoming *White-Jacket*, indicates that Duyckinck knew he had been "shut up" with final preparations for the Harper edition of that book. He may have looked over the proofs (probably with no record of the misprints he had corrected months before on the set he gave Bentley, and probably with no record of the additions he had made on that set), but he may have done nothing more than write the short preface (dated March 1850) explaining that his "man-of-war experiences and observations" were "incorporated in the present volume." Possibly also he could have been shut up in his room looking over a new edition of Cooper's *The Red Rover*, which he was happy to possess but not willing to reread. He happily enough dashed off a charming jeu d'esprit on the consonance of book content and book design which Duyckinck printed in the 16 March *Literary World* as "A Thought on Book-Binding." But he was most likely "shut up all day" working on his whaling book. Being secretive was new. Perhaps, after *Mardi*, he was uneasy because of just how high his hopes for the book were becoming. What with so many books on whaling already in print, such as J. Ross Browne's book, or the book the Harpers had published in his absence, Henry T. Cheever's *The Whale and His Captors*, perhaps he was concerned that Duyckinck might think that the marvels of whaling had already been exhausted, and therefore wanted to have a tall stack of manuscript before he talked about it very much. Surely obsessed with its composition already in March 1850, Melville did not even tell Duyckinck that he was working on the story of a whaling voyage.

As he wrote, Melville continued to fight off ominous distractions. The *Literary World* for 23 March 1850 contained a Stringer & Townsend advertisement for the forthcoming second volume of *The Living Authors of America* (no author named), which would contain over a dozen chapters including "Irving, and the Essayists"; "Hawthorne, and the Tale Tellers"; "Paulding, and the Novelists"; "Foster, Mathews, and the Gas-light School"; and two that came closer to home, "Duyckinck, and the Claquers" and "Melville, and the Romancists." The book never materialized, although at some time

Powell wrote at least part of it, the part he published, beginning that fall, in a new Manhattan paper called *Figaro!* At the end of March, the prospect of opening a book to read "Melville, and the Romancists" was an ugly threat, although what Powell eventually published on Melville, in *Figaro!* and years later in the *Daily News*, was comparatively benign.

Meanwhile, Melville's friends and acquaintances sprinkled the pages of Manhattan journalism with unseemly jibes at each other. In the 26 January 1850 *Literary World* Duyckinck had reviewed Willis's new book, *People I Have Met; or Pictures of Society and People of Mark, Drawn under a Thin Veil of Fiction.* Never one to let politeness keep him from his Christian duty to chastise corrupting literature, Duyckinck lamented that Willis's "peculiarities and individualities" would necessarily "repel simple-minded readers, of plain thoughts and warm affections." Repelling such readers was bad, but there was worse, for Willis had "fallen into the habit of taking sly occasions to astonish prudery and lift the eyelids of hypocrisy." Duyckinck declared that Willis liked "to say things as near the edge as possible, particularly in describing women." To this reproach Willis replied in kind, escalating the stakes. Two months later, on 23 March, Duyckinck condemned Willis's sketches as "occasionally disfigured by gross and inexcusable personality," then Willis in the *Home Journal* for 30 March attacked the *Literary World* as a *"journal of disappointed authors who have turned booksellers' hacks"* (a reference to those dense pages of publishers' advertisements at the back of every issue of the Duyckincks' paper), and he fleered at "the Duyckin[c]k-dom of Envy," the "kingdom of those who die of envy" because they are capable of reviewing but not of writing themselves.

The London reviews of *White-Jacket* began appearing at the end of January, even before Melville reached home. These London reviews had a profound effect on Richard Bentley, for they, and the sales they in part determined, constituted evidence on which he based decisions about the next two books Melville was to offer him. The *Sun* (28 January) started with the announcement that Melville was "indefatigable": "Hardly have we finished the perusal of one of his compositions before another is issued from the press." (Bentley later complained that Melville's books came in too rapid order for their success.) The *Athenæum* (2 February) began with a particularly telling tribute to Melville's originality: "Mr. Melville stands as far apart from any past or present marine painter in pen and ink as Turner does from the magnificent artist vilipended by Mr. Ruskin for Turner's sake — Vandervelde." Melville, the reviewer continued, was the only sea writer who had conveyed "the poetry of the Ship — her voyages and her crew" in a manner at all resembling Turner's. Seeing Melville's work as a whole (five volumes now), the writer declared that his "sea-creatures, calms and storms, belong to the . . . dreamy tone of 'The Ancient Mariner,' and have a touch of serious and suggestive picturesqueness appertaining to a world of art higher than the actor's or the scene-painter's." In *Mardi* that humour had run riot, but not unappealingly so. Now Melville had "brought his familiar" — his daemon — "into capital, practical, working order; and throwing, as his Jack o'Lantern does, a new light on the coarse, weather-beaten shapes and into the cavern-ous corners of a man-of-war, the author's pages have a tone and a relish which are alike individual and attractive." This remarkable review, one which Bent-ley had to see, confirmed for him his sense of the unique qualities — the "genius" — of the young American on whom he had been persuaded, against his business acumen, to risk two hundred pounds on top of his yet untotaled losses on *Mardi* and *Redburn*.

From *John Bull* (2 February) Bentley took a hard lesson: he should have kept a cautious eye on Melville's casual religious comments. The reviewer in that paper saw Melville as "an improving and a vastly improved writer," "no longer the wanton boy that used to give the rein to his wit and fancy, indulg-ing in refined licentiousness of description, more seductive and mischievous than open violations of decorum, and in that smart dare-devil style of remark which perverts, while it dazzles, the mind, inducing habits of levity and irreverence of thought." Melville had matured (whether through the influ-ence of time, the "salutary castigation of criticism," or other causes), but despite traces of a better attitude toward religion he was still exhibiting "far too great a freedom in touching upon sacred subjects, and, deeper and more dangerous still," exhibiting pervasively "a philosophy which ill accords with the truth of revelation." A few reviewers besides the one in *John Bull* were more profoundly offended by this and other parts of the book — for one conspicuous example, its concluding cosmological chapter on the world as a man-of-war. The reviewer in the London *Morning Post* (12 February) was aghast at Melville's irreverence: "few of the readers of this work, we think, will not be shocked at the unthinking, summary way, to say the least of it, in which the author disposes of one of the greatest subjects of human reflection, viz., the divine nature of the Founder of Christianity, when he quietly in-forms us . . . that 'Burnet and the best theologians have demonstrated that his nature was not merely human — was not that of a mere man of the world'; and we really must protest against the introduction of such matters as these, and in such a manner, into what is, and professes to be, nothing more than a sea-novel." (Bentley was to weed such irreverence out of Melville's next book.)

Various London reviews showed that one of Melville's rhetorical strat-egies had paid off — his shaming the navy of the American democracy for practices already banned from the British monarchical navy (and his last-minute tinkerings with some of these comparisons to make what he had said in the Harper edition still more palatable in the Bentley edition). Several reviewers commented approvingly on his honest acknowledgment of British superiority in some naval matters — including some passages which, Bentley remembered with satisfaction, were well-calculated additions that Melville had inserted into passages in the Harper sheets. The most favorable British review of *White-Jacket*, on the whole, was that in the March *Bentley's Miscellany* — predictable, to be sure, but significant, since it must have had the proprietor's approval. In all likelihood, it reflected not only the reviewer's literary acuity but also a sense he had somehow gotten of the vivid personal qualities of the young American who had turned up in the metropolis the previous autumn:

> Mr. Melville differs conspicuously from all other painters of life at sea. The difference between them may be not inaccurately expressed, as the difference between prose and poetry. The great charm of the marine story in the hands of such writers as Cooper, Marryatt, and Hall, is literal truthfulness, shown through just a sufficient haze of imagination, caught from the wide expanse of sky and water, to render it picturesque and effective. But Mr. Melville bathes the scene in the hues of a fanciful and reflective spirit, which gives it the interest of a creation of genius. He is everywhere original, suggestive, and individual. We follow him as if we were passing through an exciting dream. The rainbow dips and plays around us. We see the ship and the crew under the influence of an enchantment. . . .
>
> In such a book and such writing there must be great faults — the faults of a superabundant fancy and a prodigal genius. But they are as much conditions of a peculiar excellence as the rough spots in a piece of old tapestry.

For all the predominately respectful tone of the reviewers, the London reception was not such as to encourage any other British publisher to pirate *White-Jacket*, and its sales were not such as to encourage Bentley to take so great a risk as two hundred pounds on Melville again.

Without an alert brother or even an informal lookout in London (as the obliging Brodhead had been while he was secretary of legation), there was no reason that many of the English newspaper reviews of Melville's fifth book would ever have come to Herman's attention. Allan may have brought home copies of two or three London magazines with reviews of *White-Jacket*, which began reaching New York at the end of February, but Herman seems not to have been scouring the New York City reading rooms at night during these winter weeks. Furthermore, American newspapers and magazines happened to quote very few British reviews of *White-Jacket*, so what Melville learned of the British reception may have been limited pretty much to a re-printing of extracts from the *Athenæum* of 2 February in the *Albion* (2 March) and a Harper advertisement that appeared, among other places, in the *Evening Post* (19 and 20 March) and contained quotations from the *Spectator* of 2 February and from the *Atlas* and the *Literary Gazette* of 9 February. In June the New Orleans magazine *Debow's* quoted from the London *Morning Post* of 12 February, but this is not likely to have met Melville's eye. The London reviews of *White-Jacket*, in short, were important not for their effects on Melville but on Bentley.

Duyckinck and Willis were still sniping at each other when the Harper edition of *White-Jacket* was published around 20 March, two weeks after Allan supplied advance sheets to Duyckinck, who had printed "A Shore Emperor on Board a Man of War" from them in the *Literary World* of 9 March, then had reviewed *White-Jacket* at length in two installments, 16 and 23 March. The subsequent American reviews of *White-Jacket*, many of which Melville saw, were rarely as well written as the best of the British, but they were often laudatory. Duyckinck was ecstatic in the first notice in the *Literary World* (16 March): "To have the fancy and the fact united is rare in any walk, almost unknown on the sea. Hence to Herman Melville, whose mind swarms with tender, poetic, or humorous fancies, the ship is a new world, now first conquered." *White-Jacket* was "thoroughly American and democratic." Lewis Gaylord Clark in the May *Knickerbocker* rejoiced also— Melville was back "on the right ground at last," after *Mardi;* Clark had devoured *White-Jacket* in two sittings, "unavoidably protracted." Melville was not profound, but valuable: "Without the aid of much imagination, but with a daguerreotype-like naturalness of description of all which the writer saw and felt himself, and all which he saw others feel, Mr. MELVILLE has given us a volume which, in its evident truthfulness and accuracy of personal and individual delineation, reminds us continually of that admirable and justly popular work, the '*Two Years Before the Mast*' of the younger DANA."

Duyckinck had reserved "the naval reform questions" for the next week, by which time he had prepared a thoughtful, judicious view on discipline on a warship. He was not prepared to advocate that flogging be "at once and entirely abolished," but he would go so far as to say that it was "getting to be, in the nostrils of the world, everyday more and more offensive." Hiram Fuller's *Evening Mirror* (29 March), once again choosing not to link Melville to the Duyckinck clique, very respectfully treated *White-Jacket* as a book to take rank with the younger Dana's, concluding that it should be studied "by every one who feels the least interest in the honor and true interest of our country." In *Saroni's Musical Times* (30 March) a veteran of service in a man-of-war passionately testified to the truth of *White-Jacket:*

Dark as the picture appears in some parts, the author must acknowledge that he has left much the darkest colors untouched upon the pallet. Let "White-Jacket" be printed thousands of thousands of times, let a copy be attached to every village library wherever the English language is spoken, nay, let a polyglot edition be spread all over the world, in order that adventurous youths, who meditate the rash experiment which has already ruined so many, may awake from their day-dreams of "spicy islands" and "moonlit waters" and other fairy-like incidents of "a life on the ocean-wave." If after reading "White-Jacket," they be still bent upon "shipping," they will then sign the roll with their eyes wide open.

Like Duyckinck, this reviewer was not prepared to go along with Melville's demand for the immediate end of flogging: "It is a perplexing and knotty problem that our government is now attempting to solve, the problem of governing a most unruly set of men without an appliance which hitherto has been found effectual." George Ripley in the *Tribune* for 5 April took a respectful view of Melville's public service in "revealing the secrets of his prison-house" (*Hamlet*, everyone knew) and "calling the public attention to the indescribable abominations of the naval life, reeking with the rankest corruption, cruelty, and blood," especially at a time when any new light on the subject of flogging was bound to be "of more than common public interest." On 6 April the *Spirit of the Times* declared that *White-Jacket* passed the test of a "great book"—that it interests "all classes of the community": "while the ingenious narrative and abundant incident will attract the crowd of general readers, curiosity will excite the navy corps, and the facts so important and so clearly stated will appeal to our legislators."

The Boston *Christian Register* (16 April) saw nothing to object to and in fact commended the book "to those Christian parents who have young sons desirous of serving their country as midshipmen," but the old evangelical vendetta against Melville surfaced in several reviews of *White-Jacket*. The Boston *Puritan Recorder* (18 April) grudgingly admitted that it was not of such "irreligious character" as some of his others: "we discover no jack-a-nape flings at missionaries, any one of whom is worth as many of the flippant, tom-fooling writers of Melville's sort, as could be buried in a ten-acre lot." The most explicit religious objection was repeated from an English critic: after commenting on the attention American writers were receiving in London papers, the reviewer in the Richmond *Southern Literary Messenger* (April) plagiarized parts of the review in the London *Morning Post*, including the complaint about Melville's irreverent attitude toward "the divine author of our holy religion." In the *Tribune* Ripley had taken exception to Melville's failure to confine himself to what he had heard and seen, "for the moral and metaphysical reflections he sets forth in bad Carlylese, are only incumbrances to the narrative, and often become intolerable." The most ominous of the religious objections was the direct warning buried in Duyckinck's review: "In regarding . . . the spirit of things, may he not fall into the error of undervaluing their forms, lest he get into a bewildering, barren, and void scepticism!" Duyckinck probably felt he had sufficiently put his friend on notice that there were limits to his toleration of religious improprieties, but Melville's skepticism was so ingrained by now that he missed the message.

On 30 March 1850, the New York *Albion* reviewed *White-Jacket*, in the main favorably, but with a particular objection to the emphasis on the horrors of flogging: "In so able, so practical, and so large-minded an author as Herman Melville, we scarcely expected to find the 'essential dignity of man' and 'the spirit of our domestic institutions' lugged in on such a question as this. Is it consistent with the 'essential dignity,' that one man should sweep the floor of Congress, and another make laws upon it which his democratic countrymen must obey?" The reviewer quoted Melville's diplomatic praise of British discipline on ships of war "as a little set-off against the democratic institutions." This contempt for Melville's democratic excesses provides one of the few connections between Melville's progress on his manuscript and contemporary events, for (now or later) Melville wrote his reaction to this review into what became the end of the first "Knights and Squires" chapter (26) of *Moby-Dick*, a plea that when he attributes high qualities to the men on the *Pequod* the "great democratic God" will bear him out "against all mortal critics," which is to say "all mortal reviewers" (since the only critics Melville had experienced were the reviewers). (This was also the passage in which he remembered the climax of the campaign of 1844 and Gansevoort's celebration of Jackson.) No other review of *White-Jacket* is known to have provoked any reaction from Melville, who had reason, as the reviews accumulated, to be grateful that he had not been caught in literary crossfire. In March and April the time was opportune for dragging down any associate of Duyckinck or Mathews or their "you-tickle-me-and-I'll-tickle-you-school" (the sardonic insult in a 24 November 1849 article on the Powell affair in the New York *Metropolis*), but once again no reviewer of *White-Jacket* attacked Melville personally because of his association with the *Literary World* clique. He had reason to count his blessings as the reviews of *White-Jacket* accumulated.

The highest praise *White-Jacket* received in the United States came from Willis in the *Home Journal* on 13 April, under a significant heading, "AMERICAN LITERATURE," not a regular category at all, but a kind of triumphant nonce label for Melville's contribution to national writing. Melville showed "the instinct of true art" in focusing only on the "man-of-war, and what is within her." A writer who can choose only a few objects to look upon "and can keep them by the power of his own mind sufficiently long before the mind of the reader, *creates* an interest in his subject." Melville was a "literary curiosity," a man whose "perceptions are of that positive, vigorous and intense kind which amount to passion." Such a man, who *creates* an interest in any subject by the passion of his perceptions, resembles "Chaucer and Crabbe, Defoe, Charles Lamb, and Dickens, or rather he is a mixture of all without being a copy of either." In praising *White-Jacket* Willis defined the special attraction of Melville the man. Willis went on, paragraph after paragraph, rejoicing in the special essayistic qualities of Melville's mind and art, closely anticipating the special pleasures British admirers found in Melville toward the turn of the century:

> There are some things in "White Jacket" to which, we confess, an especial liking, albeit it is an enjoyment which, we suppose, must be taken a little "on the sly." Our ornate modern criticism is occasionally somewhat hard on all forms of expression and thought which do not go direct to the point. Mr. Dickens has received some especial thrashings on this account, and Mr. Melville richly deserves them if the reasoning on which they are administered holds good. We, however, differ from these dandy critics. What would become of "Hudibras," now-a-days, in the hands of these polite gentlemen? A man whose mind is full of associations, neither can, nor should speak without letting them out. His elaboration of trifles, his redundancy and often incongruity of metaphor, his quaintness of expression, what are they but parts of his suggestiveness? the fulness, the fun and humor of his soul? Men are pleased, whether critics are so, or not, with this "tracing of resemblances between things apparently dissimilar," and we venture to say that many of the latter enjoy greatly the queer things which they officially denounce.

Willis confessed his guilt for admiring one example of such an offense, Melville's "quaint elaboration of images, in so trifling a matter, as the manufacture of that celebrated 'White Jacket.'" Only Willis was subtle enough to articulate a defense of the validity of his "friend Melville's" deductions about naval abuses based not on "statements *artistically* true" but on a compound of history and romance. Melville was exercising a moral duty transcending exact facts: "Man psychologically, man as a social being, has rights and duties altogether dependent on that which cannot be weighed, measured, or even seen."

The review amounts to a tribute to the special personal and literary qualities of Melville and of the ideal Melvillean reader. Melville read it, and must have found in it the profoundest encouragement he had yet received that he should obey his "queer," eccentric impulses. In Cologne he had recognized himself as a pondering man, very much the man "whose mind is full of associations," as Willis tellingly observed. Now one of the most popular writers in America was singling out for praise Melville's essayistic chapters, his suggestive "elaboration of trifles." It may well be that Willis's praise emboldened Melville to write many passages in *Moby-Dick* that are elaborations of trifles, such as the analysis of why Ishmael goes to sea and why he goes to sea as a sailor; or Ishmael's reflections on the oil painting in the Spouter Inn; or, later, Ishmael's reflections on Father Mapple's drawing up the ladder after him into his pulpit. The pity is that we know so little of what passed personally between Melville and the American who best understood and most stoutly championed the special qualities of his mind and artistry.

In the same issue of the *Home Journal* that contained his review of *White-Jacket* (13 April), Willis belabored Duyckinck's latest explanation of his earlier comments on Willis's sensuousness: "The editor of the '*Literary World*,' as we presumed, had barked after a locomotive on its way through his extent of village, without knowing very distinctly what he was disapproving. From a broad and general accusation of 'gross and inexcusable personalities' in our writings, he comes down (in reply to a demand that he should explain) to a mention of one little story of three or four pages in our last issued volume, which he timidly defines as 'the eighteenth sketch of that collection of papers.'" The problem of allaying charges of sensuousness was complicated by Willis's decision to use his columns to defend the wife of the actor Edwin Forrest from her husband's charges that she had committed adultery — charges in which the public did not yet know Willis was himself involved. The next week Willis picked up from the *Times* of London by way of the Boston *Transcript* news that must have stung Melville with regret for his being a "ninny" four months before. The item dealt with people known to Melville — old friends of the Shaws, Abbott Lawrence and Mrs. Lawrence — and with a place he might have visited, but now never would see: "The American Minister, Mrs and Miss Lawrence, have left town on a visit to his Grace the Duke of Rutland at Belvoir Castle. — *Times.*"

The Boston *Daily Evening Transcript* on 25 March welcomed the exposé of the evil effects of the "flogging and *grogging* system." On 10 April the Boston *Post*, however, in a minutely argued disquisition (reprinted in the sister paper the Boston *Statesman* on 13 April), lectured the young author for "crudities and puerilities that would disgrace a school-boy." Melville was simply incompetent to discuss "the 'Articles of War,' the propriety or impropriety of 'Flogging in the Navy,' or the whole system of government and ceremonials of our 'National Marine.'" Sensible men of experience and judgment knew that discussion of "these great practical subjects require practical men — men of character, wisdom and experience — not men of theories, fancies and enthusiasm." The question of flogging was one that "must be settled by men of practice, by wisdom, by authority." Furthermore, in less serious passages Melville was guilty of "autobiographical twaddle." His attempts to "be smart, witty and entertaining" turn out to be "egotism, vapidness and affectation, with, here and there, a fragment of amber on its waters." This was unpleasant news for the Shaw household and the aging Melvill aunts and uncles, but the member of the family who seems most to have taken it to heart was Lizzie's half-brother Lemuel, who soon began making snide comments about Melville's having written too many books for his own good.

As Melville had expected, there were attacks by some die-hard advocates of the necessity of flogging in the navy. At Louviers, his estate up the Brandywine River from Wilmington, Delaware, Commodore Samuel F. Du Pont coordinated a brief attempt to traduce *White-Jacket* in several newspapers in Philadelphia and elsewhere. At Du Pont's behest, a notice was printed in the Philadelphia *Pennsylvanian* on 3 May, rather late, decrying the book as "a studied injustice to the American navy, that is infamous," and accusing Melville of writing a work "calculated to dishonor his country." After a time Du Pont decided that there was no point mustering the entire fleet against the book. Du Pont may not have connected the author of *White-Jacket* with the lieutenant on the *Somers* whom he had defended, and Melville probably never knew of the fury he had aroused in the man who in 1861 sunk the "Stone Fleet," an armada of American whalers, in order to block the harbor at Charleston (the subject of Melville's poem "The Stone Fleet. An Old Sailor's Lament").

During these weeks the Boston family was under intense daily strain, for Judge Shaw was presiding over a sensational Boston murder trial, in which Dr. John W. Webster, a Harvard Medical School professor, was accused of murdering his landlord, Dr. George Parkman, and dissecting the body so as to destroy it. On 1 April Shaw found him guilty of a most un-Harvard-like crime, assault and murder with malice aforethought (said the *Post* the next day) "done within the apartments of a public institution in this city, the Medical College, of which you were a professor and instructor, upon the person of a man of mature age, well known, and of extensive connections in this community, and a benefactor of that institution." Demanding that Webster rise, Shaw also rose, and addressed him at length "in a tone of profound solemnity," concluding with a sentence that Dr. Webster be hung by the neck until he was dead and an appeal that God in his infinite goodness might have mercy on the murderer's soul.

For weeks Shaw received many letters from people about the crime. Some were reasonable and even thoughtful, but some were egotistic fantasizings by cranks who had formed instant theories about the case, theorizings that showed little sense of the human suffering that marked the whole case for the judge. Some were hate letters such as nothing in his long career had prepared Shaw to understand. Many, like this one written from New York on 4 April, were deeply perturbing: "Dr Webster is not *Guilty*. For the sake of our dear Saviour do not let him be executed — Time will reveal all — and show the darkest & deepest laid scheme to ruin an innocent man — *Remember!* the crime will be proved on one, now, nearly beyond Suspicion. 'More I dare not say.' " Shaw endured for weeks an ongoing bitter lesson about the perils of notoriety and about the virulent underside of a Republic where citizens gained their information from a sensationalistic and irresponsible press. Now he could sympathize more than ever with what his son-in-law had endured from G. W. Peck. "The term 'freedom of the press,' " Melville put into the mouth of a character in *The Confidence-Man* (ch. 29), is "on a par with *freedom of Colt's revolver.*"

Some momentary comic relief came on 8 April when the *Evening Transcript* regaled Boston with fictitious comments on the profits of authorship, growing out of a report of an exorbitant sum a local publisher was said to have paid a new author: "If the young and the obscure derive such sums from the sale of their manuscripts, what may be expected of those, whose fame is already established? May we not soon hope to see Hawthorne riding in his carriage — Whipple building a chateau — Benjamin giving princely entertainments at Newport — Longfellow making a Lawrence-like donation to Harvard University — Melville keeping his yacht — and our lady writers (the unmarried ones) all run after as heiresses? It is evident, that a good time for authors is coming." This cheerful fantasy must have inspired a few apt elaborations (Lizzie in nautical garb leaving Mt. Vernon Street for the Naval Yard or Herman assisting the furbelowed and trepidatory Hope aboard the yacht). Since Lenox was on Shaw's annual circuit and in the vicinity of Pittsfield, the family would have been especially interested in other news about this time in the *Transcript:* Nathaniel Hawthorne had "lately taken up his residence in Lenox and added another celebrity to that genial atmosphere of talent and genius."

In these weeks for the first time Melville's name was commonly interlinked with Hawthorne's in print, merely by the coincidence of their books being reviewed together. In the May *Knickerbocker Magazine* appeared favorable reviews of both *White-Jacket* and *The Scarlet Letter.* Scathingly reviewing Mathews's *The Adventures of Mr. Moneypenny* in the same issue, Clark called Mathews by the name of his character, Puffer Hopkins, and treated Evert Duyckinck as Mathews's sidekick, his "*Fidus Achates*": "Now we ask any reader, who may heretofore for a moment have fancied that the 'North-American Review,' the KNICKERBOCKER, and other the like journals, had been 'too hard' upon PUFFER HOPKINS, we ask *any* reader to read, or *try* to read, at least, this latest specimen of the peculiar 'humor' of our 'American DICKENS.' Try it *once*, reader, for *our* sake, for the love of 'Old KNICK.'" Farther on Clark made room for another jibe: "WILLIS, in the *'Home Journal,'* in one of those trenchant sentences which 'bite like a serpent and sting like an adder,' says that *'The Literary World'* weekly review is a 'journal conducted by sour, disappointed, unsuccessful authors, turned booksellers' hacks.' These 'be cruel words!'" The situation was such that Clark could stand back and incite Willis and the Duyckinck crowd to attack each other.

Three months earlier, in February 1850, most likely within a week or two of his return, Melville had tried to settle down to work on his whaling book. The use he made of his whaling sources suggests, somewhat inconclusively, that during the late winter and early spring he wrote about whaling much more than about the natural history of whales. He had other whaling books at hand, but among those he turned to was Bennett's *A Whaling Voyage round the Globe.* He also drew on Francis Allyn Olmsted's *Incidents of a Whaling Voyage. To Which Are Added Observations on the Scenery, Manners and Customs, and Missionary Stations of the Sandwich and Society Islands* (New York, 1841); J. C. Hart, *Miriam Coffin, or the Whale-Fishermen: A Tale* (New York, 1834); Obed Macy, *The History of Nantucket; Being a Compendious Account of the First Settlement of the Island by the English; Together with the Rise and Progress of the Whale Fishery; and Other Historical Facts Relative to Said Island and Its Inhabitants* (Boston: Hilliard, Gray, 1835); W.A.G., *Ribs and Trucks, from Davy's Locker; Being Magazine Matter Broke Loose, and Fragments of Sundry Things Inedited* (Boston: Charles D. Strong, 1842); Captain James Colnett, *A Voyage to the South Atlantic and round Cape Horn into the Pacific Ocean, for the Purpose of Extending the Spermaceti Whale Fisheries, and Other Objects of Commerce, by Ascertaining the Ports, Bays, Harbours, and Anchoring Births, in Certain Islands and Coasts in Those Seas at Which the Ships of the British Merchants Might Be Refitted* (London, 1798); Pierre Bayle, *An Historical and Critical Dictionary* (London, 1710); and John Kitto, *A Cyclopædia of Biblical Literature* (Edinburgh, 1845).

Early in 1850 Melville also had begun to make use of information about the natural history of whales, including articles in the *Penny Cyclopædia*, especially the entry on "Whales," which cited and paraphrased whole passages from the already-standard work by Thomas Beale. The *Cyclopædia* Melville had acquired earlier, and had made much use of in his previous two books. Promptly enough he also got hold of a book the Harpers had published in his absence, late in 1849, the Reverend Henry T. Cheever's *The Whale and His Captors; or, The Whaleman's Adventures, and the Whale's Biography, as Gathered on the Homeward Cruise of the "Commodore Preble."* In "The Affidavit" (ch. 45)

Melville took from Cheever evidence for two basic points: that a whaling captain seeking a particular whale would have a chance of finding it, and that a whale could sink a ship. The purpose of that chapter, which seems to have been drafted at an early stage of the composition, was to establish the plausibility of a quest for one whale out of all the whales in the oceans and the plausibility of a catastrophe like that which befell the *Essex* — the sinking of a ship by (in all likelihood) that identical whale. The fact that Melville (or his narrator, Ishmael) says in "The Affidavit" that he had not yet learned particulars of the destruction of the *Union* by a whale may mean that he had not yet acquired, or not read all the way through, Macy's book, where they do occur.

As the weeks of spring passed Melville realized that he needed access to some basic books about whales as well as books about whaling. From the New York Society Library on 29 April he borrowed the two volumes of William Scoresby's *An Account of the Arctic Regions, with a History and Description of the Northern Whale Fishery* (Edinburgh, 1820). Much of this book proved of little use, since the viewpoint was British and since the subject was the Northern (Atlantic) fishery for the right whale, but it provided Melville with much incidental information. Furthermore, Scoresby's stuffy and pious tone proved so irritating or amusing that Melville treated him as a stooge whenever he plundered him (as he had mocked his sources ever since he honed his skills on the good missionary William Ellis while rifling his *Polynesian Researches* for *Omoo*). Probably about the time he borrowed Scoresby, he asked Putnam to get him a copy of Thomas Beale so he would not have to make do with excerpts in his other source books.

Outside on 1 May, the city's traditional moving day, walkers had to be watchful: "Every third person you meet is carrying either a looking glass, or an astral lamp, or a hall lamp, or some other little article that wont stand the jolting of the cart," "Charlemac" wrote in his letter to the Savannah *Daily Morning News* (printed on 7 May). Inside the house on Fourth Avenue, on 1 May Melville broke off working long enough to reply to a letter from Richard Henry Dana Jr. (two days after borrowing the Scoresby volumes). This letter contains his first known reference to what became *Moby-Dick* and gives a hint as to how far along he was in its composition:

> About the "whaling voyage" — I am half way in the work, & am very glad that your suggestion so jumps with mine. It will be a strange sort of a book, tho', I fear; blubber is blubber you know; tho' you may get oil out of it, the poetry runs as hard as sap from a frozen maple tree; — & to cook the thing up, one must needs throw in a little fancy, which from the nature of the thing, must be ungainly as the gambols of the whales themselves. Yet I mean to give the truth of the thing, spite of this.

This passage directly follows an account of how Edward Moxon had spoken to him in London about the gratification *Two Years before the Mast* had afforded certain people, among them the banker-poet Samuel Rogers, "who poetically appreciated the scenic sea passages, describing ice, storms, Cape Horn, & all that." To some extent, this use of "poetically" must condition Melville's use of "poetry."

Dana was just enough Melville's senior to pepper him with friendly concern that he make good use of his varied experiences in the South Seas. In 1849 Dana had suggested that he write a book about his experiences on a man-of-war, and Melville had replied on 6 October 1849 that his "hint" had, "in anticipation, been acted on" — in fact, a printed copy of the book (in the form of sheets) was before him. Again, in the letter of April 1850 to which Melville was replying, Dana had made a suggestion — this time, that Melville write a book based on his experiences as a whaleman. Once again the suggestion had jumped with (or jumped a little later than) Melville's own. The difference between the two cases is that the previous autumn Melville had made no qualifications at all: Dana had made a suggestion and could look forward to seeing just the sort of book he wanted to see. Now Dana had made a new suggestion and had to be warned that the book would *not* be just the sort he had in mind. Rather, it would be "a strange sort of a book," probably less documentary than Melville thought Dana would have hoped, and more imaginative. The aesthetic problem as Melville defined it for Dana (and himself) was how to reconcile a realistic account of whaling processes with a poetic treatment of the subject: easy to get oil from blubber, harder to get poetry from blubber. Furthermore, in cooking the thing up, working it into literary form, "one must needs throw in a little fancy" (in the sense of "imagination"), ungainly though that fancy must be, given "the nature of the thing." Yet despite all difficulties Melville meant "to give the truth of the thing," presumably the sort of realistic depiction of whaling that Dana by literary example and temperament would be expected to prefer. (A recent real story may have come to Melville's attention in one of the New York papers, for it reached Savannah on 4 May in the *Republican*, belatedly: "VESSEL WRECKED BY A WHALE," an item about the Peruvian brig *Frederic*, sunk by a whale off Porto Anna in Nicaragua on 8 July 1849.)

In this 1 May 1850 letter Melville cast Dana into the role of soul mate in recalling the "sort of Siamese link of affectionate sympathy" he had felt reading *Two Years before the Mast* after his voyage to Liverpool in 1839. He even fantasized about Dana as the ideal audience of one (if only he did not need to get money for his books): "I almost think, I should hereafter — in the case of a sea book — get my M.S.S. neatly & legibly copied by a scrivener — send you that one copy — & deem such a procedure the best publication."

This passage strikingly presages the rhapsodic language in his letter to Hawthorne on 17 November 1851: "I feel that the Godhead is broken up like the bread at the Supper, and that we are the pieces. Hence this infinite fraternity of feeling." (The comment about a scrivener is merely part of the fantasy of what Melville would do if he had endless money, rather than an oblique slight at his actual copyists.) That Melville had long needed male literary soul mates is clear from the depiction of Nord in *White-Jacket*, based on a shipmate on the *United States*, Oliver Russ, who wrote Melville in 1859 that he had named a son Herman Melville Russ before Melville had become famous; and Melville's non-literary companion in Typee, Richard Tobias Greene, persuaded his sister to do the same, perhaps before *Typee* was published, and named his own son Herman Melville Greene. Nat Willis and many others plainly felt the same winning charm in Melville's personality. (Dazzled by Gansevoort, the family tended to take Herman's character for granted.) The need to be around brilliant men had been assuaged during his voyage to England and intermittently in London, but Melville's self-imposed unsocial habits since his return had created an appetency for literary companionship that would demand to be satisfied.

Under other circumstances Willis might have been the companion Melville needed now. Their relationship was rooted in Gansevoort's free-and-easy friendship with Willis in London, and had flourished to the point of intimacy. Melville up to this point had seen much more of Willis than Dana, and at times he may have seen more of Willis than Duyckinck for long stretches: our sense of who was important in Melville's life is skewed by Duyckinck's preservation of documents. Melville and Willis were also united in the late 1840s by their public reputations for sexual experiences. While Melville had become our first literary sex symbol, Willis had become known as a sensualist, to the point that late the previous year, on 18 October 1849, he had Greeley print in the *Tribune* his defense: "since my first return to this country, and as a husband and father, my habits have been pure, and my tastes (by refinement, and without the aid of principle) are altogether above the level . . . ascribed to me." Despite this public denial, in 1848 Willis had been pursuing a liaison with the indiscriminately generous English wife of Edwin Forrest, as had his musical brother, Richard S. Willis (younger, born in Melville's year), fresh back from Europe. Such an affair Willis would not have talked to Melville about, but Willis exuded a kind of refined sensuality which Melville had knocked about enough to be sensitive to, and not offended by, and Willis found Melville alluring in person and in literary performance. The current feuding with Duyckinck was bad enough, but Willis's involvement in the Forrest divorce case was much more distressing for Melville. Willis in the *Home Journal* on 1 June 1850 attacked the veracity of an actor's affidavit that he had been intimate with Mrs. Forrest. This was too much for the muscular Forrest, who on the evening of 17 June joined with a confederate to waylay the frail Willis as he walked from his house at 198 Fourth Street toward Broadway. In the Washington Parade Ground (Washington Square) Forrest appeared from behind (Willis and others said). Under the pretext that Willis was making a motion as if to draw a weapon, Forrest knocked down the writer (ill for months with a rheumatic fever, his first biographer, Henry Beers, said, and in an unusually feeble condition of body), seized Willis's elegant cane, planted his foot on Willis's neck and beat him with the cane (or, by another report, with a gutta-percha whip). Poor Willis, at a considerable disadvantage in pulmonary capacity at any time, tried to call for police, but Forrest shouted down any would-be rescuers: "Gentlemen, this is the seducer of my wife; do not interfere."

That evening Willis was strong enough to indite a "card" (a public personal statement) which was printed in the *Herald* and other papers the next day. In it he charged that Forrest had attacked him from behind. Forrest encountered William Cullen Bryant and his son-in-law Parke Godwin on Broadway and demanded to be told who was responsible for the report in the *Evening Post* that he had struck Willis from behind. Godwin manfully took responsibility, and lived to testify that on an earlier occasion Forrest had threatened to cut Willis's damned heart out; he also lived to offer shelter to Mrs. Forrest in his house. On 20 June Greeley printed in the *Tribune* another card from Willis quoting an affidavit from an eyewitness saying that Forrest attacked from behind after lurking behind a tree close to Willis's home. The card was followed by a long letter, "The Assault on N. P. Willis," signed "A Citizen of New-York"; "Citizen" approved the skeptical tone of the *Tribune*'s earlier comments and pointed out that Forrest picked on the weakest in physique out of the half dozen accused seducers. Other testimony mounted against Forrest until on the twenty-fifth the tragedian printed his own card in the *Herald:* "I most solemnly aver, that when I first struck N. P. Willis, I stood before him, face to face, and with my hand alone felled him to the earth." On 29 June Willis devoted much space in the *Home Journal* to "MR. FORREST'S COWARDLY ASSAULT." All the dozens of newspapers of New York joined in with gleeful disapproval and skepticism of one or both sides in the controversy. Mathews got involved at once. Oakey Hall on 23 June literally "scissored" from the *Prompter,* Mathews's new magazine, part of the "very vigorous article upon Mr. Forrest's literary pretensions as an actor, written by one of our most accomplished scholars. It is just in its denunciation and severe in its truthfulness."

Such sordid controversies involving the New York literati of which he had become a part gave Melville, as the weeks passed, more and more reason to want to keep his distance from Zenzori, Hauto, Lucree, Roddi, and Pollo, those critics he had written into *Mardi* late in 1848 — more distance even from Willis and Duyckinck, of whom he was personally fond. In London he had recognized that Allan and others would account him "a ninny" for not staying on to accept the duke of Rutland's invitation, and that he would later "upbraid" himself "for neglecting such an opportunity of procuring *material.*" That summer of 1850, news spread around the United States of what the Savannah *Daily Morning News* on 31 July proclaimed in boldface and small capitals as "Massacre and Cannibalism. A ship's crew eaten by the savages of the Sandle Wood islands." Melville did not need to wait for summer to be reminded of massacres and cannibalism. Already, in the spring, in some moods it seemed obvious that he had returned all too precipitously to a discarded fragment of *Mardi*, a strange island teeming with hysterical pygmy cannibals — no place to do the work he now needed to do.

35

Pittsfield and Hawthorne

June–7 August 1850

Rural amusements invigorate the body and enliven the mind.

"Allan Melvills Book," 1796

CLINCHED TO HIS DESK from February through May or a little longer, and in the later weeks of this period frustrated by his need for supplementary whaling books, Melville by June was eager to reward himself with more than brisk walks down to the Battery. The author of *White-Jacket*, with its tribute to wanderlust, may have treated himself to one or more outings as the weather improved. Allan, Sophia, and Fanny had not been able to stop at West Point in 1848, but Allan and Sophia did tour there in 1849, and Herman seems to have taken his own chance in the spring of 1850. A casual comment in a letter Augusta wrote to Evert Duyckinck on 20 July refers to someone's, presumably Melville's, taking an excursion to West Point which had proved very interesting "in the telling." He may have had company, for Tom was home in late spring of 1850, looking for a ship. The explorers would have come back with stories of the cadets encamped on the plain (as they did June through August). There they performed their military exercises daily, as Dickens had told the world in his *American Notes*, where he marveled at the splendor of the location: "In this beautiful place: the fairest among the fair and lovely Highlands of the North River: shut in by deep green heights and ruined forts, and looking down upon the distant town of Newburgh, along a glittering path of sunlit water, with here and there a skiff, whose white sail often bends upon some new tack as sudden flaws of wind come down upon her from the gullies in the hills: hemmed in, besides, all round with memories of Washington, and events of the revolutionary war: is the Military School of America." Many Americans saw the region through Dickens's eyes, as Dickens himself had seen it through Washington Irving's. Melville had known it, from the level of riverboat decks, since his boyhood, but seems never to have explored it before.

With or without an outing to West Point, Melville was dissatisfied, but without any definite plans for the summer. He delayed a decision about a

vacation from week to week until he reached a good stopping point on the
book, which depended in part on his receiving the whaling books he had
ordered and seeing just what sort of use they might be to him. On 27 June he
still did not have his copy of Thomas Beale's *Natural History of the Sperm
Whale* but decided he could write to Richard Bentley anyway: "In the latter
part of the coming autumn I shall have ready a new work; and I write you now
to propose its publication in England." He described the book as "a romance
of adventure, founded upon certain wild legends in the Southern Sperm
Whale Fisheries, and illustrated by the author's own personal experience, of
two years & more, as a harpooneer." Having strained the truth by claiming to
have been a harpooneer, and one for that long a time, Melville went on to say
that he thought the book would be worth two hundred pounds to Bentley, or
more if he could "positively" be put "in possession of the copyright." This
optimistic suggestion Melville justified in terms of the "great novelty" of the
manuscript: "I do not know that the subject treated of has ever been worked
up by a romancer; or, indeed, by any writer, in any adequate manner." The
most significant part of the 27 June letter to Bentley is Melville's characterization of the book, which must have reflected not only his sense of it as it
then stood but also his sense of how he expected it to stand after months
more of work. As in the description to Dana, he was seeing the book as both
romantic and realistic, founded on wild legends and illustrated by personal
experience.

There seems no reason not to take seriously Melville's assurance that he
expected to have the new work ready in the latter part of the next autumn —
which would, after all, put the completion after Thanksgiving and near
Christmas, like *Omoo*, making a total of ten or eleven months for composition of a single book by a man who had written two books in four months the
year before. The reviewing of *White-Jacket* had provided an occasion for
word to reach the public about what the Duyckinck circle knew of Melville's
extraordinary productivity the summer before. Young Oakey Hall in the
New Orleans *Commercial Bulletin* (9 April) was adulatory about *White-Jacket*,
and about Melville: "Keep your eye on Herman Melville. If his present field,
or rather ocean of literature, should ever become fruitless of pursuit, he will
be famous in other fields. There is a humor, and sparkle of rhetoric in his
writings, which, if he lives to be the man equal in years to Irving, Cooper and
Paulding, will rank him as high on the chalk-notch of fame as they." Hall
declared that Melville was "a man to whom the words 'fail' and 'fag out' are
unknown," and moreover "a sturdy Knickerbocker" of whom New Yorkers
were proud. Melville's intimacy with the Duyckinck clique was thus a means
of spreading his fame, and even intimate details of his working habits.

Nothing in Melville's description to Bentley on 27 June suggested it, but he needed more scientific ballast for his personal experience than he was finding in the *Penny Cyclopædia* and in Scoresby. At last on 10 July he picked up the copy of Beale that Putnam had imported from England for him. As he had known already from the many quotations from it he had seen in other books, and perhaps from one available copy or another of the book itself, Beale would be immensely useful for information that he could quote or otherwise assimilate into the manuscript. Like the *Penny Cyclopædia*, Beale proved to contain information that Melville could manipulate so as to give the impression that he had read more reference books than had in fact come his way. When he alluded (ch. 32, "Cetology") to Scoresby, Cuvier, Hunter, and Lesson as if he had consulted them all, he was drawing quotations from a single page of Beale. Once he had his Beale to go with his borrowed Scoresby, Melville could have fallen to, eking out his manuscript with chapters or parts of chapters dealing with the natural history of the whale. He could, in short, have proved that he could write two books in the summer of 1849 and another one by the fall of 1850.

That did not happen — in large part because Melville was a family man, indulged, even pampered, but a man with responsibilities to his wife and child, his sisters and brothers, and his mother. Maria Gansevoort Melville now had few constraints on her movements other than shortage of money. Her most severe constraint, it seemed, was the need to spend as much time as possible with her darling Tom, whenever he was ashore, between ships. His arrivals always occasioned great joy in the household, and under normal circumstances Maria would have gone nowhere until he sailed. This time, recalling how very sick she had been much of the previous summer, Maria decided that she must treat herself to a vacation with her widowed sister-in-law Mary Melvill, whom she had not seen for many years, perhaps not since 1838. Mary had returned from Galena with three of her children and was staying at the farm with Robert and Susan. Saying farewell to Tom and the others in New York, Maria went to Pittsfield. In the summer of 1848 the Melvill house had been good enough for the Longfellows and the previous fall it had been good enough for ex-president John Tyler and his family, and it had always seemed like paradise to her.

Maria arrived in Pittsfield, perhaps without an escort, sometime after 6 June and before 18 June. In the past the Melvilles had always gone straight to the farm and stayed there, pretty much, for they were better acquainted with the Sedgwicks in Lenox than any Pittsfield family. The village remained unfamiliar territory, especially after the passage of so much time. What Maria encountered in 1850 was much like what a New Hampshire visitor encountered two years later when he stopped over at Pittsfield on the way to Albany, on impulse, after seeing that his train was approaching "a large and beautiful town." The Housatonic Railroad depot was a long flight of stairs below Main Street, where the street divided into "North" and "South." The New Hampshire writer was struck by the openness of the village: "Beautiful dwellings scattered around; gardens laid out with the most exquisite taste, in which every one seemed to vie with his neighbor for the finest display; and, what seemed to me better than all, they were not fenced in so as to be seen only by the privileged few, but low fences and open slatwork enabled the passer by to see and admire." In this article, printed in the Portsmouth *Journal* (21 August 1852), the visitor described encountering an acquaintance at the hotel (the Berkshire House) who drove him to the cemetery west of town, which was being completed when Maria arrived in 1850: "This is destined to become one of the most beautiful spots of the kind in that vicinity. It consists of several acres of land, diversified in surface and scenery, exhibiting hills, valleys and evergreen forests." This tract was well described, when less raw, by a mourner at former Governor Briggs's funeral in 1861: "It was a secluded spot, in the valley of the 'West Branch' (one of the streams which unite to form the Housatonic), a mile or more away from the centre of the village of Pittsfield—a very gem, set in the bosom of the mountains." The writer for the *Journal* also described the "large carriage manufactory of Messrs. J. Clapp & Son," where fifty or more men were employed in "making pleasure carriages, from the light Phaeton to the largest Family Coach," primarily for sale in New York and Boston. As the writer found, so Maria found: Pittsfield had become a bustling village.

Maria had time now to talk with her widowed sister-in-law about deaths and births and finances, and to come to terms with the unfairness of the situation in which Mary and her children still received regular income from the Melvill estate, through Judge Shaw. Maria was comfortable with Robert, whom she remembered well from his young manhood, although she was not well acquainted with his wife, who had suffered much in her years of marriage. Maria could flourish in the presence of timidity like Susan's. She shrewdly had made her plans to arrive early, before the house was crowded with summer boarders from the elite of literature and politics, and she found herself so happy that her letters home made it harder and harder for the others to stay in town. If she had consulted only her own pleasure she would have stayed all summer, but around 24 June out of "motives of delicacy" Maria had Robert put her on the train for a journey to Lansingburgh, as she wrote Augusta on 27 June. He did so ineptly, she had to say, in her description of her harrowing departure and the providential appearance of an old friend on the train:

I met Mr Ives at Richmond a few miles from Pittsfield, he seem'd surprised to meet me, I was really rejoic'd to have a companion. From the hurried manner in which I left, the car whistle sounding just as Robert & I were slowly entering the Village, we were very nearly left behind, he jumpt from the Buggy, ran up the platform overhanging the cars, & cryed out A passenger wait a moment, so amidst hissing of steam, cries of this way! this way! trunk! make haste, hurry, where do you want to go, today, step in this car, I stept in, look'd out, saw Robert & a man coming down the crook'd stairs with Lizzies big black trunk draged hurriedly between them, down they came the trunk flying off & pitched in the Baggage car any way. Robert shook hands through the window, the steam hissing louder & louder, we darted off, & Robert was lost to view.

By leaving to visit her cousin Maria Peebles in Lansingburgh when she did, Maria to her great annoyance missed a letter Augusta wrote her on 24 June telling her that some others in the family had decided to join her at Pittsfield. That letter reached her on the twenty-seventh, forwarded from Pittsfield, along with another one Augusta had mailed on the twenty-sixth, addressed to her at Lansingburgh. Fanny had been on her way to the farm when Maria left, and found herself in Pittsfield, on 27 June, motherless for one of the few times in her life. When she wrote Augusta on 27 June, Maria had regrouped. Now she was hoping to rendezvous with "Kate, Allan & Sophia, with sweet little Maria in Albany on Saturday" (the twenty-ninth) — presumably all on their way to Pittsfield, where Augusta addressed a letter to Sophia on the Sunday the thirtieth.

Just which members of the Fourth Avenue household came to Pittsfield that summer, when they arrived, and just how long they stayed is not entirely clear. Augusta's own June visit, to the Van Rensselaers at the Manor House, proved disastrous, for she carried the whooping cough back to New York with her and communicated it to both Malcolm and little Maria. Malcolm recuperated more slowly than his cousin, thereby complicating any plans for vacation. During Herman's first visit to the farm as a married man, alone, his Cousin Priscilla had commented (3 April 1848) on his manifesting "so much constancy toward the object of his *first love*, our *Berkshire* farm — as to *tear* himself from the idol of his heart" (that is to say, Lizzie) "to indulge again in the unfetter'd freedom of Batchelor ways." On that occasion the weather had forbade any free unfettered wandering such as he probably experienced late that summer. Now, if Herman could only get there, with a healthy Malcolm held by one hand and Thomas Beale by the other, he could wander all he wanted to for at least a few days. Old Zack, having become President Taylor, had died in Washington City on 9 July, so newspapers were black-bordered in New York on the tenth, when Melville picked up his Beale from London. Perhaps he did so on the way to the depot with Lizzie and Malcolm to join Sophia at Robert's: late on that day Augusta wrote to both Sophia and Lizzie there. Herman then intended to be back in New York in a week, but Allan may have decided already that he would commute back and forth as long as Sophia was content on the farm.

Tom by this time had found a vessel, the *Celestial* — technically a "ship" again, next in size to a steamer. The destination was San Francisco — exciting for Tom, since the gold fever had not abated, and vicariously exciting for Herman and the rest of the family. (The author of *Typee* and *Omoo* had been hard at work on the whaling manuscript during the months when Bayard Taylor's descriptions of California were featured in the *Tribune*, before appearing as *Eldorado* in two volumes about 11 May 1850.) No one wanted to be away from home when Tom left, but it became progressively harder, this summer, to fit everyone's schedule to his, especially since there was a huge and well-staffed house for him and "Dut" to rattle around in until the *Celestial* sailed on 16 July, under Captain Gardner. (From Cooper's *The Sea Lions* Melville already knew of the differently spelled Gardiners of Gardiner Island, that sweet morsel in the very jaws of Long Island, whose unbroken proprietorship rivaled that of the Van Rensselaers; but Tom's captain may have given his name to the captain of the *Rachel* in Herman's whaling book, after some months had passed.)

When he arrived at Robert's, Melville was keyed up, having said goodbye to Tom, who had probably already signed on his ship, although the day of sailing was still doubtful. Melville may have planned to go back to New York and work a few weeks while Lizzie and Malcolm and others in the family enjoyed the Berkshires. Then he may have decided that if he went back to New York for his manuscript he could return and settle down to a bucolic summer's writing. He and the other city Melvilles had to adjust to the changes in Aunt Mary and the Melvill cousins. The mentally impaired Henry Dearborn was there, as well as Helen Jean, Kate's "crony" in the old days, and Allan Cargill, who as a baby had been very fond of Herman and was old enough to remember him from his visit to Galena a decade earlier. Robert and Herman had known each other as children and as young adults, and had renewed their acquaintance in 1848, after their fortunes had so astonishingly diverged. Of the Melvill cousins Lizzie knew only Robert and his wife, from her visit in 1848. Hours had to be devoted to exchanging news with Aunt Mary and the cousins, for both families had to tell and retell the news of twelve years, including the circumstances of the deaths of Uncle Thomas, Julia, Gansevoort, and other losses, including one of Robert and Susan's children.

More than the changes in their relatives, the Melvilles had to adjust to a change in the status of the farm. Some rooms of the Melvill house were occupied by boarders, including an anomalously situated couple, John Rowland Morewood and his wife, Sarah, who, Herman learned, had just bought the farm. It is not clear whether or not Robert had been given title to the farm by Judge Shaw and John D'Wolf, but the money Morewood paid, sixty-five hundred dollars, went to Aunt Mary and her children, apparently in equal parts. The Morewoods, however, had no immediate plans to take possession of the property, for they were planning a lengthy trip to visit Rowland's family in England, for he was English-born. (He was called by his middle name.) In the late winter and early spring of 1848 this couple had begun to grow restless in their retreat near New York City. Morewood was a commission merchant at 14 Beaver Street with a home in Carmansville, or Fort Washington, near the site of the present George Washington Bridge. Their own "Noble looking Child" (Sarah Morewood to Ann McConnel, 21 March 1848), Willie, blue-eyed, fair, was a year older than the Melville cousins; in due course he became the husband of Allan and Sophia's "sweet little Maria."

In Carmansville, Sarah's biggest problem, as she described it in her 21 March 1848 letter to her sister-in-law, was the American phenomenon not yet named "urban sprawl" and the consequent desecration of the landscape — concerns much on the minds of many upper-middle-class and upper-class Americans by the late 1840s and early 1850s. The "march of 'improvement'" had made "such rapid strides as to make it most difficult" for them "to remain long in the Country, when its locality be at all accessible to the City." Already their view was damaged ("we now look out on brick walls — instead of green fields as we used to do"). Nothing was "exempt from the spoiler," for a railroad with its "dark stiff looking embankment" was going up along the Hudson, and the charm had fled. Driven out of their pleasant home two years later, they had purchased the Melvill place, apparently just before Herman Melville arrived there in July 1850. The news of the purchase was a shock (who had known it was for sale?) and stirred up in Herman a brew of feelings in which two of the ingredients were envy and jealousy — emotions fit for the cauldron in that passage he had memorized from *Macbeth* in his youth.

The Melville most familiar with Aunt Mary and all the Melvill cousins, Herman quickly entered into the spirit of vacation. He could now play a new and appealing role, for the fatherless boy of the 1830s had returned with wife and son as a man who had made good. Robert had been planning a wagon trip around the southern part of Berkshire County "to view the state of the crops — he being chairman of the 'Viewing Committee' of the Berkshire

Agricultural Society." This Herman jotted down in *A History of the County of Berkshire, Massachusetts* (Pittsfield, 1829), by David Dudley Field (by 1850 identified locally as "the elder" Field of that name). Melville paid seventy-five cents for the book on 16 July, relying on it for a quick review of locales, crops, and customs, for he had decided to set out two days later on the excursion with Robert. On the seventeenth he wrote home to New York about his plans for a week-long "rambling expedition," as Augusta phrased his plans in relaying the news to Evert Duyckinck on 20 July. She was already anticipating that he would have stories to tell about it as interesting as his stories about West Point. At breakfast on the eighteenth, before he and Robert set out, Aunt Mary gave him a copy of Hawthorne's *Mosses from an Old Manse*, a well-chosen gift, since in the early summer of 1850 Nathaniel Hawthorne and his wife, Sophia, and their two children, in the flush of his first popular success, with *The Scarlet Letter,* had moved into William Aspinwall Tappan and Caroline Tappan's red cottage overlooking Stockbridge Bowl outside Lenox. (People were shifting houses: the Tappans were living in the big house belonging to Sam Ward of Bond Street while they rented the Hawthornes their cottage nearby.) Other writers were in the neighborhood. Oliver Wendell Holmes, no longer the impudent youth who had poeticized the old Major Melvill, had a summer house a little east of the Melvill house, for the Wendell family had been great landowners in the Berkshires; and the novelist Catharine Sedgwick lived with her brother Charles in Lenox. As the cousins set off at eight in the morning the new cachet of the Berkshires can only have enhanced the old appeal the region had for Melville: he felt almost a native, not a tourist.

Robert had traveled as far as the Mississippi, more than once, but year by year he had dragged out a miserable existence on the farm at Pittsfield or at his wife's father's farm nearby. Herman was now a seasoned traveler who knew enough about metaphorical and literal guidebooks to take complicated pleasure in carrying the *History* of Berkshire County around with him. The truth is that some of what he was seeing was new to him. In the late 1830s his work on the farm and his duties as schoolteacher had defined his status as a workman going about a routine, never as a vacationer, however many youthful rambles he managed to make. Even now he and Robert were holding to an itinerary, which the Pittsfield *Sun* printed on 18 July: "The Committee of the Agricultural Society, ON CROPS, will commence the discharge of their duties on THURSDAY of the present week. They will go down from Lenox on the western side of the County, and return on the eastern during this week. On MONDAY next [22 JULY], they will go from Pittsfield through the eastern towns to the north, and return by Lanesborough." Acutely aware of the ironic discrepancy between keeping a London journal and a set of Berkshire memoranda, Melville memorialized the outing by making his own notes on the endpapers of the *History:* "Arrived in Lenox Meeting house on the hill, Took a round turn into the hollow — Thence to Richmond, dining at the [Eleazer] Williams' nigh the R. R. Depot. Went to a high hill in Richmond to see a crop of rye on a mountain. Fine prospect. Put up for the night at old Cap. [Caleb] Smith's in Lenox, near the Pond. Glorious place, & fine old fellow." On the nineteenth they were detained at old Smith's till noon by a severe storm — not a hardship, since Melville relished Smith ("quite a gem," he later assured Sophia Hawthorne). Then they went on to Stockbridge, and across the Housatonic, over what the locals called "the plains," and on by Monument Mountain, through Barrington to Egremont, where they put up for the night at the house of Nelson Joyner, a man Melville did not know. On Saturday the twentieth they made their way to Sheffield, where they dined at John L. Cooper's, then reached Stockbridge in time to "tea" with Luther T. Hinckley in the village before Herman caught a late train to Pittsfield.

On the wagon Herman had improved odd moments by reminding himself of names of grasses, or learning names of newly introduced varieties, for he listed these on the back flyleaf: Redtop, Ribbon Grass, Finger Grass, Orchard Grass, Hair Grass. In the back he copied out lines he ascribed to a Shaker poet:

> Let them talk of Blue Ridges
> And Natural Bridges,
> But give me the Valley of Berks: —
> There the hill-horse neighs,
> There wind the purple ways . . .

Later he or someone scraped off two more lines, losing the rhyme for "Berks." Whether or not his notes indicate uneasiness with his company, Herman now reacted to any sort of confinement (even in a wagon in the open air) with something like a panic of restlessness, and three days in a wagon with Robert was enough.

Back at the Melvill house, Herman amused the whole family by writing out a spoof agricultural report for Robert to sign, everyone recognizing that of the two schoolmaster cousins Herman had advanced farther, by now, toward the mastery of satiric prose. What Herman dashed off was a gleeful parody of the language of Progress, much to his own pleasure and that of the family, who would watch for local comment when in due course the report would be printed in the papers:

Swamps and quagmires, in which the only vegetable productions were alders and ferns, with a few cat-tails interspersed among them as decorations, are

now covered with a carpet of herds-grass and clover, and afford exuberant
crops of hay. The Committee would be sorry that any words of theirs should
give rise to suspicion that they are deficient in the milk of human kindness,
and they profess to have as great an aversion to strife as the most enthusiastic
members of the Peace Society; yet they cannot withhold their approbation of
the determination manifested by the proprietors of these swamps, to extermi-
nate the tribes of insects and reptiles, which, for ought [aught] that we know
to the contrary, had a life estate thereof from generation to generation, since
the day when Noah, with his numerous family, emerged from the Ark.

In another paragraph Melville recorded his satisfaction that farmers had
begun to embellish the "road-sides with forest trees." He waxed ammoniac
in praising the "superior construction of barns, by which not only the comfort of domestic animals is much increased, but greater conveniences for
their care, and for the accumulation of manure are attained." Saving manure
caught Melville's fancy, and he elaborated it into a vision of bounteous Nature's way with that ingredient: "The greatest pleasure may be taken by the
philosopher and naturalist, (and the farmer *should* be both,) in contemplating
that benign process by which ingredients the most offensive to the human
senses, are converted into articles that gratify the most delicate taste, and
pamper the most luxurious appetite." He was being a good cousin, for alert
readers could smile at this part of the report, and Robert could supply the
serious list of prizes that made up the bulk of the report.

Published in the Pittsfield *Culturist and Gazette* on 9 October 1850, the
report passed for what it was. On 23 October the editor, Stephen Reed,
published a lampoon from the "Bunkum Agricultural Society" signed by
"Z. Q. Factminus, Esq. *Chairman*": "Your Committee have examined a very
large number of crops, many of which were extremely fine, and have become
fully satisfied that our County can produce excellent crops, but since we have
learned but little ourselves how they can be produced, you will expect from
us nothing farther than to hold out to you encouragement from the fact that
such is the fact." This was quite all Melville's effort deserved in the form of
public acknowledgment. A century passed before Jay Leyda retrieved it from
the *Culturist and Gazette*.

On Sunday, 21 July, the day after Herman got back to the farm, he was off
again to the Shaker colony at Hancock, where he bought a copy of a recent
book, *A Summary View of the Millennial Church, or United Society of Believers,
Commonly Called Shakers*. In Manhattan, Augusta was expecting Herman to
return, alone, soon after his week-long trip with Robert, so she could "hardly
look for him before Tuesday or Wednesday," the twenty-third or twenty-
fourth, she wrote to Evert Duyckinck. Melville had not been able to schedule

the start of the vacation much in advance, and he continued to improvise during the next weeks. He also had things on his mind that his literary friends might help with. Back on the first of May, when he had written Dana, his aesthetic problem had been to boil poetry out of blubber even while telling "the truth of the thing." At some point later in the spring Melville had begun focusing on a more momentous problem, how an American writer could write of real American life with a Shakespearean intensity without imitating Shakespeare — particularly Shakespearean rhetoric. Thomas Powell in *Living Authors of America* had caught his attention with the assertion that all poets had been accused of imitation. In that passage Melville had found a welcome reminder that even Shakespeare had been charged by a contemporary with imitation, and he had carried the memory of *Groatsworth of Wit* into his further study of what critics were saying of Shakespeare.

In these first months after his return from England, Melville may have made a point of looking into editorial introductions in editions of Shakespeare such as the one he had acquired early the year before. In particular, he seems to have looked at one edited by John Payne Collier (1844). That edition contained a "History of the English Drama and Stage to the Time of Shakespeare" and a "Life of William Shakespeare." In the "History" Melville seems to have read the passage in which Collier attempted to praise Shakespeare's greatness without doing "injustice" to his predecessors and contemporaries: "He rose to eminence, and he maintained it, amid struggles for equality by men of high genius and varied talents; and with his example ever since before us, no poet of our own, or of any other country, has even approached his excellence. Shakespeare is greatest by a comparison with greatness, or he is nothing." The clearest evidence that Melville had used this edition is in the "Life," where Collier enunciated the new theory that Chettle was the author of *Groatsworth of Wit*, a theory that Melville accepted, and combined with Powell's ideas about originality and imitation.

At this stopping point in his work Melville was eager to talk about issues he had not been able to discuss with Allan and could not even broach with Robert during hours of enforced companionship. Acutely aware of his lack of formal education, Melville had eagerly availed himself the autumn before of the shipboard philosophical tutorials from his junior, George Adler; now he thought Cornelius Mathews could advise him. Mathews, after all, had been writing on English drama and writing dramas for half a decade before *Typee* appeared. Mathews was himself the dramatist Melville knew best, as well as an authority on the drama and editor of a new periodical devoted to the drama, *The Prompter*. This journal, as Oakey Hall had told his New Orleans readers in May, was published not in the usual magazine size but in the smaller size of the series known as the "Modern Standard Drama." Hall had added: "Even to non-theatrical goers there is oftentimes something fascinating in dramatic details." Melville was not just fascinated but downright bedeviled by his ambitions for his own new work, and he felt that what he needed was to consult the authority, an expert on the drama whom he could quiz about Elizabethan drama as a whole, not just Shakespearean drama. Mathews may not have been able to help him, but Melville was not unreasonable in hoping that he could.

When Melville came bounding in from the country in the last week of July, he was too late to say a final good-bye to Tom, for the *Celestial* had been cleared on the sixteenth and was on its way to San Francisco. Augusta and Allan and others in the family told him of their farewells, and Henry Thurston had details to tell him of what Tom had shown him in the interior of the vessel. Melville had been holding aloof from his city friends for many months, but now he called on Duyckinck to pick up some books for Berkshire reading, and as usual found Mathews there. One reason for thinking that he borrowed books at this time is that on 20 July Augusta thanked Duyckinck for sending over to her "Tennyson's new poem," *In Memoriam*. In Duyckinck's list of books loaned the Tennyson book just precedes a volume of the *Democratic Review* (perhaps the one containing "The Great Nation of Futurity," November 1839?), a volume of *Arcturus*, Thoreau's *Merrimack*, and Sylvester Judd's *Margaret*. Borrowing *Arcturus* reminded Melville that Duyckinck and Mathews had already been living literary lives when he was an anonymous whaler. Here he saw articles on the well-appreciated young Dana and the poorly appreciated, no longer young Hawthorne, and in between there were some intriguing unsigned comments on old English books ("the far ancestors of the present race of authors, in great Eliza's age, when literature was young and vigorous"), a highly moral article on Beaumont and Fletcher by Duyckinck (the "gross falling off" from "the heroic standard of Shakespeare" by the two playwrights was a moral, not aesthetic lapse). The Thoreau he may have borrowed because Duyckinck told him there was a section on Mount Greylock in it.

While Melville made his selections from Duyckinck's library, he raved about the Berkshires in such a way as to evoke undisguised envy in his city friends. Duyckinck looked pallid in the heat, and Mathews was a man whose "hand faltered in a ten years' use of the unresting quill," a man who had not had a "country holiday" in ten long years — since before Melville went awhaling (so Mathews wrote in a 7 September essay for the *Literary World*). Melville wanted to return various hospitalities and generosities Duyckinck had shown him (not least in the book-lending line), and he had notions of playing the host in a grand fashion. In the city he could offer whist games for the gentlemen, but on the Melvill farm he could be profligate with entertainments simply by entrusting himself to the Berkshires. Sorry that Duyckinck and Mathews had been trapped in the city while he was rambling over the gorgeous terrain, and also eager to have resident authorities on literary matters at hand, now that he had time to talk, Melville impetuously invited both of them to come up the following week, without making sure there was room for them right away at the Melvill house. (There wasn't.) Borrowed books snugly in hand, plans burgeoning in head, Melville took the train back to Pittsfield in time to spend his thirty-first birthday on the farm.

Melville welcomed the prospect of having Duyckinck's company for a few days — after all, only ten months before he had strong-armed that gentle father of three into considering, for some days, an impulsive trip abroad, during which they would have been cabined and otherwise confined together for as long as a year. Why Melville welcomed Mathews's company is harder to see. Mathews was irrefutably self-important, tactless, and officious. A chauvinist for national literature who pointed to his own dreary writings as salient examples of the great emerging American literature, Mathews struck many of his contemporaries (James Russell Lowell among them) as a grotesque figure made only for ridicule. Mathews bedecked his circular face with peculiarly unflattering eyeglasses, the size of slightly elongated bantam eggs. He was lumpy in stature and waddled when he walked; his gait was "singularly ungainly," Thomas Powell wrote in May 1851, when he also described him as having "an intellectual face, and a remarkably well-developed brow," features which suggested that he "ought to have achieved more" than he had. On 22 March 1850 Oakey Hall had given his early report on Mathews's "local novel in the humourous vein," published that day, *Money-penny* — illustrated by Darley. The novelist "rather kaleidoscopes New York society, in his quiet telling way," Hall said, but he had to admit that some readers already (before actual publication) had found fault "with the un-hingedness of its plot, now and then." Confessing this drove Hall to define why he found Mathews appealing (the spelling is that of the *Commercial Bulletin*, 2 April): "Matthews is a man, who, if he wrote as he *talked*, would stand the first of American humorous writers. His talk is as original and quaint as any man's I know of. He is a conversationalist satirist, and will talk down his enemies yet. The reason why he does'nt write as well as he talks, is that [when] his pen [is] communicating thought for him its connections and appositeness are not so rapid and *flashing* as they ought to be. He could bring back an artificial rapidity of appositeness if he would elaborate more." Most contemporary reports of Mathews's speech and behavior make him seem nothing more than an egregious, humorless, self-promoting egotist, but Melville recognized in Mathews some of the qualities young Oakey Hall saw — a man who was cursed by some missing synaptic fluid so that in speech he could (if only rarely) be brilliant, while on paper he gravitated toward ponderousness. Melville cannot have felt as companionable with Mathews as with Evert Duyckinck, but he invited him also, and he cared too much about the Berkshires to import contemptible people there.

On Friday, 2 August (the day after Melville's birthday), Evert Duyckinck and Cornelius Mathews rattled "over the 160 miles" (as Evert wrote his wife on 3 August), reaching Pittsfield at half past ten at night and putting up at the Berkshire House in Pittsfield. A Gramercy Street man, a lawyer, but a true son of Stockbridge, David Dudley Field (namesake of his father, the editor and part author of the Berkshire history Melville had just bought), was "in the cars" for part or all of the trip, and Maria Melville somehow met the strapping big-footed Field in the cars also ("a very fine looking man rather handsome," she decided); perhaps she had gone home from Lansingburgh and then had been escorted back to the Berkshires by Duyckinck and Mathews. Without consulting Melville's wishes, Field laid out a plan for the New York literary men to meet "all the celebrities of Stockbridge," a formidable contingent, Duyckinck knew. (Duyckinck caught Field's name as Dudley David, perhaps because the younger Field went by his middle name, Dudley.)

Neither of the editorial New Yorkers had been to the Berkshires before. Duyckinck woke up tasting the "pure & bracing mountain air" (as he wrote his wife on 3 August) and prepared for Melville to move his and Mathews's gear to the Melvill house, though they were to sleep in a house nearby. Taking in the reality of the place, Duyckinck began guiltily writing ecstatic descriptions of the air and scenery to his wife, Margaret, who was stewing in the city with their daughter and two little sons, and the overtaxed Mathews effused pathetic gratitude for the bucolic respite. Sarah Morewood, soon to be the mistress of the Melvill house, "in linen sack armed with a bait box and fishing rod for the finny sport" (so Evert described her), whirled the visitors and some of the others away "for an afternoon excursion to Pontusac Lake, some seven miles westward" (so Mathews wrote in "Several Days in Berkshire," *Literary World*, 24 August). You did not just drive to Pontoosuc, Duyckinck wrote his wife, "you descend upon it and wind about it and above it by pleasant roads." Lizzie, Duyckinck recorded, was in "a great flapping straw hat tied under the chin, floating about with the Zephyrs in blue, pink or lilac." Sophia was so tremendously pregnant as to attract awestruck eyes and cut off witticisms mid-course. Still, Mathews said that the "very fish lurking below couldn't bite for laughing" out of the sheer joyousness of the day.

Evert had brought along proof sheets of Appleton's edition of Wordsworth's posthumous poem, *The Prelude*, for leisure reading. But when Mathews told him that Griswold was about to publish a whole book of the poem in his next week's magazine, Evert concluded to put together hastily a review for *his* next week's paper, and somewhere in the day he found time to send a parcel to his editorial office. He boasted to his wife about being able to edit the *Literary World* at long distance, but he had not found time to do more than dip into the poem and tag a few generalities onto lavish quotations — the way Thomas Powell wrote whole volumes. Aghast at Duyckinck's doing any work at all, Melville accused him of yielding to the temptation of the alien "Yankee atmosphere" instead of submitting himself to the genuine bucolic Berkshire spirit.

Sunday was Herman and Lizzie's third wedding anniversary. Mathews recalled it as a day of delicious beauty. Hardworking people took their ease, "lying under trees — lounging in the doorway — gossiping." Maria wrote Augusta that the day was passed (by the gentlemen) "in conversation & in smoking sitting on Chairs out on the grass." No one pushed himself too hard that day. Tempted not by the Yankee atmosphere now but by "the purity and sweetness of this mountain air," air which was "simply delicious" so that "every breath" was an enjoyment, Evert indulged himself in a fantasy of moving there with his family:

> The country is a broken plain surrounded by ranges of mountains, of which from the spot where I am looking over the spires of pleasant Pittsfield the cleft two humped Saddleback is the hugest wonder. But I wont describe scenery or tell you of the dark lakes set in the hollows or the murmuring brooks of the meadows, whose cool pebbly sound is only surpassed by the breezes in the tree tops above them. I will tell you nothing of the languishing elms whose foliage swoons in the luxury of air. To tell of these things to a lady encased in hot bricks in New York would be unprovoked cruelty were I not bound to a full and faithful account of my wanderings and did I not hope to make a convert to that beautiful part of the world the country. I assure you the Poets have made no mistake. The air is balm and a great many other things.

On that same day he gave the best contemporary description of the Melvill place: "The house where we live, Melville's is a rare place — an old family mansion, wainscoted and stately, with large halls & chimneys — quite a piece of mouldering rural grandeur — The family has gone down & this is their last season. The farm has been sold. Herman Melville knows every stone & tree & will probably make a book of its features. The old lady, his aunt, shows you a vial of the Boston tea, brought home by his grandfather in his shoes from the famous Boston tea party in the harbor." In an extraordinary mood, from the teeming fullness of his head Melville had talked of making a new kind of book about the features of the place.

Melville's mood may have taken a cast from a look at the Greylock section of Thoreau's *Week on the Concord and Merrimack Rivers.* At the time the book was published in 1849 Melville had other things on his mind: the review in the *Literary World* appeared on 22 September, as he was preparing for his voyage to England. There Duyckinck had mocked Thoreau: "He deprecates churches and preachers. Will he allow us to uphold them? or does he belong to the family of Malvolios, whose conceit was so engrossing that it threatened to deprive the world of cakes and ale. 'Dost thou think that because thou readest Confucius and art a Confusion there shall be no more steeples and towers? Aye, and bells shall ring too and Bishops shall dine!'" Now, Melville was prepared to see a kindred spirit in the man who made his way up the "long and spacious valley called the Bellows," on the way to the top of what he called Saddle-back Mountain, "a road for the pilgrim to enter upon who would climb to the gates of heaven." If Thoreau could put Mount Greylock into a book, Melville could talk of putting the farm into one.

Melville's mood did not merely spring from his desire to rival and surpass the man Duyckinck thought of as a cranky imitator of Emerson. That week he had united the parts of his life — his wife and child, the other Melvilles and Melvills (even his father under the larch trees and Gansevoort rowing on the lake), his childhood servitude and his status as celebrity, neighbors he recalled from his youth and select representatives of the New York literati, kidnapped in his piratical raid on the city. For Melville, there in the amphitheater below Mount Greylock, to talk enthusiastically to a New York editor about a plan to put the farm into a book (thereby preserving in his art the buildings, trees, fields, and lake just as they went out of Melvill hands) meant he was drawing a magic circle, freehand, around the fragmented parts of his life.

Rested up from sitting on chairs on the grass, smoking benignly, on Monday the men took the train the ten or fifteen miles or so to Stockbridge. Duyckinck described it as like descending into "a lower level in a Chinese painted green saucer, with water, trees and verandahs, edged by blue mountains." Dudley Field was at the depot with a victim of his "lion lasso," Oliver Wendell Holmes, the man who had immortalized the Hero of the Tea Party. Mathews described the doctor as "a slight apparition" with "a glazed India-rubber bag in hand." Holmes's own grandfather Wendell had owned twenty-four thousand acres in the Berkshires, what Holmes at the 1844 Berkshire Jubilee called a "baronial territory." There he had visited as a child, so now he could outdo Melville with tales of carriage travel across Massachusetts in the old days. Holmes and other members of his family still summered near Pittsfield, on the road roughly parallel to the road in front of the Melvill house: the doctor was no tourist either. Rendezvous point was the Field cottage, "convenient and rambling and pitched down in the verdure."

Field got the early arrivals out of the cottage by proposing a preliminary climb, "just by way of a rehearsal, for the grand climb," Mathews recorded, "a run to the top of Sacrifice Mount, not far off." Soon after they returned, the publisher of *The Scarlet Letter*, James T. Fields (a fastidious dandy in curled whiskers and patent leather shoes designed for State Street, not mountain climbing), drove up triumphantly in a chariot for two horses with his downright juvenile bride (innocently dressed in delicate blue silk) and his still greater trophy, Nathaniel Hawthorne. Sophia Hawthorne had stayed at home with her mother and the children, Una and Julian. Fields (not Field) by preference talked of the success of *The Scarlet Letter*, but he had news for Melville and others to hear, for he had just been at Harvard, where Bayard Taylor gave the commencement poem and the surviving graduates of the year 1800, including Lemuel Shaw and the father of the poet James Russell Lowell, had laughed over their college tricks of half a century past and lamented their lost classmates, among them the painter Washington Allston. A "young whiskered" scion of the famous Stockbridge family, Henry (Harry) Sedgwick (as Duyckinck wrote his wife on 6 August), came over on horse back, and the augmented party (including Miss Jenny Field as the second female) set out in three conveyances for Monument Mountain, three miles to the east.

Hawthorne had not visited there before, although the mountain lay, in Sophia Hawthorne's words to her sister Elizabeth on 8 August, "like a head-less Sphinx," south from the piazza at their little red house above Stock-bridge Bowl. Some way up from the base of the mountain they had to abandon the wagons. Duyckinck seized the chance to fraternize with Haw-thorne, his favorite American writer besides Mathews, and strode off in ad-vance with him, "talking of the Scarlet Letter," which he had extolled in the *Literary World*. As they scrambled up the rocky summit they could not pause to admire the prospect on either side, for (Duyckinck wrote) "a black thun-der cloud from the south dragged its ragged skirts" toward them, "the thun-der rolling in the distance." They took what shelter they could against and partly under rocks (the dainty Fields pressed into "a damp underground of mosses and decay"), and Dr. Holmes, doubly resourceful, cut three branches for an umbrella and produced from his medical bag a bottle of champagne and a single silver mug for everyone to drink from. The rain slackened quickly, and Melville, still agile from his sailor years, "bestrode a peaked rock, which ran out like a bowsprit, and pulled and hauled imaginary ropes" for the "delectation" of the others (so Fields recalled), while Dr. Holmes peeped about the cliffs claiming that the heights affected him like ipecac, an emetic. "Hawthorne looked mildly about for the great Carbuncle," Duy-ckinck recorded, referring to one of the pieces in Hawthorne's *Twice-Told*

Tales. Egregiously drawing attention away from Hawthorne and toward himself, Mathews pulled out a copy of Bryant's lengthy poetic pseudo-Indian legend, "Monument Mountain," and declaimed it, all the way through — the feat of half an hour. The others forgave Mathews, and in Heidseck everyone toasted "long life to the dear old poet," now a New Yorker but native, as they all knew, to the region. They were still dry after their earnest toasts to Bryant (Melville keeping silent about his personal knowledge of the dear old poet's long memory of Gansevoort's personal criticism). Then they stoutly progressed through national poets (but only those with local connections?) at least as far as Longfellow, whose "name was mentioned over a glass of iced Champagne" ("six thousand feet above Stockbridge," Fields assured the poet of Craigie House, who after his visit in 1848 had a fair idea what the altitude really was).

The party got down the mountain and drove back to the Field cottage, where some of them donned dry articles of clothing (dainty-footed Duyckinck "boated" around in Field's big stockings and slippers). Then (as Evert wrote his wife) "came the dinner — a three hours' business from turkey to ice cream, well moistened by the way." Dr. Holmes set out to provoke everyone "by laying down various propositions of the superiority of Englishmen" over American men — the "physical differences between the present American and English men," Fields recalled long afterward. Holmes was using ideas from popular works on ethnology such as Robert Knox's *Races of Man*, the same ideas Hawthorne had just incorporated into a passage in *The Scarlet Letter* on the progressive stringiness or loss of stately port observable in modern women of English ancestry in the New World. Delightedly recognizing a worthy opponent in the little satirist, Melville "attacked him vigorously." (Part of Holmes's satire was self-directed, toward his own lack of heroic stature; when he started to address the 1844 Berkshire Jubilee the organizers had lifted him onto a table so the crowd could see the top of his head, at least.) Mathews recorded that Holmes at some point switched sides, perhaps after the "condition of American poetry" came in for something other than champagne toasts, and (drolly spoofing the chauvinists present) "gave it as his deliberate opinion and as the result of a most elaborate and searching scrutiny, that in less than twenty years it would be a common thing to grow in these United States men sixteen and seventeen feet high; and intellectual in proportion." Someone brought up the sea serpent that had recently been spotted in the New York harbor, whether or not as a specimen of what could flourish in American waters, and someone else brought up the pugnacious Henry M. Payne from Worcester, who had recently issued the intellectual equivalent of a backwoodsman's challenge, daring scientists around the world to match wits with him. While all this was ricocheting around, Hawthorne "looked on" (Duyckinck said), although Fields much later fondly claimed to recall him as stoutly taking part on the American side and as raying out "in a sparkling and unwonted manner." The thicker the witticisms came, the closer they edged toward vulgarity, until somebody on the chauvinists' side went so far as to remind the company of a remarkable bullock that could be observed by the curious at nearby Great Barrington.

Three hours might have become four, but the popularizer of history Joel Tyler Headley dropped in with his brother-in-law (famous as one of the innocent bystanders shot at the Astor Place riots) and propelled the party (the men, at least) into carriages toward a local curiosity, the Icy-Glen. (J. T. Headley, known as the author of *Napoleon and His Marshals*, had just published *Sketches and Rambles* and *Sacred Scenes and Characters*.) Duyckinck protested to his wife that it "was a merciless thing to get us off from such a dinner in the afternoon" and out to that "break in one of the hills of tumbled, huge, damp, mossy rocks in whose recesses ice is said to be found all the year round." Headley led the now somewhat tipsy and even more boisterous tourists on a "nasty and sublime" scramble. The long-legged Hawthorne kept pace with him, "with his dreamy face and dark eye," and Melville forged along with those two. The well-lubricated Duyckinck followed, feeling no pain from the hardships he was undergoing — indeed, "beaming with pleasure." The short waddling Mathews preceded the trim diminutive Holmes, and after them Fields brought up the rear of what the military-minded Headley bepunned as "this remarkable *literary column.*" Headley knew the way well enough to lead them perversely on the most difficult possible route, so as to enhance the mysterious character of the glen. Sophia Hawthorne wrote her sister Elizabeth Peabody that her husband came home describing it "as looking as if the Devil had torn his way through a rock & left it all jagged behind him" — a fair indication that Headley had misled them by the base of the rugged free-standing peaks of the Devil's Pulpit, which were thrust up to eye level from the nearest point on the mountain, a giant's leap away. Drinking and climbing had loosened Hawthorne's throat, and rather than mildly looking about for his Great Carbuncle, he called out facetious warnings that imminent destruction awaited them all.

They all survived and "came out on the peaceful fields of the Housatonic." Skirting a meadow, they crossed the river once again and arrived at the Field "cottage" on the village green. (Architectural nomenclature was shifting, and this was not a veritable little cottage like the one the Hawthornes were renting, but a more substantial square red-brick house later known as the Old Parsonage.) The guests had only to look south to see Monument Mountain testifying to their prowess at climbing. This time a tall Mrs. Sedgwick (perhaps Helen's teacher, Mrs. Charles Sedgwick) was there to quiz Duyckinck on Catharine Sedgwick's novel, *Hope Leslie*, and Maga-wisca, a character in it—a test at which he did not distinguish himself. Helen could have coached Duyckinck, but she was still in New York, despite her mother's insistence that she come and join the holiday group. Holmes es-caped cross-examination, since all the locals knew that Catharine Sedgwick had followed him as speaker at the Berkshire Jubilee six years earlier—tall enough not to have to stand on the table. At ten o'clock the Pittsfield party took the railway home, getting off not at the distant depot but at the nearby bridge, "the Cars politely stopping to accommodate them while passing the road leading to the farm" (Maria wrote to Augusta), so that after a short walk under the stars they reached the Melvill house at eleven. (Mathews immor-talized the brakeman, "friendly Conklin, who, taking pity on three roving knights of the quill, did gently pause his train at the bridge, saving us there a foot-sore tramp at midnight.") A "vigorous Creole lady & her husband" having left, Duyckinck and Mathews were bedded down in their own room at the Melvill house (surely a room that the great Longfellow had walked through, Mathews could tell himself) instead of having to grope their way to their quarters in the neighboring farm.

Monday, 5 August 1850, had been for all the participants a day to mark with a white stone (in the phrase Melville used in *The Confidence-Man*). After Hawthorne's death, most of the events of the day faded from general aware-ness and what was remembered (even during the nadir of Melville's reputa-tion) was that on that day Hawthorne and Melville met each other. In 1879 the local poet and journalist Joseph Smith, who distinguished himself from the slain Mormon leader by using two middle initials (J. E. A. Smith), even improved upon the fact with a suitable legend: "one day it chanced that when they [Hawthorne and Melville] were out on a pic-nic excursion, the two were compelled by a thunder-shower to take shelter in a narrow recess of the rocks of Monument Mountain. Two hours of enforced intercourse settled the matter. They learned so much of each other's character, and found that they held so much of thought, feeling and opinion in common, that the most inti-mate friendship for the future was inevitable." Melville had been caught off guard by the effect Nathaniel Hawthorne had on him during their snatches of conversation, even if there was no enforced intimacy of two hours to-gether in a narrow recess on Monument Mountain which so appealed to Smith. Hawthorne, just turned forty-six, was still more than handsome, so darkly gorgeous that Mathews aptly depicted him as "Mr. Noble Melan-choly," a term that Melville later relished, being a connoisseur of manly beauty himself, ever since his sailing and island-hopping years. Just now Melville was eager to validate his exalted new self-estimate by identifying another American fellow writer as comparably great, so eager that he was willing to look for that miraculous companion in the Emerson-impersonator Thoreau. Before the day was over, Melville decided Hawthorne was the most fascinating American he had ever met. Stockbridge was not London, and David Dudley Field's cottage was not Elm Court or the Erechtheum Club, but it had afforded a chance to drink and talk with literary men in Hawthorne's presence while Lizzie was safe nearby with Malcolm, instead of a guilt-tinged ocean away. Jolted out of his characteristic reserve, Melville was eager to pursue the acquaintanceship.

Jolted out of his own even more characteristic reserve, Hawthorne was also eager to pursue the acquaintanceship with Melville. For the sake of Duyckinck, his New York champion for a decade, Hawthorne might have gone so far as to ask Melville to bring his editorial guests to call on him on Thursday the eighth (for a visit timed at two hours or less), as he did. Such courtesy, for Hawthorne, was a marked favor, no more than Duyckinck had earned over the years. For Melville, Hawthorne did something phenomenal. He liked Melville so much that he asked him to spend a few days with him "before leaving these parts" (Hawthorne to Horatio Bridge, 7 August). Melville was apt to disappear into the alien New York world, so Hawthorne had to act fast if he were to see more of him. If Melville did not already know Hawthorne's reputation for reclusiveness, Duyckinck and Mathews must have told him just how remarkable such an invitation was.

Next morning, Tuesday the sixth, Duyckinck and Mathews were urged (presumably by Sarah Morewood) to visit the "best part of the scenery," Salisbury Lakes and the ascent of the Dome of the Taconic, Massachusetts's Mount Washington, but they chose to rest. Evert continued his guilty rhapsodies to his wife: "I wish you could see the view from my window now & breathe this fine air. It is warm but you do not *swelter*. If you were here with the children I could be content to remain till October." Their plans took an unexpected turn at nine in the morning when Headley showed up and stayed. He took dinner at the Melvill house and finally left at four ("rather a long visit for the first," Maria observed sternly to Augusta on the eighth), inviting the gentlemen to dine with him two days later, Thursday. The conversation may naturally have turned on scenes familiar to Headley and the Melvilles, for "J.T.H." in the 7 August 1845 *Evangelist* had published an article entitled "Saratoga Springs — Berkshire," in which Berkshire came off decidedly better ("How one can endure Saratoga Springs is a marvel to me"). Later Allan Melville made his way over from the Lenox station, prepared to stay until Monday, and exacerbated Duyckinck's tender conscience by reporting that the heat of the city was still oppressive.

Early on Wednesday the seventh Melville had a chance to read some of Hawthorne's *Mosses from an Old Manse* (two days later he wrote frankly that he had "never read it till the day before yesterday"). That morning Evert wrote George in a way that conclusively shows how thoroughly Melville had isolated himself from his city friends during the months after his return from England: "Melville has a new book mostly done — a romantic, fanciful & literal & most enjoyable presentment of the Whale Fishery — something quite new." In New York neither George nor Evert had known much if anything at all about the book in progress. At half past two a carriage and a buggy were brought up, and the Melville brothers and Duyckinck and Mathews, accompanied by Lizzie and Sophia, set off to tour the Shaker settlements in Lebanon and in nearby Hancock village, Herman driving a pair of horses in the light carriage with Lizzie and his two guests. Duyckinck described the several-mile drive to his wife: "The mountain beauty of the drive over the Taconic to Lebanon is a thing to *enjoy*. You may pass through a cloud on the summit and fancy yourself in the Ossianic Scotch Highlands and then you are out upon the sunshine of the broken valleys. You go some-where by one road and come back by another and cut across by a third." At Lebanon in the Shaker sleeping quarters Herman "saw a long handled brush at a bed head & asked its object." An old Shakeress gave him a blunt reply: "Why I guess it's for him to scratch himself with when he itches." Meanwhile the deferential Duyckinck improved the opportunity to ingratiate himself with one of the elders, Father Hilliard.

No sooner had the party left the Melvill house than Mrs. Morewood decided she could not stay behind, so she sent her English manservant into the village to hire "the handsomest Carriage he could get & *four* horses," but he could only get a pair. Then Sarah Morewood, her sisters Mrs. Ellen Brittain and Miss Lizzie Huyler, and Helen Jean Melvill drove off for Leba-non, Mrs. Morewood holding the reins. They met up with the Melville party at Hancock village in time to go all together to see the Shakers' Round Barn, around which they all had a fine race except Sophia. Allan was terrified that she might actually run, and Sophia herself was nervous at being near a barn, "rather afraid of being mistaken for a cow or an elephant" in her condition (as she wrote Augusta on the eleventh). The united parties returned together in the two carriages and the buggy. At night a nephew of Susan Melvill played the guitar and sang for the guests. While the young self-taught amateur per-formed, Melville and his guests may have talked about the idea that Melville would write something about Hawthorne. No one had a copy of the book that one could legitimately still review, *The Scarlet Letter* (think of it, the great bookman Evert Duyckinck caught with nothing but proofs of *The Prelude* in his possession!). The only Hawthorne book at hand was Aunt Mary's gift,

Mosses from an Old Manse, which had been out in the world for four years. Never too late, they decided, over cigars, and it was agreed that Melville would dash off something good (like his Parkman and Cooper reviews) while the editorial gentlemen ever so reluctantly stayed on until Monday, as a business delay, so they could carry the manuscript home.

36

Hawthorne and His *Mosses*

8 August–September 1850

A review [of *The House of the Seven Gables*], somewhat extravagant in its terms, was published in the "Literary World," and was enclosed to Hawthorne by Longfellow in this cordial note. . . . Something of the character of this notice may be gathered from the following passage in a letter of Mrs. Peabody's: — " . . . I carried the 'Literary World' to Aunt Rawlins. . . . 'No man of common-sense,' she said, 'would seriously name Mr. Hawthorne, deserving as he is of respect and admiration, in the same day with Shakspeare. Shakspeare! the greatest man that ever lived.' . . .

— It is certainly not necessary to the vindication of Hawthorne's fame to bracket him with Shakespeare; and to the man himself the idea must have appeared too absurdly monstrous to be understood otherwise than as covert satire, or at least as the ravings of well-meaning imbecility. . . .

A far more sagacious and poignant discussion of the subject was contributed by Herman Melville in a letter.

A befuddled Julian Hawthorne, in *Nathaniel Hawthorne and His Wife*, 1884

ON THURSDAY THE MELVILLE BROTHERS and the guests left at eight in the morning "in a pretty light Carriage & pair of fine horses." The "Centurion & the St's brother," Maria called the guests. In the family nicknaming, anyone named Cornelius would have been linked to the centurion in Acts 10. More curious was the way of identifying Evert Duyckinck by association with his nonverbal George, the lover of seventeenth-century English devotional poets: neither of the Duyckinck brothers made much of an impression on the mother of Gansevoort Melville. The guests did not impress Maria, but they were excited. Tingeing everything the Centurion and the Saint's brother experienced was the stimulating knowledge that Melville was going to write something about Hawthorne.

Melville and his guests returned a call the doctor-poet's brother John Wendell Holmes had made at the house (while they were away the day before?), then traveled the six miles or so to the Hawthornes' before noon. Sophia's mother, Mrs. Peabody, was there visiting, but the guests were allowed to see that Sophia Hawthorne (who reminded Duyckinck of a more robust version of Margaret Fuller) had fitted up the red farmhouse "with great taste — particularly a little room or passage or closet or oratory which looks out upon the *view* — a fresh rippling lake at the foot of descending meadows, encircled by the mountains in the distance — Fine art prints savoring of Italy hung on low walls and a fine engraving of the Transfiguration presented by Emerson" (Duyckinck wrote his wife). Hawthorne "in his nervous way" popped the corks on a couple of bottles of champagne that an admirer had sent him some time before, then walked the men down to the lake. Sophia Hawthorne ignored Allan (Melville junior, Hawthorne identified him), but she wrote her sister Elizabeth her impressions of the others: "Mr Typee is interesting in his aspect — quite. I see Fayaway in his face. Mr Matthews (Big Abel) is a very chatty gossiping body. Mr Duyckinck — a trim dutch but very gentle, agreeable gentleman."

Seeing Fayaway in Melville's face means that Sophia saw him in terms of his erotic prowess in tropical climes far more remote than the distant Cuba of her young womanhood, a young man still retaining his sailor-agility who only a few years before had done things her husband in all his wanderings through remote New England had never done. (Her husband's life, she assured her mother in September, had literally been pure "from the smallest taint of earthliness.") Specifically, Melville had reclined, according to his published record, in the stern of a canoe with a pipe-smoking Marquesan girl with whom he was not merely on good terms but on "the very best terms possible" (a nice discrimination the loving Sophia understood) and (disembarking his pilot, Kory-Kory) had paddled to the windward side, where the inventive Fayaway had suddenly stripped off her tappa draping, posed herself as a naked mast, and held up the tappa as a sail to catch the wind and propel the canoe back across the lake — a game so joyous that it had to be repeated many times. Experiencing no such sexual alertness about either Melville or Hawthorne, Duyckinck pronounced the author of *The Scarlet Letter* "a fine ghost in a case of iron — a man of genius and he looks it and lives it."

The guests stayed as long as they could before keeping their engagement at the hotel at Stockbridge, where Headley saluted them "with a volley of bottles at the dinner table." When they went on the piazza to smoke, the newsboy brought them the morning papers from New York City containing the news that the heat had broken. Before the day was over Duyckinck received a note from George Duyckinck's traveling companion in Europe, William Allen Butler, announcing his presence in nearby Great Barrington and his plans to stop over in Pittsfield on Friday long enough to get from the one depot to the other, where he planned to catch the train to Springfield.

(Having to change depots there inconvenienced travelers for the next decade as the railroads fought for a monopoly of traffic.)

Maria had written to Augusta on Thursday that Mathews and Duyckinck were staying until Monday, but Evert waited till Friday morning to notify his wife cryptically that she would have approved his delay if he had telegraphed her (an extravagance, still) his reason for staying: after dipping into the *Mosses* on Wednesday, Melville had agreed that he would find the time to write something about it for the *Literary World,* if Duyckinck stayed around. Duyckinck was delighted, particularly since in 1845 he had solicited and in 1846 had published *Mosses* in the Library of American Books, where *Typee* had appeared. For years he had promoted Hawthorne's reputation, long before and even more assiduously than he had promoted Melville's. Not only would he get an essay about the great and never sufficiently praised Hawthorne, he would get it from the hand of Melville, who for many months had been increasingly reluctant to write a real review, more reluctant than ever after *Mardi* had been stabbed so cruelly and Melville had learned the dangers of dissipating his forces on miscellaneous writing. Furthermore, Duyckinck could also vaunt himself more than ever on his prowess at editing his paper so admirably from a distance of 160 miles. If ever an editor had reason for hovering around a contributor, it was Duyckinck hovering around Melville; smug little Fields had conveyed Hawthorne about as a trophy of the Boston publishing establishment embodied behind his own curled whiskers, but Duyckinck could get into the cars for home with a tribute that would reclaim Hawthorne for the Manhattan literary patriots.

Rain delayed the elaborate picnic Mrs. Morewood had planned for Friday the ninth, quite unexpectedly affording Melville the chance they were all looking for. The man who had dashed *White-Jacket* off in "a score of sittings" found himself possessed of a long morning and the first two hours of the afternoon — almost, by his count, a full working-day. In the barn, perhaps, not at a desk, he wrote some twenty or so manuscript pages before breaking off before he had quite said his say. By his superficial praise of several of the pieces in *Mosses from an Old Manse* Melville revealed that he had started the essay without having read much of the book. He didn't need to have read much of it, since for the first part of his essay he was thumbing through Hawthorne's book and making extemporary effusive comments on the titles and sometimes the content of several of the pieces. He did not even have to copy out the quotations he wanted to use, for his marks in the book show that he left the copying to Lizzie, who had been pressed back into service.

Even his initial cursory comments led him into intense speculation about the dark half of Hawthorne's soul that might balance the commonly perceived "Indian-summer sunlight." Melville could not "altogether tell," he admitted, whether Hawthorne had "simply availed himself" of darkness "as a means to the wondrous effects he makes it to produce in his lights and shades" — that is, whether this "mystical blackness" were mere aesthetic strategy, or whether there really lurked in him "perhaps unknown to himself, a touch of Puritanic gloom." Melville went on, raptly, writing from Maria's early Dutch Reformed teachings and his own maturest reflections: "Certain it is, however, that this great power of blackness" (as Elizabeth copied his scrawl) "in him derives its force from its appeals to that Calvinistic sense of Innate Depravity and Original Sin, from whose visitations, in some shape or other, no deeply thinking mind is always & wholly free. For, in certain moods, no man can weigh this world, without throwing in something, some-how like Original Sin, to strike the uneven balance." The world was mis-taken in "its absurd misconception" of Nathaniel Hawthorne as "a pleasant writer, with a pleasant style, — a sequestered, harmless man, from whom any deep and weighty thing would hardly be anticipated: — a man who means no meanings." Propelling the essay, page by page, was the conviction that the world was equally mistaken in its absurd misconception of Herman Melville as a pleasant writer of graphic adventure stories, the lover of Fayaway, the happy dog who meant no meanings.

Quite suddenly, Melville was writing about Hawthorne the man and Shakespeare and himself. He surely had not read all of the pieces in the *Mosses* even when he finished the essay the next day, on the tenth. In the act of writing the essay, Melville expressed openly Hawthorne's impact on him, and not until he finished a draft and Lizzie had copied it for him did he protect himself by ascribing the essay to "a Virginian spending July in Vermont," and masking himself in a few passages, as when he replaced the word "me" with "the hot soil of my Southern soul": "To what infinite height of loving wonder & admiration I may yet be borne, when by repeatedly banquetting on these Mosses, I shall have thoroughly incorporated their whole stuff into my be-ing, — that, I can not tell. But already I feel that this Hawthorne has dropped germinous seeds into my soul. He expands and deepens down, the more I contemplate him; and further and further, shoots his strong New-England roots into the hot soil of my Southern soul." Such florid romantic rhetoric was not unique in reviews, and the cautious Duyckinck, once he had posses-sion of the essay, saw nothing in this language that required excision by his editorial pen.

In the essay Melville posed a formidable question he had been facing as he worked on the whaling manuscript: how was an American, a democrat, to write a tragedy equal to Shakespeare's without setting it in some heroic past or presenting it in Shakespearean rhetoric. There was a "great mistake" made even by literary chauvinists who were looking for the coming of a great

American genius: "they somehow fancy he will come in the costume of Queen Elizabeth's day, — be a writer of dramas founded upon old English history, or the tales of Boccaccio." Another aspect of the problem was how the second generation of post-revolutionary American writers, without impiety, could break with the older, more imitative generation (a set consisting of only two looming figures, Irving and Cooper). For whatever reason, Melville was laboring under absolutely no need to repudiate the influence of Cooper, the great national novelist, but in this essay he revealed his edginess about how to break away from Irving, to whom he was profoundly indebted, most recently for much of the characterization of his narrator in *Redburn* as well as incidental scenes in that book. (Six months later he wrote Duyckinck of Hawthorne's superiority: "Irving is a grasshopper to him — putting the *souls* of the two men together, I mean.") Part of the problem was that Melville was not merely imitating Irving — he shared some of the essential Irvingesque sensibility, which *would* emerge, despite any rejection of the older writer.

Into the essay Melville also poured out his aroused literary aspirations (which Holmes, the little master of barbed badinage, had so complexly challenged). He also expressed his delight upon discovering in *Mosses from an Old Manse* (and in its author) some of the repressed dark truths that were stirring in his own mind and that he had recently discerned as "craftily" said or "insinuated" by Shakespeare in the plays: "For in this world of lies, Truth is forced to fly like a sacred white doe in the woodlands; and only by cunning glimpses will she reveal herself, as in Shakespeare and other masters of the great Art of Telling the Truth, — even though it be covertly, and by snatches." Hawthorne he found to be such a truth-teller, not greater than Shakespeare, or as great, though "the difference between the two men is by no means immeasurable." This was heresy to bardolators, and Melville was cautious in pushing beyond it to insist that Shakespeare already had "been approached." Melville was not thinking of artistry but of insight: "There are minds that have gone as far as Shakespeare into the universe." Worship of Shakespeare had become dogma in supposedly democratic America: "You must believe in Shakespeare's unapproachability, or quit the country. But what sort of a belief is this for an American, a man who is bound to carry republican progressiveness into Literature, as well as into Life? Believe me, my friends, that men not very much inferior to Shakespeare, are this day being born on the banks of the Ohio. And the day will come, when you shall say who reads a book by an Englishman that is a modern?"

This passage, quite aside from its spread-eagle oratorical qualities, reveals something of Melville's reading. Everyone would have recognized his turning upside down Sydney Smith's notorious rhetorical question in the

1820 *Edinburgh Review*, familiar to him from childhood: "In the four quarters of the globe, who reads an American book?" Carrying republican progressiveness into literature as well as into life was the stuff of many a nationalistic plea, such as the famous one on "The Great Nation of Futurity," part of Melville's thinking since 1839, when he encountered it in the *Democratic Review* or a local newspaper. Shakespeare's approachability was treated, though not to his liking, in Collier, and probably other editors or commentators he had read.

Plain to the literary guests at the Melvill house was Melville's taking on Maurice Morgann, the contemporary of Dr. Johnson famous in his own time for his "Essay on the Dramatic Character of Sir John Falstaff." Morgann's reputation had been revived by several of the Romantic critics, and solidified by Charles Knight in three different books (1839, 1847, 1849). Somewhere Melville saw Morgann's controversial essay and found himself less impressed by the claim that Falstaff was no coward than by Morgann's celebration of the imperial majesty of Shakespeare's language: "When the hand of time shall have brushed off his present Editors and Commentators, and when the very name of *Voltaire*, and even the memory of the language in which he has written, shall be no more, the *Apalacian* mountains, the banks of the *Ohio*, and the plains of *Scioto* shall resound with the accents of this Barbarian: In his native tongue he shall roll the genuine passions of nature; nor shall the griefs of *Lear* be alleviated, or the charms and wit of *Rosalind* be abated by time." In the enthusiast Morgann, Melville found a man after his own heart, and in another context he might have celebrated Morgann's own celebration of Shakespeare, but he was not striving for judiciousness here, and (just as he used Sydney Smith's words against Smith) he turned one of Morgann's phrases against him in his flourish about men "this day being born on the banks of the Ohio." Halfway through his whaling book, he knew in his heart, against all reason, that one such man, capable of writing a mighty book, had been born on, or very near, the banks of the East and Hudson rivers three decades earlier.

A living example of the American literary genius for whom Young America had been calling, Hawthorne was proof that "great geniuses are parts of the times; they themselves are the times; and possess a correspondent coloring." Such authors, Melville began to analyze, do not have to bedeck their characters in Elizabethan rhetoric: "It is of a piece with the Jews, who while their Shiloh was meekly walking in their streets, were still praying for his magnificent coming; looking for him in a chariot, who was already among them on an ass. Nor must we forget, that, in his own life-time, Shakespeare was not Shakespeare, but only Master William Shakespeare of the business firm of Condell, Shakespeare & Co., proprietors of the Globe Theatre in

London; & by a courtly author, of the name of Chettle, was hooted at as an 'upstart crow' beautified 'with other birds feathers'."

When Melville referred to *Groatsworth of Wit* as by Chettle and not Greene he was following one of the best authorities rather than making a simple blunder. He picked up the association of Robert "Green" and imitation from Powell then picked up Chettle as author of *Groatsworth* from Collier then mixed the ideas of imitation and approachability into the *Mosses* essay. Always prone to put private references in his writings, Melville worked into this essay an allusion to his whaling manuscript. Declaring that "immitation is often the first charge brought against real originality," he continued: "Why this is so, there is not space to set forth here. You must have plenty of sea-room to tell the Truth in; especially, when it seems to have an aspect of newness, as America did in 1492, tho' it was then just as old, and perhaps older than Asia, only those sagatious philosophers, the common sailors, had never seen it before; swearing it was all water & moonshine there." The "truth of the thing" in the 1 May letter to Dana seemed to refer to realistic depiction of American whaling; now "Truth" and truth-telling had acquired metaphysical dimensions.

Arguing that Shakespeare would yet be equalled and even surpassed by an American, he appealed to national pride as nakedly as any polemicist of the previous decade and a half: "Let America then prize and cherish her writers; yea, let her glorify them," rather than lavishing her embraces "upon the household of an alien": "For believe it or not England, after all, is, in many things, an alien to us. China has more bowels of real love for us than she. But even were there no Hawthorne, no Emerson, no Whittier, no Irving, no Bryant, no Dana[,] no Cooper[,] no Willis (not the author of the 'Dashes', but the author of the 'Belfry Pigeon') — were there none of these, & others of like calibre among us, nevertheless, let America first praise mediocrity even, in her own children, before she praises . . . the best excellence in the children of any other land." (For Melville to include even the very popular poem by his friend Willis was to lower his standards.) Melville, as the Virginian, had an extreme example to clinch his case: "I was much pleased with a hot-headed Carolina cousin of mine, who once said, — 'If there were no other American to stand by, in Literature, — why, then, I would stand by Pop Emmons and his "Fredoniad," & till a better epic came along, swear it was not very far behind the Illiad.'"

Wound up now, incited by childhood memories of the orator on the Boston Common (whom he was confusing with Emmons's brother, the author of the *Fredoniad*), Melville at last said what he truly thought of Washington Irving: "But that graceful writer, who perhaps of all Americans has recieved the most plaudits from his own country for his productions, — that very popular & amiable writer, however good and self-reliant in many things, perhaps owes his chief reputation to the self-acknowledged imitation of a foreign model, & to the studied avoidance of all topics but smooth ones. But it is better to fail in originality, than to succeed in imitation." (Self-acknowledged was an obvious reference to Irving's tribute to Goldsmith in the preface to the life that Putnam had published in 1849 — the biography that had occasioned Powell's first attacks.) Failure, in this view, was "the true test of greatness," and the predictably successful Irving was not great: if "continual success is a proof that a man wisely knows his powers, — it is only to be added, that, in that case, he knows them to be small." Just as the ancient Romans had defined themselves in relation to the culture of the Greeks, Americans had been vaunting themselves in being successful imitators of English exemplars. Bryant was the American Wordsworth, Cooper was the American Scott, Mathews wanted agonizingly to be the American Dickens, Melville had been labeled the American Defoe. Irving, of course, was the American Goldsmith. Melville exploded: "we want no American Gold-smiths; nay, we want no American Miltons."

Once the floodgates were opened, all Melville's repressed resentment at the treatment of *Mardi* burst out, for in his mind its failure had now become the true test of its greatness, not the ecstatic acclaim of Irving's life of Gold-smith in the same year. Melville outdid all but the most extreme literary chauvinists: "While we are rapidly preparing for that political supremacy among the nations, which prophetically awaits us at the close of the present century; in a literary point of view, we are deplorably unprepared for it." Americans needed, now, to give due recognition to "the meritorious writers that are our own; — those writers, who breathe that unshackled, democratic spirit of Christianity in all things, which now takes the practical lead in this world." In response, Americans should "contemn all imitation," though it comes to them "graceful and fragrant as the morning," and "foster all orig-inality," particularly — here Melville triumphantly picked up the nominal subject of his essay — the "unimitating, and, perhaps, in his way," inimitable Nathaniel Hawthorne.

In his peroration for the part he wrote on Friday the ninth (although this was only three-quarters of the final essay, it required a peroration), Melville called upon his countrymen to join him in patriotically bestowing a "shock of recognition" upon America's still-unrecognized native authors, and specifi-cally Hawthorne. Using imagery from scientific experiments with the Ley-den jar, Melville was not talking about any shock he felt in reading Haw-thorne but about the shock Hawthorne needed to experience from worthy readers, like Melville himself, if he were to know that he was appreciated by his own country. Such generous recognition might prompt Hawthorne "to the full flower of some still greater achievement."

Melville had some food after writing all this, and by three he and Evert were in Pittsfield at the Housatonic Railroad depot to meet the Butlers in the Stockbridge cars. No one had counted on the effect his morning's work would have on his mood. Under the pretext of writing on Hawthorne, Melville had spent hours expressing the deepest hopes for his own book. Genuinely fascinated by the glamorous Hawthorne, he had written what amounted (in passages) to a passionate private message to this new friend. Writing so intimately about Hawthorne's power to arouse his literary aspirations had left him more than a little febrile—excited intellectually, emotionally, and sexually—sexual arousal being for Melville an integral part of such intensely creative phases. In this state of intense and undirected arousal Melville acted out an extraordinary display of deflected sexuality.

Lacking someone more appropriate to lavish an excess of esteem upon, Melville abducted a younger man's bride. Melville had met William A. Butler at least once, late the previous February at Clinton Place. Unacquainted with Butler's new wife, the former Mary Russell Marshall, except as Duyckinck identified her after they boarded the cars, Melville (without giving her time to become wholly assured of the identity and intentions of this "strange man with luxuriant beard") "whisked" her out of the car and into his buggy, then whirled away with her "behind a black pony of very questionable build, gait and behavior." (So Butler wrote to George Duyckinck, when safely away from Melville.) The confused and outraged bridegroom had not intended to delay long at Pittsfield, but he was left with Duyckinck in Melville's dust, and could only give chase "in a most serpentine and erratic manner in an old wagon and gray steed apparently coeval with the famous Pittsfield Elm which still shakes its gaunt skeleton branches against the sunlight." It was no fun rolling through the dust with Evert Duyckinck all the while imagining his wife somewhere ahead, in the hands of "Typee," the American writer most notorious for his sexual conquests.

Butler and Duyckinck caught up with Melville and Mrs. Butler only at the Melvill house. Three weeks later (on 31 August), Butler described the place in the Washington *National Intelligencer* as "one of those wide-halled, thick-walled, capacious and cavernous old houses that are cool in the middle of August, and warm in the midst of December." (He had never huddled in the office or the kitchen all winter long.) Melville and Duyckinck laid down to the bride and her winded bridegroom the terms of their captivity: their release was contingent upon their accepting the kind invitation to attend Mrs. Morewood's masquerade party that night. A youth of stout character as well as worldly experience that included the grand tour with George Duyckinck, young William refused "to be caught in this Berber fashion," so "shaking the Berkshire dust" from their feet he and his bride were returned to town for "waffles and muffins" before they went on to Springfield from the other depot. ("Berber" was an allusion to the season's fashionable vacation reading, Melville's imitator William Starbuck Mayo's follow-up to his successful *Kaloolah;* Oakey Hall wrote on 16 August: "Every where you go, you see people in cars and boat cabins in possession of a couple of books in orange colored binding, as striking as the dress of a Turk would be in a Locofoco mass meeting; they are the bound pages of *The Berber!* Mayo gave Putnam an original work; Putnam gives the original work an original binding.")

Butler heard of Melville's morning's work for the *Literary World* and of Mathews's plans to memorialize the visit in an essay of his own, for in his report he ventured the opinion that under the "stanch roof rafters" of the Melvill house "doubtless many lucubrations" had been "hatched into life during the warm weather, to be food for publishers and critics in the Fall." Except in the light of the aroused sexuality and literary ambitions of his morning's work, Melville's dangerous skylarking is incomprehensible. Whatever the bride thought, young Butler's feelings about Melville, the sexually licentious author of *Typee*, the subject of G. W. Peck's exhaustive analysis in the *Whig Review*, surfaced not in his essay in the *National Intelligencer* but in that paper sixteen months later. There he condemned the forecastle scene in *Moby-Dick* "with its maudlin and ribald orgies," a sufficient warning to all dark-bearded strangers that Mrs. William Allen Butler was no Sabine woman there for the seizing. (No other reviewer of *Moby-Dick*, only the proper young husband who still resented having his bride manhandled by Fayaway's lover, is known to have denounced the sexuality of the forecastle scene.)

By the time the Butlers escaped, some of the tension may have drained out of Melville's system, but at night he dressed to fit his aroused state — as a Turk. In the popular imagination, a Turk was not only sexually strange but also sexually formidable, the very pattern of an exotic predatory infidel. Conveniently, a Turk was marked outwardly by a beard such as Melville had grown after his return from England (in a draft passage for *Typee* Melville had associated a Turkish seraglio specifically with "bearded men"). A lover of clothing loose about his body ever since his days in the Pacific (so loose as in later years to confuse and offend his growing and grown daughters), Melville this evening bedecked himself or allowed the women to bedeck him as a figure society saw as sexually vigorous and threatening, turbaned and fitted with a make-do dagger or scimitar, or else a real sword left over from his uncle's noncombatant service in the War of 1812.

Having missed the high moments of the abduction scene, and remaining utterly oblivious to any sexual-aesthetic tension involving the essay Melville had started, Mathews made his own notes for a *Literary World* piece (published on 7 September), listing bucolic enjoyments not otherwise recorded: "Apple-gathering, blackberrying, raking after the cart, angling, birdsnesting" as preparation for the climactic event, "a grand fancy dress ball in the very heart of Berkshire":

> Fairy Belt [Sarah Morewood] again in motion, Fairy Belt's sisters, too, all the ladies: the village ransacked for green goggles, yellow stuff for breeches, antique hats, long-tail coats, brought down from garrets; heavy boots, of a past fashion, fished up from cellars; invitations scattered post-haste through the country; and, when evening comes, the great rooms of Broad Hall are thrown open; and thronged, in rapid procession, with Aunt Tabitha (supposed to be Fairy Belt in perfect disguise)[,] a lovely Peasant Girl, a Turk, two prim maidens (who cannot hide their roses quite so easily under chalk); an awful Yankee, with three hanks of flax for a wig — and such a length of tail in his coat! — two extraordinary waiters with cobblers — such waiters! — another Yankee, exceedingly sober-sided, and pronounced an impostor; a terrific Captain of the Pittsfield Artillery; a Spotted Man (savoring fearfully of the presence of Barnum); a Bride — oh, would she were! — and though last, not least lovely, a Highland Maiden, the Di Vernon of the Berkshire Hills.

(This was the first known use of Broad Hall as a name for the Melvill house.)

Sophia Melville gave a cooler and ironic report of the ball to Augusta, alluding to the well-known vulgarity of James Gordon Bennett's paper, where Gansevoort's gorgeous banner and gaudy speech in Newark had been celebrated:

> On Friday evening Mrs. Morewood gave a fancy dress ball to which we were all invited and went. Truly such a magnificent affair could only be properly described by one of the Herald reporters. As no one was admitted without a fancy dress I consented to be rigged up in a black dress with train and a very old fashioned hat and cap with various feathers and ribbons, said to be very becoming. Lizzie was a flower girl, Herman a Turk, Mr. Mathews a Yankee from the down-east jumping off place. Mr Duyckinck made a very neat looking waiter carrying around cherry-cobblers. Miss Dillingham as a novice, some half dozen ladies and gentlemen from the village altogether quite an amusing affair, they danced in the hall, and had supper at 12 in the dining room.

Allan, wearing a cart-frock, had paired off with Duyckinck to serve the cherry cobblers, then at supper he had distinguished himself with one of his

carefully stored up puns — "an awful pun, portentous, ill-timed, rude, unseemly, mean, inhospitable, villanous, and so complicated in its scoundrelism
as to cause the sudden and violent ejection of its maker out of a back door
into the door-yard grass at midnight," as Mathews told the story in the
7 September *Literary World*. Sophia at last took her distended body to her
room, but the others, she said, "kept it up until after one o'clock."

Rising early despite the late bedtime, Melville finished his essay on Hawthorne before ten o'clock (departure time for the picnic). His mood was
more sober, or sobered up, and oddly confessional, even to the point of
admitting that the day before he had written his article without reading all
the book:

> Twenty four hours have elapsed since writing the foregoing. I have just re-
> turned from the hay mow, charged more and more with love & admiration of
> Hawthorne. For I have just been g[l]eaning through the [M]osses, picking up
> many things here & there that had previously escaped me. I found that but to
> glean after this man, is better than to be in at the harvest of others. To be
> frank (though, perhaps, rather foolish) notwithstanding what I wrote yester-
> day of these Mosses, I had not then culled them all; but had, nevertheless,
> been sufficiently impregnated with their subtle essence, in them, as to write as
> I did.

Now he offered a theory of Hawthorne's manner of entitling his pieces so
commonplacely: "some of them are directly calculated to deceive — egregiously deceive, the superficial skimmer of pages." He himself had been
deceived, he now admitted, in the piece entitled "Young Goodman Brown,"
which he now declared to be "deep as Dante." Reading skimmingly himself,
he did not consider the possibility that Brown's accepting the devil's offer
that he could penetrate the deep mystery of sin proved his own loss of faith
but not the loss of faith of others. At last he spoke words very much like what
he now dared to hope he would hear applied to himself: "Gainsay it who will,
as I now write, I am Posterity speaking by proxy — and after times will make it
more than good, when I declare — that the American, who up to the present
day, has evinced, in Literature, the largest brain with the largest heart, that
man is Nathaniel Hawthorne."

After that Melville was ready for the drive west on the Gulf Road, allured,
Mathews coyly wrote, "by that Princess of Pic Nic, Fairy Belt." Sarah Morewood, her sister Miss Hetty Huyler, and Mathews rode (how the Centurion
sat a horse is not recorded), while Herman drove the large open wagon in
which were crowded Lizzie, Maria, Helen Jean, Duyckinck, Miss Dilling-
ham, and Joseph Smith (Sarah's discovery, the local poet, interested in her
sister Miss Huyler), besides Sarah's English manservant and the provisions.

Allan and Sophia were alone in a covered wagon they must have thought easier to control. Mathews thought the caravan looked "like a flight of Cossacks in the desert." Reaching the Gulf Road, "a woody defile, wild, strange, and primeval," they pushed on through Lanesborough, past the "ancient churchyard, thickly set with gravestones," then up Constitution Hill. Halfway up, they left off the coachman and the hamper at an inviting ledge, also leaving a courting couple in the group to help guard the contents. The rest "clambered on" to the top, where the Georgics-mindful Mathews said they sat or lay "scattered in groups like so many shepherds and shepherdesses on the mountain-top," until everyone remembered the food.

Just before they reached the ledge halfway down, an accident occurred which involved Lizzie, as Sophia wrote to Augusta. From July to December 1839 Lizzie had taken twenty-one riding lessons for which her father paid fifty cents each, but that was in the city, where people had chopped off Beacon Hill and thrown the dirt in the pond and the bay. On the rugged Berkshire terrain she had difficulty controlling her mount, as Sophia recorded: "Lizzie had mounted one of the saddle horses for a ride notwithstanding her being in a short dress. When we halted, her horse happened to be just before our wagon and it is supposed that our horse bit her's, at any rate the first thing we knew, was to see Lizzie rolling on the grass, the horse having thrown her, she jumped up unhurt, but Herman threw himself off Mr. Mathews horse which he had been riding, and they rolled over and over together." Hawthorne had dropped germinous seeds in his soul, but Herman and Lizzie were married lovers, and his reflexes were fast. What might have been disastrous turned out all right, as Sophia wrote: "As all [the horses] were standing perfectly still neither were hurt in the least. But I must needs become very much excited and nervous, quite unable to control my feelings. But in a few minutes was comparatively composed so that I had determined to remain with the party when Herman came to us and told Allan to take me home quietly."

Herman was still the older brother. Allan obeyed him and took Sophia back to the Melvill house. The rest were able to enjoy the picnic, even the tossed-about Lizzie. The picnic went on, "an excellent Feast, as in the Arabian Nights, conjured up in the wilderness," Mathews wrote. It was not a dry occasion, for they drank to "absent friends," letting "the corks dart to and fro, scaring the innocent birds from the twigs as if they had been shot at." Choosing "another of the numberless new roads winding every way," the subdued members of the "caravan-march homeward" reached Pontoosuc Lake at twilight and ambled about its banks, yet they reached home in the last of the light, only an hour after the newly cautious Allan and Sophia. After all that had happened, Lizzie was in no condition to start copying Herman's manuscript for him, even if there had been enough light.

Sunday was reserved for a visit (so Evert wrote) "to the Shakers who are then at their spasms." No one seemed to think that gawking at religious worshipers was in any way peculiar, for Herman, Lizzie, Robert, and Allan all went along hoping to see the Shakers dance, but the older Shakers suddenly decided to have a private meeting and the onlookers were told to leave. They were back at the Melvill place early in the afternoon, so Lizzie began to copy the manuscript. She finished it by the next morning, in time for Melville to add a title and a belated attribution to the imaginary vacationing Virginian. Monday afternoon, carrying the prized manuscript, Duyckinck and Mathews boarded the cars for New York City. Mathews wrote up his experiences in the jouncing cars: "Faster and faster, now that this other day of happiness is gone — the mighty city of labor and suffering draws nearer and begins its dim eclipse upon the spirit." Gawky, officious, vainglorious, ludicrous, Mathews nevertheless was suffused with a sense of having been blessed by the experiences: "Parting in mirth and free hilarity — when shall we meet again! When will any two or three of that gay company, in memory and friendly talk, revive these scenes of innocent enjoyment? Long, long in this heart at least, as on a stage, will those happy scenes be re-enacted: one by one shall those dear friends come up and glide by, smiling on us once again, waving their friendly hands, and bid us God speed on our course: — God speed all, dear friends!" Duyckinck was also deeply moved by the visit, as he wrote George on 15 August: "Ten years of repressed nature in me, suddenly exploding[,] are not to be bottled down again in a hurry."

Duyckinck also worked intermittently during the eight hours on the train so he could give his attention to his family when he reached home. In the course of preparing the manuscript for the printers he scrutinized the much-revised passage where Melville had named writers whom America should prize and cherish: "But even were there no Hawthorne, no Emerson, no Whittier, no Irving, no Bryant, no Dana[,] no Cooper[,] no Willis (not the author of the 'Dashes', but the author of the 'Belfry Pigeon') — were there none of these, & others of like calibre among us, nevertheless, let America first praise mediocrity even, in her own children." Unwilling, after the sniping that had gone on in the spring, to grant Willis any place in the honor roll, and unwilling to include a rabid abolitionist like Whittier, Duyckinck solved the problem to his satisfaction by marking through all the names of American writers and making the text read: "But even were there no strong literary individualities among us, as there are some dozen at least, nevertheless, let America first praise mediocrity even, in her own children." Duyckinck left uncensored Melville's comments on that unnamed but eminent American writer known as an imitator rather than an original genius—a lapse of courtesy and literary piety inexplicable except as a result of extreme haste and a blinding excess of pleasure in being able to publish such a tribute to Hawthorne.

During his hospitality Melville had "treated the house as his own & would suffer no payments," so he paid Robert for his guests and paid the neighbor who had provided a place to sleep until the Creole and her husband left. In Manhattan on Tuesday morning, therefore, Duyckinck got off by the new Express system a wicker basket of Heidseck (a dozen quarts for $15), the champagne that had passed muster on Monument Mountain, along with two kinds of "Segars," $3.25 for one kind and $.75 for the other. (As he knew, the sailor-author liked to vary his cigars, light and dark.) Both Duyckinck and Mathews wrote their bread-and-butter notes promptly, and Melville received them the next day and was "delighted & softened by both," although he was grieved to think they were "once more in those dreary regions" which were "*Trans-Taconic*" to him. The champagne arrived safely, twelve "beautiful babies" with uncommon intelligence in their aspect, and full of "animation & hilarity." Melville was still sightseeing, for he picked up the gift at the Express office on the fifteenth on the way back from Lebanon in a four-carriage outing devised to display the Shakers to two new boarders who had arrived in the morning. Rather than coddling the babies, Melville secured the basket at his feet and "drove off full speed"—his habitual daring and even reckless pace for twelve more years— "followed by the whole galloping procession." Mathews's gift, for Lizzie, was Mrs. Browning's poem "The Cry of the Human," in the author's hand, and he sent also a couple of gifts for Malcolm, "the boy popularly known as Barney." (He had already given Malcolm and little Maria small baskets he bought at the Shaker village.) Melville's article would appear in the next two issues of the *Literary World* with no more effort on his part, not even proofreading. Meanwhile, he could get to work on his whaling manuscript. He had just the place in mind.

Although he was still making himself available for outings, Melville had taken measures to get back to a manuscript that gave him proper sea-room to tell the truth in. His library was at Fourth Avenue, but he may have had his new whale books with him, the borrowed Scoresby, *An Account of the Arctic Regions*, and the imported Beale, *The Natural History of the Sperm Whale*, or he may have decided that he could work on narrative or essayistic chapters without any books. After Duyckinck left clutching the review of Hawthorne's *Mosses*, Melville found and reclaimed an old desk, as he wrote to his Trans-Taconic editorial friend:

I write you this from the *garret-way*, seated at that little embrasure of a window (you must remember it) which commands so noble a view of Saddle-back. — My desk is an odd one — an old thing of my Uncle the Major's, which for twelve years back has been packed away in the corn-loft over the carriage house. Upon dragging it out to day light, I found that it was covered with the marks of fowls — quite white with them — eggs had been laid in it — think of that! — Is it not typical of those other eggs that authors may be said to lay in their desks, — especially those with pigeon-holes?

Melville had written the essay on Hawthorne without the benefit of a desk, but now, always the stickler for proper equipment (whose first known fiction was published not as lines from a lap-board but as fragments from a writing-desk), he had set himself up with a memory-freighted heirloom, however soiled, and had appropriated a snug, quiet nook commanding an inspiring view, an ideal setting for him to write in. A century and a half later, the second-floor north room runs the entire width of the house, but in the sum-mer of 1850 it was divided by walls on either side of a stairway to the garret, the lowest steps of which were to the north, so that there was room for a desk in the small, isolated area, walls on either side of him, stairs starting behind him, and Greylock to the north.

Melville had most likely already invented his Ishmael as the sailor-narrator of the work in progress, a man obsessed with seeing objects and actions as puzzles to be pondered upon and resolved, if only temporarily. Ishmael himself could not have taken more pleasure than Melville in defining the problem of writing without a writing-desk then temporarily, at least, resolving it. All equipped except for his regular copyists, he may well have let the pages pile up without requisitioning Lizzie again. Yet although he had positioned himself to write greatly, he was not able to focus on his manu-script for long.

When the *Literary World* dated 17 August arrived early, with the first installment of the essay on Hawthorne (divided arbitrarily at a point that bore no relation to the author's own stopping point at the end of the first day's work), Melville wrote Duyckinck that under the circumstances the printing was far more correct than he expected, although he had spotted "one or two ugly errors" about which he was prepared to be philosophical ("no one sees them, I suppose, but myself"). (Soon he described them to Mrs. Hawthorne as "provoking.") The next day, Saturday the seventeenth, he drove over to Lenox to deliver to Hawthorne a package from Duyckinck, ignorant that it consisted of copies of all of his own books (a gift from Duyckinck, who in conversation had ascertained that Hawthorne was not in possession of any of them, not even the copy of *Typee* Duyckinck had sent to him for review in Salem). We do not know much about this visit, not even whether or not Melville showed his host and hostess the *Literary World* or whether or not Hawthorne opened the parcel while Melville was there. On this occasion, probably, Sophia Hawthorne decided that Melville as a "good authority" on the Berkshires (as she wrote her mother on 1 September) could be trusted when he said Indian summer there surpassed Indian summer anywhere else. They did formalize the invitation Hawthorne had impulsively extended on the fifth: Melville was to come to spend a few days with them "next month." To all appearances, Melville was simply enjoying his vacation and drawing it out into late August, the month he associated with his rare childhood reprieves from enforced labor in the bank or the cap and fur store.

In his old pattern of loafing summers and setting to work at the first frost, Hawthorne after Melville's call took his last long indulgence before starting his Salem romance of the Pyncheon house and family. Retreating to the barn, he lay on the new-mown hay (mown by the landlord or his hired hands) and reread *Typee*, wondering just what he had said in his review, then read *Omoo*, *Mardi*, *Redburn*, and *White-Jacket* (this last containing an incidental compliment to himself). He wrote Duyckinck on 29 August that he read the books "with a progressive appreciation of the author," having found *Mardi* a rich book, "with depths here and there that compel a man to swim for his life," "so good that one scarcely pardons the writer for not having brooded long over it, so as to make it a great deal better." Hawthorne further decided that no writer "ever put the reality before his reader more unflinchingly" than Melville had done in his last two books.

On 24 August Longfellow (saying he had "rarely seen a more appreciating and sympathising critic" than the Virginian) sent the last two issues of the *Literary World* to Hawthorne from Nahant, assuming Hawthorne might already have them but knowing that an extra set would be appreciated. As a shrewd professional whose *Evangeline* had been reviewed everywhere, controversially, in late 1847 and 1848, and as a friend with an acute awareness of Hawthorne's long failure to achieve recognition, Longfellow knew the potential value of such an appreciation in such a paper: the Virginian might single-handedly, in this propitious time after the success of *The Scarlet Letter,* confirm Hawthorne's high literary stature and define the terms by which others would appreciate him. He knew, in short, as the Hawthornes immediately did, that this was not merely one magazine article among many. From Longfellow if not another source as well (they may have subscribed), the Hawthornes received the papers, and were powerfully moved by the praise in them. They expressed their emotions according to their characters. Sophia wrote urgently to her sister Elizabeth Peabody not to wait an hour "to procure the two last numbers of 'The Literary World,' and read a new criticism on Mr. Hawthorne." Within the family she could exult without restraint: "At last some one speaks the right word of him. I have not before heard it. I have been wearied & annoyed hitherto with hearing him *compared* to Washington Irving & other American writers — & put generally *second*. At last some one dares to say what in my secret mind I have often thought — that he is only to be mentioned with the Swan of Avon — The Great Heart and the Grand Intellect combined." Wholly misled by the ascription of the essay to a Virginian, she was amused to think that the Southerner, not having seen Hawthorne, could not know in what a temple of physical beauty the heart and intellect were "enshrined."

Sophia Hawthorne was so excited that on 29 August she wrote to Evert Duyckinck declaring that she could not "speak or think of any thing" but the "extraordinary review":

> The Virginian is the first person who has ever in *print* apprehended Mr Hawthorne. I keep constantly reading over & over the inspired utterances, & marvel more & more that the word has at last been said which I have so long hoped to hear, & said so well. There is such a generous, noble enthusiasm as I have not before found in any critic of any writer. While bringing out the glory of his subject, (excuse me, but I am speaking as an indifferent person) he surrounds himself with a glory. The freshness of primeval nature is in that man, & the true Promethean fire is in him. Who can he be, so fearless, so rich in heart, of such fine intuition? Is his name altogether hidden?

After reading over Sophia's letter, Hawthorne wrote Duyckinck his opinion of Melville's books (innocent of the identity of the Virginian), then declared that the writer of the essay in the *Literary World* "is no common man; and, next to deserving his praise, it is good to have beguiled or bewitched such a man into praising me more than I deserve." (In using "bewitched" he was picking up the language Melville had used.) Among the passages that Sophia Hawthorne read and reread obsessively was one Duyckinck had unaccountably let stand in his last-minute censorship of the essay, the heretical allusion to Washington Irving, unnamed but unmistakable, as "that graceful writer" who owed "his chief reputation to the self-acknowledged imitation of a foreign model, and to the studied avoidance of all topics but smooth ones."

While Sophia Hawthorne was rhapsodic at the Virginian's exaltation of Hawthorne over the man hitherto universally acclaimed as the greatest writer America had produced, the master of Sunnyside was soon distressed, and his friend Duyckinck may well have heard from him on the subject. At the end of August Washington Irving was caught at a disadvantage. The new railroad along the east bank of the Hudson that had driven away the Morewoods ought to have been a convenience for him, since it could carry him so fast to lower Manhattan, but for months he had been aware only of its drawbacks — for in the middle of every night he was violently jolted awake by train whistles. A midsummer illness was compounded by the nightly assault, but the "salt air and sea breezes" during a week at Oyster Bay set him up again (as he wrote to Gouverneur Kemble on 7 August). He was back at Sunnyside when the *Literary World* of the seventeenth and then of the twenty-fourth arrived. Although temporarily revived by his vacation, Irving was in a generally weakened state when his nephew Pierre came upon the Virginian's calculated dispraise of the great man as a "self-acknowledged imitator" of Goldsmith. Such heresy would have been outrageous at any time, but coming, when it did, the Irvings saw it as the continuation of the onslaught from the unspeakable Powell.

The impudent article in the *Literary World* and the actual conversation young Irving had with his uncle rankled in Pierre's memory. Drawing on journals, of which only the one for the last year of Irving's life is known to survive, Pierre Irving wrote a ninety-four-page outline for his *Life and Letters of Washington Irving*. In the outline he reminded himself to include "Attack of a Thomas Powell in his 'Living authors of England' " toward the end of the 1848–49 chapter, and reminded himself to mention in the chapter on 1850 "an attack in the Herald about copyright" and in the chapter on 1851 (getting things off a few months) he remembered the pain of the attack in the *Literary World* essay on Hawthorne and his *Mosses:* "Preface to his Life of Goldsmith — 'Self-acknowledged imitator of.' " After writing these words in ink Pierre M. Irving went back at some time and above "self-acknowledged" impulsively wrote "turned against him" in pencil in the margin — a reminder that the anonymous author, Melville, had treacherously turned Irving's own words in his life of Goldsmith against him.

In his 1864 biography of his uncle, five years after the old man's death, Pierre made the connection between the anonymous 1850 essay in the *Literary World* and Powell's slanders (noting that the article appeared "some months" after the slanders). Pierre's strategy in the biography was to ignore or defuse any attacks on his uncle and to portray the writer as aloof from the give-and-take of journalism.

It was some months after this [Powell's 1849 attacks] that I mentioned to him an article I had been reading in a weekly periodical, in which the writer, evidently alluding to his [Irving's] preface in his biography of Goldsmith,

styles him, in an invidious spirit, "a self-acknowledged imitator of that author." At the close of that preface, the reader may remember he addresses
Goldsmith in the language of Dante's apostrophe to Virgil. . . .

He smiled; said he meant only to express his affectionate admiration of
Goldsmith, but it would never do for an author to acknowledge anything.
Was never conscious of an attempt to write after any model. No man of
genius ever did. From his earliest attempts, everything fell naturally from
him. His style, he believed, was as much his own as though Goldsmith had
never written — as much his own as his voice.

This was not the language of self-eulogy, but of quiet self-vindication. He
had never meant to warrant such perversion of his quotation [from Dante],
any more than Dante meant to confess himself an imitator of Virgil. There
were undoubtedly qualities of style as well as mental and moral characteristics
in which he resembled both Goldsmith and Addison, the two with whom he is
most frequently compared, while in others it would be impossible to con-
found them.

This was all benign and aloof, but the outline shows that Washington Irving
suffered greatly from what the Virginian wrote and that Pierre's account in
the biography was a deliberate alteration of the facts so that the historical
record could stand unblemished. It is curious that what bothered the Irvings
most was Melville's "turning" Washington Irving's words against him —
much the way he had turned back Sydney Smith's words against him and
Maurice Morgann's words against him.

In a letter dated August, probably late August, Irving complained of
"being very languid from the heat of the weather and the lingerings of an
indisposition" from which he was just recovering. By 27 August he had
missed two successive meetings of the board of the Astor Library because of
illness, from which he was then recovering but not recovered. The Irvings
knew enough not to make any public protests, so nothing marred the pleasure Hawthorne-lovers took in the essay.

Charles Lanman wrote Duyckinck asking what Sophia had asked — the
identity of the author. In September Duyckinck indiscreetly but kindly
loaned the sickly Augusta both the letters from the Hawthornes, and she kept
them until 30 September, when she wrote him, saying they had given her
"very great pleasure," and until that day had made her only reading since she
was taken sick — a fortnight ago, she said, although she had never fully recovered from the whooping cough she had caught at the Manor House
weeks before. She was at last ready to part with the letters:

I now return them, as if parting from a friend. Having read them, I am prepared still better to like the "old Man of the Mosses" & his loving, worshiping

wife, who knows so well how to appreciate the peculiar talents of her gifted husband, & yet can afford generously to discern them in another. She has offered a beautiful tribute to my noble-souled brother, and one who can so speak of him, has a place in my heart. Of him, no truer words were ever written than those, "the freshness of primeval nature is in that man." You love my brother, Mr Duyckinck & therefore you will pardon a sister for thus speaking.

Duyckinck had every reason to congratulate himself upon the wholly unexpected fruit of his vacation in the Berkshires, and no reason to be displeased with the three predictable pieces of literary gossip Mathews was contributing, "Several Days in Berkshire."

Allan and Sophia were both at the Melvill house with little Maria on 22 August (Allan had been commuting while Sophia stayed, much too pregnant to take the jolting cars as often as her husband did). Maria, Lizzie, and Malcolm were all there through August, although Maria was back in New York on 3 September. Helen meanwhile had gone to Coney Island with the ailing Mrs. Ives, then accompanied her home to Lansingburgh. On 29 August Augusta reported to Mary Blatchford: "Herman & Lizzie still prolong their rusticating, & are so happy among the mountains of Berkshire, that it seems impossible to tear themselves away." The thought of their moving to Pittsfield (and carrying her with them) had not crossed her mind. Meanwhile, the vacation at the Melvill house stretched on, with Lizzie a willing lagger, since she knew that if they lingered past the first week of September she would get to see her father and stepmother during the judge's regular court session in Lenox, and be able to show off Malcolm in relaxed circumstances. In early September only Herman, Lizzie, and Malcolm hung on at the Melvill house, and by this time it had crossed Melville's mind that tearing himself away from the mountains and from Hawthorne would in literal fact be "impossible."

The delay allowed Melville and Hawthorne to pursue their acquaintance. On 3 September Melville arrived in Lenox for his visit with the Hawthornes. All three of them had seen the article that preceded the second part of the essay on Hawthorne in the 24 August *Literary World*, "Several Days in Berkshire," Mathews's grateful account of how a city dweller went to the country: "Feeling the weight of brick and mortar somewhat oppressively, at the high point of the thermometer the other day, we determined, on a sudden thought, to reverse the proceedings of Sinbad, and throwing off the load, to become in our own proper person the Young Man of the Mountains of Berkshire." Melville identified the writer as Mathews (surely not to Hawthorne's surprise) and further informed them that in the latest issue, that of the thirty-first, Mathews was depicting his host as "Mr Noble Melancholy."

Sophia indulged herself in a letter to her mother after the owner of the little red house drove off with Hawthorne and Melville in his wagon. The landlord was William Aspinwall Tappan, Herman's age, son of the New York merchant and abolitionist Lewis Tappan. For three years the younger Tappan had been married to a member of Emerson's circle at Concord, Caroline Sturgis. Sophia earnestly informed her mother about her husband's temperament — "pensive perhaps," but not gloomy, "in his remote moods, like a stray Seraph, who had experienced in his own life no evil, but by the intuition of a divine Intellect saw & sorrowed over all evil." (About this time with the help of the stray Seraph she became pregnant again.)

Tappan had not wanted to meet Melville, perhaps because of Melville's reputation as a man who had indulged in sexual exploits in the South Seas and bragged about those exploits back home, perhaps because he was offended by Melville's treatment of the missionaries. In recounting Tappan's attitude, Sophia Hawthorne gave a detailed account of the impression she and her husband had formed of the writer from New York. She no longer saw only Fayaway in his face:

> I have no doubt he will be repaid by finding Mr Melville a very different man from what he imagines — & very agreable & entertaining — We find him so — a man with a true warm heart & a soul & an intellect — with life to his fingertips — earnest, sincere & reverent, very tender & *modest* — And I am not sure that he is not a very great man — but I have not quite decided upon my own opinion — I should say, I am not quite sure that I *do not think him* a very great man — for my opinion is of course as far as possible from settling the matter. He has very keen perceptive power, but what astonishes me is that his eyes are not large & deep — He seems to see every thing very accurately & how he can do so with his small eyes, I cannot tell. They are not keen eyes, either, but quite undistinguished in any way. His nose is straight & rather handsome, his mouth expressive of sensibility & emotion — He is tall & erect with an air free, brave & manly. When conversing, he is full of gesture & force, & loses himself in his subject — There is no grace nor polish — once in a while his animation gives place to a singularly quiet expression out of these eyes, to which I have objected — an indrawn, dim look, but which at the same time makes you feel — that he is at that instant taking deepest note of what is before him — It is a strange, lazy glance, but with a power in it quite unique — It does not seem to penetrate through you, but to take you into himself. I saw him look at Una so yesterday several times.

All this was written on the basis of her personal observations (supplemented by any reading she had done in his books), for his identity as the Virginian remained unrevealed. It is by all odds the fullest such description of Melville known to exist.

In Pittsfield, after putting Tappan on the cars for Albany, Hawthorne and Melville turned the wagon around and drove to dine with the household at the Melvill house (which Melville in a letter to Duyckinck on 16 August called Banyan Hall, because of its seeming to be "the old original Hall of all this neighborhood," besides being a "wide-spreading house," so that "the various outhouses seem shoots from it, that have taken root all round"). At eight Sophia's husband and their guest returned in Mr. Tappan's wagon. The low ceilings and cramped rooms of the cottage were oppressive after the Melvill mansion, but many of the furnishings were of the quaint old-fashioned sort that Melville associated with his own family houses. As she placed the furniture a few months earlier Sophia had itemized some pieces in a letter to her mother that her son, Julian, printed in *Nathaniel Hawthorne and His Wife* (1884), a book Melville owned late in his life. There was a "fairy tea-table" (a Hawthorne heirloom), a box and bowl and pitcher brought home from India by her husband's sea-captain father, an "ancient Manning chair," "the antique ottoman" that her sister had recovered, an antique center table that had lost a foot on the move, and small pieces of statuary and paintings. Melville felt comfortable there.

At some point during the next two days that Melville spent with the Hawthornes a deeper secret than Mathews's authorship of "Several Days" was disclosed to them, and Melville stood revealed as the Virginian, the man with the "freshness of primeval nature" and "the true Promethean fire," "so fearless, so rich in heart, of such fine intuition." The implication of Sophia's letter to her sister late in the month is that they "discovered" the secret, not that Melville himself revealed it. Most likely Duyckinck sent the news along with the belated second issue of the *Literary World*. What Sophia wrote to Elizabeth Peabody was based on a mixture of her reading (and repeated re-readings) of the essay and her discussions with Melville, and was more than a little ambiguous. She began: "We have discovered who wrote the Review in the Literary World. It was no other than Herman Melville himself! He had no idea when he wrote it that he should ever see Mr Hawthorne." She may have meant to assert that Melville had said to her that when he wrote it he had no idea he would ever see Hawthorne, which is not the truth, but she may have made that assumption based erroneously on the essay itself, where the "Virginian" declares that he has never seen Hawthorne and "in the chances of a quiet plantation life, remote from his haunts," perhaps never would. If Hawthorne in retrospect troubled himself about this matter at all, he had to figure Melville as having been, at their first meeting, either a man who had not yet written the essay — and subsequently disguised the fact that he had met the author of the *Mosses* before writing the essay — or else a man who had written the essay yet went through the entire day without mentioning it. Perhaps in the rush of other matters he did not focus on the problem enough even to perceive an oddity.

Sophia was quite explicit about other matters she and Melville discussed, and about his appearance and her judgment of him. While her earlier impressions of him were spontaneous, in this letter what she said of Melville was infused with her knowledge that Melville was the author of the article. He had told her that the essay she had read so many times "was too carelessly written — that he dashed it off in great haste & did not see the proof sheets, & that there was one provoking mistake in it" (which she had not noticed), "same madness of vital truth" instead of "sane madness of vital truth."

> I had some delightful conversations with him about the "sweetest Man of Mosses" after we discovered him to be the author of the Review. One interview we had upon the Verandah of Chateau Brun in the golden light of evening twilight, when the lake was like glass of a rose tint. We had been to see Caroline [Tappan], & she was obliged to go to put baby to bed, & so Mr Melville & I went out to sit in the light of setting sun. He said Mr Hawthorne was the first person whose physical being appeared to him wholly in harmony with the intellectual & spiritual. He said the sunny haze & the pensiveness, the symmetry of his face, the depth of eyes, "the gleam — the shadow — & the peace supreme" all were in exact response to the high calm intellect, the glowing, deep heart — the purity of actual & spiritual life. Mr Melville is a person of great ardor & simplicity. He is all on fire with the subject that interests him. It rings through his frame like a cathedral bell. His truth & honesty shine out at every point. At the same time he sees thing[s] artistically, as you percieve in his books. I have just read again Typee. It is a *true history*, yet how poetically told — the divine beauty of the scene, the lovely faces & forms — the peace & good will — & all this golden splendor & enchantment glowing before the dark refrain constantly brought as a background — the fear of being killed & eaten — the latent cannibalism in the olive tinted Apollos around him — the unfathomable mystery of their treatment of him.

(Chateau Brun was not the little red cottage but the much more luxurious house the Tappans were renting from Sam Ward; it survives at the site of the Tanglewood concerts.) Adoringly obsessed with her husband, Sophia saw nothing excessive in Melville's own enthusiasm. Melville must indeed have said much of what she quotes him as saying, though it is not entirely clear whether it was he or Sophia herself who had recourse to the lines from Wordsworth's "Composed upon an Evening of Extraordinary Splendour and Beauty" ("the gleam — the shadow — & the peace supreme"). Much of her description can be confirmed by other witnesses. Notably, the quality of "simplicity" coincides with Thomas Low Nichols's judgment of Melville in

1845 or so as "a simple-hearted, enthusiastic man of genius, who wrote with the consciousness of an impelling force, and with great power and beauty."

Melville impressed Sophia by showing that he knew how to respect the requirements of a fellow writer even when that man was his host (as she wrote her sister Elizabeth in October): "He was very careful not to interrupt Mr Hawthorne's mornings — when he was here. He generally walked off somewhere — & one morning he shut himself into the boudoir & read Mr Emerson's Essays in presence of our beautiful picture." The picture, an engraving of Raphael's "The Transfiguration" given them by Emerson, occasioned some stories from Hawthorne, and especially from Sophia, about their stay in the Old Manse in Concord and their acquaintance with Emerson and his followers such as Thoreau and the young William Ellery Channing. Melville had his own indirect connection with Emerson, since Lemuel Shaw as a young man had boarded with Emerson's mother and her then-young sons, and had been acquainted with Waldo before he was banned from Harvard a decade earlier, even though he had failed, perhaps because of the lack of time, to get from Emerson a letter introducing Melville to Carlyle. Melville and Hawthorne, and probably Sophia as well, were led naturally into talk of the authors the Hawthornes had known in Concord and the British writers Melville had met and others that they all wished they could meet. Sophia gave some of her attention to the children, tactfully leaving the men together, and then gave Melville some time alone with her: "In the afternoon he walked with Mr Hawthorne. He told me he was naturally so silent a man that he was complained of a great deal on this account; but that he found himself talking to Mr Hawthorne to a great extent. He said Mr Hawthorne's great but hospitable silence drew him out — that it was astonishing how *sociable* his silence was. (This Mr Emerson used to feel) He said sometimes they would walk along without talking on either side, but that even then they seemed to be very social."

After breakfast on 7 September, a Saturday, Melville went away — perhaps on foot to the Lenox station. Sophia had enjoyed her conversations with him, but she was glad to see him go, since she was tired out from having "to spend every morning from breakfast to dinner in preparing dinners & overseeing all the cooking." (She may unwittingly have been suffering the physical imbalance of very early pregnancy, all the more because on 21 September she would be forty-one.) Melville already knew that one thing he had in common with Hawthorne was the need to reconcile family duties with the sacredness of a writing routine, and his admiration of the Hawthornes as "the loveliest family he ever met with, or anyone can possibly imagine" (as his sister Augusta quoted him in a letter to Helen on 24 January 1851) had much to do with his seeing that Sophia subordinated everything else to the needs of her husband, whom she quite literally worshiped.

Hawthorne and Melville had been extraordinarily drawn to each other at their first meeting, Hawthorne so much so that he had invited Melville for this all but unprecedented visit. Writing to his old classmate Horatio Bridge about his inviting Melville, Hawthorne left unspoken what he knew his old friend would understand: the recluse had behaved wholly out of character. Now their intimacy was sealed in these prolonged afternoon walks when Hawthorne could not forget the new knowledge that Melville was the man he had "beguiled or bewitched" into praising him so much and while Melville accepted the consequences of his having written as he did, so that now Hawthorne knew that he had dropped germinous seeds into the younger man's soul, whether through his writings or his personal presence. As he talked his way through these walks in Stockbridge Bowl, Melville's old aspirations to write a great book — to take strides beyond *Mardi* — became inextricably tangled with the liberation he felt in the presence of Hawthorne's person and achievements. Meeting Hawthorne, being so quickly drawn to him, knowing that the feeling was reciprocated, writing about him so ecstatically, confirming the friendship with the final intimacy of the Hawthorne household, where he could read the precious inscribed copy of Emerson's essays in the boudoir, all this had created an incommunicable need in Melville — the need to find a way to continue writing the book within reach of this other American writer already proclaimed in the *Literary World* (no matter by whom) as one who had approached Shakespearean greatness. Just a year before, Melville had looked forward with aplomb to leaving Lizzie at the Shaws for a year, since she would have had Malcolm to console her for his absence. Now, after the conversations on the porch looking down at Stockbridge Bowl, after the walks with the nobly pensive if not melancholic romancer, he was all at once unwilling to look forward to completing his manuscript without having Hawthorne somewhere in his vicinity.

Once back at Banyan Hall, Melville probably abandoned his attempt to absorb himself in his book, since on Tuesday Lemuel and Hope Shaw were expected from Boston for three days (probably to stay at the hotel in the village) before taking rooms at the Curtis Hotel in Lenox on the thirteenth for Shaw's annual court session. In these few days Melville gave shape to his deepest ambitious urgings with a momentous decision. He would act against the advice of his *History of the County of Berkshire, Massachusetts* on the damage to the local economy wrought by borrowers: "The subject is an *old one*, indeed; but the anger is renewed from day to day. It is not the *borrowers* of money, as a general fact, upon whom the country can depend; but dependence must be placed upon the substantial and independent farmer, mechanic, and labourer. *Mortgage* is certain to prove in the general, what the word signifies, a *death-gage* to the property upon which it is fastened, and to the prosperity of the man who allows it to be fastened upon his estate." At some point Melville drew a curved line in the left margin along all the last sentence, beginning "Mortgage," but marking prudent advice was no guarantee he would take it. Very possibly Melville had spent the last several weeks chastising himself for not having known in time that the Melvill farm was to be sold; more likely, if he coveted the farm and old mansion from the moment he learned the Morewoods were buying it for sixty-five hundred dollars, he was realistic enough to acknowledge that even if he had learned earlier that it was for sale he could not have afforded to buy it.

For some time Melville had been discontent with his working conditions in Fourth Avenue, judging from Mary Blatchford's comment to Augusta on 9 January 1851 about his having longed for a "quiet place." In the three and then four weeks that Melville stayed on at the farm, weeks during which his intimacy with Hawthorne grew, he passed out of the stage where he accepted his financial situation realistically and could imagine going back to the discomforts of the noisy city. Now he was determined to have the next best thing to the Melvill farm, even if it cost more money than he had earned from all his five books together, in both England and the United States — even if it cost what the Melvill farm had brought. Within days of Shaw's arrival at Pittsfield, Melville persuaded him to advance him another three thousand dollars against Lizzie's inheritance so he could purchase Dr. John Brewster's neighboring farm, across the road from Holmes's estate, a property which was *not* among those publicly advertised in the *Sun*. He seems not to have shopped around, and he probably did not haggle over the price, which was sixty-five hundred dollars for 160 acres and a house, just what the Morewoods were paying for the Melvill house and 250 acres.

After Melville's death his old friend and first biographer, Joseph Smith, described the purchase from a local's point of view: "Mr. Melville on the 14th of September, 1850, bought of Dr. John Brewster, Sr., the farm adjoining the Broadhall estate in the rear, but which as to its buildings faces easterly on the middle road to Lenox, and so near that town that it renders access to it easy. On the farm was, and is, a large quaint old house, built in the early days of the settlement of the town, by Capt. David Bush. Mr. Melville named the place Arrowhead, from some Indian relics which were turned up in his first plowing of its soil." The details of this transaction are not wholly clear, but on 14 September the farm was transferred to Melville's name, with Brewster holding a mortgage of fifteen hundred dollars, on which Melville would pay interest of ninety dollars a year. If the whole of Shaw's new three thousand dollars went to Brewster, that leaves a discrepancy of two thousand dollars. Apparently Melville had left two thousand of the sixty-five hundred dollars unpaid, for he later referred to the portion of the purchase money, separate from the mortgage, which Brewster had agreed to wait a little while for, until Melville sold the indenture of lease on the Fourth Avenue house in New York, which Melville was sure he would do quickly, and at a substantial profit.

Lizzie, with fiscal prudence instilled in her from childhood, was the sort of person who would put a house on the market and sell it before buying a different house. Her husband was not, and he acted impulsively and extravagantly, even recklessly. Sophia Melville's pregnancy (and the birth of a healthy daughter, Florence, on 15 September) may have been forcing the family to see that the time had come to have separate establishments, but there was no urgency about the matter. Even if Sophia needed to have one of the girls' rooms for a new nursery, Augusta could always have gone indefinitely to the Manor House and Helen could have gone to visit Hope Shaw in Boston or stayed on in Lansingburgh with the ailing Mrs. Ives, who needed her, and even the younger Fanny and Kate would have been welcomed in any number of homes, no doubt including Mrs. Thurston's house on Bond Street. Temporary refuge for charming and competent young female relations in that age of prolonged, even ceremonial visits was simply not a problem, although prolonged separation would have been hard for everyone to bear. The brothers would hardly have spent so much time in the country that summer if finding a buyer for the Fourth Avenue house was uppermost on anyone's mind.

Melville's impulsive decision (in which Lizzie's opinion could hardly have mattered) took the family and friends by surprise — everyone from Cousin Priscilla in Canandaigua (who would not necessarily have been kept up to date) to the people who would in the natural course of things have been informed immediately. In all the intimate talk with Duyckinck in the Berkshires Melville had given not the slightest hint that he was thinking of moving there; Evert was the one who indulged (at least to his wife) his fantasies of settling in so magnificent and healthful a region. As the time to return to New York grew close, Melville simply could not tear himself away from the Berkshires; for all the irrationality of it, one reason, whether he admitted it or not, was that he was not willing to tear himself away from the vicinity where Hawthorne lived. He had decided that to write greatly on his manuscript he needed to have Greylock outside his study window; and he had decided, at some level of consciousness, that to write as greatly as he felt he might be able to write, he needed Hawthorne off in the other direction, nearby even if not regularly visited. Rationally Melville must have recognized that Hawthorne was merely renting the cottage and not planning to keep his family there indefinitely, but rationality was not, just now, the dominant force in Melville's life.

On Sunday, 15 September, Hope Shaw (perhaps with the judge) went to "Mr Neals Church" in Lenox (as she noted in her diary), then in the afternoon went to the Melvill house. She went back there on Monday in the stagecoach, perhaps because Malcolm had begun to feel sick the day before. On the nineteenth Lizzie was able to go with "Helen Melville" (Herman's cousin Helen Jean Melvill, who was there at the house) to dine with Hope in Lenox. On the same evening, probably, while Lizzie was occupied, Melville harnessed a horse and in the splendor of the waxing moon (a foretaste of the full astounding beauty of the harvest moon to come two days later) he set out alone to the little red cottage to tell the Hawthornes the news. Sophia reported to her sister: "he drove up one superb moonlight night & said he had bought an estate six miles from us, where he is really going to build a real towered house — an actual tower. He is married to a daughter of Judge Shaw Judge Lemuel Shaw, & has a child of year & half — Malcolm. He is of Scotch descent — of noble lineage — of the Lords of Melville & Leven, & Malcolm is a family name. So we shall have him for a neighbour." Melville may or may not have told the decent but plebeian Hawthornes that he was of noble lineage (Allan might have, on the first visit Melville made there), but he was waxing like that superb moon, ecstatic at the reality of the purchase of an "estate" and caught up in the plans for building his own vantage point for surveying the mountain ranges and valleys from the Catskills to Saddleback (and beyond, to Vermont). The man who had spent his youth in cities "pent up in lath and plaster, tied to counters, nailed to benches, clinched to desks" (*Moby-Dick*, ch. 1, "Loomings"), was going to have a vantage point for brooding over the steeples of Pittsfield, better than the crow's nest in any whaler or the back-railed tops in a man-of-war. He would soon, like Montaigne, have a writing tower, with windows toward the Catskills and Mount Greylock. It was a fantasy in which he totally believed. In his mood, anything could happen.

At the time Sophia recorded her impressions of him, Melville was intermittently in a state of nervous exaltation, a natural state for anyone part way through the writing of a great book. His emotional states owed much to the interaction between his present intense consciousness (dominated by thought of his work in progress and his intimacy with Hawthorne) and the power of his memory. Everywhere in the Berkshires were traps for what he called on 29 June the next year, in a letter to Hawthorne, his "susceptible and peradventure febrile temperament," reminders of how his life had changed, and changed again — through death (his father's, his uncle's, various cousins', his brother's), impoverishment, bodily changes, seasonal changes, his own travels, his literary achievements, his marriage. There, a boy tired from stage travel, he had witnessed the meeting between his father and the uncle he did not remember having seen before: "It was in the larch-shaded porch of the mansion looking off, under urn-shaped road-side elms, across meadows to South Mountain." He recalled, decades later, their embracing "with the unaffectedness and warmth of boys—such boys as Van Dyck painted."

He had written those emotion-laden larch trees into the opening of the essay on Hawthorne—private acknowledgment of the stunning collision of childhood and manhood. The mere act of staying in the Berkshires through much of July, all of August, then September, at such a time of psychological unfolding, would have thrown Melville intermittently into states of nervous agitation. Making a turn on a road, just as much as glancing about his uncle's old place, Melville collided with himself as a penniless and futureless boy, a sexually wondering and sexually excited youth, just as in 1849, a famous author stepping ashore in England, he had collided with his younger self, the ship's boy of 1839. Small wonder that a turbulent state flared as soon as he arrived at Pittsfield in the summer of 1850, and that it blazed higher as soon as he met the only American writer he could even provisionally consider his equal.

As a fatherless adolescent on visits to the Melvill farm or later as an eighteen-year-old schoolteacher, Melville had taken an outjutting of rock as a vantage point for brooding over the steeples of Pittsfield and the amphitheater dominated by Mount Greylock. Now he knew he would pass that outcropping whenever he took the Old Lenox Road from Arrowhead on his way to see Hawthorne. The excitement of being there, near Hawthorne, was infinitely compounded by the physical and mental arousals, the anxieties, agitations, frustrations, and temporary triumphs of the philosophical, psychological, and aesthetic struggle he was intermittently waging in his manuscript as he sat at his uncle's old desk, before that little embrasure of a window which commanded so noble a view of Saddleback.

37

Writing at Arrowhead
October 1850–Mid-January 1851

COUNTRY LIFE
Oh let me in the Country range,
'Tis there we breath[e], 'tis there we live;
Whispering winds the Poplars courting,
Swains in rustic Circles sporting;
These afford a lasting pleasure,
Without Guilt and without measure.

"Thomas Melvill's Book," 1789

AROUND THE START OF THE LAST week of September 1850, Melville was at last back home with Lizzie in New York. Their first attention went to the new baby in the house, but Herman had another purpose for the visit — to prepare for the move to Pittsfield. His old Lansingburgh friend Tertullus D. Stewart (living at 7 Fifth Avenue and running a sugar refinery at 108 Front Street) volunteered to lend him all the money to make the move, assuring him that there would be no need to worry about how soon he repaid him, but Melville did not see any need to go outside the family for money.

On 21 September Melville dined with Sir Edward Belcher and young Bayard Taylor (cousin of his companion on the *Southampton*), who had recent stories of James Fenimore Cooper and George Bancroft, with whom the pedestrian traveler had dined the night before. Some news in the papers touched Melville closely. He saw copies in various places of the 31 August *Literary World*, where Mathews celebrated "The Mountain Festival." In the second issue (7 September) of Powell's new venture, *Figaro!*, he saw the "Personal Sketch" of Nathaniel Parker Willis, whom Powell managed to link to Irving: "with regard to his politics he is, with the solitary exception of Washington Irving, the least republican his country has produced" — a result, Powell declared, of Willis's elegant, conventional, and fastidious nature. On the same day, Melville saw in the *Literary World* the Centurion's "The Grand Fancy Dress-Ball," which Mathews concluded with his heartfelt sense of the special blessing of the experience — "God speed all, dear friends!"

The gossip in the city was about Nathaniel Parker Willis's plans to repudiate city life, not about Herman Melville's plans to do the same thing. On 30 August Oakey Hall wrote this account of Willis (printed in the New Orleans *Commercial Bulletin* for 13 September):

> Willis is about retiring, for the second time, from the busy world to such rural haunts as best befit the poet. He is about resigning the notoriety of the man of fashion and crowds, for the comfort and retirement of country fame as a man of letters. . . . He has lately purchased some forty acres of land at the head of Newburg Bay, near the base of Butter Hill, a peak of the Hudson highlands. In the centre of this land runs, for about half a mile, one of the most romantic ravines that I have ever been through. I was so impressed on a recent visit to the vicinity, with its wild enchanting beauty, that, paying tribute to the Dryads and Fauns of the spot, I waded *sans bottes* the whole extent of it (for there is a charming brook in the depth of the ravine), and so explored the whole of its beauties. I counted no less than ten cascades from the river-road to the mill-dam heading the ravine, and numbered some half a dozen springs. Here, not four miles from the city of Newburg, and hemmed in by many accessories of the most unromantic utilitarianism, such as plaster mills and brick yards, one may see nature in her wildest grandeur. Mr. Willis will build almost immediately. He is in gun-shot distance from the (building) country seat of J. Tyler Headl[e]y, the biographer of military men, a *l'elèrtique*, and a cannon-shot from Downing, the Architect, and author of sundry works upon landscape gardening, rural horticulture, and kindred subjects. Literature must be above par from these tokens! When before were editors and essay writers known to purchase country seats?

Soon word got around that Melville, like Willis, was leaving town for good, and that he too had big plans for his country estate. On 23 September George Duyckinck passed the word to Joann Miller: "Herman Melville has taken us by surprize by buying a farm of 160 acres in Berkshire County. It is mostly woodland which he intends to preserve and have a road through, making it more of an ornamental place than a farm. Part of it is on a hill commanding a view of twenty miles, where he intends eventually to build. He removes at once with his mother and sisters to our great sorrow as the house was one of the pleasantest to visit at I ever came across and we are much attached to them all." The move had surprised everyone, including Herman.

On 17 October the Pittsfield *Sun* reported that the "Melvill Farm, one mile south of the village," had been purchased by John Morewood, and that the "noble mansion" was "undergoing extensive repairs," so that Mr. Morewood could take possession "on his return from Europe." It continued with the news that "Herman Melvill, Esq., the author," had purchased from Dr. J. M. Brewster "a portion of the Farm formerly owned by the late Mr. David Bush, a short distance south of the summer residence of Dr. Oliver Wendell Holmes, and contemplates the erection, at no distant day, as we understand, of 'a house to suit him' in a beautiful grove on the premises. The situation he has purchased commands one of the most extensive and splendid views in Berkshire." Independent epistolary reports from Sophia Hawthorne and George Duyckinck and this newspaper item make it clear that Melville had been talking extravagantly about his new plans. In George's letter the word "eventually" sounds the note of the beginnings of sobriety in Melville, but George's language, like Sophia Hawthorne's, reflects Melville's own. Melville had decided suddenly to move to Pittsfield; he had made up his mind he could be a gentleman farmer (more gentleman than farmer). His mother and sisters were going to live with him, not with Allan (except for Kate, who decided to stay with Allan and Sophia at least for the present). And he was going to build a house on a spectacular site commanding (even before climbing to the writing tower?) a view of twenty miles, and more. There, of course, he was going to write works of literature such as Mathews had been promoting—literary works to match the mountains, and in a world suddenly so nearly perfect the great book, once he completed it, would be sure to make him financially comfortable. He didn't need that yacht the Boston *Transcript* had joshed about; instead, he would take the money and build a real towered house in a beautiful grove, where he would write masterpiece after masterpiece.

Melville knew that moving a household was tumultuous. He could remember moving within New York City as a child, as well as stripping the house the third and second days before the terrifying day and night at the Cortlandt Street dock when he and his father had fled the city for Albany in 1830. He cannot have avoided the duties of packer, carter, and teamster during the move within Albany, or the one from Albany to Lansingburgh in 1838, or from there to New York City in 1847. Like a reasonable man Melville made up his mind to put the manuscript aside without complaint during the time it would take for him to get moved to Pittsfield and settled in. He probably pretty much resolved to sacrifice September and October. Augusta was still too weak to help, but everyone else sprang into frenzied action. Around the second or third of October (as Augusta recalled in a letter to Helen on 5 December), Helen and Fanny made a last heroic expedition to Canal Street to Arnold & Constable's, shopping for elegant silks, satin, and velvets, as well as more utilitarian items. Remembering Lansingburgh, they were determined to purchase things that would be unobtainable in Pittsfield.

The eight hours in the railway cars to Pittsfield exhausted Augusta more than anyone had expected, but a bed was apparently ready for her to lie down on, and the bustle began (or continued) around her all through the next "fortnight," as she explained when she took up her duties as correspondent on 17 October, writing to Mary Blatchford: "when there is so much disorder around one, one sympathizes with it, till there is about as much within, and then one hardly likes to trust oneself upon paper fearful of the consequences to one's epistolary reputation. — But now that I can discern something of order around me — Sweet order that goodly thing of which these poor eyes have been deprived for many long weeks — I think I can discover a corresponding something in my brain." Melville was wholly involved in trying to dispel the disorder. At this time he was putting "locks & bolts" on doors that had stood seventy years without them — a strange occupation for the man who with such admiration had proclaimed (in his first book, ch. 27) that there "was not a padlock in the valley" of the Typees.

One of the first things Melville did was to name his estate. On 17 October Augusta explained it to Mary Blatchford: "What think you of the name of our place — Arrow-head. It is so called from the number of these Indian relics which have been found." Melville may have chosen the name before he composed his first letter from the house on 6 October — a letter to Evert Duyckinck, written at an unusual time of day and on a make-do table rather than a proper desk: "Until to day I have been as busy as man could be. Every thing to be done, & scarcely any one to help me do it. But I trust that before a great while we shall be all 'to rights,' and I shall take my ease on mine mountain. For a month to come, tho', I expect to be in the open air all day, except when assisting in lifting a bedstead or a bureau." What Melville was doing outside is not clear, except that he was harvesting apples and perhaps some crops that Brewster had laid by. Luckily for everyone's attempt to establish order, they had an extraordinarily fine fall, as Melville declared to Duyckinck, writing by candlelight or lamplight, despite the pain that light caused his eyes:

> I hardly thought that I should find time or even *table* to write you this long while. But it is Sunday at last, and after a day chiefly spent in *Jacquesizing* in the woods, I sit down to do what with me is an almost unexampled thing — inditing a letter at night. It has been a most glowing & Byzantine day — the heavens reflecting the tints of the October apples in the orchard — nay, the heavens themselves looking so ripe & ruddy, that it must be harvest-home with the angels, & Charles' Wain be heaped high as Saddle-Back with Autumn's sheaves. — You should see the maples — you should see the young perennial pines — the red blazings of the one contrasting with the painted green of the other, and the wide flushings of the autumn air harmonizing

both. I tell you that sunrises and sunsets grow side by side in these woods, & momentarily moult in the falling leaves.——A hammer! yes a hammer is before me—the very one that so cruelly bruised the very finger that guides my pen. I can sentimentalise it no more.

As he expected, Melville was drawn into domestic duties, without and within the house, for several weeks. When Aunt Mary Melvill got back from visiting her sisters-in-law and the Shaws (and perhaps some of the Hobarts and Dearborns) in Boston, she checked up on the neighboring household and reported to Shaw on 17 October: "Yesterday I was at Hermans, they are all well, and the house in comfortable order Malcom is particularly hearty, and appears to have quite recovered from his lameness" (this last a transient affliction).

On 17 October, also, Augusta, "amidst noise & bustle, carpenters & locksmiths," wrote to Mary Blatchford a long letter that gives the fullest account of Arrowhead we have. (It survives in the Augusta Papers because Mary's family returned Augusta's letters after Mary died.) The weather had been "most delightful for ten days past—cloudless skies & the balmiest of air—windows & doors all open." She had never before "fully realized the glorious beauty of an October in the country," since her visits in the 1830s had been in the summer (the latest was her mid-September visit in 1837):

> It far surpasses my expectations. The scenery is magnificent. I could never have imagined anything more beautiful—more varied—in every direction, it stretches away in mountain, hill & valley, all glowing with gorgeous tints of autumn. I have no doubt we see it now under its most beautiful aspect, for I hardly think the fresh green of June can be as well suited to its wild sublimity. . . . I wish you were by my side this moment, dear Mary, to watch the changing light and shade upon the forest slope just before me—it is exquisite—The glowing scarlet of the maples contrast so brightly with the more subdued tints of their woodland sisters, & all wrapt in that soft dreamy haze which characterizes a mountain sunset—. I declare it has made even prosaic me, poetical—what then would be its effect on you. —I really believe that I could at this moment indite a sonnet.

Her description makes it plain that Herman's ecstatic love of the Berkshires was shared by others in the family. Lizzie seems to have gone along with all of her husband's plans in her usual good spirit. Indeed she may have welcomed the simpler life in the farmhouse. She knew that by living there she could count on seeing her father and stepmother every fall (and in spring, some years), when the judge's official duties would bring him to Lenox. If she needed to see them at any other time of the year, such as Thanksgiving, she could be whisked across the state of Massachusetts straight to Boston on the railroad in a third or a quarter of the time it had taken her to get home from New York City. After all, her father was the same age Herman's father would have been, and Allan Melvill had been dead almost two decades.

Kate's reason for staying in New York City may have been that she was unwilling to leave Sophia and the nurse with a small baby as well as little Maria. For the senior Maria, staying with Allan and Sophia was not a serious option, since her daughter-in-law had an extremely clear sense of how she wanted to conduct a household and no hesitation about making her desires known, a straightforward assertiveness that Allan had to apologize to his mother for, deprecatingly calling it a touch of "Aunt Catherineness" (in reference to what the family always saw as the selfish outspokenness of Uncle Herman's doughty domestic tyrant of a wife). For Maria, being with Herman and Lizzie and at least three of her daughters in Pittsfield was what she wanted, for she still saw Pittsfield as a refuge from all the woes embodied in the phrase "cholera summer." She also saw it as the opportunity to show what she could do in a garden if she had a hired man to direct, and to show how she could run a rural household with a cook and a cleaning woman. Lizzie, the assumption was, would have enough to do caring for Herman and Malcolm. There is no indication that Lizzie did not accept this view of her role, although she was, like everyone else, pitching in to make Arrowhead habitable.

Leaving some of the family behind in New York proved painful. The "Arrowheads" (as Maria was saying by 29 December of the next year) had to become accustomed to being away not only from the astringent Sophia, but also, deprivations more severe, from Allan and Kate and the two baby girls. Maria felt a peculiar stinging grief as the weeks went by, for it was the first time Kate ever resided away from her, though she had visited the Van Vechtens for weeks at a time. As Augusta wrote to Mary Blatchford on 25 November, it felt "very strange" to be at Arrowhead, parted "from Kate & the rest of our dear household in New York" — so strange that she was unable to acknowledge the severed ties by writing "*their* dear household."

The Melvilles all found that Arrowhead was in less than ideal move-in condition, and there may be an edge of defensiveness in Augusta's description of the location on 17 October: "The house itself though appearing to be in a valley, contrasted with the heights around, is in reality upon a hill & commands from every window a fine view." While Herman had set his heart on a higher location for his towered house, Augusta sensibly gave no hint now that she was thinking of Arrowhead as merely temporary. Nor did she romanticize it as a piece of mouldering grandeur like the Melvill house beyond the hill:

Our old farm house cannot boast much in point of beauty, but it is delightfully comfortable & that is all that is really necessary in the country. It is an old house, counting its seventy years or more, & though outwardly modernized, retains all its ancient appearance within. It is built after that peculiarly quaint style of architecture which places the chimney — the hugest in proportions — immediately in the centre, & the rooms around it. An arrangement so totally void of grace & beauty, must surely possess some counterbalancing advantage, but as yet I have been unable to discover it, even after having made it the subject of the most profound reflection for a fortnight — unless it be, that the heat is thus kept in the house & secured from all superfluous waste — no trifling consideration in this breezy county of Berkshire. But another view just strikes me — the economy in the matter of brick & mortar — four chimneys would most certainly require more than one — oh wise & prudent & mindful of the cost, were the generation that are gone. And very trustworthy & honest must they all of [have] been, judging from the absence of locks & bolts, for, with the exception of the two outside ones, bedroom & parlor, pantry & closet — each door stood guiltless of their sign. What would they say I wonder, could they look in upon the changes a few days have wrought, not anything very favorable, I fear for the honesty of the present generation, judging from the number of locks & bolts.

She did not enumerate rooms, but assured her friend that they had "all sorts of odd little closets, in all sorts of odd little places." The "gem of the collection" was the "one that stands in the parlor": "you have heard of 'the corner cupboard' — well this must be it. We have left it standing for its oddity, but elevate it from its ignoble use into doing duty as an 'etage[re].' In just such another, no doubt, did poor Dame Hubbard make her unsuccessful search." This was a house that could be made to work, not a house like Banyan Hall, which would immediately have enveloped them all into well-designed spaces.

When far-flung members of the family heard the astonishing news, they expressed their feelings in skepticism mingled with optimism. On 24 October, Cousin Priscilla, the day after receiving from Robert her "share of the proceeds of the *farm*-sale," wrote to Lemuel Shaw from Canandaigua about the news: "I am delighted to hear that 'Lizzie' & our other New-York friends are so pleased with their change of residence — hope they will have no cause to regret it — tho' I confess that it surprised *me* at first." Nilly Thayer wrote Augusta on 8 November from Boston:

I was much surprised in receiving your letter to find that you had so suddenly pulled up stakes & were again established elsewhere. I was in N. Y. a fortnight since & as I passed your pretty & pleasant house in the 4th Avenue I almost breathed a sigh that you were not still in the enjoyment of it. I am not romantic enough to discover any particular beauty or pleasure in the country in winter & cannot imagine the same feeling in any other & fear you will find some of the long dreary wintry days rather dull after the bustle & pleasant excitement of a city life, but I have ever given you the credit of making the best of everything. . . . I know of no lovelier spot than the beautiful mountain scenery of Pittsfield & can readily believe a greater portion of the year you will enjoy it.

Nilly had received from Augusta a description of Arrowhead much like the one received by Mary Blatchford, for she continued: "I was quite amused with your description of your old house with all its nooks & corners & old chimneys."

Cousin Priscilla also received a similar letter from Augusta (not entered in Augusta's record of correspondence), and replied on 20 November:

> *What* charitable excuse *had* your *true* cousinly regard devised for my apparent neglect? — O! I think I can *guess* — you probably fear'd that the startling announcement contained in your last, had paralized my faculties & left me powerless — but no such disastrous effect was produced — I did indeed *stare* with astonishment, as the almost *incredible* fact met my wondering eyes — & If circumstances had seconded my impulses at that moment, I could have poured forth my astonishment in eloquent strophes — but in plain prose dear coz, how *do* you enjoy the change? I presume you have become nicely established, & are giving the country a fair trial this winter, I think — & never sigh for the *dry pavements* — & brilliant sights of Broadway.

Although taken totally off guard, everyone took a realistic view of the matter, knowing that the strong character and inner resources of the Arrowhead household could make up for the loss of metropolitan gaiety.

In the New York papers Melville saw a good deal of gossip, among which it would have been hard to miss Clark's onslaughts against Mathews and Duyckinck. In the October *Knickerbocker*, Clark mercifully did not mention Mathews's "Several Days in Berkshire" when he passed along an item from Hiram Fuller of the *Evening Mirror*. The report was replete with old malice (years before, Fuller had begun calling Duyckinck and Mathews the Mutual Admiration Society) but newly tainted by virulent gossip from Thomas Powell, still feared as the author of *Living Authors of America* and the prospective author of a second series of that title. Clark was sublimely happy with his fake news item: " 'PUFFER HOPKINS' is engaged in writing his Autobiography, after the manner of LEIGH HUNT. The 'Mutual Admiration Society' have subscribed for the entire edition, with the exception of a 'presentation copy,' held in reserve. Will it embrace the notice of the writer, which we are told the author of 'The Living Authors of America' affirms was written by 'PUFFER' himself for that work? It *ought* to, surely." On 12 October the Duyckincks reprinted from the London *Athenæum* Richard Bentley's statement that he had paid Prescott, Cooper, and Melville "between £15,000 and £16,000" — enough to produce some fast derisory arithmetic at Arrowhead at the thought of an equitable three-way division of the alleged spoils — well over $25,000 for each.

In the next (November) issue of the *Knickerbocker* Clark used the titles of some of Mathews's defunct publishing ventures to ridicule his latest production, *Moneypenny:* "Think of the 'American DICKENS' coming down from 'Arcturus' on the back of a 'Behemoth,' and blowing a penny *'Whistle'* in the streets! But *that* music may have ceased before this squib is printed. Twenty unlucky 'literary' offspring of the same parent, 'gone before,' remind us that 'change' (we don't mean 'small-change') is written on all that PUFFER HOPKINS WRITES. 'Passing away! passing away,' into the dull pool of Lethe!" About this time Duyckinck would have passed on to Melville a copy of Powell's portrait of "HERMAN MELVILLE. — ROMANCIST" in the 2 November issue of *his* new periodical, *Figaro!*, although he kept a file copy of his own. Powell had written temperately throughout the essay, for a wonder, and had included one of the oddly few word-portraits his contemporaries devoted to Melville: "In person, Mr. Melville is little above the medium height, well made, with an intelligent and composed face; his manners are reserved, but courteous, and he has little of that disputatious spirit which too frequently distinguishes the *'irritable genus.'*" (The piece contained bad typographical errors such as "Jamnis" for "Junius," so Powell may have written "genius.") Powell went on: "He has observed and thought more than his writings would lead a casual reader to conclude, and his conversation is at once sensible, liberal and entertaining." Remembering how Melville had shut himself up early in the year, and how he had retreated further to the Berkshires, the scoundrel continued with bland amiability: "He very wisely avoids literary society, and devotes most of his time to literary composition."

A few years earlier, Dickens had made himself the modern writer most associated with Christmas, so in chauvinistic rivalry Mathews determined to be the writer associated with the great *American* holiday. The *Literary World* trumpeted *Chanticleer: A Thanksgiving Story of the Peabody Family*, as "A National Thanksgiving Book," ready November first. (Melville did not receive his presentation copy of it from Mathews until after New Year's.) Melville read the *Literary World* every week as "a sort of private letter" from Evert to him, he wrote on 13 December, but in the beauty of the long autumn New York City gradually faded from Melville's consciousness. He was where he wanted to be, away from the cannibal island, but he began to realize that he might, with luck, settle down to work six miles from Hawthorne, but could not pay him even one autumnal visit, no recorded visit in 1850 after that moonlit night in mid-September.

At Arrowhead from the beginning there were innumerable chores, many of which only Melville could attend to. The problem came when household chores did not end abruptly at the time Melville had allotted for them. By early November Melville was becoming torn between the need to finish settling in at Arrowhead and the compulsion to return to his book, a conflict complicated by his desire to see Hawthorne, once he had added a sufficient number of pages to his neglected manuscript. Just after the middle of the month, his sister Helen needed to catch a train for Troy at a time of day (probably late morning) which had been sacred to his literary labors in New York City. Thus drawn away from the manuscript he had just returned to, he let his irritation show. Wounded, Helen went on to visit Mrs. Ives in Lansingburgh. Writing to Helen on the twenty-second, Augusta tried to soothe her sister's injured feelings: "Herman was in such haste to be on his way home again that I thought it would not do, to ask him to wait until your train whirled out of sight, so I took his offered arm immediately, after he had seated you in the cars & we hastened down to the waggon — & there he left me to go in search of that cabinet-maker. That unfortunate cabinet-maker! He was not to be found. — And once more we returned, to find Lizzie with bedstead upturned & room emptied in readiness to receive him [the cabinet-maker] . . . but Herman did not bring him — he came himself." Herman had spoken rudely to Helen, or else his attitude had revealed his impatience toward one of the people who loved him most devotedly. Rather than rushing home to Arrowhead, Helen went down to spend Thanksgiving in New York with Kate, Allan, Sophia and the two children, who had left the Fourth Avenue house vacant and moved into a new house on Thirty-first Street near Lexington.

Lizzie, in contrast, about this time began to be "in fine spirits" as she made her preparations to take Malcolm home for Thanksgiving (so Augusta wrote to Helen on 23 November). Aunt Mary had made yet another trip to Boston, and ambitious — and disruptive — plans hinged on her return, as Augusta said to Helen in an afterthought to her letter of the twenty-third: "And I had forgotten too, Aunt Mary's return from Boston & the grand Thanksgiving we are to have. Fanny went over to the farm on Wednesday to invite our guests — Aunt Mary & Helen — Susan & Robert, Henry & Allan, Julian & little Robert, Major & the slay [sleigh] . . . Ten [eight?] guests & our own family — truly a large party. — not to be dined in the little dining room. So Herman's Library is to be thrown open for their accommodation." The

Helen invited was Cousin Helen Jean, and Allan was the replacement Allan Cargill; Julian — named for Julia Maria — and little Robert were Robert and Susan's surviving children. Herman was at that moment available, "just going to town," so that Augusta had been obliged to make her pen "fairly fly" in order to send the letter with him: no one wanted to cross him.

Wanting her husband to come with her, Lizzie held out what ought to have been sufficient inducement to the grandson of the "Last Leaf," the offer of "a Boston Thanksgiving," the only genuine variety. Augusta made clear what happened when she wrote to Mary Blatchford on 25 November: "I have just returned from a most exhilerating drive to town, where we left Lizzie with Malcolm & his nurse in the cars for Boston. — To think of her ever consenting to leave home without Herman! But these New England girls it seems, esteem it a sacred duty to eat their Thanksgiving dinner no where but beneath their father's roof, they will travel any number of miles for the sake of so doing — Their very peace of mind for the ensuing year depends upon it — and so Lizzie must — though Herman must remain." Herman, she continued, was now so engaged with his book "that he was not to be prevailed upon to leave it." When she referred to the "exhilerating" drive, Augusta meant that Herman had driven in his usual hell-for-leather style — driving like Jehu, they said in the family, driving furiously.

Augusta herself was thriving, feeling "a vigor & a bounding energy within, which have long been as strangers." She had been much out of doors during the time her brother was trying to settle down indoors, and she made it clear that nature was still cooperating with the newcomers: "Never was there a more beautiful Autumn — the 25th of November — and not a single one yet of those shuddering murky days which you promised me. Why the skies are as bright & the air as balmy to-day — as any you can have in New York. I quite begin to love our new home — & even if the dull, murky days should come, I would not weary of them, for then I should have no inducement to spend so many hours in rambling in our beautiful woods, & should have all that time for reading and the thousand things a young lady finds to do." Melville no doubt had quite begun to love his new home too, but he was torn between trivial demands and exalted ambitions. It was his job to split wood and to milk and feed the cows and the horse, but he became increasingly exasperated at not being able to establish a work routine after breakfast. Some interruptions were brought about by his stubborn masculine protectiveness, for he forbade the women to drive the wagon. This meant that every time one of them wanted to go to town or to the old Melvill house (still occupied by the aunt and cousins) she had to wait until Herman was free to drive her. Whatever work routine he did manage to establish in November was disrupted in the preparations for the "grand Thanksgiving," the most ominous feature of which was that (a day or two before the actual feast?) his library was "to be thrown open." His exasperation was compounded by the fact that having to create a makeshift dining room on the second floor made him feel humiliated. The Melvill place had a grand dining room and other stately rooms, but Arrowhead did not have a room on the first floor sufficiently large to accommodate the two households. As long as the New York house remained unsold, and as long as the whaling manuscript remained unfinished, there was no way of paying Brewster the two thousand dollars he still owed him as part of the purchase money and laying out the additional thousands it would cost to build his real towered house, one that would as a matter of course contain a real dining room where he could give Belshazzarian feasts, if he wanted to.

Thanksgiving was a stormy day, and the Melvills arrived late, "over the hills" the short bone-jolting way (Augusta wrote Helen on 5 December), everyone, including the driver, "seated upon the straw in the bottom of the great lumber wagon, & completely hidden from sight with piles of cloaks buffalos & umbrellas." They erupted into Arrowhead like sailors into a tavern. Augusta described the scene to Helen: "Such a shaking out of dresses, & such a rubbing of backs as followed!" By the time they were all "smoothed down," dinner was announced:

> Herman offering his arm to Aunt Mary, led the way, — the tribe of Melville following one by one, up that stairs of many angles — to the Library where the feast was spread. The room looked beautifully. Everything was beautifully cooked, & every one beautifully happy. And it "was beautiful to see them eat." — The evening was passed in looking at the French Portfolio through the glass, & in listening to the fortunes as told by the Sibyl Augusta from "Home Oracles." With tea handed round at 7 — & egg nog at 9, the appetites of the company were so fully satisfied that they begged they might not be asked to partake of anything more, even if it were Thanksgiving. They had done their very best.

They all appeared to enjoy themselves, Augusta concluded, and at ten "rumbled off in their cumbrous vehicle," leaving Helen Jean behind to pass a week or two with Fanny, the elder by a year and a half, and Helen Jean's crony from childhood.

Melville took comfort (and perhaps even inspiration) from domesticity. He loved his aunt and cousins, however objectively he viewed Robert, but he had just gotten his wife and child out of his way (or Lizzie and Malcolm had just gotten away from him), and tensions between creativity and domesticity were building up. Usually he behaved well enough when he had to escort one of the women. We know of one instance, apparently in mid-December,

because twenty-year-old Cousin Helen Jean described it "with much satisfaction" to her sister Priscilla, working in Canandaigua, and Priscilla in turn
relayed the report to Augusta (on 30 December). Priscilla reviewed the information that her sister Helen "one lovely evening, with Mother in company"
had gone "with Auntie & Herman to make calls in the village," Auntie being
her Aunt Maria. Priscilla continued: "I infer, very sagely, that some of the
Pittsfield gentry have cheer'd your retreat by visits of welcome — &, no
doubt, congratulate themselves *most justly*, on *such* an acquisition to their
agreable circle. Bon soir, ma cher cousin. Pleasant dreams & pleasant realities to you *one* & *all*, for the coming New Year."

Melville's domestic comforts, conflicts, and compromises became embodied in what he was writing, to the extent that crucial passages in the book,
despite its being notoriously without major female characters, dealt with the
conflict between artist and family man, and in particular the incompatible
demands of creativity and marriage. In "A Squeeze of the Hand" (ch. 94),
Melville celebrated the sense of universal benignity that arose when the
whalers sat by their great tubs squeezing lumps of sperm back into fluid:
"Squeeze! squeeze! squeeze! all the morning long; I squeezed that sperm till I
myself almost melted into it; I squeezed that sperm till a strange sort of
insanity came over me; and I found myself unwittingly squeezing my co-
laborers' hands in it, mistaking their hands for the gentle globules." Melville,
or his narrator Ishmael, concludes, on the basis of "many prolonged, repeated experiences," that man "must eventually lower, or at least shift, his
conceit of attainable felicity; not placing it anywhere in the intellect or the
fancy; but in the wife, the heart, the bed, the table, the saddle, the fire-side,
the country." However reckless he was in business, Melville was cautious in
his words, and here he was not renouncing the claims of the intellect or the
fancy, the imagination. Rather, he had concluded that if one wanted to attain
happiness in this life, the way to do it would be to renounce the intellect and
the imagination. In "The Lee Shore" (ch. 23 — placed early, but surely written late, months after "A Squeeze of the Hand"), Melville wrote out of the
book a character he had introduced to play a major role in it, Bulkington.
With Bulkington it had fared "as with the storm-tossed ship, that miserably
drives along the leeward land. The port would fain give succor; the port is
pitiful; in the port is safety, comfort, hearthstone, supper, warm blankets,
friends, all that's kind to our mortalities. But in that gale, the port, the land, is
that ship's direst jeopardy; she must fly all hospitality; one touch of land,
though it but graze the keel, would make her shudder through and through."
In this "six-inch chapter" that serves as "the stoneless grave of Bulkington,"
Melville challenges his readers: "Glimpses do ye seem to see of that mortally
intolerable truth; that all deep, earnest thinking is but the intrepid effort of

the soul to keep the open independence of her sea; while the wildest winds of heaven and earth conspire to cast her on the treacherous, slavish shore?" Here, anything like earthly felicity was to be renounced: "But as in landless-ness alone resides the highest truth, shoreless, indefinite as God — so, better is it to perish in that howling infinite, than be ingloriously dashed upon the lee, even if that were safety! For worm-like, then, oh! who would craven crawl to land!" At Thanksgiving, and for weeks afterward, Melville still hoped, however irrationally, that he could have everything — earthly felicity with Lizzie and Malcolm and the rest of the family, and the ecstasy that comes only from the highest exercise of the intellect and the imagination.

In Lansingburgh and New York during the past half dozen years, Maria Melville had been only intermittently determined to bring her second son into a life of formal piety and the hope of a life hereafter in heaven. In the Berkshires, without easy transportation to the village, she suddenly found herself relieved of the Manhattan obligation to pay visits and receive callers, although some local people sought her and her family out, one of them George T. Chapman, the new minister of the Episcopalian church Uncle Thomas had attended. Chapman proved extremely attentive to Maria and her two resident daughters, Augusta and Fanny. In her attempts to meet the local people half way, Maria began to put pressure on Herman to become part of the community, and in conservative western Massachusetts being part of the community meant going to church. With only one son under the same roof, her only child not to claim a proper relationship to God as she knew Him, she focused her prodigious attention on Herman, determined that he become a professing Christian and regular church-goer. Maria Gansevoort Melville was not the haughty aristocrat that Melville made Mary Glendin-ning, the fictional mother of Pierre, the hero of the book he wrote after his whaling book, but she was a supremely bossy woman whose reforming zeal now was focused all too sharply on her oldest living son. She had the best reasons — the safeguarding of Herman's immortal soul and the safeguarding of Herman's career, and both directly affected her and her daughters' futures.

As week after week at Arrowhead passed, Melville had to deal with the expectations of his mother and the community that he go to church on Sunday and otherwise comport himself in what he spoke and wrote as befit-ted a good citizen in a realm controlled by evangelical Christians. The his-tory of Berkshire County he bought in July had reminded him of his child-hood, when his mother shocked Cousin Julia by traveling on Sunday. He had returned to the locality where Jonathan Edwards (whose name he wrote on a back flyleaf, along with a page reference) had attempted to Christianize the remnant of Indians and to minister to the white frontier families. In the section on Stockbridge, Melville had marked a paragraph about Edwards:

"Besides the duties owed more immediately to the people, he here completed his greatest work, 'The Inquiry concerning the Freedom of the Will.' Here also he composed his treatise on Original Sin, and carried forward the 'History of Redemption,' and probably some other works." Furthermore, the *History* assured the reader that wickedness was declining in the Berkshires. Edwards of Stockbridge was still fresh in his mind when Melville later wrote to Hawthorne that he had written a wicked book. He had written much of it in the Berkshires, where before his time saintly books had been written.

Augusta was afraid to put such pressure on Herman, but her quiet daily piety, manifested in the religious verse she copied into her commonplace book, was a standing example, if not a reproach, to her older brother. On 1 December Melville attended services (at the Episcopal church, St. Stephen's). In reporting the news to Helen, Augusta revealed some of the edginess with which they had to handle Herman: "Sunday was a most lovely day. Mamma Fanny with [Cousin] Helen [Jean] & Herman went to church. Dont mention this last item (Herman's going) when you write — But I knew you would be so much pleased to hear it." It would not do for Helen to express her pleasure in a letter that Herman might read: if they were gossiping about him he might become sorry he had gone and not go again. Denominational niceties did not perturb the worshipers: if she could not go to a Dutch Reformed church, Maria was happy to go to St. Stephen's, which she had attended with her brother-in-law Thomas long before. Herman had joined the Unitarian Church of All Souls in Manhattan, for Lizzie, but knew the beautiful limestone of St. Stephen's from visiting Pittsfield in his youth, and was as comfortable there as he could be in an American church. (In his 1890 *Pontoosuc* J. E. A. Smith recalled that Oliver Wendell Holmes had worshiped there, and Herman Melville had done so "although of a different creed from the Episcopalian.") After Thanksgiving some members of the household (reduced by Lizzie and Malcolm, as well as Helen, but augmented by Cousin Helen) walked on eggshells. Maria never walked on eggshells.

At last, with his wife and child away in Boston and Thanksgiving behind him, Melville was able to establish a new routine for the remaining work on his whaling book. It helped at first that his wife and son were so happy at the Shaw house, for he did not have to feel guilty for neglecting them. Lizzie wrote that Malcolm was "very much admired in Boston," where everyone called him "a beautiful child." Everyone included Nilly, who late in 1851 asked Augusta whether Malcolm could talk yet and recalled that "he was a sweet little child last winter & seemed to have a great many winning ways." Nilly's standards for intelligible verbal communication were high, for anyone at the Shaws' 1850 Thanksgiving could have testified to Malcolm's capacity for abstract thought and the sheer volume he was capable of: "On Thanksgiving day, he was brought into the room with the des[s]ert, & being placed immediately in front of a basket of apples & grapes electrified the company by crying out at the top of his voice 'bawbiddle' 'bawbiddle.' Lizzie says that when the explanation called for, was given it seemed to afford much amusement." This is Augusta's account on 5 December to Helen, who did not have to have it explained that "bawbiddle" was Malcolm's pronunciation of strawberry, the generic word for fruit.

Helen herself, while visiting in New York during Thanksgiving week, had heard "the warbling Jenny" Lind for the second time, as Augusta acknowledged on 5 December (Augusta had not heard the Swedish sensation even once). She also reported on the task Herman had put on her, to send a package to Eli Fly. Fly had become what the times classed as a confirmed invalid—doomed and waiting in Greenbush for death to come. (The gift was guava, which the ailing Gansevoort used to require; Fly wrote Melville to thank him for it.) Helen and Kate (much missed now, by her mother and other sisters) made a foray into Canal Street for sewing supplies, reminding Augusta of the earlier hectic last-minute purchases before the removal. There was no secret about Helen's purchases for New Year's gifts: "Mamma is much pleased at the thoughts of the large type Prayer Book—as also Herman with the anticipated play, with his gutta percha toy"—a buggy whip ironically chosen so Herman could vent his megrims on the horse instead of on any passenger he might have to convey to the depot. Like Herman, Helen had a wickedly satirical streak. Canal Street was a perilous expedition, but even in Troy or Lansingburgh Helen could provide herself with items utterly unobtainable in Pittsfield, so Maria had Augusta instruct Helen to make "a bag of 6 cent cotton" and carry home in it "a half bushel of *split peas,*" dried, and quite heavy. Helen had vouched for the comfort of the house at Thirty-first Street, although without sufficient details to satisfy the Arrowhead contingent. Augusta wrote back: "but you said naught of the furniture!—Perhaps they have none!" (After New Year's Kate reported that "Sophia proves herself to be a capital housekeeper, really appearing to take pleasure in it"—Augusta's paraphrase to Hope Shaw on 7 January 1851.) Everything in Boston, New York, and Lansingburgh was under control, and off Herman's hands—except the empty unsold house on Fourth Avenue and the manuscript in his study at Arrowhead.

Putting the unsold house (and the unpaid two-thousand-dollar debt to Brewster) out of his mind as best he could, Melville on 13 December 1850 gave an account of how he spent his days, in a long letter to Evert Duyckinck, written by candlelight, the second time in two months to strain his eyes in this fashion. Having told Duyckinck that a man in the country had no news except farm gossip, he bethought himself of a genuinely disturbing occurrence of the day before, one involving Robert. Three days of Robert in an open wagon in July had been enough for Herman, who had by now written his cousin off as hopelessly shiftless and irresponsible. Literary New Yorkers such as Cooper in *The Pioneers* satirized supposedly industrious Yankees by calling them Doolittle, so Duyckinck had no doubt which cousin Melville was talking about:

> Mr Doolittle — my cousin — was crossing the R.R. track yesterday (where it runs thro the wooded part of the farm.) in his slay — *sleigh* I mean — and was followed by all three of Mrs Morewood's horses (they running at large for the sake of the air & exercise). Well: just as Doolittle got on the track with his vehicle, along comes the Locomotive — whereupon Doolittle whips up like mad & steers clear; but the frightened horses following him, they scamper off full before the engine, which hitting them right & left, tumbles one into a ditch, pitches another into a snow-bank, & chases the luckless third so hard as to come into direct contact with him, & breaks his leg clean into two peices. — With his leg "in splints" that is done up by the surgeon, the poor colt now lies in his straw, & the prayers of all good Christians are earnestly solicited in his behalf.

As Duyckinck knew, Rowland and Sarah Morewood would have this bad news awaiting them upon their return from England.

That distressing account rendered, Melville in this letter went on to define his state of mind as "a sort of sea-feeling here in the country" now that the ground was snow-covered, for when he opened his eyes in the morning, alone in the bedroom, and looked out the window it was like looking "out of a port-hole of a ship in the Atlantic," and his study as he wrote seemed "a ship's cabin," and at nights, when the shrieking of the wind woke him, he almost fancied there was "too much sail on the house," and he "had better go on the roof & rig in the chimney." His account of his writing conditions made it sound, for the moment, as near to ideal as he could have hoped:

> Do you want to know how I pass my time? — I rise at eight — thereabouts — & go to my barn — say good-morning to the horse, & give him his breakfast. (It goes to my heart to give him a cold one, but it can't be helped) Then, pay a visit to my cow — cut up a pumpkin or two for her, & stand by to see her eat it — for it's a pleasant sight to see a cow move her jaws — she does it so mildly & with such a sanctity. — My own breakfast over, I go to my work-room & light my fire — then spread my M.S.S. on the table — take one business squint at it, & fall to with a will. At 2 1/2 P.M. I hear a preconcerted knock at my door, which (by request) continues till I rise & go to the door, which serves to wean me effectively from my writing, however interested I may be. . . . My

evenings I spend in a sort of mesmeric state in my room — not being able to read — only now & then skimming over some large-printed book.

This was the routine Melville had established when he wrote the date (16 December) and the time of day into what became "The Fountain" (ch. 85 — here with the printer's error of 1851 corrected to 1850): "and yet, that down to this blessed minute (fifteen and a quarter minutes past one o'clock P.M. of this sixteenth day of December, A.D. 1850), it should still remain a problem, whether these spoutings are, after all, really water." For a good three weeks, Melville was able to hold to this schedule.

It was in June 1849, most likely, that Melville had held forth to the English egotist Powell about a work he might write on the theme of remorse, and in London he had made a number of notes in his journal about possible literary subjects including the story of the revolutionary exile Israel Potter (and no doubt had thought of many that he did not write down). The previous summer he had talked so enthusiastically about the Melvill place that Duyckinck thought he would make a book of its features. Now, in this letter of 13 December, his mind was resolutely focused on the prolonged effort to shape out his conception of the white whale, most of the time, but also assaulted from all directions by tempting subjects, more ideas for books than he could possibly write down:

> Can you send me about fifty fast-writing youths, with an easy style & not averse to polishing their labors? If you can, I wish you would, because since I have been here I have planned about that number of future works & cant find enough time to think about them separately. — But I dont know but a book in a man's brain is better off than a book bound in calf — at any rate it is safer from criticism. And taking a book off the brain, is akin to the ticklish & dangerous business of taking an old painting off a panel — you have to scrape off the whole brain in order to get at it with due safety — & even then, the painting may not be worth the trouble.

More than a year and a half after the first reviews of *Mardi* appeared, and three seasons away from the reviews of *White-Jacket*, Melville was thinking about the vulnerability of the books he had published and the one he was writing, and he was thinking, more professionally than ever before, about the compositional process. He was not speaking only of an avowedly ambitious book like *Mardi* but of any book. In something like this fevered state, now or a little earlier, he accepted an invitation to contribute to *Godey's Lady's Book*, the Philadelphia magazine that was enlisting new contributors in an effort to make it deserve "the proud title of THE LEADING PERIODICAL IN AMERICA," as it boasted in the January 1851 number. Perhaps he wanted to keep his hand in as a literary man during what was for him a very long gap between books, but more likely he was thinking mainly of earning a little money from a magazine at last, as he had never done by reviewing for his friend Duyckinck.

By 21 December 1850 Melville was still not writing at anything like top speed. That day Augusta wrote Helen (now in Lansingburgh) not to rush home to take over the copying duties: "As to Herman's M S. S. you need not hurry your return on that account, he gets on very slowly with it. As soon as he is ready for you, I will let you know." Augusta had so little news to tell, and comparatively so much time, that she indulged more than usual in badinage about the bad effects of the Knickerbocker family in Lansingburgh on Helen's spelling and about Cousin Maria Peebles's peevishness at hearing the letter in which Augusta had referred to her as "Mrs. P." Helen had been dutiful, calling on Aunt Mary in Waterford, and planning to visit Albany if the sleighing improved. She had acquired a "beautiful desk" — the sort of desk that she could hold in her lap or place on a table top, and Augusta and Fanny were so anxious to see it they jokingly said they wanted her to send it by Express. News of Arrowhead was scarce, but Augusta could report that, after a "succession of snow storms," Herman was able to give them "a sleigh ride every afternoon" or evening, a treat made difficult for everyone by their dining at the late hour of three-thirty so as to give Herman his full writing day. The destination of the sleigh ride "every eve^g" was the post office, Augusta wrote Helen on 31 December. On their return from the village they drove "round to the farm every now & then," where everyone was well — except the luckless colt, Black Quake ("All the farmers could not save him. What will Mrs. Morewood say"). Helen Jean returned to Arrowhead for the week of Christmas, then she prolonged her visit, for on 6 January Augusta wrote Helen Maria that she had been there "almost a fortnight" and that "Aunt Mary says she must take her home to-night. They are so lonely without her." In the meantime, Herman had driven members of the family over to the farm two or three times a week, and each visit had seemed "to give them" — the Melvills — "an increased pleasure."

Happily for a working man, Christmas was still not the great holiday Thanksgiving was, as the *History* of the county had reminded Herman: "Christmas is rarely observed, except by those who are Episcopalians, as it is a point generally considered as settled, that the day on which our saviour was born can not be ascertained. The day of the New Year receives some attention — but the people are more in the habit of extending their '*compliments*' through the several seasons than of confining them to any particular one." Herman had drawn a bow-shaped line in pencil in the right margin around the lines containing "Episcopalians . . . can," then signaled a note at the bottom by an *X*: "Amazingly quizzical." Maria's Dutch household was a year away from learning how to keep Christmas in the old English way, so there would be no need to throw open Herman's study again so as to feast the combined families. The tradition in the family was to give New Year's gifts, not Christmas gifts, and they may have done what Tertullus Stewart did — that is, hang stockings up on 31 December, not the night before Christmas, although the rival tradition was gaining in popularity.

   Lizzie and Malcolm were still away. Writing frequently, Lizzie explained that she was enjoying her visit so much that she was going to stay through Christmas. Her maternal news was good: "Malcolm continues to excite the admiring gaze of all visitors, & has lost all his shrinking shyness." (On 28 February 1851 Hope Shaw confirmed this praise in a letter to her nephew Sam Savage: "Malcolm is beautiful & lovely, almost too superior for this earth.") Although Herman was going so slowly, they were planning, on 21 December, to provide plenty of paper before Herman ran out, Augusta wrote to Helen: "Some time next week, we are going to make an expedition to Lee to get a supply of paper at the manufactory." The approach of Christmas was hardly to be taken into account, and the Great Union Meeting held in Pittsfield on 27 December, a Friday, passed by without Melville's joining in the denunciation of Free-Soilers as irresponsible agitators who had done their best, over the past months, to prevent the good people of the North and South from laying the slavery question permanently to rest by passing the compromise. (In December the engineer-poet and young widower John C. Hoadley, who had met Sarah Morewood the previous summer, if not any of the Melvilles, was one of some hundreds of the citizens of Pittsfield who signed a resolution supporting the Compromise of 1850, one component of which was the Fugitive Slave Bill — now law. The Melvilles knew about the young widower Hoadley, an acquaintance of Aunt Lucy's stepdaughter, and a poet, so it was only a matter of time before someone in the family encountered him.) Shutting even momentous political events out of his mind, ignoring the newspapers for the most part (a tendency made easier by the state of his eyes late in the day, when they picked up the papers), Melville focused on his manuscript, sure of the magnitude of the game he was pursuing all alone.

   On the last day of 1850 Augusta wrote to Helen, who was still visiting Mrs. Ives in Lansingburgh. The exciting news was the arrival at Arrowhead of a six-page letter from Tom in San Francisco and addressed to the Fourth Avenue house. Allan had forwarded it still sealed, for it was addressed to Maria, the one person whose mail the others did not open. There was nautical news enough to stir Herman's memories: "It is a very long letter — six pages — & gives us a particular account of his voyage to the Golden City, which they reached on the one hundred & fourth day from New York. They met with some bad weather, but doubled the Cape without any of the white squalls & tremendous gales, which, to quote his words — are 'the usual standing dishes.'" Maria responded to the letter predictably: "Mamma as you may imagine is all happiness at the thought of hearing such good news of her darling." There was news, too, of Herman's response to the letter from Tom: "Herman too seems very happy. — & so are we all. It quite gladdens our heart for the New Year."

There was tentative news of Lizzie's return: "Herman begins to be quite impatient for Lizzie's return — & last evening when he was reading a letter from her, he told us that she would be home tomorrow. But that is New Year's day — & I don't believe she's coming — For he laughed. As for Malcolm — I almost tremble for him — Herman will fairly devour him." He had needed peace, but five weeks and more was not peace but deprivation of a wife and domestic ally. In her way Lizzie buffered him from his mother's demands and criticisms, even while her presence created some special tensions with Maria. A tactile man, he also missed the wriggling warm limbs and soft cheeks of his petticoated son. There survive few verbal vignettes of Melville with young Malcolm as vivid as Augusta's previsioning: Herman would fairly eat his son up.

Early New Year's Day Robert and his brother young Allan Cargill made the traditional call on the Arrowheads, delivering a box they had picked up in the village — books for Herman from *his* brother Allan, among them Baron Cuvier's *The Animal Kingdom Arranged in Conformity with Its Organization*, which would provide a footnote for a chapter on "The Whiteness of the Whale." The irresolute Robert had not yet decided whether to leave the old Melvill house or not, and it seemed to Augusta that he was going to wait until the Morewoods decided the matter for him by arriving to take possession of it. Time was short, for they were expected in February.

Later on New Year's Day a contingent from Arrowhead and the Melvill house met Lizzie at the depot on her return from Boston with Malcolm. Augusta wrote to Helen: "Lizzie came home on Wednesday. Herman could not endure her absence with Malcolm's any longer. We went up to the depot to meet her — that is Robert & Susan & I, in his sleigh, & Herman alone in ours, to accommodate the luggage. The cars were delayed an hour beyond their time, & there we waited most patiently until past five o'clock. She is looking remarkably well, & Malcolm is even more noble [?] looking than ever." Lizzie reported that she and Malcolm had made "a very delightful visit, & received a large share of attention." The servant Mary had taken Malcolm to Nilly's, who had been so "struck with his appearance" that she wrote Augusta to that effect. In her luggage — that indestructible big black trunk Maria had borrowed in the summer — Lizzie brought back for Augusta a French perfume case and a beautiful undergarment from Nilly, on which was a collar and worked sleeves. Lizzie had conducted "unseasonable researches" and found the three "straw flats," hats, which Helen, Fanny, and Augusta had wanted, and Hope had supplied the ribbons for them. Lizzie had also brought "some little gift for each of the family at the farm — Henry & all, & they were highly gratified" — Henry being compos enough to know when he was being neglected and when he was treated properly. While in Boston, Lizzie had been thoughtful and generous as always. She may even have brought her husband some source books, for the records of the Boston Athenæum show that on 30 December 1850, when she knew she was about to return to Pittsfield, two of William Scoresby's books were charged to Shaw, *An Account of the Arctic Regions*, and *Journal of a Voyage to the Northern Whale Fishery*. (The books were returned 16 January 1851, so it is possible that Herman could have consulted them and sent them back to Boston.)

New Year's Day occasioned the fullest accounts the Arrowhead family had received of the world they had left. Allan, Sophia, and Kate held court in Sophia's parlors all New Year's Day but received "only seventeen callers," because of the distance and the fact that some friends did not yet have their new "direction" (Sophia to Augusta, 1 January 1851). The brothers from Clinton Place made a very pleasant call, Sophia said: "Messrs Duyckinck came of course, and Mr George was pleased to admire my parlors, and Evert brought me some little French trifles from the Christmas tree, for [little] Maria he said, but they were too pretty — so I placed them on my étagère — He gave Kate a little ivory thing containing a rosary." Mrs. Duyckinck's sister, Sophia coolly supposed, had "brought a quantity of such things from Paris," for the family trinket-trove of pre-purchased gifts for variable occasions. T. D. Stewart came for a long call and told them about the birth of a son on 30 December. The father bragged that the boy had "had scarcely been two hours in the world before he commenced to suck his thumb." Stewart also claimed to have had "several rows with him," which Sophia interpreted according to Herman's mock-pugnacious paternal language: "I suppose he means the same thing as Herman does when he talks about pitching in to Malcolm."

Richard Lathers called, the easier to do because he was staying with Mrs. Thurston on Bond Street. His head was full of plans for a grand house on his property in New Rochelle, Sophia said: "He leaves for Georgia in a few days and will probably be absent for several weeks. Abby will remain in town, and I hope to have her here for a week or so. Mr Lathers intends building a stone house on the hill above his present residence, which will command an extensive view, and he is making a new road to approach it which will be lined by trees." Sophia thought this brother-in-law of hers would "never be quietly settled down such a constant idea of improvement seems to fill his mind." As it turned out, he hired one of the best architects in America, Alexander Jackson Davis, who built him Winyah, which won what may have been the first American prize for architecture, at the New York Crystal Palace in 1852.

Sophia's news from the Curtis house in Brooklyn was dismaying. On the thirtieth Allan had dined at Cousin Kate's, having been across the East River on business when he called on them near dinnertime. They were "all sick," as usual: "Aunt Mary is not well and Guert confined to his room, and Kate in a peck of trouble with her servants. They did not intend to receive calls to day so Allan did not think it worth while to go to Brooklyn at all. I thought perhaps Mr. Curtis would take this opportunity of coming over but he did not." At Thirty-first Street they had made sausages from a pig Lathers had donated, and they had been eating buckwheat cakes, which made them think of Tom, who loved them, and to long for him to be there and eat some of them. (They had all been spoiled for ordinary buckwheat. Finding a supply of just the right buckwheat was a stressful challenge Herman's household confronted for many years.) Sophia and Allan were frustrated in their thoughts of Tom, for they were still waiting to learn the contents of the letter Allan had held in his hand before forwarding it unopened to his mother. Sophia knew that Helen Jean was at Arrowhead, for she sent her "best love to your Mother Herman Fanny Aunt Mary and Helen [Jean]." Augusta had borrowed one of the early numbers of *Harper's Magazine*, so Sophia reminded her that she wanted it back, so she could have the issues bound. Sophia had learned most or all of the Melvill news. Priscilla had determined to remain in Canandaigua until the spring, when she might return with Aunt Mary and Helen Jean to Galena. John and George Melvill were to precede them there in order to start a dry-goods business with their proceeds from the farm. John was expected back in Pittsfield in January on a trip to "purchase a stock" for the store (Augusta wrote to Helen on 6 January). Knowing she might not see some of the Melvills again, Sophia now invited Helen Jean to write to her, and urged Aunt Mary to visit her before going back west. Mr. Duyckinck, she added in a postscript, had "mentioned that he had received Hermans letter" (of 13 December), and Mr. Crocker, one of the callers that day, had reported on seeing Lizzie "in Boston 10 days ago, all well." Kate had written Lizzie "the other day."

It was good for the Arrowheads to learn that the minutiae of daily life in Manhattan was continuing, at a different "direction" (or address), but it was becoming impossible for Herman to devote the proper amount of concern to a source of good buckwheat when the difference between the restless Melville and the restless Lathers was obvious to those who read Sophia's letter in the parlor at Arrowhead. Lathers had the money to build a showplace—

indeed, if he wanted one, he could build a real towered house in New Rochelle from which he could look down into New York Sound. (As it turned
out, he did want one.) Unmentioned among all the quotidian details of
Sophia's report was the empty house on Fourth Avenue, which Allan had
been charged with disposing of.

Once again Melville repressed his anxieties and focused on his manuscript. His work routine was recalled much later by Lizzie and by Joseph
Smith. In a brief biographical memorandum written toward the end of the
century (now preserved in the Berkshire Athenaeum), some years after Melville's death, his widow recalled that he "Wrote White Whale or Moby Dick
under unfavorable circumstances." What had stuck in her mind for mention
was a domestic vignette of his writing routine during the Pittsfield winter of
1850–51: "would sit at his desk all day not eating any thing till four or five
o clock—then ride to the village after dark—Would be up early and out
walking before breakfast—sometimes splitting wood for exercise." Her own
memories of that winter are from 1851 only, since she did not return from
her Thanksgiving visit until the first of January—that busy day for Arrowhead and the roads near it. The family friend Joseph Smith in the Pittsfield
Evening Journal for 16 December 1891 recorded what he had picked up, at
the time or later, about Melville's routine: "his general method of literary
work was to shut himself up in his library, having his luncheon, if needed,
placed at the door in order to avoid interruption." Smith continued: "Often
he submitted his manuscript to one of his sisters for revision. Probably it
came from her hand somewhat toned down from what he left it in the heat of
composition; but not essentially changed." (On 2 January 1847 Helen had
reacted tartly on hearing of a Mr. Little who supposed she "had any hand in
Typee": "What a goose the man must be!" The sisters did not tone down
what Herman wrote.) Drawing on his memories as well as what he had heard,
Smith added: "This solitary labor continued until he was wearied, when he
would emerge from his 'den,' join in family or social intercourse, indulge in
light reading—which was not so very light; as it included much less of what
we commonly call 'light literature,' than it did of profound reviews, abstruse
philosophy in prose or verse, and the like—visit or entertain his friends, or
otherwise enjoy himself. But no more formal serious work for him until the
next morning, although, consciously or unconsciously, his mind was always
gathering material for it." Always, Melville's writing stint for the day was
followed by a wild drive to the post office in the village (the wilder for
the gutta-percha toy), and an opening of letters. Augusta wrote Helen on
31 December: "We visit the post office with such interest every eve^g & are so
disappointed if there is nothing for us." When Herman drove to the village
alone, he learned to bring even his own letters home unopened, so the

women could have the pleasure of reading to him what his weak eyes presumably found straining; it deprived him of no essential pleasure and gave him the pleasure of hearing them enjoy the news moments ahead of him.

In her 30 December letter to Augusta, Priscilla revealed that she had devoted some sympathetic thought to the way the household might be adjusting to so drastic a change of life:

> If Berkshire has shar'd in the *deep snow* with which *we* have been favor'd in Western New-York—I imagine you must feel, in your retirement, like exiles from the world. Tho' I will remember—that you all possess so many resources within yourselves, that you may be quite independent of external circumstances, for happiness—but, write me all about it, & tell me how you pass the time, & manage to vary the monotony of such retirement at this *un*-lovely season of the year—the *novelty* of such a life may be excitement enough at present—& strengthen you in the endurance of all sorts of hardships—I presume you will become great pedestrians—& in defiance of wintry elements will brave piercing winds—& penetrate trackless snows, in search of adventure.

She was right on all counts—the start of a sense of exile, the joy in outdoor physical exertion, and the inner resources, which were exemplified by family readings as the New Year began. (Augusta wrote on 16 January 1851 to Mary Blatchford that when the New York papers "failed"—were not received or did not hold everyone's interest—they took up "some interesting book.") During the long evenings the family got around to reading aloud a book Melville had brought back from England, Schiller's *Ghost-Seer*. Early in January Augusta reported that they had finished it, and "several other interesting books," unnamed. Mathews had sent Herman a copy of his new book, *Chanticleer*, regarded as a gift to all, and Lizzie brought home a complete *David Copperfield*, which everyone decided to reserve for evening reading after Helen returned. By this time Augusta was so much stronger than in the fall that she could pass the mornings "in copying Herman's M S," and still have enough energy for "sewing & reading," so that it was half past three—the time to break up such individual activity—before she knew it. The sense of exile was reduced as the religious ladies of Pittsfield continued to take notice of the young females at Arrowhead.

Duyckinck stayed in touch. In his response to Melville's expansive December letter he sent, along with Christmas delicacies, an allegorical reading of Melville's life at Arrowhead, as Augusta reported: "He calls him a Blue-Beard, who has hidden away five agreeable ladies in an icy glen, & conjures him when next he takes the key from his girdle to carry them food, to say to them, the 'sad one' particularly that New York pines for their presence."

(The sad one was Augusta herself, from her sober religious temperament and her gypsy eyes.) Helen also wrote faithfully. She had visited Mrs. Taylor in Albany (still an intimate of the family, although her character emerges only vaguely from the surviving documents), and related an anecdote about the visit so comically that Herman "laughed loudly." (He had forgiven himself for hurting Helen's feelings.) Augusta herself was so supreme a correspondent as to guarantee that returning news would sweep up against the walls of the farmhouse like snowflakes. From November 1850 through January 1851 (a good sample) she wrote these correspondents at least one letter each (several, to Kate and Helen): Kate, Sophia's mother (Rachel Hall Thurston), Teny (Justine) Van Rensselaer, Helen, Aunt Priscilla, Mary Blatchford, Lizzie, Augusta Hunter, Nilly, Allan, Tom (to be held for him in San Francisco), Sophia, Mrs. Shaw, Mrs. Ives (writing "for Mamma"), and Cousin Kate Curtis. In that period she received letters from Mary Blatchford, Teny, Nilly, Helen, Lizzie, Aunt Priscilla, Kate, Helen, Cousin Priscilla, Sophia, and from Mrs. Charles (meaning Sophia's sister-in-law, not her mother). During this time Maria and Fanny, and in January Elizabeth, wrote and received many letters as well, and even Herman probably wrote at least a few letters we know nothing of. No wonder on 16 January Augusta specified to Mary Blatchford that part of the evening routine at Arrowhead consisted of sharing the day's correspondence ("there are the letters to be read, of which we generally have two or three"). In this account of the routine she also mentioned sharing with each other "the New York papers" (most likely at least the *Tribune* and the *Herald*, the two with the best distribution system, and once a week the *Literary World*, if not other daily or weekly papers and monthly magazines).

In these early weeks of 1851 Augusta continued to copy the whaling manuscript behind Herman without feeling pressured enough to ask Helen to return to relieve her, and she had leisure enough to copy into *Orient Pearls*, her commonplace book, any poems that reflected her own literary taste. Back on 20 October 1850 she had copied her first poem there since moving to Arrowhead, "Day Dreams" by L.E.L., and that month she listed but did not copy the poem "A man should never weep?" by J. C. Hoadley—a refined, manly meditation on the shortest biblical verse, "Jesus wept," by the engineer newly resident in Pittsfield. On 3 November 1850 Augusta copied W. Gilmore Simms's "The Virgin's Grave." In January 1851 she copied "Woman's Faith," and the next month some lines from Barry Cornwall (whom Melville had met in London)—"Sadly we mourn each vanished grace, / But most of all, her voice . . ."—and "My Last Resting Place" by A.P.V.S. During her stint as copyist of the whaling book, she copied (16 February) "Yield not to Despair" and on 2 March "Farewell of the Soul to the Body," by Mrs. Sigourney. Augusta was perceptive enough to recognize her brother as noble-souled, but she did not wince at any discrepancy between what she was copying for him and what she was copying for herself.

On 9 January Mary Blatchford listed "Herman busy writing" as one of the news bulletins in Augusta's letter of 4 January: Herman had gotten back to work as soon as Lizzie and Malcolm had settled back into Arrowhead. After her socializing in Boston Lizzie was more than content to care for Malcolm and her husband, but Maria and the sisters' social lives remained a problem to the man who needed his privacy and was too worried to let them drive the horse themselves. (In their ironical way, they had named the nondescript horse Charlie in allusion to Sophia's brother Charles Thurston, the family's connoisseur of horseflesh.) They were all enjoying the sleigh-riding very much, Augusta reported to Helen on 6 January, with one major exception: "Mamma however, does not venture out very often except on Sunday — she rather fears the cold winds." Earlier in that first week of January Edward Newton's daughter had "at last called," so rich a young lady having to ration her favors. She brought along "a very fashionably dressed personage — a Mrs Buckley" and an invitation to the young Melville ladies to join a sewing society, which had been formed for the purpose of procuring funds for enlarging St. Stephen's Church. They hoped to sell their needlework at a fair "some time during the summer when the village is so full of strangers," the vacationers who had begun to flock in every year. The next meeting was on Thursday the ninth, at the house of Mr. Newton, Uncle Thomas's old companion during the long waits between church services on Sunday afternoons at the inn. Herman volunteered to drive them there at three in the afternoon and call for them at nine in the evening, two round trips.

On 8 January Allan Melville unexpectedly "burst in" upon them just after breakfast, as Augusta wrote Helen on the fourteenth: "He had been to Providence & thought he would make us a flying visit before his return to New York. Happy indeed were we to see him though wonderfully surprised. He took the Lenox stage at the depot, & stopped at the Farm with the intention of walking over the hills, but the depth of the snow precluded that idea, & so Helen [Jean] offered to drive him over. He looks very well. Says Sophia succeeds as admirably with her housekeeping. Robert & Aunt Mary came in the evening before tea & stayed until ten o'clock." Allan stayed until the next afternoon, getting his first chance to examine Arrowhead: "He really seemed to enjoy his visit, & was quite satisfied with the appearance of the house. Then it must indeed look very nicely if *he* likes it, & expresses himself satisfied. But he suggests the propriety of putting a light into that dark back stairs as he almost pitched head-foremost he said, when he was coming down to breakfast." (By "light" Allan and Augusta meant "window.")

The "great news" was that Allan, on the spot, had offered to buy Herman out of the indenture of lease on the vacant house on Fourth Avenue. Augusta was confused, not knowing whether or not he meant to move back into it, after Sophia had just demonstrated how well she could manage her new house, but he was already extremely dissatisfied with the house he had bought "so far up town." Some would-be New Year's callers, they knew, had been deterred by the remoteness of the new house, and now Allan complained that it took Sophia all day to go down to see her mother on Bond Street and return home, and as the winter closed in he had found getting to and from Wall Street more and more difficult. (The Berkshire contingent hearkened to all this with the sympathy it merited.) Augusta loaded Allan with gifts and notes to Kate and Sophia, and Herman drove him to the depot. But Herman did not after all take his sisters to the Newton house. Augusta reported to Helen on 14 January: "It was rather provoking I must confess, that the weather should be unfavorable, as we had every thing so nicely arranged to go. Robert was to take Helen [Jean], & Herman had promised to take us at three, the hour of meeting." Instead of taking his sisters, Herman decided that his trip to the depot with Allan was enough for him, in view of the inclement weather. There was no end to social interruptions, however. On 14 January the minister from St. Stephen's, Dr. Chapman, arrived unannounced with his wife and daughter. He would have caught Augusta alone (as she wrote Helen later that day), but "Mamma with Lizzie & Fanny had just returned from their sleigh-ride & were in readiness to receive them," as Herman had to be, like it or not. The Chapmans made "a very long, but very pleasant visit," according to Augusta.

Day to day, after Lizzie's return, Herman had tried to hold to the writing schedule he had achieved in December, but his household was demanding, and over the hill Aunt Mary and her household were living tentatively, not knowing precisely when they would have to vacate the house. (Living tentatively was the only way Robert knew to live.) Augusta wrote Helen Maria on 6 January that Robert had "not yet decided whether to leave Pittsfield or not. Next month however he will be obliged to." She meant that the Morewoods were due back from England in February, when Robert would have to move out of the house, whether he had decided to leave Pittsfield or not. (As it turned out, the Morewoods chose to take a safer April Atlantic passage, which proved unseasonably stormy.) Herman would not have to help with the Melvills' moving, but Helen Jean was still at Arrowhead and needing to be in close communication with her family, so he was driving to the farm two or three times a week, and everyone was stirred up by the approaching deadline and Robert's indecision. More than one of them rather dreaded Sarah Morewood's distress when she heard about Black Quake.

By 11 January Melville needed to go to Carson's "Old Red Mill" at Dalton to get "a sleigh-load of paper," and he was more eager than ever after postponing the trip two or three weeks, as Augusta wrote Helen on the fourteenth. He had to go into the village to catch the road, but once he headed toward Dalton, five or six miles to the east, the rugged terrain was exciting for him and any passengers. There never had been a possibility that he could go alone with his wife, not when the others had been cooped up in Arrowhead while Lizzie had luxuriated for weeks in the Athens of the West, so he made the occasion a family outing, with a different set of family members than he had first planned. Maria felt able to risk the winds, as Augusta described the outing to Helen: "I had almost forgot the expedition to Dalton & the paper factory. Herman took Mamma, Lizzie & Fanny there on Saturday, & I remained home to keep house. They went quite early in the morning & did not return until nearly six. Had a delightful time & Herman made us all a present of some paper & envelopes — this accounts for my using — a ruled sheet — my abomination." Driving home on 11 January 1851 Melville may have been brooding on the female operatives in the factory, thinking thoughts he could not express to the matrons and the maid in his sleigh: out of a London experience he later wrote the first half of his diptych "The Paradise of Bachelors and the Tartarus of Maids" (1855), and out of this excursion the second half.

Two days later, still protective toward his womenfolk but increasingly resentful of interruptions during his work hours, Melville decided he was making everyone else miserable (even Augusta found it provoking to relinquish going to the Newtons) and was keeping himself needlessly in a state of suppressed anger and frustration. He did the only thing he could do if he were to get any work done on the book: he suddenly lifted his prohibition against women driving Charlie, as Augusta wrote Helen on the fourteenth:

> You know Mamma has been for some time desirous that Herman should let her drive, feeling quite confident that as Charlie was so gentle that she should be able to manage him, but until yesterday, he would not listen to it. Then however, he consented that she should make an experiment, & if we returned in safety, the horse was at our service whenever we should desire it. So Mamma & I started for the [Melvill] farm, drove through the village & so to Robert's — a distance of nearly four miles, which we reached without an accident, & drove up to the door in triumph. Herman walked over in time for tea, & we returned just after 9. I should not have the slightest fear of driving him myself — for he is most easily managed. As you may imagine we are all highly delighted at the idea of being able to drive off whenever we have an inclination to taste the fresh air.

She emphasized the change to Helen: "now we shall be quite independent." For his part, Herman might get to concentrate on his manuscript. He might concentrate even better if he could have a few hours' talk with his friend in Lenox, but Hawthorne, six miles away, might as well have been on the moon, the way the autumn had gone and the early winter was going.

38

Damned by Dollars
Mid-January–1 May 1851

I bought a book called the "Manoeuvring Mother," which I read all day for
we could not go on deck, and finished before we got to Albany.

Fanny Melville to Thomas Melville, 6 July 1848

IN THE THIRD WEEK OF JANUARY Melville took advantage of the delightful
weather and made an excursion to take tea with the Sedgwicks in Lenox.
Maria had known them from the 1830s, when Helen had spent her year at
Eliza Sedgwick's school, and Lizzie had known them since the fall of 1841, at
the latest, when she accompanied the judge and her stepmother to Lenox for
the session of court, just at the time when Gansevoort had escorted Helen
there to see Mrs. Sedgwick. Now on 24 January Augusta wrote to Helen:

> We went Tuesday, immediately after dinner, Mamma Herman & Lizzie &
> myself composing the party. We followed our road in going, but preferred not
> doing so on our return, for we found it very bad & just before it enters the old
> Lenox road, so bad that we had the choice presented to us of being precipi-
> tated down a steep hill or all jumping out & walking some distance. We pre-
> ferred the latter alternative, & respectfully suggested to Herman that we
> should take the longer road when we came back. It struck six o'clock just as
> we entered the village, found the Sedgwicks at tea.

Left to himself, Melville would have taken the shorter route coming as well
as going, but, against all impulse, he was being a reasonable man, half the
time. His calm was shattered at some point in these weeks by Allan's decision
not, after all, to purchase the indenture of lease on the Fourth Avenue house,
but he masked his anxiety. At least Lizzie was with him, and late in January
she conceived their second child.

As the weeks passed Melville became increasingly frustrated at his own
"long procrastination" in visiting Hawthorne (his words to Duyckinck on
12 February). St. Stephen's Dr. Chapman could impose his presence at Arrowhead, but Melville could not see Hawthorne. What was the point of
being six miles from the American who had evinced in literature "the largest

brain with the largest heart," if he could not, now and then, see him? Having now tested the roads first to Dalton then to Lenox, Melville on 22 January, when it was so unpleasant that no one else wanted to accompany him, drove off to visit the Hawthornes. With the Hawthornes, Melville's timing was apt to be bad. In his first weeks in New York in 1837 Gansevoort had made himself the terror of the novelist Catharine Maria Sedgwick's life by calling upon her repeatedly, presuming upon his acquaintance with her brother Charles and sister-in-law Elizabeth. There was always danger Herman could do something of the same thing, for Sophia was sternly protective of her genius husband, especially so just now, when Hawthorne was only a few days away from writing the ending of *The House of the Seven Gables*.

Luckily Melville had not walked in upon an emotional scene such as an interloper might have witnessed early the year before, the time Hawthorne read aloud to his wife the last chapters of *The Scarlet Letter*. If Julian's recollection in the *Literary Digest International Book Review* in August 1926 is to be trusted, Melville arrived in "shaggy coat and bushy dark beard," companioned "by a black Newfoundland dog, shaggy like himself, good natured and simple." Julian had earlier attested to Melville's "great dog" in his *Nathaniel Hawthorne and His Wife* (1884) and again referred to one in *Hawthorne and His Circle* (1903). Melville, so tactile at this time, was just the man to keep a good barn dog; later, in "Benito Cereno," he specified Newfoundland dogs as a breed that some men just naturally take to. Julian may have remembered accurately that he and Una made "the wayfarer" delay his entrance in order to visit the grave they had dug for a dead bird, found frozen that morning during a belated migratory flight. After paying his respects to the bird, Melville was allowed to enter, and then, Julian remembered, promptly placed him and Una astride the "warm wet dog," with which both children were soon "fraternizing." The baby, meanwhile, slept in the cradle, according to Julian's recollection three quarters of a century later, but in actuality the baby was not yet born on any recorded day when Melville came through the snow to the little red cottage. Melville had found Hawthorne "buried in snow; & the delightful scenery about him, all wrapped up & tucked away under a napkin, as it were" (so he wrote Duyckinck). The surprised Hawthornes gave him, he reported (Augusta wrote Helen), "the warmest of welcomes" along with "a cold chicken." Their larder, he must have understood by this time, was always meager in comparison to the Dutch bounty of any house his mother lived in, when she was not in direst poverty. The Hawthornes entertained him (or listened to him) until late. In Julian's 1926 recollections, the "bearded improvisatore" was a magical enchanter whose stories were "more affecting than those of Queen Scheherezade." This may well have been the occasion when Melville told them so dramatic a story of his escape from the

Typees that after his departure they looked all about for the great club they all thought he had been swinging. Sensitive as he was to slights, Melville felt totally welcome.

He reached home an hour before midnight. The next day he talked happily about his visit and the prospective return visit, and displayed gifts, as Augusta reported to Helen: "Mrs Hawthorne sent Malcolm a beautiful book, 'The Grandfather's Chair,' a collection of holiday stories written by her husband, & Mr Hawthorne presented Herman with a copy of his 'Twice told tales' in two volumes. This was gladly received as an accession to his library." Melville had had a purpose beyond that of a few hours' conversation — it was to invite all of the Hawthornes "to go & spend the day at his place near Pittsfield." He may have been surprised to see that Sophia was pregnant, but what he saw, and was told, did not make him alter the invitation. He may not have realized yet that as an older mother-to-be she had notions about behavior during pregnancy rather different from Allan's Sophia, or even Lizzie. On 24 January, two days after Melville's visit to Lenox, Augusta wrote Helen:

> Herman has invited Mr & Mrs Hawthorne with their two beautiful little children to make us a visit. They are coming week after next, on Monday or Tuesday & will return the next day. We are all looking forward to this visit with great pleasure. Herman says that they are the loveliest family he ever met with, or anyone can possibly imagine. We are all delighted to hear that you will be home before they come. Herman said last evening, when your letter came, "I am glad Helen is coming home, it will make it so much pleasanter for the Hawthorne's." Now mind that you return to us with all your powers of entertainment in the happiest condition.

Fanny's being there would most likely do nothing to make the Hawthornes' stay more pleasant — not at least by anything she would say to them other than proper greetings; still painfully shy, she would happily "sit by quietly," unobserved, "noticing and marking every thing" that passed around her. Augusta was better able to converse on general matters, as Lizzie was, when anyone gave her a chance, and Maria was competent to do the family proud in any circumstances.

Herman had spoken incautiously, not realizing that to praise the Hawthornes' married life so extravagantly might have reflected upon Lizzie as an unequal partner in his own marriage, but Augusta's letter gives a sense of the pride he felt in his womenfolk, especially the Lenox-educated and Boston-wintered Helen, who through her long youth and unmarried early womanhood had continued to mother him and the younger children. Augusta noticed nothing invidious in the comment she relayed, for she was objective enough to know that Helen did indeed have social skills she herself had not set out to master and now chose not to practice: Augusta was the model for the behavior shy Fanny carried to extremes. Augusta had only to reflect on Helen's recent anecdote about Mrs. Taylor and Herman's loud laughter to acknowledge the obvious fact that, for all the differences in their experiences, Helen and Herman had inherited, or acquired, the same ironical sense of humor couched in extravagant, even flamboyant diction. (Helen had implied that she would return early in January, causing Augusta to imagine the unpleasantness if her letter notifying them of her plans went astray and that she might find herself "actually at the depot—& no Herman in waiting." Augusta amused herself with the realization that just as there was a hopeless busybody in Lansingburgh, General Viele, there was an old doctor in Pittsfield who loafed around the depot in "indefatigable attendance at all our arrivals," offering "indefatigable politeness to all distressed damsels," so at worst Helen would have a superannuated gallant at her service.)

On the mild 26 January (during the January thaw that extended from Albany to the Berkshires), the day before her husband completed *The House of the Seven Gables*, Sophia Hawthorne noted in her diary: "I read all over to myself 'The House of the Seven Gables' in manuscript. In evening wrote a note to Mr. Melville." That note postponed any visit to Arrowhead, except possibly a visit by Hawthorne to spend the day. Melville replied to Hawthorne directly, ignoring the "side-blow" of Sophia's letter and professing himself uncharmed by the lady's "syrenisims" (or syrenisms). The sleigh was ready, a bed was made, he had cut the firewood, and two chickens were already devoted to Hawthorne's nourishment, and Melville himself was keeping "the word 'Welcome' all the time" in his mouth, ready to speak as Hawthorne crossed the threshold for the first time:

> Another thing, Mr Hawthorne — Do not think you are coming to any prim nonsensical house — that is nonsensical in the ordinary way. You wont be much bored with punctilios. You may do what you please — say or say *not* what you please. And if you feel any inclination for that sort of thing — you may spend the period of your visit *in bed*, if you like — every hour of your visit.
>
> Hark — There is some excellent Montado Sherry awaiting you & some most potent Port. We will have mulled wine with wisdom, & buttered toast with story-telling & crack jokes & bottles from morning till night.

As it turned out, none of the Lenox family came at once; on 3 February Hawthorne wrote Melville postponing the visit, and on 12 February Melville wrote to Duyckinck that Hawthorne was to have made him "a day's visit" ("& I had promised myself much pleasure in getting him up in my snug room here, & discussing the Universe with a bottle of brandy & cigars"). Hawthorne had not come, "owing to sickness in his family."

In this period of suspended work on the whaling book, while Melville was awaiting the visit from Hawthorne, he received a request from Evert Duyckinck for a daguerreotype from which could be made an engraving for inclusion in his new venture, *Holden's Dollar Magazine*, and he also wanted Melville to write something for the magazine. Under other circumstances Melville might have agreed without a second thought. Duyckinck was Duyckinck, always sliding from one publishing venture to another, but Melville had changed in the last secluded months in regard to anything that smacked of self-promotion, and he had let himself realize how great a book he was writing. On 12 February he had to confront the limitations of his New York friend, who thought so little of his work or his work schedule that he renewed his customary trivial demands on his time. Unwilling to hurt Duyckinck's feelings, Melville wrote this ambivalent, pugnacious, placating response:

> How shall a man go about refusing a man? — Best be roundabout, or plumb on the mark? — I can not write the thing you want. I am in the humor to lend a hand to a friend, if I can; — but I am not in the humor to write the kind of thing you need — and I am not in the humor to write for Holden's Magazine. If I were to go on to give you all my reasons — you would pronounce me a bore, so I will not do that. You must be content to beleive that I *have* reasons, or else I would not refuse so small a thing. — As for the Daguerreotype (I spell the word right from your sheet) that's what I can not send you, because I have none. And if I had, I would not send it for such a purpose, even to you. — Pshaw! you cry — & so cry I. — "This is intensified vanity, not true modesty or anything of that sort!" — Again, I say so too. But if it be so, how can I help it. The fact is, almost everybody is having his "mug" engraved nowadays; so that this test of distinction is getting to be reversed; and therefore, to see one's "mug" in a magazine, is presumptive evidence that he's a nobody. So being as vain a man as ever lived; & beleiving that my illustrious name is famous throughout the world — I respectfully decline being *oblivionated* by a Daguerreotype (what a devel of an unspellable word!)
>
> We are all queer customers, Mr Duyckinck, you, I, & every body else in the world. So if I here seem queer to you, be sure, I am not alone in my queerness, tho' it present itself at a different port, perhaps, from other people, since every one has his own distinct peculiarity. But I trust you take me aright. If you dont' I shall be sorry — that's all.

He offered a mitigating reminder of the service he had done Duyckinck and the *Literary World* the previous August: "By the way I have recently read his [Hawthorne's] 'Twice Told Tales' (I had not read but a few of them before) I think they far exceed the 'Mosses' — they are, I fancy, an earlier vintage from his vine. Some of those sketches are wonderfully subtle. Their deeper meanings are worthy of a Brahmin."

Melville continued with the first slight disparagement of Hawthorne he had put on record, in which he could not separate the writer from the works:

> Still there is something lacking—a good deal lacking—to the plump sphericity of the man. What is that?—He does'nt patronise the butcher—he needs roast-beef, done rare.—Nevertheless, for one, I regard Hawthorne (in his books) as evincing a quality of genius, immensely loftier, & more profound, too, than any other American has shown hitherto in the printed form. Irving is a grasshopper to him—putting the *souls* of the two men together, I mean.

One other American, so went Melville's unspoken thought, might already have evinced in a *manuscript* a loftier and more profound quality of genius. Melville's need for Hawthorne's presence and example may have begun to diminish, but only Hawthorne could be counted on to understand what Melville wrote to him a little later, sometime before the middle of May, "I read Solomon more and more, and every time see deeper and deeper and unspeakable meanings in him. I did not think of Fame, a year ago, as I do now."

In mid-February, just after Herman refused to be daguerreotyped, the family at Arrowhead vicariously experienced some of the most tumultuous times Boston had felt since the earthquake just before Lizzie left for Lansingburgh—and Herman's proposal—in August 1846. On 15 February a Negro waiter named Frederick Wilkins, also known as Shadrach, was arrested there as a runaway. As a result of the previous year's Fugitive Slave Law, slaves could not flee from the South to safety anywhere in the North, for all states were required to remand any runaway slave to his or her master. It was the Compromise of 1850, of which this law was a part, that John Hoadley and many others had celebrated in Pittsfield in December. Now in Boston one of the lawyers who volunteered to defend Shadrach was Melville's friend, the younger Richard Henry Dana. This brought Dana into conflict with Lemuel Shaw, as Dana intemperately described in a letter to his brother Ned, then in Rome:

> I prepared a petition for Hab. Corp. & went before Judge Shaw. He treated me in his worst manner, & refused the writ on a series of the most frivolous pretexts you can imagine. Judge Metcalf, who was present, was much hurt & exercised by his conduct. He seemed to forget his judicial character & duties entirely, & treated me precisely as if I had asked him to sign a Free Soil petition. The best reason he gave, wh[ich] was an afterthought, would have

served him as an impeachment. The disposition shown by such men, our best citizens, shows, more than anything else, the extent to which the selfish spirit of N. England has run.

The fifteenth was a Saturday, and a Negro crowd gathered outside the courtroom, reaching all the way back into the street. When the door was unlocked to let out some abolitionist supporters of Shadrach, the crowd pushed in.

Leonard Levy in *The Law of the Commonwealth and Chief Justice Shaw* describes the scene: "Shadrach headed for the unguarded opposite exit, and as about fifteen men streamed into the room, jamming [U.S. Deputy Marshal] Riley into a corner behind the door, the marshall screamed from his place of safety, 'Shoot him! Shoot him!' But the rescuers had already escorted Shadrach out of the room, down the stairs, and into the streets. Dana, working in his office opposite the Court House, rushed to his window at the sound of shooting in time to see two huge Negroes, bearing Shadrach between them, dash off toward Cambridge 'like a black squall,' the mob cheering as they departed." Dana wrote Ned of the moments after the rescue: "Most of the men I met burst out laughing, but here & there especially among the Tariff-bigoted merchants, & the political adherents of Webster, were faces as Sour as verjuice." That particular crowd held an unusually high proportion of abolitionists, no doubt, but Dana was anything but an objective witness. Law-abiding citizens were indignant at the least, and many of them were appalled and even terrified by this defiance of the law, for the rescue of Shadrach was a direct threat to the Union, making as it did a mockery of the Compromise of 1850. Shaw's old friend Daniel Webster, now Fillmore's secretary of state, called it "a case of treason," and the hapless president called a special cabinet meeting and issued a worried proclamation.

Only a fanatical minority of the newspapers championed the rescue. Even the liberal Boston *Investigator* (which regularly celebrated Thomas Paine's, Rousseau's, and Voltaire's birthdays, and which had a grudge against Shaw for sentencing the freethinker Abner Kneeland to prison for blasphemy in 1838) declared on 26 February that "it is better to obey even a bad law, than to resist by physical force its execution." The Whig Boston *Daily Courier* and the Democratic Boston *Post* united in denouncing the radicals. The *Courier* for 17 February headlined its report "MOB LAW TRIUMPHANT" and denounced the "outrage perpetrated in this city on Saturday," lamenting the unparalleled disgrace upon Boston, when at midday "the very sanctuary of justice" was "broken into by a gang of negroes." The question was no longer confined to the execution of the Fugitive Slave Law: "The point to be determined now is, whether *any* law shall prevail in Boston." On the eighteenth the *Post* denounced Charles Sumner for his Faneuil Hall speech of

26 November 1850 against the Fugitive Slave Bill, and held him responsible for the violence in the courthouse. The *Courier* on the twenty-first returned to the attack with a vehement condemnation of "the preaching of the 'higher law' doctrine by Messrs. Charles Sumner, Theodore Parker, George Thompson, and their coadjutors." These worthies had given the community "a palpable taste of that 'higher law.'"

Other newspapers in Boston and throughout the country expressed similar shocked determination not to let the outrage be repeated. In Pittsfield, Phinehas Allen's weekly Democratic *Sun* gave the rescue little notice in the issue of the twentieth, then by the twenty-seventh the story was old news, though worth a column and a half quoted from the *Post*, half of which was itself quoted from Sumner's "attrocious" pre-Thanksgiving Faneuil Hall speech, which the *Post* blamed for the rioting. Allen made no editorial of his own about the rescue, so the matter was not pushed into the foremost of everyone's consciousness there in western Massachusetts. The Boston papers that Melville might have seen (which would not likely have included the abolitionists' *Liberator* and *Commonwealth*) all took the same condemnatory tone that caused Dana to write Ned on 2 March: "you can hardly credit the abject state of our political mercantile press." At Arrowhead through all this Melville tried to keep his focus on his manuscript, certain of its literary value, hopeful of its financial success, and unwilling, now, to take a part openly even in the most significant political crises of the young country. Milton, he decided at some point, had erred in putting political commentary into "Lycidas." Melville marked lines 115–31 and moralized: "Mark the deforming effect of the intrusion of partizan topics & feelings of the day, however serious in import, into a poem otherwise of the first order of merit."

At the end of February Melville and the women in the household all were anxious about the failure of the Fourth Avenue house to sell, month after month, despite the efforts of Allan, the lawyer in the family. The women may all have known that Dr. Brewster held a mortgage on the farm for fifteen hundred dollars, and they must have known that Melville also owed him a large sum of money, apparently two thousand dollars, which was part of the agreed purchase price of sixty-five hundred dollars, and which was to have been paid promptly out of the sum realized from the sale of the indenture of lease on the very desirably located New York house which Herman, the previous September, had been certain would sell at once. Arrowhead looked less desirable week by week as the winter revealed the worst flaws in the farmhouse. The roof was not leaking, but the cooking facilities were primitive, there was only an outdoor well, no inside kitchen pump, the parlor walls were soiled and needed fresh papering, some of the upholstered furniture looked shabbier after the move than it had in the city, and many of the rooms required painting. Outbuildings needed repair, and the barn needed at least to be painted. Herman himself was in no position to list his own needs, other than peace and quiet in which to write the book. After his exuberant optimism of the previous autumn, nothing more was heard about building a new house with a writing tower commanding a view to fill an English duke with envy — Saddleback majestic to the north, Monument Mountain to the southwest, and on clear days the familiar Catskills to the west, already memorialized in Irving's "Rip Van Winkle."

Following one of her memorable family councils, at the end of February or the very beginning of March, Maria left to visit Allan and Sophia in their new house on Thirty-first Street, far uptown. She would see Kate and her first granddaughter (after her longest separation from them), she would get acquainted with Florence, and she would scout out items for the interior renovation of Arrowhead. Melville had to interrupt his morning work routine to take her to the depot, but he did not escort her into the waiting room and keep her company and then, after the train arrived, see that she was seated comfortably and that her trunk was securely stowed. Having arrived in New York, small thanks to Herman, Maria protested ironically to Augusta: "Herman I hope returned home safe after dumping me & my trunks out so unceremoniously at the Depot — Altho we were there more than an hour before the time, he hurried off as if his life had depended upon his speed, a more ungallant man it would be difficult to find." The gallant Gansevoort, had he lived to take her to a depot, would never have treated her as Herman did. Maria simply could not imagine that "his life" — her son's creative life — might really in some sense have "depended upon his speed." His impatience meant that he had been summoned from his study at a crucial stage, say when he was a third of the way through "The Whiteness of the Whale" or halfway through "The Grand Armada." His behavior also revealed a steadily heightened anxiety about what he would do if the New York indenture of lease did not sell. Frightened himself, he was ungracious to her. It may not have occurred to her (as it readily did to Hawthorne) that a man who had lived a life of irresponsibility might be expected to feel special tensions after he took on new family responsibilities in his mid-twenties. If it did, that for her was no excuse.

What the family had decided upon in the dead of winter (with Maria more outspoken than Lizzie) was considerably scaled down from a new towered house, but would take money. The timing is odd, but in late February, or very early March at the latest, before the ground had even begun to thaw, Melville hired men to start work on a small narrow porch on the northeast corner of the house, below his study window, and to lay the foundations of a new building or new buildings (a kitchen and wood-house, at least) — jobs that required more man-hours than the same work would have taken after the spring thaw. Perhaps he found workmen ready to undertake a difficult job cheaply in an otherwise dead season. This particular piazza was oddly placed, to the north, and badly designed. It would be too narrow to put three or four big rocking chairs on and enjoy during a spring or summer rain, the way Uncle Herman could do at Gansevoort, Saratoga County, on his wide piazza. This one was not a family piazza at all: it was for Herman. If he couldn't walk his tower battlements for a 360° view, he could pace the piazza deck, only a few feet wide. If he turned away from the house each time he reached one end of the piazza, he could gaze straight toward Greylock for a moment, and he could always glance northward as he paced lengthwise. The neighbors at least would not besmear it with human ordure, as the local residents had done to Uncle Herman's piazza, although Pittsfield was already looking askance upon the author of *Typee*, who did not go to church regularly and socialize with Christians the way the author of *Typee* would do if he were truly a reclaimed sinner.

The piazza was a luxury for Herman, precipitously and expensively started when the ground was hard, but the needs of the five Melville women and the cook and the other female servant were immediate and real. (Both the servants were Irish Catholics named Mary, which in the Melville household became the generic name for the cook, under the principle that many Irish girls were named Mary and that servants stayed too short a time to warrant the family's mastering a new name each time a new one was hired. The standing danger was that the chatelaine in charge would forget that the latest Mary did not contain within her brain the collective Marial memory, but that was part of the price one paid for being servant-ridden.) As it was, the cook and the other female servant had to draw water for the family from a well outside, near the kitchen. The well needed to be fitted with a modern pump and sheltered in a separate annex (to judge from Helen's reference on 29 May 1854 to Melville's pulling up old Charlie "at the pump-room door" after a drive to the village). A new kitchen was required to replace the old one built detached from the house then subsequently connected by makeshift walls—a more solid and spacious kitchen with better storage space, better connected to the main house, and very likely equipped with a sink that had an outside drain. Perhaps the cook had demanded a more modern wood-burning stove. Other requirements were on a still less grandiose scale, such as Herman's need for a wood-house to protect the firewood, and to give him room to swing an axe indoors, if he had to, rather than to split all the wood outdoors. Inside the house, some rearrangements would be desirable, Lizzie knew by the end of February or early March. Malcolm was still sleeping in the small bedroom Herman and Lizzie shared, but they might have to annex the next cubicle on the second floor, whatever its present use, rather than sleep in a room with Malcolm and the new baby, when it came. (Any preparation for the baby was covered by Melville's phrase to Shaw in 1856: some money had been spent "making alterations.") There was always the possibility that Kate might join them, and need some space and some furniture, even if in a room shared with Fanny or Augusta. Early spring, Maria and Herman both knew, would bring the need for Herman to work his farm the way he had years ago worked the Melvill place — not the simple gardening chores, such as he and later Tommy had been accustomed to perform on a rented plot of land in Lansingburgh, but serious farm work that had to be done if horse and cow were to be kept in hay and pumpkins over winter and if Herman were to lay root vegetables away for the family. Maria knew she had to think for her son, who would procrastinate if she allowed him to. No one wanted to consider how Herman would deal with all the demands on his time.

In Pittsfield, Maria had focused not on Herman's progress on the book but on practical matters, including the renovations. On 10 March, soon after she arrived in New York City, she wrote to Augusta that she supposed the piazza was "nearly finished," and that foundations for other buildings were being laid. The day before, something had happened that led to her involvement in Herman's refusal of Evert Duyckinck's reasonable request. She and Kate had been walking up Third Avenue after church when they passed two gentlemen without noticing them at first: "one was 'Cornelius' he had been taking a walk with his brother, recognising me through my thick veil, he turned back alone grasp'd my hand warmly and upon my surprised look, he said eagerly have you forgotten me, dont you know me Mrs Melville, he walked with me a block or two asking all about Herman &c, he then said his brother was waiting for him, and as he intended to come up with Mr Duyckinck soon to pass an Eveg with us he would take his leave." When Duyckinck called at Allan and Sophia's, he mentioned his regret at not having Melville's head for the *Dollar Magazine*. This was news to Maria, most likely, and she decided to press her son to comply with the request for a daguerreotype, as she thought any sensible man would do. (Gansevoort, had he lived a little longer, willingly would have posed for any number of daguerreotypes.) On 12 March, Maria wrote to Augusta: "Mr Bancroft has sat for his portrait it will soon appear in the Dollar Magazine — Mr Duyckinck has Mr Hawthornes which will also appear in the same. Mr Duyckinck said Herman must sit to a first rate artist when he comes on — & also told me the . . . Magazine had advertized among the Portraits that of Herman Melvilles as forthcoming with other American Authors. Mr Prescott has also had his Portrait taken for Mr Duyckinck's magazine all at the expense of Mr D— & brother."

As it turned out, the *Dollar Magazine* collapsed before it was able to use Hawthorne's portrait, so Melville, even if he had posed for a daguerreotype, might never have been immortalized in the *Dollar Magazine*. That was months in the future, and what was obvious now, to Evert, to Maria, was that Herman was acting in a way inimical to his immediate best interests and to his chances for a permanent reputation as one of the most important American writers. They were being sensible, and Herman was not, as Maria concluded: "Herman with all those illustrious examples will have to do likewise, or appear very strangely stiff." Worse than that, he would be behaving self-destructively just when many people had begun to rely on him. This seemingly petty episode involving a daguerreotype stirred Melville to articulate, a few weeks later, in a letter to Hawthorne, that he had changed—he did not think about fame as he had done a year before. The writing of the whaling book was changing him, convincing him of his great powers, but making him reckless of his best interests and the best interests of his family.

In New York, Maria still had time to worry about Herman's behavior in more than one regard. She found what she should have anticipated, that there was no hope of her impressing her ways upon Sophia's household. Baby Florence was in the hands of the nurse, so the daughter of the Hero of Fort Stanwix was reduced to entertaining little Maria with anecdotes about her "little pet Malcolm," as she wrote Augusta on 10 March; little Maria looked "intelligent as if she understood every word," and at least she knew most of her letters, even if she had added few words to the half dozen she could speak at the start of the year. (In Nilly's opinion Malcolm was slow learning to talk, and Sophia herself said little Maria was backward in speech.) Making her social calls and going to church was miserable work for Maria, since the house was so remote and the weather so bad. Before long she decided that she did not think she would be apt "to select the month of March to visit New York again," as she wrote Augusta on 10 March, but she made valiant efforts to do what she needed to do. She braved the ferry to Brooklyn to visit her ailing sister-in-law Mary Chandonette Gansevoort at the Curtis house. Mary "was sitting up looking feeble," but much better than Maria had expected. Guert and Stanwix were both there, and Kate like a good niece wanted Maria to stay a week with them.

In Brooklyn or Manhattan, Maria heard of an extraordinary family drama involving their husband-and-wife cousins, John De Peyster Douw and Margaret Van Rensselaer Douw, whose domestic life Gansevoort had so admired. Margaret had thought that a daughter of the Van Rensselaers could buy anything or be granted anything by feudal right, even a divorce, which the state legislature could grant by a special act. Rebuffed, she was still determined. Maria summed up the news to Augusta on 12 March:

> Now I heard something that will surprise you Augusta. Margaret Douw came on to New York with her Father & Wilmer [Wilmot] Johnson proceeded to Philadelphia, to be married[.] Bishop Potter, Charles Cooper & one other Clergyman were applied to, but they said it was against the Canons of the Church & decline'd to officiate, while this was going on, They receive'd a telegraphic dispatch from Mrs Van Rensselaer that Depeyster had sent word he would take his daughter from Margaret if she married, so all returned home, upon this announcement.

Augusta's religious scruples against divorce were powerful, but on 17 April she wrote a fervent letter congratulating "darling Maggie" on now having one who could "appreciate the warm heart he has made his own," and would "know how to cherish the treasure he has won." Maggie responded with the assurance that she had "prayed to God earnestly" to direct her right and had received "the opinions of eight iminent lawyers," all of whom considered her proposed remarriage *"perfectly legal,* not only in Penn. but in every state in the union." In Philadelphia on 24 April Maggie went through a marriage ceremony despite the fact that Cousin John De Peyster Douw was very much alive. After the ceremony the dubiously united couple left for exile in Baltimore, where they would not be a standing humiliation to the Van Rensselaers of the Manor House.

From Manhattan, Maria also reported on Tertullus D. Stewart, who was dividing his time between Lansingburgh and New York City. Stewart had spent Sunday evening, 9 March, at Allan's, being "agreeably surprised to see 'Madame'" there (she wrote Augusta the next day). Maria quoted Stewart as saying that he would like to see Herman very much and that when at Springfield not long since he had intended to pass the night at Arrowhead "but on enquiry found no train was going on." He felt on such easy terms with the family that he would have showed up without invitation and without prior notice, if a train had been running. Badinage followed. Allan said, "You had famous eating there, that was some consolation." Stewart demurred: "No, but I had to pay for it. If I could have gone to Pittsfield, I should have had good cheer, a good bed, good company, a hearty welcome, and enjoyed myself." Unmentioned in Sophia's parlor was Stewart's tempting offer the previous fall to lend Melville whatever he needed in order to settle in Pittsfield, and, almost surely, some recent communication between Herman and Stewart, involving Herman's second thoughts about his refusal of a loan.

In March, most likely, Herman had learned that a purchaser at last had

been found for the house in town, Lewis M. Rutherford, guardian of Rutherford Stuyvesant, devisee of Peter G. Stuyvesant. For seven thousand dollars
Melville would sell "all that certain indenture of lease" he had bought in
1847. The mortgage remained five thousand dollars. Assuming the mortgage
payments had been made all along, then Herman received from this transaction two thousand dollars in cash, minus any fees. If he had been remiss in
payments or if the fees were substantial, the sum he received was correspond-
ingly less, and in fact whatever amount he received "fell short of the amount
expected to have been realized" (as he explained belatedly to his father-in-
law on 12 May 1856). Instead of having money enough to pay Brewster then
plenty left over to pay for the work already undertaken on Arrowhead, he
found himself with too little money to pay Dr. Brewster all the delayed
portion of the purchase-money, two thousand dollars (which was an obligation separate from the fifteen hundred dollar mortgage Brewster held). It
came as a crushing realization: he would need *more* money, just to pay Brewster. (It of course was not to be considered that Shaw might be repaid the two
thousand dollars *he* had advanced for the purchase of a New York house.)
Around 8 March he wrote Stewart. Stewart received the letter from Herman
on Monday the tenth, apparently, for on that day he met Allan in the street
and gave the impression that he expected to see Herman in town in a few
days, and seemed surprised when Allan told him they did not expect him for
some weeks. Aware from his encounter with Stewart that Herman was not
keeping him fully informed, Allan on 14 March cast his lawyerly eye over the
new indenture of lease for the Fourth Avenue house before sending it to
Herman for his signature. Herman seems to have behaved in confused and
perhaps contradictory ways, reluctant to break off work on his manuscript,
and procrastinating about financial matters he had no experience handling.

  With Maria interfering with afar, with Helen away and perhaps still
smarting from his rudeness to her, with Augusta concentrating on copying
the manuscript, with the newly pregnant Lizzie absorbed in caring for Malcolm, with workmen coming and going directly beneath the study window,
with it becoming obvious to him that the money from the house would not
meet his obligations and that he would, in the end, have to borrow money
from Stewart, Melville became frantic. A true son of Allan Melvill, he denied
reality and escaped — for a few days — into a literary paradise. When his day's
writing stint ended on 12 March, he harnessed Charlie to the sleigh and
drove to the little red cottage on the other side of Lenox. Sophia Hawthorne
wrote in her diary: "At dusk arrived Herman Melville from Pittsfield. He
was entertained with Champagne foam — manufactured of beaten eggs, loaf
sugar & champagne — bread & butter & cheese. He invited us all to go &
spend tomorrow at his house. My husband concluded to go with Una."

Melville remained overnight to accompany Hawthorne and Una through the snowstorm the next day for a two-day visit, Thursday the thirteenth and Friday the fourteenth. He bore home with him a precious gift from Sophia, one of the five copies the Hawthornes had just received of the engraving made by Thomas Phillibrown from the Cephas Thompson oil painting for the new edition of *Twice-Told Tales*, published on 8 March. (The engraving, subsequently framed, survives in the Berkshire Athenaeum, with a note by Lizzie on its provenance.) Hawthorne carried to Arrowhead a gift for Melville from his own library, being unable to buy something specifically for him. It was a four-volume work his own uncle had given him in 1832, *The Mariner's Chronicle; Being a Collection of the Most Interesting Narratives of Shipwrecks, Fires, Famines, and Other Calamities Incident to a Life of Maritime Enterprise*, by Archibald Duncan (1806), the more valuable to Melville for the family transmission history evident inside it. It was a thoughtful gift, since it contained many items which, for all Hawthorne knew, Melville might use in his book.

At Arrowhead the family was given a fair chance to meet Hawthorne and ample opportunity to indulge Una (who had turned seven on 3 March), but mainly Melville and Hawthorne retreated to his study, where they could look at the pile of manuscript and talk about its content and Melville's hopes for it. Hawthorne himself was an inept businessman, but better than any other man in the country he could recognize the grandeur of Melville's conception of the book he learned to call *The White Whale* (Melville may have been calling it that as well as *The Whale*), and he could listen while his host speculated about the shrewdest way of marketing the book, perhaps by offering it to publishers other than the Harpers. Never once would Hawthorne ask questions about whose money would pay for stereotyping the book, if Melville brought up that possibility, no more than he would ask whose money was paying for the food on the table at Arrowhead and paying for the renovations going on directly below the north window. The weather was good enough for Hawthorne to sit at that window, at times, and gaze at Greylock, but the men went to the barn to take refuge from the noise of the workmen and the inhibiting effects of chamberpots. It was easier in the barn, as long as the sun shone.

Some forty years later Melville received a visit from a Philadelphian, Theodore F. Wolfe, who was preparing his *Literary Shrines*, among which he wanted to include the houses of Hawthorne and Melville in the Berkshires. Melville talked freely to Wolfe about the visits between Arrowhead and the little red cottage, especially Melville's to Hawthorne. Wolfe gained the impression that Hawthorne had come more than once "to chat with the racy romancer and philosopher by the great chimney," but he learned some specifics, imperfectly remembered or imperfectly recorded, about this particular visit:

> Once he was accompanied by little Una — "Onion" he sometimes called her — and remained a whole week. . . . March weather prevented walks abroad, so the pair spent most of the week in smoking and talking metaphysics in the barn, — Hawthorne usually lounging upon a carpenter's bench. When he was leaving, he jocosely declared he would write a report of their psychological discussions for publication in a book to be called "A Week on a Work-Bench in a Barn," the title being a travesty upon that of Thoreau's then recent book, "A Week on Concord River."

Having said what could be said about the guest's hopes for *The House of the Seven Gables* and the host's hopes for *The Whale*, the men had ranged over their literary acquaintances and their prospects for helping to make a genuine national literature. A good deal of Melville's early impression of Thoreau came from the Hawthornes, as did his impression of Emerson the man. The previous year at the red cottage they had talked about Emerson, but now they talked about the Concord man who had climbed Greylock — "the most unmalleable fellow alive," although a good walking companion, Hawthorne had decided long before (in a letter to Duyckinck, 1 July 1845).

Inside, in Melville's study on Friday the fourteenth (the day Allan looked over the indenture of lease in New York City), Hawthorne wrote to Duyckinck, saying he had only to glance his eye aside "to obtain a fine snow-covered prospect of Graylock." Conscious that Duyckinck knew the Melvill house, but not Arrowhead, Hawthorne extended an invitation for Melville: "May we not hope for the pleasure of seeing you again in Berkshire, next summer? If you were to see how snug and comfortable Melville makes himself and friends, I think you would not fail." Maria had not returned from New York with brandy, but Hawthorne relished "some excellent old port and sherry wine," he wrote to G. W. Curtis on 29 April, calling Melville "an admirable fellow." Ignoring the disturbance caused by the renovations (such as he had never yet had to commission), Hawthorne had gained a good sense of the magnitude of Melville's efforts at shaping out his gigantic conception of his *White Whale* by the time his host drove him and Una back to Lenox. Melville returned to Arrowhead reassured that he had been right to risk so much to finish his book in the Berkshires, near Hawthorne.

Hawthorne's visit had been momentous for Augusta, a reward for her months of copying her brother's manuscript. The next week, 22 March, Augusta wrote Mary Blatchford, so "carried away with romance" about Arrowhead that Mary thought there "must be some enchantment about it." Herman's guest was a leading actor in the romance of Arrowhead, as Mary's response made clear: "And a visit from your beau ideal — Hawthorne — Well I know how much pleased you must have been to entertain such a guest, and how perfectly you were in your element, in endeavoring to 'draw him out' as the saying is, and favor you with the light of his genius — You were fortunate too that the presence did not disappoint you, as is too apt to be the case, when we have our expectations highly raised from fine writing." Helen had been stimulated by the romancer's presence also, but Fanny was too shy to think of drawing out someone almost her equal in shyness. Lizzie was too much her father's daughter to carry on about any particular guest more than another one.

On 21 March Herman, at Arrowhead, signed the deed for the indenture of lease on the Fourth Avenue house, but there was further talk of his going to New York City. Kate wrote to Augusta to ask if she was coming with him so they could buy her a straw hat of the proper size, the well-intentioned Lizzie having brought back something from Boston that did not quite suit. Unwilling to break off his work on the book, embarrassed at leaving his women while workmen were tromping in and out, Herman decided that Allan could handle the sale of the indenture of lease without him. In New York and left out of any consultations, Maria saw Stewart again toward the end of the month and learned that he had heard from Herman the week before. Since Melville was so reluctant to go to New York, Stewart was planning to go to Lansingburgh by way of Pittsfield. One way or another, Stewart would make it easy for Melville to accept his friendly loan. Meanwhile, Melville was inconveniencing his lawyer-brother. He had written Allan about the indenture soon after he signed it, but he had not enclosed the signed indenture as he should have done. On 28 March Maria wrote him: "Allan is waiting to hear from you, your letter reach'd him yesterday but he wants the paper." The "paper" was the signed document, which her inept second son had retained.

On 26 March Melville wrote Duyckinck: "The Spring begins to open upon Pittsfield, but slowly. I only wish that I had more day-time to spend out *in the day*; but like an owl I steal about by twilight, owing to the twilight of my eyes." He had overstrained his eyes to the point that he did not recover during brief respites, such as the one he took in order to entertain another guest at Arrowhead, the friend of his youth, Eli Fly. Too busy to spare an hour at the depot with his mother three or four weeks earlier, Melville had escorted Fly to Springfield, "so far on his way to Brattleboro'" for a water cure, most likely. As Melville explained to Duyckinck on 26 March, "He has long been a confirmed invalid, & in some small things I act a little as his agent," as in the present letter, the purpose of which was to have Duyckinck forward Fly's copies of the *Literary World* to Brattleboro instead of Greenbush and also send him the *Dollar Magazine*, the subscriptions to both of which Melville promised to pay when he got to New York. He wanted the latter subscription to begin with the March issue, he noted meticulously, not the one just out. His duties to friends were not over. Hawthorne's note on 27 March acknowledged the hospitality at Arrowhead: "Una has very delightful reminiscences of our visit to Melville Castle. So have I." Then he asked Melville to run a few errands for him in Pittsfield, a metropolis compared to Lenox.

On 26 March, a Wednesday, the day of Melville's trip to and from Springfield, Allan had taken Maria and Kate to tea at the Duyckinck house, where the topic was the poet Martin Farquhar Tupper's sensational arrival for an American visit. Melville had bought *Proverbial Philosophy* on its publication in 1846 and was familiar with the poems in that book and, by this time, still other poems by this great favorite of Queen Victoria's. The poems were astonishing to look at, unrhymed verse more like poetic books of the Bible than any modern literature, sententious, highly rhetorical, biblical in language. The Brooklyn journalist Walter Whitman had concluded from *Proverbial Philosophy* that great oracular unrhymed American poetry just might sell amazingly well, and from it Melville had learned at least that *Evangeline* was not the only model, if he ever seriously wanted to write poetry rather than merely poetic prose. Maria reported to Herman on 28 March that "Martin Farqu[h]ar Tupper went almost direct after landing to the Editor of the Evg Post," William Cullen Bryant, "and repeated four lines of poetry." She could not remember them exactly, but the gist was "that he had arrive'd on our shore with the dust of England upon his Boots and the dews of America upon his shoulders." Bryant printed some of Tupper's new poems in the 14 March *Evening Post*, including a reassuring word to America as a whole: "in your greatness shall my soul rejoice— / For you are England's nearest and most dear!"

The newspaper sensation over Tupper's visit stirred Maria profoundly, for it reminded her that she wanted her second son to be famous and pious at the same time, like Tupper. *Her* son had never addressed a Sunday evening missionary meeting at St. Bartholomew's in poetry; on the contrary, Herman had been denounced in the newspapers and magazines for his scurrilous attacks on the missionaries in *Typee* and *Omoo*. One never knew what irreverence might come from his mouth, in private or public. Duyckinck wanted Melville to be a little more committed to his politico-literary causes, a good deal more reasonable about letting himself be touted in the press (Maria did not say where she heard about Tupper's words to the editor of the *Post*, Bryant, but pretty plainly it was Duyckinck, with whom she was still commiserating over Herman's self-destructive willfulness). That fall she referred to G. P. R. James as "the great novelist," just as Tupper was a great poet. She was confident that Herman could be a successful writer, if he put his mind to it and restrained his reckless, irreverent impulses, but nothing suggests that it ever occurred to her that Herman might be or might become a writer as great as the Englishmen Tupper and G. P. R. James, or even the American Nathaniel Hawthorne.

Maria, one way or another devoting a good deal of energy to staying irritated at Herman, by now had worked herself up into a state of zealous intensity. Simultaneously she would improve Herman's theological condition and his reputation with the reviewers and her acquaintances. In December 1839 she had complacently exaggerated the money he would be able to give her annually from his job at Greenbush, but she had learned better, and since he had become an author she had taken small gifts of money from him with an undisguised mixture of gratitude for the thought and disdain for the meagerness. The one thing Herman had ever done right was to marry well. Now he needed to be told what was necessary to do, and if he would not exercise forethought, then she was able and willing to think for him, so that all he had to do was acquiesce. Knowing that the indenture of lease on the house in New York was at last sold, and assuming that Herman had some cash in hand, Maria employed the last days of her visit by planning necessary purchases. On 28 March she sent Herman a detailed set of purchases she wanted to make for Arrowhead — garden seeds and cuttings, and especially bundles of asparagus roots, which would spread so that in a few years they would have "a superabundance" of that early and healthful vegetable. (Five bundles would cost $3.75.) She had priced "oak paper" for the parlor (for which she needed to have precise measurements) and coverings for the sofas and chairs "badly soiled by misuse." Herman had requested two shades of "seegars," and a "demijohn of brandy." All this she was prepared to carry home, knowing that Allan would see her and her gear safely aboard the cars. Furthermore, she was prepared to bring a manservant back with her. As she wrote to Herman, "you cannot do without one & this is the place to procure one." She volunteered to interview new emigrants from Ireland so as to know what kind of help was available; Mary, the cook at Arrowhead, was expecting her brother on one of the emigrant ships, and, in case the brother wanted the job, she would know what the going wage was, by month or by year, and just how prepossessing an Irishman she could afford. If Herman could not be famous and pious, perhaps he could turn into a good farmer, with the proper help.

In early April, the inhabitants of Arrowhead, especially the pregnant Lizzie, were perturbed anew by newspaper reports and letters from Mt. Vernon Street, for the whole country focused its attention on Boston again when another fugitive slave, Thomas Sims, was arrested there on 3 April. Respectable Whigs and Democrats alike were determined to show that the Athens of America would uphold the Fugitive Slave Law by returning Sims to his master in Georgia. Sims was confined to a room in the courthouse reserved for use in federal cases, so that he was technically imprisoned in a federal jail, and kept closely guarded by the deputies of the U.S. marshal. As Levy says, on 4 April "Boston awoke to witness one of the most extraordinary spectacles in its existence. During the night, the Court House had been barricaded." Iron chains "had been girded entirely around the building. Its approaches were cleared by a belt of ropes and chains along the sidewalks, and heavy links stretched across its doorways." That morning officials wanting to enter the court house had to stoop under the chains, and "Chief Justice Lemuel Shaw of the Supreme Judicial Court, the great Shaw, venerated for his wisdom and for his advanced age, was among the first that morning to stoop beneath the chains." Before dawn on 12 April "a guard of three hundred armed men led the slave through the streets of the sleeping city. At Long Wharf the brig *Acron*, armed with cannon, received him." (Dana in his diary for 13 April prided himself on never having stooped under the chain: "I either jump over it, or go round to the end, & have the rope removed, wh[ich] they have at last graciously substituted for the last few links of the chain.")

The family received further news from Boston in the next days (although Augusta's correspondence log does not show that *she* received any letters from there). On 10 April Phinehas Allen quoted in the *Sun* several items from the Boston *Post*, including one from the seventh on Sims's passing "his time cheerfully in his quarters in the courthouse." (Dana's version, on 13 April, was bleaker: "Poor Sims was confined in a small room, with one half window, in the third story of the Court House, on the west side. The window was barred, & from my office, I could see him looking through the grates of his prison.") On the seventeenth Allen quoted from the Richmond *Republic*: "Fruits of the Boston Mob," which alleged that Southern gentlemen in business were trading in New York City instead of Boston — a threat calculated to strike terror on State Street. Allen also quoted from the *Post* a description of Sims's embarkation and a brief note from the New York *Herald* praising the extradition and damning "the raving & ranting of the abolition fanatics, the pettifogging of the abolition lawyers, and the resolutions and threats of Wendell Phillips, Theodore Parker, Lloyd Garrison, and other people of that stamp." Dana Jr., not mentioned, was by now himself a person "of that stamp." The *Sun* did not mention Lemuel Shaw's part in the remanding of Sims. Naturally Melville knew a good deal about this second important fugitive slave case of the year, but it did not capture his full moral attention.

In its spiritual and moral (and aesthetic) daring, the whaling book, to be sure, was intensely political, deliberately celebrating American heroes like Jackson, and more generally "that unshackled, democratic spirit of Christianity" that Melville had exalted in the essay on Hawthorne. Gansevoort Melville had stepped boldly into "the world's hustings" (*Moby-Dick*, ch. 33), seizing particular political issues and events as tickets to immediate political glory, and Herman Melville himself in some of the parts he added to the "completed" *Mardi* had fancied himself as national political commentator. That role he now renounced forever, content instead to become one of "the choice hidden handful of the Divine Inert," one of God's studiedly self-effacing "true princes of the Empire" (ch. 33). Even though he counted himself one of those "who always abhorred slavery as an atheistical iniquity," as he later wrote in the "Supplement" to *Battle-Pieces* (1866), in *Moby-Dick* (ch. 1) he asked, "Who aint a slave?" thereby shifting the focus from the immediate horrors of Negro slavery in the United States to the level of cosmic tyranny. Gansevoort in his campaigning for Polk had slept under the roof of the Hermitage, the guest of the aged Old Hickory. In *Moby-Dick* (ch. 26) Melville looked for higher shelter. If he (or his narrator Ishmael) in later portions of the book would "ascribe high qualities, though dark," would weave "tragic graces" around "meanest mariners, and renegades and castaways," he needed some defense against "mortal critics" — such as the reviewer of *White-Jacket* in the New York *Albion* (30 March 1850), who had scoffed at Melville's lugging into the issue of flogging, careless talk about "the 'essential dignity of man' and 'the spirit of our domestic institutions.'" Reacting to this rebuke, which he had read as he worked on his manuscript, Melville appealed not to the Democratic party but to the "great democratic God!" who had thundered Andrew Jackson "higher than a throne!"

Melville was not oblivious to what was going on in Boston, and not blind to the great national sin of slavery, but he was a man with obligations as a husband, father, son, son-in-law, and brother (a condition he always viewed in the light of the New Testament's absolutism). He was also a writer who just then was convinced that in the manuscript in his study he was approaching the tragic grandeur of Shakespeare's plays. (Whether he fully appreciated the comic greatness of his own book is less certain.) Melville had dealt with modern day-to-day encounters with monstrous life-forms — those encountered in the oceans of the world and those encountered in his own mind. In passing through "the great flood-gates of the wonder-world" (ch. 1) he was a child of the post-Napoleonic era, the first generation after the deciphering of the Rosetta Stone. Abandoned, he felt, by his own father and by the heavenly Father his mother believed in, he, like Ahab, battered his imagination against

natural and supernatural hieroglyphics, physical and psychological mysteries, against the puzzles that he compulsively identified and compulsively
brooded upon — from the meaning of the painting at the Spouter Inn to the
sources of the "sourceless primogenitures of the gods" (ch. 106, "Ahab's
Leg"). He was obsessed with his own need to finish his book and obsessed
with what he was learning, hour by hour, about human psychology from
observing the growth of his own mind.

Melville also now had obligations as a friend — to the former scrivener
Eli Fly, to the story-writer Nathaniel Hawthorne — and every passing day
brought him closer to the time when he would have to stop everything in
order to plow, plant, and do all the chores that had to be done at the right
time if he were to feed the family and the livestock. On Wednesday, 9 April,
he had an obligation no one let him forget: he had to be at the depot, waiting,
when the train arrived with his mother and all her purchases. She was bringing her daughter Kate, who had never seen Arrowhead, and who had become
dispirited enough for Caroline Thurston to apprise Augusta of her concerns,
in a letter Maria was carrying: "poor Kate needs the mountain air. I think she
has been far from well the last winter, but I have no doubt, a few days in the
country and the cheerful society of her sisters which she has always before
been accustomed to have, will effect a perfect cure."

It was 11 April before Melville again arrived at the Hawthorne house,
bearing the requested purchases (a bedstead and a clock), and received for his
trouble an inscribed copy of the new book, *The House of the Seven Gables*. (He
was also given a new commission, to find a pair of shoes in Pittsfield for
Julian.) During this visit Melville and Hawthorne talked about the isolation
of the winter in the Berkshires. Even Hawthorne had decided that one sometimes needed, as he wrote Duyckinck on 27 April, "a relief from too profound repose." Hawthorne had to go to Boston and Salem, and meant to do
so early in the summer, but he and Melville talked "of making an excursion"
to Manhattan, afterward. Melville had experienced London literary society,
however briefly, before cutting short his acquaintance with British writers
and other good fellows a year and a half before, but Hawthorne, just Hawthorne, was a sufficient reward for his old self-denial. It was no hardship for
Melville to have to do most of the talking when he was with his friend.

Melville may have been particularly talkative around Sophia on 12 or
14 March, or on 11 April, the last time she had seen him before she wrote to
her sister Elizabeth Peabody, on 7 May 1851. Then she described Melville as
speaking to Hawthorne "his innermost about GOD, the Devil & Life if so be
he can get at the Truth — for he is a boy in opinion — having settled nothing
as yet." She also described Melville in full flood of monologue:

> Nothing pleases me better than to sit & hear this growing man dash his
> tumultuous waves of thought up against Mr Hawthorne's great, genial, com-
> prehending silences — out of the profound of which a wonderful smile, or one
> powerful word sends back the foam & fury into a peaceful booming, calm —
> or perchance, not into a calm — but a murmuring expostulation — for there is
> never a "mush of concession" in him. Yet such a love & reverence & admira-
> tion for Mr Hawthorne as it is really beautiful to witness — & without doing
> any thing on his own part, except merely being, it is astonishing how people
> make him their innermost Father Confessor. Is it not?

But if Melville's behavior was Melvillean, Hawthorne's was consistent with
his usual behavior also. Long afterward, Joel Benton repeated a Fitz-Greene
Halleck anecdote in a memorial article on the poet in *Frank Leslie's Illustrated
Newspaper* (4 January 1868): "He said he had never met Hawthorne but once,
and that was at a table in New York: 'We happened to sit together, and I
assure you that for an hour we talked almost incessantly, although *Hawthorne
said nothing.*'" Others besides Melville found Hawthorne's silences companionable enough.

Since the previous summer Melville's own literary ambitions had been
stimulated by Hawthorne's success in the American literary marketplace, a
success about to be confirmed by *The House of the Seven Gables*. On 16 April,
apparently, Melville wrote Hawthorne a private criticism of the book Hawthorne had given him, written for what he called the Pittsfield "Secret Review," published by H. Melville, not P. Allen, the publisher of the Pittsfield
Sun. He had savored the book, he wrote Hawthorne, having spent almost an
hour in each separate gable. He praised the book in an elaboration of its
architectural title, comparing the book to "a fine old chamber, abundantly,
but still judiciously, furnished with precisely that sort of furniture best fitted
to furnish it." *The House of the Seven Gables* was a chamber dressed with rich,
old, ornate, comfortable trappings, and an "admirable sideboard, plentifully
stored with good viands"; in this inviting chamber "there is a smell as of old
wine in the pantry." So much about the pleasures afforded by the book might
have been said by any fanciful and appreciative reviewer, but what Melville
went on to say was not so much evoked by the book as by his own now
habitual tendency to see all things as problems to be brooded about, and
specifically to see the best, dark books and authors of those books as embodying problems or riddles: "in one corner" of the chamber he discerned "a dark
little black-letter volume in golden clasps, entitled 'Hawthorne: A Problem.'" If circumstances permitted, he would "like nothing better than to
devote an elaborate and careful paper to the full consideration and analysis of
the purport and significance of what so strongly characterizes all of this

author's writings." Melville recognized in Hawthorne's very American book "an awful truth" pervading one character, and he found "a certain tragic phase of humanity" embodied in Hawthorne's works as fully as in any author — of any country: "into no recorded mind has the intense feeling of the visable truth ever entered more deeply." In the essay on Hawthorne's *Mosses* Melville had claimed that "if you rightly look for it, you will almost always find that the author himself has somewhere furnished you with his own picture"; now he was conceiving of a book accessible, even hospitable, to the general reader, but containing, inconspicuously, for the acute reader, a reminder that the writer was not fully revealed in what first meets the eye. Instead, the writer was present in the pages of the book, or at some place in the pages, as a problem to tantalize even the best of such readers.

Having quite left all reference to *The House of the Seven Gables* behind him, Melville propounded what he called "the grand truth about Nathaniel Hawthorne": "He says NO! in thunder; but the Devil himself cannot make him say *yes*. For all men who say *yes*, lie; and all men who say *no*, — why, they are in the happy condition of judicious, unincumbered travellers in Europe; they cross the frontiers into Eternity with nothing but a carpet-bag, — that is to say, the Ego. Whereas those *yes*-gentry, they travel with heaps of baggage, and, damn them! they will never get through the Custom House." Here Melville checked himself, and asked mildly why "in the last stages of metaphysics a fellow always falls to *swearing* so?" He could "rip" for an hour, but he did not; instead, he merely asked Hawthorne to walk down "one of these mornings" and see him, no nonsense. The Hawthornes received the letter with intense appreciation. Sophia Hawthorne wrote to her sister Elizabeth Peabody about responses to *The House of the Seven Gables:* "Mr Lowell has written warmly— & Mr Duyckinck— & Herman Melville an extraordinary letter."

Melville's response to *The House of the Seven Gables* was grounded both in pride of personal acquaintance and in pride of shared nationality: the book had "bred great exhilaration and exultation with the remembrance that the architect of the Gables resides only six miles off, and not three thousand miles away, in England, say." Melville had himself influenced the public understanding of Hawthorne with his essay the year before, and both at the time he read *The House of the Seven Gables* and in the next months he had occasion to reflect on the direction Hawthorne's career had taken in the last two years, in relation to his own career. The still-unusual use of an American setting for a romance (despite some works by Cooper and others) was not lost upon Melville, and he began to think about placing a book of his own in a contemporary American setting, ashore rather than afloat, and embellished with Gothic trappings such as Hawthorne had used in *The House of the Seven*

Gables. Already in the *Mosses* essay Melville had said that the "great mistake seems to be, that even with those Americans who look forward to the coming of a great literary genius among us, they somehow fancy he will come in the costume of Queen Elizabeth's day, — be a writer of dramas founded upon old English history, or the tales of Boccaccio. Whereas, great geniuses are parts of the times; they themselves are the times; and possess a correspondent coloring." Into his whaling manuscript Melville worked a comparable discussion of the problems his narrator faced as a modern American "tragic dramatist": Ahab still moved before Ishmael "in all his Nantucket grimness and shagginess," but since "all outward majestical trappings and housings" were denied him, for his democratic hero he was forced to evoke a tragic sense through unaided imaginative power: "Oh, Ahab! what shall be grand in thee, it must needs be plucked at from the skies, and dived for in the deep, and featured in the unbodied air!" (ch. 33). Melville's next book, *Pierre,* would give him opportunity to write a romance founded upon recent American history and dealing with contemporary themes; whether the trappings and housings were Elizabethan or American would not be indisputably clear.

In the third and fourth weeks of April, as the protests in Boston quieted down again and as he calmed down from the excitement of reading his friend's book and writing a secret review of it, Melville at last took time to look back over the stacks of pages of his manuscript in Helen's and Augusta's handwriting in order to patch up what struck him as awkward and readily fixable and to eke out what struck him as readily augmentable. Ironically, some whaling source books he had long sought for were coming to hand when it was almost too late to use them. Knowing that Judge Shaw from his regular court sessions on Nantucket had formed friendships with prominent islanders, he had deputed his father-in-law to make some inquiries for him. In January 1851 the Nantucketer Thomas Macy sent Shaw a book Melville had heard about from "Mad Jack" Percival and others — William Lay and Cyrus M. Hussey's *A Narrative of the Mutiny, on Board the Ship Globe, of Nantucket, in the Pacific Ocean, Jan. 1824* (1828). In April 1851, too late for it to help Melville much with his whaling book, Macy laid hands on an imperfect copy of the rare *Narrative* by Owen Chase, which Melville prized despite its defects. (Thomas Macy gave Melville a copy of Obed Macy's *History of Nantucket* in July 1852, but Melville had already been plundering one copy or another by the winter of 1850–51.) Hawthorne's gift, *The Mariner's Chronicle,* consisted of tiny accounts of losses of ships in every imaginable way, even the "Destruction of the Essex by a whale," not by Owen Chase but attributed to the captain, George Pollard. The last major section consisted of ships lost by explosions, including "Blowing up of the steam frigate Fulton, at the Navy Yard, Brooklyn, June 4, 1829," a calamity Melville may actually have *heard* as a boy; and the woodcut of the wreck may well have triggered memories, for Allan Melvill may have taken the older boys to see what was left of the vessel. The woodcuts were uniformly primitive enough to be comical, especially the one depicting the unfortunate crew of the *Magpie*, who while "hanging on their boat, with the exception of two, were attacked and devoured by sharks." Under other circumstances, Melville might have made use of *The Mariner's Chronicle* in his manuscript, but there was no time.

At Arrowhead the whaling book was being talked about as if it were finished. Augusta gave that impression in her letter to Mary Blatchford on 22 March, for a month later, 22 April, Mary wrote: "So Herman has another book ready has he? Well I presume he has quiet enough, if that is all, to prepare his mind for literary meditations." Helen would have seen the irony in that last sentence, if Augusta shared the letter with her. After the indenture of lease was sold, after Hawthorne and Una then Fly had come and gone, during the excitement over the Sims case and Melville's own excitement about *The House of the Seven Gables*, Melville may have taken some moments to confront the problem of Bulkington, the Kentuckian who had loomed so tall in chapters written a twelvemonth or more earlier but had been neglected for much of the intervening time. Perhaps at this time Melville took his characteristically easy way out by writing a dismissive chapter calculated to take up about six inches in the book, "The Lee Shore." He was building shanties of chapters and essays, he called this sort of writing a little later, finishing the book up one way or another. (Unspoken was the thought that he did not have the luxury to build one fine new gable after another.) Augusta did the necessary new copying, so that in late April she and Herman were satisfied that a huge opening hunk of the manuscript was now in shape for others to see. That achieved, Melville on 25 April wrote Fletcher Harper asking for an advance on the manuscript. Almost two years earlier, on 1 July 1849, Sophia Melville unkindly had relayed to Augusta the news that her sister Helen had said a minister "looks as you do after a headache of fatigue when you have that sickly smile on your countenance." Augusta knew she wore that sickly smile when disorder about her became quite intolerable, so as soon as Herman dismissed her as his copyist, late in April, she made her escape to the Manor House, thinking the manuscript was about ready to go to press.

By the time he signed all the documents concerning the New York indenture of lease, Melville had known that he would not have enough money to pay for the renovations he had begun at Arrowhead. Since then, any small amount of disposable money from the sale of the New York house had run out fast. A Harpers' clerk brought Melville's account up to date on the twenty-ninth, and on 30 April the Harpers wrote Melville, refusing to give him an advance, citing "an extensive and expensive addition" to their plant then clinching their case with the news that his account stood with him already in their debt by "nearly seven hundred dollars." The letter was addressed to Melville in Pittsfield, but at some time Allan endorsed it "Harper & Brothers/April 30ᵗʰ 1851," and on it he wrote three sets of numbers, verifying the Harper lists of expenses in arriving at Herman's earnings from *White-Jacket*. As always in his dealings with the Harpers, Melville could not wholly rid himself of his old bitterness toward them for the damage their refusal of *Typee* had done to his spirit in 1845. Now after such a cool refusal of an advance and a haughty reminder of how deeply in debt he was, he behaved recklessly.

Vulnerable, frightened, Melville hearkened as he had not done in the fall to the easy blandishments of his old friend who had plenty of money to spare and wanted nothing more than to help the author just when he needed help, not years later. Now, money could free him to hire a typesetter for the best book he had yet written, then free him to look for the best contract a New York (or even Boston or Philadelphia) publisher might offer him for his whaling book. If Melville received the letter from the Harpers in Pittsfield on 1 May, then T. D. Stewart was apparently there, having made the stopover on the way to Lansingburgh that he had spoken of to Maria, for Melville and Stewart were together that day. On 1 May, late, after the mail was read and digested, Melville was "induced to accept" a loan from Stewart to the tune of $2050 for five years, at nine percent. (The passive construction is Melville's, in a letter to his father-in-law on 12 May 1856.) If Lizzie had known about the loan from Stewart, she would have resisted it with all her strength, indoctrinated as she had been since childhood with an absolute horror of debt.

39

The Final Dash at *The Whale*
May–September 1851

Great gains come daily to ingenious men
From that admired instrument the Pen.

"Allan Melvills Book," 1796

SOME OF THE MONEY MELVILLE borrowed from Stewart, perhaps a great deal of it, must have gone directly to Dr. Brewster to pay off the remainder of the purchase money, supplementing the inadequate amount Melville had received from the sale of the indenture of lease on the Fourth Avenue house. Leaving the plowing partially done or still untouched, Melville made an urgent trip to New York early in May — one day in the cars down, one day for business, one day in the cars for home. He arrived in Manhattan armed with Stewart's money and more obviously cumbered with a substantial portion of the manuscript. There he tested out Allan's new and inconvenient uptown house on Thirty-first Street for two nights, so as to have his one full day in the city. He had decided that the way to avoid dealing with the miserly Harpers was to have the new book printed at his own expense, so he might sell the plates to the publisher who made him the best offer.

As usual, Melville called at Clinton Place to consult with Evert Duyckinck, who may have had in the house or his office the portrait of Hawthorne by Cephas Giovanni Thompson, sent down from Boston to be engraved for the *Dollar Magazine*. Duyckinck recommended the printer who set the *Literary World*, Robert Craighead of 112 Fulton Street, whom Melville knew as the compositor for the American edition of *Typee*. Most likely without shopping for the best price, he came to terms with Craighead and left him the manuscript to set and then to make stereotype plates. His burden off his hands, he moved around the city seeing, to his pleasure, a great deal of publicity about *The House of the Seven Gables*, in the form of advertisements and reviews. Now ready to go back home, and prepared to travel light, he warned Allan and Sophia to expect him back from Arrowhead in a few weeks for a prolonged stay, to proof the sheets. Sophia was not well, as Augusta's letter of 16 May makes clear ("I hope to hear that she feels stronger, & is no longer troubled with that wearisome pain in the back. Those arms, I trust, measure a little more in circumference, & those poor wrists are not quite as thin. I can imagine what a delicately slender appearance they present draped in the fashionable undersleeve"). Not heeding Sophia's weakness, Melville took his welcome for granted: how could his presence be burdensome, since she did not cook or clean the house? He had made a flying visit indeed, for he *had* to do the spring chores, *then*, not in a week or two.

With a large section delivered to the printer, Melville's work on *The Whale* went into abeyance, its ending not yet written. In May the women at Arrowhead, Maria, Lizzie, Helen, Kate, and Fanny, were caught up in the renovations as well as Herman, who also had the farm work to perform. In her first two weeks in the safety of the Manor House, Augusta received no letter from Allan or Sophia and only one letter from the farm, as she wrote Allan on 16 May. She understood why only one of the family had written her: "They are all so busy there, that I suppose they dont feel as if they could spare the time to write often." In the fall she had made the best of the quaintness of Arrowhead, but she had suffered from certain inconveniences, and now she allowed herself to express one of the strongest traits of her nature, the longing for order. Maria was there to supervise any help they had, and to supervise Herman on those many points where her experience was greater than his. The silence from Arrowhead meant that Augusta was falling behind in her knowledge of the renovations going forward: "The whole place will have been so much improved by the time of my return, that I expect hardly to recognize it." She assumed Allan had received letters more recently than she had, so that he knew just how far they had progressed, especially since he had seen Herman. From the single letter she had received from Arrowhead she had learned of a trip Herman had by now made to New York City, as she said to Allan on 16 May: "So you had a flying visit from Herman? When does he make the longer one? That book of his, will create a great interest, I think. It is very fine." Augusta may have known before she left that Herman was planning a flying visit, or the letter from Arrowhead may have reported that Herman had already made it or was about to make it—before the sixteenth, when Augusta was writing, her use of the past tense shows. Now she was looking ahead: "How I long to have everything in beautiful order, & you & Sophia & the children there enjoying the country air."

In March and April Melville had been torn between the need to sit "clinched" to his desk and the desire to make the solid old farmhouse more comfortable. He had supervised carpenters rather than doing all the work himself, but Maria had not brought an Irishman back, and he had no hired man to help him get in the crops. Now, he simply had to surrender to the seasonal urgencies of the farm, however torn he was by the equal and opposing urgency to write the rest of his book and see it through the press. He now did field work such as he had performed at Uncle Thomas's in 1837 and for the young Londoner named Edward and his partner the Yankee James Martin on Eimeo in 1842. In the early May letter to Hawthorne (previously dated 1 June[?]) Melville described himself as having been "building and patching and tinkering away in all directions." He did some carpentry work himself, he had to plant his corn and potatoes (he intended to show Hawthorne "some famous ones by and by"), and he also had "many other things to attend to, all accumulating upon this one particular season." He plowed not with Charlie but with his ox (he had two milk cows also). He wrote: "I work myself; and at night my bodily sensations are akin to those I have so often felt before, when a hired man, doing my day's work from sun to sun." In the evening he felt "completely done up, as the phrase is" — too weary to endure the jolting horseback or wagon ride to the Hawthorne cottage and back. Nine months earlier, he remembered, rain had kept him under a roof at the Melvill place (whether in the house or the barn) on the morning that he had written the bulk of his essay on Hawthorne. Now, in early May 1851, he wrote not about Hawthorne but to him, and made his letter very long because his writing on the book was suspended and his outdoor chores were also disrupted: "It is a rainy morning; so I am indoors, and all work suspended. I feel cheerfully disposed, and therefore I write a little bluely." He was a little the worse for wear: "see my hand! — four blisters on this palm, made by hoes & hammers within the last few days."

From points here and there in this long letter one can extract some rough facts about the status of *The Whale*. Some three weeks earlier, say about 25 April, when he asked the Harpers for an advance, Melville had stopped work at a crucial point: then, he had left *The Whale* "in his flurry." Soon, but not yet, he would have to finish the manuscript: "I'm going to take him by his jaw, however, before long, and finish him up in some fashion or other." He would leave Pittsfield as soon as the crops were in: "In a week or so, I go to New York, to bury myself in a third-story room, and work and slave on my 'Whale' while it is driving through the press. *That* is the only way I can finish it now, — I am so pulled hither and thither by circumstances. The calm, the coolness, the silent grass-growing mood in which a man *ought* always to compose, — that, I fear, can seldom be mine. Dollars damn me; and the malicious Devil is forever grinning in upon me, holding the door ajar." The lack of dollars damned him to what seemed like ceaseless writing, while "the malicious Devil" hovered nearby — a pun on printer's devil, Hawthorne knew, the boy hired to snatch copy from the author's desk and run with it to press. The pun was no idle flourish, for in fact, sooner rather than later, Craighead would cry for more copy in order to finish setting and stereotyping the book. There was no possibility Melville could finish his book in anything like ideal conditions.

This long and meandering letter has proved irresistibly quotable since Julian Hawthorne first published it, without Melville's permission, in *Nathaniel Hawthorne and His Wife* (1884), without a date and with, surely, some transcriptional errors. The document itself has disappeared. Much of the opening section of the letter is devoted to intellectual ripping, in Melville's term, swearing — or preaching — on how one may assert simultaneously "an aristocracy of the brain" while being "earnest in behalf of political equality." In his bravado about his "ruthless democracy on all sides," Melville allows that Hawthorne may "possibly feel a touch of a shrink, or something of that sort." But Truth "is the silliest thing under the sun": "Try to get a living by the Truth — and go to the Soup Societies." Even Solomon, "the truest man who ever spoke," may have "a little *managed* the truth with a view to popular conservatism; or else there have been many corruptions and interpolations of the text." This was, Melville recognized, "an endless sermon," and he dropped it, as he repeatedly came down to earth from such extended flights in letters to Hawthorne. Tormentingly near to finishing the book in which he proposed, all fatuously, to make money by telling the Truth, and tormentingly kept from working on it, Melville looked, glancingly but intensely, at his intellectual life and his career — first the present condition of affairs, then the probable future, then the past.

Reordered, like the allusions to his progress on *The Whale*, a rough personal history emerges. The look backward constituted Melville's frankest surviving self-examination:

> My development has been all within a few years past. I am like one of those seeds taken out of the Egyptian Pyramids, which, after being three thousand years a seed and nothing but a seed, being planted in English soil, it developed itself, grew to greenness, and then fell to mould. So I. Until I was twenty-five, I had no development at all. From my twenty-fifth year I date my life. Three weeks have scarcely passed, at any time between then and now, that I have not unfolded within myself. But I feel that I am now come to the inmost leaf of the bulb, and that shortly the flower must fall to the mould.

He may have used "twenty-fifth" year accurately, to mean the year he spent on the *United States* under the mentorship of Jack Chase and the literary society of the afterguard or maintop, but he may have been using the term in its colloquial sense of the year before his twenty-sixth birthday, the year he returned home from the Pacific and wrote *Typee*. As to the present, he was doomed to frustration, for he could never write what he was "most moved to write." That was banned — not only banned because the missionaries and their defenders would attack it but banned because it would not pay. Forbidden to write what he most wanted to write, he could not bring himself to write "the *other* way," in a deliberate attempt to please the public. He concluded: "So the product is a final hash, and all my books are botches." He was speaking specifically about his methods of composition, remembering what he had done a few weeks before, most obviously in writing Bulkington out of a place of prominence in the book, but surely in other Herr Alexander–like sleight-of-hand operations performed so deftly that readers find nothing to boggle at in the printed text. His books were hashes partly because he habitually worked bits from other books into them, and they were botches not merely because they were bungled but because they were patched, never written sequentially, one chapter growing out of the previous chapter while determining the shape of the next, first to last, until the end. In the weeks just ahead, he had to finish *The Whale* somehow, but however competently he did the job, there seemed no point to his driving himself as hard as he knew he would do: "What's the use of elaborating what, in its very essence, is so short-lived as a modern book? Though I wrote the Gospels in this century, I should die in the gutter."

Melville's jumping ship to live briefly among Polynesian natives was not one of the great adventures in world history, but his published accounts had, perhaps inexplicably to himself, become one of the best known adventures of an English speaker in the century, so that Melville was repeatedly spoken of in the same breath with Robinson Crusoe. In Melville's own mind, the adventure of writing *Mardi* had been altogether more hazardous than the threat of cannibalism he described in *Typee* and the actual imprisonment he described in *Omoo*. Melville now decided that the adventure of writing *Moby-Dick* was itself one of the great American adventures. It was, after all, the most daring and prolonged aesthetic adventure that had ever been conducted in the hemisphere in the English language, and he had rightly determined that his Miltonically dubious battle had to be fought on his best approximation to the plains of heaven, the amphitheater stretched out below Mount Greylock. As he drew *Moby-Dick* to a hastily written close, what was on his mind, along with the narrative under his pen, was the astonishing adventure he had been witnessing for many months, the psychological development that had followed hard upon the intellectual development he recorded in *Mardi*.

Mindful of the reviewers of *Mardi*, *Redburn*, and *White-Jacket* who had pronounced that nothing he had written subsequently compared to the freshness and originality of *Typee*—not even *Omoo*—he now lamented the nature of his reputation and the way he might go down in history, being careful to ignore the obvious fact that many readers thought of him primarily as Fayaway's lover, and a sexual libertine: "What 'reputation' H. M. has is horrible. Think of it! To go down to posterity is bad enough, any way; but to go down as a 'man who lived among the cannibals'! When I speak of posterity, in reference to myself, I only mean the babies who will probably be born in the moment immediately ensuing upon my giving up the ghost. I shall go down to some of them, in all likelihood. 'Typee' will be given to them, perhaps, with their gingerbread." Alternating for weeks between vainglory and terror, Melville knew how greatly he had written in *The Whale* but he could not forget how badly he had misjudged the way *Mardi* would be received. He could not tell anything like the "Truth" of his financial morass to Hawthorne — that he was on the rack, day by day, doing farm work and not reading proof, revising, and composing the still unwritten ending of the book that had to make money, lest he find himself out of a career and even out of a house. Lemuel Shaw might not let him, his mother, sisters, wife, Malcolm, and the unborn child die in the gutter, or a ditch on the way toward the village, but the same collateral, Arrowhead, was twice-mortgaged, in effect, to different creditors, and besides the $1500 that he owed Dr. Brewster on the farm, he owed roughly $2750 more, taking his debt to the Harpers together with his new debt to Stewart.

In the early May letter to Hawthorne, Melville said he intended to return to New York in a week or so. By the time he left for New York, he had received word that on 20 May the Hawthorne's child, Rose, had been born; Lizzie was just halfway through her own pregnancy. When Melville left, he took the rest of the manuscript, his writing materials, and Helen, for he needed her to copy behind him — she copying in a guest room on the second floor, most likely, within sound of the babies, he writing in Allan's third-story room, under the roof, on bad days an ovenlike cell, when he was not making the trip to and from the compositor's plant at the southern tip of the island. For some days around the first week of June, Abby and Richard Lathers stayed at Allan's house also, during construction of Winyah, in New Rochelle.

Then Melville was jolted out of his briefly renewed concentration on the book. On the afternoon of Tuesday, 10 June, Aunt Mary Chandonette Gansevoort died at George and Catherine Curtis's house in Brooklyn. Maria had visited her in March without realizing how near she was to death. When news of the death came, Augusta felt she had to return to Arrowhead the next Saturday rather than remain at the Manor House, for she knew that the more conventional of the "Dutch people" there would be shocked if she did not wear the full mourning that she could not afford to buy. She had feared something was wrong when Cuyler Van Vechten arrived at the Manor House on Wednesday before breakfast, so she had a moment to prepare herself for bad news. It was some relief that Cuyler was going down for the funeral and could carry her letter to Cousin Kate. Even Uncle Peter had gone down, on the night boat on the eleventh, although a headache prevented Aunt Susan's accompanying him. Mamma, it was understood, could not go, being in charge of running Arrowhead, while Kate and Fanny helped care for Malcolm and the very uncomfortable Lizzie, pregnant and suffering horribly from her allergies. Helen, Herman, and Allan represented the Melvilles at the funeral, perhaps with Sophia, although she was still unwell. Augusta reasonably suggested that Helen should stay on with Cousin Kate a few days, if Herman could "spare" her. She did not volunteer to come down and take over the copying, but she added: "How does Herman's book progress — tell me something about it in your next letter."

The death triggered in Herman and Helen old and painful memories, for they could remember Mary Ann Chandonette Gansevoort from their earliest childhood (Helen could even remember Uncle Leonard, dead so long that of the other living Melville children only Herman may have had faint memories of him). For long periods Aunt Mary and her younger children had been part of the large North Market Street household in Albany. Now Helen and Herman recalled how they had long associated Aunt Mary with primordial mysteries, for she had been with Maria Melvill in New York City for Catherine's birth in 1825 and had been in the house of the Hero of Fort Stanwix for the death of Catherine Van Schaick Gansevoort in 1830. Herman recalled being the only Melville to accompany Uncle Peter to the Common Albany Cemetery in the summer of 1832, when the ocean-tossed body of Aunt Mary's son Peter Leonard Gansevoort was at last put into the earth. Herman as recently as March 1849 had ranged about the Navy Yard in Charlestown with Guert, and Helen and Cousin Kate Curtis had remained close, long after Guert had played the cavalier to Helen and Lizzie in Boston. Even Allan, the master of the Thirty-first Street house, had dutifully kept up the connection, despite his private expressions, years past, of disrespect toward his aunt.

Herman and Helen, and even Allan, were more pained than comforted by Uncle Peter's unexpected attendance at the funeral of his sister-in-law, for the sight of him stirred up more memories, not least of the lawsuit George Curtis had filed against him, and the lengthy saga of the spoons, symbols of Uncle Peter's selfishness. Augusta had been sufficiently reminded the month before of Uncle Peter's total estrangement from Mary Ann Chandonette Gansevoort: he had not even known of her illness when Augusta told him, and the fact that Augusta had a chance to tell him was in itself astonishing, for his attention to her was so unexpected as to be suspect: what devious motive lay behind his display of avuncular devotion? Was it shame at his knowledge that his second wife had told Augusta the latest financial news, news that Augusta had relayed to Allan on 16 May: "Did you know that Uncle had sold Grandmamma's house to Mr Delesan? Aunt Susan told me of it this morning, & said that he had received $13000 for it." It was Grandmamma's house, but Uncle Peter pocketed the money from its sale. If Uncle Peter had shared the $13,000, even a portion of it, with his sister Maria, Herman might not have abased himself to Tertullus Stewart on the first of May. The death of Mrs. Leonard Gansevoort in such conditions, in her son-in-law's home in Brooklyn, not in her own home, or a home owned by one of her sons, irresistibly evoked memories in Herman and Helen of how the widows had been exiled to Lansingburgh and Waterford, east of the sun and west of the moon, and how the children of the widows had been deprived of schooling just when they had to have it, if they were to benefit from it at all. If their mothers' lives had been different, Guert Gansevoort might have behaved another way in November and December 1842, and Herman Melville might not have found himself in the middle of 1851 deeply in debt. Aunt Mary might even have been buried by the side of her husband in Albany, as Catherine Van Vechten vividly remembered had been her wish, not put down alone into the strange earth of Brooklyn. At this death there was very little Herman and the other mourners could look back on in joy.

Melville released Helen so she could manage the Brooklyn house while Cousin Kate and her husband got out of the house of death for a few days. On 14 June, two days after the funeral, Melville returned the two volumes of Scoresby to the New York Society Library, after keeping them for thirteen and a half months. He was done with putting factual whaling information into the book, at least. When Craighead proved more concerned with regular jobs like printing the Duyckincks' *Literary World* than with a private special job like *The Whale*, Melville became increasingly "wearied with the long delay of the printers" (as he wrote Hawthorne on 29 June) and "disgusted with the heat and dust of the babylonish brick-kiln of New York." (For months even New Yorkers had been complaining about the dust. On 8 April Sophia's sister-in-law Caroline, Charles Thurston's wife, had suggested half seriously, in a letter to Augusta, that gentlemen would have to start wearing veils because of the terrible dust kicked up by sewer-laying and street-paving.) Carrying a bundle of proofs, probably galleys, Melville "came back to the country to feel the grass — and end the book reclining on it" if he could, he wrote Hawthorne on 29 June. That was something of a wild hope, since the book was "only half through the press." And it was not finished: "Shall I send you a fin of the *Whale* by way of a specimen mouthful? The tail is not yet cooked — though the hell-fire in which the whole book is broiled might not unreasonably have cooked it all ere this. This is the book's motto (the secret one), — Ego non baptiso te in nomine — but make out the rest yourself."

Melville was recalling Francis Palgrave's essay on "Superstition and Knowledge," which he had read in the July 1823 issue of the *Quarterly Review* or elsewhere. On a blank leaf in the seventh volume of his Shakespeare (Geoffrey Sanborn showed in 1992), Melville jotted down phrases from Palgrave about the "raving madness" of witch-hunters such as the German persecutors who convicted priests "of baptising in the following form: — Ego non baptizo te in nomine Patris et Filii et Spiritus Sancti — sed in nomine Diaboli." In echoing to Hawthorne this witch-hunter's formula, Melville was anticipating that reviewers might respond to his prophetic truth-telling by treating him once again as a devilish opponent of Christianity. Any of his dark passages, however splendid, might be seized upon by witch-hunting reviewers who, from the time the man of the *Evangelist* rose against him in 1846, had sought to drive him from authorship. (Acknowledging their power, in 1856 he thought of dedicating *The Confidence-Man* to "victims of Auto de Fe.")

In this 29 June letter, forgetting just when and what he had written to Hawthorne last, Melville recapitulated the work of the spring and early summer: "Since you have been here, I have been building some shanties of houses (connected with the old one) and likewise some shanties of chapters and essays. I have been plowing and sowing and raising and painting and printing and praying, — and now begin to come out upon a less bustling time, and to enjoy the calm prospect of things from a fair piazza at the north of the old farm house here." Melville was torn between mundane responsibilities for overseeing printing (which he had never before had to deal with) and the obligation (however exalted) to write the "tail," the last chapters of *Moby-Dick*, including those on the final chase, as well as the necessity of going over the proofs to make whatever small insertions and other adjustments he could reasonably make in order to harmonize, as well as he could, a book written over many months in such different circumstances under such differing impulses. In the process he overlooked a good many words that Helen and Augusta had miscopied from his manuscript along with many of his own blunders in transcription (as when he took an old-style *s* for an *f*), and he left a good many anomalies, such as whether the *Pequod* had a capstan or a windlass, whether the crew numbered thirty or more than forty, whether Radney was a Vineyarder or a Nantucketer, whether Tashtego at one point and Queequeg at another should have been sleeping in the forecastle with the men instead of aft, and he left, as well, at least one powerfully introduced character, Bulkington, who seems, in the book as published, vestigial from some earlier plan.

Melville was tantalizingly near to being free of the book, but the remaining work he described was serious enough: reading and correcting proof for the second half of the book, and writing the final chapters. In the 29 June letter he more or less invited Hawthorne to come and spend a day, if he could and if he wanted to, and when he was "quite free" of his "present engagements" Melville was going to treat himself to a ride to Lenox and a visit with Hawthorne: "Have ready a bottle of brandy, because I always feel like drinking that heroic drink when we talk ontological heroics together." It was "rather a crazy letter in some respects," he recognized, and asked Hawthorne to "ascribe it to the intoxicating effects of the latter end of June operating upon a very susceptible and peradventure febrile temperament." At least he had emerged from the melancholic mood and thoughts that had struck him in the spring: "This most persuasive season has now for weeks recalled me from certain crotchetty and over doleful chimaeras, the like of which men like you and me and some others, forming a chain of God's posts round the world, must be content to encounter now and then, and fight them the best way we can." He was profoundly frustrated — nearly done with a book he knew was great, but denied the time to make it as good as he might have made it; free enough from plowing and haying to think of visiting his friend, but not free enough to saddle up and ride the six miles to see him.

The "present engagements" included the Fourth of July visit planned by Lemuel and Hope Shaw. Five months pregnant (and suffering so badly from her annual "rose cold" that she spent half her time with her face in a wet towel), on 30 June Lizzie wrote to her father that Herman would be at the depot with the chariot on Thursday, 3 July. She was writing in "a great hurry between daylight and dark," so that she could hardly guide her pen, and miserable from the intense heat for the past two days. It was cheering to know that the Berkshire heat would not last. Herman wanted to write great books at his own pace, in that calm, that coolness, that "silent grass-growing mood in which a man *ought* always to compose," but he also wanted to play the host at Arrowhead. His indulgent father-in-law had made it possible for him to live there, but he could not bring himself to tell Shaw about the loan he had taken from T. D. Stewart, so henceforth a measure of fearful guilt and irrational resentment was intermixed with the genuinely filial emotions Herman felt for the judge. There was no more thought of a towered house, although the quaint farmhouse of the crooked and cramped stairs was never going to be as grand as the Melvill house he knew so well. That house was in the hands, now, of comparative strangers, for the Morewoods had at last taken possession. Arrowhead at least was his, and now it was fit to receive guests in.

The Berkshires had become steadily more popular as a vacation spot during the 1840s, and Robert Melvill for once had been practical in thinking he would find lodgers if he turned the Melvill place into a resort. To all the former residents of the Fourth Avenue house, it now seemed that Morewood's buying that estate and Melville's purchasing Arrowhead had sealed the Berkshires as a notable summering place. Charles Thurston and Allan were taken with what they knew from Allan's brief visit and from Maria's stories. Both of them, as early as April, began longing to vacation in the Berkshires. On 8 April, in a letter Maria carried home to Augusta, Charles's seriously ill wife, Caroline, had written: "Allan is so much engrossed with thoughts of the country that he can scarcely content himself in the city — and my good husband, has the same feeling to a certain extent, & what changes another year may bring about it is impossible to foresee." She meant that she herself might die. Charlie took her for a brief stay at a boardinghouse in Pittsfield in June, before the peak of the season, when Herman and Helen were both away in New York.

On 30 June Allan wrote to Helen, who was still running the house for Kate and George Curtis in Brooklyn, while they were away. Tom's ship, the *Celestial*, had arrived on the twenty-ninth — without Tom. Sophia's young brother Henry Thurston, now eighteen, had boarded her and found that his chum had left the ship "at San Francisco where he is engaged in lightering" (working on a barge in the bay, unloading ships that could not anchor at the wharves) "making $15 a day" — a fabulous salary. Allan did not know what truth there was to the report, but planned on going on board himself to check. He was mainly concerned with plans for going to and from Pittsfield. He had determined that George Curtis had not reported in at his office, and on that basis had decided that George and Cousin Kate might stay away until after 4 July, Friday. That complicated things, for he had plans for Helen, who seemed to be stuck in Brooklyn. On the first of July, a Tuesday, Allan arrived in Pittsfield with the still ailing Sophia, planning to take her back for a dental appointment the next Tuesday by the first train (leaving the two babies and the nurse at Arrowhead). He counted on Helen's leaving the house of mourning in Brooklyn to accompany Sophia back to Pittsfield on the ninth. On 2 July, Sophia's brother Charles and his wife, Carrie, were to return to Pittsfield, where they had arranged to board at the Reed place. (Charlie was serious about this vacation: he was taking his horse with him.) As promised, Herman was at the depot "in the chariot" on Thursday the third of July to pick up Judge Shaw and Hope Shaw, who stayed on through Monday morning.

Some of the family went to the public celebration of Independence Day, where the Pittsfield poet, the young widower John C. Hoadley, read his newly composed poem, "The Union." Lizzie would not have ventured out, but she and Herman remembered that Hoadley was oddly connected to them through Aunt Lucy's stepdaughter. On that occasion, momentous for the entire family, Hoadley met Catherine Melville, who by then had fully recovered her health and spirits in the society of Augusta and Fanny. Better for him that he should have met Helen, but good for the family that he met Catherine, at least. In the constant motion of the household, the Shaws left for Boston early on 7 July. Later that day Melville inscribed in his copy of Burton's *Anatomy of Melancholy* a poignant discovery Allan had made, a faint signature, "A. Melvill": "I bought this book more than four years ago at Gowans' Store in New York. Today, Allan in looking at it, first detected the above pencil signature of my father's; who, — as it now appears — must have had the book, with many others, sold at auction, at least twenty-five years ago. — Strange!" Strange, but not so strange as the transformation of the docile boy (who seemed to have chosen commerce as a profession) into a writer with powerful affinities to Burton and other great writers of the seventeenth century. For many months, Melville had hardly taken the time to make such a reflection anywhere but in his manuscript, or in a few revelatory letters to Hawthorne. He really was nearing the end of work on the book.

About 15 July, as Melville was finishing his book, Hawthorne put a private message for him into his *A Wonder-Book for Boys and Girls:* "On the hither side of Pittsfield sits Herman Melville, shaping out the gigantic conception of his 'White Whale,' while the gigantic shape of Graylock looms upon him from his study-window." In February 1851 Hawthorne had sat in that study, looking out that window, while nearby lay the manuscript of *The Whale*, or, as Hawthorne remembered it, *The White Whale*. That was the dominant image Hawthorne carried away from the visit — the great white whale in relation to the physical grandeur of the mountain to the north. By the time Hawthorne wrote his compliment into his own book, Melville had finished the last chapters and the epilogue of *The Whale* and had capped everything with his prefatory "Extracts," for which he had combed his whaling sources.

Before 20 July, Melville received Richard Bentley's letter of 3 July containing a generous offer of £150 on account of half profits in notes at three and six months. He accepted the offer on the twentieth, advising on the progress: "I am now passing thro' the press, the closing sheets of my new work; so that I shall be able to forward it to you in the course of two or three weeks — perhaps a little longer." Two years before, on 20 July 1849, Melville had confidently assured Bentley: "ere long, doubtless, we shall have something of an international law — so much desired by all American writers — which shall settle this matter upon the basis of justice. The only marvel is, that it does not now exist." Now Melville despaired of seeing American approval of an international copyright in his time, since only the interested parties, British publishers and the American authors, desired its passage, and he retreated from his stance of literary nationalism: "Who are the authors? — A handful. And what influence have they to bring to bear upon any question whose settlement must necessarily assume a political form? — They can bring scarcely any influence whatever. This country & nearly all its affairs are governed by sturdy backwoodsmen — noble fellows enough, but not at all literary, & who care not a fig for any authors except those who write those most saleable of all books nowadays — ie — the newspapers, & magazines." Keeping his career alive had meant becoming obligated to Judge Shaw for $5000, to Brewster for the $1500 mortgage, and being in debt to his American publisher for some $700 and to a friend for $2050 — not to mention $1000 and more that Bentley had lost by publishing Melville's previous three books. No lingering exuberance could make Melville exaggerate the growth in "the number of cultivated, catholic men" in America who might be counted on to support a national literature: "they are nothing in comparison with the overwhelming majority who care nothing about it." Melville mailed this letter, along with the signed agreement, on 29 July.

Melville finished the Craighead proofs of *The Whale* before he wrote Hawthorne again on 22 July, but "one way and another," he was "not yet a disengaged man"; he was busy with various unspecified things, "not incessantly" but enough to require his "frequent tinkerings," and it was "the height of the haying season" ("my nag is dragging me home his winter's dinners all the time"). He was going to be free "very soon," and knew how he wanted to celebrate: "the earliest good chance I get, I shall roll down to you. My dear fellow-being, we — that is, you and I — must hit upon some little bit of vagabondism, before Autumn comes. Graylock — we must go and vagabondize there. But ere we start we must dig a deep hole and bury all the Blue Devils, there to abide till the Last Day" — the Blue Devils, like Ishmael's hypos, being Melville's equivalent of what was later called simply the blues. Hawthorne had taken many a stroll with Thoreau, and had headed across country with Emerson, but Melville never got to vagabondize with him, and indeed never got off alone with him for the smallest tramp through his beloved Berkshires, other than around the little red farmhouse; in March there had been so much snow that they had not even walked away from the barn onto the rest of the 160 acres of Arrowhead.

Instead, the house began to fill up with other guests, with attendant strains. Kate's household compulsion for precision (far more extreme than Augusta's love of order) grated on Sophia, to the point that Kate thought her sister-in-law had taken "a positive dislike" to her this summer at Arrowhead (a comment quoted by Maria to Augusta, 6 March 1852). Sam Shaw arrived from Cambridge on 22 July, and six days later Melville invited Duyckinck and his brother to come to Arrowhead any time after 5 August, preferably 6 August: "Come, and give yourself a week's holyday on the hay-mow." On 29 July Samuel Savage (mustachioed in Central American style) arrived at Arrowhead and amused himself with his cousin Sam Shaw; the voyeuristic interest provided by the Shakers in Lebanon remained undiminished. While the boys were there Mrs. Morewood gave a costume party in honor of a sister's wedding. Cornelius Mathews was there in spirit and in the form of three toasts that he had sent, one a slightly vulgar comment on the latest dress of feminists: "*Pittsfield beauty* — may it ever be in bloom, but never in bloomer." In "A Petit Fancy Party in Berkshire," by "Miantonomah," the local poet and journalist Joseph Smith, in imitation of Mathews's celebration of last year's masked ball, wrote up the festivities for the 7 August Boston *Evening Transcript*, first giving an idyllic description of the setting, in which he alluded to distinguished prior lodgers there such as ex-president Tyler and Professor Longfellow:

> Some mile or so from the village of Pittsfield is a romantically beautiful estate, adjoining those of Hermann Melville and Oliver Wendell Holmes. Its splendid overview of the North Berkshire valley, stretching away to "Greylock cloud-girdled on his Mountain throne," its silver lakelet, its woods and walks, have made it long noted among the beautiful sites of the country. The fine square old mansion, half hid among its trees, has often been the haunt of dignified statesmen and no less dignified men of letters, and dignified belles as well — *belles lettres*, a witty friend overlooking me suggests. It is now the residence of our kind-hearted friends, Mr and Mrs M., and the very home of "free-hearted hospitality."

In pushing herself into a frenetic season of partying Sarah Morewood may have been literally feverish, each afternoon and evening, from early stages of tuberculosis, but she kept the focus off herself. In the *Evening Transcript* Joseph Smith complimented her on "that rare talent which she so preeminently possesses of putting her guests at ease." (The party may have been given on 1 August. If so, Melville himself did not attend, for he had other plans.)

That day, 1 August, Melville celebrated his thirty-second birthday by making an unannounced visit to Hawthorne, who just then was keeping Bachelors' Hall with five-year-old Julian (just the age of *Mosses from an Old Manse*), Sophia having left with Una to display the baby to the Peabody and Hawthorne families. Hawthorne made this account in his journal:

> Returning to the Post office got Mr. Tappan's mail and my own and proceeded homeward, but clambered over the fence and sat down in Love Grove

to read the papers. While thus engaged, a cavalier on horseback came along
the road, and saluted me in Spanish; to which I replied by touching my hat,
and went on with the newspaper. But the cavalier renewing his salutation, I
regarded him more attentively, and saw that it was Herman Melville! So,
hereupon, Julian and I hastened to the road, where ensued a greeting, and we
all went homeward together, talking as we went. Soon, Mr Melville alighted,
and put Julian into the saddle; and the little man was highly pleased, and sat
on the horse with the freedom and fearlessness of an old equestrian, and had a
ride of at least a mile homeward.

Hawthorne prevailed upon the black servant Mrs. Peters to make tea and
Melville drank a cup, "but was afraid to drink much, because it would keep
him awake." He was strung taut without caffeine. After supper, Hawthorne
put Julian to bed, and when the men were alone they smoked cigars in the
house, where the ban on nicotine was absolute. Unlike caffeine, nicotine was
soothing, not overstimulating, and both men relaxed into profound communion with each other, as Hawthorne recorded: "Melville and I had a talk
about time and eternity, things of this world and of the next, and books, and
publishers, and all possible and impossible matters, that lasted pretty deep
into the night, and if the truth must be told, we smoked cigars even within
the sacred precincts of the sitting room. At last, he arose, and saddled his
horse (whom we had put into the barn) and rode off for his own domicile; and
I hastened to make the most of what little sleeping-time remained for me."
Melville, a cherisher of miserly delights, may not have told Hawthorne that
his "Buenos dias, señor" celebrated his birthday. He rode home with it
all arranged that during the visit from the Duyckincks he would drive the
chariot over and take Hawthorne and Julian home with him for at least one
night, Hawthorne's counter-offer to Melville's suggestion that they spend
several days at Arrowhead.

The next day Melville went off with the two Samuels and "explored a
neighboring mountain," Lizzie told her stepmother. Four days later, on
6 August, Allan Melville escorted Evert and George Duyckinck to the "cars"
in New York City and then entrusted them with "a fat cask and a couple of
demijohns" (as Evert wrote his wife the next day). From Bridgeport they
took the train up "the pleasant valley of the Housatonic," and the Duyckinck
brothers had the pleasure of seeing on the platform at Stockbridge the British novelist G. P. R. James and his family. The immensely popular writer —
endlessly parodied, already, as the man who opened a novel with a dramatic
depiction of a solitary horseman — had earlier descended upon the ruggedly
scenic Hell Gate, place of luxury rural estates at the northern tip of Manhattan Island, then had unaccountably decided to settle by Negro Pond in

Stockbridge. Melville met the Duyckincks at Pittsfield and took them to Arrowhead in his wagon. George was new to the Berkshire hospitality of the Melvilles, and Evert went with "inward misgivings" about the "probable effects of a second visit to Berkshire" (Evert to his wife, 7 August): last year had been too good to be repeated. Apprehensions allayed, he wrote his wife (left home with the boys and the daughter) that Berkshire in 1851 had "stood the glare of an after-noon sun, fire proof." Evert may have passed the Brewster house in 1850 without especially noticing it, and it was not to be compared to the Melvill place, whose rooms even the Longfellows of Craigie House thought were big enough, but the brothers were welcomed into "the daughter-full house."

"Mrs Melville" fussed over the Duyckincks and gave them the compliment of a little northern room, the window "looking out over a miraculous range of meadow and mountains." (This was Maria, not the seven-months-pregnant Lizzie.) To his wife Evert described Arrowhead as "different from, but quite such an affair as Miss Campbell's — an old improved farm house with just such quiet order and management." This was high compliment, for Evert had tender memories of the decorous, well-managed home in bucolic Springfield, New Jersey, of his Aunt Campbell, who died just after he visited her in the summer of 1847. Now he wrote:

> George & myself have a choice room together and (with many apologies from Mrs M) one bedstead, which you may call a field bedstead, if size has anything to do with calling them so. It is much the way we should have affairs in the country if we all turned out together — simple and excellent with country nature and city taste. You must have a peep at this region to believe the lightness and purity of the air, the fragrant coolness and the blue and purple distances in which it is set. The grounds would satisfy an English nobleman — for the noble maples and elms and the various wooded seclusions and outlooks and all for the price of a bricked in city enclosure of 25 x 100!

Or 25 x 93, as in the Fourth Avenue house, now occupied by strangers, Duyckinck might have said. Evert had journeyed with the notion of conducting some business, and at the first opportunity "said a great deal for Redfield" to Melville in the hope of enticing the whale book to the publishing company his brother-in-law had a financial interest in. Melville knew some of Redfield's adult books, such as Oakey Hall's letters from New Orleans to Manhattan, but he may have associated the firm with volumes more in Malcolm's line, "Redfield's Toy-books," which the *Tribune* (1 June 1850) had touted as a series "divided into four parts of several Lilliputian volumes each," ideal books for babes. Melville thought he had written more of a Brobdingnagian sort of book, and Duyckinck had to report to his wife that "it appears to have been concluded" that the Harpers would publish it after all.

What ensued was a second idyll in the Berkshires, fit to rank with that of the previous August. Year after year, perhaps in 1848, certainly throughout the 1850s (even allowing for summers when Melville was laid up with illnesses) and on through 1863, Melville continued to explore the neighboring mountains — and lakes and rivers and valleys, often with members of his family, often with literary or artistic notables. These excursions of 1851 deserve special attention for what they show of Melville between the time he finished *The Whale* and the time he shipped the sheets to Bentley, and for what they show of his relationship with Hawthorne. The presence of Hawthorne added incalculably to the value some of the excursions held for Melville and his guests. Just as Cornelius Mathews in 1850 had been profoundly grateful for the Berkshire holiday, in 1851 the Duyckincks both knew at the time that they were having an experience to be cherished all their lives.

On Thursday the seventh Melville put himself and his guests at the disposal of Sarah Morewood, who was "characteristically packed up for a picnic on the mountains" along with her sister Ellen Brittain (in a rakish worsted jersey), and two other young women, Mrs. Pollock from England and Miss Henderson from Cincinnati (Evert to his wife, 8 August). The Morewood party, augmented by Joseph Smith, rendezvoused at Arrowhead for dinner (the midday meal) and the addition of a wagon to the means of conveyance. Duyckinck described the day: "The morning had been warm and the afternoon was showery, clouds and shadows being the moving scenery to the permanent staging of the hills." The whole party took refuge from a rainstorm in a barn, without consulting the owner. "Mr. M" "spied out the loft" (the still-nimble Melville, not Rowland Morewood, who was in the city, and who never engaged in such athletic enterprises). Everyone ascended out of the muck, "dislodging the hens that were nestled here and there in the warm dry hay, the rain pattering its musical accompaniment on the roof." The last year Cornelius Mathews had gone nowhere without the appropriate poem in his pockets, and this year Smith had with him a poem of his own composition, "a stout MSS of heroic measure, a glorification of the United States in particular with a polite slanging of all other nations in general," as Duyckinck described it. This turned out to be a poem of the Revolution, subtitled from Thomas Paine: "On Onota's Graceful Shore: A Ballad of the Times That Tried Men's Souls." Rather than embarrassing the now-modest author by calls to recite his composition, the high-spirited Melville read the poem for him, with due emphasis, and with appropriate asides such as "Great!" "Glorious!" and "By Jove that's tremendous!" Done mean-spiritedly or archly, this performance could have wrecked the day and alienated the poet forever, but Melville charmed all the people in the loft (except the hapless English woman, who bore the Yankee vainglory as best she could). However, the exiled fowls in a corner "cackled a series of noisy resolutions, levelled at the party. 'Turn em out!' was the cry. The author impelled by the honor of his poem charged fearlessly, scattered the critics of the pit, clasping the most obstinate bodily and 'rushing' her a rapid descent below." This, Duyckinck concluded, was the ludicrous side. The other side was that Smith was "a thoughtful sensible man." Melville made full amends by letting Smith play guide to the whole party to "the Ashley Pond or Washington Lake." Getting there required "an endless ascent by the side of deep gorges, on the summit of the Hoosac," from which they could look back "to the distant sublimities of cloud & mountain of the Taghconic." The beauty made the city folk acutely aware that the flat brick-kiln of lower Manhattan was only a quarter of the way through the August doldrums.

Next day, 8 August, a Friday, the drive to Hawthorne's in "a barouche" (Hawthorne's word in his notebooks for what Maria called a chariot) and a pair of horses reminded Evert and impressed George with a sense of the majestic terrain that surrounded Melville. (The drive shook Melville into private thoughts, for this lacked a day being a year from that ecstatic rainy Friday morning he had shut himself up to write about Hawthorne and his *Mosses from an Old Manse*.) In Evert Duyckinck's account, the way to Hawthorne's "was a fine mountain drive to be succeeded during the day, by an unending series of blue mountain distances and fine woodland paths — for many of these shaded fenceless roads would be fine avenues on a gentleman's estate." In fact Melville for months had only rarely seen more than was visible between his own property and the village. The men took the "old road to Lenox," a route now obscure, probably starting through Melville's woods (passable in summer), a little out of the way, so that they went by "the Melville House of last year." The road also took them past "the rock upon which he [Melville] used to linger overlooking the fair plateau on which Pittsfield rears its homes and steeples." Melville had pointed this out to them as they went by (unless he had indicated it to Evert the previous August). In adolescence and very young manhood Melville had sought out this vantage point for brooding speculation. From there he could trace the route of the stagecoach he and his father took from Boston in 1828, when, at what was now the Morewood house, he saw his uncle for the first time (so he misremembered). His exiled uncle haunted him still, in field, house, or village, as did his own earlier self.

They passed the church at Lenox, situated "at a distance from the village overlooking it from a hill top." It was gossip-worthy, for the side of the tower that faced Lenox was newly graced with a clock with a huge dial, a gift from the notorious Fanny Kemble Butler (who had been in Lenox to welcome the Hawthornes, but had gone abroad before Melville arrived in July 1850). They arrived without incident (George wrote Joann Miller on 9 August) at the "small red house with a fine lake shut in by mountains a few rods back of his rear windows, with no other residence in sight." With Sophia still gone with the daughters, Hawthorne was in a state of fluttery helplessness in domestic matters. He had expected his callers and had vaguely hoped to provide dinner for them, but upon their arrival (not having made previous inventory), Hawthorne found "nothing whatever in the house," and he worked no miracle of the loaves and fishes. The guests, however, saved the situation by proposing a ride and a picnic, having come provided with "sundry napkined parcels and a jolly black bottle." Thus inspired, Hawthorne brought out his last bottle of champagne from the case sent him by an admirer the previous year. Every casual tourist to the Berkshires had been to see the Shakers, but Hawthorne the recluse had not, although before his marriage he had been a great cross-country walker, so they drove him with his son to Lebanon—an all-male outing, the Hawthorne males comprising the oldest and the youngest.

Hawthorne's subsequent account called that Friday "admirable" and treated the start matter-of-factly: "We took the road over the mountains toward Hudson, and by and by came to a pleasant grove, where we alighted and arranged matters for our pic-nic." This was the old trading road, over which goods had been hauled to the Hudson River for decades, and it was easy traveling. The Duyckincks were in separate tizzies. Evert watched Julian, seeing in him "the girl of the Scarlet Letter though a boy," and magnified their scouting of a good place to picnic into a contest to pick the grove "of all groves." In the selected spot they uncorked bottles and "in fine Spanish al fresco style" passed "the noontide hours under still maples and beeches—with good talk. Away then westward." George was equally convinced that Julian, who was incessantly "tumbling and gamboling" about his father, was "drawn to the life in the Scarlet Letter," but he was also taken with Hawthorne's manly beauty ("He is a very handsome man his portrait not doing him full justice"—the portrait that had reigned for a time in Clinton Place), even while feeling a little dashed at Hawthorne's living up to his reputation with "a sort of hesitating manner and a peculiar half timid smile."

The Duyckincks, Melville, and Hawthorne found some of the Shakers busy mowing their "carefully groomed fields," and at Hancock the visitors saw "the great circular barn where the winter cattle feed with their heads all to the huge hay mow in the centre" and "trod the neat quiet avenues whose stillness might be felt." The decorous Evert Duyckinck renewed his acquaintance with old Father Hilliard, who then opened the big house to them. Duyckinck admired its "oiled and polished pine floors" as being "elegant in spite of Shakerdom," and was surprised that the twenty-year-old glazed finish of the white walls looked "as pure as yesterday's work." Hawthorne responded quite differently to their inspection of the sleeping apartments. In each chamber (he wrote in his journal) "were two particularly narrow beds, hardly wide enough for one sleeper, but in each of which," according to Father Hilliard (whom Hawthorne identified only as "an old elder"), "two people slept." Disgusted, Hawthorne recorded that the only "bathing or washing conveniences" were in the entry, not the chambers, and consisted only of a sink and washbowl, "where all their attempts at purification were to be performed." For Hawthorne, this proved that "all their miserable pretence of cleanliness and neatness," manifested in the "floors and walls of polished wood, and plaster as smooth as marble," amounted to "the thinnest superficiality." The Shakers were "a filthy set," without facilities for washing their bodies—bodies that were huddled, hours each night, next to other bodies: "And then their utter and systematic lack of privacy; their close junction of man with man, and supervision of one man over another—it is hateful and disgusting to think of." By "supervision" Hawthorne referred to their performing all their poor attempts at cleaning themselves in full view of at least one other man. Genuinely appalled, Hawthorne consoled himself that the sect would become extinct—the sooner the better. Having lived in forecastles, Melville experienced no such instinctive horror, and Duyckinck, always a bookman, mildly commented: "You see no flowers in the sisters' rooms but a volume of unreadable theology (of its kind) with a pair of crossed spectacles by its side on a small table."

They left early enough, around five, but Melville's geographical expertise failed them, and delayed their getting home. Evert was nonjudgmental, merely saying that they returned "by a round about way coming upon the mountain view of Richmond looking through intervals of the distant summits to the blue range of the Catskills." Hawthorne said forthrightly, remembering Puck and Ariel, that they "mistook the road," and "went up hill and down, through unknown regions, over at least twice as much ground as there was any need," but he acknowledged that it was by far "the most picturesque ride" he had taken in Berkshire. Stockbridge Bowl "by some witchcraft," Hawthorne said, "had utterly vanished," but by the time they passed through Lenox it was "beyond twilight," and they were lighted by the full moon. The Hawthorne males communed silently as they neared home, Julian ecstatic that Melville, the man who had let him ride horseback the week before, was letting him ride up front (and hold the reins at times). Hawthorne recorded:

"The little man behaved himself still like an old traveller; but sometimes he looked round at me from the front seat (where he sat between Herman Melville and Evert Duyckinck), and smiled at me with a peculiar expression, and put back his hand to touch me." When they "drew up at the little gate of this old red house," rural courtesy required that Hawthorne ask the men in to take tea while the horses rested. Hawthorne went to "Highwood" (the house Sophia called Chateau Brun), where Caroline Tappan gave him not only the sugar he requested but also "a pot of raspberry jam, and some little bread-cakes," his own bread being "sour." With this considerable assistance, for once Mrs. Peters outdid herself: "Tea, bread and butter, dropt eggs, little bread-cakes, raspberry jam." Afterward the men smoked and talked until ten, and the conventional and reclusive host found it hard to part with his visitors: "It was a most beautiful night, with full, rich, cloudless moonlight, so that I would rather have ridden the six miles to Pittsfield, than have gone to bed." It was what George called it, a day of days. Next morning Hawthorne asked Julian whether he had a good time: "he answered with great enthusiasm in the affirmative, and that he wanted to go again, and that he loved Mr Melville as well as me, and as mamma, and as Una." For Melville the winsome Julian was a foretaste of the pleasures he might have with Malcolm in another three years.

At Arrowhead, Allan and *his* Sophia had arrived while Herman and the Duyckincks were with Hawthorne, and the next morning Sarah Morewood issued an invitation for "a general gathering at the old mansion" on that evening, Saturday the ninth (as Evert wrote to his wife two days later). On that Saturday morning the Arrowheads regrouped over a copy of Smith's article on the last Morewood party in the Boston *Daily Evening Transcript* of two days before, as Duyckinck wrote his wife, "all about Mrs M's family— Mrs B of Louisville is Mrs Barter—Miss H is Miss Hetty Huyler engaged to said Smith—Mrs B is Mrs Britten, sister—Mrs V W—Van Winkle another sister—Mr T is Capt Taylor of last years fancy ball—Mr M is Mr C[or-nelius] M[athews] &c &c." Showers may have reduced the attendance at Mrs. Morewood's Saturday night musical party, but among those who came was "Miss Newton the heiress of the village," whom Melville knew as the daughter of Uncle Thomas's courtly acquaintance, as well as "Miss Dilling-ham, a Miss Taylor and Mrs Pollock." After midnight Melville drove his party home through his wood, "the moon riding supreme over the opening meadow."

On Sunday, 10 August, some of them drove over to Lebanon for the Shaker services—"a ghastly scene," the Episcopalian Evert thought: "A glass eyed preacher was holding forth like an escaped maniac. His sermon was a clumsy impudent, disgusting affair, sufficiently so at times to have driven the ladies from the house." To his wife Evert reported that the minister "talked about the whore of Babylon and said her daughters were the protestant sects &c and called that scarlet lady 'a peculiar character.'" But the worst vulgarity and grossness of the fellow was not to be repeated to his wife. Melville's group did not identify with the rest of the "audience," which consisted mainly of "the city fashionables from Columbian Hall" (the old and lavish summer resort), who came there for entertainment, expecting "some pretty strong doses" of criticism from these Shaker expounders. The Melville party stayed for the dance ("long and protracted," and characterized by what Duyckinck described as ludicrous hand shaking, palms up, as if "weighing some imaginary groceries in each hand").

On Monday the visitors were "under marching orders" to be ready for "the grand excursion of the week to Saddleback, Williamstown &c, by railway &c.," Evert wrote his wife, making a cautious disclaimer of the enjoyment he was having: "We leave at 11 with the Morewood troupe and shall go, for a day or two picnicking about in strolling fashion. The weather is of crystal purity & all promises well; but though all this is worth packing away in one's memory, as a possession for life, I count the hours till my return to you and the children." The "Morewood troupe" consisted of the hostess, her sister Ellen Brittain, Mrs. Pollock (the Englishwoman), Miss Henderson from Cincinnati, and what Duyckinck called "an adjacent clergyman," George Entler, all equipped "with the best Pic-nic-ian appliances." The Arrowhead contingent included Herman, Augusta, and Allan and Sophia as well as the Duyckincks. The combined provisions were formidable, as Evert itemized them: "There is to be an indefinite supply of roasted cold chicken, say for a party of ten 3 or 4 pair of Berkshires; item the leg of a Berkshire pig diced into sandwiches; item tongue, head illimitable. Any odd jars of brandy fruit. A dozen of champagne may be disposed of which evaporates so speedily on the top of a mountain that they should be supported by a liberal allowance of Port, Cognac and Jamaica. With this and a party of very good natured people — a pack of cards so you can get through the night." The railroad took them along with their gear to North Adams, where they may have gone by foot to Williamstown to avoid a crooked stage contractor. There they divided. Mrs. Morewood, Sophia, Mrs. Pollock, Evert Duyckinck, and Herman, at least, started the ascent in a four-seated wagon pulled by four horses, then went horseback or on foot — "*three* miles of the toughest bog and stumbling which could well be got up by the forces of mountain torrents, the rotting of mists, snows and ever falling vegetation. The last mile of that is tough." So Sarah Morewood described the ascent. Duyckinck described the beauty of the northerly side of Greylock, but was appalled that the Yankees had "done their best" to despoil the region with cotton factories and by scraping "the hills to lay bare the nakedness of New England sandhills, piling up therewith a hideous embankment for a railway straight through the centre."

They rested late in the day, some of them gathering wildflowers, when shouts echoed "like the yells of red men." Demonstrating to Sarah and the others that he still possessed "the agility of a well trained sailor," Melville climbed a tall tree and from a "dangerously insecure" seat hallooed back till they were joined by those who had come by way of Williamstown — perhaps Augusta, Ellen Brittain, George Entler, and one or two others. They passed the night in the ramshackle observatory erected for scientific purposes by Williams College but subsequently despoiled by the local Yankees (equally hard on nature and works of man), who "broke the instruments and have well nigh plucked the building of its boards and stairways so that it's now a wind and rain penetrated and in important parts, a trembling affair." There was no view except by ascending the "crazy boards," and then (Evert wrote) "you see a near picture of sublime mountain desolation, and your distant acquaintances of Berkshire, the 'Dome' of the Taconic, Monument Mt, the Pontoosac Lake &c &c with Vermont at your back, New York and the Catskills on the right, the Green Mountains chain on the left blue and thinly veiled in the afternoon heat." In the rarefied air Melville split wood expertly and contrived to make a functioning fireplace from the roots of a huge decaying stump. The pyramid of flame reminded Evert of "the signal fires of Scott, of gypsy encampments, of martyrs at the stake." The women wrapped themselves in buffalo robes last used for winter sleighing parties, and the men, at least, drank great quantities of alcohol until after the late red moonrise.

They all stretched in a row on quilts and buffalo, but Mrs. Morewood kept up badinage about Evert's position alongside of the English lady until he said "Morewood has murdered sleep." Allan snored all night, but Augusta sat bolt upright counting the number of rats that passed over the coverlets, and Evert looked all night "at the moonlight through the broken roof, glad at its gradual entry into the dawn." They laid out the supper-stained cloth for breakfast, and Melville and the clergyman cooked two fowls bought in North Adams. They sweetened the water (two dollars a pail to the Yankee guides) with rinsings of the cherry jar. Then they descended, Sarah and George straying aside to pick wild strawberries and yellow raspberries. Evert was dazzled by the fragrance of the fields of raspberries and the exquisite shape of the stem of strawberries Sarah later displayed.

At North Adams they had to deal with an ugly bit of Yankee sharp practice in which the driver and sheriff conspired to shake down the tourists. The sheriff told Melville he was arrested and had to go along with him.

MELVILLE: "Where?"

SHERIFF: "Why, to the hotel and settle."

MELVILLE: "You have no business to take me to the hotel — I have had no demand. Where is your bill?"

SHERIFF: "[Such and such and] my fees."

MELVILLE: "Your arrest is worth nothing — make your demand."

Allan, refreshed by his innocent sleep and a good breakfast, lit into the crooked pair with lawyerese, and the rest of the party gave them plenty of "downright English." When they finally reached home in the heat of the day, Mrs. Morewood suggested that everyone rendezvous at the lake for an afternoon fishing party — this although she was expecting her husband to arrive at night with a party of fresh visitors for midnight supper. By Wednesday, 13 August, Evert, exhausted by Mrs. Morewood's "maelstrom of Hospitality," stayed behind while she took George off with her troop for boating on Pontoosuc, before the promised evening's entertainment, "a *quiet* card party at her house which means champagne & dancing till I hope not daylight as we leave here at 5 in the morning to ride 10 miles to the cars at West Stockbridge for Hudson." Somehow, in the next week or so Alfred Morewood was conceived.

After the Duyckincks left on the fourteenth the Melvilles were less put to the test to provide their share of Berkshire hospitality. When Allan and Sophia left, around Tuesday the nineteenth, Herman saw them aboard the cars, having learned his lesson. (The train passed close enough to Arrowhead for Sophia to be waving her pocket handkerchief toward the house just as a cat she had carried aboard soiled her shawl and dress and ran away.) On 24 August Melville invited Sam Savage to come back for a few days: "You can not take us by surprise. There is no one with us now: nor do we anticipate any visitors at present — but yourself." He offered Sam some consolation for his troubles with choice of livelihood: "It is — or seems to be — a wise sort of thing, to realise that all that happens to a man in this life is only by way of joke, especially his misfortunes, if he have them. And it is also worth bearing in mind, that the joke is passed round pretty liberally & impartially, so that not very many are entitled to fancy that they in particular are getting the worst of it. — In this way, I doubt not, the three old gossips comforted their unfortunate friend Job. But do you, Samuel, be as patient as he." The stoical mood was that of his narrator in "Loomings," the first chapter of his forthcoming book. A few days later (in a letter mailed 30 August) Melville invited Evert Duyckinck to stop by on a trip he was planning to make with the magnate James Beekman, in more or less serious search for country estates, or more precisely something "uniting town & country" (as Evert had written to George the previous year, 15 August 1850). Lizzie by this time was late in her seventh month, but Melville did not hesitate to assure Duyckinck that he and Beekman could stay overnight then go to see Hawthorne and return for dinner, "for this house belongs to travellers, & we occupants but stewards." On the thirtieth he rode over to see Hawthorne, uninvited, and upset Sophia and her guest, the Swedish writer Fredrika Bremer, who was disconsolate at having anyone intrude on her hours with Hawthorne. They all four had tea, the two women upset and frustrated at Melville's unwelcome presence, then they sat and watched the lightning and conversed, with more electrical tensions than Melville had heretofore felt in the little red house.

Just when Melville got Rowland Morewood and Sam Savage to witness his signature on the contract Bentley had sent him (on 13 August) is hard to say, since their signatures are not dated and Mrs. Morewood, at least, was in Manhattan by the first of September. Sam Savage probably came back by Arrowhead on the way to Boston before the Morewoods left. Most likely, Melville sent the fully signed contract back to Bentley in his lost letter of 5 September (a Friday), and about that time sent Allan the corrected set of proofs to forward to England — without bothering to see even that the outright corrections he had marked on those proofs were also made in the American text. On 10 September Allan forwarded the final Craighead proofs to Bentley. Two days later, on 12 September, as Melville's attorney, Allan signed a contract with the Harpers containing the provision that they publish *The Whale* from the plates in the possession of R. Craighead. Within a few days Herman had determined to change the title to *Moby-Dick*, perhaps after someone protested that Harpers had published *The Whale and His Captors* only two years earlier, and he had decided to dedicate the book to Nathaniel Hawthorne. In his draft (undated) of a letter explaining these changes to Bentley, Allan made the first known criticism of the book after it was given its new name: "Moby-Dick is a legitimate title for the book, being the name given to a particular whale who if I may so express myself is the hero of the volume." Allan also apprised Bentley that his brother was drawing upon the publisher by the next steamer two drafts, one at three and one at six months, from 22 September, the date they had decided Bentley would receive the proofs. This financial arrangement suited Bentley, but although Allan's letter reached London in time for Bentley to get in the dedication, it arrived too late for the title to be changed, so the three-volume work remained *The Whale* in England and the one-volume work became *Moby-Dick* in the United States.

On 12 or 19 September Melville warned Sarah Morewood away from *Moby-Dick*: "Concerning my own forthcoming book — it is off my hands, but must cross the sea before publication here. Dont you buy it — dont you read it, when it does come out, because it is by no means the sort of book for you. It is not a peice of fine feminine Spitalfields silk—but is of the horrible texture of a fabric that should be woven of ships' cables & hausers. A Polar wind blows through it, & birds of prey hover over it. Warn all gentle fastidious people from so much as peeping into the book—on risk of a lumbago & sciatics." He thanked her for two books she had sent him, Harriet Martineau's *The Hour and the Man* and Edward Bulwer-Lytton's *Zanoni*, but explained that at present the Fates had plunged him "into certain silly thoughts and wayward speculations" which would prevent him, for a time, from reading them. When other people talked about his new book they meant his whaling book, but in his own mind his new book was the work in which he would explore his hero's psychology in a way that would allow him to expatiate on what he had learned about himself in the last several years, especially what he had learned about his own thought processes while writing *Moby-Dick*. Melville was meditating a new book that would surpass his book about whales. He had heard of Krakens.

40

Melville in Triumph

The Whale and the Kraken,
September–November 1851

Lord, when shall we be done growing? As long as we have anything more to
do, we have done nothing. So, now, let us add Moby Dick to our blessing[s?],
and step from that. Leviathan is not the biggest fish; — I have heard of
Krakens.

Melville to Hawthorne, 17 November 1851

SEPTEMBER AT ARROWHEAD began with unwonted quietude, partly because
Sarah Morewood (if not also her husband) left around the first of the month
for a stay in New York City. Herman got the last of the revised proofs for
Bentley off to Allan days before the Shaws arrived on 13 September, for
the judge's annual session in Lenox. The next day Melville paid John M.
Brewster ninety dollars, one year's interest on the mortgage. Later that
month Maria went to visit her cousin Maria Peebles in Lansingburgh. Having drawn his drafts upon Bentley, Herman sent his mother a note and a
"*delicate* enclosure," which she received on Monday the twenty-second. She
considered what Herman sent her "altogether inadequate," as she wrote
Augusta, but, rather grimly, she hoped "for better times." Meanwhile, she
was improving her own opportunities, having seen the Van Vechtens in
Albany once, and expecting to go again. During her first visit to Albany,
Maria and her cousin Catherine Gansevoort Van Vechten had walked up
Washington Street to the Gansevoort house, where they saw all of Peter's
family except Henry, who was away at Andover. The thirteen thousand dollars from the sale of Melville's grandmother's house (the figure Augusta
learned from Aunt Susan and reported to Allan on 16 May) was all Peter's to
keep, and a portion of it was enough to allow Peter and Susan to make the
new dwelling into a great city residence. As it was described in a clipping
from an unidentified Albany newspaper (23 January 1918), there were parlors on either side of the entrance hall, the west parlor reserved for solemn
occasions, the east parlor for entertaining company through the fall and
winter: "Here were several family portraits by Gilbert Stuart and much fine
old furniture. Here were cases of books and china and on the walls and

mantel a general air pervading of inheritance from the past." Peter possessed treasures of family silver and numerous paintings of his colonial ancestors, including paintings by the artist whom twentieth-century scholars came to identify as the "Gansevoort Limner." The elegant octagonal dining room, entered through the east parlor, led to a much used little breakfast room still further to the east, with Dutch black and white tile on the floor. Across the hall from it was the study, from which one could enter the west parlor. In the spring and summer the garden, reached through the octagonal dining room, became the center of living and entertainment: "And a charming old garden it was, as thick with trees and high shrubs that its end was concealed until you had walked the full length to find it." On Maria's arrival at her brother's house no such charm was apparent, for renovations were in progress, as she wrote to Augusta on 25 September: "The whole house was in disorder, putting in Gas fixtures, water closets, baths, Hot & Cold water in the pantry & bed rooms, &c, & a Kitchen Range below, you may suppose they must have been in great disorder." She and Catherine Van Vechten stayed for dinner (the midday meal) despite these disruptive modernizations.

The next week Maria gave Herman ample warning that on the twenty-ninth he was to be in Pittsfield at the depot with Charlie to meet the east-bound afternoon train. While waiting for her in the village Herman bought the October issue of *Harper's New Monthly Magazine* in order to see his appetizer for *Moby-Dick*, "The Town-Ho's Story" (ch. 54), which the family took as proof that they had to subscribe to the new periodical (as Allan had already done), and to begin assembling the issues they had missed, since from month to month, the Harpers should be promoting Herman's new book in the magazine. For his part, reading over "The Town-Ho's Story" had reassured Herman of the grandeur of his achievement. Whatever Maria thought, her son was himself sure that "better times" were arriving.

On 12 September Augusta received a letter from Nilly Van Rensselaer Thayer with an account of her vacation at Newport: "We took a little tiny cottage in a most beautiful location and have been living most delightfully." Nilly had not heard of Lizzie's second pregnancy, but she knew from her parents that Augusta had taken refuge in the Manor House during the construction and renovation at Arrowhead, and in her letter of 9 September she asked if Augusta found the farmhouse comfortable now, adding: "I have often thought of you this summer, & imagined you rambling about, & enjoying to the utmost your beautiful mountain home. I know you have your beautiful scenery & the happiness of being surrounded by those you love to appreciate it with you. After all there is nothing like mountain scenery for me, partly owing I suppose to early associations. The ocean is truly grand too. I wish I could show you this beautiful moon light night, the spot we have selected for our future summer's home." The granddaughter of the last Patroon could build a vacation house wherever she wanted, of course, a freedom not lost on the residents of Arrowhead.

Houses and family fortunes, as always, were on everyone's mind. Augusta had returned in mid-June with stories from the Manor House, especially Mr. Van Rensselaer's great coup in remedying a lamentable cash shortage. Herman and Helen had been in New York then, and thereafter Herman had been in perpetual motion, what with finishing his book and playing host. With the news from Nilly reminding everyone of the Van Rensselaers, there was time for Augusta to recount to the whole family what she had reported to Allan in her 16 May letter. Stephen Van Rensselaer had lately made an "advantageous sale":

> They are to introduce the Tivoli water into the city, for which privelege, & the necessary land for the Reservoirs, the city have paid him 150 000 dollars. That has enabled him to pay up those heavy debts, & remove many of his anxieties arising from the anti-rent troubles. Then too, he has been engaged for some time in filling up his low lands bordering on the river & converting them into lumber yards & docks—which rent to such advantage, that this first year they brought him in $30,000. All these little particulars, I have treasured up in my memory, thinking they might interest you. Such things generally pass immediately out of my mind. They are making preparations to alter the patroon's bridge, so as to place it more on a direct line with the Troy road.

All "these little particulars," Augusta knew, were precisely the sort of monetary details that fascinated Allan. Other gossip had concerned the mayor's family. The Van Vechtens were thinking of sending Cuyler to Europe, now that he was "more of an exquisite than ever." (In the minds of the Melvilles, to think of the pampered Cuyler was to think of his less fortunate twin, their adored Tom—the sort of contrast Melville worked up in his next book, *Pierre*, between his hero and the foppish and Europeanized cousin Glendinning Stanly.) Catherine Van Vechten Hurlbut was missing Judge Hurlbut very much, since he was "passing a fortnight at his place in the country," having "given up all business" to be "a gentleman of leisure." Cousin Hetty Ten Eyck had "given up her house, & removed, with her furniture to Whitehall, where she is to live." Augusta continued: "Leonard is there, but the other boys are scattered. Anthony boards at the Mansion House, & practices law, but every one says he is worth nothing—Jacob is in California, Clinton in Mr Corning's store, & Cuyler [Ten Eyck] at Paige's Furnace." Arrowhead, the House of the Seven Gables, Whitehall, the Manor House, Albany's Washington Street mansion, the Thirty-first Street house, country estates, seaside cottages—member by member the family was house obsessed, as Herman brooded over novelesque settings for the early action of his next book.

In "Glimpses of Berkshire Scenery" in the *Literary World* (27 September 1851) Evert Duyckinck placed Melville in geographical relation to Catharine Sedgwick and Nathaniel Hawthorne: "Miss Sedgwick, as is well known to all readers of American literature, is there, and near by arose for the world, doubtless, first painted on the mists of the valley, the vision of The House with the Seven Gables. Herman Melville, in the vistas of his wood and the long prospective glance from his meadows to the mountains, blends the past and the future on his fancy-sprinkled page." What Duyckinck meant by referring to Melville's blending the past and the future is not obvious, but perhaps Melville had dropped new hints of using the Berkshires as the setting for a historical novel such as the story of Israel Potter. In this he would be following others, notably Thoreau in his *Week* and Hawthorne in his "Ethan Brand" (1850), based on his 1830s notebooks of his stay in North Adams. Just the year before, Melville had talked to Evert Duyckinck about making a book of the features of the Melvill place. Perhaps he was thinking of writing a minute study of a real American farm, perhaps of writing a piece of fiction set in the grandeur of the Berkshires. Even earlier, in 1849, he may have been thinking about using the terrain near Pittsfield in his story of the revolutionary beggar Israel Potter, for when he at last wrote it he moved his hero's birthplace from Rhode Island to the western Massachusetts he was familiar with.

Fresh from the tensions of waiting for the New York City house to sell, recently angered by the Harpers' refusal to give him a further advance, anxious and guilt-struck, at times, about his secret debt to Stewart, Melville was even more keenly alert than in *Redburn* to the gulf that stretched between impoverished families and their prosperous relatives. Having written into the first chapter of *Moby-Dick* an allusion to his whaleman's coming from an old established family in the land like the Van Rensselaers, he was ready to project himself into a fictional world of wealth and privilege. Melville's next work after the whaling book proved for most readers to be a startling departure—not a sea fiction but a novel about an aristocratic American family, placed, at the opening, in a grand house in a mountainous American landscape (where Saddle Meadows is based on Greylock, or Saddleback). The plot Melville resolved on for *Pierre* required that he move the setting across the state border into New York, the land of his cousins the Van Rensselaers, and along with Saddleback he exported there the little red cottage above Stockbridge Bowl as the Ulver house, where the mysterious Isabel Banford had taken refuge.

As he started *Pierre*, Melville knew that he had gambled his and his

family's future on his certainty that *Moby-Dick* would sell amazingly well —
would sell, for instance, like the many pirated editions of *David Copperfield,*
the recent Dickens sensation. During these weeks of waiting for the book to
be published and for the baby to be born, Melville harvested apples and (in
his own cider press?) made cider, some of which he sent to Allan before
5 November. Melville had hired a man, David, an Irishman plucked fresh off
the boat; this is the David whom Malcolm called his friend late in 1852. With
David's help Melville laid the crops by. Melville had been bookwriter, farmer,
host, proofreader, woodcutter — rushing from one task to another. From a
phrase his mother used, he seems to have set apart some of the property as
"Arrowhead farm" (Maria to Augusta, 5 November) and arranged to have
someone else work it in 1852.

Yet Melville's fall chores and his whirl of thoughts and speculations were
not wholly incompatible with socializing, especially out of doors, for during
the last weeks of Lizzie's pregnancy Melville took advantage of the good
weather to make a series of excursions, several of which may well have fed
into his new book. Joseph Smith in his memoir of Melville (25 January 1892)
quoted lavishly from the description of the Terror Stone or Memnon Stone
in *Pierre,* then as local historian he corrected the novelist, denying Melville's
fictional claim that Pierre was the discoverer of what he identified as the
Balance Rock near Lanesboro:

> To reach it Pierre had no occasion to plunge madly or otherwise, through
> miles of original forest, for there had not been a forest within a mile of it for
> more than a century. The last relics of one were a few beeches, chestnuts and
> maples, whose bark was thickly inscribed with the names or initials of genera-
> tions of visitors. Sorry we are to say it, but these too have mostly disappeared.
>
> The true story of the Memnon naming is this: One charming summer day,
> Mr. Melville, passing with his accustomed party of merry ladies and gentle-
> men, over smooth roads, came to the rock, and there had their usual picnic.
> While the party were enjoying their woodland meal one of the ladies crept
> into that fearful recess under the rock into which no man dare venture. And
> soon there issued from its depths sweet and mysterious music. This cunning
> priestess had hidden there a magnificent music box whose delicious strains
> must still be remembered, by some in Pittsfield and New York. This myste-
> rious music completed in Mr. Melville's mind the resemblance to the Egyp-
> tian Memnon suggested by the size and form of the rock. And voila — Pierre's
> Memnon!

The bold owner of the music box was Sarah Morewood, returned to the
Melvill (now Morewood) property for the autumn.

In his earlier version of the story (in *Taghconic,* 1852, a collection celebrating the locale, written by Smith and some of the Morewood circle) Smith alleged that "a hand which has written many a witty and clever volume" inscribed "MEMNON" on a tree near the rock and that the visitors on this particular picnic left a broken champagne bottle behind. This picnic at the Balance Rock may have been the one on 26 September, when Melville was in the Morewood party that drove to Lake Pontoosuc (a little south of the rock). A strong wind had whipped the water into "white crested waves — giving it a miniature sea look — which the wind among the Pine trees made still more perfect." It was then Melville said to Sarah that "each time he came there he found the place possessing new charms for him."

On 2 October the Morewoods arrived at a field between the village and Arrowhead in time for the plowing contest during the annual Pittsfield Cattle Show and Fair, joining "a rush of persons — horses — wagons, carts and all sorts of movable vehicles such a Broadway of confusion and excitement" (as Sarah wrote George Duyckinck on 8 October): "A large field filled with carriages and gayly dressed people — a band of merry music playing in the open space — horses & oxen with ploughs turning up the new earth as by magic." Around eleven o'clock Melville and three of his sisters (Helen, Augusta, and Fanny) joined the party for a walk ("the journey on foot which we performed before nightfall will surprise you when you hear about it," Sarah wrote George).

During some of these autumnal outings the walkers reminisced to each other about episodes from the summer's activities, when city visitors were present. On 27 October Sarah wrote to George Duyckinck: "The excursion to Greylock is not forgotten here but often recalled in an amusing way — by Mr Herman or myself — In some of our long walks we have taken a spyglass with us so as to bring nearer to us the Tower and its associations." The neighbors went on a number of such walks, as Sarah specified in the same letter: "I suppose you have seen Miss Augusta Melville since she came to your city — and if so have heard from her an account of our last walk of ten miles or more." Augusta had gone to visit Allan and Sophia three weeks into October, apparently not waiting for the birth of the new baby. Sarah added of Augusta: "I am sorry she has left here as I found her a pleasanter companion than any of her sisters are. She is warm hearted too and more romantic than most people suppose her to be."

Waiting for book and baby kept rough pace. The title page of *Moby-Dick* was deposited on 18 October in the copyright office of the Southern District of New York. The London edition, *The Whale*, was published on 18 October, although Melville had no way of knowing this. At three in the afternoon on 22 October Melville wrote a brief note to his father-in-law, then drove into the village to mail it: "Your daughter is the mother of another little boy — a fine fellow—born between 1 & 2 o'clock P.M. to day. Mother & child are doing very well." When Melville wrote Evert Duyckinck two weeks later he was not quite certain of the name: "The boy you enquire about is well. His name will probably be 'Stanwix' for some account of which, Vide *Stone's Life of Brandt*, where mention is made of how this lad's great grandfather spent his summers in the Revolutionary War before Saratoga came into being—I mean Saratoga Springs & Pavilions." In an *Index Rerum* Gansevoort Melville had plundered a copy of William Leete Stone's *Life of Joseph Brant* for references to the Hero of Fort Stanwix: the "spirited correspondence between Gates & [Peter Gansevoort]. on his assuming the command of the Northern department in June 1776," "his gallant defence of Fort Stanwix," the information that he "had determined to attempt cutting his way through St Leger's superior force, rather than surrender." Such incidents were apparently fresh in Melville's mind from his own reading of Stone, whom he may have consulted in preparation for naming the baby, before or after he knew it was a boy.

To Duyckinck, naturally enough, given the conventions of the time, Melville said nothing about the alarming situation already apparent at Arrowhead; even Melville may not yet have focused on how serious matters were. The pregnancy had been hard on Lizzie, and the birth was followed by severe complications. On 3 November Sarah sent two serving girls through the woods with a lantern after the women of Arrowhead had all retired to their rooms; they carried "Blancmange for Lizzy" (and an invitation to Helen "to go to town next morning to see the menagerie & to spend a few days with her"). In a letter to Augusta on 5 November, Maria pronounced Sarah a "woman of kind impulses," but "very imprudent to send two young girls through forest so late at night," since "the note & Blancmange would have kept until morning." A charitable if superficial interpretation is that Sarah was concerned about Lizzie and that the invitation to Helen was secondary. As for Maria, her own competence in giving birth and caring for children led her, in these years, to be intolerant of mothers whom she regarded as less efficient and less self-disciplined than she had been.

The baby was named (after some hesitation) Stanwix. On 5 November, Maria wrote Augusta, who was still with Allan and Sophia: " 'Stanwix' is small and thin, but a bright little thing, his dark eyes looking about so wise, he is also very little trouble, sleeping a good deal & having a famous appetite. He will soon be plump and I hope [h]is big nose very like Stanwix Gansevoort's whom he much resembles, will stand still, while the rest of him is growing— How do you like the name." Three years earlier Augusta had been the force behind the choice of the name Malcolm. "Stanwix," although irrevocably attached to Melville's first cousin, his long-dead Uncle Leonard's and just-dead Aunt Mary's rather slow son, may have been Maria's choice, or Herman's, but it was a propitiatory tribute to the glorious military past of Maria's father. Maria's brother Leonard's son had proved unworthy of the name, but her grandson could become worthy of it, despite his unfortunate nose.

Maria Melville also reported further medical details to Augusta: "Lizzie is not so well is very much troubled with her bosom, Mrs Proctor just now told me that she feared a gathering in one, if it could not be scattered. She is very nervous being constitutionally so, and now being so weak, with loss of appetite, that a sheet had to be placed on the wall to cover the paper the figures of which seem'd to her in motion." Knowing that Hope Savage Shaw was inadequate by character and education to have trained a daughter, Maria always assumed Lizzie could not be as competent in a given situation as her own indubitably well-trained daughters, but the precision of her description makes clear the extremity of Lizzie's present nervousness. From much of this strain Melville may well have buffered himself. The family way was to leave the sick and the children to the care of women, while men got out of the way. Melville had harvested apples and made cider. After Stanwix's birth, perhaps after Lizzie's new suffering had begun, he had taken himself into his woods "with axe, wedge, & beetle," and had brought enough fuel home to fill his wood-house, a simple precaution, none too beforehand, since by 7 November, as he reported to Duyckinck, he had "in full blast our great dining-room fire-place, which swallows down cords of wood as a whale does boats." He also reported that he had had his "dressing-gown patched up," his way of saying that he was newly costumed for his winter's stint of writing and was either thinking about his new book or engaged in writing it.

Whether he named Stanwix to please his mother or because he had been brooding about his Gansevoort grandfather, or whether he began brooding about his grandfather after naming the boy, he wrote some Gansevoort family material into early parts of his book in describing his hero Pierre Glendinning's grandfather Pierre and old Pierre's phaeton:

> Now needs must grand old Pierre take a morning drive; he rides no more with the old gray steed. He has a phaeton built, fit for a vast General, in whose sash three common men might hide. Doubled, trebled are the huge S shaped leather springs; the wheels seem stolen from some mill; the canopied seat is like a testered bed. From beneath the old archway, not one horse, but two, every morning now draw forth old Pierre, as the Chinese draw their fat god Josh, once every year from out his fane. (bk. 2, ch. 3)

This phaeton was a fictional replica of the one belonging to his uncle Peter, and before that to General Peter Gansevoort, an almost colossal trophy of an age of giants.

Melville appropriated the phaeton along with the physique of his grand-father. "The grandfather of Pierre measured six feet four inches in height," he declared, correcting or artistically improving upon the description of his grandfather Gansevoort in Thomas J. Rogers's *New American Biographical Dictionary*, which emphasized that when the Hero raised a company of gren-adiers before the Revolution he imposed a height code, "every man being at least six feet in height," while his own person "was noble and majestic, (his height being six feet, three inches.)." Rogers (which is to say, Uncle Peter, the real author of the entry) had concluded by extolling the Hero: "He was regardless of wealth, and plain and unostentatious in his habits of life: as a republican, he was firm in principle, and inflexible in practice; maintaining through life, the most pure and unimpeachable moral and political integrity. Above all, general Gansevoort was a christian." On that last long-familiar assertion Melville now elaborated a complex portrayal of just how a warrior, a man who "had annihilated two Indian savages by making reciprocal blud-geons of their heads," might be perceived as "a sweet-hearted, charitable Christian," a "fit image of his God." In *White-Jacket* Melville had pointed to the irony of the presence of a minister of the prince of peace being enlisted in the service of a man-of-war. The passage in *Pierre*, rather than being simply satirical toward the un-Christlike practice of nominal Christianity, now pro-pelled forward a major theme of the book, the outright impracticability of Christianity. Melville planted his clues in plain sight for anyone who knew the Bible thoroughly and tried to take it seriously, that is, literally, for he ended his introduction of grand old Pierre Glendinning with an allusion to the Sermon on the Mount, where Jesus had preached turning the other cheek to a foe who had smote one cheek already rather than making recipro-cal bludgeons of the heads of your enemies.

The months of summer and early fall had passed with much vagabondiz-ing on Melville's part, but not with his preferred companion, Hawthorne. Sophia Hawthorne recovered "very slowly from her recent confinement," her husband wrote on 12 June to "Grace Greenwood" (Sara Jane Clarke). The pregnancies of his wife's and Melville's had overlapped for almost four months, but the differences in the ages of the couples was obvious in Haw-thorne's describing the baby, Rose, as the child of his age, the last he expected to have. In June and July Hawthorne had been working steadily on his *A Wonder-Book*, and although Melville showed up unexpectedly while Sophia was away with her two daughters in August, the two men had not, after all, gone vagabondizing together. As far as we know, nothing took Melville to Stockbridge Bowl.

By the late summer and early fall Hawthorne was casting about for alter-natives to the cramped cottage, which would be more uncomfortable than ever with a new baby beginning to crawl about during the dead of winter. Fanny Kemble, still out of the country, had offered her larger house at Lenox at the same rent he was paying, and he also considered buying a house in eastern Massachusetts. Then in the first week of September his landlords, the Tappans, precipitated his decision by insulting Una, Julian, and Hawthorne himself. The family had assumed that they were entitled to pick currants from the bushes and fruits from the trees on the property, but this fall the Tappans belatedly let them know that no such rights went with the mere rental of the cottage. Another man could have laughed off the contretemps, but this slight misunderstanding, so ineptly handled by the Tappans, determined the prideful Hawthorne to leave the Berkshires as soon as he could. He had never liked the harsh winters, but now the whole stay in the Berkshires was soured for him. On 13 September in a letter to James T. Fields he declared himself secretly "sick to death of Berkshire," and reluctant to spend another winter there: "The air and climate do not agree with my health at all; and, for the first time since I was a boy, I have felt languid and dispirited, during almost my whole residence here." In mid-September he went to scout out houses in West Newton, and then visited Salem before returning to Lenox. By late October, about the time of Stanwix's birth, the Hawthornes had concluded to take up residence in Sophia's sister Mary's house in West Newton on 1 December, for Mary had decided to go to Washington with her husband, Horace Mann (a new U.S. Representative), during the session of Congress.

The last week of October, the feckless Ellery Channing, Thoreau's friend who had poeticized Fayaway, descended on Lenox, trying to impose himself on the Tappans despite Caroline Sturgis Tappan's peculiar effort to foist him off on the less well equipped Hawthornes. From Lenox on 30 October Channing wrote his long-suffering wife, Ellen, Margaret Fuller's sister, claiming that he had found Hawthorne changed for the worse, having "suffered much living in this place." By then Channing had knocked enough about the village to understand that it was "given evidently to criticism," and that Hawthorne was uncomfortable knowing he was the subject of hostile comment: "His ways not the ways of the world have attracted the attention of the people; his habit of not calling on people, & his having written some books have made him a lion. I do not know that he has felt this, but I think he has felt his lack of society. . . . He has lived here I know not exactly how long . . . & I suppose he has hardly seen a face beyond that of his wife and his children, a difficult life truly to live." The irresponsible Channing, like his friend Thoreau an appreciator of the grandeur of the scenery, reflected on Hawthorne's peculiar unhappiness in paradise: "One cannot explain why some people are miserable where others would be happy." Hawthorne talked to him of coming back to Concord, where he had lived in the Old Manse, and possibly buying a place there, after the stay in West Newton. Channing seems not to have strolled over to Arrowhead, although he must have been curious to see "Tommo." Even the egregious Channing may have been uneasy about the reaction Melville might have had to his versifying *Typee* so long ago.

The little red cottage turned a blank face to one passerby this fall, as recounted in a letter a new resident of Lenox wrote home to Windsor, Vermont, for printing in his hometown *Journal* (12 December 1851), from which it was reprinted in the Lowell *Weekly Journal and Courier* of 19 December 1851:

> In a spot of unrivalled loveliness on the Northern shore of the Mountain Mirror stands a small, uninviting, insignificant, red house, with green window blinds, and one single pine tree before it. One might pass it at almost any time of the day, and think it vacant; the doors would all be shut, the blinds all closed, and the single pine tree would look as sullen as if it were conscious of its loneliness. There would be no path to the gate, and no knocker on the door, and one would immediately conclude that the red house of the two gables was shut against the resort of men — and he would not be far from right, for there lives Nathaniel Hawthorne.

This account may have been written just after the Hawthornes had moved out in late November, although it hardly presented a brighter face even before the Hawthornes had moved out like thieves in the night. At no time in the past year and a half had the house shown much sign of animation to prying passersby. Hawthorne himself repeatedly decried the cottage ("the ugliest little old red farm-house," he had called it in a letter of 29 April 1851), and in the summer and fall of 1851 he had kept himself at home in that ugliness, except during his trip east.

During the fall any thoughts Hawthorne had of making an excursion, except for walks with the self-invited Ellery Channing, were centered on the offer of Charles Sedgwick, the clerk of the Massachusetts Supreme Court and Catharine Sedgwick's brother, to drive him over to see the English novelist G. P. R. James. Aside from his participation in the packing, Hawthorne had to think about his two forthcoming books, *A Wonder-Book* and *The Snow-Image*, his final gleaning of earlier pieces. He dated his preface to *The Snow-Image* 1 November, three days after Ellery Channing drew him out for a walk, but his work on the collection was not over, for two days later he was facing the exasperating prospect of having to re-create from memory part of "My Kinsman, Major Molineux," if he and Fields could not lay hand on a copy of the gift annual in which it had appeared, *The Token* of 1832.

Furthermore, he was so short of money that he would be unable to pay for his move to West Newton until Ticknor & Fields advanced him a hundred dollars (for convenience, to a Pittsfield bank). Notoriously ungregarious at best, Hawthorne had not made himself available to Sedgwick for an impromptu excursion together to James's place on Negro Pond in Stockbridge. The upshot was that Sedgwick, as the time neared for Hawthorne to leave the little red cottage, decided that the only thing to do was to throw a party, midweek (on 4 November, a Tuesday), with only a couple of days' notice, so he could at least gather James, Hawthorne, and Melville at his hearth one time. However this gathering was described to the invited guests, it was a farewell party for Hawthorne.

The Melvilles received their invitation on Monday, 3 November, in the correct form of a note to the dowager Mrs. Melville from her old friend Eliza Sedgwick (whom Herman by this time associated with her grandfather Jonathan Edwards). Maria picked it up at the post office when she drove with Herman to the village after breakfast (perhaps a sign that he had not established a writing routine on *Pierre*). Maria wrote Augusta on 5 November: "it contained an invitation for me to come to tea on tuesday eveg wishing me to extend the invitation to Mr & Mrs Herman Melville & my daughters, or any friend or friends we might have with us, from Mrs Sedgwick as an inducement to come so far we were to meet the James's from Stockbridge & a few friends." The note probably specified that the Hawthornes were invited, since the note to the Hawthornes specified that *Melville* was invited. Lizzie's sufferings were not recognized as great enough to hold the others back, given Maria's desire to meet the English novelist and Herman's intense need to let Hawthorne know that *Moby-Dick* was due out any day: "Herman said he would take us at once and seem'd pleased. As we were to be there at seven or lose our tea, we started from home at half past five. It was very *Cold muffs were brought down & Buffaloes.* . . . However we had a pleasant drive to Lenox Herman being in excellent spirits."

Before this party the Melvilles may not have learned that the Hawthornes were preparing to move. If they knew, this would at least give Melville a chance to see Hawthorne before he left the Berkshires. Herman drove straight to the Sedgwick house, so some of them knew where to go. When they last visited in January, the house may have sat in its original rather cramped position in the village of Lenox, but within the past year it had been moved to "a charming situation at a little distance, on the brow of the hill," where it commanded "a vast and beautifully-varied prospect," and where over the next years additions were made to the novelist-sister Catharine's wing of the house, notably "a broad and well-inclosed piazza, looking to the south over twenty miles of valley, meadow, lake, and hill, to the blue Taghkonic range, in southernmost Berkshire." (Thus Mary Elizabeth Dewey in her 1872 *Life and Letters of Catharine M. Sedgwick*.)

The Sedgwicks allowed the Melvilles a moment to arrange their "dress" after alighting, and before encountering "Mr Hawthorne, and all the Sedgwicks," including of course the novelist. That night Maria had a dose of how eccentric and willful two writers besides her son could be, for Hawthorne came alone and G. P. R. James's wife came without him: "Mr & Mrs Sedgwick on the entrance of Mrs James both asked for her husband, she slowly & very quietly said, Mr James beg'd me to say that he had 'commenced a new book to day,' & could not break out on any account. . . . Our disappointment was very great at not seeing the great novelist, Mr Hawthorne was induced to come to meet Herman — On asking for his wife he said they went out alternate, he took charge of the children when his wife went out. They could not both be spared together." The fact that Melville was in such good spirits may mean that he had not heard of Hawthorne's plans to leave Lenox. Once he learned of Hawthorne's imminent departure he must have become far more agitated about it than Sedgwick had been, since he had been playing out in his mind a scene he would enact any week now — an exultant ride over to the little red cottage with a presentation copy of *Moby-Dick*. Still, James's absence, as well as Sophia's, meant that it was easier for Melville and Hawthorne to confer a little over Hawthorne's plans and Melville's responses to them. Melville had a seriously sick wife and a new book on the brain if not on the page, but before the evening was out he conveyed his sense that they had to say good-bye properly, not in a moment's public chat at someone else's tea party, and he confessed to Hawthorne how frustrated he would feel if his book came out just too late for him to carry a presentation copy to Hawthorne. (This he could say without mentioning the dedication.) The last recorded image of the night is of Charles Sedgwick looking out at his departing guests and calling out that the snow was beginning to fall.

A day or two later Hawthorne received his first copies of *A Wonder-Book* and sent one at once — not to Herman but to Malcolm Melville, knowing that the father would see the pre-publication compliment to the whaling book that he had written into a late chapter months earlier, an acknowledgment to his friend that he knew the grandeur of his struggle to shape out "the gigantic conception of his 'White Whale,' while the gigantic shape of Graylock looms upon him from his study-window." Written in the summer, this was the first time the title of the book, in any form (*The White Whale*, *The Whale*, *Moby-Dick*), had been mentioned in any other book.

Moby-Dick was still unpublished when news reached the east coast from the Pacific that (on 20 August) the whaleship *Ann Alexander* had been sunk by a whale. The source of the news was an item in the Panama *Herald* of

16 October: "We have just received the following thrilling account of the destruction of the whale ship Ann Alexander, Capt. John S. Deblois, of New Bedford, by a large sperm whale. . . . A similar circumstance has never been known to occur but once in the whole history of whale-fishing, and that was the destruction of the ship Essex." Around 5 November Evert Duyckinck sent Melville a clipping about this *Ann Alexander* catastrophe. Melville's 7 November reply shows how compartmentalized his life had become:

> Your letter received last night had a sort of stunning effect on me. . . . the Whale had almost completely slipped me for the time (& I was the merrier for it) when Crash! comes Moby Dick himself (as you justly say) & reminds me of what I have been about for part of the last year or two. It is really & truly a surprising coincidence — to say the least. I make no doubt it *is* Moby Dick himself, for there is no account of his capture after the sad fate of the Pequod about fourteen years ago. — Ye Gods! What a Commentator is this Ann Alexander whale. What he has to say is short & pithy & very much to the point. I wonder if my evil art has raised this monster.

Melville did not say so to Duyckinck, but long before he may have heard of the ship or met someone who had left the *Ann Alexander.* It had touched at the outer harbor of Honolulu in mid-April 1843, shortly before he got there. In early November 1851 the news of the sinking created a sensation in the newspapers, and then after the middle of the month it created a good deal of misapprehension among a few of the reviewers of *Moby-Dick* (who remarked on the coincidental timing of the news account and the book) and some reviewers of *The Whale* (who assumed the industrious Melville had written up the three volumes on the basis of the news story). A fitting sequel emerged, as time passed. On 6 May 1854 the Honolulu *Friend* trumpeted: "TAKEN AT LAST." Captain Deblois had reported to Chaplain Damon (still the editor of the *Friend*) that in 1852 the *Rebecca Sims* had taken the whale that sank his ship, the proof being two harpoons in it marked "Ann Alexander." The whale's head was found seriously injured, and contained pieces of timbers of the *Ann Alexander.*

Thus announced by the Panama *Herald, Moby-Dick* arrived in Pittsfield, most likely a few copies at once. Melville by rights should have received copies three or four days before the official publication date of 14 November (a Friday), since copies were in bookdealers' and editors' hands in Albany and Boston by the twelfth at the latest. Their arrival was, after all, providential: if they had been delayed very much longer he would not have been able to hand a presentation copy to the man to whom he had dedicated it in token of admiration of his genius. Given the fact that Lizzie was in horrific pain but still nursing Stanwix, and given the difficulty of getting Hawthorne to pay a visit even in the best of circumstances, Melville could not consider asking Hawthorne to come to Pittsfield. Neither was Melville welcome at the upside-down little red cottage. Sophia was nursing Rose and letting the two older children run wild, so Ellery Channing thought: "she has none of the means whereby elegance & refinement may be shed over the humblest apartment. Her children brought up in the worst way for visitors, by themselves, & never having been to school, have of course nothing but bad manners. They break in when not required, & are not in fact either handsome or attractive." Melville was far more relaxed around Una and Julian than Channing was, but nevertheless Sophia was packing for the move to West Newton and in the best of circumstances she was a hostess with a meager larder whose efforts to entertain her husband's few guests always left her exhausted. Melville may never have realized that his visits wore Sophia out (admire him though she did), but he was sensitive at least to the awkwardness of imposing himself on Hawthorne in a cold little house turned topsy-turvy.

But the men had agreed they must meet if they could, and as soon as he received his first copies of *Moby-Dick* Melville drove over to invite Hawthorne to a formal farewell dinner at Curtis's hotel in Lenox. Melville took the wagon rather than riding, so he could pick his friend up, though in any case once he arrived they could walk into the village if they felt like it. This may have been on Friday the fourteenth — the official publication date. The year before, Melville had refused to let Duyckinck and Mathews pay Robert Melvill for room and board, but instead had paid himself, knowing that the man who feasted his friends (even on borrowed money) could feel as much a king as Belshazzar. He still had money, either from the drafts on Bentley or the loan from Stewart (on 1 November he had paid Stewart $92.25, the first six months' interest on the loan of $2050, a loan he had every expectation of repaying with the profits from his new book). Melville paid for his own publication party, to which he invited a solitary guest.

Since Shaw and the other judges stayed at the inn during their sessions, Melville had long known the proprietor, William Curtis, once the lad put in charge of driving the actress Fanny Kemble Butler about. A kindred spirit to Melville, Curtis habitually drove daringly, even recklessly, on narrow, precipitous mountain roads. The name Jehu was applied to both Curtis and Melville from their driving furiously. The hotel was unnervingly close to the jail where Uncle Thomas had been intermittently imprisoned, but for Melville all of the Berkshires was haunted by one memory or another. Melville arranged to be served a little late, so he and his guest could linger in the dining room with liquor and cigars long after the hotel's guests had completed their repasts and departed.

The longer the authors lingered on alone in the dining room, the more the locals buzzed with gossip about them. Lenoxites, still inhabitants of the shire town, prided themselves in being much more sophisticated than the yokels who comprised the population of Pittsfield. Nevertheless, they were, as Ellery Channing had found, unforgiving of Hawthorne's reclusiveness, convinced that he had been disdainful of them and their town when he had been there a year and a half without going to church or any other public functions. Everyone knew from gossip just what grotesque lengths Hawthorne would go to in his efforts to avoid company: more than one caller had glimpsed the writer fleeing away from the back of the house. Many of the inhabitants of Lenox had not glimpsed Hawthorne at all—frustrating, since he had become a genuine celebrity only during his months in the Berkshires. Now almost no one knew that he was in the process of leaving: even the Tappans were in no position to talk about his plans for departure, since their tactlessness had helped to drive him away. Hawthorne, in short, had not proved to be the sort of man who arrived with éclat, straightaway made himself a boon companion and a valued citizen, and at last was sent on his way with a public farewell and the keys to the city.

"Maherbal," the new Lenox resident who had begun sending letters home to Vermont, submitted his report tardily (dated 10 January 1852). It was printed in the Windsor *Journal* on 16 January 1852:

> As may be gathered from the fact that Melville dedicated his book lately published to Nathaniel Hawthorne, "in admiration of his genius," the two distinguished writers of fiction are personal friends—not however familiar, intimate friends by any means—for if the complaints on the part of the Pittsfield people with regard to the exclusiveness of the one, and the representations of Maherbal in the *Journal* concerning the social character of the other, are to be taken as conclusive in the matter, they seem to be alike strangers to any thing like familiarity of social intercourse. Not very long ago, the author of the "Scarlet Letter" and the author of "Typee," having, in some unaccountable way, gotten a mutual desire to see one another, as if neither had a home to which he could invite the other, made arrangements in a very formal manner to dine together at a hotel in this village. What a solemn time they must have had, those mighty conjurors in the domain of the imagination, all alone in the dining-room of the hotel! In the small talk of the flippant beaux and light-headed belles of Berkshire, the solemn attempt of two of the greatest characters of which the county could boast, towards an acquaintance, was made a subject of infinite merriment.

Although the best people of Lenox, the Sedgwicks, and the Fields of Stockbridge, certainly, were aware that Melville and Hawthorne were friends, this was wholly unknown to the local celebrity watchers. None of the villagers had any way of knowing even that Hawthorne had praised *Typee* in 1846 and that Melville had celebrated Hawthorne's *Mosses from an Old Manse* the year before, since the essay in the *Literary World* was unsigned.

As far as older Lenoxites were concerned, Melville was the nephew of the longtime resident of the jail. To them, and to the younger onlookers, he was now the recluse of Pittsfield — the man who drove hell-for-leather into the village for his mail and hell-for-leather home, the man who had scarcely seen the inside of a church since he had moved to the Berkshires, the man whose womenfolk were now reduced to driving themselves to social gatherings. Hawthorne was the even more peculiar recluse of Stockbridge Bowl, the man who might be glimpsed ducking behind trees and rocks when encountered out of doors. A wit could have made jokes by fantasizing about what would happen if these two celebrities accidentally collided with each other, but the reality of their seeking each other out was hilarious beyond price. A number of lucky Lenoxites actually had the privilege of seeing the somber author of Puritan adultery, punishment, penance, and penitence, *The Scarlet Letter,* stretch his long legs under the same table as the shorter legs of the author of the sensualist's handbook, *Typee!* (Which limb, they might well wonder, had pained the runaway so, and had the natives, female, or was it male, massaged only that afflicted limb, or both those limbs, now under the table in Curtis's dining room?) Two such opposites, the Lenoxites thought, united only by reclusiveness, the young author of a guidebook to sexuality before the Fall of Man and the older author of a guidebook to Puritan sin and punishment! Think of the irony — these strangers to each other, suddenly "having, in some unaccountable way, gotten a mutual desire to see one another"! Then, as if that were not extraordinary enough, arranging to fulfill that desire in public, in a hotel, as if they were travelers forced to dine away from home! Hotel dining rooms were for travelers! No one had ever heard of any two local residents dining together in Lenox at a hotel, much less two such diverse recluses! The celebrity hounds who peeked into the dining room assumed they were witnessing a grotesquely awkward occasion — the day in which two of the most idiosyncratic and private men in the area made a public, solemn, and awkward attempt at establishing an acquaintance. For days or weeks afterward, Melville and Hawthorne would be the cause of "infinite merriment" in "the small talk of the flippant beaux and light-headed belles of Berkshire."

During the hours of the early afternoon, the men had been absorbed in each other, pretty much, but after all Hawthorne had something of the Hawkeye about him, as he had been told at North Adams long before, and Melville had a way of noticing when members of the public were gawking at him. The memory of this occasion or other experiences with the effects of celebrity tinged what Melville wrote long afterward, in 1870, about his Uncle Thomas and Edward Newton — that their "exchange of salutations" in the Pittsfield tavern "presented a picture upon which the indigenous farmers there assembled, gazed with eager interest, and a kind of homely awe," affording them "a peep into a world as unknown to them as the Vale of Cashmere to the Esquimaux I[n]dian." Having by then taken the measure of village malignity, he wrote: "To the ensuing conversation, also, they listened with the look of steers astonished in the pasture at the camel of the menagerie passing by on the road." In that reminiscence he was responding to experiences of his own as well as that of his uncle and the local magnate. In the country you "cannot do a single thing you like," William Hazlitt wrote in his essay on Wordsworth's *Excursion*, "without being subject to impertinent curiosity"; Melville in the early 1860s fervently endorsed that passage, "True True True." Never had Melville been gaped at so intrusively as during this meeting with Hawthorne. Yet as lovers of Shakespeare both men knew the philanthropic virtue of being the source of wit in other men (and in women, such as the Berkshire belles), and Melville may have been all but oblivious to the gawking at the time. What mattered was that he and Hawthorne were alone in the room with each other.

There were onlookers aplenty, but no eavesdroppers to record their conversation. Decades later Melville wrote into the *Billy Budd* manuscript a closeted interview between Captain Vere and Billy — an interview the secrets of which the narrator does not reveal. At some well-chosen moment Melville took out the book whose publication they had both been awaiting and handed his friend an inscribed copy of *Moby-Dick*, the first presentation copy. In no other way could Hawthorne have had a copy so soon, one that he had read by the fifteenth or sixteenth, in time to have written a letter Melville received on the sixteenth. Here, in the dining room, Hawthorne for the first time saw the extraordinary dedication and tribute to his genius — the first book anyone had dedicated to him. Never demonstrative, he was profoundly moved. Alone with the author, he could open the book in his nervous way (more nervous even than normally), and get from his friend a guided tour of the organization of the thing now in print, and even sample a few paragraphs that caught his eye or that the author eagerly pointed out to him, perhaps even some passages he had seen in manuscript in Melville's study.

Hawthorne could see enough to acknowledge anew his own admiration for the genius of the author of this book, so queerly named for an enormous sperm whale, *Moby-Dick*. The flippant beaux and the light-headed belles were witnessing a sacred occasion in American literary life, as the men lingered at the table, drinking, soothed into ineffable socialities, obscured at times from view by their tobacco smoke. They lingered long after the dining room had emptied, each reverential toward the other's genius, each aware that when they met again, in West Newton, in Boston, or wherever their Fates might bring them together, they would not fall at once into these present terms of intimacy. Inevitably, Hawthorne, the one who was taking leave, was looking forward, while Melville at moments was looking back at his decision to finish his book near this older writer, but at other moments he was living intensely in the present, a moment he might have been robbed of if the book had been delayed, the time when his friend held in his hand his farewell gift, the printed and bound book, a tangible token of Melville's admiration for his genius.

Take it all in all, this was the happiest day of Melville's life.

Genealogical Charts

M E L V I L L [E]

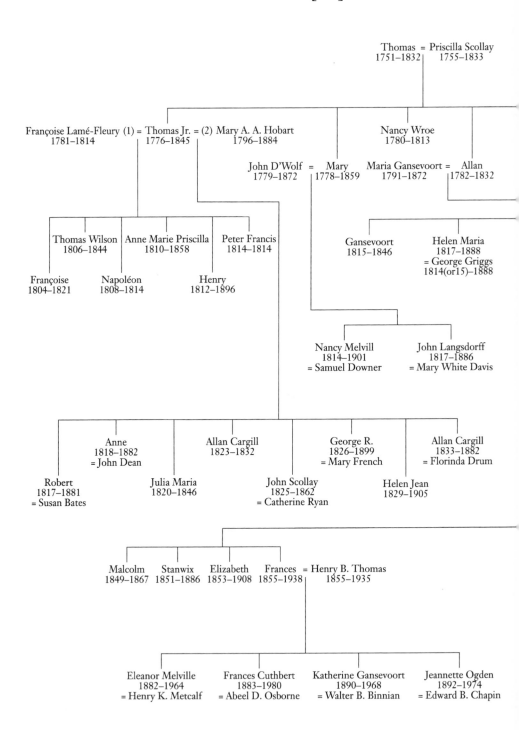

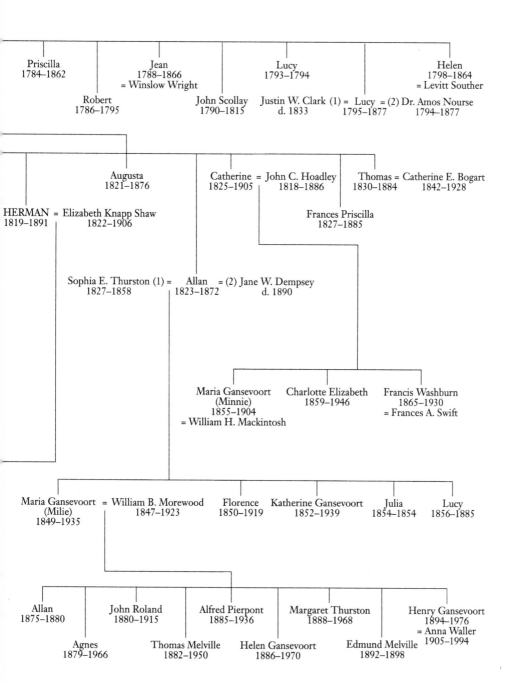

Priscilla
1784–1862

Robert
1786–1795

Jean
1788–1866
= Winslow Wright

John Scollay
1790–1815

Lucy
1793–1794

Justin W. Clark (1) = Lucy = (2) Dr. Amos Nourse
d. 1833   1795–1877   1794–1877

Helen
1798–1864
= Levitt Souther

Augusta
1821–1876

Catherine = John C. Hoadley
1825–1905   1818–1886

Thomas = Catherine E. Bogart
1830–1884   1842–1928

HERMAN = Elizabeth Knapp Shaw
1819–1891   1822–1906

Frances Priscilla
1827–1885

Sophia E. Thurston (1) =   Allan   = (2) Jane W. Dempsey
1827–1858   1823–1872   d. 1890

Maria Gansevoort
(Minnie)
1855–1904
= William H. Mackintosh

Charlotte Elizabeth
1859–1946

Francis Washburn
1865–1930
= Frances A. Swift

Maria Gansevoort = William B. Morewood
(Milie)   1847–1923
1849–1935

Florence
1850–1919

Katherine Gansevoort
1852–1939

Julia
1854–1854

Lucy
1856–1885

Allan
1875–1880

Agnes
1879–1966

John Roland
1880–1915

Thomas Melville
1882–1950

Alfred Pierpont
1885–1936

Helen Gansevoort
1886–1970

Margaret Thurston
1888–1968

Edmund Melville
1892–1898

Henry Gansevoort
1894–1976
= Anna Waller
1905–1994

GANSEVOORT

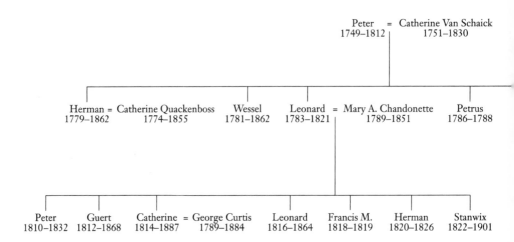

Peter = Catherine Van Schaick
1749–1812   1751–1830

Herman = Catherine Quackenboss   Wessel   Leonard = Mary A. Chandonette   Petrus
1779–1862   1774–1855   1781–1862   1783–1821   1789–1851   1786–1788

Peter   Guert   Catherine = George Curtis   Leonard   Francis M.   Herman   Stanwix
1810–1832   1812–1868   1814–1887   1789–1884   1816–1864   1818–1819   1820–1826   1822–1901

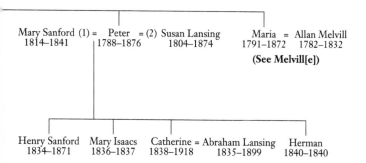

Mary Sanford (1) = Peter = (2) Susan Lansing   Maria = Allan Melvill
  1814–1841 |1788–1876   1804–1874   1791–1872 1782–1832

(See Melvill[e])

Henry Sanford Mary Isaacs Catherine = Abraham Lansing Herman
  1834–1871   1836–1837   1838–1918   1835–1899   1840–1840

Documentation

Page by page, this book is composed from nineteenth-century manuscripts and periodicals more than from printed works (other than those in *The Writings of Herman Melville*). The hundreds of quotations from nineteenth-century periodicals are all dated in the text, and locating them is further simplified now that the items in the largest category of such quotations are all reprinted in the 1995 *Herman Melville: The Contemporary Reviews*, ed. Brian Higgins and Hershel Parker (cited under Melville studies, below). While much information is provided in the text, fuller documentation is supplied here, in three main sections. In the first, I acknowledge, chapter by chapter, some basic historical and biographical studies I have drawn on and acknowledge also some benefactors, academic and otherwise. I also comment a few times on my reading of the available evidence. The second section deals with my quotations from manuscripts and the third with my use of Melville studies and other printed sources, aside from nineteenth-century periodicals. As a coda I include a note on the status of *The New Melville Log*, on which this biography is based.

Special Sources, Benefactors, and Notes on Evidence

[Ch. 1] Page 2: The description of Melville's great-grandfather John Scollay is from Wesley S. Griswold in *The Night the Revolution Began* (Battleboro: Stephen Greene Press, 1972). 6: Here and in other early chapters Alice P. Kenney (below) is my source for information about the Gansevoort estate at Gansevoort, New York, including the challenges to Herman Gansevoort's possession of it. 9: Haskell Springer (below) printed Allan Melvill's letter to the earl of Leven and Melville. 19: Melville's copy of Milton's poems is at Princeton.

[Ch. 2] 28–32: I have seen a few of the pieces of furniture described here, but I rely mainly on various family lists, such as Elizabeth Shaw Melville's "Memoranda" printed in Merton M. Sealts Jr., *The Early Lives of Melville* (below), and the inventory of the house at Gansevoort, N.Y., made after the death of Melville's sister Frances (Berkshire Athenaeum). The items in the Gansevoort house on Market Street in Albany are derived in part from a copy of an early typed inventory in Jay Leyda's papers (supplied by Victor Paltsits?) of the furniture in the estate of Catherine Gansevoort Lansing; in part from items mentioned by Huybertie Pruyn Hamlin (below); in part from items mentioned in a clipping in the Berkshire Athenaeum from an

unidentified Albany newspaper of 23 January 1918; and in part from objects
in museums. The regimental flag of Melville's Gansevoort grandfather is
displayed in the Albany Institute of History and Art and is described in
Regimental Colors in the War of the Revolution, by Gherardi Davis (New York:
Gilliss Press, 1907).

[Ch. 3] 63: Dr. Henry A. Murray and Charles Olson long were aware of
the letter in the Massachusetts Historical Society from Thomas Melvill Jr. to
Lemuel Shaw about Mrs. A. M. A. and Mrs. B.; after the publication of that
letter by Amy Puett Emmers (below), Dr. Murray enlisted Harvey Myerson
and Eugene Taylor as coauthors of "Allan Melvill's By-blow," *Melville Society
Extracts* 61 (February 1985), 1–6.

[Ch. 4] 72: Allan Melvill's set of Spenser, later heavily marked by Herman
Melville, is owned by Priscilla Ambrose; I report Melville's marginalia in this
set more fully in my second volume. 78: Harrison Hayford provided me with
his notes on family documents in the Suffolk County Probate Office, including the will of Thomas Melvill Sr.

[Ch. 5] 85: Alice P. Kenney is the source for Peter Gansevoort's courtship
of Mary Sanford and their negotiating over where to live. 92: I take from
William H. Gilman's 1951 book (below) the reference to a clipping on the
Albany Young Men's Association in a scrapbook in the Harmanus Bleecker
Library (now the Albany Public Library). In my possession are two foot-long
filing boxes of Gilman's notes for his Yale dissertation (1947); relying on
these notes, I have taken into account a good many family letters I have not
seen (mainly in the Gansevoort-Lansing Collection of the New York Public
Library). 92: Aware of errors elsewhere in the printed text of Gansevoort
Melville's lost 1834 diary, I emend "may come in contact with it" in the
comments on a story by T. S. Surr to "may come in conflict with it." 95: The
description of the house at 3 Clinton Square derives from Gilman's notes and
photographs as well as his book. 101: Here and elsewhere in the early chapters I quote Melville's memoir of Thomas Melvill Jr. from Merton M. Sealts's
article in the *Harvard Library Bulletin* (1987), cited below.

[Ch. 6] 110–12, 122–24: Melville's letters to the editor of the Albany
Microscope are in the issues of 24 Feb., 17, 24, and 31 March 1838 (the first
two signed "Philologian," the second two "Philologean"), and are printed in
the *Correspondence* volume of the Northwestern-Newberry (NN) Edition of
The Writings of Herman Melville, as are the related letters. Jay Leyda found
the Philo Logos letters (in the apparently unique copy at the New York State
Library) just in time to share them with Gilman and to include them in *The
Melville Log* (below), but in his haste he put the 14 April 1837 letter about
Melville in 1838, thereby misleading Leon Howard (below).

[Ch. 9] 169: Stanton Garner (below) discovered the autobiographical account of Clarissa Emely Gear Hobbs (below), from which I take the Hezekiah H. Gear–Thomas Melvill Jr. dialogue.

[Ch. 10] 185: The information about the salvaging of the cenotaphs from the burnt Seaman's Bethel in New Bedford and about pilgrimages there by readers of *Moby-Dick* was supplied by Chris Fauske from clippings the Bostonian music critic Philip Hale (1854–1934) placed in a copy of the 1892 United States Book Company *Moby-Dick* (Special Collections, the library of the University of New Hampshire, Durham). 185: The description of the *Acushnet* by the owners is in the National Archives, Department of Commerce, as quoted in the *Log*. 187–88: Melville's notes on what his shipmate Henry F. Hubbard told him about the crew of the *Acushnet* are best dated and transcribed in "Melville's *Acushnet* Crew Memorandum," in the Northwestern-Newberry edition of *Moby-Dick*. 196: Melville's notes in his copy of Owen Chase are best reproduced and transcribed in "Melville's Memoranda in Chase's *Narrative of the Essex*," in the Northwestern-Newberry edition of *Moby-Dick*. The 1951 *Log* includes most of the ships' logs quoted in ch. 10; the log of the *Coquette* (p. 202) is at the Nantucket Historical Association.

[Ch. 11] 213: The journal kept on the *Potomac* is quoted from Mary Malloy (below), and verified by John Koza, Phillips Library, Peabody & Essex Museum, Salem, Massachusetts.

[Ch. 12] 219: For this chapter Harrison Hayford provided photocopies and microfilm of the documents about the mutiny on the *Lucy Ann* and Melville's stay in Tahiti (including documents printed in the 1969 Hendricks House edition of *Omoo*). 228: Rita Gollin (below) found the Libbey memoir in the *Shaker Manifesto* (January-December 1878).

[Ch. 13] 242: The verbatim testimony about the *Somers* hangings is from Henry G. Langley (below).

[Ch. 14] 271: Wilson Heflin's typescript "Introduction" to *White-Jacket* (below) records his discovery that Lieutenant James Lardner recalled that Melville was stationed "in the After-Guard" on the *United States*, "not in the Main top."

[Ch. 15] 309: Samuel Shaw, third son of Lemuel Shaw, in his article in *Memorial Biographies* (below), records his father's early thoughts on literary pursuits and his schoolteaching. 309: My portrayal of the Harper brothers derives in part from Charlotte Hoadley's telling recollections of Melville's private comments on the Harpers (quoted in ch. 19 and ch. 23), in part from Richard Henry Dana's depiction of the way they gained the copyright to his *Two Years before the Mast* ("An Autobiographical Sketch," in the first volume of his *Journal*, below). It differs markedly from that in the history of Harper & Brothers by J. Henry Harper (below), for whom his grandfather Fletcher was modest, private, and conspicuous for noble manliness, while the others (in an 1877 tribute he quoted) were "the cheery James, the indomitable John, the gracious Wesley."

[Ch. 16] 322: Most of my precise physical descriptions of politicians and editors derive from a single source, the galleries of illustrations in John Niven, *Martin Van Buren: The Romantic Age of American Politics* (New York: Oxford Univ. Press, 1983). 330: My comments on Jesus' traveling toward the United States derive from Lydia Maria Child's article in the Boston *Courier*, reprinted in the *Liberator* of 25 October 1844 (and quoted in my account of Melville's homecoming in the 1995 *Resources for American Literary Study*, below).

[Ch. 17] 346: My depiction of Kate Melville's compulsive behavior is influenced by a comment in an undated clipping in the Berkshire Athenaeum from the *Ledger* (no city given): "Mrs. Hoadley is all precision, and is unhappy if she has to eat off a table cloth all awry, or sit in front of a castor, that is not in the proper geometrical position."

[Ch. 18] 359: I use Hayford's set of the National Archives file of Gansevoort Melville's 1845 recommendations for office.

[Ch. 19] 374: Fanny Melville's copy of *Voices of the Night* survives because in the 1950s Mrs. Paul Barden managed to rescue it from a load of trash tossed out of the Manor House in Gansevoort and bound for the dump. It was cheaply bound together with several novels, including *Jane Eyre*, the whole misstamped "NOVELS" on the spine. Responsible as well as alert, Mrs. Barden later donated the unwieldy object to the Lansingburgh Historical Society, headquartered in the house on River Street that Maria Melville rented (now disguised by Victorian renovations).

[Ch. 20] 400: I refer to *The Marquesan Journal of Edward Robarts, 1797–1824* (Honolulu: Univ. Press of Hawaii, 1974); its editor, Greg Dening, cites a still-unpublished Marquesan journal by W. P. Crook, copy in the Mitchell Library, Sydney.

[Ch. 22] 437: Weed's indiscreet (and somewhat imprecise) revelations are in his *Autobiography* (below).

[Ch. 23] 457: For separating fact from fiction in *Omoo* I rely primarily on the documents Hayford provided me (most of which he printed in the Hendricks House *Omoo*), but I also use Wilson Heflin's study of contemporary annotations in a first edition of *Omoo* in St. John's College Library (typescript in Jay Leyda's papers). 462–63: For the description of Bond Street I draw on Richard Lathers's *Reminiscences* (below) and on Henry T. Tuckerman's memoir of Dr. John W. Francis (below). 465: Tuckerman's "Reminiscences of Fitz-Greene Halleck" (below) is the source for Halleck's firmly-set jaw. 471: The physical description of Charles Fenno Hoffman by

William Keese is from his *John Keese: Wit and Litterateur* (New York: D. Appleton, 1883), and is quoted from Homer F. Barnes (below).

[Ch. 24] 476: James F. Beard's comments on Cooper's finances are from *The Letters and Journals of James Fenimore Cooper* (6 vols., Cambridge: Harvard Univ. Press, 1960–68), vol. 4, pp. 435–36. 483: John Romeyn Brodhead's "pretty sharp letter" is in Birss (below).

[Ch. 25] 499: Photocopies from the bookdealer Kent Bicknell, Sandonton, N.H., are the source of what I say about Melville's copy of Bennett's *Narrative of a Whaling Voyage*. 500: Alice P. Kenney is the source for the judgment against the Gansevoorts of Gansevoort.

[Ch. 26] 529: The Parisian look of Bond Street in the 1840s is from Henry T. Tuckerman's 1865 memoir of Dr. John W. Francis. 535: The information about Charles Fenno Hoffman's spoof letters between Secretary of War William L. Marcy and General Zachary Taylor is from Homer F. Barnes (below), but I have redated them from the impossible 1845 to late 1846. 540: The account of Judge Shaw's student friendships is from his son Samuel Shaw's "Lemuel Shaw" (below). 544: Two other people who may have attended the wedding are Mr. and Mrs. William Baldwin; Elizabeth Shaw wrote out an invitation to them on 21 July 1847 (now in the Houghton Library of Harvard University). 545: The account of Judge Shaw's ascent of Mount Washington in 1816 is from Samuel Shaw's "Lemuel Shaw" (below).

[Ch. 27] 553: It was William H. Gilman who discovered in the New York City Book of Conveyances (498, pp. 183–85) what I say about Melville's indenture of lease on the house on Fourth Avenue. 563: The record of tea time is from *American Life: A Narrative of Two Years' City and Country Residence in the United States* (London[?]: Bolton Percey, 1843), by the observant but reticent author known only as "Mrs. Felton."

[Ch. 28] 570: The description of the café in Warren Street is from Tuckerman's "Reminiscences of Fitz-Greene Halleck" (below). 583: For Augusta Melville's copy of *Jane Eyre*, retrieved by Mrs. Paul Barden, see p. 428 and the note to p. 374 above (in the paragraph on ch. 19).

[Ch. 29] 601: I quote Richard Henry Dana Jr. on Melville from the *Log* or Dana's *Journal* (below), but for Dana's letters about politics I rely on transcriptions made at the Massachusetts Historical Society in 1962 for my dissertation, particularly Dana's review of current history in his 21 July 1848 letter to his brother Edmund, then in Heidelberg. 602: Tuckerman's account of Halleck's love of Fort Lee is in his 1868 "Reminiscences" (below).

[Ch. 30] 616: Melville's annotated set of Shakespeare is at the Houghton Library, Harvard; see in the Northwestern-Newberry edition of *Moby-Dick* "Melville's Notes (1849–51) in a Shakespeare Volume," and see Geoffrey

Sanborn (below). 618: As indicated earlier, Melville's Milton is at Princeton. 619: The comments on *Mardi* by Richard Bentley's reader are in Horth (below). 632: Cooper on the literati's blithe petition to Macready is from vol. 6 of *The Letters and Journals of James Fenimore Cooper* (cited in the note for ch. 24, above).

[Ch. 31] 645: Background on Powell is in the "Historical Note" to the Northwestern-Newberry edition of *Moby-Dick*, which draws on my long-delayed *Herman Melville and the Powell Papers* (below). 648: Melville's reading of *Amadis de Gaul* is unattested, but he and others in his family knew the poetry of Sir Walter Scott, who in the introductory epistle to "Marmion" alludes to Amadis's fighting the Necromancer for Oriana. Elizabeth Shaw Melville was Oriana, or Orianna, the heroine of a romance; Herman Melville was the knight, soon to fare forth to do battle. 652: For Gaines and Bercaw on Melville's use of the *Penny Cyclopædia*, see below; Bercaw credits Wilson Heflin with pointing out Melville's use of the entry on "Skeleton."

[Ch. 32] Most of this chapter is retold from the 1849–50 section of the Northwestern-Newberry edition of Melville's *Journals* (1989), ed. Howard Horsford with Lynn Horth.

[Ch. 33] 694: In contemporary accounts of the *Globe* mutiny the name Mulgrave Islands was applied to some atolls in the Marshall Islands.

[Ch. 35] 732: The description of the Pittsfield cemetery at Briggs's funeral is from William C. Richards, *Great in Goodness: A Memoir of George N. Briggs, Governor of the Commonwealth of Massachusetts from 1844–1851* (Boston: Gould, 1867). 736: Melville's copy of the *History of the County of Berkshire* is in the Berkshire Athenaeum. 741: The May 1851 article on Mathews by Powell is in *Figaro!*; Powell threatened to print an essay on Duyckinck about the same time, but that piece is not in Duyckinck's own rapidly disintegrating file (Newspaper Division, New York Public Library). The other known files of *Figaro!*, at the Library of Congress, Harvard, and the Newberry, are all shorter than the NYPL file, but there are some scattered late issues (in larger format) at the New-York Historical Society. In 1951 Jay Leyda rightly intuited that Powell's announced essay on Melville might have appeared in a newspaper; the article on Duyckinck is a prize well worth the seeking. 743: The description of Sunday, 4 August 1850, takes some details from Cornelius Mathews, "Several Days in Berkshire," Part I, "Introductory," *Literary World* (24 August 1850). 744: The description of the outing to Monument Mountain is constructed from several documents: Evert Duyckinck to his brother, George, 7 August 1850; Evert Duyckinck to his wife, 6 August 1850; Sophia Hawthorne to her sister Elizabeth Peabody, 8 August 1850; Cornelius Mathews, "Several Days in Berkshire," *Literary World* (Part II, "The Mountain Festival," 31 August 1850); James T. Fields, *Yesterdays with Authors* (below); Hawthorne's *American Notebooks* (below); Joel T. Headley, "Berkshire Scenery," New York *Observer* (14 September 1850); Henry Dwight Sedgwick, "Reminiscences of Literary Berkshire," *Century Magazine* (August 1895); and, among the documents acquired by the New York Public Library in 1983, Maria Melville to Augusta Melville, 8 August 1850.

[Ch. 36] 756: On the analogy of the "sacred White Dog" in *Moby-Dick* (ch. 42) and other associations of white and sacred in Melville (not least a godlike albino whale), I edgily make the white doe in Melville's essay on Hawthorne "sacred" instead of "scared," the word as copied by Melville's wife. In Melville, Truth is apt to be holy, even if secretive; as narrator he calls *Pierre* (bk. 5, ch. 7) "this book of sacred truth." The word "scared," plausible but less fraught with Melvillean meanings, I take to be one of the unspecified "ugly errors" or "provoking" mistakes Melville said were in the printed text. 770: After I discovered an account of how the Irvings reacted when the anonymous essay on Hawthorne in the *Literary World* of 24 August 1850 reached Sunnyside, Wayne R. Kime directed me to Pierre Irving's outline for his biography of his uncle in the Berg Collection of the New York Public Library. The younger Irving's angry notations on the anonymous author of the essay on Hawthorne are in my *Herman Melville and the Powell Papers* (below).

[Ch. 37] 782: Thomas Melvill Jr.'s penmanship exercise book is at the Houghton Library, Harvard, a recent gift from Jean Melvill. 787: Maria Melville in a letter to Augusta, 6 March 1852, alludes to her son Allan's frequent filial deprecation of his wife's Aunt Catherine-like behavior. 791: In Augusta Melville's 23 November 1850 letter to her sister Helen I transcribe the guest list as concluding with "Major and the slay," meaning the horse and the "sleigh" (the farm wasn't home without a Major Melvill on the premises?). This makes eight guests for the table in Melville's study, not ten. Dodgy, ironic family humor is a bane of the literal-minded transcriber and biographer; another bane is arithmetic never meant to withstand the scrutiny of the centuries.

[Ch. 38] 812: In the epigraph for the chapter, the book Fanny Melville read was in all likelihood a cheap tiny-print double-columned American edition of *The Manoeuvring Mother* (London: H. Colburn, 1842), a three-decker by Charlotte Campbell Bury (1775–1861), lady-in-waiting when Queen Caroline was the Princess of Wales; the font used in the American editions of British novels Mrs. Barden salvaged (see note on ch. 19, above) is cruelly small. 813: Gansevoort Melville's pestering Catharine Maria Sedgwick is from Eliza Sedgwick to Catharine Sedgwick (15 January 1838), Sedgwick family papers in the Massachusetts Historical Society. 824: Information about the sale of the indenture of lease on the Fourth Avenue house (as in ch. 27) is from William H. Gilman.

[Ch. 39] 847: In the surviving manuscript fragments of *The Confidence-Man* is the notation: "Dedicated to victims of Auto da Fe"; I enlarged a facsimile of it as the "unofficial dedication" in the Norton Critical Edition (New York: W. W. Norton, 1971). 860: Sarah Morewood's account of "That Excursion to Greylock," is in Joseph E. A. Smith, *Taghconic; or, Letters and Legends about Our Summer Home* (Boston: Redding, 1852).

[Ch. 40] 865: The 23 January 1918 clipping about Peter Gansevoort's house on Washington Street is in the Berkshire Athenaeum. 874: Ellery Channing's letters to his wife, Ellen Fuller Channing, are from "The Selected Letters of William Ellery Channing the Younger (Part Two)," ed. Francis B. Dedmond, *Studies in the American Renaissance* (1990). 875: In 1987 at the Boston Public Library I came across an intriguing description of the Hawthorne cottage reprinted in a Lowell paper, a letter originally written from Lenox by "Maherbal" for the Windsor, Vermont *Journal*. After I had sought the *Journal* for five years, Richard E. Winslow III, an authority on provincial New England newspapers, located a file for me. Predictably, the correspondent had written other letters home, one of which was unpredictably valuable — the one describing the sensation created in Lenox by the meeting of Hawthorne and Melville in the dining room of a hotel. As I explain in a 1995 article in *Resources for American Literary Study*, my final scene in this volume is an imaginative reconstruction, based on Maherbal's letter and other evidence. 882: Melville's vehement annotations about country people are in his copy of William Hazlitt's *Lectures on the English Poets* (New York: Derby & Jackson, 1859), owned by William Reese.

Throughout, I took numerous hints from Jay Leyda's private correspondence and notes for the third edition of the *Log*, notably two typescripts Wilson Heflin had sent him (below). Cuyler Reynolds (below) and Alice P. Kenney were indispensable for family relationships. The Berkshire Athenaeum's Gansevoort Genealogical Tree, intricately branched and fruit-laden, was invaluable for dates used in the Index (such as the birthdate of Hun or Hunn Gansevoort) as well as in the text.

Quotations from Manuscripts

Rather than footnoting each of the hundreds of quotations from nineteenth-century manuscripts, I have cited them in a chart of correspondents, below. Leon Howard's 1951 *Herman Melville: A Biography* (below) contained no documentation because it was timed to appear with Jay Leyda's *The Melville Log*, on which it was based. My biography is also complexly related to the

Log, which Leyda charged me with continuing into a third edition. As I explain in the preface, by mid-1988 the "*Log*" I used was the version in my computer, corrected and augmented from day to day. This ever-varying digitized *Log* facilitated the editing of the Northwestern-Newberry edition of Melville's *Correspondence* (1993), and it was the digitized version, still further enlarged, from which I drafted most episodes in this biography. In arriving at accurate dates for newly discovered manuscripts (and for redating some long-known documents) my most important tool was the sheer mass of transcriptions of new manuscripts, but the surviving portion of Augusta Melville's record of her correspondence — intact for the period of the composition of *Moby-Dick* — was nothing less than a godsend. Even for long-known family letters I have found it impracticable to cite the 1951 *Log* since the working version of *The New Melville Log* contains many corrections and additions to documents in the 1951 edition and contains additional letters from correspondents already in that edition.

Often enough letters from a particular person to another survive in only one archive, or else the bulk of one side of a correspondence survives in only one archive. As it happens, any known letter from Maria Gansevoort Melville to her daughter Augusta is in the Gansevoort-Lansing Collection of the New York Public Library. Almost all letters from Thomas Melvill Jr. to Lemuel Shaw are in the Shaw Collection of the Massachusetts Historical Society, but a few of the most important letters are at Harvard. When a letter or a few letters are preserved apart from the body of the correspondence, I identify the location in a parenthetical comment in the chart below, and sometimes also identify its present anomalous location in the text, as in the case of the 16 May 1851 letter from Augusta Melville to her brother Allan about the completion of *Moby-Dick* (recently deposited at Arrowhead by Anna Morewood, the widow of one of Allan's grandsons). Letters from Lemuel Shaw are found in several collections, but a letter from Lemuel Shaw identified as a draft can be assumed (unless otherwise specified) to have remained in Shaw's possession and to have been preserved in the Shaw Collection of the Massachusetts Historical Society; similarly, anything identified as a draft written by Peter Gansevoort can be assumed (unless otherwise specified) to be in the New York Public Library, Gansevoort-Lansing Collection. In my chart of correspondents I have cited the 1951 *Log* a few times for isolated manuscripts I have not yet seen, such as passages from the diary of Stephen Reynolds. (In the absence of a daily Honolulu newspaper for 1843, such a diary is a good bet for dating more precisely the arrival of news of the *Somers*.)

In my chart of correspondents (which includes some documents concerning them) I make a few slight corrections of institutional datings and identifications, as when I ascribe letters not to Millie Van Rensselaer Thayer but to the actual Cornelia (Nilly) Van Rensselaer Thayer. I date in the text all manuscripts I quote from, and I call attention there to anomalies, such as an important letter filed and microfilmed wrong because Lemuel Shaw himself misdated it by a decade.

Abbreviations

Arrowhead Berkshire County Historical Society, Pittsfield, Massachusetts

BA The Berkshire Athenaeum, Pittsfield, Massachusetts

Extracts Frederick and Joyce Deveau Kennedy's articles (below) in the Melville Society newsletter

HCL-M The Houghton Library, Manuscript Department, Harvard University (Melville family material is shelfmarked bMS Am 188–bMS Am 188.7)

MHS-D The Massachusetts Historical Society, Dana Collection

MHS-S The Massachusetts Historical Society, Lemuel Shaw Collection

NA-S The National Archives, State Department

NYPL-Berg Henry W. and Albert A. Berg Collection, The New York Public Library, Astor, Lenox, and Tilden Foundations

NYPL-D Duyckinck Collection, Rare Books and Manuscripts Division, The New York Public Library, Astor, Lenox, and Tilden Foundations

NYPL-GL Gansevoort-Lansing Collection, Rare Books and Manuscripts Division, The New York Public Library, Astor, Lenox, and Tilden Foundations.

Chart of Correspondents

Jedediah Auld to George Duyckinck and William Allen Butler NYPL-D

Joel Barlow to Thomas Jefferson (Thomas Melvill Jr.'s copy in his letter to Lemuel Shaw, 3 Feb. 1834) MHS-S

Mary Blatchford to Augusta Melville NYPL-GL

John R. Brodhead's diary *Log*

James Buchanan to Louis McLane *Log* (3 and 13 Dec. 1845: *The Works of James Buchanan*, vol. 6 [1909])

James Buchanan to Gansevoort Melville (diplomatic passport, copy with later notations by Buchanan) NA-S

William Allen Butler to Evert A. Duyckinck NYPL-GL

David Cargill to Thomas Melvill Sr. HCL-M

John Cramer to James K. Polk *Correspondence of James K. Polk* (below)

William E. Cramer to Gansevoort Melville NYPL-GL

Edwin W. Croswell to James K. Polk *Correspondence of James K. Polk* (below)

Richard Henry Dana Jr. to Edmund Dana MHS-D

Richard Henry Dana Jr. to Richard Henry Dana Sr. MHS-D

Catherine Dix to an unidentified correspondent *Log*

Margaret (Maggie) Van Rensselaer Douw to Augusta Melville NYPL-GL

Evert A. Duyckinck's diary NYPL-D (for 1847: Yannella and Yannella, below)

Evert A. Duyckinck's record of books lent NYPL-D

Evert A. Duyckinck to George Long Duyckinck NYPL-D

Evert A. Duyckinck to Margaret Panton Duyckinck NYPL-D

Evert A. Duyckinck to Nathaniel Hawthorne (letterbook) NYPL-D

George Duyckinck to Joann Miller NYPL-D

George Duyckinck to Rosalie Miller NYPL-D

James T. Fields to Henry Wadsworth Longfellow *Log*

Eli James Murdock Fly to Peter Gansevoort NYPL-GL

Gansevoort Genealogical Tree BA

Catherine Quackenboss Gansevoort to Peter Gansevoort NYPL-GL

Catherine Van Schaick Gansevoort (copy of will, 1 March 1831) BA

Elizabeth Gansevoort (later Ogden) to Augusta Melville NYPL-GL

Guert Gansevoort to Mary Ann Chandonette Gansevoort NYPL-GL

Henry Sanford Gansevoort to Catherine Gansevoort (Melville's cousin Kitty, later
     Catherine Gansevoort Lansing) NYPL-GL

Herman Gansevoort's "Checkbook and Remembrancer, 1823–1832" NYPL-GL

Herman Gansevoort to Peter Gansevoort NYPL-GL

Hunn (or Hun) Gansevoort to Stanwix Gansevoort NYPL-GL

Mary Ann Chandonette Gansevoort to Catherine Quackenboss Gansevoort NYPL-
     GL

Mary Ann Chandonette Gansevoort to Peter Gansevoort NYPL-GL (2 January
     1843: quoted from Hayford, *The Somers Mutiny Affair*, below)

Mary Ann Chandonette Gansevoort to Stanwix Gansevoort NYPL-GL

Mary Sanford Gansevoort to Peter Gansevoort NYPL-GL

Mary Sanford Gansevoort to Edward Sanford NYPL-GL

Peter Gansevoort to William C. Bouck (draft) NYPL-GL

Peter Gansevoort to Catherine Van Schaick Gansevoort NYPL-GL

Peter Gansevoort to Guert Gansevoort (draft) NYPL-GL

Peter Gansevoort to Herman Gansevoort NYPL-GL

Peter Gansevoort to Leonard Gansevoort NYPL-GL

Peter Gansevoort to Mary Sanford Gansevoort NYPL-GL

Peter Gansevoort to Allan Melvill (typed copy of 14 June 1825) BA and HCL-M

Peter Gansevoort to Maria Gansevoort Melvill (Melville) NYPL-GL

Peter Gansevoort to Thomas Melvill Jr. NYPL-GL

Peter Gansevoort to Lemuel Shaw (draft) NYPL-GL

Peter Gansevoort to Lemuel Shaw MHS-S

Joseph Greenleaf to Peter Gansevoort NYPL-GL

George Griggs to Augusta Melville NYPL-GL

J. George Harris to George Bancroft Massachusetts Historical Society–Bancroft Collection

Sophia Hawthorne to Evert A. Duyckinck NYPL-GL

Sophia Hawthorne to Elizabeth Peabody (her mother) NYPL-Berg

Sophia Hawthorne to Elizabeth Peabody (her sister) NYPL-Berg

John J. Hill to Peter Gansevoort NYPL-GL

Charlotte Hoadley to Victor Hugo Paltsits New-York Historical Society

Augusta Whipple Hunter to Augusta Melville NYPL-GL

Pierre Irving's outline for his biography of Washington Irving NYPL-Berg

Richard Lathers to Allan Melville (a fragment, 24 April 1848) BA

Frances (Fanny) Appleton Longfellow to Nathan Appleton *Log*

Henry Wadsworth Longfellow to Nathaniel Hawthorne *Log*

Robert H. McCurdy to John M. Clayton NA-S

Louis McLane to James Buchanan *Log* (18 May 1846: NA-S)

Philip Marett to Lemuel Shaw MHS-S

Cornelius Mathews to Elizabeth Shaw Melville HCL-M

Allan Melvill's diary for 1800–1831 HCL-M

Allan Melvill's penmanship exercise book Reese Collection

Allan Melvill's "Recapitulations of Voyages and Travels from 1800 to 1822 both inclusive" NYPL-GL

Allan Melvill to "a business associate in Paris" (letterbook) NYPL-GL

Allan Melvill to J. S. Cast HCL-M

Allan Melvill to Cyrus Chenery NYPL-GL

Allan Melvill to the earl of Leven and Melville Scottish Record Office (quoted from Springer, below)

Allan Melvill to Catherine Van Schaick Gansevoort (14 Oct. 1826) BA

Allan Melvill to Guert Gansevoort NYPL-GL

Allan Melvill to Peter Gansevoort NYPL-GL (BA: 6 Feb., 29 Aug., 23 Nov. 22; 26 Apr., 19 June 1823; 9 June, 7 Sept. 1825; 21 Jan. 26, 8 April, 15 April, 4 Sept., 26 Sept. 1826; 11 Oct., 15 Dec. 1827. HCL-M: 18 Sept., 26 Sept. 1820; 10 May 1824)

Allan Melvill to Joseph Greenleaf NYPL-GL

Allan Melvill to Augusta Melvill (Melville) (1830 — not part of the Augusta Papers) NYPL-GL

Allan Melvill to Maria Gansevoort Melvill NYPL-GL (BA: 28 July 1818)

Allan Melvill to Thomas Melvill Sr. NYPL-GL (BA: 12 Sept. 1829; HCL-M: 4 Dec. 1830)

Allan Melvill to Lemuel Shaw MHS-S (some letters of 1804 are in HCL-M)

Allan Melvill to Thomas W. Melvill *Log*

Allan Melvill to Robert Swan (copy) BA

Anne Melvill to Augusta Melville NYPL-GL

Helen Melvill (Souther) to Lemuel Shaw HCL-M

Julia Maria Melvill to Augusta Melville NYPL-GL

Mary Ann Augusta Hobart Melvill (Mrs. Thomas Melvill Jr.) to Lemuel
Shaw MHS-S

Nancy Wroe Melvill to Lemuel Shaw Social Law Library, Boston

Priscilla Melvill (later, sometimes, Melville) to her cousin Augusta Melville NYPL-
GL

Priscilla Melvill (Melville) to Lemuel Shaw MHS-S

Robert Melvill to Lemuel Shaw MHS-S

Robert Melvill to Lemuel Shaw and John D'Wolf MHS-S

Thomas Melvill Jr.'s *Self Interpreting Bible* HCL-M

Thomas Melvill Jr. to George N. Briggs BA

Thomas Melvill Jr. to Peter Gansevoort NYPL-GL

Thomas Melvill Jr. to Allan Melvill MHS-S

Thomas Melvill Jr. to his parents, Thomas Melvill Sr. and Priscilla Scollay Melvill
HCL-M

Thomas Melvill Jr. to Lemuel Shaw MHS-S (HCL-M: 15, 27, 29 Jan. 1832; 8 Nov.
1836)

Thomas Melvill Jr. to Lemuel Shaw and John D'Wolf MHS-S

Thomas W. Melvill to Allan Melvill NYPL-GL

Allan Melville's autobiographical sketch (July 1843) BA

Allan Melville to Richard Bentley (draft) HCL-M (quoted from Northwestern-
Newberry *Moby-Dick*, p. 671)

Allan Melville to Evert A. Duyckinck NYPL-D

Allan Melville to Helen Maria Melville NYPL-GL

Augusta Melville's commonplace book, "Orient Pearls at Random Strung" BA

Augusta Melville's composition (the epigraph to ch. 6) NYPL-GL

Augusta Melville's correspondence record, 1849–54 NYPL-GL

Augusta Melville's "Excursions" (1852) Reese Collection

Augusta Melville to Mary Blatchford NYPL-GL

Augusta Melville to Margaret (Maggie) Van Rensselaer Douw NYPL-GL

Augusta Melville to Evert A. Duyckinck NYPL-D

Augusta Melville to Susan Lansing Gansevoort NYPL-GL

Augusta Melville to Allan Melville BA (12 August 1839; 16 May 1851 at Arrowhead)

Augusta Melville to Elizabeth Shaw Melville (27 Jan. 1849) HCL-M

Augusta Melville to Helen Maria Melville NYPL-GL

Augusta Melville to Catherine Van Schaick (her second cousin) New York State
Library

Elizabeth Shaw Melville to Samuel H. Savage *Extracts* 33 (12–18 Sept. 1847; 3 April
1848: *Extracts* 39)

Elizabeth Shaw Melville to Hope Savage Shaw HCL-M

Elizabeth Shaw Melville to Lemuel Shaw MHS-S (21 August 1847; 30 June 1851 at HCL-M)

Frances (Fanny) Priscilla Melville, essay, "Myself" NYPL-GL

Frances (Fanny) Priscilla Melville to Thomas Melville NYPL-GL

Gansevoort Melville's diplomatic passport NA-S

Gansevoort Melville's file of recommendations from politicians in 1845 NA-S

Gansevoort Melville's list of naval battles of the War of 1812 (on an envelope addressed to "Miss Melvill," inserted in an *Index Rerum*) BA

Gansevoort Melville to James Buchanan NA-S

Gansevoort Melville to William E. Cramer NYPL-GL (part of Augusta Melville Papers)

Gansevoort Melville to Peter Gansevoort NYPL-GL

Gansevoort Melville to Andrew Jackson Jackson Papers, Library of Congress (copies supplied by Carl Randall Cluff)

Gansevoort Melville to Col. Samuel Medary *Log*

Gansevoort Melville to Allan Melville BA

Gansevoort Melville to Catherine Melville (his sister) BA (only 20 July 1842)

Gansevoort Melville to Thomas Melville HCL-M (BA: 29 Jan. 1840; 28 May 1841; 14 May, 19 Sept. 1842)

Gansevoort Melville to John Murray *Log*

Gansevoort Melville to James K. Polk *Correspondence of James K. Polk* (below)

Gansevoort Melville to Lemuel Shaw MHS-S (HCL-M: 11 Jan. 1841; Social Law Library, Boston: 14 August 1841)

Helen Maria Melville to Peter Gansevoort NYPL-GL

Helen Maria Melville to Augusta Melville NYPL-GL

Helen Maria Melville to Augustus Van Schaick Univ. of Virginia–Barrett Collection (quoted from Northwestern-Newberry *Correspondence*)

Herman Melville to John M. Clayton NA-S (see Steven Olsen-Smith and Hershel Parker, below)

Maria Gansevoort Melville's account book for 1834–35 Reese Collection

Mortgage between Maria Gansevoort Melville and the N.Y. Life Ins. & Trust Co. *Log*

Maria Gansevoort Melville to Catherine Van Schaick Gansevoort NYPL-GL (BA: 28 Dec. 1826)

Maria Gansevoort Melville to her niece Catherine (Kitty) Gansevoort (24 May 1866) NYPL-GL

Maria Gansevoort Melville to Herman Gansevoort NYPL-GL

Maria Gansevoort Melville to Peter Gansevoort NYPL-GL (BA: 24 Dec. 1822; HCL-M: 11 March, 29 Dec. 1824)

Maria Gansevoort Melville to her son Allan Melville BA

Maria Gansevoort Melville to Augusta Melville NYPL-GL

Maria Gansevoort Melville to Gansevoort Melville NYPL-GL

Maria Gansevoort Melville to Hope Savage Shaw MHS-S

Maria Gansevoort Melville to Lemuel Shaw MHS-S (HCL-M: 20 June 1833)

Maria Gansevoort Melville to Conrad Ten Eyck NYPL-GL

Sophia Thurston Melville to Augusta Melville NYPL-GL

Sarah Huyler Morewood to George Long Duyckinck NYPL-D

Sarah Huyler Morewood to Ann McConnel William and Ruth Morewood Collection

John Murray to Gansevoort Melville *Log*

Nelson & Addoms to Peter Gansevoort *Log*

Amos Nourse to Lemuel Shaw MHS-S (HCL-M: 23, 29 July 1847)

Ellen Astor Oxenham to Augusta Melville NYPL-GL

Captain John Percival to Lemuel Shaw MHS-S

Gideon Pillow to George Bancroft Massachusetts Historical Society–Bancroft Collection

James K. Polk's diary *Log*

William H. Polk to Gansevoort Melville *Log*

Thomas Powell to Evert A. Duyckinck NYPL-D

Stephen Reynolds's diary *Log*

Ida Russell to Richard Henry Dana Jr. Dana, *Journal* (below)

Mary Sanford (see Mary Sanford Gansevoort)

Frederick Saunders's manuscript recollections NYPL (quoted from *Log*)

Samuel H. Savage to Hope Savage Shaw (30 April 1847) *Extracts* 35

Samuel H. Savage to Lemuel Shaw Jr. (Lem) *Extracts* 35

Elizabeth Shaw (see Elizabeth Shaw Melville)

Hope Savage Shaw's diary MHS-S

Hope Savage Shaw to Samuel H. Savage *Extracts* 31 (17 March 1849: *Extracts* 39)

Hope Savage Shaw to Lemuel Shaw MHS-S

John Oakes Shaw to Lemuel Shaw MHS-S

Lemuel Shaw to Benjamin R. Curtis (draft) MHS-S

Lemuel Shaw to Peter Gansevoort NYPL-GL

Lemuel Shaw to Robert Melvill (draft) MHS-S

Lemuel Shaw to Maria Gansevoort Melville NYPL-GL

Lemuel Shaw to Hope Savage Shaw MHS-S (HCL-M: 10 Oct. 1847)

Lemuel Shaw to John Oakes Shaw (draft) MHS-S

Lemuel Shaw to Susannah Shaw (his mother) MHS-S

Lemuel Shaw Jr. (Lem) to Samuel H. Savage (13 August 1847) *Extracts* 39

Samuel Shaw to Lemuel Shaw MHS-S

William Gilmore Simms to Evert A. Duyckinck *Log*

The Reverend Lowell Smith's diary *Log*

James Stevenson to Peter Gansevoort NYPL-GL

Bayard Taylor to Mary Agnew *Log*

Cornelia (Nilly) Van Rensselaer Thayer to Augusta Melville NYPL-GL

Caroline (Mrs. Charles) Thurston to Augusta Melville NYPL-GL

Sophia Thurston (see Sophia Thurston Melville)

Timothy Upham to A. P. Upshur Naval Records

Cornelia (Nilly) Van Rensselaer to Augusta Melville (see Cornelia [Nilly] Van Rens-
    selaer Thayer)

Margaret Van Rensselaer to Augusta Melville (see Margaret [Maggie] Van Rensselaer
    Douw)

John Van Schaick to Maria Gansevoort Melville NYPL-GL

Augusta Whipple to Augusta Melville (see Augusta Whipple Hunter)

William H. Wilcox's journal kept aboard the *United States* (transcribed by David
    Maxwell and Adriaen Morse, under the direction of Professor R. D. Madison)
    United States Naval Academy Museum

Wiley & Putnam to Allan Melville (and their account with Herman Melville) HCL-
    M

Melville Studies and Other Printed Sources

Unless otherwise specified, quotations from Melville's works are from *The Writings of Herman Melville* (Evanston and Chicago: Northwestern University Press and The Newberry Library), General Editor Harrison Hayford, Associate General Editor Hershel Parker, Bibliographical Editor G. Thomas Tanselle. Thirteen volumes of the NN Edition (as it is known) have appeared between 1968 and 1996. Since chapters in Melville's books are short, I identify quotations by chapter numbers, not page numbers. I locate passages in the draft of Melville's first book by citing the NN *Typee* page numbers where revised forms of the passages appear; and I cite NN page numbers to locate spots where passages in the draft pages would have fit if they had been retained. I name my source in the text whenever I quote from a surviving manuscript passage or from a specific early edition (such as the first American printing of *Typee*). In this volume, all quotations from letters by or to Melville are in the NN *Correspondence* except for those printed in the 1995 article by Steven Olsen-Smith and Hershel Parker (below). In the text is the new and old evidence which led me to redate to early May 1851 Melville's letter to Hawthorne customarily dated as around 1 June 1851. (Hayford concurs in this redating, made too late to go into the *Correspondence*.) Letters by Melville and to Melville are so short that I identify them only by their dates. Transcriptions of Melville's marginalia are from actual copies of his books, except that I have relied on Jay Leyda's 1951 *Log* for marginalia on Shakespeare's plays and on a photocopy for Melville's markings in Frederick

Debell Bennett's newly discovered *Narrative of a Whaling Voyage* (see the note on ch. 25, above).

For the location of books owned by Melville I have relied on the 1988 edition of Merton M. Sealts Jr.'s *Melville's Reading* and his 1990 supplement, except for a few very recent discoveries, such as the Bennett book. I have made much use of three "Historical Notes" in the editorial sections of volumes of *The Writings of Herman Melville*, my own in *Redburn*, Willard Thorp's in *White-Jacket*, and the one in *Moby-Dick* by all three editors, as well as other editorial sections in *Moby-Dick*, *Correspondence*, and *Journals* (from which I have quoted only the first, Melville's "Journal Of a Voyage from New York to London 1849"). When I quote only once or twice from a published source, such as Dickens's first edition of *American Notes* (1842), I include in the text a citation full enough for a reader to track the item down.

Alden, Carroll Storrs. *Lawrence Kearny: Sailor Diplomat*. Princeton: Princeton Univ. Press, 1936.

Barnes, Homer F. *Charles Fenno Hoffman*. New York: AMS Press, 1966 (a photofacsimile of the 1930 Columbia Univ. Press edition).

Bercaw, Mary K. "The Infusion of Useful Knowledge: Melville and *The Penny Cyclopaedia*." *Melville Society Extracts* 70 (September 1987), 9–13.

——. *Melville's Sources*. Evanston: Northwestern Univ. Press, 1987. (Bercaw provides "a checklist, keyed to Melville's works, of all the sources scholars have suggested Melville used.")

Birss, John H. " 'A Mere Sale to Effect,' with Letters of Herman Melville." *New Colophon* 1 (July 1948), 239–55.

Bryant, John. "Melville, 'Little Henry,' and the Process of Composition: A Peep at the *Typee* Fragment." *Melville Society Extracts* 67 (September 1986), 1–4.

Burg, B. R. *An American Seafarer in the Age of Sail: The Erotic Diaries of Philip C. Van Buskirk, 1851–1870*. New Haven: Yale Univ. Press, 1994.

Busch, Briton Cooper. *Whaling Will Never Do For Me: The American Whaleman in the Nineteenth Century*. Lexington: Univ. of Kentucky Press, 1994.

Casey, Janet Galligani. "New Letters of Gansevoort Melville: 1845–1846." *Studies in the American Renaissance* (1991), 141–50 (the letters are to Henry W. Ellsworth).

Dana, Richard Henry. *The Journal of Richard Henry Dana, Jr.* 3 vols. Ed. Robert F. Lucid. Cambridge: Harvard Univ. Press, 1968.

Davis, Merrell R. *Melville's "Mardi": A Chartless Voyage*. New Haven: Yale Univ. Press, 1952.

Davis, Merrell, and Harrison Hayford. "Melville as Office-Seeker." *Modern Language Quarterly* 10 (June 1949), 168–83; (September 1949), 377–88.

Drake, Francis S. *Tea Leaves: Being a Collection of Letters and Documents Relating to the*

Shipment of Tea to the American Colonies in the Year 1773, by the East India Tea Company. Boston: Crane, 1884.

D'Wolf, John. *A Voyage to the North Pacific and a Journey through Siberia, more than Half a Century Ago*. Cambridge: Welch, Bigelow, 1861. Ed. Harold M. Turner. Bristol, R.I.: Rulon-Miller Books, 1983.

Emmers, Amy Puett. "New Crosslights on the Illegitimate Daughter in *Pierre*." *Critical Essays on Herman Melville's "Pierre; or, The Ambiguities."* Ed. Brian Higgins and Hershel Parker. Boston: G. K. Hall, 1983. 237–40. (Originally printed as "Melville's Closet Skeleton: A New Letter about the Illegitimacy Incident in *Pierre*." *Studies in the American Renaissance* [1977], 339–43.)

Exman, Eugene. *The House of Harper: One Hundred and Fifty Years of Publishing*. New York: Harper & Row, 1967.

Fields, James T. *Yesterdays with Authors*. Boston: J. R. Osgood, 1872.

Gaines, Kendra. "A Consideration of an Additional Source for Melville's *Moby-Dick*." *Extracts* 29 (January 1977), 6–12.

Garner, Stanton. "The Picaresque Career of Thomas Melvill, Junior: Part II." *Melville Society Extracts* (May 1985), 1, 4–10.

Gilman, William H. *Melville's Early Life and "Redburn."* New York: New York Univ. Press, 1951.

Gollin, Rita K. "The Quondam Sailor and Melville's *Omoo*." *American Literature* 48 (March 1976), 75–79.

Hamlin, Huybertie Pruyn. *An Albany Girlhood*. Ed. Alice P. Kenney. Albany: Washington Park Press, 1990.

Hansen-Taylor, Marie, and Horace E. Scudder, eds. *Life and Letters of Bayard Taylor*. Boston: Houghton, Mifflin, 1884.

Harper, J. Henry. *The House of Harper: A Century of Publishing in Franklin Square*. New York: Harper & Brothers, 1912.

Hawthorne, Nathaniel. *The American Notebooks*. Ed. Claude M. Simpson. Columbus: Ohio State Univ. Press, 1972.

——. *The Letters, 1843–1853*. Ed. Thomas Woodson, L. Neal Smith, and Norman Holmes Pearson. Columbus: Ohio State Univ. Press, 1985.

Hayes, Kevin, and Hershel Parker. *Checklist of Melville Reviews*. Evanston: Northwestern Univ. Press, 1991.

Hayford, Harrison. See Merrell R. Davis.

Hayford, Harrison. "Melville and Hawthorne: A Biographical Study." Ph.D. dissertation, Yale Univ., 1946.

——. "The Sailor Poet of *White-Jacket*." *Boston Public Library Quarterly* 3 (July 1951), 221–28.

——. *The Somers Mutiny Affair*. Englewood Cliffs: Prentice-Hall, 1959.

——. Sections of the introduction and notes to *Omoo*. Ed. Harrison Hayford and Walter Blair. New York: Hendricks House, 1969.

Heflin, Wilson L. "Herman Melville's Whaling Years." Ph.D. dissertation, Vanderbilt Univ., 1952. (Mary K. Bercaw Edwards and Thomas Heffernan are preparing an edition of this classic study from the manuscript Heflin left unfinished, a revision incorporating the results of three decades of additional research.)

———. "An Introduction to Herman Melville's *White-Jacket*." Typescript (for Lieutenant James Lardner's recollection of Melville on the *United States*).

———. "A Man-of-War Button Divides Two Cousins." *Boston Public Library Quarterly* 3 (January 1951), 51–60.

———. "New Light on Herman Melville's Cruise in the *Charles and Henry*." *Historic Nantucket* 22 (October 1974), 6–27. Reprinted, Glassboro: The Melville Society, 1976. (Important for the list of books in the ship's library.)

———. "Sources from the Whale-Fishery and 'The Town-Ho's Story.'" *Artful Thunder: Versions of the Romantic Tradition in American Literature in Honor of Howard P. Vincent.* Kent: Kent State Univ. Press, 1975. 163–76. (Guided by Heflin, I went to the Honolulu *Friend* for the account of Luther Fox.)

———. Untitled talk on the authenticity of *Omoo* delivered at a meeting of the Melville Society at Princeton in 1973, based on study of contemporary annotations in a first edition of *Omoo* in St. John's College Library. (This typescript, in Jay Leyda's papers, is the source of my information about Alexander Simpson and Samuel Marcy in ch. 12.)

Higgins, Brian, and Hershel Parker. *Herman Melville: The Contemporary Reviews.* New York: Cambridge Univ. Press, 1995.

Hobbs, Clarissa Emely Gear. "The Galena Frontier." *Journal of the Illinois State Historical Society* 17 (1974), 611–714.

Horth, Lynn. "Richard Bentley's Place in Melville's Literary Career." *Studies in the American Renaissance* (1992), 229–45.

Irving, Pierre. *The Life and Letters of Washington Irving.* 4 vols. New York: G. P. Putnam, 1862–64.

Howard, Leon. *Herman Melville: A Biography.* Berkeley: Univ. of California Press, 1951.

Irving, Washington. *Letters.* Vol. 4 (1846–1859). Ed. Ralph M. Aderman, Herbert L. Kleinfield, and Jenifer S. Banks. Boston: Twayne, 1982.

Kennedy, Frederick and Joyce Deveau. "Additions to the *Melville Log*." *Extracts* 31 (1977), 4–8.

———. "Elizabeth and Herman (Part 1)." *Extracts* 33 (1978), 4–12.

———. "Elizabeth and Herman (Part 2)." *Melville Society Extracts* 34 (1978), 3–8.

———. "Elizabeth Shaw Melville and Samuel Hay Savage, 1847–1853." *Melville Society Extracts* 39 (1979), 1–7.

———. "Herman Melville and Samuel Hay Savage." *Melville Society Extracts* 35 (1978), 1–10.

———. "Some Naval Officers React to *White-Jacket*: An Untold Story." *Melville Society Extracts* 41 (1980), 3–11.

Kenney, Alice P. *An Albany Girlhood* (see Huybertie Pruyn Hamlin).

——. *The Gansevoorts of Albany: Dutch Patricians in the Upper Hudson Valley.* Syracuse: Syracuse Univ. Press, 1969.

Kring, Walter D., and Jonathan S. Carey. "Two Discoveries Concerning Herman Melville." *Proceedings of the Massachusetts Historical Society* 87 (1975), 137–41. (See also Yannella and Parker, below.)

Langley, Henry G. *Proceedings of the Naval Court Martial in the case of Alexander Slidell Mackenzie, a Commander in the Navy of the United States, &c. including the Charges and Specifications of Charges, preferred against him by the Secretary of the Navy. To which is annexed, An Elaborate Review, by James Fennimore [sic] Cooper.* New York: Langley, 1844; Delmar, N.Y.: Scholars' Facsimiles & Reprints, 1992.

Lathers, Richard. *Reminiscences of Richard Lathers: Sixty Years of a Busy Life in South Carolina, Massachusetts and New York.* Ed. Alvan F. Sanborn. New York: Grafton Press, 1907.

Levy, Leonard W. *The Law of the Commonwealth and Chief Justice Shaw.* Cambridge: Harvard Univ. Press, 1957.

Leyda, Jay. "An Albany Journal by Gansevoort Melville." *Boston Public Library Quarterly* 2 (October 1950), 327–47.

——. *The Melville Log: A Documentary Life of Herman Melville, 1819–1891.* New York: Harcourt Brace, 1951; 2d ed., with a supplement, New York: Gordian Press, 1969.

Libbey, William G. "Autobiography of a Quondam Sailor." *Shaker Manifesto* (January–December 1878).

Long, David F. *"Mad Jack": The Biography of Captain John Percival, USN, 1779–1862.* Westport: Greenwood Press, 1993.

Malloy, Mary. "'Bound to the Marquesas': Tommo Runs Away." *Melville Society Extracts* 82 (September 1990), 1, 3–6.

Metcalf, Eleanor Melville. *Herman Melville: Cycle and Epicycle.* Cambridge: Harvard Univ. Press, 1953.

Munroe, John A. *Louis McLane: Federalist and Jacksonian.* New Brunswick: Rutgers Univ. Press, 1973.

Olsen-Smith, Steven. "Herman Melville's Planned Work on Remorse." *Nineteenth-Century Literature* 50 (March 1996), 489–500.

Olsen-Smith, Steven, and Hershel Parker. "Three New Melville Letters: Procrastination and Passports." *Melville Society Extracts* 102 (September 1995), 8–12.

Parker, Hershel. See Kevin Hayes; Brian Higgins; Steven Olsen-Smith; Donald Yannella.

Parker, Hershel. "Biography and Responsible Uses of the Imagination: Three Episodes from Melville's Homecoming in 1844." *Resources for American Literary Study* 21 (June 1995), 16–42.

——. "Gansevoort Melville's Role in the Campaign of 1844." *The New-York Historical Society Quarterly* 49 (April 1965), 143–73.

——. *Herman Melville and the Powell Papers.* Unpublished (described in the NN *Moby-Dick* "Historical Note").

——. "Melville and Politics." Ph.D. dissertation, Northwestern Univ., 1963.

——. "*The New Melville Log*: A Progress Report and an Appeal." *Modern Language Studies* 20 (Winter 1990), 53–66.

——, ed. *Gansevoort Melville's 1846 London Journal and Letters from England, 1845.* New York: New York Public Library, 1966.

Paston, George (Emily Morse Symonds). *At John Murray's: Records of a Literary Circle, 1843–1892.* London: John Murray, 1932.

Polk, James K. *Correspondence of James K. Polk.* Vol. 8 (September-December 1844). Ed. Wayne Cutler, with Robert G. Hall II and Jayne C. Defiore. Knoxville: Univ. of Tennessee Press, 1993.

Reynolds, Cuyler. *Hudson-Mohawk Genealogical and Family Memoirs.* 4 vols. New York: Lewis Historical Publishing Co., 1911.

Sanborn, Geoffrey. "The Name of the Devil: Melville's Other 'Extracts' for *Moby-Dick*." *Nineteenth-Century Literature* 47 (September 1992), 212–35.

Sealts, Merton M., Jr. *The Early Lives of Melville: Nineteenth-Century Biographical Sketches and Their Authors.* Madison: Univ. of Wisconsin Press, 1974.

——. *Melville's Reading.* Columbia: Univ. of South Carolina Press, 1988. Also "A Supplementary Note to *Melville's Reading* (1988)." *Melville Society Extracts* 80 (February 1990), 5–10. (This work lists books known to have been owned by Melville or otherwise to have been available to him. Although two volumes of Todd's *Index Rerum* owned by Gansevoort Melville, preserved in the Berkshire Athenaeum, are listed in *Melville's Reading* as #526a, the books and periodicals I cite from them are *not* listed by Sealts.)

——. "Thomas Melville, Jr., in *The History of Pittsfield*." *Harvard Library Bulletin* 35 (1987), 201–17.

Shaw, Samuel. "Lemuel Shaw." *Memorial Biographies.* Vol. 4. Boston: The New England Historic Genealogical Society, 1885.

Smith, Joseph E. A. "Herman Melville." Pittsfield *Evening Journal* (October 1891-January 1892), as reprinted in Sealts's *Early Lives.*

—— [Godfrey Greylock, pseud.]. *Taghconic; or, Letters and Legends about Our Summer Home.* Boston: Redding, 1852.

——. *Taghconic: The Romance and Beauty of the Hills.* Boston: Lee & Shepard, 1879.

Springer, Haskell. "The Scottish Connection." *Extracts* 42 (May 1980), 15–16.

Starbuck, Alexander. *History of the American Whale Fishery from its Earliest Inception to the Year 1876.* Waltham, Mass.: Starbuck, 1876; facsimile reprint, Secaucus: Castle, 1989. (Essential for its chronological table "showing returns of whaling vessels sailing from American ports.")

Tuckerman, Henry T. Introduction. *Old New York*. By Dr. John W. Francis. New York: W. J. Widdleton, 1865.

———. "Reminiscences of Fitz-Greene Halleck." *Lippincott's Magazine* 1 (January 1868).

Vincent, Howard P. *The Tailoring of Melville's "White-Jacket."* Evanston: Northwestern Univ. Press, 1970.

Weaks, Mabel C. "Some Ancestral Lines of Herman Melville as Traced in Funeral and Memorial Spoons." *New York Genealogical and Biographical Record* 80 (October 1949), 194–98.

Weed, Thurlow. *The Autobiography of Thurlow Weed*. Boston: Houghton, Mifflin, 1883.

Wolfe, Theodore. *Literary Shrines: The Haunts of Some Famous American Authors*. Philadelphia: J. B. Lippincott, 1897.

Yannella, Donald, and Hershel Parker. *The Endless, Winding Way in Melville: New Charts by Kring and Carey*. Glassboro: The Melville Society, 1981. (Yannella and Parker gave wide publicity to the 1975 Kring-Carey article about the Melvilles' marital crisis of 1867 by reprinting it in a pamphlet distributed to all members of the Melville Society and many libraries. The pamphlet also contains commentary and supplementary material by Kring and commentaries by Melvilleans, including some who had known Melville's daughter and his older granddaughters.)

Yannella, Donald, and Kathleen Malone Yannella. "Evert A. Duyckinck's 'Diary: May 29–November 8, 1847.'" *Studies in the American Renaissance* 2 (1978), 207–58.

The New Melville Log

The Gordian Press intends to issue Jay Leyda and Hershel Parker's *The New Melville Log* in parts, beginning with two or three volumes running from Melville's birth in 1819 to the publication of *Moby-Dick* in 1851. For this volume of my biography, *Herman Melville: 1819–1851*, therefore, fuller quotations from specific documents (arranged in chronological order) as well as lavish contextual documentation should be available before the end of the second millennium.

Index

829; *Evening Star*, 151; *Family Magazine*, 233; *Figaro!* 713, 782, 790; *Frank Leslie's Illustrated Newspaper*, 834; *Gazette and Times*, 371, 414, 471, 514; *Harper's New Monthly Magazine*, 804, 866; *Herald*, 204, 205, 270, 283, 324, 328, 332, 334, 335, 337, 339, 340, 424, 538, 592, 632, 691, 705, 708, 727, 762, 770, 807, 831; *Holden's Dollar Magazine*, 709, 816, 822–823, 829, 839; *Home Journal*, 266, 354, 400, 518, 566–567, 571–572, 585, 626, 707–708, 713, 718–720, 723, 726–727; *Hunt's Merchant's Magazine*, 441; *Illustrated Magazine of Literature and Art*, 409; *Journal of Commerce*, 319, 391; *Knickerbocker*, 181, 469, 478, 479, 499, 688, 690, 695, 716, 722, 789, 790; *Literary Digest International Book Review*, 813; *Literary World*, 110, 481, 489, 492, 498, 510, 512, 609–610, 616, 620–622, 624, 626–627, 642, 697–698, 705, 709–713, 716, 718, 720, 723, 742–745, 752, 754, 761–763, 766–772, 774, 777, 782, 790, 807, 816, 828, 839, 846, 868, 881; *Metropolis*, 718; *Morning Courier and New-York Enquirer*, 163–164, 316, 410, 417, 418, 419, 436, 437, 441, 442, 530–531, 533, 538–539; *Morning News*, 372, 410, 411, 413, 437, 441, 442, 482, 638; *National Anti-Slavery Standard*, 441; *National Press*, 397, 399, 471; *Plebeian and Democrat*, 332, 333, 334, 339, 377; *Prompter*, 727, 739 (see also *Prompter's Whistle*); *Prompter's Whistle*, 790; *Putnam's Monthly Magazine*, 200, 201, 389, 477; *Republic*, 316; *Saroni's Musical Times*, 716–717; *Scientific American*, 298; *Spirit of the Times*, 363, 510, 570–571, 626, 695, 717; *Subterranean*, 414, 426; *Sunday Times & Noah's Weekly Messenger*, 511; *Tribune*, 180, 266, 299, 316, 326, 335, 413, 441, 529–531, 538–541, 557–558, 566, 581, 604–607, 609, 617, 631, 633, 637, 660, 683, 690–691, 708–709, 717, 726–727, 734, 807, 854; *United States Magazine and Democratic Review*, 154, 181, 535, 550–552, 608, 633–634, 653, 708–709, 740, 757; *Weekly Mirror*, 335, 355, 439, 441, 453, 471, 478, 479, 489, 517, 539; *Working Man's Advocate*, 180; *Yankee Doodle*, 478, 528, 535–539, 558, 573
New York Crystal Palace (1852), 804
New-York Historical Society, 605

New-York Male High School, 42, 45
New York Society Library, 576, 724, 846
New York State Bank (Albany), 68
Nichols, Thomas Low (1815–1901), 333, 377, 379, 410, 471, 570, 775–776; *Forty Years of American Life*, 171–176, 378
Nicol, John, *The Life and Adventures*, 653
North, Christopher. *See* Wilson, John
North Conway, N.H., 545
Norton, Edward. *See* Russ, Oliver
Nottingham, Eng., *Review and General Advertiser*, 503
Nourse, Amos (1794–1877; M's uncle), 542–543
Nourse, Lucy Melvill (1795–1877; Mrs. Amos; M's aunt), 46, 49, 56, 542
Nukahiva, Marquesas Islands, 211, 274. *See also* Marquesas Islands; *Typee*; Typee valley

O'Connell, Daniel (1775–1847), 557
O'Conor, Charles (1804–1884), 359
Ohio (U.S. receiving ship), 293, 294, 310
Olmsted, Francis Allyn, *Incidents of a Whaling Voyage*, 209–210, 244–246, 248–249
Olsen-Smith, Steven, 647
Olson, Charles (1910–1970), 64
Omoo, 151; authenticity, 457–458, 630, 649, 662, 663, 709, 724; autobiographical basis for, 219–229; compared to *Typee*, 503, 504, 507, 510, 511, 512; composition, 403–404, 451, 453–458, 459; Lima, Peru, road described, 280; losses on, Murray's, 575; M anticipates sales, 566; M separates *Mardi* from *Typee* and *Omoo*, 576, 589–590, 613; M tells story used in, 381–382; preface, 490; prose style, 453–455, 518; publication, 444, 470–471, 481–484, 498–499, 502; reception, 502–509, 510–515, 517–521, 524, 530–534, 538–539, 550–552, 557–559, 566–567, 674, 843; sources, 455–457, 467, 698
Oneida, N.Y., periodicals: *Chief*, 328; *Herald*, 471
Ontario (whaleship), 204
Ontario Tow Boat, 4, 21, 279, 561
Oregon question, 382, 390–391
Oregon Trail, The. See Parkman, Francis, *The California and Oregon Trail*
Ossian. *See* Macpherson, James
O'Sullivan, John L. (1813–1895), 410, 535
Oxenham, Mrs. Ellen Astor, 464, 488

Library of Congress Cataloging-in-Publication Data

Parker, Hershel.
   Herman Melville : a biography / Hershel Parker.
       p.   cm.
   Includes bibliographical references (p.   ) and index.
   Contents: v. 1. 1819–1851.
   ISBN 0-8018-5428-8 (hc : alk. paper)
   1. Melville, Herman, 1819–1891 — Biography.   2.
Novelists, American — 19th century — Biography.   I. Title.
PS2386.P37   1997
813'.3 — dc20
[B]   96-18984